UNIVERSITY CASEBOOK SERIES®

LEGISLATION

INTERPRETING AND DRAFTING STATUTES, IN THEORY AND PRACTICE

JANE C. GINSBURG
Morton L. Janklow Professor
of Literary and Artistic
Property Law
Columbia University School
of Law

DAVID S. LOUK, PH.D.
Academic Fellow
Columbia University School
of Law

Illustrations by
Adine Varah, Esq.

FOUNDATION
PRESS

University Casebook Series is a trademark registered in the U.S. Patent and Trademark Office.

© 2021 LEG, Inc. d/b/a West Academic
    444 Cedar Street, Suite 700
    St. Paul, MN 55101
    1-877-888-1330

Printed in the United States of America

ISBN: 978-1-64708-268-0

In our constitutional system in which Congress, the people's branch, is charged with enacting laws, how Congress makes its purposes known—through text and reliable accompanying materials—should be respected, lest the integrity of legislation be undermined. The experience of the executive branch in interpreting statutes can be helpful to courts. And practical ways should be pursued to further the objective of promoting statutory understanding. With greater sensitivity to the workings of the branches in the lawmaking process, we will be closer to realizing Publius's (most likely Madison's) vision in *The Federalist* No. 62: "A good government implies two things: first, fidelity to the object of government, which is the happiness of the people[;] secondly, a knowledge of the means by which the object can be best attained."

Robert A. Katzmann, *Judging Statutes* (2014)

To the memory of

Ruth Bader Ginsburg

PREFACE

This casebook serves a course in legislation and statutory interpretation and drafting, the process of enacting, implementing and interpreting our nation's laws. In contrast to law courses grounded in the common law, the study of legislation is primarily a text-based enterprise. While students tend to adapt readily to case law analysis, they often find statutory interpretation less congenial. Cases tell stories; statutes enunciate rules. And the enunciation may be extremely opaque. Perhaps because statutory text lacks both the human drama and the expository charm of case law, casebooks on legislation and statutory interpretation, rather than confronting students directly with the statutory text, have often presented issues of interpretation principally through judicial opinions that construe the statutes in question.

This casebook recasts the study of legislation in several respects. First, it trains the students' focus on the statutes themselves. Extensive excerpts from the statute(s) at issue precede most judicial opinions construing the statute(s). The casebook directs students to work their way through the text on its own terms before grappling with judicial readings. Moreover, the later chapters of the casebook offer case studies not only on the statutory text itself, but also (where relevant) the legislative history associated with the statute's enactment, as well as agency or executive branch interpretations of the statute rendered in the form of rules, guidance, or opinion letters. Practicing lawyers who work with statutes and administrative materials that interpret and implement them will often confront these documents in the absence of prior judicial constructions—when the text is still open to a range of plausible interpretations. These case studies assist readers in understanding the process by which the potential interpretations or applications narrow over the course of the interpretive process until a prevailing view emerges, often the result of an accretion of judicial (and sometimes administrative) decisions interpreting the text over time and as applied to new and evolving problems.

Second, this casebook invites students to assess leading approaches to statutory interpretation from the standpoint of *method*. Courts interpret statutes against the backdrop of legislative supremacy, and legislatures rarely set out a detailed hierarchy of prescribed methods for the interpretation of statutes. Thus, in contrast to the judicial exposition of common-law rules, judicial statutory interpretation entails the use of interpretive methods whose legitimacy or authority are almost always open to debate. This casebook regularly prompts students to assess the (often unstated) empirical and jurisprudential assumptions that courts make when employing these methods. The materials thus encourage readers to decipher the text in order to understand the problem to which the statutory text responds and the ways the text addresses the problem, as well as to examine critically how a variety of interpretive methods yield often conflicting answers.

Third, this casebook emphasizes not only the interpretation of language but also its usage. Throughout, the casebook leads the reader to examine a statute's choice of words and structure and to consider other choices legislators (and administrative agencies) could have made to address the problem at hand. Part VIII provides the student several opportunities to evaluate the range of considerations and tradeoffs that comprise the exercise of negotiating and drafting legislation, as applied to several relatable, "inspired by real life" policy issues. In addition, when taught with the aid of the accompanying teaching materials for instructors, this casebook is the first designed specifically so that instructors may enable students to take an active role in learning the process of drafting, implementing, and interpreting statutes. The additional exercises call upon students to work in groups, successively taking on the roles of legislators, administrative agency regulators, and courts. Students first draft a statute in response to a problem drawn from "real life," then, as regulators, consider how to implement another group's draft statute, and finally, as judges, interpret another group's statute by applying it to a specific fact pattern, employing doctrinal canons and methods of interpretation in the course of drafting a judicial opinion (or opinions). We have found that the process of "learning by doing" not only improves students' understanding of drafting, implementing, and interpreting statutes, but also enhances their appreciation of the difficulties entailed in each stage of those processes.

Finally, we hope a course and casebook like these—which encourage students not only to critique the work of others' but also to attempt solutions of their own—will constantly prompt the student to ask whether the interplay among, legislative, administrative, and judicial interventions has yielded a socially desirable result. The legislative enterprise demands the input (though not always the cooperation) of all three branches of government. In this sense, the study of legislation and statutory interpretation is, indirectly, also a study in civics: how the democratic will manifests itself in the enactment, enforcement, and interpretation of law. We hope readers of this casebook will remain mindful throughout that, while each case may concern a particular problem facing specific litigants, every member of society is a stakeholder in the legislative enterprise, and every lawyer will have opportunities to contribute to its improvement or impairment.

Many thanks to our excellent research assistants: Alison Hung and Vineet Surapaneni, Columbia Law School Class of 2022; as well as Emily Gerry, Columbia Law School Class of 2020; and Robert Kohler, Evan Rocher, and Sankeerth Saradhi, Columbia Law School Class of 2021. We are also grateful to the teaching assistants who helped us develop and refine the drafting exercises in the Teachers' Manual: Daniel Rosenfeld, Columbia Law School Class of 2019; Emily Gerry, Will Hayes, Virginia Hill Butler, Andrea Nishi, and Vladislav Shafran, Columbia Law School

Class of 2020; and Benjamin Covington, Randy Kreider, Robert Koehler, Lorena Rodriguez, Sankeerth Saradhi, Samuel Weitzman, Jillian Williams, and Tanner Zumwalt, Columbia Law School Class of 2021. We wish especially to recognize three scholars whose contributions significantly influenced this casebook's design and enhanced the authors' understanding of the field: Bill Eskridge, Abbe Gluck, and the Honorable Robert A. Katzmann. Thanks also to Columbia colleagues for advice and suggestions over the years, as well as to Jessica Copland for administrative support.

JANE C. GINSBURG
DAVID S. LOUK

September 2020

SUMMARY OF CONTENTS

TABLE OF CONTENTS

TABLE OF CASES

The principal cases are in bold type.

UNIVERSITY CASEBOOK SERIES®

LEGISLATION

INTERPRETING AND DRAFTING
STATUTES, IN THEORY AND
PRACTICE

PART I

THE PROCESS OF ENACTING STATUTES

A. OVERVIEW OF LEGISLATION AND THE LEGISLATIVE PROCESS*

1. THE GENERALITY OF LEGISLATION

The drafting and interpretation of legislation call on skills and analyses different from those honed in the adjudicative process covered in traditional law school common law courses like Torts and Contracts. While case law begins with particular controversies, legislation imposes a general rule. Where case law analysis calls on the lawyer to move upward from specific facts to a general principle to discern how the solution in one case can guide the resolution of another, the interpretation of legislation requires reasoning from the general to the specific, to determine whether and how a rule claiming wide application in fact governs an individual controversy.

Moreover, legislation does not simply declare rules; it expresses them in specific language. With legislation, every word (indeed, every punctuation mark) counts. As the late Edwin W. Patterson wrote:

> A proposition of case law may be correctly stated in several different ways, each of which is equally "official." A statute (proposition of legislation) is stated as an exclusive official

* This section is substantially adapted from Jane C. Ginsburg and David S. Louk, LEGAL METHODS: CASE ANALYSIS AND STATUTORY INTERPRETATION 30–64 (5th ed. 2020).

wording of the rule. Case law is flexible; legislation is (textually) rigid.

Noel Thomas Dowling, Edwin Wilhite Patterson and Richard R.B. Powell, Materials for Legal Method 15 (1946).

Statutory interpretation requires working with the words of the statute. Their meaning may be uncertain, but their presence is not. Interpreting the text should not mean rewriting or paraphrasing it. Courts inevitably have great latitude in determining the meaning and application of statutory language in concrete situations, but only the legislature is authorized to change a statute's wording by the process of amendment. (As some of the cases will show, however, courts may not always sharply draw the line between interpreting a statute and rewriting that statute.)

To some extent, the methods of case analysis and statutory interpretation converge. Judges interpret statutes, and their accumulated interpretations become, in effect, the case law of the statutes. Once a court has given a statute a particular interpretation, the principle of *stare decisis* applies to that interpretation: Lower courts in that jurisdiction are as bound by the interpretation as they would be had the rendering court resolved an issue of common law. Of course, the legislator is not bound by the court's interpretation: It is free to amend the statute to impart a different meaning to the text. (On legislative responses to prior judicial interpretations of statutes, see *infra* Section VII.C of this Casebook.)

2. TYPES OF LEGISLATION

Legislative precepts are prescribed general rules expressed in authoritative verbal form. The statutes enacted by Congress and state legislatures are legislation of the classic and most familiar kind. In the present section, however, the term "legislation" denotes not only federal and state statutes but also other types of general legal rules comprising administrative regulations, municipal ordinances and the like. Even the Constitution of the United States or a state constitution is "legislation" in this broad sense, although of higher political and legal obligation than "ordinary" legislation. A constitution, too, is a rule-prescribing instrument, one which expresses in authoritative form the general rules, or principles, that govern the exercise of political power in an organized society and safeguard individual interests from unwarranted governmental intrusion.

Because of the wide dispersion of law-making power in the United States—the constitutional division of legislative authority between the national government and the states and the delegation of subordinate legislative power to administrative agencies and, in the states, to city councils and other municipal bodies—American legislation is an aggregate of precepts from many sources. This mix often gives rise to conflicting directions; a state statute, for example, may be or seem in conflict with existing federal legislation or a state administrative regulation with a municipal ordinance on the same subject. Individuals and corporations, and so the lawyers advising them, often confront the problem of what to do when one lawmaker has commanded certain behavior and another lawmaker has ordered a quite different course of action. In determining which of two competing legislative commands is the one to be obeyed, or to be given controlling force by a court in a litigated case, the manifest first step is to consider the degree of authority with which each of the two lawmakers spoke to the subject at hand. The types of legislation briefly sketched in the following paragraphs therefore follow our legal system's hierarchy of legislative norms, from most to least authoritative.

a.   THE CONSTITUTION OF THE UNITED STATES

The Constitution sets out the norms that govern the distribution of political powers in our society and the ways in which—and purposes for which—the institutions vested with those powers are to exercise them. In our legal order, the Constitution is "law," and law of the highest authoritativeness and obligation. Even a deliberately enacted federal statute can be challenged in the courts as beyond the legislative power delegated to the Congress by the Constitution or as violative of some provision of the Bill of Rights or other constitutional guarantee of individual interests against impairment by government action. Similarly, the Constitution of the United States, as "supreme Law of the Land," is the ultimate authority to which to refer to determine the validity of state and municipal legislation. The Constitution, in its inception, related almost entirely to the structure and operations of the national (or "federal") government, but since the adoption of the Reconstruction Amendments (the Thirteenth, Fourteenth and Fifteenth Amendments) in the years following the Civil War, most of the Constitution's prescriptions have borne equally on state legislation and to action taken by state and local officials.

b.   FEDERAL STATUTES

Article I, Section 1 of the Constitution of the United States provides that "all legislative Powers herein granted shall be vested in a Congress of the United States." The powers so granted to Congress are enumerated in considerable detail in Article I, Section 8, which concludes with a broadly worded grant of authority to "make all Laws which shall be necessary and proper for carrying into Execution the foregoing Powers." What are the constitutional and legal consequences when Congress, as it has done quite often, enacts a statute which, although clearly within the scope of its law-making authority under Article I, Section 8, conflicts directly with existing state legislation or state constitutional provisions?

The "supremacy clause" (Article VI, paragraph 2) of the Constitution supplies the answer.

The supremacy clause, one of the key provisions of the Constitution, provides in full as follows:

This Constitution, and the Laws of the United States which shall be made in Pursuance thereof; and all Treaties made, or which shall be made, under the Authority of the United States, shall be the supreme Law of the Land; and the Judges in every State shall be bound thereby, any Thing in the Constitution or Laws of any State to the Contrary notwithstanding.

The words are carefully chosen and their meaning and effect clear. A federal statute "made in pursuance" of the Constitution is a part of "the supreme Law of the Land" and so supersedes any state constitutional provision, state statute or other type of state legislation.

c.   TREATIES

Article II, Section 2 of the Constitution provides that the President shall have power, by and with the Advice and Consent of the Senate, to make Treaties, provided two-thirds of the Senators present concur.

A treaty in its essence is a diplomatic instrument, a compact between nations, and it may seem strange to see treaties included in an inventory of the types of legislation. Nonetheless, there are a few circumstances in which a treaty made by the President with the advice and consent of the Senate has much the same legal effect as a federal statute. Suppose, for example, that a treaty between the United States and some other nation provides that the citizens of each country shall be fully entitled to inherit property or to engage in all kinds of business in the other country. By the explicit terms of the supremacy clause of the Constitution of the United States, just considered in its relation to federal statutes, this treaty is a part of the "supreme law of the land" and so is superior in legal authoritativeness to any type of state legislation. The citizens of the nation with whom the supposed treaty was made are thus entitled to inherit property or to engage in any kind of business in State X, even if State X has a statute or state constitutional provision restricting the inheritance of property or the carrying on of designated kinds of business to American citizens. The place of treaties and the treaty power in our constitutional system raises many complex questions, some of them of lively contemporary importance, but these questions must be left to later courses in International Law and Constitutional Law. It is sufficient now to note the possibility that a treaty may have an incidental side-effect as federal legislation, either directly (if it is self-executing) or indirectly through federal implementing legislation.

d.   STATE CONSTITUTIONS

State constitutions existed before the drafting of the Constitution of the United States. Almost all of the thirteen original states adopted constitutions in 1776 or 1777. These first state constitutions and those adopted early in the 19th century were much like the Constitution of the United States in content and style, that is, they were largely confined to essential matters like basic governmental structure and the definition and distribution of political powers, or of individual rights, and generally expressed in terms of broad principles or standards as distinguished from narrowly stated rules.

Every state has its constitution, and the typical state constitution of today is a far bulkier document and is likely to deal at length and in very specific terms with subjects like school and police administration, lotteries, state and municipal budgeting, the tenure of civil service employees, and the powers to be exercised by irrigation and sewer districts. Such explicit and detailed provisions are written into a state constitution for the manifest purpose of making it impossible for a subsequent state legislature to change the law on the subject by simple statutory enactment. It is far harder politically to amend a state constitution than to repeal or amend a statute; a two-thirds majority in each house of the state legislature is commonly required to propose a state constitutional amendment, and an amendment so proposed must typically be approved by popular referendum which may, in its turn, require more than a simple-majority vote of the electorate.

State statutes are, of course, subject to challenge in the courts on federal constitutional grounds, but, because of the great specificity of most state constitutions, the state constitutional barrier may be the more difficult one to overcome. A state statute that would unquestionably pass Supreme Court scrutiny as consistent with the Constitution of the United States can nonetheless be held invalid by a state court of last resort as a violation of some provision of the local state constitution. And that will be a final and conclusive determination because the Supreme Court of the United States is not superior in authority to state courts on questions of state law.

e.   STATE STATUTES

It is sometimes said that state statutes are less important in the day-to-day work of lawyers than they once were, because federal regulatory activity has vastly expanded. To say this is to overlook two other developments during approximately the same time: (1) the extension and intensification of state controls, imposed by or based on statutes, in such areas as consumer protection, environmental management, and equal employment opportunity; and (2) the increasing tendency of state legislatures to intervene in traditional private law fields by replacing old case law rules with new and presumably more up-to-date legislative norms.

The effectiveness of a state statutory provision as an authoritative rule may be challenged in court on one or more of several grounds: that it violates some more or less explicit prohibition in the Constitution of the United States, that it contravenes some provision of the state constitution, or that it conflicts with some more authoritative federal statute, treaty or administrative regulation. But it is misleading to concentrate too much on the possible vulnerability of state statutes to constitutional challenge. Ninety percent or more of the statutes enacted by a busy state legislature at one of its sessions will raise no serious question of federal or state constitutional law. The lawyer's work in dealing with state statutes is chiefly a work of interpretation, of determining the meaning and effect of enacted statutory language for specific cases and counseling situations.

f.   MUNICIPAL ORDINANCES

The rules enacted by the legislative branch of a local or "municipal" unit of government are authoritative precepts of legislation within the unit's territorial limits. These prescribed rules of local legislative origin are commonly called "ordinances" (to distinguish them from the "statutes" enacted by Congress and the state legislatures), and that is what we shall call them here, even though they sometimes bear another name (*e.g.*, "by-law"). A municipal ordinance is, of course, legally ineffective if inconsistent with a higher norm of federal law or with a provision of the state constitution and is usually, but not always, inferior in authoritativeness to a conflicting state statute—"not always" because many state constitutions contain so-called "home rule" provisions which, to one or another extent, may empower cities and other municipal units to enact ordinances, on a few designated subjects, that are not vulnerable to disapproval or modification by the state legislature. Insofar as the law-making power of the municipal unit comes to it by statutory delegation from the state legislature, however, the rule prescribed by a municipal ordinance must yield to the conflicting direction of a state statute and may, like an administrative regulation, be repealed or modified by subsequent action of the legislature.

g.   NOTE ON UNIFORM CODES

One way to systematize the law and make it uniform across state jurisdictions is to reduce the common law to statutory form and seek adoption by state legislators. The Uniform Commercial Code (UCC), developed and monitored by the American Law Institute (ALI) in collaboration with the National Conference of Commissioners on Uniform State Laws (NCCUSL), represents the most successful of such efforts.[1] The UCC is a comprehensive code aimed at simplifying and

---

[1]   Other ALI proposals for law reform include model statutory formulations such as the Model Code of Evidence, the Model Penal Code, a Model Code of Pre-Arraignment Procedure, a Model Land Development Code, and a proposed Federal Securities Code. In 2012, the Council approved several new projects including Restatements of consumer contracts law, American

standardizing (rather than restating) most aspects of commercial law. You are likely to study sections of the UCC closely in your contracts class. Helping to promote commerce between states by making it simpler to pursue transactions in various jurisdictions, the Code covers the sales of goods, commercial paper, bank deposits and collections, letters of credit, investment securities, and secured transactions. The UCC which took ten years to complete and another 14 years before it was enacted across the country[2] is generally viewed as one of the most important developments in American law. It has been enacted (with some local variations) in 49 states and in the District of Columbia and the Virgin Islands, as well as partially in Louisiana.[3]

In addition to collaborating with the ALI on the UCC, the NCCUSL has drafted more than 200 uniform laws on numerous subjects and in various fields of law since its organization in 1892. The conference comprises more than 300 lawyers, judges and law professors, appointed by the states as well as the District of Columbia, Puerto Rico and the U.S. Virgin Islands, to "draft proposals for uniform and model laws on subjects where uniformity is desirable and practicable, and work toward their enactment in legislatures."[4] Uniform acts include the Uniform Probate Code, the Uniform Child Custody Jurisdiction Act, the Uniform Partnership Act, the Uniform Anatomical Gift Act, the Uniform Limited Partnership Act, and the Uniform Interstate Family Support Act.[5] Recently promulgated uniform acts include the Uniform Foreign-Country Money Judgments Recognition Act, the Uniform Representation of Children in Abuse, Neglect, and Custody Proceedings Act, and the Uniform Rules Relating to Discovery of Electronically Stored Information.[6] The Conference can only propose laws, and no uniform law is effective until adopted by a state legislature. For example, as of April 2019, New York has enacted more than 78 Uniform Acts since 1897.[7]

More recently, conservative and progressive organizations have also been involved in preparing model laws, first on the right (the American Legislative Exchange Council, or "ALEC"), and, more recently and in response, on the left (originally the American Legislative and Issue Campaign Exchange, or "ALICE," now known as the State Innovation

---

Indian law, and intentional torts to persons. The ALI also plans on updating the Restatement of the Foreign Relations Law of the United States and the Model Penal Code's provisions on sexual assault and related offenses. *See* https://www.ali.org/media/filer_public/be/2d/be2d7c2d-58c6-427d-b5ce-a2176cc072a0/annual-report-2019-web.pdf.

[2]   *See* http://www.uniformlaws.org.

[3]   *See* Uniform Commercial Code, Uniform Law Commission, https://www.uniformlaws.org/acts/ucc.

[4]   *See* http://www.uniformlaws.org.

[5]   The texts of all acts and drafts can be found at the Uniform Law Commission's website: http://www.uniformlaws.org/acts/overview.

[6]   *See* http://www.uniformlaws.org.

[7]   *See* Richard B. Long, Uniform State Laws: Where Do They Come From and Why Do They Matter, NYSBA J., Apr. 2019, 32–35, https://nysba.org/NYSBA/Publications/Bar%20Journal/PastIssues2000present/2019/NYSBA%20Journal%C3%84pril%202019_WEB.pdf.

Exchange, or "SIX"). In contrast to the ALI and the NCCUSL, these organizations prepare model legislation to achieve specifically conservative or progressive policy objectives. Because many state legislatures operate on a part-time basis and sit for only a few months in any two-year legislative term, model legislation has proven to be an extremely effective way to implement state-level legal change at a rapid pace by providing state legislators with ready-made draft bills, though not without some controversy.[8]

3. THE LEGISLATIVE PROCESS

We now consider legislative institutions and processes to assist in the understanding of legislative law.

a. INTRODUCTION

Of all the professional tasks a lawyer is asked to perform, one of the most frequent is that of interpreting legislation and the regulations implementing legislation. She may be called on for interpretation, for example, as counsel advising clients of their rights under statutes, or as advocate urging, or defending against, a statutory claim, or as a judge or administrator ruling on the application of legislative language, or as a scholar explaining or appraising its significance.

As you read the following discussion of the stages of the federal legislative process, it may be helpful to keep in view some general and specific questions. As a general question, a reader might well ask himself at each stage—what does this aspect of the legislature or its procedures disclose about the nature of the legislative institution, about the special advantages and disadvantages of legislative lawmaking and its part in the American legal system? More specifically, and with an eye to the practical use of the process, he should also ask himself the legislative advocate's (lobbyist's) question—what can be done at this stage to speed a bill on its way or obstruct its advance? The effort to answer this last question will surely shed light on the more general question first suggested. Finally, with an eye to interpretive considerations, it is instructive to ask—what does this phase of the process yield in the way of records of legislative deliberations and where are they to be found? What is or should be the weight of these particular records in the search for "legislative intent"? (And as you will see, some jurists resist seeking legislative intent beyond the enacted text of the statute itself.)

b. STRUCTURE, POWERS, AND FUNCTIONS OF CONGRESS

The primary function of Congress is to make laws. All the legislative power entrusted by the Constitution to the national government is

---

[8]   *See* Molly Jackman, ALEC's Influence over Lawmaking in State Legislatures, Brookings Institute, Dec. 6, 2013, https://www.brookings.edu/articles/alecs-influence-over-lawmaking-in-state-legislatures/; Mary Whisner, *There Oughta Be A Law-A Model Law*, 106 Law Libr. J. 125 (2014); Barak Orbach, *Invisible Lawmaking*, 79 U. Chi. L. Rev. Dialogue 1 (2012).

conferred upon the Congress in Article I, Section 1. The enumeration of Congress's legislative powers in Article I, Section 8 of the Constitution—including familiar powers to tax, borrow, and spend, to regulate commerce, to provide for defense and for the general welfare, etc.—merely sketches the underpinning of the vast power Congress today wields. On this constitutional foundation of granted powers, generously construed by the courts, Congress legislates today for the ongoing needs of a huge government establishment and for substantive concerns as diverse as tariffs, public lands, currency, sale of securities, transportation, highways, aviation, healthcare, nuclear energy, space exploration, urban renewal, communications, environmental protection, social security, welfare, housing, education, anti-discrimination, industrial safety, wages and hours, labor-management relations, agriculture, intellectual property, foreign aid, defense, national security, armed services, and so forth. Its responsibilities for public finance, for taxes and other revenue, for borrowing and for appropriations inevitably require it to scrutinize and deal with an enormous range of activities embracing all those just mentioned by way of illustration and others too numerous to itemize. Lawyers, in particular, should be mindful too that Congressional responsibilities include the revision and updating of the substantial body of federal statute law, to say nothing of "back-up" work in dealing with unsatisfactory lawmaking or interpretation by judicial and administrative agencies. Beyond all these aspects of general legislation, there is a continuing and not negligible concern with private legislation in settlement, for example, of individual claims against the government or individual immigration or naturalization cases, or on behalf of other causes of particular interest to individual legislators.[9]

Lawmaking is not the only function of Congress or of Senators and Representatives. There is too, for example, the conduct of investigations—commonly in aid of lawmaking and often in pursuit of another major Congressional concern, that of checking on the administration of the laws. The Legislative Reorganization Act of 1946 focused a spotlight on this last concern and called for "continuous oversight" by Congressional committees of the administrative arms of government. Such checking seemed to the sponsors and has seemed to many since to be particularly necessary at a time when the speed and complexity of modern industrial society have required Congress to delegate much power to administrators. "Oversight" permits Congress to appraise administrative performance and to revise the machinery and rules and to provide funds for administrative activity as appropriate.

In recent decades, the legislative branch has also undertaken oversight of the White House. First during the Nixon Administration, and more recently during the Clinton and Trump Administrations,

---

⁹ *See, e.g.,* to approve an application for compassionate use of a gene therapy (https://www.congress.gov/bill/116th-congress/house-bill/2855); several bills waiving time limits to allow the President of the United States to award Medals of Honor and Purple Hearts posthumously (*e.g.,* https://www.congress.gov/bill/116th-congress/house-bill/238).

Congress has reasserted powers to investigate potential illegality taking place not only in the President's official capacity, but also in his capacity as a private citizen. *See* Trump v. Mazars USA, LLP, 140 S.Ct. 2019, 207 L.Ed.2d 951 (2020) (holding that House committees are not required to demonstrate a specific need for records they seek from the President in his private capacity nor to show that the records were demonstrably critical to a legislative purpose).

c. SOURCE AND DEVELOPMENT OF LEGISLATIVE PROPOSALS

John V. Sullivan, "How Our Laws Are Made," H. Doc. 110–49 (2007) (excerpt):

Sources of ideas for legislation are unlimited and proposed drafts of bills originate in many diverse quarters. Primary among these is the idea and draft conceived by a Member. This may emanate from the election campaign during which the Member had promised, if elected, to introduce legislation on a particular subject. The Member may have also become aware after taking office of the need for amendment to or repeal of an existing law or the enactment of a statute in an entirely new field.

In addition, the Member's constituents, either as individuals or through citizen groups, may avail themselves of the right to petition and transmit their proposals to the Member. The right to petition is guaranteed by the First Amendment to the Constitution. Similarly, state legislatures may "memorialize" Congress to enact specified federal laws by passing resolutions to be transmitted to the House and Senate as memorials. If favorably impressed by the idea, a Member may introduce the proposal in the form in which it has been submitted or may redraft it. In any event, a Member may consult with the Legislative Counsel of the House or the Senate to frame the ideas in suitable legislative language and form.

In modern times, the "executive communication" has become a prolific source of legislative proposals. The communication is usually in the form of a message or letter from a member of the President's Cabinet, the head of an independent agency, or the President himself, transmitting a draft of a proposed bill to the Speaker of the House of Representatives and the President of the Senate. Despite the structure of separation of powers, Article II, Section 3, of the Constitution imposes an obligation on the President to report to Congress from time to time on the "State of the Union" and to recommend for consideration such measures as the President considers necessary and expedient. Many of these executive communications follow on the President's message to Congress on the state of the Union. The communication is then referred to the standing committee or committees having jurisdiction of the subject matter of the proposal. The chairman or the ranking minority member of the relevant committee often introduces the bill, either in the form in which it was received or with desired changes. This practice is usually followed even when the majority of the House and the President are not of the same political party, although there is no constitutional or statutory requirement that a bill be introduced to effectuate the recommendations.

The most important of the regular executive communications is the annual message from the President transmitting the proposed budget to Congress. The President's budget proposal, together with testimony by officials of the various branches of the government before the Appropriations Committees of the House and Senate, is the basis of the several appropriation bills that are drafted by the Committees on Appropriations of the House and Senate.

The drafting of statutes is an art that requires great skill, knowledge, and experience. In some instances, a draft is the result of a study covering a period of a year or more by a commission or committee designated by the President or a member of the Cabinet. The Administrative Procedure Act and the Uniform Code of Military Justice are two examples of enactments resulting from such studies. In addition, congressional committees sometimes draft bills after studies and hearings covering periods of a year or more.

d.   INTRODUCTION AND REFERENCE

Once the drafting of the legislative proposal has been completed and the bill is ready for Congressional consideration, it is necessary to take the appropriate formal steps to lay it before the Congress—*i.e.,* to introduce the bill in one or both chambers. Only a Representative can introduce legislation in the House of Representatives, only a Senator in the Senate. Thus the supporters of a proposal must find one or more sponsors in one or both chambers to assume responsibility for the bill and accomplish its introduction.

The choice of a sponsor or sponsors can be important. Sponsorship may represent a burdensome commitment and sponsors not infrequently have a degree of power over the fate of a measure. The sponsor identified with a bill is assumed to have taken a position in its favor (to avoid this, members sometimes insist on adding the phrase "by request" to the notice of their sponsorship) and frequently must defend this position in correspondence, in the Congress and in public discussion and in meeting proposals for amendment. From the proponents' point of view it is vital to know whether a potential sponsor or sponsors is truly in favor of the proposal. Will she take her commitment seriously? Is she strategically placed—say as a member of the Congressional leadership or as chair of a standing committee (or, at least, as an influential member of it) and as a member of the majority party—so as to make her support most telling? Is she a tenacious and effective fighter if there are storms in the offing, as, for example, New York's Senator Wagner was in sponsoring the National Labor Relations Act and the Social Security Act? Significant Administration bills, which account for much of Congressional time and effort, are commonly introduced by the chairs of the committees or subcommittees concerned with the subject-matter or, especially if the committee's support is in question, by a leader of the President's party in Congress. Multiple sponsorship of bills is possible in both houses. Whether co-sponsorship is desirable or not in a given case may depend on the circumstances. Dilution of responsibility and prestige must be weighed against a possible broadening of the base of support.

Once the issue of sponsorship has been settled, the sponsor or one of them introduces the legislative proposal. Assume that the proposal is to begin its legislative career in the House. In this case introduction involves nothing more than dropping the proposed bill, with the sponsor's name endorsed upon it, into the hopper at the clerk's desk in the chamber of the House of Representatives. Although there is no opportunity for sponsors to make statements as they introduce legislation in the House, sponsors must insert an explanatory statement about their bills in the Congressional Record at some time on the day of introduction.[10] In the Senate, the sponsor may make a statement about the bill, if she is present on the floor of the Senate and is recognized. If the bill is ultimately enacted, the statement made about it by the Senate sponsor at the time of Senate introduction, and the explanatory remarks of the House sponsor sometime after House introduction, will be components of the bill's legislative history that the courts may weigh in ascertaining legislative intent. Lawyers need to be aware that such materials will generally be found in the Congressional Record.

The first action on our bill after introduction is an important one: the referring of the bill to the appropriate House standing committee for consideration. The committees and their operation will be discussed in some detail in section f, below. For the moment it is enough to point out that bills are normally referred to whichever of the numerous House standing committees has jurisdiction, under House rules, of the bill's subject-matter. *See* Table, *infra* p. 19. A sponsor may request a desired reference. The decision on reference, usually a routine one, is made by the Speaker with the assistance of the Parliamentarian and is recorded in the Congressional Record. From time to time difficult problems of choice arise where bills arguably fall within the jurisdiction of more than one committee. Occasionally, a disputed reference, when the Speaker's

---

[10] Since the 112th Congress, sponsors are required at the time of introduction to include "a statement of constitutional authority indicating why Congress has the authority to enact the proposed bill or joint resolution." Mark J. Oleszek, Cong. Research Serv., R44001, *Introducing a House Bill or Resolution* 4 (2017). The bill clerk will not accept a bill if it lacks this statement. *Id.*

ruling is not accepted, has led to a floor fight and a decision by the House itself.

116TH CONGRESS
2D SESSION

H. R. 5946

To preserve knowledge and promote education about jazz in the United States and abroad.

IN THE HOUSE OF REPRESENTATIVES

FEBRUARY 21, 2020

Ms. JACKSON LEE introduced the following bill; which was referred to the Committee on House Administration, and in addition to the Committee on Education and Labor, for a period to be subsequently determined by the Speaker, in each case for consideration of such provisions as fall within the jurisdiction of the committee concerned

---

A BILL

To preserve knowledge and promote education about jazz in the United States and abroad.

1   *Be it enacted by the Senate and House of Representa-*

2   *tives of the United States of America in Congress assembled,*

3   **SECTION 1. SHORT TITLE.**

4   This Act may be cited as the "National Jazz Preser-

5   vation, Education, and Promulgation Act of 2020".

A House rule calls on the Speaker to refer bills in such a way that, as far as may be, each committee that has jurisdiction over any provision of a bill will have responsibility for considering and reporting on that provision. This may be accomplished by having committees consider legislation concurrently or successively, or by dividing up the bill, or by creating a special ad hoc committee with members drawn from the various standing committees interested in the measure.

In the Senate, the reference process is much the same as in the House, with the decision on reference being made by the presiding officer at the time. Under the Senate rules any controversy as to jurisdiction is to be decided by the presiding officer (subject to an appeal) in favor of that committee which has jurisdiction over the subject matter which predominates in the bill. Upon motion by both the Majority and Minority Leaders or their designees, the bill may be referred to two or more committees jointly or sequentially and may be divided up between the committees.

After introduction and reference, the proposed bill is given a number and sent to the Government Printing Office. The next morning printed copies are available in the Senate and House document rooms.[11] The print of the bill following introduction appears as indicated by the example above. The designation—H.R.1524 (note that H.R. means House of Representatives)—will often be used to refer to the bill thereafter. Had it been a Senate bill the designation would have been the letter "S" followed by the bill number.

e.   READING THE BILL

As you become accustomed to seeing or reading bills or statutes, you will note that their structure commonly contains such elements as these (items 1, 2, 4, and 8 always being present):

1.   *Identifying Designation*—"H.R." or "S." and a number for federal bills, "Chapter" or "Public Law" and a number for federal statutes. State bills have comparable designations.

2.   *Title*—This succinctly states the subject or aim of the legislation.

3.   *Preamble*—This is found mainly in older legislation. Utilizing one or more "whereas" clauses, a preamble typically has purposes similar to those of the now more widely used Legislative Findings, Purpose or Policy (see below).

4.   *Enacting Clause*—This states that the legislature adopts as law what follows.

5.   *Short Title*—This gives an easy "handle" or name to the legislation.

6.   *Legislative Findings, Purpose or Policy*—This embraces some or all of the following: The reasons or the occasion for the legislation, or the facts found as a basis for it, or arguments for its adoption or constitutionality. Unlike a preamble, it is a part of the Act, since it follows the enacting clause, and, unlike a preamble, it is frequently carried into codifications.

---

[11] The GPO is required by law to print copies of public bills, as well as of joint resolutions. *See* 44 U.S.C. § 706.

7. *Definitions*—These save repetition and attempt to clarify meaning. Sometimes they are found at the end of a bill or statute.

8. *Purview*—This is the main body of the law containing the administrative, substantive and remedial provisions, etc.

9. *Standard Clauses*—These may comprehend all or some of the following commonly encountered types of clauses:

    a. Severability Clause—This is a clause that keeps the remaining provisions of the bill or statute in force if any portion of it is judicially declared void or unconstitutional.

    b. Saving Clause—This is a clause exempting from coverage something that would otherwise be included. Colloquially, this kind of clause is also referred to as a "grandfathering" clause. It is generally used in a repealing act to preserve rights and claims that would otherwise be lost.

    c. Repealer Clause—This may be (1) a general repealer repealing in general terms all laws inconsistent with the legislation in question, or (2) a specific schedule explicitly listing laws repealed or (3) both.

    d. Effective Date Clause—This designates the time when the legislation takes effect.

We have spoken only of bills but it is well to note that legislative action by the Congress or its chambers can take other legislative forms. These include joint resolutions, designated as "H.J.Res." or "S.J.Res.," which go through the same legislative process as bills, including signature by the President, and have the same effect, except in the case of joint resolutions proposing constitutional amendments which must be approved by two-thirds of each house and are not signed by the President. There is little, if any, practical difference between bills and those joint resolutions that do not propose constitutional amendments and these forms are sometimes used interchangeably. The bill form tends to be used routinely for general legislation. The Joint Resolution tends to be used for miscellaneous special cases such as authorizing invitations to foreign governments, or extending statutes due to expire.

There are, in addition, concurrent resolutions, designated as "H.Con.Res." or "S.Con.Res.," which are not submitted to the President and so are not equal in status or legal effect to bills or joint resolutions. They are not used for general legislation but normally deal with matters affecting only the Congress and express principles, opinions and purposes of the two Houses. And there are, finally, simple resolutions, designated "H.Res." and "S.Res.," which are promulgated by one House only and deal with concerns of the enacting House such as the establishment of a committee or the expression of the sense of one House on some public or intra-mural issue.

Joint and Concurrent Resolutions, like enacted bills, are printed in the Statutes at Large after adoption; simple resolutions are not but may be found in the Congressional Record. The Library of Congress's congress.gov website has the text of bills and resolutions going back to the 101st Congress.[12]

f.   THE COMMITTEE STAGE

John V. Sullivan, "How Our Laws Are Made," H.Doc. 110–49 (2007) (excerpt):

> Perhaps the most important phase of the legislative process is the action by committees. The committees provide the most intensive consideration to a proposed measure as well as the forum where the public is given their opportunity to be heard. A tremendous volume of work, often overlooked by the public, is done by the Members in this phase. There are, at present, 20 standing committees in the House and 16 in the Senate as well as several select committees. In addition, there are four standing joint committees of the two Houses, with oversight responsibilities but no legislative jurisdiction. The House may also create select committees or task forces to study specific issues and report on them to the House. A task force may be established formally through a resolution passed by the House or informally through organization of interested Members by the House leadership.
>
> Each committee's jurisdiction is defined by certain subject matter under the rules of each House and all measures are referred accordingly. For example, the Committee on the Judiciary in the House has jurisdiction over measures relating to judicial proceedings and 18 other categories, including constitutional amendments, immigration policy, bankruptcy, patents, copyrights, and trademarks. In total, the rules of the House and of the Senate each provide for over 200 different classifications of measures to be referred to committees. Until 1975, the Speaker of the House could refer a bill to only one committee. In modern practice, the Speaker may refer an introduced bill to multiple committees for consideration of those provisions of the bill within the jurisdiction of each committee concerned. Except in extraordinary circumstances, the Speaker must designate a primary committee of jurisdiction on bills referred to multiple committees. The Speaker may place time limits on the consideration of bills by all committees, but usually time limits are placed only on additional committees to which a bill has been referred following the report of the primary committee.
>
> In the Senate, introduced measures and House-passed measures are referred to the one committee of preponderant

---

[12] *See* https://www.congress.gov.

jurisdiction by the Parliamentarian on behalf of the Presiding Officer. By special or standing order, a measure may be referred to more than one committee in the Senate.

Membership on the various committees is divided between the two major political parties. The proportion of the Members of the minority party to the Members of the majority party is determined by the majority party, except that half of the members on the Committee on Standards of Official Conduct are from the majority party and half from the minority party. The respective party caucuses nominate Members of the caucus to be elected to each standing committee at the beginning of each Congress. Membership on a standing committee during the course of a Congress is contingent on continuing membership in the party caucus that nominated a Member for election to the committee. If a Member ceases to be a Member of the party caucus, a Member automatically ceases to be a member of the standing committee.

Members of the House may serve on only two committees and four subcommittees with certain exceptions. However, the rules of the caucus of the majority party in the House provide that a Member may be chairman of only one subcommittee of a committee or select committee with legislative jurisdiction, except for certain committees performing housekeeping functions and joint committees.

A Member usually seeks election to the committee that has jurisdiction over a field in which the Member is most qualified and interested. For example, the Committee on the Judiciary traditionally is populated with numerous lawyers.

Members rank in seniority in accordance with the order of their appointment to the full committee and the ranking majority member with the most continuous service is often elected chairman. The rules of the House require that committee chairmen be elected from nominations submitted by the majority party caucus at the commencement of each Congress. No Member of the House may serve as chairman of the same standing committee or of the same subcommittee thereof for more than three consecutive Congresses, except in the case of the Committee on Rules.

The rules of the House provide that a committee may maintain no more than five committees, but may have an oversight committee as a sixth. The standing rules allow a greater number of subcommittees for the Committees on Appropriations and Oversight and Government Reform. In addition, the House may grant leave to certain committeess [sic] to establish additional subcommittees during a given Congress.

Each committee is provided with a professional staff to assist it in the innumerable administrative details involved in the consideration of bills and its oversight responsibilities. For standing committees, the professional staff is limited to 30 persons appointed by a vote of the committee. Two-thirds of the committee staff are selected by a majority vote of the majority committee members and one-third of the committee staff are selected by a majority vote of minority committee members. All staff appointments are made without regard to race, creed, sex, or age. Minority staff requirements do not apply to the Committee on Standards of Official Conduct because of its bipartisan nature. The Committee on Appropriations has special authority under the rules of the House for appointment of staff for the minority.

Standing House Committees, 116th Congress (2019–2021)

Committee	Total Members	D	R	No. of Subcom.
Agriculture	47	26	21	6
Appropriations	53	30	23	12
Armed Services	58	32	26	6
Budget	36	22	14	0
Education and Labor	52	30	22	5
Energy and Commerce	54	30	24	6
Ethics	10	5	5	0
Financial Services	60	34	26	6
Foreign Relations	47	26	21	6
Homeland Security	31	18	13	6
House Administration	9	6	3	1
Judiciary	41	24	17	5
Natural Resources	44	25	19	5
Oversight and Government Reform	42	24	18	5
Rules	13	9	4	3
Science, Space and, Technology	39	227	17	5
Small Business	24	14	10	5
Transportation and Infrastructure	67	37	30	6
Veterans' Affairs	28	16	12	5
Ways and Means	42	25	17	6

Select Committees of the House

Permanent Select Committee on Intelligence

Select Committee on the Climate Crisis

Select Committee on the Modernization of Congress

Standing Senate Committees, 116th Congress (2019–2021)

Committee	Total Members	R	D	No. of Subcom.
Agriculture	20	11	9	5
Appropriations	31	16	15	12
Armed Services	27	14	13	7
Banking, Housing, and Urban Affairs	25	13	12	5
Budget	21	11	10	0
Commerce, Science, and Transportation	26	14	12	6
Energy and Natural Resources	20	11	9	4
Environment and Public Works	21	11	10	4
Finance	28	15	13	6
Foreign Relations	22	12	10	7
Health, Education, Labor, and Pensions	23	12	11	3
Homeland Security and Governmental Affairs	14	8	6	3
Judiciary	22	12	10	6
Rules and Administration	19	10	9	0
Small Business and Entrepreneurship	19	10	8	0
Veterans' Affairs	17	9	8	0

Select Committees of the Senate

Select Committee on Ethics

Select Committee on Intelligence

Special Committee on Aging

Committee on Indian Affairs

Joint Committees

Joint Economic Committee

Joint Committee on the Library

Joint Committee on Printing

Joint Committee on Taxation

What happens when a bill has been referred to a standing committee? In most cases, the standing committee chairman will refer the bill to a subcommittee for consideration, if the committee has subcommittees, as most do. Also, copies will often be transmitted to the executive departments or agencies with a request for their views. One must remark at this point, on the power of the committee as a whole and the power of the standing committee chair in particular. Only a small percentage of bills referred to committees is reported out. The power the committee possesses to block or to report legislation, with or without amendment—and we shall later see further reasons for its life and death powers—helps to make the committee a crucial factor in almost any bill's history.

The Committee chair has other practical powers stemming from her other functions—such as calling and presiding over meetings and hearings, setting the agenda, developing and controlling staff, negotiating for floor consideration, designating the floor manager for the bill and participating in conference proceedings. In turn, the subcommittee chair will have major power over the fate of the bill and much to say, subject to the power of the full committee and its chair, over whether the measure is to languish or be pursued with more or less vigor. The subcommittee's decision to table or to endorse or to reshape is often accepted by the full committee and ultimately by the Congress. The Appropriations Committees, for example, regularly endorse the work of their subcommittees. Thus, the work of a very few Senators or Representatives and of the chair may be decisive. The extraordinary fragmentation of Congressional power becomes evident.

Whether the bill is considered by the full committee or a subcommittee, and especially if it is a significant bill and in some degree controversial, the chair or subcommittee chair as the case may be will probably decide to hold public hearings on it; he or she has much discretion over whether and how such hearings will be conducted. With the staff, who are subject to his or her control, the chair concerned will schedule the hearings, give notice, plan the pattern of witnesses, and issue requests to testify or, perhaps, subpoenas. On the appointed hearing day, an official reporter will be present to record testimony. After introductory statements by committee or subcommittee members, the Senators and Representatives who seek to be heard will receive preference as witnesses; officials of the executive departments or agencies may also then be heard, as well as the representatives of interest groups and other private persons. Prepared statements will often be submitted and witnesses will be questioned. Owing to the multiple burdens of committee work that affect legislators, the hearing may be only sparsely attended by members of the sponsoring committee or subcommittee.

The purposes of hearings may vary widely depending on the measure and the aims of the legislators. If well organized by the chair and staff to that end, they can serve as a valuable means for gathering information and for testing the proposal's impact on segments of the public. In this aspect it is instructive to compare the modest research and data-gathering capability of the courts to the capabilities of Congressional committees, with their staffs, their access to the Congressional Research Service and the Offices of Legislative Counsel, and their access through hearings and otherwise to the expertise of governmental and private sources. But hearings are not always well managed to serve this informational purpose and may be used to serve, instead or in addition, such other purposes as mobilizing public support or opposition, providing publicity for legislators, stalling the legislative progress of a bill, furnishing a "safety valve" for disturbances, and so forth.

After the hearings, the hard work begins on the bill. A transcript of the hearings is made available. With the help of staff, other data, analyses and drafts are assembled. The legislators then meet, with or without preliminary caucusing and with staff personnel and sometimes representatives of governmental departments (and sometimes representatives of private interests) in attendance. They discuss the bill and any amendments and decide whether and on what terms to report it out. If the vote is to table, that will often be the end of a bill unless pressures in the full committee (in the case of a bill first considered by a subcommittee) or in the chamber as a whole can force a different result. If the bill is not tabled, the next step is to "mark up" the bill and it will often receive its definitive shape in the course of compromises and negotiations on this level at the hands of members and staff and drafters. Note must be taken here of the ease with which a proposal can be blocked by a strategically placed minority at this stage—unless the pressures against it can be overcome by intense pressures in its behalf.

When a bill is reported out, with or without amendment, by a subcommittee, it must run the gauntlet of the full committee, which typically has regular meeting days on which subcommittee reports are taken up. Sometimes the subcommittee's work will be accepted; at other times, the whole process of hearings and "marking up" or revision will be repeated in the full committee, which in any event must ultimately vote on its own to table the bill or to report it in some form. Again, there is opportunity for delay and defeat and much may depend on the attitude and practice of the full committee chair toward the proposal. From the standpoint of the lobbyist, of course, the subcommittee and committee phases of action are key points for the application of favorable or adverse pressures and the same is apt to be true at other points of the process where a small number of persons exercise great power over a measure's progress.

Notice at the committee stage that three kinds of documents emerge that may be vital elements in the legislative history of the bill when its meaning is later sought by lawyers, administrators, judges or by the public. The first of these is the hearings, if they are printed and made generally available to the Congress and the public.[13] These may contain important clues to the impact or sense of legislative provisions, especially, for example, when amendments are made in response to points made at the hearings. The second is the different versions of the bill considered by the committee. Changes in language between the bill as referred to the committee and the bill as reported out may shed significant light on the bill's final meaning. The third and perhaps most important document at this stage is the full committee's formal report accompanying the bill when it is transmitted by the committee to the chamber as a whole. This formal report normally discusses the purposes of and reasons for the bill and analyzes its provisions. Committee amendments are indicated and communications from the executive regarding the bill are commonly incorporated in the report. There may be a minority report—*i.e.*, dissenting views—on the same bill. Both the committee report (which will be given a number) and the bill as reported will be printed up and made available promptly after filing. The report has special significance for interpretive purposes, representing, as it does, an expression of views about the bill by the Congressional group charged with detailed knowledge and responsibility. It constitutes a prime source of information about the bill for the members of Congress as well, a source to which they can refer as a basis for their vote. So important is it for this purpose that House and Senate normally require that committee reports be available to the membership for several days before consideration of the measures to which they are addressed.

We have been considering the committee stage in relation to a bill. But if it is to become law, the bill must somehow be laid before the chambers themselves to be voted on and approved by the membership as a whole. In the House, serious risks of delay and obstruction attend the process of getting to the floor but rigid, expeditious procedures speed it to its fate thereafter; on the other hand, in the Senate, getting to the floor is notably less difficult, but serious risks of delay and obstruction arise in connection with floor consideration.

g.   FLOOR ACTION ON THE BILL

i.   *On the House Floor*

Let us look first at the patterns of floor action in the House. Assuming the bill is important and controversial, it will in all probability, as we saw, be the subject of a special rule from the Rules Committee. Even bills privileged in their own right, such as revenue bills, not infrequently are brought before the House by preference under a special rule from the Rules Committee limiting the terms of debate. The initial step then in the floor proceedings on our bill—unlike privileged bills or

---

[13] A printed version of the hearings may not be available until many months after the hearings have taken place. Each committee, however, posts the hearing transcripts on its website shortly after the hearing.

bills coming up on the Private or Consent or Discharge Calendar or Suspension of the Rules or as District of Columbia business—will be the Speaker's recognition of a member of the Rules Committee to call up the rule relating to our bill. Special rules of this kind may be debated for an hour but the debate does not normally consume the allotted time and such rules are often adopted without difficulty by voice vote. Following is an example of a typical special rule, of the "open" kind, for a bill on the Union Calendar:

> *Resolved,* That upon the adoption of this resolution it shall be in order to move that the House resolve itself into the Committee of the Whole House on the State of the Union for the consideration of the bill (H.R. ___) to (here insert the purpose of the bill). After general debate, which shall be confined to the bill and shall continue not to exceed two hours, to be equally divided and controlled by the chairman and ranking minority member of the Committee on ___, the bill shall be read for amendment under the five-minute rule. At the conclusion of the consideration of the bill for amendment, the Committee shall rise and report the bill to the House with such amendments as may have been adopted, and the previous question shall be considered as ordered on the bill and amendments thereto to final passage without intervening motion except one motion to recommit.

The text of the resolution is of great importance as it sets the pattern for what follows.

Upon adoption of the special rule the House resolves itself into the Committee of the Whole House on the State of the Union. This step, applicable to most significant pieces of legislation, has a number of consequences. In essence it makes less formal, and speeds, the action of the House. In the Committee of the Whole, the House can operate with a quorum of 100 members (as against 218 for the House itself). Time-consuming yea and nay votes are avoided. For the deliberations of the Committee of the Whole, the Speaker steps down from the chair, appointing another chairman in her place.

As the above special rule indicates, the next step in relation to our bill is general debate. The time the rule allows is equally divided between (a) the bill's floor manager, who is normally the chair of the responsible standing committee or subcommittee, and, (b) his or her principal opponent, who is usually a ranking minority member of the same committee or subcommittee. The floor manager speaks first, followed by his or her opposite number. Both yield time to others for further speeches regarding the bill. Note once again the pervasive role of the standing committee and its leaders in the legislative process.

Following the general debate, the bill is open to amendment, committee amendments having priority. The sponsor of an amendment has five minutes to explain and support his or her amendment; additional time requires unanimous consent. The floor manager has five minutes to respond. If other members want time to discuss an amendment, they offer fictional or pro forma amendments (motions to "strike the last word") as a basis for receiving five minutes of speaking time. Members of the standing committee are also entitled to preference in recognition. Debate on an amendment can continue for some little time under this system and may be closed by unanimous consent or by motion requiring a majority vote. While there are possibilities for delay in House procedure, there is no real opportunity to stop a bill or amendment from being voted on.

Votes on amendments in the Committee of the Whole may be voice votes. If the vote is close or doubtful, a vote by division (proponents and opponents stand in turn to be counted) may be demanded. A roll call vote may be had if the division reveals the lack of a quorum.

The amending stage is crucial in the progress of a bill. The amendments offered may be and often are of such character as to change the bill substantially or weaken it drastically. Their adoption might undermine such support for the bill as already exists. In any case, the skill, dedication and prestige of the floor manager may make the difference between success and failure in warding off crippling revisions. Once again it is appropriate to point to the life and death role of the committee personnel who, having addressed the bill in the committee itself and championed it before the Rules Committee, are now proponents for the bill on the floor. The support or opposition of the bill's standing committee proponents with respect to a particular amendment may influence a member of Congress' vote on the amendment. In theory, doubts should be resolved in favor of the committee that has done the detailed work on the bill. If the committee represents a cross-section of the House, it may have foreseen and met the need to compromise adequately the divergent interests represented in the full House. Weight may attach, too, to the position of the leadership; and in the case of amendments proposed by minority party spokespersons, party loyalty may play a role. Incidentally, one of the most difficult tasks of those managing bills is to see that needed supporters are available on the floor when critical votes are taken.

Note, for purposes of later comparison with the Senate, that amendments put forward in the Committee of the Whole must be germane to the bill and to that portion of the bill they purport to revise. It may be possible to tack a non-germane amendment to a bill when the Rules Committee's special rule waives points of order against the bill or when the amendment concerned has specifically been made in order.

Not only is the bill open to amendment under the procedures we have been discussing, but it is also possible—though rare—to kill the bill in its entirety if a motion to strike the enacting clause is offered and sustained. If this preferential motion—which must be considered at once and allows ten minutes of debate—is upheld in the Committee of the Whole, the

Committee rises and reports back to the full House which then has an opportunity to vote on the same question. If the full House sustains the defeat, the bill is killed; if not, the House resolves itself back into Committee of the Whole and resumes debate.

The process of amending the bill in Committee of the Whole, if not limited by the provisions of the special rule, will normally continue until there are no amendments left to consider, but it may be brought to an end by a unanimous consent agreement or by a motion disposed of by majority vote. Here, too, the inexorable march and expedition of House procedures deserve comparison with the Senate.

When the process of reading the bill for amendment has concluded, the Committee of the Whole rises, its action is reported to the House itself, the Speaker resumes the chair, the quorum requirement is once again 218 members, and the House itself takes over consideration at this point. Note again the terms of the special rule, *supra*, governing the remaining steps, and these steps will generally be quite similar as a practical matter even when a privileged measure—such as an appropriation bill—is being considered without a special rule. Under the rule the "previous question" is deemed ordered, a highly privileged procedure which calls for final vote forthwith on the merits.

The House itself now takes up without debate the amendments, if any, reported by the Committee of the Whole and usually, though not necessarily, votes on them en bloc. Amendments rejected in Committee of the Whole are not reported and, in practice, they are lost and may not be voted on again. Once the amendments approved in Committee of the Whole have been voted on by the House—and the House commonly approves the work of the Committee of the Whole—the question before the House is the adoption of the amended bill itself. After vote on engrossment and third reading of the bill a member of the opposition may make a motion to recommit the bill to the original standing committee with or without instructions. If such a motion without instructions carries, the bill is stopped *pro tem* and goes back to the committee which may however report it back again at some later date for another attempt at passage. If the motion is made and approved with instructions to amend the bill in specified ways—often ways that were defeated in the Committee of the Whole—and to report forthwith, the bill as revised by the standing committee in accordance with the instructions is reported back to the House and put to a vote. When the motion to recommit is defeated, as it normally is, the question before the House becomes the final passage of the bill. The final vote will be a roll-call vote if one fifth of the members so demand.

House floor procedure, taken as a whole, is notable then for the power it gives the majority, the continuing power exercised by the committee, the short shrift (*e.g.*, the 5-minute rule, the "previous question") given to dilatory tactics and to efforts to block a final vote. While the amending process can be used to delay and perhaps destroy, such action is subject to majority approval and is part and parcel of the ongoing Congressional task of reconciling divergent interests as a basis for social action.

ii.   On the Senate Floor

Compare the operation of the Senate when it takes up a bill on the floor, especially its handling of amendments and the limitation of debate. Commonly a bill will come before the Senate pursuant to a unanimous consent arrangement worked out by the majority leader in consultation with the minority leader and other interested Senators. Failing that, a motion may be made to take up the bill. Such a motion is vulnerable to the filibuster tactic (see below). Pursuant to such a motion, if adopted, or to a unanimous consent agreement, floor consideration of the bill begins—usually with an opening statement by the floor manager who will probably be either the responsible subcommittee chair or, especially on major bills, the chair of the standing committee itself. Members of the committee will most likely be on hand on the floor at this point and the opposition will be led by the appropriate ranking minority committee member. There is no reserved time for general debate as in the House and the amendment of the bill is in order at once. Committee amendments are taken up first, then non-committee amendments. This amendment stage is no less critical, no less dependent on the skill and prestige of the floor managers, than it is in the House. Note, however, that in contrast to the House, where the requirement of germaneness regulates the amending process, in the Senate an amendment to a bill need not be germane to a bill, unless it is a general appropriation bill.

The central characteristic of Senate floor procedure that differentiates it from that of the House and, indeed, from that of most other legislative bodies, is the difficulty of limiting debate. At this time, there are only three ways in which debate may close. First, when all Senators have said all they wish to say on a proposal the debate will come to a halt. Second, there is the possibility of a unanimous consent agreement to limit debate on a particular measure. Even on many relatively controversial bills, the discussion is ended pursuant to such agreements. But such a device is not available to close debate against the wishes of even a single Senator. Absent unanimous consent, or the exhaustion of all desires to speak, the only recourse is the so-called cloture rule.

John V. Sullivan, "How Our Laws Are Made," H. Doc. 110–49 (2007) (excerpt):

On occasion, Senators opposed to a measure may extend debate by making lengthy speeches or a number of speeches at various stages of consideration intended to prevent or defeat action on the measure. This is the tactic known as "filibustering." Debate may be closed, however, if 16 Senators sign a motion to that effect and the motion is carried by three-fifths of the Senators duly chosen and sworn. Such a motion is voted on one hour after the Senate convenes, following a quorum call on the next day after a day of session has intervened. This procedure is called "invoking cloture." In 1986, the Senate amended its rules to limit "post-cloture" consideration to 30 hours. "Post-cloture," a Senator may speak for not more than one hour and may yield all or a part of that time to the majority or minority floor managers of the bill under consideration or to the Majority or Minority leader. The Senate may increase the time for "post-cloture" debate by a vote of three-fifths of the Senators duly chosen and sworn. After the time for debate has expired, the Senate may consider only amendments actually pending before voting on the bill.

There has been much argument over the merits of unlimited debate, or filibustering, and the weak cloture rule. On the one hand, the arguments made have cited the importance of unfettered debate in at least one chamber and have stressed the desirability of assuring that legislation with drastic consequences cannot be adopted by ruthless majorities over the intense opposition of a numerous minority. On the other hand there have been arguments based on the desirability of a majority's being ultimately able to prevail in a democratic society. The upshot of the present rule certainly is, in any case, to allow an intense minority to prevail, to block action, unless an extraordinary majority can be mobilized on the other side. And this state of affairs has pervasive implications for Senate procedure and decision-making. A majority cannot act if a large and determined minority opposes. The filibuster and threat of filibuster—even by individuals—offer a tremendous weapon for extracting concessions and compromises in legislative bargaining, especially in the crowded hours before sessions draw to a close. The difficulty of building winning coalitions is greatly increased. The further dispersion of already dispersed Congressional power should be plain enough to any observer.

The Senate conducts a great deal of business, nonetheless, without encountering the occasional barrier of an actual filibuster. Assuming the bill is a part of such normal business, it will come in due course to a vote. Unlike the House, the Senate does not deliberate in a Committee of the Whole, but it conducts its voting as the House does—by voice, by division and, on the request of one-fifth of a quorum, by roll-call (the yeas and nays). Roll-call votes, due to the chamber's smaller size, are easier and more frequent in the Senate.

When the vote has been taken, any Senator on the prevailing side may move to reconsider it within two days. In order to make the result definite and final, this motion to reconsider is generally made promptly after the final vote and another Senator moves to table the motion while the supporters of the final vote are still on hand. Tabling the motion has the effect of making the final vote conclusive; it usually is approved by voice vote. Once in a while, after a close vote, a change of heart or the arrival of new troops can dramatically upset the result. In the House, as we saw, it is common for the opponents of a bill to move to recommit; the same motion is possible in the Senate, but infrequent. Generally, when the motion to reconsider is tabled, the Senate's deliberations—short of conference—on a bill are finished. Such deliberations, it should now be apparent, are far more flexible and leisurely than the House's, more prone to delay and liable as well to serious minority obstruction.

The student of votes in the Congressional Record will note references to "pairs." The practice of pairing is followed in both chambers. Pairing permits absent, or otherwise nonvoting, Senators to record their position. Thus, two absent Senators on opposite sides may "pair" with each other and their positions will be noted but will not be counted in the voting tallies.

iii. The Congressional Record

Lawyers investigating the history of bills, and other students of the legislative process will inevitably make extensive use of the Congressional Record, which reports the floor proceedings of Congress and contains other information as well. The Record has been published since 1873. Before that time the proceedings of Congress were published in the Annals of Congress (1789–1824), the Register of Debates (1824–1837) and the Congressional Globe (1833–1873). The modern Record is published daily while Congress is in session and is also available online.[14] Bound volumes appear later. The bound volumes do not necessarily match the daily edition exactly and, as to both, it must be noted that the Record purports only to be "substantially a verbatim report of proceedings." Unfortunately, the practice of Representatives and Senators in revising or extending their remarks or inserting undelivered speeches has marred the accuracy of the Record as a transcript of what occurred on the floor. A modest step was taken on March 1, 1978 in both House and Senate toward identifying in the Record materials not actually uttered on the floor. Now, in the House section of the Congressional Record, undelivered speeches and other extraneous material are printed in a different type style to distinguish them from speeches actually given on the Floor; in the Senate section, statements or insertions that are not spoken by a Senator from the Floor are preceded by a "bullet." However, because in the Senate, with unanimous consent, remarks are printed as if spoken, the system adopted falls far short of enabling the reader reliably to know how much of what is printed was in fact said in debate. Although only substantially verbatim, the Record is the best source available and lawyers must learn to make effective use of it. It is necessary to remember that the Record fulfills many purposes for the legislator besides that of providing an accurate record for judicial use. A glance at its pages seasoned with articles,

---

[14] *See* https://www.congress.gov/congressional-record.

occasional speeches, editorials, etc. and at its swollen Appendix will give some idea of the problem. But it does provide a record of some kind of the floor proceedings, the texts of amendments (which may also be available separately and may be crucial for interpretive purposes), and conference reports, and it contains indices invaluable to the researcher such as the Daily Digest, and, in the permanent edition, the History of Bills and Resolutions. In the Congressional Record and in the headings of bills, one peculiarity appears (particularly in the Senate proceedings) which should be mentioned. That is the phenomenon of the "legislative day." Because the Senate is apt to recess, rather than adjourn, from day to day and because recessing overnight does not trigger a new legislative day when the Senate reconvenes in the morning, the Senate may be still operating on a legislative day, begun much earlier, which does not coincide with the calendar day. In the study of the rules this can be important as they may provide for lapses of time in terms of legislative days or calendar days and the difference must be noted.

h.   INTER-HOUSE COORDINATION

The House and Senate, acting successively or concurrently in accordance with the procedures already described, may adopt identical measures. When they do, there is nothing to prevent or delay presentation of the legislation to the President for his signature. The same is true, even when the chambers pass different versions of a bill, if one chamber is willing, without more, to accept the other's version.

When the differences between the chambers regarding a bill are controversial in character, however, and neither chamber is, or seems, likely to yield its position, special action to compose differences may be needed. Normally a conference will be requested. Conferees or managers from each chamber are appointed by, respectively, the Speaker of the House and the presiding officer of the Senate. At least three conferees—but there may be more—are designated in each chamber. In selecting them, the presiding officer generally follows the recommendations of the appropriate standing committee chair. Each chamber's team of conferees or managers is very likely to include senior members of the standing committee. Such persons as the standing committee chair, the ranking majority and minority members, the appropriate subcommittee chair and the ranking minority subcommittee member will probably be selected. A House rule provides that in appointing conference committee members the Speaker "shall appoint no less than a majority of members who generally supported the House position as determined by the Speaker." Another rule requires the Speaker, to the extent feasible, to name as conferees the authors of the principal amendments to the proposed bill. Both political parties are commonly represented on the committee, with the majority party having the larger representation. Because the Senate and House delegations vote separately on all questions arising in the conference committee and because a majority of each delegation must approve every action, it is not essential that the two delegations be of the same size and they frequently are not. Note here, as elsewhere in the federal legislative process the pervasive influence of the standing committee and its chair.

The designated conferees meet to discuss the bill, typically under great pressure to reach an accommodation and often under great pressure of time. On rare occasions, conference delegations operate under direction from the parent chamber, but generally there are no instructions. The conferees are generally free to negotiate and resolve all matters in dispute between the chambers, although House rules restrict the power of House conferees to agree to non-germane Senate amendments. The conferees may trade off Senate provisions against House provisions and vice versa; they may seek a middle ground between the Senate and House provisions. They may not add new provisions or change provisions already agreed on by both chambers. Nonetheless they have, in practice, substantial leeway to compose differences; moreover, it is difficult to enforce strict limitations. Sometimes, one chamber will have amended a bill originating in the other by striking out all that follows the enacting clause and inserting its own provisions. When such an amendment "in the nature of a substitute" comes before the conference, the conferees have the entire subject matter before them and are much freer to make changes, even to draw a new bill. In such cases, the conferees may not include in their report matter not committed to them by either house; but they may include matter which is a germane modification of subjects in disagreement.

The deliberations of a small group with a large measure of power over the shape and fate of a controversial bill are a natural target for pressure from special interests for this or that modification of the bill's provisions. By any yardstick, the conference is crucial for a bill, and any experienced lobbyist cannot fail to be aware of this. Once more there is a major opportunity for blocking action.

As the figures quoted earlier suggest, conference committees are usually able to arrive at some sort of accommodation of Senate-House differences and to agree on provisions to be recommended to the chambers. If the chambers cannot be thus brought to agreement, the bill is lost. Assuming, however, that the conferees do concur in recommendations for adjusting the differences, they incorporate these recommendations in a report which must be signed by a majority of each delegation of the conferees and filed with their respective houses. The dissenting managers have no authority to file statements of minority views. The recommendations are accompanied by a statement on the part of the managers explaining the effect of actions recommended. The conference report containing the recommendations and statement is made available in print separately and in the Congressional Record. As a document representing the late and detailed views of representatives of both chambers it is a very important aid to judicial interpretation of the enacted bill.

The engrossed bill and amendments, together with a copy of the report of the conference committee, are transmitted to the chamber which is to act first on the conference report (normally to the house other than the one requesting the conference). Whichever chamber takes up the conference report, it represents a matter of high privilege. In the House of Representatives, for example, the report and bill do not need help from the Rules Committee to reach the floor quickly.

The chamber first approving the conference report sends the documents to the other house for final action. When both chambers have approved the conference bill it is sent to the enrolling clerk of the chamber in which the bill had its origin. It is then ready for the last stage of its journey to enactment.

i.   EXECUTIVE ACTION

When the bill has weathered the stages of committee review, of getting to the floor, of floor consideration, of inter-house coordination, it faces at least one more critical test—that of Presidential review. In fact, the President's concern with an important bill is not something that merely springs into being at the end of the long process just described. When discussing the sources of legislation, we noted the President's major role as an initiator of enactments. Through public statements and personal communications, through Cabinet members, staff aides, administrative agency officials and otherwise, the President maintains active contact with the Congress in regard to bills important to him as they make their way forward from stage to stage of the process. His participation in that process comes to a climax or focus, however, when the moment arrives for exercise of the power to approve or veto conferred on him by the Constitution.

Once the bill is approved in identical form by both House and Senate, it is transmitted to the enrolling clerk of the chamber in which it originated, who undertakes the often complex and difficult task of preparing the so-called enrolled bill, incorporating as accurately as may be all amendments adopted along the way. The enrolled bill is printed and when the proper committee approves the bill as truly enrolled, it is transmitted for signature first to the Speaker of the House, then to the President of the Senate. When both have affixed their signatures to the enrolled bill, it is delivered to the White House and a receipt is secured for it. This delivery is normally regarded as presentation to the President and as triggering the start of the ten-day period allowed for Presidential action by the Constitution. Occasionally, in the past, when a President has had to be absent for an extended period—as Wilson was in 1919 and as Franklin D. Roosevelt was some decades later—the step of delivery to the White House has been deferred for a time so as not to trigger the ten-day period at an inconvenient moment.

The President has several choices in dealing with a bill presented to him. If he decides to approve the measure, he may do so affirmatively by signing it, or passively, if Congress is still in session at the end of ten days following presentation, by leaving it unsigned. In either case the bill becomes a law. In neither of these cases does the Constitution require any statement by the President. By the mid-twentieth century, special occasions arose—for example, President Truman's approval of the Hobbs Anti-Racketeering Act of 1946 and the Portal-to-Portal Act of 1947—when the chief executive upon approving a bill sent a formal message to Congress explaining his approval and discussing the provisions of the legislation concerned. Whether or not there is a formal communication to Congress, the President may in any case issue a more or less detailed public statement on signing the bill, a practice that has become more regular in recent decades. President George W. Bush frequently filed "signing statements" with signed bills, in which he asserted that the Constitution gives him the right to ignore certain sections of the bills. Although President Bush was not the first president to use signing statements, his use of signing statements functioned to assert his authority as President to "supervise the unitary executive branch" and to undertake an independent determination as to the constitutionality of legislative enactments, a practice that his predecessors Ronald Reagan, George H.W. Bush, and Bill Clinton also engaged in. President Obama also occasionally issued signing statements, albeit with less frequency; President Trump has resumed the practice of regular issuance of signing statements.

If the President objects to a bill, the Constitution provides that within ten days after presentation "he shall return it, with his objections to the House in which it shall have originated, who shall enter the objections at large on their Journal and proceed to reconsider it." The President's veto may be overridden by a two-thirds vote of both Senate and House. In that event the bill becomes a law; without such overriding it does not. There is also the possibility of a "pocket veto." This occurs when the President fails to sign a measure and Congress adjourns before the end of the ten-day period allowed for Presidential action. In this case the bill is lost; Congress has no opportunity to override the veto. When the President vetoes by returning a bill to Congress, there is an obligatory Presidential message that goes with it. Although such a message is not required with a "pocket veto," it has been a Presidential practice to give the press and the public a full statement of reasons for each "pocket veto."

How is the decision made to veto or approve a bill? At the point where an enrolled bill is presented to the President, the Legislative Reference Division of the President's Office of Management and Budget undertakes a searching review process. Copies of the bill are sent to the executive departments and agencies concerned with its provisions and their recommendations are sought within forty-eight hours as to whether the

President should veto or approve. While this may sound like a short period for response, it must be remembered that the departments and agencies in question will generally have been active in the legislative process on the bill—*e.g.*, providing expert views and aid to the Congressional committees in hearings and otherwise—and so will commonly be very familiar with the measure. When agency responses are received, the Legislative Reference Division has several days to prepare its own "enrolled bill memorandum" for the chief executive. In that memorandum will be the arguments advanced by the agencies for and against the bill, together with the Division's own analysis and recommendations. In the end the President must weigh all this argumentation in relation to his perception of the national interest, his programs and promises, his obligations, his party position, the counsels of staff and other close advisers, and so forth. Note that the lobbying pressures on the President and his advisers may be as intense at this point as they are at earlier critical points in the legislative process. Note also that the President with his national constituency and his own objectives and resources, brings to the decisional process still another perspective from that applied by the Senators and Representatives who have previously passed on it.

One way or another, the President must decide. Much of the time, the decision is to approve. The number of Presidential vetoes is not in fact very large in comparison to the total number of bills which are presented for signature and become law without exercise of the veto power. But the number of vetoes should not be taken as an index of the veto power's importance. The existence of the veto power and the threat of its possible use extend the President's influence throughout the legislative process. His position must be reckoned with by proponents and opponents at every stage. Here is one more center of power in the panorama of dispersed and divided powers that the Federal legislative processes offer to view. Here is one more opportunity to block action.

If the decision is to approve, and unless the President allows the bill to become law without his signature, there may be more or less elaborate signing ceremonies. Notice of the signing is generally sent by message to the chamber where the bill originated and that chamber informs the other. The action is noted in the Congressional Record.

If the President vetoes a bill, other than by "pocket veto," the bill and his veto message are, as we saw, returned to the chamber of origin. A vetoed bill returned to the Congress in this way is accorded high privilege (there is no need for recourse to the Rules Committee in the House) and will generally be disposed of quickly. Amendments are not in order; in the House, only a limited time is allowed for debate. If there is no real possibility the veto may be overridden, the bill may be tabled or sent back to committee. Otherwise the question is put, "Shall the bill pass, the objections of the President to the contrary notwithstanding?" To override the veto, each chamber must separately vote to do so by a vote of at least two-thirds of those present, a quorum being required to be on hand. A negative vote kills the bill and if it occurs in the first chamber a message is normally sent to the other advising of the decision that the bill is not to pass.

If the President signs the bill or allows it to become law without signature, or if the chambers vote to override a veto, then, as the case may be, the President or the chamber last voting to override will transmit the bill to the General Services Administration for publication. There, a public law number will be given to the bill (the public law number contains the number of the enacting Congress and a number indicating the order in which the bill was adopted as compared with other enactments by the same Congress). The bill is forthwith made available in published form. First, it is made available as a slip law in unbound pamphlet form printed by offset process from the enrolled bill. Later, this and other new laws will be published in bound volumes of the Statutes at Large, an official authoritative compilation containing the laws of each Congress in the chronological order of their enactment.

Later also, the bill will be incorporated in the United States Code, a compilation consolidating and codifying the general and permanent laws of the United States and arranging them by subject-matter under 50 titles. Congress's Office of the Law Revision Counsel transmutes the enacted statute at large into specific and segmented provisions of the U.S. Code; often left out altogether are important portions of the bill, such as the legislative findings and purposes—which may help to clarify the legislative purpose and intent of the statute.[15] Notwithstanding the possibility that portions of the statute may be lost in transmutation, for most lawyers, the Code is a much more readily usable research tool than the chronologically arranged Statutes at Large. Certain titles of the Code have been enacted into positive law in an ongoing codification effort; as to these titles the Code is the official and authoritative source of the statute law. The Statutes at Large and the Revised Statutes (an early compilation of the laws in force as of Dec. 1, 1873) remain the official and authoritative source, however, for laws not included in these titles. These versions of the bill—the slip law, the text in the Statutes at Large, the version in the U.S. Code—are primary sources for lawyers working with legislation. Other materials, such as veto or approval messages, may be of high importance as aids to understanding the bill, now a statute, when it comes before lawyers, courts or administrators for interpretation. Many of these materials are located on the Library of Congress's congress.gov website. This collection includes bills, resolutions, public laws, Senate and House Roll Call Votes, the Congressional Record, committee reports, and treaties.[16]

---

[15] *See* Jarrod Shobe, *Enacted Legislative Findings and Purposes*, 86 U. Chi. L. Rev. 669, 673 (2019).

[16] *See* http://congress.gov.

B. LEGISLATIVE ENACTMENT AND STATUTORY INTERPRETATION

The preceding traditional overview of the federal legislative process not only provides a glimpse into "how the sausage is made," but also bears on the work of lawyers and judges. This is because what one understands about the process of drafting and enacting a statute may inform how one interprets the resulting text. Political developments and contemporary scholarship, however, offer a more nuanced, not to say jaundiced portrait of the legislative process. As you review the following accounts, consider whether or how they should influence statutory interpretation.

1. ORTHODOX LAWMAKING: "VETOGATES," "LOGROLLING," AND CITIZEN LAWMAKING

Discussion of the President's veto power in the previous section provides one prominent example of the power a legislative actor may possess to stall or kill a bill. Numerous Madisonian "checks and balances" at both the federal and state levels characterize the American system of government. Such checks reduce the ease with which lawmakers can change the status quo by creating choke points that define the contours of legislative negotiations. The political science literature on institutional decisionmaking generally uses the terms "veto points," "veto players," and "vetogates" interchangeably; all three terms describe a person or institutional body that must consent in order for legislation to be passed.

a. VETOGATES

Many scholars emphasize that one way to understand the meaning of statutes is to examine the coalitions that enacted them; the vetogates through which the drafted bills had to pass; and the revealed preferences of legislators on the road to enactment:

> Our starting point is the analogy between legislation and contracts. In the case of legislation, parties to a statutory contract are the members of the legislative coalition that enacted the statute, and the contract is an agreement over public policy. . . . Positive political theory can make a significant contribution to overcoming the difficulties encountered in filling in gaps in the legislative contract, in part by focusing attention on several important features of the legislative process. One is a sharper conceptualization of the notion of "statutory intent." [We approach] the intent of a statute [as an effort to] to codify the agreement of the enacting coalition with respect to the policy adopted, in part so that members of the enacting coalition can know more precisely the nature of their agreement and in part to convey instructions to agencies and courts. Statutes are most assuredly not embodiments of the objectives of any particular person, but a compromise among numerous political actors. The

structure and process of legislative enactment allocate influence to the relevant actors (including the President) and sometimes accord greater weight to some over others, depending on the specific circumstances surrounding the legislation.

A positive political theory approach suggests that the major lines of compromise result from bargains among veto players in the legislative process. The preferences of veto players are most influential in determining policy bargains, and, therefore, their preferences must be ascertained in order to uncover the implicit agreement underlying the explicit statutory language.

A positive political theory approach also offers guidance in sorting out meaningful or sincere evaluations of legislative language from strategic or opportunistic posturing by legislators or the President. Positive theory provides an analytical framework for sorting through statements about a bill at various stages of the bargaining process to separate statements that are likely to reveal relevant information about the agreement of the enacting coalition from more opportunistic attempts by members to gain personal advantage in the way courts will interpret statutes after the fact.

We derive two general and several specific implications from our application of positive political theory to the problem of building a normative framework for statutory interpretation. First, positive political theory leads us to look at the structure of the legislative process—as embodied in the Constitution and in House and Senate rules—to identify veto gates. Not all coalition members are equally important in determining the content of legislation; positive political theory points to the members who control the various veto gates as crucial to understanding legislative intent. Second, positive political theory shows us that not all statements made by members of Congress and the President are created equal. When talk is cheap—when members of Congress or the President cannot be held accountable for their statements about a bill by members of the coalition—its information content is not reliable.

These two general points imply several specific interpretive canons. The first is that consequential statements and actions have priority over inconsequential ones. The second canon, following from the first, is that decisions by legislators to reject language provide useful negative inferences about statutes. The third canon is that the totality of the legislative history conveys important information about whose preferences were most consequential in shaping the coalitional agreement. That is, in the sequence of veto points through which a statute must pass, some are likely to be much closer calls than others, and at these stages the details of the coalitional agreement are most profoundly shaped. The fourth canon is that because the President has a constitutionally granted role in the legislative process, statutory interpretation must take the President's preferences into account and must accord them considerable weight if the President possessed a credible veto threat over the statute in question.

McNollGast, *Positive Canons: The Role of Legislative Bargains in Statutory Interpretation*, 80 Geo. L.J. 705 (1992).

At the federal level, Professor Bill Eskridge has highlighted the specific vetogates through which "a bill becomes a law":

The bicameralism and presentment requirements of Article I, Section 7 of the US Constitution provide the starting point for a comprehensive account of statutory enactment: a bill does not become a law unless it is accepted in the same form by (a) the House of Representatives, (b) the Senate, and (c) the President (unless his veto can be overridden by two-thirds of each chamber). The requirements of Article I, Section 7 are supplemented by Article I, Section 5, Clause 2, which provides that "[e]ach House may determine the Rules of its Proceedings."

Both the House and the Senate have adopted rules of their proceedings that create multiple opportunities in each chamber for opponents to kill proposed legislation. Combining Sections 5 and 7 of Article I yields a process that looks very complex indeed, with at least nine major points where bills can be vetoed, usually without the need to secure a majority vote against the bill. Consider this common scenario, where a bill originates in the House of Representatives.

Vetogate 1: House Committee. When a bill is introduced in the House, the Speaker must refer it to the appropriate committee (House Rule XII(2)). The committee chair decides whether to schedule hearings, markup sessions and even votes (House Rule XI(2)(c)). Although a majority of the committee's membership can compel the chair to schedule a bill, this rarely occurs. Hence, if the chair opposes the bill, believes more study is needed on the matter, or is pessimistic that the bill has sufficient political support down the road, the bill will die in committee.

Vetogate 2: House Rules Committee. A bill reported by a House committee will not be considered by the chamber unless the Rules Committee expedites its consideration through a special rule, voted upon by the full chamber. This traffic cop authority vests the Rules Committee with veto power similar to that of the substantive committee. In practice, the Rules Committee does the bidding of the Speaker of the House and so is typically an instrument by which the majority party dictates the House agenda. Thus, if the party leadership does not support the bill or, more likely, wants to press other matters ahead of this bill, then they can veto that bill through their control of the Rules Committee.

Vetogate 3: House Floor Consideration. On the floor of the House, a proposed bill faces new challenges. The most common challenge is that opponents will propose amendments that either weaken the bill or (less often) strengthen it so much that the bill will lose its majority support (killer amendments). Hence, even a measure that enjoys the support of a majority of the House may be either weakened or even defeated through the strategic deployment of amendments.

Vetogate 4: Senate Committee. The Senate Rules do not require the Majority Leader to refer bills to committee (Senate Rule XVII), but the Senate practice is to do so. As in the House, the chair of the relevant Senate committee (or subcommittee) can usually kill the bill, subject to petition by a majority of the committees members (Senate Rule XXVI(3)). So add this as another vetogate, where even measures with majority support can be delayed or even killed.

Vetogate 5: Unanimous Consent Agreement. Unlike the House, the Senate has no rules committee that recommends expedited scheduling. Instead, the Senate expedites bills and organizes their debate according to unanimous consent agreements negotiated by the Majority Leader (Senate Rule XII(4)). If one senator objects, of course, the agreement is not unanimous. Theoretically, one senator can kill or delay even major legislation, and a determined minority can usually do so.

Vetogate 6: Filibusters. Senators can often talk a bill to death through the now-notorious filibuster; filibusters may occur on motion to proceed with a bill, but the famous ones are those seeking to block final votes on bills. Under the Senates standing rules, as amended in 1975, 60 votes can cut off debate; conversely, a minority of 41 senators can and, with increasing frequency, do block legislation (Senate Rule XXII(2)).

Vetogate 7: Conference Committee. Article I, Section 7 requires that legislation be adopted in the same form by both chambers. Hence, any inconsistencies adopted by the second chamber must either be accepted by the first or must be resolved through a conference committee. Not only do conference committees edit out provisions that enjoyed majority support in one of the chambers, but in recent years, scholars have shown that such committees are deleting provisions adopted in both chambers.

Vetogate 8: Conference Bill Consideration by House and Senate. Even when conferees from the House and Senate reach agreement as to the final product, both chambers must vote for that product. Although few bills die at this stage, some do, either because time runs out in the congressional session or there are too many problems with the final product for a majority in one chamber to accept it.

Vetogate 9: Presentment to the President. Under Article I, Section 7, once presented with an enrolled bill, the President has 10 days (not including Sundays) to sign it or veto it. If the President vetoes the bill, it is returned to Congress, where the veto can be overridden by two-thirds of those voting in each chamber. If the veto is overridden, the bill then becomes law without the President's signature. The most common scenario is one in which the President's veto is followed by congressional adjustment of the proposed legislation, either to accommodate the President or to secure votes needed to override the veto or both.

Although one would expect greater party polarization to result in gridlock during periods of divided or closely contested government, as has been characteristic of this country, polarization sometimes makes legislation easier, but only if the two parties can reach agreement on what to enact. Thus, the hurdles for major legislation have often been reduced through deals worked out by congressional, executive, and/or party officials through legislator-executive "summits," as well as legislative caucuses or conference committees. What political scientist Barbara Sinclair [has] call[ed] "unorthodox lawmaking" allows many pieces of important legislation (especially budgetary and tax legislation) to bypass one or more vetogates. Combine Sinclair's insight with the changes in the House and the Senate, and the operative vetogates model for most major legislation after 1980 is a simpler one involving three preference points: the consensus position of the party controlling the House, the filibuster median in the Senate, and the President. . . .

William N. Eskridge Jr., *Vetogates and American Public Law*, 31 J. Law, Econ. & Org. 756 (2012).

As Professor Eskridge notes, in highly partisan environments, fewer (but more significant) vetogates restrict the path of legislative enactment. Similar vetogates operate at the state level; in particular, many states have supermajority rules for the passage of budgets or any legislation that raises taxes. These rules, like the filibuster in the U.S. Senate, can enable a minority party to block policy changes supported by a clear majority. For example, from 1933 to 2010 California had a supermajority requirement for the passage of its state budget, which created a minority-party vetogate and enabled minority-party legislators to impede passage of the state budget; not coincidentally, during this period California experienced several crippling government shutdowns when partisan squabbling led to both sides digging in and refusing to compromise. Vetogates are thus both a feature and a bug: they ensure that legislation is not enacted with undue haste, but they also make the legislative process more susceptible to negotiation failure.

b. LOGROLLING AND OTHER DYNAMICS IN LEGISLATIVE NEGOTIATIONS

Failure to enact legislation depends in large part on legislators' comfort with the status quo. Thus, one must also be mindful of the presence or absence of what one of this Casebook's co-authors has described as legislative "default rules." In legal fields like contracts and property, default rules operate to fill gaps in incomplete agreements and serve as the baseline outcome that contracting parties must negotiate to alter. The party more comfortable with the default outcome has an inherent advantage in negotiations, for they have less incentive to negotiate around the default.

As in contract and property law, default rules also exist in legislation: most enacted legislation remains in place indefinitely absent subsequent amendment or judicial overturning. Two notable exceptions exist, however. First, legislatures sometimes enact what are known as "sunset laws," temporary statutes that stipulate a fixed expiration date. Second, the vast majority of appropriations legislation lacks defaults; when a state or federal budget expires, no default rules exist to prevent at least a partial government shutdown in the absence of continued funding.

Two political science models of legislative negotiations—the logrolling model and the game-of-chicken model—capture how coalition dynamics in legislative negotiations can affect the path for how a bill becomes a law, and also how the status quo may affect bargaining positions. The following excerpt highlights these dynamics in the budgetmaking context, although similar dynamics apply to all legislative efforts:

> Of the two major political-science models of legislative negotiations, the logrolling model probably best describes the majority of legislative negotiations over the course of United States history. In particular, the logrolling model tends to describe legislative negotiations more accurately when minority party discipline is weak and when a majority party coalition is relatively easy to assemble. In order to pass a budget under the logrolling model, the majority coalition offers enticements to swing members of the majority party as well as moderate members of the minority party in order to induce them to support the majority coalition's budget. Since individual

legislators represent their geographic regions and not just their parties, the majority coalition can induce compromise by offering "pork" for legislators' home districts. The resulting budget will thus usually be a compromise between the preferences of the majority party leadership and the preferences of the most centrist members of both the majority and minority parties.

Under this model, the majority party leadership's influence often depends on how easily it can assemble a coalition amongst party members. It also depends on how cohesive the interests of the minority party members are, and whether the intensity of preference among them is weak enough that the majority can offer sufficient concessions to obtain agreement. If the majority party leadership has multiple prospective coalition partners among the centrist members of the majority and minority parties, then the majority party leadership may pass a budget closer to its true preference. Conversely, if the majority party leadership must secure the votes of nearly every potential swing vote, then it may be forced to agree to many of these legislators' demands.

In times of divided government, the key to successful logrolling will typically be the moderate members of the minority party; these legislators might be enticed to vote with the majority party coalition in order to get a modified version of the majority's budget through the chamber controlled by the minority party. For instance, the contrasts between the repeal of the "Don't Ask, Don't Tell" policy and the passage of the ACA are instructive recent examples of the differences between logrolling when there are many moderate minority party members to choose from, and logrolling when the majority coalition has almost no options from which to pick. Ahead of the repeal of Don't Ask, Don't Tell in the fall of 2010, Senate Democrats needed to win over only a handful of moderate Republicans amongst a number of possible choices to achieve a cloture-proof 60-member supermajority coalition. Once a filibuster-proof coalition had been assembled, several additional moderate Republicans ultimately joined the vote anyway, likely so they could be part of a seemingly inevitable winning coalition. In contrast, uniform Republican opposition to the ACA forced Democrats to pass the bill without a single Republican vote in the Senate. Democrats had to achieve unanimous support among their caucus of 60 to overcome cloture, requiring significant concessions to the most centrist members of their own party to form the coalition. . . .

The repeal of Don't Ask, Don't Tell teaches that when minority party discipline is weak and individual members of the minority party vote based on their own preferences, the majority party can usually entice some members of the minority to form a coalition without significant concessions. This can be especially true of budget making, since the process consists of numerous smaller policy choices ... among many different programs. Individual politicians will have far stronger preferences about some fiscal policy choices than others, so when minority party discipline is weak, the majority party can usually form a coalition to pass a budget.

In contrast to the logrolling model, the game-of-chicken model tends to describe negotiations when minority party discipline is strong, and vetogates necessitate at least some minority party support. If the majority party cannot entice a sufficient number of centrist members of the minority parties to break ranks, then the majority party may need to negotiate with the leadership of the minority party itself in the hope of forging a bipartisan compromise budget. Party-line voting can thus turn budget negotiations into a partisan game of chicken where neither party can peel away enough members of the opposition in order to form a coalition capable of passing a budget without the cooperation of the other party's leadership. Budget negotiations that follow the game-of-chicken model are far more likely to result in negotiation failure because compromise outcomes are more difficult to achieve. Even if every player would prefer a compromise to the default outcome, they may still fail to reach a compromise, triggering the default in spite of their preferences. . . .

David Scott Louk and David Gamage, *Preventing Government Shutdowns: Designing Default Rules for Budgets*, 86 U. Colo. L. Rev. 181 (2015).

Given these dynamics, appropriations legislation thus can be an especially fraught setting for legislative negotiation, because individual legislators can attach unrelated substantive amendments (known as riders) to "must pass" appropriations bills in order to secure their vote, effectively holding the majority coalition hostage. While logrolling negotiations generally present a lower risk of negotiation failure, logrolling is still susceptible to the accumulation of unpopular legislative amendments, because individual legislators can extract concessions favorable to their constituencies but unfavorable to the majority of voters in order to get their support for a bill.

c.   SINGLE SUBJECT RULES AND THE LEGISLATIVE PROCESS

In recognition of the unwanted legislative consequences that stem from logrolling and game-of-chicken negotiations, numerous states have enacted "single subject rules" into their state constitutions that require that any enacted piece of legislation concerns only a single subject. Easily justified in theory, single subject rules prove difficult to enforce in practice, in large part because what constitutes a "single subject' is open to significant debate. The following case, *Commonwealth v. Neiman*, highlights the difficulties state courts encounter when interpreting the ambit of a statute and in policing the boundaries of a single legislative subject.

Commonwealth v. Neiman
Supreme Court of Pennsylvania, 2013.
624 Pa. 53, 84 A.3d 603 (2013).

■ JUSTICE TODD. [JUSTICES SAYLOR, EAKIN, BAER, and MCCAFFERY join the opinion.]

In this appeal, we consider whether Act 152 of 2004 ("Act 152"), which makes various amendments to the Judicial Code, violates the "single subject" rule of Article III, Section 3 of the Pennsylvania Constitution .... For reasons detailed at greater length herein, we conclude that Act 152 does violate Article III, Section 3, since its various provisions do not all relate to a single unifying subject. . . .

I.   Background

We begin with a discussion of the legislative history of Act 152, as it is necessary to understand the basis of the constitutional questions at issue. The legislation which ultimately became Act 152 of 2004 originated in the Pennsylvania State Senate on January 29, 2003 with the introduction of Senate Bill 92 of 2003, P.N. 0091. ("S.B. 92, P.N. 91"). This eight-page bill had two sections amending Section 8103 of the Judicial Code, 42 Pa.C.S.A. § 8103, governing deficiency judgment procedures in the courts of common pleas after an execution sale of real property. The first section set a six-month statute of limitations for certain judgment creditors or debtors to file a valuation petition for real property purchased at an execution sale, while the second section established, *inter alia,* deficiency judgment procedures when parcels of real property are located in more than one county. This bill was passed by the Senate Judiciary Committee on February 11, 2003, and, thereafter, was considered by the full Senate three separate times, with final passage in the Senate occurring on March 5, 2003.

S.B. 92, P.N. 91 was then sent to the House of Representatives, and, after being approved by the House Judiciary Committee without amendment, it was considered twice by the full House. After the second consideration, S.B. 92, P.N. 91 was referred to the House Appropriations Committee, which re-reported it on July 15, 2003, without amendment, for final consideration by the full House. However, during its final consideration on the House floor, the bill was amended to add two sections, one creating a separate chapter in Title 42 to govern eviction proceedings between landlords and tenants, and another section amending the Municipal Police Jurisdiction Act to establish the jurisdiction of county park police in counties of the third class. This altered legislation was redesignated S.B. 92, P.N. 1105. The full House voted to pass this version of the bill on July 15, 2003, and it was sent to the Senate for further consideration.

The bill remained in the Senate Rules Committee from July 17, 2003 until May 11, 2004, whereupon the committee made two alterations to the bill, changing its listing of sponsoring senators and changing the chapter and statutory designations for the proposed landlord/tenant act. The Rules Committee reported the altered version, now numbering 21 pages, to the full Senate as S.B. 92, P.N. 1614, which, in turn, recommitted it back to the Rules Committee on May 17, 2004.

After this recommitment, the bill underwent significant revision. Although the Rules Committee retained the aforementioned provisions related to deficiency judgments and county park police jurisdiction, it deleted all of the landlord-tenant chapters, redesignated the bill S.B. 92, P.N. 1995, and added 15 new sections—spanning 38 additional pages—which accomplished the following substantive legal changes: (1) established a two-year limitation for asbestos actions; (2) amended the Crimes Code to create various criminal offenses for individuals subject to sexual offender registration requirements who fail to comply; (3) amended the provisions of the Sentencing Code which govern "Registration of Sexual Offenders"; (4) added the offenses of luring and institutional sexual assault to the list of enumerated offenses which require a 10-year period of registration and established local police notification procedures for out-of-state sexual offenders who move to Pennsylvania; (5) directed the creation of a searchable computerized database of all registered sexual offenders ("database"); (6) amended the duties of the Sexual Offenders Assessment Board ("SOAB"); (7) allowed a sentencing court to exempt a lifetime sex offender registrant, or a sexually violent predator registrant, from inclusion in the database after 20 years if certain conditions are met; (8) established mandatory registration and community notification procedures for sexually violent predators; (9) established community notification requirements for a "common interest community"—such as a condominium or cooperative— of the presence of a registered sexually violent predator; (10) conferred immunity on unit owners' associations of a common interest community for good faith distribution of information obtained from the database; (11) directed the Pennsylvania State Police to publish a list of approved registration sites to collect and transmit fingerprints and photographs of all sex offenders who register at those sites; and (12) mandated the Pennsylvania Attorney General to conduct annual performance audits of state or local agencies who participate in the administration of Megan's Law, and, also, required registered sex offenders to submit to fingerprinting and being photographed when registering at approved registration sites. S.B. 92, P.N. 1995 was reported out of the Rules

Committee on November 19, 2004 and approved by the full Senate that same day.

S.B. 92, P.N. 1995 was sent to the House on November 20, 2004, and that body voted to approve it on that date. The bill was sent to then-Governor Rendell who signed it on November 24, 2004, at which time it became Act 152 of 2004.

Appellant's criminal prosecution giving rise to this appeal originated after Act 152 became law, and its provisions were applied by the trial court therein. In October 2005, Appellant was arrested for various sexual offenses against two young girls—ages 7 and 10—committed over a two-year period from 2003–2005. Appellant proceeded to a jury trial on those charges and was convicted on March 8, 2007, after which the trial court ordered Appellant to be assessed by the SOAB. . . . At his sentencing hearing, the trial court . . . and sentenced him to an aggregate sentence of 13½ to 27 years imprisonment. The trial court further ruled that Appellant was a sexually violent predator and, thus, the sex offender registration and reporting provisions of Act 152 applied to him.

Appellant filed a timely notice of appeal [and raised] . . . . a claim that the legislature's passage of Act 152 violated Article III, Section 3 of the Pennsylvania Constitution because it contained multiple topics which were not germane to a single subject. . . . The trial court rejected this claim, finding that "the provisions of [Act 152] are sufficiently related and germane to a single subject, the amendments of [Title 42]." On appeal to the Superior Court, that tribunal deemed Appellant's Article III, Section 3 challenge sufficiently important to certify for *en banc* review, and, ultimately, ruled . . . Act 152 violated Article III, Section 3. In reaching its decision, the court extensively discussed our Court's rulings in *City of Philadelphia v. Com.*, 575 Pa. 542 (2003) ("*City of Philadelphia* ") (holding that, in order to ascertain whether legislation violates Article III, Section 3, the various provisions added during the legislative process must be examined to determine if they are germane to the overarching subject of the legislation) and *Pennsylvanians Against Gambling Expansion Fund Inc. v. Com.*, 583 Pa. 275, 877 A.2d 383 (2005) ("*PAGE*") (concluding that the majority of the provisions of the Gaming Act did not violate single subject rule of Article III, Section 3, since they were germane to one subject—the regulation of gaming; however, provisions that were not germane to the subject of gaming were stricken). Pursuant to the principles articulated in these cases, the court . . . . opined that there was "little relationship" between the amendments to Megan's Law and the provisions of Act 152 amending the deficiency judgment statutes, nor, in the court's view, was there any apparent way to harmonize the other subjects of the bill involving the establishment of statutes of limitations and county police jurisdiction. Following the issuance of the Superior Court's decision, the General Assembly applied to the Superior Court for permission to intervene for the purpose of defending the constitutionality of Act 152 .... Subsequently, Appellant petitioned for allowance of appeal, which we granted. . . .

II. Single Subject Rule of Article III, Section 3

We begin by addressing the question of whether Act 152 violates Article III, Section 3 of the Pennsylvania Constitution. Appellant, reciting the extensive transformation and expansion of Act 152 during the legislative process described above, argues that its various final provisions amending Megan's Law, deficiency judgment procedures, county park police jurisdiction, and the statute of limitations for asbestos claims "have no unifying relationship such that they can be brought into a common focus." Appellant notes that the Superior Court also could discern no substantial relationship between the dissimilar topics of these amendments. Appellant analogizes Act 152 to the legislation struck down by our Court in *City of Philadelphia,* which, likewise, significantly expanded from its initial form to final passage to include a wide variety of divergent topics. Appellant contends that this lack of germaneness of Act 152's differing provisions to a single subject renders the entirety of the act violative of Article III, Section 3.

Appellee, the Commonwealth, responds by highlighting the fact that each of the provisions of Act 152 offer civil remedies. Specifically, it notes that the Megan's Law amendments provide a civil remedy to the Commonwealth by allowing monitoring of sexually violent offenders. The deficiency judgment and asbestos claim sections establish time periods and procedures for civil suits seeking relief, and the portion delineating the jurisdiction of county police expands civil remedies by allowing officers acting outside of this established jurisdiction to be potentially subjected to lawsuits for their actions. The Commonwealth thus posits that all of these provisions are germane to the single subject of "refining civil remedies," and, as a result, Appellant cannot carry his heavy burden of proof to overcome the presumption of the act's constitutionality.

The General Assembly argues that Act 152 complies with Article III, Section 3 since all of its provisions relate to the "single subject of judicial remedies and sanctions." The General Assembly posits that the Megan's Law amendments imposing the public registration obligation are remedial, and so too are the deficiency judgment procedures and the statute of limitations provision for asbestos-related claims, since both establish set processes by which litigants can pursue judicial remedies. The General Assembly asserts that the portions of Act 152 setting county park police jurisdiction are related to the Megan's Law amendments because municipal police are sometimes called upon to participate in the administration of the provisions of Megan's Law, as they are the recipients of information from the state police regarding the address of the residence, place of employment or school of registered sex offenders and must also provide notifications to the public regarding the presence of a sexually violent predator in their neighborhood. . . .

In conducting our review, we are guided by the principle that "acts passed by the General Assembly are strongly presumed to be constitutional, including the manner in which they were passed." *Pennsylvania State Ass'n of Jury Comm'rs v. Com.*, 64 A.3d 611, 618 (Pa.2013). Thus, a statute will not be found unconstitutional "unless it clearly, palpably, and plainly violates the Constitution." *Id.* If there is any doubt as to whether a challenger has met this high burden, then we will resolve that doubt in favor of the statute's constitutionality. *Id.*

As our Court has emphasized, the single subject rule of Article III, Section 3 was first included by the framers of our Commonwealth's organic charter in 1864, and then readopted as part of the 1874 Constitution, in order to effectuate "the electorate's overall goal of curtailing legislative practices that it viewed with suspicion." *City of Philadelphia,* 575 Pa. at 574. In particular, there were two legislative practices the framers and the electorate sought to eliminate with their adoption of Article III, Section 3. The first involved the insertion into a single bill of a number of distinct and independent subjects of legislation in order to deliberately hide the real purpose of the bill. [*PAGE*], 583 Pa. at 295. The second was the practice of "logrolling" which involves "embracing in one bill several distinct matters, none of which could singly obtain the assent of the legislature, and procuring its passage by combining the minorities who favored the individual matters to form a majority that would adopt them all." *City of Philadelphia,* 575 Pa. at 575.

Our Court has additionally observed that Article III, Section 3 serves other salutary purposes furthering the efficiency of the legislative process. The requirement that each piece of legislation pertain to only one subject creates a greater likelihood that it will receive a more considered and thorough review by legislators than if it is aggregated with other pieces of legislation pertaining to different topics into a singular "omnibus bill," thereby creating a "jumbling together of incongruous subjects." [Citations.] Additionally, and significantly, "the single subject requirement proscribe[s] the inclusion of provisions into legislation without allowing for 'fair notice to the public and to legislators of the existence of the same.' " *PAGE,* 583 Pa. at 295. It, thus, provides a vital assurance to residents of this Commonwealth that they will be able to make their views and wishes regarding a particular piece of legislation known to their duly elected representatives its final passage, and it concomitantly ensures that those representatives will be adequately apprised of the full scope and impact of a legislative measure before being required to cast a vote on it.

Accordingly, our Court has interpreted Article III, Section 3 as mandating that a final bill enacted by the General Assembly meet two specific criteria: "First, the title of the bill must clearly express the substance of the proposed law. . . . Second, the differing topics within the bill must be 'germane' to each other." *Jury Comm'rs,* 64 A.3d at 616. Presently, Appellant does not assert that the title of Act 152 does not adequately give notice of its contents; rather, the crux of his challenge is that Act 152 did not meet the second portion of this test, *i.e.*, that the various subjects of Act 152 were not germane to a single subject.

In determining "germaneness," our Court has acknowledged that some degree of deference to the General Assembly's prerogative to amend legislation is required, due to the normal fluidity inherent in the legislative process, and, thus, we have deemed it is appropriate for a reviewing court to hypothesize a "reasonably broad topic" which would unify the various provisions of a final bill as enacted. *City of Philadelphia,* 575 Pa. at 577. However, our Court has also stressed the "reasonable" aspect of any proposed hypothetical unifying topic, in recognition of the fact that Article III, Section 3 would be rendered nugatory if such hypothetical topics were too expansive. *PAGE,* 583 Pa. at 296. We observed that, "no two subjects are so wide apart that they may not be brought into a common focus, if the point of view be carried back far enough." [Citation.] Consequently, in determining whether a proposed unifying subject is sufficiently narrow so as to pass muster under Article III, Section 3, our Court must examine the various subjects contained within a legislative enactment and determine whether they have a nexus to a common purpose. Stated another way, our task is to ascertain whether the various components of the enactment are part of "a unifying scheme to accomplish a single purpose." *City of Philadelphia,* 575 Pa. at 579.

In this regard, the mere fact that a piece of legislation amends a particular title of the Pennsylvania Consolidated Statutes, as in *City of Philadelphia,* or amends a particular article of a codified body of statutes such as the County Code, like the legislation in *Jury Comm'rs,* will not automatically fulfill the requirements of Article III, Section 3, as our rulings in those cases established. Thus, in the case at bar, the Superior Court properly determined that, merely because all of the various components of Act 152 amended "Title 42," this does not establish its compliance with Article III, Section 3.

Likewise, the proposed unifying subjects for Act 152 offered by the Commonwealth ("refining civil remedies or relief") and the General Assembly ("judicial remedies and sanctions") are far too expansive to satisfy Article III, Section 3, as such subjects are virtually boundless in that they could encompass, respectively, civil court proceeding which could be brought in the courts of this Commonwealth, and power of the judiciary to impose sanctions on, or order the payment of damages by, a party to civil litigation. We therefore decline to endorse such broad suggested topics, as they would have the effect of "render[ing] the safeguards of [Article III,] Section 3 inert." *PAGE,* 583 Pa. at 296.

Further, upon considered reflection, we cannot discern any other common nexus for the myriad disparate provisions of Act 152, inasmuch as we can see no reasonable basis under which deficiency judgment procedures, asbestos statutes of limitations, county police jurisdiction, and sexual offender registration requirements act together as "a unifying scheme to accomplish a single purpose." *City of Philadelphia.* Because there is simply no common focus to all of Act 152's provisions, this case presents a situation akin to that which existed in our decisions in *City of Philadelphia* and *Jury Comm'rs,* in which we rejected, in turn, the proposed unifying subjects of "municipalities" and "powers of county commissioners" as being too broad, and, thus, violative of the single subject rule. As a result, we are constrained to conclude that Act 152 clearly, palpably, and plainly violates Article III, Section 3 of the Constitution and, consequently, we affirm the Superior Court's ruling in this regard. . . .

Accordingly, the order of the Superior Court is hereby reversed and the entirety of Act 152 is stricken as violative of Article III, Section 3 of our Constitution. . . .

■ CHIEF JUSTICE CASTILLE files a dissenting opinion.

The Majority Opinion provides a reasonable analysis of the constitutional issue presented herein. Nevertheless, while I find the question of single subject legislation to be close, I respectfully believe that the Act in question is not so clearly, plainly and palpably unconstitutional that the presumption of constitutionality attending its passage has been defeated. Hence, I respectfully dissent. My reasons follow. . . . Mindful of the highly deferential nature of our review, I would hold that the various provisions of Act 152 are germane to the subject of refining civil remedies, a category that is sufficiently narrow for the purposes of the single-subject rule. Thus, in my view, the law, as enacted by the General Assembly, does not violate Article III, Section 3 of the Pennsylvania Constitution.

Initially, I recognize that the general purpose of Article III is to encourage open, deliberative, and accountable government by placing procedural restraints on the legislative process. The provision was born of a desire to curb prior legislative abuses. Thus, one of the purposes that Section 3 of Article III serves is to restrain "log-rolling" in its several forms, including the practice of drafting one bill whose passage is procured by combining several distinct minority-supported matters to form a majority that would adopt them all, or the practice of attaching to a popular bill certain to pass riders that would not become law standing on their own. *City of Philadelphia v. Commonwealth,* 575 Pa. 5426 (2003). To some degree, however, any law passing through the enactment process is the result of salutary legislative compromise and the single-subject rule is not intended to completely discourage such compromise. The dangers that Article III, Section 3 seeks to avoid are the passage of intentionally disguised or hidden legislation, of legislation that serves special interests and does not reflect the will of the majority, as expressed through their elected representatives. "Also, a bill addressing a single topic is more likely to obtain a considered review than one addressing many subjects." *Id.*

Striking the balance between fidelity to the intent and purpose of Article III, Section 3 and allowing legislative processes to operate reasonably unimpeded has proven complicated. As the Court described in *City of Philadelphia,* Article III, Section 3 jurisprudence has undergone a certain ebb and flow since the beginning of the Twentieth Century. 838 A.2d at 587–88. In more recent expressions, the Court has recognized that, to have meaning, procedural limitations such as those in Section 3 of Article III must set reasonable restrictions on the breadth of topics covered in a bill "as otherwise virtually all legislation, no matter how diverse in substance, would meet the single-subject requirement." [Citations.] But, to be reasonable, the restrictions must also include sufficient flexibility to avoid "pedantic" management of the General Assembly's labors and permit efficiency and compromise in the legislative process. [Citations.] . . .

In light of these considerations, while I find the question to be exceedingly close, I do not believe that Act 152 clearly, plainly and palpably violates the single subject restriction. Initially, I accept the explanations of the Commonwealth and of the General Assembly that refinement of civil remedies, in the present context, is a sufficiently narrow legislative topic. The topic encompasses a manageable category of issues selected for inclusion and outlined in the Judicial Code. That the law amends primarily one title is not, of course, dispositive of the inquiry—as the Majority concludes also. Nevertheless, this fact is relevant to our inquiry because the very reason Pennsylvania laws are consolidated within the same title is because they generally have some close kinship. Moreover, it is not beyond cavil that the General Assembly would seek to remedy perceived gaps within the topic of statutory civil remedies at one time, via the same statute, for the purposes of efficiency and in order to ensure consistency.

I recognize that the issue of refining civil remedies may not be as narrow as "gaming" was in the context of the Court's decision in *PAGE,* but, at least in my view, neither is it as broad as the topic of "municipalities" was in the context of the decision in *City of Philadelphia* or the topic of "powers of county commissioners" was in the context of the decision in *Jury Commissioners.* Thus, in *City of Philadelphia,* the Court held that the subject of "municipalities" was too broad where used to describe provisions as different as restricting the political activities of police officers; authorizing parking authorities to undertake mixed-use development projects; imposing a citizenship requirement for board members of business improvement districts; transferring authority over Philadelphia's taxis and limousines from the Public Utility Commission to the Philadelphia Parking Authority; repealing Section 209(k) of the Pennsylvania Intergovernmental Cooperation Authority Act; and authorizing municipalities to hold gifts in trust. 838 A.2d at 589. In *Jury Commissioners,* the Court held that the subject "powers of county commissioners" was defined too broadly where it included permitting certain counties to abolish the office of jury commissioner; authorizing imposition of an excise tax on the rental of motor vehicles by counties of the first class; providing for regional renaissance initiatives; and creating procedures for commissioners of counties of the third through eighth class to sell personal property and surplus farm products. 64 A.3d at 613 n. 1. Meanwhile, the topic of "gaming" was deemed appropriate by the unanimous Court in *PAGE,* where it included creation of the Gaming Control Board; establishment of policies and procedures for gaming licenses for the installation and operation of slot machines; provisions to assist Pennsylvania's horse racing industry through other gaming; and provisions for administration and enforcement of the gaming law. 877 A.2d at 396.

Act 152 has nineteen sections; of these, Sections 2 and 5 add a period of limitations for the commencement of a civil action to the procedure for execution of deficiency judgments otherwise addressed in Sections 8103 and 5522 of the Judicial Code, and amend Section 8103 to address primarily deficiency judgments in relation to collateral located in more than one county. Sections 3 and 4 delete and add, respectively, a period of limitations for the commencement of a civil action to the procedure for recovering damages for injury caused by exposure to asbestos. Section 6 amends the definition of "primary jurisdiction," in relation to police officers. Finally, Sections 1 and 7 through 19 amend Megan's Law registration requirements—a civil regulatory scheme—and create criminal sanctions to enforce the requirements of that regulatory scheme. The Megan's Law provisions address registration requirements, assessment, verification, and notification procedures, and distributions of responsibility for the administration of the Megan's Law notification system.

On the available spectrum, I find that the question of refining civil remedies, as defined in the present case, certainly is broad, but not unreasonably so, particularly in view of our precedent. All nineteen provisions of Act 152 amend aspects of existing categories of civil remedies, remedies that are already part of the Judicial Code. The Judicial Code supplies the outside parameters for which judicial remedies and what aspects of these remedies the statute addresses. Accordingly, in my view, the subject of refining judicial remedies—in the context of the statute before us—is not "boundless" as the Majority holds. Moreover, each of the component parts of Act 152 is germane to the subject so described. Two provisions amend definitions of terms for the purposes of the Judicial Code; several of the provisions describe periods of limitation for commencing particular types of actions; and the remaining provisions undertake substantial reconstruction of civil remedy schemes, including by creating a related enforcement mechanism within the Criminal Code.

Reasonable minds could certainly differ on the question of whether Act 152 exceeds the limits of the single-subject doctrine. Ultimately, however, mindful of the constitutional presumption and the requirement that the provision must stand unless it clearly, plainly and palpably violated the Constitution, I would uphold the constitutionality of Act 152 as against this Article III, Section 3 single-subject challenge.

NOTES AND QUESTIONS

1.   The majority rejects the argument that because Act 152 amended only Title 42 of Pennsylvania's Consolidated Statutes ("Judiciary and Judicial Procedure"), it concerns a single subject. Why shouldn't legislation that amends only a single title of a state code be considered *per se* evidence that it concerns only a single subject? Does it matter that Title 42 sets out rules of judicial procedure that apply to a wide array of distinct and substantive legislative provisions?

2.   The dissent in *Neiman* notes that one purpose for Pennsylvania's single subject rule is to police efforts to subvert the legislative process by disguising or hiding legislation serving special interests. Based on the majority's review of the legislative history, is Act 152 susceptible to such accusations? To the degree this is the chief evil the single subject rule seeks to prevent, should courts focus more on a statute's legislative process and history than on whether its contents form a tidy single subject? Can you think of circumstances where seemingly disparate provisions may be enacted in good faith in the form of a single statute?

3.   As with most states' single subject rules, Pennsylvania's rule appears premised in part on the idea that logrolling is a preventable ailment of the legislative process. Yet as the dissent notes, not all agree with this dim view of logrolling; indeed, as Professor Michael Gilbert has argued, logrolling may be a salutary aspect of the legislative process:

> The single subject rule was designed to: (1) prevent "logrolling," the process of combining multiple proposals, some or all of which command only minority support, into an omnibus bill that will receive majority support; (2) eliminate "riders," unpopular provisions that are attached to otherwise popular bills; and (3) improve political transparency, both for citizens and politicians. . . . [But] logrolling results from exchange; legislators trade votes to garner support for their favored provisions. This process always leaves a majority of legislators better off, though it may cause severe harm to a minority. In contrast, riders do not result from exchange but rather a manipulation of legislative procedures. Well-placed legislators can attach self-serving measures to otherwise popular bills, and they need not offer anything to the measures' opponents. Consequently, riding always leaves a majority of legislators worse off, though it may yield a significant benefit to a minority. Finally, . . . confining acts to a single subject can cut against political transparency[, because r]igidly separating bills can make it difficult to grasp the compromises that underpin legislation.

... [T]he single subject rule should not be used to prevent logrolling. Logrolls can be socially beneficial or harmful, and courts cannot possibly filter one from the other on a case-by-case basis. Doing so would require more information than courts will ever possess. A better approach is to adopt a presumption for or against logrolling and apply it in every case. . . . [L]ogrolling tends to be beneficial and . . . judicial intervention in this area causes more harm than good.

In contrast to logrolling, riding should be eliminated under the auspices of the single subject rule. As with logrolls, riders can be socially beneficial or harmful, and courts cannot reliably distinguish one from the other. The solution to this problem is to adopt a presumption for or against riders and apply it consistently. . . . [R]iding tends to be deleterious, and the presumption against it in single subject jurisprudence is appropriate.

To operationalize these concepts, I . . . develop a test that enables judges to distinguish logrolling from riding. In brief, the test instructs judges to parse a statute challenged on single subject grounds into its "functionally related" components. Courts must then ask the following question about each component: assuming all legislators adhere to their promises, if this component were removed and voted upon separately, would it receive majority support? If the answer is no, the component is a rider, and the bill violates the single subject rule. The basic insight is that independently popular measures and components of a logroll always command majority support. Therefore, they will always pass the test. Riders, on the other hand, never command majority support and will fail.

The test further requires courts to consider whether the bill's title captures all of the issues that it touches upon. These considerations are captured by the following definition of a single subject: A bill can be said to embrace but one subject when all of its components command majority support due to their individual merits or legislative bargaining and the title gives notice of the bill's contents.

Michael D. Gilbert, *Single Subject Rules and the Legislative Process*, 67 U. Pitt. L. Rev. 803 (2006).

Based on what you know about its legislative history, would the Pennsylvania law in question in *Neiman* pass this test? Does its title seem accurately to describe its contents? Do you share Professor Gilbert's view that only riders—but not logrolling—are unfavorable consequences of the legislative process?

2. UNORTHODOX LAWMAKING

The traditional legislative process, where legislators logroll and negotiate to achieve a bill acceptable to the majority coalition as well as moderate members of the minority coalition, might be called the "orthodox," or *Schoolhouse Rock!* version of how a bill becomes a law. In some states, as well as at the federal level, the *Schoolhouse Rock!* legislative environment has given way to forms of *unorthodox* lawmaking, a term first coined by political scientist Barbara Sinclair.[17] Unorthodox lawmaking not only has consequences for positive political science theories, but also for theories of statutory drafting and interpretation, as legal scholars have noted. Unorthodox lawmaking takes many forms:

> The Patient Protection and Affordable Care Act of 2010 (ACA) is a 2700-page statute worked on by five congressional committees; it delegates not to a single federal agency but to multiple federal agencies, as well as to states, quasi-public actors, and an independent commission, to which it outsourced the controversial question of cutting Medicare. The Supreme Court recently called it "inartful[ly] drafted" and lacking "the type of care and deliberation that one might expect of such significant legislation." . . .

> In December 2014, Congress enacted a $1.104 trillion spending bill to avert a government shutdown. . . . Among them was a provision that quietly undid a controversial mandate in the Dodd-Frank Act—with "no hearings, . . . and no chance for debate . . . in the last days of a lame-duck Congress."

> And so it seems that the *Schoolhouse Rock!* cartoon version of the conventional legislative process is dead. It may never have accurately described the lawmaking process in the first place. . . . Just as the now-textbook 1970s model was once itself revolutionary, ours is again a world of . . . "unorthodox lawmaking" . . . . These unorthodoxies are everywhere and they are not exceptions. They are the *new* textbook process. . . . [I]t would be a return to the *Schoolhouse Rock!* fiction to fail to appreciate the sheer variety of deviations from the textbook process that fall under the general umbrella of unorthodox policymaking. Omnibus bills and rules are different from emergency bills and rules; both are different from unorthodox delegations; and so on. . . .

> **[1. Omnibus Bills:]** Omnibus legislation is the most familiar type of unorthodox lawmaking . . . . From a statutory interpretation standpoint, omnibus bills pose particular challenges for common doctrinal assumptions of legislative perfection: These are often long and messy bills. They may have errors or linguistic inconsistencies that statutory interpretation doctrine does not usually tolerate. Legislative history for

---

[17] *See* Barbara Sinclair, Unorthodox Lawmaking: New Legislative Processes in the U.S. Congress (1st ed. 1997)

omnibus bills also is often outdated, because parts of such bills often are drafted years before—as part of earlier, failed bills that later are bundled into an omnibus package as part of a bigger deal. Sometimes omnibus legislative history is simply nonexistent, because many omnibus bills bypass the committee stage, where reports are typically produced. . . .

There is no single definition of omnibus legislation, but there is consensus that legislation that "packages together several measures into one or combines diverse subjects into a single bill" fits the label, as do so-called "money bills," including omnibus appropriations bills and budget bills. Some experts, including Sinclair, add to this definition legislation that is "usually highly complex and long" and that takes on numerous issues, even within a single subject area—for example the 800-page Clean Air Act and the 2,700-page health reform statute, the ACA. Omnibus legislation has "proliferated" since the 1970s. . . .

[2. Emergency Legislation:] Like omnibus bills, emergency legislation often bypasses conventional process, including committee deliberation and report writing. The [Authorization for the Use of Military Force (AUMF)], for example, passed Congress just three days after the September 11 attacks, without going through the foreign relations committees in the House and Senate. Instead, the majority and minority leaders of both chambers conducted the negotiations, and the AUMF was drafted jointly by White House and congressional lawyers beginning just hours after the attacks. As a result, there is no formal legislative history for the AUMF that can be found in committee reports or conference reports, and there was minimal floor debate. . . .

[3. Automatic Lawmaking Processes:] Congress has increasingly resorted to what might be called *automatic lawmaking processes*. Automatic lawmaking processes establish procedures that effectively make law without Congress having to do anything other than set up the initial framework. These procedures both overcome the structural vetogates that Congress has created for itself to intentionally slow down lawmaking in most instances—vetogates such as the multistage legislative process or specialized debate and amendment rules— and also allow legislators to avoid having to engage with particularly controversial issues. . . .

[4. The President as Legislator:] In the textbook account of legislation, the President is understood as the last stop (the signature) in the Article I, Section 7 path to formal law. . . . In contrast, the unorthodox President takes on aspects of Congress, shaping legislation and sometimes using executive tools to manipulate the congressional process itself. . . .

Understanding the unorthodox President also reveals important gaps in legal doctrine. Courts do not generally conceive of the President as a statutory interpreter, or as an agency. . . .

Signing Statements.—The most familiar example of President as simultaneous legislator and regulator comes when the President issues "signing statements" at the moment of enacting legislation. These statements sometimes give specific, often controversial, interpretations to disputed statutory provisions and even read sections out of the legislation entirely. . . . How should we view this activity? Is it part of the legislative process itself? After all, the bill would not exist if the President had not signed it without a veto override. Or do we view it as part of implementation? . . .

President as Legislation Substitute.—Modern Presidents also have increasingly used executive orders and memoranda as *substitutes* for failed domestic-policy legislative efforts. We might call this *quasi-legislation.* Here, the President may take liberties in construing the expanse of delegation, interpreting statutes to authorize administrative action that was not foreseen by the enacting Congress. . . . For [example], President Clinton issued a controversial directive to the FDA to interpret the Food, Drug, and Cosmetic Act to regulate tobacco. While these moves have been recognized as part of the modern age of "presidential administration," their place as part of the President's *legislative* role has received much less engagement. . . .

[5. Outside Drafters:] [U]northodox drafters outside of government . . . [such as l]obbyists and private and nonprofit interest groups . . . loom large in the day-to-day work of legislation, as do certain entities inside of Congress itself, such as the Congressional Budget Office (CBO): All of these actors regularly draft, review, and advise on bills, but the legal literature about statutory interpretation and legislation doctrine rarely grapples with their roles. . . .

[One Cause of Unorthodox Lawmaking—Gridlock:]

The increase of legislative gridlock over the last several decades is well documented. Sinclair's path-breaking work identifies a hostile political climate and gridlock as key causal factors that have altered the context in which Congress functions. . . . [G]ridlock often leads to legislative bundling and a high degree of legislative punting on Congress's side. This in turn leads to more overlapping delegations to agencies—because more committees are involved in the legislative deal—and often more utilization of unorthodox delegates, like states and private actors. These unorthodox delegations are in a sense the ultimate punt of a controversial topic: They move the implementation outside of the federal government altogether. Moreover, as work in political science substantiates, when the President is a member of a different party, majorities in Congress may prefer to have legislation implemented by the states rather than by an executive branch with different views.

The massive legislative deals that now typify major legislation also mean that agencies have to use more creative regulatory strategies to deal with the unexpected ambiguities, errors, and other complexities that may come with omnibus bills or with bills that do not go through the complete multi-stage legislative process. The ambiguities often attendant to such legislation also can create opportunities for opponents to seize on "inartful drafting"—as in the recent ACA challenge—to try to impede agency implementation. This, in turn, may even incentivize more unorthodox rulemaking by the agency.

Finally, sometimes Congress cannot break through the gridlock, motivating a different kind of unorthodox rulemaking entirely. . . . [A]gencies themselves have jumped into the gap in such circumstances—frequently led by the President—adapting a statute in innovative ways to solve problems not necessarily anticipated at the time of the statute's passage. . . .

Abbe R. Gluck, Anne Joseph O'Connell, and Rosa Po, *Unorthodox Lawmaking, Unorthodox Rulemaking*, 115 Colum. L. Rev. 1789 (2015).

3. CITIZEN LAWMAKING

In addition to legislation enacted through the representative process, many states allow one or more forms of citizen lawmaking. Direct democratic legislating—in the form of ballot measures, initiatives, and referenda—enable citizens to enact or ratify proposed legislation directly via the ballot box. Citizen lawmaking empowers the voting public to overcome the vetogates that may stall popular legislation in state legislatures. These forms of lawmaking rose to prominence during the Progressive Era of the early Twentieth Century to give more power to citizens and weaken the grip that the wealthy held on state representatives. No analog exists at the federal level, and little evidence suggests the framers of the U.S. Constitution anticipated any role for citizens to participate directly in the lawmaking process. This is perhaps unsurprising given that a majority of U.S. citizens—including nearly all women, Blacks, and white males without property—were denied the right to vote at the nation's founding. The framers, moreover, provided only for the direct election of Representatives; Senators were not directly elected until the Seventeenth Amendment (1913), and the Electoral College operates such that the President still is not directly elected by the people.

Notwithstanding the benefits of citizen lawmaking, statutes enacted through ballot initiatives may suffer from similar problems as statute enacted through representative lawmaking: drafters may have ulterior motives for enacting legislation; those voting on it may fail to understand fully its meaning and effect; and opportunities exist to insert unrelated (and unpopular) provisions into a popular measure in order to ensure its passage.

For these reasons, in most states single-subject rules apply not only to statutes enacted by legislatures but also to those enacted through citizen lawmaking processes. While the chief evil that single-subject rules for representative lawmaking seeks to prevent is logrolling, a statute enacted through direct democratic procedures presents a different concern: whether a ballot measure is sufficiently transparent as to its aims, scope, and effect. Yet citizen lawmaking is also susceptible to the possibility that an unrelated (and possibly unpopular) rider may be added to an otherwise coherent (and popular) ballot. At the same time, such initiatives may overreach by seeking to amend a wide swath of a state's laws. The following case study highlights the perils and possibilities of citizen lawmaking against the backdrop of a single subject rule for state initiatives.

a.   CASE STUDY ON CITIZEN LAWMAKING TO ENSURE LEGISLATOR RESPONSIVENESS AND TO CONTROL LEGISLATOR SELF-INTEREST

The Texts to Be Construed: Proposition 24: Legislators' Compensation, Reapportionment, Initiative Constitutional Amendment

Before you read *Senate of the State of California v. Jones*, review the following voter-proposed ballot initiative at issue in the case. What do you think the purpose of this initiative is? How does it accomplish that purpose? Do you think each of the parts of this initiative are "reasonably germane to each other?" Could you articulate a succinct principle that explains how these provisions are all reasonably related?

Let the Voters Decide Act of 2000
(Submitted to appear on the March 7, 2000 California state election ballot).

SECTION 1. *Title*

This measure shall be known and may be cited as "Let The Voters Decide Act of 2000."

SECTION 2. *Findings and Declarations of Purpose*

The People of the State of California find and declare that:

(a) Our Legislature should be responsive to the demands of the citizens of the state of California and not the self-interest of individual legislators. We demand that our representative system of government be fair to all, open to public scrutiny, free of conflicts of interest and dedicated to the principle that government derives its powers from the consent of the governed.

(b)　Legislators should not be entitled to raise their own pay or draw their own districts without obtaining approval of the voters.

(c)　Therefore the voters enact reforms which include:

1)　Salary Reform. The recent controversial pay raises must be repealed and the voters must approve any future increases;

2)　No Pay if Budget is Late. Legislators should not be paid when they fail to pass a state budget on time;

3)　Fair Reapportionment. Legislators must not have the unrestricted ability to draw the boundaries of their own legislative districts and the districts of our congressional representatives, offices to which they might aspire, for their own self-interest and the voters must have an opportunity to approve any redistricting plan adopted by the Legislature.

SECTION 3. *Compensation of Legislators*

Article III, Section 8, Subdivision (g) of the California Constitution is amended to read:

(g)　*Beginning in the session immediately following the adoption of this Act, the annual salary of all Members of the Legislature shall be reduced to $75,000.* ~~On or before December 3, 1990, the commission shall, by a single resolution adopted by a majority of the membership of the commission, establish the annual salary and the medical, dental, insurance, and other similar benefits of state officers. The annual salary and benefits specified in that resolution shall be effective on and after December 3, 1990.~~

Thereafter, at or before the end of each fiscal year, the commission, ~~shall,~~ by a single resolution adopted by a majority of the membership of the commission, *may recommend to the Legislature an adjustment of* ~~adjust~~ the annual salary and the medical, dental, insurance, and other similar benefits of state officers. The annual salary and benefits specified in the resolution shall be effective <u>on and after the first Monday of the next December</u> *if approved by a statute, passed by roll call vote entered into the journal, a majority of each house of the Legislature concurring and approved by the voters as a Legislative measure at the next regular election.*

SECTION 4. *Legislative Travel and Living Expenses*

Subdivision (b) of Section 4 of Article IV of the California Constitution is amended to read:

(b)　Travel and living expenses for Members of the Legislature in connection with their official duties shall ~~be prescribed by statute passed by roll call vote entered in the journal, two-thirds of the membership of each house concurring.~~ *not exceed $75 per day.* A

Member may not receive travel and living expenses during the times that the Legislature is in recess. ~~for more than three calendar days, unless the Member is traveling to or from, or is in attendance at, any meeting of a committee of which he or she is a member, or a meeting, conference, or other legislative function or responsibility as authorized by the rules of the house of which he or she is a member, which is held at a location at least 20 miles from his or her place of residence.~~ *In no case, shall a Member receive travel and living expenses for more than 120 days per year. The amount paid for travel and living expenses may be increased if approved by a statute, passed by roll call vote entered into the journal, a majority of each house of the Legislature concurring and approved by the voters as a Legislative measure at the next regular election.*

SECTION 5. *Timely Budget*

Subdivision (h) of section 12 of Article IV is added to read:

(h) Notwithstanding any other provision in this constitution, including Sections 4 and 8 of Article III and Sections 4 and 12(c) of this article, in any year in which the budget bill is not passed by the legislature by midnight on June 15, each Member of the Legislature shall forfeit any salary and reimbursement for travel or living expenses during any regular or special session for the period from midnight on June 15 until the day that the budget bill is presented to the Governor. No forfeited salary and travel and living expenses shall be paid retroactively. The amount forfeited can be approved for payment if approved by a statute, passed by roll call vote entered into the journal, a majority of each house of the Legislature concurring and approved by the voters as a Legislative measure at the next regular election.

SECTION 6. *Fair Reapportionment*

Article XXI of the California Constitution is amended to read:

Section 1. In the year following the year in which the national census is taken under the direction of Congress at the beginning of each decade, the ~~Legislature~~ *Supreme Court* shall, adjust the boundary lines of the Senatorial, Assembly, Congressional, and Board of Equalization districts in conformance with the following standards:

(a) Each member of the Senate, Assembly, Congress, and the Board of Equalization shall be elected from a single-member district.

(b) The population of all districts of a particular type shall be reasonably equal *in compliance with Federal law.*

(c) Every district shall be contiguous *and as compact as possible.*

(d) Districts of each type shall be numbered consecutively commencing at the northern boundary of the state and ending at the southern boundary.

(e) The geographical integrity of any city, county, or city and county, or of any geographical region shall be respected to the extent possible ~~without violating the requirements of any other subdivision of this section~~.

The Supreme Court shall appoint a panel of Special Masters made up of retired federal and state judges reflecting the cultural and ethnic diversity of California to hold public hearings to receive the presentation of evidence and argument from the public with respect to proposed plans of reapportionment.

Section 2. The reapportionment plans adopted by the Supreme Court shall be submitted to the voters for approval at the next regular election. The plans shall be used for all elections unless and until rejected by the voters.

SECTION 7. *Severability*

If any part of the measure or the application to any person or circumstance is held invalid, the invalidity shall not affect other provisions or applications which reasonably can be given effect without the invalid provision or application.

Senate of the State of California v. Jones

Supreme Court of California, 1999.
21 Cal.4th 1142, 988 P.2d 1089 (1999).

■ GEORGE, C.J. [to which MOSK, J., BAXTER, J., WERDEGAR, J., and CHIN, J., concur.]

[A]rticle II, section 8(d), explicitly provides that "[a]n initiative measure embracing more than one subject *may not be submitted to the electors* or have any effect" (italics added) . . . .

On April 5, 1999, the proponent submitted the above initiative measure to the Attorney General,[and] the Attorney General issued a title and a summary of the chief purpose and points of the measure that ultimately became Proposition 24. The title provided by the Attorney General reads: "Legislators' Compensation, Reapportionment, Initiative Constitutional Amendment[,]" and the summary briefly enumerates a number of the specific proposals contained in the initiative measure. . . .

On October 28, 1999, petitioners filed this proceeding directly in this court, asserting that the initiative measure "is procedurally defective and unconstitutional" and thus should not be allowed to appear on the March 7, 2000, election ballot. . . . [T]he petition maintains that the measure violates the single-subject rule set forth in article II, section 8(d). The petition asserts that the measure "embraces at least two very different subjects: [1] state officers' pay and [2] the redistricting of Congressional,

Assembly, Senate, and Board of Equalization seats." . . . [T]he petition [also] asserts that the initiative measure, as set forth in the petitions that were circulated to qualify the measure for the ballot, contained numerous misleading statements and omissions that were reasonably likely to have misled the electors who signed the circulated petitions. . . . As we shall explain, because we conclude that the initiative measure violates the single-subject rule and for this reason may not be submitted to the electors, we need not reach the question[ ] . . . whether its allegedly misleading aspects are sufficient, in themselves, to warrant an order withholding the measure from the ballot.

The constitutional provision limiting initiative measures to a single subject was added to the California Constitution initially in 1948, in apparent response to a lengthy, multifaceted initiative provision that recently had been the source of considerable controversy. [Citation.] The ballot argument in favor of the proposed single-subject amendment explained that the principal purpose of the amendment was to attempt to avoid confusion of either voters or petition signers and to prevent the subversion of the electorate's will. [Citation.] . . . In articulating the proper standard to guide analysis in this context, the governing decisions establish that " ' "[a]n initiative measure does not violate the single-subject requirement if, despite its varied collateral effects, *all of its parts are 'reasonably germane'* to each other," and to the general purpose or object of the initiative.' " [Citation.] . . .

As the proponent of Proposition 24 correctly observes, over the past half-century the great majority of appellate decisions that have addressed single-subject challenges to initiative measures have found that the challenged measures satisfied the single-subject rule. In two decisions of relatively recent vintage, however, the Court of Appeal concluded in each instance that the challenged initiative measure violated the single-subject requirement. ([*California Trial Lawyers Assn. v. Eu* (1988) ["*CTLA*"]], 200 Cal.App.3d 351, 245 Cal.Rptr. 916; [*Chemical Specialties Manufacturers Assn., Inc. v. Deukmejian* (1991)], 227 Cal.App.3d 663, 278 Cal.Rptr. 128.) As we shall explain, these decisions provide important guidance with respect to the proper application of the single-subject rule embodied in article II, section 8(d), and demonstrate that the rule is neither devoid of content nor as "toothless" as some legal commentaries have suggested. [Citations.]

In *CTLA*, the petitioners brought a preelection single-subject challenge against an initiative measure entitled the "Insurance Cost Control Initiative of 1988." Although the initiative was lengthy, virtually all of its provisions were reasonably germane to the subject of controlling the cost of insurance. However, one provision of the initiative measure— which the Court of Appeal noted was "located inconspicuously at pages 52 and 53 of the [120-page] typewritten measure" [citation]—bore no relation to that subject, but would have added a section to the Insurance Code providing insurance companies (and others) protection from future campaign contribution regulations that might be specifically targeted at insurers. In attempting to defend the measure against the petitioner's single-subject challenge, the insurers argued that because the initiative at issue "deals generally with the regulation of insurance industry practices and [the campaign contribution provision] relates to a specific aspect of those practices, the latter section ipso facto satisfies the 'reasonably germane' test." [Citation.]

The Court of Appeal in *CTLA* rejected the insurers' argument on two grounds: "First, the express purpose of the initiative is to control the cost of insurance, not generally to regulate the practices of the insurance industry. Second, we cannot accept the implied premise of [the insurers'] analysis, *i.e.*, that any two provisions, no matter how functionally unrelated, nevertheless comply with the constitution's single-subject requirement so long as they have in common an effect on any aspect of the business of insurance. Contemporary society is structured in such a way that the need for and provision of insurance against hazards and losses pervades virtually every aspect of life. [The insurers'] approach would permit the joining of enactments so disparate as to render the constitutional single-subject limitation nugatory." [Citation.] Observing that, in its view, "the initiative is a paradigm of the potentially deceptive combinations of unrelated provisions at which the constitutional limitation on the scope of initiative is aimed" [citation], the Court of Appeal concluded that the measure violated the single-subject rule and issued an order directing the respondent election officials to refrain from taking any action to place the matter on the ballot.

In *Chemical Specialties,* the Court of Appeal addressed a single-subject challenge to a measure, entitled the "Public's Right to Know Act" (Proposition 105 on the November 1988 ballot), that was different in form from the measure at issue in *CTLA.* Unlike the initiative in *CTLA,* Proposition 105 did not contain one unrelated provision inserted within a lengthy proposition addressing a separate subject, but instead contained a series of diverse provisions that ostensibly were related by the circumstance that each provision required public disclosure of some information. Proposition 105 mandated separate disclosure requirements for (1) household toxic products, (2) senior's health insurance, (3) nursing homes, (4) statewide initiative or referendum campaigns, and (5) sales of stock or securities for corporations doing business with South Africa, requiring the disclosure of different information in each of these areas. [Citations.]

Although the supporters of Proposition 105 asserted that all of its provisions were reasonably germane to the single subject of "public disclosure" or "truth-in-advertising," the Court of Appeal in *Chemical Specialties* rejected that argument, finding that such a subject was clearly one of "excessive generality" [citation] and was "so broad that a virtually unlimited array of provisions could be considered germane thereto and joined in this proposition, essentially obliterating the constitutional requirement." [Citation.] Instead, the Court of Appeal concluded that "[i]n actuality, the measure seeks to reduce toxic pollution, protect seniors from fraud and deceit in the issuance of insurance policies, raise the health and safety standards in nursing homes, preserve the integrity of the election process, and fight apartheid; well-intentioned objectives but not reasonably related to one another for purposes of the single-subject rule." [Citation.] Accordingly, the court in *Chemical Specialties* found that the measure violated the single-subject rule and could not properly be given any effect.

In the present case, petitioners contend that the initiative measure here at issue exhibits many of the same fundamental flaws as the measures found invalid in *CTLA* and *Chemical Specialties*. Petitioners maintain that like the provision in *Chemical Specialties,* Proposition 24 "combines salary changes for legislators and constitutional officers with the subject of redistricting, two unrelated concepts that can only be linked by a concept so broad it could mean almost anything." And petitioners further assert that like the measure in *CTLA*, Proposition 24 contains an " 'unnatural combination of provisions . . . dealing with more than one subject' " [, citation,] that have been joined together simply for improper tactical purposes, a combination that strikes at the heart of the single-subject rule's purpose of minimizing voter confusion and deception. As we shall explain, after reviewing the specific provisions of Proposition 24, we agree with petitioners' claim that the measure at issue "embrac[es] more than one subject" within the meaning of the constitutional single-subject rule. . . .

As petitioners acknowledge, although sections 3, 4, and 5 of the initiative would make a number of distinct changes with respect to the compensation of legislators and other state officers, under our precedents it appears that these provisions are reasonably germane to the subject of state officers' compensation, and properly could be joined together in a single initiative. As petitioners point out, however, the other, very significant change in the state Constitution that would be implemented by section 6 of Proposition 24—transferring the power of reapportionment from the Legislature to this court—involves an entirely different subject; reapportionment clearly is unrelated to the subject of state officers' salaries or compensation. We agree with petitioners that, when viewed from a realistic and commonsense perspective, the provisions of Proposition 24 appear to embrace at least two distinct subjects—state officers' compensation and reapportionment.

In responding to petitioners' claim that Proposition 24 embraces more than one subject, the proponent initially argues in his opposition that "[t]he various parts of Proposition 24 are reasonably germane to the general purpose of the initiative. In summary, the initiative identifies a single problem that has plagued the Legislature for decades and proposes a single solution—voter involvement." *In essence, the proponent seeks to justify the joinder of these disparate subjects on the theory that because each of the substantive sections of Proposition 24 contains a provision for voter approval, "voter approval" properly may be viewed as the single subject to which all of the measure's provisions are reasonably germane.*

This argument is analogous to, and demonstrates the same fundamental flaw as, the unsuccessful argument that was proffered by the proponents of Proposition 105 in *Chemical Specialties*. As noted above, in that case it was claimed that the diverse provisions dealing with toxic household products, senior's health insurance, nursing homes, initiative or referendum advertising, and businesses dealing with South Africa, were reasonably germane to the single subject of "public disclosure" or "truth-in-advertising," because each of the provisions proposed to require public disclosure of some information as a remedy or solution to a problem in each of the separate fields covered by the proposition. As we have seen, the court in *Chemical Specialties* rejected this argument, finding that the proffered subject was a subject of excessive generality and was "so broad that a virtually unlimited array of provisions could be considered germane thereto and joined in this proposition, essentially obliterating the constitutional requirement." (*Chemical Specialties, supra,* 227 Cal.App.3d at p. 671, 278 Cal.Rptr. 128.) The same reasoning applies here to the proponent's suggestion that the measure at issue satisfies the single-subject rule because each one of its varied sections includes a requirement of voter approval of various determinations covered by the section. As petitioners observe, *under the proponent's proposed approach, a measure would satisfy the single-subject rule even if it contained separate provisions requiring voter approval for laws dealing with "fisheries, student class-size reduction, and securities fraud."* We agree with the Court of Appeal in *Chemical Specialties* that acceptance of such a theory would "essentially obliterat[e] the constitutional requirement."

In his return, the Secretary of State suggests that the provisions of Proposition 24 can be found to be reasonably germane to a similar but ostensibly somewhat narrower subject—"voter approval of political issues." The return, however, provides no definition of the term "political issues," a phrase that could well encompass the entire range of matters dealt with by the political system. In any event, this suggestion exhibits the same flaw as the proponent's argument. When the drafters of an initiative measure join separate provisions dealing with *otherwise unrelated* "political issues" in a single initiative, the initiative cannot be found to satisfy the single-subject rule simply because each provision imposes a requirement of voter approval, any more than if each provision contained a remedy of money damages or a remedy of injunctive relief.

The proponent alternatively maintains that all of the provisions of Proposition 24 are reasonably germane to the objective of dealing with the problem of "legislative self-interest." As the proponent observes, one of the purposes of the proposition, as described in its findings and declaration of purpose, is to combat "the self-interest of individual legislators." (Prop.24, § 2, subd. (a).) In this regard, the measure explicitly declares: "Legislators should not be entitled to raise their own pay or draw their own districts without obtaining approval of the voters." (*Id.*, § 2, subd. (b).)

We need not determine in this case whether an initiative matter that includes provisions dealing with a number of subject matter areas as diverse as legislator salaries and reapportionment would satisfy the single-subject requirement if each of the separate areas addressed by the provision poses a potential conflict of interest between the personal interests of legislators and the public interest. Even if we were to assume that the theme or objective of remedying "legislative self-interest" is not excessively broad and would permit the combination of such otherwise unrelated proposals, the initiative before us cannot properly be defended on this basis. Although the text of Proposition 24 obscures this point, in reality, under existing law, members of the Legislature do *not* control their own salaries (and thus cannot "raise their own pay," as the initiative implies).

Under a specific provision approved by the voters in 1990, the California Constitution currently assigns that task to the California Citizens Compensation Commission, a commission whose members are appointed by the Governor (without legislative confirmation) for six-year terms and may not be current or former state officials or employees. [Citation.] Thus, Proposition 24 would not operate to limit a preexisting authority of legislators to set their own salaries, but on the contrary would reduce the authority of the independent citizens' commission that was established in 1990 to set such salaries, transforming the commission from a body that *establishes* legislator salaries and benefits to one that simply *recommends* the appropriate compensation. Furthermore, in contrast to the initiative's professed objective, this section of Proposition 24 actually would reinvest state legislators with a direct role in the process of setting legislative salaries, albeit at the same time subjecting the legislative decision to the approval of the voters. . . .

Although the circumstances identified by the proponent may well demonstrate that this provision of Proposition 24 is reasonably related to the objective of reducing legislators' salaries, they do not demonstrate that the proposed change is directed at, or reasonably can be explained as responsive to, the subject of "legislator self-interest." As the proponent's argument itself recognizes, the 1990 proposition criticized by the proponent removed ("divorced") the authority to set legislators' salaries (as well as the salaries of other state officers) from the legislators themselves, and transferred such authority to an independent commission. . . . [T]he members of the commission may not be legislators or former legislators, are appointed by the Governor (without legislative confirmation) for six-year terms, and include persons with expertise in the setting of public officer salaries.

The circumstance that the Citizens Compensation Commission has increased the annual salary of state legislators from $49,000 to $99,000 over the past eight years may simply reflect that the current figure is a fairer and more accurate measure of the appropriate compensation for such officers, taking into consideration the substantial responsibilities of the particular office and the salaries currently paid to other public officials in this state with comparable positions and responsibilities. [Citation.] The proponent of Proposition 24 objects to the commission's salary determination, believing that a lower figure is appropriate and that any future adjustments should be subject to voter approval. Such dissatisfaction with the commission's work product, however, does not demonstrate that the relevant provision of Proposition 24 is directed at a problem arising out of *a conflict of interest of legislators.* . . .

Finally, the proponent contends that Proposition 24 may not properly be found to violate the single-subject rule because other initiative measures that have been upheld by this court in previous cases were assertedly much broader and contained more numerous and more diverse provisions than those included in Proposition 24. . . . [W]hile the initiative measure at issue in *Legislature v. Eu,* contained a number of seemingly distinct measures (imposing term limits, reducing legislative expenditures, and limiting legislative pensions), the court, in concluding that the measure did not violate the single-subject rule, observed that "[t]he unifying theme or common purpose of Proposition 140 is incumbency reform" [citation] and found that each of "the separate aspects of [the measure] relate to the furtherance of [this] common purpose." [Citation.] The court explained that the various provisions of the initiative were aimed at "making an extended career in public office both less available and less attractive to incumbent legislators" [citation]; the term limits provisions of the measure rendered an extended career less available to incumbent legislators, and the provisions limiting legislative expenditures and reducing legislative pensions were related both to making such an extended career less available and less attractive. The provisions of Proposition 24 exhibit no similar unifying theme or common purpose, with respect to "incumbency reform" or any other shared objective, but instead simply combine a measure that would transfer the reapportionment authority from the Legislature to this court with unrelated provisions that would make various changes pertaining to the compensation of legislators and other state officers.

In sum, we conclude that the initiative measure challenged in this case violates the single-subject rule. The portion of Proposition 24 that proposes to transfer the power of reapportionment from the Legislature, where it traditionally has resided, to the Supreme Court, itself involves a most fundamental and far-reaching change in the law. Assuming (contrary to petitioners' separate contention that we do not reach) that the transfer of this traditional legislative power to this court does not rise to the level of a constitutional revision that never may be accomplished by initiative but only by a constitutional convention or legislative submission, the proposal to adopt such a significant change nonetheless clearly represents a separate "subject" within the meaning of the single-subject rule upon which a clear expression of the voters' intent is essential. To permit the drafters of an initiative petition to combine a provision transferring the power of reapportionment from the Legislature to this court with unrelated provisions relating to legislators' pay would inevitably create voter confusion and obscure the electorate's intent with regard to each of the separate subjects included within the initiative, undermining the basic objectives sought to be achieved by the single-subject rule.

Because we have concluded that Proposition 24 embraces more than one subject, article II, section 8(d), provides that the measure "may not be submitted to the electors. . . ." . . . A peremptory writ of mandate shall issue, directing respondents to refrain from taking any steps to place Proposition 24 on the March 7, 2000, election ballot or to include the measure in the ballot pamphlet.

■ Dissenting Opinion by KENNARD, J. [in which BROWN, J., concurred.]

I dissent. I cannot join the majority in its hasty decision to declare invalid, and to remove from the March 2000 election ballot, an initiative measure, Proposition 24, for which more than a million California voters have signed petitions. Because this challenge to Proposition 24 presents issues that are close and difficult, and because there has been inadequate time to give these issues the thoughtful attention and deliberation they deserve, I have not attempted to determine whether Proposition 24 is valid or invalid. Rather, consistent with this court's decision under similar circumstances in *Brosnahan v. Eu* (1982) [citation], I would deny the peremptory writ of mandate without prejudice to deciding these issues if and when the electorate enacts Proposition 24.

The court's rush to decision has been extraordinary. On October 28, 1999, this court received and filed the petition for writ of mandate challenging Proposition 24. This court then learned that a decision on the merits would need to issue by Monday, December 13, the deadline for finalizing ballot materials. Nonetheless, on November 10 this court issued an order, in which I did not join, establishing an expedited briefing schedule and directing respondents to show cause and present oral argument on Wednesday, December 8. Only eight court days elapsed between the filing of the final party brief (November 24) and oral argument. Only three court days elapsed between oral argument and the filing of the decision, which is final immediately. Only once before, and that was 50 years ago and under very different circumstances, has this court decided the merits of a preelection single-subject challenge to an initiative. Never before has this court invalidated an initiative measure for violation of the single-subject rule. Never before has this court decided such complex issues so quickly with so little justification for haste. . . .

Is it clear beyond a doubt that Proposition 24 violates the single-subject rule? Hardly. The majority opinion takes more than 10,000 words and 34 pages (in slip opinion format) to decide the issue. As I explain below, the initiative proponents, who insist that the initiative does not violate the single-subject rule as this court has consistently interpreted it, have presented plausible arguments that the majority does not persuasively rebut and that this court has not had time to fully consider.

To avoid unduly interfering with the right of initiative, this court has held that the single-subject rule should be "construed liberally." [Citation.] An initiative measure satisfies the single-subject rule " ' "if, despite its varied collateral effects, all of its parts are 'reasonably germane' to each other," and to the general purpose or object of the initiative.' " [Citations.] It is not necessary that each of the measure's provisions "effectively interlock in a functional relationship," but only that "the various provisions are reasonably related to a common theme or purpose." [Citations.]

Two of the matters that Proposition 24 addresses—legislators' salaries and reapportionment—at first blush may seem separate and unrelated. But the initiative's proponents (by which I mean both the respondents in this proceeding and the amici curiae who have filed briefs supporting Proposition 24) present coherent and substantial arguments suggesting that this first impression may well be mistaken because all the initiative's provisions are reasonably germane to a single subject within the meaning of this court's past decisions. . . .

According to the proponents, the common theme or purpose to which all of Proposition 24's various provisions are reasonably related is voter control of basic conditions of state legislators' employment. They argue that the basic conditions of any employment agreement are compensation and job security. Legislators' salaries and per diem reimbursements are their compensation. Reapportionment of legislative districts determines their opportunities for reelection, and hence job security. The proponents argue that because legislators work for the people of California, the people are in essence their employers and should have the final say, which they do not now have, on these basic employment conditions.

The proponents offer arguments to explain why each of Proposition 24's various provisions is reasonably related to the common purpose of establishing voter control over the most basic employment conditions, compensation and job security. . . . [R]equiring this court in the first instance to draw up redistricting plans for legislative, Board of Equalization, and congressional districts, with the plans to then be submitted to the voters for approval, will ensure that the voters choose their legislators rather than the legislators choosing their voters.

The proponents acknowledge that Proposition 24 will significantly affect not only legislators, but also other constitutional officers. They offer substantial arguments in defense of this aspect of Proposition 24.

First, the proponents argue that since term limits for state legislators went into effect, legislators whose terms have expired have increasingly moved to occupy other elective or appointive offices in state government. Thus, all but two of the state constitutional officers whose salaries are now set by the California Citizens Compensation Commission are former legislators. Thus, they argue, effective control of legislators' compensation requires control of the compensation of these officers also. In a similar vein, the proponents argue that because congressional seats and positions on the Board of Equalization are attractive career moves for California legislators, those legislators should not control reapportionment of the districts for those offices, but instead this court should determine reapportionment, subject to voter approval.

Alternatively, the proponents argue that Proposition 24's impact on compensation and districting for persons other than California legislators may be defended as permissible collateral effects. [Citation.] The constitutional provision under which the California Citizens Compensation Commission sets legislators' salaries (Cal. Const., art. III, § 8) includes legislators within the larger category of "state officers." Rather than drastically rewriting the provision to distinguish legislators from other state officers, the drafters of Proposition 24 accepted the provision as written and made the minimum changes necessary to vest in the voters, rather than the Commission, final authority over these salary increases.

In the same way, the state constitutional provision governing reapportionment (Cal. Const., art. XXI) lumps together state legislative, congressional, and Board of Equalization districts and imposes a single set of reapportionment for all alike. The proponents argue that rather than drastically rewriting the provision to sever state legislative district reapportionment from reapportionment for congressional and Board of Equalization districts, the drafters merely accepted the existing classification and adopted the most economical changes necessary to give the electorate final reapportionment authority over state legislative districts. Under this view, therefore, the effects on other districts are accidental or "collateral." . . .

Act in haste, repent at leisure. This court may well regret its precipitous decision in this case, and the unfortunate precedent it sets. Absent compelling circumstances requiring a preelection ruling—and such circumstances are absent here—a challenge to an initiative raising even moderately complex issues should not be decided before the election if doing so requires an expedited proceeding that sacrifices this court's normal deliberative process.

My vote here is not a vote for or against the validity of Proposition 24. Neither is it a vote for or against the current test under which this court evaluates single-subject challenges. . . . My vote is a vote for careful judicial deliberation of complex issues of substantial importance to the people of this state. The prudent and correct course here is to defer decision on the validity of Proposition 24 until after the March 2000 election. Abandoning judicial restraint, the majority has sacrificed the prime judicial virtue of careful deliberation.

NOTES AND QUESTIONS

1.   The majority sided with the petitioners in concluding that reforming state officer pay and redistricting state electoral districts were "two very different subjects," and it rejected the proponents' arguments that all of the provisions were "reasonably germane to each other" since they concerned "voter involvement" and/or "voter approval of political issues." Both unifying principles, the majority concluded, were too vague. Are they? Do you think the purpose section of Proposition 24 provides a coherent rationale for why these provisions should exist in a single ballot measure?

2.   The majority also rejected the proponents' alternative unifying principle of combatting the problem "legislative self-interest" because at least one of the provisions affected non-legislative state officers. Do you think evidence that an initiative may have an incidental effect on unrelated state officers is sufficient to establish the initiative violates the single-subject rule? What of the dissent's objection to this argument?

3.   At the outset, the majority notes that the single-subject rule exists for the principal purpose to "avoid confusion of either voters or petition signers and to prevent the subversion of the electorate's will." Having read the text of Proposition 24, do you think it runs the risk of inducing either harm?

4.   Recall Section 7 of Proposition 24—not mentioned by either the majority or the dissent—which anticipates the need to sever a problematic provision from the Act while allowing the rest of the Act to remain in effect. Had the Court not blocked the proposition from being placed on the ballot altogether, and instead allowed it to be voted on and enacted, how do you think the Court could have severed the offending aspects from the rest of the bill? Following the majority's rationale, should only Section 6 have been struck? Keep these questions in mind as you read Section VII.B, *infra*, on severability provisions in legislation.

5.   As articulated by the California Supreme Court, California's single subject rule for ballot initiatives appears to have comparable goals, and similar applications, to Pennsylvania's single subject rule for legislatively enacted statutes discussed in *Neiman, supra*. Yet given how different these lawmaking processes are, can the same rule be justified for both kinds of lawmaking? Professors Robert Cooter and Michael Gilbert are skeptical, and instead argue that single subject rules should apply differently for initiatives enacted through citizen lawmaking:

> [W]e develop a new theory of interpretation for the single subject rule. The theory rests on the claim that "subjects" cannot be defined with logic and should instead be framed in light of voters' preferences and the democratic process. . . . [O]ur democratic process theory posits that "subject" means a set of policy proposals over which a majority of voters have insufficiently separable preferences. To give meaning to this phrase, "insufficiently

separable preferences," we first explain its opposite, "sufficiently separable preferences." A voter has sufficiently separable preferences for two policy proposals when she can decide how to vote on each without knowing whether the other will become law.

The clearest case of sufficient separability occurs when a voter understands the proposals to be completely independent. To illustrate, imagine two policy proposals, one that would implement no-fault insurance for car accidents and another that would permit politicians who receive contributions from interest groups to participate in governmental decisions affecting those groups. Most voters probably have sufficiently separable preferences for these proposals. Their vote on the first is unaffected by whether the second becomes law and vice versa.

Short of being completely independent, a voter also has sufficiently separable preferences for two policy proposals when those proposals are only weakly conjoined. Proposals are weakly conjoined when they weakly complement or weakly substitute for one another. . . . To illustrate, imagine two proposals, one of which would ban pesticide X and the other of which would ban pesticide Y. If growers can easily switch between X and Y, then passing only one proposal would slightly decrease pesticide use, and passing both proposals would dramatically decrease pesticide use. An environmentalist might support each proposal on its own, but either one would be more attractive to her if the other one also passed. As defined above, this environmentalist has "sufficiently separable preferences" for the proposals.

Now we turn from sufficiently to insufficiently separable preferences. A voter has insufficiently separable preferences for two policy proposals when she cannot decide how to vote on one without knowing whether the other will become law. This occurs in two circumstances: when the proposals are strong complements, such that the voter only votes for one if she is certain also to get the other; and when the proposals are strong substitutes, such that the voter only votes for one if she is certain not to get the other.

We illustrate insufficiently separable preferences over proposals that strongly substitute for each other: Imagine two proposals, one that would reduce property tax rates and another that would leave property tax rates unchanged but exempt half of the value of every home from taxation. If a voter wants to reduce property taxes but believes that passing both measures would have disastrous consequences for the state budget, that voter has insufficiently separable preferences over these proposals. She cannot decide how to vote on one without knowing whether the other will pass. . . .

According to the democratic process theory, the single subject rule aims to separate policy proposals over which most voters have separable preferences and unite policy proposals over which most voters have inseparable preferences. Citizens can express their support for or opposition to proposals over which they have separable preferences by voting on them in isolation. Combining such proposals violates the single subject rule. Conversely, voters cannot express their support for or opposition to proposals over which they have inseparable preferences by voting on them in isolation. Therefore, a sound democratic process permits citizens to consider such proposals simultaneously, and combining them does not violate the single subject rule. . . .

[O]ur theory of the single subject rule is also descriptive: It clarifies existing jurisprudence by explaining in a precise way what judges are already trying to accomplish with the rule. We support this assertion with examples. In trying to articulate their test for single subject compliance, California courts state that all of the provisions of a challenged ballot proposition must be "reasonably germane" to one another. If most voters have inseparable preferences over the proposals contained in a ballot measure—and therefore cannot decide whether they support one proposal without knowing whether the other will become law—then surely the proposals qualify as "reasonably germane."

Robert D. Cooter & Michael D. Gilbert, *Single A Theory of Direct Democracy and the Single Subject Rule*, 110 Colum. L. Rev. 687 (2010).

Applying the Cooter-Gilbert test to *Jones*, were the policy proposals contained in Proposition 24 ones for which voters would be likely to have separable or inseparable preferences? How might a court undertake such an assessment?

PART II

THE INTERPRETATION OF STATUTES—AN OVERVIEW

A. STATING AND RESOLVING STATUTORY ISSUES

1. FINDING AND STATING ISSUES OF STATUTORY LAW

To interpret and apply a statute, you must work with its precise language. This proposition may seem obvious, but it marks an essential change of emphasis from the methods of caselaw analysis with which students become familiar in most beginning law school classes. While the rule of law derived from a case or from a line of cases can be stated in many different forms of language, each of which may constitute an acceptable statement, a statutory rule of law exists in only one authorized version. Moreover, confronting statutes after acquiring some facility with common-law reasoning can be jarring. Recounted in or underlying every case is a story; the judges' opinions offer at the same time examples from which a legal rule can be derived and applied to a concrete problem (thus giving both the story and its moral). Statutes, by contrast, are embodied in fixed text unrelieved by anecdote (though the legislative process that produced the text can sometimes prove picaresque). Accordingly, the interpretive technique calls not for telling a tale, but for perceiving a problem. What problem does the statutory text respond to? How does the text address the problem? Does it satisfactorily solve the problem? Does the text create new problems, perhaps inadvertently? You might, at least at first, liken statutory text to pieces of a puzzle: you can't solve the puzzle by redesigning the pieces, you have to work to fit together the pieces you're given.

The Problem Cases in this Section are designed to give you practice in statutory analysis and in the statement of statutory issues. The vital lesson to derive from the preparation and discussion of these Problem Cases is this: *You must state the issue in a case of statutory interpretation to include an exact quotation of the precise terms of the statute with respect to which the question of statutory applicability arises*: DO NOT PARAPHRASE THE STATUTE! As to each Problem Case—and, later, as to each statute examined in this Part—you must be prepared to give an accurate and precise answer to the question: "What does the statute *say,* exactly, with respect to the legal problem at hand?" Accordingly, you should analyze and discuss the following Problem Cases solely on the basis of the words of the statutes at issue. When you are studying a judicial opinion that construes a statute (as you will be doing in the following sections of this Casebook), first practice reading and rereading the text of the statute itself. Only after you are familiar with the precise statutory language on its own terms should you turn to its judicial exposition.

NOTE: THE IMPORTANCE OF THE TEXT

The remarks of Erwin N. Griswold, then Solicitor General of the United States, in his discussion on "Appellate Advocacy," 26 The Record of the Association of the Bar of the City of New York 342 (1971), underscore the importance to lawyers of finding and precisely stating statutory issues. Solicitor General Griswold urged that advocates "orient the court" at the beginning of any oral argument on appeal. As a part of "orienting" the court, he recommended that counsel focus the issue for the judges, commenting as follows:

> [L]et the court see—and I mean "see"—the exact language with which they have to deal. Tell them, right at the beginning: "The statutory language involved appears at page 4 of my brief. Though the clause is a somewhat long one, the issue turns, I believe, on the proper construction or effect of words in two lines near the top of the page." Give the court time to find the two lines, and then read the words to them. At this point, the eye can be as important as the ear in oral argument, and the court will follow all of the rest of your argument much better if you have taken pains to tell them exactly what it is about, and where to find the words if they want to look at them again.
>
> In the years when I was a law teacher, I suppose that my most famous classroom remark was "Look at the statute"—or "What does the statute say?" Over the years, I have had literally hundreds of my former students write me and say that this was the most

important thing they learned in law school. There is something about the student, and some oral advocates, too, which leads them to think great thoughts without ever taking the time and care to see just exactly what they are thinking about. Now I would not suggest that the court would make such a mistake. But courts are accustomed to think in terms of concrete, rather specific cases. The oral advocate takes a great step in advancing his cause, I think, if, right at the beginning of his argument, after the procedural setting has been established, he tells the court exactly what the case is about, including specific reference to any statutory language which must be construed or evaluated in bringing the case to a decision. With orientation, the court finds moorings. It is no longer cast adrift on the great sea of all the law. If you can get the court moored to the question as you see it, and so that they see it clearly and distinctly, you may be off to a good start towards leading them to decide the case your way.

The following problem cases provide an initial opportunity to find your moorings in statutory texts.

PROBLEM CASES

Problem Case No. 1

Humphrey Hume was born in England of English parents in 1940 and came to the United States in 1960. He has never become a naturalized citizen of the United States.

In 1969, Hume was indicted on a charge of willfully destroying valuable federal property (Selective Service files) earlier in that year in the course of militant anti-war protest activity. He was tried shortly afterward and found guilty by a jury and then sentenced to imprisonment for a year and a day. He served his sentence as required.

Two and a half years ago, Hume drove a motor vehicle on behalf of a labor union engaged in demonstrations against certain West Coast grape growers. In the course of one demonstration his vehicle struck and killed a bystander. Hume was indicted for manslaughter, based on negligent and reckless operation (without intent to injure the victim) of a motor vehicle in violation of state law. On his plea of guilty he was sentenced to imprisonment by state authorities for a term of two years. He served his sentence and was recently released from the penitentiary. Thereupon deportation proceedings were commenced against him under Section 241(a) of the Immigration and Nationality Act of 1952, 66 Stat. 204, 8 U.S.C.A. Sec. 1251(a).

Section 241(a) of the Immigration and Nationality Act of 1952 (as modified for the purpose of this Problem Case) provides as follows:

    (a)   Any alien in the United States shall, upon the order of the Attorney General, be deported who—

       (4)   is hereafter convicted of a crime involving moral turpitude committed within five years after entry and either sentenced to confinement or confined therefor in a prison or corrective

institution for a year or more, or who hereafter at any time after entry is more than once convicted of a crime involving moral turpitude.

After a procedurally correct deportation hearing, Hume has now been ordered deported and taken into custody for that purpose. He seeks *habeas corpus* in a District Court of the United States on the ground that Section 241(a) does not authorize his deportation.

State the issue or issues of statutory interpretation raised by this case, noting as to each issue the *precise language* of the statute with respect to which the question of statutory applicability arises.

Problem Case No. 2

A. A sign posted at the entry to a public path by order of the New Coda City Council states: "Pedestrians only. No bikes." Which of the following are prohibited from or permitted on the path? Why?

  1. A cyclist dismounts and walks her bicycle.

  2. A roller skater.

  3. A skate boarder.

  4. A pedestrian pushing a baby carriage.

  5. A jogger pushing a 3-wheeled high-speed baby stroller.

  6. A jogger.

B. Uncertainty about the meaning of the 'Pedestrians only. No bikes.' sign has prompted the New Coda City Council to try again. This time, it has added pictograms to its revision of the prohibition.

Photo by Zach Horton, Columbia Law School Class of 2021. Used with permission.

Has the revised version resolved the ambiguities of the prior sign? Has it introduced new ambiguities?

Problem Case No. 3

The Growers' Irrigation Company (hereinafter called the "Company") owns, maintains and operates within the State of New Coda an irrigation system consisting of four large storage reservoirs and 400 miles of irrigation canals. More than 100,000 acres of New Coda farmland, owned by many different farmers, are irrigated with water furnished by the Company. The water distributed by the Company is diverted from streams in New Coda during the non-irrigation season and runs through canals into the Company's reservoirs. During the irrigation season, this water is released from the reservoirs, carried through the Company's canals, and delivered to the lateral irrigation ditches of the farmers.

Sugar beets, corn, peas and beans are grown on the land irrigated. Virtually all of the sugar beets are processed into refined sugar in plants operated within New Coda, and large amounts of the corn, peas, and beans are canned in factories within New Coda. More than 75% of the refined sugar and canned vegetables is shipped in interstate commerce to purchasers outside New Coda.

There are 1,000 shares of authorized capital stock in the Company, all of which shares are owned by farmers in the irrigation area of New Coda. Each share of stock entitles the owner thereof to a 1/1,000th share of the property of the Company and of the total supply of water available during the irrigation season. The expenses necessary to the operation of the irrigation system are borne by annual assessments levied on the Company's stockholders, and the proceeds of the assessments constitute the Company's sole source of income. Payment of the assessment on his shares of stock is a condition precedent to the right of a stockholder to receive water for his farm during the irrigation season. The Company does not sell water to persons other than stockholders.

The Company employs 16 reservoir tenders, who take care of the diverting and storage of water during the non-irrigation season and attend the conduct of water through the Company's canals and into the lateral ditches of the farmers during the irrigation season. These reservoir tenders do not look after the lateral ditches of the farmers; in fact, they do not go at all on to the farmers' property. The Company pays its reservoir tenders a flat wage rate of $3 per hour, irrespective of the number of hours worked during any week. During the irrigation season, the 16 reservoir tenders work considerably more than 40 hours a week.

The Administrator of the Wage and Hour Division of the Department of Labor has now filed a complaint in the United States District Court for the State of New Coda, charging that the Company is violating the federal Fair Labor Standards Act by failing to pay the 16 reservoir tenders time-and-a-half for overtime. The Administrator's complaint asks that the District Court issue an injunction against the Company restraining continued violation of the Act.

The Fair Labor Standards Act (as modified and renumbered for the purposes of this Problem Case) provides, in pertinent part, as follows:

Section 1: *Declaration of Policy.* The Congress finds that the existence, in industries engaged in commerce, of labor conditions detrimental to the maintenance of minimum standards of living causes commerce and the channels of commerce to be used to spread such detrimental labor conditions among the workers of the several States.

Section 2: No employer shall employ any employee who is engaged in commerce or in the production of goods for commerce for a workweek longer than 40 hours unless such employee receives compensation for his employment in excess of the hours above specified at a rate not less than one and one-half times the regular pay rate at which he is employed.

Section 3: The provisions of Section 2 of this Act shall not apply with respect to: (1) any employee employed in a bona fide executive, administrative, or professional capacity; (2) any employee engaged in any retail or service establishment the greater part of whose selling or servicing is done within the State; (3) any employee employed in agriculture; or (4) any individual employed in handling, packing, storing, or canning agricultural commodities for market.

Section 4: *Definitions.*

(a) "Commerce" means trade, commerce, transportation, transmission, or communication among the several States or from any State to any place outside thereof.

(b) "Employer" includes any person acting directly or indirectly in the interest of an employer in relation to an employee but shall not include the United States or any State or political subdivision of a State.

(c) "Employee" includes any individual employed by an employer.

(d) "Agriculture" includes farming and all its branches and includes any practices performed by a farmer or on a farm as incident to or in conjunction with farming operations, including preparation for market and delivery to storage or to market.

(e) "Goods" means wares, products, commodities, merchandise or articles or subjects of commerce of any character whatsoever.

(f) "Produced" means produced, manufactured, mined, handled, or in any other manner worked on in any State; and for the purposes of this Act an employee shall be deemed to have been engaged in the production of goods if such employee was employed in any process or occupation necessary to the production of goods in any State.

The Growers' Irrigation Company moves to dismiss the Administrator's injunction action on the ground that the Company's activities are not within the area of coverage of the Fair Labor Standards Act.

State the issues of statutory interpretation raised by this case, noting as to each issue the *precise language* of the statute with respect to which the question of statutory applicability arises.

Problem Case No. 4

Prior to 1949, no anti-discrimination legislation had ever been enacted in the State of New Coda. During its 1949 session, the State Legislature passed the following statute, which was approved by the Governor and became effective June 1, 1949:

An Act to protect all citizens in the enjoyment of their civil rights.

Be it enacted by the Legislature of the State of New Coda:

Section 1: This statute may be cited as "The Anti-Discrimination Act of 1949."

Section 2: All persons within the jurisdiction of this State shall be entitled to the full and equal accommodations, advantages, facilities and privileges of inns, restaurants, hotels, eating-houses, bath-houses, barber shops, theatres, music halls, public conveyances on land and water, and all other places of public accommodation or amusement, subject only to conditions and limitations applicable alike to all citizens.

Section 3: Any person who shall violate any of the provisions of the foregoing section by denying to any citizen, except for reasons applicable alike to all citizens of every race, creed or color, and regardless of race, creed or color, the full enjoyment of any of the accommodations, advantages, facilities or privileges in said section enumerated, or by aiding or inciting such denial, shall for every such offense be subject to a fine of not more than $5,000, or to imprisonment for not more than one year, or to both such fine and such imprisonment.

Dr. Claudius Smythe, a retired physician, is the sole owner of a rest home for persons recovering from major operations or from severe illnesses. The rest home is situated in one of the rural counties of the State of New Coda. It has a maximum capacity of fifteen convalescents. For some time, all financial and other business details have been handled by Rufus DeLong, who serves as the rest home's resident manager. Recently, DeLong wrote and distributed to all physicians in New Coda advertisements describing the rest home. At the specific direction of Dr. Smythe, DeLong included in the advertisements the following statement:

Admission Policy: It is the policy of the Smythe Rest Home to admit *white* patients only. Applications from non-white persons will not be considered.

No non-white person was ever actually turned away by the Smythe Rest Home; in fact, there is no record of any application to the rest home ever having been received from a non-white person.

Early this year, the Smythe Rest Home's advertisement was called to the attention of the prosecuting attorney of the county in which the rest home is situated. Dr. Smythe was promptly indicted for violation of the Anti-

Discrimination Act of 1949. After trial before a jury, Dr. Smythe was convicted and fined $1,500. He appeals to the appropriate appellate court of the State of New Coda.

State the issue or issues of statutory interpretation raised by Dr. Smythe's appeal, noting as to each issue the *precise language* of the statute with respect to which the question of statutory applicability arises.

Problem Case No. 5: California Civil Code 3344.1 (as amended 2007)

(a) (1)   Any person who uses a deceased personality's name, voice, signature, photograph, or likeness, in any manner, on or in products, merchandise, or goods, or for purposes of advertising or selling, or soliciting purchases of, products, merchandise, goods, or services, without prior consent from the [heirs], shall be liable for any damages sustained by the person or persons injured as a result thereof. . . .

(2)   For purposes of this subdivision, a play, book, magazine, newspaper, musical composition, audiovisual work, radio or television program, single and original work of art, work of political or newsworthy value, or an advertisement or commercial announcement for any of these works, shall not be considered a product, article of merchandise, good, or service if it is fictional or nonfictional entertainment, or a dramatic, literary, or musical work. . . .

(b)   The rights recognized under this section are property rights, freely transferable or descendible, in whole or in part, by contract or by means of any trust or any other testamentary instrument, ... and . . . shall vest in the persons entitled to these property rights under the testamentary instrument of the deceased personality effective as of the date of his or her death. In the absence of an express transfer in a testamentary instrument of the deceased personality's rights in his or her name, voice, signature, photograph, or likeness, a provision in the testamentary instrument that provides for the disposition of the residue of the deceased personality's assets shall be effective to transfer the rights recognized under this section in accordance with the terms of that provision. The rights established by this section shall also be freely transferable or descendible by contract, trust, or any other testamentary instrument by any subsequent owner of the deceased personality's rights as recognized by this section. Nothing in this section shall be construed to render invalid or unenforceable any contract entered into by a deceased personality during his or her lifetime by which the deceased personality assigned the rights, in whole or in part, to use his or her name, voice, signature, photograph or likeness . . .

(g)   No action shall be brought under this section by reason of any use of a deceased personality's name, voice, signature, photograph, or likeness occurring after the expiration of 70 years after the death of the deceased personality.

(h)   As used in this section, "deceased personality" means any natural person whose name, voice, signature, photograph, or likeness has commercial value at the time of his or her death, whether or not during the lifetime of that natural person the person used his or her name, voice, signature, photograph, or likeness on or in products, merchandise or goods, or for purposes of advertising or selling, or solicitation of purchase of, products, merchandise, goods, or services. A "deceased personality" shall include, without limitation, any such natural person who has died within 70 years prior to January 1, 1985.

(i)   As used in this section, "photograph" means any photograph or photographic reproduction, still or moving, or any video tape or live television transmission, of any person, such that the deceased personality is readily identifiable. A deceased personality shall be deemed to be readily identifiable from a photograph when one who views the photograph with the naked eye can reasonably determine who the person depicted in the photograph is.

(j)   For purposes of this section, a use of a name, voice, signature, photograph, or likeness in connection with any news, public affairs, or sports broadcast or account, or any political campaign, shall not constitute a use for which consent is required under subdivision (a). . . .

(m) The remedies provided for in this section are cumulative and shall be in addition to any others provided for by law.

(n)   This section shall apply to the adjudication of liability and the imposition of any damages or other remedies in cases in which the liability, damages, and other remedies arise from acts occurring directly in this state. . . .

QUESTIONS

Your client, Edsel Parsley, Jr., is the son and sole heir of the deceased famous eponymous rock star. He asks you to explain what the statute means, and how it works. For example:

1.   Pablita Metisse made a series of cubist portraits of Parsley in the 1960s. She has for many years licensed the images for reproduction and sale on a variety of products, including posters, wall calendars, and t-shirts. What claims, if any, might Parsley Jr. have against Metisse?

2.   Of all Parsley's hit songs, "Red Leather Boots" has proven the most loved and most enduring. Nick Nack Emporium has been producing and selling a novelty item, a red leather key chain in the form of a boot, with a microchip that plays a digitally remastered clip of Parsley singing the opening bars of "Red Leather Boots." Does Parsley Jr. have a claim under this statute?

3.   During Parsley's lifetime, his business manager, Sergeant Sanders, handled all Parsley's affairs, including concert and club appearances and endorsements. He has contacted Parsley Jr. to inform him that, in light of his relationship with Parsley Sr., Sergeant Sanders has sole authority to exercise Parsley's post-mortem rights. What is the basis of Sanders' claim, and is it valid?

4.   Andy Varhol is a famous artist who creates silk screens of dead celebrities, including Parsley. He mass produces these silk screens and sells them to art dealers. The Varhol images have received extensive press coverage, and have come to be considered current cultural icons. Andy has

never sought permission from Parsley Jr. Does the latter have a claim under the statute?

5.   Parsley Sr.'s brother, Syd, was also a famous singer, and in fact, he was probably a better musician and more famous than Parsley Sr. at one point. However, a series of personal scandals left Syd unpopular and broke, and by the time he passed away, not many people remembered Syd or his music. A few years ago, Syd's music was rediscovered by the underground music community, and now it has regained popularity among mainstream music fans. Vendors have followed suit, and now t-shirts and posters are being sold in California with Syd's face on them. Are these vendors liable to Syd's heirs under the statute?

Problem Case No. 6: California and New York State Eavesdropping Statutes

Cal. Penal Code

§ 632. Eavesdropping on or recording confidential communications

(a)   A person who, intentionally and without the consent of all parties to a confidential communication, uses an electronic amplifying or recording device to eavesdrop upon or record the confidential communication, whether the communication is carried on among the parties in the presence of one another or by means of a telegraph, telephone, or other device, except a radio, shall be punished by a fine not exceeding two thousand five hundred dollars ($2,500) per violation, or imprisonment in a county jail not exceeding one year, or in the state prison, or by both that fine and imprisonment.

(b)   For the purposes of this section, "person" means an individual, business association, partnership, corporation, limited liability company, or other legal entity, and an individual acting or purporting to act for or on behalf of any government or subdivision thereof, whether federal, state, or local, but excludes an individual known by all parties to a confidential communication to be overhearing or recording the communication.

(c)   For the purposes of this section, "confidential communication" means any communication carried on in circumstances as may reasonably indicate that any party to the communication desires it to be confined to the parties thereto, but excludes a communication made in a public gathering or in any legislative, judicial, executive, or administrative proceeding open to the public, or in any other circumstance in which the parties to the communication may reasonably expect that the communication may be overheard or recorded.

§ 637. Disclosure of telegraphic or telephonic message; punishment; exception

Every person not a party to a telegraphic or telephonic communication who willfully discloses the contents of a telegraphic or telephonic message, or any part thereof, addressed to another person, without the permission of that person, unless directed so to do by the lawful order of a court, is punishable by imprisonment . . . , or in a county jail not exceeding one year, or by fine not exceeding five thousand dollars ($5,000), or by both that fine and imprisonment.

§ 637.2. Civil action by person injured; injunction

(a) Any person who has been injured by a violation of this chapter may bring an action against the person who committed the violation for the greater of the following amounts:

(1) Five thousand dollars ($5,000) per violation.

(2) Three times the amount of actual damages, if any, sustained by the plaintiff. . . .

New York Penal Law

§ 250.00 Eavesdropping; definitions of terms

The following definitions are applicable to this article:

1. "Wiretapping" means the intentional overhearing or recording of a telephonic or telegraphic communication by a person other than a sender or receiver thereof, without the consent of either the sender or receiver, by means of any instrument, device or equipment. The normal operation of a telephone or telegraph corporation and the normal use of the services and facilities furnished by such corporation pursuant to its tariffs or necessary to protect the rights or property of said corporation shall not be deemed "wiretapping."

2. "Mechanical overhearing of a conversation" means the intentional overhearing or recording of a conversation or discussion, without the consent of at least one party thereto, by a person not present thereat, by means of any instrument, device or equipment.

3. "Telephonic communication" means any aural transfer made in whole or in part through the use of facilities for the transmission of communications by the aid of wire, cable or other like connection between the point of origin and the point of reception (including the use of such connection in a switching station) furnished or operated by any person engaged in providing or operating such facilities for the transmission of communications and such term includes any electronic storage of such communications.

4. "Aural transfer" means a transfer containing the human voice at any point between and including the point of origin and the point of reception.

5. "Electronic communication" means any transfer of signs, signals, writing, images, sounds, data, or intelligence of any nature transmitted in whole or in part by a wire, radio, electromagnetic, photoelectronic or photo-optical system, but does not include:

(a) any telephonic or telegraphic communication; or

(b) any communication made through a tone only paging device; or

(c) any communication made through a tracking device consisting of an electronic or mechanical device which permits the tracking of the movement of a person or object; or

(d) any communication that is disseminated by the sender through a method of transmission that is configured so that such communication is readily accessible to the general public.

6. "Intercepting or accessing of an electronic communication" and "intentionally intercepted or accessed" mean the intentional acquiring, receiving, collecting, overhearing, or recording of an electronic communication, without the consent of the sender or intended receiver thereof, by means of any instrument, device or equipment, except when used by a telephone company in the ordinary course of its business or when necessary to protect the rights or property of such company.

7. "Electronic communication service" means any service which provides to users thereof the ability to send or receive wire or electronic communications.

8. "Unlawfully" means not specifically authorized pursuant to article seven hundred or seven hundred five of the criminal procedure law for the purposes of this section and sections 250.05, 250.10 . . . of this article.

§ 250.05 Eavesdropping

A person is guilty of eavesdropping when he unlawfully engages in wiretapping, mechanical overhearing of a conversation, or intercepting or accessing of an electronic communication.

Eavesdropping is a . . . felony.

§ 250.10 Possession of eavesdropping devices

A person is guilty of possession of eavesdropping devices when, under circumstances evincing an intent to use or to permit the same to be used in violation of section 250.05, he possesses any instrument, device or equipment designed for, adapted to or commonly used in wiretapping or mechanical overhearing of a conversation.

Possession of eavesdropping devices is a . . . misdemeanor.

QUESTIONS

Do either the California or New York Eavesdropping Statutes cover the following situations?

1. Online retailer Amaze-on sells a voice-controlled Gotcha speaker that, when turned on, listens and records all ambient sounds nearby it. Gotcha's sound recordings are uploaded to Amaze-on's cloud server, though the recordings are inaccessible to the owner of the device that recorded them. A homeowner who keeps a Gotcha on at all times in her living room invites a friend over, and the Gotcha listens to their conversation. The friend is unaware of the Gotcha's presence. Has either Amaze-on or the host violated either statute? Does it matter whether the host is aware of, and consented to, Gotcha's background recording and storage practices?

2. A parent keeps a baby monitor that looks like a teddy bear in his child's bedroom; the monitor records both video and audio in the room. While the parent is out at dinner, a babysitter puts the child to bed by reading her a bedtime story in the child's bedroom. Has the parent violated either statute if he fails to inform the babysitter about the baby monitor's recording?

3. A police officer pulls over a driver whose car has one taillight out. An observer nearby, concerned about possible police brutality, surreptitiously records the police officer's interactions with the driver of the car. The observer feels the driver was treated very rudely (and possibly verbally abusively) by the police officer, so unbeknownst to both the driver and officer, she posts the recording to her Facepalm social media account to expose the local police department. Has she violated either statute by either recording and/or posting the interaction?

4. A group of policymakers meet to discuss important current affairs issues under "Chatham House Rules" (where the broad contents of the meeting can be disclosed but no statement can be attributed to any particular participant). Unbeknownst to the group, one participant records the conversation. He later plays it for a journalist, who posts the recording online. Has either the recording participant or the leaking journalist violated either statute? Would it matter if the recording was of a conference call rather than an in-person gathering?

5. Three individuals are on a Swype video chat. One of the participants, who is recording the video chat without the knowledge of the other two participants, leaves the room for another meeting midway through the call, and does not return. Nevertheless, he secretly keeps the recording going; the recording captures a conversation between the other two about how unlikeable he is. Has he violated either statute by keeping the recording going?

6. A wife secretly records her deaf husband's sign language conversations over Swype video chat with a deaf ex-girlfriend who lives overseas. Has the wife violated either statute? Does it matter if at any point during the conversation either the husband or the ex-girlfriend speaks out loud?

7.   A celebrity gossip website gains access to a celebrity's cell phone text messages without his permission and posts excerpts of the text messages online. Has the gossip website violated either statute?

2.   RESOLVING STATUTORY ISSUES—A GENERAL VIEW

Heydon's Case

Court of Exchequer, 1584.
3 Coke 7a, 76 Eng.Rep. 637.

[The technique of identifying the problem to which the statutory text responds is usually traced back to this case. Sir Edward Coke (later Lord Chief Justice of England and Wales) stated the much-quoted "Doctrine of Heydon's Case" as follows:]

And it was resolved by them [the judges], that for the sure and true interpretation of all statutes in general (be they penal or beneficial, restrictive or enlarging of the common law) four things are to be discerned and considered—

1st. What was the common law before the making of the Act.

2nd. What was the mischief and defect for which the common law did not provide.

3rd. What remedy the Parliament hath resolved and appointed to cure the disease of the commonwealth.

And 4th. The true reason of the remedy, and then the office of all the Judges is always to make such construction as shall suppress the mischief, and advance the remedy, and to suppress subtle inventions of evasion for continuance of the mischief, and *pro privato commodo*, and to add force and life to the cure and remedy, according to the true intent of the makers of the Act, *pro bono publico.* . . .

QUESTION

What assumptions about sources of law underlie the "Doctrine of Heydon's Case"? How valid are these assumptions today, especially when interpreting federal statutes?

———————

In applying statutes, courts traditionally often looked to "the intent of the legislature" to resolve doubts as to the meaning or legal effect of statutory language, as *Heydon's Case* articulates. In your study of the cases in this Casebook, you will find that the effort to ascertain the "legislative intent" is, on many occasions, quite as difficult and subtle an operation as is the parallel case law task of arriving at the "holding" of a case.

Consider the range of problems that may arise when deciding particular cases by reference to the general commands of statutes. A legislative direction must be expressed in words, and words are notoriously inexact and imperfect symbols for the communication of ideas. In addition, one must reckon with the inexhaustible variety of the facts to which such words could be applied. To determine from the language of an enactment the "legislative intent," in the sense of a pre-existing understanding of the lawmakers as to the statute's construction in relation to a particular issue, may involve semantic problems of very great difficulty.

Even more difficult are the cases in which the interpretive issue before the court is one which was not, and perhaps could not have been, foreseen, even in the most general outline, by the legislators responsible for the enactment. In such cases, the "interpreting" judge must perform the originative function of deciding whether to assign the statute a meaning or legal effect which it did not possess before the court's decision. Cardozo saw this with his characteristic clarity when he wrote:*

> Interpretation is often spoken of as if it were nothing but the search and the discovery of a meaning which, however obscure and latent, had none the less a real and ascertainable pre-existence in the legislator's mind. The process is, indeed, that at times, but it is often something more.

There are a number of other questions or considerations related to the methods of statutory interpretation which you should keep in mind in analyzing the materials to come. What light do these cases and other materials shed on the nature and application of legislative intent or other basic approaches to interpretation? What, if anything, does this case or excerpt reveal as to the types and causes of statutory ambiguity? What, if any, intrinsic and extrinsic aids to interpretation, or interpretative rules or maxims, do the judges employ in a given case, and what conclusions would you draw as to these aids' value and use? What lessons emerge from these materials for purposes of advocacy in subsequent statutory cases? Note, incidentally, that the materials in this Casebook provide many illustrations of the different types of statutory enactments one may expect to encounter in law practice.

B. METHODS OF STATUTORY INTERPRETATION—AN OVERVIEW

In the court-centered domain of the common law, judges are the undisputed authorities of the law's content, developed over time through the case method. By contrast, statutes derive their legitimacy from the

---

* The Nature of the Judicial Process 14 (1921).

democratically elected legislators who enacted them. Those subject to the law must then interpret those enactments so that their conduct complies with the law, and when two or more parties disagree about the terms of such compliance, courts are called upon to resolve the disagreement. Hence the tension: courts retain "the last word" as to a law's meaning, but legislatures, not courts, produce the law's content (including, sometimes, statutes that override courts' prior interpretations, as discussed in Section VII.C, *infra*). Describing judges as "faithful agents" of the legislature helps to reconcile potentially conflicting institutional competences. Viewed this way, when courts interpret statutes, they should seek to apply the broad statutory command of the legislature to the specific circumstances of the case. Yet because statutory provisions are often ambiguous, and because a specific set of facts may present a court with a situation not clearly anticipated by the statute's drafters (nor clearly answered by the statute's text), courts regularly draw on sources and methods of interpretation beyond the "plain text" of the statutory provision itself in order to resolve the apparent ambiguity. Once the interpreter seeks answers beyond the "plain text," however, she may need to provide a rationale for the particular source or method she uses to derive meaning from the text. (And as you will see, even seemingly straightforward sources of meaning such as dictionaries can raise numerous complications.)

1.   A TYPOLOGY OF STATUTORY INTERPRETATION METHODS

One way to examine questions of statutory interpretation is to scrutinize prevailing interpretative approaches *as methods* and to consider the justifications (both stated and unstated) for their application. One may categorize legal methods of interpretation on the basis of three broad sources of authority:

a.   THE DRAFTER'S INTENDED MEANING

First, some interpretive methods seek to identify the drafters' *intended* meaning of the statute. These methods derive their legitimacy in part from the concept of legislative supremacy itself. Since democratically elected legislative bodies enact statutes on the basis of popular mandate, the interpreter should endeavor to understand what that popular will—as manifested through the legislature—sought to accomplish in enacting the statute. (Recall the inquiry prescribed in *Heydon's Case, supra*: "What remedy the Parliament hath resolved and appointed to cure the disease of the commonwealth. . . . [and t]he true reason of the remedy[?]") "Intended meaning" subdivides into two further categories:

> *(a)   Drafters' Purpose (or* Objective *Intent):* This approach seeks to elucidate the goals of the statute, often evidenced by the statute's "findings" or "purpose" section. This may involve a holistic reading of the statutory scheme in order to identify the

"evil" or "mischief" sought to be remedied—as articulated above in *Heydon's Case*—or to ascertain the regulatory scheme the legislature sought to put in place.

(b) Drafters' Intentions (or Subjective *Intent):* A second, related approach focuses on specific drafters' intentions as articulated by individual legislators or in documents prepared by the legislative committee(s) responsible for drafting the statute. These materials, which document the "legislative history" of the bill on its way to becoming a statute, purport to elucidate the drafters' specific intention(s) as to how the statute should operate, as well as what they intended it to mean. These materials include comments made in committee reports, floor statements, and committee testimony, often in the form of explanations from the drafters that elaborate on the (too often ambiguous) statutory text they have prepared. Non-drafting legislators and their staff members frequently rely on these materials to understand the effect the bill they are voting is intended to have. As you will read later, some scholars and jurists emphasize that legislators rely more heavily on these materials than the text of the statute itself when seeking to understand the statute's meaning prior to enacting it.

b.   THE REASONABLE READER'S UNDERSTANDING

By contrast, many interpretive methods instead focus on the meaning of the statute as the statute's *reasonable reader* might understand it. These methods generally purport to seek the "ordinary" meaning of the statutory term or phrase at issue, drawing on evidence of customary linguistic usage, syntax, and semantics. Many judicial "canons of construction" derive from broadly applicable syntactic and semantic rules for deriving meaning from text, as you will see in the next subsection. Because only the bare statutory text itself was enacted into law—and not the accompanying legislative history materials—these methods derive much of their legitimacy from bicameralism and presentment (the formal process of enacting the text of the statute), the public availability of that text, and the presumption that the statute's text (and often the text alone) must communicate the legislature's meaning. "Textualist" jurists like Justice Robert Jackson and Justice Antonin Scalia have often remarked that "[w]e do not inquire what the *legislature* meant; we ask only what the *statute* means."* For a variety of jurisprudential and methodological reasons discussed throughout this Part and Part III, *infra*, these jurists are skeptical of the value of ascertaining drafters' intentions, and prefer instead to focus on the meaning of the drafters' words.

---

*   Antonin Scalia, A Matter of Interpretation: Federal Courts and the Law 23 (Amy Gutmann ed., 1997) (emphasis added).

Interpretive methods grounded in the reasonable reader's understanding align along two further axes, those of temporality and sophistication:

Temporality

(a) *The* Original *Reasonable Reader's Understanding:* This is the meaning of the statutory term or phrase as it would have been understood by the reasonable reader at the time of the statute's enactment.

(b) *The* Present-Day *Reasonable Reader's Understanding:* This is the meaning of the statutory term or phrase as understood by the *present-day* reasonable reader of the statute at the time the interpretive problem arises.

As with all linguistic usage, the meaning commonly attributed to statutory terms or phrases may change over time. These contrasting approaches highlight the choice between giving a term or phrase its commonly understood meaning at the time of the statute's enactment, or instead its contemporary meaning at the time the interpretive question arises.

In some instances, the statute *itself* may indicate whether to interpret its meaning historically or dynamically. For example, in Business Electronics Corp. v. Sharp Electronics Corp., 485 U.S. 717, 732 (1988), the Supreme Court recognized that "[t]he Sherman Act adopted the term 'restraint of trade' along with its dynamic potential. It invokes the common law itself, and not merely the static content that the common law had assigned to the term in 1890. . . . The changing content of the term 'restraint of trade' was well recognized at the time the Sherman Act was enacted." Thus, the present-day reasonable reader's understanding of a "restraint of trade" might prevail over the common understanding of a "restraint of trade" at the time the statute was enacted.

Sophistication

A second axis concerns the reasonable reader's presumed degree of sophistication or specialization:

(a) *The Reasonable* Generalist *Reader's Understanding:* This is commonly referred to as the "ordinary" meaning that a member of the public might attribute to the term or phrase in question. Judges often turn to dictionaries or other depositories of general linguistic usage to ascertain the "ordinary" meaning of a term.

(b) *The Reasonable* Specialist *Reader's Understanding:* As you will see, while the audience for many statutes is presumed to be members of the general public, some statutory provisions address a more specialized audience or linguistic community. In those circumstances, interpretive methods may seek to ascertain the meaning of a word or phrase as understood by the more specialized community of readers, such as lawyers. Interpretive aids such as *Black's Law Dictionary* may identify the meaning of a legal term of art that may differ from that term's ordinary meaning. In other circumstances, judges have sought evidence of the linguistic usage of specialists in fields such as intellectual property or bankruptcy.

Thus, when drawing on methods that seek the reasonable reader's understanding, the interpreter will assume (either tacitly or expressly) *both* a temporality *and* a level of sophistication of the presumed reader. Consider again the term "restraint of trade" from *Sharp Electronics Corp., supra*: is that term's meaning more likely to be reflected by what an ordinary reader would understand it means today, or what a lawyer or other common-law literate reader likely thought it meant at the time of the statute's passage?

Note that if methods that yield the reasonable reader's interpretation are to be *dispositive*, there can be only *one* reasonable reading of the statute. Otherwise, if the statute is susceptible to multiple reasonable understandings, the reasonable reader approach will not, *on its own*, resolve the interpretive question. In some instances, interpreters who employ the reasonable reader approach thus may beg the question: what makes one particular hypothetical reader's understanding *reasonable*, and another's *unreasonable*? If the reasonable ordinary reader believes a "restraint of trade" means one thing, and a reasonable law-literate reader believes another, whose meaning should prevail? As you will see throughout this Casebook, in many cases judges disagree about a statute's "ordinary" or "plain" meaning. Sometimes they also disagree about whether the presumed reader should be a generalist reader or a specialist reader; in other instances, some focus more on the term's meaning during its period of enactment, others on its evolving present-day meaning.

If presumptively reasonable *judges* often disagree about the "ordinary" or "plain" meaning of a statutory term or phrase, one may wonder how often only one single, reasonable "ordinary" or "plain" meaning will emerge from a statutory term or phrase. Some interpretive settings expressly acknowledge the inherent ambiguity of many statutory texts. For example, prevailing practices in administrative law anticipate the possibility of multiple reasonable interpretations: in certain circumstances, *any* reasonable reading may suffice when courts review an administrative agency's proposed construction of an ambiguous statutory provision. However, if two readers can arrive at distinct yet reasonable understandings of the statute's meaning outside of the context of agency interpretations of statutes, then what makes one reader's understanding more legally persuasive than another's?

c.   RULE-OF-LAW-BASED METHODS OF INTERPRETATION

Perhaps because judges often disagree about what the legislature intended the statute to mean, or about what a reasonable reader might understand it to mean, they often turn to a third set of interpretive methods. Some "canons of construction" draw on jurisprudential tenets that guide the interpreter in deciding on the *legal* meaning or effect of the statutory text. These methods serve as fundamental rules for legal interpretation, and they derive their legitimacy primarily from long-standing rule-of-law principles that undergird our federal, common-law legal system.

Most "substantive" canons of interpretation you will encounter in this Part do not necessarily reflect either the drafters' intended meaning or the reasonable reader's understanding. Canons such as the "clear notice rule," the "rule of lenity," the doctrines of "constitutional avoidance" and "void for vagueness," and the "presumption against retroactive application" are instead grounded in fundamental legal principles like fair notice, reasonable reliance, and separation of powers. For this reason, substantive canons sometimes come under attack because they are hard to justify on faithful agency grounds alone, because they are sometimes in tension with both legislative supremacy *and* popular understanding. Nevertheless, these methods prove to be remarkably enduring (and well received) among judges across the interpretive spectrum. Perhaps for this reason, judges generally do not disagree about *whether* to apply these substantive methods in at least some circumstances; instead, disagreements arise concerning *when* and *how* they apply.

2.   APPLYING LEGAL METHODS OF STATUTORY INTERPRETATION

Courts regularly draw on all three sets of methods to arrive at a chosen interpretation, often shoring up the weaknesses in reasoning of one set of methods with support from another. As you read the cases in this Casebook, look for instances in which judges either expressly or implicitly rely on rule-of-law methods as a form of tie-breaker for deciding between competing potential drafters' intended meanings or reasonable readers' understandings of the statute.

For instance, the opinions rendered in the appellate and Supreme Court decisions in *Johnson v. Southern Pacific Co.*, below, expose many different methods of statutory interpretation. As you study the opinions, try to identify the different interpretive techniques and devices employed.

BUT, before you read any of the judicial analysis, concentrate first on the facts of the case and on the language of the statute:

— What happened in this case?

— What does the statute say (verbatim)?

— How does the statute apply to these facts?

Consider how *you* would rule on Johnson's claim under the statute. Only then should you turn to the courts' treatment of his claim.

————————

The Southern Pacific Co. was operating passenger trains between San Francisco and Ogden, Utah. It habitually drew a dining car in these trains. Such a car formed a part of a train leaving San Francisco, and ran through to Ogden, where it was ordinarily turned and put into a train going west to San Francisco. On August 5, 1900, the east-bound train was so late that it was not practicable to get the dining car into Ogden in time to place it in the next west-bound train, and it was therefore left on a side track at Promontory, Utah, to be picked up by the west-bound train when it arrived. While it was standing on this track the conductor of an interstate freight train which arrived there was directed to take this dining car to a turntable, turn it, and place it back upon the side track so that it would be ready to return to San Francisco. The conductor instructed his crew to carry out this direction. The plaintiff, Johnson, the head brakeman, undertook to couple the freight engine to the dining car for the purpose of carrying out the conductor's order. The freight engine and the eight-wheel dining car involved were the property of defendant railroad company. The freight engine, regularly used in interstate hauling of standard eight-wheel freight cars, was equipped with a Janney coupler, which would couple automatically with another Janney coupler, and the dining car was provided with a Miller automatic hook; but the Miller hook would not couple automatically with the Janney coupler, because it was on the same side, and would pass over it. Johnson knew this, and undertook to make the coupling by means of a link and pin. He knew that it was a difficult coupling to make, and that it was necessary to go between the engine and the car to accomplish it, and that it was dangerous to do so. Nevertheless, he went in between the engine and the car without objection or protest and tried three times to make the coupling. He failed twice; the third time his hand was caught and crushed so that it became necessary to amputate his hand above the wrist.

Johnson brought an action for damages for personal injury against the railroad. The case was tried in the Circuit Court of the United States for the District of Utah. At the trial, Southern Pacific, after the plaintiff had rested, moved the court to instruct the jury to find in defendant's favor. The motion was granted and the jury found a verdict accordingly on which judgment was entered. Plaintiff carried the case to the Circuit Court of Appeals for the Eighth Circuit.

Defendant contended in the district and circuit courts that it was not liable for the injury on the ground that plaintiff, under the rules of the common law, had "assumed the risk" involved in coupling the dining car and locomotive. Plaintiff Johnson, on the other hand, contended that at the time of the injury defendant was violating a federal statute (*infra*) in respect to the dining car and locomotive concerned, and that by reason of such violation plaintiff, under this statute, was not to be deemed to have assumed the risk. It was acknowledged that the locomotive possessed a power driving-wheel brake, that there were train brakes and appliances for operating a train brake system as required and that there was no failure, as to either vehicle, to provide the requisite grab irons or drawbars.

Railway Safety Appliance Act
52 Cong. Ch. 196, March 2, 1893, 27 Stat. 531.

The text of the federal statute relied on by plaintiff, which was in effect at the time of the injury and at all times pertinent to this problem, is set out herewith as it appears in the Statutes at Large (27 Stat. 531):

Chap. 196.—An act to promote the safety of employees and travelers upon railroads by compelling common carriers engaged in interstate commerce to equip their cars with automatic couplers and continuous brakes and their locomotives with driving-wheel brakes, and for other purposes.

Sec. 1. *Be it enacted by the Senate and House of Representatives of the United States of America in Congress assembled,* That from and after the first day of January, eighteen hundred and ninety-eight, it shall be unlawful for any common carrier engaged in interstate commerce by railroad to use on its line any locomotive engine in moving interstate traffic not equipped with a power driving-wheel brake and appliances for operating the train-brake system, or to run any train in such traffic after said date that has not a sufficient number of cars in it so equipped with power or train brakes that the engineer on the locomotive drawing such train can control its speed without requiring brakemen to use the common hand brake for that purpose.

Sec. 2.   That on and after the first day of January, eighteen hundred and ninety-eight, it shall be unlawful for any such common carrier to haul or permit to be hauled or used on its line any car used in moving interstate traffic not equipped with couplers coupling automatically by impact, and which can be uncoupled without the necessity of men going between the ends of the cars.

Sec. 3.   That when any person, firm, company, or corporation engaged in interstate commerce by railroad shall have equipped a sufficient number of its cars so as to comply with the provisions of section one of this act, it may lawfully refuse to receive from connecting lines of road or shippers any cars not equipped sufficiently, in accordance with the first section of this act, with such power or train brakes as will work and readily interchange with the brakes in use on its own cars, as required by this act.

Sec. 4.   That from and after the first day of July, eighteen hundred and ninety-five, until otherwise ordered by the Interstate Commerce Commission, it shall be unlawful for any railroad company to use any car in interstate commerce that is not provided with secure grab irons or handholds in the ends and sides of each car for greater security to men in coupling and uncoupling cars.

Sec. 5.   That within ninety days from the passage of this act the American Railway Association is authorized hereby to designate to the Interstate Commerce Commission the standard height of drawbars for freight cars, measured perpendicular from the level of the tops of the rails to the centers of the drawbars, for each of the several gauges of railroads in use in the United States, and shall fix a maximum variation from such standard height to be allowed between the drawbars of empty and loaded cars. Upon their determination being certified to the Interstate Commerce Commission, said Commission shall at once give notice of the standard fixed upon to all common carriers, owners, or lessees engaged in interstate commerce in the United States by such means as the Commission may deem proper. But should said association fail to determine a standard as above provided, it shall be the duty of the Interstate Commerce Commission to do so, before July first, eighteen hundred and ninety-four, and immediately to give notice thereof as aforesaid. And after July first, eighteen hundred and ninety-five, no cars, either loaded or unloaded, shall be used in interstate traffic which do not comply with the standard above provided for.

Sec. 6.   That any such common carrier using any locomotive engine, running any train, or hauling or permitting to be hauled or used on its line any car in violation of any of the provisions of this act, shall be liable to a penalty of one hundred dollars for each and every such violation, to be recovered in a suit or suits to be brought by the United States district attorney in the district court of the United States having jurisdiction in the locality where such violation shall have been committed, and it shall be the duty of such district attorney to bring such suits upon duly verified information being lodged with him of such violation having occurred. And it shall also be the duty of the Interstate Commerce Commission to lodge with the proper district attorneys information of any such violations as may come to its knowledge: *Provided,* that nothing in this act contained shall apply to trains composed of four-wheel cars or to locomotives used in hauling such trains.

Sec. 7.   That the Interstate Commerce Commission may from time to time upon full hearing and for good cause extend the period within which any common carrier shall comply with the provisions of this act.

Sec. 8.   That any employee of any such common carrier who may be injured by any locomotive, car, or train in use contrary to the provision of this act shall not be deemed thereby to have assumed the risk thereby occasioned, although continuing in the employment of such carrier after the unlawful use of such locomotive, car, or train had been brought to his knowledge.

Approved, March 2, 1893.

Johnson v. Southern Pacific Co.
Circuit Court of Appeals for the Eighth Circuit, 1902.
117 Fed. 462, reversed 196 U.S. 1, 25 S.Ct. 158, 49 L.Ed. 363 (1904).

■ SANBORN, CIRCUIT JUDGE [joined by LOCHREN, DISTRICT JUDGE], after stating the case . . .

Under the common law the plaintiff assumed the risks and dangers of the coupling which he endeavored to make, and for that reason he is estopped from recovering the damages which resulted from his undertaking. He was an intelligent and experienced brakeman, familiar with the couplers he sought to join, and with their condition, and well aware of the difficulty and danger of his undertaking, so that he falls far within the familiar rules that the servant assumes the ordinary risk and dangers of the employment upon which he enters, so far as they are known to him, and so far as they would have been known to one of his age, experience, and capacity by the use of ordinary care, and that the risks and dangers of coupling cars provided with different kinds of well-known couplers, bumpers, brakeheads and deadwoods are the ordinary risks and dangers of a brakeman's service. [Citations.]

This proposition is not seriously challenged, but counsel base their claim for a reversal of the judgment below upon the position that the plaintiff was relieved of this assumption of risk, and of its consequences, by the provisions of the act of Congress of March 2, 1893 (27 Stat. c. 196, p. 531). The title of that act, and the parts of it that are material to the consideration of this contention are these: [see *supra*]

The first thought that suggests itself to the mind upon a perusal of this law, and a comparison of it with the facts of this case, is that this statute has no application here, because both the dining car and the engine were equipped as this act directs. The car was equipped with Miller couplers which would couple automatically with couplers of the same construction upon cars in the train in which it was used to carry on interstate commerce, and the engine was equipped with a power driving wheel brake such as this statute prescribes. To overcome this difficulty, counsel for the plaintiff persuasively argues that this is a remedial statute; that laws for the prevention of fraud, the suppression of a public wrong, and the bestowal of a public good are remedial in their nature, and should be liberally construed, to prevent the mischief and to advance the remedy, notwithstanding the fact that they may impose a penalty for their violation; and that this statute should be so construed as to forbid the use of a locomotive as well as a car which is not equipped with an automatic coupler. In support of this contention he cites Suth. St. Const. § 360; Wall v. Platt, 169 Mass. 398, 48 N.E. 270; Taylor v. U.S., 3 How. 197, 11 L.Ed. 559; and other cases of like character. The general propositions which counsel quote may be found in the opinions in these cases, and in some of them they were applied to the particular facts which those actions presented. But the interpolation in this act of Congress by construction of an ex post facto provision that it is, and ever since January 1, 1898, has been unlawful for any common carrier to use any engine in interstate traffic that is or was not equipped with couplers coupling automatically, and that any carrier that has used or shall use an engine not so equipped has been and shall be liable to a penalty of $100 for every violation of this provision, is too abhorrent to the sense of justice and fairness, too rank and radical a piece of judicial legislation, and in violation of too many established and salutary rules of construction, to commend itself to the judicial reason or conscience.

The primary rule for the interpretation of a statute or a contract is to ascertain, if possible, and enforce, the intention which the legislative body that enacted the law, or the parties who made the agreement, have expressed therein. But it is the intention expressed in the law or contract, and that only, that the courts may give effect to. They cannot lawfully assume or presume secret purposes that are not indicated or expressed by the statute itself and then enact provisions to accomplish these supposed intentions. While ambiguous terms and doubtful expressions may be interpreted to carry out the intention of a legislative body which a statute fairly evidences, a secret intention cannot be interpreted into a statute which is plain and unambiguous, and which does not express it. The legal presumption is that the legislative body expressed its intention, that it intended what is expressed, and that it intended nothing more. [Citation.] Construction and interpretation have no place or office where the terms of a statute are clear and certain, and its meaning is plain. In such a case they serve only to create doubt and to confuse the judgment. When the language of a statute is unambiguous, and its meaning evident, it must be held to mean what it plainly expresses, and no room is left for construction [Citations.]

This statute clearly prohibits the use of any engine in moving interstate commerce not equipped with a power driving wheel brake, and the use of any car not equipped with automatic couplers, under a penalty of $100 for each offense; and it just as plainly omits to forbid, under that or any penalty, the use of any car which is not equipped with a power driving wheel brake, and the use of any engine that is not equipped with automatic couplers. This striking omission to express any intention to prohibit the use of engines unequipped with automatic couplers raises the legal presumption that no such intention existed, and prohibits the courts from importing such a purpose into the act, and enacting provisions to give it effect. The familiar rule that the expression of one thing is the exclusion of others points to the same conclusion. Section 2 of the act does not declare that it shall be unlawful to use any engine or car not equipped with automatic couplers, but that it shall be unlawful only to use any car lacking this equipment. This clear and concise definition of the unlawful act is a cogent and persuasive argument against the contention that the use without couplers of locomotives, hand cars, or other means of conducting interstate traffic, was made a misdemeanor by this act. Where the statute enumerates the persons, things, or acts affected by it, there is an implied exclusion of all others. Suth. St. Const. § 227. And when the title of this statute and its first section are again read; when it is perceived that it was not from inattention, thoughtlessness, or forgetfulness; that it was not because locomotives were overlooked or out of mind, but that it was advisedly and after careful consideration of the equipment which they should have, that Congress forbade the use of cars alone without automatic couplers; when it is seen that the title of the act is to compel common carriers to "equip their cars with automatic couplers . . . and their locomotives with driving wheel brakes"; that the first section makes it unlawful to use locomotives not equipped with such brakes, and the second section declares it to be illegal to use cars without automatic couplers,—the argument becomes unanswerable and conclusive.

Again, this act of Congress changes the common law. Before its enactment, servants coupling cars used in interstate commerce without automatic couplers assumed the risk and danger of that employment, and carriers were not liable for injuries which the employés suffered in the discharge of this duty. Since its passage the employés no longer assume this risk, and, if they are free from contributory negligence, they may recover for the damages they sustain in this work. A statute which thus changes the common law must be strictly construed. The common or the general law is not further abrogated by such a statute than the clear import of its language necessarily requires. Shaw v. Railroad Co., 101 U.S. 557, 565, 25 L.Ed. 892; Fitzgerald v. Quann, 109 N.Y. 441, 445, 17 N.E. 354; Brown v. Barry, 3 Dall. 365, 367, 1 L.Ed. 638. The language of this statute does not require the abrogation of the common law that the servant assumes the risk of coupling a locomotive without automatic couplers with a car which is provided with them.

Moreover, this is a penal statute, and it may not be so broadened by judicial construction as to make it cover and permit the punishment of an act which is not denounced by the fair import of its terms. The acts which this statute declares to be unlawful, and for the commission of which it imposes a penalty, were lawful before its enactment, and their performance subjected to no penalty or liability. It makes that unlawful which was lawful before its passage, and it imposes a penalty for its performance. Nor is this penalty a mere forfeiture for the benefit of the party aggrieved or injured. It is a penalty prescribed by the statute, and recoverable by the government. It is, therefore, under every definition of the term, a penal statute. The act which lies at the foundation of this suit—the use of a locomotive which was not equipped with a Miller hook to turn a car which was duly equipped with automatic couplers—was therefore unlawful or lawful as it was or was not forbidden by this statute. That act has been done. When it was done it was neither forbidden nor declared to be unlawful by the express terms of this law. There is no language in it which makes it unlawful to use in interstate commerce a locomotive engine which is not equipped with automatic couplers. The argument of counsel for the plaintiff is, however, that it falls within the mischief which congress was seeking to remedy, and hence it should be construed to make this act unlawful because it falls within the mischief which congress was seeking to remedy, and hence it should be presumed that the legislative body intended to denounce this act as much as that which it forbade by the terms of the law. An ex post facto statute which would make such an innocent act a crime would be violative of the basic principles of Anglo-Saxon jurisprudence. An ex post facto construction which has the same effect is equally abhorrent to the sense of justice and of reason. The mischief at which a statute was leveled, and the fact that other acts which it does not denounce are within the mischief, and of equal atrocity with those which it forbids, do not raise the presumption that the legislative body which enacted it had the intention, which the law does not express, to prohibit the performance of the acts which it does not forbid. Nor will they warrant a construction which imports into the statute such a prohibition. The intention of the legislature and the meaning of a penal statute must be found in the language actually used, interpreted according to its fair and usual meaning, and not in the evils which it was intended to remedy, nor in the assumed secret intention of the lawmakers to accomplish that which they did not express. [Citation.]

The decision and opinion of the Supreme Court in U.S. v. Harris, 177 U.S. 305, 309, is persuasive—nay, it is decisive—in the case before us. The question there presented was analogous to that here in issue. It was whether Congress intended to include receivers managing a railroad among those who were prohibited from confining cattle, sheep, and other animals in cars more than 28 consecutive hours without unloading them for rest, water, and feeding, under "An act to prevent cruelty to animals while in transit by railroad or other means of transportation," approved March 3, 1873, and published in the Revised Statutes as sections 4386, 4387, 4388, and 4389. This statute forbids the confinement of stock in

cars by any railroad company engaged in interstate commerce more than
28 consecutive hours, and prescribes a penalty of $500 for a violation of
its provisions. The plain purpose of the act was to prohibit the
confinement of stock while in transit for an unreasonable length of time.
The confinement of cattle by receivers operating a railroad was as
injurious as their confinement by a railroad company, and the argument
for the United States was that, as such acts committed by receivers were
plainly within the mischief Congress was seeking to remedy, the
conclusion should be that it intended to prohibit receivers, as well as
railroad companies, from the commission of the forbidden acts, and hence
that receivers were subject to the provisions of the law. The Supreme
Court conceded that the confinement of stock in transit was within the
mischief that Congress sought to remedy. But it held that as the act did
not, by its terms, forbid such acts when committed by receivers, it could
not presume the intention of Congress to do so, and import such a
provision into the plain terms of the law. Mr. Justice Shiras, who
delivered the unanimous opinion of the court, said:

> "Giving all proper force to the contention of the counsel for the
> government, that there has been some relaxation on the part of
> the courts in applying the rule of strict construction to such
> statutes, it still remains that the intention of a penal statute
> must be found in the language actually used, interpreted
> according to its fair and obvious meaning. It is not permitted to
> courts, in this class of cases, to attribute inadvertence or
> oversight to the legislature when enumerating the classes of
> persons who are subjected to a penal enactment, nor to depart
> from the settled meaning of words or phrases in order to bring
> persons not named or distinctly described within the supposed
> purpose of the statute."

He cited with approval the decision of the Supreme Court in Sarlls
v. United States, 152 U.S. 570, 575, to the effect that lager beer was not
included within the meaning of the term "spirituous liquors" in the penal
statute found in section 2139 of the Revised Statutes, and closed the
discussion with the following quotation from the opinion of Chief Justice
Marshall in United States v. Wiltberger, 5 Wheat. 76, 5 L.Ed. 37:

> "The rule that penal statutes are to be construed strictly is
> perhaps not much less old than construction itself. It is founded
> on the tenderness of the law for the rights of individuals, and on
> the plain principle that the power of punishment is vested in the
> legislative, and not in the judicial, department. It is the
> legislature, not the court, which is to define a crime and ordain
> its punishment. It is said that, notwithstanding this rule, the
> intention of the lawmaker must govern in the construction of
> penal as well as other statutes. But this is not a new,
> independent rule, which subverts the old. It is a modification of
> the ancient maxim, and amounts to this: that, though penal

statutes are to be construed strictly, they are not to be construed so strictly as to defeat the obvious intention of the legislature. The maxim is not to be applied so as to narrow the words of the statute, to the exclusion of cases which those words, in their ordinary acceptation, or in that sense in which the legislature ordinarily used them, would comprehend. The intention of the legislature is to be collected from the words they employ. Where there is no ambiguity in the words, there is no room for construction. The case must be a strong one, indeed, which would justify a court in departing from the plain meaning of words,—especially in a penal act,—in search of an intention which the words themselves did not suggest. To determine that a case is within the intention of a statute, its language must authorize us to say so. It would be dangerous, indeed, to carry the principle that a case which is within the reason or mischief of a statute is within its provisions, so far as to punish a crime not enumerated in the statute, because it is of equal atrocity or of a kindred character with those which are enumerated. If this principle has ever been recognized in expounding criminal law, it has been in cases of considerable irritation, which it would be unsafe to consider as precedents forming a general rule in other cases."

The act of March 2, 1893, is a penal statute, and it changes the common law. It makes that unlawful which was innocent before its enactment, and imposes a penalty, recoverable by the government. Its terms are plain and free from doubt, and its meaning is clear. It declares that it is unlawful for a common carrier to use in interstate commerce a car which is not equipped with automatic couplers, and it omits to declare that it is illegal for a common carrier to use a locomotive that is not so equipped. As Congress expressed in this statute no intention to forbid the use of locomotives which were not provided with automatic couplers, the legal presumption is that it had no such intention, and provisions to import such an intention into the law and to effectuate it may not be lawfully enacted by judicial construction. The statute does not make it unlawful to use locomotives that are not equipped with automatic couplers in interstate commerce, and it did not modify the rule of the common law under which the plaintiff assumed the known risk of coupling such an engine to the dining car.

There are other considerations which lead to the same result. If we are in error in the conclusion already expressed, and if the word "car," in the second section of this statute, means locomotive, still this case does not fall under the law, (1) because both the locomotive and the dining car were equipped with automatic couplers; and (2) because at the time of the accident they were not "used in moving interstate traffic."

For the reasons which have been stated, this statute may not be lawfully extended by judicial construction beyond the fair meaning of its language. There is nothing in it which requires a common carrier engaged in interstate commerce to have every car on its railroad equipped with the same kind of coupling, or which requires it to have every car equipped with a coupler which will couple automatically with every other coupler with which it may be brought into contact in the usual course of business upon a great transcontinental system of railroads. If the lawmakers had intended to require such an equipment, it would have been easy for them to have said so, and the fact that they made no such requirement raises the legal presumption that they intended to make none.

Nor is the reason for their omission to do so far to seek or difficult to perceive. There are several kinds or makes of practical and efficient automatic couplers. Some railroad companies use one kind; others have adopted other kinds. Couplers of each kind will couple automatically with others of the same kind or construction. But some couplers will not couple automatically with couplers of different construction. Railroad companies engaged in interstate commerce are required to haul over their roads cars equipped with all these couplers. They cannot relieve themselves from this obligation or renounce this public duty for the simple reason that their cars or locomotives are not equipped with automatic couplers which will couple with those with which the cars of other roads are provided, and which will couple with equal facility with those of their kind. These facts and this situation were patent to the congress when it enacted this statute. It must have known the impracticability of providing every car with as many different couplers as it might meet upon a great system of railroads, and it made no such requirement. It doubtless knew the monopoly it would create by requiring every railroad company to use the same coupler, and it did not create this monopoly. The prohibition of the statute goes no farther than to bar the handling of a car "not equipped with couplers coupling automatically by impact and which can be uncoupled without the necessity of men going between the ends of the car." It does not bar the handling and use of a car which will couple automatically with couplers of its kind because it will not also couple automatically with couplers of all kinds, and it would be an unwarrantable extension of the terms of this law to import into it a provision to this effect. A car equipped with practical and efficient automatic couplers, such as the Janney couplers or the Miller hooks, which will couple automatically with those of their kind, fully and literally complies with the terms of the law, although these couplers will not couple automatically with automatic couplers of all kinds or constructions. The dining car and the locomotive were both so equipped. Each was provided with an automatic coupler which would couple with those of its kind, as provided by the statute, although they would not couple with each other. Each was accordingly equipped as the statute directs, and the defendant was guilty of no violation of it by their use.

Again, the statute declares it to be unlawful for a carrier "to haul or permit to be hauled or used on its line any car used in moving interstate traffic not equipped," etc. It is not, then, unlawful, under this statute, for a carrier to haul a car not so equipped which is either used in intrastate traffic solely, or which is not used in any traffic at all. It would be no violation of the statute for a carrier to haul an empty car not used to move any interstate traffic from one end of its railroad to the other. It would be no violation of the law for it to haul such a car in its yards, on its side track, to put it into its trains, to move it in any manner it chose. It is only when a car is "used in moving interstate traffic" that it becomes unlawful to haul it unless it is equipped as the statute prescribes. On the day of this accident the dining car in this case was standing empty on the side track. The defendant drew it to a turntable, turned it, and placed it back upon the side track. The accident occurred during the performance of this act. The car was vacant when it went to the turntable, and vacant when it returned. It moved no traffic on its way. How could it be said to have been "used in moving interstate traffic" either while it was standing on the side track, or while it was going to and returning from the turntable? . . .

[In a part of the opinion omitted here, the court argues that its conclusion that the dining car was not "used in moving interstate traffic" is dictated not only by rules of construction earlier referred to, but by limitations on the power of Congress.]

The fact that such cars have been or will be so used does not constitute their use in moving interstate traffic, because the prohibition is not of the hauling of cars that have been or will be used in such traffic, but only of those used in moving that traffic. . . . Neither the empty dining car standing upon the side track, nor the freight engine which was used to turn it at the little station in Utah, was then used in moving interstate traffic, within the meaning of this statute, and this case did not fall within the provisions of this law.

The judgment below must accordingly be affirmed, and it is so ordered.

■ THAYER, CIRCUIT JUDGE[, concurring in part and concurring in the judgment]. I am unable to concur in the conclusion, announced by the majority of the court, that the act of Congress of March 2, 1893 (27 Stat. 531, c. 196), does not require locomotive engines to be equipped with automatic couplers; and I am equally unable to concur in the other conclusion announced by my associates that the dining car in question at the time of the accident was not engaged or being used in moving interstate traffic.

In my judgment, it is a very technical interpretation of the provisions of the act in question, and one which is neither in accord with its spirit nor with the obvious purpose of the lawmaker, to say that Congress did not intend to require engines to be equipped with automatic couplers. The statute is remedial in its nature; it was passed for the protection of human life; and there was certainly as much, if not greater, need that engines should be equipped to couple automatically, as that ordinary cars should be so equipped, since engines have occasion to make couplings more frequently. In my opinion, the true view is that engines are included by the words "any car," as used in the second section of the act. The word "car" is generic, and may well be held to comprehend a locomotive or any other similiar [sic] vehicle which moves on wheels; and especially should it be so held in a case like the one now in hand, where no satisfactory reason has been assigned or can be given which would probably have influenced Congress to permit locomotives to be used without automatic coupling appliances.

I am also of opinion that, within the fair intent and import of the act, the dining car in question at the time of the accident was being hauled or used in interstate traffic. The reasoning by which a contrary conclusion is reached seems to me to be altogether too refined and unsatisfactory to be of any practical value. It was a car which at the time was employed in no other service than to furnish meals to passengers between Ogden and San Francisco. It had not been taken out of that service, even for repairs or for any other use, when the accident occurred, but was engaged therein to the same extent that it would have been if it had been hauled through to Ogden, and if the accident had there occurred while it was being turned to make the return trip to San Francisco. The cars composing a train which is regularly employed in interstate traffic ought to be regarded as used in that traffic while the train is being made up with a view to an immediate departure on an interstate journey as well as after the journey has actually begun. I accordingly dissent from the conclusion of the majority of the court on this point.

While I dissent on the foregoing propositions, I concur in the other view which is expressed in the opinion of the majority, to the effect that the case discloses no substantial violation of the provisions of the act of Congress, because both the engine and the dining car were equipped with automatic coupling appliances. In this respect the case discloses a compliance with the law, and the ordinary rule governing the liability of the defendant company should be applied. The difficulty was that the car and engine were equipped with couplers of a different pattern, which would not couple, for that reason, without a link. Janney couplers and Miller couplers are in common use on the leading railroads of the country, and Congress did not see fit to command the use of either style of automatic coupler to the exclusion of the other, while it must have foreseen that, owing to the manner in which cars were ordinarily handled and exchanged, it would sometimes happen, as in the case at bar, that cars having different styles of automatic couplers would necessarily be brought in contact in the same train. It made no express provision for such an emergency, but declared generally that, after a certain date, cars should be provided with couplers coupling automatically. The engine and dining car were so equipped in the present instance, and there was no such violation of the provisions of the statute as should render the defendant company liable to the plaintiff by virtue of the provisions contained in the eighth section of the act. In other words, the plaintiff assumed the risk of making the coupling in the course of which he sustained the injury. On this ground I concur in the order affirming the judgment below.

Johnson v. Southern Pacific Co.

Supreme Court of the United States, 1904.
196 U.S. 1, 25 S.Ct. 158, 49 L.Ed. 363.

Error and Certiorari to the Circuit Court of Appeals for the Eighth Circuit.

■ Statement by MR. CHIEF JUSTICE FULLER:

Johnson brought this action in the district court of the first judicial district of Utah against the Southern Pacific Company to recover damages for injuries received while employed by that company as a brakeman. The case was removed to the circuit court of the United States for the district of Utah by defendant on the ground of diversity of citizenship.

The facts were briefly these: August 5, 1900, Johnson was acting as head brakeman on a freight train of the Southern Pacific Company, which was making its regular trip between San Francisco, California, and Ogden, Utah. On reaching the town of Promontory, Utah, Johnson was directed to uncouple the engine from the train and couple it to a dining car, belonging to the company, which was standing on a side track, for the purpose of turning the car around preparatory to its being picked up and put on the next westbound passenger train. The engine and the dining car were equipped, respectively, with the Janney coupler and the Miller hook, so called, which would not couple together automatically by impact, and it was, therefore, necessary for Johnson, and he was ordered, to go between the engine and the dining car, to accomplish the coupling. In so doing Johnson's hand was caught between the engine bumper and the dining car bumper, and crushed, which necessitated amputation of the hand above the wrist.

On the trial of the case, defendant, after plaintiff had rested, moved the court to instruct the jury to find in its favor, which motion was granted, and the jury found a verdict accordingly, on which judgment was entered. Plaintiff carried the case to the circuit court of appeals for the eighth circuit, and the judgment was affirmed. [54 C.C.A. 508, 117 Fed. 462.]

■ MR. CHIEF JUSTICE FULLER delivered the [unanimous] opinion of the court:

. . . The plaintiff claimed that he was relieved of assumption of risk under common-law rules by the act of Congress of March 2, 1893 (27 Stat.

at L. 531, chap. 196, U.S.Comp.Stat.1901, p. 3174), entitled "An Act to Promote the Safety of Employees and Travelers upon Railroads by Compelling Common Carriers Engaged in Interstate Commerce to Equip their Cars with Automatic Couplers and Continuous Brakes and their Locomotives with Driving-Wheel Brakes, and for Other Purposes."

The issues involved questions deemed of such general importance that the government was permitted to file a brief and be heard at the bar.

The act of 1893 provided: [see *supra*]

The circuit court of appeals held, in substance, Sanborn, J., delivering the opinion and Lochren, J., concurring, that the locomotive and car were both equipped as required by the act, as the one had a power driving-wheel brake and the other a coupler; that § 2 did not apply to locomotives; that at the time of the accident the dining car was not "used in moving interstate traffic;" and, moreover, that the locomotive, as well as the dining car, was furnished with an automatic coupler, so that each was equipped as the statute required if § 2 applied to both. Thayer, J., concurred in the judgment on the latter ground, but was of opinion that locomotives were included by the words "any car" in the 2d section, and that the dining car was being "used in moving interstate traffic."

We are unable to accept these conclusions, notwithstanding the able opinion of the majority, as they appear to us to be inconsistent with the plain intention of Congress, to defeat the object of the legislation, and to be arrived at by an inadmissible narrowness of construction.

The intention of Congress, declared in the preamble and in §§ 1 and 2 of the act, was "to promote the safety of employees and travelers upon railroads by compelling common carriers engaged in interstate commerce to equip their cars with automatic couplers and continuous brakes and their locomotives with driving-wheel brakes," those brakes to be accompanied with "appliances for operating the train-brake system;" and every car to be "equipped with couplers coupling automatically by impact, and which can be uncoupled without the necessity of men going between the ends of the cars," whereby the danger and risk consequent on the existing system was averted as far as possible.

The present case is that of an injured employee, and involves the application of the act in respect of automatic couplers, the preliminary question being whether locomotives are required to be equipped with such couplers. And it is not to be successfully denied that they are so required if the words "any car" of the 2d section were intended to embrace, and do embrace, locomotives. But it is said that this cannot be so because locomotives were elsewhere, in terms, required to be equipped with power driving-wheel brakes, and that the rule that the expression of one thing excludes another applies. That, however, is a question of intention, and as there was special reason for requiring locomotives to be equipped with power driving-wheel brakes, if it were also necessary that locomotives should be equipped with automatic couplers, and the word "car" would cover locomotives, then the intention to limit the equipment of locomotives to power driving-wheel brakes, because they were separately mentioned, could not be imputed. Now it was as necessary for the safety of employees in coupling and uncoupling that locomotives should be equipped with automatic couplers as it was that freight and passenger and dining cars should be; perhaps more so, as Judge Thayer suggests, "since engines have occasion to make couplings more frequently."

And manifestly the word "car" was used in its generic sense. There is nothing to indicate that any particular kind of car was meant. Tested by context, subject-matter, and object, "any car" meant all kinds of cars running on the rails, including locomotives. And this view is supported by the dictionary definitions and by many judicial decisions, some of them having been rendered in construction of this act. [Citations.]

The result is that if the locomotive in question was not equipped with automatic couplers, the company failed to comply with the provisions of the act. It appears, however, that this locomotive was in fact equipped with automatic couplers, as well as the dining car; but that the couplers on each, which were of different types, would not couple with each other automatically, by impact, so as to render it unnecessary for men to go between the cars to couple and uncouple.

Nevertheless, the circuit court of appeals was of opinion that it would be an unwarrantable extension of the terms of the law to hold that where the couplers would couple automatically with couplers of their own kind, the couplers must so couple with couplers of different kinds. But we think that what the act plainly forbade was the use of cars which could not be coupled together automatically by impact, by means of the couplers actually used on the cars to be coupled. The object was to protect the lives and limbs of railroad employees by rendering it unnecessary for a man operating the couplers to go between the ends of the cars; and that object would be defeated, not necessarily by the use of automatic couplers of different kinds, but if those different kinds would not automatically couple with each other. The point was that the railroad companies should be compelled, respectively, to adopt devices, whatever they were, which would act so far uniformly as to eliminate the danger consequent on men going between the cars.

If the language used were open to construction, we are constrained to say that the construction put upon the act by the circuit court of appeals was altogether too narrow.

This strictness was thought to be required because the common-law rule as to the assumption of risk was changed by the act, and because the act was penal.

The dogma as to the strict construction of statutes in derogation of the common law only amounts to the recognition of a presumption against an intention to change existing law; and as there is no doubt of that intention here, the extent of the application of the change demands at least no more rigorous construction than would be applied to penal laws. And, as Chief Justice Parker remarked, conceding that statutes in derogation of the common law are to be construed strictly, "They are also to be construed sensibly, and with a view to the object aimed at by the legislature." Gibson v. Jenney, 15 Mass. 205.

The primary object of the act was to promote the public welfare by securing the safety of employees and travelers; and it was in that aspect remedial; while for violations a penalty of $100, recoverable in a civil action, was provided for, and in that aspect it was penal. But the design to give relief was more dominant than to inflict punishment, and the act might well be held to fall within the rule applicable to statutes to prevent fraud upon the revenue, and for the collection of customs,—that rule not requiring absolute strictness of construction. [Citations.]

Moreover, it is settled that "though penal laws are to be construed strictly, yet the intention of the legislature must govern in the construction of penal as well as other statutes; and they are not to be construed so strictly as to defeat the obvious intention of the legislature." [Citation.] . . .

Tested by these principles, we think the view of the circuit court of appeals, which limits the 2d section to merely providing automatic couplers, does not give due effect to the words "coupling automatically by impact, and which can be uncoupled without the necessity of men going between the cars," and cannot be sustained.

We dismiss, as without merit, the suggestion which has been made, that the words "without the necessity of men going between the ends of the cars," which are the test of compliance with § 2, apply only to the act of uncoupling. The phrase literally covers both coupling and uncoupling; and if read, as it should be, with a comma after the word "uncoupled," this becomes entirely clear. [Citations.]

The risk in coupling and uncoupling was the evil sought to be remedied, and that risk was to be obviated by the use of couplers actually coupling automatically. True, no particular design was required, but, whatever the devices used, they were to be effectively interchangeable. Congress was not paltering in a double sense. And its intention is found "in the language actually used, interpreted according to its fair and obvious meaning." United States v. Harris, 177 U.S. 309.

That this was the scope of the statute is confirmed by the circumstances surrounding its enactment, as exhibited in public documents to which we are at liberty to refer. [Citations.]

President Harrison, in his annual messages of 1889, 1890, 1891, and 1892, earnestly urged upon Congress the necessity of legislation to obviate and reduce the loss of life and the injuries due to the prevailing method of coupling and braking. In his first message he said: "It is competent, I think, for Congress to require uniformity in the construction of cars used in interstate commerce, and the use of improved safety appliances upon such trains. Time will be necessary to make the needed changes, but an earnest and intelligent beginning should be made at once. It is a reproach to our civilization that any class of American workmen should, in the pursuit of a necessary and useful vocation, be subjected to a peril of life and limb as great as that of a soldier in time of war."

And he reiterated his recommendation in succeeding messages, saying in that for 1892: "Statistics furnished by the Interstate Commerce Commission show that during the year ending June 30, 1891, there were forty-seven different styles of car couplers reported to be in use, and that during the same period there [were] 2,660 employees killed and 26,140 injured. Nearly 16 per cent of the deaths occurred in the coupling and uncoupling of cars, and over 36 per cent of the injuries had the same origin."

The Senate report of the first session of the Fifty-second Congress (No. 1049) and the House report of the same session (No. 1678) set out the numerous and increasing casualties due to coupling, the demand for protection, and the necessity of automatic couplers, coupling interchangeably. The difficulties in the case were fully expounded and the result reached to require an automatic coupling by impact so as to render it unnecessary for men to go between the cars; while no particular device or type was adopted, the railroad companies being left free to work out the details for themselves, ample time being given for that purpose. The law gave five years, and that was enlarged, by the Interstate Commerce Commission as authorized by law, two years, and subsequently seven months, making seven years and seven months in all.

The diligence of counsel has called our attention to changes made in the bill in the course of its passage, and to the debates in the Senate on the report of its committee. 24 Cong. Rec., pt. 2, pp. 1246, 1273 et seq. These demonstrate that the difficulty as to interchangeability was fully in the mind of Congress, and was assumed to be met by the language which was used. The essential degree of uniformity was secured by providing that the couplings must couple automatically by impact without the necessity of men going between the ends of the cars.

In the present case the couplings would not work together; Johnson was obliged to go between the cars; and the law was not complied with.

March 2, 1903, 32 Stat. 943, c. 976, an act in amendment of the act of 1893 was approved, which provided, among other things, that the provisions and requirements of the former act "shall be held to apply to common carriers by railroads in the Territories and the District of Columbia and shall apply in all cases, whether or not the couplers brought together are of the same kind, make, or type;" and "shall be held to apply to all trains, locomotives, tenders, cars, and similar vehicles used on any railroad engaged in interstate commerce."

This act was to take effect September first, nineteen hundred and three, and nothing in it was to be held or construed to relieve any common carrier "from any of the provisions, powers, duties, liabilities, or requirements" of the act of 1893, all of which should apply except as specifically amended.

As we have no doubt of the meaning of the prior law, the subsequent legislation cannot be regarded as intended to operate to destroy it. Indeed, the latter act is affirmative, and declaratory, and, in effect, only construed and applied the former act. [Citations.] This legislative recognition of the scope of the prior law fortifies and does not weaken the conclusion at which we have arrived.

Another ground on which the decision of the circuit court of appeals was rested remains to be noticed. That court held by a majority that, as the dining car was empty and had not actually entered upon its trip, it was not used in moving interstate traffic, and hence was not within the act. The dining car had been constantly used for several years to furnish meals to passengers between San Francisco and Ogden, and for no other purpose. On the day of the accident the eastbound train was so late that it was found that the car could not reach Ogden in time to return on the next westbound train according to intention, and it was therefore dropped off at Promontory, to be picked up by that train as it came along that evening. . . .

Confessedly this dining car was under the control of Congress while in the act of making its interstate journey, and in our judgment it was equally so when waiting for the train to be made up for the next trip. It was being regularly used in the movement of interstate traffic, and so within the law.

Finally, it is argued that Johnson was guilty of such contributory negligence as to defeat recovery, and that, therefore, the judgment should be affirmed. But the circuit court of appeals did not consider this question, nor apparently did the circuit court, and we do not feel constrained to inquire whether it could have been open under § 8, or, if so, whether it should have been left to the jury, under proper instructions.

The judgment of the Circuit Court of Appeals is reversed; the judgment of the Circuit Court is also reversed, and the cause remanded to that court with instructions to set [aside] the verdict, and award a new trial.

NOTES AND QUESTIONS

1.   While *Johnson* arose at the beginning of the twentieth century, the same statutory provisions at issue in *Johnson* continue to demand judicial construction. Consider the following more recent decision:

Porter v. Bangor & Aroostook Railroad Co., 75 F.3d 70 (1st Cir. 1996)

■ ALDRICH, SENIOR CIRCUIT JUDGE.

Mark J. Porter, an experienced brakeman employed by defendant Bangor & Aroostook Railroad Co., injured his back on October 1, 1992, while adjusting a rusty car coupler device that had previously failed to couple automatically with another car. He seeks recovery under the Federal Safety Appliance Act (FSAA), 45 U.S.C. § 2,[1] a statute that has been ruled to impose liability without fault, San Antonio & Aransas Pass Railway Company v. Wagner, 241 U.S. 476 (1916), when a violation contributed in any degree to an employee's injuries. Carter v. Atlantic & St. Andrews Bay Ry. Co., 338 U.S. 430, 434–35 (1949). . . . In response to special questions the jury found that defendant had violated the FSAA but that the failure was not a cause of plaintiff's injury. . . . After denial of plaintiff's motion for new trial . . . , the court entered judgment for defendant. Plaintiff appeals. We affirm.

Plaintiff . . . faces the substantial obstacle of a jury finding of no causal connection between the violation and the injury. Recognizing this burden, he takes the bull by the horns and argues that, the violation and injury having been established, the jury not merely should have found, but was required to find a causal connection between them as matter of law.

Plaintiff's contention takes two forms. First, he says the jury's finding that defendant violated the FSAA means that the coupling equipment was defective. Thus plaintiff strained his back working on defective coupler equipment; hence he was within the statute. We do not agree. There is nothing especially dangerous in coupling devices themselves, the statutory reach is the coupling maneuver. As the Court said in the early case of Johnson v. Southern Pacific Co., 196 U.S. 1, 19 (1904), "The risk in coupling and uncoupling was the evil sought to be remedied. . . . " Although plaintiff speaks about having to go between the ends of the cars, it was not for coupling, but in preparation for coupling. One must go behind, viz., between the cars, to align the drawbars before commencing the coupling operation.[2] If, as here, the cars are safely separated and not in motion, readying is not coupling, and does not involve the special coupling risks. What could be the reason, or purpose, for requiring special protection for this isolated activity? It is true that other circuits appear to have read the FSAA more broadly, see Clark v. Kentucky & Indiana Terminal Railroad, 728 F. 2d 307 (6th

---

[1] "It shall be unlawful for any common carrier engaged in interstate commerce by railroad to haul or permit to be hauled or used on its line any car . . . not equipped with couplers coupling automatically by impact, and which can be uncoupled without the necessity of men going between the ends of the cars." 45 U.S.C. § 2 (1893) (repealed 1994) (current version at 49 U.S.C. § 20302).

[2] Plaintiff himself testified that the drawbars can swing, and must sometimes be lined up in order to meet, a procedure he performed routinely every day. See Goedel v. Norfolk & Western Railway Co., 13 F.3d 807, 809 (4th Cir. 1994).

Cir. 1984) (collecting cases), but they give no answer to our question. We can think of none. Plaintiff had no FSAA case.

In light of the prior decision, *Johnson,* is the First Circuit's analysis persuasive? Is the court's distinction between going between railroad cars in order to couple them, and going between the cars in order to *prepare* to couple them, a convincing interpretation of the statutory language? Of the statute's "intent"?

2.   Note that the previous question asked if, *in light of a prior decision,* a subsequent court (bound by the prior court's authority) correctly interpreted the statute. While many different individuals and entities may engage in statutory interpretation, the *authoritative* interpreters of statutes are almost always courts. (For the interpretations of administrative agencies, see *infra* Part V, and for other audiences, see *infra* Section IV.C.) Under the doctrine of precedent, when a court has interpreted a statute, it and dependent lower courts are bound by that interpretation (unless or until the legislature amends the statute in response to prior judicial interpretations, see *infra* Part VII). Hence, were a case like *Johnson* to arise in a federal district court after the Supreme Court's decision, the judge would not be free to rule that the statute tolerates equipment of cars with automatic couplers that do not in fact couple automatically to each other. By the same token, distinguishing cases on their facts remains a tool in analyzing whether a prior judicial interpretation of a statute determines the case at hand. Thus, the First Circuit was able to rule that *Johnson* did not control the application of the FSAA to brakeman Porter, because *Johnson* involved an injury sustained in the act of coupling; by contrast, Porter was hurt not while coupling railroad cars, but merely while preparing to engage in the act of coupling railroad cars.

3.   For another controversy involving application of the Federal Safety Appliance Act to an accident involving misaligned drawbars, as well as a pictorial catalogue of automatic couplers, see Goedel v. Norfolk & Western Railway Co., 13 F.3d 807 (4th Cir. 1994).

3.   CANONS OF STATUTORY CONSTRUCTION

Both the Eighth Circuit and the Supreme Court in *Johnson* invoked a variety of maxims to aid their interpretation of the Railway Safety Appliance Act. Sometimes these principles, known as "canons of construction," which often take the form of maxims or even Latin phrases, appear to be opposed. For example, the canon favoring narrow interpretation of a "penal" statute and the canon counseling expansive interpretation of a "remedial" statute are both canons that bear on a statute designed to remedy a problem by imposing sanctions on those who violate the new norm. Sometimes different courts appear to apply the *same* canon of construction, yet reach different conclusions.

How helpful *are* canons of construction? What is their relationship to statutory text? Should we assume that legislatures enact statutes against the backdrop of the canons, and thus take into account, or are at least aware of, the interpretive lenses through which judges will study the statutory language? Is there an accepted repertory of canons?* Is there an accepted hierarchy of canons? Do we need an answer to both of those questions before we can attribute to a legislature an understanding or an expectation of how courts will interpret the language it enacts? Does it make any difference whether canons of construction are implicitly part of the legislative package, or instead are imposed by judges as a reasonable or "ordinary" way of understanding language or resolving legal ambiguity? In the latter event, are canons any more reliable or useful than other extratextual aids to interpretation?

Professor Karl Llewellyn famously lampooned the canons of construction during a period in which many legal realists considered canons of construction to be window dressing that permitted judges to reach their preferred outcomes. Llewellyn did so in part by arguing that the canons themselves are often contradictory:

> When it comes to presenting a proposed construction in court, there is an accepted conventional vocabulary. As in argument over points of case-law, the accepted convention still, unhappily requires discussion as if only one single correct meaning could exist. Hence there are two opposing canons on almost every point. . . .

CANONS OF CONSTRUCTION

Statutory interpretation still speaks a diplomatic tongue. Here is some of the technical framework for maneuver.

THRUST	BUT	PARRY
1. A statute cannot go beyond its text.		1. To effect its purpose a statute may be implemented beyond its text.
2. Statutes in derogation of the common law will not be extended by construction.		2. Such acts will be liberally construed if their nature is remedial. . . .

---

* Professors William Eskridge and Philip Frickey have catalogued canons of construction extracted from Supreme Court decisions from the 1986 through 1993 Terms. Their illuminating listing is set out in *Appendix: The Rehnquist Court's Canons of Statutory Construction*, in WILLIAM N. ESKRIDGE, JR., PHILIP P. FRICKEY AND ELIZABETH GARRETT, LEGISLATION AND STATUTORY INTERPRETATION, 375–83 (Foundation Press, Concepts and Insights series, 2000). More recently, the late Justice Antonin Scalia and lexicographer Bryan Garner produced a comprehensive, though also controversial, compendium of canons in their treatise, *Reading Law. See* ANTONIN SCALIA & BRYAN GARNER, READING LAW: THE INTERPRETATION OF LEGAL TEXTS (2012). (*See infra* Section III.A.2.a for Judge Richard Posner's trenchant assessment of the textualist approach that treatise espouses.)

6. Statutes *in pari materia* must be construed together

6. A statute is not *in pari materia* if its scope and aim are distinct or where a legislative design to depart from the general purpose or policy of previous enactments may be apparent.

7. A statute imposing a new penalty or forfeiture, or a new liability or disability, or creating a new right of action will not be construed as having a retroactive effect.

7. Remedial statutes are to be liberally construed and if a retroactive interpretation will promote the ends of justice, they should receive such construction. . . .

9. Definitions and rules of construction contained in an interpretation clause are part of the law and binding.

9. Definitions and rules of construction in a statute will not be extended beyond their necessary import nor allowed to defeat intention otherwise manifested. . . .

11. Titles do not control meaning; preambles do not expand scope; section headings do not change language.

11. The title may be consulted as a guide when there is doubt or obscurity in the body; preambles may be consulted to determine rationale, and thus the true construction of terms; section headings may be looked upon as part of the statute itself.

12. If language is plain and unambiguous it must be given effect.

12. Not when literal interpretation would lead to absurd or mischievous consequences or thwart manifest purpose. . . .

16. Every word and clause must be given effect.

16. If inadvertently inserted or if repugnant to the rest of the statute, they may be rejected as surplusage.

17. The same language used repeatedly in the same connection is presumed to bear the same meaning throughout the statute.

17. This presumption will be disregarded where it is necessary to assign different meanings to make the statute consistent.

18. Words are to be interpreted according to the proper grammatical effect of their arrangement within the statute.

18. Rules of grammar will be disregarded where strict adherence would defeat purpose. . . .

Karl N. Llewellyn, *Remarks on the Theory of Appellate Decision and the Rules or Canons About How Statutes Are to be Construed*, 3 Vand. L. Rev. 395 (1950).

Llewellyn's skepticism of the canons was widely shared at mid-century. Today, however, the canons have found new life, especially among modern-day textualists. Consider the Harvard Law School Dean John Manning's discussion of the role of canons of construction:

Karl Llewellyn largely persuaded two generations of academics that the canons of construction were not to be taken seriously. His point was simple: The canons are indeterminate, and judges use them to justify reasoning by other means. . . . [But] a large and growing number of academics (and academics-turned-judges) now believe in the utility of canons of construction. . . . Modern textualists, who tend to be formalist in orientation, understandably favor the use of canons, particularly the traditional linguistic canons. Justice Scalia, for instance, argue[d] that many such canons are "so commonsensical that, were [they] not couched in Latin, you would find it hard to believe that anyone could criticize them." And Judge Easterbrook, a formalist with a law and economics twist, defends canons "as off-the-rack provisions that spare legislators the costs of anticipating all possible interpretive problems and legislating solutions for them." . . . [T]hese scholars . . . have sought to revive . . . the idea that a system of established rules of construction might make the process of statutory interpretation more predictable, effective, and even legitimate.

This intellectual development raises two questions. First, why have canons of construction recently gone from laughingstock to the subject of serious academic inquiry? And why do textualists and pragmatists, who think so differently about most questions of statutory interpretation, now share enthusiasm for the once maligned idea of such canons of construction? . . . Although he is not usually identified with this trend, Llewellyn's view of the canons nicely complemented an emerging scholarly consensus that, contrary to prior realist scholarship, judges could meaningfully resolve textual ambiguity by consulting the legislature's intent or purpose, to be derived in no small part from legislative history. Conversely, his impact began to wane in the 1980s, when influential textualist and pragmatist scholars revived (for quite different reasons) broader realist claims about the inaccessibility and unreliability of legislative intent and purpose as organizing principles in statutory construction. . . .

In economists' terms, canons of construction and intent or purpose are substitutes, rather than complements. . . . Textualists believe that the statutory text will often be determinate and decisive, and that intent or purpose derived from the legislative history are unreliable guides for resolving statutory doubts. They want clearly established background rules of construction to guide legislators and interpreters in decoding textual commands. Pragmatists have less faith in the statutory text, but also question whether intent and purpose can effectively address its deficiencies. They favor the rationalization and harmonization of rules of construction to provide judges with guidelines for addressing indeterminacy and for doing so in ways that promote socially and institutionally beneficial outcomes. . . . In short, the canons' revival may be the flip side of a growing perception that the early realists were correct in arguing that it is hard to get inside "Congress's mind."

John F. Manning, *Legal Realism & the Canons' Revival*, 5 Green Bag 283, 283–85 (2002).

Canons of construction generally fall into two broad categories: (a) "linguistic" canons, which purport to explain how meaning follows from prevailing linguistic usage; and (b) "substantive" canons, which purport to set out legal rules or first principles for arriving at a legal meaning of a statutory provision. While linguistic canons chiefly aid in identifying the reasonable reader's understanding of the statutory term or phrase in question, the application of many linguistic canons will also depend on claims or assumptions about the legislative drafters' intentions. By contrast, substantive canons often yield statutory meanings that may not reflect either the drafters' seeming intended meaning or the reasonable reader's understanding. Some examples of each:

a. EXAMPLES OF LINGUISTIC CANONS

Ejusdem Generis: This linguistic canon, named for the Latin phrase meaning "of the same kind," instructs that "[w]here general words follow specific words in a statutory enumeration, the general words are construed to embrace only objects similar in nature to those objects enumerated by the preceding specific words." Circuit City Stores, Inc. v. Adams, 532 U.S. 105, 114–15 (2001). In *Circuit City Stores*, for instance, the Court interpreted a portion of the Federal Arbitration Act (FAA) that excludes from the FAA's coverage "contracts of employment of seamen, railroad employees, or any other class of workers engaged in foreign or interstate commerce." 9 U.S.C. § 1. In deciding whether this exclusion applied to *all* workers engaged in foreign and interstate commerce, or only to those workers engaged in the transportation industry, a majority of the Supreme Court drew on the *ejusdem generis* canon to conclude that the inclusion of "seamen" and "railroad employees"—workers engaged in transportation industries—narrowed the meaning of the term "other class of workers" to those workers who are also engaged in transportation industries. Whether this canon should have dispositive effect is often open to debate; as the dissent in *Circuit City Stores* cautioned, "Like many interpretive canons, . . . *ejusdem generis* is a fallback, and if there are good reasons not to apply it, it is [to be] put aside." *Id.* at 138 (Stevens, J., dissenting).

Expressio Unius Est Exclusio Alterius: This linguistic canon, named for the Latin phrase meaning "the explicit mention of one (thing) is the exclusion of another," provides that "when the items expressed are members of an 'associated group or series,' [the interpreter may] infer[ ] that items not mentioned were excluded by deliberate choice, not inadvertence." Barnhart v. Peabody Coal Co., 537 U.S. 149, 168 (2003). Although a linguistic canon grounded in the reasonable reader's understanding of the text of the statute, the application of *expressio unius* may be limited to circumstances in which its application conforms to evidence of the legislative drafters' intent. For example in *Barnhart*, and more recently in *Marx v. General Revenue Corp.*, the U.S. Supreme Court noted that the "*expressio unius* canon does not apply 'unless it is fair to suppose that Congress considered the unnamed possibility and meant to say no to it.' " 568 U.S. 371, 381 (2013) (quoting *Barnhart*, 537 U.S. at 168).

Whether such a supposition is "fair" will often depend on other evidence of the drafters' intended meaning or purpose in enacting the statute, including whether there is evidence they "considered the unnamed possibility." Recall, for example, that in *Johnson v. Southern Pacific Co.*, *supra*, the Eighth Circuit and the Supreme Court reached opposite conclusions about whether the absence of an *express* requirement for the use of automatic couplers shed light on whether the statute as a whole required their use. Consider the degree to which different views about the relevance of the statute's broad purpose and the drafters' specific intent influenced the courts' conflicting intuitions about the application of *expressio unius*.

Rule Against Superfluities: Also known as the "surplusage canon" or the "antiredundancy canon," this rule reflects the judicial assumption, as articulated in *Bailey v. United States, infra* Section VII.B.1, that when a legislative body uses multiple terms to modify a noun, or sets out multiple action verbs that trigger liability or culpability, "Congress use[d] [different] terms because it intended each term to have a particular, nonsuperfluous meaning." 516 U.S. 137, 146 (1995). That is, where two competing interpretations of a term or phrase are plausible, but one interpretation would render its meaning redundant or "mere surplusage" in light of other provisions in the same statute, the surplusage canon instructs the interpreter to select the meaning that would avoid the redundancy. As with many other linguistic canons, the U.S. Supreme Court has added the proviso that "our hesitancy to construe statutes to render language superfluous does not require us to avoid surplusage at all costs. It is appropriate to tolerate a degree of surplusage rather than adopt a textually dubious construction that threatens to render the entire provision a nullity." United States v. Atl. Research Corp., 551 U.S. 128, 137 (2007).

The surplusage canon's legitimacy rests in no small part on the assumption that legislators (and their aides) aspire to avoid redundancy in drafting. However, when Professors Abbe Gluck and Lisa Schultz Bressman surveyed congressional drafters, they reported that redundancy is often not only inevitable, but *intentional*:

> . . . [Drafters] pointed out that the political interests of the audience often demand redundancy. They told us, for example, that "sometimes politically for compromise they must include certain words in the statute—that senator, that constituent, that lobbyist wants to see that word"; similarly, they said that "sometimes the lists are in there to satisfy groups, certain phrases are needed to satisfy political interests and they might overlap" or that "sometimes you have it in there because someone had to see their phrase in the bill to get it passed."

> Common sense tells us that, despite the popularity of this rule with judges, there is likely to be redundancy, especially in exceedingly long statutes. But what respondents told us was different from that common-sense assumption: namely, that even in short statutes—indeed, even within single sections of statutes—that terms are often purposefully redundant to satisfy audiences other than courts. . . .

Abbe R. Gluck & Lisa Schultz Bressman, *Statutory Interpretation from the Inside: An Empirical Study of Congressional Drafting, Delegation, and the Canons: Part I*, 65 Stan. L. Rev. 901 (2013).

Last Antecedent Rule: This linguistic canon instructs that where a statutory provision "include[s] a list of terms or phrases followed by a limiting clause, the limiting clause or phrase should ordinarily be read as modifying only the noun or phrase that it immediately follows." Lockhart v. United States, 136 S.Ct. 958, 962 (2016) (citation omitted), *infra* Section III.B.1. In *Lockhart*, for example, the majority concluded that in a list of prior convictions "related to aggravated sexual assault, sexual abuse, or abusive sexual conduct *involving a minor or ward*," the modifier "involving a minor or ward" applied only to the last antecedent— a prior conviction for abusive sexual conduct. *Id.* at 963–64. However, structural or contextual evidence may "rebut the last antecedent inference." *Id.* at 962.

Series-Qualifier Canon: The series-qualifier canon yields the opposite inference of the last antecedent rule. This canon holds that in circumstances where the modifying clause appears at the end of a *single, integrated list*, "the exact opposite is usually true: . . . the modifying phrase refers alike to each of the list's terms." *Lockhart*, 136 S.Ct. at 970 (Kagan, J., dissenting). Whether a list can be said to be a "single, integrated list" that calls for the series-qualifier canon, or simply "a list of terms or phrases" that calls for the last antecedent rule, is not always clear. In *Lockhart*, the majority applied the last antecedent rule to reach one meaning, while the dissent applied the series-qualifier canon to yield the other meaning. (One could view the disagreement in *Lockhart* as tailor-made evidence supporting Professor Llewelyn's skepticism that the canons of construction do much more than provide a plausible basis for confirming the interpreter's pre-existing interpretive inclinations.)

b.   EXAMPLES OF SUBSTANTIVE CANONS

Rule of Lenity: This substantive canon instructs that "when there are two rational readings of a criminal statute, one harsher than the other, [the interpreter is] to choose the harsher only when [the legislature] has spoken in clear and definite language." McNally v. United States, 483 U.S. 350, 359–60 (1987). The lenity rule has an esteemed normative basis: as articulated by the dissent in *Muscarello v. United States, infra* Section III.B.3.b, "[t]his policy embodies the instinctive distaste against men languishing in prison unless the lawmaker has clearly said they should." 524 U.S. at 150 (Ginsburg, J., dissenting) (citation omitted). This rule does not purport to reveal the conduct that the legislative drafters *intended* to prohibit, nor what the drafters *thought* their language would convey, but instead provides a rule-of-law basis for deciding between "two rational readings" of a statutory provision. In this way, the rule of lenity functions as a kind of tie-breaker in circumstances where two reasonable readers of a criminal statute could reach opposite conclusions as to the meaning of the prohibition at issue.

While judges seem to be in near-unanimous agreement that the rule applies in at least some circumstances, they often disagree vigorously about *when* it should apply. The lenity rule's application depends in large part on (a) the degree of ambiguity necessary for it to trigger; and (b) whether the interpreter must exhaust all other methods of interpretation before triggering it. For example, the majority in *Muscarello* bluntly rejected the rule's application because "[t]he simple existence of some statutory ambiguity . . . is not sufficient to warrant application of that rule, for most statutes are ambiguous to some degree." *Id.* at 138.

What degree of ambiguity is necessary? One scholar has suggested that the Supreme Court has provided at least *four* arguably meaningfully distinct articulations of the degree of ambiguity necessary to trigger the rule: (1) where it is not "unambiguously correct" that the statute penalizes the defendant's conduct; (2) where "reasonable doubt" remains after exhausting other methods; (3) where a court is left with "no more than a guess" as to the provision's meaning; and (4) where "grievous ambiguity" remains.[*]

Clear Notice Rule: An analog to the rule of lenity for the interpretation of civil statutes, the clear notice rule applies in certain circumstances, such as in interpreting statutes in which Congress sets particular terms for the disbursal of federal money to the States. The U.S. Supreme Court has said, as in *Arlington Central School District Board of Education v. Murphy, infra* Section IV.C.1, that "when Congress attaches conditions to a State's acceptance of federal funds, the conditions must be set out 'unambiguously.'" 548 U.S. 291, 296 (2006) (citation omitted). Like its criminal-law cousin the rule of lenity, the clear notice rule's application risks begging the question of the extent or degree of ambiguity that the interpreter may tolerate before employing the rule as a tiebreaker to narrow the reach of a requirement accompanying federal funds. The clear notice rule thus raises questions about the relative clarity one may expect from legislative drafters—after all, as the *Muscarello* majority noted, many statutes are ambiguous *to some degree*. The clear notice rule may also raise questions of audience: if the statute must furnish clear notice to state officials, what level of sophistication should those officials be presumed to have in order that the provision in question be clear *to them*? The same level of sophistication as judges? As laypeople? As state officials with more expertise than laypeople but less expertise than judges?

Presumption Against Statutory Retroactivity: This longstanding presumption instructs courts to "decline[ ] to give retroactive effect to statutes burdening private rights unless Congress

---

[*] *See* Daniel Ortner, *The Merciful Corpus: The Rule of Lenity, Ambiguity and Corpus Linguistics*, 25 B.U. Pub. Int. L.J. 101, 103–04 (2016).

had made clear its intent." Landgraf v. USI Film Prod., 511 U.S. 244, 270 (1994), *infra* Section VI.B. This presumption serves to protect reliance interests: as noted in *Landgraf*, this presumption "has consistently been explained by reference to the unfairness of imposing new burdens on persons after the fact," particularly where new provisions affect contractual or property rights, "matters in which predictability and stability are of prime importance." *Id.* at 270–71. As you will see in *Martin v. Hadix, Vartelas v. Holder, infra* Section VI.B, and *AT&T Corp. v. Noreen Hulteen, infra* Section VII.C.3, the presumption often requires identifying the "retroactivity event" or action whose legal consequences would change unfavorably for the actor were the statute to apply to acts completed before the statute's enactment. As with the clear notice rule, this presumption also raises difficult questions about precisely how "clear" Congress must be in specifying the retroactivity event or moment in question.

Constitutional Avoidance: Among the Supreme Court's preferred substantive canons, the canon of constitutional avoidance instructs that "[w]hen the validity of an act of the Congress is drawn in question, and even if a serious doubt of constitutionality is raised, it is a cardinal principle that this Court will first ascertain whether a construction of the statute is fairly possible by which the question may be avoided." Crowell v. Benson, 285 U.S. 22, 62 (1932). Like other substantive canons, this presumption serves an important rule-of-law function—in this case, reducing the likelihood that the Court will be required to reach a constitutional question in order to resolve the statutory interpretation problem. Courts endeavor to avoid ruling on a statute's constitutionality because once the court has ruled that Congress exceeded its power or violated some constitutional prescription, Congress cannot have a "do-over." By contrast, if Congress disagrees with a court's interpretation of a statute, Congress can revise the statute to make its intentions clear. As with other substantive canons, the rule of constitutional avoidance is almost universally accepted in theory; controversy arises concerning when and how it should apply. In recent years, some members of the U.S. Supreme Court have argued that the constitutional avoidance canon should "come[ ] into play only when, after the application of ordinary textual analysis, the statute is found to be susceptible of more than one construction. In the absence of more than one plausible construction, the canon simply has no application." Jennings v. Rodriguez, 138 S.Ct. 830, 842 (2018) (citations omitted). A skeptic might contend that this articulation of the rule simply begs the question of deciding whether multiple "plausible" constructions are possible.

Void-for-Vagueness Doctrine: As much a doctrine as a canon, the constitutional prohibition against vagueness stands to protect the ancient principle of legality, *nulla poena sine lege*: there can be no penalty without law. This principle is reflected in the U.S. Supreme Court's oft-quoted recitation that "a statute which either forbids or requires the doing of an act in terms so vague that men of common intelligence must necessarily guess at its meaning and differ as to its application, violates the first essential of due process of law." Connally v. General Constr. Co., 269 U.S. 385, 391 (1926). The reader may already detect a tension between this doctrine and the above-mentioned canon of constitutional avoidance, for even a vague criminal prohibition has straightforward applications. For example, while it may be open for debate whether the poisoning of another is a "crime of violence," the battery of another indisputably is. Should a statute that augments penalties for a "crime of violence" be stuck down as unconstitutionally void for vagueness even if its application in at least some circumstances (battery) is quite straightforward, just because in other circumstances (poisoning) it is not? Under what circumstances should evidence of a criminal statute's set of clear applications be sufficient to withstand attacks related to vagueness as to its peripheral applications? Keep this tension in mind as you encounter *Johnson v. United States, infra* Section III.A.2.c. That section also explains the distinction between an ambiguous statutory prohibition, where the rule of lenity may be of use, and a vague statutory provision, where it will often be of little assistance.

Presumption Against Ineffectiveness: This canon stands for the principle that an interpretation of a statutory provision that would hinder the manifest purpose of the statute should be avoided where the statute is amenable to an alternative interpretation. Or, as articulated by the Texas Supreme Court, "It is recognized that a statute is to be construed with reference to its manifest object, and if the language is susceptible of two constructions, one of which will carry out and the other defeat such manifest object, it should receive the former construction." Citizens Bank of Bryan v. First State Bank, Hearne, 580 S.W.2d 344, 348 (Tex. 1979). In his academic writing, Justice Antonin Scalia endorsed this canon on the following grounds: "This canon follows inevitably from the facts that (1) interpretation always depends on context, (2) context always includes evident purpose, and (3) evident purpose always includes effectiveness." Antonin Scalia & Bryan Garner, Reading Law: The Interpretation of Legal Texts 63 (2012). As discussed in Section III.A.2.a, *infra*, a close cousin of this canon is the anti-self-destruction principle, which cautions against a literal interpretation of a provision that would cause the statutory scheme to self-destruct.

Absurd Results Canon: As articulated in *Holy Trinity Church, infra* Section II.B, the absurd results canon recognizes that "frequently words of general meaning are used in a statute, words broad enough to include an act in question, and yet a consideration of . . . the absurd results which follow from giving such broad meaning to the words, makes it unreasonable to believe that the legislator intended to include the particular act." 143 U.S. at 459. To some degree, this canon depends on the (perhaps questionable) assumption that legislative drafters always seek to avoid the possibility of producing results that some might consider "absurd." In the criminal law context, the absurdity doctrine is sometimes justified on the basis that a criminal prohibition whose interpretation yields an absurd result is unlikely to have provided sufficient notice to members of the general public. Of course, whether a given result is "absurd" may itself be a matter of vigorous disagreement. *E.g.*, Public Citizen v. U.S. Dep't of Justice, 491 U.S. 440, 470–74 (1989) (Kennedy, J., concurring in the judgment).

QUESTION

The Eighth Circuit and Supreme Court opinions in *Johnson* employ a variety of canons both "linguistic" and "substantive." They also invoke other sources of statutory meaning (see the "Typology" of approaches, *supra*). Go back through the *Johnson* decisions to identify where in the opinions the various canons appear. What other kinds of statutory interpretation methods and sources figure in each opinion? What can you infer about the consequences of resorting to some methods or sources, as opposed to others? Do you find some interpretive devices more persuasive than others? Why?

C. TWO PREVAILING APPROACHES TO INTERPRETATION: PURPOSIVISM AND TEXTUALISM

John Manning endorses application of the canons of statutory construction as a means to illuminate ambiguous text without recourse to the extratextual aid of legislative history. Dictionaries offer another preferred "textualist" interpretative aid. (Several of the decisions you will soon encounter in the casebook make varying use of dictionaries.) As the *Johnson* case itself illustrates, however, strict textualism risks producing robotic results that rankle common sense (at least the common sense that some judges intuit, and that they, perhaps wishfully, attribute to legislators).

Of course, not every case presents such a stark disagreement between the seeming purpose of the statute and the strict construction of the relevant statutory text as in *Johnson*. Nevertheless, these two approaches, respectively known as purposivism and textualism, are the prevailing theories of contemporary statutory interpretation. As Dean Manning has helpfully explained, debates about purposivism and textualism operate on two levels: the first concerns a disagreement about the methods judges should prioritize when interpreting statutes, and the second concerns a disagreement about the role common-law judges should play in a constitutional system of legislative supremacy in which the legislature, not the judiciary, makes the law:

> For a not inconsiderable part of our history, the Supreme Court held that the "letter" (text) of a statute must yield to its "spirit" (purpose) when the two conflicted. Traditionally, the Court's "purposivism" rested on the following intuitions: In our constitutional system, federal courts act as faithful agents of Congress; accordingly, they must ascertain and enforce Congress's commands as accurately as possible. Statutes are active instruments of policy, enacted to serve some background purpose or goal. Ordinarily, a statutory text will adequately reflect its intended purpose. Sometimes, however, the text of a particular provision will seem incongruous with the statutory purpose reflected in various contextual cues—such as the overall tenor of the statute, patterns of policy judgments made in related legislation, the "evil" that inspired Congress to act, or express statements found in the legislative history. Since legislators act under the constraints of limited resources, bounded foresight, and inexact human language, unanticipated problems of fit have long been viewed as unavoidable. It is said that just as individuals sometimes inadvertently misstate their intended meaning, so too does Congress. Accordingly, the Court long assumed that when the clear import of a statute's text deviated sharply from its purpose, (1) Congress must have expressed its true intentions imprecisely, and (2) a judicial faithful agent could properly adjust the enacted text to capture what Congress would have intended had it expressly confronted the apparent mismatch between text and purpose.

> Near the close of the twentieth century, however, the "new textualism" challenged the prevailing judicial orthodoxy by arguing that the Constitution, properly understood, requires judges to treat the clear import of an enacted text as conclusive, even when the text fits poorly with its apparent background purposes. The textualist critique—which took shape largely in judicial opinions written by Justice Scalia and Judge

Easterbrook—initially stressed two related themes: First, textualists emphasized that the statutory text alone has survived the constitutionally prescribed process of bicameralism and presentment. Accordingly, they argued that when a statute is clear in context, purposivist judges disrespect the legislative process by relying upon unenacted legislative intentions or purposes to alter the meaning of a duly enacted text.

Second, building upon the intent skepticism of the legal realists, the new textualists contended that the purposivist judge's aspiration to identify and rely upon the actual intent of any multimember lawmaking body is fanciful. In brief, textualists have contended that the final wording of a statute may reflect an otherwise unrecorded legislative compromise, one that may—or may not—capture a coherent set of purposes. A statute's precise phrasing depends, moreover, on often untraceable procedural considerations, such as the sequence of alternatives presented (agenda manipulation) or the effect of strategic voting (including logrolling). Given the opacity, complexity, and path dependency of this process, textualists believe that it is unrealistic for judges ever to predict with accuracy what Congress would have "intended" if it had expressly confronted a perceived mismatch between the statutory text and its apparent purpose. In place of traditional conceptions of "actual" legislative intent, modern textualists urge judges to focus on what they consider the more realistic— and objective—measure of how "a skilled, objectively-reasonable user of words" would have understood the statutory text in context.' . . .

The distinction between textualism and purposivism is not, as is often assumed, cut-and-dried. Properly understood, textualism is not and could not be defined either by a strict preference for enacted text over unenacted context, or by a wholesale rejection of the utility of purpose. Because the meaning of language depends on the way a linguistic community uses words and phrases in context, textualists recognize that meaning can never be found exclusively within the enacted text. This feature of textualism, moreover, goes well beyond the often subconscious process of reading words in context in order to pinpoint the "ordinary" meaning of a word that may mean several things in common parlance. Rather, because legal communication often entails the use of specialized conventions, textualists routinely consult unenacted sources of context whose contents might be obscure to the ordinary reader without further inquiry. Moreover, because textualists understand that speakers use language purposively, they recognize that evidence of purpose (if derived from sources other than the legislative history) may also form an appropriate ingredient of the context used to define the text.

Conversely, certain features of purposivism reflect textualist practices and assumptions more deeply than textualists sometimes acknowledge. . . . [M]any important conceptual similarities were already present in the (now canonical) mid-twentieth-century account of purposivism developed in the Legal Process materials of Professors Hart and Sacks. Although Legal Process purposivists believe that interpretation entails the attribution of purpose, they do not deny that semantic meaning of the text casts light—perhaps the most important light—on the purposes to be attributed. Nor do they deny that, in such a pursuit, the judge should carefully consult the technical conventions that distinctively pertain to legalese. Perhaps most important, much like modern textualists, Hart-and-Sacks-style purposivists recognize that a judge's task, properly conceived, is not to seek actual legislative intent; rather, their method of interpretation poses the objective question of how a hypothetical "reasonable legislator" (as opposed to a real one) would have resolved the problem addressed by the statute. . . .

[Nevertheless, s]ignificant practical and theoretical differences persist between textualists and purposivists. Why? Each side gives priority to different elements of statutory context. Textualists give primacy to the semantic context—evidence about the way a reasonable person conversant with relevant social and linguistic practices would have used the words. Purposivists give precedence to policy context—evidence that goes to the way a reasonable person conversant with the circumstances underlying enactment would suppress the mischief and advance the remedy. This difference accounts for the distinct questions that each methodology poses for the hypothetical reasonable interpreter. As noted, textualists ask how "a skilled, objectively reasonable user of words" would have understood the text, in the circumstances in which it was uttered. Legal Process purposivists ask how "reasonable persons pursuing reasonable purposes reasonably" would have resolved the policy issue addressed by the words.

Ultimately, the justifications for their disparate preferences are rooted in competing understandings of the legislative process as it relates to the constitutional ideal of legislative supremacy. Purposivists in the Legal Process tradition think it unrealistic and arbitrary to suppose that Congress collectively knows or cares about the semantic detail of often complex statutes. For them, enforcing the overarching policy of a statute rather than the minutiae of its semantic detail better serves legislative supremacy while also promoting the independently valuable aims of policy coherence and adaptability of the law to unforeseen circumstances.

Textualists (again, myself included) believe that the purposivist approach disregards the central place of legislative compromise embedded in both the constitutional structure and the corresponding congressional rules of legislative procedure. Textualists contend that once one gives up the idea of ascertaining subjective legislative intent, as Legal Process purposivists do, legislative supremacy is most meaningfully served by attributing to legislators the understanding that a reasonable person conversant with applicable conventions would attach to the enacted text in context. From that starting point, textualists argue that purposivism cannot deal adequately with legislative compromise because semantic detail, in the end, is the only effective means that legislators possess to specify the limits of an agreed-upon legislative bargain. When interpreters disregard clear contextual clues about semantic detail, it becomes surpassingly difficult for legislative actors to agree reliably upon terms that give half a loaf. . . .

John F. Manning, *What Divides Textualists from Purposivists?*, 106 Colum. L. Rev. 70, 71–92 (2006).

The degree of agreement or disagreement among legislators may vary depending on the statute they seek to enact; this, naturally, will influence the degree of specificity of the statutory enactment. To this end, Judge Pierre N. Leval of the U.S. Court of Appeals for the Second Circuit has identified the kinds of statutes that properly call for purely textualist interpretations, and those that demand a more wide-ranging and purposivist analysis. In his view, textual ambiguity need not be seen as a shortcoming to be overcome by reference to static text-fillers, whether lexicographic or drawn from legislative history. Rather, ill-defined terms might instead be deemed invitations to judicial elaboration, in a dynamic process of partnership between legislators who design the frame, and judges who fill in the picture.

A View from the Bench

How should these statutes be understood? How far-reaching are the rights they establish? What is the pertinence to them of the old common law decisions? To answer those questions, it is useful to divide statutes into two admittedly oversimplified categories.

1. Micromanager Statutes

One category is what I shall call a *micromanager* statute. In passing a micromanager statute, the legislature undertakes not only to establish policies, but to make the rules that will govern all the questions that will arise in the enforcement of these policies. Such statutes are generally quite lengthy and detailed. The best example of such a statute is probably the Internal Revenue Code. The passage of a micromanager statute may well, depending on the legislature's intent, relegate to the dustbin all prior decisional law in the area, which may be seen as superseded.

It is fashionable in speaking of statutory interpretation to say that the only interpretive source a court should use is a dictionary. That maxim is most appropriate for micromanager statutes, because, at least in theory, the text undertakes to answer all the questions that may arise. Thus, an understanding of the words used in the text of the statute will produce an answer to the problem in litigation.

2.   Delegating Statutes

The other category is what I shall call a *delegating* statute. The legislature states its policy in generalized terms but intentionally delegates to the courts a considerable interpretive role. Delegating statutes can be of two basic types.

a.   Statutes Adopting Common Law

At the furthest remove from the micromanager statute is the statute which does nothing more than give statutory recognition to a body of law previously developed by the courts. Such statutes neither establish new rules nor set new policies. They do not change the law, even in the smallest degree. Their sole purpose is a highly respectable one—to place a reference to the particular body of doctrine in statute books so as to enable those searching for law to discover there at least a reference to that body of rules which previously could be found only by a common law search through the volumes of court opinions. Such statutes often express themselves circumspectly. A single word— murder, larceny, embezzlement, for example—may stand for the full complexity of the doctrine's development. Alternatively, the statute may undertake a fairly detailed summary of the law, or of some of its provisions. Regardless, however, of whether the text is detailed or consists of only a vague generalized reference to the body of doctrine, if the intention of the statute was not to make law but to give recognition in statutory form to a previously developed body of court-made law, proper interpretation of the statute demands that it be so understood.

Furthermore, as the enactment of such a statute is not intended to, and should not, alter the future development of doctrine, such a statute preserves in the court the function by which it developed the body of rules newly given statutory recognition. The court's dynamic function, by which it previously created and shaped the law, is not superseded; it continues to operate, notwithstanding that the law is now expressed in statutory form. As new questions arise, the courts' answers to these questions should be derived from the same considerations that governed the development of the doctrine, rather than from the words chosen by the legislature to summarize or represent that doctrine. Those words were not intended as exercises of the legislature's power to create law.

b. New Policy

The second class of *delegating* statute falls somewhere between the micromanager statute and the statute adopting common law. Such a statute, which I shall call a *new policy* statute, is created when the legislature enacts a new policy but does so in vague, imprecise terms. The legislature recognizes that innumerable questions of interpretation will arise as experience unfolds and delegates to the courts the task of answering those questions in the light of experience and the legislative objective for which the statute was passed. A paradigm example is the Sherman Act. Such an enactment has, on the one hand, some similarity to the micromanager statute in that court interpretations should seek to advance the policy enacted by the legislature. In this respect such statutes are quite unlike enactments of common law, as to which the legislature expresses no policy objective other than to give statutory recognition to a court-developed doctrine, so that future court decisions should be guided by the same principles which guided the courts prior to the enactment. On the other hand, statutes of the *new policy* type are similar to common law adopting statutes and unlike micromanager statutes in that they are delegating. Rather than undertaking to answer the problems expected to arise, the legislature refrains from trying to anticipate and solve such problems; it formulates vague policy statements and delegates responsibility to the courts to work out the problems as they arise.

The proposition that courts should approach the task of interpretation armed only with a dictionary is wholly inappropriate to delegating statutes. The words of the statute simply will not provide the answers and were not intended by the legislature to do so. In passing delegating statutes, legislatures recognize that they function together with courts in a law-making partnership, each having its proper role. As to delegating statutes of the new policy type, the legislature relies on the courts, as experience unfolds, to use their good judgment to do the fine-tuning, to establish contours and boundaries to achieve the legislature's objective. The courts' interpretive rulings, of course, are always subject to legislative correction. As to delegating statutes of the type adopting common law, the legislature delegates to the courts the continued exercise of the function they always performed: the continued development of the common law doctrine in the light of the policies that always drove its development, without regard for the particular words chosen by the legislature to summarize the development.

Needless to say, statutes can be and often are hybrids—partially micromanaging while partially delegating, partially preserving a common law tradition while partially superseding it.

Pierre N. Leval, *Trademark: Champion of Free Speech*, 27 Colum. J. L. & The Arts 187, 196–98 (2004).

QUESTIONS

1. Consider the *Johnson* case: Would you call the Federal Railway Safety Appliance Act a "Micromanager" or a "Delegating" statute? Some of both? Which, if any, portions call for development of judge-made standards in tandem with the statutory rules? As you work through the statutory language in the other cases in this Casebook, consider the extent to which the micromanager/delegating distinction helps you analyze the statute's application to the controversy at hand.

2. Are Dean Manning's and Judge Leval's approaches to statutory interpretation reconcilable? How would a strict textualist interpret a "delegating statute" adopting the common law? One adopting a new policy?

The *Holy Trinity Church* case, *infra*, remains a landmark decision in the study of statutory interpretation, though it has come to stand for different precepts at different times. Before you read the opinions of the trial court and the Supreme Court, work your way through the statute whose meaning the courts were construing. What is the statute's purpose? How does the statute achieve that objective? What conduct violates the statute? Who is liable? For what penalties? Is the text coherent, or are there inconsistencies in the way the statute addresses the problem it seeks to resolve?

Alien Contract Labor Law

48 Cong. Ch. 164, February 26, 1885, 23 Stat. 332.

Chap. 164.—An act to prohibit the importation and migration of foreigners and aliens under contract or agreement to perform labor in the United States, its Territories, and the District of Columbia.

[Sec. 1.] Be it enacted by the Senate and House of Representatives of the United States in Congress assembled, That from and after the passage of this act it shall be unlawful for any person, company, partnership, or corporation, in any manner whatsoever, to prepay the transportation, or in any way assist or encourage the importation or migration of any alien or aliens, any foreigner or foreigners, into the United States, its

Territories, or the District of Columbia, under contract or agreement, parol or special, express or implied, made previous to the importation or migration of such alien or aliens, foreigner or foreigners, to perform labor or service of any kind in the United States, its territories, or the District of Columbia.

Sec. 2. That all contracts or agreements, express or implied, parol, or special, which may hereafter be made by and between any person, company, partnership, or corporation, and any foreigner or foreigners, alien or aliens, to perform labor or service or having reference to the performance of labor or service by any person in the United States, its territories or the District of Columbia, previous to the migration or importation of the person or persons whose labor or service is contracted for into the United States, shall be utterly void and of no effect.

Sec. 3. That for every violation of any of the provisions of section one of this act, the person, partnership, company or corporation violating the same, by knowingly assisting, encouraging or soliciting the migration or importation of any alien or aliens, foreigner or foreigners, into the United States, its Territories or the District of Columbia, to perform labor or service of any kind under contract or agreement, express or implied, parol or special, with such alien or aliens, foreigner or foreigners, previous to becoming residents or citizens of the United States, shall forfeit and pay for every such offense the sum of one thousand dollars, which may be sued for and recovered by the United States or by any person who shall first bring his action therefor including any such alien or foreigner who may be a party to any such contract or agreement, as debts of like amount are now recovered in the circuit courts of the United States; the proceeds to be paid into the Treasury of the United States; and separate suits may be brought for each alien or foreigner who may be a party to any such contract or agreement aforesaid. And it shall be the duty of the district attorney of the proper district to prosecute every such suit at the expense of the United States.

Sec. 4. That the master of any vessel who shall knowingly bring within the United States on any such vessel, and land, or permit to be landed, from any foreign port or place, any alien laborer, mechanic, or artisan who, previous to embarkation on such a vessel, had entered into contract or agreement, parol or special, express or implied, to perform labor or service in the United States, shall be deemed guilty of a misdemeanor, and on conviction thereof, shall be punished by a fine of not more than five hundred dollars for each and every such alien laborer, mechanic or artisan so brought as aforesaid, and may also be imprisoned for a term not exceeding six months.

Sec. 5. That nothing in this act shall be construed as to prevent any citizen or subject of any foreign country temporarily residing in the United States, either in private or official capacity, from engaging, under contract or otherwise, persons not residents or citizens of the United States to act as private secretaries, servants or domestics for such foreigner temporarily residing in the United States as aforesaid, nor shall this act be so construed as to prevent any person, persons, partnership, or corporation from engaging, under contract or agreement, skilled workman in foreign countries to perform labor in the United States in or upon any new industry not at present established in the United States: *Provided*, That skilled labor for that purpose cannot be otherwise obtained; nor shall the provisions of this act apply to professional actors, artists, lecturers, or singers, nor to persons employed strictly as personal or domestic servants: *Provided*, That nothing in this act shall be construed as prohibiting any individual from assisting any member of his family or any relative or personal friend, to migrate from any foreign country to the United States, for the purpose of settlement here.

Sec. 6. That all laws or parts of laws conflicting herewith be, and the same are hereby, repealed.

Approved, February 26, 1885.

QUESTIONS

1. Section 1 makes it illegal for anyone in the United States to form a contract with an alien made prior to his or her arrival, and Section 2 voids any such contracts. Why do you think Congress was concerned about contracts formed only *prior* to arrival?

2. Section 3 makes clear that only the person or persons forming the contract with the alien are liable. Why do you think Congress did not also impose liability on the alien?

3. Sections 4 and 5 seem to provide greater specificity as to the types of positions and services that Congress sought to prevent imported aliens from performing. Why do you think some positions or services were prohibited, while others expressly exempted from such prohibitions? Can you think of other ways Congress might have enumerated what conduct was to be permitted and prohibited?

United States v. Church of the Holy Trinity

United States Circuit Court for the Southern District of New York, 1888.
36 Fed. 303, reversed, 143 U.S. 457, 12 S.Ct. 511, 36 L.Ed. 226 (1892).

■ WALLACE, J. This suit is brought to recover a penalty of $1,000 imposed by the act of congress of February 26, 1885, (23 St. at Large, 332,) upon every person or corporation offending against its provisions by knowingly encouraging the migration of any alien into the United States "to perform labor or service of any kind under contract or agreement, express or implied," previously made with such alien. The defendant, a religious corporation, engaged one Warren, an alien residing in England, to come here and take charge of its church as a pastor. The act makes it the duty of the United States district attorney to bring suit to enforce the penalty prescribed. The demurrer interposed to the complaint raises the single question whether such a contract as was made in this case is within the terms of the act. In other words, the question is whether congress intended to prohibit the migration here of an alien who comes pursuant to a contract with a religious society to perform the functions of a minister of the gospel, and to subject to the penalty the religious society making the contract and encouraging the migration of the alien minister. The act is entitled "An act to prohibit the importation and migration of foreigners and aliens under contract or agreement to perform labor in the United States." It was, no doubt, primarily the object of the act to prohibit the introduction of assisted immigrants, brought here under contracts previously made by corporations and capitalists to prepay their passage and obtain their services at low wages for limited periods of time. It was a measure introduced and advocated by the trades union and labor associations, designed to shield the interests represented by such organizations from the effects of the competition in the labor market of foreigners brought here under contracts having a tendency to stimulate immigration and reduce the rates of wages. Except from the language of the statute there is no reason to suppose a contract like the present to be within the evils which the law was designed to suppress; and, indeed, it would not be indulging a violent supposition to assume that no legislative body in this country would have advisedly enacted a law framed so as to cover a case like the present. Nevertheless, where the terms of a statute are plain, unambiguous, and explicit, the courts are not at liberty to go outside of the language to search for a meaning which it does not reasonably bear in the effort to ascertain and give effect to what may be imagined to have been or not to have been the intention of congress. Whenever the will of congress is declared in ample and unequivocal language, that will must be absolutely followed, and it is not admissible to resort to speculations of policy, nor even to the views of members of congress in debate, to find reasons to control or modify the statute. U.S. v. Railroad Co., 91 U.S. 72. If it were permissible to narrow the provisions of the act to correspond with the purport of the title, and restrain its operation to cases in which the alien is assisted to come here under contract "to perform labor," there might be room for interpretation; and the restricted meaning might possibly be given to the word "labor" which signifies the manual work of the laborer, as distinguished from the work of the skilled artisan, or the professional man. But no rule in the construction of statutes is more familiar than the one to the effect that the title cannot be used to extend or restrain positive provisions in the body of the act. In Hadden v. Collector, 5 Wall. 107, it is said: "The title of an act furnishes little aid in the construction of its provisions." The encouragement of migration prohibited by the first section is of aliens under contract or agreement previously made "to perform labor or service of any kind in the United States." The contracts which are declared to be void by the second section are contracts "having reference to the performance of labor or service by any person in the United States" previous to the migration of the alien. The penalty imposed by the third section is imposed on the person or corporation encouraging the migration of the alien under a contract or agreement previously made "to perform labor or service of any kind." No more comprehensive terms could have been employed to include every conceivable kind of labor or avocation, whether of the hand or brain, in the class of prohibited contracts; and, as if to emphasize and make more explicit the intention that the words "labor or service" should not be taken in any restricted sense, they are followed by the words "of any kind." Every kind of industry, and every employment, manual or intellectual, is embraced within the language used. If it were possible to import a narrower meaning than the natural and ordinary one to the language of these sections, the terms of the fifth section would forbid the attempt. That section is a proviso withdrawing from the operation of the act several classes of persons and contracts. Foreigners residing here temporarily, who may engage private secretaries; persons desirous of establishing a new industry not then existing in the United States, who employ skilled workmen therein; domestic servants; and a limited professional class, are thereby exempted from its provisions. The last clause of the proviso is: "Nor shall the provisions of this act apply to professional actors, artists, lecturers, or singers, nor to persons employed strictly as personal or domestic servants." If, without this exemption, the act would apply to this class of persons, because such persons come here under contracts for labor or service, then clearly it must apply to ministers, lawyers, surgeons, architects, and all others who labor in any professional calling. Unless congress supposed the act to apply to the excepted classes, there was no necessity for the proviso. The office of a proviso is generally to restrain an enacting clause, and to except something which would otherwise have been within it. Wayman v. Southard, 10 Wheat. 30; Minis v. U.S., 15 Pet. 423. In the language of the authorities: "A proviso carves special exemptions only out of the enacting clauses." U.S. v. Dickson, 15 Pet. 165; Ryan v. Carter, 93 U.S. 83. Giving effect to this well-settled rule of statutory interpretation, the proviso is equivalent to a declaration that contracts to perform professional services except those of actors, artists, lecturers, or singers, are within the prohibition of the preceding sections.

The argument based upon the fourth section of the act has not been overlooked. That section subjects to fine and imprisonment any master of a vessel who knowingly brings within the United States any alien "laborer, mechanic, or artisan," who has previously entered into any contract to perform labor or service in the United States. This section is wholly independent of the others, and the difference in the persons described may reasonably be referred to an intention to mitigate the severity of the act in its application to masters of vessels. The demurrer is overruled.

Holy Trinity Church v. United States

Supreme Court of the United States, 1892.
143 U.S. 457, 12 S.Ct. 511, 36 L.Ed. 226.

In error to the circuit court of the United States for the southern district of New York.

■ MR. JUSTICE BREWER delivered the [unanimous] opinion of the court.

Plaintiff in error is a corporation duly organized and incorporated as a religious society under the laws of the state of New York. E. Walpole Warren was, prior to September, 1887, an alien residing in England. In that month the plaintiff in error made a contract with him, by which he was to remove to the city of New York, and enter into its service as rector and pastor; and, in pursuance of such contract, Warren did so remove and enter upon such service. It is claimed by the United States that this contract on the part of the plaintiff in error was forbidden by chapter 164, 23 St. p. 332; and an action was commenced to recover the penalty prescribed by that act. The circuit court held that the contract was within the prohibition of the statute, and rendered judgment accordingly, (36 Fed.Rep. 303,) and the single question presented for our determination is whether it erred in that conclusion.

The first section describes the act forbidden, and is in these words:

"Be it enacted by the senate and house of representatives of the United States of America, in congress assembled, that from and after the passage of this act it shall be unlawful for any person, company, partnership, or corporation, in any manner whatsoever, to prepay the transportation, or in any way assist or encourage the importation or migration, of any alien or aliens, any foreigner or foreigners, into the United States, its territories, or the District of Columbia, under contract or agreement, parol or special, express or implied, made previous to the importation or migration of such alien or aliens, foreigner or foreigners, to perform labor or service of any kind in the United States, its territories, or the District of Columbia."*

It must be conceded that the act of the corporation is within the letter of this section, for the relation of rector to his church is one of service, and implies labor on the one side with compensation on the other. Not only are the general words "labor" and "service" both used, but also, as it were to guard against any narrow interpretation and emphasize a breadth of meaning, to them is added "of any kind;" and, further, as noticed by the circuit judge in his opinion, the fifth section, which makes specific exceptions, among them professional actors, artists, lecturers, singers, and domestic servants, strengthens the idea that every other kind of labor and service was intended to be reached by the first section. While there is great force to this reasoning, we cannot think congress intended to denounce with penalties a transaction like that in the present case. It is a familiar rule that a thing may be within the letter of the statute and yet not within the statute, because not within its spirit nor within the intention of its makers. This has been often asserted, and the Reports are full of cases illustrating its application. This is not the substitution of the will of the judge for that of the legislator; for frequently words of general meaning are used in a statute, words broad enough to include an act in question, and yet a consideration of the whole legislation, or of the circumstances surrounding its enactment, or of the absurd results which follow from giving such broad meaning to the words, makes it unreasonable to believe that the legislator intended to include the particular act. . . .

In U.S. v. Kirby, 7 Wall. 482, 486, the defendants were indicted for the violation of an act of congress providing "that if any person shall knowingly and willfully obstruct or retard the passage of the mail, or of any driver or carrier, or of any horse or carriage carrying the same, he shall, upon conviction, for every such offense, pay a fine not exceeding one hundred dollars." The specific charge was that the defendants knowingly and willfully retarded the passage of one Farris, a carrier of the mail, while engaged in the performance of his duty, and also in like manner retarded the steam-boat Gen. Buell, at that time engaged in carrying the mail. To this indictment the defendants pleaded specially that Farris had been indicted for murder by a court of competent authority in Kentucky; that a bench-warrant had been issued and placed in the hands of the defendant Kirby, the sheriff of the county, commanding him to arrest Farris, and bring him before the court to answer to the indictment; and that, in obedience to this warrant, he and the other defendants, as his posse, entered upon the steam-boat Gen. Buell and arrested Farris, and used only such force as was necessary to accomplish that arrest. The question as to the sufficiency of this plea was certified to this court, and it was held that the arrest of Farris upon the warrant from the state court was not an obstruction of the mail, or the retarding of the passage of a carrier of the mail, within the meaning of the act. In its opinion the court says: "All laws should receive a sensible construction. General terms should be so limited in their application as not to lead to injustice, oppression, or an absurd consequence. It will always, therefore, be presumed that the legislature intended exceptions to its language which would avoid results of this character. The reason of the law in such cases should prevail over its letter. The common sense of man approves the judgment mentioned by Puffendorf, that the Bolognian law which enacted 'that whoever drew blood in the streets should be punished with the utmost severity,' did not extend to the surgeon who opened the vein of a person that fell down in the street in a fit. The same common sense accepts the ruling, cited by Plowden, that the statute of 1 Edw. II., which enacts that a prisoner who breaks prison shall be guilty of felony, does not extend to a prisoner who breaks out when the prison is on fire, 'for he is not to be hanged because he would not stay to be burnt.' And we think that a like common sense will sanction the ruling we make, that the act of congress which punishes the obstruction or retarding of the passage of the mail, or of its carrier, does not apply to a case of temporary detention of the mail caused by the arrest of the carrier upon an indictment for murder." . . .

Among other things which may be considered in determining the intent of the legislature is the title of the act. We do not mean that it may be used to add to or take from the body of the statute, (Hadden v. Collector, 5 Wall. 107) but it may help to interpret its meaning. In the case of U.S. v. Fisher, 2 Cranch 358, 386, CHIEF JUSTICE MARSHALL said: "On the influence which the title ought to have in construing the enacting clauses, much has been said, and yet it is not easy to discern the point of difference between the opposing counsel in this respect. Neither party contends that the title of an act can control plain words in the body of the statute; and neither denies that, taken with other parts, it may assist in removing ambiguities. Where the intent is plain, nothing is left to construction. Where the mind labors to discover the design of the legislature, it seizes everything from which aid can be derived; and in such case the title claims a degree of notice, and will have its due share of consideration." . . .

It will be seen that words as general as those used in the first section of this act were by that decision limited, and the intent of congress with respect to the act was gathered partially, at least, from its title. Now, the title of this act is, "An act to prohibit the importation and migration of foreigners and aliens under contract or agreement to perform labor in the United States, its territories, and the District of Columbia." Obviously the thought expressed in this reaches only to the work of the manual laborer, as distinguished from that of the professional man. No one reading such a title would suppose that congress had in its mind any purpose of staying the coming into this country of ministers of the gospel, or, indeed, of any class whose toil is that of the brain. The common understanding of the terms "labor" and "laborers" does not include preaching and preachers, and it is to be assumed that words and phrases are used in their ordinary meaning. So whatever of light is thrown upon the statute by the language of the title indicates an exclusion from its penal provisions of all contracts for the employment of ministers, rectors, and pastors.

Again, another guide to the meaning of a statute is found in the evil which it is designed to remedy; and for this the court properly looks at contemporaneous events, the situation as it existed, and as it was pressed upon the attention of the legislative body. U.S. v. Railroad Co., 91 U.S. 72, 79. The situation which called for this statute was briefly but fully stated by Mr. Justice Brown when, as district judge, he decided the case of U.S. v. Craig, 28 Fed. Rep. 795, 798: "The motives and history of the act are matters of common knowledge. It had become the practice for large capitalists in this country to contract with their agents abroad for the shipment of great numbers of an ignorant and servile class of foreign laborers, under contracts by which the employer agreed, upon the one hand, to prepay their passage, while, upon the other hand, the laborers agreed to work after their arrival for a certain time at a low rate of wages. The effect of this was to break down the labor market, and to reduce other laborers engaged in like occupations to the level of the assisted immigrant. The evil finally became so flagrant that an appeal was made to congress for relief by the passage of the act in question, the design of which was to raise the standard of foreign immigrants, and to discountenance the migration of those who had not sufficient means in their own hands, or those of their friends, to pay their passage."

It appears, also, from the petitions, and in the testimony presented before the committees of congress, that it was this cheap, unskilled labor which was making the trouble, and the influx of which congress sought to prevent. It was never suggested that we had in this country a surplus of brain toilers, and, least of all, that the market for the services of Christian ministers was depressed by foreign competition. Those were matters to which the attention of congress, or of the people, was not directed. So far, then, as the evil which was sought to be remedied interprets the statute, it also guides to an exclusion of this contract from the penalties of the act.

A singular circumstance, throwing light upon the intent of congress, is found in this extract from the report of the senate committee on education and labor, recommending the passage of the bill: "The general facts and considerations which induce the committee to recommend the passage of this bill are set forth in the report of the committee of the house. The committee report the bill back without amendment, although there are certain features thereof which might well be changed or modified, in the hope that the bill may not fail of passage during the present session. Especially would the committee have otherwise recommended amendments, substituting for the expression, 'labor and service,' whenever it occurs in the body of the bill, the words 'manual labor' or 'manual service,' as sufficiently broad to accomplish the purposes of the bill, and that such amendments would remove objections which a sharp and perhaps unfriendly criticism may urge to the proposed legislation. The committee, however, believing that the bill in its present form will be construed as including only those whose labor or service is manual in character, and being very desirous that the bill become a law before the adjournment, have reported the bill without change." Page 6059, Congressional Record, 48th Cong. And, referring back to the report of the committee of the house, there appears this language: "It seeks to restrain and prohibit the immigration or importation of laborers who would have never seen our shores but for the inducements and allurements of men whose only object is to obtain labor at the lowest possible rate, regardless of the social and material well-being of our own citizens, and regardless of the evil consequences which result to American laborers from such immigration. This class of immigrants care nothing about our institutions, and in many instances never even heard

of them. They are men whose passage is paid by the importers. They come
here under contract to labor for a certain number of years. They are
ignorant of our social condition, and, that they may remain so, they are
isolated and prevented from coming into contact with Americans. They
are generally from the lowest social stratum, and live upon the coarsest
food, and in hovels of a character before unknown to American workmen.
They, as a rule, do not become citizens, and are certainly not a desirable
acquisition to the body politic. The inevitable tendency of their presence
among us is to degrade American labor, and to reduce it to the level of
the imported pauper labor." Page 5359, Congressional Record, 48th Cong.

We find, therefore, that the title of the act, the evil which was
intended to be remedied, the circumstances surrounding the appeal to
congress, the reports of the committee of each house, all concur in
affirming that the intent of congress was simply to stay the influx of this
cheap, unskilled labor. . . .

The judgment will be reversed, and the case remanded for further
proceedings in accordance with this opinion.

NOTES AND QUESTIONS

1. How clear was it that the words of the statute encompassed the services
of the Rev. E. Walpole Warren? Consider that, when the contract labor
statute was enacted, in 1885, the predominant meaning of the word "labor"
was "physical toil," and "service" generally was understood to mean
"domestic service," rather than professional services (referred to in the
plural). On the other hand, contemporary dictionaries also included broader
meanings for these terms. *See* William N. Eskridge, Jr., *Textualism: The
Unknown Ideal?*, 96 Mich. L. Rev. 1509, 1518, 1533 (1998). Does the
exemption clause's coverage of "persons employed strictly as personal or
domestic servants" suggest what meaning should apply to "service of any
kind"?

2. Is it relevant that the meaning of the word "lecturer" has evolved from
its 16th-century meaning of "preacher" to its current secular connotation?*
If, as the Oxford English Dictionary suggests, both meanings were still
current in the late-nineteenth century, how should we interpret the contract
labor statute's clause excluding "lecturers" from the statute's coverage? As a
general matter, if judges are to consult dictionaries in aid of interpretation,
should they not ensure that the dictionary they peruse offers definitions
contemporaneous with the statute under scrutiny? Keep these questions in
mind as you read *MCI Telecommunications v. AT&T*, *infra* Section III.B.3.a,
and *New Prime Inc. v. Oliveira*, *infra* Section VI.A.

3. For an account of the history of the contract labor statute and the
prosecution of the Holy Trinity Church under it, as well as different
approaches to the Supreme Court's use of legislative history, *compare* Carol
Chomsky, *Unlocking the Mysteries of Holy Trinity: Spirit, Letter, and History*

---

* Thanks to Prof. William Eskridge and to Josephine Coakley, Columbia JD 2004, for
direction concerning the etymology of the words "lecturer," "lectureship," and "lecture."

in Statutory Interpretation, 100 Colum. L. Rev. 901 (2000), *with* Adrian Vermeule, *Legislative History and the Limits of Judicial Competence: the Story of Holy Trinity Church*, 50 Stan. L. Rev. 1833 (1998).

4.   Contrast the nature of the problem posed for the Court in the principal case with that posed in *United States v. Kirby* (discussed in the *Holy Trinity Church* case, *supra*) and consider the result reached in the *Kirby* decision and the quoted justifications offered for that result. What other reasonable justifications, if any, might have been given? What are the implications of *Kirby* for the judicial function in interpretation?

5.   Compare Riggs v. Palmer, 115 N.Y. 506, 22 N.E. 188 (1889). In that case, the beneficiary under a will had murdered the testator and then claimed the property pursuant to the will's provisions. The question was whether the beneficiary could have the property in such circumstances. It was acknowledged that the statute regulating the making, proof and effect of wills and the devolution of property did not deal with "murdering heirs." If literally construed, the statute would award the property to the murderer.

> The relevant statute provided:

> N.Y. Rev. Stat § 3.1.42 (1882): No will in writing, except in the cases herein after mentioned, nor any part thereof, shall be revoked, or altered, otherwise than by some other will in writing, or some other writing of the testator, declaring such revocation or alteration, and executed with the same formalities with which the will itself was required by law to be executed; or unless such will be burnt, torn, cancelled, obliterated or destroyed, with the intent and for the purpose of revoking the same, by the testator himself, or by another person in his presence, by his direction and consent; and when so done by another person, the direction and consent of the testator, and the fact of such injury or destruction, shall be proved by at least two witnesses.

The Court however ruled that the murderer was not entitled to the property. Inter alia, the Court stated:

> The purpose of [the statutes concerned] was to enable testators to dispose of their estates to the objects of their bounty at death, and to carry into effect their final wishes legally expressed; and in considering and giving effect to them this purpose must be kept in view. It was the intention of the law-makers that the donees in a will should have the property given to them. But it never could have been their intention that a donee who murdered the testator to make the will operative should have any benefit under it. . . .

> What could be more unreasonable than to suppose that it was the legislative intention in the general laws passed for the orderly, peaceable and just devolution of property, that they should have operation in favor of one who murdered his ancestor that he might speedily come into the possession of his estate? Such an intention is inconceivable. We need not, therefore, be much troubled by the general language contained in the laws.

Besides, all laws as well as all contracts may be controlled in their operation and effect by general, fundamental maxims of the common law. No one shall be permitted to profit by his own fraud, or to take advantage of his own wrong, or to found any claim upon his own iniquity, or to acquire property by his own crime. These maxims are dictated by public policy, have their foundation in universal law administered in all civilized countries, and have nowhere been superseded by statutes.

United States v. Marshall

United States Court of Appeals for Seventh Circuit, 1990.
908 F.2d 1312, *aff'd sub nom.* Chapman v. U.S., 500 U.S. 453,
111 S.Ct. 1919, 114 L.Ed.2d 524 (1991).

[Reargued In Banc May 30, 1990, before BAUER, CHIEF JUDGE, and CUMMINGS, WOOD, JR., CUDAHY, POSNER, COFFEY, FLAUM, EASTERBROOK, RIPPLE, MANION, and KANNE, CIRCUIT JUDGES.]

■ EASTERBROOK, CIRCUIT JUDGE.

. . . [W]e must resolve . . . [w]hether 21 U.S.C. § 841(b)(1)(A)(v) and (B)(v), which set mandatory minimum terms of imprisonment—five years for selling more than one gram of a "mixture or substance containing a detectable amount" of LSD, ten years for more than ten grams—exclude the weight of a carrier medium. . . .

I

According to the Sentencing Commission, the LSD in an average dose weighs 0.05 milligrams. Twenty thousand pure doses are a gram. But 0.05 mg is almost invisible, so LSD is distributed to retail customers in a carrier. Pure LSD is dissolved in a solvent such as alcohol and sprayed on paper or gelatin; alternatively the paper may be dipped in the solution. After the solvent evaporates, the paper or gel is cut into one-dose squares and sold by the square. Users swallow the squares or may drop them into a beverage, releasing the drug. Although the gelatin and paper are light, they weigh much more than the drug. Marshall's 11,751 doses weighed 113.32 grams; the LSD accounted for only 670.72 mg of this, not enough to activate the five-year mandatory minimum sentence, let alone the ten-year minimum. The ten sheets of blotter paper carrying the 1,000 doses Chapman and confederates sold weighed 5.7 grams; the LSD in the paper did not approach the one-gram threshold for a mandatory minimum sentence. This disparity between the weight of the pure LSD and the weight of LSD-plus-carrier underlies the defendants' arguments.

A

If the carrier counts in the weight of the "mixture or substance containing a detectable amount" of LSD, some odd things may happen. Weight in the hands of distributors may exceed that of manufacturers and wholesalers. Big fish then could receive paltry sentences or small fish draconian ones. Someone who sold 19,999 doses of pure LSD (at 0.05 mg per dose) would escape the five-year mandatory minimum of § 841(b)(1)(B)(v) and be covered by § 841(b)(1)(C), which lacks a minimum term and has a maximum of "only" 20 years. Someone who sold a single hit of LSD dissolved in a tumbler of orange juice could be exposed to a ten-year mandatory minimum. Retailers could fall in or out of the mandatory terms depending not on the number of doses but on the medium: sugar cubes weigh more than paper, which weighs more than gelatin. One way to eliminate the possibility of such consequences is to say that the carrier is not a "mixture or substance containing a detectable amount" of the drug. Defendants ask us to do this. . . .

It is not possible to construe the words of § 841 to make the penalty turn on the net weight of the drug rather than the gross weight of carrier and drug. The statute speaks of "mixture or substance containing a detectable amount" of a drug. "Detectable amount" is the opposite of "pure"; the point of the statute is that the "mixture" is not to be converted to an equivalent amount of pure drug. . . .

[The 7th Circuit *en banc* majority concluded that despite these arguably anomalous results, the LSD carrier came within the statutory term "mixture or substance containing a detectable amount."]

■ POSNER, CIRCUIT JUDGE, joined by BAUER, CHIEF JUDGE, and WOOD, JR., and CUDAHY, CIRCUIT JUDGES, dissenting.

. . . LSD is a potentially dangerous drug, especially for psychotics (whom it can drive to suicide). Hoffman, LSD: My Problem Child 67–71 (1983). But many things are dangerous for psychotics. No one believes that LSD is a more dangerous drug than heroin or cocaine (particularly crack cocaine). The general view is that it is *much* less dangerous. Cox, *et al.*, Drugs and Drug Abuse: A Reference Text 313–15 (1983). There is no indication that Congress believes it to be more dangerous, or more difficult to control. The heavy sentences that the law commands for minor traffickers in LSD are the inadvertent result of the interaction among a statutory procedure for measuring weight, adopted without understanding how LSD is sold; a decision to specify harsh mandatory minimum sentences for drug traffickers, based on the weight of the drug sold; and a decision (gratuitous and unreflective, as far as I can see) by the framers of the Guidelines to key punishment to the statutory measure of weight, thereby amplifying Congress's initial error and ensuring that the big dealer who makes or ships the pure drug will indeed receive a shorter sentence than the small dealer who handles the stuff in its street form. As the wholesale value of LSD may be as little as 35 cents a dose (Report 1988: The Supply of Illicit Drugs to the United States 52 (National Narcotics Intelligence Consumers Comm.1989)), a seller of five sugar cubes could be subject to a mandatory minimum prison term of ten years for selling $2 worth of illegal drugs. Dean received six years (no parole, remember) for selling $73 worth. The irrationality is quite bad enough if we confine our attention to LSD sold on blotter paper, since the weight of blotter paper varies considerably, making punishment turn on a factor that has no relation to the dosages or market values of LSD.

Well, what if anything can we judges do about this mess? The answer lies in the shadow of a jurisprudential disagreement that is not less important by virtue of being unavowed by most judges. It is the disagreement between the severely positivistic view that the content of law is exhausted in clear, explicit, and definite enactments by or under express delegation from legislatures, and the natural lawyer's or legal pragmatist's view that the practice of interpretation and the general terms of the Constitution (such as "equal protection of the laws") authorize judges to enrich positive law with the moral values and practical concerns of civilized society. Judges who in other respects have seemed quite similar, such as Holmes and Cardozo, have taken opposite sides of this issue. Neither approach is entirely satisfactory. The first buys political neutrality and a type of objectivity at the price of substantive injustice, while the second buys justice in the individual case at the price of considerable uncertainty and, not infrequently, judicial willfulness. It is no wonder that our legal system oscillates between the approaches. The positivist view, applied unflinchingly to this case, commands the affirmance of prison sentences that are exceptionally harsh by the standards of the modern Western world, dictated by an accidental, unintended scheme of punishment nevertheless implied by the words (taken one by one) of the relevant enactments. The natural law or pragmatist view leads to a freer interpretation, one influenced by norms of equal treatment; and let us explore the interpretive possibilities here. One is to interpret "mixture or substance containing a detectable amount of [LSD]" to exclude the carrier medium—the blotter paper, sugar or gelatin cubes, and orange juice or other beverage. That is the course we rejected in *United States v. Rose,* [citation], as have the other circuits. I wrote *Rose,* but I am no longer confident that its literal interpretation of the statute, under which the blotter paper, cubes, etc. are "substances" that "contain" LSD, is inevitable. The blotter paper, etc. are better viewed, I now think, as carriers, like the package in which a kilo of cocaine comes wrapped or the bottle in which a fifth of liquor is sold.

Interpreted to exclude the carrier, the punishment schedule for LSD would make perfectly good sense; it would not warp the statutory design. The comparison with heroin and cocaine is again illuminating. The statute imposes the five-year mandatory minimum sentence on anyone who sells a substance or mixture containing a hundred grams of heroin, equal to 10,000 to 20,000 doses. One gram of pure LSD, which also would trigger the five-year minimum, yields 20,000 doses. The comparable figures for cocaine are 3250 to 50,000 doses, placing LSD in about the middle. So Congress may have wanted to base punishment for the sale of LSD on the weight of the pure drug after all, using one and ten grams of the pure drug to trigger the five-year and ten-year minima (and corresponding maxima—twenty years and forty years). This interpretation leaves "substance or mixture containing" without a referent, so far as LSD is concerned. But we must remember that Congress used the identical term in each subsection that specifies the quantity of a drug that subjects the seller to the designated minimum and maximum punishments. In thus automatically including the same term in each subsection, Congress did not necessarily affirm that, for each and every drug covered by the statute, a substance or mixture containing the drug *must* be found. . . .

[The dissent of JUDGE CUMMINGS, joined by CHIEF JUDGE BAUER and CIRCUIT JUDGES WOOD, JR., CUDAHY, and POSNER, has been omitted.]

NOTES

1.   In Chapman v. United States, 500 U.S. 453 (1991), the Supreme Court adopted the position of the Seventh Circuit majority in *Marshall* that the mandatory minimum prison term statute should be interpreted to include the weight of the LSD carrier in calculating the weight of the "mixture or substance containing a detectable amount" of the drug.

2.   The two broad trends in statutory interpretation that Judge Posner recognizes in *United States v. Marshall* are by no means limited to the construction of criminal statutes. The sequence of decisions in this book, from *Johnson v. Southern Pacific* to *Holy Trinity Church* and onward, also demonstrate courts' "jurisprudential disagreement" over the interpretation of statutes.

PART III

INTERPRETIVE APPROACHES EMPHASIZING TEXT

A. INTERPRETING A STATUTE "ON ITS FACE"

The Statute on its Face

Babb v. Wilkie

Supreme Court of the United States, 2020.
140 S.Ct. 1168, 206 L.Ed.2d 432.

■ JUSTICE ALITO delivered the opinion of the Court[, in which CHIEF JUSTICE ROBERTS, JUSTICE GINSBURG,* JUSTICE BREYER, JUSTICE SOTOMAYOR, JUSTICE KAGAN, JUSTICE GORSUCH, and JUSTICE KAVANAUGH joined.]

---

* Editors' Note: JUSTICE GINSBURG joined all but footnote 3 of the opinion, which has been omitted here.

The federal-sector provision of the Age Discrimination in Employment Act of 1967 (ADEA), 88 Stat. 74, 29 U.S.C. § 633a(a), provides (with just a few exceptions) that "personnel actions" affecting individuals aged 40 and older "shall be made free from any discrimination based on age." We are asked to decide whether this provision imposes liability only when age is a "but-for cause" of the personnel action in question.

We hold that § 633a(a) goes further than that. The plain meaning of the critical statutory language ("made free from any discrimination based on age") demands that personnel actions be untainted by any consideration of age. This does not mean that a plaintiff may obtain all forms of relief that are generally available for a violation of § 633a(a), including hiring, reinstatement, backpay, and compensatory damages, without showing that a personnel action would have been different if age had not been taken into account. To obtain such relief, a plaintiff must show that age was a but-for cause of the challenged employment decision. But if age discrimination played a lesser part in the decision, other remedies may be appropriate.

I

Noris Babb, who was born in 1960, is a clinical pharmacist at the U.S. Department of Veterans Affairs Medical Center in Bay Pines, Florida. Babb brought suit in 2014 against the Secretary of Veterans Affairs (hereinafter VA), claiming that she had been subjected to age and sex discrimination, as well as retaliation for engaging in activities protected by federal anti-discrimination law. Only her age-discrimination claims are now before us.

Those claims center on the following personnel actions. First, in 2013, the VA took away Babb's "advanced scope" designation, which had made her eligible for promotion on the Federal Government's General Scale from a GS-12 to a GS-13. Second, during this same time period, she was denied training opportunities and was passed over for positions in the hospital's anticoagulation clinic. Third, in 2014, she was placed in a new position, and while her grade was raised to GS-13, her holiday pay was reduced. All these actions, she maintains, involved age discrimination, and in support of her claims, she alleges, among other things, that supervisors made a variety of age-related comments.

The VA moved for summary judgment and offered non-discriminatory reasons for the challenged actions, and the District Court granted that motion. Evaluating each of Babb's claims under the burden-shifting framework outlined in *McDonnell Douglas Corp. v. Green*, 411 U.S. 792 (1973), the court found that Babb had established a prima facie case [that the challenged actions were the result of employment discrimination due to her age], that the Secretary had proffered legitimate reasons [unrelated to the plaintiff's age] for the challenged actions, and that no jury could reasonably conclude that those reasons were pretextual [bases for excusing discriminatory actions].

Babb appealed, contending that the District Court should not have used the *McDonnell Douglas* framework because it is not suited for "mixed motives" claims. She argued that under the terms of the ADEA's federal-sector provision, a personnel action is unlawful if age is a factor in the challenged decision. As a result, she explained that even if the VA's proffered reasons were not pretextual, it would not necessarily follow that age discrimination played no part.

The Eleventh Circuit panel that heard Babb's appeal found that her argument was "foreclosed" by Circuit precedent but added that it might have agreed with her if it were "writing on a clean slate." [Citation.]

We granted certiorari, [citation], to resolve a Circuit split over the interpretation of § 633a(a).

II

That provision of the ADEA states in relevant part: "All personnel actions affecting employees or applicants for employment who are at least 40 years of age . . . shall be made free from any discrimination based on age." 29 U.S.C. § 633a(a).

The Government interprets this provision to impose liability only when age is a but-for cause of an employment decision. According to the Government, even if age played a part in such a decision, an employee or applicant for employment cannot obtain any relief unless it is shown that the decision would have been favorable if age had not been taken into account. This interpretation, the Government contends, follows both from the meaning of the statutory text and from the "default rule" that we have recognized in other employment discrimination cases, namely, that recovery for wrongful conduct is generally permitted only if the injury would not have occurred but for that conduct. [Citation.]

Babb interprets the provision differently. She maintains that its language prohibits any adverse consideration of age in the decision-making *process*. Accordingly, she argues proof that age was a but-for cause of a challenged employment decision is not needed.

A

Which interpretation is correct? To decide, we start with the text of the statute, [citation], and as it turns out, it is not necessary to go any further. The plain meaning of the statutory text shows that age need not be a but-for cause of an employment decision in order for there to be a violation of § 633a(a). To explain the basis for our interpretation, we will first define the important terms in the statute and then consider how they relate to each other.

1

Section 633a(a) concerns "personnel actions," and while the ADEA does not define this term, its meaning is easy to understand. The Civil Service Reform Act of 1978, which governs federal employment, broadly defines a "personnel action" to include most employment-related decisions, such as appointment, promotion, work assignment, compensation, and performance reviews. [Citation.] That interpretation is consistent with the term's meaning in general usage, and we assume that it has the same meaning under the ADEA.

Under § 633a(a), personnel actions must be made "free from" discrimination. The phrase "free from" means "untainted" or "[c]lear of (something which is regarded as objectionable)." Webster's Third New International Dictionary 905 (def. 4(a)(2)) (1976); 4 Oxford English Dictionary 521 (def. 12) (1933); *see also* American Heritage Dictionary 524 (def. 5(a)) (1969) (defining "free" "used with from" as "[n]ot affected or restricted by a given condition or circumstance"); Random House Dictionary of the English Language 565 (def. 12) (1966) (defining "free" as "exempt or released from something specified that controls, restrains, burdens, etc."). Thus, under § 633a(a), a personnel action must be made "untainted" by discrimination based on age, and the addition of the term "any" ("free from *any* discrimination based on age") drives the point home. And as for "discrimination," we assume that it carries its " 'normal definition,' " which is " 'differential treatment.' " [Citation.]

Under § 633a(a), the type of discrimination forbidden is "discrimination based on age," and "[i]n common talk, the phrase 'based on' indicates a but-for causal relationship." [Citations.] Therefore, § 633a(a) requires that age be a but-for cause of the discrimination alleged.

What remains is the phrase "shall be made." "[S]hall be made" is a form of the verb "to make," which means "to bring into existence," "to produce," "to render," and "to cause to be or become." Random House Dictionary of the English Language, at 866. Thus, "shall be made" means "shall be produced," etc. And the imperative mood, denoting a duty, *see* Black's Law Dictionary 1233 (5th ed. 1979), emphasizes the importance of avoiding the taint.

2

So much for the individual terms used in § 633a(a). What really matters for present purposes is the way these terms relate to each other. Two matters of syntax are critical. First, "based on age" is an adjectival phrase that modifies the noun "discrimination." It does not modify "personnel actions." The statute does not say that "it is unlawful to take personnel actions that are based on age"; it says that "personnel actions . . . shall be made free from any discrimination based on age." § 633a(a). As a result, age must be a but-for cause of discrimination— that is, of differential treatment—but not necessarily a but-for cause of a personnel action itself.

Second, "free from any discrimination" is an adverbial phrase that modifies the verb "made." *Ibid.* Thus, "free from any discrimination" describes how a personnel action must be "made," namely, in a way that is not tainted by differential treatment based on age. If age discrimination plays any part in the way a decision is made, then the decision is not made in a way that is untainted by such discrimination.

This is the straightforward meaning of the terms of § 633a(a), and it indicates that the statute does not require proof that an employment decision would have turned out differently if age had not been taken into account.

To see what this entails in practice, consider a simple example. Suppose that a decision-maker is trying to decide whether to promote employee A, who is 35 years old, or employee B, who is 55. Under the employer's policy, candidates for promotion are first given numerical scores based on non-discriminatory factors. Candidates over the age of 40 are then docked five points, and the employee with the highest score is promoted. Based on the non-discriminatory factors, employee A (the 35-year-old) is given a score of 90, and employee B (the 55-year-old) gets a score of 85. But employee B is then docked 5 points because of age and thus ends up with a final score of 80. The decision-maker looks at the candidates' final scores and, seeing that employee A has the higher score, promotes employee A.

This decision is not "made" "free from any discrimination" because employee B was treated differently (and less favorably) than employee A (because she was docked five points and A was not). And this discrimination was "based on age" because the five points would not have been taken away were it not for employee B's age.

It is true that this difference in treatment did not affect the outcome, and therefore age was not a but-for cause of the decision to promote employee A. Employee A would have won out even if age had not been considered and employee B had not lost five points, since A's score of 90 was higher than B's initial, legitimate score of 85. But under the language of § 633a(a), this does not preclude liability. . . .

C

We are not persuaded by the argument that it is anomalous to hold the Federal Government to a stricter standard than private employers or state and local governments. That is what the statutory language dictates, and if Congress had wanted to impose the same standard on all employers, it could have easily done so.

As first enacted, the ADEA "applied only to actions against private employers." [Citation.] In 1974, "Congress expanded the scope of the ADEA" to reach both state and local governments and the Federal Government. [Citation.] To cover state and local governments, Congress simply added them to the definition of an "employer" in the ADEA's private-sector provision, *see* 29 U.S.C. § 630(b), and Congress could have easily done the same for the Federal Government. Indeed, the first proposal for expansion of the ADEA to government entities did precisely that. [Citation.]

But Congress did not choose this route. Instead, it "deliberately prescribed a distinct statutory scheme applicable only to the federal sector," [citation], and in doing so, it eschewed the language used in the private-sector provision, § 623(a). [Citation.] We generally ascribe significance to such a decision. [Citation.] . . . In any event, "where, as here, the words of [a] statute are unambiguous, the " 'judicial inquiry is complete.' ' " [Citation.]

D

While Babb can establish that the VA violated § 633a(a) without proving that age was a but-for cause of the VA's personnel actions, she acknowledges—and we agree—that but-for causation is important in determining the appropriate remedy. It is bedrock law that "requested relief" must "redress the alleged injury." [Citation.] Thus, § 633a(a) plaintiffs who demonstrate only that they were subjected to unequal consideration cannot obtain reinstatement, backpay, compensatory damages, or other forms of relief related to the end result of an employment decision. To obtain such remedies, these plaintiffs must show that age discrimination was a but-for cause of the employment outcome.

Although unable to obtain such relief, plaintiffs are not without a remedy if they show that age was a but-for cause of differential treatment in an employment decision but not a but-for cause of the decision itself. In that situation, plaintiffs can seek injunctive or other forward-looking relief. Determining what relief, if any, is appropriate in the present case is a matter for the District Court to decide in the first instance if Babb succeeds in showing that § 633a(a) was violated.

* * *

The judgment of the United States Court of Appeals for the Eleventh Circuit is reversed, and the case is remanded for further proceedings consistent with this opinion.

It is so ordered.

[The concurring opinion of JUSTICE SOTOMAYOR, joined by JUSTICE GINSBURG, has been omitted.]

■ JUSTICE THOMAS, dissenting.

Until now, the rule for pleading a claim under a federal antidiscrimination statute was clear: A plaintiff had to plausibly allege that discrimination was the but-for cause of an adverse action, unless the statute's text unequivocally replaced that standard with a different one. Today, however, the Court departs from this rule, concluding that the federal-sector provision of the Age Discrimination in Employment Act of 1967 (ADEA) imposes liability if an agency's personnel actions are at all tainted by considerations of age. This rule is so broad that a plaintiff could bring a cause of action even if he is ultimately promoted or hired over a younger applicant. This novel "any consideration" standard does serious damage to our interpretation of antidiscrimination statutes and disrupts the settled expectations of federal employers and employees. I therefore respectfully dissent.

I

A

In my view, the default rule of but-for causation applies here because it is not clearly displaced by the text of the ADEA's federal-sector provision. Though the Court engages at length with the provision's text, it barely acknowledges our default rule, which undergirds our antidiscrimination jurisprudence. Because the interpretation of an antidiscrimination statute must be assessed against the backdrop of this default rule, I begin by describing the rule in detail.

We have explained that "[c]ausation in fact—*i.e.,* proof that the defendant's conduct did in fact cause the plaintiff's injury—is a standard requirement of any tort claim," including claims of discrimination. [Citation.] "In the usual course, this standard requires the plaintiff to show that the harm would not have occurred in the absence of—that is, but for—the defendant's conduct." [Citation.] But-for causation is "the background against which Congress legislate[s]," and it is "the default rul[e Congress] is presumed to have incorporated, absent an indication to the contrary in the statute itself." [Citation.] We have recognized as much when interpreting 42 U.S.C. § 1981's prohibition against racial discrimination in contracting, [citation], Title VII's retaliation provision, [citation], and the private-sector provision of the ADEA, [citation].

Given this established backdrop, the question becomes whether the federal-sector provision of the ADEA contains sufficiently clear language to overcome the default rule. The provision states: "All personnel actions affecting employees or applicants for employment who are at least 40 years of age . . . shall be made free from any discrimination based on age." 29 U.S.C. § 633a(a).

I agree with the Court that discrimination means differential treatment, that "based on" connotes a but-for relationship, and that "to make" typically means to produce or to become. But I disagree with the Court's overall interpretation of how these terms fit together. Specifically, the Court believes that " 'based on age' " modifies only " 'discrimination,' " not " 'personnel actions.' " From this, the Court concludes that the plain meaning of the text "demands that personnel actions be untainted by any consideration of age."

In my view, however, the provision is also susceptible of the Government's interpretation, *i.e.,* that the entire phrase "discrimination based on age" modifies "personnel actions." Under this reading, as the Government explains, the provision "prohibits agencies from engaging in 'discrimination *based on* age' in the making of personnel actions." Because the only thing being "made" in the statute is a "personnel action," it is entirely reasonable to conclude that age must be the but-for cause of that personnel action.

At most, the substantive mandate against discrimination in § 633a(a) is ambiguous. And it goes without saying that an ambiguous provision does not contain the clear language necessary to displace the default rule. Accordingly, I would hold that the default rule of but-for causation applies here.

B

The Court attempts to downplay the sweeping nature of its novel "any consideration" rule by discussing the limited remedies available under that rule. . . . [T]he Court implausibly concludes that, in the federal-sector provision of the ADEA, Congress created a novel "any consideration" causation standard but remained completely silent as to what remedies were available under that new rule. Just as implausibly, the Court assumes from this congressional silence that Congress intended for judges to craft a remedial scheme in which the available relief would vary depending on the inflicted injury, using an as-yet-unknown scheme.

I would not follow such an unusual course. We have stated in the past that we must "read [the ADEA] the way Congress wrote it." [Citation.] The federal-sector provision contains no clear language displacing the default rule, and Congress has demonstrated that it knows how to do so when it wishes. [Citations.] Rather than supplementing a novel rule with a judicially crafted remedy, I would infer from the textual silence that Congress wrote the ADEA to conform to the default rule of but-for causation. . . .

QUESTIONS

1. The majority's opinion exemplifies a textualist approach to interpretation that emphasizes the "plain meaning" of the statutory text, drawing on dictionary definitions of the "individual terms used in § 633(a)," as well as "matters of syntax." The majority does not stop there, however, for it proceeds to consider an objection to the resulting "plain meaning": that it would be anomalous to hold the Federal Government to a stricter standard than other employers. It does so, moreover, by referencing the legislative history of the statute. How would you classify that method of interpretation? Should the stricter standard matter if the text is plain? Why address that objection at all?

2. Although the majority interprets the statute according to what it says is the "plain meaning" of the statutory text, that plain meaning does not fully resolve the legal question at issue. Even if age need not be a but-for cause of an adverse personnel action, the Court acknowledges that "but-for causation is important in determining the appropriate remedy." On this basis, it concludes that without establishing but-for causation, a plaintiff may not receive "reinstatement, backpay, compensatory damages, or other forms of relief." Is this a hollow victory for the plaintiff? Even if the remedies are

limited, can you think of other benefits of this ruling for prospective plaintiffs? Is there legal significance to prevailing in a lawsuit even if your remedies are quite circumscribed?

3. The dissent argues that the ADEA text in question is not sufficiently clear to displace the Court's long-established "default rule of but-for causation" for employment discrimination claims under federal law. Recall the typology of interpretive methods in Section II.B.1 of this Casebook. What is the basis for the claim that a court-imposed default rule should prevail absent evidence that it has been "clearly displaced by the text"? Does the presumption further the drafters' aims for the ADEA? Does it draw on the reasonable reader's understanding of the provision? Or, is it grounded in a rule-of-law principle? If the latter, can you articulate what that rule-of-law principle might be?

4. In Part II.A.2 of its opinion, the majority argues that syntax and grammar support its construction of the statutory provision in question. While the opinion's previous section utilized multiple dictionaries, the majority does not cite any authorities to support its invocation of syntax and grammar. What authorities, if any, could a court point to when utilizing grammar in its reasoning? Are rules of grammar universally understood— and accepted? If so, how can the dissent reasonably disagree with the majority's construction of the provision?

5. The majority concludes its argument by finding that, where "the words of [a] statute are unambiguous, the ' "judicial inquiry is complete." ' " How does the majority conclude that the statute is unambiguous? Do you think it's possible to reach such a conclusion without looking at all to the statute's legislative history?

6. The dissent asserts that the majority "assumes from . . . congressional silence that Congress intended for judges to craft a remedial scheme." Can a statute, unambiguous or not, have unspecified gaps that courts can fill? What problem does the dissent have with allowing courts to read law into congressional silence?

1. THE "PLAIN MEANING RULE"

Cases like *Holy Trinity Church, supra* Section II.C, highlight tensions between giving the narrow linguistic meaning to a statutory text (often referred to as the "literal meaning"), which could lead to undesirable results seemingly at odds with the purpose of its enactment, and a purposivist interpretation of the statute, which would avoid the undesirable result, but at the expense of the statute's seemingly literal meaning. For many statutory interpretation controversies, however, the distinction between legislative text and legislative intent is not so stark. Indeed, all too often, a straightforward meaning emerges neither from the statute's literal meaning nor from an examination of the legislative intent behind its enactment.

As a result, the statutory interpreter must decide which sources and methods of interpretation to prioritize, and the reasons for doing so. The predominant judicial approach to statutory interpretation has long sought guidance from extrinsic as well intrinsic sources of interpretation. For example, in the course of interpreting the ordinary meanings of the statutory words at issue, courts often consult extratextual aids like legislative history, and inquire into the social context that gave rise to the legislation. (The Supreme Court's opinion in *Johnson v. S. Pacific,* *supra* Section II.B.2, exemplifies this approach.) By contrast, some of the older cases, and a strain of more recent decisions in the mode of "the new textualism" popularized by jurists like Justice Antonin Scalia, reject the resort to certain extratextual aids *on principle* in circumstances where they perceive that the "plain meaning" of the words alone suffices to ascertain the statutory meaning. (*See, e.g.,* the 8th Circuit's opinion in *Johnson.*) According to this view, for all intents and purposes, the legislature "meant what [it] said, and said what [it] meant."* (And—as some of the decisions imply—if the legislature did not mean what it said, it is for the legislature, and not the courts, to correct its misstatement.)

When courts exclude evidence of statutory purpose because the text itself conveys a plain meaning, they often do so on the basis of the "Plain Meaning Rule." This rule rests on the foundational premise that the meaning of a statutory term is indeed "plain." But plainness may be in the eye of the beholder; what may seem clear to one reader may appear ambiguous to another. The context in which a statement is made, however, can clarify—or change—the meaning. For example, in some parts of the English-speaking world, when people meet, they simply say:

Q.: "How are you?"

A.: "How are you?"

And they will leave it at that. They do not expect an answer. The words, through custom, have lost their plain meaning and are now used as greetings. The same question asked by a physician in an examination room will get a different answer. Once again, custom and context supply the "meaning," as even textualists—per Dean Manning, *supra*—acknowledge.

Context can also fill the gaps in semantic meaning when a statement, taken literally, appears incomplete. Many statements leave much to assumption. For example, if one office-worker asks her co-worker if he has a stapler, it is usually not because the inquirer seeks to compile an inventory of the co-worker's equipment, but because she wishes to borrow the stapler. To provide the answer, "I do," and nothing more, would respond to what the speaker, in context, sought. Moreover, the asker also assumes that the loaned stapler will include staples. To supply an empty stapler would respond literally to the request, but would "clearly" not offer what the borrower sought.

In order to understand a statement, we often need to know its purpose. Consider a sign posted in a classroom: "NO COFFEE." What is

---

* Theodor Seuss Geisel (Dr. Seuss), Horton Hatches the Egg (1940).

this supposed to mean? If a student brings in a sealed can of ground coffee, has she violated the rule indicated by the sign? What if she brings in a cup of tea? What do we know about this rule? Is it intended to keep classrooms clean? If so, one can infer that it prohibits bringing in cups of the coffee beverage. If that is the purpose of the rule, should one infer by extension a prohibition on other beverages? All other beverages? What about other potential sources of classroom untidiness, such as candy bars? Loose notebook paper? Eraser shavings—erasers?

What if the classroom at issue were located in the Macrobiotic Institute of America, an institution whose creed bans artificial stimulants, such as caffeine? Does the prohibition take on a different meaning now? What purpose do you now infer? What meaning follows from it? The Plain Meaning Rule has venerable roots, and variable applications. The following oft-cited judicial statement indicates the function and effect of this approach to statutory interpretation:

> The general rule is perfectly well settled that, where a statute is of doubtful meaning and susceptible upon its face of two constructions, the court may look into prior and contemporaneous acts, the reasons which induced the act in question, the mischiefs intended to be remedied, the extraneous circumstances, and the purpose intended to be accomplished by it, to determine its proper construction. But where the act is clear upon its face, and when standing alone it is fairly susceptible of but one construction, that construction must be given to it. * * * The whole doctrine applicable to the subject may be summed up in the single observation that prior acts may be referred to *solve* but not to *create* an ambiguity.

Hamilton v. Rathbone, 175 U.S. 414 (1899).

In the following case, the majority and dissent disagree on the plainness of the meaning of the term in question. Consider what methods they apply to decide whether the term is plain, as well as what the significance of such a finding is.

Yates v. United States

Supreme Court of the United States, 2015.
574 U.S. 528, 135 S.Ct. 1074, 1919 L.Ed.2d 64.

■ JUSTICE GINSBURG announced the judgment of the Court and delivered an opinion, in which . . . CHIEF JUSTICE [ROBERTS], JUSTICE BREYER, and JUSTICE SOTOMAYOR join.

John Yates, a commercial fisherman, caught undersized red grouper in federal waters in the Gulf of Mexico. To prevent federal authorities from confirming that he had harvested undersized fish, Yates ordered a crew member to toss the suspect catch into the sea. For this offense, he was charged with, and convicted of, violating 18 U.S.C. § 1519, which provides:

"Whoever knowingly alters, destroys, mutilates, conceals, covers up, falsifies, or makes a false entry in any record, document, or tangible object with the intent to impede, obstruct, or influence the investigation or proper administration of any matter within the jurisdiction of any department or agency of the United States or any case filed under title 11, or in relation to or contemplation of any such matter or case, shall be fined under this title, imprisoned not more than 20 years, or both."

Yates was also indicted and convicted under § 2232(a), which provides:

"DESTRUCTION OR REMOVAL OF PROPERTY TO PREVENT SEIZURE.—Whoever, before, during, or after any search for or seizure of property by any person authorized to make such search or seizure, knowingly destroys, damages, wastes, disposes of, transfers, or otherwise takes any action, or knowingly attempts to destroy, damage, waste, dispose of, transfer, or otherwise take any action, for the purpose of preventing or impairing the Government's lawful authority to take such property into its custody or control or to continue holding such property under its lawful custody and control, shall be fined under this title or imprisoned not more than 5 years, or both."

Yates does not contest his conviction for violating § 2232(a), but he maintains that fish are not trapped within the term "tangible object," as that term is used in § 1519.

Section 1519 was enacted as part of the Sarbanes-Oxley Act of 2002 [citation], legislation designed to protect investors and restore trust in financial markets following the collapse of Enron Corporation. A fish is no doubt an object that is tangible; fish can be seen, caught, and handled, and a catch, as this case illustrates, is vulnerable to destruction. But it would cut § 1519 loose from its financial-fraud mooring to hold that it encompasses any and all objects, whatever their size or significance, destroyed with obstructive intent. Mindful that in Sarbanes-Oxley, Congress trained its attention on corporate and accounting deception and cover-ups, we conclude that a matching construction of § 1519 is in order: A tangible object captured by § 1519, we hold, must be one used to record or preserve information.

I

On August 23, 2007, the Miss Katie, a commercial fishing boat, was six days into an expedition in the Gulf of Mexico. . . . Engaged in a routine offshore patrol to inspect both recreational and commercial vessels, Officer John Jones . . . decided to board the Miss Katie to check on the vessel's compliance with fishing rules. . . .

Upon boarding the Miss Katie, Officer Jones noticed three red grouper that appeared to be undersized hanging from a hook on the deck.

At the time, federal conservation regulations required immediate release of red grouper less than 20 inches long. Violation of those regulations is a civil offense punishable by a fine or fishing license suspension. [Citation.]

Suspecting that other undersized fish might be on board, Officer Jones proceeded to inspect the ship's catch, setting aside and measuring only fish that appeared to him to be shorter than 20 inches. After separating the fish measuring below 20 inches from the rest of the catch by placing them in wooden crates, Officer Jones directed Yates[, the captain,] to leave the fish, thus segregated, in the crates until the Miss Katie returned to port. . . .

Four days later, after the Miss Katie had docked in Cortez, Florida, Officer Jones measured the fish contained in the wooden crates. This time, however, the measured fish, although still less than 20 inches, slightly exceeded the lengths recorded on board. Jones surmised that the fish brought to port were not the same as those he had detected during his initial inspection. Under questioning, one of the crew members admitted that, at Yates's direction, he had thrown overboard the fish Officer Jones had measured at sea, and that he and Yates had replaced the tossed grouper with fish from the rest of the catch.

. . . On May 5, 2010, [Yates] was indicted for destroying property to prevent a federal seizure, in violation of § 2232 (a), and for destroying, concealing, and covering up undersized fish to impede a federal investigation, in violation of § 1519.[1] By the time of the indictment, the minimum legal length for Gulf red grouper had been lowered from 20 inches to 18 inches. *See* 50 C.F.R. § 622.37(d)(2)(iv) (effective May 18, 2009). No measured fish in Yates's catch fell below that limit. The record does not reveal what civil penalty, if any, Yates received for his possession of fish undersized under the 2007 regulation. *See* 16 U.S.C. § 1858(a).

Yates was tried on the criminal charges in August 2011. . . . For violating § 1519 and § 2232(a), the court sentenced Yates to imprisonment for 30 days, followed by supervised release for three years. For life, he will bear the stigma of having a federal felony conviction. . . .

II

The Sarbanes-Oxley Act, all agree, was prompted by the exposure of Enron's massive accounting fraud and revelations that the company's outside auditor, Arthur Andersen LLP, had systematically destroyed potentially incriminating documents. The Government acknowledges that § 1519 was intended to prohibit, in particular, corporate document-shredding to hide evidence of financial wrongdoing. . . .

---

[1] Yates was also charged with making a false statement to federal law enforcement officers, in violation of 18 U.S.C. § 1001(a)(2). That charge, on which Yates was acquitted, is not relevant to our analysis.

In the Government's view, § 1519 extends beyond the principal evil motivating its passage. The words of § 1519, the Government argues, support reading the provision as a general ban on the spoliation of evidence, covering all physical items that might be relevant to any matter under federal investigation.

Yates urges a contextual reading of § 1519, tying "tangible object" to the surrounding words, the placement of the provision within the Sarbanes-Oxley Act, and related provisions enacted at the same time, in particular § 1520 and § 1512(c)(1). Section 1519, he maintains, targets not all manner of evidence, but records, documents, and tangible objects used to preserve them, *e.g.*, computers, servers, and other media on which information is stored.

We agree with Yates and reject the Government's unrestrained reading. "Tangible object" in § 1519, we conclude, is better read to cover only objects one can use to record or preserve information, not all objects in the physical world.

A

The ordinary meaning of an "object" that is "tangible," as stated in dictionary definitions, is "a discrete . . . thing," Webster's Third New

International Dictionary 1555 (2002), that "possess[es] physical form," Black's Law Dictionary 1683 (10th ed. 2014). From this premise, the Government concludes that "tangible object," as that term appears in § 1519, covers the waterfront, including fish from the sea.

Whether a statutory term is unambiguous, however, does not turn solely on dictionary definitions of its component words. Rather, "[t]he plainness or ambiguity of statutory language is determined [not only] by reference to the language itself, [but as well by] the specific context in which that language is used, and the broader context of the statute as a whole." *Robinson v. Shell Oil Co.*, 519 U.S. 337, 34 (1997). [Citation.] Ordinarily, a word's usage accords with its dictionary definition. In law as in life, however, the same words, placed in different contexts, sometimes mean different things.

We have several times affirmed that identical language may convey varying content when used in different statutes, sometimes even in different provisions of the same statute. . . .

. . . [A]lthough dictionary definitions of the words "tangible" and "object" bear consideration, they are not dispositive of the meaning of "tangible object" in § 1519.

Supporting a reading of "tangible object," as used in § 1519, in accord with dictionary definitions, the Government points to the appearance of that term in Federal Rule of Criminal Procedure 16. That Rule requires the prosecution to grant a defendant's request to inspect "tangible objects" within the Government's control that have utility for the defense.

Rule 16's reference to "tangible objects" has been interpreted to include any physical evidence. [Citation.] Rule 16 is a discovery rule designed to protect defendants by compelling the prosecution to turn over to the defense evidence material to the charges at issue. In that context, a comprehensive construction of "tangible objects" is fitting. In contrast, § 1519 is a penal provision that refers to "tangible object" not in relation to a request for information relevant to a specific court proceeding, but rather in relation to federal investigations or proceedings of every kind, including those not yet begun. *See Commissioner v. National Carbide Corp.*, 167 F.2d 304, 306 (C.A.2 1948) (Hand, J.) ("words are chameleons, which reflect the color of their environment"). Just as the context of Rule 16 supports giving "tangible object" a meaning as broad as its dictionary definition, the context of § 1519 tugs strongly in favor of a narrower reading.

B

Familiar interpretive guides aid our construction of the words "tangible object" as they appear in § 1519.

We note first § 1519's caption: "Destruction, alteration, or falsification of records in Federal investigations and bankruptcy." That heading conveys no suggestion that the section prohibits spoliation of any and all physical evidence, however remote from records. Neither does the title of the section of the Sarbanes-Oxley Act in which § 1519 was placed, § 802: "Criminal penalties for altering documents." [Citation.] Furthermore, § 1520, the only other provision passed as part of § 802, is titled "Destruction of corporate audit records" and addresses only that specific subset of records and documents. While these headings are not commanding, they supply cues that Congress did not intend "tangible object" in § 1519 to sweep within its reach physical objects of every kind, including things no one would describe as records, documents, or devices closely associated with them. [Citation.] If Congress indeed meant to make § 1519 an all-encompassing ban on the spoliation of evidence, as the dissent believes Congress did, one would have expected a clearer indication of that intent. . . .

The contemporaneous passage of § 1512(c)(1), which was contained in a section of the Sarbanes-Oxley Act discrete from the section embracing § 1519 and § 1520, is also instructive. Section 1512(c)(1) provides:

"(c) Whoever corruptly—

"(1) alters, destroys, mutilates, or conceals a record, document, or other object, or attempts to do so, with the intent to impair the object's integrity or availability for use in an official proceeding

"shall be fined under this title or imprisoned not more than 20 years, or both."

The legislative history reveals that § 1512(c)(1) was drafted and proposed after § 1519. [Citation.] The Government argues, and Yates does not dispute, that § 1512(c)(1)'s reference to "other object" includes any and every physical object. But if § 1519's reference to "tangible object" already included all physical objects, as the Government and the dissent contend, then Congress had no reason to enact § 1512(c)(1): Virtually any act that would violate § 1512(c)(1) no doubt would violate § 1519 as well, for § 1519 applies to "the investigation or proper administration of any matter within the jurisdiction of any department or agency of the United States . . . or in relation to or contemplation of any such matter," not just to "an official proceeding."

The Government acknowledges that, under its reading, § 1519 and § 1512(c)(1) "significantly overlap." [Citation.] Nowhere does the Government explain what independent function § 1512(c)(1) would serve if the Government is right about the sweeping scope of § 1519. We resist a reading of § 1519 that would render superfluous an entire provision passed in proximity as part of the same Act. [Citation.]

The words immediately surrounding "tangible object" in § 1519— "falsifies, or makes a false entry in any record [or] document"—also cabin the contextual meaning of that term. As explained in *Gustafson v. Alloyd Co.*, 513 U.S. 561, 575 (1995), we rely on the principle of *noscitur a sociis*—a word is known by the company it keeps—to "avoid ascribing to one word a meaning so broad that it is inconsistent with its accompanying words, thus giving unintended breadth to the Acts of Congress." [Citation.] . . .

"Tangible object" is the last in a list of terms that begins "any record [or] document." The term is therefore appropriately read to refer, not to any tangible object, but specifically to the subset of tangible objects involving records and documents, *i.e.*, objects used to record or preserve information. [Citation.]

This moderate interpretation of "tangible object" accords with the list of actions § 1519 proscribes. The section applies to anyone who "alters, destroys, mutilates, conceals, covers up, falsifies, or makes a false entry in any record, document, or tangible object" with the requisite obstructive intent. The last two verbs, "falsif[y]" and "mak[e] a false entry in," typically take as grammatical objects records, documents, or things used to record or preserve information, such as logbooks or hard drives. [Citation.] It would be unnatural, for example, to describe a killer's act of wiping his fingerprints from a gun as "falsifying" the murder weapon. But it would not be strange to refer to "falsifying" data stored on a hard drive as simply "falsifying" a hard drive. Furthermore, Congress did not include on § 1512(c)(1)'s list of prohibited actions "falsifies" or "makes a false entry in." [Citation.] That contemporaneous omission also suggests that Congress intended "tangible object" in § 1519 to have a narrower scope than "other object" in § 1512(c)(1).

A canon related to *noscitur a sociis*, *ejusdem generis*, counsels: "Where general words follow specific words in a statutory enumeration, the general words are [usually] construed to embrace only objects similar in nature to those objects enumerated by the preceding specific words." [Citation.] . . . Just so here. Had Congress intended "tangible object" in § 1519 to be interpreted so generically as to capture physical objects as dissimilar as documents and fish, Congress would have had no reason to refer specifically to "record" or "document." The Government's unbounded reading of "tangible object" would render those words misleading surplusage.

Having used traditional tools of statutory interpretation to examine markers of congressional intent within the Sarbanes-Oxley Act and § 1519 itself, we are persuaded that an aggressive interpretation of "tangible object" must be rejected. It is highly improbable that Congress would have buried a general spoliation statute covering objects of any and every kind in a provision targeting fraud in financial record-keeping. . . .

C

Finally, if our recourse to traditional tools of statutory construction leaves any doubt about the meaning of "tangible object," as that term is used in § 1519, we would invoke the rule that "ambiguity concerning the ambit of criminal statutes should be resolved in favor of lenity." [Citation.] That interpretative principle is relevant here, where the

Government urges a reading of § 1519 that exposes individuals to 20-year prison sentences for tampering with *any* physical object that *might* have evidentiary value in *any* federal investigation into *any* offense, no matter whether the investigation is pending or merely contemplated, or whether the offense subject to investigation is criminal or civil. . . .

For the reasons stated, we resist reading § 1519 expansively to create a coverall spoliation of evidence statute, advisable as such a measure might be. Leaving that important decision to Congress, we hold that a "tangible object" within § 1519's compass is one used to record or preserve information. The judgment of the U.S. Court of Appeals for the Eleventh Circuit is therefore reversed, and the case is remanded for further proceedings.

It is so ordered.

■ JUSTICE ALITO, concurring in the judgment.

This case can and should be resolved on narrow grounds. And though the question is close, traditional tools of statutory construction confirm that John Yates has the better of the argument. Three features of 18 U.S.C. § 1519 stand out to me: the statute's list of nouns, its list of verbs, and its title. Although perhaps none of these features by itself would tip the case in favor of Yates, the three combined do so.

Start with the nouns. Section 1519 refers to "any record, document, or tangible object." The *noscitur a sociis* canon instructs that when a statute contains a list, each word in that list presumptively has a "similar" meaning. [Citation.] A related canon, *ejusdem generis*, teaches that general words following a list of specific words should usually be read in light of those specific words to mean something "similar." [Citation.] Applying these canons to § 1519's list of nouns, the term "tangible object" should refer to something similar to records or documents. A fish does not spring to mind—nor does an antelope, a colonial farmhouse, a hydrofoil, or an oil derrick. All are "objects" that are "tangible." But who wouldn't raise an eyebrow if a neighbor, when asked to identify something similar to a "record" or "document," said "crocodile"?

This reading, of course, has its shortcomings. For instance, this is an imperfect *ejusdem generis* case because "record" and "document" are themselves quite general. And there is a risk that "tangible object" may be made superfluous—what is similar to a "record" or "document" but yet is not one? An e-mail, however, could be such a thing. [Citation.] An e-mail, after all, might not be a "document" if, as was "traditionally" so, a document was a "piece of paper with information on it," not "information stored on a computer, electronic storage device, or any other medium." Black's Law Dictionary 587–588 (10th ed. 2014). E-mails might also not be "records" if records are limited to "minutes" or other formal writings "designed to memorialize [past] events." *Id.*, at 1465. A hard drive, however, is tangible and can contain files that are precisely akin to even these narrow definitions. Both "record" and "document" can be read more expansively, but adding "tangible object" to § 1519 would ensure beyond question that electronic files are included. . . .

Next, consider § 1519's list of verbs: "alters, destroys, mutilates, conceals, covers up, falsifies, or makes a false entry in." Although many of those verbs could apply to nouns as far-flung as salamanders, satellites, or sand dunes, the last phrase in the list—"makes a false entry in"—makes no sense outside of filekeeping. How does one make a false entry in a fish? "Alters" and especially "falsifies" are also closely associated with filekeeping. . . .

Again, the Government is not without a response. One can imagine Congress trying to write a law so broadly that not every verb lines up with every noun. But failure to "line up" may suggest that something has gone awry in one's interpretation of a text. Where, as here, each of a statute's verbs applies to a certain category of nouns, there is some reason to think that Congress had that category in mind. . . .

Finally, my analysis is influenced by § 1519's title: "Destruction, alteration, or falsification of records in Federal investigations and bankruptcy." This too points toward filekeeping, not fish. . . . The title is especially valuable here because it reinforces what the text's nouns and verbs independently suggest—that no matter how other statutes might be read, this particular one does not cover every noun in the universe with tangible form.

Titles, of course, are also not dispositive. Here, if the list of nouns did not already suggest that "tangible object" should mean something similar to records or documents, especially when read in conjunction with § 1519's peculiar list of verbs with their focus on filekeeping, then the title would not be enough on its own. In conjunction with those other two textual features, however, the Government's argument, though colorable, becomes too implausible to accept.

■ JUSTICE KAGAN, with whom JUSTICE SCALIA, JUSTICE KENNEDY, and JUSTICE THOMAS join, dissenting.

. . . This case raises the question whether the term "tangible object" means the same thing in § 1519 as it means in everyday language—any object capable of being touched. The answer should be easy: Yes. The term "tangible object" is broad, but clear. Throughout the U.S. Code and many States' laws, it invariably covers physical objects of all kinds. And in § 1519, context confirms what bare text says: All the words surrounding "tangible object" show that Congress meant the term to have a wide range. That fits with Congress's evident purpose in enacting § 1519: to punish those who alter or destroy physical evidence—any physical evidence—with the intent of thwarting federal law enforcement. . . .

I

When Congress has not supplied a definition, we generally give a statutory term its ordinary meaning. [Citation.] As the plurality must acknowledge, the ordinary meaning of "tangible object" is "a discrete thing that possesses physical form. A fish is, of course, a discrete thing that possesses physical form. *See generally* Dr. Seuss, *One Fish Two Fish Red Fish Blue Fish* (1960). So the ordinary meaning of the term "tangible object" in § 1519, as no one here disputes, covers fish (including too-small red grouper).

That interpretation accords with endless uses of the term in statute and rule books as construed by courts. Dozens of federal laws and rules of procedure (and hundreds of state enactments) include the term "tangible object" or its first cousin "tangible thing"—some in association with documents, others not. [Citation.] To my knowledge, no court has ever read any such provision to exclude things that don't record or preserve data; rather, all courts have adhered to the statutory language's ordinary (*i.e.*, expansive) meaning. . . .

That is not necessarily the end of the matter; I agree with the plurality (really, who does not?) that context matters in interpreting statutes. We interpret particular words "in their context and with a view to their place in the overall statutory scheme." [Citation.] And sometimes that means, as the plurality says, that the dictionary definition of a disputed term cannot control. [Citation.] But this is not such an occasion, for here the text and its context point the same way. Stepping back from the words "tangible object" provides only further evidence that Congress said what it meant and meant what it said.

Begin with the way the surrounding words in § 1519 reinforce the breadth of the term at issue. Section 1519 refers to "any" tangible object, thus indicating (in line with that word's plain meaning) a tangible object "of whatever kind." Webster's Third New International Dictionary 97 (2002). This Court has time and again recognized that "any" has "an expansive meaning," bringing within a statute's reach all types of the item (here, "tangible object") to which the law refers. And the adjacent laundry list of verbs in § 1519 ("alters, destroys, mutilates, conceals, covers up, falsifies, or makes a false entry") further shows that Congress wrote a statute with a wide scope. Those words are supposed to ensure— just as "tangible object" is meant to—that § 1519 covers the whole world of evidence-tampering, in all its prodigious variety. . . .

The words "record, document, or tangible object" in § 1519 also track language in 18 U.S.C. § 1512, the federal witness-tampering law covering (as even the plurality accepts) physical evidence in all its forms. Section 1512, both in its original version (preceding § 1519) and today, repeatedly uses the phrase "record, document, or other object"—most notably, in a provision prohibiting the use of force or threat to induce another person to withhold any of those materials from an official proceeding. [Citation.] That language encompasses no less the bloody knife than the incriminating letter, as all courts have for decades agreed. [Citation.] And typically "only the most compelling evidence" will persuade this Court that Congress intended "nearly identical language" in provisions dealing with related subjects to bear different meanings. [Citation.] Context thus again confirms what text indicates.

And legislative history, for those who care about it, puts extra icing on a cake already frosted. Section 1519, as the plurality notes, was enacted after the Enron Corporation's collapse, as part of the Sarbanes-Oxley Act of 2002. [Citation.] But the provision began its life in a separate bill, and the drafters emphasized that Enron was "only a case study exposing the shortcomings in our current laws" relating to both "corporate and criminal" fraud. . . .

As Congress recognized in using a broad term, giving immunity to those who destroy non-documentary evidence has no sensible basis in penal policy. A person who hides a murder victim's body is no less culpable than one who burns the victim's diary. A fisherman, like John Yates, who dumps undersized fish to avoid a fine is no less blameworthy than one who shreds his vessel's catch log for the same reason. Congress thus treated both offenders in the same way. It understood, in enacting § 1519, that destroying evidence is destroying evidence, whether or not that evidence takes documentary form.

II

. . . The plurality's analysis starts with § 1519's title: "Destruction, alteration, or falsification of records in Federal investigations and bankruptcy." That's already a sign something is amiss. I know of no other case in which we have begun our interpretation of a statute with the title, or relied on a title to override the law's clear terms. Instead, we have followed "the wise rule that the title of a statute and the heading of a section cannot limit the plain meaning of the text."

The reason for that "wise rule" is easy to see: A title is, almost necessarily, an abridgment. Attempting to mention every term in a statute "would often be ungainly as well as useless"; accordingly, "matters in the text . . . are frequently unreflected in the headings." [Citation.] Section 1519's title refers to "destruction, alteration, or falsification" but not to mutilation, concealment, or covering up, and likewise mentions "records" but not other documents or objects. Presumably, the plurality would not refuse to apply § 1519 when a person only conceals evidence rather than destroying, altering, or falsifying it; instead, the plurality would say that a title is just a title, which cannot "undo or limit" more specific statutory text. [Citation.] The same holds true when the evidence in question is not a "record" but something else whose destruction, alteration, etc., is intended to obstruct justice. . . .

The plurality's third argument, relying on the surplusage canon, at least invokes a known tool of statutory construction—but it too comes to nothing. Says the plurality: If read naturally, § 1519 "would render superfluous" § 1512(c)(1), which Congress passed "as part of the same act." But that is not so: Although the two provisions significantly overlap, each applies to conduct the other does not. The key difference between the two is that § 1519 protects the integrity of "matter[s] within the jurisdiction of any [federal] department or agency" whereas § 1512(c)(1) safeguards "official proceeding[s]" as defined in § 1515(a)(1)(A). Section 1519's language often applies more broadly than § 1512(c)(1)'s, as the plurality notes. For example, an FBI investigation counts as a matter within a federal department's jurisdiction, but falls outside the statutory definition of "official proceeding" as construed by courts. [Citation.] But conversely, § 1512(c)(1) sometimes reaches more widely than § 1519. For example, because an "official proceeding" includes any "proceeding before a judge or court of the United States," § 1512(c)(1) prohibits tampering with evidence in federal litigation between private parties. [Citation.] By contrast, § 1519 wouldn't ordinarily operate in that context because a federal court isn't a "department or agency." So the surplusage canon doesn't come into play. Overlap—even significant overlap—abounds in the criminal law. . . .

Getting nowhere with surplusage, the plurality switches canons, hoping that *noscitur a sociis* and *ejusdem generis* will save it. . . . But understood as this Court always has, the canons have no such transformative effect on the workaday language Congress chose.

As an initial matter, this Court uses *noscitur a sociis* and *ejusdem generis* to resolve ambiguity, not create it. . . . [w]hen words have a clear definition, and all other contextual clues support that meaning, the canons cannot properly defeat Congress's decision to draft broad legislation. [Citation.]

Anyway, assigning "tangible object" its ordinary meaning comports with *noscitur a sociis* and *ejusdem generis* when applied, as they should be, with attention to § 1519's subject and purpose. Those canons require identifying a common trait that links all the words in a statutory phrase. [Citation.] In responding to that demand, the plurality characterizes records and documents as things that preserve information—and so they are. But just as much, they are things that provide information, and thus potentially serve as evidence relevant to matters under review. And in a statute pertaining to obstruction of federal investigations, that evidentiary function comes to the fore. The destruction of records and documents prevents law enforcement agents from gathering facts relevant to official inquiries. And so too does the destruction of tangible objects—of whatever kind. Whether the item is a fisherman's ledger or an undersized fish, throwing it overboard has the identical effect on the administration of justice. [Citation.] For purposes of § 1519, records, documents, and (all) tangible objects are therefore alike.

Indeed, even the plurality can't fully credit its *noscitur /ejusdem* argument. The same reasoning would apply to every law placing the word "object" (or "thing") after "record" and "document." But as noted earlier, such statutes are common[.] . . . The plurality accepts that in those laws "object" means object; its argument about superfluity positively depends on giving § 1512(c)(1) that broader reading. What, then, is the difference here? The plurality proposes that some of those statutes describe less serious offenses than § 1519. How and why that distinction affects application of the *noscitur a sociis* and *ejusdem generis* canons is left obscure: Count it as one more of the plurality's never-before-propounded, not-readily-explained interpretive theories. [Citation.] But in any event, that rationale cannot support the plurality's willingness to give "object" its natural meaning in § 1512, which (like § 1519) sets out felonies with penalties of up to 20 years. [Citation.] The canons, in the plurality's interpretive world, apparently switch on and off whenever convenient.

And the plurality's invocation of § 1519's verbs does nothing to buttress its canon-based argument. The plurality observes that § 1519 prohibits "falsif[ying]" or "mak[ing] a false entry in" a tangible object, and no one can do those things to, say, a murder weapon (or a fish). But of course someone can alter, destroy, mutilate, conceal, or cover up such a tangible object, and § 1519 prohibits those actions too. The Court has never before suggested that all the verbs in a statute need to match up with all the nouns. [Citation.] And for good reason. It is exactly when Congress sets out to draft a statute broadly—to include every imaginable variation on a theme—that such mismatches will arise. To respond by narrowing the law, as the plurality does, is thus to flout both what Congress wrote and what Congress wanted. . . .

III

If none of the traditional tools of statutory interpretation can produce today's result, then what accounts for it? The plurality offers a clue when it emphasizes the disproportionate penalties § 1519 imposes if the law is read broadly. . . . That brings to the surface the real issue: overcriminalization and excessive punishment in the U.S. Code.

. . . The plurality omits from its description of § 1519 the requirement that a person act "knowingly" and with "the intent to impede, obstruct, or influence" federal law enforcement. And in highlighting § 1519's maximum penalty, the plurality glosses over the absence of any prescribed minimum. (Let's not forget that Yates's sentence was not 20 years, but 30 days.) Congress presumably enacts laws with high maximums and no minimums when it thinks the prohibited conduct may run the gamut from major to minor. . . . Most district judges, as Congress knows, will recognize differences between such cases . . . and will try to make the punishment fit the crime. Still and all, I tend to think, for the reasons the plurality gives, that § 1519 is a bad law—too broad and undifferentiated, with too-high maximum penalties, which give prosecutors too much leverage and sentencers too much discretion. And I'd go further: In those ways, § 1519 is unfortunately not an outlier, but an emblem of a deeper pathology in the federal criminal code.

But whatever the wisdom or folly of § 1519, this Court does not get to rewrite the law. . . . If judges disagree with Congress's choice, we are perfectly entitled to say so—in lectures, in law review articles, and even in dicta. But we are not entitled to replace the statute Congress enacted with an alternative of our own design.

I respectfully dissent.

QUESTIONS

1.   How do the plurality and the dissent use the statute's context to illuminate the meaning of the phrase "tangible object"?

2.   Compare the use of the statutes' titles to limit the scope of their operative language in *Holy Trinity Church* and in *Yates*. Which, if any, treatment seems to you more persuasive and why?

3.   The dissent claims that its interpretation "fits with Congress's evident purpose in enacting § 1519: to punish those who alter or destroy physical evidence—any physical evidence—with the intent of thwarting federal law enforcement." *Is* it so evident that that was Congress's purpose? Recall that § 1519 was enacted as part of the Sarbanes-Oxley Act, with the heading "Destruction, alteration, or falsification *of records* in Federal investigations and bankruptcy" (emphasis added). What methods does the dissent employ to conclude that its broader reading of Congress's purpose was "evident?" Do those methods yield a meaning that is any more evident than the methods employed by the plurality or concurrence?

4.   Does it matter that § 1519 was passed as part of Sarbanes-Oxley, a statute seeking to deter white-collar financial crimes, but codified into the U.S. Code alongside other provisions related to the general obstruction of justice, 18 U.S.C. §§ 1501–21? Which context do you find more illuminating, and why?

5.   Under the plurality and concurrence's approaches, must the information that the defendant "knowingly alters, destroys, mutilates, conceals, covers up, falsifies, or makes a false entry in any record, document, or tangible object with the intent to impede, obstruct, or influence the investigation [of]" relate to financial records? What if Captain Yates had cast overboard together with the grouper the ledger recording their size?

6.   If the plurality and concurring opinions allow fish and other tangible objects not "used to record or preserve information" to escape § 1519's net, can they be said to be rewriting the statute?

NOTE: IS THE PLAIN MEANING RULE "PLAIN"?

The Plain Meaning Rule functions to exclude certain methods or sources of statutory meaning when, but only when, the meaning of the statute is "plain." For example, the dissent contended in *Yates* that the ordinary meaning of the term "tangible object" was "plain;" the Court therefore should have followed "the wise rule that the title of a statute and the heading of a section cannot limit the plain meaning of the text." What makes this rule so wise? Because the application of the Plain Meaning Rule has legal significance only when it excludes otherwise illuminating interpretive sources, Professors William Baude and Ryan Doerfler have questioned the circumstances where courts, invoking the Plain Meaning Rule, can justify excluding information that would tend to help clarify the meaning of a statute:

> The plain meaning rule says that otherwise-relevant information about statutory meaning is forbidden when the statutory text is plain or unambiguous. To see the rule in action, we need not look far. Consider one of the Court's recent and entertaining statutory interpretation cases, *Yates v United States*, in which [the dissent] invoked "the wise rule that the title of a statute and the heading of a section cannot limit the plain meaning of the text. . . ."

> Upon closer examination, there is something puzzling about the plain meaning rule. There are reasons to consider all pertinent information. There are reasons to categorically discard certain kinds of pertinent information. But why consider it only *sometimes*? . . .

> [W]hy make otherwise-relevant information only *conditionally* admissible? If legislative history is truly bad evidence of statutory meaning, shouldn't it be ignored both when the meaning is plain and when it is less than clear? Conversely, if it is good evidence, shouldn't we always at least *look* at it, even when the text seems pretty clear on its own? Why should legislative history's admissibility depend on the evidence we get from another source, like the text? . . .

> [O]ne might be able to construct a justification for considering pertinent information only sometimes—but such a limit makes sense only if that "sometimes" is connected to some epistemic or other practical end. What makes little sense is a blanket prohibition against considering pertinent nontextual information if statutory language is "clear." This is especially so if the courts' main concern is interpretive *accuracy*—that is, getting it right. Courts justify adherence to the plain meaning rule as a way to avoid interpretive mistakes, but the rule seems ill-suited to the task. . . .

A. Cost Efficiency

The plain meaning rule might make sense for evidence that is probative but also expensive to collect or consider.

Note that a cost-efficiency story for the plain meaning rule is still a little tricky. . . . [T]he cost-efficiency justification for the plain meaning rule would have to justify the *conditional* exclusion of evidence. Some scholars have argued, for example, that most nontextual evidence should be *categorically* excluded in part on cost-efficiency grounds. That kind of categorical argument, of course, is too strong to yield the plain meaning rule. Rather, a cost-efficiency justification for the plain meaning rule would require a particular ratio of costs and accuracies such that the extra evidence is too costly when A is clear, but not *so* costly that it is prohibitive when A is unclear. Again, this is *possible*, but would require a more precise quantification of the decision costs of considering different kinds of evidence than we have seen.

A cost-efficiency justification for the plain meaning rule is at least conceivable for some classes of evidence .... Legislative history, for example, might be time-consuming for courts to consider. ... In this respect, legislative history contrasts sharply with, say, titles or section headings, which are easy for courts to consider. It is hard for us to imagine any cost-exclusion justification for excluding those kinds of materials.

B. Bias

Perhaps the plain meaning rule could make sense for certain kinds of evidence that have both potential value but also a hard-to-assess sort of bias. ... It seems at least conceivable to us that something like the practical consequences of a statutory interpretation might fit this model. Judges might well be committed to the view that practical consequences are relevant but of secondary importance to more standard legal materials like text and so on. On the other hand, judges might also worry that once they take into account practical considerations, it is hard to think clearly about anything else, and hard to resist the urge to start reinterpreting the standard materials to match the consequences the judges want to see. ...

C. Legal Convention

An alternative justification, of sorts, might proceed in a more legalistic way: judges should follow the plain meaning rule because it is a rule, and judges should follow the rules. We recognize that this argument sounds hilariously circular—where did the rule *come from?*—but we think a version of it can be made to work.

One way is by focusing on the "law of interpretation." This argument requires us first to accept that rules of statutory interpretation can be set by law, in which case they need not be justified on first-order normative grounds. ... Under this argument, maybe the plain meaning rule is simply a common-law rule of statutory interpretation.

Perhaps Congress knows about the plain meaning rule and intends (or means) that its work should be interpreted through the rule. ... [R]ecent empirical research by Professors Abbe Gluck and Lisa Schultz Bressman has suggested that Congress does not know very much about the Supreme Court's statutory interpretation rules, suggesting that we should be hesitant to justify interpretive rules purely on the basis of expectations. ...

D. Public-Facing Explanation

It is also possible that there is a difference between a court's own reasoning process and the reasoning process it presents to the audience of its opinions. Or, to put a finer point on it, maybe the plain meaning doctrine is a public lie or, more generously, an oversimplification. . . .

Under this justification, then, it is not actually true that outside information is ignored when the meaning is plain. Rather, judges think that the outside information will change the purely textual result only in an unusual case, and when the information does not change the result, it is better to pretend that it *could not* have changed the result. . . .

Why might a court do this? Perhaps it does not fully trust its audience. When presenting its textual argument to nonjudges and even lay people, who are not as steeped in the court's conventions of statutory interpretation, it makes sense to speak in accessible shorthand. . . .

E. Predictability and Consistency

Additionally, the plain meaning rule might make sense— under certain extremely specific assumptions—if one were willing to trade *accuracy* for *predictability*. Suppose, for example, that a regulated private party cares not very much about whether she has the meaning of the statute "right" in the abstract, but cares a great deal about whether she correctly guesses how a judge will interpret the statute. That party might prefer that the range of considerations for a judge be limited in cases in which one consideration—the text—points clearly in one direction. . . .

[T]his justification requires some tricky assumptions. It is not enough to argue—as many have—that text is a useful coordinating point. That argument would be more likely to point toward textualism across the board. Rather, it requires an argument that text is only *sometimes* useful as a coordinating point. The underlying intuition seems to be that when the text is plain, the coordinating function is strong and the loss in accuracy is weak, but when the text is less plain, we should flip to emphasizing accuracy over coordination.

Maybe that argument could work, but it rests on several empirical assumptions. . . . [One] required assumption is that the plain meaning *threshold* is itself reasonably plain—in other words, that most interpreters can agree on which textual meanings are plain. . . . The current evidence suggests that this assumption is false—that is, the plain meaning threshold is highly vulnerable to dispute (good faith and otherwise). . . .

CONCLUSION

[W]e come neither to praise the plain meaning rule nor to bury it. Our main aim is to challenge those who use the rule to consider and explain why they think nontextual evidence is relevant at some times but not at others—and to show all readers that the challenge is harder to answer than they might have first thought.

William Baude & Ryan D. Doerfler, *The (Not So) Plain Meaning Rule*, 84 U. Chi. L. Rev. 539 (2017) (excerpt).

2.   LITERALISM AND ITS LIMITS

In addition to the problems Professors Baude and Doerfler identify with limiting a statute's meaning to the "plain" meaning of the relevant text in question, the literal application of statutory texts presents an additional quandary: how to put the literal meaning into practice. After all, even when the *meaning* of a statutory phrase appears "plain," its *application* to specific circumstances may not be so straightforward. If the application of a statutory text's plain meaning yields ambiguous outcomes, how should courts resolve the ambiguity of the statute's *application*? What extra-textual devices might courts draw on when crafting a resolution?

Consider, for example, the following sections of the Immigration and Nationality Act, which concern the unlawful procurement of citizenship or naturalization status, and the U.S. Supreme Court's efforts to interpret as well as to apply the statute in *Maslenjak v. United States*, *infra*. Before you read the Supreme Court's application of this statute, work your way through the statute whose meaning the courts were construing. What do you think is the purpose of these statutory provisions? How do they achieve those objectives? What conduct violates them? Who is liable, and for what penalties? Is the text coherent, or are there inconsistencies in the way the statute addresses the problem it seeks to resolve?

Immigration and Nationality
United States Code, Title 8, Chapter 12.

§ 1427   Requirements of naturalization

(a) Residence

No person, except as otherwise provided in this title, shall be naturalized unless such applicant, (1) immediately preceding the date of filing his application for naturalization has resided continuously, after being lawfully admitted for permanent residence, within the United States for at least five years and during the five years immediately preceding the date of filing his application has been physically present therein for periods totaling at least half of that time[,] and who has resided within the State or within the district of the Service in the United States in which the applicant filed the application for at least three months, (2) has resided continuously within the United States from the date of the application up to the time of admission to citizenship, and (3) during all the periods referred to in this subsection has been and still is a person of good moral character, attached to the principles of the Constitution of the United States, and well disposed to the good order and happiness of the United States.

§ 1451. Revocation of naturalization

(e) Citizenship unlawfully procured

When a person shall be convicted under section 1425 of Title 18 of knowingly procuring naturalization in violation of law, the court in which such conviction is had shall thereupon revoke, set aside, and declare void the final order admitting such person to citizenship, and shall declare the certificate of naturalization of such person to be canceled. Jurisdiction is hereby conferred on the courts having jurisdiction of the trial of such offense to make such adjudication.

Crimes: Nationality and Citizenship

United States Code, Title 18, Chapter 69.

§ 1425. Procurement of citizenship or naturalization unlawfully

(a) Whoever knowingly procures or attempts to procure, contrary to law, the naturalization of any person, or documentary or other evidence of naturalization or of citizenship; . . .

Shall be fined under this title or imprisoned not more than 25 years (if the offense was committed to facilitate an act of international terrorism (citation)), 20 years (if the offense was committed to facilitate a drug trafficking crime (citation)), 10 years (in the case of the first or second such offense, if the offense was not committed to facilitate such an act of international terrorism or a drug trafficking crime), or 15 years (in the case of any other offense), or both.

§ 1015. Naturalization, citizenship or alien registry

(a) Whoever knowingly makes any false statement under oath, in any case, proceeding, or matter relating to, or under, or by virtue of any law of the United States relating to naturalization, citizenship, or registry of aliens . . . . [s]hall be fined under this title or imprisoned not more than five years, or both.

Maslenjak v. United States

Supreme Court of the United States, 2017.
137 S.Ct. 1918, 198 L.Ed.2d 460.

■ JUSTICE KAGAN delivered the opinion of the Court[, in which CHIEF JUSTICE ROBERTS, JUSTICE KENNEDY, JUSTICE GINSBURG, JUSTICE BREYER, and JUSTICE SOTOMAYOR joined].

A federal statute, 18 U.S.C. § 1425(a), makes it a crime to "knowingly procure[ ], contrary to law, the naturalization of any person."

And when someone is convicted under § 1425(a) of unlawfully procuring her own naturalization, her citizenship is automatically revoked. *See* 8 U.S.C. § 1451(e). In this case, we consider what the Government must prove to obtain such a conviction. We hold that the Government must establish that an illegal act by the defendant played some role in her acquisition of citizenship. When the illegal act is a false statement, that means demonstrating that the defendant lied about facts that would have mattered to an immigration official, because they would have justified denying naturalization or would predictably have led to other facts warranting that result.

I

Petitioner Divna Maslenjak is an ethnic Serb who resided in Bosnia during the 1990's, when a civil war between Serbs and Muslims divided the new country. In 1998, she and her family (her husband Ratko Maslenjak and their two children) met with an American immigration official to seek refugee status in the United States. Interviewed under oath, Maslenjak explained that the family feared persecution in Bosnia from both sides of the national rift. Muslims, she said, would mistreat them because of their ethnicity. And Serbs, she testified, would abuse them because her husband had evaded service in the Bosnian Serb Army by absconding to Serbia—where he remained hidden, apart from the family, for some five years. Persuaded of the Maslenjaks' plight, American officials granted them refugee status, and they immigrated to the United States in 2000.

Six years later, Maslenjak applied for naturalization. Question 23 on the application form asked whether she had ever given "false or misleading information" to a government official while applying for an immigration benefit; question 24 similarly asked whether she had ever "lied to a[ ] government official to gain entry or admission into the United States." Maslenjak answered "no" to both questions, while swearing under oath that her replies were true. She also swore that all her written answers were true during a subsequent interview with an immigration official. In August 2007, Maslenjak was naturalized as a U.S. citizen.

But Maslenjak's professions of honesty were false: In fact, she had made up much of the story she told to immigration officials when seeking refuge in this country. Her fiction began to unravel at around the same time she applied for citizenship. In 2006, immigration officials confronted Maslenjak's husband Ratko with records showing that he had not fled conscription during the Bosnian civil war; rather, he had served as an officer in the Bosnian Serb Army. And not only that: He had served in a brigade that participated in the Srebrenica massacre—a slaughter of some 8,000 Bosnian Muslim civilians. Within a year, the Government convicted Ratko on charges of making false statements on immigration documents. The newly naturalized Maslenjak attempted to prevent Ratko's deportation. During proceedings on that matter, Maslenjak admitted she had known all along that Ratko spent the war years not secreted in Serbia but fighting in Bosnia.

As a result, the Government charged Maslenjak with knowingly "procur[ing], contrary to law, [her] naturalization," in violation of 18 U.S.C. § 1425(a). According to the Government's theory, Maslenjak violated § 1425(a) because, in the course of procuring her naturalization, she broke another law: 18 U.S.C. § 1015(a), which prohibits knowingly making a false statement under oath in a naturalization proceeding. The false statements the Government invoked were Maslenjak's answers to questions 23 and 24 on the citizenship application (stating that she had not lied in seeking refugee status) and her corresponding statements in the citizenship interview. Those statements, the Government argued to the District Court, need not have affected the naturalization decision to support a conviction under § 1425(a). The court agreed: Over Maslenjak's objection, it instructed the jury that a conviction was proper so long as the Government "prove[d] that one of the defendant's statements was false"—even if the statement was not "material" and "did not influence the decision to approve [her] naturalization." The jury returned a guilty verdict; and the District Court, based on that finding, stripped Maslenjak of her citizenship. *See* 8 U.S.C. § 1451(e).

The United States Court of Appeals for the Sixth Circuit affirmed the conviction. As relevant here, the Sixth Circuit upheld the District Court's instructions that Maslenjak's false statements need not have influenced the naturalization decision. If, the Court of Appeals held, Maslenjak made false statements violating § 1015(a) and she procured naturalization, then she also violated § 1425(a)—irrespective of whether the false statements played any role in her obtaining citizenship. That decision created a conflict in the Circuit Courts. We granted certiorari to resolve it, . . . and we now vacate the Sixth Circuit's judgment.

II

A

Section 1425(a), the parties agree, makes it a crime to commit some other illegal act in connection with naturalization. But the parties dispute the nature of the required connection. Maslenjak argues that the relationship must be "causal" in kind: A person "procures" her naturalization "contrary to law," she contends, only if a predicate crime in some way "contribut[ed]" to her gaining citizenship. By contrast, the Government proposes a basically chronological link: Section 1425(a), it urges, "punishes the commission of other violations of law in the course of procuring naturalization"—even if the illegality could not have had any effect on the naturalization decision. We conclude that Maslenjak has the better of this argument.

We begin, as usual, with the statutory text. In ordinary usage, "to procure" something is "to get possession of" it. Webster's Third New International Dictionary 1809 (2002); accord, Black's Law Dictionary

1401 (10th ed. 2014) (defining "procure" as "[t]o obtain (something), esp. by special effort or means"). So to "procure . . . naturalization" means to obtain naturalization (or, to use another word, citizenship). The adverbial phrase "contrary to law," wedged in between "procure" and "naturalization," then specifies how a person must procure naturalization so as to run afoul of the statute: in contravention of the law—or, in a word, illegally. Putting the pieces together, someone "procure[s], contrary to law, naturalization" when she obtains citizenship illegally.

What, then, does that whole phrase mean? The most natural understanding is that the illegal act must have somehow contributed to the obtaining of citizenship. Consider if someone said to you: "John obtained that painting illegally." You might imagine that he stole it off the walls of a museum. Or that he paid for it with a forged check. Or that he impersonated the true buyer when the auction house delivered it. But in all events, you would imagine illegal acts in some kind of means-end relation—or otherwise said, in some kind of causal relation—to the painting's acquisition. If someone said to you, "John obtained that painting illegally, but his unlawful acts did not play any role in his obtaining it," you would not have a clue what the statement meant. You would think it nonsense—or perhaps the opening of a riddle. That is because if no illegal act contributed at all to getting the painting, then the painting would not have been gotten illegally. And the same goes for naturalization. If whatever illegal conduct occurring within the naturalization process was a causal dead-end—if, so to speak, the ripples from that act could not have reached the decision to award citizenship—then the act cannot support a charge that the applicant obtained naturalization illegally. The conduct, though itself illegal, would not also make the obtaining of citizenship so. To get citizenship unlawfully, we understand, is to get it through an unlawful means—and that is just to say that an illegality played some role in its acquisition.

The Government's contrary view—that § 1425(a) requires only a "violation[ ] of law in the course of procuring naturalization"—falters on the way language naturally works. Return for a moment to our artwork example. Imagine this time that John made an illegal turn while driving to the auction house to purchase a painting. Would you say that he had "procured the painting illegally" because he happened to violate the law in the course of obtaining it? Not likely. And again, the same is true with respect to naturalization. Suppose that an applicant for citizenship fills out the necessary paperwork in a government office with a knife tucked away in her handbag (but never mentioned or used). She has violated the law—specifically, a statute criminalizing the possession of a weapon in a federal building. *See* 18 U.S.C. § 930. And she has surely done so "in the course of" procuring citizenship. But would you say, using English as you ordinarily would, that she has "procure[d]" her citizenship "contrary to law" (or, as you would really speak, "illegally")? Once again, no. That is because the violation of law and the acquisition of citizenship are in that example merely coincidental: The one has no causal relation to the other.

The Government responds to such examples by seeking to define them out of the statute, but that effort falls short for multiple reasons. According to the Government, the laws to which § 1425(a) speaks are only laws "pertaining to naturalization." But to begin with, that claim fails on its own terms. The Government's proposed limitation has no basis in § 1425(a)'s text (which refers to "law" generally); it is a *deus ex machina*—rationalized only by calling it "necessary," and serving only to get the Government out of a tight interpretive spot. Indeed, the Government does not really buy its own argument: At another point, it asserts that an applicant for citizenship can violate § 1425(a) by bribing a government official—even though the law against that conduct has nothing in particular to do with naturalization. *See* 18 U.S.C. § 201(b)(1). And still more important, the Government's (sometime) carve-out does nothing to alter the linguistic understanding that gives force to the examples the Government would exclude—and that applies just as well to every application that would remain. Laws pertaining to naturalization, in other words, are subject to the same rules of language usage as laws concerning other subjects. And under those rules, as we have shown, § 1425(a) demands a means-end connection between a legal violation and naturalization. Take § 1015(a)'s bar on making false statements in connection with naturalization—the prototypical § 1425(a) predicate, and the one at issue here. If such a statement (in an interview, say) has no bearing at all on the decision to award citizenship, then it cannot render that award—as § 1425(a) requires—illegally gained.

The broader statutory context reinforces that point, because the Government's reading would create a profound mismatch between the requirements for naturalization on the one hand and those for denaturalization on the other. [Citation.] The immigration statute requires all applicants for citizenship to have "good moral character," and largely defines that term through a list of unlawful or unethical behaviors. 8 U.S.C. §§ 1427(a)(3), 1101(f).

On the Government's theory, some legal violations that do not justify denying citizenship under that definition would nonetheless justify *revoking* it later. Again, false statements under § 1015(a) offer an apt illustration. The statute's description of "good moral character" singles out a specific class of lies—"false testimony for the purpose of obtaining [immigration] benefits"—as a reason to deny naturalization. 8 U.S.C. § 1101(f)(6). By contrast, "[w]illful misrepresentations made for other reasons, such as embarrassment, fear, or a desire for privacy, were not deemed sufficiently culpable to brand the applicant as someone who lacks good moral character"—and so are not generally disqualifying. [Citation]. But under the Government's reading of § 1425(a), a lie told in the naturalization process—even out of embarrassment, fear, or a desire for privacy—would always provide a basis for rescinding citizenship. The

Government could thus take away on one day what it was required to give the day before.

And by so wholly unmooring the revocation of citizenship from its award, the Government opens the door to a world of disquieting consequences—which we would need far stronger textual support to believe Congress intended. Consider the kinds of questions a person seeking citizenship confronts on the standard application form. Says one: "Have you **EVER** been . . . in any way associated with[ ] any organization, association, fund, foundation, party, club, society, or similar group[?]" [Citation.] Asks another: "Have you **EVER** committed . . . a crime or offense for which you were **NOT** arrested?" Suppose, for reasons of embarrassment or what-have-you, a person concealed her membership in an online support group or failed to disclose a prior speeding violation. Under the Government's view, a prosecutor could scour her paperwork and bring a § 1425(a) charge on that meager basis, even many years after she became a citizen. That would give prosecutors nearly limitless leverage—and afford newly naturalized Americans precious little security. Small wonder that Congress, in enacting § 1425(a), did not go so far as the Government claims. The statute it passed, most naturally read, strips a person of citizenship not when she committed any illegal act during the naturalization process, but only when that act played some role in her naturalization.

B

That conclusion leaves us with a more operational question: How should § 1425(a)'s requirement of causal influence apply in practice, when charges are brought under that law?[4]

Because the proper analysis may vary with the nature of the predicate crime, we confine our discussion of that issue to the kind of underlying illegality alleged here: a false statement made to government officials. Such conduct can affect a naturalization decision in a single, significant way—by distorting the Government's understanding of the facts when it investigates, and then adjudicates, an application. So the issue a jury must decide in a case like this one is whether a false statement sufficiently altered those processes as to have influenced an award of citizenship.

The answer to that question, like the naturalization decision itself, turns on objective legal criteria. Congress has prescribed specific

---

[4]   JUSTICE GORSUCH would stop before answering that question, (opinion concurring in part and concurring in judgment), but we think that such a halfway-decision would fail to fulfill our responsibility to both parties and courts. The Government needs to know what prosecutions to bring; defendants need to know what defenses to offer; and district courts need to know how to instruct juries. Telling them only "*§ 1425(a)* has something to do with causation" would not much help them make those decisions. And we are well-positioned to provide further guidance. The parties have had every opportunity to address the nature of the statute's causal standard, and both gave us considered views about how the law should work in practice. Moreover, many lower courts have already addressed those same issues—including one that has called this Court's failure to provide clear guidance "maddening[ ]." [Citations.]

eligibility standards for new citizens, respecting such matters as length of residency and "physical[ ] presen[ce]," understanding of English and American government, and (as previously mentioned) "good moral character," with all its many specific components. *See* 8 U.S.C. §§ 1423(a), 1427(a); [citation]. Government officials are obligated to apply that body of law faithfully—granting naturalization when the applicable criteria are satisfied, and denying it when they are not. [Citation.] And to ensure right results are reached, a court can reverse such a determination, at an applicant's request, based on its "own findings of fact and conclusions of law." 8 U.S.C. § 1421(c). The entire system, in other words, is set up to provide little or no room for subjective preferences or personal whims. Because that is so, the question of what any individual decisionmaker might have done with accurate information is beside the point: The defendant in a § 1425(a) case should neither benefit nor suffer from a wayward official's deviations from legal requirements. Accordingly, the proper causal inquiry under § 1425(a) is framed in objective terms: To decide whether a defendant acquired citizenship by means of a lie, a jury must evaluate how knowledge of the real facts would have affected a reasonable government official properly applying naturalization law.

If the facts the defendant misrepresented are themselves disqualifying, the jury can make quick work of that inquiry. In such a case, there is an obvious causal link between the defendant's lie and her procurement of citizenship. To take an example: An applicant for citizenship must be physically present in the United States for more than half of the five-year period preceding her application. *See* 8 U.S.C. § 1427(a)(1). Suppose a defendant misrepresented her travel history to convey she had met that requirement, when in fact she had not. The Government need only expose that lie to establish that she obtained naturalization illegally—for had she told the truth instead, the official would have promptly denied her application. Or consider another, perhaps more common case stemming from the "good moral character" criterion. *See* § 1427(a)(3); [citation]. That phrase is defined to exclude any person who has been convicted of an aggravated felony. *See* § 1101(f)(8). If a defendant falsely denied such a conviction, she too would have gotten her citizenship by means of a lie—for otherwise the outcome would have been different. In short, when the defendant misrepresents facts that the law deems incompatible with citizenship, her lie must have played a role in her naturalization.

But that is not the only time a jury can find that a defendant's lie had the requisite bearing on a naturalization decision. For even if the true facts lying behind a false statement would not "in and of themselves justify denial of citizenship," they could have "led to the discovery of other facts which would" do so. [Citation.] We previously addressed that possibility when considering the civil statute that authorizes the Government to revoke naturalization. [Citation.]

As we explained in that context, a person whose lies throw investigators off a trail leading to disqualifying facts gets her citizenship by means of those lies—no less than if she had denied the damning facts at the very end of the trail.

When relying on such an investigation-based theory, the Government must make a two-part showing to meet its burden. As an initial matter, the Government has to prove that the misrepresented fact was sufficiently relevant to one or another naturalization criterion that it would have prompted reasonable officials, "seeking only evidence concerning citizenship qualifications," to undertake further investigation. [Citation.] If that much is true, the inquiry turns to the prospect that such an investigation would have borne disqualifying fruit. As to that second link in the causal chain, the Government need not show definitively that its investigation would have unearthed a disqualifying fact (though, of course, it may). Rather, the Government need only establish that the investigation "would predictably have disclosed" some legal disqualification. [Citation.] If that is so, the defendant's misrepresentation contributed to the citizenship award in the way we think § 1425(a) requires.

That standard reflects two real-world attributes of cases premised on what an unhindered investigation would have found. First is the difficulty of proving that a hypothetical inquiry would have led to some disqualifying discovery, often several years after the defendant told her lies. As witnesses and other evidence disappear, the Government's effort to reconstruct the course of a "could have been" investigation confronts ever-mounting obstacles. [Citation.] Second, and critical to our analysis, is that the defendant—not the Government—bears the blame for that evidentiary predicament. After all, the inquiry cannot get this far unless the defendant made an unlawful false statement and, by so doing, obstructed the normal course of an investigation. [Citations.]

Section 1425(a) is best read to take those exigencies and equities into account, by enabling the Government (as just described) to rest on disqualifications that a thwarted investigation predictably would have uncovered. A yet-stricter causal requirement, demanding proof positive that a disqualifying fact would have been found, sets the bar so high that "we cannot conceive that Congress intended" that result. [Citation.] And nothing in the statutory text requires that approach. While § 1425(a) clearly imports some kind of causal or means-end relation, Congress left that relation's precise character unspecified. [Citation.] The open-endedness of the statutory language allows, indeed supports, our adoption of a demanding but still practicable causal standard.

Even when the Government can make its two-part showing, however, the defendant may be able to overcome it. Section 1425(a) is not a tool for denaturalizing people who, the available evidence indicates, were actually qualified for the citizenship they obtained. When addressing the civil denaturalization statute, this Court insisted on a similar point: We provided the defendant with an opportunity to rebut the Government's case "by showing, through a preponderance of the evidence, that the statutory requirement as to which [a lie] had a natural tendency to produce a favorable decision was in fact met." [Citation.] Or said otherwise, we gave the defendant a chance to establish that she was qualified for citizenship, and held that she could not be denaturalized if she did so—even though she concealed or misrepresented facts that suggested the opposite. And indeed, all our denaturalization decisions share this crucial feature: We have never read a statute to strip citizenship from someone who met the legal criteria for acquiring it. [Citations.] We will not start now. Whatever the Government shows with respect to a thwarted investigation, qualification for citizenship is a complete defense to a prosecution brought under § 1425(a).

III

Measured against all we have said, the jury instructions in this case were in error. As earlier noted, the District Court told the jury that it could convict based on any false statement in the naturalization process (*i.e.*, any violation of § 1015(a)), no matter how inconsequential to the ultimate decision. But as we have shown, the jury needed to find more than an unlawful false statement. Recall that Maslenjak's lie in the naturalization process concerned her prior statements to immigration officials: She swore that she had been honest when applying for admission as a refugee, but in fact she had not. The jury could have convicted if that earlier dishonesty (*i.e.*, the thing she misrepresented when seeking citizenship) were itself a reason to deny naturalization— say, because it counted as "false testimony for the purpose of obtaining [immigration] benefits" and thus demonstrated bad moral character. Or else, the jury could have convicted if (1) knowledge of that prior dishonesty would have led a reasonable official to make some further investigation (say, into the circumstances of her admission), (2) that inquiry would predictably have yielded a legal basis for rejecting her citizenship application, and (3) Maslenjak failed to show that (not withstanding such an objective likelihood) she was in fact qualified to become a U.S. citizen. This jury, however, was not asked to—and so did not—make any of those determinations. Accordingly, Maslenjak was not convicted by a properly instructed jury of "procur[ing], contrary to law, [her] naturalization."

The Government asserts that any instructional error in this case was harmless. "Had officials known the truth," the Government asserts, "it would have affected their decision to grant [Maslenjak] citizenship." Unsurprisingly, Maslenjak disagrees. In keeping with our usual practice, we leave that dispute for resolution on remand. [Citation.]

For the reasons stated, we vacate the judgment of the Court of Appeals and remand the case for further proceedings consistent with this opinion.

It is so ordered.

■ JUSTICE GORSUCH, with whom JUSTICE THOMAS joins, concurring in part and concurring in the judgment.

The Court holds that the plain text and structure of the statute before us require the Government to prove causation as an element of conviction: The defendant's illegal conduct must, in some manner, cause her naturalization. I agree with this much and concur in Part II-A of the Court's opinion to the extent it so holds. And because the jury wasn't instructed at all about causation, I agree too that reversal is required.

But, respectfully, there I would stop. In an effort to "operational[ize]" the statute's causation requirement, the Court says a great deal more, offering, for example, two newly announced tests, the second with two more subparts, and a new affirmative defense—all while indicating that some of these new tests and defenses may apply only in some but not all cases. The work here is surely thoughtful and may prove entirely sound. But the question presented and the briefing before us focused primarily on whether the statute contains a *materiality* element, not on the contours of a *causation* requirement. So the parties have not had the chance to join issue fully on the matters now decided. And, of course, the lower courts have not had a chance to pass on any of these questions in the first instance. Most cited by the Court have (again) focused only on the materiality (not causation) question; none has tested the elaborate operational details advanced today; and at least one has found our prior unilateral and fractured foray into a related statute in *Kungys v. United States,* 485 U.S. 759 (1988), "maddening[ ]."

Respectfully, it seems to me at least reasonably possible that the crucible of adversarial testing on which we usually depend, along with the experience of our thoughtful colleagues on the district and circuit benches, could yield insights (or reveal pitfalls) we cannot muster guided only by our own lights. So while I agree with the Court that the parties will need guidance about the details of the statute's causation requirement, I have no doubt that the Court of Appeals, with aid of briefing from the parties, can supply that on remand. Other circuits may improve that guidance over time too. And eventually we can bless the best of it. For my part, I believe it is work enough for the day to recognize that the statute requires some proof of causation, that the jury instructions here did not, and to allow the parties and courts of appeals to take it from there as they usually do. This Court often speaks most wisely when it speaks last.

■ JUSTICE ALITO, concurring in the judgment.

We granted review in this case to decide whether "a naturalized American citizen can be stripped of her citizenship in a criminal proceeding based on an immaterial false statement." The answer to that question is "no." Although the relevant criminal statute, 18 U.S.C. § 1425(a), does not expressly refer to the concept of materiality, the critical statutory language effectively requires proof of materiality in a case involving false statements. The statute makes it a crime for a person to "procure" naturalization "contrary to law." In false statement cases, then, the statute essentially imposes the familiar materiality requirement that applies in other contexts. That is, a person violates the statute by procuring naturalization through an illegal false statement which has a "natural tendency to influence" the outcome—that is, the obtaining of naturalization. [Citation.]

Understood in this way, Section 1425(a) does not require proof that a false statement actually had some effect on the naturalization decision. The operative statutory language—"procure" naturalization "contrary to law"—imposes no such requirement.

Here is an example. Eight co-workers jointly buy two season tickets to see their favorite football team play. They all write their names on a piece of paper and place the slips in a hat to see who will get the tickets for the big game with their team's traditional rival. One of the friends puts his name in twice, and his name is drawn. I would say that he "procured" the tickets "contrary to" the rules of the drawing even though he might have won if he had put his name in only once.

Here is another example. A runner who holds the world's record in an event wants to make sure she wins the gold medal at the Olympics, so she takes a performance enhancing drug. She wins the race but fails a drug test and is disqualified. The second-place time is slow, and sportswriters speculate that she would have won without taking the drug. But it would be entirely consistent with standard English usage for the race officials to say that she "procured" her first-place finish "contrary to" the governing rules.

As these examples illustrate—and others could be added—the language of 18 U.S.C. § 1425(a) does not require that an illegal false statement have a demonstrable effect on the naturalization decision. Instead, the statute applies when a person makes an illegal false statement to obtain naturalization, and that false statement is material to the outcome. I see no indication that Congress meant to require more.

One additional point is worth mentioning. Section 1425(a) not only makes it a crime to procure naturalization contrary to law; it applies equally to any person who "attempts to procure, contrary to law. . . . naturalization." Therefore, if a defendant knowingly performs a substantial act that he or she thinks will procure naturalization, that is sufficient for conviction. [Citation.]

NOTES AND QUESTIONS

1. Did the Court's resort to dictionary definitions of "to procure" definitively answer the question of the statute's plain meaning? If you think it did, why do you suppose the Court went on to consider hypothetical outcomes of the competing interpretations? Could the Court not have stopped at the plain meaning definition?

2.   The Court claims that it is understandable that one might lie about membership in a club when seeking citizenship. Is this persuasive? Why shouldn't the government have a right to ask such a question and expect an honest answer as a condition of granting citizenship?

3.   Justice Alito contends that here, like most false statement cases, the more appropriate inquiry is whether the lie was *material* to the citizenship decision, not whether it *actually* affected it. What does "material" mean here? How can a statement be "material" if it bears no causal relationship to the outcome? What are the arguments for and against imposing a materiality standard instead of one rooted in causality?

4.   Reread footnote 4 and Section II.B of the majority opinion—the portions Justices Thomas and Gorsuch declined to join. Should the Court provide guidance to lower courts on the application of section 1425(a) to future, unknown cases? How helpful is the guidance provided? Is Justice Gorsuch's argument—that the lower courts should resolve these issues in the first instance—more satisfying? Consider that if the Court had not provided such guidance, the lower court would have had to do so. Imagine that the lower court did, and did so in a manner that nevertheless resulted in a conviction for Maslenjak. If Maslenjak were dissatisfied with the lower court's application of the causation test, her only resort would be to appeal her case back to the Supreme Court again. Is there an argument that judicial economy (not to mention individual liberty) is better served by the Court providing the lower courts with guidance?

5.   Relying on the Supreme Court's guidance that Maslenjak's false statements had to have sufficiently altered the citizenship processes as to have influenced the award of citizenship, Maslenjak's counsel argued on remand that the trial court was in error when it instructed that the jury could find Maslenjak in violation of the statute if "one of [her] statements was false," even if the "false statement did not influence the decision to approve [her] naturalization." United States v. Maslenjak, 943 F.3d 782, 786 (6th Cir. 2019). The Sixth Circuit agreed, concluding that the trial court's instructional error was not harmless because the government had not proven beyond a reasonable doubt that a properly instructed jury would have found that Maslenjak's misrepresentations could disqualify her from receiving citizenship or would have prevented investigators from learning disqualifying facts about her application. *Id.* The court accordingly vacated Maslenjak's convictions and remanded to the district court for a new trial.

Small v. United States

Supreme Court of the United States, 2005.
544 U.S. 385, 125 S.Ct. 1752, 161 L.Ed.2d 651.

■ JUSTICE BREYER delivered the opinion of the Court[, joined by JUSTICE STEVENS, JUSTICE O'CONNOR, JUSTICE SOUTER, and JUSTICE GINSBURG].

The United States Criminal Code makes it "unlawful for any person . . . who has been *convicted in any court* of, a crime punishable by imprisonment for a term exceeding one year . . . to . . . possess . . . any firearm." 18 U.S.C. § 922(g)(1) (emphasis added).

The question before us focuses upon the words "convicted in any court." Does this phrase apply only to convictions entered in any domestic court or to foreign convictions as well? We hold that the phrase encompasses only domestic, not foreign, convictions.

I

In 1994 petitioner, Gary Small, was convicted in a Japanese court of having tried to smuggle several pistols, a rifle, and ammunition into Japan. Small was sentenced to five years' imprisonment. After his release, Small returned to the United States, where he bought a gun from a Pennsylvania gun dealer. Federal authorities subsequently charged Small under the "unlawful gun possession" statute here at issue. Small pleaded guilty while reserving the right to challenge his conviction on the ground that his earlier conviction, being a foreign conviction, fell outside the scope of the illegal gun possession statute. The Federal District Court rejected Small's argument, as did the Court of Appeals for the Third Circuit. Because the Circuits disagree about the matter, we granted certiorari. [Citations.]

II

A

The question before us is whether the statutory reference "convicted in *any* court" includes a conviction entered in a *foreign* court. The word "any" considered alone cannot answer this question. In ordinary life, a speaker who says, "I'll see any film," may or may not mean to include films shown in another city. In law, a legislature that uses the statutory phrase " 'any person' " may or may not mean to include " 'persons' " outside "the jurisdiction of the state." [Citations.] Thus, even though the word "any" demands a broad interpretation, [citation], we must look beyond that word itself.

In determining the scope of the statutory phrase we find help in the "commonsense notion that Congress generally legislates with domestic concerns in mind." [Citation.] This notion has led the Court to adopt the legal presumption that Congress ordinarily intends its statutes to have domestic, not extraterritorial, application. [Citations.] That presumption would apply, for example, were we to consider whether this statute prohibits unlawful gun possession abroad as well as domestically. And, although the presumption against extraterritorial application does not apply directly to this case, we believe a similar assumption is appropriate when we consider the scope of the phrase "convicted in any court" here.

For one thing, the phrase describes one necessary portion of the "gun possession" activity that is prohibited as a matter of domestic law. For another, considered as a group, foreign convictions differ from domestic convictions in important ways. Past foreign convictions for crimes punishable by more than one year's imprisonment may include a conviction for conduct that domestic laws would permit, for example, for engaging in economic conduct that our society might encourage. . . . They would include a conviction from a legal system that is inconsistent with an American understanding of fairness. *See, e.g.,* U.S. Dept. of State, Country Reports on Human Rights Practices for 2003, Submitted to the House Committee on International Relations and the Senate Committee on Foreign Relations, 108th Cong., 2d Sess., 702–705, 1853, 2023 (Joint Comm. Print 2004) (describing failures of "due process" and citing examples in which "the testimony of one man equals that of two women"). And they would include a conviction for conduct that domestic law punishes far less severely. *See, e.g.,* Singapore Vandalism Act, ch. 108, §§ 2, 3, III Statutes of Republic of Singapore, pp. 257–258 (imprisonment for up to three years for an act of vandalism). Thus, the key statutory phrase "convicted in any court of, a crime punishable by imprisonment for a term exceeding one year" somewhat less reliably identifies dangerous individuals for the purposes of U.S. law where foreign convictions, rather than domestic convictions, are at issue.

In addition, it is difficult to read the statute as asking judges or prosecutors to refine its definitional distinctions where foreign convictions are at issue. To somehow weed out inappropriate foreign convictions that meet the statutory definition is not consistent with the statute's language; it is not easy for those not versed in foreign laws to accomplish; and it would leave those previously convicted in a foreign court (say, of economic crimes) uncertain about their legal obligations. *Cf.* 1 United States Sentencing Commission, Guidelines Manual § 4A1.2(h) (Nov.2004) ("[S]entences resulting from foreign convictions are not counted" as a "prior sentence" for criminal history purposes).

These considerations, suggesting significant differences between foreign and domestic convictions, do not dictate our ultimate conclusion. Nor do they create a "clear statement" rule, imposing upon Congress a special burden of specificity. . . . They simply convince us that we should apply an ordinary assumption about the reach of domestically oriented statutes here—an assumption that helps us determine Congress' intent where Congress likely did not consider the matter and where other indicia of intent are in approximate balance. [Citation.] We consequently assume a congressional intent that the phrase "convicted in any court" applies domestically, not extraterritorially. But, at the same time, we stand ready to revise this assumption should statutory language, context, history, or purpose show the contrary.

B

We have found no convincing indication to the contrary here. The statute's language does not suggest any intent to reach beyond domestic convictions. Neither does it mention foreign convictions nor is its subject matter special, say, immigration or terrorism, where one could argue that foreign convictions would seem especially relevant. To the contrary, if read to include foreign convictions, the statute's language creates anomalies.

For example, the statute creates an exception that allows gun possession despite a prior conviction for an antitrust or business regulatory crime. 18 U.S.C. § 921(a)(20)(A). In doing so, the exception speaks of "Federal or State" antitrust or regulatory offenses. If the phrase "convicted in any court" generally refers only to domestic convictions, this language causes no problem. But if "convicted in any court" includes foreign convictions, the words "Federal or State" prevent the exception from applying where a *foreign* antitrust or regulatory conviction is at issue. An individual convicted of, say, a Canadian antitrust offense could not lawfully possess a gun, Combines Investigation Act, 2 R.S.C.1985, ch. C-34, §§ 61(6), (9), but a similar individual convicted of, say, a New York antitrust offense, could lawfully possess a gun.

For example, the statute specifies that predicate crimes include "a misdemeanor crime of domestic violence." 18 U.S.C. § 922(g)(9). Again, the language specifies that these predicate crimes include only crimes that are "misdemeanor[s] under Federal or State law." § 921(a)(33)(A). If "convicted in any court" refers only to domestic convictions, this language creates no problem. If the phrase also refers to foreign convictions, the language creates an apparently senseless distinction between (covered) domestic relations misdemeanors committed within the United States and (uncovered) domestic relations misdemeanors committed abroad.

For example, the statute provides an enhanced penalty where unlawful gun possession rests upon three predicate convictions for a "serious drug offense." § 924(e)(1) (2000 ed., Supp. II). Again the statute defines the relevant drug crimes through reference to specific federal crimes and with the words "offense under State law." §§ 924(e)(2)(A)(i), (ii) (2000 ed.). If "convicted in any court" refers only to domestic convictions, this language creates no problem. But if the phrase also refers to foreign convictions, the language creates an apparently senseless distinction between drug offenses committed within the United States (potentially producing enhanced punishments) and similar offenses committed abroad (not producing enhanced punishments).

For example, the statute provides that offenses that are punishable by a term of imprisonment of up to two years, and characterized under state law as misdemeanors, are not predicate crimes. § 921(a)(20). This exception is presumably based on the determination that such state crimes are not sufficiently serious or dangerous so as to preclude an individual from possessing a firearm. If "convicted in any court" refers only to domestic convictions, this language creates no problem. But if the phrase also refers to foreign convictions, the language creates another apparently senseless distinction between less serious crimes (misdemeanors punishable by more than one year's imprisonment) committed within the United States (not predicate crimes) and similar offenses committed abroad (predicate crimes). These illustrative examples taken together suggest that Congress did not consider whether the generic phrase "convicted in any court" applies to domestic as well as foreign convictions.

The statute's lengthy legislative history confirms the fact that Congress did not consider whether foreign convictions should or should not serve as a predicate to liability under the provision here at issue. Congress did consider a Senate bill containing language that would have restricted predicate offenses to domestic offenses. *See* S.Rep. No. 1501, 90th Cong., 2d Sess., 31 (1968) (defining predicate crimes in terms of "Federal" crimes "punishable by a term of imprisonment exceeding one year" and crimes "determined by the laws of the State to be a felony"). And the Conference Committee ultimately rejected this version in favor of language that speaks of those "convicted in any court of, a crime punishable by a term of imprisonment exceeding one year," § 928(g)(1). *See* H.R. Conf. Rep. No.1956, 90th Cong., 2d Sess., 28–29 (1968), U.S. Code Cong. & Admin. News 1968, 4426, 4428. But the history does not suggest that this language change reflected a congressional view on the matter before us. Rather, the enacted version is simpler and it avoids potential difficulties arising out of the fact that States may define the term "felony" differently. And as far as the legislative history is concerned, these latter virtues of the new language fully explain the change. Thus, those who use legislative history to help discern congressional intent will see the history here as silent, hence a neutral factor, that simply confirms the obvious, namely, that Congress did not consider the issue. Others will not be tempted to use or to discuss the history at all.

The statute's purpose *does* offer some support for a reading of the phrase that includes foreign convictions. As the Government points out, Congress sought to " 'keep guns out of the hands of those who have demonstrated that they may not be trusted to possess a firearm without becoming a threat to society.' [Citations.] And, as the dissent properly notes, one convicted of a serious crime abroad may well be as dangerous as one convicted of a similar crime in the United States.

The force of this argument is weakened significantly, however, by the empirical fact that, according to the Government, since 1968, there have probably been no more than "10 to a dozen" instances in which such a foreign conviction has served as a predicate for a felon-in-possession prosecution. This empirical fact reinforces the likelihood that Congress, at best, paid no attention to the matter.

C

In sum, we have no reason to believe that Congress considered the added enforcement advantages flowing from inclusion of foreign crimes, weighing them against, say, the potential unfairness of preventing those with inapt foreign convictions from possessing guns. *See supra,* at 1755. The statute itself and its history offer only congressional silence. Given the reasons for disfavoring an inference of extraterritorial coverage from a statute's total silence and our initial assumption against such coverage, *see supra,* at 1756, we conclude that the phrase "convicted in any court" refers only to domestic courts, not to foreign courts. Congress, of course, remains free to change this conclusion through statutory amendment.

For these reasons, the judgment of the Third Circuit is reversed, and the case is remanded for further proceedings consistent with this opinion.

It is so ordered.

[THE CHIEF JUSTICE took no part in the decision of this case.]

■ JUSTICE THOMAS, with whom JUSTICE SCALIA and JUSTICE KENNEDY join, dissenting.

. . . In concluding that "any" means not what it says, but rather "a subset of any," the Court distorts the plain meaning of the statute and departs from established principles of statutory construction. I respectfully dissent.

I

In December 1992, Small shipped a 19-gallon electric water heater from the United States to Okinawa, Japan, ostensibly as a present for someone in Okinawa. Small had sent two other water heaters to Japan that same year. Thinking it unusual for a person to ship a water tank from overseas as a present, Japanese customs officials searched the heater and discovered 2 rifles, 8 semiautomatic pistols, and 410 rounds of ammunition[.]

The Japanese Government indicted Small on multiple counts of violating Japan's weapons-control and customs laws. Each offense was punishable by imprisonment for a term exceeding one year. Small was tried before a three-judge court in Naha, Japan, convicted on all counts on April 14, 1994, and sentenced to 5 years' imprisonment with credit for 320 days served. He was paroled on November 22, 1996, and his parole terminated on May 26, 1998.

A week after completing parole for his Japanese convictions, on June 2, 1998, Small purchased a 9-millimeter SWD Cobray pistol from a firearms dealer in Pennsylvania. Some time later, a search of his residence, business premises, and automobile revealed a .380-caliber Browning pistol and more than 300 rounds of ammunition. This prosecution ensued.

II

. . . "Read naturally, the word 'any' has an expansive meaning, that is, 'one or some indiscriminately of whatever kind.'" *United States v. Gonzales,* 520 U.S. 1, 5 (1997) (quoting Webster's Third New International Dictionary 97 (1976) (hereinafter Webster's 3d)); [citations]). No exceptions appear on the face of the statute; "[n]o modifier is present, and nothing suggests any restriction," *Lewis v. United States,* 445 U.S. 55, 60 (1980), on the scope of the term "court." *See Gonzales, supra,* at 5, (statute referring to " 'any other term of imprisonment' " includes no "language limiting the breadth of that word, and so we must read [the statute] as referring to all 'term[s] of imprisonment' "). The broad phrase "any court" unambiguously includes all judicial bodies with jurisdiction to impose the requisite conviction—a conviction for a crime punishable by imprisonment for a term of more than a year. . . .

Of course, the phrase "any court," like all other statutory language, must be read in context. [Citation.] The context of § 922(g)(1), however, suggests that there is no geographic limit on the scope of "any court." By contrast to other parts of the firearms-control law that expressly mention only state or federal law, "any court" is not qualified by jurisdiction. *See* 18 U.S.C. § 921(a)(20) (excluding certain "Federal or State offenses" from the definition of "crime punishable by imprisonment for a term exceeding one year"); § 921(a)(33)(A)(i) (defining a "misdemeanor crime of domestic violence" by reference to "Federal or State law"). Congress' explicit use of "Federal" and "State" in other provisions shows that it specifies such restrictions when it wants to do so. . . .

III

Faced with the inescapably broad text, the Court narrows the statute by assuming that the text applies only to domestic convictions; criticizing the accuracy of foreign convictions as a proxy for dangerousness; finding that the broad, natural reading of the statute "creates anomalies"; and suggesting that Congress did not consider whether foreign convictions counted. None of these arguments is persuasive.

A

The Court first invents a canon of statutory interpretation—what it terms "an ordinary assumption about the reach of domestically oriented statutes"—to cabin the statute's reach. This new "assumption" imposes a clear statement rule on Congress: Absent a clear statement, a statute refers to nothing outside the United States. The Court's denial that it has created a clear statement rule is implausible. After today's ruling, the only way for Congress to ensure that courts will construe a law to refer to foreign facts or entities is to describe those facts or entities specifically as foreign. If this is not a "special burden of specificity," I am not sure what is.

The Court's innovation is baseless. The Court derives its assumption from the entirely different, and well-recognized, canon against extraterritorial application of federal statutes: "It is a longstanding principle of American law that legislation of Congress, unless a contrary intent appears, is meant to apply only within the territorial jurisdiction of the United States." *EEOC v. Arabian American Oil Co.,* 499 U.S. 244, 248 (1991) (internal quotation marks omitted). But the majority rightly concedes that the canon against extraterritoriality itself "does not apply directly to this case." Though foreign as well as domestic convictions trigger § 922(g)(1)'s prohibition, the statute criminalizes gun possession in this country, not abroad. In prosecuting Small, the Government is enforcing a domestic criminal statute to punish domestic criminal conduct. [Citation.]

The extraterritoriality cases cited by the Court . . ., restricting federal statutes from reaching conduct *beyond U.S. borders,* lend no support to the Court's unprecedented rule restricting a federal statute from reaching conduct *within U.S. borders.*

We have, it is true, recognized that the presumption against extraterritorial application of federal statutes is rooted in part in the "commonsense notion that Congress generally legislates with domestic concerns in mind." [Citation.] But my reading of § 922(g)(1) is entirely true to that notion: Gun possession in this country is surely a "domestic concern." We have also consistently grounded the canon in the risk that extraterritorially applicable U.S. laws could conflict with foreign laws, for example, by subjecting individuals to conflicting obligations. *Arabian American Oil Co., supra,* at 248. That risk is completely absent in applying § 922(g)(1) to Small's conduct. . . .

B

In support of its narrow reading of the statute, the majority opines that the natural reading has inappropriate results. . . . The Court's claim that foreign convictions punishable by imprisonment for more than a year "somewhat less reliably identif[y] dangerous individuals" than domestic convictions is untenable. In compiling examples of foreign convictions that might trigger § 922(g)(1), the Court constructs a parade of horribles. Citing laws of the Russian Soviet Federated Socialist Republic, Cuba, and Singapore, it cherry-picks a few egregious examples of convictions unlikely to correlate with dangerousness, inconsistent with American intuitions of fairness, or punishable more severely than in this country. This ignores countless other foreign convictions punishable by more than a year that serve as excellent proxies for dangerousness and culpability. . . . The Court also ignores the facts of this very case: A week after completing his sentence for shipping two rifles, eight semiautomatic pistols, and hundreds of rounds of ammunition into Japan, Small bought a gun in this country. It was eminently reasonable for Congress to use convictions punishable by imprisonment for more than a year—foreign no less than domestic—as a proxy for dangerousness.

Contrary to the majority's assertion, it makes sense to bar people convicted overseas from possessing guns in the United States. The Court casually dismisses this point with the observation that only " '10 to a dozen' " prosecutions under the statute have involved foreign convictions as predicate convictions. The rarity of such prosecutions, however, only refutes the Court's simultaneous claim that a parade of horribles will result if foreign convictions count. Moreover, the Court does not claim that any of these few prosecutions has been based on a foreign conviction inconsistent with American law. As far as anyone is aware, the handful of prosecutions thus far rested on foreign convictions perfectly consonant with American law, like Small's conviction for international gunrunning.

The Court has no answer for why including foreign convictions is unwise, let alone irrational.

C

The majority worries that reading § 922(g)(1) to include foreign convictions "creates anomalies" under other firearms-control provisions. It is true, as the majority notes, that the natural reading of § 922(g)(1) affords domestic offenders more lenient treatment than foreign ones in some respects: A domestic antitrust or business regulatory offender could possess a gun, while a similar foreign offender could not; the perpetrator of a state misdemeanor punishable by two years or less in prison could possess a gun, while an analogous foreign offender could not. In other respects, domestic offenders would receive harsher treatment than their foreign counterparts: One who committed a misdemeanor crime of domestic violence in the United States could not possess a gun, while a similar foreign offender could; and a domestic drug offender could receive a 15-year mandatory minimum sentence for unlawful gun possession, while a foreign drug offender could not.

These outcomes cause the Court undue concern. They certainly present no occasion to employ, nor does the Court invoke, the canon against absurdities. We should employ that canon only "where the result of applying the plain language would be, in a genuine sense, absurd, *i.e.,* where it is quite impossible that Congress could have intended the result . . . and where the alleged absurdity is so clear as to be obvious to most anyone." [Citations.]

Here, the "anomalies" to which the Court points are not absurd. They are, at most, odd; they may even be rational. For example, it is not senseless to bar a Canadian antitrust offender from possessing a gun in this country, while exempting a domestic antitrust offender from the ban. Congress might have decided to proceed incrementally and exempt only antitrust offenses with which it was familiar, namely, domestic ones. In any event, the majority abandons the statute's plain meaning based on results that are at most incongruous and certainly not absurd. . . .

Even assuming that my reading of the statute generates anomalies, the majority's reading creates ones even more dangerous. As explained above, the majority's interpretation permits those convicted overseas of murder, rape, assault, kidnaping, terrorism, and other dangerous crimes to possess firearms freely in the United States. Meanwhile, a person convicted domestically of tampering with a vehicle identification number, 18 U.S.C. § 511(a)(1), is barred from possessing firearms. The majority's concern with anomalies provides no principled basis for choosing its interpretation of the statute over mine.

D

The Court hypothesizes "that Congress did not consider whether the generic phrase 'convicted in any court' applies to domestic as well as foreign convictions," and takes that as license to restrict the clear breadth of the text. Whether the Court's empirical assumption is correct is anyone's guess. Regardless, we have properly rejected this method of guesswork-as-interpretation. In *Beecham v. United States,* 511 U.S. 368 (1994), we interpreted other provisions of the federal firearms laws to mean that a person convicted of a federal crime is not relieved of the firearms disability unless his civil rights have been restored under federal (as opposed to state) law. We acknowledged the possibility "that the phrases on which our reading of the statute turns . . . were accidents of statutory drafting," *id.,* at 374; and we observed that some legislators might have read the phrases differently from the Court's reading, "or, more likely, . . . never considered the matter at all." We nonetheless adhered to the unambiguous meaning of the statute. [Citations.] Here, as in *Beecham,* "our task is not the hopeless one of ascertaining what the legislators who passed the law would have decided had they reconvened to consider [this] particular cas[e]," 511 U.S., at 374, but the eminently more manageable one of following the ordinary meaning of the text they enacted. That meaning includes foreign convictions.

The Court's reliance on the absence of any discussion of foreign convictions in the legislative history is equally unconvincing. Reliance on explicit statements in the history, if they existed, would be problematic enough. Reliance on silence in the history is a new and even more dangerous phenomenon. [Citation.]

I do not even agree, moreover, that the legislative history is silent. As the Court describes, the Senate bill that formed the basis for this legislation was amended in Conference, to change the predicate offenses from " 'Federal' crimes" punishable by more than one year's imprisonment and "crimes 'determined by the laws of a State to be a felony' " to conviction " 'in any court of, a crime punishable by a term of imprisonment exceeding one year.' " The Court seeks to explain this change by saying that "the enacted version is simpler and . . . avoids potential difficulties arising out of the fact that States may define the term 'felony' differently." But that does not explain why all limiting reference to "Federal" and "State" was eliminated. The revised provision would have been just as simple, and would just as well have avoided the potential difficulties, if it read "convicted in any Federal or State court of a crime punishable by a term of imprisonment exceeding one year." Surely that would have been the natural change if expansion beyond federal and state convictions were not intended. The elimination of the limiting references suggests that not *only* federal and state convictions were meant to be covered. . . .

. . . I respectfully dissent.

QUESTIONS

1. The majority refers to "the legal presumption that Congress ordinarily intends its statutes to have domestic, not extraterritorial, application." Why do you think this presumption against extraterritorial application exists? Do

you agree with the majority that a similar presumption should apply to 18 U.S.C. § 922(g)(1)? Why or why not?

2. The majority argues that interpreting the statute to include foreign convictions creates "anomalies" and draws "a senseless distinction" between crimes committed domestically and the same offenses committed abroad. Are you persuaded that these anomalies justify the employment of the absurdity canon, or might these distinctions be acceptable or even reasonable, as Justice Thomas suggests in his dissent?

3. The dissent argues that the statutory phrase "any court" is unambiguous, "inescapably broad," and has a plain, "natural" meaning. Do you agree that the majority impermissibly narrows and distorts the meaning of the text?

4. Both the majority and the dissent examine the statute's context and legislative history for guidance, but they reach different conclusions. Does this disagreement undermine the usefulness of inferring context from extra-statutory sources? Do the conflicting lessons drawn from context and legislative history support the Plain Meaning Rule precept that courts should not look beyond the "literal" meaning of the text when interpreting a statute? Or, mindful that, as in *Yates*, two reasonable readers can reach different conclusions as to the meaning of the text, should one conclude that neither text nor context is likely to be determinative on its own?

a.   LOOKING BEYOND THE "PLAIN" TEXT: INTERPRETIVE TECHNIQUES IN STATUTORY INTERPRETATION

The previous materials should have illustrated that few statutes reveal a truly "plain" meaning; more often, courts look to a variety of aids to interpretation. And even when two judges both seek the "ordinary meaning" of the statutory term or phrase in question, they may disagree about which of several plausible meanings is the "ordinary" one.

The interpretative techniques discussed above, as well as the use of dictionaries, canons of construction, and corpus linguistics surveyed in Section III.B.3, below, are often called "textual" methods because they seek to resolve interpretive questions by looking to the common meanings and linguistic usage of the words and phrases in the statutory text. In many circumstances, however, there may be practical impediments to giving the words or phrases in the statute their "literal" meaning.

Indeed, in most circumstances, a court will seek to understand the statutory provision at issue by reference to any number of legal methods, many of which look beyond the meaning of the words or phrases in the text of the contested provision itself, including by reference to:

a.   a statutory definitions section, an intra-statutory solution (*see, e.g., McBoyle v. United States* and *Lozman v. City of Riviera Beach, Fla, infra*);

b. related provisions in the same statute, an intra-statutory canon known as the "whole statute" canon (*see, e.g., Holy Trinity, supra; King v. Burwell* and *Peacock v. Lubbock Compress Co., infra*);

c. related and potentially similar, contrasting, or conflicting provisions in *other* statutes, an inter-statutory canon known as the "whole code" canon, which draws on materials from other related statutes (*see, e.g., Alaska Steamship Co. v. United States, Tennessee Valley Authority v. Hill,* and *U.S. Forest Service v. Cowpasture River Preservation Society, infra*);

d. dictionaries, corpus linguistics, and other evidence of linguistic usage, which are extra-statutory sources of linguistic meaning that examine statutory text against the backdrop of ordinary usage and that attribute to the legislature an intent, or at least an imputed practice, of using words according to their commonly understood meanings (*see infra* Section III.B.3, "Sources of Ordinary Meaning");

e. canons of construction (as in *Lockhart v. United States, infra*), some of which, like the plain meaning rule discussed *Yates, supra,* or the clear notice rule, discussed in *Arlington Central School District Board of Education v. Murphy, infra,* are substantive canons developed by *courts,* not by elected legislators;

f. context stated in or inferable from the statute, for example from titles and purpose clauses, a technique which may be implicit in b. and c. (as discussed in *Johnson, Holy Trinity,* and *Yates, supra*); and/or

g. context supplied by extra-statutory sources such as the legislative history of the statute's enactment (*see, e.g., Johnson* and *Holy Trinity, supra*).

Finally, courts sometimes consider not only methods of interpretation, but also the *consequences* of interpretation (recall Question 1 following *Maslenjak* as well as Question 2 following *Small*). Chief Justice Marshall long ago recognized that limits may exist to the application of the literal meaning of the statute:

> Where words conflict with each other, where the different clauses of an instrument bear upon each other, and would be inconsistent unless the natural and common import of words be varied, construction becomes necessary, and a departure from the obvious meaning of words is justifiable. But if, in any case, the plain meaning of a provision, not contradicted by any other provision in the same instrument, is to be disregarded, because we believe the framers of that instrument could not intend what they say, it must be one in which the absurdity and injustice of applying the provision to the case would be so monstrous that all mankind would, without hesitation, unite in rejecting the application.

Sturges v. Crowninshield, 4 Wheat. 122, 202, 4 L.Ed. 529, 550 (1819).

In some circumstances, courts may choose to depart from the "obvious meaning of words" not only where such meaning would produce a "monstrous" result in a given case, but also where literal application of the text may effectively lead the statute to "self-destruct." While similar in ethos, the "absurd results" canon and the "anti-self-destruction" canon arise from distinct concerns. The anti-self-destruction canon, a variation on the presumption against ineffectiveness (*see supra* Section II.B.3), cautions against interpreting a statute in such a manner as to destroy the evident or core purpose of the statute *generally*. By contrast, the absurd results canon applies in circumstances in which the statute's application may yield an absurd or bizarre result *in the particular case*. The interpreter typically applies the absurd results canon only in fringe cases where the overarching statutory scheme itself is not implicated, regardless of the outcome in the case. Recall the interpretive inquiry in *Holy Trinity*: even though the Supreme Court declined to apply the statutory prohibition in question to the Episcopal priest because it would have yielded an "absurd" result, no doubt remained that the statute applied to a core set of cases—manual laborers, for example.

In these next cases, consider the reasons why it may (or may not) be appropriate for courts to look beyond the "plain" meaning of the text itself and apply other interpretive techniques. As you read each opinion, strive to identify and articulate the other methods and sources courts draw on, as well as their basis for doing so. For the statutes in question, consider whether the plain meaning urged upon the statutory text is indeed "plain," and if you think it is, whether its application in those cases would meet Chief Justice Marshall's "absurdity and injustice" test or would cause the statute to "self-destruct."

King v. Burwell

Supreme Court of the United States, 2015.
576 U.S. 473, 135 S.Ct. 2480, 192 L.Ed.2d 483.

■ CHIEF JUSTICE ROBERTS delivered the opinion of the Court[, in which JUSTICE KENNEDY, JUSTICE GINSBURG, JUSTICE BREYER, JUSTICE SOTOMAYOR, and JUSTICE KAGAN joined].

The Patient Protection and Affordable Care Act adopts a series of interlocking reforms designed to expand coverage in the individual health insurance market. First, the Act bars insurers from taking a person's health into account when deciding whether to sell health insurance or how much to charge. Second, the Act generally requires each person to maintain insurance coverage or make a payment to the Internal Revenue Service. And third, the Act gives tax credits to certain people to make insurance more affordable.

In addition to those reforms, the Act requires the creation of an "Exchange" in each State—basically, a marketplace that allows people to compare and purchase insurance plans. The Act gives each State the opportunity to establish its own Exchange, but provides that the Federal Government will establish the Exchange if the State does not. . . .

An Exchange may be created in one of two ways. First, the Act provides that "[e]ach State shall . . . establish an American Health Benefit Exchange . . . for the State." *Ibid*. Second, if a State nonetheless chooses not to establish its own Exchange, the Act provides that the Secretary of Health and Human Services "shall . . . establish and operate such Exchange within the State." § 18041(c)(1).

The issue in this case is whether the Act's tax credits are available in States that have a Federal Exchange rather than a State Exchange. The Act initially provides that tax credits "shall be allowed" for any "applicable taxpayer." 26 U.S.C. § 36B(a). The Act then provides that the amount of the tax credit depends in part on whether the taxpayer has enrolled in an insurance plan through "an Exchange *established by the State* under section 1311 of the Patient Protection and Affordable Care Act [hereinafter 42 U.S.C. § 18031]." 26 U.S.C. §§ 36B(b)–(c) (emphasis added). . . .

[T]he [relevant] IRS Rule provides that a taxpayer is eligible for a tax credit if he enrolled in an insurance plan through "an Exchange," [citation], which is defined as "an Exchange serving the individual market . . . regardless of whether the Exchange is established and operated by a State . . . or by HHS," [citation]. . . .

When analyzing an agency's interpretation of a statute, we often apply the two-step framework announced in *Chevron* [citation]. <u>Under that framework, we ask whether the statute is ambiguous and, if so, whether the agency's interpretation is reasonable.</u> [Citation.] This approach "is premised on the theory that a statute's ambiguity constitutes an implicit delegation from Congress to the agency to fill in the statutory gaps." [Citation.] "In extraordinary cases, however, there may be reason to hesitate before concluding that Congress has intended such an implicit delegation." [Citation.]

This is one of those cases. The tax credits are among the Act's key reforms, involving billions of dollars in spending each year and affecting the price of health insurance for millions of people. Whether those credits are available on Federal Exchanges is thus a question of deep "economic and political significance" that is central to this statutory scheme; had Congress wished to assign that question to an agency, it surely would have done so expressly. [Citation.] It is especially unlikely that Congress would have delegated this decision to the *IRS,* which has no expertise in crafting health insurance policy of this sort. [Citation.] This is not a case for the IRS.

It is instead our task to determine the correct reading of Section 36B. If the statutory language is plain, we must enforce it according to its terms. [citation] But oftentimes the "meaning—or ambiguity—of certain words or phrases may only become evident when placed in context."

[citation] So when deciding whether the language is plain, we must read the words "in their context and with a view to their place in the overall statutory scheme." [Citation.] Our duty, after all, is "to construe statutes, not isolated provisions." [Citation.]

We begin with the text of Section 36B. As relevant here, Section 36B allows an individual to receive tax credits only if the individual enrolls in an insurance plan through "an Exchange established by the State under [42 U.S.C. § 18031]." In other words, three things must be true: First, the individual must enroll in an insurance plan through "an Exchange." Second, that Exchange must be "established by the State." And third, that Exchange must be established "under [42 U.S.C. § 18031]." We address each requirement in turn.

First, all parties agree that a Federal Exchange qualifies as "an Exchange" for purposes of Section 36B. [Citation.] Section 18031 provides that "[e]ach State shall ... establish an American Health Benefit Exchange ... for the State." § 18031(b)(1). Although phrased as a requirement, the Act gives the States "flexibility" by allowing them to "elect" whether they want to establish an Exchange. § 18041(b). If the State chooses not to do so, Section 18041 provides that the Secretary "shall ... establish and operate *such Exchange* within the State." § 18041(c)(1) (emphasis added).

By using the phrase "such Exchange," Section 18041 instructs the Secretary to establish and operate the *same* Exchange that the State was directed to establish under Section 18031. *See* Black's Law Dictionary 1661 (10th ed. 2014) (defining "such" as "That or those; having just been mentioned"). In other words, State Exchanges and Federal Exchanges are equivalent—they must meet the same requirements, perform the same functions, and serve the same purposes. Although State and Federal Exchanges are established by different sovereigns, Sections 18031 and 18041 do not suggest that they differ in any meaningful way. A Federal Exchange therefore counts as "an Exchange" under Section 36B.

Second, we must determine whether a Federal Exchange is "established by the State" for purposes of Section 36B. At the outset, it might seem that a Federal Exchange cannot fulfill this requirement. After all, the Act defines "State" to mean "each of the 50 States and the District of Columbia"—a definition that does not include the Federal Government. 42 U.S.C. § 18024(d). But when read in context, "with a view to [its] place in the overall statutory scheme," the meaning of the phrase "established by the State" is not so clear. [Citation.]

After telling each State to establish an Exchange, Section 18031 provides that all Exchanges "shall make available qualified health plans to qualified individuals." 42 U.S.C. § 18031(d)(2)(A). Section 18032 then defines the term "qualified individual" in part as an individual who "resides in the State that established the Exchange." § 18032(f)(1)(A). And that's a problem: If we give the phrase "the State that established the Exchange" its most natural meaning, there would be *no* "qualified individuals" on Federal Exchanges. But the Act clearly contemplates that there will be qualified individuals on *every* Exchange. As we just mentioned, the Act requires all Exchanges to "make available qualified health plans to qualified individuals"—something an Exchange could not do if there were no such individuals. § 18031(d)(2)(A). And the Act tells the Exchange, in deciding which health plans to offer, to consider "the interests of qualified individuals . . . in the State or States in which such Exchange operates"—again, something the Exchange could not do if qualified individuals did not exist. § 18031(e)(1)(B). This problem arises repeatedly throughout the Act. *See, e.g.,* § 18031(b)(2) (allowing a State to create "one Exchange . . . for providing . . . services to both qualified individuals and qualified small employers," rather than creating separate Exchanges for those two groups).[1]

These provisions suggest that the Act may not always use the phrase "established by the State" in its most natural sense. Thus, the meaning of that phrase may not be as clear as it appears when read out of context.

Third, we must determine whether a Federal Exchange is established "under [42 U.S.C. § 18031]." This too might seem a requirement that a Federal Exchange cannot fulfill, because it is Section 18041 that tells the Secretary when to "establish and operate such Exchange." But here again, the way different provisions in the statute interact suggests otherwise.

The Act defines the term "Exchange" to mean "an American Health Benefit Exchange established under section 18031." § 300gg–91(d)(21). If we import that definition into Section 18041, the Act tells the Secretary to "establish and operate such 'American Health Benefit Exchange established under section 18031.' " That suggests that Section 18041 authorizes the Secretary to establish an Exchange under Section 18031, not (or not only) under Section 18041. Otherwise, the Federal Exchange, by definition, would not be an "Exchange" at all. [Citation.]

This interpretation of "under [42 U.S.C. § 18031]" fits best with the statutory context. All of the requirements that an Exchange must meet are in Section 18031, so it is sensible to regard all Exchanges as established under that provision. In addition, every time the Act uses the word "Exchange," the definitional provision requires that we substitute the phrase "Exchange established under section 18031." If Federal Exchanges were not established under Section 18031, therefore, literally none of the Act's requirements would apply to them. Finally, the Act repeatedly uses the phrase "established under [42 U.S.C. § 18031]" in situations where it would make no sense to distinguish between State

---

[1] The dissent argues that one would "naturally read instructions about qualified individuals to be inapplicable to the extent a particular Exchange has no such individuals." [Citation.] But the fact that the dissent's interpretation would make so many parts of the Act "inapplicable" to Federal Exchanges is precisely what creates the problem. It would be odd indeed for Congress to write such detailed instructions about customers on a State Exchange, while having nothing to say about those on a Federal Exchange.

and Federal Exchanges. *See, e.g.,* 26 U.S.C. § 125(f)(3)(A) (2012 ed., Supp. I) ("The term 'qualified benefit' shall not include any qualified health plan . . . offered through an Exchange established under [42 U.S.C. § 18031]"); 26 U.S.C. § 6055(b)(1)(B)(iii)(I) (2012 ed.) (requiring insurers to report whether each insurance plan they provided "is a qualified health plan offered through an Exchange established under [42 U.S.C. § 18031]"). A Federal Exchange may therefore be considered one established "under [42 U.S.C. § 18031]."

The upshot of all this is that the phrase "an Exchange established by the State under [42 U.S.C. § 18031]" is properly viewed as ambiguous. The phrase may be limited in its reach to State Exchanges. But it is also possible that the phrase refers to *all* Exchanges—both State and Federal—at least for purposes of the tax credits. If a State chooses not to follow the directive in Section 18031 that it establish an Exchange, the Act tells the Secretary to establish "such Exchange." § 18041. And by using the words "such Exchange," the Act indicates that State and Federal Exchanges should be the same. But State and Federal Exchanges would differ in a fundamental way if tax credits were available only on State Exchanges—one type of Exchange would help make insurance more affordable by providing billions of dollars to the States' citizens; the other type of Exchange would not.[2]

The conclusion that Section 36B is ambiguous is further supported by several provisions that assume tax credits will be available on both State and Federal Exchanges. . . .

Petitioners and the dissent respond that the words "established by the State" would be unnecessary if Congress meant to extend tax credits to both State and Federal Exchanges. [Citation.] But "our preference for avoiding surplusage constructions is not absolute." [Citation.] And specifically with respect to this Act, rigorous application of the canon does not seem a particularly useful guide to a fair construction of the statute.

The Affordable Care Act contains more than a few examples of inartful drafting. (To cite just one, the Act creates three separate Section 1563s. *See* 124 Stat. 270, 911, 912.) Several features of the Act's passage contributed to that unfortunate reality. Congress wrote key parts of the Act behind closed doors, rather than through "the traditional legislative process." [Citation.] And Congress passed much of the Act using a complicated budgetary procedure known as "reconciliation," which limited opportunities for debate and amendment, and bypassed the

---

[2] The dissent argues that the phrase "such Exchange" does not suggest that State and Federal Exchanges "are in all respects equivalent." In support, it quotes the Constitution's Elections Clause, which makes the state legislature primarily responsible for prescribing election regulations, but allows Congress to "make or alter such Regulations." Art. I, § 4, cl. 1. No one would say that state and federal election regulations are in all respects equivalent, the dissent contends, so we should not say that State and Federal Exchanges are. But the Elections Clause does not precisely define what an election regulation must look like, so Congress can prescribe regulations that differ from what the State would prescribe. The Affordable Care Act does precisely define what an Exchange must look like, however, so a Federal Exchange cannot differ from a State Exchange.

Senate's normal 60-vote filibuster requirement. [Citation.] As a result, the Act does not reflect the type of care and deliberation that one might expect of such significant legislation. [Citation.]

Anyway, we "must do our best, bearing in mind the fundamental canon of statutory construction that the words of a statute must be read in their context and with a view to their place in the overall statutory scheme." [Citation.] After reading Section 36B along with other related provisions in the Act, we cannot conclude that the phrase "an Exchange established by the State under [Section 18031]" is unambiguous. . . .

Given that the text is ambiguous, we must turn to the broader structure of the Act to determine the meaning of Section 36B. "A provision that may seem ambiguous in isolation is often clarified by the remainder of the statutory scheme . . . because only one of the permissible meanings produces a substantive effect that is compatible with the rest of the law." [Citation.] Here, the statutory scheme compels us to reject petitioners' interpretation because it would destabilize the individual insurance market in any State with a Federal Exchange, and likely create the very "death spirals" that Congress designed the Act to avoid. [Citation.][3] . . .

It is implausible that Congress meant the Act to operate in this manner. [Citation.] Congress made the guaranteed issue and community rating requirements applicable in every State in the Nation. But those requirements only work when combined with the coverage requirement and the tax credits. So it stands to reason that Congress meant for those provisions to apply in every State as well.[4]

Petitioners respond that Congress was not worried about the effects of withholding tax credits from States with Federal Exchanges because "Congress evidently believed it was offering states a deal they would not refuse.". . . Section 18041 refutes the argument . . . . [and] provides that,

---

[3]   The dissent notes that several other provisions in the Act use the phrase "established by the State," and argues that our holding applies to each of those provisions. [citation] But "the presumption of consistent usage readily yields to context," and a statutory term may mean different things in different places. [citation] That is particularly true when, as here, "the Act is far from a chef d'oeuvre of legislative draftsmanship." [citation] Because the other provisions cited by the dissent are not at issue here, we do not address them.

[4]   The dissent argues that our analysis "show[s] only that the statutory scheme contains a flaw," one "that appeared as well in other parts of the Act." For support, the dissent notes that the guaranteed issue and community rating requirements might apply in the federal territories, even though the coverage requirement does not. The confusion arises from the fact that the guaranteed issue and community rating requirements were added as amendments to the Public Health Service Act, which contains a definition of the word "State" that includes the territories, 42 U.S.C. § 201(f), while the later-enacted Affordable Care Act contains a definition of the word "State" that excludes the territories, § 18024(d). The predicate for the dissent's point is therefore uncertain at best.

The dissent also notes that a different part of the Act "established a long-term-care insurance program with guaranteed-issue and community-rating requirements, but without an individual mandate or subsidies." True enough. But the fact that Congress was willing to accept the risk of adverse selection in a comparatively minor program does not show that Congress was willing to do so in the general health insurance program—the very heart of the Act. Moreover, Congress said expressly that it wanted to avoid adverse selection in the *health* insurance markets. § 18091(2)(I).

if a State elects not to establish an Exchange, the Secretary "shall . . . establish and operate such Exchange within the State." 42 U.S.C. § 18041(c)(1)(A). The whole point of that provision is to create a federal fallback in case a State chooses not to establish its own Exchange. Contrary to petitioners' argument, Congress did not believe it was offering States a deal they would not refuse—it expressly addressed what would happen if a State *did* refuse the deal. . . .

Petitioners' arguments about the plain meaning of Section 36B are strong. But while the meaning of the phrase "an Exchange established by the State under [42 U.S.C. § 18031]" may seem plain "when viewed in isolation," such a reading turns out to be "untenable in light of [the statute] as a whole." [Citation.] In this instance, the context and structure of the Act compel us to depart from what would otherwise be the most natural reading of the pertinent statutory phrase.

Reliance on context and structure in statutory interpretation is a "subtle business, calling for great wariness lest what professes to be mere rendering becomes creation and attempted interpretation of legislation becomes legislation itself." [Citation.] For the reasons we have given, however, such reliance is appropriate in this case, and leads us to conclude that Section 36B allows tax credits for insurance purchased on any Exchange created under the Act. Those credits are necessary for the Federal Exchanges to function like their State Exchange counterparts, and to avoid the type of calamitous result that Congress plainly meant to avoid. . . .

■ JUSTICE SCALIA, with whom JUSTICE THOMAS and JUSTICE ALITO joins, dissenting. . . .

Perhaps sensing the dismal failure of its efforts to show that "established by the State" means "established by the State or the Federal Government," the Court tries to palm off the pertinent statutory phrase as "inartful drafting." This Court, however, has no free-floating power "to rescue Congress from its drafting errors." [Citation.] Only when it is patently obvious to a reasonable reader that a drafting mistake has occurred may a court correct the mistake. The occurrence of a misprint may be apparent from the face of the law, as it is where the Affordable Care Act "creates three separate Section 1563s." But the Court does not pretend that there is any such indication of a drafting error on the face of § 36B. The occurrence of a misprint may also be apparent because a provision decrees an absurd result—a consequence "so monstrous, that all mankind would, without hesitation, unite in rejecting the application." [Citation.] But § 36B does not come remotely close to satisfying that demanding standard. It is entirely plausible that tax credits were restricted to state Exchanges deliberately—for example, in order to encourage States to establish their own Exchanges. We therefore have no authority to dismiss the terms of the law as a drafting fumble.

The Court's decision reflects the philosophy that judges should endure whatever interpretive distortions it takes in order to correct a supposed flaw in the statutory machinery. That philosophy ignores the American people's decision to give *Congress* "[a]ll legislative Powers" enumerated in the Constitution. Art. I, § 1. They made Congress, not this Court, responsible for both making laws and mending them. This Court holds only the judicial power—the power to pronounce the law as Congress has enacted it. We lack the prerogative to repair laws that do not work out in practice, just as the people lack the ability to throw us out of office if they dislike the solutions we concoct. We must always remember, therefore, that "[o]ur task is to apply the text, not to improve upon it." [Citation.]

Trying to make its judge-empowering approach seem respectful of congressional authority, the Court asserts that its decision merely ensures that the Affordable Care Act operates the way Congress "meant [it] to operate." First of all, what makes the Court so sure that Congress "meant" tax credits to be available everywhere? Our only evidence of what Congress meant comes from the terms of the law, and those terms show beyond all question that tax credits are available only on state Exchanges. More importantly, the Court forgets that ours is a government of laws and not of men. That means we are governed by the terms of our laws, not by the unenacted will of our lawmakers. "If Congress enacted into law something different from what it intended, then it should amend the statute to conform to its intent [Citation.] In the meantime, this Court "has no roving license . . . to disregard clear language simply on the view that . . . Congress 'must have intended' something broader." [Citation.]

Even less defensible, if possible, is the Court's claim that its interpretive approach is justified because this Act "does not reflect the type of care and deliberation that one might expect of such significant legislation." It is not our place to judge the quality of the care and deliberation that went into this or any other law. A law enacted by voice vote with no deliberation whatever is fully as binding upon us as one enacted after years of study, months of committee hearings, and weeks of debate. Much less is it our place to make everything come out right when Congress does not do its job properly. It is up to Congress to design its laws with care, and it is up to the people to hold them to account if they fail to carry out that responsibility.

Rather than rewriting the law under the pretense of interpreting it, the Court should have left it to Congress to decide what to do about the Act's limitation of tax credits to state Exchanges. If Congress values above everything else the Act's applicability across the country, it could make tax credits available in every Exchange. If it prizes state involvement in the Act's implementation, it could continue to limit tax credits to state Exchanges while taking other steps to mitigate the economic consequences predicted by the Court. If Congress wants to accommodate both goals, it could make tax credits available everywhere while offering new incentives for States to set up their own Exchanges.

And if Congress thinks that the present design of the Act works well enough, it could do nothing. Congress could also do something else altogether, entirely abandoning the structure of the Affordable Care Act. The Court's insistence on making a choice that should be made by Congress both aggrandizes judicial power and encourages congressional lassitude. . . .

NOTES AND QUESTIONS

1.   The majority assesses the phrase "an Exchange established by the State" not as a free-standing clause to be interpreted in isolation, but as a technical provision whose meaning should be informed by the usage and meaning of its individual terms elsewhere in the statute. The dissent, by contrast, urges that the term be given its "plain" meaning as a free-standing phrase. Should it matter who the primary audience for this provision is? Given everything you know about the text of the ACA, do you think Congress had "ordinary" readers in mind when drafting the statute? Should the likely audience of the statute influence how courts interpret it? Keep this question in mind when you encounter Section IV.B, *infra*.

2.   Recall from the typology of interpretive methods in Section II.B.1, *supra*, that many understand the role of courts interpreting statutes as "faithful agents" of the legislature. Do you think the approach recommended by the dissent can be described as "faithful"? Why or why not?

3.   The interpretive problem at issue in *King v. Burwell* exemplifies statutory problems that can arise from unorthodox lawmaking procedures. Indeed, as Professor Abbe Gluck has explained, the issue in *King* arose because lawmaking often involves combining different versions of a statute drafted by separate committees; the results frequently are in discord:

> [T]he ACA is a textbook example of the modern trend toward nontextbook, or "unorthodox," lawmaking, and *King* stakes out new ground by recognizing the special challenges that trend poses for the Court. Nevertheless, the Court does not actually discuss where the four words at issue came from. . . . The issue in *King* comes from the merger of committee drafts of the ACA. Two committees in the Senate—the Finance Committee and the Health, Education, Labor and Pensions Committee (HELP)—shared primary jurisdiction over most of the subject matter and so each drafted a version of the ACA. The final version used the Finance bill as its primary template, but there were important elements of the HELP bill incorporated when the drafts were merged. In particular, the *consequences* section of the ACA—what happens if a state elects not to establish its own exchange—was taken from the HELP bill, which provided for a federal fallback exchange, with subsidies. One reason that the HELP bill was a necessary model here was that the Finance bill had *no concept* of a federally run exchange at all: that bill included only "state exchanges" and provided that if a state failed to operate its own exchange, HHS would have to contract with a nongovernmental entity to run those exchanges in the

states. The Finance Committee markup repeatedly referred to those nongovernmental-entity fallback exchanges as "state exchanges."

Perhaps the Government viewed this explanation as too complicated for the Court, or perhaps there was a fear of acknowledging something that had the odor of mistake, but it explains why the statute looks the way it does. As noted, Justice Scalia's dissent rejects a mistake story: "What are the odds," he asks, "that the same slip of the pen occurred in seven separate places? . . . If there was a mistake here, context suggests it was a substantive mistake in designing this part of the law, not a technical mistake in transcribing it." In fact, because under the Finance bill, none of the exchanges was to be federally run, all the provisions retained from Finance had that state-exclusive language. All but one of the references in the final ACA to "exchange established by the state" that the dissent mentions came from the Finance draft and none came from the HELP draft. This also explains what the challengers argued was inexplicable, namely, how the federal government could be thought to be operating a "state exchange." That is precisely what the Finance bill had told the federal government to set up: the Finance bill's fallback exchanges were state exchanges operated by outsiders.

Ideally, the lingering Finance language would have been clarified once the provisions modeled on the HELP bill were merged into the draft. Staffers have reported that they expected to have that opportunity, as the textbook legislative process would have permitted. Under the conventional process, after the Senate vote, the bill would have moved to and through the House and then been cleaned up and harmonized in the two-chamber Conference Committee before a final vote by each chamber. . . .

[H]owever, Conference never occurred. After combining the two Senate drafts, the Senate moved to what was at the time thought to be a preliminary vote on the bill. The House also drafted its own version of the ACA, which notably made *federal* exchanges—with subsidies—the default option. The expectation was that differences over the exchange structure would be worked out later, before the final vote. But one month after the Senate vote, Senator Kennedy, who had died several months earlier, was replaced by Republican Scott Brown, depriving the Democrats of their critical sixtieth vote in support of the ACA. (Sixty is the magic number in the Senate because sixty votes are required to close debate and move to a vote on the merits.) Without sixty votes, the Senate Democrats lost flexibility to later amend the version enacted by the Senate in December 2009—whether to clean it up or to include items expected to be demanded by the House—because any amendment would require the same sixty-vote process of getting to a vote on the merits, and it was clear that the ACA obstructionists would filibuster. As a result, the House had no choice but to accept the Senate draft as final, and there was no Conference to eliminate imperfections.

As the *King* majority notes, Congress did utilize a different procedure—a budget procedure known as reconciliation—to pass a law a week after the ACA was enacted that, among other provisions, included amendments to the ACA and allowed some concessions to the House. Reconciliation was useful under the circumstances because it suspends the Senate filibuster rules to facilitate the enactment of legislation. Because it is part of the budget process, however, reconciliation is strictly limited to budget-related provisions, and thus only certain House demands (for instance, its desire to lower the "Cadillac tax") could be accomplished through this procedure. Ordinary cleanup could not.

It is worth noting that the one and only provision in the ACA that refers to the notion of an "exchange under section . . . 1321(c)" (the federally operated exchange provision) was added in reconciliation and expressly assumes the availability of subsidies on federally run exchanges, because it requires section 1321 exchanges to report them. The Court has long recognized the particular importance of changes made at the very last stage of the legislative process. The *King* majority, however, in lamenting that, as a result of the ACA's unconventional legislative process, "the Act does not reflect the type of care and deliberation that one might expect of such significant legislation," generally treated the use of reconciliation as a pathology rather than as a source of insight.

So, was it a "mistake," an "amalgamation" error, a "term of art" retained from the Finance draft, or just ambiguity? The statutory history illustrates that these concepts are a lot more complicated than the Court has previously understood them to be. It certainly does not seem to be the kind of *"substantive* mistake in designing this part of the law" that Justice Scalia surmises. Justice Scalia's cynicism about a seven-time "slip of the pen" rests on the fiction that Congress drafts statutes front to back, and always has the opportunity to perfect them. These assumptions, as detailed below, are replicated in most of the Court's statutory interpretation doctrines. The ACA's procedural history—and as well the history of most other modern statutes—does not fit that narrative. . . .

Abbe R. Gluck, *Imperfect Statutes, Imperfect Courts: Understanding Congress's Plan in the Era of Unorthodox Lawmaking*, 129 Harv. L. Rev. 62 (2015).

NOTE: DOES TEXTUALISM HOBBLE LEGISLATION?

In his review of *Reading Law*, a book by Justice Antonin Scalia and lawyer and lexicographer Bryan A. Garner, Judge Posner expressed skepticism regarding whether textualism furthers either political neutrality or judicial objectivity in the interpretation of statutory language. As you read the following excerpt, ask yourself how the views expressed in the book review are related to the reasoning of Judge Posner's dissent in *Marshall* in Section II.C, *supra*, and Justice Scalia's dissent in *King v. Burwell*:

> The passive view of the judicial role is aggressively defended in a new book by Justice Antonin Scalia and the legal lexicographer Bryan Garner. They advocate what is best described as textual originalism, because they want judges to "look for meaning in the governing text, ascribe to that text the meaning that it has borne from its inception, and reject judicial speculation about both the drafters' extra-textually derived purposes and the desirability of the fair reading's anticipated consequences." This austere interpretive method leads to a heavy emphasis on dictionary meanings, in disregard of a wise warning issued by Judge Frank Easterbrook, who though himself a self-declared textualist advises that "the choice among meanings [of words in statutes] must have a footing more solid than a dictionary—which is a museum of words, an historical catalog rather than a means to decode the work of legislatures." . . . [T]ext as such may be politically neutral, but textualism is conservative.
>
> A legislature is thwarted when a judge refuses to apply its handiwork to an unforeseen situation that is encompassed by the statute's aim but is not a good fit with its text. Ignoring the limitations of foresight, and also the fact that a statute is a collective product that often leaves many questions of interpretation to be answered by the courts because the legislators cannot agree on the answers, the textual originalist demands that the legislature think through myriad hypothetical scenarios and provide for all of them explicitly rather than rely on courts to be sensible. In this way, textualism hobbles legislation—and thereby tilts toward "small government" and away from "big government," which in modern America is a conservative preference.
>
> Scalia and Garner insist that legal terms be given their original meaning lest the intent of the legislators or the constitution-makers be subverted by unforeseen linguistic changes. . . .
>
> The decisive objection to the quest for original meaning, even when the quest is conducted in good faith, is that judicial historiography rarely dispels ambiguity. Judges are not competent historians. Even real historiography is frequently indeterminate, as real historians acknowledge. To put to a judge a question that he cannot answer is to evoke "motivated thinking," the form of cognitive delusion that consists of credulously accepting the evidence that supports a preconception and of peremptorily rejecting the evidence that contradicts it. . . .
>
> It is possible to glean from judges who actually are loose constructionists the occasional paean to textualism, but it is naïve to think that judges believe everything they say, especially when speaking *ex cathedra* (that is, in their judicial opinions). Judges

tend to deny the creative—the legislative—dimension of judging, important as it is in our system, because they do not want to give the impression that they are competing with legislators, or engaged in anything but the politically unthreatening activity of objective, literal-minded interpretation, using arcane tools of legal analysis. The fact that loose constructionists sometimes publicly endorse textualism is evidence only that judges are, for strategic reasons, often not candid.

Richard A. Posner, *The Spirit Killeth, But the Letter Giveth Life*, New Republic, Sept. 13, 2012, at 18 (reviewing Antonin Scalia & Brian A. Garner, Reading Law: The Interpretation of Legal Texts (2012)).

Posner alleges that textualism calls for "austere" and "conservative" interpretive methods that "hobble" legislation. Is this necessarily always so? For example, as you will see in *Commonwealth v. Welosky* in Section III.E.1, *infra*, sometimes the literal interpretation of the statutory text yields the *broader* application, and extratextual methods yield the *narrower*, more conservative result.

Certainly, Posner's critique appears to apply in at least some circumstances: in *King*, for example, the dissent's textually driven approach would seem to cause the statute to self-destruct. (Ironically, Scalia and Garner, in *Reading Law*, include the presumption against ineffectiveness among the "fundamental principles" of statutory interpretation). The majority, by contrast, suggests that where a statutory phrase is susceptible to multiple reasonable interpretations of the phrase's "ordinary" meaning, a court should avoid interpreting the statute in a way that produces a "death spiral," the very "calamitous result" the statute was enacted to avoid.

b.   SCRIVENER'S ERRORS

Perhaps the most straightforward way to read statutes is to read their text literally. As you have already seen in *Holy Trinity*, however, literal readings of statutory texts sometimes produce counter-intuitive or absurd results when applied to circumstances that seem beyond what the legislature had in mind. After all, drafters cannot possibly anticipate every conceivable application of a proposed statute, let alone draft a response to them. Yet as *King v. Burwell* illustrates, literal application of a word or phrase can produce anomalous results *even within* the circumstances Congress directly confronted.

A different problem emerges, however, when a statutory text seems in error *on its face*. If so, should a court conclude that the seemingly erroneous text must be a "scrivener's error"? As you read these next cases, consider the policy consequences either of applying the literal text without regard to the (possibly) absurd results that follow, or of attempting a judicial "fix" to the statute so as to avoid those absurd results. Does it matter how severe the absurd result will be? Moreover, should courts consider whether the scrivener's error results in a windfall benefit to opportunistic litigants?

United States v. Locke

Supreme Court of the United States, 1985.
471 U.S. 84, 105 S.Ct. 1785, 85 L.Ed.2d 64.

■ JUSTICE MARSHALL delivered the opinion of the Court [in which CHIEF JUSTICE BURGER, JUSTICE WHITE, JUSTICE BLACKMUN, JUSTICE REHNQUIST, and JUSTICE O'CONNOR joined].

From the enactment of the general mining laws in the 19th century until 1976, those who sought to make their living by locating and developing minerals on federal lands were virtually unconstrained by the fetters of federal control. The general mining laws, 30 U.S.C. § 22 *et seq.*, still in effect today, allow United States citizens to go onto unappropriated, unreserved public land to prospect for and develop certain minerals. . . .

By the 1960's, it had become clear that this 19th-century laissez-faire regime had created virtual chaos with respect to the public lands. . . .

After more than a decade of studying this problem in the context of a broader inquiry into the proper management of the public lands in the modern era, Congress in 1976 enacted the [Federal Land Policy and Management Act (FLPMA)]. Section 314 of the Act establishes a federal recording system that is designed both to rid federal lands of stale mining claims and to provide federal land managers with up-to-date information that allows them to make informed land management decisions.

[The text of 43 U.S.C. § 1744 provides, in relevant part, as follows:

"Recordation of Mining Claims

"(a) Filing requirements

"The owner of an unpatented lode or placer mining claim located prior to October 21, 1976, shall, within the three-year period following October 21, 1976 and prior to December 31 of each year thereafter, file the instruments required by paragraphs (1) and (2) of this subsection . . . .

"(1) File for record in the office where the location notice or certificate is recorded either a notice of intention to hold the mining claim (including but not limited to such notices as are provided by law to be filed when there has been a suspension or deferment of annual assessment work), an affidavit of assessment work performed thereon, on a detailed report provided by section 28–1 of title 30, relating thereto.

"(2) File in the office of the Bureau designated by the Secretary a copy of the official record of the instrument filed or recorded pursuant to paragraph (1) of this subsection, including a description of the location of the mining claim sufficient to locate the claimed lands on the ground.]

For claims located before FLPMA's enactment, the federal recording system imposes two general requirements. First, the claims must initially be registered with the BLM by filing, within three years of FLPMA's enactment, a copy of the official record of the notice or certificate of location. [Citation.] Second, in the year of the initial recording, and "prior to December 31" of every year after that, the claimant must file with state officials and with BLM a notice of intention to hold the claim, an affidavit of assessment work performed on the claim, or a detailed reporting form. [Citation.] Section 314(c) of the Act provides that failure to comply with either of these requirements "shall be deemed conclusively to constitute an abandonment of the mining claim . . . by the owner." [Citation.]

The second of these requirements—the annual filing obligation—has created the dispute underlying this appeal. Appellees, four individuals engaged "in the business of operating mining properties in Nevada," purchased in 1960 and 1966 10 unpatented mining claims on public lands near Ely, Nevada. . . . Throughout the period during which they owned the claims, appellees complied with annual state-law filing and assessment work requirements. In addition, appellees satisfied FLPMA's initial recording requirement by properly filing with BLM a notice of location, thereby putting their claims on record for purposes of FLPMA.

At the end of 1980, however, appellees failed to meet on time their first annual obligation to file with the Federal Government. After allegedly receiving misleading information from a BLM employee,[7] appellees waited until December 31 to submit to BLM the annual notice of intent to hold or proof of assessment work performed required under § 314(a) of FLPMA, 43 U.S.C. § 1744(a). As noted above, that section requires these documents to be filed annually "prior to December 31." Had appellees checked, they further would have discovered that BLM regulations made quite clear that claimants were required to make the annual filings in the proper BLM office "on or before December 30 of each calendar year." [Citation.] Thus, appellees' filing was one day too late.

---

[7] An affidavit submitted to the District Court by one of appellees' employees stated that BLM officials in Ely had told the employee that the filing could be made at the BLM Reno office "on or before December 31, 1980." Affidavit of Laura C. Locke ¶ 3. The 1978 version of a BLM question and answer pamphlet erroneously stated that the annual filings had to be made "on or before December 31" of each year. Staking a Mining Claim on Federal Lands 9–10 (1978). Later versions have corrected this error to bring the pamphlet into accord with the BLM regulations that require the filings to be made "on or before December 30."

JUSTICE STEVENS and JUSTICE POWELL seek to make much of this pamphlet and of the uncontroverted evidence that appellees were told a December 31 filing would comply with the statute. [Citation.] However, at the time appellees filed in 1980, BLM regulations and the then-current pamphlets made clear that the filing was required "on or before December 30." Thus, the dissenters' reliance on this pamphlet would seem better directed to the claim that the United States was equitably estopped from forfeiting appellees' claims, given the advice of the BLM agent and the objective basis the 1978 pamphlet provides for crediting the claim that such advice was given. The District Court did not consider this estoppel claim. Without expressing any view as to whether, as a matter of law, appellees could prevail on such a theory, [Citation.] we leave any further treatment of this issue, including fuller development of the record, to the District Court on remand.

This fact was brought painfully home to appellees when they received a letter from the BLM Nevada State Office informing them that their claims had been declared abandoned and void due to their tardy filing. In many cases, loss of a claim in this way would have minimal practical effect; the claimant could simply locate the same claim again and then rerecord it with BLM. In this case, however, relocation of appellees' claims, which were initially located by appellees' predecessors in 1952 and 1954, was prohibited by the Common Varieties Act of 1955, 30 U.S.C. § 611; that Act prospectively barred location of the sort of minerals yielded by appellees' claims. Appellees' mineral deposits thus escheated to the Government.

After losing an administrative appeal, appellees filed the present action in the United States District Court for the District of Nevada. . . . [T]he Government was obliged, in the District Court's view, to provide individualized notice to claimants that their claims were in danger of being lost, followed by a post-filing-deadline hearing at which the claimants could demonstrate that they had not, in fact, abandoned a claim. Alternatively, the District Court held that the 1-day late filing "substantially complied" with the Act and regulations. . . .

Before the District Court, appellees asserted that the § 314(a) requirement of a filing "prior to December 31 of each year" should be construed to require a filing "on or before December 31." Thus, appellees argued, their December 31 filing had in fact complied with the statute, and the BLM had acted ultra vires in voiding their claims. . . .

It is clear to us that the plain language of the statute simply cannot sustain the gloss appellees would put on it. As even counsel for appellees conceded at oral argument, § 314(a) "is a statement that Congress wanted it filed by December 30th. I think that is a clear statement . . . ." [Citation.]. While we will not allow a literal reading of a statute to produce a result "demonstrably at odds with the intentions of its drafters," [citation], with respect to filing deadlines a literal reading of Congress' words is generally the only proper reading of those words. To attempt to decide whether some date other than the one set out in the statute is the date actually "intended" by Congress is to set sail on an aimless journey, for the purpose of a filing deadline would be just as well served by nearly any date a court might choose as by the date Congress has in fact set out in the statute. "Actual purpose is sometimes unknown," [citation], and such is the case with filing deadlines; as might be expected, nothing in the legislative history suggests why Congress chose December 30 over December 31, or over September 1 (the end of the assessment year for mining claims, 30 U.S.C. § 28), as the last day on which the required filings could be made. But "[d]eadlines are inherently arbitrary," while fixed dates "are often essential to accomplish necessary results." [Citation.] Faced with the inherent arbitrariness of filing deadlines, we must, at least in a civil case, apply by its terms the date fixed by the statute. . . .

Moreover, BLM regulations have made absolutely clear since the enactment of FLPMA that "prior to December 31" means what it says. As the current version of the filing regulations states:

"The owner of an unpatented mining claim located on Federal lands . . . have filed or caused to have been filed *on or before December 30* of each calendar year . . . evidence of annual assessment work performed during the previous assessment year or a notice of intention to hold the mining claim.". . . .

In so saying, we are not insensitive to the problems posed by congressional reliance on the words "prior to December 31." [Citation.] But the fact that Congress might have acted with greater clarity or foresight does not give courts a *carte blanche* to redraft statutes in an effort to achieve that which Congress is perceived to have failed to do. "There is a basic difference between filling a gap left by Congress' silence and rewriting rules that Congress has affirmatively and specifically enacted." [Citation.] Nor is the Judiciary licensed to attempt to soften the clear import of Congress' chosen words whenever a court believes those words lead to a harsh result. [Citation.] On the contrary, deference to the supremacy of the Legislature, as well as recognition that Congressmen typically vote on the language of a bill, generally requires us to assume that "the legislative purpose is expressed by the ordinary meaning of the words used." [Citation.] "Going behind the plain language of a statute in search of a possibly contrary congressional intent is 'a step to be taken cautiously' even under the best of circumstances." [Citation.] When even after taking this step nothing in the legislative history remotely suggests a congressional intent contrary to Congress' chosen words, and neither appellees nor the dissenters have pointed to anything that so suggests, any further steps take the courts out of the realm of interpretation and place them in the domain of legislation. The phrase "prior to" may be clumsy, but its meaning is clear. Under these circumstances, we are obligated to apply the "prior to December 31" language by its terms. [Citations.] . . .

We therefore hold that BLM did not act ultra vires in concluding that appellees' filing was untimely. . . . [T]he District Court held that, even if the statute required a filing on or before December 30, appellees had "substantially complied" by filing on December 31. We cannot accept this view of the statute.

The notion that a filing deadline can be complied with by filing sometime after the deadline falls due is, to say the least, a surprising notion, and it is a notion without limiting principle. If 1-day late filings are acceptable, 10-day late filings might be equally acceptable, and so on in a cascade of exceptions that would engulf the rule erected by the filing deadline; yet regardless of where the cutoff line is set, some individuals will always fall just on the other side of it. Filing deadlines, like statutes of limitations, necessarily operate harshly and arbitrarily with respect to individuals who fall just on the other side of them, but if the concept of a filing deadline is to have any content, the deadline must be enforced. "Any less rigid standard would risk encouraging a lax attitude toward filing dates," [Citation.]. A filing deadline cannot be complied with, substantially or otherwise, by filing late—even by one day. . . .[14]

[The opinions of JUSTICE O'CONNOR, concurring, and JUSTICE POWELL, dissenting, have been omitted.]

■ JUSTICE STEVENS, with whom JUSTICE BRENNAN joins, dissenting.

The Court's opinion is contrary to the intent of Congress . . . and unjustly creates a trap for unwary property owners. First, the choice of the language "prior to December 31" when read in context in 43 U.S.C. § 1744(a) is, at least, ambiguous, and, at best, "the consequence of a legislative *accident,* perhaps caused by nothing more than the unfortunate fact that Congress is too busy to do all of its work as carefully as it should." [Citation.] In my view, Congress actually intended to authorize an annual filing at any time prior to the close of business on December 31st, that is, prior to the end of the calendar year to which the filing pertains. Second, even if Congress irrationally intended that the applicable deadline for a calendar year should end *one day before* the end of the calendar year that has been recognized since the amendment of the Julian Calendar in 8 B.C., it is clear that appellees have substantially complied with the requirements of the statute, in large part because the Bureau of Land Management has issued interpreting regulations that recognize substantial compliance. . . .

Congress enacted § 314 of the Federal Land Policy and Management Act to establish for federal land planners and managers a federal recording system designed to cope with the problem of stale claims, and to provide "an easy way of discovering which Federal lands are subject to either valid or invalid mining claim locations." I submit that the appellees' actions in this case did not diminish the importance of these congressional purposes; to the contrary, their actions were entirely consistent with the statutory purposes, despite the confusion created by the "inartful draftsmanship" of the statutory language.

---

[14] Since 1982, BLM regulations have provided that filings due on or before December 30 will be considered timely if postmarked on or before December 30 and received by BLM by the close of business on the following January 19. Appellees and the dissenters attempt to transform this regulation into a blank check generally authorizing "substantial compliance" with the filing requirements. We disagree for two reasons. First, the regulation was not in effect when appellees filed in 1980; it therefore cannot now be relied on to validate a purported "substantial compliance" in 1980. Second, that an agency has decided to take account of holiday mail delays by treating as timely filed a document postmarked on the statutory filing date does not require the agency to accept all documents hand-delivered any time before January 19. The agency rationally could decide that either of the options in this sort of situation—requiring mailings to be received by the same date that hand-deliveries must be made or requiring mailings to be postmarked by that date—is a sound way of administering the statute. Justice STEVENS further suggests that BLM would have been well within its authority to promulgate regulations construing the statute to allow for December 31 filings. Assuming the correctness of this suggestion, the fact that two interpretations of a statute are equally reasonable suggests to us that the agency's interpretation is sufficiently reasonable as to be acceptable.

A careful reading of § 314 discloses at least three respects in which its text cannot possibly reflect the actual intent of Congress. First, the description of what must be filed in the initial filing and subsequent annual filings is quite obviously garbled. Read literally, § 314(a)(2) seems to require that a notice of intent to hold the claim and an affidavit of assessment work performed on the claim must be filed "on a detailed report provided by § 28–1 of Title 30." One must substitute the word "or" for the word "on" to make any sense at all out of this provision. This error should cause us to pause before concluding that Congress commanded blind allegiance to the remainder of the literal text of § 314.

Second, the express language of the statute is unambiguous in describing the place where the second annual filing shall be made. If the statute is read inflexibly, the owner must "file in the office of the Bureau" the required documents. Yet the regulations that the Bureau itself has drafted, quite reasonably, construe the statute to allow filing in a mailbox, provided that the document is actually received by the Bureau prior to the close of business on January 19 of the year following the year in which the statute requires the filing to be made. A notice mailed on December 30, 1982, and received by the Bureau on January 19, 1983, was filed "in the office of the Bureau" during 1982 within the meaning of the statute, but one that is hand-delivered to the office on December 31, 1982, cannot be accepted as a 1982 "filing."

The Court finds comfort in the fact that the implementing regulations have eliminated the risk of injustice. [Citation.] But if one must rely on those regulations, it should be apparent that the meaning of the statute itself is not all that obvious. To begin with, the regulations do not use the language "prior to December 31;" instead, they use "on or before December 30 of each year." The Bureau's drafting of the regulations using this latter phrase indicates that the meaning of the statute itself is not quite as "plain," [citation], as the Court assumes; if the language were plain, it is doubtful that the Bureau would have found it necessary to change the language at all. Moreover, the Bureau, under the aegis of the Department of the Interior, once issued a pamphlet entitled "Staking a Mining Claim on Federal Lands" that contained the following information:

> "Owners of claims or sites located on or before Oct. 21, 1976, have until Oct. 22, 1979, to file evidence of assessment work performed the preceding year or to file a notice of intent to hold the claim or site. Once the claim or site is recorded with BLM, *these documents must be filed on or before December 31 of each subsequent year.*" (emphasis added).

"Plain language," indeed.

There is a more important reason why the implementing regulations cannot be supportive of the result the Court reaches today: the Bureau's own deviation from the statutory language in its mail-filing regulation. [Citation.] If the Bureau had issued regulations expressly stating that a

December 31 filing would be considered timely—just as it has stated that a mail filing received on January 19 is timely—it is inconceivable that anyone would question the validity of its regulation. It appears, however, that the Bureau has more power to interpret an awkwardly drafted statute in an enlightened manner consistent with Congress' intent than does this Court.[11]

In light of the foregoing, I cannot believe that Congress intended the words "prior to December 31 of each year" to be given the literal reading the Court adopts today. The statutory scheme requires periodic filings on a calendar-year basis. The end of the calendar year is, of course, correctly described either as "prior to the close of business on December 31," or "on or before December 31," but it is surely understandable that the author of § 314 might inadvertently use the words "prior to December 31" when he meant to refer to the end of the calendar year. As the facts of this case demonstrate, the scrivener's error is one that can be made in good faith. The risk of such an error is, of course, the greatest when the reference is to the end of the calendar year. That it was in fact an error seems rather clear to me because no one has suggested any rational basis for omitting just one day from the period in which an annual filing may be made, and I would not presume that Congress deliberately created a trap for the unwary by such an omission.

It would be fully consistent with the intent of Congress to treat any filing received during the 1980 calendar year as a timely filing for that year. Such an interpretation certainly does not interfere with Congress' intent to establish a federal recording system designed to cope with the problem of stale mining claims on federal lands. The system is established, and apparently, functioning. Moreover, the claims here were *active;* the Bureau was well aware that the appellees intended to hold and to operate their claims. . . .

I respectfully dissent.

NOTES AND QUESTIONS

1.   The majority warns that "the fact that Congress might have acted with greater clarity or foresight does not give courts a *carte blanche* to redraft statutes in an effort to achieve that which Congress is perceived to have failed to do." Is the dissent's proposed judicial fix an effort to act in a "*carte blanche*" manner? Could you construct a limiting principle for fixes of the kind the dissent proposes?

---

[11] The Court, *ante,* criticizes my citation of the BLM regulations to demonstrate that the agency has itself departed from the "plain" statutory language by allowing mail filings to be received by January 19. In the same breath, the Court acknowledges that the agency is not bound by the "plain" language in "administering the statute." The mail-delivery deadline makes it clear that the Court's judicially created "up-to-date" statutory purpose is utterly lacking in foundation. The agency's adoption of the January 19th deadline illustrates that it does not need the information by December 30; that it is not bound by the language of the provision; and that substantial compliance does not interfere with the agency's statutory functions or with the intent of Congress.

2. The dissent suggests (not unreasonably) that the BLM's practice of accepting mailed filings up to January 19 of the following year indicates that the December 30 deadline is susceptible to some flexibility, at least as enforced. If courts are concerned primarily with being "faithful agents" of *the legislature*, should the practices of the agency enforcing the statute in question influence how courts interpret it? Keep this question in mind as you read Part V, Agency Interpretations of Statutes, *infra*.

3. In contrast to common law disputes, in which judges have a relatively free hand, in statutory interpretation cases judges are limited to declaring the correct legal meaning of the statute, and usually doing nothing more. How satisfying is the outcome here, where the Court concluded that December 30 was the legal deadline but also acknowledged that BLM representatives had informed the Lockes that they could file on December 31, and they apparently acted on that reliance? When interpreting a statute, should courts have any leeway to make an exception on the basis of the special circumstances of the instant case?

4. In *Locke*, the apparent scrivener's error redounded to the detriment of ordinary citizens. Should it matter which party benefits from the error, especially if the statutory error seems to invite opportunistic conduct by private parties? Consider this factor as you read the next case, *In re Adamo*.

In re Adamo

United States Court of Appeals for the Second Circuit, 1980.
619 F.2d 216.

■ BARTELS, DISTRICT JUDGE[, joined by LUMBARD and MANSFIELD, CIRCUIT JUDGES]:

This is an appeal from a judgment of the United States District Court for the Western District of New York, Burke, J., affirming the discharge by the Bankruptcy Court of certain student loan obligations in proceedings brought on by twenty-one voluntary petitions in bankruptcy. The sole question for review is the effect of the repeal by Congress of Section 439A of the Higher Education Act of 1965, as amended, 20 U.S.C. § 1087–3, pertaining to dischargeability of student loans, on petitions in bankruptcy commenced but not disposed of prior to the date of such repeal.

The pertinent facts are undisputed. Each of the loans here involved is either owed to or guaranteed by appellant New York State Higher Education Services Corporation ("NYSHESC"), and each was reinsured to appellant by the United States Office of Education by agreements entered into pursuant to the Higher Education Act of 1965, as amended, 20 U.S.C. §§ 1071 et seq. At the time the twenty-one voluntary petitions in bankruptcy were filed, § 1087–3 of Title 20 provided, in part, as follows:

(a) A debt which is a loan insured or guaranteed under the authority of this part may be released by a discharge in bankruptcy under the Bankruptcy Act only if such discharge is granted after the five-year period . . . beginning on the date of commencement of the repayment period of such loan, except that prior to the expiration of that five-year period, such loan may be released only if the court in which the proceeding is pending determines that payment from future income or other wealth will impose an undue hardship on the debtor or his dependents.

(b) Subsection (a) of this section shall be effective with respect to any proceedings begun under the Bankruptcy Act on or after September 30, 1977.

This provision was subsequently repealed effective November 6, 1978, however, by Section 317 of the Bankruptcy Reform Act of 1978 ("BRA"), Pub. L. 95–598,[2] and was replaced . . . by Section 523(a)(8), as amended by Pub. L. 96–56, [which] provides:

(a) A discharge under section 727, 1141, or 1328(b) of this title does not discharge an individual debtor from any debt . . .

(8) for an educational loan made, insured, or guaranteed by a governmental unit, or made under any program funded in whole or in part by a governmental unit or a nonprofit institution of higher education, unless—

(A) such loan first became due before five years . . . before the date of the filing of the petition; or

(B) excepting such debt from discharge under this paragraph will impose an undue hardship on the debtor and the debtor's dependents; . . .

Under section 402(a) of the BRA, this replacement provision did not become effective until October 1, 1979, approximately eleven months after the effective date of the repeal of its predecessor, 20 U.S.C. § 1087–3.[3] According to appellant, this interruption in the rule of nondischargeability of student loans constitutes a loophole through which certain student loan debtors now attempt to escape their repayment obligations.

The Bankruptcy Court disposed of all of the twenty-one petitions by two identical memorandum decisions and orders dated March 16 and April 5, 1979, respectively, holding that because the petitions were considered and resolved after the repeal of 20 U.S.C. § 1087–3 but before the effective date of 11 U.S.C. § 523(a)(8), the Bankruptcy Court no

---

[2] Section 317 of the Bankruptcy Reform Act of 1978 ("BRA") provides that "Section 439A of part B of title IV of the Higher Education Act of 1965 (20 U.S.C. § 1087–3) is repealed." The effective date of this section appears in section 402(d) of the BRA, which provides that "(t)he amendments made by sections 217, 218, 230, 247, 302, 314(j), 317, 327, 328, 338, and 411 of this Act shall take effect on the date of enactment of this Act."

[3] Section 402(a) of the BRA provides that "[e]xcept as otherwise provided in this title, this Act shall take effect on October 1, 1979."

longer had jurisdiction "to determine that the subject bankrupts are not entitled to a discharge, since the law which exists at the time of this decision has no provision for the denial of the discharge of student loans." Accordingly, Bankruptcy Judge Hayes ordered that the student loan debts in question be discharged. His decision was affirmed by the district court in a brief order on September 27, 1979, and this appeal followed. . . .

We conclude that the hiatus between the repeal of section 1087–3 of Title 20 and the effective date of its successor provision, 11 U.S.C. § 523(a)(8), was purely a manifestation of congressional inadvertence and that to follow blindly the plain meaning of the statute without regard to the obvious intention of Congress would create an absurd result in accord with neither established principles of statutory construction nor common sense. Accordingly, the decisions of the district court and the bankruptcy court below must be reversed.

Analysis of the legislative history of the BRA supports appellant's contention that the failure of the effective dates of the repeal and replacement statutes to coincide resulted from a mistake of Congress. Section 1087–3 of Title 20 of the United States Code was enacted in 1976 to prevent abuse of the bankruptcy laws by students petitioning for bankruptcy immediately upon graduation without attempting to realize the potential increased earning capacity which education may provide. [Citation.] By creating a special exception from discharge for education loans, Congress hoped to insure a more realistic view of a student's ability to repay the debt.

During the 95th Congress, however, bankruptcy reform legislation was introduced in the House of Representatives which included the repeal of section 1087–3 in order to "restore the law to where it had been before the 1976 amendment . . ." H.Rep. 95–595, 95th Cong., 1st Sess., 132, *reprinted in* [1978] U.S.Code Cong. & Admin.News, pp. 5787, 6093. This repeal provision, which was to take effect on the date of enactment of the legislation, was predicated upon the view that student abuses were not as widespread as had been thought and, therefore, did not warrant special treatment under the bankruptcy laws. This sentiment did not prevail, however, and when the legislation H.R. 8200 was reintroduced for further consideration in early 1978, the House, by amendment to section 523(a)(8) of the bill, adopted a replacement provision making nondischargeable educational loans insured or guaranteed under Part B of Title IV of the Higher Education Act of 1965, *supra.*

Similar bankruptcy reform legislation was introduced in the Senate in October 1977 as S. 2266. While § 317 of S. 2266 also provided for the repeal of 20 U.S.C. § 1087–3, the bill contained a more comprehensive replacement provision in section 523(a)(8) excepting from discharge any debt for an educational loan. The effective date of both sections 317 and 523(a)(8) was October 1, 1979. The differences between the House and Senate versions of the relevant provisions were resolved by the conference committee in September 1978. Because the Senate members would not acquiesce to the limited nondischargeability provision contained in H.R. 8200, the committee amended the House bill by broadening the scope of section 523(a)(8) to make nondischargeable all educational loans owing to or insured or guaranteed by a governmental unit or a nonprofit institution of higher education. The committee failed, however, to notice that the section repealing 20 U.S.C. § 1087–3 as of the date of enactment remained in the House bill. Thus, as subsequently approved by Congress and signed into law by the President, the BRA contained the House repeal provision and, due to the insistence of the Senate conferees, a broad replacement provision, the effective dates of which did not coincide. There is no indication in the history of the BRA that Congress intended to legislate such an inconsistency or that it sought for some unexpressed reason to create an approximately eleven-month hiatus for the benefit of student loan debtors.

The inadvertence of this action was subsequently acknowledged by the Senate Committee on the Judiciary . . . .

> The gap in coverage of a prohibition on the discharge in bankruptcy of loans made under the Guaranteed Student Loan Program resulting from the early repeal of section 349A (sic) is very undesirable and totally inadvertent. . . . [An] inadvertent "gap" [was] created when the applicable section of the Higher Education Act of 1965 prohibiting discharge of student loans was repealed as of November 6, 1978, and its replacement section in Title II was not made effective until October 1, 1979. Congress obviously did not mean to create a gap and at all times held to the principle of nondischargeability of student loans . . . .[7]

Although such an interpretation by a subsequent Congress is not necessarily controlling, it may be useful in determining the intention of an earlier Congress. [Citation.]

The language of the BRA gives further credence to this interpretation. In addition to the obvious significance of the inclusion of a more comprehensive exception provision in section 523(a)(8) of the BRA than had existed previously in section 1087–3 of Title 20 U.S.C., the BRA also includes a "savings" provision in section 403(a) which preserves the

---

[7] . . . The remarks of various members of Congress . . . confirm the conclusion of the Senate Judiciary Committee quoted above. Senator DeConcini (D.Ariz.), principal sponsor and floor manager for the BRA in the Senate, explained the intent of Congress with respect to . . . the BRA:

> . . . [T]he Bankruptcy Reform Act . . . inadvertently created a "gap" in provisions of existing law concerning nondischargeability of student loans in a bankruptcy case. Public Law 95–598 repealed provisions in the Higher Education Act making student loans nondischargeable. It was the intent to merely shift the location of the nondischargeability provision from the Higher Education Act to the Bankruptcy Code, 11 U.S.C. However, . . . a "gap" was created between November 6, 1978, and October 1, 1979, when it can be argued that there is no nondischargeability provision in the law although it clearly was not the intent of Congress to have created such a gap.

125 Cong. Rec. S. 9160 (daily ed. July 11, 1979). . . .

substantive rights of the parties to actions commenced prior to the effective date of the BRA. Section 403(a) provides as follows:

> A case commenced under the Bankruptcy Act, and all matters and proceedings in or relating to any such case, shall be conducted and determined under such Act as if this Act had not been enacted, and the substantive rights of parties in connection with any such bankruptcy case, matter or proceeding shall continue to be governed by the law applicable to such case, matter or proceeding as if the Act had not been enacted.

Because this section, together with the BRA as a whole, did not become effective until October 1, 1979, it is not dispositive of this appeal. However, we consider it persuasive evidence of Congress' desire not to impair the rights of parties to actions commenced under the old Bankruptcy Act.

Finally, we note the apparent absurdity of a construction of the BRA which, for no discernible reason, would permit the discharge of student loans by debtors who, by sheer chance, have their bankruptcy petitions adjudicated during the eleven-month gap. Both before and after this period, nondischargeability has been and will continue to be the rule; absent an explicit statement of intent by Congress to provide a period of "amnesty" for student loan debtors, to recognize the repeal of section 1087–3 before giving effect to either section 523(a)(8) of the BRA or the savings provision in section 403(a) would, it seems to us, effectuate a legislative mistake prejudicial to the substantive rights of appellant.

The result of an obvious mistake should not be enforced, particularly when it "overrides common sense and evident statutory purpose." . . . It is a well established principle of statutory construction that a statute should not be applied strictly in accord with its literal meaning where to do so would pervert its manifest purpose. Nowhere has this principle been expressed more eloquently than by Judge Learned Hand in his concurring opinion in *Guiseppi v. Walling*, 144 F.2d 608, 624 (2d Cir.1944), where he stated:

> There is no surer way to misread any document than to read it literally; in every interpretation we must pass between Scylla and Charybdis; and I certainly do not wish to add to the barrels of ink that have been spent in logging the route. As nearly as we can, we must put ourselves in the place of those who uttered the words, and try to divine how they would have dealt with the unforeseen situation; and, although their words are by far the most decisive evidence of what they would have done, they are by no means final. [Citation.]

In this case, a literal application of the effective date of section 317 of the BRA, repealing 20 U.S.C. § 1087–3, would require us to disregard its intended purpose.[9] We hold, therefore, that the premature repeal of

---

[9]   "[F]or the letter killeth but the spirit giveth life." 2 Corinthians 3.6.

section 1087–3 is of no effect with respect to proceedings commenced prior to the effective date of the BRA on October 1, 1979. Accordingly, the decision of the district court is hereby reversed, and the petitions at bar are remanded to the bankruptcy court for further proceedings in accordance with this opinion.

NOTES AND QUESTIONS

1.   In re Hogan, 707 F.2d 209, 210 n.2 (5th Cir. 1983), also concerned the "inadvertent gap" created by the repeal and effective dates of the Bankruptcy Reform Act:

> The disposition of this case is compelled by *In the Matter of Williamson*. To preserve our institutional integrity, we must adhere to the precedent established by a prior panel. We cannot do so, however, without expressing our concern that in following the lead of our colleagues of the other circuits we have used a rule of statutory construction to effectively enact a law the Congress did not adopt. There is no ambiguity in the two statutes. The courts have strained to rectify congressional inadvertence by saying, in effect, that one statute is effective 11 months longer than Congress said it was. *See, e.g.*, Carnegia v. Georgia Higher Educ. Assistance Corp., 691 F.2d 482 (11th Cir. 1982); *In the Matter of Williamson*; Wisconsin Higher Educ. Aids Bd. v. Lipke, 630 F.2d 1225 (7th Cir. 1980); *In re Adamo, cert. denied sub nom* Williams v. New York State Higher Educ. Servs. Corp., 449 U.S. 843 (1980); In re Hawes,

No. B78–28 (D.N.J. 1979), *aff'd per curiam*, 633 F.2d 210 (3d Cir. 1980).

The result of these cases comports with one's sense of fairness, and would draw our votes if we were operating in a legislative setting. But we are not. In underscoring our concern, we highlight our apprehension that the course we have chosen to pursue has taken us over the line which separates legislative interpretation from legislating. We therefore caution those who would read this opinion to signal that such interpretative glossing will come easily in the future. It will not.

2. Independent Ins. Agents v. Clarke, 955 F.2d 731 (D.C. Cir. 1992), involved the inadvertent repeal of § 92 of the National Bank Act. Section 92 permitted any national bank, or its branch, located in a community of not more than 5,000 inhabitants to sell insurance to customers outside that community. Although early provisions of Title 12 of the United States Code included § 92, the 1952 U.S.C. and subsequent editions omitted it, with a note indicating that Congress had repealed the section in 1918. The parties in the case did not raise the issue of the validity of § 92, but, assuming the section to be applicable, differed as to its interpretation.

The Court of Appeals, acting *sua sponte,* held that § 92 had been repealed in 1918, notwithstanding the perception of Congress, other courts, and the Comptroller of the Currency that the section remained in effect. The court rejected arguments that the deletion of § 92 was the result of mistake in punctuation (in this case, the misplacement of quotation marks around restated text of the statute, which excluded the language at issue) and that its repeal should therefore be ignored. The court stated:

> We recognize that, in order to give effect to a clear congressional intent, federal courts have assumed a rather broad responsibility for correcting flaws in the language and punctuation of federal statutes. There is a point, however, beyond which a court cannot go without trespassing on the exclusive prerogatives of the legislative branch.

> We believe we are at that point. It is one thing for a court to bend statutory language to make it achieve a clearly stated congressional purpose; it is quite another for a court to reinstate a law that, intentionally or unintentionally, Congress has stricken from the statute books. If the deletion of section 92 was a mistake, it is one for Congress to correct, not the courts.

Id. at 739. The Supreme Court reversed, holding that § 92 was not repealed in 1918. Writing for a unanimous Court, Justice Souter concluded that the deletion of the section "was a simple scrivener's error, a mistake made by someone unfamiliar with the law's object and design. . . . The true meaning of the . . . Act is clear beyond question, and so we repunctuate." United States National Bank of Oregon v. Independent Ins. Agents, 508 U.S. 439, 462 (1993).

3. Can you reconcile the different approaches of the Second Circuit in *In re Adamo* and the D.C. Circuit in *Independent Insurance Agents v. Clarke*?

NOTE: CORRECTING "PLAIN" ERRORS IN STATUTORY TEXT

If the meaning is indeed "plain," why *shouldn't* a court "countenance" applying the plain meaning to the statute even where it leads to "absurd or futile results plainly at variance with the policy of the legislation as a whole"? How does a court know what is "the policy of the legislation as a whole," and which application of the statute is "plainly at variance" with that policy? As we have seen (and will see again), discerning a coherent policy underlying legislation is not always an easy task, though it is usually possible to ascertain *some* policy objective. In some circumstances, however, the statutory text is so flawed that one cannot articulate *any* policy under which the wording would make sense. The following is an example of an error in legislative drafting ascribable only to inadvertence.

Amalgamated Transit Union Local 1309 v. Laidlaw Transit Services, Inc., 435 F.3d 1140 (9th Cir.), rehearing en banc denied, 448 F.3d 1092 (9th Cir. 2006), involved the interpretation of a provision of the Class Action Fairness Act.

The statute, 28 USC 1453(c)(1), provides:

[A] court of appeals may accept an appeal from an order of a district court granting or denying a motion to remand a class action to the State court from which it was removed if application is made to the court of appeals not less than 7 days after entry of the order.

The three-judge panel held that the "not less than" provision in the statute must mean "not more than."

We remain somewhat troubled that, in contrast to most statutory construction cases where we are usually asked to construe the meaning of an ambiguous phrase or word, we are here faced with the task of striking a word passed on by both Houses of Congress and approved by the President, and replacing it with a word of the exact opposite meaning. We nonetheless agree with the Tenth Circuit, the only other circuit to address this issue, that there is no apparent logical reason for the choice of the word "less" in the statute, use of the word "less" is, in fact, illogical and contrary to the stated purpose of the provision, and the statute should therefore be read to require that an application to appeal under § 1453(c)(1) must be filed-in accordance with the requirements of FRAP 5—not more than 7 days after the district court's order.

The Circuit Court denied rehearing en banc, with 6 dissenters discussing and rejecting both the "scrivener's error" and "absurd results" doctrines.

Which approach shows more deference to Congress: judicial correction of inadvertent errors in a law in accordance with congressional intent, or application of the law as enacted by Congress?

For a comparative law perspective, consider, **France, Cassation Chambre Criminelle, decision of March 8, 1930**, D.1930.I.101, note Voirin.

The law in question forbade descending from a train "*when* it has completely stopped" (emphasis supplied). Apparently, the legislature intended to forbid descending from a train *before* it has completely stopped. The defendant descended from a still-moving train, and was fined for this conduct. He claimed that he had not violated the law, but had in fact obeyed it to the letter (though it is doubtful he knew of the drafting error in the penal code at the time he got off the train). The Cour de cassation rejected the appeal from the lower court's decision upholding the fine, on the ground that the lower court was entitled to interpret the text as forbidding defendant's act.

The commentary of Professor Pierre Voirin justifies the result on the ground that there was evidence "intrinsic" to the text of the law to indicate that the legislature intended to prohibit descent from still-moving trains. (It appears that other provisions of the same law must have supported that interpretation, though he does not quote them.) He distinguishes judicial error-correction based on "intrinsic" evidence of statutory intent from "extrinsic" evidence of legislative error. He finds the latter illegitimate.

He evokes a then-recent High Court decision in which the Cour de cassation ruled as if a provision of the civil code concerning the guardians of minors had not been repealed, when in fact it had: "Even if it occurred unintentionally and unbeknown to the legislature, the repeal nonetheless occurred in fact, and nothing in the current text of the civil code permits one to avoid that result, for the general principle, from which the repealed provision derogated, remaining in effect, barred any room for interpretation."

Professor Voirin then explores the consequences of allowing "extrinsic" considerations, such as the judges' conviction that the legislature made a mistake, to justify courts' error-correction:

> If the interpreter could correct texts that are enacted, promulgated, and published in the regular fashion, on the pretext of giving effect to the true will of the legislature, when this intent is discerned exclusively by extrinsic information, that would be the end of the guarantees that the formalities of legislative or administrative procedure assure to citizens. And once embarked on this slope, no doubt we will manage to declare without effect the formulation of some laws whose terms each Assembly will have voted, by giving a very different meaning to those words, for in fact there will have been no "legislative intent."

Do these criticisms sound familiar? Should it make a difference to the defendant's criminal liability in the train case that the textual error could be corrected based on other provisions of the same statute, even though defendant's conduct comported perfectly with the precisely applicable provision? Would your answer be the same if defendant faced only civil liability?

c. TEXTUAL VAGUENESS AND THE VOID FOR VAGUENESS DOCTRINE

In addition to difficulties resulting from literal meanings that seem to strain plausibility, the opposite problems often confront statutory interpreters: statutory provisions that are so ambiguous or vague as to have no straightforward application whatsoever. While the terms "ambiguous" and "vague" are often used as synonyms in casual conversation, their legal meanings are quite distinct.

An ambiguous term or phrase is one that is susceptible to multiple reasonable interpretations. For example, a "seizure" may refer to a medical episode or the attempt to detain a suspect, and "arms" may refer to weapons or limbs. In many cases, the words surrounding a homonym clarify which meaning obtains: when we are told the "police officer seized the subject," we do not think she induced him to shake violently, and if a citizen claims he has a "constitutional right to bear arms," he is probably not referring to the right to wear a tank top (though he *might* be if he claimed a right to "bare arms"). Precisely because a term or phrase is sometimes susceptible to multiple reasonable meanings, the rule of lenity can serve as a tiebreaker in deciding on the *best* meaning by breaking the tie in favor of the defendant. And once the ambiguity is resolved, the interpretive problem is resolved, too: for example, in the wake of *Yates v. United States, supra,* no longer must commercial fishermen risk the wrath of the Sarbanes-Oxley Act for tossing their undersized catch overboard.

By contrast, a vague term or phrase is one for which multiple interpreters may agree about its conceptual meaning but who nevertheless disagree (or are at least uncertain) about how that term or phrase should be applied across a range of individual cases. For instance, as you will see below, two interpreters agree on what it means, conceptually, "to annoy" someone, and yet may reasonably disagree—or at least have great difficulty in deciding—whether a particular kind of conduct is "annoying." Even if we decide that spitting on someone is annoying, that doesn't answer whether poking that person is. And even if poking is annoying, is eyerolling? Coughing rudely? Interrupting? This kind of persistent indeterminacy across a range of borderline cases means that a single effort at interpretation may be unable to definitively resolve all permissible applications of the statutory term or phrase in question. Deciding that spitting is annoying doesn't necessarily establish that interrupting is. While vague statutory terms tend to be infrequent, where they arise, problems with their application tend to persist, eluding conclusive interpretive resolution.

As *Johnson v. United States* illustrates, when a legislature sets out a criminal prohibition in such a vague manner as to raise *repeated* problems in its interpretation and application, potential due process concerns arise related to the persistent inability of the statutory text to provide fair notice.

Johnson v. United States

Supreme Court of the United States, 2015.
576 U.S. 591, 135 S.Ct. 2551, 192 L.Ed.2d 569.

■ JUSTICE SCALIA delivered the opinion of the Court[, in which CHIEF JUSTICE ROBERTS, JUSTICE GINSBURG, JUSTICE BREYER, JUSTICE SOTOMAYOR, and JUSTICE KAGAN joined].

Under the Armed Career Criminal Act of 1984, a defendant convicted of being a felon in possession of a firearm faces more severe punishment if he has three or more previous convictions for a "violent felony," a term defined to include any felony that "involves conduct that presents a serious potential risk of physical injury to another." 18 U.S.C. § 924(e)(2)(B). We must decide whether this part of the definition of a violent felony survives the Constitution's prohibition of vague criminal laws.

I

Federal law forbids certain people—such as convicted felons, persons committed to mental institutions, and drug users—to ship, possess, and receive firearms. § 922(g). In general, the law punishes violation of this ban by up to 10 years' imprisonment. § 924(a)(2). But if the violator has three or more earlier convictions for a "serious drug offense" or a "violent felony," the Armed Career Criminal Act increases his prison term to a minimum of 15 years and a maximum of life. § 924(e)(1); [citation.] The Act defines "violent felony" as follows:

"any crime punishable by imprisonment for a term exceeding one year . . . that—

"(i) has as an element the use, attempted use, or threatened use of physical force against the person of another; or

"(ii) is burglary, arson, or extortion, involves use of explosives, *or otherwise involves conduct that presents a serious potential risk of physical injury to another*." § 924(e)(2)(B) (emphasis added).

The closing words of this definition, italicized above, have come to be known as the Act's residual clause. Since 2007, this Court has decided four cases attempting to discern its meaning. We have held that the residual clause (1) covers Florida's offense of attempted burglary, *James v. United States*, 550 U.S. 192; (2) does *not* cover New Mexico's offense of driving under the influence, *Begay v. United States*, 553 U.S. 137 (2008); (3) does *not* cover Illinois' offense of failure to report to a penal institution, *Chambers v. United States*, 555 U.S. 1224 (2009); and (4) does cover Indiana's offense of vehicular flight from a law-enforcement officer, *Sykes v. United States*, 564 U.S. 1 (2011). In both *James* and *Sykes*, the Court rejected suggestions by dissenting Justices that the residual clause violates the Constitution's prohibition of vague criminal laws. [Citations.] This case involves the application of the residual clause to another crime, Minnesota's offense of unlawful possession of a short-barreled shotgun. Petitioner Samuel Johnson is a felon with a long criminal record. In 2010, the Federal Bureau of Investigation began to monitor him because of his involvement in a white-supremacist organization that the Bureau suspected was planning to commit acts of terrorism. During the investigation, Johnson disclosed to undercover agents that he had manufactured explosives and that he planned to attack "the Mexican consulate" in Minnesota, "progressive bookstores," and " 'liberals.' " Johnson showed the agents his AK-47 rifle, several semiautomatic firearms, and over 1,000 rounds of ammunition.

After his eventual arrest, Johnson pleaded guilty to being a felon in possession of a firearm in violation of § 922(g). The Government requested an enhanced sentence under the Armed Career Criminal Act. It argued that three of Johnson's previous offenses—including unlawful possession of a short-barreled shotgun, *see* Minn. Stat. § 609.67 (2006)—qualified as violent felonies. The District Court agreed and sentenced Johnson to a 15-year prison term under the Act. The Court of Appeals affirmed. We granted certiorari to decide whether Minnesota's offense of unlawful possession of a short-barreled shotgun ranks as a violent felony under the residual clause. We later asked the parties to present reargument addressing the compatibility of the residual clause with the Constitution's prohibition of vague criminal laws.

II

The Fifth Amendment provides that "[n]o person shall ... be deprived of life, liberty, or property, without due process of law." Our cases establish that the Government violates this guarantee by taking away someone's life, liberty, or property under a criminal law so vague that it fails to give ordinary people fair notice of the conduct it punishes, or so standardless that it invites arbitrary enforcement. [Citation.] (1983). The prohibition of vagueness in criminal statutes "is a well-recognized requirement, consonant alike with ordinary notions of fair play and the settled rules of law," and a statute that flouts it "violates the first essential of due process." [Citation.] These principles apply not only to statutes defining elements of crimes, but also to statutes fixing sentences. [Citation.]

In *Taylor v. United States*, 495 U.S. 575, 600 (1990), this Court held that the Armed Career Criminal Act requires courts to use a framework known as the categorical approach when deciding whether an offense "is burglary, arson, or extortion, involves use of explosives, or otherwise involves conduct that presents a serious potential risk of physical injury to another." Under the categorical approach, a court assesses whether a crime qualifies as a violent felony "in terms of how the law defines the offense and not in terms of how an individual offender might have committed it on a particular occasion." *Begay, supra*, at 141.

Deciding whether the residual clause covers a crime thus requires a court to picture the kind of conduct that the crime involves in "the ordinary case," and to judge whether that abstraction presents a serious potential risk of physical injury. *James, supra,* at 208. The court's task goes beyond deciding whether creation of risk is an element of the crime. That is so because, unlike the part of the definition of a violent felony that asks whether the crime "has *as an element* the use . . . of physical force," the residual clause asks whether the crime "*involves conduct*" that presents too much risk of physical injury. What is more, the inclusion of burglary and extortion among the enumerated offenses preceding the residual clause confirms that the court's task also goes beyond evaluating the chances that the physical acts that make up the crime will injure someone. The act of making an extortionate demand or breaking and entering into someone's home does not, in and of itself, normally cause physical injury. Rather, risk of injury arises because the extortionist might engage in violence *after* making his demand or because the burglar might confront a resident in the home *after* breaking and entering.

We are convinced that the indeterminacy of the wide-ranging inquiry required by the residual clause both denies fair notice to defendants and invites arbitrary enforcement by judges. Increasing a defendant's sentence under the clause denies due process of law.

A

Two features of the residual clause conspire to make it unconstitutionally vague. In the first place, the residual clause leaves grave uncertainty about how to estimate the risk posed by a crime. It ties the judicial assessment of risk to a judicially imagined "ordinary case" of a crime, not to real-world facts or statutory elements. How does one go about deciding what kind of conduct the "ordinary case" of a crime involves? "A statistical analysis of the state reporter? A survey? Expert evidence? Google? Gut instinct?" [Citation.] To take an example, does the ordinary instance of witness tampering involve offering a witness a bribe? Or threatening a witness with violence? Critically, picturing the criminal's behavior is not enough; as we have discussed, assessing "potential risk" seemingly requires the judge to imagine how the idealized ordinary case of the crime subsequently plays out. . . . The residual clause offers no reliable way to choose between these competing accounts of what "ordinary" attempted burglary involves.

At the same time, the residual clause leaves uncertainty about how much risk it takes for a crime to qualify as a violent felony. It is one thing to apply an imprecise "serious potential risk" standard to real-world facts; it is quite another to apply it to a judge-imagined abstraction. By asking whether the crime "*otherwise* involves conduct that presents a serious potential risk," moreover, the residual clause forces courts to interpret "serious potential risk" in light of the four enumerated crimes—burglary, arson, extortion, and crimes involving the use of explosives. These offenses are "far from clear in respect to the degree of risk each poses." *Begay,* 553 U.S., at 143. Does the ordinary burglar invade an occupied home by night or an unoccupied home by day? Does the typical extortionist threaten his victim in person with the use of force, or does he threaten his victim by mail with the revelation of embarrassing personal information? By combining indeterminacy about how to measure the risk posed by a crime with indeterminacy about how much risk it takes for the crime to qualify as a violent felony, the residual clause produces more unpredictability and arbitrariness than the Due Process Clause tolerates.

This Court has acknowledged that the failure of "persistent efforts . . . to establish a standard" can provide evidence of vagueness. [Citation.] Here, this Court's repeated attempts and repeated failures to craft a principled and objective standard out of the residual clause confirm its hopeless indeterminacy. The present case, our fifth about the meaning of the residual clause, opens a new front of uncertainty. When deciding whether unlawful possession of a short-barreled shotgun is a violent felony, do we confine our attention to the risk that the shotgun will go off by accident while in someone's possession? Or do we also consider the possibility that the person possessing the shotgun will later use it to commit a crime? The inclusion of burglary and extortion among the enumerated offenses suggests that a crime may qualify under the residual clause even if the physical injury is remote from the criminal act. But how remote is too remote? Once again, the residual clause yields no answers. . . .

It has been said that the life of the law is experience. Nine years' experience trying to derive meaning from the residual clause convinces us that we have embarked upon a failed enterprise. Each of the uncertainties in the residual clause may be tolerable in isolation, but "their sum makes a task for us which at best could be only guesswork." [Citation.] Invoking so shapeless a provision to condemn someone to prison for 15 years to life does not comport with the Constitution's guarantee of due process.

B

The Government and the dissent claim that there will be straightforward cases under the residual clause, because some crimes clearly pose a serious potential risk of physical injury to another. True enough, though we think many of the cases the Government and the dissent deem easy turn out not to be so easy after all. Consider just one of the Government's examples, Connecticut's offense of "rioting at a correctional institution." *See United States* v. *Johnson*, 616 F. 3d 85 (2d Cir. 2010). That certainly sounds like a violent felony—until one realizes that Connecticut defines this offense to include taking part in "any disorder, disturbance, strike, riot or other organized disobedience to the rules and regulations" of the prison. Conn. Gen. Stat. § 53a–179b(a) (2012). Who is to say which the ordinary "disorder" most closely resembles—a full-fledged prison riot, a food-fight in the prison cafeteria, or a "passive and nonviolent [act] such as disregarding an order to move," *Johnson*, 616 F. 3d, at 95 (Parker, J., dissenting)?

In all events, although statements in some of our opinions could be read to suggest otherwise, our *holdings* squarely contradict the theory that a vague provision is constitutional merely because there is some conduct that clearly falls within the provision's grasp. For instance, we have deemed a law prohibiting grocers from charging an "unjust or unreasonable rate" void for vagueness—even though charging someone a thousand dollars for a pound of sugar would surely be unjust and unreasonable. *L. Cohen Grocery Co.*, 255 U.S., at 89. We have similarly deemed void for vagueness a law prohibiting people on sidewalks from "conduct[ing] themselves in a manner annoying to persons passing by"— even though spitting in someone's face would surely be annoying. *Coates* v. *Cincinnati*, 402 U.S. 611 (1971). These decisions refute any suggestion that the existence of *some* obviously risky crimes establishes the residual clause's constitutionality.

Resisting the force of these decisions, the dissent insists that "a statute is void for vagueness only if it is vague in all its applications." It claims that the prohibition of unjust or unreasonable rates in *L. Cohen Grocery* was "vague in all applications," even though one can easily envision rates so high that they are unreasonable by any measure. It seems to us that the dissent's supposed requirement of vagueness in all applications is not a requirement at all, but a tautology: If we hold a statute to be vague, it is vague in all its applications (and never mind the reality). If the existence of some clearly unreasonable rates would not save the law in *L. Cohen Grocery*, why should the existence of some clearly risky crimes save the residual clause? . . .

Finally, the dissent urges us to save the residual clause from vagueness by interpreting it to refer to the risk posed by the particular conduct in which the defendant engaged, not the risk posed by the ordinary case of the defendant's crime. In other words, the dissent suggests that we jettison for the residual clause (though not for the enumerated crimes) the categorical approach adopted in *Taylor*, *see* 495 U.S., at 599–602 . . . . *Taylor* had good reasons to adopt the categorical approach, reasons that apply no less to the residual clause than to the enumerated crimes. *Taylor* explained that the relevant part of the Armed Career Criminal Act "refers to 'a person who . . . has three previous convictions' for—not a person who has committed—three previous violent felonies or drug offenses." 495 U.S., at 600. This emphasis on convictions indicates that "Congress intended the sentencing court to look only to the fact that the defendant had been convicted of crimes falling within certain categories, and not to the facts underlying the prior convictions." *Ibid. Taylor* also pointed out the utter impracticability of requiring a sentencing court to reconstruct, long after the original conviction, the conduct underlying that conviction. For example, if the original conviction rested on a guilty plea, no record of the underlying facts may be available. "[T]he only plausible interpretation" of the law, therefore, requires use of the categorical approach. *Id.*, at 602. . . .

C

That brings us to *stare decisis*. This is the first case in which the Court has received briefing and heard argument from the parties about whether the residual clause is void for vagueness. In *James*, however, the Court stated in a footnote that it was "not persuaded by [the principal dissent's] suggestion . . . that the residual provision is unconstitutionally vague." 550 U.S., at 210, n. 6. In *Sykes*, the Court again rejected a dissenting opinion's claim of vagueness. 564 U.S., at 15–16.

The doctrine of *stare decisis* allows us to revisit an earlier decision where experience with its application reveals that it is unworkable. *Payne* v. *Tennessee*, 501 U.S. 808, 827. Experience is all the more instructive when the decision in question rejected a claim of unconstitutional vagueness. Unlike other judicial mistakes that need correction, the error of having rejected a vagueness challenge manifests itself precisely in subsequent judicial decisions: the inability of later opinions to impart the predictability that the earlier opinion forecast. Here, the experience of the federal courts leaves no doubt about the unavoidable uncertainty and arbitrariness of adjudication under the residual clause. Even after *Sykes* tried to clarify the residual clause's meaning, the provision remains a "judicial morass that defies systemic solution," "a black hole of confusion and uncertainty" that frustrates any effort to impart "some sense of order and direction." *United States* v. *Vann*, 660 F. 3d 771, 787 (4th Cir. 2011) (Agee, J., concurring).

This Court's cases make plain that [even decisions rendered after full adversarial presentation may have to yield to the lessons of subsequent experience. Although it is a vital rule of judicial self-government, *stare decisis* does not matter for its own sake. It matters because it "promotes the evenhanded, predictable, and consistent development of legal principles." *Payne, supra,* at 827. Decisions under the residual clause have proved to be anything but evenhanded, predictable, or consistent. Standing by *James* and *Sykes* would undermine, rather than promote, the goals that *stare decisis* is meant to serve.

We hold that imposing an increased sentence under the residual clause of the Armed Career Criminal Act violates the Constitution's guarantee of due process. Our contrary holdings in *James* and *Sykes* are overruled. Today's decision does not call into question application of the Act to the four enumerated offenses, or the remainder of the Act's definition of a violent felony.

We reverse the judgment of the Court of Appeals for the Eighth Circuit and remand the case for further proceedings consistent with this opinion.

It is so ordered.

[The opinion of Justice Kennedy, concurring in the judgment, has been omitted.]

■ JUSTICE THOMAS, concurring in the judgment.

I agree with the Court that Johnson's sentence cannot stand. But rather than use the Fifth Amendment's Due Process Clause to nullify an Act of Congress, I would resolve this case on more ordinary grounds. Under conventional principles of interpretation and our precedents, the offense of unlawfully possessing a short-barreled shotgun does not constitute a "violent felony" under the residual clause of the Armed Career Criminal Act (ACCA). . . .

In relevant part, ACCA defines a "violent felony" as a "crime punishable by imprisonment for a term exceeding one year" that either

"(i) has as an element the use, attempted use, or threatened use of physical force against the person of another; or

"(ii) is burglary, arson, or extortion, involves use of explosives, or otherwise involves conduct that presents a serious potential risk of physical injury to another." 18 U.S.C. § 924(e)(2)(B).

The offense of unlawfully possessing a short-barreled shotgun neither satisfies the first clause of this definition nor falls within the enumerated offenses in the second. It therefore can constitute a violent felony only if it falls within ACCA's so-called "residual clause"—*i.e.*, if it "involves conduct that presents a serious potential risk of physical injury to another." § 924(e)(2)(B)(ii).

To determine whether an offense falls within the residual clause, we consider "whether the conduct encompassed by the elements of the offense, in the ordinary case, presents a serious potential risk of injury to another." [Citation.] . . . In light of the elements of and reported convictions for the unlawful possession of a short-barreled shotgun, this crime does not "involv[e] conduct that presents a serious potential risk of physical injury to another," § 924(e)(2)(B)(ii). The acts that form the basis of this offense are simply too remote from a risk of physical injury to fall within the residual clause.

Standing alone, the elements of this offense—(1) unlawfully (2) possessing (3) a short-barreled shotgun—do not describe inherently dangerous conduct. As a conceptual matter, "simple possession [of a firearm], even by a felon, takes place in a variety of ways (*e.g.*, in a closet, in a storeroom, in a car, in a pocket) many, perhaps most, of which do not involve likely accompanying violence." [Citation.] These weapons also can be stored in a manner posing a danger to no one, such as unloaded, disassembled, or locked away. By themselves, the elements of this offense indicate that the ordinary commission of this crime is far less risky than ACCA's enumerated offenses.

Reported convictions support the conclusion that mere possession of a short-barreled shotgun does not, in the ordinary case, pose a serious risk of injury to others. A few examples suffice. In one case, officers found the sawed-off shotgun locked inside a gun cabinet in an empty home.

[Citation.] In another, the firearm was retrieved from the trunk of the defendant's car. [Citation.] In still another, the weapon was found missing a firing pin. [Citation.] In these instances and others, the offense threatened no one.

The Government's theory for why this crime should nonetheless qualify as a "violent felony" is unpersuasive. Although it does not dispute that the unlawful possession of a short-barreled shotgun can occur in a nondangerous manner, the Government contends that this offense poses a serious risk of physical injury due to the connection between short-barreled shotguns and other serious crimes. As the Government explains, these firearms are "weapons not typically possessed by law-abiding citizens for lawful purposes, [citation], are instead primarily intended for use in criminal activity. In light of that intended use, the Government reasons that the ordinary case of this possession offense will involve the *use* of a short-barreled shotgun in a serious crime, a scenario obviously posing a serious risk of physical injury.

But even assuming that those who unlawfully possess these weapons typically intend to use them in a serious crime, the risk that the Government identifies arises not from the act of possessing the weapon, but from the act of using it. Unlike attempted burglary (at least of the type at issue in *James*) or intentional vehicular flight—conduct that by itself often or always invites a dangerous confrontation—possession of a short-barreled shotgun poses a threat *only* when an offender decides to engage in additional, voluntary conduct that is not included in the elements of the crime. Until this weapon is assembled, loaded, or used, for example, it poses no risk of injury to others in and of itself. The risk of injury to others from mere possession of this firearm is too attenuated to treat this offense as a violent felony. I would reverse the Court of Appeals on that basis. . . .

■ JUSTICE ALITO, dissenting.

The Court is tired of the Armed Career Criminal Act of 1984 (ACCA) and in particular its residual clause. Anxious to rid our docket of bothersome residual clause cases, the Court is willing to do what it takes to get the job done. So brushing aside *stare decisis*, the Court holds that the residual clause is unconstitutionally vague even though we have twice rejected that very argument within the last eight years. The canons of interpretation get no greater respect. Inverting the canon that a statute should be construed if possible to avoid unconstitutionality, the Court rejects a reasonable construction of the residual clause that would avoid any vagueness problems, preferring an alternative that the Court finds to be unconstitutionally vague. And the Court is not stopped by the well-established rule that a statute is void for vagueness only if it is vague in all its applications. While conceding that some applications of the residual clause are straightforward, the Court holds that the clause is now void in its entirety. The Court's determination to be done with residual clause cases, if not its fidelity to legal principles, is impressive. . . .

III

The residual clause is not unconstitutionally vague.

A

The Fifth Amendment prohibits the enforcement of vague criminal laws, but the threshold for declaring a law void for vagueness is high. "The strong presumptive validity that attaches to an Act of Congress has led this Court to hold many times that statutes are not automatically invalidated as vague simply because difficulty is found in determining whether certain marginal offenses fall within their language." [Citation.] Rather, it is sufficient if a statute sets out an "ascertainable standard." [Citation.] A statute is thus void for vagueness only if it wholly "fails to provide a person of ordinary intelligence fair notice of what is prohibited, or is so standardless that it authorizes or encourages seriously discriminatory enforcement." [Citation.]

The bar is even higher for sentencing provisions. The fair notice concerns that inform our vagueness doctrine are aimed at ensuring that a " 'person of ordinary intelligence [has] a reasonable opportunity to know what is prohibited, so that he may act accordingly.' " *Hoffman Estates v. Flipside, Hoffman Estates, Inc.*, 455 U.S. 489, 498 (1982) (quoting *Grayned v. City of Rockford*, 408 U.S. 104, 108 (1972)). The fear is that vague laws will " 'trap the innocent.' " 455 U.S., at 498. These concerns have less force when it comes to sentencing provisions, which come into play only after the defendant has been found guilty of the crime in question. Due process does not require, as Johnson oddly suggests, that a "prospective criminal" be able to calculate the precise penalty that a conviction would bring. [Citation]; *see Chapman v. United States*, 500 U.S. 453, 467–468 (1991) (concluding that a vagueness challenge was "particularly" weak "since whatever debate there is would center around the appropriate sentence and not the criminality of the conduct").

B

ACCA's residual clause unquestionably provides an ascertainable standard. It defines "violent felony" to include any offense that "involves conduct that presents a serious potential risk of physical injury to another." 18 U.S.C. § 924(e)(2)(B)(ii). That language is by no means incomprehensible. Nor is it unusual. There are scores of federal and state laws that employ similar standards. . . . If all these laws are unconstitutionally vague, today's decision is not a blast from a sawed-off shotgun; it is a nuclear explosion.

Attempting to avoid such devastation, the Court distinguishes these laws primarily on the ground that almost all of them "require gauging the riskiness of conduct in which an individual defendant engages *on a particular occasion*." . . . . [A]ccording to the Court, ACCA's residual clause is unconstitutionally vague because its standard must be applied to "an idealized ordinary case of the crime" and not, like the vast majority of the laws in the Solicitor General's appendix, to "real-world conduct." ACCA, however, makes no reference to "an idealized ordinary case of the crime." That requirement was the handiwork of this Court in *Taylor* v. *United States,* 495 U.S. 575 (1990). And as I will show, the residual clause can reasonably be interpreted to refer to "real-world conduct."

C

When a statute's constitutionality is in doubt, we have an obligation to interpret the law, if possible, to avoid the constitutional problem. *See, e.g., Edward J. DeBartolo Corp. v. Florida Gulf Coast Building & Constr. Trades Council,* 485 U.S. 568, 575 (1988). As one treatise puts it, "[a] statute should be interpreted in a way that avoids placing its constitutionality in doubt." A. Scalia & B. Garner, Reading Law: The Interpretation of Legal Texts § 38, p. 247 (2012). This canon applies fully when considering vagueness challenges. . . .

The Court all but concedes that the residual clause would be constitutional if it applied to "real-world conduct." Whether that is the *best* interpretation of the residual clause is beside the point. What matters is whether it is a reasonable interpretation of the statute. And it surely is that.

First, this interpretation heeds the pointed distinction that ACCA draws between the "element[s]" of an offense and "conduct." Under § 924(e)(2)(B)(i), a crime qualifies as a "violent felony" if one of its "element[s]" involves "the use, attempted use, or threatened use of physical force against the person of another." But the residual clause, which appears in the very next subsection, § 924(e)(2)(B)(ii), focuses on "conduct"—specifically, "conduct that presents a serious potential risk of physical injury to another." The use of these two different terms in § 924(e) indicates that "conduct" refers to things done during the commission of an offense that are not part of the elements needed for conviction. Because those extra actions vary from case to case, it is natural to interpret "conduct" to mean real-world conduct, not the conduct involved in some Platonic ideal of the offense.

Second, as the Court points out, standards like the one in the residual clause almost always appear in laws that call for application by a trier of fact. This strongly suggests that the residual clause calls for the same sort of application.

Third, if the Court is correct that the residual clause is nearly incomprehensible when interpreted as applying to an "idealized ordinary case of the crime," then that is telling evidence that this is not what Congress intended. When another interpretation is ready at hand, why should we assume that Congress gave the clause a meaning that is impossible—or even, exceedingly difficult—to apply? . . .

E

Even if the categorical approach is used in residual clause cases, however, the clause is still not void for vagueness. "It is well established that vagueness challenges to statutes which do not involve First Amendment freedoms must be examined" on an as-applied basis. [Citation.] "Objections to vagueness under the Due Process Clause rest on the lack of notice, and hence may be overcome in any specific case where reasonable persons would know that their conduct is at risk." [Citation.] Thus, in a due process vagueness case, we will hold that a law is facially invalid "only if the enactment is impermissibly vague in *all* of its applications." [Citation.] . . .

The Court's treatment of this issue is startling. Its facial invalidation precludes a sentencing court that is applying ACCA from counting convictions for even those specific offenses that this Court previously found to fall within the residual clause. [Citations.] Still worse, the Court holds that vagueness bars the use of the residual clause in other cases in which its applicability can hardly be questioned. Attempted rape is an example. [Citation.] Can there be any doubt that "an idealized ordinary case of th[is] crime" "involves conduct that presents a serious potential risk of physical injury to another"? How about attempted arson, attempted kidnapping, solicitation to commit aggravated assault, possession of a loaded weapon with the intent to use it unlawfully against another person possession of a weapon in prison, or compelling a person to act as a prostitute? Is there much doubt that those offenses "involve conduct that presents a serious potential risk of physical injury to another"?

Transforming vagueness doctrine, the Court claims that we have never actually *held* that a statute may be voided for vagueness only when it is vague in all its applications. But that is simply wrong. In *Hoffman Estates*, we reversed a Seventh Circuit decision that voided an ordinance prohibiting the sale of certain items. *See* 455 U.S., at 491. The Seventh Circuit struck down the ordinance because it was "unclear in *some* of its applications," but we reversed and emphasized that a law is void for vagueness "only if [it] is impermissibly vague in all of its applications." *Id.*, at 494–495; [citation]. Applying that principle, we held that the "facial challenge [wa]s unavailing" because "at least some of the items sold . . . [we]re covered" by the ordinance. *Id.*, at 500. These statements were not dicta. They were the holding of the case. Yet the Court does not even mention this binding precedent.

IV

Because I would not strike down ACCA's residual clause, it is necessary for me to address whether Johnson's conviction for possessing a sawed-off shotgun qualifies as a violent felony. Under either the categorical approach or a conduct-specific inquiry, it does.

A

The categorical approach requires us to determine whether "the conduct encompassed by the elements of the offense, in the ordinary case, presents a serious potential risk of injury to another." [Citation.] ... Under these principles, unlawful possession of a sawed-off shotgun qualifies as a violent felony. . . . [S]awed-off shotguns are "not typically possessed by law-abiding citizens for lawful purposes." Instead, they are uniquely attractive to violent criminals. Much easier to conceal than long-barreled shotguns used for hunting and other lawful purposes, short-barreled shotguns can be hidden under a coat, tucked into a bag, or stowed under a car seat. And like a handgun, they can be fired with one hand—except to more lethal effect. These weapons thus combine the deadly characteristics of conventional shotguns with the more convenient handling of handguns. . . .

Congress' treatment of sawed-off shotguns confirms this judgment. As the Government's initial brief colorfully recounts, sawed-off shotguns were a weapon of choice for gangsters and bank robbers during the Prohibition Era. In response, Congress enacted the National Firearms Act of 1934, which required individuals possessing certain especially dangerous weapons—including sawed-off shotguns—to register with the Federal Government and pay a special tax. 26 U.S.C. §§ 5845(a)(1)–(2). The Act was passed on the understanding that "while there is justification for permitting the citizen to keep a pistol or revolver for his own protection without any restriction, there is no reason why anyone except a law officer should have a . . . sawed-off shotgun." H. R. Rep. No. 1780, 73d Cong., 2d Sess., 1 (1934). As amended, the Act imposes strict registration requirements for any individual wishing to possess a covered shotgun, see, e.g., §§ 5822, 5841(b), and illegal possession of such a weapon is punishable by imprisonment for up to 10 years. See §§ 5861(b)–(d), 5871. It is telling that this penalty exceeds that prescribed by federal law for quintessential violent felonies. It thus seems perfectly clear that Congress has long regarded the illegal possession of a sawed-off shotgun as a crime that poses a serious risk of harm to others. . . .

B

If we were to abandon the categorical approach, the facts of Johnson's offense would satisfy the residual clause as well. According to the record in this case, Johnson possessed his sawed-off shotgun while dealing drugs. When police responded to reports of drug activity in a parking lot, they were told by two people that "Johnson and another individual had approached them and offered to sell drugs." The police then searched the vehicle where Johnson was seated as a passenger, and they found a sawed-off shotgun and five bags of marijuana. Johnson admitted that the gun was his.

Understood in this context, Johnson's conduct posed an acute risk of physical injury to another. Drugs and guns are never a safe combination. If one of his drug deals had gone bad or if a rival dealer had arrived on the scene, Johnson's deadly weapon was close at hand. . . . A judge or jury could thus conclude that Johnson's offense qualified as a violent felony.

There should be no doubt that Samuel Johnson was an armed career criminal. His record includes a number of serious felonies. And he has been caught with dangerous weapons on numerous occasions. That this case has led to the residual clause's demise is confounding. I only hope that Congress can take the Court at its word that either amending the list of enumerated offenses or abandoning the categorical approach would solve the problem that the Court perceives.

NOTES AND QUESTIONS

1.   As noted in the discussion preceding *Johnson*, vague statutory terms do not present borderline application problems in *every* instance (*i.e.*, no member of the Court in *Johnson* would have disputed that detonating an explosive device in a crowded plaza would have raised a "serious potential risk of physical injury"). In dissent, Justice Alito contends that the canon of constitutional avoidance instructs courts to interpret statutes in a manner that renders them constitutional, where possible. Does this canon necessarily conflict with the void for vagueness doctrine? Any vague concept has some number of non-borderline cases, after all, so couldn't a court apply the statute to at least those small number of non-vague applications to save the statute as a whole? If the canon of constitutional avoidance conflicts with the void for vagueness doctrine, which should prevail, and why? Should it depend on the circumstances of the statute? The frequency of the borderline cases? The severity of the consequences of running afoul of the vague provision?

2.   Many statutes have terms that could be considered vague, such as any statute making reference to a "crime of violence." Yet numerous statutes reference violent crimes without being struck down as unconstitutionally void for vagueness. What do you think made ACCA's residual clause different or especially troublesome? Should it matter whether a statute is likely to raise issues of vagueness in only 2% of its probable applications as opposed to 20% of them?

3.   As noted above, ambiguous terms or phrases generally do not raise persistent interpretive problems: if a statute prohibits "robbing a bank," the interpreter need only decide whether the conduct prohibited is the taking of water from riverbank or the taking of money from a commercial bank.* Once a court decides which "bank" is at issue, the ambiguity is generally settled for good. (Though as you will see with *Smith*, *Bailey*, and *Watson* in Section VII.B, courts can sometimes inadvertently *create* new statutory ambiguity in the effort to resolve it!)

By contrast, difficult borderline issues remain even as a vague expression continues to be interpreted over time. This means that a vague statute may be susceptible to recurring trouble, just as ACCA's residual

---

* This example is borrowed from Ralf Poscher, *Ambiguity and Vagueness in Legal Interpretation*, in The Oxford Handbook of Language and Law (Lawrence M. Solan and Peter M. Tiersma eds., 2012).

clause necessitated five distinct Supreme Court decisions in less than a decade. Justice Alito criticizes the majority for jettisoning *stare decisis* and the Court's first four decisions—which found that specific crimes fell within the residual clause prohibition—by striking down the statutory provision as a whole. Does the void for vagueness doctrine present a special exception to statutory *stare decisis*? After all, if a court finds the same allegedly vague provision to be susceptible to recurring interpretive difficulties, doesn't the accretion of such cases evince an especially problematic instance of statutory vagueness? (Recall the majority's observation that failure after "persistent efforts . . . to establish a standard" can provide evidence of vagueness.) Alternatively, if the court has succeeded in applying (or not applying) the vague term to the conduct in question in each individual case, can the term really be said to be vague? Or is vagueness a problem, as the majority suggests, not because the statute wholly defies application, but because it constantly requires revisiting the interpretation in order to apply the statute to a new situation? On this view, due process concerns underlie the notion of "void for vagueness": if, even after several attempts to articulate the bounds of a prohibition, a court still has not clarified precisely what conduct the statute targets, the statute can never be said to give sufficiently fair notice to the general public.

d. TEXTUAL AMBIGUITY AND THE RULE OF LENITY

Ambiguous statutory provisions raise distinct but related problems: often, multiple compelling (and conflicting) interpretations may apply to the same statutory term or phrase. One way of deciding between competing meanings of *criminal* statutes is to invoke one of the oldest and most venerated substantive canons, the rule of lenity. As described above in Section II.A.3, judges and courts at all levels, state and federal, accept the rule. While the canon has near unanimous acceptance, judges frequently disagree about when to apply it, either because the statute is not sufficiently ambiguous as to warrant it, or because its application is not appropriate in the given case.

In *United States v. Thompson/Ctr. Arms Co.*, 504 U.S. 505 (1992), the Supreme Court invoked the rule of lenity in its interpretation of an ambiguous tax statute with potential criminal consequences. The Court considered whether a gun manufacturer "makes" a firearm regulated under the National Firearms Act (NFA) when it packages a pistol with a kit that can convert the pistol into an unregulated long-barreled rifle (not subject to regulation under the NFA) or a short-barreled rifle (subject to regulation).

Section 5821(a) of the NFA imposed a $200 tax "for each firearm" which would "be paid by the person making the firearm," 26 U.S.C. § 5821(b). In addition, the NFA required the "manufacturer, importer, and maker" of each firearm to obtain approval from the Secretary of the Treasury, § 5822, and to register each firearm with the Secretary. § 5841. Any firearm maker who failed to comply with the NFA could face criminal penalties of up to 10 years' imprisonment or a fine of up to

$10,000, or both. § 5871. As the Court summarized it, the NFA further defined specific terms as follows:

> The word "firearm" is used as a term of art in the NFA. It means, among other things, "a rifle having a barrel or barrels of less than 16 inches in length. . . ." § 5845(a)(3). "The term 'rifle' means a weapon designed or redesigned, made or remade, and intended to be fired from the shoulder and designed or redesigned and made or remade to use the energy of the explosive in a fixed cartridge to fire only a single projectile through a rifled bore for each single pull of the trigger, and shall include any such weapon which may be readily restored to fire a fixed cartridge." § 5845(c). . . . The NFA provides that "[t]he term 'make', and the various derivatives of such word, shall include manufacturing (other than by one qualified to engage in such business under this chapter), putting together, altering, any combination of these, or otherwise producing a firearm." § 5845(i).

Thompson/Center Arms Company manufactured the "Contender," a pistol that, when paired with a kit containing a shoulder stock and 21-inch barrel, could be converted into a long-barreled gun or, if the pistol's barrel was left on the gun, a short-barreled rifle. Thompson/Center applied to the Bureau of Alcohol, Tobacco and Firearms for approval to "make, use and segregate as a single unit," § 5822, a package consisting of the Contender pistol and the conversion kit and paid the $200 tax. Thompson/Center subsequently sued for a refund, arguing that the registered unit was not a firearm under the NFA.

Writing for the plurality, Justice Souter argued that that statute was ambiguous as to whether the "making" of the regulated firearm included the manufacture of kits that could possibly be used to assemble a regulated firearm (in this case, a short-barreled rifle), or if it included only the manufacture of kits that would be useless except for the assembly of a regulated firearm. The plurality concluded that the statute's language, structure, and legislative history did not provide any definitive guidance, but that the rule of lenity resolved the ambiguity:

> After applying the ordinary rules of statutory construction, then, we are left with an ambiguous statute. The key to resolving the ambiguity lies in recognizing that although it is a tax statute that we construe now in a civil setting, the NFA has criminal applications that carry no additional requirement of willfulness. [Citations.] Making a firearm without approval may be subject to criminal sanction, as is possession of an unregistered firearm and failure to pay the tax on one, 26 U.S.C. §§ 5861, 5871. It is proper, therefore, to apply the rule of lenity and resolve the ambiguity in Thompson/Center's favor. [Citations.] Accordingly, we conclude that the Contender pistol and carbine kit when packaged together by Thompson/Center

have not been "made" into a short-barreled rifle for purposes of the NFA.

Four justices dissented, arguing that the NFA's provisions were unambiguous and that Congress clearly intended for a weapon like the Contender kit to fall within the scope of the NFA's definition of "firearm." Writing for the dissent, Justice Stevens added that even if the statute were ambiguous, it was inappropriate to apply to rule of lenity in construing the NFA, which, in this civil context, was effectively a tax statute:

> The main function of the rule of lenity is to protect citizens from the unfair application of ambiguous punitive statutes. Obviously, citizens should not be subject to punishment without fair notice that their conduct is prohibited by law. The risk that this respondent would be the victim of such unfairness, is, however, extremely remote. . . .

> The Court, after acknowledging that this case involves "a tax statute" and its construction "in a civil setting," nevertheless proceeds to treat the case as though it were a criminal prosecution. In my view, the Court should approach this case like any other civil case testing the Government's interpretation of an important regulatory statute. This statute serves the critical objective of regulating the manufacture and distribution of concealable firearms—dangerous weapons that are a leading cause of countless crimes that occur every day throughout the Nation. This is a field that has long been subject to pervasive governmental regulation because of the dangerous nature of the product and the public interest in having that danger controlled. The public interest in carrying out the purposes that motivated the enactment of this statute is, in my judgment and on this record, far more compelling than a mechanical application of the rule of lenity.

You will encounter further disagreement about the rule of lenity's application later in this chapter, including in the next case.

B. LINGUISTIC MEANINGS, "ORDINARY" AND EXTRAORDINARY

1. LINGUISTIC CANONS OF CONSTRUCTION

Lockhart v. United States

Supreme Court of the United States, 2016.
136 S.Ct. 958, 194 L.Ed.2d 48.

■ JUSTICE SOTOMAYOR delivered the opinion of the Court[, in which THE CHIEF JUSTICE, JUSTICE KENNEDY, JUSTICE THOMAS, JUSTICE GINSBURG, JUSTICE ALITO joined] . . . .

I

In April 2000, Avondale Lockhart was convicted of sexual abuse in the first degree under N.Y. Penal Law Ann. § 130.65(1) (West Cum. Supp. 2015). The crime involved his then-53-year-old girlfriend. [Citation.] Eleven years later, Lockhart was indicted in the Eastern District of New York for attempting to receive child pornography in violation of 18 U.S.C. § 2252(a)(2) and for possessing child pornography in violation of § 2252(a)(4)(b). Lockhart pleaded guilty to the possession offense and the Government dismissed the receipt offense.

Lockhart's presentence report calculated a guidelines range of 78 to 97 months for the possession offense. But the report also concluded that Lockhart was subject to § 2252(b)(2)'s mandatory minimum because his prior New York abuse conviction related "to aggravated sexual abuse, sexual abuse, or abusive sexual conduct involving a minor or ward." [Citation.]

Lockhart objected, arguing that the statutory phrase "involving a minor or ward" applies to all three listed crimes: "aggravated sexual abuse," "sexual abuse," and "abusive sexual conduct." He therefore contended that his prior conviction for sexual abuse involving an adult fell outside the enhancement's ambit. The District Court rejected Lockhart's argument and applied the mandatory minimum. The Second Circuit affirmed his sentence.

II

Section 2252(b)(2) reads in full:

"Whoever violates, or attempts or conspires to violate [18 U.S.C. § 2252(a)(4)] shall be fined under this title or imprisoned not more than 10 years, or both, but . . . if such person has a prior conviction under this chapter, chapter 71, chapter 109A, or chapter 117, or under section 920 of title 10 (article 120 of the Uniform Code of Military Justice), or under the laws of any State relating to aggravated sexual abuse, sexual abuse, or abusive sexual conduct involving a minor or ward, or the production, possession, receipt, mailing, sale, distribution, shipment, or transportation of child pornography, such person shall be fined under this title and imprisoned for not less than 10 years nor more than 20 years."

This case concerns that provision's list of state sexual-abuse offenses. The issue before us is whether the limiting phrase that appears at the end of that list—"involving a minor or ward"—applies to all three predicate crimes preceding it in the list or only the final predicate crime. We hold that "involving a minor or ward" modifies only "abusive sexual conduct," the antecedent immediately preceding it. Although § 2252(b)(2)'s list of state predicates is awkwardly phrased (to put it charitably), the provision's text and context together reveal a straightforward reading. A timeworn textual canon is confirmed by the structure and internal logic of the statutory scheme.

A

Consider the text. When this Court has interpreted statutes that include a list of terms or phrases followed by a limiting clause, we have typically applied an interpretive strategy called the "rule of the last antecedent." *See* Barnhart v. Thomas, 540 U.S. 20, 26 (2003). The rule provides that "a limiting clause or phrase . . . should ordinarily be read as modifying only the noun or phrase that it immediately follows." *Ibid.*; *see also* Black's Law Dictionary 1532–1533 (10th ed. 2014) ("[Q]ualifying words or phrases modify the words or phrases immediately preceding them and not words or phrases more remote, unless the extension is necessary from the context or the spirit of the entire writing"); A. Scalia & B. Garner, Reading Law: The Interpretation of Legal Texts 144 (2012).

This Court has applied the rule from our earliest decisions to our more recent. [Citations.] The rule reflects the basic intuition that when a modifier appears at the end of a list, it is easier to apply that modifier only to the item directly before it. That is particularly true where it takes more than a little mental energy to process the individual entries in the list, making it a heavy lift to carry the modifier across them all. For example, imagine you are the general manager of the Yankees and you are rounding out your 2016 roster. You tell your scouts to find a defensive catcher, a quick-footed shortstop, or a pitcher from last year's World Champion Kansas City Royals. It would be natural for your scouts to confine their search for a pitcher to last year's championship team, but to look more broadly for catchers and shortstops.

Applied here, the last antecedent principle suggests that the phrase "involving a minor or ward" modifies only the phrase that it immediately follows: "abusive sexual conduct." As a corollary, it also suggests that the phrases "aggravated sexual abuse" and "sexual abuse" are not so constrained.

Of course, as with any canon of statutory interpretation, the rule of the last antecedent "is not an absolute and can assuredly be overcome by other indicia of meaning." Barnhart, 540 U.S., at 26; [citation]. For instance, take " 'the laws, the treaties, and the constitution of the United States.' [Citation.] (KAGAN, J., dissenting). A reader intuitively applies "of the United States" to "the laws," "the treaties" and "the constitution" because (among other things) laws, treaties, and the constitution are often cited together, because readers are used to seeing "of the United States" modify each of them, and because the listed items are simple and parallel without unexpected internal modifiers or structure. Section 2252(b)(2), by contrast, does not contain items that readers are used to seeing listed together or a concluding modifier that readers are accustomed to applying to each of them. And the varied syntax of each item in the list makes it hard for the reader to carry the final modifying clause across all three.

More importantly, here the interpretation urged by the rule of the last antecedent is not overcome by other indicia of meaning. To the contrary, § 2252(b)(2)'s context fortifies the meaning that principle commands.

B

Our inquiry into § 2252(b)(2)'s context begins with the internal logic of that provision. Section 2252(b)(2) establishes sentencing minimums and maximums for three categories of offenders. The first third of the section imposes a 10-year maximum sentence on offenders with no prior convictions. The second third imposes a 10-year minimum and 20-year maximum on offenders who have previously violated a federal offense listed within various chapters of the Federal Criminal Code. And the last third imposes the same minimum and maximum on offenders who have previously committed state "sexual abuse, aggravated sexual abuse, or abusive sexual conduct involving a minor or ward" as well as a number of state crimes related to the possession and distribution of child pornography.

Among the chapters of the Federal Criminal Code that can trigger § 2252(b)(2)'s recidivist enhancement are crimes "under . . . chapter 109A." Chapter 109A criminalizes a range of sexual-abuse offenses involving adults or minors and wards. And it places those federal sexual-abuse crimes under headings that use language nearly identical to the language § 2252(b)(2) uses to enumerate the three categories of state sexual-abuse predicates. The first section in Chapter 109A is titled "Aggravated sexual abuse." 18 U.S.C. § 2241. The second is titled "Sexual abuse." § 2242. And the third is titled "Sexual abuse of a minor or ward." § 2243. Applying the rule of the last antecedent, those sections mirror precisely the order, precisely the divisions, and nearly precisely the words used to describe the three state sexual-abuse predicate crimes in § 2252(b)(2): "aggravated sexual abuse," "sexual abuse," and "abusive sexual conduct involving a minor or ward."

This similarity appears to be more than a coincidence. We cannot state with certainty that Congress used Chapter 109A as a template for the list of state predicates set out in § 2252(b)(2), but we cannot ignore the parallel, particularly because the headings in Chapter 109A were in place when Congress amended the statute to add § 2252(b)(2)'s state sexual-abuse predicates.

If Congress had intended to limit each of the state predicates to conduct "involving a minor or ward," we doubt it would have followed, or thought it needed to follow, so closely the structure and language of Chapter 109A.[3] The conclusion that Congress followed the federal template is supported by the fact that Congress did nothing to indicate that offenders with prior federal sexual-abuse convictions are more culpable, harmful, or worthy of enhanced punishment than offenders with nearly identical state priors. We therefore see no reason to interpret § 2252(b)(2) so that "[s]exual abuse" that occurs in the Second Circuit courthouse triggers the sentence enhancement, but "sexual abuse" that occurs next door in the Manhattan municipal building does not.

III

A

Lockhart argues, to the contrary, that the phrase "involving a minor or ward" should be interpreted to modify all three state sexual-abuse predicates. He first contends, as does our dissenting colleague, that the so-called series-qualifier principle supports his reading. This principle, Lockhart says, requires a modifier to apply to all items in a series when such an application would represent a natural construction.

This Court has long acknowledged that structural or contextual evidence may "rebut the last antecedent inference." [Citations.] Lockhart attempts to identify contextual indicia that he says rebut the rule of the last antecedent, but those indicia hurt rather than help his prospects. He points out that the final two state predicates, "sexual abuse" and "abusive sexual conduct," are "nearly synonymous as a matter of everyday speech." And, of course, anyone who commits "aggravated sexual abuse" has also necessarily committed "sexual abuse." So, he posits, the items in the list are sufficiently similar that a limiting phrase could apply equally to all three of them.

But Lockhart's effort to demonstrate some similarity among the items in the list of state predicates reveals far too much similarity. The three state predicate crimes are not just related on Lockhart's reading; they are hopelessly redundant. Any conduct that would qualify as "aggravated sexual abuse ... involving a minor or ward" or "sexual abuse ... involving a minor or ward" would also qualify as "abusive

---

[3] The dissent points out that § 2252(b)(2) (2012 ed.) did not also borrow from the heading of the fourth section in Chapter 109A (or, we note, from the fifth, sixth, seventh, or eighth sections) in defining its categories of state sexual-abuse predicates. But the significance of the similarity between the three state predicates in § 2252(b)(2) and the wording, structure, and order of the first three sections of Chapter 109A is not diminished by the fact that Congress stopped there (especially when the remaining sections largely set out derivations from, definitions of, and penalties for the first three). *See, e.g.,* § 2244 (listing offenses derived from §§ 2241, 2242, and 2243); § 2245 (creating an enhancement for offenses under Chapter 109A resulting in death); § 2246 (listing definitions).

sexual conduct involving a minor or ward." We take no position today on the meaning of the terms "aggravated sexual abuse," "sexual abuse," and "abusive sexual conduct," including their similarities and differences. But it is clear that applying the limiting phrase to all three items would risk running headlong into the rule against superfluity by transforming a list of separate predicates into a set of synonyms describing the same predicate. *See* Bailey v. United States, 516 U.S. 137, 146 (1995) ("We assume that Congress used two terms because it intended each term to have a particular, nonsuperfluous meaning").

Applying the limiting phrase "involving a minor or ward" more sparingly, by contrast, preserves some distinction between the categories of state predicates by limiting only the third category to conduct "involving a minor or ward." We recognize that this interpretation does not eliminate all superfluity between "aggravated sexual abuse" and "sexual abuse." [Citation.] But there is a ready explanation for the redundancy that remains: It follows the categories in Chapter 109A's federal template. We see no similar explanation for Lockhart's complete collapse of the list.

The dissent offers a suggestion rooted in its impressions about how people ordinarily speak and write. The problem is that, as even the dissent acknowledges, § 2252(b)(2)'s list of state predicates is hardly intuitive. No one would mistake its odd repetition and inelegant phrasing for a reflection of the accumulated wisdom of everyday speech patterns. It would be as if a friend asked you to get her tart lemons, sour lemons, or sour fruit from Mexico. If you brought back lemons from California, but your friend insisted that she was using customary speech and obviously asked for Mexican fruit only, you would be forgiven for disagreeing on both counts.

Faced with § 2252(b)(2)'s inartful drafting, then, do we interpret the provision by viewing it as a clear, commonsense list best construed as if conversational English? Or do we look around to see if there might be some provenance to its peculiarity? With Chapter 109A so readily at hand, we are unpersuaded by our dissenting colleague's invocation of basic examples from day-to-day life. Whatever the validity of the dissent's broader point, this simply is not a case in which colloquial practice is of much use. Section 2252(b)(2)'s list is hardly the way an average person, or even an average lawyer, would set about to describe the relevant conduct if they had started from scratch. . . .

D

Finally, Lockhart asks us to apply the rule of lenity. We have used the lenity principle to resolve ambiguity in favor of the defendant only "at the end of the process of construing what Congress has expressed" when the ordinary canons of statutory construction have revealed no satisfactory construction. [Citation.] That is not the case here. To be sure, Lockhart contends that if we applied a different principle of statutory construction—namely, his "series-qualifier principle"—we would arrive at an alternative construction of § 2252(b)(2). But the arguable availability of multiple, divergent principles of statutory construction cannot automatically trigger the rule of lenity. Cf. Llewellyn, Remarks on the Theory of Appellate Decision and the Rules or Canons About How Statutes Are To Be Construed, 3 Vand. L. Rev. 395, 401 (1950) ("[T]here are two opposing canons on almost every point"). Here, the rule of the last antecedent is well supported by context and Lockhart's alternative is not. We will not apply the rule of lenity to override a sensible grammatical principle buttressed by the statute's text and structure.

* * *

We conclude that the text and structure of § 2252(b)(2) confirm that the provision applies to prior state convictions for "sexual abuse" and "aggravated sexual abuse," whether or not the convictions involved a minor or ward. We therefore hold that Lockhart's prior conviction for sexual abuse of an adult is encompassed by § 2252(b)(2). The judgment of the Court of Appeals, accordingly, is affirmed.

So ordered.

■ JUSTICE KAGAN, with whom JUSTICE BREYER joins, dissenting.

Imagine a friend told you that she hoped to meet "an actor, director, or producer involved with the new Star Wars movie." You would know immediately that she wanted to meet an actor from the Star Wars cast—not an actor in, for example, the latest Zoolander. Suppose a real estate agent promised to find a client "a house, condo, or apartment in New York." Wouldn't the potential buyer be annoyed if the agent sent him information about condos in Maryland or California? And consider a law imposing a penalty for the "violation of any statute, rule, or regulation relating to insider trading." Surely a person would have cause to protest if punished under that provision for violating a traffic statute. The reason in all three cases is the same: Everyone understands that the modifying phrase—"involved with the new Star Wars movie," "in New York," "relating to insider trading"—applies to each term in the preceding list, not just the last.

That ordinary understanding of how English works, in speech and writing alike, should decide this case. Avondale Lockhart is subject to a 10-year mandatory minimum sentence for possessing child pornography if, but only if, he has a prior state-law conviction for "aggravated sexual abuse, sexual abuse, or abusive sexual conduct involving a minor or ward." 18 U.S.C. § 2252(b)(2). The Court today, relying on what is called the "rule of the last antecedent," reads the phrase "involving a minor or ward" as modifying only the final term in that three-item list. But properly read, the modifier applies to each of the terms—just as in the examples above. That normal construction finds support in uncommonly clear-cut legislative history, which states in so many words that the three predicate crimes all involve abuse of children. And if any doubt remained, the rule of lenity would command the same result: Lockhart's prior conviction for sexual abuse of an adult does not trigger § 2252(b)(2)'s mandatory minimum penalty. I respectfully dissent.

I

Begin where the majority does—with the rule of the last antecedent. This Court most fully discussed that principle in Barnhart v. Thomas, 540 U.S. 20 (2003), which considered a statute providing that an individual qualifies as disabled if "he is not only unable to do his previous work but cannot, considering his age, education, and work experience, engage in any other kind of substantial gainful work *which exists in the national economy.*" [Citation.] The Court held, invoking the last-antecedent rule, that the italicized phrase modifies only the term "substantial gainful work," and not the term "previous work" occurring earlier in the sentence. Two points are of especial note. First, *Barnhart* contained a significant caveat: The last-antecedent rule "can assuredly be overcome by other indicia of meaning." [Citation.] Second, the grammatical structure of the provision in *Barnhart* is nothing like that of the statute in this case: The modifying phrase does not, as here, immediately follow a list of multiple, parallel terms. That is true as well in the other instances in which this Court has followed the rule. [Citations.]

Indeed, this Court has made clear that the last-antecedent rule does not generally apply to the grammatical construction present here: when "[t]he modifying clause appear[s] . . . at the end of a single, integrated list." [Citation.] Then, the exact opposite is usually true: As in the examples beginning this opinion, the modifying phrase refers alike to each of the list's terms. A leading treatise puts the point as follows: "When there is a straightforward, parallel construction that involves all nouns or verbs in a series," a modifier at the end of the list "normally applies to the entire series." A. Scalia & B. Garner, Reading Law: The Interpretation of Legal Texts 147 (2012); compare *id.*, at 152 ("When the syntax involves something other than [such] a parallel series of nouns or verbs," the modifier "normally applies only to the nearest reasonable referent"). That interpretive practice of applying the modifier to the whole list boasts a fancy name—the "series-qualifier canon," *see* Black's Law Dictionary 1574 (10th ed. 2014)—but, as my opening examples show, it reflects the completely ordinary way that people speak and listen, write and read.[1]

---

[1]   The majority's baseball example reads the other way only because its three terms are not parallel. The words "catcher" and "shortstop," but not "pitcher," are qualified separate and apart from the modifying clause at the end of the sentence: "Pitcher" thus calls for a modifier of its own, and the phrase "from the Kansas City Royals" answers that call. Imagine the sentence is slightly reworded to refer to a "defensive catcher, quick-footed shortstop, or hard-throwing pitcher from the Kansas City Royals." Or, alternatively, suppose the sentence referred simply to a "catcher, shortstop, or pitcher from the Kansas City Royals." Either way, all three players must come from the Royals—because the three terms (unlike in the majority's sentence) are a parallel series with a modifying clause at the end.

Even the exception to the series-qualifier principle is intuitive, emphasizing both its common-sensical basis and its customary usage. When the nouns in a list are so disparate that the modifying clause does not make sense when applied to them all, then the last-antecedent rule takes over. Suppose your friend told you not that she wants to meet "an actor, director, or producer involved with Star Wars," but instead that she hopes someday to meet "a President, Supreme Court Justice, or actor involved with Star Wars." Presumably, you would know that she wants to meet a President or Justice even if that person has no connection to the famed film franchise. But so long as the modifying clause "is applicable as much to the first and other words as to the last," this Court has stated, "the natural construction of the language demands that the clause be read as applicable to all." Paroline v. United States, 134 S.Ct. 1710, 1721, [citation]. In other words, the modifier then qualifies not just the last antecedent but the whole series.

As the majority itself must acknowledge, this Court has repeatedly applied the series-qualifier rule in just that manner. In *Paroline*, for example, this Court considered a statute requiring possessors of child pornography to pay restitution to the individuals whose abuse is recorded in those materials. The law defines such a victim's losses to include "medical services relating to physical, psychiatric, or psychological care; physical and occupational therapy or rehabilitation; necessary transportation, temporary housing, and child care expenses; lost income; attorneys' fees, as well as other costs incurred; and any other losses suffered by the victim as a proximate result of the offense." 18 U.S.C. §§ 2259(b)(3)(A)–(F) (lettering omitted). The victim bringing the lawsuit invoked the last-antecedent rule to argue that the modifier at the end of the provision—"as a proximate result of the offense"—pertained only to the last item in the preceding list, and not to any of the others. [Citation.] But the Court rejected that view: It recited the "canon[ ] of statutory construction," derived from the "natural" use of language, that "[w]hen several words are followed by a clause" that can sensibly modify them all, it should be understood to do so. *Ibid.* Thus, the Court read the proximate-cause requirement to cover each and every term in the list.

United States v. Bass, 404 U.S. 336 (1971), to take just one other example, followed the same rule. There, the Court confronted a statute making it a crime for a convicted felon to "receive[ ], possess[ ], or transport[ ] in commerce or affecting commerce . . . any firearm." [Citation.] The Government contended that the modifying clause—"in commerce or affecting commerce"—applied only to "transport" and not to "receive" or "possess." But the Court rebuffed that argument. "[T]he natural construction of the language," the Court recognized, "suggests that the clause 'in commerce or affecting commerce' qualifies all three antecedents in the list." [Citation.] Relying on longstanding precedents endorsing such a construction, the Court explained: "Since 'in commerce or affecting commerce' undeniably applies to at least one antecedent, and since it makes sense with all three, the more plausible construction here is that it in fact applies to all three." [Citations].

That analysis holds equally for § 2252(b)(2), the sentencing provision at issue here. The relevant language—"aggravated sexual abuse, sexual abuse, or abusive sexual conduct involving a minor or ward"—contains a "single, integrated list" of parallel terms (*i.e.*, sex crimes) followed by a modifying clause. [Citation.] Given the close relation among the terms in the series, the modifier makes sense "as much to the first and other words as to the last." [Citation.] In other words, the reference to a minor or ward applies as well to sexual abuse and aggravated sexual abuse as to abusive sexual conduct. (The case would be different if, for example, the statute established a mandatory minimum for any person previously convicted of "arson, receipt of stolen property, or abusive sexual conduct involving a minor or ward.") So interpreting the modifier "as applicable to all" the preceding terms is what "the natural construction of the language" requires. [Citation.]

The majority responds to all this by claiming that the "inelegant phrasing" of § 2252(b)(2) renders it somehow exempt from a grammatical rule reflecting "how people ordinarily" use the English language. But to begin with, the majority is wrong to suggest that the series-qualifier canon is only about "colloquial" or "conversational" English. In fact, it applies to both speech and writing, in both their informal and their formal varieties. Here is a way to test my point: Pick up a journal, or a book, or for that matter a Supreme Court opinion—most of which keep "everyday" colloquialisms at a far distance. You'll come across many sentences having the structure of the statutory provision at issue here: a few nouns followed by a modifying clause. And you'll discover, again and yet again, that the clause modifies every noun in the series, not just the last—in other words, that even (especially?) in formal writing, the series-qualifier principle works.[2] And the majority is wrong too in suggesting that the "odd repetition" in § 2252(b)(2)'s list of state predicates causes the series-qualifier principle to lose its force. The majority's own made-

---

[2] Too busy to carry out this homework assignment? Consider some examples (there are many more) from just the last few months of this Court's work. In OBB Personenverkehr AG v. Sachs, 577 U.S. ___, ___, 136 S.Ct. 390, 395, 193 L.Ed.2d 269 (2015), this Court described a lawsuit as alleging "wrongful arrest, imprisonment, and torture by Saudi police." In James v. Boise, 577 U.S. ___, ___, 136 S.Ct. 685, 686–687, ___ L.Ed.2d ___ (2016) (per curiam) (quoting Martin v. Hunter's Lessee, 1 Wheat. 304, 348, 4 L.Ed. 97 (1816)), this Court affirmed that state courts must follow its interpretations of "the laws, the treaties, and the constitution of the United States." In Musacchio v. United States, 577 U.S. ___, ___, 136 S.Ct. 709, 715, ___ L.Ed.2d ___ (2016) (quoting Reed Elsevier, Inc. v. Muchnick, 559 U.S. 154, 166, 130 S.Ct. 1237, 176 L.Ed.2d 18 (2010)), this Court noted that in interpreting statutes it looks to the "text, context, and relevant historical treatment of the provision at issue." In FERC v. Electric Power Supply Assn., 577 U.S. ___, ___, 136 S.Ct. 760, 774, ___ L.Ed.2d ___ (2016), this Court applied a statute addressing "any rule, regulation, practice, or contract affecting [a wholesale] rate [or] charge." And in Montanile v. Board of Trustees of Nat. Elevator Industry Health Benefit Plan, 577 U.S. ___, ___, 136 S.Ct. 651, 655, ___ L.Ed.2d ___ (2016), this Court interpreted an employee benefits plan requiring reimbursement "for attorneys' fees, costs, expenses or damages claimed by the covered person." In each case, of course, the italicized modifying clause refers to every item in the preceding list. That is because the series-qualifier rule reflects how all of us use language, in writing and in speech, in formal and informal contexts, all the time.

up sentence proves that much. If a friend asked you "to get her tart lemons, sour lemons, or sour fruit from Mexico," you might well think her list of terms perplexing: You might puzzle over the difference between tart and sour lemons, and wonder why she had specifically mentioned lemons when she apparently would be happy with sour fruit of any kind. But of one thing, you would have no doubt: Your friend wants some produce *from Mexico*; it would not do to get her, say, sour lemons from Vietnam. However weird the way she listed fruits—or the way § 2252(b)(2) lists offenses—the modifying clause still refers to them all.

The majority as well seeks refuge in the idea that applying the series-qualifier canon to § 2252(b)(2) would violate the rule against superfluity. Says the majority: "Any conduct that would qualify as 'aggravated sexual abuse . . . involving a minor or ward' or 'sexual abuse . . . involving a minor or ward' would also qualify as 'abusive sexual conduct involving a minor or ward.'" But that rejoinder doesn't work. "[T]he canon against superfluity," this Court has often stated, "assists only where a competing interpretation gives effect to every clause and word of a statute." [Citations.] And the majority's approach (as it admits) produces superfluity too—and in equal measure. Now (to rearrange the majority's sentence) any conduct that would qualify as "abusive sexual conduct involving a minor or ward" or "aggravated sexual abuse" would also qualify as "sexual abuse." In other words, on the majority's reading as well, two listed crimes become subsets of a third, so that the three could have been written as one. And indeed, the majority's superfluity has an especially odd quality, because it relates to the modifying clause itself: The majority, that is, makes the term "involving a minor or ward" wholly unnecessary. Remember the old adage about the pot and the kettle? That is why the rule against superfluity cannot excuse the majority from reading § 2252(b)(2)'s modifier, as ordinary usage demands, to pertain to all the terms in the preceding series. . . .

III

As against the most natural construction of § 2252(b)(2)'s language, . . . the majority relies on a structural argument. The federal sexual-abuse predicates in § 2252(b)(2), the majority begins, are described as crimes "under . . . Chapter 109A," and that chapter "criminalizes a range of sexual-abuse offenses involving adults *or* minors." Once again, the majority cannot say that this fact alone resolves the question presented, given the many times (just discussed) that Congress opted to make federal crimes, but not equivalent state crimes, predicates for § 2252(b)(2)'s mandatory minimums. But the majority claims to see more than that here: The headings of the sections in Chapter 109A, it contends, "mirror precisely the order . . . and nearly precisely the words used to describe" the state predicate crimes at issue. The majority "cannot state with certainty," but hazards a guess that Congress thus used Chapter 109A "as a template for the list of state predicates"—or, otherwise said, that Congress "followed" the "structure and language of Chapter 109A" in defining those state-law offenses.

But § 2252(b)(2)'s state predicates are not nearly as similar to the federal crimes in Chapter 109A as the majority claims. That Chapter includes the following offenses: "Aggravated sexual abuse," § 2241, "Sexual abuse," § 2242, "Sexual abuse of a minor or ward," § 2243, and "Abusive sexual contact," § 2244. The Chapter thus contains *four* crimes—one more than found in § 2252(b)(2)'s list of state offenses. If the drafters of § 2252(b)(2) meant merely to copy Chapter 109A, why would they have left out one of its crimes? The majority has no explanation. And there is more. Suppose Congress, for whatever hard-to-fathom reason, wanted to replicate only Chapter 109A's first three offenses. It would then have used the same language, referring to "the laws of any State relating to aggravated sexual abuse, sexual abuse, or sexual abuse of a minor or ward." (And had Congress used that language, the phrase "of a minor or ward" would clearly have applied only to the third term, to differentiate it from the otherwise identical second.) But contra the majority, that is not what § 2252(b)(2)'s drafters did. Rather than repeating the phrase "sexual abuse," they used the phrase "abusive sexual conduct" in the list's last term—which echoes, if anything, the separate crime of "abusive sexual contact" (included in Chapter 109A's *fourth* offense, as well as in other places in the federal code, *see, e.g.,* 10 U.S.C. § 920(d)). The choice of those different words indicates, yet again, that Congress did not mean, as the majority imagines, to duplicate Chapter 109A's set of offenses. . . .

The majority seems to think that view somehow consistent with its own hypothesis that Chapter 109A served as a "template" for § 2252(b)(2)'s state predicates; in responding to one of Lockhart's arguments, the majority remarks that the state predicates might have a "generic" meaning, distinct from Chapter 109A's, But if that is so, the majority's supposed template is not much of a template after all. The predicate state offenses would "follow" or "parallel" Chapter 109A in a single respect, but not in any others—that is, in including sexual abuse of adults, but not in otherwise defining wrongful sexual conduct (whether concerning adults or children). The template, one might say, is good for this case and this case only. And the majority has no theory for why that should be so: It offers not the slimmest explanation of how Chapter 109A can resolve today's question but not the many issues courts will face in the future involving the meaning of § 2252(b)(2)'s state predicate offenses. That is because no rationale would make sense. . . .

IV

Suppose, for a moment, that this case is not as clear as I've suggested. . . . This Court has a rule for how to resolve genuine ambiguity in criminal statutes: in favor of the criminal defendant. As the majority puts the point, the rule of lenity insists that courts side with the defendant "when the ordinary canons of statutory construction have revealed no satisfactory construction." [Citations.] At the very least, that principle should tip the scales in Lockhart's favor, because nothing the majority has said shows that the modifying clause in § 2252(b)(2) unambiguously applies to only the last term in the preceding series.

But in fact, Lockhart's case is stronger. Consider the following sentence, summarizing various points made above: "The series-qualifier principle, the legislative history, and the rule of lenity discussed in this opinion all point in the same direction." Now answer the following question: Has only the rule of lenity been discussed in this opinion, or have the series-qualifier principle and the legislative history been discussed as well? Even had you not read the preceding 16-plus pages, you would know the right answer—because of the ordinary way all of us use language. That, in the end, is why Lockhart should win.

QUESTIONS

1.   Consider the typology of interpretive methods in Section II.B.1, *supra*. Most linguistic canons like the rule of the last antecedent and the series qualifier canon may derive legitimacy either from background rules of semantics and syntax that legislative drafters are presumed to know (and use) when drafting statutes, and/or on the basis of prevailing linguistic practices reasonable readers of statutory texts employ when interpreting statutory texts. Can you identify where in the dueling opinions the majority and dissent employ arguments grounded in drafters' intent and arguments grounded in the reasonable reader's understanding to bolster the application of their preferred linguistic canons?

2.   Although the thrust of the disagreement between the majority and the dissent concerns the application of competing linguistic canons, the majority and dissent also disagree about the applicability of the rule of lenity, a *substantive* canon. On what basis does the rule of lenity derive its legitimacy? Is it best described as a rule-of-law background assumption, or as a tie-breaker when the application of linguistic canons yields a deadlock?

3.   Recall Professor Karl Llewellyn's infamous "thrust/parry" typology of canons and counter-canons referenced by the majority and excerpted in Section II.B.3, *supra*. Is a canon of construction rendered ineffective as an interpretive aid if there exists a counter-canon that yields the opposite meaning? Can you articulate a principled basis for preferring a particular canon over its counter-canon?

4.   The dissent argues that the series qualifier canon should apply in part because it "reflects the completely ordinary way that people speak and listen, write and read." Should the "completely ordinary way" in which people employ language be the standard by which judges evaluate the utility of linguistic canons? How would you determine which linguistic canons reflect how people ordinarily speak, listen, write, and read? Consider statutes like the Affordable Care Act discussed in *King v. Burwell*, *supra*. Is there any indication Congress drafted the ACA in a manner in which "completely ordinary people" write and read? If not, how might one justify the reliance on such canons?

5.   In discussing the last antecedent principle, the majority concedes that the principle can be overcome by "other indicia of meaning." What other indicia of meaning does the majority consider—or fail to consider?

2. STATUTORY DEFINITIONS SECTIONS

Rather than leave problems with the definitions of statutory terms entirely to their readers, many statutes include a section that provides definitions of some of the key statutory terms. Often, however, definitions sections can lead to ambiguities of their own.

McBoyle v. United States

Supreme Court of the United States, 1931.
283 U.S. 25, 51 S.Ct. 340, 75 L.Ed. 816.

■ MR. JUSTICE HOLMES delivered the [unanimous] opinion of the Court.

The petitioner was convicted of transporting from Ottawa, Illinois, to Guymon, Oklahoma, an airplane that he knew to have been stolen, and was sentenced to serve three years' imprisonment and to pay a fine of $2,000. The judgment was affirmed by the Circuit Court of Appeals for the Tenth Circuit. 43 F.(2d) 273. A writ of certiorari was granted by this Court on the question whether the National Motor Vehicle Theft Act applies to aircraft. Act of October 29, 1919, c. 89; 41 Stat. 324; U.S. Code, Title 18, § 408. That Act provides: "Sec. 2. That when used in this Act: (a) The term 'motor vehicle' shall include an automobile, automobile truck, automobile wagon, motor cycle, or any other self-propelled vehicle not designed for running on rails; . . . Sec. 3. That whoever shall transport or cause to be transported in interstate or foreign commerce a motor vehicle, knowing the same to have been stolen, shall be punished by a fine of not more than $5,000, or by imprisonment of not more than five years, or both."

Section 2 defines the motor vehicles of which the transportation in interstate commerce is punished in § 3. The question is the meaning of the word "vehicle" in the phrase "any other self-propelled vehicle not designed for running on rails." No doubt etymologically it is possible to use the word to signify a conveyance working on land, water or air, and sometimes legislation extends the use in that direction, *e.g.*, land and air, water being separately provided for, in the Tariff Act, September 22, 1922, c. 356, § 401(b), 42 Stat. 858, 948. But in everyday speech "vehicle" calls up the picture of a thing moving on land. Thus in Rev. Stats. § 4, intended, the Government suggests, rather to enlarge than to restrict the definition, vehicle includes every contrivance capable of being used "as a means of transportation on land." And this is repeated, expressly excluding aircraft, in the Tariff Act, June 17, 1930, c. 997, § 401(b); 46 Stat. 590, 708. So here, the phrase under discussion calls up the popular picture. For after including automobile truck, automobile wagon and motor cycle, the words "any other self-propelled vehicle not designed for running on rails" still indicate that a vehicle in the popular sense, that is a vehicle running on land, is the theme. It is a vehicle that runs, not something, not commonly called a vehicle, that flies. Airplanes were well known in 1919, when this statute was passed; but it is admitted that they were not mentioned in the reports or in the debates in Congress. It is impossible to read words that so carefully enumerate the different forms of motor vehicles and have no reference of any kind to aircraft, as including airplanes under a term that usage more and more precisely confines to a different class. The counsel for the petitioner have shown that the phraseology of the statute as to motor vehicles follows that of earlier statutes of Connecticut, Delaware, Ohio, Michigan and Missouri, not to mention the late Regulations of Traffic for the District of Columbia, Title 6, c. 9, § 242, none of which can be supposed to leave the earth.

Although it is not likely that a criminal will carefully consider the text of the law before he murders or steals, it is reasonable that a _fair warning_ should be given to the world in language that the common world will understand, of what the law intends to do if a certain line is passed. To make the warning fair, so far as possible the line should be clear. When a rule of conduct is laid down in words that evoke in the common mind only the picture of vehicles moving on land, the statute should not be extended to aircraft, simply because it may seem to us that a similar policy applies, or upon the speculation that, if the legislature had thought of it, very likely broader words would have been used. United States v. Thind, 261 U.S. 204, 209.

Judgment reversed.

Lozman v. City of Riviera Beach, Fla.

Supreme Court of the United States, 2013.
568 U.S. 115, 133 S.Ct. 735, 184 L.Ed.2d 604.

■ JUSTICE BREYER delivered the opinion of the Court[, joined by CHIEF JUSTICE ROBERTS, JUSTICE SCALIA, JUSTICE THOMAS, JUSTICE GINSBURG, JUSTICE ALITO, and JUSTICE KAGAN].

The Rules of Construction Act defines ["vessel" as follows: "The word 'vessel' includes every description of watercraft or other artificial contrivance used, or capable of being used, as a means of transportation on water."] 1 U.S.C. § 3. The question before us is whether petitioner's floating home (which is not self-propelled) falls within the terms of that definition.

In answering that question we focus primarily upon the phrase "capable of being used." This term encompasses "practical" possibilities, not "merely . . . theoretical" ones. Stewart v. Dutra Constr. Co., 543 U.S. 481, 496 (2005). We believe that a reasonable observer, looking to the home's physical characteristics and activities, would not consider it to be designed to any practical degree for carrying people or things on water. And we consequently conclude that the floating home is not a "vessel."

I

In 2002 Fane Lozman, petitioner, bought a 60-foot by 12-foot floating home. The home consisted of a house-like plywood structure with French doors on three sides. It contained a sitting room, bedroom, closet, bathroom, and kitchen, along with a stairway leading to a second level with office space. An empty bilge space underneath the main floor kept it afloat. After buying the floating home, Lozman had it towed about 200 miles to North Bay Village, Florida, where he moored it and then twice more had it towed between nearby marinas. In 2006 Lozman had the home towed a further 70 miles to a marina owned by the city of Riviera Beach (City), respondent, where he kept it docked.

After various disputes with Lozman and unsuccessful efforts to evict him from the marina, the City brought this federal admiralty lawsuit *in rem* against the floating home. It sought a maritime lien for dockage fees and damages for trespass. [Citation.]

Lozman, acting *pro se,* asked the District Court to dismiss the suit on the ground that the court lacked admiralty jurisdiction. After summary judgment proceedings, the court found that the floating home was a "vessel" and concluded that admiralty jurisdiction was consequently proper. The judge then conducted a bench trial on the merits and awarded the City $3,039.88 for dockage along with $1 in nominal damages for trespass. On appeal the Eleventh Circuit affirmed. It agreed with the District Court that the home was a "vessel." In its view, the home was "capable" of movement over water and the owner's subjective intent to remain moored "indefinitely" at a dock could not show the contrary.

Lozman sought certiorari. In light of uncertainty among the Circuits about application of the term "capable" we granted his petition. Compare De La Rosa v. St. Charles Gaming Co., 474 F.3d 185, 187 (C.A.5 2006) (structure is not a "vessel" where "physically," but only "theoretical[ly]," "capable of sailing," and owner intends to moor it indefinitely as floating casino), with Board of Comm'rs of Orleans Levee Dist. v. M/V Belle of Orleans, 535 F.3d 1299, 1311–1312 (C.A.11 2008) (structure is a "vessel" where capable of moving over water under tow, "albeit to her detriment," despite intent to moor indefinitely). *See also* 649 F.3d, at 1267 (rejecting views of Circuits that " 'focus on the intent of the shipowner' ")....

III

A

We focus primarily upon the statutory phrase "capable of being used . . . as a means of transportation on water." 1 U.S.C. § 3. The Court of Appeals found that the home was "capable" of transportation because it could float, it could proceed under tow, and its shore connections (power cable, water hose, rope lines) did not " 'rende[r]' " it "practically incapable of transportation or movement." 649 F.3d, at 1266 (quoting Belle of Orleans, *supra*, at 1312). At least for argument's sake we agree with the Court of Appeals about the last-mentioned point, namely that Lozman's shore connections did not " 'render' " the home " 'practically incapable of transportation.' " But unlike the Eleventh Circuit, we do not find these considerations (even when combined with the home's other characteristics) sufficient to show that Lozman's home was a "vessel."

The Court of Appeals recognized that it had applied the term "capable" broadly. Indeed, it pointed with approval to language in an earlier case, Burks v. American River Transp. Co., 679 F.2d 69 (C.A.5 1982), in which the Fifth Circuit said:

" 'No doubt the three men in a tub would also fit within our definition, and one probably could make a convincing case for Jonah inside the whale.' " 649 F.3d, at 1269 (brackets omitted) (quoting Burks, *supra*, at 75).

But the Eleventh Circuit's interpretation is too broad. Not *every* floating structure is a "vessel." To state the obvious, a wooden washtub, a plastic dishpan, a swimming platform on pontoons, a large fishing net, a door taken off its hinges, or Pinocchio (when inside the whale) are not "vessels," even if they are "artificial contrivance[s]" capable of floating, moving under tow, and incidentally carrying even a fair-sized item or two when they do so. Rather, the statute applies to an "artificial contrivance . . . capable of being used . . . *as a means of transportation on water*." 1 U.S.C. § 3 (emphasis added). "[T]ransportation" involves the "conveyance (of things or persons) from one place to another." 18 Oxford English Dictionary 424 (2d ed. 1989) (OED). [Citation.] And we must apply this definition in a "practical," not a "theoretical," way. Stewart, *supra*, at 496, 125 S.Ct. 1118. Consequently, in our view a structure does not fall within the scope of this statutory phrase unless a reasonable observer, looking to the home's physical characteristics and activities, would consider it designed to a practical degree for carrying people or things over water.

B

. . . But for the fact that it floats, nothing about Lozman's home suggests that it was designed to any practical degree to transport persons or things over water. It had no rudder or other steering mechanism. Its hull was unraked, and it had a rectangular bottom 10 inches below the water. It had no special capacity to generate or store electricity but could obtain that utility only through ongoing connections with the land. Its small rooms looked like ordinary nonmaritime living quarters. And those inside those rooms looked out upon the world, not through watertight portholes, but through French doors or ordinary windows. . . .

Lozman's home differs significantly from an ordinary houseboat in that it has no ability to propel itself. Cf. 33 CFR § 173.3 (2012) ("Houseboat means a *motorized* vessel . . . designed primarily for multi-purpose accommodation spaces with low freeboard and little or no foredeck or cockpit" (emphasis added)). Lozman's home was able to travel over water only by being towed. Prior to its arrest, that home's travel by tow over water took place on only four occasions over a period of seven years. And when the home was towed a significant distance in 2006, the towing company had a second boat follow behind to prevent the home from swinging dangerously from side to side. . . .

In a word, we can find nothing about the home that could lead a reasonable observer to consider it designed to a practical degree for "transportation on water."

C

. . . The Court's reasoning in Stewart also supports our conclusion. We there considered the application of the statutory definition to a dredge. 543 U.S., at 494. The dredge was "a massive floating platform" from which a suspended clamshell bucket would "remov[e] silt from the ocean floor," depositing it "onto one of two scows" floating alongside the dredge. *Id.*, at 484. Like more traditional "seagoing vessels," the dredge had, *e.g.*, "a captain and crew, navigational lights, ballast tanks, and a crew dining area." *Ibid.* Unlike more ordinary vessels, it could navigate only by "manipulating its anchors and cables" or by being towed. *Ibid.* Nonetheless it did move. In fact it moved over water "every couple of hours." *Id.*, at 485.

We held that the dredge was a "vessel." We wrote that § 3's definition "merely codified the meaning that the term 'vessel' had acquired in general maritime law." *Id.*, at 490. We added that the question of the "watercraft's use 'as a means of transportation on water' is . . . practical," and not "merely . . . theoretical." *Id.*, at 496. And we pointed to cases holding that dredges ordinarily "served a waterborne transportation function," namely that "in performing their work they carried machinery, equipment, and crew over water." *Id.*, at 491–492 (citing, *e.g.*, Butler v. Ellis, 45 F. 2d 951, 955 (4th Cir. 1930)).

As the Court of Appeals pointed out, in Stewart we also wrote that § 3 "does not require that a watercraft be used *primarily* for that [transportation] purpose," 543 U.S., at 495; that a "watercraft need not be in motion to qualify as a vessel," *ibid.*; and that a structure may qualify as a vessel even if attached—but not "permanently" attached—to the land or ocean floor. *Id.*, at 493–494. We did not take these statements, however, as implying a universal set of sufficient conditions for application of the definition. Rather, they say, and they mean, that the statutory definition *may* (or may not) apply—not that it *automatically must* apply—where a structure has some other *primary* purpose, where it is stationary at relevant times, and where it is attached—but not permanently attached—to land.

After all, a washtub is normally not a "vessel" though it does not have water transportation as its primary purpose, it may be stationary much of the time, and it might be attached—but not permanently attached—to land. . . .

IV

Although we have focused on the phrase *"capable* of being used" for transportation over water, the statute also includes as a "vessel" a structure that is *actually* "used" for that transportation. 1 U.S.C. § 3 (emphasis added). And the City argues that, irrespective of its design, Lozman's floating home was *actually* so used. We are not persuaded by its argument.

We are willing to assume for argument's sake that sometimes it is possible actually to use for water transportation a structure that is in no practical way designed for that purpose. But even so, the City cannot show the actual use for which it argues. Lozman's floating home moved only under tow. Before its arrest, it moved significant distances only twice in seven years. And when it moved, it carried, not passengers or cargo, but at the very most (giving the benefit of any factual ambiguity to the City) only its own furnishings, its owner's personal effects, and personnel present to assure the home's safety. This is far too little *actual* "use" to bring the floating home within the terms of the statute. *See* Evansville, 271 U.S., at 20–21 (wharfboat not a "vessel" even though "[e]ach winter" it "was towed to [a] harbor to protect it from ice"); *see also* Roper v. United States, 368 U.S. 20, 23 (1961) ("Unlike a barge, the S.S. *Harry Lane* was not moved in order to transport commodities from one location to another").

V

For these reasons, the judgment of the Court of Appeals is reversed.

It is so ordered.

■ JUSTICE SOTOMAYOR, with whom JUSTICE KENNEDY joins, dissenting.

I agree with much of the Court's reasoning. Our precedents fully support the Court's reasoning that the Eleventh Circuit's test is overinclusive; that the subjective intentions of a watercraft's owner or designer play no role in the vessel analysis of 1 U.S.C. § 3; and that an objective assessment of a watercraft's purpose or function governs whether that structure is a vessel. The Court, however, creates a novel and unnecessary "reasonable observer" reformulation of these principles and errs in its determination, under this new standard, that the craft before us is not a vessel. Given the underdeveloped record below, we should remand. Therefore, I respectfully dissent.

I

The relevant statute, 1 U.S.C. § 3, "sweeps broadly." Stewart v. Dutra Constr. Co., 543 U.S. 481, 494 (2005). It provides that "[t]he word 'vessel' includes every description of watercraft or other artificial contrivance used, or capable of being used, as a means of transportation on water." This broad phrasing flows from admiralty law's long recognition that vessels come in many shapes and sizes. *See* E. Benedict, American Admiralty § 218, p. 121 (1870 ed.) ("[V]essel, is a general word, many times used for any kind of navigation"); M. Cohen, Admiralty Jurisdiction, Law, and Practice 232 (1883) ("[T]he term 'vessel' shall be understood to comprehend every description of vessel navigating on any sea or channel, lake or river . . .").

Our test for vessel status has remained the same for decades: "Under § 3, a 'vessel' is any watercraft practically capable of maritime transportation. . . ." Stewart, 543 U.S., at 497. At its core, vessel status has always rested upon the objective physical characteristics of a vessel (such as its structure, shape, and materials of construction), as well as its usage history. But over time, several important principles have guided both this Court and the lower courts in determining what kinds of watercraft fall properly within the scope of admiralty jurisdiction.

Consider the most basic of requirements. For a watercraft to be "practically capable" of maritime transportation, it must first be "capable" of such transportation. Only those structures that can simultaneously float and carry people or things over water are even presumptively within § 3's reach. Stopping here, as the Eleventh Circuit essentially did, results in an overinclusive test. Section 3, after all, does not drag every bit of floating and towable flotsam and jetsam into admiralty jurisdiction. Rather, the terms "capable of being used" and "practical" have real significance in our maritime jurisprudence.

"[A] water craft is not 'capable of being used' for maritime transport in any meaningful sense if it has been permanently moored." Stewart, 543 U.S., at 494. So, . . . a watercraft whose objective physical connections to land "evidence a permanent location" does not fall within § 3's ambit. [Citation.] Put plainly, structures "permanently affixed to shore or resting on the ocean floor," Stewart, 543 U.S., at 493–494, have never been treated as vessels for the purposes of § 3.

Our precedents have also excluded from vessel status those watercraft "rendered practically incapable of transportation or movement." *Id.*, at 494. Take the easiest case, a vessel whose physical characteristics have been so altered as to make waterborne transportation a practical impossibility. [Citation.] The longstanding admiralty exception for "dead ships," those watercraft that "require a major overhaul" for their "reactivation," also falls into this category.

[Citation.] Likewise, ships that "have been withdrawn from the water for extended periods of time" in order to facilitate repairs and reconstruction may lose their status as vessels until they are rendered capable of maritime transport. Stewart, 543 U.S., at 496, 125 S.Ct. 1118.... Finally, our maritime jurisprudence excludes from vessel status those floating structures that, based on their physical characteristics, do not "transport people, freight, or cargo from place to place" as one of their purposes. Stewart, 543 U.S., at 493. "Purpose," in this context, is determined solely by an objective inquiry into a craft's function. "[N]either size, form, equipment nor means of propulsion are determinative factors upon the question of [vessel status]," though all may be considered. The Robert W. Parsons, 191 U.S. 17, 30 (1903). Moreover, in assessing a particular structure's function, we have consistently examined its past and present activities. Of course, a seaborne craft is not excluded from vessel status simply because its "primary purpose" is not maritime transport. Stewart, 543 U.S., at 497. We held as much in Stewart when we concluded that a dredge was a vessel notwithstanding that its "primary purpose" was "dredging rather than transportation." *Id.*, at 486, 495. So long as one purpose of a craft is transportation, whether of cargo or people or both, § 3's practical capability requirement is satisfied. . . .

In sum, our precedents offer substantial guidance for how objectively to determine whether a watercraft is practically capable of maritime transport and thus qualifies as a § 3 vessel. First, the capacity to float and carry things or people is an obvious prerequisite to vessel status. Second, structures or ships that are permanently moored or fixed in place are not § 3 vessels. Likewise, structures that are practically incapable of maritime transport are not vessels ... [*e.g.*, dead ships]. Third, those watercraft whose physical characteristics and usage history reveal no maritime transport purpose or use are not § 3 vessels.

II

... The majority errs ... in concluding that the purpose component of the § 3 test is whether "a reasonable observer, looking to the [craft]'s physical characteristics and activities, would not consider it to be designed to any practical degree for carrying people or things on water." This phrasing has never appeared in any of our cases and the majority's use of it, despite its seemingly objective gloss, effectively (and erroneously) introduces a subjective component into the vessel-status inquiry.

For one thing, in applying this test the majority points to some characteristics of Lozman's craft that have no relationship to maritime transport, such as the style of the craft's rooms or that "those inside those rooms looked out upon the world, not through water-tight portholes, but through French doors or ordinary windows." The majority never explains why it believes these particular esthetic elements are important for determining vessel status. In fact, they are not. Section 3 is focused on whether a structure is "used, or capable of being used, as a means of transportation on water." By importing windows, doors, room style, and other esthetic criteria into the § 3 analysis, the majority gives our vessel test an "I know it when I see it" flavor. [Citation.] But that has never been nor should it be the test . . . .

The majority's treatment of the craft's past voyages is also strange. The majority notes that Lozman's craft could be and was, in fact, towed over long distances, including over 200 miles at one point. But the majority determines that, given the design of Lozman's craft, this is "far too little *actual* 'use' to bring the floating home within the terms of the statute." This is because "when it moved, it carried, not passengers or cargo, but at the very most (giving the benefit of any factual ambiguity to the City) only its own furnishings, its owner's personal effects, and personnel present to assure the home's safety."

I find this analysis confusing. The majority accepts that the record indicates that Lozman's craft traveled hundreds of miles while "carrying people or things." But then, in the same breath, the majority concludes that a "reasonable observer" would nonetheless conclude that the craft was not "designed to any practical degree for carrying people or things on water." The majority fails to explain how a craft that apparently did carry people and things over water for long distances was not "practically capable" of maritime transport.

This is not to say that a structure capable of such feats is necessarily a vessel. A craft like Lozman's might not be a vessel, for example, if it could only carry its owner's clothes and personal effects, or if it is only capable of transporting itself and its appurtenances. [Citation.] But if such a craft can carry large appliances (like an oven or a refrigerator) and all of the other things we might find in a normal home in addition to the occupants of that home, as the existing record suggests Lozman's craft may have done, then it would seem to be much more like a mobile home . . . . The simple truth is that we know very little about the craft's capabilities and what did or did not happen on its various trips. By focusing on the little we do know for certain about this craft (*i.e.*, its windows, doors, and the style of its rooms) in determining whether it is a vessel, the majority renders the § 3 inquiry opaque and unpredictable.

Indeed, the little we do know about Lozman's craft suggests only that it was an unusual structure. A surveyor was unable to find any comparable craft for sale in the State of Florida. Lozman's home was neither obviously a houseboat, as the majority describes such ships, nor clearly a floating home. The only clear difference that the majority identifies between these two kinds of structures is that the former are self-propelled, while the latter are not. But even the majority recognizes that self-propulsion has never been a prerequisite for vessel status. Consequently, it is unclear why Lozman's craft is a floating home, why all floating homes are not vessels, or why Lozman's craft is not a vessel. If windows, doors, and other esthetic attributes are what take Lozman's craft out of vessel status, then the majority's test is completely malleable.

If it is the craft's lack of self-propulsion, then the majority's test is unfaithful to our longstanding precedents. [Citation.] If it is something else, then that something is not apparent from the majority's opinion. . . .

III

With a more developed record, Lozman's craft might be distinguished from the houseboats in those lower court cases just discussed. For example, if Lozman's craft's previous voyages caused it serious damage, then that would strongly suggest that it lacked a maritime transportation purpose or function. There is no harm in remanding the case for further factfinding along the lines described above, cautioning the lower courts to be aware that features of Lozman's "incomparable" craft, may distinguish it from previous precedents. At most, such a remand would introduce a relatively short delay before finally ending the years-long battle between Lozman and the city of Riviera Beach.

. . . [N]umerous maritime industries rely heavily on clear and predictable legal rules for determining which ships are vessels. The majority's distorted application of our settled law to the facts of this case frustrates these ends. . . .

IV

It is not clear that Lozman's craft is a § 3 vessel. It is clear, however, that we are not in a good position to make such a determination based on the limited record we possess. The appropriate response is to remand the case for further proceedings in light of the proper legal standard. The Court resists this move and in its haste to christen Lozman's craft a nonvessel delivers an analysis that will confuse the lower courts and upset our longstanding admiralty precedent. I respectfully dissent.

QUESTIONS

1.   As the majority acknowledged, the meaning of the term "vessel" might, depending on the circumstances, include everything from a wooden washtub to a plastic dishpan to a door taken off its hinges. How should judges decide what the proper context should be?

In particular, are any of the following "vessels"?

— A surfboard

— A swimming pool raft

— An inflatable life raft

— A non self-propelled barge used for transporting goods

— Boats used for amusement park rides such as "Splash Mountain"

2.   Recall the verb the Rules of Construction Act uses in defining a vessel: "The word 'vessel' *includes* every description of watercraft or other artificial contrivance used, or capable of being used, as a means of transportation on water" (emphasis added). Consider the following drafting guidance provided

in Section VIII.A.2, *infra*: " 'Means' is used in the definition if the definition restricts or limits the meaning of a word. 'Includes' is used if the definition extends the meaning. . . . In some cases a drafter may not want to define a word or phrase completely and exactly, yet may want to make certain that the word or phrase *includes* all the specific cases in mind." Understood this way, "includes" is *extensive* and introduces *non-exclusive* specific cases that fall within the definition. Does this understanding of "includes" suggest other objects could constitute a "vessel" beyond those "watercraft or other artificial contrivance used, or capable of being used, as a means of transportation on water?" Does this understanding of how "includes" is used in defining a "vessel" strengthen the majority's or the dissent's interpretation? Should this understanding of "includes" be read in tandem with other canons of construction? For example, would the *noscitur a sociis* canon bolster the majority's interpretation?

3. SOURCES OF "ORDINARY" MEANING

Concepts like "literal purview" or "plain meaning" are not self-evident and often beg important questions of meaning. First, these concepts conceal the predicate question of *how* to determine whether the language of the statute is indeed "plain," or whether a particular phrase has a "literal" meaning at all. Second, they obscure the appropriate sources an interpreter may consult when deciding if a meaning is "plain." Legislators sometimes simplify these inquiries by including a definitions section (although as we have seen, statutory definitions do not always dispel interpretive doubt). Otherwise, courts must look elsewhere to determine the meaning of the term or phrase in question. Courts often use "plain meaning" and "ordinary meaning" interchangeably; note, for example, how the dissent in *Yates, supra,* suggested that if the ordinary meaning of the term "tangible object" was readily apparent, then that meaning was "plain," and no deeper inquiry was warranted. What makes a meaning "plain"? That a term or phrase has such a clear and definite meaning *as used in ordinary speech* as to convey a single and conclusive *legal* meaning? And if the meaning is not "plain," to what should the interpreter turn? Consider this question as you read the following section of the Freedom of Information Act (FOIA). FOIA is the statutory scheme that governs the release of government documents, subject to a number of exceptions:

Freedom of Information Act
United States Code, Title 5, Chapter 5.

§ 552   Public information; agency rules, opinions, orders, records, and proceedings

(a) Each agency shall make available to the public information as follows: . . .

(b) This section does not apply to matters that are—. . .

(4) trade secrets and commercial or financial information obtained from a person and privileged or confidential; . . .

(6) personnel and medical files and similar files the disclosure of which would constitute a clearly unwarranted invasion of personal privacy;

(7) records or information compiled for law enforcement purposes, but only to the extent that the production of such law enforcement records or information

  (A) could reasonably be expected to interfere with enforcement proceedings,

  (B) would deprive a person of a right to a fair trial or an impartial adjudication,

  (C) could reasonably be expected to constitute an unwarranted invasion of personal privacy,

  (D) could reasonably be expected to disclose the identity of a confidential source, including a State, local, or foreign agency or authority or any private institution which furnished information on a confidential basis, and, in the case of a record or information compiled by criminal law enforcement authority in the course of a criminal investigation or by an agency conducting a lawful national security intelligence investigation, information furnished by a confidential source,

  (E) would disclose techniques and procedures for law enforcement investigations or prosecutions, or would disclose guide-lines for law enforcement investigations or prosecutions if such disclosure could reasonably be expected to risk circumvention of the law, or

  (F) could reasonably be expected to endanger the life or physical safety of any individual; . . .

QUESTIONS

1. Section 552(b) lists information not subject to disclosure in response to FOIA requests. Do you discern common themes or concerns underlying the various exceptions?

2. Who are the beneficiaries of non-disclosures under exception (7)(D)?

3. How do the exceptions collectively treat "person" "personal" and "personnel"? What inferences can you draw?

Federal Communications Commission
v. AT&T Inc.

Supreme Court of the United States, 2011.
562 U.S. 397, 131 S.Ct. 1177, 179 L.Ed.2d 132.

■ CHIEF JUSTICE ROBERTS delivered the opinion of the Court[, in which all other Members joined, except JUSTICE KAGAN, who took no part in the consideration or decision of the case.]

The Freedom of Information Act requires federal agencies to make records and documents publicly available upon request, unless they fall within one of several statutory exemptions. One of those exemptions covers law enforcement records, the disclosure of which "could reasonably be expected to constitute an unwarranted invasion of personal privacy." 5 U.S.C. § 552(b)(7)(C). The question presented is whether corporations have "personal privacy" for the purposes of this exemption.

I

The Freedom of Information Act request at issue in this case relates to an investigation of respondent AT&T Inc., conducted by the Federal Communications Commission. AT&T participated in an FCC-administered program—the E-Rate (or Education-Rate) program—that was created to enhance access for schools and libraries to advanced telecommunications and information services. In August 2004, AT&T voluntarily reported to the FCC that it might have overcharged the Government for services it provided as part of the program.

The FCC's Enforcement Bureau launched an investigation. As part of that investigation, AT&T provided the Bureau various documents, including responses to interrogatories, invoices, emails with pricing and billing information, names and job descriptions of employees involved, and AT&T's assessment of whether those employees had violated the company's code of conduct. The FCC and AT&T resolved the matter in December 2004 through a consent decree in which AT&T—without conceding liability—agreed to pay the Government $ 500,000 and to institute a plan to ensure compliance with the program.

Several months later, CompTel—"a trade association representing some of AT&T's competitors"—submitted a FOIA request seeking " '[a]ll pleadings and correspondence' " in the Bureau's file on the AT&T investigation. AT&T opposed CompTel's request, and the Bureau issued a letter-ruling in response.

The Bureau concluded that some of the information AT&T had provided (including cost and pricing data, billing-related information, and identifying information about staff, contractors, and customer representatives) should be protected from disclosure under FOIA Exemption 4, which relates to "trade secrets and commercial or financial information," 5 U.S.C. § 552(b)(4). The Bureau also decided to withhold other information under FOIA Exemption 7(C). Exemption 7(C) exempts "records or information compiled for law enforcement purposes" that "could reasonably be expected to constitute an unwarranted invasion of personal privacy." § 552(b)(7)(C). The Bureau concluded that "individuals identified in [AT&T's] submissions" have "privacy rights" that warrant protection under Exemption 7(C). The Bureau did not, however, apply that exemption to the corporation itself, reasoning that "businesses do not possess 'personal privacy' interests as required" by the exemption.

On review the FCC agreed with the Bureau. The Commission found AT&T's position that it is "a 'private corporate citizen' with personal privacy rights that should be protected from disclosure that would 'embarrass' it . . . within the meaning of Exemption 7(C) . . . at odds with established [FCC] and judicial precedent." It therefore concluded that "Exemption 7(C) has no applicability to corporations such as [AT&T]."

AT&T sought review in the Court of Appeals for the Third Circuit, and that court rejected the FCC's reasoning. Noting that Congress had defined the word "person" to include corporations as well as individuals, 5 U.S.C. § 551(2), the court held that Exemption 7(C) extends to the "personal privacy" of corporations, since "the root from which the statutory word [personal] . . . is derived" is the defined term "person." 582 F.3d at 497. As the court explained, "[i]t would be very odd indeed for an adjectival form of a defined term not to refer back to that defined term." The court accordingly ruled "that FOIA's text unambiguously indicates that a corporation may have a 'personal privacy' interest within the meaning of Exemption 7(C)."

The FCC petitioned this Court for review of the Third Circuit's decision and CompTel filed as a respondent supporting petitioners. We granted certiorari, and now reverse.

II

Like the Court of Appeals below, AT&T relies on the argument that the word "personal" in Exemption 7(C) incorporates the statutory definition of the word "person." The Administrative Procedure Act defines "person" to include "an individual, partnership, corporation, association, or public or private organization other than an agency." 5 U.S.C. § 551(2). Because that definition applies here, the argument goes, "personal" must mean relating to those "person[s]": namely, corporations and other entities as well as individuals. This reading, we are told, is dictated by a "basic principle of grammar and usage." [Citation.] According to AT&T, "[b]y expressly defining the noun 'person' to include corporations, Congress *necessarily* defined the adjective form of that noun—'personal'—also to include corporations."

We disagree. Adjectives typically reflect the meaning of corresponding nouns, but not always. Sometimes they acquire distinct meanings of their own. The noun "crab" refers variously to a crustacean and a type of apple, while the related adjective "crabbed" can refer to handwriting that is "difficult to read," Webster's Third New International Dictionary 527 (2002); "corny" can mean "using familiar and stereotyped formulas believed to appeal to the unsophisticated," *id.,* at 509, which has little to do with "corn," *id.,* at 507 ("the seeds of any of the cereal grasses used for food"); and while "crank" is "a part of an axis bent at right angles," "cranky" can mean "given to fretful fussiness," *id.,* at 530.

Even in cases such as these there may well be a link between the noun and the adjective. "Cranky" describes a person with a "wayward" or "capricious" temper, *see* 3 Oxford English Dictionary 1117 (2d ed. 1989) (OED), which might bear some relation to the distorted or crooked angular shape from which a "crank" takes its name. That is not the point. What is significant is that, in ordinary usage, a noun and its adjective form may have meanings as disparate as any two unrelated words. The FCC's argument that "personal" does not, in fact, derive from the English word "person," but instead developed along its own etymological path, simply highlights the shortcomings of AT&T's proposed rule.

"Person" is a defined term in the statute; "personal" is not. When a statute does not define a term, we typically "give the phrase its ordinary meaning." *Johnson v. United States,* 559 U.S. 133 (2010). "Personal" ordinarily refers to individuals. We do not usually speak of personal characteristics, personal effects, personal correspondence, personal influence, or personal tragedy as referring to corporations or other artificial entities. This is not to say that corporations do not have correspondence, influence, or tragedies of their own, only that we do not use the word "personal" to describe them.

Certainly, if the chief executive officer of a corporation approached the chief financial officer and said, "I have something personal to tell you," we would not assume the CEO was about to discuss company business. Responding to a request for information, an individual might say, "that's personal." A company spokesman, when asked for information about the company, would not. In fact, we often use the word "personal" to mean precisely the *opposite* of business-related: We speak of personal expenses and business expenses, personal life and work life, personal opinion and a company's view.

Dictionaries also suggest that "personal" does not ordinarily relate to artificial "persons" such as corporations. *See, e.g.,* 7 OED 726 (1933) ("[1] [o]f, pertaining to . . . the individual person or self," "individual; private; one's own," "[3] [o]f or pertaining to one's person, body, or figure," "[5] [o]f, pertaining to, or characteristic of a person or self-conscious being, as opposed to a thing or abstraction"); 11 OED at 599–600 (2d ed. 1989) (same); Webster's Third New International Dictionary 1686 (1976) ("[3] relating to the person or body"; "[4] relating to an individual, his character, conduct, motives, or private affairs"; "[5] relating to or characteristic of human beings as distinct from things"); *ibid.* (2002) (same).

AT&T dismisses these definitions, correctly noting that "personal"—at its most basic level—simply means "[o]f or pertaining to a particular person." Webster's New International Dictionary 1828 (2d ed. 1954). The company acknowledges that "in non-legal usage, where a 'person' is a human being, it is entirely unsurprising that the word 'personal' is used to refer to human beings." But in a watered-down version of the "grammatical imperative" argument, AT&T contends that "person"—in common *legal* usage—is understood to include a corporation. "Personal" in the same context therefore can and should have the same scope, especially here in light of the statutory definition.

The construction of statutory language often turns on context, [citation], which certainly may include the definitions of related words. But here the context to which AT&T points does not dissuade us from the ordinary meaning of "personal." We have no doubt that "person," in a legal setting, often refers to artificial entities. The Dictionary Act makes that clear. 1 U.S.C. § 1 (defining "person" to include "corporations, companies, associations, firms, partnerships, societies, and joint stock companies, as well as individuals"). But AT&T's effort to ascribe a corresponding legal meaning to "personal" again elides the difference between "person" and "personal."

When it comes to the word "personal," there is little support for the notion that it denotes corporations, even in the legal context. AT&T notes that corporations are "protected by the doctrine of 'personal' jurisdiction," but that phrase refers to jurisdiction *in personam*, as opposed to *in rem*, not the jurisdiction "of a person." The only other example AT&T cites is an 1896 case that referred to the " 'personal privilege' " of a corporation. [Citation.] These examples fall far short of establishing that "personal" here has a legal meaning apart from its ordinary one, even if "person" does. [Citation.]

Regardless of whether "personal" can carry a special meaning in legal usage, "when interpreting a statute . . . we construe language . . . in light of the terms surrounding it." [Citation.] Exemption 7(C) refers not just to the word "personal," but to the term "personal privacy." § 552(b)(7)(C); [citation]. AT&T's effort to attribute a special legal meaning to the word "personal" in this particular context is wholly unpersuasive.

AT&T's argument treats the term "personal privacy" as simply the sum of its two words: the privacy of a person. Under that view, the defined meaning of the noun "person," or the asserted specialized legal meaning, takes on greater significance. But two words together may assume a more particular meaning than those words in isolation. We understand a golden cup to be a cup made of or resembling gold. A golden boy, on the other hand, is one who is charming, lucky, and talented. A golden opportunity is one not to be missed. "Personal" in the phrase "personal privacy" conveys more than just "of a person." It suggests a type of privacy evocative of human concerns—not the sort usually associated with an entity like, say, AT&T.

Despite its contention that "[c]ommon legal usage" of the word "person" supports its reading of the term "personal privacy," AT&T does not cite a single instance in which this Court or any other (aside from the Court of Appeals below) has expressly referred to a corporation's "personal privacy." Nor does it identify any other statute that does so. On the contrary, treatises in print around the time that Congress drafted the exemptions at hand reflect the understanding that the specific concept of "personal privacy," at least as a matter of common law, did not apply to corporations. . . .

AT&T concludes that the FCC has simply failed to demonstrate that the phrase "personal privacy" "necessarily *excludes* the privacy of corporations." [AT&T Brief], at 31–32 (emphasis added). But construing statutory language is not merely an exercise in ascertaining "the outer limits of [a word's] definitional possibilities," *Dolan v. Postal Service*, 546 U.S. 481, 486, 126 S.Ct. 1252, 163 L. Ed. 2d 1079 (2006). AT&T has given us no sound reason in the statutory text or context to disregard the ordinary meaning of the phrase "personal privacy."

III

The meaning of "personal privacy" in Exemption 7(C) is further clarified by the rest of the statute. Congress enacted Exemption 7(C) against the backdrop of pre-existing FOIA exemptions, and the purpose and scope of Exemption 7(C) becomes even more apparent when viewed in this context. [Citation.] The phrase "personal privacy" first appeared in the FOIA exemptions in Exemption 6, enacted in 1966, eight years before Congress enacted Exemption 7(C). *See* 80 Stat. 250, codified as amended at 5 U.S.C. § 552(b)(6). Exemption 6 covers "personnel and medical files and similar files the disclosure of which would constitute a clearly unwarranted invasion of personal privacy." § 552(b)(6). Not only did Congress choose the same term in drafting Exemption 7(C), it also used the term in a nearly identical manner.

Although the question whether Exemption 6 is limited to individuals has not come to us directly, we have regularly referred to that exemption as involving an "individual's right of privacy." [Citations.] AT&T does not dispute that "identical words and phrases within the same statute should normally be given the same meaning," [citation], but contends that "if Exemption 6 does not protect corporations, it is because [it] applies only to 'personnel and medical files and similar files,'" not because of the term "personal privacy." Yet the significance of the pertinent phrase—"the disclosure of which would constitute a clearly unwarranted invasion of personal privacy," § 552(b)(6)—cannot be so readily dismissed. Without it, Exemption 6 would categorically exempt "personnel and medical files" as well as any "similar" file. Even if the scope of Exemption 6 is also limited by the types of files it protects, the "personal privacy" phrase importantly defines the particular subset of that information Congress sought to exempt. [Citation.] And because Congress used the same phrase in Exemption 7(C), the reach of that phrase in Exemption 6 is pertinent in construing Exemption 7(C).

In drafting Exemption 7(C), Congress did not, on the other hand, use language similar to that in Exemption 4. Exemption 4 pertains to "trade secrets and commercial or financial information obtained from a person and privileged or confidential." 5 U.S.C. § 552(b)(4). This clearly applies to corporations—it uses the defined term "person" to describe the source of the information—and we far more readily think of corporations as having "privileged or confidential" documents than personally private ones. So at the time Congress enacted Exemption 7(C), it had in place an exemption that plainly covered a corporation's commercial and financial information, and another that we have described as relating to "individuals." The language of Exemption 7(C) tracks the latter.

* * *

We reject the argument that because "person" is defined for purposes of FOIA to include a corporation, the phrase "personal privacy" in Exemption 7(C) reaches corporations as well. The protection in FOIA against disclosure of law enforcement information on the ground that it would constitute an unwarranted invasion of personal privacy does not extend to corporations. We trust that AT&T will not take it personally.

The judgment of the Court of Appeals is reversed.

It is so ordered.

a. DICTIONARY DEFINITIONS

The Court's approach in *FCC v. AT&T* exemplifies a common method courts employ when seeking the "ordinary meaning" of a statutory term: the resort to dictionary definitions of the term in question. Indeed, the Court fairly readily dismissed AT&T's argument that the Court should look to the statute's definitions section, which defined "person" to include *corporate* persons, in order to divine the statutory meaning of "personal." Rather, the Court emphasized that the meaning of the adjective "personal" had "acquire[d a] distinct meaning[ ] of [its] own." Would it always be unreasonable for a related statutory definition to inform the interpretation of an ambiguous term?

The Court also reached its conclusion by centering the interpretive inquiry on the meaning of the statutory phrase *"personal privacy"*—not the word "personal" as defined or used in isolation. As you will see later in this subsection, that phrase is an example of a linguistic "collocation" in which two words that frequently appear together may take on a more specific or contextual meaning than when either word is used on its own. As you read the next subsection, consider whether dictionary definitions are as useful when interpreting a statutory *phrase* as opposed to an individual word, given that most dictionary definitions provide definitions only of individual words. Consider also whether a central task for an interpreter is to decide whether the interpretive inquiry should be to define a *word* or a *phrase*. For example, as you will see in *Muscarello v. U.S., infra*, the majority focused its interpretive inquiry primarily on the meaning of the statutory word "carries," while the dissent focused instead on the statutory phrase "carries *a firearm*." Thus, whether an interpreter chooses to "zoom in" or "zoom out" may itself be dispositive of the meaning to give to a statutory provision.

NOTE: DICTIONARIES: OBJECTIVE? AUTHORITATIVE? BIASED?

Dictionaries may be a useful source of "ordinary" meaning because they are widely available (including online), and they generally seek to reflect how language is ordinarily used. At a minimum, then, dictionaries might be said to capture how the reasonable lay reader would understand the meaning of the statute in question. Nevertheless, dictionaries are not themselves neutral depositaries of word meanings and usages. The editors of dictionaries make conscious choices about whether to exclude, include, or prioritize one meaning or usage of a word over another—or even to include a word at all. As essayist David Foster Wallace famously documented in a 2001 article in *Harper's*, lexicographic Usage Wars have in recent decades become as heated as judicial debates about textualism and purposivism:

> Did you know that probing the seamy underbelly of U.S. lexicography reveals ideological strife and controversy and intrigue and nastiness and fervor . . . ? For instance, did you know that some modern dictionaries are notoriously liberal and others notoriously conservative, and that certain conservative dictionaries were actually conceived and designed as corrective responses to the "corruption" and "permissiveness" of certain liberal dictionaries? That the oligarchic device of having a special "Distinguished Usage Panel . . . of outstanding professional speakers and writers" is an attempted compromise between the forces of egalitarianism and traditionalism in English, but that most linguistic liberals dismiss

the Usage Panel as mere sham-populism . . .? Did you know that U.S. lexicography even *had* a seamy underbelly? . . .

We regular citizens tend to go to The Dictionary for authoritative guidance. Rarely, however, do we ask ourselves who decides what gets in The Dictionary or what words or spellings or pronunciations get deemed "substandard" or "incorrect." Whence the authority of dictionary-makers to decide what's OK and what isn't? Nobody elected them, after all. And simply appealing to precedent or tradition won't work, because what's considered correct changes over time. In the 1600s, for instance, the second-singular pronoun took a singular conjugation—"You is." . . . English itself changes over time; if it didn't, we'd all still be talking like Chaucer. Who's to say which changes are natural and which are corruptions? . . .

You'd sure know lexicography had an underbelly if you read the little introductory essays in modern dictionaries . . . . They're salvos in the Usage Wars that have been under way ever since editor Philip Gove first sought to apply the value-neutral principles of structural linguistics to lexicography in *Webster's Third*. Gove's famous response to conservatives who howled when *Webster's Third* endorsed *OK* and described *ain't* as "used orally in most parts of the U.S. by many cultivated speakers [*sic*]" was this: "A dictionary should have no traffic with . . . artificial notions of correctness or superiority. It should be descriptive and not prescriptive." These terms stuck and turned epithetic, and linguistic conservatives are now formally known as Prescriptivists and linguistic liberals as Descriptivists.

Descriptivists . . . . tend to be hard-core academics, mostly linguists or Comp theorists. Loosely organized under the banner of structural (or "descriptive") linguistics, they are doctrinaire positivists . . . . In this age of technology, [some] Descriptivists contend, it's the Scientific Method—clinically objective, value-neutral, based on direct observation and demonstrable hypothesis—that should determine both the content of dictionaries and the standards of "correct" English. Because language is constantly evolving, such standards will always be fluid. Gove's now classic introduction to *Webster's Third* outlines this type of Descriptivism's five basic edicts:

"1—Language changes constantly;

2—Change is normal;

3—Spoken language is the language;

4—Correctness rests upon usage;

5—All usage is relative."

These principles look *prima facie* OK—commonsensical and couched in the bland simple s.-v.-o, prose of dispassionate Science—

but in fact they're vague and muddled and it takes about three seconds to think of reasonable replies to each one of them, viz.:

1—OK, but how much and how fast?

2—Same thing. Is Heraclitean flux as normal or desirable as gradual change? Do some changes actually serve the language's overall pizzazz better than others? And how many people have to deviate from how many conventions before we say the language has actually changed? Fifty percent? Ten percent? Where do you draw the line? Who draws the line?

3—This is an old claim, at least as old as Plato's *Phaedrus*. And it's specious. If Derrida and the infamous Deconstructionists have done nothing else, they've debunked the idea that speech is language's primary instantiation. Plus consider the weird arrogance of Gove's (3) [with respect to] correctness. Only the most mullahlike Prescriptivists care very much about spoken English; most Prescriptive usage guides concern Standard *Written* English.

4—Fine, but whose usage? Gove's (4) begs the whole question. What he wants to suggest here, I think, is a reversal of the traditional entailment-relation between abstract rules and concrete usage: Instead of usage ideally corresponding to a rigid set of regulations, the regulations ought to correspond to the way real people are actually using the language. Again, fine, but which people? Urban Latinos? Boston Brahmins? Rural Midwesterners? Appalachian Neogaelics?

5—*Huh?* If this means what it seems to mean, then it ends up biting Gove's whole argument in the ass. (5) appears to imply that the correct answer to the above "which people?" is: "All of them!" And it's easy to show why this will not stand up as a lexicographical principle. The most obvious problem with [Descriptivist ambitions] is that not everything can go in The Dictionary. Why not? Because you can't observe every last bit of every last native speaker's "language behavior," and even if you could, the resultant dictionary would weigh 4 million pounds and have to be updated hourly. The fact is that any lexicographer is going to have to make choices about what gets in and what doesn't. And these choices are based on . . . what? And now we're right back where we started. . . .

There's an even more important way Descriptivists are wrong in thinking that the Scientific Method is appropriate to the study of language: . . . [Language] is both *human* and fundamentally *normative*. . . . To understand this, you have only to accept the proposition that language is by its very nature public. [Norms, after all, are just practices people have agreed on as optimal ways of doing things for certain purposes. They're not laws, but they're not laissez-faire, either.] Norms-wise, let's keep in mind that language didn't come into being because our hairy ancestors were sitting around the veldt with nothing better to do. Language was invented to serve certain specific purposes: "That mushroom is poisonous";

"Knock these two rocks together and you can start a fire"; "This shelter is mine!" And so on. Clearly, as linguistic communities evolve over time, they discover that some ways of using language are "better" than others—meaning better with respect to the community's purposes. . . . The whole point of norms is to help us evaluate our actions (including utterances) according to what we as a community have decided our real interests and purposes are. . . .

David Foster Wallace, *Tense Present*, Harper's (April 2001).

The question of whether usage authorities are, or should be, engaged in "value judgment" is not a uniquely English-language phenomenon, either. Consider this recent controversy:

[Ghent U]niversity in Belgium has refused demands to "immediately" strip its website of Flemish sign-language videos displaying stereotypical and anti-Semitic symbols for Jews, saying it was merely hosting a dictionary of signs without adding "value judgment." . . .

According to the Flemish dictionary, there are four ways to sign the word "Jewish": by stroking the chin; by stroking an imagined goatee; by mimicking bilateral pipe curls with the fingers; and by moving a hooked finger over the face—symbolizing a hooked nose. . . .

[T]he university . . . . said that it had discussed the complaints with the researchers who created the dictionary [and] in a statement on Friday . . . , the university described the controversy as a purely "scientific issue."

It said that in creating the dictionary, researchers merely "register and describe the signs that are used in the Flemish sign language." It added: "They don't take position on these signs, and don't cast a value judgment on them. This is what lexicographers do." . . .

The Flemish Sign Language Center, which helped create the dictionary in 1999 and is responsible for updating its content, said in a statement that . . . "We don't decide ourselves whether or not a sign has its place in the dictionary[.]" . . .

But in many dictionaries of sign languages around the world, including of American Sign Language in the United States, the sign for "Jewish" is simply a stroke under the chin. . . .

Milan Schreuer, *University Denounced for Showing Sign Language for 'Jewish' as a Hooked Nose*, New York Times (Sept. 20, 2019), available at https://www.nytimes.com/2019/09/20/world/europe/belgium-sign-language-jews.html.

Keep these debates about the proper place of dictionaries—and the authorities who develop them—in mind as you read the following case, as well as the cases in the next sections of this Part.

MCI Telecommunications Corp. v. American Tel. & Tel. Co.

Supreme Court of the United States, 1994.
512 U.S. 218, 114 S.Ct. 2223, 129 L.Ed.2d 182.

■ JUSTICE SCALIA delivered the opinion of the Court[, in which CHIEF JUSTICE REHNQUIST, JUSTICE KENNEDY, JUSTICE THOMAS, and JUSTICE GINSBURG joined].

Section 203(a) of Title 47 of the United States Code requires communications common carriers to file tariffs with the Federal Communications Commission, and § 203(b) authorizes the Commission to "modify" any requirement of § 203. These cases present the question whether the Commission's decision to make tariff filing optional for all nondominant long-distance carriers is a valid exercise of its modification authority.

I

... When Congress created the Commission in 1934, AT & T, through its vertically integrated Bell system, held a virtual monopoly over the Nation's telephone service. The Communications Act of 1934, 48 Stat. 1064, as amended, authorized the Commission to regulate the rates charged for communication services to ensure that they were reasonable and nondiscriminatory. The requirements of § 203 that common carriers file their rates with the Commission and charge only the filed rate were the centerpiece of the Act's regulatory scheme.

... By 1979, competition in the provision of long-distance service was well established, and some urged that the continuation of extensive tariff filing requirements served only to impose unnecessary costs on new entrants and to facilitate collusive pricing. The Commission held hearings on the matter, *see Competitive Carrier Notice of Inquiry and Proposed Rulemaking,* 77 F.C.C.2d 308 (1979), following which it issued a series of rules that have produced this litigation.

The *First Report and Order,* 85 F.C.C.2d 1, 20–24 (1980), distinguished between dominant carriers (those with market power) and nondominant carriers—in the long-distance market, this amounted to a distinction between AT & T and everyone else—and relaxed some of the filing procedures for nondominant carriers, *id.,* at 30–49. In the *Second Report and Order,* 91 F.C.C.2d 59 (1982), the Commission entirely eliminated the filing requirement for resellers of terrestrial common carrier services. This policy of optional filing, or permissive detariffing, was extended to all other resellers, and to specialized common carriers, including petitioner MCI Telecommunications Corp., by the *Fourth Report and Order,* 95 F.C.C.2d 554 (1983), and to virtually all remaining categories of nondominant carriers by the *Fifth Report and Order,* 98 F.C.C.2d 1191 (1984). . . .

On August 7, 1989, AT & T filed a complaint, pursuant to the third-party complaint provision of the Communications Act, 47 U.S.C. § 208(a), which alleged that MCI's collection of unfiled rates violated §§ 203(a) and (c). MCI responded that the *Fourth Report* was a substantive rule, and so MCI had no legal obligation to file rates. AT & T rejoined that . . . if the *Fourth Report and Order* established a substantive rule, it was in excess of statutory authority. The Commission . . . refused to address . . . AT & T's contention that the rule was ultra vires, announcing instead a proposed rulemaking to consider that question. [Citation.] . . .

[T]he Commission released a Report and Order from the rulemaking proceeding commenced in response to AT & T's complaint. *See In re Tariff Filing Requirements for Interstate Common Carriers,* 7 FCC Rcd 8072 (1992), stayed pending further notice, 7 FCC Rcd 7989 (1992). That is the Report and Order at issue in this case. The Commission, relying upon the § 203(b) authority to "modify" . . . determined that its permissive detariffing policy was within its authority under the Communications Act. AT & T filed a motion with the District of Columbia Circuit seeking summary reversal of the Commission's order. . . . We granted the petitions and consolidated them.

II

Section 203 of the Communications Act contains both the filed rate provisions of the Act and the Commission's disputed modification authority. It provides in relevant part:

"(a) Filing; public display.

"Every common carrier, except connecting carriers, shall, within such reasonable time as the Commission shall designate, file with the Commission and print and keep open for public inspection schedules showing all charges . . ., whether such charges are joint or separate, and showing the classifications, practices, and regulations affecting such charges. . . .

"(b) Changes in schedule; discretion of Commission to *modify* requirements. . . .

"(2) The Commission may, in its discretion and for good cause shown, *modify* any requirement made by or under the authority of this section either in particular instances or by general order applicable to special circumstances or conditions except that the Commission may not require the notice period specified in paragraph (1) to be more than one hundred and twenty days. . . ." [emphasis added]

The dispute between the parties turns on the meaning of the phrase "modify any requirement" in § 203(b)(2). Petitioners argue that it gives the Commission authority to make even basic and fundamental changes in the scheme created by that section. We disagree. The word "modify"—like a number of other English words employing the root "mod-" (deriving from the Latin word for "measure"), such as "moderate," "modulate," "modest," and "modicum"—has a connotation of increment or limitation. Virtually every dictionary we are aware of says that "to modify" means to change moderately or in minor fashion. *See, e.g.,* Random House

Dictionary of the English Language 1236 (2d ed. 1987) ("to change somewhat the form or qualities of; alter partially; amend"); Webster's Third New International Dictionary 1452 (1981) ("to make minor changes in the form or structure of: alter without transforming"); 9 Oxford English Dictionary 952 (2d ed. 1989) ("[t]o make partial changes in; to change (an object) in respect of some of its qualities; to alter or vary without radical transformation"); Black's Law Dictionary 1004 (6th ed. 1990) ("[t]o alter; to change in incidental or subordinate features; enlarge; extend; amend; limit; reduce").

In support of their position, petitioners cite dictionary definitions contained in, or derived from, a single source, Webster's Third New International Dictionary 1452 (1981) (Webster's Third), which includes among the meanings of "modify," "to make a basic or important change in."[2] Petitioners contend that this establishes sufficient ambiguity to entitle the Commission to deference in its acceptance of the broader meaning, which in turn requires approval of its permissive detariffing policy. [Citation.] In short, they contend that the courts must defer to the agency's choice among available dictionary definitions, citing *National Railroad Passenger Corporation v. Boston & Maine Corp.*, 503 U.S. 407, 418 (1992).

But *Boston & Maine* does not stand for that proposition. That case involved the question whether the statutory term "required" could only mean "demanded as essential" or could also mean "demanded as appropriate." In holding that the latter was a permissible interpretation, to which [judicial] deference was owed, the opinion did not rely exclusively upon dictionary definitions, but also upon contextual indications, *see* 503 U.S., at 417–419,—which in the present cases, as we shall see, contradict petitioners' position. Moreover, when the *Boston & Maine* opinion spoke of "alternative dictionary definitions," *ibid.*, it did not refer to what we have here: one dictionary whose suggested meaning contradicts virtually all others. It referred to alternative definitions *within the dictionary cited* (Webster's Third, as it happens), which was not represented to be the *only* dictionary giving those alternatives. To the contrary, the Court said "these alternative interpretations are as old as the jurisprudence of this Court," *id.*, at 419, citing *McCulloch v. Maryland*, 4 Wheat. 316 (1819). *See also* Webster's New International

---

2   Petitioners also cite Webster's Ninth New Collegiate Dictionary 763 (1991), which includes among its definitions of "modify," "to make basic or fundamental changes in often to give a new orientation to or to serve a new end." They might also have cited the eighth version of Webster's New Collegiate Dictionary 739 (1973), which contains that same definition; and Webster's Seventh New Collegiate Dictionary 544 (1963), which contains the same definition as Webster's Third New International Dictionary quoted in text. The Webster's New Collegiate Dictionaries, published by G. & C. Merriam Company of Springfield, Massachusetts, are essentially abridgments of that company's Webster's New International Dictionaries, and recite that they are based upon those lengthier works. The last New Collegiate to be based upon Webster's Second New International, rather than Webster's Third, does not include "basic or fundamental change" among the accepted meanings of "modify." *See* Webster's New Collegiate Dictionary 541 (6th ed. 1949).

Dictionary 2117 (2d ed. 1934); 2 New Shorter Oxford English Dictionary 2557 (1993) (giving both alternatives).

Most cases of verbal ambiguity in statutes involve, as *Boston & Maine* did, a selection between accepted alternative meanings shown as such by many dictionaries. One can envision (though a court case does not immediately come to mind) having to choose between accepted alternative meanings, one of which is so newly accepted that it has only been recorded by a single lexicographer. (Some dictionary must have been the very first to record the widespread use of "projection," for example, to mean "forecast.") But what petitioners demand that we accept as creating an ambiguity here is a rarity even rarer than that: a meaning set forth in a single dictionary (and, as we say, its progeny) which not only *supplements* the meaning contained in all other dictionaries, but *contradicts* one of the meanings contained in virtually all other dictionaries. Indeed, contradicts one of the alternative meanings contained in the out-of-step dictionary itself—for as we have observed, Webster's Third itself defines "modify" to connote *both* (specifically) major change *and* (specifically) minor change. It is hard to see how that can be. When the word "modify" has come to mean *both* "to change in some respects" *and* "to change fundamentally" it will in fact mean *neither* of those things. It will simply mean "to change," and some adverb will have to be called into service to indicate the great or small degree of the change.

If that is what the peculiar Webster's Third definition means to suggest has happened—and what petitioners suggest by appealing to Webster's Third—we simply disagree. "Modify," in our view, connotes moderate change. It might be good English to say that the French Revolution "modified" the status of the French nobility—but only because there is a figure of speech called understatement and a literary device known as sarcasm. And it might be unsurprising to discover a 1972 White House press release saying that "the Administration is modifying its position with regard to prosecution of the war in Vietnam"—but only because press agents tend to impart what is nowadays called "spin." Such intentional distortions, or simply careless or ignorant misuse, must have formed the basis for the usage that Webster's Third, and Webster's Third alone, reported.[3] It is perhaps gilding the lily to add this: In 1934, when the Communications Act became law—the most relevant time for determining a statutory term's meaning, [citation], Webster's Third was not yet even contemplated. To our knowledge *all* English dictionaries provided the narrow definition of "modify," including those published by

---

[3]   That is not an unlikely hypothesis. Upon its long-awaited appearance in 1961, Webster's Third was widely criticized for its portrayal of common error as proper usage. *See, e.g.,* Follett, Sabotage in Springfield, 209 Atlantic 73 (Jan. 1962); Barzun, What is a Dictionary? 32 The American Scholar 176, 181 (spring 1963); Macdonald, The String Unwound, 38 The New Yorker 130, 156–157 (Mar. 1962). An example is its approval (without qualification) of the use of "infer" to mean "imply": "infer" "5: to give reason to draw an inference concerning: HINT <did not take part in the debate except to ask a question inferring that the constitution must be changed—Manchester Guardian Weekly>." Webster's Third New International Dictionary 1158 (1961).

G. & C. Merriam Company. *See* Webster's New International Dictionary 1577 (2d ed. 1934); Webster's Collegiate Dictionary 628 (4th ed. 1934). We have not the slightest doubt that is the meaning the statute intended.

Beyond the word itself, a further indication that the § 203(b)(2) authority to "modify" does not contemplate fundamental changes is the sole exception to that authority which the section provides. One of the requirements of § 203 is that changes to filed tariffs can be made only after 120 days' notice to the Commission and the public. § 203(b)(1). The *only* exception to the Commission's § 203(b)(2) modification authority is as follows: "except that the Commission may not require the notice period specified in paragraph (1) to be more than one hundred and twenty days." Is it conceivable that the statute is indifferent to the Commission's power to eliminate the tariff-filing requirement entirely for all except one firm in the long-distance sector, and yet strains out the gnat of extending the waiting period for tariff revision beyond 120 days? We think not. The exception is not as ridiculous as a Lilliputian in London only because it is to be found in Lilliput: in the small-scale world of "modifications," it is a big deal. . . .

[T]he Commission's permissive detariffing policy can be justified only if it makes a less than radical or fundamental change in the Act's tariff-filing requirement. The Commission's attempt to establish that no more than that is involved greatly understates the extent to which its policy deviates from the filing requirement, and greatly undervalues the importance of the filing requirement itself.

To consider the latter point first: For the body of a law, as for the body of a person, whether a change is minor or major depends to some extent upon the importance of the item changed to the whole. Loss of an entire toenail is insignificant; loss of an entire arm tragic. The tariff-filing requirement is, to pursue this analogy, the heart of the common-carrier section of the Communications Act. In the context of the Interstate Commerce Act, which served as its model, [citation,] this Court has repeatedly stressed that rate filing was Congress's chosen means of preventing unreasonableness and discrimination in charges. . . .

Bearing in mind, then, the enormous importance to the statutory scheme of the tariff-filing provision, we turn to whether what has occurred here can be considered a mere "modification." The Commission stresses that its detariffing policy applies only to nondominant carriers, so that the rates charged to over half of all consumers in the long-distance market are on file with the Commission. It is not clear to us that the proportion of customers affected, rather than the proportion of carriers affected, is the proper measure of the extent of the exemption (of course *all* carriers in the long-distance market are exempted, except AT & T). But even assuming it is, we think an elimination of the crucial provision of the statute for 40% of a major sector of the industry is much too extensive to be considered a "modification." What we have here, in reality, is a fundamental revision of the statute, changing it from a scheme of rate regulation in long-distance common-carrier communications to a scheme of rate regulation only where effective competition does not exist. That may be a good idea, but it was not the idea Congress enacted into law in 1934. . . .

The judgment of the Court of Appeals is

Affirmed.

■ JUSTICE O'CONNOR took no part in the consideration or decision of [this case].

■ JUSTICE STEVENS, with whom JUSTICE BLACKMUN and JUSTICE SOUTER join, dissenting.

. . . According to the Court, the term "modify," as explicated in all but the most unreliable dictionaries, rules out the Commission's claimed authority to relieve nondominant carriers of the basic obligation to file tariffs. Dictionaries can be useful aids in statutory interpretation, but they are no substitute for close analysis of what words mean as used in a particular statutory context. *Cf. Cabell v. Markham,* 148 F.2d 737, 739 (2d Cir. 1945) (Hand, J.). Even if the sole possible meaning of "modify" were to make "minor" changes, further elaboration is needed to show why the detariffing policy should fail. The Commission came to its present policy through a series of rulings that gradually relaxed the filing requirements for nondominant carriers. Whether the current policy should count as a cataclysmic or merely an incremental departure from the § 203(a) baseline depends on whether one focuses on particular carriers' obligations to file (in which case the Commission's policy arguably works a major shift) or on the statutory policies behind the tariff-filing requirement (which remain satisfied because market constraints on nondominant carriers obviate the need for rate filing). When § 203 is viewed as part of a statute whose aim is to constrain monopoly power, the Commission's decision to exempt nondominant carriers is a rational and "measured" adjustment to novel circumstances—one that remains faithful to the core purpose of the tariff-filing section. *See* Black's Law Dictionary 1198 (3d ed. 1933) (defining "modification" as "A change; an alteration which introduces new elements into the details, or cancels some of them, but leaves *the general purpose and effect of the subject-matter* intact").

The Court seizes upon a particular sense of the word "modify" at the expense of another, long-established meaning that fully supports the Commission's position. That word is first defined in Webster's Collegiate Dictionary 628 (4th ed. 1934) as meaning "to limit or reduce in extent or degree."[5] The Commission's permissive detariffing policy fits comfortably

---

[5]   *See also* 9 Oxford English Dictionary 952 (2d ed. 1989) ("2. To alter in the direction of moderation or lenity; to make less severe, rigorous, or decided; to qualify, tone down. . . . 1610 Donne *Pseudomartyr* 184 'For so Mariana modefies his Doctrine, that the Prince should not execute any Clergy man, though hee deser[v]e it' "); Random House Dictionary of the English Language 1236 (2d ed. 1987) ("5. to reduce or lessen in degree or extent; moderate; soften; *to modify one's demands*"); Webster's Third New International Dictionary 1452 (1981) ("1: to make

within this common understanding of the term. The FCC has in effect adopted a general rule stating that "if you are dominant you must file, but if you are nondominant you need not." The Commission's partial detariffing policy—which excuses nondominant carriers from filing *on condition that* they remain nondominant—is simply a relaxation of a costly regulatory requirement that recent developments had rendered pointless and counterproductive in a certain class of cases.

... Whatever the best reading of § 203(b)(2), the Commission's reading cannot in my view be termed unreasonable. It is informed (as ours is not) by a practical understanding of the role (or lack thereof) that filed tariffs play in the modern regulatory climate and in the telecommunications industry.... We should sustain its eminently sound, experience-tested, and uncommonly well-explained judgment.

I respectfully dissent.

NOTE

In **United States v. Costello**, 666 F.3d 1040 (7th Cir. 2012), Judge Posner considered whether the defendant, who allowed her boyfriend to live with her while knowing he was in the United States without authorization, had violated a statute criminalizing the knowing "harboring" of an unauthorized alien. The government's argument relied heavily on dictionary definitions:

> The actual definition of "to harbor" that the government has found in these dictionaries and urges us to adopt is "to shelter," which is not synonymous with "to provide a place to stay." "To shelter" has an aura of protectiveness, as in taking "shelter" from a storm. To shelter is to provide a refuge. "Sheltering" doesn't seem the right word for letting your boyfriend live with you....

> [D]ictionaries must be used as sources of statutory meaning only with great caution. "Of course it is true that the words used, even in their literal sense, are the primary, and ordinarily the most reliable, source of interpreting the meaning of any writing: be it a statute, a contract, or anything else. But it is one of the surest indexes of a mature and developed jurisprudence not to make a fortress out of the dictionary; but to remember that statutes always have some purpose or object to accomplish, whose sympathetic and imaginative discovery is the surest guide to their meaning." *Cabell v. Markham,* 148 F.2d 737, 739 (2d Cir. 1945) (L. Hand, J.)....

> Dictionary definitions are acontextual, whereas the meaning of sentences depends critically on context, including all sorts of

---

more temperate and less extreme: lessen the severity of; ... 'traffic rules were *modified* to let him pass'"); Webster's New Collegiate Dictionary 739 (1973) ("1. to make less extreme; MODERATE"); Webster's Seventh New Collegiate Dictionary 544 (1963) (same); Webster's Seventh New International Dictionary 1577 (2d ed. 1934) ("2. To reduce in extent or degree; to moderate; qualify; lower; as, to *modify* heat, pain, punishment"); N. Webster, American Dictionary of the English Language (1828) ("To moderate; to qualify; to reduce in extent or degree. Of his grace\He *modifies* his first severe decree. *Dryden*").

background understandings. . . . We doubt that the government would argue that a hospital emergency room that takes in a desperately ill person whom the hospital staff knows to be an illegal alien would be guilty of harboring, although it fits the government's definition of the word.

A Google search . . . of several terms in which the word "harboring" appears—a search based on the supposition that the number of hits per term is a rough index of the frequency of its use—reveals the following:

"harboring fugitives": 50,800 hits

"harboring enemies": 4,730 hits

"harboring refugees": 4,820 hits

"harboring victims": 114 hits

"harboring flood victims": 0 hits

"harboring victims of disasters": 0 hits . . .

"harboring Jews": 19,100 hits

"harboring guests": 184 hits

"harboring victims of persecution": 0 hits

It is apparent from these results that "harboring," as the word is actually used, has a connotation—which "sheltering," and *a fortiori* "giving a person a place to stay"—does not, of deliberately safeguarding members of a specified group from the authorities, whether through concealment, movement to a safe location, or physical protection. This connotation enables one to see that the emergency staff at the hospital may not be "harboring" an alien when it renders emergency treatment even if he stays in the emergency room overnight, that giving a lift to a gas station to an alien with a flat tire may not be harboring, that driving an alien to the local office of the Department of Homeland Security to apply for an adjustment of status to that of lawful resident may not be harboring, that inviting an alien for a "one night stand" may not be attempted harboring, that placing an illegal alien in a school may not be harboring (*cf. Plyler v. Doe,* 457 U.S. 202 (1982)), and finally that allowing your boyfriend to live with you may not be harboring, even if you know he shouldn't be in the United States.

Judge Manion disagreed with Judge Posner's conclusion as to the ordinary meaning of the term "harboring," and dissented:

[T]he court rejects the ordinary definition of the term "harboring" and asserts that the facts cannot support Costello's conviction even when considering a more exacting definition of "harboring"; thus, the court would reverse Costello's conviction. I disagree, and conclude that the plain language of the statute and the stipulated facts support the conviction of harboring. . . .

Contrary to the court's assertion, the ordinary meaning of "harboring" certainly includes "providing shelter to." This was a common understanding of the term when the term "harbor" was first added to the statute in 1917, and when the statute was amended and the term retained in 1952. *See* Webster's New International Dictionary of the English Language 981 (1917) ("harbor" defined as "[t]o afford lodging to; to entertain as a guest; to shelter; to receive; to give refuge to"); Webster's New Collegiate Dictionary 376 (John P. Bethel et al., eds. 1953) ("harbor" defined as "to entertain as a guest; to shelter; to give a refuge to"). . . .

As we [have] noted [previously], " 'conceal,' 'harbor,' and 'shield from detection' have independent meanings, and thus a conviction can result from committing (or attempting to commit) any one of the three acts." Perhaps if Costello had shooed her boyfriend out the back door when the police were approaching from the front, she could be accused of shielding. Or if she had hidden him in the basement under a pile of laundry when federal agents showed up with a search warrant, she could also be charged with concealing. But she neither shielded nor concealed; instead, she provided shelter to her boyfriend, and nothing more is required to charge her with harboring under the statute.

QUESTIONS

1. Do you agree with Judge Posner's critique of the relative utility of dictionaries? Does his use of Google search results reveal more or less about the contextual meaning of the word "harbor"? What sources are legitimate for a judge to consult when seeking the meaning of a word in a statute? Should there be any limits placed on how many, and what kinds of, sources judges can consult? Would your answer be different for criminal statutes than for technical, regulatory statutes? Remember this last point when you read *Muscarello v U.S., infra.*

2. Recall David Foster Wallace's description of the notable role that *Webster's Third* played in leading to a split among descriptive and prescriptive lexicographers. In preparing *Webster's Third*, its editor sought to capture language as actually used in present-day colloquial communication, rather than as it had been used in the past, or as prescribed as appropriate by expert lexicographers. When a court turns to a dictionary in search of the definition of a statutory term, does it matter whether that dictionary's editor has sought to emphasize meanings based on language as it is actually used or as it is acceptably used according to a subset of experts in linguistic usage? Would it matter whether one seeks the "ordinary" or "specialized" meaning of a word or phrase? Do these choices depend on assumptions about legislative drafters' intentions when drafting statutes?

3. What kind of authority do dictionaries have as sources of *legal* knowledge? After all, lexicographers are not elected by the public, nor delegated lawmaking authority by legislatures. Recall the typology of interpretive methods from Section II.B.1, *supra*. In theory, one may justify the use of dictionaries on at least several grounds, including: (a) they reveal the intended meaning of a term *as used by legislative drafters*; (b) they reveal the meaning *that members of the public* most frequently associate with a term; and/or (c) they reveal a meaning that the interpreter believes would most satisfactorily resolve the *legal* dispute at issue, whether or not it purports to represent either the legislature's intention or the public's understanding. What kind of empirical or normative assumptions underlie each of these claims to authority?

4. As highlighted in Section VIII.A.2, *infra,* the State of Oregon's appellate courts have indicated they will use *Webster's Third New International Dictionary, Unabridged,* to determine the meaning of a word if there is no statutory definition or well-defined legal meaning. Can you articulate arguments in support of this approach? What are some potential problems with adopting a specific dictionary? Is your assessment influenced by the preceding excerpts highlighting controversies over *Webster's Third* and the Flemish sign-language dictionary?

5. Dictionaries may not always resolve problems of linguistic ambiguity. After all, dictionary definitions, like statutory definitions sections, often contain their own vague or ambiguous words. As Judge Raymond Randolph of the U.S. Court of Appeals for the District of Columbia has observed:

> [C]iting to dictionaries creates a sort of optical illusion, conveying the existence of certainty—or "plainness"—when appearance may be all there is. Lexicographers define words with words. Words in the definition are defined by more words, as are those words. The trail may be endless; sometimes, it is circular. Using a dictionary definition simply pushes the problem back. . . .
>
> Dictionary citing in judicial opinions, and the plain meaning rule itself, imply that the meanings of the words used in a statute equal the meaning of the statute. This is demonstrably false . . . . Of course, one must comprehend the words in a statute in order to comprehend the statute, just as one must comprehend the letters in a word in order to comprehend the word. A statute, however, cannot be understood merely by understanding the words in it. Judge Easterbrook thinks dictionaries are like "word museums." I think they are also like "word zoos." One can observe an animal's features in the zoo, but one still cannot be sure how the animal will behave in its native surroundings. The same is true of words in a text.

A. Raymond Randolph, *Dictionaries, Plain Meaning, and Context in Statutory Interpretation,* 17 Harv. J.L. & Pub. Pol'y 71 (1994).

6. If dictionaries supposedly aid in revealing the intended meaning of a term as used by legislative drafters, should it matter whether legislative drafters themselves rely on dictionaries when drafting? In surveying dozens of legislative drafters, Abbe Gluck and Lisa Schultz Bressman found that dictionaries do not play a significant role in most legislative drafting:

> *"No one uses a freaking dictionary"*
>
> More than 50% of our respondents said that dictionaries are never or rarely used when drafting. This finding stands in stark juxtaposition with the frequent and increasing use of dictionaries

by the Supreme Court in statutory interpretation cases. Although the Court has always looked to dictionaries in some statutory cases, scholars have documented that the Court's use of this interpretive tool recently has risen dramatically: the Court used dictionaries in 225 opinions from 2000 to 2010, compared to just sixteen opinions in the 1960s.

Our respondents were aware of this judicial trend, but told us that it nevertheless did not affect their practice. Several specifically referenced Justice Scalia—acknowledging that the Court frequently uses dictionaries but noting that they remain mostly irrelevant to the drafting process. As one respondent put it (while laughing): "Scalia is a bright guy, but no one uses a freaking dictionary." Another noted more delicately: "This question presumes that legislative staff have dictionaries. I have tried to get an OED but people over at finance say we aren't spending money to buy you a dictionary. And no Black's Law Dictionary either."

The Court's rationale for dictionary consultation, however, may assume that Congress does use dictionaries or at least would welcome their use by judges. . . .

Abbe R. Gluck & Lisa Schultz Bressman, *Statutory Interpretation from the Inside: An Empirical Study of Congressional Drafting, Delegation, and the Canons: Part I*, 65 Stan. L. Rev. 901 (2013).

b.   OTHER SOURCES OF ORDINARY USAGE AND MEANING

Muscarello v. United States

Supreme Court of the United States, 1998.
524 U.S. 125, 118 S.Ct. 1911, 141 L.Ed.2d 111.

■ JUSTICE BREYER delivered the opinion of the Court[, joined by JUSTICE STEVENS, JUSTICE O'CONNOR, JUSTICE KENNEDY, and JUSTICE THOMAS].

A provision in the firearms chapter of the federal criminal code imposes a 5-year mandatory prison term upon a person who "uses or carries a firearm" "during and in relation to" a "drug trafficking crime." 18 U.S.C. § 924(c)(1). The question before us is whether the phrase "carries a firearm" is limited to the carrying of firearms on the person. We hold that it is not so limited. Rather, it also applies to a person who knowingly possesses and conveys firearms in a vehicle, including in the locked glove compartment or trunk of a car, which the person accompanies.

The question arises in two cases, which we have consolidated for argument. [The defendant] in the first case, Frank J. Muscarello, unlawfully sold marijuana, which he carried in his truck to the place of sale. Police officers found a handgun locked in the truck's glove compartment. During plea proceedings, Muscarello admitted that he had "carried" the gun "for protection in relation" to the drug offense, though he later claimed to the contrary, and added that, in any event, his "carrying" of the gun in the glove compartment did not fall within the scope of the statutory word "carries."

[The defendants] in the second case, Donald Cleveland and Enrique Gray-Santana, placed several guns in a bag, put the bag in the trunk of a car, and then traveled by car to a proposed drug-sale point, where they intended to steal drugs from the sellers. Federal agents at the scene stopped them, searched the cars, found the guns and drugs, and arrested them.

In both cases the Courts of Appeals found that [the defendants] had "carried" the guns during and in relation to a drug trafficking offense. [Citation.] We granted certiorari to determine whether the fact that the guns were found in the locked glove compartment, or the trunk, of a car, precludes application of § 924(c)(1). We conclude that it does not.

A

We begin with the statute's language. The parties vigorously contest the ordinary English meaning of the phrase "carries a firearm." Because they essentially agree that Congress intended the phrase to convey its ordinary, and not some special legal, meaning, and because they argue the linguistic point at length, we too have looked into the matter in more than usual depth. Although the word "carry" has many different meanings, only two are relevant here. When one uses the word in the first, or primary, meaning, one can, as a matter of ordinary English, "carry firearms" in a wagon, car, truck, or other vehicle that one accompanies. When one uses the word in a different, rather special, way, to mean, for example, "bearing" or (in slang) "packing" (as in "packing a gun"), the matter is less clear. But, for reasons we shall set out below, we believe Congress intended to use the word in its primary sense and not in this latter, special way.

Consider first the word's primary meaning. The Oxford English Dictionary gives as its first definition "convey, originally by cart or wagon, hence in any vehicle, by ship, on horseback, etc." 2 Oxford English Dictionary 919 (2d ed. 1989); *see also* Webster's Third New International Dictionary 343 (1986) (first definition: "move while supporting (as in a vehicle or in one's hands or arms)"); The Random House Dictionary of the English Language Unabridged 319 (2d ed. 1987) (first definition: "to take or support from one place to another; convey; transport").

The origin of the word "carries" explains why the first, or basic, meaning of the word "carry" includes conveyance in a vehicle. *See* The Barnhart Dictionary of Etymology 146 (1988) (tracing the word from Latin "carum," which means "car" or "cart"); 2 Oxford English Dictionary, *supra*, at 919 (tracing the word from Old French "carier" and the late Latin "carricare," which meant to "convey in a car"); The Oxford Dictionary of English Etymology 148 (C. Onions ed.1966) (same); The Barnhart Dictionary of Etymology, *supra*, at 143 (explaining that the term "car" has been used to refer to the automobile since 1896).

The greatest of writers have used the word with this meaning. *See, e.g.*, the King James Bible, 2 Kings 9:28 ("His servants carried him in a chariot to Jerusalem"); *id.*, Isaiah 30:6 ("They will carry their riches upon the shoulders of young asses"). Robinson Crusoe says, "with my boat, I carry'd away every Thing." D. Defoe, Robinson Crusoe 174 (J. Crowley ed. 1972). And the owners of Queequeg's ship, Melville writes, "had lent him a [wheelbarrow], in which to carry his heavy chest to his boarding-house." H. Melville, Moby Dick 43 (U. Chicago 1952). . . .

These examples do not speak directly about carrying guns. But there is nothing linguistically special about the fact that weapons, rather than drugs, are being carried. Robinson Crusoe might have carried a gun in his boat; Queequeg might have borrowed a wheelbarrow in which to carry, not a chest, but a harpoon. And, to make certain that there is no special ordinary English restriction (unmentioned in dictionaries) upon the use of "carry" in respect to guns, we have surveyed modern press usage, albeit crudely, by searching computerized newspaper databases—both the New York Times database in Lexis/Nexis, and the "US News" database in Westlaw. We looked for sentences in which the words "carry," "vehicle," and "weapon" (or variations thereof) all appear. We found thousands of such sentences, and random sampling suggests that many, perhaps more than one third, are sentences used to convey the meaning at issue here, *i.e.*, the carrying of guns in a car. . . .

Now consider a different, somewhat special meaning of the word "carry"—a meaning upon which the linguistic arguments of petitioners and the dissent must rest. The Oxford English Dictionary's twenty-sixth definition of "carry" is "bear, wear, hold up, or sustain, as one moves about; habitually to bear about with one." 2 Oxford English Dictionary, *supra*, at 921. Webster's defines "carry" as "to move while supporting," not just in a vehicle, but also "in one's hands or arms." Webster's Third New International Dictionary, *supra*, at 343. And Black's Law Dictionary defines the entire phrase "carry arms or weapons" as

> "To wear, bear or carry them upon the person or in the clothing or in a pocket, for the purpose of use, or for the purpose of being armed and ready for offensive or defensive action in case of a conflict with another person." Black's Law Dictionary 214 (6th ed. 1990).

These special definitions, however, do not purport to limit the "carrying of arms" to the circumstances they describe. No one doubts that one who bears arms on his person "carries a weapon." But to say that is not to deny that one may also "carry a weapon" tied to the saddle of a horse or placed in a bag in a car.

Nor is there any linguistic reason to think that Congress intended to limit the word "carries" in the statute to any of these special definitions. To the contrary, all these special definitions embody a form of an important, but secondary, meaning of "carry," a meaning that suggests support rather than movement or transportation, as when, for example, a column "carries" the weight of an arch. 2 Oxford English Dictionary, *supra*, at 919, 921. In this sense a gangster might "carry" a gun (in colloquial language, he might "pack a gun") even though he does not move from his chair. It is difficult to believe, however, that Congress intended to limit the statutory word to this definition—imposing special punishment upon the comatose gangster while ignoring drug lords who drive to a sale carrying an arsenal of weapons in their van.

We recognize, as the dissent emphasizes, that the word "carry" has other meanings as well. But those other meanings, (*e.g.*, "carry all he knew," "carries no colours") are not relevant here. And the fact that speakers often do not add to the phrase "carry a gun" the words "in a car" is of no greater relevance here than the fact that millions of Americans did not see Muscarello carry a gun in his truck. The relevant linguistic facts are that the word "carry" in its ordinary sense includes carrying in a car and that the word, used in its ordinary sense, keeps the same meaning whether one carries a gun, a suitcase, or a banana.

Given the ordinary meaning of the word "carry," it is not surprising to find that the Federal Courts of Appeals have unanimously concluded that "carry" is not limited to the carrying of weapons directly on the person but can include their carriage in a car. [Citation.]

B

[The Court then] conclude[d] that neither the statute's basic purpose nor its legislative history support circumscribing the scope of the word "carry" by applying an "on the person" limitation.

This Court has described the statute's basic purpose broadly, as an effort to combat the "dangerous combination" of "drugs and guns." [Citation.] . . .

From the perspective of any such purpose (persuading a criminal "to leave his gun at home") what sense would it make for this statute to penalize one who walks with a gun in a bag to the site of a drug sale, but to ignore a similar individual who, like defendant Gray-Santana, travels to a similar site with a similar gun in a similar bag, but instead of walking, drives there with the gun in his car? How persuasive is a punishment that is without effect until a drug dealer who has brought his gun to a sale (indeed has it available for use) actually takes it from the trunk (or unlocks the glove compartment) of his car? It is difficult to say that, considered as a class, those who prepare, say, to sell drugs by placing guns in their cars are less dangerous, or less deserving of punishment, than those who carry handguns on their person. . . .

C

We are not convinced by petitioners' remaining arguments to the contrary. First, they say that our definition of "carry" makes it the equivalent of "transport." Yet, Congress elsewhere in related statutes used the word "transport" deliberately to signify a different, and broader, statutory coverage. The immediately preceding statutory subsection, for example, imposes a different set of penalties on one who, with an intent to commit a crime, "ships, transports, or receives a firearm" in interstate commerce. 18 U.S.C. § 924(b). Moreover, § 926A specifically "entitles" a person "not otherwise prohibited ... from transporting, shipping, or receiving a firearm" to "transport a firearm ... from any place where he may lawfully possess and carry" it to "any other place" where he may do so. Why, petitioners ask, would Congress have used the word "transport," or used both "carry" and "transport" in the same provision, if it had intended to obliterate the distinction between the two?

The short answer is that our definition does not equate "carry" and "transport." "Carry" implies personal agency and some degree of possession, whereas "transport" does not have such a limited connotation and, in addition, implies the movement of goods in bulk over great distances. [Citation.] If Smith, for example, calls a parcel delivery service, which sends a truck to Smith's house to pick up Smith's package and take it to Los Angeles, one might say that Smith has shipped the package and the parcel delivery service has transported the package. But only the truck driver has "carried" the package in the sense of "carry" that we believe Congress intended. Therefore, "transport" is a broader category that includes "carry" but also encompasses other activity.

The dissent refers to § 926A and to another statute where Congress used the word "transport" rather than "carry" to describe the movement of firearms. 18 U.S.C. §§ 925(a)(2)(B). According to the dissent, had Congress intended "carry" to have the meaning we give it, Congress would not have needed to use a different word in these provisions. But as we have discussed above, we believe the word "transport" is broader than the word "carry."

And, if Congress intended "carry" to have the limited definition the dissent contends, it would have been quite unnecessary to add the proviso in § 926A requiring a person, to be exempt from penalties, to store her firearm in a locked container not immediately accessible. *See* § 926A (exempting from criminal penalties one who transports a firearm from a place where "he may lawfully possess and carry such firearm" but not exempting the "transportation" of a firearm if it is "readily accessible or is directly accessible from the passenger compartment of such transporting vehicle"). The statute simply could have said that such a person may not "carry" a firearm. But, of course, Congress did not say this because that is not what "carry" means.

As we interpret the statutory scheme, it makes sense. Congress has imposed a variable penalty with no mandatory minimum sentence upon a person who "transports" (or "ships" or "receives") a firearm knowing it will be used to commit any "offense punishable by imprisonment for [more than] one year," § 924(b), and it has imposed a 5-year mandatory minimum sentence upon one who "carries" a firearm "during and in relation to" a "drug trafficking crime," § 924(c). The first subsection imposes a less strict sentencing regime upon one who, say, ships firearms by mail for use in a crime elsewhere; the latter subsection imposes a mandatory sentence upon one who, say, brings a weapon with him (on his person or in his car) to the site of a drug sale. . . .

. . . [P]etitioners say that our reading of the statute would extend its coverage to passengers on buses, trains, or ships, who have placed a firearm, say, in checked luggage. . . . In our view, this argument does not take adequate account of other limiting words in the statute—words that make the statute applicable only where a defendant "carries" a gun *both* "during *and* in relation to" a drug crime. § 924(c)(1) (emphasis added). Congress added these words in part to prevent prosecution where guns "played" no part in the crime. [Citation.]

Once one takes account of the words "during" and "in relation to," it no longer seems beyond Congress' likely intent, or otherwise unfair, to interpret the statute as we have done. If one carries a gun in a car "during" and "in relation to" a drug sale, for example, the fact that the gun is carried in the car's trunk or locked glove compartment seems not only logically difficult to distinguish from the immediately accessible gun, but also beside the point.

At the same time, the narrow interpretation creates its own anomalies. The statute, for example, defines "firearm" to include a "bomb," "grenade," "rocket having a propellant charge of more than four ounces," or "missile having an explosive or incendiary charge of more than one-quarter ounce," where such device is "explosive," "incendiary," or delivers "poison gas." 18 U.S.C. § 921(a)(4)(A). On petitioners' reading, the "carry" provision would not apply to instances where drug lords, engaged in a major transaction, took with them "firearms" such as these, which most likely could not be carried on the person.

. . . [P]etitioners [also] argue that we should construe the word "carry" to mean "immediately accessible." And, as we have said, they point out that several Circuit Courts of Appeals have limited the statute's scope in this way. [Citations.] That interpretation, however, is difficult to square with the statute's language, for one "carries" a gun in the glove compartment whether or not that glove compartment is locked. Nothing in the statute's history suggests that Congress intended that limitation. And, for reasons pointed out above, we believe that the words "during" and "in relation to" will limit the statute's application to the harms that Congress foresaw.

Finally, petitioners and the dissent invoke the "rule of lenity." The simple existence of some statutory ambiguity, however, is not sufficient to warrant application of that rule, for most statutes are ambiguous to some degree. Cf. *Smith*, 508 U.S. at 239 ("The mere possibility of articulating a narrower construction . . . does not by itself make the rule of lenity applicable"). " 'The rule of lenity applies only if, "after seizing everything from which aid can be derived," . . . we can make "no more than a guess as to what Congress intended." ' " [Citation.] To invoke the rule, we must conclude that there is a " ' "grievous ambiguity or uncertainty" ' in the statute." [Citation.] Certainly, our decision today is based on much more than a "guess as to what Congress intended," and there is no "grievous ambiguity" here. The problem of statutory interpretation in this case is indeed no different from that in many of the criminal cases that confront us. Yet, this Court has never held that the rule of lenity automatically permits a defendant to win. . . .

For these reasons, we conclude that [defendants]' conduct falls within the scope of the phrase "carries a firearm." The decisions of the Courts of Appeals are affirmed.

It is so ordered.

■ JUSTICE GINSBURG, with whom . . . CHIEF JUSTICE [REHNQUIST], JUSTICE SCALIA, and JUSTICE SOUTER join, dissenting.

. . . It is uncontested that § 924(c)(1) applies when the defendant bears a firearm, *i.e.*, carries the weapon on or about his person "for the purpose of being armed and ready for offensive or defensive action in case of a conflict." Black's Law Dictionary 214 (6th ed. 1990) (defining the phrase "carry arms or weapons"). The Court holds that, in addition, "carries a firearm," in the context of § 924(c)(1), means personally transporting, possessing, or keeping a firearm in a vehicle, anyplace in a vehicle.

Without doubt, "carries" is a word of many meanings, definable to mean or include carting about in a vehicle. But that encompassing definition is not a ubiquitously necessary one. Nor, in my judgment, is it a proper construction of "carries" as the term appears in § 924(c)(1). In line with . . . the principle of lenity the Court has long followed, I would confine "carries a firearm," for § 924(c)(1) purposes, to the undoubted meaning of that expression in the relevant context. I would read the words to indicate not merely keeping arms on one's premises or in one's vehicle, but bearing them in such manner as to be ready for use as a weapon.

I

A

I note first what is at stake for petitioners. The question before the Court "is not whether possession of a gun [on the drug offender's premises or in his car, during and in relation to commission of the offense,] means a longer sentence for a convicted drug dealer. It most certainly does. . . . Rather, the question concerns which sentencing statute governs the precise length of the extra term of punishment," § 924(c)(1)'s "blunt 'mandatory minimum'" five-year sentence, or the more finely tuned "sentencing guideline statutes, under which extra punishment for drug-related gun possession varies with the seriousness of the drug crime." United States v. McFadden, 13 F.3d 463, 466 (C.A.1 1994) (Breyer, C. J., dissenting).

Accordingly, there would be no "gap," no relevant conduct "ignored," were the Court to reject the Government's broad reading of § 924(c)(1). To be more specific, as cogently explained on another day by today's opinion writer:

"The special 'mandatory minimum' sentencing statute says that anyone who 'uses or carries' a gun 'during and in relation to any . . . drug trafficking crime' must receive a mandatory five-year prison term added on to his drug crime sentence. 18 U.S.C. § 924(c). At the same time, the Sentencing Guidelines, promulgated under the authority of a different statute, 28 U.S.C. § 994, provide for a two-level (*i.e.*, a 30% to 40%) sentence enhancement where a 'firearm . . . was possessed' by a drug offender, U.S. S. G. § 2D1.1(b)(1), unless the possession clearly was not 'connected with the [drug] offense.' " *McFadden*, 13 F.3d at 467 (Breyer, C. J., dissenting).

In Muscarello's case, for example, the underlying drug crimes involved the distribution of 3.6 kilograms of marijuana, and therefore carried a base offense level of 12. *See* United States Sentencing Commission, Guidelines Manual § 2D1.1(a)(3) (Nov. 1995). After adjusting for Muscarello's acceptance of responsibility, *see id.*, § 3E1.1(a), his final offense level was 10, placing him in the 6-to-12 month sentencing range. *See id.*, ch. 5, pt. A. The two-level enhancement for possessing a firearm, *id.*, § 2D1.1(b)(1), would have increased his final offense level to 12 (a sentencing range of 10 to 16 months). In other words, the less rigid (tailored to "the seriousness of the drug crime," *McFadden*, 13 F.3d at 466) Guidelines regime would have added four months to Muscarello's prison time, in contrast to the five-year minimum addition the Court's reading of § 924(c)(1) mandates.

In sum, drug traffickers will receive significantly longer sentences if they are caught traveling in vehicles in which they have placed firearms. The question that divides the Court concerns the proper reference for enhancement in the cases at hand, the Guidelines or § 924(c)(1).

B

Unlike the Court, I do not think dictionaries,[2] surveys of press reports,[3] or the Bible[4] tell us, dispositively, what "carries" means

---

[2] I note, however, that the only legal dictionary the Court cites, Black's Law Dictionary, defines "carry arms or weapons" restrictively.

[3] Many newspapers, the New York Times among them, have published stories using "transport," rather than "carry," to describe gun placements resembling petitioners'. *See, e.g.*, Atlanta Constitution, Feb. 27, 1998, p. 9D, col. 2 ("House members last week expanded gun laws by allowing weapons to be *carried into restaurants or transported anywhere in cars.*"); Chicago Tribune, June 12, 1997, sports section, p. 13 ("Disabled hunters with permission to hunt from a standing vehicle would be able to *transport a shotgun in an all-terrain vehicle* as long as the gun is unloaded and the breech is open."); Colorado Springs Gazette Telegraph, Aug. 4, 1996, p. C10 (British gun laws require "locked steel cases bolted onto a car for *transporting guns from home to shooting range.*"); Detroit News, Oct. 26, 1997, p. D14 ("It is unlawful to *carry afield or transport a rifle . . .* or shotgun if you have buckshot, slug, ball loads, or cut shells in possession except while traveling directly to deer camp or target range with firearm not readily available to vehicle occupants."); N. Y. Times, July 4, 1993, p. A21, col. 2 ("The gun is supposed to be *transported unloaded*, in a locked box in the trunk."); Santa Rosa Press Democrat, Sept. 28, 1996, p. B1 ("Police and volunteers ask that participants . . . *transport [their guns] to the fairgrounds* in the trunks of their cars."); Worcester Telegram & Gazette, July 16, 1996, p. B3 ("Only one gun can be turned in per person. *Guns transported in a vehicle* should be locked in the trunk.") (emphasis added in all quotations).

[4] The translator of the Good Book, it appears, bore responsibility for determining whether the servants of Ahaziah "carried" his corpse to Jerusalem. Compare *ante*, with, *e.g.*, The New English Bible, 2 Kings 9:28 ("His servants *conveyed* his body to Jerusalem."); Saint Joseph Edition of the New American Bible ("His servants *brought* him in a chariot to Jerusalem."); Tanakh: The Holy Scriptures ("His servants *conveyed* him in a chariot to Jerusalem."); *see also*

embedded in § 924(c)(1). On definitions, "carry" in legal formulations could mean, inter alia, transport, possess, have in stock, prolong (carry over), be infectious, or wear or bear on one's person. At issue here is not "carries" at large but "carries a firearm." The Court's computer search of newspapers is revealing in this light. Carrying guns in a car showed up as the meaning "perhaps more than one third" of the time. One is left to wonder what meaning showed up some two thirds of the time. Surely a most familiar meaning is, as the Constitution's Second Amendment ("keep and *bear* Arms") (emphasis added) and Black's Law Dictionary, at 214, indicate: "wear, bear, or carry . . . upon the person or in the clothing or in a pocket, for the purpose . . . of being armed and ready for offensive or defensive action in a case of conflict with another person."

On lessons from literature, a scan of Bartlett's and other quotation collections shows how highly selective the Court's choices are. If "the greatest of writers" have used "carry" to mean convey or transport in a vehicle, so have they used the hydra-headed word to mean, inter alia, carry in one's hand, arms, head, heart, or soul, sans vehicle. Consider, among countless examples:

> "He shall gather the lambs with his arm, and carry them in his bosom." The King James Bible, Isaiah 40:11.

> "And still they gaz'd, and still the wonder grew, That one small head could carry all he knew." O. Goldsmith, The Deserted Village, ll. 215–216, in The Poetical Works of Oliver Goldsmith 30 (A. Dobson ed. 1949).

> "There's a Legion that never was 'listed, That carries no colours or crest." R. Kipling, The Lost Legion, st. 1, in Rudyard Kipling's Verse, 1885–1918, p. 222 (1920).

> "There is a homely adage which runs, 'Speak softly and carry a big stick; you will go far.'" T. Roosevelt, Speech at Minnesota State Fair, Sept. 2, 1901, in J. Bartlett, Familiar Quotations 575:16 (J. Kaplan ed. 1992).[6]

These and the Court's lexicological sources demonstrate vividly that "carry" is a word commonly used to convey various messages. Such references, given their variety, are not reliable indicators of what Congress meant, in § 924(c)(1), by "carries a firearm."

---

id., Isaiah 30:6 ("They *convey* their wealth on the backs of asses."); The New Jerusalem Bible ("They *bear* their riches on donkeys' backs.") (emphasis added in all quotations).

[6] Popular films and television productions provide corroborative illustrations. In "The Magnificent Seven," for example, O'Reilly (played by Charles Bronson) says: "You think I am brave because I carry a gun; well, your fathers are much braver because they carry responsibility, for you, your brothers, your sisters, and your mothers." *See* http://us.imdb.com/M/search_quotes?for=carry. And in the television series "M*A*S*H," Hawkeye Pierce (played by Alan Alda) presciently proclaims: "I will not carry a gun. . . . I'll carry your books, I'll carry a torch, I'll carry a tune, I'll carry on, carry over, carry forward, Cary Grant, cash and carry, carry me back to Old Virginia, I'll even 'hari-kari' if you show me how, but I will not carry a gun!" *See* http://www.geocities.com/Hollywood/8915/mashquotes.html.

C

Noting the paradoxical statement, " 'I use a gun to protect my house, but I've never had to use it,' " the Court in *Bailey*, 516 U.S. at 143, emphasized the importance of context—the statutory context. Just as "uses" was read to mean not simply "possession," but "active employment," so "carries," correspondingly, is properly read to signal the most dangerous cases—the gun at hand, ready for use as a weapon. It is reasonable to comprehend Congress as having provided mandatory minimums for the most life-jeopardizing gun-connection cases (guns in or at the defendant's hand when committing an offense), leaving other, less imminently threatening, situations for the more flexible guidelines regime.[8] As the Ninth Circuit suggested, it is not apparent why possession of a gun in a drug dealer's moving vehicle would be thought more dangerous than gun possession on premises where drugs are sold: "A drug dealer who packs heat is more likely to hurt someone or provoke someone else to violence. A gun in a bag under a tarp in a truck bed [or in a bedroom closet] poses substantially less risk." [Citation.][9]

For indicators from Congress itself, it is appropriate to consider word usage in other provisions of Title 18's chapter on "Firearms." . . . Section 925(a)(2)(B), for example, provides that no criminal sanction shall attend "the transportation of [a] firearm or ammunition carried out to enable a person, who lawfully received such firearm or ammunition from the Secretary of the Army, to engage in military training or in competitions." . . . In describing when and how a person may travel in a vehicle that contains his firearm without violating the law, §§ 925(a)(2)(B) and 926A use "transport," not "carry," to "imply personal agency and some degree of possession."[10] . . . [U]nder § 925(a)(2)(B), one could carry his gun to a car, transport it to the shooting competition, and use it to shoot targets. Under the conditions of § 926A, one could transport her gun in a car, but under no circumstances could the gun be readily accessible while she travels in the car. "Courts normally try to read language in different, but related, statutes, so as best to reconcile those statutes, in light of their

---

[8]   The Court reports that the Courts of Appeals "have unanimously concluded that 'carry' is not limited to the carrying of weapons directly on the person." In *Bailey*, however, the Government's argument based on a similar observation did not carry the day. . . .

[9]   The "Firearms" statutes indicate that Congress, unlike the Court, recognizes that a gun in the hand is indeed more dangerous than a gun in the trunk. *See, e.g.,* 18 U.S.C. § 926A (permitting the transportation of firearms in a vehicle, but only if "neither the firearm nor any ammunition being transported is readily accessible or is directly accessible from the passenger compartment of such transporting vehicle").

[10]   The Court asserts that " 'transport' is a broader category that includes 'carry' but encompasses other activity." "Carry," however, is not merely a subset of "transport" A person seated at a desk with a gun in hand or pocket is carrying the gun, but is not transporting it. Yes, the words "carry" and "transport" often can be employed interchangeably, as can the words "carry" and "use." . . . Without doubt, Congress is alert to the discrete meanings of "transport" and "carry" in the context of vehicles, as the Legislature's placement of each word in § 926A illustrates. The narrower reading of "carry" preserves discrete meanings for the two words, while in the context of vehicles the Court's interpretation of "carry" is altogether synonymous with "transport." Tellingly, when referring to firearms traveling in vehicles, the "Firearms" statutes routinely use a form of "transport"; they never use a form of "carry."

purposes and of common sense." *McFadden*, 13 F.3d at 467 (Breyer, C. J., dissenting). So reading the "Firearms" statutes, I would not extend the word "carries" in § 924(c)(1) to mean transports out of hand's reach in a vehicle.

II

Section 924(c)(1), as the foregoing discussion details, is not decisively clear one way or another. The sharp division in the Court on the proper reading of the measure confirms, "at the very least, . . . that the issue is subject to some doubt. Under these circumstances, we adhere to the familiar rule that, 'where there is ambiguity in a criminal statute, doubts are resolved in favor of the defendant.'" [Citation.] . . . "Carry" bears many meanings, as the Court and the "Firearms" statutes demonstrate. The narrower "on or about [one's] person" interpretation is hardly implausible nor at odds with an accepted meaning of "carries a firearm."

Overlooking that there will be an enhanced sentence for the gun-possessing drug dealer in any event, the Court asks rhetorically: "How persuasive is a punishment that is without effect until a drug dealer who has brought his gun to a sale (indeed has it available for use) actually takes it from the trunk (or unlocks the glove compartment) of his car?" Correspondingly, the Court defines "carries a firearm" to cover "a person who knowingly possesses and conveys firearms [anyplace] in a vehicle . . . which the person accompanies." Congress, however, hardly lacks competence to select the words "possesses" or "conveys" when that is what the Legislature means.[14] Notably in view of the Legislature's capacity to speak plainly, and of overriding concern, the Court's inquiry pays scant attention to a core reason for the rule of lenity: "Because of the seriousness of criminal penalties, and because criminal punishment usually represents the moral condemnation of the community, legislatures and not courts should define criminal activity. This policy embodies 'the instinctive distaste against men languishing in prison unless the lawmaker has clearly said they should.'" [Citation.]

* * *

The narrower "on or about [one's] person" construction of "carries a firearm" . . . respects the Guidelines system by resisting overbroad readings of statutes that deviate from that system." [Citation.] It fits plausibly with other provisions of the "Firearms" chapter, and it adheres to the principle that, given two readings of a penal provision, both consistent with the statutory text, we do not choose the harsher construction. The Court, in my view, should leave it to Congress to speak

---

[14] *See, e.g.*, 18 U.S.C.A. § 924(a)(6)(B)(ii) (Supp. 1998) ("if the person sold . . . a handgun . . . to a juvenile knowing . . . that the juvenile intended to *carry or otherwise possess* . . . the handgun . . . in the commission of a crime of violence"); 18 U.S.C. § 926A ("may lawfully *possess and carry* such firearm to any other place where he may lawfully *possess and carry* such firearm"); § 929(a)(1) ("uses or *carries a firearm and is in possession* of armor piercing ammunition"); § 2277 ("brings, *carries, or possesses* any dangerous weapon") (emphasis added in all quotations).

" 'in language that is clear and definite' " if the Legislature wishes to impose the sterner penalty. [Citation.] . . .

QUESTIONS

1. Do you agree with the majority that the "primary" meaning of "carry" means to " 'carry . . .' in a wagon, car, truck, or other vehicle"? When interpreting a statutory phrase, should the "primary" meaning of one word in that phrase be dispositive if there are alternative plausible meanings? How should the interpreter decide which, if any, of these plausible meanings is the "plain" meaning? To be "plain," must the word's meaning be "ubiquitously necessary"? What difference should the "rule of lenity" make in deciding whether to interpret the term broadly or narrowly?

2. To what extent is the plain meaning of a term determined by which dictionary or other sources of linguistic usage the interpreter chooses as his reference? If leading dictionaries provide competing definitions, or if the term is commonly used to convey different ideas, could the interpreter reasonably conclude that a "plain" meaning exists at all? Would a judge applying the plain meaning rule in this manner be said to be more or less deferential to the legislature?

3. The dissent points out that "Congress . . . hardly lacks the competence to select the words 'possess' or 'conveys' when that is what the legislature means." What inference should one draw from Congress's use of related but distinct words across a single statute? Recall the typology of interpretive methods in Section II.B.1, *supra*. Does this evidence of nuanced and varied word selection shed light on what *the legislative drafters' intended* the statutory phrase in question to mean, or what the *reasonable reader* should infer the statute to mean? Note that the latter method attributes to the "reasonable reader" the capacity to parse an entire statute carefully in order to understand the meaning of a single term or phrase. (And recall Part II's opening salvo that one must always *read* the statute closely, and not paraphrase it!)

NOTE: "CORPUS LINGUISTICS"

As we have seen, dictionaries have inherent limits as sources of ordinary meaning. An emerging alternative method, known as "corpus linguistics," seeks to capture more holistically the contextual ordinary meanings and usage of words. Justice Thomas R. Lee of the Utah Supreme Court is a leading advocate of this method, and has argued that compared to dictionary definitions written by a small number of experts, corpus linguistics analysis provides a more systematic survey of linguistic usage and a more representative account of "ordinary" meaning in contemporary practice:

> When we speak of *ordinary* meaning, we are asking an empirical question—about the sense of a word or phrase that is most likely implicated in a given linguistic context. Linguists have developed computer-aided means of answering such questions. We propose to import those methods into the modern theory and

practice of interpretation, and we identify problems in the methods that the law has been using to address these issues.

Our proposed methodology is a set of tools utilized in a field called corpus linguistics. Corpus linguists study language through data derived from large bodies—corpora—of naturally occurring language. They look for patterns in meaning and usage in large databases of actual written language. And we think their methods may easily be adapted in a manner that will allow us to conceptualize and measure the "standard picture" in a much more careful way. . . .

Is a woman who allows her boyfriend—an undocumented immigrant—to sleep at her apartment guilty of harboring an alien under a federal statute criminalizing that act? . . . *Costello* involved a statutory term broad enough to encompass both parties' positions. Sometimes harbor refers to the mere act of providing shelter, but it may also indicate the sort of sheltering that is aimed at concealment. How is the court to decide which sense is the ordinary one? Writing for the majority, Judge Posner recognized the deficiencies of standard methods—principally, dictionaries—in answering that question. So he proceeded to a search for data, and he did so using the tool that is perhaps most familiar to us today. He performed a Google search.

Is this the best we can do? . . . [There are] theoretical and operational deficiencies in the law's search for ordinary meaning. . . .

The case law embraces a startlingly broad range of senses of ordinary meaning. When judges speak of ordinary meaning, they often seem to be speaking to a question of relative frequency—as in a point on the following continuum:

POSSIBLE→COMMON→MOST FREQUENT→EXCLUSIVE

At the left end of the continuum is the idea of a possible or linguistically permissible meaning—a sense of a word or phrase that is attested in a known body of written or spoken language. A meaning is a possible one if we can say that "you can use that word in that way" (as attested by evidence that other people have used the word in that way in the past). Yet a possible meaning may be an uncommon or unnatural sense of a given term. In that case, we might note that a given sense of a term is not common in a given linguistic setting, even if it is possible to speak that way. And even a common sense of a term might not be the most frequent use of it in a certain context.

The notion of plain meaning adds the final point to the continuum. When courts speak of plain meaning (as a concept distinct from ordinary meaning) they generally mean to "denote obvious meaning" or "meaning that is clear." A plain—obvious or clear—meaning would be more than most frequent. It would be nearly exclusive. . . .

Judge Posner rejects a dictionary-based approach to ordinary meaning in Costello. . . . Judge Posner turns to Google to get a "rough index of the frequency of [harboring's] use." This approach is innovative. But it is far from perfect.

Google might seem to be a good source for data-driven analysis of language usage. . . . Yet we still see a range of problems in Judge Posner's approach.

First is the black box of the Google algorithm. Google searches "are sorted according to a complex and unknown algorithm (with full listings of all results usually not permitted) so we do not know what biases are being introduced." Google returns can vary by geography, by time of day, and from day to day. Google search results are thus rather unscientific, if we understand good science as including replicability.

Second are problems with the Google search engine: the fact that it does not allow us to search only for verb forms of harbor and that it will not allow us to look at a particular speech community or period of time (only contemporary web pages, even if their content was first published in the past). If we are interested in knowing the ordinary use of harbor as a verb among ordinary English speakers at the time of the enactment of the statute at issue (1917), Google cannot give us that kind of parsed data.

In light of these search engine problems, Judge Posner formulated his own set of search terms—comparing hit counts for phrases like "harboring fugitives" and "harboring guests." But this innovation introduces a third set of problems: Judge Posner gives no basis for his chosen set of search terms, and the terms he chose seem likely to affect the outcome.

Finally, even setting aside the problems discussed above, the hit counts that Judge Posner relies on may not be indicative of ordinariness in the sense of frequency of usage. Judge Posner implies that relative hit counts are an indication of frequency of usage in our ordinary language. But that may not hold. Google hit counts are based on the total number of web pages, not the total number of occurrences of a given phrase. . . . So hit counts may not be a reliable indication of ordinariness, even if we could overcome the other problems identified here.

We think Judge Posner was onto something in seeking an empirical method of measurement, but we also think his Google search was inadequate. . . .

Corpus linguistic tools can be employed to measure ordinary meaning as conceptualized in this Article. . . . Linguistic corpora come in a number of varieties, each tailored to suit the needs of a particular set of empirical questions about language use. . . .

Linguistic corpora can perform a variety of tasks that cannot be performed by human linguistic intuition alone. . . . [C]orpora can be used to measure the statistical frequency of words and word senses in a given speech community and over a given time period. Whether we regard the ordinary meaning of a given word to be the possible, common, or the most common sense of that word in a given context, linguistic corpora allows us to determine empirically where a contested sense of a term falls on that continuum.

Corpora can also show collocation, "which is the tendency of words to be biased in the way they co-occur." As we have seen, words are often interpreted according to the semantic environment in which they are found. A collocation program can show the possible range of linguistic contexts in which a word typically appears and can provide useful information about the range of possible meanings and sense divisions.

Corpora also have a concordance or key word in context ("KWIC") function, which allows their users to review a particular word or phrase in hundreds of contexts, all on the same page of running text. This allows a corpus user to evaluate words in context systematically. . . .

[The authors then ran the term "harbor" through several prominent corpora databases:]

[W]e examined 140 concordance lines in which harbor occurred in the same environment as fugitives, terrorists, criminals, aliens, and refugees. Of these, twenty-three instances of harbor referred to concealment while thirty-two referred to shelter. In an additional eighty-three instances, the distinction could not be determined by context. There were also three instances of unrelated senses of harbor. In the COHA, there were only three clear-cut cases of the shelter sense. The remaining five instances of harbor could not be determined by context. . . .

This data raises more questions than it answers. With respect to frequency, we would be hard-pressed to say that either the shelter meaning or the conceal meaning of harbor are the most common. We might say that both are common meanings, and they are both certainly possible and attested meanings. But where more than half of the instances of harbor are unclear as to whether they include shelter or concealment or both, it is hard to state from the standpoint of frequency what the ordinary meaning actually is. . . .

Such are the data. But what to make of them? Do corpus data yield means of measuring ordinary meaning? We think the answer is a resounding yes—with a few caveats. Certainly, the answer is yes by comparison with existing means of measurement. If ordinary meaning is an empirical construct—and we think it is—then corpus analysis is superior to an intuitive guess (or, worse, crediting a dictionary or a word's etymology). . . .

Thomas R. Lee & Stephen C. Mouritsen, *Judging Ordinary Meaning*, 127 Yale L.J. 788 (2018)

The authors acknowledge that corpus linguistics will not always yield a "most frequent," let alone "exclusive," ordinary meaning of a statutory term or phrase. Does this suggest an inherent problem with their proposed approach? Or, alternatively, might it suggest that many statutory terms and phrases simply do not have a "most frequent" or "exclusive" ordinary meaning? Perhaps corpus linguistics may be more useful when the interpreter seeks the "prototypical" meaning of a term or phrase. For example, just as the dissent in *Muscarello* suggested, when one hears "*carry a firearm*," the prototypical image that the phrase evokes is carriage on the person—*i.e.*, "pack[ing] heat"—even if one could permissibly, and even commonly, use the phrase "*carry* a firearm" to refer to transporting a firearm in one's truck. If so, might corpus linguistics be most usefully employed as a way to rule out the Plain Meaning Rule in circumstances where an analysis of various corpora turn up no such single "plain" meaning, but rather several common or plausible meanings?

As a method of legal interpretation, corpus linguistics also raises questions about the objectivity of source selection and access. Adherents such as Lee and Mouritsen argue, perhaps rightly, that the resort to corpus linguistics is at least as objective as the resort to dictionaries, and is more likely to yield a useful "ordinary meaning." Yet whereas any ordinary reader of English can (relatively) easily resort to a dictionary (online or otherwise), corpus linguistics requires access to sophisticated databases—or "corpora"—of evidence of common usage. It also requires knowledge of how to derive meaning correctly from these vast corpora. (And we should not forget the potential selection bias in the composition of the corpora.) However accurate corpus linguistics may be as a method of obtaining the ordinary meaning of a word or phrase, might its costs outweigh its benefits for all but the most diligent and sophisticated statutory readers?

Other scholars are less sanguine than Lee and Mouritsen about the possibility that corpus linguistics can bring greater objectivity to the interpretation of statutes, given issues of access and selection bias:

> Just as a legal interpreter resorting to a dictionary must choose a particular dictionary to use, so too must the user of corpus linguistics techniques choose a corpus to search. The choice of corpus is subjective because it is not constrained by any principle that suggests why one corpus rather than another should be chosen. . . . [T]here is nothing internal to a particular corpus that requires its use in certain circumstances. Likewise, there is nothing about a particular term or phrase that tells the interpreter which corpus to use when searching for its meaning. As a result, simply by opting for a corpus search, the user of corpus linguistics techniques introduces a subjective element into the interpretive process.

Corpus usage confirms that the choice of corpus is subjective: corpus users rely on multiple or different corpora without articulating a standard for determining when one corpus would be appropriate and another would not be appropriate. Take Lee and Mouritsen's searches for the terms "vehicle," "carry," and "interpreter" in their work advocating the adoption of corpus techniques. Lee and Mouritsen rely on searches in the News on the Web (NOW) Corpus and the Corpus of Historical American English (COHA) without describing why either or both of these corpora are appropriate for their searches and despite the significant differences between the texts found in these corpora. The NOW Corpus, for example, contains not only news sources, but also online magazines with subjects as diverse as video games, cricket, and fashion. And the origin of these web sources? The NOW Corpus includes texts that come not only from the United States, but, unless specifically excluded by the researcher, texts from markedly different linguistic communities, like India, Nigeria, Singapore, Kenya, Pakistan, and the Philippines, among others. The COHA, by contrast, includes different kinds of texts, including movie scripts and poetry.

Some proponents of corpus linguistics techniques acknowledge that they must choose a corpus, but minimize the significance of the choice by suggesting that it is driven by a distinction between "ordinary" words and legal terms of art. If the word under consideration is an "ordinary" one, they search for it in a general corpus, like the COHA, the COCA, or the NOW Corpus; by contrast, if it is a legal term of art, some intimate that interpreters should use a still-hypothetical specialized legal corpus. However, framing the choice of corpus as a choice between an ordinary term and a legal term of art does not eliminate its subjectivity; it merely substitutes one subjective decision for another. The determination that a word is ordinary itself reflects a subjective decision because there is not an objective way to distinguish between ordinary words and legal terms of art. As linguists have noted, the line between legal terms of art and ordinary words is indistinct at best. David Mellinkoff notes that not every word "that has the sound of the law is a term of art." Conversely, many words that sound ordinary, because they are used in nonlegal settings, also have specialized legal meanings. For these reasons, the "difference between legal terms and words of ordinary language is relative and hard to define." Even linguists who are more optimistic about the possibility of identifying legal terms of art recognize the significant disagreement over what constitutes a legal term. Because choosing to designate a statutory term ordinary rather than legal does not appear to be "reliably constrained," the choice between a general corpus and a still-hypothetical specialized legal corpus is subjective.

Evan C. Zoldan, *Corpus Linguistics and the Dream of Objectivity*, 50 Seton Hall L. Rev. 401 (2019).

————————

Although corpus linguistics has captured the attention of and sparked debate among scholars and judges alike, the editors were unable, as of May 2020, to find a case—state or federal—in which the use of corpus linguistics was dispositive to the outcome. While in some cases judges have disagreed about whether to draw on corpus linguistics as an interpretive method, both those using corpus linguistics and those declining to do so have thus far appeared to reach the same conclusions as to statutory meaning.

For instance, in **State v. Rasabout**, 356 P.3d 1258 (Utah 2015), Utah Supreme Court Justice Thomas R. Lee (author of the excerpt above) proposed that the Court draw on corpus linguistics research to determine the meaning of a state statute that prohibited the unlawful "discharge" of a firearm. *Rasabout* concerned whether twelve shots fired from a single firearm constituted a single, merged "discharge," or twelve distinct (and separably punishable) "discharge[s]." All members of the *Rasabout* Court agreed that each fired shot constituted a distinct "discharge" in violation of the statute, but they disagreed about the propriety of Justice Lee's *sua sponte* use of corpus linguistics research to yield that result. In particular, Chief Justice Matthew B. Durrant wrote separately to "applaud Justice Lee for his thoughtful exploration of corpus linguistics as a potential additional tool for our statutory interpretation tool box," but noted that "an analysis conducted using our long-established methods of statutory construction" yielded the same sufficiently determinative meaning anyway. *Id.* at 1269–70. Chief Justice Durrant further expressed concern about the use of corpus linguistics "where it has not been argued by the parties," given that "a *sua sponte* venture into such territory may be fraught with the potential for error," especially if the "respective sides in the dispute [are not able] to challenge each other's [or the Court's] database, methodologies, and conclusions." *Id.* at 1270. Durrant also doubted that the benefits of such an approach would outweigh the costs, particularly since the employment of corpus linguistics research yielded an identical outcome to traditional tools of statutory interpretation.

A similar debate arose more recently in Wilson v. Safelite Group, Inc., 930 F.3d 429 (6th Cir. 2019). The Sixth Circuit Court of Appeals reached a unanimous decision but disagreed about the interpretive propriety and validity of corpus linguistics research in the interpretation of a federal statute. *See id.* at 439–45 (Judge Amul R. Thapar advocating in favor of corpus linguistics research); *id.* at 445–48 (Judge Jane B. Stranch resisting its application).

If corpus linguistics has thus far seemed only to confirm outcomes equally reached by way of traditional interpretive methods, does this suggest that its utility in helping judges determine the "ordinary meaning" of a term or phrase may be limited? Or, is the method simply too difficult or too costly (or too new) for judges and litigants to adopt with much success? Although it remains to be seen whether corpus linguistics will become a widely accepted tool in the statutory interpretation toolkit, its utility as a legal method is not necessarily limited to statutory interpretation alone. For example, in determining whether a term claimed as a trademark has lost its brand name significance to the consuming public and has become "generic" (a fate that befell, for example, "aspirin," "dry ice," and "escalator"), courts may find corpus linguistics techniques to be helpful in assessing a word's relative "genericness":

> [Under prevailing trademark law,] U.S. courts look to the "primary significance of the [disputed] term in the minds of the consuming public" to determine a word's status as a trademark. In gauging such primary significance, the courts currently give substantial weight to consumer surveys and record evidence of mark usage. . . .
>
> Corpora are simply compilations of record evidence, which . . . is already frequently accepted by the courts. The principal advantage of corpora is that when they are designed to be representative of the language of the population of interest, neither generic nor trademark uses should be disproportionately likely to be included in the analysis, unlike typical record evidence, which may be handpicked so as to overrepresent one kind of usage. When corpora are large enough, they can be used to make meaningful, quantitative measurements of usage of a disputed mark. Further, corpora are analyzed in accordance with principles of corpus linguistics (*e.g.*, . . . data are gathered from sources containing usage by or usage indicative of the understanding of potential consumers of the product whose mark is in question, etc.).
>
> In addition to these characteristics, corpus-based analyses have other distinct advantages that may capture the attention of courts, including the relative ease of their replication, the ability to capture language in natural rather than artificial environments, and cost effectiveness.

Quentin J. Ullrich, *Corpora in the Courts: Using Textual Data to Gauge Genericness and Trademark Validity*, 108 TMR 989 (2018).

PART IV

INTERPRETIVE APPROACHES EMPHASIZING CONTEXT

A. INTERPRETING STATUTES IN LIGHT OF THE "EVIL SOUGHT TO BE REMEDIED"

In contrast to textualism, which derives statutory meaning primarily from the statutory text alone, purposivism prioritizes contextual evidence that sheds light on the statute's purpose and meaning, sometimes even over the "literal" meaning of a specific word or phrase when taken out of context. Purposivists proceed from the premise that legislatures enact statutes in response to societal problems; ascertaining "the evil to be remedied" can provide the key to understanding the legislative solution. The context of a statute's passage, then, may shed important light on its meaning. To supply that context, courts might look to the state of the law before passage of the statute to discern what the new law was enacted to change. Recall Sir Edward Coke's inquiries in *Heydon's Case, supra* Section II.A.2: "What was the common law before the making of the Act? What was the mischief and defect for which the common law did not provide?"

More controversial, at least for some jurists, is "legislative history," that is, "extratextual sources" generated through the legislative process—such as prior versions of the bill that became a law, as well as the committee reports, hearings, floor statements, and other documentation of the bill's journey from proposal to passage. The following cases will address these and other sources of purpose and context for legislative enactments.

Moskal v. United States

Supreme Court of the United States, 1990.
498 U.S. 103, 111 S.Ct. 461, 112 L.Ed.2d 449.

■ JUSTICE MARSHALL delivered the opinion of the Court[, in which CHIEF JUSTICE REHNQUIST, JUSTICE WHITE, JUSTICE BLACKMUN, and JUSTICE STEVENS joined].

The issue in this case is whether a person who knowingly procures genuine vehicle titles that incorporate fraudulently tendered odometer readings receives those titles "knowing [them] to have been *falsely made.*" 18 U.S.C. § 2314 (emphasis added). We conclude that he does.

[Editors' Note: the statute at issue, 18 U.S.C. § 2314, provided in part:

"Whoever, with unlawful or fraudulent intent, transports in interstate or foreign commerce any falsely made, forged, altered, or counterfeited securities or tax stamps, knowing the same to have been falsely made, forged, altered, or counterfeited; . . . .

Shall be fined not more than $10,000 or imprisoned not more than ten years, or both."

For purposes of § 2314, "securities" are defined to include any "valid . . . motor vehicle title."]

I

Petitioner Raymond Moskal participated in a "title-washing" scheme. Moskal's confederates purchased used cars in Pennsylvania, rolled back the cars' odometers, and altered their titles to reflect those lower mileage figures. The altered titles were then sent to an accomplice in Virginia, who submitted them to Virginia authorities. Those officials, unaware of the alterations, issued Virginia titles incorporating the false mileage figures. The "washed" titles were then sent back to Pennsylvania, where they were used in connection with car sales to unsuspecting buyers. Moskal played two roles in this scheme: He sent altered titles from Pennsylvania to Virginia; he received "washed" titles when they were returned.

ODOMETER SCRUBBING

The Government indicted and convicted Moskal under 18 U.S.C. § 2314 for receiving two washed titles, each recording a mileage figure that was 30,000 miles lower than the true number. Section 2314 imposes fines or imprisonment on anyone who, "with unlawful or fraudulent intent, transports in interstate . . . commerce any falsely made, forged, altered, or counterfeited securities . . . , knowing the same to have been falsely made, forged, altered or counterfeited." On appeal, Moskal maintained that the washed titles were nonetheless genuine and thus not "falsely made." The Court of Appeals disagreed, finding that "the purpose of the term 'falsely made' was to . . . prohibit the fraudulent introduction into commerce of falsely made documents regardless of the precise method by which the introducer or his confederates effected their lack of authenticity." [Citation.]

Notwithstanding the narrowness of this issue, we granted certiorari to resolve a divergence of opinion among the Courts of Appeals. [Citation]. We now affirm petitioner's conviction.

II

As indicated, § 2314 prohibits the knowing transportation of "falsely made, forged, altered, or counterfeited securities" in interstate commerce. Moskal acknowledges that he could have been charged with violating this provision when he sent the Pennsylvania titles to Virginia, since those titles were "altered" within the meaning of § 2314. But he insists that he did not violate the provision in subsequently receiving the washed titles from Virginia because, although he was participating in a fraud (and thus no doubt had the requisite intent under § 2314), the washed titles themselves were not "falsely made." He asserts that when a title is issued by appropriate state authorities who do not know of its falsity, the title is "genuine" or valid as the state document it purports to be and therefore not "falsely made."

Whether a valid title that contains fraudulently tendered odometer readings may be a "falsely made" security for purposes of § 2314 presents a conventional issue of statutory construction, and we must therefore determine what scope Congress intended § 2314 to have. Moskal, however, suggests a shortcut in that inquiry. Because it is *possible* to read the statute as applying only to forged or counterfeited securities, and because *some* courts have so read it, Moskal suggests we should simply resolve the issue in his favor under the doctrine of lenity. [citation].

In our view, this argument misconstrues the doctrine. We have repeatedly "emphasized that the 'touchstone' of the rule of lenity 'is statutory ambiguity.' " [Citation.] Stated at this level of abstraction, of course, the rule "provides little more than atmospherics, since it leaves open the crucial question—almost invariably present—of *how much* ambiguousness constitutes . . . ambiguity." [Citation].

Because the meaning of language is inherently contextual, we have declined to deem a statute "ambiguous" for purposes of lenity merely because it was *possible* to articulate a construction more narrow than that urged by the Government. [Citation.] Nor have we deemed a division of judicial authority automatically sufficient to trigger lenity. [Citation.] If that were sufficient, one court's unduly narrow reading of a criminal statute would become binding on all other courts, including this one. Instead, we have always reserved lenity for those situations in which a reasonable doubt persists about a statute's intended scope even *after* resort to "the language and structure, legislative history, and motivating policies" of the statute. [Citation.] Examining these materials, we conclude that § 2314 unambiguously applies to Moskal's conduct.

A

"In determining the scope of a statute, we look first to its language," [citation], giving the "words used" their "ordinary meaning," [citation]. We think that the words of § 2314 are broad enough, on their face, to encompass washed titles containing fraudulently tendered odometer readings. Such titles are "falsely made" in the sense that they are made to contain false, or incorrect, information.

Moskal resists this construction of the language on the ground that the state officials responsible for issuing the washed titles did not know that they were incorporating false odometer readings. We see little merit in this argument. As used in § 2314, "falsely made" refers to the character of the securities being transported. In our view, it is perfectly consistent with ordinary usage to speak of the security as *being* "falsely made" regardless of whether the party responsible for the physical production of the document *knew* that he was making a security in a manner that incorporates false information. Indeed, we find support for this construction in the nexus between the *actus reus* and *mens rea* elements of § 2314.* Because liability under the statute depends on *transporting* the "falsely made" security with unlawful or fraudulent intent, there is no reason to infer a scienter requirement for the act of falsely making itself.[2]

Short of construing "falsely made" in this way, we are at a loss to give *any* meaning to this phrase independent of the other terms in § 2314, such as "forged" or "counterfeited." By seeking to exclude from § 2314's scope any security that is "genuine" or valid, Moskal essentially equates "falsely made" with "forged" or "counterfeited." His construction therefore violates the established principle that a court should " 'give effect, if possible, to every clause and word of a statute.' " [Citation.]

Our conclusion that "falsely made" encompasses genuine documents containing false information is supported by Congress' purpose in enacting § 2314. Inspired by the proliferation of interstate schemes for passing counterfeit securities, [citation], Congress in 1939 added the clause pertaining to "falsely made, forged, altered or counterfeited securities" as an amendment to the National Stolen Property Act. 53 Stat. 1178. Our prior decisions have recognized Congress' "general intent" and "broad purpose" to curb the type of trafficking in fraudulent securities that often depends for its success on the exploitation of interstate commerce. In *United States v. Sheridan,* 329 U.S. 379 (1946), we explained that Congress enacted the relevant clause of § 2314 in order to "com[e] to the aid of the states in detecting and punishing criminals whose offenses are complete under state law, but who utilize the channels of interstate commerce to make a successful getaway and thus make the state's detecting and punitive processes impotent." *Id.,* at 384. This, we concluded, "was indeed one of the most effective ways of preventing further frauds." *Ibid.; see also McElroy v. United States,* 455 U.S. 642, 655 (1982) (rejecting a narrow reading of § 2314 that was at odds with Congress' "broad purpose" and that would "undercut sharply . . . federal prosecutors in their effort to combat crime in interstate commerce").

We think that "title-washing" operations are a perfect example of the "further frauds" that Congress sought to halt in enacting § 2314. As Moskal concedes, his title-washing scheme is a clear instance of fraud involving securities. And as the facts of this case demonstrate, title

---

* Editors' Note: *Actus reus* and *mens rea* are terms of art in criminal law: *actus reus* refers to the conduct that is an element of the crime, whereas *mens rea* refers to the mental state of the accused when engaged in the conduct at issue.

[2] Indeed, we offer no view on how we would construe "falsely made" in a statute that punished the *act* of false making and that specified no scienter requirement. [Citation.]

washes involve precisely the sort of fraudulent activities that are dispersed among several States in order to elude state detection.

Moskal draws a different conclusion from this legislative history. Seizing upon the references to counterfeit securities, petitioner finds no evidence that "the 1939 amendment had anything at all to do with odometer rollback schemes." We think petitioner misconceives the inquiry into legislative purpose by failing to recognize that Congress sought to attack a category of fraud. At the time that Congress amended the National Stolen Property Act, counterfeited securities no doubt constituted (and may still constitute) the most prevalent form of such interstate fraud. The fact remains, however, that Congress did not limit the statute's reach to "counterfeit securities" but instead chose the broader phrase "falsely made, forged, altered, *or* counterfeited securities," which was consistent with its purpose to reach a class of frauds that exploited interstate commerce.

This Court has never required that every permissible application of a statute be expressly referred to in its legislative history. . . .

Our precedents concerning § 2314 specifically reject constructions of the statute that limit it to *instances* of fraud rather than the *class* of fraud encompassed by its language. For example, in *United States v. Sheridan,* the defendant cashed checks at a Michigan bank, drawn on a Missouri account, with a forged signature. The Court found that such conduct was proscribed by § 2314. In reaching that conclusion, the Court noted Congress' primary objective of reaching counterfeiters of corporate securities but nonetheless found that the statute covered check forgeries "done by 'little fellows' who perhaps were not the primary aim of the congressional fire." 329 U.S., at 390. "Whether or not Congress had in mind primarily such small scale transactions as Sheridan's," we held, "his operation was covered literally and we think purposively. Had this not been intended, appropriate exception could easily have been made." *Ibid.* In explaining that conclusion, we stated further:

"Drawing the [forged] check upon an out-of-state bank, knowing it must be sent there for presentation, is an obviously facile way to delay and often to defeat apprehension, conviction and restoration of the ill-gotten gain. There are sound reasons therefore why Congress would wish not to exclude such persons [from the statute's reach], among them the very ease with which they may escape the state's grasp." *Id.,* at 391.

In *McElroy v. United States,* we similarly rejected a narrow construction of § 2314. The defendant used blank checks that had been stolen in Ohio to buy a car and a boat in Pennsylvania. Defendant conceded that the checks he had thus misused constituted "forged securities" but maintained his innocence under the federal statute because the checks were not yet forged when they were transported across state boundaries. The Court acknowledged that "Congress could have written the statute to produce this result," *id.,* 455 U.S. at 656, but rejected such a reading as inconsistent with Congress' "broad purpose" since it would permit "a patient forger easily [to] evade the reach of federal law," *id.,* at 655. Moreover, because we found the defendant's interpretation to be contradicted by Congress' intent in § 2314 and its predecessors, we also rejected the defendant's plea for lenity: "[A]lthough 'criminal statutes are to be construed strictly . . . this does not mean that every criminal statute must be given the narrowest possible meaning in complete disregard of the purpose of the legislature.' " *Id.,* at 658, [citation.] We concluded that the defendant had failed to "raise significant questions of ambiguity, for the statutory language and legislative history . . . indicate that Congress defined the term 'interstate commerce' more broadly than the petitioner contends." 455 U.S., at 658.

Thus, in both *Sheridan* and *McElroy,* defendants who admittedly circulated fraudulent securities among several States sought to avoid liability by offering a reading of § 2314 that was narrower than the scope of its language and of Congress' intent, and in each instance we rejected the proffered interpretation. Moskal's interpretation in the present case rests on a similarly cramped reading of the statute's words, and we think it should likewise be rejected as inconsistent with Congress' general purpose to combat interstate fraud. "[F]ederal criminal statutes that are intended to fill a void in local law enforcement should be construed broadly." [Citation.]

To summarize our conclusions as to the meaning of "falsely made" in § 2314, we find both in the plain meaning of those words and in the legislative purpose underlying them ample reason to apply the law to a fraudulent scheme for washing vehicle titles.

B

Petitioner contends that such a reading of § 2314 is nonetheless precluded by a further principle of statutory construction. "[W]here a federal criminal statute uses a common-law term of established meaning without otherwise defining it, the general practice is to give that term its common-law meaning." United States v. Turley, 352 U.S. 407, 411 (1957). Petitioner argues that, at the time Congress enacted the relevant clause of § 2314, the term "falsely made" had an established common-law meaning equivalent to forgery. As so defined, "falsely made" excluded authentic or genuine documents that were merely false in content. Petitioner maintains that Congress should be presumed to have adopted this common-law definition when it amended the National Stolen Property Act in 1939 and that § 2314 therefore should be deemed not to cover washed vehicle titles that merely contain false odometer readings. We disagree for two reasons.

First, . . . [the Court concluded that the common-law meaning of "false made" was not universally agreed upon].

Our second reason for rejecting Moskal's reliance on the "common-law meaning" rule is that, as this Court has previously recognized, Congress' general purpose in enacting a law may prevail over this rule of statutory construction. In *Taylor v. United States,* 495 U.S. 575 (1990), we confronted the question whether "burglary," when used in a sentence enhancement statute, was intended to take its common-law meaning. We declined to apply the "common-law meaning" rule, in part, because the common-law meaning of burglary was inconsistent with congressional purpose. "The arcane distinctions embedded in the common-law definition [of burglary]," we noted, "have little relevance to modern law-enforcement concerns." *Id.,* at 593 (footnote omitted). [Citations].

We reach a similar conclusion here. The position of those common-law courts that defined "falsely made" to exclude documents that are false only in content does not accord with Congress' broad purpose in enacting § 2314—namely, to criminalize trafficking in fraudulent securities that exploits interstate commerce. We conclude, then, that it is far more likely that Congress adopted the common-law view of "falsely made" that encompasses "genuine" documents that are false in content.

Affirmed.

JUSTICE SOUTER took no part in the consideration or decision of this case.

■ JUSTICE SCALIA, with whom JUSTICE O'CONNOR and JUSTICE KENNEDY join, dissenting.

Today's opinion succeeds in its stated objective of "resolv[ing] a divergence of opinion among the Courts of Appeals." It does that, however, in a manner that so undermines generally applicable principles of statutory construction that I fear the confusion it produces will far exceed the confusion it has removed.

I

The Court's decision rests ultimately upon the proposition that, pursuant to "ordinary meaning," a "falsely made" document includes a document which is genuinely what it purports to be, but which contains information that the maker knows to be false, or even information that the maker does not know to be false but that someone who causes him to insert it knows to be false. It seems to me that such a meaning is quite *extra*-ordinary. Surely the adverb preceding the word "made" naturally refers to the manner of making, rather than to the nature of the product made. An inexpensively made painting is not the same as an inexpensive painting. A forged memorandum is "falsely made"; a memorandum that contains erroneous information is simply "false."

One would not expect general-usage dictionaries to have a separate entry for "falsely made," but some of them do use precisely the phrase "to make falsely" to define "forged." *See, e.g.,* Webster's New International Dictionary 990 (2d ed. (1945); Webster's Third New International Dictionary 891 (1961). The Court seeks to make its interpretation plausible by the following locution: "Such titles are 'falsely made' in the sense that they are made to contain false, or incorrect, information." This sort of word-play can transform virtually anything into "falsely made."

Thus: "The building was falsely made in the sense that it was made to contain a false entrance." This is a far cry from "ordinary meaning."

That "falsely made" refers to the manner of making is also evident from the fifth clause of § 2314, which forbids the interstate transportation of "any tool, implement, or thing used or fitted to be used in falsely making, forging, altering, or counterfeiting any security or tax stamps." This obviously refers to the tools of counterfeiting, and not to the tools of misrepresentation.

The Court maintains, however, that giving "falsely made" what I consider to be its ordinary meaning would render the term superfluous, offending the principle of construction that if possible each word should be given some effect. [Citation.] The principle is sound, but its limitation ("if possible") must be observed. It should not be used to distort ordinary meaning. Nor should it be applied to the obvious instances of iteration to which lawyers, alas, are particularly addicted—such as "give, grant, bargain, sell, and convey," "aver and affirm," "rest, residue, and remainder," or "right, title, and interest." *See generally* B. Garner, A Dictionary of Modern Legal Usage 197–200 (1987). The phrase at issue here, "falsely made, forged, altered, or counterfeited," is, in one respect at least, uncontestedly of that sort. As the United States conceded at oral argument, and as any dictionary will confirm, "forged" and "counterfeited" mean the same thing. *See, e.g.,* Webster's 2d, *supra,* at 607 (defining to "counterfeit" as to "forge," and listing "forged" as a synonym of the adjective "counterfeit"), *id.,* at 990 (defining to "forge" as to "counterfeit," and listing "counterfeit" as a synonym of "forge"). Since iteration is obviously afoot in the relevant passage, there is no justification for extruding an unnatural meaning out of "falsely made" simply in order to avoid iteration. The entire phrase "falsely made, forged, altered, or counterfeited" is self-evidently not a listing of differing and precisely calibrated terms, but a collection of near synonyms which describes the product of the general crime of forgery.

II

Even on the basis of a layman's understanding, therefore, I think today's opinion in error. But in declaring that understanding to be the governing criterion, rather than the specialized legal meaning that the term "falsely made" has long possessed, the Court makes a mistake of greater consequence. The rigid and unrealistic standard it prescribes for establishing a specialized legal meaning, and the justification it announces for ignoring such a meaning, will adversely affect many future cases.

The Court acknowledges, as it must, the doctrine that when a statute employs a term with a specialized legal meaning relevant to the matter at hand, that meaning governs. As Justice Jackson explained for the Court in *Morissette v. United States,* 342 U.S. 246, 263 (1952):

"[W]here Congress borrows terms of art in which are accumulated the legal tradition and meaning of centuries of practice, it presumably knows and adopts the cluster of ideas that were attached to each borrowed word in the body of learning from which it was taken and the meaning its use will convey to the judicial mind unless otherwise instructed. In such a case, absence of contrary direction may be taken as satisfaction with widely accepted definitions, not as departure from them."

Or as Justice Frankfurter more poetically put it: "[I]f a word is obviously transplanted from another legal source, whether the common law or other legislation, it brings its soil with it." *Some Reflections on the Reading of Statutes*, 47 Colum. L. Rev. 527, 537 (1947).

We have such an obvious transplant before us here. Both Black's Law Dictionary and Ballentine's Law Dictionary contain a definition of the term "false making." The former reads as follows:

"*False making.* An essential element of forgery, where material alteration is not involved. Term has reference to manner in which writing is made or executed rather than to its substance or effect. A falsely made instrument is one that is fictitious, not genuine, or in some material particular something other than it purports to be and without regard to truth or falsity of facts stated therein." Black's Law Dictionary 602 (6th ed. 1990).

Ballentine's is to the same effect. *See* Ballentine's Law Dictionary 486 (2d ed. 1948). "Falsely made" is, in other words, a term laden with meaning in the common law, because it describes an essential element of the crime of forgery. Blackstone defined forgery as "the *fraudulent making* or alteration of a writing to the prejudice of another man's right." 4 W. Blackstone, Commentaries 245 (1769) (emphasis added). The most prominent 19th-century American authority on criminal law wrote that "[f]orgery, at the common law, is the *false making* or materially altering, with intent to defraud, of any writing which, if genuine, might apparently be of legal efficacy or the foundation of a legal liability." 2 J. Bishop, Criminal Law § 523, p. 288 (5th ed. 1872) (emphasis added). The distinction between "falsity in execution" (or "false making") and "falsity of content" was well understood on both sides of the Atlantic as marking the boundary between forgery and fraud.

"The definition of forgery is not, as has been suggested in argument, that every instrument containing false statements fraudulently made is a forgery; but . . . that every instrument which fraudulently purports to be that which it is not is a forgery. . . ." *Queen v. Ritson*, L.R. 1 Cr.Cas.Res. 200, 203 (1869).

"The term *falsely,* as applied to making or altering a writing in order to make it forgery, has reference not to the contracts or tenor of the writing, or to the fact stated in the writing . . . but it implies that the paper or writing is false, not genuine, fictitious, not a true writing, without regard to the truth or falsity of the statement it contains." *State v. Young,* 46 N.H. 266, 270 (1865) (emphasis in original).

In 1939, when the relevant portion of § 2314 was enacted, the States and the Federal Government had been using the "falsely made" terminology for more than a century in their forgery statutes. [Citations.] More significantly still, the most common statutory definition of forgery had been a formulation employing precisely the four terms that appear in § 2314: falsely make, alter, forge, and counterfeit. [Citations.] By 1939, several federal courts and eight States had held that the formula "falsely make, alter, forge or counterfeit" did not encompass the inclusion of false information in a genuine document. [Citations.]

Commentators in 1939 were apparently unanimous in their understanding that "false making" was an element of the crime of forgery, and that the term did not embrace false contents. . . .

I think it plain that "falsely made" had a well-established common-law meaning at the time the relevant language of § 2314 was enacted—indeed, that the entire formulary phrase "falsely made, forged, altered, or counterfeited" had a well-established common-law meaning; and that that meaning does not support the present conviction. . . .

[Part III, discussing prior federal cases interpreting the term "falsely made" in related statutes, has been omitted.]

IV

The Court acknowledges the principle that common-law terms ought to be given their established common-law meanings, but asserts that the principle is inapplicable here because the meaning of "falsely made" I have described above "was not universal." For support it cites three cases and an A.L.R. annotation. . . . If such minimal "divergence"—by States with statutes that did not include the term "falsely made" (*see supra,* at 473)—is sufficient to eliminate a common-law meaning long accepted by virtually all the courts and by apparently all the commentators, the principle of common-law meaning might as well be frankly abandoned.

The Court's second reason for refusing to give "falsely made" its common-law meaning is that "Congress' general purpose in enacting a law may prevail over this rule of statutory construction." That is undoubtedly true in the sense that an explicitly stated statutory purpose that contradicts a common-law meaning (and that accords with another, "ordinary" meaning of the contested term) will prevail. The Court, however, means something quite different. What displaces normal principles of construction here, according to the Court, is "Congress' broad purpose in enacting § 2314—namely, to criminalize trafficking in fraudulent securities that exploits interstate commerce." *Ibid.* But that analysis does *not* rely upon any explicit language, and is simply question-begging. The whole issue before us here is how "broad" Congress' purpose in enacting § 2314 was. Was it, as the Court simply announces, "to criminalize trafficking in fraudulent securities"? Or was it to exclude trafficking in *forged* securities? The answer to that question is best sought by examining the language that Congress used—here, language that Congress has used since 1790 to describe not fraud but forgery, and that we reaffirmed bears that meaning as recently as 1962 . . . . It is perverse to find the answer by assuming it, and then to impose that answer upon the text.

The "Congress' broad purpose" approach is not supported by the authorities the Court cites. . . .

We should have rejected the argument in precisely those terms today. Instead, the Court adopts a new principle that can accurately be described as follows: "Where a term of art has a plain meaning, the Court will divine the statute's purpose and substitute a meaning more appropriate to that purpose."

NOTES AND QUESTIONS

1.   The majority invokes the "rule against superfluities," a canon that counsels the interpreter to give, where possible, each statutory term an independent (non-redundant) meaning. The dissent contends that the "where possible" proviso excludes the rule's application in circumstances, as here, where doing so would contradict the term's ordinary meaning. In indulging the legal fiction that Congress drafts statutes concisely, the "rule against superfluities" may impose a counter-factual coherence on the text. Recall the findings of Professors Gluck and Bressman, discussed in Section II.B.3.a *supra*, that legislative drafters often *purposefully* introduce superfluous language into legislation. Redundancy can supply the "belt and suspenders" to understanding a provision even when the rest of the text is (sometimes deliberately) opaque. By contrast, the rule against superfluities may enable courts, in the guise of finding independent meaning, to read the statute to say what they think it "ought" to say.

2.   The majority considers and rejects the defendant's (and the dissent's) argument that the narrower meaning of "falsely made" as making a forgery appropriately corresponds to the common-law meaning of the term at the time of the statute's enactment. Recall the typology of interpretive methods in Section II.B.1, *infra*. This question implicates considerations of both temporality and generality. First, the argument to attribute to the term its common-law meaning suggests that the *legal* meaning of the term will not necessarily be the same as the ordinary (read: lay) understanding of that term. Second, the argument suggests that evidence of meaning should be restricted to the era during and immediately prior to the statute's enactment. But what does evidence of the enacting era's *legal* (as opposed to ordinary) meaning reveal? Is it probative of the drafters' intent in using that term according to its common-law origins? Or does it show the reasonable (albeit *law-literate*) reader's understanding of the term at the time of its enactment? What clues should the modern-day interpreter look to when deciding whether to give the term its legal or ordinary meaning, and its enacting-era or present-day meaning? Keep these questions in mind as you read *New Prime, Inc. v. Oliveira, infra* Section VI.A.

Like the interpretive dispute in *Yates v. United States*, *supra* Section III.A.1, the controversy in the following case concerns a provision of the Sarbanes-Oxley Act, which not only responded to corporate mischief, but whose interpretation has created much of its own. Section 806 of Sarbanes-Oxley is entitled "Protection for Employees of Publicly Traded Companies Who Provide Evidence of Fraud," and is codified as § 1514A of Title 18 of the United States Code. As you examine this provision, consider: Who does the statute protect? What acts does the statute protect? What acts does it prohibit? By who? What do you think was the evil to which Congress was responding?

Civil action to protect against retaliation in fraud cases

(a) WHISTLEBLOWER PROTECTION FOR EMPLOYEES OF PUBLICLY TRADED COMPANIES.—No company with a class of securities registered under section 12 of the Securities Exchange Act of 1934 (15 U.S.C. § 78*l*), or that is required to file reports under section 15(d) of the Securities Exchange Act of 1934 (15 U.S.C. § 78*o*(d)), or any officer, employee, contractor, subcontractor, or agent of such company, may discharge, demote, suspend, threaten, harass, or in any other manner discriminate against an employee in the terms and conditions of employment because of any lawful act done by the employee—

  (1) to provide information, cause information to be provided, or otherwise assist in an investigation regarding any conduct which the employee reasonably believes constitutes a violation of section 1341 [mail fraud], 1343 [wire fraud], 1344 [bank fraud], or 1348 [securities or commodities fraud], any rule or regulation of the Securities and Exchange Commission, or any provision of Federal law relating to fraud against shareholders, when the information or assistance is provided to or the investigation is conducted by [a federal agency, Congress, or supervisor] . . . .

Lawson v. FMR LLC

Supreme Court of the United States, 2014.
571 U.S. 429, 134 S.Ct. 1158, 188 L.Ed.2d 158.

■ JUSTICE GINSBURG delivered the opinion of the Court[, in which CHIEF JUSTICE ROBERTS, JUSTICE BREYER, and JUSTICE KAGAN joined, and in which JUSTICE SCALIA and JUSTICE THOMAS joined in principal part].

To safeguard investors in public companies and restore trust in the financial markets following the collapse of Enron Corporation, Congress enacted the Sarbanes-Oxley Act of 2002 [citation omitted]. A provision of the Act, 18 U.S.C. § 1514A, protects whistleblowers. Section 1514A, at the time here relevant, instructed:

"No [public] company . . ., or any officer, employee, contractor, subcontractor, or agent of such company, may discharge, demote, suspend, threaten, harass, or in any other manner discriminate against an employee in the terms and conditions of employment because of [whistleblowing or other protected activity]." § 1514A(a) (2006).

This case concerns the definition of the protected class: Does § 1514A shield only those employed by the public company itself, or does it shield as well employees of privately held contractors and subcontractors—for example, investment advisers, law firms, accounting enterprises—who perform work for the public company?

We hold, based on the text of § 1514A, the mischief to which Congress was responding, and earlier legislation Congress drew upon, that the provision shelters employees of private contractors and subcontractors, just as it shelters employees of the public company served by the contractors and subcontractors. We first summarize our principal reasons, then describe this controversy and explain our decision more comprehensively.

Plaintiffs below, petitioners here, are former employees of private companies that contract to advise or manage mutual funds. The mutual funds themselves are public companies that have no employees. Hence, if the whistle is to be blown on fraud detrimental to mutual fund investors, the whistleblowing employee must be on another company's payroll, most likely, the payroll of the mutual fund's investment adviser or manager.

Taking the allegations of the complaint as true, both plaintiffs blew the whistle on putative fraud relating to the mutual funds and, as a consequence, suffered adverse action by their employers. Plaintiffs read § 1514A to convey that "[n]o . . . contractor . . . may . . . discriminate against [its own] employee [for whistleblowing]." We find that reading consistent with the text of the statute and with common sense. Contractors are in control of their own employees, but are not ordinarily positioned to control someone else's workers. Moreover, we resist attributing to Congress a purpose to stop a contractor from retaliating against whistleblowers employed by the public company the contractor serves, while leaving the contractor free to retaliate against its own employees when they reveal corporate fraud.

In the Enron scandal that prompted the Sarbanes-Oxley Act, contractors and subcontractors, including the accounting firm Arthur Andersen, participated in Enron's fraud and its coverup. When employees of those contractors attempted to bring misconduct to light, they encountered retaliation by their employers. The Sarbanes-Oxley Act contains numerous provisions aimed at controlling the conduct of accountants, auditors, and lawyers who work with public companies.

[citations omitted] Given Congress' concern about contractor conduct of the kind that contributed to Enron's collapse, we regard with suspicion construction of § 1514A to protect whistleblowers only when they are employed by a public company, and not when they work for the public company's contractor.

Congress borrowed § 1514A's prohibition against retaliation from the wording of the 2000 Wendell H. Ford Aviation Investment and Reform Act for the 21st Century (AIR 21), 49 U.S.C. § 42121. That Act provides: "No air carrier or contractor or subcontractor of an air carrier may discharge an employee or otherwise discriminate against an employee with respect to compensation, terms, conditions, or privileges of employment" when the employee provides information regarding violations "relating to air carrier safety" to his or her employer or federal authorities. § 42121(a)(1). AIR 21 has been read to cover, in addition to employees of air carriers, employees of contractors and subcontractors of the carriers. Given the parallel statutory texts and whistleblower protective aims, we read the words "an employee" in AIR 21 and in § 1514A to have similar import.

I

A

The Sarbanes-Oxley Act of 2002 (Sarbanes-Oxley or Act) aims to "prevent and punish corporate and criminal fraud, protect the victims of such fraud, preserve evidence of such fraud, and hold wrongdoers accountable for their actions." Of particular concern to Congress was abundant evidence that Enron had succeeded in perpetuating its massive shareholder fraud in large part due to a "corporate code of silence"; that code, Congress found, "discourage[d] employees from reporting fraudulent behavior not only to the proper authorities, such as the FBI and the SEC, but even internally." When employees of Enron and its accounting firm, Arthur Andersen, attempted to report corporate misconduct, Congress learned, they faced retaliation, including discharge. As outside counsel advised company officials at the time, Enron's efforts to "quiet" whistleblowers generally were not proscribed under then-existing law. Congress identified the lack of whistleblower protection as "a significant deficiency" in the law, for in complex securities fraud investigations, employees "are [often] the only firsthand witnesses to the fraud." [Citations omitted.]

Section 806 of Sarbanes-Oxley addresses this concern. [*See* provision reproduced before opinion.] . . .

B

Petitioners Jackie Hosang Lawson and Jonathan M. Zang (plaintiffs) separately initiated proceedings under § 1514A against their former employers, privately held companies that provide advisory and management services to the Fidelity family of mutual funds. . . . [A]s is common in the mutual fund industry, the Fidelity funds themselves have no employees. Instead, they contract with investment advisers like respondents to handle their day-to-day operations, which include making investment decisions, preparing reports for shareholders, and filing reports with the Securities and Exchange Commission (SEC). . . .

Lawson worked for FMR for 14 years, eventually serving as a Senior Director of Finance. She alleges that, after she raised concerns about certain cost accounting methodologies, believing that they overstated expenses associated with operating the mutual funds, she suffered a series of adverse actions, ultimately amounting to constructive discharge. Zang was employed by FMR for eight years, most recently as a portfolio manager for several of the funds. He alleges that he was fired in retaliation for raising concerns about inaccuracies in a draft SEC registration statement concerning certain Fidelity funds. . . .

FMR moved to dismiss the suits, arguing, as relevant, that neither plaintiff has a claim for relief under § 1514A. FMR is privately held, and maintained that § 1514A protects only employees of public companies— *i.e.*, companies that either have "a class of securities registered under section 12 of the Securities Exchange Act of 1934," or that are "required to file reports under section 15(d)" of that Act. § 1514A(a).[3] In a joint order, the District Court rejected FMR's interpretation of § 1514A and denied the dismissal motions in both suits. [citation omitted]

On interlocutory appeal, a divided panel of the First Circuit reversed. The Court of Appeals majority acknowledged that FMR is a "contractor" within the meaning of § 1514A(a), and thus among the actors prohibited from retaliating against "an employee" who engages in protected activity. The majority agreed with FMR, however, that "an employee" refers only to employees of public companies and does not cover a contractor's own employees. Judge Thompson dissented. In her view, the majority had "impose[d] an unwarranted restriction on the intentionally broad language of the Sarbanes-Oxley Act" and "bar[red] a significant class of potential securities-fraud whistleblowers from any legal protection." [Citations omitted.] . . .

We granted certiorari to resolve the division of opinion on whether § 1514A extends whistleblower protection to employees of privately held contractors who perform work for public companies.

II

A

In determining the meaning of a statutory provision, "we look first to its language, giving the words used their ordinary meaning." *Moskal v. United States*, 498 U.S. 103, 108 (1990) (citation and internal quotation marks omitted). As Judge Thompson observed in her dissent from the Court of Appeals' judgment, "boiling [§ 1514A(a)] down to its relevant syntactic elements, it provides that 'no . . . contractor . . . may discharge

---

[3]   Here, as just noted, the public company has no employees.

... an employee.'" [citation omitted] The ordinary meaning of "an employee" in this proscription is the contractor's own employee.

FMR's interpretation of the text requires insertion of "of a public company" after "an employee." But where Congress meant "an employee of a public company," it said so: With respect to the actors governed by § 1514A, the provision's interdictions run to the officers, employees, contractors, subcontractors, and agents "of such company," *i.e.*, a public company. § 1514A(a). Another anti-retaliation provision in Sarbanes-Oxley provides: "[A] broker or dealer and persons employed by a broker or dealer who are involved with investment banking activities may not, directly or indirectly, retaliate against or threaten to retaliate against any securities analyst *employed by that broker or dealer or its affiliates . . . .*" 15 U.S.C. § 78*o*–6(a)(1)(C) (emphasis added). In contrast, nothing in § 1514A's language confines the class of employees protected to those of a designated employer. Absent any textual qualification, we presume the operative language means what it appears to mean: A contractor may not retaliate against its own employee for engaging in protected whistleblowing activity.[7]

Section 1514A's application to contractor employees is confirmed when we enlarge our view from the term "an employee" to the provision as a whole. The prohibited retaliatory measures enumerated in § 1514A(a)—discharge, demotion, suspension, threats, harassment, or discrimination in the terms and conditions of employment—are commonly actions an employer takes against its own employees. Contractors are not ordinarily positioned to take adverse actions against employees of the public company with whom they contract. FMR's interpretation of § 1514A, therefore, would shrink to insignificance the provision's ban on retaliation by contractors. . . .

FMR urges that Congress included contractors in § 1514A's list of governed actors simply to prevent public companies from avoiding liability by employing contractors to effectuate retaliatory discharges. FMR describes such a contractor as an "ax-wielding specialist," illustrated by George Clooney's character in the movie *Up in the Air*. [citation omitted] As portrayed by Clooney, an ax-wielding specialist is a contractor engaged only as the bearer of the bad news that the employee has been fired; he plays no role in deciding who to terminate. If the company employing the ax-wielder chose the recipients of the bad tidings for retaliatory reasons, the § 1514A claim would properly be directed at the company. Hiring the ax-wielder would not insulate the company from liability. Moreover, we see no indication that retaliatory ax-wielding specialists are the real-world problem that prompted Congress to add contractors to § 1514A.

---

[7] We need not decide in this case whether § 1514A also prohibits a contractor from retaliating against an employee of one of the other actors governed by the provision.

Moving further through § 1514A to the protected activity described in subsection (a)(1), we find further reason to believe that Congress presumed an employer-employee relationship between the retaliator and the whistleblower. Employees gain protection for furnishing information to a federal agency, Congress, or "a person with supervisory authority over *the employee* (or such other person working for *the employer* who has the authority to investigate, discover, or terminate misconduct)." § 1514A(a)(1) (emphasis added). And under § 1514A(a)(2), employees are protected from retaliation for assisting "in a proceeding filed or about to be filed (*with any knowledge of the employer*) relating to an alleged violation" of any of the enumerated fraud provisions, securities regulations, or other federal law relating to shareholder fraud. § 1514A(a)(2) (emphasis added). The reference to employer knowledge is an additional indicator of Congress' expectation that the retaliator typically will be the employee's employer, not another entity less likely to know of whistleblower complaints filed or about to be filed.

Section 1514A's enforcement procedures and remedies similarly contemplate that the whistleblower is an employee of the retaliator. . . .

Regarding remedies, § 1514A(c)(2) states that a successful claimant shall be entitled to "reinstatement with the same seniority status that the employee would have had, but for the discrimination," as well as "the amount of back pay, with interest." As the Solicitor General, for the United States as amicus curiae, observed, "It is difficult, if not impossible, to see how a contractor or subcontractor could provide those remedies to an employee of a public company." [citation omitted] The most sensible reading of § 1514A's numerous references to an employer-employee relationship between the respondent and the claimant is that the provision's protections run between contractors and their own employees. . . .

[Were the other view of § 1514A's reach to prevail, there would be a substantial gap in its coverage:] Contractors' employees would be disarmed; they would be vulnerable to retaliation by their employers for blowing the whistle on a scheme to defraud the public company's investors, even a scheme engineered entirely by the contractor. Not only would mutual fund advisers and managers escape § 1514A's control. Legions of accountants and lawyers would be denied § 1514A's protections. Instead of indulging in fanciful visions of whistleblowing babysitters and the like, the dissent might pause to consider whether a Congress, prompted by the Enron debacle, would exclude from whistleblower protection countless professionals equipped to bring fraud on investors to a halt.

B

We turn next to two textual arguments made by FMR. First, FMR urges that "an employee" must be read to refer exclusively to public company employees to avoid the absurd result of extending protection to the personal employees of company officers and employees, *e.g.*, their housekeepers or gardeners. [citation omitted] Plaintiffs and the Solicitor General do not defend § 1514A's application to personal employees. They argue, instead, that the prohibition against an "officer" or "employee" retaliating against "an employee" may be read as imposing personal liability only on officers and employees who retaliate against other public company employees. FMR calls this reading "bizarre," for it would ascribe to the words "an employee" in § 1514A(a) "one meaning if the respondent is an 'officer' and a different meaning if the respondent is a 'contractor.'"

We agree with FMR that plaintiffs and the Solicitor General offer an interpretation at odds with the text Congress enacted. If, as we hold, "an employee" includes employees of contractors, then grammatically, the term also includes employees of public company officers and employees. Nothing suggests Congress' attention was drawn to the curiosity its drafting produced. The issue, however, is likely more theoretical than real. Few housekeepers or gardeners, we suspect, are likely to come upon and comprehend evidence of their employer's complicity in fraud. In any event, FMR's point is outweighed by the compelling arguments opposing FMR's contention that "an employee" refers simply and only to public company employees.

Second, FMR argues that the statutory headings support the exclusion of contractor employees from § 1514A's protections. Although § 1514A's own heading is broad ("Civil action to protect against retaliation in fraud cases"), subsection (a) is captioned "Whistleblower Protection for Employees of Publicly Traded Companies." Similarly, the relevant public law section, § 806 of Sarbanes-Oxley, is captioned "Protection for Employees of Publicly Traded Companies Who Provide Evidence of Fraud." The Court of Appeals described the latter two headings as "explicit guides" limiting protection under § 1514A to employees of public companies. [Citations omitted.]

This Court has placed less weight on captions. In Trainmen v. Baltimore & Ohio R. Co., we explained that where, as here, "the [statutory] text is complicated and prolific, headings and titles can do no more than indicate the provisions in a most general manner." 331 U. S. 519, 528 (1947). The under-inclusiveness of the two headings relied on by the Court of Appeals is apparent. The provision indisputably extends protection to employees of companies that file reports with the SEC pursuant to § 15(d) of the 1934 Act, even when such companies are not "publicly traded." And the activity protected under § 1514A is not limited to "provid[ing] evidence of fraud"; it also includes reporting violations of SEC rules or regulations. § 1514A(a)(1). As in *Trainmen*, the headings here are "but a short-hand reference to the general subject matter" of the provision, "not meant to take the place of the detailed provisions of the text." 331 U. S. at 528. Section 1514A is attended by numerous indicators that the statute's prohibitions govern the relationship between a contractor and its own employees; we do not read the headings to "undo or limit" those signals. *Id.* at 529.

III

A

Our textual analysis of § 1514A fits the provision's purpose. It is common ground that Congress installed whistleblower protection in the Sarbanes-Oxley Act as one means to ward off another Enron debacle. And . . . "Congress plainly recognized that outside professionals— accountants, law firms, contractors, agents, and the like—were complicit in, if not integral to, the shareholder fraud and subsequent cover-up [Enron] officers . . . perpetrated." Indeed, the Senate Report demonstrates that Congress was as focused on the role of Enron's outside contractors in facilitating the fraud as it was on the actions of Enron's own officers. [Citations omitted.]

Also clear from the legislative record is Congress' understanding that outside professionals bear significant responsibility for reporting fraud by the public companies with whom they contract, and that fear of retaliation was the primary deterrent to such reporting by the employees of Enron's contractors. Congressional investigators discovered ample evidence of contractors demoting or discharging employees they have engaged who jeopardized the contractor's business relationship with Enron by objecting to Enron's financial practices. [Citations omitted.]

In the same vein, two of the four examples of whistle-blower retaliation recounted in the Senate Report involved outside professionals retaliated against by their own employers. Emphasizing the importance of outside professionals as "gatekeepers who detect and deter fraud," the Senate Report concludes: "Congress must reconsider the incentive system that has been set up that encourages accountants and lawyers who come across fraud in their work to remain silent." From this legislative history, one can safely conclude that Congress enacted § 1514A aiming to encourage whistleblowing by contractor employees who suspect fraud involving the public companies with whom they work.

. . . Although lawyers and accountants are subject to extensive regulations and sanctions throughout Sarbanes-Oxley, no provision of the Act other than § 1514A affords them protection from retaliation by their employers for complying with the Act's reporting requirements. In short, we cannot countenance the position advanced by FMR and the dissent, that Congress intended to leave these professionals vulnerable to discharge or other retaliatory action for complying with the law.

B

Our reading of § 1514A avoids insulating the entire mutual fund industry from § 1514A, as FMR's and the dissent's "narrower construction" would do. As companies "required to file reports under section 15(d) of the Securities Exchange Act of 1934," 18 U.S.C. § 1514A(a), mutual funds unquestionably are governed by § 1514A. Because mutual funds figure prominently among such report-filing companies, Congress presumably had them in mind when it added to "publicly traded companies" the discrete category of companies "required to file reports under section 15(d)."

Virtually all mutual funds are structured so that they have no employees of their own; they are managed, instead, by independent investment advisers. The United States investment advising industry manages $14.7 trillion on behalf of nearly 94 million investors. These investment advisers, under our reading of § 1514A, are contractors prohibited from retaliating against their own employees for engaging in whistleblowing activity. This construction protects the "insiders [who] are the only firsthand witnesses to the [shareholder] fraud." Under FMR's and the dissent's reading, in contrast, § 1514A has no application to mutual funds, for all of the potential whistleblowers are employed by the privately held investment management companies, not by the mutual funds themselves. [Citations omitted.] . . .

[A]ffording whistleblower protection to mutual fund investment advisers is crucial to Sarbanes-Oxley's endeavor to "protect investors by improving the accuracy and reliability of corporate disclosures made pursuant to the securities laws." As plaintiffs observe, these disclosures are written, not by anyone at the mutual funds themselves, but by employees of the investment advisers. "Under FMR's [and the dissent's] proposed interpretation of section 1514A, FMR could dismiss any FMR employee who disclosed to the directors of or lawyers for the Fidelity funds that there were material falsehoods in the documents being filed by FMR with the SEC in the name of those funds." It is implausible that Congress intended to leave such an employee remediless. [Citations omitted.]

C

. . . The dissent's fears that household employees and others, on learning of today's decision, will be prompted to pursue retaliation claims, and that OSHA will find them meritorious under § 1514A, seem to us unwarranted. If we are wrong, however, Congress can easily fix the problem by amending § 1514A explicitly to remove personal employees of public company officers and employees from the provision's reach. But it would thwart Congress' dominant aim if contractors were taken off the hook for retaliating against their whistleblowing employees, just to avoid the unlikely prospect that babysitters, nannies, gardeners, and the like will flood OSHA with § 1514A complaints.

Plaintiffs and the Solicitor General observe that overbreadth problems may be resolved by various limiting principles. . . . Finally, the Solicitor General suggests that we need not determine the bounds of § 1514A today, because plaintiffs seek only a "mainstream application" of the provision's protections. We agree. Plaintiffs' allegations fall squarely within Congress' aim in enacting § 1514A. Lawson alleges that she was constructively discharged for reporting accounting practices that overstated expenses associated with managing certain Fidelity mutual funds. This alleged fraud directly implicates the funds' shareholders: "By inflating its expenses, and thus understating its profits, [FMR] could potentially increase the fees it would earn from the mutual funds, fees ultimately paid by the shareholders of those funds." Zang alleges that he was fired for expressing concerns about inaccuracies in a draft registration statement FMR prepared for the SEC on behalf of certain Fidelity funds. The potential impact on shareholders of false or misleading registration statements needs no elaboration. If Lawson and Zang's allegations prove true, these plaintiffs would indeed be "firsthand witnesses to [the shareholder] fraud" Congress anticipated § 1514A would protect. [Citations omitted.] . . .

IV

. . . For the reasons stated, we hold that 18 U.S.C. § 1514A whistleblower protection extends to employees of contractors and subcontractors. The judgment of the U.S. Court of Appeals for the First Circuit is therefore reversed, and the case is remanded for further proceedings consistent with this opinion.

It is so ordered.

■ JUSTICE SCALIA, with whom JUSTICE THOMAS joins, concurring in principal part and concurring in the judgment.

I agree with the Court's conclusion that 18 U.S.C. § 1514A protects employees of private contractors from retaliation when they report covered forms of fraud. As the Court carefully demonstrates, that conclusion logically flows from § 1514A's text and broader context. I therefore join the Court's opinion in principal part.

I do not endorse, however, the Court's occasional excursions beyond the interpretative terra firma of text and context, into the swamps of legislative history. Reliance on legislative history rests upon several frail premises. First, and most important: That the statute means what Congress intended. It does not. Because we are a government of laws, not of men, and are governed by what Congress enacted rather than by what it intended, the sole object of the interpretative enterprise is to determine what a law says. Second: That there was a congressional "intent" apart from that reflected in the enacted text. On most issues of detail that come before this Court, I am confident that the majority of Senators and Representatives had no views whatever on how the issues should be resolved—indeed, were unaware of the issues entirely. Third: That the views expressed in a committee report or a floor statement represent those of all the Members of that House. Many of them almost certainly did not read the report or hear the statement, much less agree with it— not to mention the Members of the other House and the President who signed the bill.

. . . I do not agree with the Court's acceptance of the possible validity of the Government's suggestion that "§ 1514A protects contractor employees only to the extent that their whistleblowing relates to 'the contractor . . . fulfilling its role as a contractor for the public company.'"

[citation omitted] Although that "limiting principl[e]," may be appealing from a policy standpoint, it has no basis whatsoever in the statute's text. So long as an employee works for one of the actors enumerated in § 1514A(a) and reports a covered form of fraud in a manner identified in § 1514(a)(1)–(2), the employee is protected from retaliation.

For all the other reasons given by the Court, the statute's text is clear, and I would reverse the judgment of the Court of Appeals and remand the case.

■ JUSTICE SOTOMAYOR, with whom JUSTICE KENNEDY and JUSTICE ALITO join, dissenting. . . .

The Court's interpretation gives § 1514A a stunning reach. As interpreted today, the Sarbanes-Oxley Act authorizes a babysitter to bring a federal case against his employer—a parent who happens to work at the local Walmart (a public company)—if the parent stops employing the babysitter after he expresses concern that the parent's teenage son may have participated in an Internet purchase fraud. And it opens the door to a cause of action against a small business that contracts to clean the local Starbucks (a public company) if an employee is demoted after reporting that another nonpublic company client has mailed the cleaning company a fraudulent invoice.

Congress was of course free to create this kind of sweeping regime that subjects a multitude of individuals and private businesses to litigation over fraud reports that have no connection to, or impact on, the interests of public company shareholders. But because nothing in the text, context, or purpose of the Sarbanes-Oxley Act suggests that Congress actually wanted to do so, I respectfully dissent.

I

Although the majority correctly starts its analysis with the statutory text, it fails to recognize that § 1514A is deeply ambiguous. Three indicators of Congress' intent clearly resolve this ambiguity in favor of a narrower interpretation of § 1514A: the statute's headings, the statutory context, and the absurd results that follow from the majority's interpretation.

A

[T]he statute is ambiguous. The majority is correct that it may be read broadly, to create a cause of action both for employees of public companies and for employees of the enumerated public company representatives. But the statute can also be read more narrowly, to prohibit the public company and the listed representatives—all of whom act on the company's behalf—from retaliating against just the public company's employees. . . .

The majority responds by suggesting that the narrower interpretation could have been clearer if Congress had added the phrase " 'of a public company' after 'an employee.' " Fair enough. But Congress could more clearly have dictated the majority's construction of the statute, too: It could have specified that public companies and their officers, employees, contractors, subcontractors, and agents may not retaliate against "their own employees." In any case, that Congress could have spoken with greater specificity in both directions only underscores that the words Congress actually chose are ambiguous. To resolve this ambiguity, we must rely on other markers of intent.

<h2 style="text-align:center">B</h2>

We have long held that where the text is ambiguous, a statute's titles can offer "a useful aid in resolving [the] ambiguity." FTC v. Mandel Brothers, Inc., 359 U.S. 385, 388–89 (1959). Here, two headings strongly suggest that Congress intended § 1514A to apply only to employees of public companies. First, the title of § 806—the section of the Sarbanes-Oxley Act that enacted § 1514A—speaks clearly to the scope of employees protected by the provision: "Protection for Employees of Publicly Traded Companies Who Provide Evidence of Fraud." [citation omitted] Second, the heading of § 1514A(a) reinforces that the provision provides "[w]histleblower protection for employees of publicly traded companies." . . .

Recognizing that Congress chose headings that are inconsistent with its interpretation, the majority notes that the Court has "placed less weight on captions." But where the captions favor one interpretation so decisively, their significance should not be dismissed so quickly. As we have explained, headings are important " 'tools available for the resolution of a doubt' about the meaning of a statute." Almendarez-Torres v. United States, 523 U.S. 224, 234 (1998).

<h2 style="text-align:center">C</h2>

<h3 style="text-align:center">1</h3>

Statutory context confirms that Congress intended § 1514A to apply only to employees of public companies. To start, the Sarbanes-Oxley Act as a whole evinces a clear focus on public companies. . . .

When Congress wanted to depart from the Act's public company focus to regulate private firms and their employees, it spoke clearly. For example, § 307 of the Act ordered the Securities and Exchange Commission (SEC) to issue rules "setting forth minimum standards of professional conduct for attorneys appearing and practicing before the [SEC]," including a rule requiring outside counsel to report violations of the securities laws to public company officers and directors. 15 U.S.C. § 7245. Similarly, Title I of the Act created the Public Company Accounting Oversight Board (PCAOB) and vested it with the authority to register, regulate, investigate, and discipline privately held outside accounting firms and their employees. §§ 7211–7215. And Title V required the SEC to adopt rules governing outside securities analysts when they make public recommendations regarding securities. § 78o–6.

Section 1514A, by contrast, does not unambiguously cover the employees of private businesses that contract with public companies or the employees of individuals who work for public companies. . . . Yet as the rest of the Sarbanes-Oxley Act demonstrates, if Congress had really wanted § 1514A to impose liability upon broad swaths of the private sector, it would have said so more clearly. . . .

D

1

Finally, the majority's reading runs afoul of the precept that "interpretations of a statute which would produce absurd results are to be avoided if alternative interpretations consistent with the legislative purpose are available." Griffin v. Oceanic Contractors, Inc., 458 U.S. 564, 575 (1982). The majority's interpretation transforms § 1514A into a sweeping source of litigation that Congress could not have intended. As construed by the majority, the Sarbanes-Oxley Act regulates employment relationships between individuals and their nannies, housekeepers, and caretakers, subjecting individual employers to litigation if their employees claim to have been harassed for providing information regarding any of a host of offenses. If, for example, a nanny is discharged after expressing a concern to his employer that the employer's teenage son may be participating in some Internet fraud, the nanny can bring a § 1514A suit. The employer may prevail, of course, if the nanny cannot prove he was fired "because of" the fraud report. § 1514A. But there is little reason to think Congress intended to sweep such disputes into federal court. . . .

Finally, it must be noted that § 1514A protects the reporting of a variety of frauds—not only securities fraud, but also mail, wire, and bank fraud. By interpreting a statute that already protects an expansive class of conduct also to cover a large class of employees, today's opinion threatens to subject private companies to a costly new front of employment litigation. Congress almost certainly did not intend the statute to have that reach. . . .

The Court's interpretation of § 1514A undeniably serves a laudatory purpose. By covering employees of every officer, employee, and contractor of every public company, the majority's interpretation extends § 1514A's protections to the outside lawyers and accountants who could have helped prevent the Enron fraud.

But that is not the statute Congress wrote. Congress envisioned a system in which public company employees would be covered by § 1514A, and in which outside lawyers, investment advisers, and accountants would be regulated by the SEC and PCAOB. Congress did not envision a system in which employees of other private businesses—such as cleaning and construction company workers who have little interaction with investor-related activities and who are thus ill suited to assist in detecting fraud against shareholders—would fall within § 1514A. Nor, needless to say, did it envision § 1514A applying to the household employees of millions of individuals who happen to work for public companies—housekeepers, gardeners, and babysitters who are also poorly positioned to prevent fraud against public company investors. And to the extent § 1514A may have been underinclusive as first drafted, Congress has shown itself capable of filling in any gaps. [citing sections of the Dodd-Frank Wall Street Reform and Consumer Protection Act]

The Court's decision upsets the balance struck by Congress. Fortunately, just as Congress has added further protections to the system it originally designed when necessary, so too may Congress now respond to limit the far-reaching implications of the Court's interpretation.[12] But because that interpretation relies on a debatable view of § 1514A's text, is inconsistent with the statute's titles and its context, and leads to absurd results that Congress did not intend, I respectfully dissent.

QUESTIONS

1.   Which of the following groups mentioned in the *Lawson* opinions are protected by § 1514A under the Court's decision:

     (a)   employees of mutual fund investment advisors;

     (b)   outside firms providing legal and accounting services;

     (c)   consultants, such as the one portrayed by George Clooney in the movie *Up in the Air*, who are contracted to fire employees; and/or

     (d)   "personal" or "household" employees of individuals who work for public companies

2.   What is the dissent's strongest argument that § 1514A should not be read to protect the plaintiffs? Is the statute ambiguous?

3.   Is this an appropriate application of the absurd results canon? How absurd is it that Congress would write a statute that could be read to protect household employees against retaliation for reporting securities, mail, wire, and bank fraud to federal officials? Does 1514A protect a nanny who reports violations of maximum hour laws (assuming these exist)?

4.   Does the absurd results canon apply with equal weight when the statutory interpretation determines the fate of the parties to the case, as in *Holy Trinity*, and when the alleged absurd result affects a hypothetical situation not in fact before the Court?

5.   What do you think of the concurrence's observations regarding legislative intent? What arguments—in the majority and dissent—do the concurring Justices object to?

---

[12] Congress could, for example, limit § 1514A to contractor employees in only those professions that can assist in detecting fraud on public company shareholders, or it could restrict the fraud reports that trigger whistleblower protection to those that implicate the interests of public company investors.

6. The majority appears to reject limiting principles ("plaintiffs and the Solicitor General offer an interpretation at odds with the text Congress enacted"); yet it does not clearly hold that § 1514A protects personal employees ("we need not determine the bounds of § 1514A today, because plaintiffs seek only a 'mainstream application' of the provision's protections"). If you were advising personal employees planning on reporting their employer's securities, mail, wire, or bank fraud, what would you tell them regarding whether a court would protect them under § 1514A? What parts of the majority opinion would support protection? Does the concurrence support protection for your clients?

1. CASE STUDY: THE BABY VERONICA CONTROVERSY

As discussed above, courts may seek to uncover either (a) the specific intent of the legislators regarding the particular statutory provision in question, and/or (b) whether the problem before the court appears to fall within the scope of the broader purpose the legislation sought to accomplish through its enactment.

As you read the Indian Child Welfare Act of 1978 and the case of *Adoptive Couple v. Baby Girl*, consider the grounds for disagreement about the broad purpose of the legislation, as well as the different methods the majority and dissent draw on to determine that purpose.

The Text to Be Construed: The Indian Child Welfare Act of 1978
United States Code, Title 25, Chapter 21.

§ 1901. Congressional findings

Recognizing the special relationship between the United States and the Indian tribes and their members and the Federal responsibility to Indian people, the Congress finds—

(1) that clause 3, section 8, article I of the United States Constitution provides that "The Congress shall have Power . . . To regulate Commerce . . . with Indian tribes" and, through this and other constitutional authority, Congress has plenary power over Indian affairs;

(2) that Congress, through statutes, treaties, and the general course of dealing with Indian tribes, has assumed the responsibility for the protection and preservation of Indian tribes and their resources;

(3) that there is no resource that is more vital to the continued existence and integrity of Indian tribes than their children and that the United States has a direct interest, as trustee, in protecting Indian children who are members of or are eligible for membership in an Indian tribe;

(4)   that an alarmingly high percentage of Indian families are broken up by the removal, often unwarranted, of their children from them by nontribal public and private agencies and that an alarmingly high percentage of such children are placed in non-Indian foster and adoptive homes and institutions; and

(5)   that the States, exercising their recognized jurisdiction over Indian child custody proceedings through administrative and judicial bodies, have often failed to recognize the essential tribal relations of Indian people and the cultural and social standards prevailing in Indian communities and families.

§ 1902. Congressional declaration of policy

The Congress hereby declares that it is the policy of this Nation to protect the best interests of Indian children and to promote the stability and security of Indian tribes and families by the establishment of minimum Federal standards for the removal of Indian children from their families and the placement of such children in foster or adoptive homes which will reflect the unique values of Indian culture, and by providing for assistance to Indian tribes in the operation of child and family service programs.

§ 1903. Definitions

For the purposes of this chapter, except as may be specifically provided otherwise, the term—

(1)   "child custody proceeding" shall mean and include—. . .

(ii)   "termination of parental rights" which shall mean any action resulting in the termination of the parent-child relationship; . . .

(iv)   "adoptive placement" which shall mean the permanent placement of an Indian child for adoption, including any action resulting in a final decree of adoption. . . .

(2)   "extended family member" shall be as defined by the law or custom of the Indian child's tribe or, in the absence of such law or custom, shall be a person who has reached the age of eighteen and who is the Indian child's grandparent, aunt or uncle, brother or sister, brother-in-law or sister-in-law, niece or nephew, first or second cousin, or stepparent;

(3)   "Indian" means any person who is a member of an Indian tribe, or who is an Alaska Native and a member of a Regional Corporation as defined in 1606 of title 43;

(4)   "Indian child" means any unmarried person who is under age eighteen and is either (a) a member of an Indian tribe or (b) is eligible for membership in an Indian tribe and is the biological child of a member of an Indian tribe;

(5) "Indian child's tribe" means (a) the Indian tribe in which an Indian child is a member or eligible for membership or (b), in the case of an Indian child who is a member of or eligible for membership in more than one tribe, the Indian tribe with which the Indian child has the more significant contacts;

(6) "Indian custodian" means any Indian person who has legal custody of an Indian child under tribal law or custom or under State law or to whom temporary physical care, custody, and control has been transferred by the parent of such child; . . .

(8) "Indian tribe" means any Indian tribe, band, nation, or other organized group or community of Indians recognized as eligible for the services provided to Indians by the Secretary because of their status as Indians, including any Alaska Native village as defined in section 1602(c) of title 43;

[Editors' Note: ICWA does not further define "Indian." Nor does ICWA further define Indian "status" through enrollment in an Indian Tribe. The list of the 573 federally recognized Indian Tribes is published at Federal Register/Vol. 84, No. 22 p. 1200/Friday, Feb. 1, 2019/Notices. Indian tribes determine their own rules for tribal membership. According to the Department of the Interior:

> Tribal enrollment criteria are set forth in tribal constitutions, articles of incorporation or ordinances. The criterion varies from tribe to tribe, so uniform membership requirements do not exist.

> Two common requirements for membership are lineal decendency from someone named on the tribe's base roll or relationship to a tribal member who descended from someone named on the base roll. (A "base roll" is the original list of members as designated in a tribal constitution or other document specifying enrollment criteria.) Other conditions such as tribal blood quantum, tribal residency, or continued contact with the tribe are common.

U.S. Department of the Interior, "Tribal enrollment process," http://www.doi.gov/tribes/enrollment.cfm]

(9) "parent" means any biological parent or parents of an Indian child or any Indian person who has lawfully adopted an Indian child, including adoptions under tribal law or custom. It does not include the unwed father where paternity has not been acknowledged or established; . . .

(11) "Secretary" means the Secretary of the Interior; and

(12) "tribal court" means a court with jurisdiction over child custody proceedings and which is either a Court of Indian Offenses, a court established and operated under the code or custom of an Indian tribe, or any other administrative body of a tribe which is vested with authority over child custody proceedings.

§ 1911. Indian tribe jurisdiction over Indian child custody proceedings . . .

(b) Transfer of proceedings; declination by tribal court

In any State court proceeding for the foster care placement of, or termination of parental rights to, an Indian child not domiciled or residing within the reservation of the Indian child's tribe, the court, in the absence of good cause to the contrary, shall transfer such proceeding to the jurisdiction of the tribe, absent objection by either parent, upon the petition of either parent or the Indian custodian or the Indian child's tribe: *Provided,* That such transfer shall be subject to declination by the tribal court of such tribe.

(c) State court proceedings; intervention

In any State court proceeding for the foster care placement of, or termination of parental rights to, an Indian child, the Indian custodian of the child and the Indian child's tribe shall have a right to intervene at any point in the proceeding. . . .

§ 1912. Pending court proceedings

(a) Notice; time for commencement of proceedings; additional time for preparation

In any involuntary proceeding in a State court, where the court knows or has reason to know that an Indian child is involved, the party seeking the foster care placement of, or termination of parental rights to, an Indian child shall notify the parent or Indian custodian and the Indian child's tribe, by registered mail with return receipt requested, of the pending proceedings and of their right of intervention. If the identity or location of the parent or Indian custodian and the tribe cannot be determined, such notice shall be given to the Secretary in like manner, who shall have fifteen days after receipt to provide the requisite notice to the parent or Indian custodian and the tribe. No foster care placement or termination of parental rights proceeding shall be held until at least ten days after receipt of notice by the parent or Indian custodian and the tribe or the Secretary: *Provided,* That the parent or Indian custodian or the tribe shall, upon request, be granted up to twenty additional days to prepare for such proceeding.

(b) Appointment of counsel

In any case in which the court determines indigency, the parent or Indian custodian shall have the right to court-appointed counsel in any removal, placement, or termination proceeding. The court may, in its discretion, appoint counsel for the child upon a finding that such appointment is in the best interest of the child. Where State law makes no provision for appointment of counsel in such proceedings, the court shall promptly notify the Secretary upon appointment of counsel, and the Secretary, upon certification of the presiding judge, shall pay reasonable fees and expenses out of funds which may be appropriated pursuant to section 13 of this title. . . .

(d) Remedial services and rehabilitative programs; preventive measures

Any party seeking to effect a foster care placement of, or termination of parental rights to, an Indian child under State law shall satisfy the court that active efforts have been made to provide remedial services and rehabilitative programs designed to prevent the breakup of the Indian family and that these efforts have proved unsuccessful. . . .

(f) Parental rights termination orders; evidence; determination of damage to child

No termination of parental rights may be ordered in such proceeding in the absence of a determination, supported by evidence beyond a reasonable doubt, including testimony of qualified expert witnesses, that the continued custody of the child by the parent or Indian custodian is likely to result in serious emotional or physical damage to the child.

§ 1913. Parental rights; voluntary termination

(a) Consent; record; certification matters; invalid consents

Where any parent or Indian custodian voluntarily consents to a foster care placement or to termination of parental rights, such consent shall not be valid unless executed in writing and recorded before a judge of a court of competent jurisdiction and accompanied by the presiding judge's certificate that the terms and consequences of the consent were fully explained in detail and were fully understood by the parent or Indian custodian. The court shall also certify that either the parent or Indian custodian fully understood the explanation in English or that it was interpreted into a language that the parent or Indian custodian understood. Any consent given prior to, or within ten days after, birth of the Indian child shall not be valid. . . .

(c) Voluntary termination of parental rights or adoptive placement; withdrawal of consent; return of custody

In any voluntary proceeding for termination of parental rights to, or adoptive placement of, an Indian child, the consent of the parent may be withdrawn for any reason at any time prior to the entry of a final decree of termination or adoption, as the case may be, and the child shall be returned to the parent.

(d) Collateral attack; vacation of decree and return of custody; limitations

After the entry of a final decree of adoption of an Indian child in any State court, the parent may withdraw consent thereto upon the grounds that consent was obtained through fraud or duress and may petition the court to vacate such decree. Upon a finding that such consent was obtained through fraud or duress, the court shall vacate such decree and return the child to the parent. No adoption which has been effective for at least two years may be invalidated under the provisions of this subsection unless otherwise permitted under State law. . . .

§ 1915. Placement of Indian children

(a) Adoptive placements; preferences

In any adoptive placement of an Indian child under State law, a preference shall be given, in the absence of good cause to the contrary, to a placement with (1) a member of the child's extended family; (2) other members of the Indian child's tribe; or (3) other Indian families. . . .

§ 1921. Higher State or Federal standard applicable to protect rights of parent or Indian custodian of Indian child

In any case where State or Federal law applicable to a child custody proceeding under State or Federal law provides a higher standard of protection to the rights of the parent or Indian custodian of an Indian child than the rights provided under this subchapter, the State or Federal court shall apply the State or Federal standard. . . .

§ 1931. Grants for on or near reservation programs and child welfare codes

(a) Statement of purpose; scope of programs

The Secretary is authorized to make grants to Indian tribes and organizations in the establishment and operation of Indian child and family service programs on or near reservations and in the preparation and implementation of child welfare codes. The objective of every Indian child and family service program shall be to prevent the breakup of Indian families and, in particular, to insure that the permanent removal of an Indian child from the custody of his parent or Indian custodian shall be a last resort. Such child and family service programs may include, but are not limited to—

(1) a system for licensing or otherwise regulating Indian foster and adoptive homes;

(2) the operation and maintenance of facilities for the counseling and treatment of Indian families and for the temporary custody of Indian children;

(3) family assistance, including homemaker and home counselors, day care, afterschool care, and employment, recreational activities, and respite care;

(4) home improvement programs;

(5) the employment of professional and other trained personnel to assist the tribal court in the disposition of domestic relations and child welfare matters;

(6) education and training of Indians, including tribal court judges and staff. in skills relating to child and family assistance and service programs;

(7) a subsidy program under which Indian adoptive children may be provided support comparable to that for which they would be eligible as foster children, taking into account the appropriate State standards of support for maintenance and medical needs; and

(8) guidance, legal representation, and advice to Indian families involved in tribal, State, or Federal child custody proceedings. . . .

§ 1932. Grants for off-reservation programs for additional services

The Secretary is also authorized to make grants to Indian organizations to establish and operate off-reservation Indian child and family service programs which may include, but are not limited to—

(1) a system for regulating, maintaining, and supporting Indian foster and adoptive homes, including a subsidy program under which Indian adoptive children may be provided support comparable to that for which they would be eligible as Indian foster children, taking into account the appropriate State standards of support for maintenance and medical needs;

(2) the operation and maintenance of facilities and services for counseling and treatment of Indian families and Indian foster and adoptive children;

(3) family assistance, including homemaker and home counselors, day care, afterschool care, and employment, recreational activities, and respite care; and

(4) guidance, legal representation, and advice to Indian families involved in child custody proceedings.

QUESTIONS

1. If you were advising an unrelated, non-Indian couple looking to adopt an Indian child, what sections of ICWA would be most relevant? What information would you need in order to advise the couple of the steps necessary to undertake the adoption?

2. What aspects of your answer will vary between States? Between Indian Tribes? What information will be generally applicable to all adoptions from a particular Tribe in a particular State, and what will depend on the circumstances of the particular Indian child?

3. Once an adoption has taken place, when, if ever, could you assure your clients that it is irrevocable? If an adoption is complete under state law, under what circumstances could it still be revoked under ICWA, and who would have the right or opportunity to do so?

4. Look at the declaration of policy in § 1902. Could the policies it expresses ever be in tension? If so, does ICWA accommodate one policy more than another?

Adoptive Couple v. Baby Girl

Supreme Court of the United States, 2013.
570 U.S. 637, 133 S.Ct. 2552, 186 L.Ed.2d 729.

■ JUSTICE ALITO delivered the opinion of the Court[, in which CHIEF JUSTICE ROBERTS, JUSTICE KENNEDY, JUSTICE THOMAS, and JUSTICE BREYER joined].

This case is about a little girl (Baby Girl) who is classified as an Indian because she is 1.2% (3/256) Cherokee. Because Baby Girl is classified in this way, the South Carolina Supreme Court held that certain provisions of the federal Indian Child Welfare Act of 1978 required her to be taken, at the age of 27 months, from the only parents she had ever known and handed over to her biological father, who had attempted to relinquish his parental rights and who had no prior contact with the child. The provisions of the federal statute at issue here do not demand this result.

Contrary to the State Supreme Court's ruling, we hold that 25 U.S.C. § 1912(f)—which bars involuntary termination of a parent's rights in the absence of a heightened showing that serious harm to the Indian child is likely to result from the parent's "continued custody" of the child—does not apply when, as here, the relevant parent never had custody of the child. We further hold that § 1912(d)—which conditions involuntary termination of parental rights with respect to an Indian child on a showing that remedial efforts have been made to prevent the "breakup of the Indian family"—is inapplicable when, as here, the parent abandoned the Indian child before birth and never had custody of the child. Finally, we clarify that § 1915(a), which provides placement preferences for the adoption of Indian children, does not bar a non-Indian family like Adoptive Couple from adopting an Indian child when no other eligible candidates have sought to adopt the child. We accordingly reverse the South Carolina Supreme Court's judgment and remand for further proceedings.

I

"The Indian Child Welfare Act of 1978 (ICWA), 92 Stat.3069, 25 U.S.C. §§ 1901–1963, was the product of rising concern in the mid-1970's over the consequences to Indian children, Indian families, and Indian tribes of abusive child welfare practices that resulted in the separation of large numbers of Indian children from their families and tribes through adoption or foster care placement, usually in non-Indian homes." Mississippi Band of Choctaw Indians v. Holyfield, 490 U.S. 30, 32 (1989). Congress found that "an alarmingly high percentage of Indian families [were being] broken up by the removal, often unwarranted, of their children from them by nontribal public and private agencies." § 1901(4). This "wholesale removal of Indian children from their homes" prompted Congress to enact the ICWA, which establishes federal standards that govern state-court child custody proceedings involving Indian children.

Id., at 32, 36 (internal quotation marks omitted); *see also* § 1902 (declaring that the ICWA establishes "minimum Federal standards for the removal of Indian children from their families").

Three provisions of the ICWA are especially relevant to this case. First, "[a]ny party seeking" an involuntary termination of parental rights to an Indian child under state law must demonstrate that "active efforts have been made to provide remedial services and rehabilitative programs designed to prevent the breakup of the Indian family and that these efforts have proved unsuccessful." § 1912(d). Second, a state court may not involuntarily terminate parental rights to an Indian child "in the absence of a determination, supported by evidence beyond a reasonable doubt, including testimony of qualified expert witnesses, that the continued custody of the child by the parent or Indian custodian is likely to result in serious emotional or physical damage to the child." § 1912(f). Third, with respect to adoptive placements for an Indian child under state law, "a preference shall be given, in the absence of good cause to the contrary, to a placement with (1) a member of the child's extended family; (2) other members of the Indian child's tribe; or (3) other Indian families." § 1915(a).

II

In this case, Birth Mother (who is predominantly Hispanic) and Biological Father (who is a member of the Cherokee Nation) became engaged in December 2008. One month later, Birth Mother informed Biological Father, who lived about four hours away, that she was pregnant. . . . The couple's relationship deteriorated, and Birth Mother broke off the engagement in May 2009. In June, Birth Mother sent Biological Father a text message asking if he would rather pay child support or relinquish his parental rights. Biological Father responded via text message that he relinquished his rights.

Birth Mother then decided to put Baby Girl up for adoption. Because Birth Mother believed that Biological Father had Cherokee Indian heritage, her attorney contacted the Cherokee Nation to determine whether Biological Father was formally enrolled. The inquiry letter misspelled Biological Father's first name and incorrectly stated his birthday, and the Cherokee Nation responded that, based on the information provided, it could not verify Biological Father's membership in the tribal records.

Working through a private adoption agency, Birth Mother selected Adoptive Couple, non-Indians living in South Carolina, to adopt Baby Girl. . . . [After the birth,] Adoptive Couple initiated adoption proceedings in South Carolina a few days later, and returned there with Baby Girl. After returning to South Carolina, Adoptive Couple allowed Birth Mother to visit and communicate with Baby Girl.

It is undisputed that, for the duration of the pregnancy and the first four months after Baby Girl's birth, Biological Father provided no financial assistance to Birth Mother or Baby Girl, even though he had the ability to do so. Indeed, Biological Father "made no meaningful attempts to assume his responsibility of parenthood" during this period.

Approximately four months after Baby Girl's birth, Adoptive Couple served Biological Father with notice of the pending adoption. (This was the first notification that they had provided to Biological Father regarding the adoption proceeding.) Biological Father signed papers stating that he accepted service and that he was "not contesting the adoption." But Biological Father later testified that, at the time he signed the papers, he thought that he was relinquishing his rights to Birth Mother, not to Adoptive Couple.

Biological Father contacted a lawyer the day after signing the papers, and subsequently requested a stay of the adoption proceedings. In the adoption proceedings, Biological Father sought custody and stated that he did not consent to Baby Girl's adoption. Moreover, Biological Father took a paternity test, which verified that he was Baby Girl's biological father.

A trial took place in the South Carolina Family Court in September 2011, by which time Baby Girl was two years old. The Family Court concluded that Adoptive Couple had not carried the heightened burden under § 1912(f) of proving that Baby Girl would suffer serious emotional or physical damage if Biological Father had custody. The Family Court therefore denied Adoptive Couple's petition for adoption and awarded custody to Biological Father. On December 31, 2011, at the age of 27 months, Baby Girl was handed over to Biological Father, whom she had never met.

The South Carolina Supreme Court affirmed the Family Court's denial of the adoption and the award of custody to Biological Father. . . .

III

It is undisputed that, had Baby Girl not been 3/256 Cherokee, Biological Father would have had no right to object to her adoption under South Carolina law. . . .

A

Section 1912(f) addresses the involuntary termination of parental rights with respect to an Indian child. Specifically, § 1912(f) provides that "[n]o termination of parental rights may be ordered in such proceeding in the absence of a determination, supported by evidence beyond a reasonable doubt, . . . that the *continued* custody of the child by the parent or Indian custodian is likely to result in serious emotional or physical damage to the child." (Emphasis added.) The South Carolina Supreme Court held that Adoptive Couple failed to satisfy § 1912(f) because they did not make a heightened showing that Biological Father's "*prospective* legal and physical custody" would likely result in serious damage to the child. [Citation.] That holding was error.

INTERPRETING STATUTES IN LIGHT OF THE "EVIL
SOUGHT TO BE REMEDIED"   343

Section 1912(f) conditions the involuntary termination of parental rights on a showing regarding the merits of "*continued* custody of the child by the parent." (Emphasis added.) The adjective "continued" plainly refers to a pre-existing state. As Justice SOTOMAYOR concedes, "continued" means "[c]arried on or kept up without cessation" or "[e]xtended in space without interruption or breach of conne[ct]ion." Compact Edition of the Oxford English Dictionary 909 (1981 reprint of 1971 ed.) (Compact OED); *see also* American Heritage Dictionary 288 (1981) (defining "continue" in the following manner: "1. To go on with a particular action or in a particular condition; persist. . . . 3. To remain in the same state, capacity, or place"); Webster's Third New International Dictionary 493 (1961) (Webster's) (defining "continued" as "stretching out in time or space esp. without interruption"); Aguilar v. FDIC, 63 F. 3d 1059, 1062 (11th Cir. 1995) (per curiam) (suggesting that the phrase "continue an action" means "go on with . . . an action" that is "preexisting"). The term "continued" also can mean "resumed after interruption." Webster's 493; *see* American Heritage Dictionary 288. The phrase "continued custody" therefore refers to custody that a parent already has (or at least had at some point in the past). As a result, § 1912(f) does not apply in cases where the Indian parent never had custody of the Indian child. . . .

Our reading of § 1912(f) comports with the statutory text demonstrating that the primary mischief the ICWA was designed to counteract was the unwarranted removal of Indian children from Indian families due to the cultural insensitivity and biases of social workers and state courts. The statutory text expressly highlights the primary problem that the statute was intended to solve: "an alarmingly high percentage of Indian families [were being] broken up by the *removal*, often unwarranted, of their children from them by nontribal public and private agencies." § 1901(4)(emphasis added); *see also* § 1902 (explaining that the ICWA establishes "minimum Federal standards for the *removal* of Indian children from their families" (emphasis added)); *Holyfield*, 490 U. S., at 32–34. And if the legislative history of the ICWA is thought to be relevant, it further underscores that the Act was primarily intended to stem the unwarranted removal of Indian children from intact Indian families. *See, e.g.*, H. R. Rep. No. 95–1386, p. 8 (1978) (explaining that, as relevant here, "[t]he purpose of [the ICWA] is to protect the best interests of Indian children and to promote the stability and security of Indian tribes and families by establishing minimum Federal standards for the *removal* of Indian children from their families and the placement of such children in foster or adoptive homes" (emphasis added)); *id.*, at 9 (decrying the "wholesale separation of Indian children" from their Indian families); *id.*, at 22 (discussing "the removal" of Indian children from their parents pursuant to §§ 1912(e) and (f)). In sum, when, as here, the adoption of an Indian child is voluntarily and lawfully initiated by a non-Indian parent with sole custodial rights, the ICWA's primary goal of preventing the unwarranted removal of Indian children and the dissolution of Indian families is not implicated. . . .

B

Section 1912(d) provides that "[a]ny party" seeking to terminate parental rights to an Indian child under state law "shall satisfy the court that active efforts have been made to provide remedial services and rehabilitative programs designed to *prevent the breakup of the Indian family* and that these efforts have proved unsuccessful." (Emphasis added.) The South Carolina Supreme Court found that Biological Father's parental rights could not be terminated because Adoptive Couple had not demonstrated that Biological Father had been provided remedial services in accordance with § 1912(d). [Citation.] We disagree.

Consistent with the statutory text, we hold that § 1912(d) applies only in cases where an Indian family's "breakup" would be precipitated by the termination of the parent's rights. The term "breakup" refers in this context to "[t]he discontinuance of a relationship," American Heritage Dictionary 235 (3d ed. 1992), or "an ending as an effective entity," Webster's 273 (defining "breakup" as "a disruption or dissolution into component parts: an ending as an effective entity"). *See also* Compact OED 1076 (defining "break-up" as, inter alia, a "disruption, separation into parts, disintegration"). But when an Indian parent abandons an Indian child prior to birth and that child has never been in the Indian parent's legal or physical custody, there is no "relationship" that would be "discontinu[ed]"—and no "effective entity" that would be "end[ed]"—by the termination of the Indian parent's rights. In such a situation, the "breakup of the Indian family" has long since occurred, and § 1912(d) is inapplicable.

Our interpretation of § 1912(d) is, like our interpretation of § 1912(f), consistent with the explicit congressional purpose of providing certain "standards for the *removal* of Indian children from their families." § 1902 (emphasis added); *see also, e.g.,* § 1901(4); *Holyfield,* 490 U. S., at 32–34. In addition, the B[ureau of] I[ndian] A[ffairs]'s Guidelines confirm that remedial services under § 1912(d) are intended "to alleviate the need to *remove* the Indian child from his or her parents or Indian custodians," not to facilitate a *transfer* of the child to an Indian parent. *See* 44 Fed. Reg., at 67592 (emphasis added). . . .

The Indian Child Welfare Act was enacted to help preserve the cultural identity and heritage of Indian tribes, but under the State Supreme Court's reading, the Act would put certain vulnerable children at a great disadvantage solely because an ancestor—even a remote one— was an Indian. As the State Supreme Court read §§ 1912(d) and (f), a biological Indian father could abandon his child in utero and refuse any support for the birth mother—perhaps contributing to the mother's decision to put the child up for adoption—and then could play his ICWA trump card at the eleventh hour to override the mother's decision and the child's best interests. If this were possible, many prospective adoptive parents would surely pause before adopting any child who might possibly qualify as an Indian under the ICWA. Such an interpretation would raise equal protection concerns, but the plain text of §§ 1912(f) and (d) makes clear that neither provision applies in the present context. Nor do § 1915(a)'s rebuttable adoption preferences apply when no alternative party has formally sought to adopt the child. We therefore reverse the judgment of the South Carolina Supreme Court and remand the case for further proceedings not inconsistent with this opinion.

It is so ordered.

[The concurring opinions of JUSTICE THOMAS and JUSTICE BREYER have been omitted.]

■ JUSTICE SOTOMAYOR, with whom JUSTICE GINSBURG and JUSTICE KAGAN join, and with whom JUSTICE SCALIA joins in part, dissenting.

A casual reader of the Court's opinion could be forgiven for thinking this an easy case, one in which the text of the applicable statute clearly points the way to the only sensible result. In truth, however, the path from the text of the Indian Child Welfare Act of 1978 (ICWA) to the result the Court reaches is anything but clear, and its result anything but right.

The reader's first clue that the majority's supposedly straightforward reasoning is flawed is that not all Members who adopt its interpretation believe it is compelled by the text of the statute (Thomas, J., concurring); nor are they all willing to accept the consequences it will necessarily have beyond the specific factual scenario confronted here. The second clue is that the majority begins its analysis by plucking out of context a single phrase from the last clause of the last subsection of the relevant provision, and then builds its entire argument upon it. That is not how we ordinarily read statutes. The third clue is that the majority openly professes its aversion to Congress' explicitly stated purpose in enacting the statute. The majority expresses concern that reading the Act to mean what it says will make it more difficult to place Indian children in adoptive homes, but the Congress that enacted the statute announced its intent to stop "an alarmingly high percentage of Indian families [from being] broken up" by, among other things, a trend of "plac[ing][Indian children] in non-Indian . . . adoptive homes." 25 U.S.C. § 1901(4). Policy disagreement with Congress' judgment is not a valid reason for this Court to distort the provisions of the Act. Unlike the majority, I cannot adopt a reading of ICWA that is contrary to both its text and its stated purpose. I respectfully dissent.

I

. . .

A

Better to start at the beginning and consider the operation of the statute as a whole. ICWA commences with express findings. Congress recognized that "there is no resource that is more vital to the continued existence and integrity of Indian tribes than their children," 25 U.S.C. § 1901(3), and it found that this resource was threatened. State authorities insufficiently sensitive to "the essential tribal relations of Indian people and the cultural and social standards prevailing in Indian communities and families" were breaking up Indian families and moving Indian children to non-Indian homes and institutions. *See* §§ 1901(4)–(5). As § 1901(4) makes clear, and as this Court recognized in Mississippi Band of Choctaw Indians v. Holyfield, 490 U. S. 30, 33 (1989), adoptive placements of Indian children with non-Indian families contributed significantly to the overall problem. *See* § 1901(4) (finding that "an alarmingly high percentage of [Indian] children are placed in non-Indian . . . adoptive homes"). Consistent with these findings, Congress declared its purpose "to protect the best interests of Indian children and to promote the stability and security of Indian tribes and families by the establishment of minimum Federal standards" applicable to child custody proceedings involving Indian children. § 1902. Section 1903 then goes on to establish the reach of these protections through its definitional provisions. . . .

II

The majority's textually strained and illogical reading of the statute might be explicable, if not justified, if there were reason to believe that it avoided anomalous results or furthered a clear congressional policy. But neither of these conditions is present here. . . .

B

On a more general level, the majority intimates that ICWA grants Birth Father an undeserved windfall: in the majority's words, an "ICWA trump card" he can "play . . . at the eleventh hour to override the mother's decision and the child's best interests." The implicit argument is that Congress could not possibly have intended to recognize a parent-child relationship between Birth Father and Baby Girl that would have to be legally terminated (either by valid consent or involuntary termination) before the adoption could proceed.

But this supposed anomaly is illusory. In fact, the law of at least 15 States did precisely that at the time ICWA was passed. And the law of a number of States still does so. The State of Arizona, for example, requires that notice of an adoption petition be given to all "potential father[s]" and that they be informed of their "right to seek custody." Ariz. Rev. Stat. §§ 8–106(G)–(J) (West Supp. 2012). In Washington, an "alleged father['s]" consent to adoption is required absent the termination of his parental rights, Wash. Rev. Code §§ 26.33.020(1), 26.33.160(1)(b) (2012); and those rights may be terminated only "upon a showing by clear, cogent, and convincing evidence" not only that termination is in the best interest of the child and that the father is withholding his consent to adoption contrary to child's best interests, but also that the father "has failed to perform parental duties under circumstances showing a substantial lack of regard for his parental obligations," § 26.33.120(2).

Without doubt, laws protecting biological fathers' parental rights can lead—even outside the context of ICWA—to outcomes that are painful and distressing for both would be adoptive families, who lose a much wanted child, and children who must make a difficult transition. *See, e.g., In re Adoption of Tobias D.*, 2012 Me. 45, ¶ 27, 40 A. 3d 990, 999 (recognizing that award of custody of 2½-year-old child to biological father under applicable state law once paternity is established will result in the "difficult and painful" necessity of "removing the child from the only home he has ever known"). On the other hand, these rules recognize that biological fathers have a valid interest in a relationship with their child. And children have a reciprocal interest in knowing their biological parents. *See Santosky*, 455 U. S., at 760–761, n. 11 (describing the foreclosure of a newborn child's opportunity to "ever know his natural parents" as a "los[s] [that] cannot be measured"). These rules also reflect the understanding that the biological bond between a parent and a child is a strong foundation on which a stable and caring relationship may be built. Many jurisdictions apply a custodial preference for a fit natural parent over a party lacking this biological link. [Citations] Cf. Smith v. Organization of Foster Families For Equality & Reform, 431 U. S. 816, 845 (1977) (distinguishing a natural parent's "liberty interest in family privacy," which has its source "in intrinsic human rights," with a foster parent's parallel interest in his or her relationship with a child, which has its "origins in an arrangement in which the State has been a partner from the outset"). This preference is founded in the "presumption that fit parents act in the best interests of their children." *Troxel v. Granville*, 530 U. S. 57, 68 (2000) (plurality opinion). " '[H]istorically [the law] has recognized that natural bonds of affection [will] lead parents' " to promote their child's well-being. *Ibid.* (quoting Parham v. J. R., 442 U.S. 584, 602 (1979)).

Balancing the legitimate interests of unwed biological fathers against the need for stability in a child's family situation is difficult, to be sure, and States have, over the years, taken different approaches to the problem. Some States, like South Carolina, have opted to hew to the constitutional baseline established by this Court's precedents and do not require a biological father's consent to adoption unless he has provided financial support during pregnancy. [Citation.] Other States, how-ever, have decided to give the rights of biological fathers more robust protection and to afford them consent rights on the basis of their biological link to the child. At the time that ICWA was passed, as noted, over one-fourth of States did so.

ICWA, on a straightforward reading of the statute, is consistent with the law of those States that protected, and protect, birth fathers' rights more vigorously. This reading can hardly be said to generate an anomaly. ICWA, as all acknowledge, was "the product of rising concern . . . [about] abusive child welfare practices that resulted in the separation of large numbers of Indian children from their families." *Holyfield*, 490 U. S., at

32. It stands to reason that the Act would not render the legal status of an Indian father's relationship with his biological child fragile, but would instead grant it a degree of protection commensurate with the more robust state-law standards.

C

The majority also protests that a contrary result to the one it reaches would interfere with the adoption of Indian children. This claim is the most perplexing of all. A central purpose of ICWA is to "promote the stability and security of Indian . . . families," 25 U.S.C. § 1902, in part by countering the trend of placing "an alarmingly high percentage of [Indian] children . . . in non-Indian foster and adoptive homes and institutions." § 1901(4). The Act accomplishes this goal by, first, protecting the familial bonds of Indian parents and children; and, second, establishing placement preferences should an adoption take place, *see* § 1915(a). ICWA does not interfere with the adoption of Indian children except to the extent that it attempts to avert the necessity of adoptive placement and makes adoptions of Indian children by non-Indian families less likely. The majority may consider this scheme unwise. But no principle of construction licenses a court to interpret a statute with a view to averting the very consequences Congress expressly stated it was trying to bring about. Instead, it is the " 'judicial duty to give faithful meaning to the language Congress adopted in the light of the evident legislative purpose in enacting the law in question.' " [Citation.]

The majority further claims that its reading is consistent with the "primary" purpose of the Act, which in the majority's view was to prevent the dissolution of "intact" Indian families. We may not, however, give effect only to congressional goals we designate "primary" while casting aside others classed as "secondary"; we must apply the entire statute Congress has written. While there are indications that central among Congress' concerns in enacting ICWA was the removal of Indian children from homes in which Indian parents or other guardians had custody of them, *see, e.g.,* §§ 1901(4), 1902, Congress also recognized that "there is no resource that is more vital to the continued existence and integrity of Indian tribes than their children," § 1901(3). As we observed in *Holyfield*, ICWA protects not only Indian parents' interests but also those of Indian tribes. *See* 490 U. S., at 34, 52. A tribe's interest in its next generation of citizens is adversely affected by the placement of Indian children in homes with no connection to the tribe, whether or not those children were initially in the custody of an Indian parent.

Moreover, the majority's focus on "intact" families begs the question of what Congress set out to accomplish with ICWA. In an ideal world, perhaps all parents would be perfect. They would live up to their parental responsibilities by providing the fullest possible financial and emotional support to their children. They would never suffer mental health problems, lose their jobs, struggle with substance dependency, or encounter any of the other multitudinous personal crises that can make it difficult to meet these responsibilities. In an ideal world parents would never become estranged and leave their children caught in the middle. But we do not live in such a world. Even happy families do not always fit the custodial-parent mold for which the majority would reserve IWCA's substantive protections; unhappy families all too often do not. They are families nonetheless. Congress understood as much. ICWA's definitions of "parent" and "termination of parental rights" provided in § 1903 sweep broadly. They should be honored. . . .

The majority opinion turns § 1912 upside down, reading it from bottom to top in order to reach a conclusion that is manifestly contrary to Congress' express purpose in enacting ICWA: preserving the familial bonds between Indian parents and their children and, more broadly, Indian tribes' relationships with the future citizens who are "vital to [their] continued existence and integrity." § 1901(3). The majority casts Birth Father as responsible for the painful circumstances in this case, suggesting that he intervened "at the eleventh hour to override the mother's decision and the child's best interests." I have no wish to minimize the trauma of removing a 27-month old child from her adoptive family. It bears remembering, however, that Birth Father took action to assert his parental rights when Baby Girl was four months old, as soon as he learned of the impending adoption. As the South Carolina Supreme Court recognized, " '[h]ad the mandate of . . . ICWA been followed [in 2010], . . . much potential anguish might have been avoided[;] and in any case the law cannot be applied so as automatically to "reward those who obtain custody, whether lawfully or otherwise, and maintain it during any ensuing (and protracted) litigation.' " [Citation.]

The majority's hollow literalism distorts the statute and ignores Congress' purpose in order to rectify a perceived wrong that, while heartbreaking at the time, was a correct application of federal law and that in any case cannot be undone. Baby Girl has now resided with her father for 18 months. However difficult it must have been for her to leave Adoptive Couple's home when she was just over 2 years old, it will be equally devastating now if, at the age of 3½, she is again removed from her home and sent to live halfway across the country. Such a fate is not foreordained, of course. But it can be said with certainty that the anguish this case has caused will only be compounded by today's decision.

I believe that the South Carolina Supreme Court's judgment was correct, and I would affirm it. I respectfully dissent.

■ JUSTICE SCALIA, dissenting.

I join JUSTICE SOTOMAYOR's dissent except as to one detail. I reject the conclusion that the Court draws from the words "continued custody" in 25 U.S.C. § 1912(f) not because "literalness may strangle meaning," but because there is no reason that "continued" must refer to custody in the past rather than custody in the future. I read the provision as requiring the court to satisfy itself (beyond a reasonable doubt) not merely that initial or temporary custody is not "likely to result in serious emotional or physical damage to the child," but that continued custody is not likely to do so. *See* Webster's New International Dictionary 577 (2d ed. 1950) (defining "continued" as "[p]rotracted in time or space, esp. without interruption; constant"). For the reasons set forth in JUSTICE SOTOMAYOR's dissent, that connotation is much more in accord with the rest of the statute.

While I am at it, I will add one thought. The Court's opinion, it seems to me, needlessly demeans the rights of parenthood. It has been the constant practice of the common law to respect the entitlement of those who bring a child into the world to raise that child. We do not inquire whether leaving a child with his parents is "in the best interest of the child." It sometimes is not; he would be better off raised by someone else. But parents have their rights, no less than children do. This father wants to raise his daughter, and the statute amply protects his right to do so. There is no reason in law or policy to dilute that protection.

NOTES AND QUESTIONS

1. The majority and dissent identify different principal evils to be remedied by the statute. Recall the typology of interpretive methods in Section III.A.2.a, *supra*. Which methods do the majority and dissent draw upon to determine what those evils were?

2. What relevance, if any, is the percentage (3/256th) of Baby Veronica's Cherokee heritage to the application of the statute?

3. To what extent do you think normative objectives informed the majority's textualist interpretation? Would the majority's textualist methods of interpretation reach the same result even if one did not share the majority's view that Congress's "primary" goal was to preserve only *intact* Indian families?

4. For further information about ICWA and the families embroiled in the "Baby Veronica" controversy, listen to this podcast: https://www.wnyc studios.org/story/more-perfect-presents-adoptive-couple-v-baby-girl.

B. INTERPRETING A STATUTE IN LIGHT OF LEGISLATIVE HISTORY

When courts speak of "legislative history," they generally refer to materials produced during a statute's drafting process—the committee reports, floor debates, proposed alterations and amendments, and legislator statements—that may collectively shed light on the specific intent of Congress in enacting legislation. The materials below highlight the potential benefits and risks of relying on these materials when interpreting statutes.

Securities and Exchange Commission v. Robert Collier & Co.

United States Court of Appeals for the Second Circuit, 1935.
76 F.2d 939.

Appeal from the District Court of the United States for the Southern District of New York.

Suit by the Securities & Exchange Commission against Robert Collier & Co., Inc., and others, to enjoin the defendants under the Securities Act of 1933. From a decree dismissing the bill (10 F.Supp. 95), plaintiff appeals.

■ Before L. HAND, SWAN, and AUGUSTUS N. HAND, CIRCUIT JUDGES.

■ L. HAND, CIRCUIT JUDGE. The single question presented by this appeal is whether the Securities and Exchange Commission, created under section 4(a) of title 1 of the Securities Exchange Act of 1934, section 78d, tit. 15, U.S. Code, 15 U.S.C.A. § 78d, may appear in the District Court by its own solicitor and file a bill under section 20(b)* of the Securities Act (15 U.S.C.A. § 77t, subd. (b)), or whether it must appear by the Attorney General, or a district attorney. The defendants and the judge thought that the situation fell within our decision in Sutherland v. International Insurance Co., 43 F.2d 969; the Commission insists that section 20(b) is an exception to the general rule. Though we had before us section 20(b) without any knowledge of its amendments in committee, we might still have held that the contrast between the diction of the two clauses was enough to turn the scale against a tradition of even such long standing as that on which the defendants rely. There would have been strong reasons for supposing that so striking a change in expression could only have proceeded from a deliberate difference of intent, no matter how inveterate the contrary usage. But if that be doubtful, the change in the section on its way through Congress makes the intent entirely plain. When first introduced, the two clauses were in identical language. "Whenever it shall appear to the Commission" (at that time the Federal Trade Commission), "that the practices investigated constitute a fraud . . . it shall transmit such evidence as may be available" to "the Attorney General who may in his discretion bring an action. . . . The Commission may transmit such evidence as may be available concerning such acts and practices to the Attorney General who may, in his

---

  * Editors' Note:

    (b) Whenever it shall appear to the Commissioner that any person is engaged or about to engage in any acts or practices which constitute or will constitute a violation of the provisions of this subchapter, or of any rule or regulation prescribed under the authority thereof, it may in its discretion, bring an action in any district court of the United States, United States court of any Territory, or the Supreme Court of the District of Columbia to enjoin such acts or practices, and upon a proper showing a permanent or temporary injunction or restraining order shall be granted without bond. The Commission may transmit such evidence as may be available concerning such acts or practices to the Attorney General who may, in his discretion, institute the necessary criminal proceedings under this sub-chapter. * * *

discretion institute the necessary criminal proceedings under this sub-chapter." Hearings on H.R. 4314, 73d Congress, 1st Session, p. 6; Hearings on S.R. 875, p. 7. As the bill then stood, its intent was therefore to follow the ancient custom and deny to the Commission control over civil, as well as criminal, prosecutions. During the hearings before the committees, the chief counsel of the Federal Trade Commission, Robert E. Healey, testified; we quote the relevant passages in the margin.* It was after this that the first clause was changed to its present form. We cannot see how any one can doubt what was the purpose of both committees in this amendment, though it is quite true that they said nothing about it in their reports. Healey was not a casual interloper; he was the person chiefly responsible for the prosecution of the new functions about to be conferred, at least so far as they touched legal questions. There cannot be the least question that in fact it was at his suggestion that the change was made and that it was intended to allow the Commission complete autonomy in civil prosecutions. The committees' intent may be irrelevant in construing the section, but the evidence of it as a fact is incontrovertible.

The defendants suggest that the purpose may have been limited to giving power to the Commission to decide when suits should be begun, but yet to require district attorneys to conduct them. Congress has indeed done just that on occasion. Section 12(1) tit. 49, U.S. Code, 49 U.S.C.A. § 12(1); section 413, tit. 33, U.S. Code (33 U.S.C.A. § 413); section 486, tit. 28, U.S. Code (28 U.S.C.A. § 486). But the resulting situation is certainly undesirable administratively, and whenever it has been prescribed, the language has been express. It is extremely unlikely that such a halfway measure should have been here intended. The original

---

* "This bill provides that if the Commission discovers fraud and misrepresentation in connection with the sale of securities, it shall bring that information to the attention of the Attorney General, who shall proceed by injunction to stop that fraud and also to prosecute the guilty person criminally. My suggestion is where there is such a condition existing that Congress by this bill should say to the Attorney General, 'Punish them,' and then say to the Federal Trade Commission, 'Stop them.' I would amend this bill to provide for giving the power to apply for injunctions to the Commission. It is not wise to leave it to us to submit the information to the Attorney General. If we get the information why should we not use it and go after the fellow right then and there and get the injunction against him continuing to sell the stock? Why should we tell the Attorney General about it so he can seek the injunction? We should tell the Attorney General about it so that he can punish them, but why divide the responsibility? Why create such a magnificent buck-passing opportunity as that?

"Now if this Commission is competent to go out and get these facts,—and I will tell you I think that we are,—and if not, there are two vacancies down there, two vacancies that are just yearning to be filled, by some deserving Democrats,—I tell you I believe that we should be allowed to stop the practice. I submit to you gentlemen, first, if this Commission is on to its job and it finds these fellows selling stock by fraud or misrepresentation, we should be given the power to apply to the courts for an injunction and the prosecuting power should be left to the Attorney General where it belongs." [Hearings on H.R. 4312, 73rd Cong., 1st Sess. pp. 240, 241].

"I wish to offer the suggestion that in the section of this bill which provides that the power of injunction shall be given, that provision be made that if the Commission which is charged with the administration of the bill finds people acting contrary to law or in defiance of the Act, that Commission and not the Attorney General will proceed to ask for an injunction. I would suggest that it is unwise to divide the responsibility and to encounter the delay that would come if we have to send our stuff to the Attorney General. Let him prosecute criminally, let us proceed to stop them." [Hearings on S. 875, 73rd Cong., 1st Sess. p. 226.]

bill gave power to the Attorney General not only to decide when to sue, but necessarily to conduct the suit. The amendment was in form at least a transfer of the total power; unless some good reason to the contrary appears, it ought to be construed as total, not as leaving the Commission subject to a public officer whom they could not control. . . .

Finally, it is said that we should not regard the testimony of a witness before the committees; that it is not even as relevant as speeches on the floor of either house, which courts will not consider at all. [Citation.] It would indeed be absurd to suppose that the testimony of a witness by itself could be used to interpret an act of Congress; we are not so using it. The bill was changed in a most significant way; we are concerned to learn why this was done; we find that it can most readily be explained, and indeed cannot naturally be explained on any other assumption than by supposing that the committees assented to a request from the very agency to whom the new functions were to be committed. To close our eyes to this patent and compelling argument would be the last measure of arid formalism. The amendments of a bill in committee are fertile sources of interpretation, [citation]. It is of course true that members who vote upon a bill do not all know, probably very few of them know, what has taken place in committee. On the most rigid theory possibly we ought to assume that they accept the words just as the words read, without any background of amendment or other evidence as to their meaning. But courts have come to treat the facts more really; they recognize that while members deliberately express their personal position upon the general purposes of the legislation, as to the details of its articulation they accept the work of the committees; so much they delegate because legislation could not go on in any other way.

Decree reversed.

QUESTIONS

1.   How did the change in the Section in the course of its enactment make the Congressional intent "entirely plain"? Is this meaning of intent the subjective intent of individual drafters, the objective intent evident in the statutory purpose, or both? Does it, or should it, matter?

2.   In what respect does the contrast in diction of the two clauses indicate a deliberate difference of intent?

3.   Under what theory did the court solve the problem of the transference of the committee intent to Congress?

4.   As the court noted, the change in the legislation was due to "a request from the very agency to whom the new functions were to be committed," and that same agency, the SEC, was involved in the subsequent case at hand. As the discussion of legislative history in *Robert Collier & Co.* reflects, agencies are often involved in drafting statutes that later give rise to interpretive disputes in which they are parties. Where this is the case, should a court treat an agency statement about the interpretation of such a statute with greater authority? Keep this question in mind in Section III.F, *infra*.

5. In Zuber v. Allen, 396 U.S. 168 (1969), quoted favorably in Garcia v. United States, 469 U.S. 70, 76 (1984), the Supreme Court stated, per Justice Harlan: "We consider our conclusions in no way undermined by the colloquy on the floor between Senator Copeland and Senator Murphy upon which the dissent places such emphasis. A committee report represents the considered and collective understanding of those Congressmen involved in drafting and studying proposed legislation. Floor debates reflect at best the understanding of individual Congressmen. It would take extensive and thoughtful debate to detract from the plain thrust of a committee report in this instance." 396 U.S. at 186. In a dissenting opinion, Justice Black took issue with the majority's treatment of the floor debates, observing that "anyone acquainted with the realities of the United States Senate knows that the remarks of the floor manager [Senator Murphy] are taken by other Senators as reflecting the views of the committee itself." Justice Rehnquist, dissenting in the case of Simpson v. United States, 435 U.S. 6, 17–18 (1978), made the following statement about this matter more broadly:

> The decisions of this Court have established that some types of legislative history are substantially more reliable than others. The report of a joint conference committee of both Houses of Congress, for example, or the report of a Senate or a House committee, is accorded a good deal more weight than the remarks even of the sponsor of a particular portion of a bill on the floor of the chamber. (Citations omitted.) It is a matter of common knowledge that at any given time during the debate, particularly a prolonged debate, of a bill the members of either House in attendance on the Floor may not be great, and it is only these members or those who later read the remarks in the Congressional Record, who will have the benefit of the Floor remarks. In the last analysis, it is the statutory language embodied in the enrolled bill which Congress enacts, and that must be our first reference point in interpreting its meaning.

The Court has also noted that "oral testimony of . . . individual Congressmen, unless very precisely directed to the intended meaning of particular words in a statute, can seldom be expected to be as precise as the enacted language itself." Regan v. Wald, 468 U.S. 222, 237 (1984).

In Chrysler Corp. v. Brown, 441 U.S. 281, 311 (1979), Justice Rehnquist's opinion for a virtually unanimous Court went still further, arguing that "[t]he remarks of a single legislator, even the sponsor, are not controlling in analyzing legislative history . . . [such remarks] must be considered with the Reports of both Houses and the statements of other Congressmen" as well as with the statute in question.

Subsequently, in Barnhart v. Sigmon Coal Company, 534 U.S. 438 (2002), Justice Thomas writing for a majority of six Justices wrote:

> Floor statements from two Senators cannot amend the clear and unambiguous language of a statute. We see no reason to give greater weight to the views of two Senators than to the collective votes of both Houses, which are memorialized in the unambiguous statutory text. Moreover, were we to adopt this form of statutory

interpretation, we would be placing an obligation on Members of Congress not only to monitor their colleague's floor statements but to read every word of the Congressional Record including written explanations inserted into the record. This we will not do. The only "evidence" that we need rely on is the clear statutory text.

Although these statements reflect a growing disfavor of relying on Floor Statements among members of the Court, that view has not been entirely shared. Justice Stevens, writing in dissent in *Barnhart*, argued that ignoring Floor Statements that provide convincing evidence of Congressional intent may lead to arbitrary results:

> This case raises the question whether clear evidence of coherent congressional intent should inform the Court's construction of a statutory provision that seems, at first blush, to convey an incoherent message. Today a majority of the Court chooses to disregard that evidence and instead, adheres to an interpretation of the statute that produces absurd results. Two Members of Congress—both sponsors of the legislation at issue—have explained that the statute does not mandate such results, and the agency charged with administering the statute agrees. As a partner of the other two branches of Government, we should heed their more reasonable interpretation of Congress' objectives.

Note that Justice Stevens' dissent refers to the Court's role in interpreting legislation as one of "partnership" with the other branches of government. Based on the decisions you have studied so far, does this characterization accurately capture the approach of the current Supreme Court? Of its predecessors? How would you describe the Court's role? Keep these inquiries in mind as you work through the other materials in this Part.

For a summary of the use of legislative intent in statutory interpretation and a discussion of what weight to give floor statements in particular, see Lori L. Outzs, *A Principled Use of Congressional Floor Speeches in Statutory Interpretation*, 28 Colum. J.L. & Soc. Probs. 297 (1995).

NOTE: *BANK ONE CHICAGO* AND THE ONGOING DEBATE OVER LEGISLATIVE HISTORY

The ongoing debate over the use and misuse of legislative history received particularly sharp treatment in **Bank One Chicago, N.A. v. Midwest Bank & Trust Company**, 516 U.S. 264 (1996), in which Justices Scalia and Stevens offered strongly contrasting assessments:

■ JUSTICE SCALIA, concurring in part and concurring in the judgment.

I agree with the Court's opinion, except that portion of it which enters into a discussion of the drafting history of § 4010. In my view a law means what its text most appropriately conveys, whatever the Congress that enacted it might have "intended." The law is what the law says, and we should content ourselves with reading it rather than psychoanalyzing those who enacted it. *See* United States v. Public Util. Comm'n of Cal., 345 U.S. 295, 319 (1953) (Jackson, J., concurring). Moreover, even if subjective intent rather than textually expressed intent were the touchstone, it is a fiction of Jack-and-the-Beanstalk proportions to assume that more than a handful of those Senators and Members of the House who voted for the final version of the Expedited Funds Availability Act, and the President who signed it, were, when they took those actions, aware of the drafting evolution that the Court describes; and if they were, that their actions in voting for or signing the final bill show that they had the same "intent" which that evolution suggests was in the minds of the drafters.

JUSTICE STEVENS acknowledges that this is so, but asserts that the intent of a few committee members is nonetheless dispositive because legislators are "busy people," and "most members [of Congress] are content to endorse the views of the responsible committees." I do not know the factual basis for that assurance. Many congressional committees tend not to be representative of the full house, but are disproportionately populated by Members whose constituents have a particular stake in the subject matter—agriculture, merchant marine and fisheries, science and technology, etc. I think it quite unlikely that the House of Representatives would be "content to endorse the views" that its Agriculture Committee would come up with if that committee knew (as it knows in drafting Committee Reports) that those views need not be moderated to survive a floor vote. And even more unlikely that the Senate would be "content to endorse the views" of the House Agriculture Committee. But assuming JUSTICE STEVENS is right about this desire to leave details to the committees, the very first provision of the Constitution forbids it. Article I, Section 1 provides that "all legislative Powers herein granted shall be vested in a Congress of the United States, which shall consist of a Senate and a House of Representatives." It has always been assumed that these powers are nondelegable—or, as John Locke put it, that legislative power consists of the power "to make laws, . . . not to make legislators." J. Locke, Second Treatise of Government 87 (R. Cox ed. 1982). No one would think that the House of Representatives could operate in such fashion that only the broad outlines of bills would be adopted by vote of the full House, leaving minor details to be written, adopted, and voted upon, only by the cognizant committees. Thus, if legislation consists of forming an "intent" rather than adopting a text (a proposition with which I do not agree), Congress cannot leave the formation of that intent to a small band of its number, but must, as the Constitution says, form an intent of the Congress. There is no escaping the point: Legislative history that does not represent the intent of the whole Congress is nonprobative; and legislative history that does represent the intent of the whole Congress is fanciful.

Our opinions using legislative history are often curiously casual, sometimes even careless, in their analysis of what "intent" the legislative history shows. [Citation.] Perhaps that is because legislative history is in any event a make-weight; the Court really makes up its mind on the basis of other factors. Or perhaps it is simply hard to maintain a rigorously analytical attitude, when the point of departure for the inquiry is the fairyland in which legislative history reflects what was in "the Congress's mind."

In any case, it seems to me that if legislative history is capable of injecting into a statute an "intent" that its text alone does not express, the drafting history alluded to in today's opinion should have sufficed to win this case for respondent. It shows that interbank liability was not merely omitted from subsection (a), entitled "Civil liability." It was removed from that subsection, simultaneously with the addition of subsection (f), 12 U.S.C. § 4010(f), which gave the Federal Reserve Board power to "impose on or allocate among depository institutions the risks of loss and liability in connection with any aspect of the payment system" (language that is at least as compatible with adjudication as with rulemaking). Now if the only function of this new subsection (f) had been to give the Board rulemaking power, there would have been no logical reason to eliminate interbank disputes from the "Civil liability" subsection, whose basic prescription (banks are civilly liable for violations of the statute or of rules issued under the statute)[1] applies no less in the interbank than in the bank-customer context. Nor can the removal of interbank disputes from subsection (a) be explained on the ground that Congress had decided to apply different damages limits to those disputes. The former subsection (a), in both House and Senate versions, already provided varying damages limits for individual suits and class actions, *see* S. 790, 100th Cong., 1st Sess., § 609(a) (1987); H.R.Rep. No. 100–52, pp. 10–11 (1987), and it would have been logical to set forth the newly desired interbank variation there as well, leaving to the new subsection (f) only the conferral of rulemaking authority. Or, if it were thought essential to "consolidate" all the details of interbank disputes in subsection (f), it would still not have been necessary to specifically exclude interbank disputes from the general "civil liability" pronouncement of subsection (a). The prologue of that subsection, "except as otherwise provided in this section," would have made it clear that interbank civil liability was limited as set forth in subsection (f). The most plausible explanation for specifically excluding interbank disputes from the "Civil liability" subsection when subsection (f) was added—and for avoiding any reference to "civil liability" in subsection (f) itself—is an intent to commit those disputes to a totally different regime, *i.e.*, to Board adjudication rather than the normal civil-liability regime of the law courts.[2]

Today's opinion does not consider this argument, but nonetheless refutes it (in my view) conclusively. After recounting the drafting history, the Court states that "*nothing in § 4010(f)'s text* suggests that Congress meant

---

[1]   The Senate version of subsection (a) did not refer to violations of rules, *see* S. 790, 100th Cong., 1st Sess., § 609(a) (1987), but it was the House version of subsection (a), *see* H.R. Rep. No. 100–52, p. 10 (1987), which did specifically mention rules, that was retained.

[2]   I have explained why the "consolidation" explanation developed by Justice Stevens, does not ring true. Even if it did, however, it would not be accurate to say that the legislative history thus provides "the answer to an otherwise puzzling aspect of the statutory text," *ibid.* What Justice Stevens calls "the answer" (viz., the wish to consolidate all the interbank provisions in one section) is no more evident from the legislative history than it is from the face of the statute itself. Nothing in the legislative history says "we will consolidate interbank matters in a new subsection (f)"; Justice Stevens simply surmises, from the fact that the final text contains such consolidation, that consolidation was the reason for excluding interbank disputes from subsection (a). What investigation of legislative history has produced, in other words, is not an answer (that, if there is one, is in the text), but rather the puzzlement to which an answer is necessary: why were interbank disputes eliminated from subsection (a) when subsection (f) was adopted? Being innocent of legislative history, I would not have known of that curious excision if the Court's opinion had not told me. Thus, legislative history has produced what it usually produces: more questions rather than more answers.

the Federal Reserve Board to function as both regulator and adjudicator in interbank controversies." (emphasis added). Quite so. The text's the thing. We should therefore ignore drafting history without discussing it, instead of after discussing it.

■ JUSTICE STEVENS, concurring.

Given the fact that the Expedited Funds Availability Act was a measure that easily passed both houses of Congress, JUSTICE SCALIA is quite right that it is unlikely that more than a handful of legislators were aware of the Act's drafting history. He is quite wrong, however, to conclude from that observation that the drafting history is not useful to conscientious and disinterested judges trying to understand the statute's meaning.

Legislators, like other busy people, often depend on the judgment of trusted colleagues when discharging their official responsibilities. If a statute such as the Funds Availability Act has bipartisan support and has been carefully considered by committees familiar with the subject matter, Representatives and Senators may appropriately rely on the views of the committee members in casting their votes. In such circumstances, since most members are content to endorse the views of the responsible committees, the intent of those involved in the drafting process is properly regarded as the intent of the entire Congress.

In this case, as the Court and JUSTICE SCALIA agree, the statutory text of § 4010 supports petitioner's construction of the Act. However, the placement of the authorization for interbank litigation in subsection (f) rather than subsection (a) lends some support to the Court of Appeals' interpretation. When Congress creates a cause of action, the provisions describing the new substantive rights and liabilities typically precede the provisions describing enforcement procedures; subsection (f) does not conform to this pattern. The drafting history, however, provides a completely satisfactory explanation for this apparent anomaly in the text.

JUSTICE SCALIA nevertheless views the Court's reference to this history as unwise. As he correctly notes, the simultaneous removal of the provision for interbank liability from subsection (a) and the addition of a new subsection (f) support another inference favoring the Court of Appeals' construction of the statute: that the drafters intended to relegate the resolution of interbank disputes to a different tribunal. JUSTICE SCALIA is mistaken, however, in believing that this inference provides the "most plausible explanation" for the change. In my judgment the Court has correctly concluded that the most logical explanation for the change is a decision to consolidate the aspects of § 4010 that relate to interbank disputes—liability limits and rulemaking authority—in the same subsection. Thus, the net result of the inquiry into drafting history is to find the answer to an otherwise puzzling aspect of the statutory text.

I must also take exception to JUSTICE SCALIA's psychoanalysis of judges who examine legislative history when construing statutes. He confidently asserts that we use such history as a make-weight after reaching a conclusion on the basis of other factors. I have been performing this type of work for more than 25 years and have never proceeded in the manner

JUSTICE SCALIA suggests. It is quite true that I have often formed a tentative opinion about the meaning of a statute and thereafter examined the statute's drafting history to see whether the history supported my provisional conclusion or provided a basis for revising it. In my judgment, a reference to history in the Court's opinion in such a case cannot properly be described as a "make-weight." That the history could have altered my opinion is evidenced by the fact that there are significant cases, such as Green v. Bock Laundry Machine Co., 490 U.S. 504 (1989), in which the study of history did alter my original analysis. In any event, I see no reason why conscientious judges should not feel free to examine all public records that may shed light on the meaning of a statute.

Finally, I would like to suggest that JUSTICE SCALIA may be guilty of the transgression that he ascribes to the Court. He has confidently asserted that the legislative history in this case and in Wisconsin Public Intervenor v. Mortier, 501 U.S. 597 (1991), supports a result opposite to that reached by the Court. While I do not wish to reargue the *Mortier* case, I will say that I remain convinced that a disinterested study of the entire legislative history supports the conclusion reached by the eight-member majority of the Court. Even if his analysis in both cases is plausible, it is possible that JUSTICE SCALIA's review of the history in *Mortier* and in this case may have been influenced by his zealous opposition to any reliance on legislative history in any case. In this case, as in *Mortier*, his opinion is a fine example of the work product of a brilliant advocate.[2] It is the Court's opinion, however, that best sets forth the reasons for reversing the judgment of the Court of Appeals.

JUSTICE BREYER has authorized me to say that he agrees with the foregoing views.

QUESTIONS

1.   Recall Question 3 following *S.E.C. v. Robert Collier & Co.*, *supra*, asking you to articulate the theory underlying Judge Hand's transference of the House Committee's intent to the entire enacting Congress. What are the views of the opinion writers in *Bank One* concerning transference of intent? Whose views do you find most persuasive?

2.   Inquiries into legislative history are not usually clear-cut, but instead require balancing the evidence in support of conflicting interpretations. In Justice Scalia's view, one can characterize "the use of legislative history as the equivalent of entering a crowded cocktail party and looking over the heads of the guests for one's friends. . . . The legislative history of [the Act in question] contains a variety of diverse personages, a selected few of whom— its 'friends'—the Court has introduced to us in support of its result. But there are many other faces in the crowd, most of which, I think, are set against today's result." Conroy v. Aniskoff, 507 U.S. 511 (1993) (Scalia, J., concurring in the judgment). Does this critique discredit legislative history per se, or

---

[2]   Justice Jackson, whose opinion in United States v. Public Util. Comm'n of Cal., 345 U.S. 295 (1953), Justice Scalia cites, was also a brilliant advocate. Like Justice Scalia, he recognized the danger of indiscriminate use of legislative history, but unlike Justice Scalia he also recognized that it can be helpful in appropriate cases. See Schwegmann Brothers v. Calvert Distillers Corp., 341 U.S. 384, 395–396 (1951).

simply its selective citation? Is there a difference? Could the same accusation be made when selecting from among dictionary definitions or canons of construction?

NOTE

Chief Judge Robert A. Katzmann of the U.S. Court of Appeals for the Second Circuit has written extensively about the relationship between Congress and the Courts. In particular, he has advocated that the judiciary enhance its understanding of the process through which legislation is drafted and enacted. Drawn from his book, *Judging Statutes*, this excerpt identifies some of the important dynamics legislators face when drafting legislation, and in particular the important role that legislative history plays *for legislators* when shepherding a drafted bill to passage:

> Since the early nineteenth century, congressional committees have been central to lawmaking. Without committees, Congress could not function. . . . Congressional staffs, on committees or in the personal offices of legislators, assist members in their legislative work in every facet of activity. Today there are some 130 standing committees and subcommittees of various kinds in the House and 98 in the Senate. Some committees are authorizing committees, charged with making substantive policy as well as recommending spending levels to fund programs in their jurisdiction. . . .

> In the 111th Congress, 383 public bills were enacted, with a total of 7,617 pages, averaging 19.89 pages per statute. In the House of Representatives, 6,677 bills were introduced (including joint resolutions), and 861 passed, with a .129 ratio of bills passed to bills introduced. In the Senate, 4,101 bills were introduced and 176 bills passed, with a ratio of .043 bills passed to bills introduced.31 Additionally, the Senate held 2,374 committee and subcommittee hearings. . . . In recent decades, Congress has more frequently enacted legislation through large omnibus bills or resolutions, packing together a wide range of disparate issues. The omnibus mechanism is a departure from the traditional approach of handling individual pieces of legislation. In part, Congress uses omnibus bills to facilitate passage of overdue measures. For example, in 2009, 2010, 2011, and 2014, Congress packaged appropriations bills into a single omnibus bill, reducing opportunities for further delay as opposed to considering each bill individually. Because it is generally subject to an up-and-down vote, the massive omnibus bill masks differences over contentious measures included in the legislation that might not have passed if considered individually as stand-alone bills.

> Congressional life is marked by incredible pressure—such as the pressures of the permanent campaign for reelection, raising funds, balancing work in Washington and time in the district, balancing committee and floor work in an environment of increasing polarization, and balancing work and family

responsibilities. It is also now more intense than in the past. Consider these statistics: In 1955, the number of recorded votes in the House was 147; in the 111th Congress (2009–2010), it was 991 and 664 respectively . . . . In 1955, the number of recorded votes in the Senate was 88; in the 111th Congress (2009–2010), it was 400 and 307, respectively . . . . At times, these votes take place in the dead of night, especially as the legislative session moves at a frenetic pace to recess or end of the session. In 1955–1956, Congress was in session 227 days; from 2007 to 2012, the average was 323 days. In the House, the session day consisted of an average of 7.4 and 5.3 hours per day in the 111th and 112th Congress, respectively, as compared to 4.1 hours per day in 1955–1956. In the Senate, the session day consisted of 7.1 and 6.3 hours per day in the 111th and 112th Congress, respectively, as compared to 6.1 hours per day in 1955–1956. In 1955–1956, the average total of committee assignments for members of the House was 3.0; in 2011–2012, it was 5.3 (1.7 standing committee assignments, 3.4 subcommittee assignments, and .20 other committee assignments). Similarly, in the Senate, the average number of committee assignments was 7.9 in 1955–1956; in 2011–2012, it was 12.9 (3.4 standing committee assignments, 8.6 subcommittee assignments, and .9 other committee assignments).

The key point is that the expanding, competing demands on legislators' time reduce opportunities for reflection and deliberation. In that circumstance, beyond the work of their own committees of which legislators have direct knowledge, members operate in a system in which they rely on the work of colleagues on other committees. Members of Congress accept the trustworthiness of statements made by their colleagues on other committees, especially those charged with managing the bill, about what the proposed legislation means. They cannot read every word of the bills they vote upon, and, indeed, reading every word is often not particularly instructive, to the degree bills contain language amending the United States Code or enacted statutes. For example, a legislator unfamiliar with the Hobby Protection Act in its codified or statutory version might have a hard time understanding this provision in a bill that the House adopted in July 2013:

The Hobby Protection Act (15 U.S.C. § 2101 et seq.) is amended—

(1)   in section 2—

(A) in subsection (b), by inserting ", or the sale in commerce" after "distribution in commerce";

(B) by redesignating subsection (d) as subsection (e) and inserting after subsection (c) the following:

"(d) Provision of Assistance or Support—It shall be a violation of subsection (a) or (b) for a person to provide substantial assistance or support to any manufacturer, importer, or seller if that person knows or should have known that the manufacturer, importer, or seller is engaged in any act or practice that violates subsection (a) or (b).”; and

(C) in subsection (e) (as so redesignated), by striking “and (b)” and inserting “(b), and (d)”;

(2) in section 3—

(A) by striking “If any person” and inserting “(a) In General— If any person”;

(B) by striking “or has an agent” and inserting “, has an agent, transacts business, or wherever venue is proper under section 1391 of title 28, United States Code”; and

(C) by adding at the end the following:

“(b) Trademark Violations—If the violation of section 2 (a) or (b) or a rule under section 2(c) also involves unauthorized use of registered trademarks belonging to a collectibles certification service, the owner of such trademarks shall have, in addition to the remedies provided in subsection (a), all rights provided under sections 34, 35, and 36 of the Trademark Act of 1946 (15 U.S.C. 1116, 1117, and 1118) for violations of such Act.”; . . .

Legislators and their staffs become educated about the bill by reading the materials produced by the committees and conference committees from which the proposed legislation emanates. These materials include, for example, committee reports, conference committee reports, and the joint statements of conferees who drafted the final bill.

Committee reports accompanying bills have long been important means of informing the whole chamber about proposed legislation; they are often the primary means by which staffs brief their principals before voting on a bill. To facilitate deliberation, Congress was concerned from its earliest days that its proceedings be published, consistent with the constitutional requirement that a journal be kept. With the advent of the committee system, reports of committee activity were delivered orally, but, in the House by the period 1830–1860, and in the Senate by 1900, it was also commonplace for committee reports accompanying proposed legislation to be disseminated to the full chamber so that members could have a fuller appreciation of the bills on which they were called on to vote. Committee reports are generally circulated at least two calendar days before legislation is considered on the floor. Those reports provide members and their staffs with explanatory material about a bill’s context, purposes, policy implications, and details, as well as information about who the committee supporters of a particular bill are and about possible minority views. Conference committee reports represent the views of legislators from both chambers who are charged with reconciling bills that have passed both the House and the Senate and presenting them for final legislative consideration. Members and their staffs will also hear from interest groups—including groups they find credible—and the executive branch about particular bills. The system works because committee members and their staffs will lose influence with their colleagues as to future bills if they do not accurately represent the bills under consideration within their jurisdiction. Indeed, staffers would risk losing their jobs if they were to mislead legislators as to the details of legislation and accompanying reports.

Although any legislator can introduce a bill, it is the committee of jurisdiction that generally processes the proposed measure. In drafting bills, legislators look to multiple sources. In his memoir, the late Senator Edward M. Kennedy wrote that "[n]inety-five percent of the nitty-gritty work of drafting and even negotiating is now done by staff," marking "an enormous shift of responsibility over the past forty or fifty years." Ninety-five percent, observed veteran journalist Robert Kaiser, the author of a rich saga of the passage of the Dodd-Frank Act, "might underestimate staff members' share of the work." Committees are aided by professional drafters in each chamber's office of legislative counsel; these drafters are trained in the nuances of statute writing. Although legislators and their staffs are not required to consult with legislative counsel, doing so is prudent because a poorly drafted bill can lead to all manner of problems for agencies and courts charged with interpreting the statute. Typically, a committee staffer will contact the office for assistance in framing the bill so that it is technically correct. Those who work as legislative counsel think of the committees as clients. Their role is not to offer views about the merits of a particular proposal; it is to determine how best to commit the bill's purposes to writing.

Not all bills originate from the committees themselves. Some originate with the executive branch; others from interest groups, lobbyists, businesses, and state and local governments. These various interests may assist in drafting bills as well, but not necessarily with the care that each chamber's office of legislative counsel provides. Not all bills are drafted in the committee; bills can also be drafted, or at least substantially revised, on the floor and in conference committee. In the Senate, flexible procedures allow senators to draft bills in the course of debate. When bills are drafted on the floor, for example, the pressures of time mean that legislators do not generally check with the legislative counsel, and thus there is more likely to be problematic drafting language. In conference committee, the pressure to come to closure and pass a bill can compromise technical precision.

... The statutemaking process, as legislators and staffs understand it, involves not just the text of legislation, but also quite importantly legislative history—such as the reports and debates associated with the legislative text. As I described earlier, committee reports and conference committee reports accompanying bills can provide guidance to legislators in the enactment process. Legislative history accompanying legislation can also be helpful by providing direction to agencies as to how to interpret and implement legislation. Scholars . . . have more recently shown how Congress operates within a milieu of rules, norms, and practices— including importantly the applicability of legislative history. The degree to which these norms and practices shape both the drafting process and also legislative expectations about how laws should be understood is not commonly known within the judiciary—a matter to which I return later in this book when I discuss judicial interpretation of statutes.

* * *

What relevance does this whirlwind survey of Congress and lawmaking have for the interpretation of statutes? The point is a simple one. The laws of Congress are the product of often complex institutional processes, which engage legislators, staff, and other interests with stakes in the outcome. Having a basic understanding of legislative lawmaking can only better prepare judges to undertake their interpretive responsibilities. . . .

Robert A. Katzmann, Judging Statutes 13–22 (2014).

C. INTERPRETING A STATUTE IN LIGHT OF ITS AUDIENCES

Chief Judge Katzmann's discussion of the role that legislative history can play as an aid for legislators voting on pending legislation raises important related questions: who are the audiences of a statute, and how do those audiences determine what the statute means? Chief Judge Katzmann has suggested that an important and underexamined audience for a bill's legislative history is the non-drafting legislators who must understand what the drafted bill accomplishes before deciding whether to vote for it. Yet other audiences may look primarily to the enacted statutory text, rather than the legislative history. And some audiences—such as the administrative agency tasked with implementing the legislation—are likely to focus on *both*.

One of this Casebook's co-authors has written about precisely this issue: depending on the audience of the statute in question, and the circumstances in which that audience may be called upon to interpret it, the selection and prioritization of interpretive methods may (and in practice does) reasonably vary:

"IDENTIFY THE AUDIENCE.—Decide who is supposed to get the message." So instructs the U.S. House of Representatives' legislative drafting manual. This advice is common to many statutory drafting guides, which emphasize that a statute's audience should influence a statute's structure, style, and terminology. Different audiences have varied levels of legal fluency and background knowledge, and distinct audiences have very different modes of interacting with a given statutory scheme. It would be foolish to draft a playground ordinance in the same manner as a multinational corporate tax provision. For statutory drafting, at least, audience considerations appear to be a central concern.

When it comes to the interpretation of statutes, however, important considerations of audience often go overlooked in statutory interpretation debates. In using the term "audience," I mean to focus on the range of legal actors whose behavior may be altered as a result of a statutory enactment. These include audiences that are actively engaged in understanding statutory meaning, as well as those passively affected by statutory rules, and also include the many third parties whom the law conscripts to transmit legal knowledge to the affected audience(s). Not all statutes communicate to their respective audiences in the same manner: some statutes establish specific rules that regulate the conduct of lay audiences like the general public, while other statutes set out broad mandates to specialized government audiences, who implement them through subsequent regulation and enforcement.

Despite these differences, when it comes to methods of interpretation (*i.e.*, semantic and syntactic canons of construction, evidence of linguistic usage, and extratextual sources of statutory meaning), judges often treat all statutes, and all statutory audiences, homogeneously. They deploy the same tools and rules of interpretation to decipher a firearms carriage rule with direct application to the general public as they do to decode technical statutory language directing federal agencies to implement the Affordable Care Act.[7]

A common trope in discussions of statutory interpretation theory is that American judges lack a principled method of interpreting statutes . . . . [and] judges tend to apply interpretive methods inconsistently such that even sophisticated litigants cannot predict which canons of construction, dictionaries, or sources of meaning may apply in any given case. And the prevailing dialogue seems to offer no obvious path forward; Abbe Gluck recently concluded that debates between textualism and purposivism have "taken us as far as they can go."

An important reason that these debates have largely run aground, I argue, is that the leading theories of statutory interpretation, textualism and purposivism, are as much theories about how *judges* should behave vis-à-vis the legislatures as they are theories about the interpretation and implementation of statutory texts. Textualist and purposivist theories are largely motivated by faithful-agent concerns that arise due to the inherent tension of common-law judges interpreting statutes enacted by democratically accountable legislatures. Anxiety about legislative supremacy has been called "a shibboleth in discourse about statutory interpretation." A core disagreement between these approaches is not just about the meaning and interpretation of text but also a debate about how to *judge* it: textualism and purposivism *both* "seek to provide a superior way for federal judges to fulfill their presumed duty as Congress's faithful agents." Indeed, it has been said that the "fundamental question" for statutory interpretation is "whether courts should view themselves as faithful agents of the legislature or as independent cooperative partners."

Problematically, judges tend to disagree just as much about theories of judging as they do about theories of interpretation. Many debates ostensibly about how to interpret statutes (*i.e.*, which canons of construction and sources of statutory meaning to prioritize) thus transform into debates about how to judge

---

[7] *Compare* Muscarello v. United States, 524 U.S. 125 (1998) (majority and dissent employing, among other methods and canons: consistent usage presumption, dictionary definitions, legislative history, legislative intent, ordinary meaning, plain meaning, rule against superfluity, statutory context, statutory purpose, statutory scheme/structure, whole act, whole code, and the legal significance of semantic ambiguity), *with* King v. Burwell, 135 S.Ct. 2480 (2015) (majority and dissent employing, among other methods and canons: dictionary definitions, legislative history, legislative intent, ordinary meaning, plain meaning, rule against superfluity, statutory context, statutory purpose, statutory scheme/structure, whole act, whole code, and the legal significance of semantic ambiguity).

statutes, fixating on separation-of-powers concerns related to the proper rule of the courts vis-à-vis legislatures. . . .

Debates about judicial faithful agency often overshadow other equally pressing aspects of statutory interpretation theory. These include providing an account of how statutes communicate meaning to, and alter the behavior of, relevant audiences, and the proper role of judicial interpretive theory in enhancing a statute's capacity to ensure its relevant audiences get (and effectuate) the statutory message. . . . Scott Shapiro has helpfully analogized laws to specific social plans. On this account, the individuals and/or entities subject to laws—what I call statutory audiences—give functional meaning to these statutory plans through implementation and practice. This, of course, is why many legislative drafters are mindful of the intended audience when they draft statutes—for the social plan to be effective, the audience must be able to get the message.

Inherent in the nature of statutory enactments is that they will inevitably be incomplete social plans—the communication can only be completed through responsive action. This is because statutory texts communicate in a manner distinct from other forms of linguistic communication. In contrast to the speech acts of individual speakers, legislation constitutes a form of collective speech act that is typically the result of one or more compromises. Legislative compromises often result in incomplete decisions about the precise legal content of the enacted legislation.

In addition, statutory plans as a form of communication may be strategically and intentionally under-specified. As a result, cooperative assumptions in ordinary conversation about how speakers conventionally convey information—for example, that the speaker intends to convey her message with specificity and precision—often does not apply in the case of legislative speech acts. The unique dynamics associated with the production of legislative "speech" are especially important when making assumptions about the sufficiency of the communicative content conveyed by legislative texts. In many conversational contexts, the audience may assume the speaker seeks, through choice of language, intentional omission or ambiguity, and implicatures that suggest something different is meant than what was literally said, to provide the sufficient quality and quantity of information necessary to convey her meaning.

In legislative contexts, however, textual underspecification, redundancy, and contradiction—both intentional and unintentional—are common features of legislative texts, in single statutes and across them. Among other things, this may diminish just how much implied content can be reasonably derived from legislative speech acts, with semantically enriched content subject to debatable and competing inferences about how broadly or narrowly to read the statutory text. Despite this, legislated "speech" often necessitates that the audience—those implementing legislative plans—must fill larger gaps as compared to instructions given in interpersonal communication between individuals.

Moreover, in contrast to most conversational communicative contexts between speaker and audience, the legislative context is inherently impersonal. Legislators address an audience comprised largely of those not personally known (or sometimes even anticipated) by the legislature. Thus, both the precise execution of the plans themselves, as well as those who implement them, may be unknown at the time the broad plan is enacted. . . .

The upshot of this is twofold. First, notions of judicial "faithful agency" may often have limited utility when courts are tasked with attributing legal meaning to ambiguous statutory texts—there may simply not be an objective answer as to what either the legislature "intended" or what the text "means." Rather, the legal meaning of statutes will often have to be developed through post-enactment implementation and interpretation, or what Scott Soames calls "precisifying." To the degree this is so, then judicial choices about which substantive canons and interpretive methods to prioritize function to provide a legal grammar for how statutory audiences are expected to engage with statutes, at least as much as these choices function as an act of discovering the "plain" or "objective" meaning of the text itself.

A second upshot is that while courts and government officials play an important role in precisifying statutory meaning, statutes are also directed at other audiences, who also play an important role in precisifying statutory meaning. Thus, for statutes to function in their essential capacity as a means to implement social plans and coordinate societal behavior, in at least some circumstances the uncertainty about statutory meaning must also be resolved (and resolvable) by [those] statutory audiences. . . .

Of course, not all statutory provisions seek to communicate or alter behavior in the same manner, nor with respect to the same audiences. . . . [Professor] Meir Dan-Cohen [ha]s observ[ed] that an "acoustic separation" often exists between conduct rules and decision rules embedded in the criminal law. Whereas conduct rules are specific statutory provisions that directly address (and seek to expressly alter) the actions of lay audiences, decision rules are aimed at guiding the (often discretionary) enforcement decisions of government officials, and thus may have little to say directly to the public at large.

This distinction—between statutory provisions that delegate authority to government officials and those that directly regulate the conduct of members of the public more broadly—is essential to my theory of statutory audience. As [Professor] Ed Rubin has described, statutes have both "transitive" and "intransitive" modes of communication and application. Transitive statutes state the precise rule to be applied, which means that the relevant statutory audiences might be thought to be put on notice simply by the enactment of the rule itself. Given their direct application, transitive statutory provisions may raise heightened concerns about notice and the possibility of textual ambiguity or vagueness.[71] These kinds of statutory provisions may also require judges to treat the statutory communication as "complete," for rule of law reasons [related to due process and fair notice] . . .

By contrast, intransitive statutes merely set out the mechanism by which subsequent rules shall be developed— usually by government officials, such as administrative agencies. As a practical matter, "the ultimate target of the [intransitive] statute cannot know what behavior the statute will require." In these circumstances, the capacity for the affected audience to derive notice from the statutory text itself may be of less concern, because no such notice can be derived from the text alone since the legislative communication is incomplete. The legal rule that will modify the audience's behavior will instead derive from an administrative adjudication, regulation, or guidance document promulgated by the agency in accordance with administrative law and in furtherance of the intransitive statutory delegation. So long as the statute provides a sufficient textually-enriched basis to guide the officials addressed with implementing it, whether the statutory text alone provides clear notice, or gives specific instructions to the audiences it seeks to regulate, may be of less concern than for transitive provisions. . . . [T]here may be good reasons to prioritize different interpretive methods depending

---

[71] Drawing a clear distinction between ambiguity and vagueness is essential to understanding how statutes can give notice to relevant audiences. Whereas a term is ambiguous if it is susceptible to two different, but potentially overlapping meanings (such as the word "blue" conveying both the color and the mood), a term is vague if among the range of normal applications of the term are borderline cases separating instances in which the term clearly applies and when it clearly doesn't (such as the word "tall"). . . . Statutory ambiguity is an unavoidable aspect of many statutes, but statutory vagueness can raise essential rule-of-law concerns, at least for criminal statutes directed at the general public. In other circumstances, intentionally vague regulatory plans may provide an agency with a wide berth in which to implement a range of potential policymaking objectives.

on whether the relevant audience is regulated by a direct conduct rule or an instransitive statutory delegation.

. . . Because statutes address distinct audiences in different ways, courts play a crucial role in helping statutory audiences (and their interpreters) translate and derive meaning from underspecified and often-ambiguous statutory enactments. How a judge chooses to interpret a legal text will affect that text's legal meaning just as much as the semantic meaning of the text itself. The semantic meaning derived from "bare" text is not always synonymous with the legal meaning a judge may attribute to it. A statute's legal meaning can be derived not only from the statute's semantic content, but also from contextual content associated with that statute, such as evidence of the enacting legislature's intentions—collectively, its communicative content.

Most crucially, the legal content of a statute is also not synonymous with its communicative content. When judges apply substantive canons like the rule of lenity, clear notice rules, or the plain meaning rule, they specify the legal meaning that shall be derived from the statutory text. That meaning may not be the meaning that one or more of its drafters intended, nor the semantic meaning most commonly associated with the term or phrase in question (to the degree one can be clearly ascertained). In this sense, judicial interpretation provides the authoritative lens through which to view the statutory text, framing and shaping the meaning(s) that others may permissibly derive from that text.

Understood this way, judicial rules of interpretation function as a kind of legal grammar: they provide guidance for deriving legal meaning from oft-underspecified statutory text. [J]udges['] . . . opinions not only resolve particular . . . interpretive disputes, but also provide interpretive rules and rationales that can have secondary effects for future cases. (This, of course, assumes such rules are justified on the basis of more than the mere ad-hoc whims of the particular judge(s).) Most canons of construction seem to derive their authority from the presumption that they apply across statutes. If so, then their application will necessarily have the effect of altering how future audiences may be expected to understand and interpret legal texts that present similar ambiguities. . . .

My thesis . . . is that statutes communicate in distinct ways and to varied audiences, and so different tools of interpretation may be more appropriate for transitive statutes than for intransitive ones, and for statutes addressed primarily at some kinds of audience than others. Moreover, most statutes are directed at multiple audiences, so a central task for many statutory interpretation questions should be to identify the principal audience at issue, which will often clarify what the statute means, how it applies, and which normative concerns should prevail when they conflict. . . .

David S. Louk, *The Audiences of Statutes*, 105 Cornell L. Rev. 137 (2020).

QUESTIONS

1. Consider the distinction between transitive conduct rules and intransitive decision rules as articulated in the excerpt. Although this distinction may be purely descriptive, it also has potential normative significance. For example, are the practical concerns about ambiguity the same for criminal prohibitions as they are for legislative delegations to administrative agencies? If not, should ambiguity be more (or less) tolerated for statutes directed primary at one audience than for statutes directed primarily at another? Recall that the rule of lenity and the void-for-vagueness doctrines—which guard, respectively, against undue ambiguity or vagueness—apply only for statutes carrying criminal penalties. Does this suggest ambiguity and vagueness are less problematic for civil statutes or statutes directed primarily at government bureaucrats?

2. Chief Judge Katzmann has observed that ambiguity can be the "solvent of disagreement, at least temporarily,"[*] for legislators often draft statutory language imprecisely on purpose, in order to facilitate the bill's passage. Thus a statute may be *intentionally* ambiguous, either because legislators cannot agree on the precise range of possible applications, or because legislators would prefer to "pass the buck" to the law's enforcers to help refine the statute's meaning across a range of reasonable applications over time. In these circumstances, should courts prioritize different methods of interpretation than they might when interpreting a statute for which they believe a "true" meaning of the statutory text exists? When the statutory text appears intentionally ambiguous or open-ended, should judges give more weight to the interpretations of the enforcing agency? Keep these questions in mind as you read Part V, Agency Interpretations of Statutes. Consider also how, if at all, intentional ambiguity alters the normative force of interpretive canons such as the "plain meaning rule," the "evil sought to be remedied," or the "clear notice rule," as discussed in *Arlington Central School District v. Murphy, infra.*

1. CASE STUDY: CHILDREN WITH SPECIAL EDUCATION NEEDS

Statutes often regulate the conduct of several distinct and separate audiences, each of which have their own interests, capacities, and concerns. Given this, it is possible—and sometimes probable—that different audiences may encounter a statute in a very different light. Consider a question of statutory interpretation raised by an amendment

---

[*] *See* Robert A. Katzmann, Judging Statutes 47 (2014) (citing Herbert Kaufman, The Administrative Behavior of Federal Bureau Chiefs (1981)).

to the Individuals with Disabilities Education Act (IDEA) as part of the Handicapped Children's Protection Act of 1986.

The Text to Be Construed: Handicapped Children's Protection Act of 1986

The Statute as Drafted:

SHORT TITLE

SECTION 1. This Act may be cited as the "Handicapped Children's Protection Act of 1986".

AWARD OF ATTORNEYS' FEES

SEC. 2. Section 615(e)(4) of the Education of the Handicapped Act is amended by inserting "(A)" after the paragraph designation and by adding at the end thereof the following new subparagraphs:

"(B) In any action or proceeding brought under this subsection, the court, in its discretion, may award reasonable attorneys' fees as part of the costs to the parents or guardian of a handicapped child or youth who is the prevailing party.

"(C) For the purpose of this subsection, fees awarded under this subsection shall be based on rates prevailing in the community in which the action or proceeding arose for the kind and quality of services furnished. No bonus or multiplier may be used in calculating the fees awarded under this subsection.

"(D) No award of attorneys' fees and related costs may be made in any action or proceeding under this subsection for services performed subsequent to the time of a written offer of settlement to a parent or guardian, if—

"(i) the offer is made within the time prescribed by Rule 68 of the Federal Rules of Civil Procedure or, in the case of an administrative proceeding, at any time more than ten days before the proceeding begins;

"(ii) the offer is not accepted within ten days; and

"(iii) the court or administrative officer finds that the relief finally obtained by the parents or guardian is not more favorable to the parents or guardian than the offer of settlement.

"(E) Notwithstanding the provisions of subparagraph (D), an award of attorneys' fees and related costs may be made to a parent or guardian who is the prevailing party and who was substantially justified in rejecting the settlement offer.

"([F]) Whenever the court finds that—

"(i) the parent or guardian, during the course of the action or proceeding, unreasonably protracted the final resolution of the controversy;

"(ii) the amount of the attorneys' fees otherwise authorized to be awarded unreasonably exceeds the hourly rate prevailing in the community for similar services by attorneys of reasonably comparable skill, experience, and reputation; or

"(iii) the time spent and legal services furnished were excessive considering the nature of the action or proceeding,

the court shall reduce, accordingly, the amount of the attorneys' fees awarded under this subsection.

"(G) The provisions of subparagraph (F) shall not apply in any action or proceeding if the court finds that the State or local educational agency unreasonably protracted the final resolution of the action or proceeding or there was a violation of section 615 of this Act." . . .

GAO STUDY OF ATTORNEYS' FEES PROVISION

SEC. 4. (a) The Comptroller General of the United States, through the General Accounting Office, shall conduct a study of the impact of the amendments to the Education of the Handicapped Act made by section 2 of this Act. Not later than June 30, 1989, the Comptroller General shall submit a report containing the findings of such study to the Committee on Education and Labor of the House of Representatives and the Committee on Labor and Human Resources of the Senate. The Comptroller General shall conduct a formal briefing for such Committees on the status of the study not later than March 1, 1988. Such report shall include the information described in subsection (b).

(b) The report authorized under subsection (a) shall include the following information:

(1) The number, in the aggregate and by State, of written decisions under sections "615(b)(2) and (c) transmitted to State advisory panels under section 615(d)(4) for fiscal years 1984 through 1988, the prevailing party in each such decision, and the type of complaint. For fiscal year 1986, the report shall designate which decisions concern complaints filed after the date of the enactment of this Act.

(2) The number, in the aggregate and by State, of civil actions brought under section 615(e)(2), the prevailing party in each action, and the type of complaint for fiscal years 1984 through 1988. For fiscal year 1986 the report shall designate which decisions concern complaints filed after the date of enactment.

(3) Data, for a geographically representative selective sample of States, indicating (A) the specific amount of attorneys' fees, costs, and expenses awarded to the prevailing party, in each action and proceeding under section 615(e)(4)(B) from the date of the enactment of this Act through fiscal year 1988, and the range of such fees, costs, and expenses awarded in the actions and proceedings under such section, categorized by type of complaint and (B) for the same sample as in (A) the number of hours spent by personnel, including attorneys and consultants, involved in the action or proceeding, and expenses incurred by the parents and the State educational agency and local educational agency.

(4) Data, for a geographically representative sample of States, on the experience of educational agencies in resolving complaints informally under section 615(b)(2), from the date of the enactment of this Act through fiscal year 1988. . . .

In the next section, consider how you might approach this problem of statutory interpretation differently depending on the audience of which you are a member:

a. A LEGISLATOR DECIDING WHETHER TO ENACT THE STATUTE

Imagine that you are a member of the U.S. House of Representatives who has no particular experience with, or strong views about, education issues—your campaign platform, and the chief concerns of your district, lie elsewhere. Last summer, you and your colleagues approved amendments to the Individuals with Disabilities Education Act (IDEA)* as part of the Handicapped Children's Protection Act (HCPA)—one of over 500 votes you cast that year. The amendments respond to your colleagues' concerns that although the IDEA guarantees an adequate education to all special needs children at no cost to parents or guardians, parents and guardians have often had to pay out of pocket for costs associated with demonstrating their children's special education needs. These costs include hiring expensive qualified experts who can attest, in court, to a child's special education needs.

Prior to the vote, sponsors of the bill indicated that the HCPA would amend the IDEA to ensure that the attorney's fee award provided under the IDEA would "include[ ] expenses of expert witnesses [and] the reasonable costs of any study, report, test, or project which is found to be necessary for the preparation of the parents' or guardian's due process hearing, state administrative review or civil action; as well as traditional costs and expenses incurred in the course of litigating a case." H.R. REP. NO. 99–296, at 6 (1985) (Comm. Rep.). This amendment would ensure that a parent or guardian with a legitimate claim would not have to pay

---

* Editors' Note: At the time the legislation was enacted, the act now known as the IDEA was referred to as the "Education for All Handicapped Children Act." For simplicity's sake, it will be referred to as the IDEA throughout.

out of pocket for an expert to vouch for their child's special education needs. After adoption by unanimous consent, the bill was then sent to conference, where members of both houses resolved the remaining differences between the House and Senate versions of the bill.

The conference has reconciled the two bills and provided a Conference Report clarifying the changes ahead of a final vote on the HCPA. Your legislative aid has provided you with the Conference Report, which contains both the revised bill and the joint committee's statement about the reconciled bill. Your chief of staff has indicated that you have roughly 10 minutes to read the materials and decide whether to support the revised HCPA before you must attend a meeting with constituents who have flown all the way to D.C. from your faraway district.

The Accompanying Conference Report*:

JOINT EXPLANATORY STATEMENT OF THE COMMITTEE OF CONFERENCE

The managers on the part of the House and the Senate at the conference on the disagreeing votes of the two Houses on the amendment of the House to the bill (S. 415) . . . . The differences between the Senate bill and the House amendment and the substitute agreed to in the conference, are noted below, except for clerical corrections, conforming changes made necessary by agreements reached by the conferees, and minor drafting and clarifying changes.

1. The Senate bill provides for "a reasonable attorney's fee."

The House amendment provides for "reasonable attorneys' fees."

The Senate recedes.

2. With slightly different wording, both the Senate bill and the House amendment provide for the awarding of attorneys' fees in addition to costs.

The Senate recedes to the House and the House recedes to the Senate with an amendment clarifying that "the court, in its discretion, may award reasonable attorneys' fees as part of the costs . . ." This change in wording incorporates the Supreme Court *Marek v. Chesny* decision (87 L. Ed. 2d 1).

The conferees intend that the term "attorneys' fees as part of the costs" include reasonable expenses and fees of expert witnesses and the reasonable costs of any test or evaluation which is found to be necessary for the preparation of the parent or guardian's case in the action or proceeding, as well as traditional costs incurred in the course of litigating a case.

---

* H.R. REP. NO. 99–687 (1986) (Conf. Rep.).

3.   The Senate bill provides for the award of attorney's fees "to a parent or legal representative."

The House amendment provides for the award of attorneys' fees "to the parents or guardian."

The Senate recedes. . . .

6.   The House amendment, but not the Senate bill, provides for a GAO study of the impact of the bill authorizing the awarding of fees and costs.

The Senate recedes to the House with an amendment expanding the data collection requirements of the GAO study to include information regarding the amount of funds expended by local educational agencies and state educational agencies on civil actions and administrative proceedings. . . .

11. The House amendment, but not the Senate bill, includes an anti-retaliation provision.

The House recedes. It is the conferees' intent that no person may discharge, intimidate, retaliate, threaten, coerce, or otherwise take an adverse action against any person because such person has filed a complaint, testified, furnished information, assisted or participated in any manner in a meeting, hearing, review, investigation, or other activity related to the administration of, exercise of authority under, or right secured by part B of EHA. The term "person" the first time it is used means a state educational agency, local educational agency, intermediate educational unit or any official or employee thereof. . . .

QUESTIONS

1.   The revised bill does not expressly identify how the Committee altered the bill from the prior version the House approved last year. To identify the salient changes since you voted on it, how useful is text of the revised bill compared to the conference report's explanation of the changes?

2.   In deciding whether to continue to support the bill, which portions of the above texts, if any, would you find most useful in identifying what the revised bill seeks to achieve?

3.   Would you be more likely to consult a dictionary to understand the meaning of an ambiguous term in the amended bill, or would you instead refer first to the Committee Report's explanation as to what that term means?

b.   A BENEFICIARY SEEKING RELIEF UNDER THE STATUTE

Suppose you are the parent of a special needs child who is not receiving an adequate education in his traditional classroom. You know that your son is entitled to a free and appropriate education under federal law, but after discussions with both your child's teacher and his principal, the school has declined to accommodate your son's needs, and the district will not transfer him to a special education classroom in another school.

In considering your options, you speak to a local attorney who tells you that you may initiate an administrative action against the district, which could lead to your filing a federal civil lawsuit if the district proves obstinate. The attorney offers to take your case for free on a contingency basis, for she will be awarded attorney's fees if you prevail in an action brought against the district. However, she requires a retainer of $10,000 to cover the costs of an early childhood development consultant whose needs assessment of your child will be critical for you to prevail. The attorney indicates that if you win, it is probable that a judge may ultimately award you the costs of the expert's assessment. After some internet research, you discover that parents and guardians of special needs children who are represented by an attorney and an expert witness are almost twice as likely to prevail in IDEA actions brought against school districts. *See* U.S. Gov't Accountability Office, GAO/HRD–90–22BR, Special Education: The Attorney Fees Provision of Public Law 99–372 26 (1990).

Below is an excerpted portion of New York State's Procedural Safeguards Notice, a notice that the IDEA requires each state to furnish on an annual basis to every parent or guardian of a disabled child. *See* New York State Education Department, Procedural Safeguards Notice, July 2017, available at http://www.p12.nysed.gov/specialed/formsnotices/documents/NYSEDProceduralSafeguardsNoticeJuly2017v2.pdf. Among other rights, the Procedural Safeguards Notice informs parents about their rights under the IDEA to an independent educational evaluation for their child, at no cost to the parent:

... INDEPENDENT EDUCATIONAL EVALUATIONS

34 CFR section 300.502; 8 NYCRR section 200.5(g)

General

As described below, you have the right to obtain an independent educational evaluation (IEE) of your child if you disagree with the evaluation of your child that was obtained by your school district.

If you request an IEE, the school district must provide you with information about where you may obtain one and about the school district's criteria that apply to IEEs.

Definitions

Independent educational evaluation means an evaluation conducted by a qualified examiner who is not employed by the school district responsible for the education of your child.

Public expense means that the school district either pays for the full cost of the evaluation or ensures that the evaluation is otherwise provided at no cost to you, consistent with the provisions of Part B of IDEA, which allow each state to use whatever State, local, federal and private sources of support are available in the State to meet the requirements of Part B of IDEA.

Parent right to evaluation at public expense

You have the right to an IEE of your child at public expense if you disagree with an evaluation of your child obtained by your school district, subject to [certain] conditions. . . .

You are entitled to only one IEE of your child at public expense each time your school district conducts an evaluation of your child with which you disagree. . . .

Requests for evaluations by impartial hearing officers

If an impartial hearing officer requests an IEE of your child as part of a due process hearing, the cost of the evaluation must be at public expense. . . .

* * *

While it is clear that as a parent you are entitled to the initial IEE of your child at public expense in preparing for the administrative hearing, the Notice is silent as to whether you can expect the district to cover the costs of the expert's participation in a possible federal civil suit.

QUESTIONS

1. As a parent, how likely would you be to press your child's case in court if you would have to cover the costs of the expert's fees yourself?

2. The statute's purpose—to ensure an adequate education for special needs children at no cost to their parent or guardian—seems undermined if an expert assessment and involvement in the civil suit doubles your likelihood of success, and yet the costs associated are not covered under the statute's fee and cost-shifting provision. As a parent, what reasons would you have to think the assessment should be covered? What methods of interpretation, if any, would support your conclusion?

c.   A STATE OFFICIAL COMPLYING WITH THE STATUTE

Imagine that you are the Deputy General Counsel of the New York State Education Department. Your responsibilities include overseeing the State's compliance with federal education laws, including the IDEA. Under the IDEA, New York State has received at least $1.2 billion in grant allocations from the federal government during each of the past five years. In exchange for the grant funding, New York State and its subdivisions must comply with a number of IDEA procedural requirements, including the provision of an administrative hearing for any parent or guardian who brings an action alleging that their local school district has failed to provide their child with a free and appropriate special education. Such an administrative proceeding can be costly and time-consuming, especially if it fails to resolve the dispute, leading to an even more costly federal lawsuit. It also usually requires the involvement of an expensive special education consultant who assesses the child's needs. While the IDEA requires the local school district to cover the costs of the consultant's assessment and testimony as part of the administrative proceeding, the district need not cover the costs of further assessments (or testimony) undertaken as part of any subsequent federal lawsuit.

The U.S. Supreme Court has just granted cert in a case that will decide whether prevailing parents in federal suits may include expert witness fees among "reasonable attorneys' fees as part of the costs" that may be awarded to prevailing parents under the statutes. These fees can range from between $5,000 and $20,000, depending on the case, and thus far most federal district courts have included them in the fee awards they have granted.

The Governor has asked your opinion on whether New York State should join either of two competing *amicus curiae* briefs to be filed before the Court. One brief argues that expert witness fees should be included among the "reasonable attorneys' fees as part of the costs," the other argues that they should not be included. In addition, the Governor has also asked whether you think New York should continue to accept IDEA grants if the Supreme Court holds that the IDEA fee-shifting provision includes expert witness fees. Although the state does not gather data on the total annual costs the state incurs in paying for the attorney's fee and expert witness fee awards of prevailing parents, you know that last year, parents in New York State prevailed in approximately 200 administrative actions and in 1 civil action brought under the IDEA. *See* GAO Special Education: The Attorney Fees Provision of Public Law 99–372, GAO/HRD–90–22BR, at 63. In each, it is probable that an award of expert witness fees would be in the $5,000–$20,000 range. Should you decline to accept IDEA fees, the state would lose at least $1.2 billion in federal grants per year.

QUESTIONS

1.   What factors do you consider, and how would you decide? How great would the costs have to be for covering expert witness fees in IDEA litigation in your state before you would advise the Governor to decline IDEA grants altogether?

2.   If you were uncertain about the statute's meaning, to what would you turn? The text of the statute? The legislative history? Guidance from the U.S. Department of Education? The term's use in other federal statutes? Judicial decisions in the lower federal courts?

d.   A JUDGE INTERPRETING THE STATUTE

You are a busy district court judge on the Southern District of New York, with a docket of over 500 cases filed per year. *See* Comparison of Districts Within the Second Circuit—12-Month Period Ending September 30, 2019, available at https://www.uscourts.gov/sites/default/files/data_tables/fcms_na_distcomparison0930.2019.pdf. You and your three law clerks each work at least 60 hours a week just to maintain your docket load. You are required by law to report the number of outstanding motions yet to be resolved every six months, and every judge in your district receives monthly statistics indicating both the number of outstanding motions and the number of active cases on each judge's docket, so you are especially motivated to keep your numbers down. The cases on your docket require you to resolve complicated merits questions on the papers, conduct trials, sentence federal criminals, and adjudicate discovery disputes between highly contentious corporate commercial litigants. (You also sit by designation on the U.S. Court of Appeals for the Second Circuit several times per year.) Among the cases on your docket are a number of motions to shift attorney's fees to prevailing parties under several dozen federal statutes that awards a reasonable attorney's fee to the prevailing party.

Such fee award petitions are usually presented in the form of a separate motion filed at the end of what is often protracted litigation, just as the case is otherwise ready to be closed and removed from your docket. In your decade on the bench, you have repeatedly encountered statutory provisions that grant you the discretion to "award reasonable attorneys' fees as part of the costs" to the prevailing party, and in nearly every instance in your experience, such an award has *excluded* expert witness fees.

In the instant case, the attorney for the prevailing petitioner contends that the legislative history of *this* statute—the IDEA—suggests that "reasonable attorneys' fees as part of the costs" should include expert witness fees. The district has opposed this position, arguing that the U.S. Supreme Court has on several occasions considered an almost identical phrase in other federal fee-shifting statutes and each time has held that the term of art excludes expert witness fees.

QUESTION

How influential do you find this legislative history? Does it matter to you that several Supreme Court precedents have adopted the contrary interpretation as applied to similar provisions in other federal statutes? Would your views of the statute's meaning be influenced by the knowledge that carefully considering the legislative history will require a special first-impression merits opinion that will take at least a week for you and your law clerk's time to research, write, and edit?

Arlington Central School District
Board of Education v. Murphy

Supreme Court of the United States, 2006.
548 U.S. 291, 126 S.Ct. 2455, 165 L.Ed.2d 526.

■ JUSTICE ALITO delivered the opinion of the Court[, in which CHIEF JUSTICE ROBERTS, JUSTICE SCALIA, JUSTICE KENNEDY, and JUSTICE THOMAS joined].

The Individuals with Disabilities Education Act (IDEA or Act) provides that a court "may award reasonable attorneys' fees as part of the costs" to parents who prevail in an action brought under the Act. 111 Stat. 92, 20 U.S.C. § 1415(i)(3)(B). We granted certiorari to decide whether this fee-shifting provision authorizes prevailing parents to recover fees for services rendered by experts in IDEA actions. We hold that it does not.

I

Respondents Pearl and Theodore Murphy filed an action under the IDEA on behalf of their son, Joseph Murphy, seeking to require petitioner Arlington Central School District Board of Education to pay for their son's private school tuition for specified school years. Respondents prevailed in the District Court, and the Court of Appeals for the Second Circuit affirmed.

As prevailing parents, respondents then sought . . . fees for the services of an educational consultant, Marilyn Arons, who assisted respondents throughout the IDEA proceedings. The District Court . . . held that only the value of Arons' time spent between the hearing request and the ruling in respondents' favor could properly be considered charges incurred in an "action or proceeding brought" under the Act, [citation]. This reduced the maximum recovery to $8,650. The District Court also held that Arons, a nonlawyer, could be compensated only for time spent on expert consulting services, not for time spent on legal representation, but it concluded that all the relevant time could be characterized as falling within the compensable category, and thus allowed compensation for the full $8,650.

The Court of Appeals for the Second Circuit affirmed. [Citation.] Acknowledging that other Circuits had taken the opposite view, the Court of Appeals for the Second Circuit held that "Congress intended to and did authorize the reimbursement of expert fees in IDEA actions." [Citation.] The court began by discussing two decisions of this Court holding that expert fees could not be recovered as taxed costs under particular cost- or fee-shifting provisions. *See Crawford Fitting Co. v. J.T. Gibbons, Inc.*, 482 U.S. 437 (1987) (interpreting Fed. Rule Civ. Proc. 54(d) and 28 U.S.C. § 1920); *West Virginia Univ. Hospitals, Inc. v. Casey*, 499 U.S. 83 (1991) (interpreting 42 U.S.C. § 1988 (1988 ed.)). According to these decisions, the court noted, a cost- or fee-shifting provision will not be read to permit a prevailing party to recover expert fees without

" 'explicit statutory authority' indicating that Congress intended for that sort of fee-shifting." [Citation.]

Ultimately, though, the court was persuaded by a statement in the Conference Committee Report relating to 20 U.S.C. § 1415(i)(3)(B) and by a footnote in *Casey* that made reference to that Report. [Citation.] Based on these authorities, the court concluded that it was required to interpret the IDEA to authorize the award of the costs that prevailing parents incur in hiring experts. . . . We now reverse.

II

Our resolution of the question presented in this case is guided by the fact that Congress enacted the IDEA pursuant to the Spending Clause. [Citation.] Like its statutory predecessor, the IDEA provides federal funds to assist state and local agencies in educating children with disabilities "and conditions such funding upon a State's compliance with extensive goals and procedures." [Citation.]

Congress has broad power to set the terms on which it disburses federal money to the States, [citation], but when Congress attaches conditions to a State's acceptance of federal funds, the conditions must be set out "unambiguously," [citations]. "[L]egislation enacted pursuant to the spending power is much in the nature of a contract," and therefore, to be bound by "federally imposed conditions," recipients of federal funds must accept them "voluntarily and knowingly." [Citation.] States cannot knowingly accept conditions of which they are "unaware" or which they are "unable to ascertain." Thus, in the present case, we must view the IDEA from the perspective of a state official who is engaged in the process of deciding whether the State should accept IDEA funds and the obligations that go with those funds. We must ask whether such a state official would clearly understand that one of the obligations of the Act is the obligation to compensate prevailing parents for expert fees. In other words, we must ask whether the IDEA furnishes clear notice regarding the liability at issue in this case.

III

A

In considering whether the IDEA provides clear notice, we begin with the text. We have "stated time and again that courts must presume that a legislature says in a statute what it means and means in a statute what it says there." [Citation.] When the statutory "language is plain, the sole function of the courts—at least where the disposition required by the text is not absurd—is to enforce it according to its terms."[Citations.]

The governing provision of the IDEA, 20 U.S.C. § 1415(i)(3)(B), provides that "[i]n any action or proceeding brought under this section, the court, in its discretion, may award reasonable attorneys' fees as part of the costs" to the parents of "a child with a disability" who is the "prevailing party." While this provision provides for an award of "reasonable attorneys' fees," this provision does not even hint that acceptance of IDEA funds makes a State responsible for reimbursing prevailing parents for services rendered by experts.

Respondents contend that we should interpret the term "costs" in accordance with its meaning in ordinary usage and that § 1415(i)(3)(B) should therefore be read to "authorize reimbursement of all costs parents incur in IDEA proceedings, including expert costs."

This argument has multiple flaws. For one thing, as the Court of Appeals in this case acknowledged, " 'costs' is a term of art that generally does not include expert fees." [Citation.] The use of this term of art, rather than a term such as "expenses," strongly suggests that § 1415(i)(3)(B) was not meant to be an open-ended provision that makes participating States liable for all expenses incurred by prevailing parents in connection with an IDEA case—for example, travel and lodging expenses or lost wages due to time taken off from work. Moreover, contrary to respondents' suggestion, § 1415(i)(3)(B) does not say that a court may award "costs" to prevailing parents; rather, it says that a court may award reasonable attorney's fees "as part of the costs" to prevailing parents. This language simply adds reasonable attorney's fees incurred by prevailing parents to the list of costs that prevailing parents are otherwise entitled to recover. This list of otherwise recoverable costs is obviously the list set out in 28 U.S.C. § 1920, the general statute governing the taxation of costs in federal court, and the recovery of witness fees under § 1920 is strictly limited by § 1821, which authorizes travel reimbursement and a $40 per diem. Thus, the text of 20 U.S.C. § 1415(i)(3)(B) does not authorize an award of any additional expert fees, and it certainly fails to provide the clear notice that is required under the Spending Clause.

Other provisions of the IDEA point strongly in the same direction. While authorizing the award of reasonable attorney's fees, the Act contains detailed provisions that are designed to ensure that such awards are indeed reasonable. *See* §§ 1415(i)(3)(C)–(G). The absence of any comparable provisions relating to expert fees strongly suggests that recovery of expert fees is not authorized. Moreover, the lack of any reference to expert fees in § 1415(d)(2) gives rise to a similar inference. This provision, which generally requires that parents receive "a full explanation of the procedural safeguards" available under § 1415 and refers expressly to "attorneys' fees," makes no mention of expert fees.

B

Respondents contend that their interpretation of § 1415(i)(3)(B) is supported by a provision of the Handicapped Children's Protection Act of 1986 that required the General Accounting Office (GAO) to collect certain data [citation] (hereinafter GAO study provision), but this provision is of little significance for present purposes. The GAO study provision directed the Comptroller General, acting through the GAO, to compile data on, among other things: "(A) the specific amount of attorneys' fees, costs, and expenses awarded to the prevailing party" in IDEA cases for a particular period of time, and (B) "the number of hours spent by personnel, including attorneys and consultants, involved in the action or proceeding, and expenses incurred by the parents and the State educational agency and local educational agency. [Citation.]

Subparagraph (A) would provide some support for respondents' position if it directed the GAO to compile data on awards to prevailing parties of the expense of hiring consultants, but that is not what subparagraph (A) says. Subparagraph (A) makes no mention of consultants or experts or their fees.[1]

Subparagraph (B) similarly does not help respondents. Subparagraph (B), which directs the GAO to study "the number of hours spent [in IDEA cases] by personnel, including . . . consultants," says nothing about the award of fees to such consultants. Just because Congress directed the GAO to compile statistics on the hours spent by consultants in IDEA cases, it does not follow that Congress meant for States to compensate prevailing parties for the fees billed by these consultants.

Respondents maintain that "Congress' direction to the GAO would be inexplicable if Congress did not anticipate that the expenses for 'consultants' would be recoverable," [citation,] but this is incorrect. There are many reasons why Congress might have wanted the GAO to gather data on expenses that were not to be taxed as costs. Knowing the costs incurred by IDEA litigants might be useful in considering future procedural amendments (which might affect these costs) or a future amendment regarding fee shifting. And, in fact, it is apparent that the GAO study provision covered expenses that could not be taxed as costs. . . .

In sum, the terms of the IDEA overwhelmingly support the conclusion that prevailing parents may not recover the costs of experts or consultants. Certainly the terms of the IDEA fail to provide the clear notice that would be needed to attach such a condition to a State's receipt of IDEA funds.

---

[1] Because subparagraph (A) refers to both "costs" and "expenses" awarded to prevailing parties and because it is generally presumed that statutory language is not superfluous, it could be argued that this provision manifests the expectation that prevailing parties would be awarded certain "expenses" not included in the list of "costs" set out in 28 U.S.C. § 1920 and that expert fees were intended to be among these unenumerated "expenses." This argument fails because, whatever expectation this language might seem to evidence, the fact remains that neither 20 U.S.C. § 1415 nor any other provision of the IDEA authorizes the award of any "expenses" other than "costs." Recognizing this, respondents argue not that they are entitled to recover "expenses" that are not "costs," but that expert fees *are* recoverable "costs." As a result, the reference to awards of both "expenses" and "costs" does not support respondents' position. The reference to "expenses" may relate to IDEA actions brought in state court, § 1415(i)(2)(A), where "expenses" other than "costs" might be receivable. Or the reference may be surplusage. While it is generally presumed that statutes do not contain surplusage, instances of surplusage are not unknown.

IV

Thus far, we have considered only the text of the IDEA, but perhaps the strongest support for our interpretation of the IDEA is supplied by our decisions and reasoning in *Crawford Fitting*, [citation,] and *Casey*, [citation]. In light of those decisions, we do not see how it can be said that the IDEA gives a State unambiguous notice regarding liability for expert fees.

In *Crawford Fitting*, the Court rejected an argument very similar to respondents' argument that the term "costs" in § 1415(i)(3)(B) should be construed as an open-ended reference to prevailing parents' expenses. It was argued in *Crawford Fitting* that Federal Rule of Civil Procedure 54(d), which provides for the award of "costs" to a prevailing party, authorizes the award of costs not listed in 28 U.S.C. § 1821. [Citation.] The Court held, however, that Rule 54(d) does not give a district judge "discretion to tax whatever costs may seem appropriate"; rather, the term "costs" in Rule 54(d) is defined by the list set out in § 1920. [Citation.] Because the recovery of witness fees, *see* § 1920(3), is strictly limited by § 1821, the Court observed, a broader interpretation of Rule 54(d) would mean that the Rule implicitly effected a partial repeal of those provisions. [Citation.] But, the Court warned, "[w]e will not lightly infer that Congress has repealed §§ 1920 and 1821, either through Rule 54(d) or any other provision not referring explicitly to witness fees." [Citation.]

The reasoning of *Crawford Fitting* strongly supports the conclusion that the term "costs" in 20 U.S.C. § 1415(i)(3)(B), like the same term in Rule 54(d), is defined by the categories of expenses enumerated in 28 U.S.C. § 1920. This conclusion is buttressed by the principle, recognized in *Crawford Fitting*, that no statute will be construed as authorizing the taxation of witness fees as costs unless the statute "refer[s] explicitly to witness fees." [Citation.] ("[A]bsent explicit statutory or contractual authorization for the taxation of the expenses of a litigant's witness as costs, federal courts are bound by the limitations set out in 28 U.S.C. § 1821 and § 1920").

Our decision in *Casey* confirms even more dramatically that the IDEA does not authorize an award of expert fees. In *Casey*, as noted above, we interpreted a fee-shifting provision, 42 U.S.C. § 1988, the relevant wording of which was virtually identical to the wording of 20 U.S.C. § 1415(i)(3)(B). Compare *ibid.* (authorizing the award of "reasonable attorneys' fees as part of the costs" to prevailing parents) with 42 U.S.C. § 1988 (1988 ed.) (permitting prevailing parties in certain civil rights actions to be awarded "a reasonable attorney's fee as part of the costs"). We held that § 1988 did not empower a district court to award expert fees to a prevailing party. [Citation.] To decide in favor of respondents here, we would have to interpret the virtually identical language in 20 U.S.C. § 1415 as having exactly the opposite meaning. Indeed, we would have to go further and hold that the relevant language in the IDEA *unambiguously means* exactly the opposite of what the nearly identical language in 42 U.S.C. § 1988 was held to mean in *Casey*.

The Court of Appeals, as noted above, was heavily influenced by a *Casey* footnote, [citation,] but the court misunderstood the footnote's meaning. The text accompanying the footnote argued, based on an analysis of several fee-shifting statutes, that the term "attorney's fees" does not include expert fees. [Citation.] In the footnote, we commented on petitioners' invocation of the Conference Committee Report relating to 20 U.S.C. § 1415(i)(3)(B), which stated: " 'The conferees intend[ed] that the term "attorneys' fees as part of the costs" include reasonable expenses and fees of expert witnesses and the reasonable costs of any test or evaluation which is found to be necessary for the preparation of the . . . case.' " [Citation.] This statement, the footnote commented, was "an apparent effort to *depart* from ordinary meaning and to define a term of art." [Citation.] The footnote did not state that the Conference Committee Report set out the correct interpretation of § 1415(i)(3)(B), much less that the Report was sufficient, despite the language of the statute, to provide the clear notice required under the Spending Clause. The thrust of the footnote was simply that the term "attorneys' fees," standing alone, is generally not understood as encompassing expert fees. Thus, *Crawford Fitting* and *Casey* strongly reinforce the conclusion that the IDEA does not unambiguously authorize prevailing parents to recover expert fees.

V

Respondents make several arguments that are not based on the text of the IDEA, but these arguments do not show that the IDEA provides clear notice regarding the award of expert fees.

Respondents argue that their interpretation of the IDEA furthers the Act's overarching goal of "ensur[ing] that all children with disabilities have available to them a free appropriate public education," 20 U.S.C. § 1400(d)(1)(A), as well as the goal of "safeguard[ing] the rights of parents to challenge school decisions that adversely affect their child." These goals, however, are too general to provide much support for respondents' reading of the terms of the IDEA. The IDEA obviously does not seek to promote these goals at the expense of all other considerations, including fiscal considerations. Because the IDEA is not intended in all instances to further the broad goals identified by respondents at the expense of fiscal considerations, the goals cited by respondents do little to bolster their argument on the narrow question presented here.[3]

Finally, respondents vigorously argue that Congress clearly intended for prevailing parents to be compensated for expert fees. They rely on the legislative history of § 1415 and in particular on the following statement in the Conference Committee Report, discussed above: "The

---

[3] Respondents note that a GAO report stated that expert witness fees are reimbursable expenses. But this passing reference in a report issued by an agency not responsible for implementing the IDEA is plainly insufficient to provide clear notice regarding the scope of the conditions attached to the receipt of IDEA funds.

conferees intend that the term 'attorneys' fees as part of the costs' include reasonable expenses and fees of expert witnesses and the reasonable costs of any test or evaluation which is found to be necessary for the preparation of the . . . case." [Citation.]

Whatever weight this legislative history would merit in another context, it is not sufficient here. Putting the legislative history aside, we see virtually no support for respondents' position. Under these circumstances, where everything other than the legislative history overwhelmingly suggests that expert fees may not be recovered, the legislative history is simply not enough. In a Spending Clause case, the key is not what a majority of the Members of both Houses intend but what the States are clearly told regarding the conditions that go along with the acceptance of those funds. Here, in the face of the unambiguous text of the IDEA and the reasoning in *Crawford Fitting* and *Casey,* we cannot say that the legislative history on which respondents rely is sufficient to provide the requisite fair notice. . . .

We reverse the judgment of the Court of Appeals for the Second Circuit and remand the case for further proceedings consistent with this opinion.

It is so ordered.

■ JUSTICE GINSBURG, concurring in part and concurring in the judgment.

I agree, in the main, with the Court's resolution of this case, but part ways with the Court's opinion in one respect. The Court extracts from *Pennhurst State School and Hospital v. Halderman,* 451 U.S. 1, 17 (1981), a "clear notice" requirement, and deems it applicable in this case because Congress enacted the Individuals with Disabilities Education Act (IDEA), as it did the legislation at issue in *Pennhurst,* pursuant to the Spending Clause. That extraction, in my judgment, is unwarranted. *Pennhurst's* "clear notice" requirement should not be unmoored from its context. The Court there confronted a plea to impose "an unexpected condition for compliance—a new [programmatic] obligation for participating States." [Citation.] The controversy here is lower key: It concerns not the educational programs IDEA directs school districts to provide, but "the remedies available against a noncomplying [district]."

The Court's repeated references to a Spending Clause derived "clear notice" requirement are questionable on other grounds as well. For one thing, IDEA was enacted not only pursuant to Congress' Spending Clause authority, but also pursuant to § 5 of the Fourteenth Amendment. [Citation.] Furthermore, no "clear notice" prop is needed in this case given the twin pillars on which the Court's judgment securely rests. First, as the Court explains, the specific, attorneys'-fees-oriented, provisions of IDEA, [citation,] overwhelmingly support the conclusion that prevailing parents may not recover the costs of experts or consultants." Those provisions place controls on fees recoverable for attorneys' services, without mentioning costs parents might incur for other professional services and controls geared to those costs. Second, as the Court develops, prior decisions closely in point "strongly suppor[t]," even "confir[m] . . . dramatically," today's holding that IDEA trains on attorneys' fees and does not authorize an award covering amounts paid or payable for the services of an educational consultant. [Citations.]

For the contrary conclusion, JUSTICE BREYER's dissent relies dominantly on a Conference Report stating the conferees' view that the term "attorneys' fees as part of the costs" includes "expenses and fees of expert witnesses" and payments for tests necessary for the preparation of a case. [Citation.] Including costs of consultants and tests in § 1415(i)(3)(B) would make good sense in light of IDEA's overarching goal, *i.e.,* to provide a "free appropriate public education" to children with disabilities, § 1400(d)(1)(A). But Congress did not compose § 1415(i)(3)(B)'s text,[2] as it did the texts of other statutes too numerous and varied to ignore, to alter the common import of the terms "attorneys' fees" and "costs" in the context of expense-allocation legislation. [Citations.] Given the constant meaning of the formulation "attorneys' fees as part of the costs" in federal legislation, we are not at liberty to rewrite "the statutory text adopted by both Houses of Congress and submitted to the President," [citation,] to add several words Congress wisely might have included. The ball, I conclude, is properly left in Congress' court to provide, if it so elects, for consultant fees and testing expenses beyond those IDEA and its implementing regulations already authorize,[3] along with any specifications, conditions, or limitations geared to those fees and expenses Congress may deem appropriate. Cf. § 1415(i)(3)(B)–(G); § 1415(d)(2)(L) (listing only attorneys' fees, not expert or consulting fees, among the procedural safeguards about which school districts must inform parents).

In sum, although I disagree with the Court's rationale to the extent that it invokes a "clear notice" requirement tied to the Spending Clause, I agree with the Court's discussion of IDEA's terms, and of our decisions

---

[2]   At the time the Conference Report was submitted to the Senate and House, sponsors of the legislation did not mention anything on the floor about expert or consultant fees. They were altogether clear, however, that the purpose of the legislation was to "reverse" this Court's decision in Smith v. Robinson, 468 U.S. 992, 104 S.Ct. 3457, 82 L.Ed.2d 746 (1984). In Smith, the Court held that, under the statute as then designed, prevailing parents were not entitled to attorneys' fees. See 132 Cong. Rec. 16823 (1986) (remarks of Sen. Weicker) ("In adopting this legislation, we are rejecting the reasoning of the Supreme Court in Smith versus Robinson."); *id.,* at 16824 (remarks of Sen. Kerry) ("This vital legislation reverses a U.S. Supreme Court decision Smith versus Robinson [.]"); *id.,* at 17608–17609 (remarks of Rep. Bartlett) ("I support those provisions in the conference agreement that, in response to the Supreme Court decision in . . . Smith versus Robinson, authoriz[e] the awarding of reasonable attorneys' fees to parents who prevail in special education court cases."); *id.,* at 17609 (remarks of Rep. Biaggi) ("This legislation clearly supports the intent of Congress back in 1975 and corrects what I believe was a gross misinterpretation of the law. Attorneys' fees should be provided to those individuals who are being denied access to the educational system.").

[3]   Under 34 CFR § 300.502(b)(1) (2005), a "parent has the right to an independent educational evaluation at public expense if the parent disagrees with an evaluation obtained by the public agency."

in *Crawford* and *Casey*. Accordingly, I concur in part in the Court's opinion, and join the Court's judgment.

[The dissenting opinion of JUSTICE SOUTER has been omitted.]

■ JUSTICE BREYER, with whom JUSTICE STEVENS and JUSTICE SOUTER join, dissenting.

. . . Unlike the Court, I believe that the word "costs" includes, and authorizes payment of, the costs of experts. The word "costs" does not define its own scope. Neither does the phrase "attorneys' fees as part of costs." But Members of Congress did make clear their intent by, among other things, approving a Conference Report that specified that "the term 'attorneys' fees as part of the costs' include[s] reasonable expenses and fees of expert witnesses and the reasonable costs of any test or evaluation which is found to be necessary for the preparation of the parent or guardian's case in the action or proceeding." [Citation.] No Senator or Representative voiced *any* opposition to this statement in the discussion preceding the vote on the Conference Report—the last vote on the bill before it was sent to the President. I can find no good reason for this Court to interpret the language of this statute as meaning the precise opposite of what Congress told us it intended.

I

There are two strong reasons for interpreting the statutory phrase to include the award of expert fees. First, that is what Congress said it intended by the phrase. Second, that interpretation furthers the IDEA's statutorily defined purposes.

A

Congress added the IDEA's cost-shifting provision when it enacted the Handicapped Children's Protection Act of 1986 (HCPA), 100 Stat. 796. Senator Lowell Weicker introduced the relevant bill in 1985. [Citation.] As introduced, it sought to overturn this Court's determination that the then-current version of the IDEA (and other civil rights statutes) did not authorize courts to award attorney's fees to prevailing parents in IDEA cases. [Citation.] The bill provided that " '[i]n any action or proceeding brought under this subsection, the court, in its discretion, may award a reasonable attorney's fee as part of the costs to a parent or legal representative of a handicapped child or youth who is the prevailing party.' " [Citation.]

After hearings and debate, several Senators introduced a new bill in the Senate that would have put a cap on attorney's fees for legal services lawyers, but at the same time would have explicitly authorized the award of "a reasonable attorney's fee, reasonable witness fees, and *other reasonable expenses of the civil action,* in addition to the costs to a parent . . . who is the prevailing party." [Citation.] While no Senator objected to the latter provision, some objected to the cap. [Citation.] A bipartisan group of Senators, led by Senators Hatch and Weicker, proposed an alternative bill that authorized courts to award " 'a reasonable attorney's fee in addition to the costs to a parent' " who prevailed. [Citations.]

Senator Weicker explained that the bill

"will enable courts to compensate parents for *whatever reasonable costs they had to incur to fully secure what was guaranteed to them by the [Education of the Handicapped Act].* As in other fee shifting statutes, it is our intent that such awards will include, at the discretion of the court, reasonable attorney's fees, *necessary expert witness fees, and other reasonable expenses which were necessary for parents to vindicate their claim to a free appropriate public education for their handicapped child.*" [Citation] (emphasis added).

Not a word of opposition to this statement (or the provision) was voiced on the Senate floor, and S. 415 passed without a recorded vote. [Citation.]

The House version of the bill also reflected an intention to authorize recovery of expert costs. Following the House hearings, the Committee on Education and Labor produced a substitute bill that authorized courts to " 'award reasonable attorneys' fees, *expenses, and costs*' " to prevailing parents. [Citation.] The House Report stated:

"The phrase 'expenses and costs' includes *expenses of expert witnesses; the reasonable costs of any study, report, test, or project which is found to be necessary for the preparation of the parents' or guardian's due process hearing, state administrative review or civil action;* as well as traditional costs and expenses incurred in the course of litigating a case (*e.g.*, depositions and interrogatories)." [Citation (emphasis added).]

No one objected to this statement. By the time H.R. 1523 reached the floor, another substitute bill was introduced. [Citation.] This new bill did not change in any respect the text of the authorization of expenses and costs. It did add a provision, however, that directed the General Accounting Office (GAO)—now known as the Government Accountability Office, *see* note following 31 U.S.C. § 731 (2000 ed., Supp.IV)—to study and report to Congress on the fiscal impact of the cost-shifting provision. [Citation.] The newly substituted bill passed the House without a recorded vote. [Citation.]

Members of the House and Senate (including all of the primary sponsors of the HCPA) then met in conference to work out certain differences. At the conclusion of those negotiations, they produced a Conference Report, which contained the text of the agreed-upon bill and a "Joint Explanatory Statement of the Committee of Conference." [Editors' Note: a portion of this statement has been excerpted, *supra*.] The Conference accepted the House bill's GAO provision with "an amendment expanding the data collection requirements of the GAO study to include information regarding the amount of funds expended by local educational agencies and state educational agencies on civil actions and administrative proceedings." [Citation.] And it accepted (with minor changes) the cost-shifting provisions provided in both the Senate and House versions. The conferees explained:

> ... "*The conferees intend that the term 'attorneys' fees as part of the costs' include reasonable expenses and fees of expert witnesses and the reasonable costs of any test or evaluation which is found to be necessary for the preparation of the parent or guardian's case in the action or proceeding, as well as traditional costs incurred in the course of litigating a case.*" [Citation.]

The Conference Report was returned to the Senate and the House. A motion was put to each to adopt the Conference Report, and both the Senate and the House agreed to the Conference Report by voice votes. [Citation.] No objection was raised to the Conference Report's statement that the cost-shifting provision was intended to authorize expert costs. I concede that "sponsors of the legislation did not mention anything on the floor about expert or consultant fees" at the time the Conference Report was submitted. But I do not believe that silence is significant in light of the fact that *every* Senator and *three of the five* Representatives who spoke on the floor had previously *signed his name* to the Conference Report—a Report that made Congress' intent clear on the first page of its explanation. [Citation.] And every Senator and Representative who took the floor preceding the votes voiced his strong support for the Conference Report. [Citation.] The upshot is that Members of both Houses of Congress voted to adopt both the statutory text before us and the Conference Report that made clear that the statute's words include the expert costs here in question.

B

The Act's basic purpose further supports interpreting the provision's language to include expert costs. The IDEA guarantees a "free" and "appropriate" public education for "all" children with disabilities. 20 U.S.C. § 1400(d)(1)(A) (2000 ed., Supp.V); *see also* § 1401(9)(A) (defining "free appropriate public education" as one "provided at public expense," "without charge"); § 1401(29) (defining "special education" as "specially designed instruction, at *no cost* to parents, to meet the unique needs of a child with a disability" (emphasis added)).

Parents have every right to become involved in the Act's efforts to provide that education; indeed, the Act encourages their participation. § 1400(c)(5)(B) (IDEA "ensur[es] that families of [disabled] children have meaningful opportunities to participate in the education of their children at school"). It assures parents that they may question a school district's decisions about what is "appropriate" for their child. And in doing so, they may secure the help of experts. § 1415(h)(1) (parents have "the right to be accompanied and advised by counsel and by individuals with special knowledge or training with respect to the problems of children with disabilities"); [citations.]

The practical significance of the Act's participatory rights and procedural protections may be seriously diminished if parents are unable to obtain reimbursement for the costs of their experts. In IDEA cases, experts are necessary. [Citation] (detailing findings of study showing high correlation between use of experts and success of parents in challenging school district's plan); [citations].

Experts are also expensive. [Citation] (collecting District Court decisions awarding expert costs ranging from $200 to $7,600, and noting three reported cases in which expert awards exceeded $10,000). The costs of experts may not make much of a dent in a school district's budget, as many of the experts they use in IDEA proceedings are already on the staff. [Citation.] But to parents, the award of costs may matter enormously. Without potential reimbursement, parents may well lack the services of experts entirely. [Citations.]

In a word, the Act's statutory right to a "free" and "appropriate" education may mean little to those who must pay hundreds of dollars to obtain it. That is why this Court has previously avoided interpretations that would bring about this kind of result. . . . [W]e [have] explained: "IDEA was intended to ensure that children with disabilities receive an education that is both appropriate and free. To read the provisions of § 1401(a)(18) to bar reimbursement in [such] circumstances . . . would defeat this statutory purpose." [Citation.]

To read the word "costs" as requiring successful parents to bear their own expenses for experts suffers from the same problem. Today's result will leave many parents and guardians "without an expert with the firepower to match the opposition," [citation], a far cry from the level playing field that Congress envisioned.

II

The majority makes essentially three arguments against this interpretation. It says that the statute's purpose and "legislative history is simply not enough" to overcome: (1) the fact that this is a Spending Clause case; (2) the text of the statute; and (3) our prior cases which hold that the term "costs" does not include expert costs. I do not find these arguments convincing.

A

At the outset the majority says that it "is guided by the fact that Congress enacted the IDEA pursuant to the Spending Clause." "In a Spending Clause case," the majority adds, "the key is not what a majority of the Members of both Houses intend but what the States are clearly told regarding the conditions that go along with the acceptance of those funds." . . .

I agree that the statute on its face does not *clearly* tell the States that they must pay expert fees to prevailing parents. But I do not agree that the majority has posed the right question. For one thing, we have repeatedly examined the nature and extent of the financial burdens that the IDEA imposes without reference to the Spending Clause or any "clear-statement rule." [Citations.] Those cases did not ask whether the statute "furnishes clear notice" to the affirmative obligation or liability at issue.

For another thing, neither *Pennhurst* nor any other case suggests that *every spending detail* of a Spending Clause statute must be spelled out with unusual clarity. To the contrary, we have held that *Pennhurst's* requirement that Congress "unambiguously" set out "a condition on the grant of federal money" does *not* necessarily apply to legislation setting forth "*the remedies available against a noncomplying State.*" [Citation.] We have added that *Pennhurst* does not require Congress "specifically" to "identify" and "proscribe *each* condition in [Spending Clause] legislation." [Citations.] And we have denied any implication that "suits under Spending Clause legislation are suits in contract, or that contract-law principles apply to *all* issues that they raise." [Citation.]

. . . [T]he basic objective of *Pennhurst's* clear-statement requirement does not demand textual clarity in respect to every detail. That is because ambiguity about the precise nature of a statutory program's details—particularly where they are of a kind that States might have anticipated—is rarely relevant to the basic question: Would the States have accepted the Federal Government's funds *had they only known* the nature of the accompanying conditions? Often, the later filling-in of details through judicial interpretation will not lead one to wonder whether funding recipients would have agreed to enter the basic program at all. Given the nature of such details, it is clear that the States would have entered the program regardless. At the same time, to view each statutory detail of a highly complex federal/state program (involving, say, transportation, schools, the environment) simply through the lens of linguistic clarity, rather than to assess its meanings in terms of basic legislative purpose, is to risk a set of judicial interpretations that can prevent the program, overall, from achieving its basic objectives or that might well reduce a program in its details to incoherence.

This case is about just such a detail. . . .

B

If the Court believes that the statute's language is unambiguous, I must disagree. The provision at issue says that a court "may award reasonable attorneys' fees as part of the costs" to parents who prevail in an action brought under the Act. 20 U.S.C. § 1415(i)(3)(B). The statute neither defines the word "costs" nor points to any other source of law for a definition. And the word "costs," alone, says nothing at all about which costs fall within its scope.

Neither does the statutory phrase—"as part of the costs to the parents of a child with a disability who is the prevailing party"—taken in its entirety unambiguously foreclose an award of expert fees. I agree that, read literally, that provision does not clearly grant authority to award any costs at all. And one might read it, as the Court does, as referencing another federal statute, 28 U.S.C. § 1920, which provides that authority. [Citations.] But such a reading is not inevitable. The provision (indeed, the entire Act) says nothing about that other statute. And one can, consistent with the language, read the provision as both embodying a general authority to award costs while also specifying the inclusion of "reasonable attorneys' fees" as part of those costs (as saying, for example, that a court "may award reasonable attorneys' fees as part of [a] costs [award]").

This latter reading, while linguistically the less natural, is legislatively the more likely. The majority's alternative reading, by cross-referencing only the federal general cost-awarding statute (which applies solely *in federal courts*), would produce a jumble of different cost definitions applicable to similar IDEA administrative and state-court proceedings in different States. [Citation.] This result is particularly odd, as all IDEA actions must begin in state due process hearings, where the federal cost statute clearly does not apply, and the overwhelming majority of these actions are never appealed to *any* court. . . . [Citation.] And when parents do appeal, they can file their actions in either state or federal courts. [Citation.]

Would Congress "obviously" have wanted the content of the word "costs" to vary from State to State, proceeding to proceeding? Why? At most, the majority's reading of the text is plausible; it is not the only possible reading.

C

The majority's most persuasive argument does not focus on either the Spending Clause or lack of statutory ambiguity. Rather, the majority says that "costs" is a term of art. In light of the law's long practice of excluding expert fees from the scope of the word "costs," along with this Court's cases interpreting the word similarly in other statutes, the "legislative history is simply not enough."

I am perfectly willing to assume that the majority is correct about the traditional scope of the word "costs." . . . Regardless, here the statute itself indicates that Congress did not intend to use the word "costs" as a term of art. . . . If Congress intended the word "costs" in § 2 to authorize an award of only those costs listed in the federal cost statute, why did it use the word "expenses" in § 4(b)(3)(A) as part of the "amount . . . awarded to the prevailing party"? When used as a term of art, after all, "costs" does not cover expenses. Nor does the federal costs statute cover any expenses, at least not any that Congress could have wanted the GAO to study. [Citation.]

Further, why did Congress, when asking the GAO (in the statute itself) to study the "number of hours spent by personnel," include among those personnel both attorneys *"and consultants"*? Who but experts could those consultants be? Why would Congress want the GAO to study the hours that those experts "spent," unless it thought that it would help keep track of the "costs" that the statute imposed?

. . . We *know* what Congress intended the GAO study to cover. It *told* the GAO in its Conference Report that the word "costs" included the costs of experts. And, not surprisingly, the GAO made clear that it understood precisely what Congress asked it to do. In its final report, the GAO wrote: "Parents can receive reimbursement from state or local education agencies for some or all of their attorney fees *and related expenses* if they are the prevailing party in part or all of administrative hearings or court proceedings. *Expert witness fees, cost of tests or evaluations found to be necessary during the case, and court costs for services rendered during administrative and court proceedings are examples of reimbursable expenses.*" GAO, Briefing Report to Congressional Requesters, Special Education: The Attorney Fees Provision of Public Law 99–372 (GAO/HRD–90–22BR), p. 13 (Nov.1989) (emphasis added), online at http://archive.gao.gov/d26t7/140084.pdf. At the very least, this amounts to *some* indication that Congress intended the word "costs," not as a term of art, not as it was used in the statutes at issue in *Casey* and *Crawford Fitting,* but rather as including certain additional "expenses." If that is so, the claims of tradition, of the interpretation this Court has given other statutes, cannot be so strong as to prevent us from examining the legislative history. And that history could not be more clear about the matter: Congress intended the statutory phrase "attorneys' fees as part of the costs" to include the costs of experts.

III

For the reasons I have set forth, I cannot agree with the majority's conclusion. Even less can I agree with its failure to consider fully the statute's legislative history. That history makes Congress' purpose clear. And our ultimate judicial goal is to interpret language in light of the statute's purpose. Only by seeking that purpose can we avoid the substitution of judicial for legislative will. Only by reading language in its light can we maintain the democratic link between voters, legislators, statutes, and ultimate implementation, upon which the legitimacy of our constitutional system rests. . . .

For these reasons, I respectfully dissent.

NOTES AND QUESTIONS

1. The majority invoked the "clear notice rule" because Congress enacted the IDEA under its Spending Clause authority. On this basis, the majority concluded that the statute must be viewed "from the perspective of a state official who is engaged in the process of deciding whether the State should accept IDEA funds and the obligations that go with those funds. We must ask whether such a state official would clearly understand that one of the obligations of the Act is the obligation to compensate prevailing parents for expert fees." Is there reason to think that such officials may (or may be allowed to) interpret the statutory provision differently than, say, members

of Congress, parents of disabled children, the federal Department of Education, and/or federal judges? From which perspective does the dissent seem inclined to view the statutory phrase in question? What about the concurrence?

2.   If the majority is right to interpret the statutory text differently in light of a prioritized audience, what obligation, if any, do judges have to appreciate how that audience is likely to understand a statute's meaning? In the case of the IDEA provision in question, the majority likely underestimated the knowledge and sophistication of the most plausible audience, which is state-level education officials who engage directly with the Department of Education in understanding the IDEA's requirements and deciding whether to accept conditioned federal funds. Local educators are not the state officials directly involved in the states' decision to consent to IDEA requirements; rather, since at least 1970, the IDEA has mandated that states establish advisory councils that advise both local officials and state education agencies as to requirements under the IDEA. What kind of empirical examination, if any, should judges engage in to decide how a statute gives notice to that audience? Does it matter if their empirical claim about the audience's likely understanding may be unsupported by evidence? Should it matter if notice is provided by extratextual means that these officials are likely to reference anyway, such as legislative history or agency guidance?

3.   Expecting or requiring that a term or phrase have a consistent meaning across all federal statutes seems implausible as a descriptive account of how Congress drafts statutes. Indeed, as Professors Abbe Gluck and Lisa Bressman have found in surveying legislative drafters, congressional staffers generally have no such expectations:

> . . . Although more than 93% of our respondents affirmed that the "goal" is for statutory terms to have consistent meanings throughout, our respondents emphasized time and again the significant organizational barriers that the committee system, bundled legislative deals, and lengthy, multidrafter statutes pose to the realistic operation of those rules.

> Our respondents told us that congressional committees are "islands" that limit communication between committees drafting different parts of the same statutes and that, because of the increasing tendency to legislate through omnibus or otherwise "unorthodox" legislative vehicles, most major statutes are now conglomerations of multiple committees' separate work. . . .

> For the same reasons, our respondents also vigorously disputed that the first cousin of the whole act rule—the "whole code rule," under which courts construe terms across different statutes consistently—reflects how Congress drafts or even how it tries to draft. Specifically, only 9% of respondents told us that drafters often or always intend for terms to apply consistently across statutes that are unrelated by subject matter.

> This presumption of consistent usage, we would note, is widely accepted in the federal courts. Indeed, leading commentators have

called it one of the most important and consistently applied textual default rules, and it has been employed by textualists and purposivists alike. In the October 2011 Term of the Supreme Court alone, the whole act rule was used in at least three cases, and the leading case for the principle has been cited in at least 118 federal cases since 1995. To our knowledge, however, courts have never considered the role that committee jurisdiction plays when applying the rule, and courts have rarely focused on the type of statutory vehicle.

We also note that, given the institutional factors that our respondents identified, application of the consistent-usage presumption is unlikely to exert any positive influence on the drafting process. This suggestion runs contrary to popular arguments that a strict textual approach may incentivize Congress to draft more carefully. Justice Scalia's new book offers a typical example of such an argument in support of the consistent-usage rule:

> The canons . . . promote better drafting. When it is widely understood in the legal community that, for example, a word used repeatedly in a document will be taken to have the same meaning throughout . . . you can expect those who prepare legal documents competently to draft accordingly.

Such arguments, however, depend on the absence of other barriers to such "better" drafting. Almost all of our respondents told us that consistent term usage was the "goal" or what "should be," but they still told us that the rule was unlikely to hold because of the way that Congress is organized.

Abbe R. Gluck & Lisa Schultz Bressman, *Statutory Interpretation from the Inside: An Empirical Study of Congressional Drafting, Delegation, and the Canons: Part I*, 65 Stan. L. Rev. 901 (2013).

4. If consistent usage presumptions are difficult to justify in terms of the drafters' *intended* meaning, can they be justified on other grounds? For example, should law-literate reasonable readers like judges and lawyers be able to *expect* that a legal term of art means the same thing throughout the federal code? (Maybe not: see *Yates v. United States, supra* Section III.A.1: "In law as in life, . . . the same words, placed in different contexts, sometimes mean different things.") Should it matter whether other non-legal audiences might also be expected to engage with federal statutes from time to time? Or is it sufficient to answer that a client's legal counsel should be expected to do the interpreting? If so, does such an answer assume the widespread availability of affordable legal services?

D. INTERPRETING A STATUTE IN LIGHT OF RELATED STATUTES OR PROVISIONS

Peacock v. Lubbock Compress Company

United States Court of Appeals for the Fifth Circuit, 1958.
252 F.2d 892.

■ JOHN R. BROWN, CIRCUIT JUDGE[, joined by HUTCHESON, CHIEF JUDGE, and JONES, CIRCUIT JUDGE].

This whole case turns on one word. Does the word "and" mean *and*? Does it mean *or*? May it have been primarily used as a comma?

The question arises in connection with an FLSA [Fair Labor Standards Act] suit for overtime wages brought by three night watchmen against the Compress Company who, admittedly, was subject to the Act, and had employed them for eighty-four hours each week at a wage in excess of the minimum hourly rate (75 cents) but without payment of overtime. The dispute narrows down to Section 207(c) with emphasis on the few words italicized:

"In the case of an employer engaged in the first processing of milk, buttermilk, whey, skimmed milk, or cream into dairy products, *or in the ginning and compressing of cotton*, or in the processing of cottonseed, or in the processing of sugar beets, sugar-beet molasses, sugarcane, or maple sap, into sugar * * * the provisions of subsection (a) * * * (29 U.S.C.A. § 207(a) requiring overtime) shall not apply to his employees in any place of employment where he is so engaged * * *." 29 U.S.C.A. § 207(c), Section 7 of the Act.

The statute, of course, says "ginning *and* compressing of cotton." If it is conjunctive, the watchmen are right, the Compress is wrong, and the cause must be reversed. This is so because it is admitted that the Compress Company is engaged exclusively in compressing cotton and never has engaged in the activity of ginning cotton or a combination of ginning and compressing. Actually, it cuts much deeper since it is an acknowledged undisputed fact of the cotton industry that compressing is an operation entirely removed from ginning and that the two are never carried on together. To read it literally here is to read it out of the statute.

But the word "and" is not a word with a single meaning, for chameleonlike, it takes its color from its surroundings. Nor has the law looked upon it as such. It is ancient learning, recorded authoritatively for us nearly one hundred years ago, echoing that which had accumulated in the previous years and forecasting that which was to come,[1] that, "In the

---

[1] Hundreds of cases are conveniently collected in Vol. 3, Words and Phrases, under the title word "And," at page 569, and see especially pages 583–593 under the heading of "Civil Statutes." Whatever the particular meaning attributed to the word or words may be in each of these collected cases, the universal test may be summarized. The words "and" and "or" when used in a statute are convertible, as the sense may require. A substitution of one for the other

construction of statutes, it is the duty of the Court to ascertain the clear intention of the legislature. In order to do this, Courts are often compelled to construe 'or' as meaning 'and,' and again 'and' as meaning 'or.' " United States v. Fisk, 70 U.S. 445, 448 (1866), and *see* Heydon's Case, 3 Co. 7a (1584).

In searching then for the Congressional purpose, there appears to be no basis for concluding that the exemption was to be confined to those engaging in *both* ginning and compressing. Indeed, the contrary appears. The great concern of Congress was to exempt agriculture as such from the Act. Maneja v. Waialua Agricultural Co., 349 U.S. 254. Once it set out to shore up that basic exclusion, certain operation such as those defined in Section 207(c) were specifically removed so far as *hours* were concerned, and other operations of the kind described in 213(a)(10) within the area of production to be defined administratively were taken[2] out from the Act as to both *hours* and *wages*. The latter, Section 213(a)(10), note 2, *supra*, was to make certain that for services described in it, the small farms forced to use nearby independent contractors, or the like, would not be worse off than larger integrated farms equipped with their own facilities.[3] In that Section, Congress did not even find it necessary to use the descriptive term "cotton." So long as the operation is within the area of production as promulgated, the 213(a)(10) exemption applies to ginning of cotton, the compressing of cotton, or either one or both of them.

Of course the two sections, 207(c) and 213(a)(10) are not complementary and are intended to, and do, accomplish different objectives. Maneja v. Waialua Agricultural Co., *supra*. But if either of the two activities, ginning *or* compressing, was such as to warrant exemption within the geographical-population limits of the area of production, [citation,] from the whole Act, it seems highly improbable[4] that Congress

---

is frequently resorted to in the interpretation of statutes, when the evident intention of the lawmaker requires it.

   [2] 29 U.S.C.A. § 213(a)(10): "The provisions of sections 206 and 207 * * * (29 U.S.C.A. §§ 206, 207) shall not apply with respect to * * * (10) any individual employed within the area of production (as defined by the Administrator), engaged in handling, packing, storing, *ginning*, *compressing*, pasteurizing, drying, preparing in their raw or natural state, or canning of agricultural or horticultural commodities for market, or in making cheese or butter or other dairy products." (Emphasis supplied.)

   [3] Maneja v. Waialua Agricultural Co., 349 U.S. 254, 268,: "Thus, for example, the cotton farmer without a gin was placed on an equal footing with farms who ginning their own cotton, since each could have their cotton ginned by employees who were covered by neither the wage nor the hour provisions of the Act."

   [4] Maneja v. Waialua Agricultural Co., 349 U.S. 254, 267: That case involved the processing of sugar cane into sugar. The Court's reference to "cotton ginning" alone and not in conjunction with compressing indicates, however, that it saw no decisive significance in the coupling word "and". To the suggested argument that the express exemption in § 207(c) from overtime liabilities was a deliberate choice by Congress to limit relief to overtime, the Court said: "But we cannot be sure of this, because § 7(c) (207(c)) includes similar exemptions for operations like cotton ginning, which also come within the agricultural exemption if performed by the farmer on his own crops. More significant is the omission of sugar milling from the exemption provided by § 13(a)(10), § 213(a)(10), from various processing operations performed within the area of production."

in mentioning the two again deliberately set out to prescribe a standard impossible to meet as to the hours-overtime exemption of 207(c).

If Congress did not intend the Section 207(c) exemption to apply to those same operations described in 213(a)(10) "ginning, compressing," all it had to do was to omit altogether any reference to this activity in 207(c). To accomplish any such assumed objective, it was not necessary for Congress to go at it by the roundabout method of appearing to grant it only to take it away by the prerequisite of a dual combination of "ginning and compressing" of cotton.[5]

For us to conclude that Congress meant "and" in a literal conjunctive sense is to determine that Congress meant in fact to grant no relief. To do this is to ignore realities, for Congress has long been acutely aware of the manifold problems of the production, marketing and distribution of cotton. The commodity is one of the most important in the complex pattern of farm parity and production control legislation. It is inconceivable that Congress legislated in ignorance of the distinctive nature of the physical operations of ginning of cotton as compared to the compressing of cotton, or that, with full consciousness of these practicable considerations, it meant to lay down a standard which could not be met in fact.

Literalism gives way in the face of such considerations. [Citations omitted]. Under Section 207(c), the ginning of cotton, the compressing of cotton, the performance of either or both is exempt from the overtime provisions of the Act.

Affirmed.

QUESTIONS

1. How does section 213(a)(10) of the Fair Labor Standards Act help illuminate the meaning of section 207(c) of the same statute? Section 207(c) concerns restrictions on hours worked, while section 213(a)(10) exempts certain agriculture-related businesses from both minimum wages and hours limitations. Is it reasonable to expect that legislative drafters, when drafting a given statutory provision, attend to how similar language appears elsewhere in the statute?

2. A literal reading of the relevant provision of the Fair Labor Standards Act would have exempted from an obligation to pay overtime only employers of workers engaged in the combined activity of both ginning and compressing cotton; it would have required payment of overtime of workers engaged separately in either of those activities. The employer's preferred construction of the statute, reading "and" as "or," thus substantially broadened the scope of the employers' exemption. Given the significantly different meanings and effects of "and" and "or," as well as the overall purpose of the FLSA to

---

[5] The sparse legislative history on the point as set forth in the briefs is unilluminating. Apparently in its original form, Senate Bill 2475, 75th Congress, granted the overtime exemption for "the ginning and bailing of cotton." The "bailing" is an integral part of the "ginning" process. In Committee "compressing and storing" of cotton was added.

improve workers' conditions, why was it appropriate for the court to substitute "or" for "and"? Is the court's interpretation any more or less problematic than interpolating a comma in *Johnson v. Southern Pacific*, or than ignoring the repeal of the bankruptcy provisions in *Adamo*?

1. CASE STUDY: PROTECTING THE NATIONAL PARK SYSTEM WHILE LEASING ACCESS TO FEDERAL LAND RESOURCES

Among the areas of federal law that implicate a mosaic of overlapping statutes is the regulation of public lands. As the following case study illustrates, laws governing use and management of public lands will occasionally come into conflict, requiring courts to make sense of several distinct but interrelated statutes to resolve the interpretive conflict.

The Texts to Be Construed: **The National Trails System Act, The Park Service Organic Act, The Mineral Leasing Act, and The Wild and Scenic Rivers Act**

Before you read *United States Forest Serv. v. Cowpasture River Preservation Association*, review the following statutory provisions referenced in the majority and dissenting opinions, and consider these questions:

- What is/are the objective(s) of these statutes?
- Whom do these statutes empower, and to do what?
  - The Weeks Act?
  - The National Trails System Act?
  - The Park Service Organic Act?
  - The Mineral Leasing Act?
  - The Wild and Scenic Rivers Act?
- Do you notice any overlap between provisions? Any conflicts, or inconsistencies?
- Based on your reading of the statutes, who has authority over the Appalachian Trail? Over the lands that the Trail crosses? Is there a difference?
- Does the Trail fall under the "lands in the National Park System" carve-out in 30 U.S.C. § 185(b)(1)? Why or why not?

The Weeks Act
United States Code, Title 16, Chapter 2.

§ 521.   Lands acquired to be reserved, held, and administered as national forest lands; designation

Subject to the provisions of section 519 of this title the lands acquired under this Act shall be permanently reserved, held, and administered as national forest lands.[1] . . . [T]he Secretary of Agriculture may from time to time divide the lands acquired under this Act into such specific national forests and so designate the same as he may deem best for administrative purposes.

§ 472.   Laws affecting national forest lands

The Secretary of the Department of Agriculture shall execute or cause to be executed all laws affecting public lands reserved . . . after such lands have been so reserved, excepting such laws as affect the surveying, prospecting, locating, appropriating, entering, relinquishing, reconveying, certifying, or patenting of any of such lands.

[Note: What is now known as the George Washington National Forest was established as a national forest in 1918. The Secretary of Agriculture delegated the authority to administer national forest lands to the United States Forest Service. 36 CFR § 200.3(b)(2)(i) (2019).]

National Trails System Act
United States Code, Title 16, Chapter 27.

§ 1244. National scenic and national historic trails

(a) Establishment and designation; administration

National scenic and national historic trails shall be authorized and designated only by Act of Congress. There are hereby established the following National Scenic and National Historic Trails:

> **(1)** The Appalachian National Scenic Trail, a trail of approximately two thousand miles extending generally along the Appalachian Mountains from Mount Katahdin, Maine, to Springer Mountain, Georgia. Insofar as practicable, the right-of-way for such trail shall comprise the trail depicted on the maps identified as "Nationwide System of Trails, Proposed Appalachian Trail, NST-AT-101-May 1967", which shall be on file and available for public inspection in the office of the Director of the National Park Service. Where practicable, such rights-of-way shall include lands protected for it under agreements in effect as of October 2, 1968, to which Federal agencies and States were parties. The Appalachian Trail

---

[1]   Section 519 authorizes the Secretary of Agriculture to offer for sale as homesteads "small areas of land chiefly valuable for agriculture [that] may of necessity or by inadvertence be included in tracts acquired under this Act," as long as the occupation of such areas for agricultural purposes does not damage the forests.

shall be administered primarily as a footpath by the Secretary of the Interior, in consultation with the Secretary of Agriculture.

§ 1246. Administration and development of national trails system

(a) Consultation of Secretary with other agencies; transfer of management responsibilities; selection of rights-of-way; criteria for selection; notice; impact upon established uses

(1)(A)   The Secretary charged with the overall administration of a trail pursuant to section 1244(a) of this title shall, in administering and managing the trail, consult with the heads of all other affected State and Federal agencies. Nothing contained in this chapter shall be deemed to transfer among Federal agencies any management responsibilities established under any other law for federally administered lands which are components of the National Trails System. . . .

(2)   Pursuant to section 1244(a) of this title, the appropriate Secretary shall select the rights-of-way for national scenic and national historic trails and shall publish notice of the availability of appropriate maps or descriptions in the Federal Register: Provided, That in selecting the rights-of-way full consideration shall be given to minimizing the adverse effects upon the adjacent landowner or user and his operation. Development and management of each segment of the National Trails System shall be designed to harmonize with and complement any established multiple-use plans for that specific area in order to insure continued maximum benefits from the land. The location and width of such rights-of-way across Federal lands under the jurisdiction of another Federal agency shall be by agreement between the head of that agency and the appropriate Secretary. In selecting rights-of-way for trail purposes, the Secretary shall obtain the advice and assistance of the States, local governments, private organizations, and landowners and land users concerned. . . .

(d) Use and acquisition of lands within exterior boundaries of areas included within right-of-way

Within the exterior boundaries of areas under their administration that are included in the right-of-way selected for a national recreation, national scenic, or national historic trail, the heads of Federal agencies may use lands for trail purposes and may acquire lands or interests in lands by written cooperative agreement, donation, purchase with donated or appropriated funds or exchange.

(e) Right-of-way lands outside exterior boundaries of federally administered areas; cooperative agreements or acquisition; failure to agree or acquire; agreement or acquisition by

Secretary concerned; right of first refusal for original owner upon disposal

Where the lands included in a national scenic or national historic trail right-of-way are outside of the exterior boundaries of federally administered areas, the Secretary charged with the administration of such trail shall encourage the States or local governments involved (1) to enter into written cooperative agreements with landowners, private organizations, and individuals to provide the necessary trail right-of-way, or (2) to acquire such lands or interests therein to be utilized as segments of the national scenic or national historic trail: Provided, That if the State or local governments fail to enter into such written cooperative agreements or to acquire such lands or interests therein after notice of the selection of the right-of-way is published, the appropriate Secretary may (i) enter into such agreements with landowners, States, local governments, private organizations, and individuals for the use of lands for trail purposes, or (ii) acquire private lands or interests therein by donation, purchase with donated or appropriated funds or exchange in accordance with the provisions of subsection (f) of this section: Provided further, That the appropriate Secretary may acquire lands or interests therein from local governments or governmental corporations with the consent of such entities. The lands involved in such rights-of-way should be acquired in fee, if other methods of public control are not sufficient to assure their use for the purpose for which they are acquired: Provided, That if the Secretary charged with the administration of such trail permanently relocates the right-of-way and disposes of all title or interest in the land, the original owner, or his heirs or assigns, shall be offered, by notice given at the former owner's last known address, the right of first refusal at the fair market price.

Park Service Organic Act

United States Code, Title 54.

Subtitle I.   National Park System

§ 100101. Promotion and regulation

(a) **In general.**—The Secretary, acting through the Director of the National Park Service, shall promote and regulate the use of the National Park System by means and measures that conform to the fundamental purpose of the System units, which purpose is to conserve the scenery, natural and historic objects, and wild life in the System units and to provide for the enjoyment of the scenery, natural and historic objects, and wild life in such manner and by such means as will leave them unimpaired for the enjoyment of future generations.

(b) **Declarations.**—

(1) **1970 declarations.**—Congress declares that—

(A) the National Park System, which began with establishment of Yellowstone National Park in 1872, has since grown to include superlative natural, historic, and recreation areas in every major region of the United States and its territories and possessions;

(B) these areas, though distinct in character, are united through their interrelated purposes and resources into one National Park System as cumulative expressions of a single national heritage;

(C) individually and collectively, these areas derive increased national dignity and recognition of their superb environmental quality through their inclusion jointly with each other in one System preserved and managed for the benefit and inspiration of all the people of the United States; and

(D) it is the purpose of this division to include all these areas in the System and to clarify the authorities applicable to the System.

(2) 1978 reaffirmation.—Congress reaffirms, declares, and directs that the promotion and regulation of the various System units shall be consistent with and founded in the purpose established by subsection (a), to the common benefit of all the people of the United States. The authorization of activities shall be construed and the protection, management, and administration of the System units shall be conducted in light of the high public value and integrity of the System and shall not be exercised in derogation of the values and purposes for which the System units have been established, except as directly and specifically provided by Congress.

§ 100102. Definitions

In this title:

(1) Director.—The term "Director" means the Director of the National Park Service.

(2) National Park System.—The term "National Park System" means the areas of land and water described in section 100501 of this title.

(3) Secretary.—The term "Secretary" means the Secretary of the Interior.

(4) Service.—The term "Service" means the National Park Service.

(5) System.—The term "System" means the National Park System.

(6) System unit.—The term "System unit" means one of the areas described in section 100501 of this title.

§ 100501. Areas included in System

The System shall include any area of land and water administered by the Secretary, acting through the Director, for park, monument, historic, parkway, recreational, or other purposes.

Mineral Leasing Act

United States Code, Title 30, Chapter 3A.

§ 181. Lands subject to disposition; persons entitled to benefits; reciprocal privileges; helium rights reserved

Deposits of coal, phosphate, sodium, potassium, oil, oil shale, gilsonite (including all vein-type solid hydrocarbons), or gas, and lands containing such deposits owned by the United States, including those in national forests, but excluding lands acquired under the Appalachian Forest Act, approved March 1, 1911 (36 Stat. 961), and those in incorporated cities, towns, and villages and in national parks and monuments, those acquired under other Acts subsequent to February 25, 1920, and lands within the naval petroleum and oil-shale reserves, except as hereinafter provided, shall be subject to disposition in the form and manner provided by this chapter to citizens of the United States, or to associations of such citizens, or to any corporation organized under the laws of the United States, or of any State or Territory thereof, or in the case of coal, oil, oil shale, or gas, to municipalities. Citizens of another country, the laws, customs, or regulations of which deny similar or like privileges to citizens or corporations of this country, shall not by stock ownership, stock holding, or stock control, own any interest in any lease acquired under the provisions of this chapter.

The term "oil" shall embrace all nongaseous hydrocarbon substances other than those substances leasable as coal, oil shale, or gilsonite (including all vein-type solid hydrocarbons).

The term "combined hydrocarbon lease" shall refer to a lease issued in a special tar sand area pursuant to section 226 of this title after November 16, 1981.

The term "special tar sand area" means (1) an area designated by the Secretary of the Interior's orders of November 20, 1980 (45 FR 76800–76801) and January 21, 1981 (46 FR 6077–6078) as containing substantial deposits of tar sand.

The United States reserves the ownership of and the right to extract helium from all gas produced from lands leased or otherwise granted under the provisions of this chapter, under such rules and regulations as shall be prescribed by the Secretary of the Interior: Provided further, That in the extraction of helium from gas produced from such lands it shall be so extracted as to cause no substantial delay in the delivery of gas produced from the well to the purchaser thereof, and that extraction of helium from gas produced from such lands shall maintain the lease as if the extracted helium were oil and gas.

§ 185. Rights-of-way for pipelines through Federal lands

(a) Grant of authority

Rights-of-way through any Federal lands may be granted by the Secretary of the Interior or appropriate agency head for pipeline purposes for the transportation of oil, natural gas, synthetic liquid or gaseous fuels, or any refined product produced therefrom to any applicant possessing the qualifications provided in section 181 of this title in accordance with the provisions of this section.

(b) Definitions

(1) For the purposes of this section "Federal lands" means all lands owned by the United States except lands in the National Park System, lands held in trust for an Indian or Indian tribe, and lands on the Outer Continental Shelf. A right-of-way through a Federal reservation shall not be granted if the Secretary or agency head determines that it would be inconsistent with the purposes of the reservation.

(2) "Secretary" means the Secretary of the Interior.

(3) "Agency head" means the head of any Federal department or independent Federal office or agency, other than the Secretary of the Interior, which has jurisdiction over Federal lands.

Wild and Scenic Rivers Act
United States Code, Title 16, Chapter 28.

§ 1281. Administration . . .

(c) Areas administered by National Park Service and Fish and Wildlife Service

Any component of the national wild and scenic rivers system that is administered by the Secretary of the Interior through the National Park Service shall become a part of the national park system, and any such component that is administered by the Secretary through the Fish and Wildlife Service shall become a part of the national wildlife refuge system. The lands involved shall be subject to the provisions of this chapter and the Acts under which the national park system or national wildlife system, as the case may be, is administered, and in case of conflict between the provisions of this chapter and such Acts, the more restrictive provisions shall apply. The Secretary of the Interior, in his administration of any component of the national wild and scenic rivers system, may utilize such general statutory authorities relating to areas of the national park system and such general statutory authorities otherwise available to him for recreation and preservation purposes and for the conservation and management of natural resources as he deems appropriate to carry out the purposes of this chapter.

§ 1277. Land acquisition . . .

(e) Transfer of jurisdiction over federally owned property to appropriate Secretary

The head of any Federal department or agency having administrative jurisdiction over any lands or interests in land within the authorized boundaries of any federally administered component of the national wild and scenic rivers system designated in section 1274 of this title or hereafter designated for inclusion in the system by Act of Congress is authorized to transfer to the appropriate secretary jurisdiction over such lands for administration in accordance with the provisions of this chapter. Lands acquired by or transferred to the Secretary of Agriculture for the purposes of this chapter within or adjacent to a national forest shall upon such acquisition or transfer become national forest lands.

United States Forest Service v. Cowpasture River Preservation Association

Supreme Court of the United States, 2020.
140 S.Ct. 1837, 207 L.Ed.2d 186.

■ JUSTICE THOMAS delivered the opinion of the Court[, in which CHIEF JUSTICE ROBERTS, JUSTICE BREYER, JUSTICE ALITO, JUSTICE GORSUCH, and JUSTICE KAVANAUGH joined, and in which JUSTICE GINSBURG joined except as to Part III-B-2].

We granted certiorari in these consolidated cases to decide whether the United States Forest Service has authority under the Mineral Leasing Act, 30 U.S.C. § 181 *et seq.*, to grant rights-of-way through lands within national forests traversed by the Appalachian Trail. We hold that the Mineral Leasing Act does grant the Forest Service that authority and therefore reverse the judgment of the Court of Appeals for the Fourth Circuit.

I

A

In 2015, petitioner Atlantic Coast Pipeline, LLC (Atlantic) filed an application with the Federal Energy Regulatory Commission to construct and operate an approximately 604-mile natural gas pipeline extending from West Virginia to North Carolina. The pipeline's proposed route traverses 16 miles of land within the George Washington National Forest. The Appalachian National Scenic Trail (Appalachian Trail or Trail) also crosses parts of the George Washington National Forest.

To construct the pipeline, Atlantic needed to obtain special use permits from the United States Forest Service for the portions of the pipeline that would pass through lands under the Forest Service's jurisdiction. In 2018, the Forest Service issued these permits and granted a right-of-way that would allow Atlantic to place a 0.1-mile segment of pipe approximately 600 feet below the Appalachian Trail in the George Washington National Forest.

B

Respondents Cowpasture River Preservation Association, Highlanders for Responsible Development, Shenandoah Valley Battlefields Foundation, Shenandoah Valley Network, Sierra Club, Virginia Wilderness Committee, and Wild Virginia filed a petition for review in the Fourth Circuit. They contended that the issuance of the special use permit for the right-of-way under the Trail, as well as numerous other aspects of the Forest Services regulatory process, violated the Mineral Leasing Act (Leasing Act), 41 Stat. 437, 30 U.S.C. § 181 *et seq.*, the National Environmental Policy Act of 1969, 83 Stat. 852, 42 U.S.C. § 4321 *et seq.*, the National Forest Management Act of 1976, 90 Stat. 2952, 16 U.S.C. § 1604, and the Administrative Procedure Act, 5 U.S.C. § 500 *et seq.* Atlantic intervened in the suit.

The Fourth Circuit vacated the Forest Service's special use permit after holding that the Leasing Act did not empower the Forest Service to grant the pipeline right-of-way beneath the Trail. As relevant here, the court concluded that the Appalachian Trail had become part of the National Park System because, though originally charged with the Trails administration, 16 U. S. C. § 1244(a)(1), the Secretary of the Interior delegated that duty to the National Park Service, 34 Fed. Reg. 14337 (1969). In the Fourth Circuit's view, this delegation made the Trail part of the National Park System because the Trail was now "an area of land . . . administered by the Secretary [of the Interior] acting through the Director [of the National Park Service]." 54 U.S.C. § 100501. Because it concluded the Trail was now within the National Park System, the court held that the Trail was beyond the authority of "the Secretary of the Interior or appropriate agency head" to grant pipeline rights-of-way under the Leasing Act. 30 U.S.C. § 185(a).

II

These cases involve the interaction of multiple federal laws. We therefore begin by summarizing the relevant statutory and regulatory background.

A

Congress enacted the Weeks Act in 1911, Pub. L. 61–435, 36 Stat. 961, which provided for the acquisition of lands for inclusion in the National Forest System, *see* 16 U.S.C. §§ 516–517. The Weeks Act also directed that lands acquired for the National Forest System "shall be permanently reserved, held, and administered as national forest lands." § 521. Though Congress initially granted the Secretary of Agriculture the authority to administer national forest lands, § 472, the Secretary has delegated that authority to the Forest Service, 36 CFR 200.3(b)(2)(i) (2019).

What is now known as the George Washington National Forest was established as a national forest in 1918, *see* Proclamation No. 1448, 40 Stat. 1779, and renamed the George Washington National Forest in 1932, Exec. Order No. 5867. No party here disputes that the George Washington National Forest was acquired for inclusion in the National Forest System and that it is under the jurisdiction of the Forest Service. *See* 16 U.S.C. § 1609.

B

Enacted in 1968, the National Trails System Act (Trails Act), among other things, establishes national scenic and national historic trails. 16 U.S.C. § 1244(a). *See* 82 Stat. 919, codified at 16 U.S.C. § 1241 *et seq.* The Appalachian Trail was one of the first two trails created under the Act. § 1244(a)(1).

Under the statute, the Appalachian Trail "shall be administered primarily as a footpath by the Secretary of the Interior, in consultation with the Secretary of Agriculture." *Ibid.* The statute empowers the Secretary of the Interior to establish the location and width of the Appalachian Trail by entering into "rights-of-way" agreements with other federal agencies as well as States, local governments, and private landowners. §§ 1246(a)(2), (d), (e). However, the Trails Act also contains a proviso stating that "[n]othing contained in this chapter shall be deemed to transfer among Federal agencies any management responsibilities established under any other law for federally administered lands which are components of the National Trails System." § 1246(a)(1)(A).

The Trails Act currently establishes 30 national historic and national scenic trails. *See* §§ 1244(a)(1)–(30). It assigns responsibility for most of those trails to the Secretary of the Interior. *Ibid.* Though the Act is silent on the issue of delegation, the Department of the Interior has delegated the administrative responsibility over each of those trails to either the National Park Service or the Bureau of Land Management, both of which are housed within the Department of the Interior. [Citation]. Currently, the National Park Service administers 21 trails, the Bureau of Land Management administers 1 trail, and the two agencies co-administer 2 trails. The Secretary of Interior delegated his authority over the Appalachian Trail to the National Park Service in 1969. 34 Fed. Reg. 14337.

C

In 1920, Congress passed the Leasing Act, which enabled the Secretary of the Interior to grant pipeline rights-of-way through "public lands, including the forest reserves," § 28, 41 Stat. 449. Congress amended the Leasing Act in 1973 to provide that not only the Secretary of the Interior but also "any appropriate agency head" may grant

"[r]ights-of-way through any Federal lands . . . for pipeline purposes."
Pub. L. 93–153, 87 Stat. 576, codified at 30 U.S.C. § 185(a). Notably, the
1973 amendment also defined "Federal lands" to include "all lands owned
by the United States, except lands in the National Park System, lands
held in trust for an Indian or Indian tribe, and lands on the Outer
Continental Shelf." 87 Stat. 577, codified at 30 U.S.C. § 185(b). In 1970,
Congress defined the National Park System as "any area of land and
water now and hereafter administered by the Secretary of the Interior,
through the National Park Service for park, monument, historic,
parkway, recreational, or other purposes." § 2(b), 84 Stat. 826, codified at
54 U.S.C. § 100501.

III

We are tasked with determining whether the Leasing Act enables
the Forest Service to grant a subterranean pipeline right-of-way some
600 feet under the Appalachian Trail. To do this, we first focus on the
distinction between the lands that the Trail traverses and the Trail itself,
because the lands (not the Trail) are the object of the relevant statutes.

Under the Leasing Act, the "Secretary of the Interior or appropriate
agency head" may grant pipeline rights-of-way across "Federal *lands*." 30
U.S.C. § 185(a) (emphasis added). The Forest Service is an "appropriate
agency head" for "Federal lands" over "which [it] has jurisdiction."
§ 185(b)(3). As stated above, it is undisputed that the Forest Service has
jurisdiction over the "Federal lands" within the George Washington
National Forest. The question before us, then, becomes whether these
lands within the forest have been removed from the Forest Service's
jurisdiction and placed under the Park Service's control because the Trail
crosses them. If no transfer of jurisdiction has occurred, then the lands
remain National Forest lands, *i.e.*, "Federal lands" subject to the grant of
a pipeline right-of-way. If, on the other hand, jurisdiction over the lands
has been transferred to the Park Service, then the lands fall under the
Leasing Acts carve-out for "*lands* in the National Park System," thus
precluding the grant of the right-of-way. § 185(b)(1) (emphasis added).

We conclude that the lands that the Trail crosses remain under the
Forest Service's jurisdiction and, thus, continue to be "Federal lands"
under the Leasing Act.

A

We begin our analysis by examining the interests and authority
granted under the Trails Act. Pursuant to the Trails Act, the Forest
Service entered into "right-of-way" agreements with the National Park
Service "for [the] approximately 780 miles of Appalachian Trail route
within national forests," including the George Washington National
Forest. 36 Fed. Reg. 2676 (1971); *see also* 16 U.S.C. § 1246(a)(2); 36 Fed.
Reg. § 19805. These "right-of-way" agreements did not convert "Federal
lands" into "lands" within the "National Park System."

1

A right-of-way is a type of easement. In 1968, as now, principles of property law defined a right-of-way easement as granting a nonowner a limited privilege to "use the lands of another." [Citations.] Specifically, a right-of-way grants the limited "right to pass . . . through the estate of another." Black's Law Dictionary 1489 (4th ed. 1968). Courts at the time of the Trails Act's enactment acknowledged that easements grant only nonpossessory rights of use limited to the purposes specified in the easement agreement. [Citation.] And because an easement does not dispossess the original owner, [citation], "a possessor and an easement holder can simultaneously utilize the same parcel of land," [citation]. Thus, it was, and is, elementary that the grantor of the easement retains ownership over "the land itself." [Citation.] Stated more plainly, easements are not land, they merely burden land that continues to be owned by another. [Citation.]

If analyzed as a right-of-way between two private landowners, determining whether any land had been transferred would be simple. If a rancher granted a neighbor an easement across his land for a horse trail, no one would think that the rancher had conveyed ownership over that land. . . . Likewise, when a company obtains a right-of-way to lay a segment of pipeline through a private owner's land, no one would think that the company had obtained ownership over the land through which the pipeline passes.

Although the Federal Government owns all lands involved here, the same general principles apply. We must ascertain whether one federal agency has transferred jurisdiction over lands—meaning "jurisdiction to exercise the incidents of ownership"—to another federal agency. [Citation.] The Trails Act refers to the granted interests as "rights-of-way", both when describing agreements with the Federal Government and with private and state property owners. 16 U.S.C. §§ 1246(a)(2), (e). When applied to a private or state property owner, "right-of-way" would carry its ordinary meaning of a limited right to enjoy another's land. Nothing in the statute suggests that the term adopts a more expansive meaning when the right is granted to a federal agency, and we "do not lightly assume that Congress silently attaches different meanings to the same term in the same . . . statute," [citation]. Accordingly, as would be the case with private or state property owners, a right-of-way between two agencies grants only an easement across the land, not jurisdiction over the land itself.

The dissent notes that the Federal Government has referred to the Trail as an "area" and a "unit" and has described the Trail in terms of "acres." In the dissent's view, this indicates that the Trail and the land are the same. This is not so. Like other right-of-way easements, the Trail burdens "a particular parcel of land." [Citation] It is thus not surprising that the Government might refer to the Trail as an "area," much as one might mark out on his property the "area" of land burdened by a sewage easement. The fact remains that the land and the easement are still separate.

The dissent also cites provisions of the Trails Act that discuss "lands" to be included in the Trail. But this, too, is consistent with our conclusion that the Trail is an easement. Like all easements, the parcel of land burdened by the easement has particular metes and bounds. [Citations] In fact, without such descriptions, parties to an easement agreement would be unable to understand their rights or enforce another party's obligations under the easement agreement. Thus, there is nothing noteworthy about the fact that the Trails Act discusses whether particular lands should be included within the metes and bounds of the tracts of land burdened by the easement. In short, none of the characterizations identified by the dissent changes the fact that the burden on the land and the land itself remain separate.

In sum, read in light of basic property law principles, the plain language of the Trails Act and the agreement between the two agencies did not divest the Forest Service of jurisdiction over the lands that the Trail crosses. It gave the Department of the Interior (and by delegation the National Park Service) an easement for the specified and limited purpose of establishing and administering a Trail, but the land itself remained under the jurisdiction of the Forest Service. To restate this conclusion in the parlance of the Leasing Act, the lands that the Trail crosses are still "Federal lands," 30 U.S.C. § 185(a), and the Forest Service may grant a pipeline right-of-way through them just as it granted a right-of-way for the Trail. Sometimes a complicated regulatory scheme may cause us to miss the forest for the trees, but at bottom, these cases boil down to a simple proposition: A trail is a trail, and land is land.

2

The various duties described in the Trails Act reinforce that the agency responsible for the Trail has a limited role of administering a trail easement, but that the underlying land remains within the jurisdiction of the Forest Service. The Trails Act states that the Secretary of the Interior (and by delegation the National Park Service) shall "administe[r]" the Trail "primarily as a footpath." 16 U.S.C. § 1244(a)(1). The Secretary is charged with designating Trail uses, providing Trail markers, and establishing interpretative and informational sites "to present information to the public about the [T]rail." § 1246(c). He also has the authority to pass regulations governing Trail protection and good conduct and can regulate the "protection, management, development, and administration of the Trail." § 1246(i). Though the Trails Act states that the responsible agency shall "*provide* for" the maintenance of the Trail, § 1246(h)(1) (emphasis added), it is the Forest Service that performs the necessary physical work. As the Government explained at oral argument (and as respondents did not dispute), "[i]f a tree falls on forest lands over the trail, it's the Forest Service that's responsible for it. You don't call the nine [National] Park Service employees at Harpers

Ferry [in West Virginia] and ask them to come out and fix the tree." These statutory duties refer to the Trail easement, not the lands over which the easement passes.

The dissent resists this conclusion by asserting that the National Park Service "administers" the Trail, and that so long as that is true, the Trail is land within the National Park System. But the National Park Service does not administer the "land" crossed by the Trail. It administers the Trail as an easement—an easement that is separate from the underlying land.

3

Finally, Congress has used unequivocal and direct language in multiple statutes when it wished to transfer land from one agency to another, just as one would expect if a property owner conveyed land in fee simple to another private property owner. In the Wild and Scenic Rivers Act, for instance, which was enacted the same day as the Trails Act, Congress specified that "[a]ny component of the national wild and scenic rivers system that is administered by the Secretary of the Interior through the National Park Service *shall become a part of the [N]ational [P]ark [S]ystem.*" § 10(c), 82 Stat. 916, codified at 16 U.S.C. § 1281(c) (emphasis added). That statute also explicitly permits the head of an agency "to transfer to the appropriate secretary *jurisdiction over such lands.*" § 6(e), 82 Stat. 912–913, codified at 16 U.S.C. § 1277(e) (emphasis added). . . . The fact that Congress chose to speak in terms of rights-of-way in the Trails Act, rather than in terms of land transfers, reinforces the conclusion that the Park Service has a limited role over only the Trail, not the lands that the Trail crosses. . . .

For these reasons, we hold that the Trails Act did not transfer jurisdiction of the lands crossed by the Trail from the Forest Service to the Department of the Interior. It created a trail easement and gave the Department of the Interior the administrative responsibilities concomitant with administering the Trail as a trail. Accordingly, because the Department of the Interior had no jurisdiction over any lands, its delegation to the National Park Service did not convert the Trail into "*lands* in the National Park System," 30 U.S.C. § 185(b)(1) (emphasis added)—*i.e.*, an "*area of land* . . . administered by the Secretary [of the Interior] acting through the Director [of the National Park Service]." 54 U.S.C. § 100501 (emphasis added). The Forest Service therefore retained the authority to grant Atlantic a pipeline right-of-way.

B

[Editors' Note: Part III.B.1 has been omitted, in which the majority addresses respondents' arguments that the National Park Service administers the Trail and therefore also the land underneath it. In Part III.B.2, also omitted, the majority cautions that the respondents' interpretation would have "striking implications" for federalism and private property rightsholders; JUSTICE GINSBURG declined to join this portion of the opinion.]

* * *

We hold that the Department of the Interior's decision to assign responsibility over the Appalachian Trail to the National Park Service did not transform the land over which the Trail passes into land within the National Park System. Accordingly, the Forest Service had the authority to issue the permit here.

For the foregoing reasons, we reverse the judgment of the Court of Appeals and remand the cases for further proceedings consistent with this opinion.

It is so ordered.

■ JUSTICE SOTOMAYOR, with whom JUSTICE KAGAN joins, dissenting.

The majority's complicated discussion of private-law easements, footpath maintenance, differently worded statutes, and policy masks the simple (and only) dispute here. Is the Appalachian National Scenic Trail "lan[d] in the National Park System"? 30 U.S.C. § 185(b)(1). If it is, then the Forest Service may not grant a natural-gas pipeline right-of-way that crosses the Trail on federally owned land. So says the Mineral Leasing Act, and the parties do not disagree. [Citations.]

By definition, lands in the National Park System include "any area of land" administered by the Park Service for "park, monument, historic, parkway, recreational, or other purposes." 54 U.S.C. § 100501. So says the National Park Service Organic Act, and the parties agree. [Citations.]

The Appalachian Trail, in turn, is "administered" by the Park Service to ensure "outdoor recreation" and to conserve "nationally significant scenic, historic, natural, or cultural qualities." §§ 3(b), 5(a)(1), 82 Stat. 919–920; *see also* 34 Fed. Reg. 14337 (1969). So say the National Trails System Act and relevant regulations, and again the parties agree. [Citations.]

Thus, as the Government puts it, the only question here is whether parts of the Appalachian Trail are "lands" within the meaning of those statutes. [Citation.] Those laws, a half century of agency understanding, and common sense confirm that the Trail is land, land on which generations of people have walked. Indeed, for 50 years the "Federal Government has referred to the Trail" as a "unit" of the National Park System. [S]ee Part I-C, *infra*. A "unit" of the Park System is by definition either "land" or "water" in the Park System. 54 U.S.C. §§ 100102(6), 100501. Federal law does not distinguish "land" from the Trail any more than it distinguishes "land" from the many monuments, historic buildings, parkways, and recreational areas that are also units of the Park System. Because the Trail is land in the Park System, "no federal agency" has "authority under the Mineral Leasing Act to grant a pipeline right-of-way across such lands." [Citation.]

By contrast, today's Court suggests that the Trail is not "land" in the Park System at all. The Court strives to separate "the lands that the Trail traverses" from "the Trail itself," reasoning that the Trail is simply an "easement," "not land." In doing so, however, the Court relies on anything except the provisions that actually answer the question presented. Because today's Court condones the placement of a pipeline that subverts the plain text of the statutes governing the Appalachian Trail, I respectfully dissent.

I

Petitioner Atlantic Coast Pipeline, LLC, seeks to construct a natural-gas pipeline across the George Washington National Forest. The proposed route traverses 21 miles of national forests and requires crossing 57 rivers, streams, and lakes within those forests. [Citations.] The plan calls for "clearing trees and other vegetation from a 125-foot right of way (reduced to 75 feet in wetlands) through the national forests, digging a trench to bury the pipeline, and blasting and flattening ridgelines in mountainous terrains." [Citation.]. Construction noise will affect Appalachian Trail use 24 hours a day. Atlantic's machinery (including the artificial lights required to work all night) will dim the stars visible from the Trail. As relevant here, at one stretch the pipeline would cross the Trail.

A

Three interlocking statutes foreclose this proposal. The Mineral Leasing Act authorizes the Secretary of the Interior "or appropriate agency head" to grant rights-of-way for natural-gas pipelines "through any Federal lands." 30 U.S.C. § 185(a); *see also* § 185(q) (governing renewals of pre-existing pipeline rights-of-way across Federal lands). "For the purposes of" § 185, however, " 'Federal lands' " exclude "lands in the National Park System." § 185(b). Thus, as all acknowledge, if a proposed pipeline would cross any land in the Park System, then no federal agency would have "authority under the Mineral Leasing Act to grant" a "right-of-way across" that land. [Citations.]

Although the Mineral Leasing Act does not define "lands in the National Park System," the Park Service Organic Act does. Under the Organic Act, the Park System and any "unit" of the Park System "include any area of land and water administered by the Secretary" of the Interior, "acting through the Director" of the Park Service, for "park, monument, historic, parkway, recreational, or other purposes." 54 U.S.C. §§ 100102, 100501. That definition is sweeping; whether land or water, "any area" so "administered" by the Park Service is in the Park System. § 100501.

In turn, the National Trails System Act of 1968 (Trails Act), 82 Stat. 919, provides that the Appalachian Trail "shall be administered" "by the Secretary of the Interior" to "provide for maximum outdoor recreation potential and for the conservation and enjoyment" of "nationally significant scenic, historic, natural, or cultural qualities." §§ 3(b), 5(a)(1), *id.*, at 919–920; *see also* 16 U.S.C. §§ 1242(a)(2), 1244(a)(1). The Trails Act provides that the Secretary of the Interior has authority to "grant easements and rights-of-way," among other things, "under" the Appalachian Trails surface. § 9(a), 82 Stat. 925; *see also* 16 U.S.C. § 1248(a). In 1969, the Secretary of the Interior assigned all these powers to the Park Service, naming it the Trail's "land administering bureau." 34 Fed. Reg. 14337. Since then, the Federal Government has consistently identified the Trail as a " 'unit' " of, and thus land in, the National Park System. 54 U.S.C. §§ 100102(6), 100501.

By statutory definition, the Appalachian Trail is land in the National Park System, and the Mineral Leasing Act does not permit pipeline rights-of-way across it. . . .

C

Agency practice confirms this conclusion. For a half century the Park Service has acknowledged that the Appalachian Trail is a unit of (and land in) the Park System. Recall that a year after the Trails Acts enactment, the Secretary of Interior named the Park Service the "land administering bureau" for the Appalachian Trail. 34 Fed. Reg. 14337. In 1972, the Park Service identified the Trail as a "recreational are[a]" that it "administered." National Park Service (NPS), National Parks & Landmarks 88 (capitalization deleted). Similarly, as the administrator of that land, the Park Service issued regulations for the Trail under the umbrella, "Areas of the National Park System." 36 CFR pt. 7 (1983) (capitalization deleted); *see also id.*, § 7.100; 48 Fed. Reg. 30252 (1983). When it did so, the Park Service explained that "[t]hese regulations will be utilized to fulfill the statutory purposes of units of the National Park System." 36 CFR § 1.1; 48 Fed. Reg. 30275. All those terms—land, area, administer, recreation, unit of the National Park System—trace the Organic Acts definition of land in the Park System. *See, e.g.*, 54 U.S.C. §§ 100102(6), 100501.

More recently, a 2005 Park Service history stated that the Appalachian Trail was "brought into the National Park System" by the Trails Act and that, with the Trail's "inclusion in the System, the [Park Service] became responsible for its protection and maintenance within federally administered areas." NPS, The National Parks: Shaping the System § 77. A 2006 Park Service handbook stated that "[s]everal components of the National Trails System which are administered by the [Park] Service," including the Appalachian Trail, "have been designated as units of the national park system and are therefore managed as national park areas." NPS, Management Policies 2006, 9.2.2.7, p. 134. A 2016 Park Service index similarly listed the Trail as "a unit of the National Park System." NPS, The National Parks: Index 2012–2016, p. 142 (NPS Index).

Still taking cues from statutory text, the Park Service continues to refer to the Appalachian Trail as land in the Park System. Just last year, the Park Service issued a reference manual describing the Appalachian

Trail as a "land protection project" that has been "formally declared [a] uni[t] of the National Park System." NPS, National Trails System: Reference Manual § 45, pp. 28, 221 (2019) (NPS, Reference Manual). The Park Service's compendium of regulations similarly explains that the General Authorities Act "brought all areas administered by the [Park Service] into one National Park System." NPS, Appalachian Trail Superintendents Compendium § 2 (2019). Even the Park Services recent budget justification to Congress identified the Appalachian Trail as a "Park Base Uni[t]," a "Park Uni[t]," and a national "par[k]." Dept. of Interior, Budget Justifications and Performance Information—Fiscal Year 2020: National Park Service, at Overview-16, ONPS-89, -105 (Budget Justifications) (capitalization deleted).

The Government has even brought this understanding to bear against private citizens. For example, the Government (including the Park Service and the Forest Service) filed a damages lawsuit against an individual, invoking the Organic Act and asserting that a segment of the Appalachian Trail passing through Forest Service lands was a unit of the National Park System. *See* Record in United States v. Reed, No. 1:05-cv-00010 (WD Va.), Doc. 1, p. 2 ("The United States . . . has established the Appalachian National Scenic Trail . . . as [a] uni[t] of the National Park Service"). In that case, the Government obtained a jury verdict against someone who had caused a fire on a Trail segment that was, as the Government alleged, land in the Park System. [Citation.]

Here, at least before they reached this Court, both the Park Service and Forest Service explained in proceedings below that the Trail is land in the Park System. The Park Service noted that the Appalachian Trail is a "protected corridor (a swath of land averaging about 1,000 feet in width . . .)" that the Park Service "administers." Thus, the Park Service detailed, "the entire Trail corridor" is a "park unit." *Ibid.* For its part, the Forest Service acknowledged that the Park Service "is the lead federal administrator agency for the entire [Appalachian Trail], regardless of land ownership." Again, this statement echoes the Organic Acts definition of land in the Park System, *see* 54 U.S.C. § 100501, further reflecting that the Trail is land in the Park System.

The agencies' common ground does not stop there. The Park Service's Land Resources Division estimates that the Appalachian Trail corridor constitutes nearly 240,000 acres. [Citations.] In its own management plan, the Forest Service explained that the Secretary of the Interior "administer[s] in the George Washington National Forest about 9,000 acres." *Ibid.* Acres of land, that is.

As federally owned land administered by the Park Service, the Trail segment that Atlantic aims to cross is exempt from the Mineral Leasing Acts grant of right-of-way authority.

II

The Court resists this conclusion for three principal reasons. Each tries to detach the Appalachian Trail from land, but none adheres to the plain text and history described above.

A

First, the Court posits that the Forest Service granted the Park Service only an "easement" for the Trails route through the George Washington National Forest. Because private-law "easements are not land," the Court reasons, nothing "divest[ed] the Forest Service of jurisdiction over the lands that the Trail crosses."

That reasoning is self-defeating. Despite recognizing that the Park Service "administers the Trail," the Court insists that this administration excludes "the underlying land" constituting the Trail. But the Court does not disclose how the Park Service could administer the Trail without administering the land that forms it.

Neither does the Court explain how the Trail could be a unit of the Park System if it is not land. The Court declares that the Trails status as a System "unit" does not "indicat[e] that the Trail and the land are the same." But the Court cites no statutory authority for this view. Nor could it. The Organic Act says the opposite: A " 'System unit' " is by definition "land" or "water." 54 U.S.C. §§ 100102(6), 100501. Unless the Court means to imply that the Appalachian Trail is water, the Trail must be land in the Park System. Indeed, the Courts atextual reading unsettles much of the Park System as we know it. Other System units include the Booker T. Washington National Monument, George Washingtons birthplace, the Harriet Tubman Underground Railroad National Historical Park, the Blue Ridge Parkway, and the Golden Gate National Recreation Area. [Citations.] These monuments, houses, roads, and recreational areas are just as much land in the Park System as is a foot trail worn into the earth.

The Court's analysis of private-law easements is also unconvincing. In the Court's words, a private-law easement is "a limited privilege" granted to "a nonowner" of land. (adding that "the grantor of [an] easement retains ownership" over the land and that "easements are not land, they merely burden land that continues to be owned by another). But as the Court recognizes, "the Federal Government owns all lands involved here," so private law is inapposite. Precisely because the Government owns all the lands at issue, it makes little sense to ask whether the Government granted itself an easement over its own land under state-law principles. Between agencies of the Federal Government, federal statutory commands, not private-law analogies, govern.

In any event, the Trails Act provides that the "rights-of-way" for the Appalachian Trail "shall include lands protected for it where practicable." 16 U.S.C. § 1244(a)(1); cf. §§ 1246(d) (listing the "areas . . . included" in a right-of-way); 1246(e) (providing that the Government may "acquire such lands or interests therein to be utilized as segments of" a trail and that "lands involved in such rights-of-way should be acquired in fee"). Thus, even with a so-called "easement" through a federal forest, the Park Service still administers land "acquire[d]" and "protected" for the Trail. That is why the Park Service refers to the Trail as a "swath of land"; why the Forest Service admits that the Park Service administers those "acres," Forest Service Land Plan 4-42; and why the Secretary of the Interior has authority to grant rights-of-way "under" the Trails surface, § 1248(a).

Tellingly, the Court recognizes that § 1248(a) "extends a positive grant of authority to the agency responsible for the Trail." Indeed. That only scratches the surface. The Park Service may control what happens under the Trail consistent with "units of the national park system." § 1246(i). The Park Service also determines which "uses along the trail" to permit, § 1246(c), and provides for the Trail's "protection, management, development, and administration," § 1246(i). But under the Court's atextual reading of the relevant statutes, the agency tasked with protecting the Trail (and empowered to grant rights-of-way under it) could be excluded from determining whether a pipeline bores across the Trail. The Court's interpretation means that the Mineral Leasing Act would not even stop Atlantic from building a pipeline on top of an undisputed unit of the Park System. That cannot be right.

The Court also appears to assume that the Park Service's administrative jurisdiction over lands making up the Appalachian Trail must be mutually exclusive with the Forest Service's jurisdiction. *See ante* (focusing on whether "jurisdiction over the lands" making up the Trail was "transferred," "convert[ed]," or "divest[ed]"). But this is not a zero-sum inquiry. The question is "not whether those portions of the [Appalachian Trail] were removed from the George Washington National Forest; the question is whether they were added to the National Park System." [Citation.] As explained above, the lands making up the Appalachian Trail were indeed added to the National Park System.

That the Trail may fall within both the Forest System and the Park System is not surprising. The Trails Act recognizes that two agencies may have overlapping authority over the Appalachian Trail. *See* 16 U.S.C. § 1244(a)(1) (giving the Secretary of the Interior administrative authority "in consultation with the Secretary of Agriculture"); § 1246(a)(2) ("Development and management of each segment of the National Trails System shall be designed to harmonize with and complement any established multiple-use plans for that specific area"). So too the Mineral Leasing Act contemplates that multiple agencies may share authority over federally owned land implicated in proposed rights-of-way. *See* 30 U.S.C. § 185(c). The Court appears to recognize this point, but does not follow it to its logical conclusion: that land may be in both the Park Service and the Forest Service and thus excluded from the Mineral Leasing Act's right-of-way authority. The Mineral Leasing Acts carve-out simply asks whether the federally owned land is in the Park System at all. *See* § 185(b). If it is, then (as the parties recognize) the Mineral Leasing Act does not permit pipelines to cross that park land. . . .

B

Second, the Court maintains that Congress should have used "unequivocal and direct language" had it intended for the Trail to be land in the Park System. The Court cites the Wild and Scenic Rivers Act (Rivers Act) . . ., noting that Congress "failed to enact similar language in the Trails Act." But as the Government explained, "[m]agic words such as transfer jurisdiction are unnecessary." [Citation]

Indeed, . . . [this] example lends the Court much support. Certainly the Rivers Act, 82 Stat. 906, stated that any component of the Rivers System would "become a part of" the National Park System. § 10(c), *id.*, at 916. But this shows that Congress has many means to make land a unit of the Park System. Congress charted another path for the Appalachian Trail by enacting the General Authorities Act, a statute just as explicit as the Rivers Act. Again, it was after the Park Service had become the Trails land administering bureau, 34 Fed. Reg. 14337, that Congress provided that any area of land . . . now or hereafter administered by the Secretary of the Interior through the National Park Service is land in the Park System, 2(b), 84 Stat. 826; *see also* 54 U.S.C. 100102(2), (6), 100501. Resembling the Rivers Act, the General Authorities Act unambiguously provided that a component of the Trails System would become land in the National Park System. . . .

* * *

Today's outcome is inconsistent with the language of three statutes, longstanding agency practice, and common sense. The Park Service administers acres of land constituting the Appalachian Trail for scenic, historic, cultural, and recreational purposes. §§ 3(b), 5(a)(1), 82 Stat. 919–920; 34 Fed. Reg. 14337. "[A]ny area of land" so "administered" by the Park Service is a unit of and thus land in the National Park System. 54 U.S.C. §§ 100102(6), 100501. The Mineral Leasing Act does not permit natural-gas pipelines across such federally owned lands. 30 U.S.C. § 185(b). Only Congress, not this Court, should change that mandate.

I respectfully dissent.

QUESTIONS

1. The majority and the dissenting constructions of the relevant provisions of the Mineral Leasing Act rely heavily on interpretations of other (related) statutes. What are the benefits of such an approach? Potential pitfalls?

2. The interpretations of the majority and the dissent focus on the same three statutes: the Mineral Leasing Act, the Park Service Organic Act, and the National Trails System Act. How do they reach such different results? How does the review of the same statutes that you conducted before you read

the Supreme Court's decision compare with the majority and dissenting opinions?

3.   The majority's analysis turns, in large part, on the distinction it draws between the land that the Trail crosses and the Trail itself. Are you convinced? On which provisions of which statutes do you base your conviction (or lack of it)?

2.   WHEN LEGISLATIVE APPROPRIATIONS SEEM TO FURTHER THE STATUTORY PURPOSE

In addition to interpreting a statute in light of related statutes regulating the same subject matter, one may also look to Congress's choices in appropriating funds to further the statute's goals. Consider how Congress's funding choices influence the Court's interpretation in the following case.

Alaska Steamship Co. v. United States

Supreme Court of the United States, 1933.
290 U.S. 256, 54 S.Ct. 159, 78 L.Ed. 302.

Certiorari to review the affirmance of a judgment dismissing a suit against the United States under the Tucker Act.

■ MR. JUSTICE STONE delivered the opinion of the Court.

In this suit, brought under the Tucker Act, 24 Stat. 505, in the District Court for Western Washington, petitioner sought compensation at an agreed rate for the transportation of certain destitute seamen from Ketchikan, Alaska, to Seattle, under the provisions of § 4578 R.S., as amended, 46 U.S.C.A. § 679. That section imposes on masters of United States vessels homeward bound the duty, upon request of consular officers, to receive and carry destitute seamen to the port of destination at such compensation not exceeding a specified amount as may be agreed upon by the master with a consular officer, and authorizes the consular officer to issue certificates for such transportation, "which certificates shall be assignable for collection." By § 4526 R.S., 17 Stat. 269, as amended December 21, 1898, 30 Stat. 755, 46 U.S.C.A. § 593, seamen, whose term of service is terminated by loss or wreck of their vessel, are "destitute seamen," and are required to be transported as provided in § 4578.

The demand in the present case was for compensation for the transportation of the crew of the S.S. Depere, owned by petitioner, which had been wrecked on the Alaska coast and for that reason had been unable to complete her voyage. The crew was received and carried to Seattle on petitioner's S.S. Yukon, on certificate of the deputy customs collector of Alaska that he had agreed with the master for their transportation at a specified rate. The Comptroller General refused payment upon the certificate on the sole ground that it was the duty of petitioner to transport to the United States the crew of its own wrecked vessel, and that the Congressional appropriation for the relief of American seamen was not available to compensate the owner for performing that duty. Judgment of the district court dismissing the complaint, 60 F.2d 135, was affirmed by the Court of Appeals for the Ninth Circuit, on the ground that the certificate of the deputy collector authorizing the transportation did not satisfy the requirement of the statute that the certificate should be that of a consular officer. 63 F.2d 398. This court granted certiorari.

The government, conceding that the statute by long administrative practice has been construed as authorizing payment for transportation of seamen from Alaska on the certificate of deputy customs collectors, insists that it does not authorize payment to the owner for the transportation of the crew of his own wrecked vessel and that such has been its administrative construction.

1.   If the statutory language is to be taken literally, the certificate, which by R.S. § 4578 is authority for the transportation and evidence of the right of the vessel to compensation, must be that of a consular officer. Deputy collectors of customs are not consular officers and there are no consular officers in Alaska. If the right to compensation is dependent upon certification by a consular officer the statutes providing for transportation of destitute seamen can be given no effect in Alaska. But the meaning of this provision must be ascertained by reading it with related statutes and in the light of a long and consistent administrative practice.

Since 1792 the statutes of the United States have made provision for the return of destitute seamen to this country upon suitable action taken by consular officers of the United States. And since 1803 the government has undertaken to compensate for their transportation. Beginning in 1896, Congress has made provision for the relief of American seamen shipwrecked in Alaska in annual appropriation bills for the maintenance of the diplomatic and consular service. The appropriation bill for that year, 29 Stat. 186, and every later one has extended the benefits of the appropriation for the relief of American seamen in foreign countries to "American seamen shipwrecked in Alaska." The appropriation for 1922 and 1923, c. 204, 42 Stat. 599, 603; c. 21, 42 Stat. 1068, 1072, contained the proviso, not appearing in previous acts, that no part of the appropriation should be available for payment for transportation in excess of a specified rate agreed upon by a consular officer and the master of the vessel. The proviso did not appear in subsequent appropriation acts, but by Act of January 3, 1923, 43 Stat. 1072, it was transferred to its proper place in the shipping laws, where it now appears in § 680 of Title 46 of the United States Code. The Act of 1929, 45 Stat. 1098, applicable when the seamen in the present case were transported, appropriated $70,000 "for relief, protection and burial of American seamen in foreign countries, in the Panama Canal Zone, and in the Philippine Islands, and shipwrecked American seamen in the Territory of Alaska, in the Hawaiian Islands, in Porto Rico and in the Virgin Islands." By the amendment of R.S. § 5226 of December 21, 1898, 30 Stat. 755, 46 U.S.C.A., § 593, it was provided that where the service of a seaman terminates by reason of the loss or wreck of the vessel, "he shall not be entitled to wages for any period beyond such termination of the service and shall be considered as a destitute seaman, and shall be treated and transported to port of shipment," as provided in R.S. § 4578. No exception is made in the case of transportation of seamen from Alaska or other dependencies of the United States.

Thus, from 1896 to the present time, there has been a definite obligation on the part of the government to provide transportation for shipwrecked seamen without reference to the place where shipwrecked, and funds have been annually appropriated for the purpose of carrying out that obligation in the case of seamen shipwrecked in Alaska. As appears from the findings of the trial court, not challenged here, the appropriations have been expended for the transportation of shipwrecked seamen from Alaska, in conformity to a practice established and consistently followed at least since 1900. Certificates for the transportation of shipwrecked seamen have been regularly signed and issued by the collector of customs or the deputy collector in Alaska upon forms provided by the Bureau of Navigation of the Department of Commerce. That Bureau, which has a general superintendence over merchant seamen of the United States, 46 U.S.C.A., §§ 1 and 2, has regularly supplied its customs officials and its agents in Alaska with these forms, with instructions that they were to be used in arranging transportation of shipwrecked seamen to the United States, as provided by the sections of the statute to which reference has been made. The stipulated amounts due for the transportation, as certified, have been regularly paid without objection upon presentation of the certificate to the disbursing officer of the United States.

Courts are slow to disturb the settled administrative construction of a statute long and consistently adhered to. [Citations.] This is especially the case where, as here, the declared will of the legislative body could not be carried out without the construction adopted. That construction must be accepted and applied by the courts when, as in the present case, it has received Congressional approval, implicit in the annual appropriations over a period of thirty-five years, the expenditure of which was effected by resort to the administrative practice, and in amendments by Congress to the statutes relating to transportation of destitute seamen without modification of that practice. [Citations]

2.   The rejection of petitioner's claim by the Comptroller General rests upon the supposed duty of the owner to transport to the home port the seamen of its own wrecked vessel. Diligent search by counsel of the ancient learning of the admiralty has failed to disclose the existence of any such duty. . . .

The rulings of the Comptroller General rest upon a proposition so plainly contrary to law and so plainly in conflict with the statute as to leave them without weight as administrative constructions of it. [Citation]

Reversed.

QUESTION

Recall the Supreme Court's use of legislative history in *Holy Trinity Church*, in which it relied on a committee report to conclude that Congress had not intended to bring "brain toilers" within the scope of the immigration prohibition on contract labor. In the report, the committee acknowledged that the statute as written could be read to include "brain toilers," but feared that time constraints would prevent redrafting the bill with more precise language. Nevertheless, some might be troubled by the Court's reliance on statements from the committee's unenacted clarification. By contrast, in *Alaska Steamship* the Court relied on subsequent legislation to clarify the meaning of the destitute seaman statute, insofar as it applied to repatriations from Alaska. Is the Court on firmer ground in clarifying Congress' intent when it interprets a statute in light of *subsequent* (enacted) legislation that seems to inform the prior statute's meaning, as opposed to interpreting a statute in reliance on (unenacted) statements contemporaneous with the bill's passage?

3. WHEN LEGISLATIVE APPROPRIATIONS SEEM TO UNDERMINE THE STATUTORY PURPOSE

When Congress's subsequent appropriations choices seem to support its earlier legislative enactment, conflict rarely ensues. But what if Congress's subsequent appropriations seem to hinder, rather than support, the prevailing understanding of the statute's meaning and application? The following case considers whether Congress's subsequent, and seemingly contradictory, appropriations decisions should influence a Court's understanding of the meaning of Congress's earlier statutory enactment.

Tennessee Valley Authority v. Hill

Supreme Court of the United States, 1978.
437 U.S. 153, 98 S.Ct. 2279, 57 L.Ed.2d 117.

■ CHIEF JUSTICE BURGER delivered the opinion of the Court[, in which JUSTICE BRENNAN, JUSTICE STEWART, JUSTICE WHITE, JUSTICE MARSHALL, and JUSTICE STEVENS joined].

The questions presented in this case are (a) whether the Endangered Species Act of 1973 requires a court to enjoin the operation of a virtually completed federal dam—which had been authorized prior to 1973—when, pursuant to authority vested in him by Congress, the Secretary of the Interior has determined that operation of the dam would eradicate an endangered species; and (b) whether continued congressional appropriations for the dam after 1973 constituted an implied repeal of the Endangered Species Act, at least as to the particular dam.

I

The Little Tennessee River originates in the mountains of northern Georgia and flows through the national forest lands of North Carolina into Tennessee, where it converges with the Big Tennessee River near Knoxville. The lower 33 miles of the Little Tennessee takes the river's clear, free-flowing waters through an area of great natural beauty....

In this area of the Little Tennessee River the Tennessee Valley Authority, a wholly owned public corporation of the United States, began constructing the Tellico Dam and Reservoir Project in 1967, shortly after Congress appropriated initial funds for its development. Tellico is a multipurpose regional development project designed principally to stimulate shoreline development, generate sufficient electric current to heat 20,000 homes, and provide flatwater recreation and flood control, as well as improve economic conditions in "an area characterized by underutilization of human resources and outmigration of young people."[*] Hearings on Public Works for Power and Energy Research Appropriation Bill, 1977, before a Subcommittee of the House Committee on Appropriations, 94th Cong., 2d Sess., pt. 5, p. 261 (1976). Of particular relevance to this case is one aspect of the project, a dam which TVA determined to place on the Little Tennessee, a short distance from where the river's waters meet with the Big Tennessee. When fully operational, the dam would impound water covering some 16,500 acres—much of which represents valuable and productive farmland—thereby converting the river's shallow, fast-flowing waters into a deep reservoir over 30 miles in length.

The Tellico Dam has never opened, however, despite the fact that construction has been virtually completed and the dam is essentially ready for operation. Although Congress has appropriated monies for Tellico every year since 1967, progress was delayed, and ultimately stopped, by a tangle of lawsuits and administrative proceedings. [The opinion describes prior legal challenges unrelated to the present controversy.] [A] discovery was made in the waters of the Little Tennessee which would profoundly affect the Tellico Project. Exploring the area around Coytee Springs, which is about seven miles from the mouth of the river, a University of Tennessee ichthyologist, Dr. David A.

---

[*] Editors' Note: The Subcommittee on Public Works of the House Committee on Appropriations asked TVA Chairman Aubrey J. Wagner to submit a statement detailing TVA's approach to the Tellico Project and arguing that ongoing litigation should have no impact on the House's appropriations for the Tellico Project: "The act was not intended to supplant an agency's primary responsibilities . . . . We are doing our best to preserve the snail darter, and the results to date have been very encouraging. We cannot guarantee that the transplant will ultimately be a success. In any event, however, we believe the Tellico project must be completed on schedule. . . . We ask the committee to approve the $9.7 million requested by the President to complete the project."

Etnier, found a previously unknown species of perch, the snail darter, or *Percina (Imostoma) tanasi*. This three-inch, tannish-colored fish, whose numbers are estimated to be in the range of 10,000 to 15,000, would soon engage the attention of environmentalists, the TVA, the Department of the Interior, the Congress of the United States, and ultimately the federal courts, as a new and additional basis to halt construction of the dam.

Until recently the finding of a new species of animal life would hardly generate a cause célèbre. This is particularly so in the case of darters, of which there are approximately 130 known species, 8 to 10 of these having been identified only in the last five years. The moving force behind the snail darter's sudden fame came some four months after its discovery, when the Congress passed the Endangered Species Act of 1973 (Act), 87 Stat. 884, 16 U.S.C. § 1531 *et seq.* (1976 ed.). This legislation, among other things, authorizes the Secretary of the Interior to declare species of animal life "endangered" and to identify the "critical habitat" of these creatures. When a species or its habitat is so listed, the following portion [of § 7] of the Act—relevant here—becomes effective:

> "The Secretary [of the Interior] shall review other programs administered by him and utilize such programs in furtherance of the purposes of this chapter. All other Federal departments and agencies shall, in consultation with and with the assistance of the Secretary, utilize their authorities in furtherance of the purposes of this chapter by carrying out programs for the conservation of endangered species and threatened species listed pursuant to section 1533 of this title and *by taking such action necessary to insure that actions authorized, funded, or carried out by them do not jeopardize the continued existence of such endangered species and threatened species or result in the destruction or modification of habitat of such species* which is determined by the Secretary, after consultation as appropriate with the affected States, to be critical." 16 U.S.C. § 1536 (1976 ed.) (emphasis added).

In January 1975, the respondents in this case and others petitioned the Secretary of the Interior to list the snail darter as an endangered species. After receiving comments [from] various interested parties, including TVA and the State of Tennessee, the Secretary formally listed the snail darter as an endangered species on October 8, 1975. [Citation.]*

---

* Editors' Note: Following Hill's petition to U.S. Fish and Wildlife Service to list the snail darter as an endangered species, the agency invited comment on its proposed rulemaking listing the snail darter as endangered. The agency received 16 comments, of which 4 were in opposition, including a letter from TVA. TVA's letter raised specific objections to the rulemaking, including: "1. Listing of [the snail darter] would have no valid basis since the taxonomic status of the fish has not been determined . . . . [2.] There has been no systematic or adequate study of the range of this fish. . . . 3. Listing . . . would not enhance the likelihood that this fish would survive and therefore would not further the purpose of the Endangered Species Act. . . . 4. For the foregoing reasons, it is clear that the [Act] does not require, nor indeed does it permit, the Secretary [of the Interior's] proposed listing. In light of this we do not believe that the Fish and Wildlife

In so acting, it was noted that "the snail darter is a living entity which is genetically distinct and reproductively isolated from other fishes." [Citation.] More important for the purposes of this case, the Secretary determined that the snail darter apparently lives only in that portion of the Little Tennessee River which would be completely inundated by the reservoir created as a consequence of the Tellico Dam's completion. [Citation.] The Secretary went on to explain the significance of the dam to the habitat of the snail darter:

> "[T]he snail darter occurs only in the swifter portions of shoals over clean gravel substrate in cool, low-turbidity water. Food of the snail darter is almost exclusively snails which require a clean gravel substrate for their survival. *The proposed impoundment of water behind the proposed Tellico Dam would result in total destruction of the snail darter's habitat.*" [Citation] (emphasis added).

Subsequent to this determination, the Secretary declared the area of the Little Tennessee which would be affected by the Tellico Dam to be the "critical habitat" of the snail darter. [Citation.] Using these determinations as a predicate, and notwithstanding the near completion of the dam, the Secretary declared that pursuant to § 7 of the Act, "all Federal agencies must take such action as is necessary to insure that actions authorized, funded, or carried out by them do not result in the destruction or modification of this critical habitat area." [Citation.] This notice, of course, was pointedly directed at TVA and clearly aimed at halting completion or operation of the dam. . . .

TVA conducted a search of alternative sites which might sustain the fish, culminating in the experimental transplantation of a number of snail darters to the nearby Hiwassee River. However, the Secretary of the Interior was not satisfied with the results of these efforts, finding that TVA had presented "little evidence that they have carefully studied the Hiwassee to determine whether or not" there were "biological and other factors in this river that [would] negate a successful transplant." [Citation.]

Meanwhile, Congress had also become involved in the fate of the snail darter. Appearing before a Subcommittee of the House Committee on Appropriations in April 1975—some seven months before the snail darter was listed as endangered—TVA representatives described the discovery of the fish and the relevance of the Endangered Species Act to the Tellico Project. [Citations.] At that time TVA presented a position which it would advance in successive forums thereafter, namely, that the Act did not prohibit the completion of a project authorized, funded, and substantially constructed before the Act was passed. TVA also described its efforts to transplant the snail darter, but contended that the dam

---

Service should inject itself into the longstanding controversy surrounding the wisdom of the Tellico project." 40 Fed. Reg. 47505.

should be finished regardless of the experiment's success. Thereafter, the House Committee on Appropriations, in its June 20, 1975, Report, stated the following in the course of recommending that an additional $29 million be appropriated for Tellico:

"The *Committee* directs that the project, for which an environmental impact statement has been completed and provided the Committee, should be completed as promptly as possible . . . ."

Congress then approved the TVA general budget, which contained funds for continued construction of the Tellico Project. In December 1975, one month after the snail darter was declared an endangered species, the President signed the bill into law. [Citation.]

In February 1976, . . . respondents filed the case now under review, seeking to enjoin completion of the dam and impoundment of the reservoir on the ground that those actions would violate the Act by directly causing the extinction of the species *Percina (Imostoma) tanasi*. . . . The District Court found that closure of the dam and the consequent impoundment of the reservoir would "result in the adverse modification, if not complete destruction, of the snail darter's critical habitat," making it "highly probable" that "the continued existence of the snail darter" would be "jeopardize[d]." Despite these findings, the District Court declined to embrace the plaintiffs' position on the merits: that once a federal project was shown to jeopardize an endangered species, a court of equity is compelled to issue an injunction restraining violation of the Endangered Species Act.

In reaching this result, the District Court stressed that the entire project was then about 80% complete and, based on available evidence, "there [were] no alternatives to impoundment of the reservoir, short of scrapping the entire project." The District Court also found that if the Tellico Project was permanently enjoined, "[s]ome $53 million would be lost in nonrecoverable obligations," meaning that a large portion of the $78 million already expended would be wasted. The court also noted that the Endangered Species Act of 1973 was passed some seven years after construction on the dam commenced and that Congress had continued appropriations for Tellico, with full awareness of the snail darter problem. Assessing these various factors, the District Court concluded:

"At some point in time a federal project becomes so near completion and so incapable of modification that a court of equity should not apply a statute enacted long after inception of the project to produce an unreasonable result. . . . Where there has been an irreversible and irretrievable commitment of resources by Congress to a project over a span of almost a decade, the Court should proceed with a great deal of circumspection."

To accept the plaintiffs' position, the District Court argued, would inexorably lead to what it characterized as the absurd result of requiring "a court to halt impoundment of water behind a fully completed dam if an endangered species were discovered in the river on the day before such impoundment was scheduled to take place. We cannot conceive that Congress intended such a result." [Citation.]

Less than a month after the District Court decision, the Senate and House Appropriations Committees recommended the full budget request of $9 million for continued work on Tellico. In its Report accompanying the appropriations bill, the Senate Committee stated:

"During subcommittee hearings, TVA was questioned about the relationship between the Tellico project's completion and the November 1975 listing of the snail darter (a small 3-inch fish which was discovered in 1973) as an endangered species under the Endangered Species Act. TVA informed the Committee that it was continuing its efforts to preserve the darter, while working towards the scheduled 1977 completion date. TVA repeated its view that the Endangered Species Act did not prevent the completion of the Tellico project, which has been under construction for nearly a decade. The subcommittee brought this matter, as well as the recent U. S. District Court's decision upholding TVA's decision to complete the project, to the attention of the full Committee. *The Committee does not view* the Endangered Species Act as prohibiting the completion of the Tellico project at its advanced stage and directs that this project be completed as promptly as possible in the public interest." [Citation.] (Emphasis added.)

On June 29, 1976, both Houses of Congress passed TVA's general budget, which included funds for Tellico; the President signed the bill on July 12, 1976. [Citation.]

Thereafter, in the Court of Appeals, respondents argued that the District Court had abused its discretion by not issuing an injunction in the face of "a blatant statutory violation." ... The Court of Appeals accepted the District Court's finding that closure of the dam would result in the known population of snail darters being "significantly reduced if not completely extirpated." TVA, in fact, had conceded as much in the Court of Appeals, but argued that "closure of the Tellico Dam, as the last stage of a ten-year project, falls outside the legitimate purview of the Act if it is rationally construed." Disagreeing, the Court of Appeals held that the record revealed a prima facie violation of § 7 of the Act, namely that TVA had failed to take "such action ... necessary to insure" that its "actions" did not jeopardize the snail darter or its critical habitat.

The reviewing court thus rejected TVA's contention that the word "actions" in § 7 of the Act was not intended by Congress to encompass the terminal phases of ongoing projects. Not only could the court find no "positive reinforcement" for TVA's argument in the Act's legislative history, but also such an interpretation was seen as being "inimical to . . . its objectives." . . . As far as the Court of Appeals was concerned, it made no difference that Congress had repeatedly approved appropriations for Tellico, referring to such legislative approval as an "advisory opinio[n]" concerning the proper application of an existing statute. In that court's view, the only relevant legislation was the Act itself, "[t]he meaning and spirit" of which was "clear on its face." . . . [T]he Court of Appeals ruled that the District Court had erred by not issuing an injunction. . . .

Following the issuance of the permanent injunction, members of TVA's Board of Directors appeared before Subcommittees of the House and Senate Appropriations Committees to testify in support of continued appropriations for Tellico. The Subcommittees were apprised of all aspects of Tellico's status, including the Court of Appeals' decision. TVA reported that the dam stood "ready for the gates to be closed and the reservoir filled," and requested funds for completion of certain ancillary parts of the project, such as public use areas, roads, and bridges. As to the snail darter itself, TVA commented optimistically on its transplantation efforts, expressing the opinion that the relocated fish were "doing well and ha[d] reproduced."

Both Appropriations Committees subsequently recommended the full amount requested for completion of the Tellico Project. In its June 2, 1977, Report, the House Appropriations Committee stated:

> "It is *the Committee's view* that the Endangered Species Act was not intended to halt projects such as these in their advanced stage of completion, and [the Committee] strongly recommends that these projects not be stopped because of misuse of the Act." [Citation.] (Emphasis added.)

As a solution to the problem, the House Committee advised that TVA should cooperate with the Department of the Interior "to relocate the endangered species to another suitable habitat so as to permit the project to proceed as rapidly as possible." Toward this end, the Committee recommended a special appropriation of $2 million to facilitate relocation of the snail darter and other endangered species which threatened to delay or stop TVA projects. Much the same occurred on the Senate side, with its Appropriations Committee recommending both the amount requested to complete Tellico and the special appropriation for transplantation of endangered species. Reporting to the Senate on these measures, the Appropriations Committee took a particularly strong stand on the snail darter issue:

> "This *committee has not viewed* the Endangered Species Act as preventing the completion and use of these projects which were well under way at the time the affected species were listed as endangered. If the act has such an effect which is contrary to *the Committee's understanding* of the intent of Congress in enacting the Endangered Species Act, funds should be appropriated to

allow these projects to be completed and their benefits realized in the public interest, the Endangered Species Act notwithstanding." [Citation.] (Emphasis added.)

TVA's budget, including funds for completion of Tellico and relocation of the snail darter, passed both Houses of Congress and was signed into law on August 7, 1977.

We granted certiorari ... to review the judgment of the Court of Appeals.

II

We begin with the premise that operation of the Tellico Dam will either eradicate the known population of snail darters or destroy their critical habitat.... [U]nder § 4(a)(1) of the Act, the Secretary of the Interior is vested with exclusive authority to determine whether a species such as the snail darter is "endangered" or "threatened" and to ascertain the factors which have led to such a precarious existence. By § 4(d) Congress has authorized—indeed commanded—the Secretary to "issue such regulations as he deems necessary and advisable to provide for the conservation of such species." [Citation.] As we have seen, the Secretary promulgated regulations which declared the snail darter an endangered species whose critical habitat would be destroyed by creation of the Tellico Dam. Doubtless petitioner would prefer not to have these regulations on the books, but there is no suggestion that the Secretary exceeded his authority or abused his discretion in issuing the regulations. Indeed, no judicial review of the Secretary's determinations has ever been sought and hence the validity of his actions are not open to review in this Court.

Starting from the above premise, [w]ould TVA be in violation of the Act if it completed and operated the Tellico Dam as planned? For the reasons stated hereinafter, we hold that question[ ] must be answered in the affirmative.

(A)

It may seem curious to some that the survival of a relatively small number of three-inch fish among all the countless millions of species extant would require the permanent halting of a virtually completed dam for which Congress has expended more than $100 million. The paradox is not minimized by the fact that Congress continued to appropriate large sums of public money for the project, even after congressional Appropriations Committees were apprised of its apparent impact upon the survival of the snail darter. We conclude, however, that the explicit provisions of the Endangered Species Act require precisely that result.

One would be hard pressed to find a statutory provision whose terms were any plainer than those in § 7 of the Endangered Species Act. Its very words affirmatively command all federal agencies "to *insure* that actions *authorized, funded,* or *carried out* by them do not *jeopardize* the continued existence" of an endangered species or *"result* in the destruction or modification of habitat of such species . . . ." [Citation.] (Emphasis added.) This language admits of no exception. Nonetheless, petitioner urges, as do the dissenters, that the Act cannot reasonably be interpreted as applying to a federal project which was well under way when Congress passed the Endangered Species Act of 1973. To sustain that position, however, we would be forced to ignore the ordinary meaning of plain language. It has not been shown, for example, how TVA can close the gates of the Tellico Dam without "carrying out" an action that has been "authorized" and "funded" by a federal agency. Nor can we understand how such action will "*insure*" that the snail darter's habitat is not disrupted. Accepting the Secretary's determinations, as we must, it is clear that TVA's proposed operation of the dam will have precisely the opposite effect, namely the *eradication* of an endangered species.

Concededly, this view of the Act will produce results requiring the sacrifice of the anticipated benefits of the project and of many millions of dollars in public funds. But examination of the language, history, and structure of the legislation under review here indicates beyond doubt that Congress intended endangered species to be afforded the highest of priorities.

When Congress passed the Act in 1973, it was not legislating on a clean slate. [The Court describes earlier, less extensive federal statutes enacted to protect endangered species.] Despite the fact that the [earlier] legislation represented "the most comprehensive of its type to be enacted by any nation" up to that time, Congress was soon persuaded that a more expansive approach was needed if the newly declared national policy of preserving endangered species was to be realized. By 1973, when Congress held hearings on what would later become the Endangered Species Act of 1973, it was informed that species were still being lost at the rate of about one per year, [citation], and "the pace of disappearance of species" appeared to be "accelerating." [Citation.] Moreover, Congress was also told that the primary cause of this trend was something other than the normal process of natural selection:

> "[M]an and his technology has [*sic*] continued at any ever-increasing rate to disrupt the natural ecosystem. This has resulted in a dramatic rise in the number and severity of the threats faced by the world's wildlife. The truth in this is apparent when one realizes that half of the recorded extinctions of mammals over the past 2,000 years have occurred in the most recent 50-year period." 1973 House Hearings 202 (statement of Assistant Secretary of the Interior).

. . . The legislative proceedings in 1973 are, in fact, replete with expressions of concern over the risk that might lie in the loss of *any* endangered species. . . . Congress was concerned about the *unknown* uses that endangered species might have and about the *unforeseeable* place such creatures may have in the chain of life on this planet.

In shaping legislation to deal with the problem thus presented, Congress started from the finding that "[t]he two major causes of extinction are hunting and destruction of natural habitat." [Citation.] Of these twin threats, Congress was informed that the greatest was destruction of natural habitats; [citations]. . . . Virtually every bill introduced in Congress during the 1973 session responded to this concern by incorporating language similar, if not identical, to that found in the present § 7 of the Act. These provisions were designed, in the words of an administration witness, "for the first time [to] *prohibit* [a] federal agency from taking action which does jeopardize the status of endangered species," [citation]; furthermore, the proposed bills would "*direc[t]* all . . . Federal agencies to utilize their authorities for carrying out programs *for the protection* of endangered animals." [Citation.] (Emphasis added.)

As it was finally passed, the Endangered Species Act of 1973 represented the most comprehensive legislation for the preservation of endangered species ever enacted by any nation. Its stated purposes were "to provide a means whereby the ecosystems upon which endangered species and threatened species depend may be conserved," and "to provide a program for the conservation of such . . . species . . . ." [Citation.] In furtherance of these goals, Congress expressly stated in § 2(c) that "all Federal departments and agencies *shall* seek *to conserve endangered species* and threatened species . . . ." [Citation.] (Emphasis added.) Lest there be any ambiguity as to the meaning of this statutory directive, the Act specifically defined "conserve" as meaning "to use and the use of *all methods and procedures which are necessary* to bring *any endangered species or threatened species* to the point at which the measures provided pursuant to this chapter are no longer necessary." [Citation.] (Emphasis added.) . . .

Section 7 of the Act, which of course is relied upon by respondents in this case, provides a particularly good gauge of congressional intent. . . . [Prior] legislation qualified the obligation of federal agencies by stating that they should seek to preserve endangered species only "*insofar as is practicable and consistent with the[ir] primary purposes* . . ." . . . This type of language did not go unnoticed by those advocating strong endangered species legislation. A representative of the Sierra Club, for example, attacked the use of the phrase "consistent with the primary purpose" in proposed [legislation], cautioning that the qualification "could be construed to be a declaration of congressional policy that other agency purposes are necessarily more important than protection of endangered species and would always prevail if conflict were to occur." [Citation.]

What is very significant in this sequence is that the final version of the 1973 Act carefully omitted all of the reservations described above. In the bill which the Senate initially approved (S. 1983), however, the version of the current § 7 merely required federal agencies to "carry out such programs *as are practicable* for the protection of species listed . . . ."

[Citation.] (Emphasis added.) By way of contrast, the bill that originally passed the House, H.R. 37, contained a provision which was essentially a mirror image of the subsequently passed § 7—indeed all phrases which might have qualified an agency's responsibilities had been omitted from the bill. In explaining the expected impact of this provision in H.R. 37 on federal agencies, the House Committee's Report states:

> "This subsection *requires* the Secretary and the heads of all other Federal departments and agencies to use their authorities in order to carry out programs for the protection of endangered species, and it further *requires* that those agencies take *the necessary action* that will *not jeopardize* the continuing existence of endangered species or result in the destruction of critical habitat of those species." [Citation.] (Emphasis added.)

Resolution of this difference in statutory language, as well as other variations between the House and Senate bills, was the task of a Conference Committee. [Citation.] The Conference Report, [citation], basically adopted the Senate bill; but the conferees rejected the Senate version of § 7 and adopted the stringent, mandatory language in H.R. 37. While the Conference Report made no specific reference to this choice of provisions, the House manager of the bill, Representative Dingell, provided an interpretation of what the Conference bill would require, making it clear that the mandatory provisions of § 7 were not casually or inadvertently included:

> "[Section 7] substantially amplifie[s] the obligation of [federal agencies] to take steps within their power to carry out the purposes of this act. A recent article . . . illustrates the problem which might occur absent this new language in the bill. It appears that the whooping cranes of this country, perhaps the best known of our endangered species, are being threatened by Air Force bombing activities along the gulf coast of Texas. Under existing law, the Secretary of Defense has some discretion as to whether or not he will take the necessary action to see that this threat disappears . . . . [O]nce the bill is enacted, [the Secretary of Defense] *would be required to take the proper steps.* . . .

> "Another example . . . [has] to do with the continental population of grizzly bears which may or may not be endangered, but which is surely threatened. . . . Once this bill is enacted, the appropriate Secretary, whether of Interior, Agriculture or whatever, *will have to take action* to see that this situation is not permitted to worsen, and that these bears are not driven to extinction. The purposes of the bill included the conservation of the species and of the ecosystems upon which they depend, and *every agency of government is committed* to see that those purposes are carried out. . . . [T]he agencies of Government can no longer plead that they can do nothing about

it. *They can, and they must. The law is clear."* [Citation.] (Emphasis added.)

It is against this legislative background that we must measure TVA's claim that the Act was not intended to stop operation of a project which, like Tellico Dam, was near completion when an endangered species was discovered in its path. While there is no discussion in the legislative history of precisely this problem, the totality of congressional action makes it abundantly clear that the result we reach today is wholly in accord with both the words of the statute and the intent of Congress. The plain intent of Congress in enacting this statute was to halt and reverse the trend toward species extinction, whatever the cost. This is reflected not only in the stated policies of the Act, but in literally every section of the statute. . . . In addition, the legislative history undergirding § 7 reveals an explicit congressional decision to require agencies to afford first priority to the declared national policy of saving endangered species. The pointed omission of the type of qualifying language previously included in endangered species legislation reveals a conscious decision by Congress to give endangered species priority over the "primary missions" of federal agencies.

It is not for us to speculate, much less act, on whether Congress would have altered its stance had the specific events of this case been anticipated. In any event, we discern no hint in the deliberations of Congress relating to the 1973 Act that would compel a different result than we reach here. Indeed, the repeated expressions of congressional concern over what it saw as the potentially enormous danger presented by the eradication of *any* endangered species suggest how the balance would have been struck had the issue been presented to Congress in 1973.

Furthermore, it is clear Congress foresaw that § 7 would, on occasion, require agencies to alter ongoing projects in order to fulfill the goals of the Act. Congressman Dingell's discussion of Air Force practice bombing, for instance, obviously pinpoints a particular activity— intimately related to the national defense—which a major federal department would be obliged to alter in deference to the strictures of § 7. . . .

One might dispute the applicability of these examples to the Tellico Dam by saying that in this case the burden on the public through the loss of millions of unrecoverable dollars would greatly outweigh the loss of the snail darter. But neither the Endangered Species Act nor Art. III of the Constitution provides federal courts with authority to make such fine utilitarian calculations. On the contrary, the plain language of the Act, buttressed by its legislative history, shows clearly that Congress viewed the value of endangered species as "incalculable." Quite obviously, it would be difficult for a court to balance the loss of a sum certain—even $100 million—against a congressionally declared "incalculable" value, even assuming we had the power to engage in such a weighing process, which we emphatically do not.

In passing the Endangered Species Act of 1973, Congress was also aware of certain instances in which exceptions to the statute's broad sweep would be necessary. Thus, § 10, 16 U.S.C. § 1539 (1976 ed.), creates a number of limited "hardship exemptions," none of which would even remotely apply to the Tellico Project. In fact, there are no exemptions in the Endangered Species Act for federal agencies, meaning that under the maxim *expressio unius est exclusio alterius*, we must presume that these were the only "hardship cases" Congress intended to exempt. [Citation.]

Notwithstanding Congress' expression of intent in 1973, we are urged to find that the continuing appropriations for Tellico Dam constitute an implied repeal of the 1973 Act, at least insofar as it applies to the Tellico Project. In support of this view, TVA points to the statements found in various House and Senate Appropriations Committees' Reports; . . . those Reports generally reflected the attitude of the *Committees* either that the Act did not apply to Tellico or that the dam should be completed regardless of the provisions of the Act. Since we are unwilling to assume that these latter Committee statements constituted advice to ignore the provisions of a duly enacted law, we assume that these Committees believed that the Act simply was not applicable in this situation. But even under this interpretation of the Committees' actions, we are unable to conclude that the Act has been in any respect amended or repealed.

There is nothing in the appropriations measures, as passed, which states that the Tellico Project was to be completed irrespective of the requirements of the Endangered Species Act. . . . To find a repeal of the Endangered Species Act under these circumstances would surely do violence to the " 'cardinal rule . . . that repeals by implication are not favored.' " [Citations.] In practical terms, this "cardinal rule" means that "[i]n the absence of some affirmative showing of an intention to repeal, the only permissible justification for a repeal by implication is when the earlier and later statutes are irreconcilable." [Citation.]

The doctrine disfavoring repeals by implication "applies with full vigor when . . . the subsequent legislation is an *appropriations* measure." [Citation.] This is perhaps an understatement since it would be more accurate to say that the policy applies with even *greater* force when the claimed repeal rests solely on an Appropriations Act. . . . Not only would this lead to the absurd result of requiring Members to review exhaustively the background of every authorization before voting on an appropriation, but it would flout the very rules the Congress carefully adopted to avoid this need. House Rule XXI(2), for instance, specifically provides:

"No appropriation shall be reported in any general appropriation bill, or be in order as an amendment thereto, for any expenditure not previously authorized by law, unless in continuation of appropriations for such public works as are already in progress. *Nor shall any provision in any such bill or amendment thereto changing existing law be in order.*" (Emphasis added.) . . .

Perhaps mindful of the fact that it is "swimming upstream" against a strong current of well-established precedent, TVA argues for an exception to the rule against implied repealers in a circumstance where, as here, Appropriations Committees have expressly stated their "understanding" that the earlier legislation would not prohibit the proposed expenditure. We cannot accept such a proposition. Expressions of committees dealing with requests for appropriations cannot be equated with statutes enacted by Congress, particularly not in the circumstances presented by this case. . . .

Quite apart from the foregoing factors, we would still be unable to find that in this case "the earlier and later statutes are irreconcilable," [citation]; here it is entirely possible "to regard each as effective." [Citation.] The starting point in this analysis must be the legislative proceedings leading to the 1977 appropriations since the earlier funding of the dam occurred prior to the listing of the snail darter as an endangered species. In all successive years, TVA confidently reported to the Appropriations Committees that efforts to transplant the snail darter appeared to be successful; this surely gave those Committees some basis for the impression that there was no direct conflict between the Tellico Project and the Endangered Species Act. Indeed, the special appropriation for 1978 of $2 million for transplantation of endangered species supports the view that the Committees saw such relocation as the means whereby collision between Tellico and the Endangered Species Act could be avoided. It should also be noted that the Reports issued by the Senate and House Appropriations Committees in 1976 came within a month of the District Court's decision in this case, which hardly could have given the Members cause for concern over the possible applicability of the Act. This leaves only the 1978 appropriations, the Reports for which issued after the Court of Appeals' decision now before us. At that point very little remained to be accomplished on the project; the Committees understandably advised TVA to cooperate with the Department of the Interior "to relocate the endangered species to another suitable habitat so as to permit the project to proceed as rapidly as possible." [Citation.] It is true that the *Committees* repeated their earlier expressed "view" that the Act did not prevent completion of the Tellico Project. Considering these statements in context, however, it is evident that they " 'represent only the personal views of these legislators,' " and "however explicit, [they] cannot serve to change the legislative intent of Congress expressed before the Act's passage."

Having determined that there is an irreconcilable conflict between operation of the Tellico Dam and the explicit provisions of § 7 of the

Endangered Species Act, we must now consider what remedy, if any, is appropriate. . . . Congress has spoken in the plainest of words, making it abundantly clear that the balance has been struck in favor of affording endangered species the highest of priorities, thereby adopting a policy which it described as "institutionalized caution."

Our individual appraisal of the wisdom or unwisdom of a particular course consciously selected by the Congress is to be put aside in the process of interpreting a statute. Once the meaning of an enactment is discerned and its constitutionality determined, the judicial process comes to an end. We do not sit as a committee of review, nor are we vested with the power of veto. We agree with the Court of Appeals that in our constitutional system the commitment to the separation of powers is too fundamental for us to pre-empt congressional action by judicially decreeing what accords with "common sense and the public weal." Our Constitution vests such responsibilities in the political branches.

Affirmed.

■ MR. JUSTICE POWELL, with whom MR. JUSTICE BLACKMUN joins, dissenting.

The Court today holds that § 7 of the Endangered Species Act requires a federal court, for the purpose of protecting an endangered species or its habitat, to enjoin permanently the operation of any federal project, whether completed or substantially completed. This decision casts a long shadow over the operation of even the most important projects, serving vital needs of society and national defense, whenever it is determined that continued operation would threaten extinction of an endangered species or its habitat. This result is said to be required by the "plain intent of Congress" as well as by the language of the statute.

In my view § 7 cannot reasonably be interpreted as applying to a project that is completed or substantially completed when its threat to an endangered species is discovered. Nor can I believe that Congress could have intended this Act to produce the "absurd result"—in the words of the District Court—of this case. If it were clear from the language of the Act and its legislative history that Congress intended to authorize this result, this Court would be compelled to enforce it. It is not our province to rectify policy or political judgments by the Legislative Branch, however egregiously they may disserve the public interest. But where the statutory language and legislative history, as in this case, need not be construed to reach such a result, I view it as the duty of this Court to adopt a permissible construction that accords with some modicum of common sense and the public weal. . . .

II

Today the Court, like the Court of Appeals below, adopts a reading of § 7 of the Act that gives it a retroactive effect and disregards 12 years of consistently expressed congressional intent to complete the Tellico Project. With all due respect, I view this result as an extreme example of a literalist construction, not required by the language of the Act and adopted without regard to its manifest purpose. Moreover, it ignores established canons of statutory construction.

A

The starting point in statutory construction is, of course, the language of § 7 itself. [Citation.] I agree that it can be viewed as a textbook example of fuzzy language, which can be read according to the "eye of the beholder." The critical words direct all federal agencies to take "such action [as may be] necessary to insure that actions authorized, funded, or carried out by them do not jeopardize the continued existence of . . . endangered species . . . or result in the destruction or modification of [a critical] habitat of such species . . . ." Respondents—as did the Sixth Circuit—read these words as sweepingly as possible to include all "actions" that any federal agency ever may take with respect to any federal project, whether completed or not.

The Court today embraces this sweeping construction. Under the Court's reasoning, the Act covers every existing federal installation, including great hydroelectric projects and reservoirs, every river and harbor project, and every national defense installation—however essential to the Nation's economic health and safety. The "actions" that an agency would be prohibited from "carrying out" would include the continued operation of such projects or any change necessary to preserve their continued usefulness. The only precondition, according to respondents, to thus destroying the usefulness of even the most important federal project in our country would be a finding by the Secretary of the Interior that a continuation of the project would threaten the survival or critical habitat of a newly discovered species of water spider or amoeba.

"[F]requently words of general meaning are used in a statute, words broad enough to include an act in question, and yet a consideration of the whole legislation, or of the circumstances surrounding its enactment, or of the absurd results which follow from giving such broad meaning to the words, makes it unreasonable to believe that the legislator intended to include the particular act." *Church of the Holy Trinity,* [citation]. The result that will follow in this case by virtue of the Court's reading of § 7 makes it unreasonable to believe that Congress intended that reading. Moreover, § 7 may be construed in a way that avoids an "absurd result" without doing violence to its language.

The critical word in § 7 is "actions" and its meaning is far from "plain." It is part of the phrase: "actions authorized, funded or carried out." In terms of planning and executing various activities, it seems evident that the "actions" referred to are not all actions that an agency can ever take, but rather actions that the agency is *deciding whether* to authorize, to fund, or to carry out. In short, these words reasonably may be read as applying only to *prospective actions, i. e.,* actions with respect to which the agency has reasonable decisionmaking alternatives still available, actions *not yet* carried out. At the time respondents brought this lawsuit, the Tellico Project was 80% complete at a cost of more than $78 million. The Court concedes that as of this time and for the purpose of deciding this case, the Tellico Dam Project is "completed" or "virtually completed and the dam is essentially ready for operation," [citation]. Thus, under a prospective reading of § 7, the action already had been "carried out" in terms of any remaining reasonable decisionmaking power. [Citations.]

This is a reasonable construction of the language and also is supported by the presumption against construing statutes to give them a retroactive effect. . . . [T] he "presumption is very strong that a statute was not meant to act retrospectively, and it ought never to receive such a construction if it is susceptible of any other." This is particularly true where a statute enacts a new regime of regulation. . . .

Similarly under § 7 of the Endangered Species Act, at some stage of a federal project, and certainly where a project has been completed, the agency no longer has a reasonable choice simply to abandon it. When that point is reached, as it was in this case, the presumption against retrospective interpretation is at its strongest. The Court today gives no weight to that presumption.

B

The Court recognizes that the first purpose of statutory construction is to ascertain the intent of the legislature. [Citation.] The Court's opinion reviews at length the legislative history, with quotations from Committee Reports and statements by Members of Congress. The Court then ends this discussion with curiously conflicting conclusions. . . .

If the relevant Committees that considered the Act, and the Members of Congress who voted on it, had been aware that the Act could be used to terminate major federal projects authorized years earlier and nearly completed, or to require the abandonment of essential and long-completed federal installations and edifices, we can be certain that there would have been hearings, testimony, and debate concerning consequences so wasteful, so inimical to purposes previously deemed important, and so likely to arouse public outrage. The absence of any such consideration by the Committees or in the floor debates indicates quite clearly that no one participating in the legislative process considered these consequences as within the intendment of the Act.

As indicated above, this view of legislative intent at the time of enactment is abundantly confirmed by the subsequent congressional actions and expressions. We have held, properly, that post-enactment statements by individual Members of Congress as to the meaning of a statute are entitled to little or no weight. [Citation.] The Court also has recognized that subsequent Appropriations Acts themselves are not necessarily entitled to significant weight in determining whether a prior statute has been superseded. [Citation.] But these precedents are inapposite. There was no effort here to "bootstrap" a post-enactment view of prior legislation by isolated statements of individual Congressmen. Nor is this a case where Congress, without explanation or comment upon the statute in question, merely has voted apparently inconsistent financial support in subsequent Appropriations Acts. Testimony on this precise issue was presented before congressional committees, and the Committee Reports for three consecutive years addressed the problem and affirmed their understanding of the original congressional intent. We cannot assume—as the Court suggests—that Congress, when it continued each year to approve the recommended appropriations, was unaware of the contents of the supporting Committee Reports. All this amounts to strong corroborative evidence that the interpretation of § 7 as not applying to completed or substantially completed projects reflects the initial legislative intent. [Citations.]

III

I have little doubt that Congress will amend the Endangered Species Act to prevent the grave consequences made possible by today's decision. Few, if any, Members of that body will wish to defend an interpretation of the Act that requires the waste of at least $53 million, [citation], and denies the people of the Tennessee Valley area the benefits of the reservoir that Congress intended to confer. There will be little sentiment to leave this dam standing before an empty reservoir, serving no purpose other than a conversation piece for incredulous tourists.

But more far reaching than the adverse effect on the people of this economically depressed area is the continuing threat to the operation of every federal project, no matter how important to the Nation. If Congress acts expeditiously, as may be anticipated, the Court's decision probably will have no lasting adverse consequences. But I had not thought it to be the province of this Court to force Congress into otherwise unnecessary action by interpreting a statute to produce a result no one intended.

[The dissent of JUSTICE REHNQUIST has been omitted.]

NOTES AND QUESTIONS

1.   Can you reconcile the Court's treatment of appropriations bills in *TVA v. Hill* and *Alaska Steamship*?

2.   Recall Dean John Manning's discussion in Section II.C, *supra*, concerning the major grounds of disagreement between textualists and purposivists. Textualists tend to view courts as acting as "faithful agents" of the legislature when they respect the enacted text as conclusive, even when the text fits poorly against the statute's apparent purpose, a view Judge Posner rather pointedly criticized in Section III.A.2.a, *supra*. By contrast, purposivists emphasize that courts can act as faithful agents when they serve more as "cooperative partners" of the legislature by ensuring that adherence to the text does not disregard the policy context that motivated the statute's enactment. Which, in your opinion, best characterizes the approach taken by the *TVA v. Hill* majority? By the dissent? What

interpretive methods do they draw on to support their preferred resolutions of the problems arising in this case?

3.   The majority claims that "the ordinary meaning of [the] plain language" of Section 7 of the ESA required its holding. Recall that the plain meaning rule rejects the resort to extratextual sources when the meaning of the statutory text is "plain." If the text was so clear, why do you think the majority dedicated such lengthy efforts to reviewing the legislative history of the ESA and the appropriations authorizations for the Dam? Why do you think the majority did not invoke the plain meaning rule and stop at the text of the statute itself?

4.   Would a court disinclined to consult legislative history come to the same conclusion as the majority? Consider this question again after reading Part V, Agency Interpretations of Statutes, and the case study on the Endangered Species Act and *Babbitt v. Sweet Home* (1995).

5.   The preceding questions highlight an important shift in statutory interpretation jurisprudence in the decades since the Burger Court's decision in *TVA v. Hill*. In large part, the Justices of the Warren Court and the Burger Court tended to draw readily on any interpretive methods and sources that would shed light on a given interpretive problem before the Court. For instance, all Justices on the Burger Court readily resorted to legislative history to ascertain the meaning of ambiguous statutory provisions, as evinced by the majority and dissenting opinions in *TVA v. Hill*. Following Justice Scalia's appointment to the Court, however, debates about the propriety of particular interpretive methods (especially legislative history) have increasingly become as heated as the underlying disagreements about the meaning of the statutory texts themselves, as evinced in *Bank One Chicago*, *supra* Section IV.B, by the colloquy between Justice Scalia and Justice Stevens, both of whom fully agreed on the outcome! What advantages—and disadvantages—can you identify in the more pragmatic interpretive approaches taken by the members of the Burger Court in *TVA v. Hill*?

6.   However pragmatic the Justices' interpretive approaches in *TVA v. Hill* may have been, the Court's decision in the end was starkly formalist, concluding that although stopping the Dam at near completion may have been nonsensical in the extreme, Section 7 of the ESA demanded it. Such formalism, of course, is easier to swallow if the legislature can readily amend the statute to correct problems in the prior version of the text. Indeed, commentators have noted that all nine Justices deciding *TVA v. Hill* seemed openly to expect Congress to overrule the Court's decision. Professor Elizabeth Garrett has interpreted "the tone of the final paragraphs" of Chief Justice Burger's majority opinion as suggesting he "would not characterize the rules as sensible," and Justice Powell's dissent was even clearer in expressing the view that Congress would amend the ESA to correct the "grave consequences made possible by today's decision." Sure enough, Congress acted swiftly to amend the ESA by creating an administrative process to provide for exemptions from the Act. See Elizabeth Garrett, *The Story of TVA v. Hill (1978): Congress Has the Last Word, in* Statutory Interpretation Stories 58–91 (Eskridge, Frickey & Garrett eds. 2011). Do you think the Court's expectation that Congress would revise the statute influenced the Court in its decision in *TVA v. Hill*? Should it have?

7.   Contrast the formalism of the outcome in *TVA v. Hill* with the formalism of the dissent's position in *King v. Burwell*, *supra* Section III.A.2.a. Are the consequences of formalism any harder to stomach if it is well known that a congressional remedy is *not* likely to be forthcoming, as the dissent no doubt knew in *Burwell*? Should that background knowledge affect how courts resolve interpretive ambiguity in statutes, even at the margins? To that end, do you think the lack of a probable legislative remedy at least partially motivated Judge Posner's critique of the *Burwell* dissent's formalism, or are there principled grounds for objection regardless of the availability of a legislative "fix?" Keep this dynamic in mind when you consider legislative overrides of judicial interpretations in Section VII.C.2, *infra*.

8.   As the Court's discussion of the legislative history of the ESA as well as the Dam's appropriations indicates, legislative history contains not only documentary evidence of various legislators' involvement in drafting and developing a given statute, but also the relevant agencies' participation. Professor Jarrod Shobe has identified how agency legislative history can be an underappreciated source of extratextual evidence of the statute's purpose and meaning:

> Much like congressional legislative history, agency legislative history comes in many different forms, . . . [and] the various types of agency legislative history have influenced statutory interpretation. While scholars have rarely discussed the existence of agency legislative history, courts have, albeit infrequently and quietly, used agency legislative history as part of interpretation for many decades. . . .
>
> [There are] two broad types of agency-Congress communications that are part of the history of a piece of legislation[:] informal agency-Congress legislative communications, like phone calls and emails between staffers, . . . [and] formal written or spoken communications with Congress, which are generally documented and often publicly available. . . .
>
> Agencies communicate with Congress during the legislative process in ways beyond drafting and revising legislation, yet these types of legislative communications have gone almost entirely unnoticed in legal literature. Agencies engage in various types of formal communications with Congress to express opinions about legislation, to raise issues with legislation, and to suggest changes to legislation. . . .
>
> Another way in which agencies participate in the legislative process is through testimony in congressional hearings. Congress regularly invites agencies to testify about particular issues or proposed legislation. This testimony is drafted within an agency the same way a legislative proposal would be: the relevant bureau creates a draft and then that draft goes through an internal agency clearance process and OMB clearance before it is submitted to

Congress. This testimony is therefore meant to reflect official administration policy. . . .

Scholars and judges already consider congressional hearings to be a type of legislative history, since hearings are almost always publicly available. However, scholars have not emphasized the importance of agency testimony. Because agencies are closely involved in drafting and revising legislation, their testimony is likely to be informative and accurate in explaining how legislation is intended to work. It is also very likely that committee members form their opinions on legislation based on how it is described by agencies and rely on representations made by agencies of how legislation will be carried out after enactment. . . .

Agency legislative analysis also commonly occurs during agency testimony in congressional hearings. Because this testimony is recorded in the Congressional Record and therefore always publicly available, courts have unsurprisingly cited to it frequently, most commonly when the agency was also involved in drafting the legislation. . . . For example, in *Tennessee Valley Authority v. Hill*, the famous snail darter case, the Supreme Court looked to testimony by various officials from the Department of Interior to support its broad reading of protections for endangered species under the Endangered Species Act. . . .

Jarrod Shobe, *Agency Legislative History*, 68 Emory L.J. 283 (2018).

You have already seen the important roles agencies can play in drafting legislation, as well as the role agency legislative history may play in informing subsequent judicial interpretations of such legislation. *See SEC v. Robert Collier & Co.*, Section IV.B, *supra*. As you read the next Part on agency interpretations of statutes, be on the lookout for other examples of agency involvement in statutory drafting, and evidence of agency legislative history in the judicial interpretations of those statutes.

PART V

AGENCY INTERPRETATIONS OF STATUTES

A. OVERVIEW OF THE ADMINISTRATIVE LAW PROCESS

No study of legislation would be complete without a review of perhaps the most important statutory interpreters outside of courts: administrative agencies. Administrative agencies interpret and apply statutes when they conduct adjudicatory proceedings which, for the parties involved, are essentially indistinguishable from court proceedings. Administrative agencies also interpret statutes when they promulgate rules, which for almost all intents and purposes, function with the same force of law as the statutes they interpret. They also provide (often non-binding) guidance to regulated parties as to what the law means, and how the agency will apply it. Finally, agencies also develop expertise in the meaning of the statutes they administer because they are often involved in drafting and updating legislation relevant to their regulatory ambit.

Although the federal courts are the interpreters of last resort for federal statutes, in many areas of law, agencies—not courts—engage in the bulk of the interpretation of statutes. Accordingly, courts have considered, whether and how to defer to the interpretations of administrative agencies overseeing and implementing statutes. The following provides an overview of these administrative functions in the U.S. legal system.

1. BACKGROUND AND HISTORY

Ronald M. Levin and Jeffrey S. Lubbers, Administrative Law and Process in a Nutshell 1–3 (6th ed. 2017), offer the following observations on the reasons for establishing administrative agencies (instead of relying on the courts and the legislature):

> Administrative agencies usually are created to deal with current crises or to redress serious social problems. Throughout the modern era of administrative regulation, which began in the late nineteenth century, the government's response to a public demand for action has often been to establish a new agency, or to grant new powers to an existing bureaucracy. Near the turn of the century, agencies like the Interstate Commerce Commission and the Federal Trade Commission were created in an attempt to control the anticompetitive conduct of monopolies and powerful corporations. . . . In the 1960's when the injustices of poverty and racial discrimination became an urgent national concern, the development of programs designed to redress these grievances expanded the scope of government administration. More recently, increased public concern about risks to human health and safety and threats to the natural environment, as well as national security concerns, have resulted in new agencies and new regulatory programs.

> The primary reason why administrative agencies have so frequently been called upon to deal with such diverse social problems is the great flexibility of the regulatory process. In comparison to courts or legislatures or elected executive officials, administrative agencies have several institutional strengths that equip them to deal with complex problems. Perhaps the most important of these strengths is specialized staffing: an agency is authorized to hire people with whatever mix of talents, skills and experience it needs to get the job done. Moreover, because the agency has responsibility for a limited area of public policy, it can develop the expertise that comes from continued exposure to a problem area. . . .

> However, these potential strengths of the administrative process can also be viewed as a threat to other important values. Administrative "flexibility" may simply be a mask for unchecked power, and in our society unrestrained government power has

traditionally been viewed with great and justifiable suspicion. Thus, the fundamental policy problem of the administrative process is how to design a system of checks which will minimize the risks of bureaucratic arbitrariness and overreaching, while preserving for the agencies the flexibility they need to act effectively.

For the historical context of the shift in lawmaking from legislatures to administrative agencies, consider the following developments traced in 1 Kristin E. Hickman & Richard J. Pierce, Jr., Administrative Law Treatise § 1.4 (6th ed. 2019):

> [T]he powers and roles of agencies increased and expanded significantly in the twentieth century. Peter Strauss has illustrated the change by comparing the Federal Railway Safety Appliances Act of 1893 with the National Traffic and Motor Vehicle Safety Act of 1966. *See* Peter L. Strauss, Legislative Theory and the Rule of Law: Some Comments on Rubin, 89 Colum. L. Rev. 427, 428–30 (1989). In both instances, Congress responded to the widespread perception that the then-dominant form of transportation was unsafe. Its 1966 response differed significantly, however, from its 1893 response. In the process of enacting the Federal Railway Safety Appliances Act, Congress debated and resolved the major policy issues concerning rail safety. Congress specified detailed safety rules in the statute itself. By contrast, in passing the Motor Vehicle Safety Act 70 years later, Congress debated and resolved none of the major policy issues. Rather, Congress instructed an agency to pursue motor vehicle safety subject only to loosely-worded general guidance in the statute, delegating broad policymaking discretion to the agency. Many contend that the scope and degree of government intervention and the complexity of modern society have combined to make it impossible for legislature to resolve most policy disputes by statute. . . .

For a broad perspective about the early development of American administrative law, one must seek help from a leading legal and social historian, such as James Willard Hurst. In his book, Law and Social Order in the United States 35–41 (1977), Hurst declared:

> One can plot a curve of statute law that begins at a modest and yet substantial level, rises considerably from the 1830's to the 1880's, then shows a marked increase of pitch and takes off into an ascending line, which in the 1970's shows no sign of turning down. . . . From the 1880's, but most markedly from the take-off decade of 1905–1915, the regulatory component of statute law became much more prominent and added considerably to the volume of legislation, a shift of emphasis that brought a new type of

statute law concerning organized relationships. The focus changed from enabling organized action to injecting more public management or supervision of affairs and providing more sustained, specialized means of defining and enforcing public policy. Symbolic of this turn of affairs were the statutes creating the modern federal and state administrative apparatus; typical was the shift from factory safety laws that simply commanded employers to provide safe work places to law implemented by provision for administrative rulemaking and inspection. . . . United States legal history began with distrust of and hence deliberate restriction of executive power and with only rudimentary administrative machinery. . . . Well into the last quarter of the nineteenth century legislative processes—especially in the states—were crude. Legislators worked with little experience and little precedent to guide their jobs; sessions were short; legislators were part-time amateurs at public policy making; only slowly did a standing committee system develop. . . . Our chart will show [no] great contribution to the body of law from executive offices or administrative agencies until the 1890's. . . . We can plot major executive administrative contributions from the decade 1905–1915, which first saw the grant of substantial rule-making, rule-enforcement, and adjudicative powers to executive offices and independent administrative agencies. . . . Indeed, by the mid-twentieth century the curve for administrative legislation perhaps topped that for statute law: by the 1950's lawyers with business clients and individuals with demands on the increasing service functions of government had to turn more to administrative rule books than to statute books to locate the legal frame of reference for their affairs.

Elihu Root, in a 1916 address as President of the American Bar Association, made a statement that could hardly be improved upon with the hindsight of nearly a century later:

There is one special field of law development which has manifestly become inevitable. We are entering upon the creation of a body of administrative law quite different in its machinery, its remedies, and its necessary safeguards from the old methods of regulation by specific statutes enforced by the courts. As any community passes from simple to complex conditions, the only way in which government can deal with the increased burdens thrown upon it is by the delegation of power to be exercised in detail by subordinate agents, subject to the control of general directions prescribed by superior authority. The necessities of our situation have already led to an extensive employment of that method. . . . Before these agencies the old doctrine prohibiting the delegation of legislative power has virtually retired from the field and given up the fight. There will be no withdrawal from these experiments. We shall go on; we shall expand them, whether we approve theoretically or not, because such agencies furnish protection to rights and obstacles to wrongdoing which under our new social and industrial conditions cannot be practically accomplished by the old and simple procedure of legislatures and courts as in the last generation.

Elihu Root, Public Service by the Bar: Address by Elihu Root as President of the American Bar Association at the Annual Meeting in Chicago 14–15, reprinted in 41 A.B.A.R. 355[,] (1916). In his clarity of perception, Elihu Root may have been a generation or more ahead of other leaders of the bar. At the same time, he uttered important words of caution:

If we are to continue a government of limited powers, these agencies of regulation must themselves be regulated. The limits of their power over the citizen must be fixed and determined. The rights of the citizen against them must be made plain. A system of administrative law must be developed, and that with us is still in its infancy, crude and imperfect.

Id. at 15.

2. ADMINISTRATIVE ADJUDICATION

The courts are our society's traditional instrumentalities for the authoritative disposition of controversies and, at the start of the 20th century, seemed to have a virtual monopoly of the public business of dispute-settlement. But just as legislation has made great inroads into what were once the largely exclusive preserves of the case law, administrative agencies like the National Labor Relations Board and the Federal Trade Commission have come to exercise powers of adjudication in many areas of American social and economic life.

The following are examples of disputes remitted to administrative adjudication. If a person has a disputed claim for federal retirement benefits, he or she does not begin by going to court to sue on it; the claim will be judged and authoritatively determined, at least as a matter of first instance, by an adjudicatory official in the Social Security Administration. A power company that wishes to construct a nuclear reactor applies for the required license not to a court but to the Nuclear Regulatory Commission, which, after proper hearing and deliberation by its atomic safety and licensing board, will grant or deny the application.

Administrative agencies entrusted with power to hear and pass upon claims, applications and charges of law violation are found everywhere in the federal governmental structure, sometimes as divisions within cabinet departments, sometimes as independent regulatory establishments. Quantitatively, far more controversies are decided by federal administrative agencies than by all the federal courts.*

Administrative adjudication has similarly been a growth industry in the state and local governments. Administrative bodies are empowered to issue or refuse, and to revoke or suspend, the licenses required to engage in a wide variety of professions and businesses. Workers' compensation commissions hear and decide claims arising from industrial accidents, and public utility commissions pass on applications for rate increases submitted by gas, light and water companies. Every municipal government has its administrative complex of local tax boards, licensing officials, zoning appeals boards and the like, all performing in one way or another the essentially judicial function—or quasi-judicial function—of hearing and deciding particular claims, charges and disputes. The decisions reached by federal, state and local administrative agencies are, to one or another extent, subject to judicial review in the (regular) courts, but the scope of this review is usually limited and constitutes not a retrial of the case or claim but an inquiry into whether the administrative adjudicative agency has acted illegally, arbitrarily or without sufficient evidence to support its findings.

In the early part of the twentieth century, many lawyers looked with distrust and hostility on the proliferation of administrative agencies and the extension of their decision-making powers. Despite this, the growing consensus seemed to be that administrative adjudication was inevitable, given the vastly increased range of government's regulatory and public welfare programs, and, being here to stay, should be ordered and regularized. The great step in this direction, so far as the federal agencies are concerned, was the enactment in 1946 of the Administrative Procedure Act, codified at 5 U.S.C. §§ 551 *et seq.* By this Act, passed by the unanimous vote of both houses of Congress, the adjudicative processes of the federal agencies were largely "judicialized," that is, subjected to uniform procedural standards designed to secure fairness in the hearing, determination and review of particular cases. Section 554 supplies the broad rules of procedure that agencies must follow when

---

* *See, e.g.,* Judith Resnik, *Migrating, Morphing, and Vanishing: The Empirical and Normative Puzzles of Declining Trial Rates in Courts,* 1 J. Empirical Legal Stud. 783, 799 (2004) (finding that the SSA, INS, Board of Veterans Appeals, and EEOC conducted 720 thousand hearings in 2001, compared to 85 thousand federal trials). Adjudication Research, a joint project of the Administrative Conference of the US and Stanford Law School, collects data on administrative processes. *See* http://acus.law.stanford.edu. During the most recently available year for which data are available, FY2013, there were 1,790,052 administrative adjudication hearings across all agencies. By contrast, in 2013 a total of 363,914 civil and criminal cases were filed in the federal district courts. District court filings declined a few percentage points a year from 2013–2016, spiked 10% in 2017, fell 16% in 2018, then continued the low single-digit decline in 2019. *See* https://www.uscourts.gov/statistics-reports/analysis-reports/federal-judicial-caseload-statistics.

engaging in adjudication required by statute. Section 554 also sets out the rights held by parties before administrative hearings, as well as all other interested parties. Many states have enacted similar legislation to regularize the processes of administrative adjudication in the state and local governments. More recently, a new generation of scholars and jurists have raised renewed questions about the legitimacy and legality of such practices.*

3. RULE PROMULGATION

a. FEDERAL ADMINISTRATIVE REGULATIONS

Administrative adjudication is an important element in the contemporary American pattern of controversy-settlement. But administrative agencies do not only apply law in particular cases; they also make law, and the general rules formulated and prescribed by the agencies constitute a major ingredient of American law. Dozens of federal agencies, some established as independent commissions and others as more or less separate branches within cabinet departments, regulate large segments of business and social life. Congress often entrusts an agency with subordinate rulemaking authority, subordinate in the sense that the regulations made and issued by an administrative agency must be within the scope of the authority Congress delegates to it.

Regulations prescribed by a federal agency within the scope of its delegated rule-making power are authoritative norms of the legal order and, assuming the constitutional validity of the underlying federal statute, superior in authoritativeness to state law. Thus a properly issued regulation of the Securities and Exchange Commission, the National Labor Relations Board, or the Food and Drug Administration has legal effect everywhere in the United States, and any conflicting rule on the same subject in a state's case law or statutes, or even in its constitution, must yield to the superior authority of the federal regulation. The Administrative Procedure Act ("the APA"), 5 U.S.C. § 551 *et seq.*, governs the rulemaking processes of the federal administrative agencies, like their adjudicatory processes. Depending on the particular statutory instruction to the agency, an agency may engage in either "formal" or "informal" rulemaking. Under the APA, what is known as "formal" rulemaking is made "on the record after an opportunity for an agency hearing." 5 U.S.C. § 553(c); Sections 556 and 557 set out the rules for such hearings. By contrast, an agency may undertake "informal" rulemaking by complying with the "notice-and-comment" provisions of Section 553, which afford members of the public the right to be given

---

* Prominent critics include: Philip Hamburger, Is Administrative Law Unlawful? (2014); Richard Epstein, The Dubious Morality of Modern Administrative Law (2020); Joseph Postell, Bureaucracy in America: The Administrative States' Challenge to Constitutional Government (2017); David Schoenbrod, Power Without Responsibility: How Congress Abuses the People through Delegation (1995); Gary Lawson, *The Rise and Rise of the Administrative State*, 107 HARV. L. REV. 1231 (1994).

notice of proposed rules as well as the opportunity participate in rulemaking through the submission of data, views, and arguments. While the agency must respond to the major threads of the public's comments, the APA does not require that the agency actually change course in response to significant objections.

Rules promulgated through formal and informal rulemaking are considered "legislative" (or "substantive") rules, and so are accorded a weight similar to legislation. But under the APA, agencies can also promulgate "interpretative rules, general statements of policy, or rules of agency organization, procedure, or practice" without undergoing notice-and-comment rulemaking or providing a hearing. Interpretative rules (commonly referred to as "interpretive rules") and other forms of agency guidance can serve as the agency's official understanding of a particular statutory provision, but because an agency need not undertake formal or informal rulemaking to promulgate interpretive rules or guidance, these interpretations are generally accorded less weight by reviewing courts. As you will see later in this Part, the nature of the rule, and the rulemaking procedure that produced it, may be important considerations in deciding the weight to accord to the agency's interpretation of a statute. Finally, note also that interpretive rules can provide interpretations of an agency's own rules (both legislative and interpretive), meaning that agency rules may sometimes constitute interpretations of interpretations!

Congress mandates publication of administrative regulations in a daily and official gazette called the Federal Register, and further requires that regulations be systematically arranged and codified, by a continuing process, in the Code of Federal Regulations. Law school courses on Administrative Law intensively examine the rule-making functions of administrative agencies, as well as their adjudicatory and executive (largely enforcement) functions.

b.   STATE ADMINISTRATIVE REGULATIONS

State governments have vested administrative agencies with the provision of public services and the supervision of private activity. The list of regulated activities differs from state to state, reflecting differences in economic conditions and in prevailing political attitudes, but it is everywhere a long list. State and local agencies and officials prescribe regulations on an enormous variety of subjects: agriculture, civil service, fishing, horse racing, water resources and zoning, to mention just a few. State administrative regulations, in their vast aggregate, loom large in the picture of American legislation.

B. AGENCY INTERPRETATIONS OF STATUTES

Many statutes task administrative agencies with implementing complex regulatory schemes on the basis of relatively bare statutory instructions. While legislative delegations to administrative agencies may provoke constitutional questions about the separation of powers, they also raise important and unique interpretive issues for courts. For most regulatory statutes, the relevant agencies do the bulk of the interpretive work in the course of administering statutes, and policy considerations often inform these interpretations. Under what circumstances should courts defer to agency interpretations, especially when agencies interpret statutes in light of policy considerations for which agencies—and not courts—possess the relevant expertise? Should these factors influence the manner in which courts interpret statutes directed primarily at agencies? This section explores these tensions.

1. JUDICIAL DEFERENCE TO AGENCY INTERPRETATIONS OF STATUTES

Perhaps the most important question for courts reviewing agency interpretations of statutes is the weight to accord the agency's interpretation, particularly when the court might on its own have adopted a different interpretation. Properly speaking, when a court defers to the agency, it adopts the agency's interpretation *even if* the court believes a different interpretation might be preferable; so long as the agency's interpretation is *reasonable*, the court will let the agency's interpretation carry the day. Agencies no doubt have greater expertise than courts as to the substantive *policy* considerations at stake when deciding how to implement a given statutory scheme; nevertheless, Article III courts retain the final say as to the legal meaning of the statute in question. In the wake of the emergence of numerous and prominent federal administrative agencies during the New Deal era—and prior to the enactment of the APA in 1946—courts faced increasingly frequent difficulties in deciding how to review an agency policy determination that also put forward a particular interpretation of the relevant statute, as well as how much weight—if any—to give the agency's determination as to the statute's meaning. During this period, the Supreme Court developed what became known as "*Skidmore* deference," so named for the doctrine that arose from the following case:

Skidmore et al. v. Swift & Co.
Supreme Court of the United States, 1944.
323 U.S. 134, 65 S.Ct. 161, 89 L.Ed. 124.

■ MR. JUSTICE JACKSON delivered the [unanimous] opinion of the Court.

Seven employees of the Swift and Company packing plant at Fort Worth, Texas, brought an action under the Fair Labor Standards Act, 29 U.S.C.A. s 201 et seq., to recover overtime, liquidated damages, and attorneys' fees, totalling approximately $77,000. The District Court rendered judgment denying this claim wholly, and the Circuit Court of Appeals for the Fifth Circuit affirmed.

It is not denied that the daytime employment of these persons was working time within the Act. . . . Under their oral agreement of employment, however, petitioners undertook to stay in the fire hall on the Company premises, or within hailing distance, three and a half to four nights a week. This involved no task except to answer alarms, either because of fire or because the sprinkler was set off for some other reason. No fires occurred during the period in issue, the alarms were rare, and the time required for their answer rarely exceeded an hour. . . . The trial court found . . . as a 'conclusion of law' that 'the time plaintiffs spent in the fire hall subject to call to answer fire alarms does not constitute hours worked, for which overtime compensation is due them under the Fair Labor Standards Act, as interpreted by the Administrator and the Courts,' and in its opinion . . . observed, 'of course we know pursuing such pleasurable occupations or performing such personal chores does not constitute work.' The Circuit Court of Appeals affirmed.

. . . [W]e hold that no principle of law found either in the statute or in Court decisions precludes waiting time from also being working time. We have not attempted to, and we cannot, lay down a legal formula to resolve cases so varied in their facts as are the many situations in which employment involves waiting time. Whether in a concrete case such time falls within or without the Act is a question of fact to be resolved by appropriate findings of the trial court. [Citation.] . . . We do not minimize the difficulty of such an inquiry where the arrangements of the parties have not contemplated the problem posed by the statute. But it does not differ in nature or in the standards to guide judgment from that which frequently confronts courts where they must find retrospectively the effect of contracts as to matters which the parties failed to anticipate or explicitly to provide for.

Congress did not utilize the services of an administrative agency to find facts and to determine in the first instance whether particular cases fall within or without the Act. Instead, it put this responsibility on the courts. [Citation.] But it did create the office of Administrator, impose upon him a variety of duties, endow him with powers to inform himself of conditions in industries and employments subject to the Act, and put on him the duties of bringing injunction actions to restrain violations. Pursuit of his duties has accumulated a considerable experience in the problems of ascertaining working time in employments involving periods of inactivity and a knowledge of the customs prevailing in reference to their solution. From these he is obliged to reach conclusions as to conduct without the law, so that he should seek injunctions to stop it, and that within the law, so that he has no call to interfere. He has set forth his views of the application of the Act under different circumstances in an interpretative bulletin and in informal rulings. They provide a practical guide to employers and employees as to how the office representing the public interest in its enforcement will seek to apply it. [Citation.]

The Administrator thinks the problems presented by inactive duty require a flexible solution, rather than the all-in or all-out rules respectively urged by the parties in this case, and his Bulletin endeavors to suggest standards and examples to guide in particular situations. . . . In general, the answer depends 'upon the degree to which the employee is free to engage in personal activities during periods of idleness when he is subject to call and the number of consecutive hours that the employee is subject to call without being required to perform active work.' 'Hours worked are not limited to the time spent in active labor but include time given by the employee to the employer.' . . . [T]he conclusion of the Administrator, as expressed in the brief amicus curiae, is that the general tests which he has suggested point to the exclusion of sleeping and eating time of these employees from the work-week and the inclusion of all other on-call time. . . .

There is no statutory provision as to what, if any, deference courts should pay to the Administrator's conclusions. And, while we have given them notice, we have had no occasion to try to prescribe their influence. The rulings of this Administrator are not reached as a result of hearing adversary proceedings in which he finds facts from evidence and reaches conclusions of law from findings of fact. They are not, of course, conclusive, even in the cases with which they directly deal, much less in those to which they apply only by analogy. They do not constitute an interpretation of the Act or a standard for judging factual situations which binds a district court's processes, as an authoritative pronouncement of a higher court might do. But the Administrator's policies are made in pursuance of official duty, based upon more specialized experience and broader investigations and information than is likely to come to a judge in a particular case. They do determine the policy which will guide applications for enforcement by injunction on behalf of the Government. Good administration of the Act and good judicial administration alike require that the standards of public enforcement and those for determining private rights shall be at variance only where justified by very good reasons. The fact that the Administrator's policies and standards are not reached by trial in adversary form does not mean that they are not entitled to respect. This Court has long given considerable and in some cases decisive weight to Treasury Decisions and to interpretative regulations of the Treasury and of other bodies that were not of adversary origin.

We consider that the rulings, interpretations and opinions of the Administrator under this Act, while not controlling upon the courts by reason of their authority, do constitute a body of experience and informed judgment to which courts and litigants may properly resort for guidance. The weight of such a judgment in a particular case will depend upon the thoroughness evident in its consideration, the validity of its reasoning, its consistency with earlier and later pronouncements, and all those factors which give it power to persuade, if lacking power to control.

... [I]n this case, although the District Court referred to the Administrator's Bulletin, its evaluation and inquiry were apparently restricted by its notion that waiting time may not be work, an understanding of the law which we hold to be erroneous. Accordingly, the judgment is reversed and the cause remanded for further proceedings consistent herewith.

The Court's observation in *Skidmore*, that the agency has the "power to persuade, if [not the] power to control" the final interpretation of a statute within its enforcement power, became known over time as "*Skidmore* deference." After *Skidmore*, a court reviewing an agency's interpretation considered "the thoroughness evident in its consideration, the validity of its reasoning, its consistency with earlier and later pronouncements, and all those factors which give it power to persuade." Nevertheless, the Court in *Skidmore* also recognized that "[t]here is no statutory provision as to what, if any, deference courts should pay to the Administrator's conclusions." *Skidmore* was decided two years before Congress enacted the Administrative Procedure Act, 5 U.S.C. §§ 551 *et seq.*, which governs the procedures for administrative agencies implementing—and interpreting—federal law. It also provides for judicial review of "final agency action," *id.* § 704. Despite this, the APA's judicial review provisions are *also* silent as to what deference, if any, courts should pay to an agency's interpretation of a statute it implements. That question was answered, at least in part, in the landmark 1984 case *Chevron v. Natural Resources Defense Council*.

Chevron implicates important tensions between agency expertise and judicial supremacy that are often at the heart of many questions about agency interpretations of statutes. When reviewing agency interpretations of statutes, courts will often need to resolve a series of related, and often nested, questions raised in the cases in the following section:

1.   What signals must Congress give to indicate that the agency may regulate with the force of law, and, in the event of ambiguity, who (between the agency and the court) decides the scope of the agency's authority? As you will soon learn, this is what is known as the "*Chevron* Step Zero" inquiry, named after *Chevron*, *infra*. *Chevron* Step Zero was first formally elaborated in a later case, *United States v. Mead*, *infra* (about tariff rates for binders, of all things!). Depending on the degree of ambiguity of the statute, questions sometimes arise about whether the court or the agency should decide if the statute delegates authority to regulate with the force of law to the agency, as in *City of Arlington v. FCC*, *infra* (cell tower permits).

2.   If the agency has *some* kind of lawmaking authority, but the nature of that authority is ambiguous, are the agency's actions reasonably within the bounds of the delegation Congress has given it, or

are they so sweeping as to require a clear statement from Congress that the agency may act in such sweeping fashion? Although infrequently applied, this is known as the "Major Questions" doctrine, and as you will see, when the Court does apply it, it has done so in instances of especially high-profile agency activity such as *MCI v. AT&T* (telecommunications rate modifications) and *King v. Burwell* (state insurance exchanges), *supra*, and *FDA v. Brown & Williamson Tobacco, infra* (tobacco regulation). As you will see, some scholars question whether this doctrine should survive in the wake of the U.S. Supreme Court's ruling in *City of Arlington.*

3.   If the agency *does* have undisputed lawmaking authority in this area, are Congress's instructions to the agency sufficiently clear as to require the agency to act in a particular fashion, and if so, has the agency so acted? This is known as the *"Chevron* Step One" inquiry, a question considered at length in the case study on *Babbitt v. Sweet Home, infra* (incidental takings under the Endangered Species Act).

4.   Finally, if Congress's instructions to the agency *are* ambiguous, are the agency's interpretation and application permissible or reasonable constructions of the statute? This is known as the *"Chevron* Step Two" inquiry, which raises questions about whether the agency's interpretation warrants deference even when it conflicts with a lower court's prior interpretation, as in *National Cable & Telecommunications Assoc. v. Brand X Internet Services, infra* (regulatory treatment of internet service providers).

A reasonable reader may query whether these questions are entirely distinct; as you will encounter in this Part, judges often disagree about precisely which of these questions is at issue; in particular, much hangs on deciding just how clear Congress's instructions must be, and just how ambiguous its delegation is.

Chevron, U.S.A., Inc. v. Natural Resources Defense Council, Inc.

Supreme Court of the United States, 1984.
467 U.S. 837, 104 S.Ct. 2778, 81 L.Ed.2d 694.

■ JUSTICE STEVENS delivered the opinion of the Court[, in which CHIEF JUSTICE BURGER, JUSTICE BRENNAN, JUSTICE WHITE, JUSTICE BLACKMUN, and JUSTICE POWELL joined].

In the Clean Air Act Amendments of 1977, Pub.L. 95–95, 91 Stat. 685, Congress enacted certain requirements applicable to States that had not achieved the national air quality standards established by the Environmental Protection Agency (EPA) pursuant to earlier legislation. The amended Clean Air Act required these "nonattainment" States to establish a permit program regulating "new or modified major stationary sources" of air pollution. Generally, a permit may not be issued for a new or modified major stationary source unless several stringent conditions are met. The EPA regulation promulgated to implement this permit requirement allows a State to adopt a plantwide definition of the term "stationary source." Under this definition, an existing plant that contains several pollution-emitting devices may install or modify one piece of equipment without meeting the permit conditions if the alteration will not increase the total emissions from the plant. The question presented by these cases is whether EPA's decision to allow States to treat all of the pollution-emitting devices within the same industrial grouping as though they were encased within a single "bubble" is based on a reasonable construction of the statutory term "stationary source."

I

The EPA regulations containing the plantwide definition of the term stationary source were promulgated on October 14, 1981. 46 Fed. Reg. 50766. Respondents filed a timely petition for review in the United States Court of Appeals for the District of Columbia Circuit pursuant to 42 U.S.C. § 7607(b)(1).[4] The Court of Appeals set aside the regulations. *Natural Resources Defense Council, Inc. v. Gorsuch*, 685 F.2d 718 (D.C. Cir. 1982).

The court observed that the relevant part of the amended Clean Air Act "does not explicitly define what Congress envisioned as a 'stationary source,' to which the permit program . . . should apply," and further stated that the precise issue was not "squarely addressed in the legislative history." *Id.*, at 273, 685 F.2d, at 723. In light of its conclusion that the legislative history bearing on the question was "at best contradictory," it reasoned that "the purposes of the nonattainment program should guide our decision here." *Id.*, at 276, n. 39, 685 F.2d, at 726, n. 39.[5] Based on two of its precedents concerning the applicability of the bubble concept to certain Clean Air Act programs, the court stated that the bubble concept was "mandatory" in programs designed merely to maintain existing air quality, but held that it was "inappropriate" in programs enacted to improve air quality. *Id.*, at 276, 685 F.2d, at 726. Since the purpose of the permit program—its "raison d'être," in the court's view—was to improve air quality, the court held that the bubble concept was inapplicable in these cases under its prior precedents. *Ibid.* It therefore set aside the regulations embodying the bubble concept as contrary to law. We . . . now reverse.

---

[4]   Petitioners, Chevron U.S.A. Inc., American Iron and Steel Institute, American Petroleum Institute, Chemical Manufacturers Association, Inc., General Motors Corp., and Rubber Manufacturers Association were granted leave to intervene and argue in support of the regulation.

[5]   The court remarked in this regard:

"We regret, of course, that Congress did not advert specifically to the bubble concept's application to various Clean Air Act programs, and note that a further clarifying statutory directive would facilitate the work of the agency and of the court in their endeavors to serve the legislators' will." 685 F.2d at 726 n.39.

The basic legal error of the Court of Appeals was to adopt a static judicial definition of the term "stationary source" when it had decided that Congress itself had not commanded that definition. . . .

II

When a court reviews an agency's construction of the statute which it administers, it is confronted with two questions. First, always, is the question whether Congress has directly spoken to the precise question at issue. If the intent of Congress is clear, that is the end of the matter; for the court, as well as the agency, must give effect to the unambiguously expressed intent of Congress.[9] If, however, the court determines Congress has not directly addressed the precise question at issue, the court does not simply impose its own construction on the statute, as would be necessary in the absence of an administrative interpretation. Rather, if the statute is silent or ambiguous with respect to the specific issue, the question for the court is whether the agency's answer is based on a permissible construction of the statute.

The power of an administrative agency to administer a congressionally created . . . program necessarily requires the formulation of policy and the making of rules to fill any gap left, implicitly or explicitly, by Congress. Morton v. Ruiz, 415 U.S. 199, 231 (1974). If Congress has explicitly left a gap for the agency to fill, there is an express delegation of authority to the agency to elucidate a specific provision of the statute by regulation. Such legislative regulations are given controlling weight unless they are arbitrary, capricious, or manifestly contrary to the statute. Sometimes the legislative delegation to an agency on a particular question is implicit rather than explicit. In such a case, a court may not substitute its own construction of a statutory provision for a reasonable interpretation made by the administrator of an agency.

We have long recognized that considerable weight should be accorded to an executive department's construction of a statutory scheme it is entrusted to administer, and the principle of deference to administrative interpretations

> has been consistently followed by this Court whenever decision as to the meaning or reach of a statute has involved reconciling conflicting policies, and a full understanding of the force of the statutory policy in the given situation has depended upon more than ordinary knowledge respecting the matters subjected to agency regulations. [Citation.]. . . If this choice represents a reasonable accommodation of conflicting policies that were committed to the agency's care by the statute, we should not disturb it unless it appears from the statute or its legislative

---

[9] The judiciary is the final authority on issues of statutory construction and must reject administrative constructions which are contrary to clear congressional intent. *See, e.g.,* FEC v. Democratic Senatorial Campaign Committee, 454 U.S. 27, 32 (1981) [further citations omitted]. If a court, employing traditional tools of statutory construction, ascertains that Congress had an intention on the precise question at issue, that intention is the law and must be given effect.

history that the accommodation is not one that Congress would have sanctioned." United States v. Shimer, 367 U.S. 374, 382, 383 (1961).

Accord Capital Cities Cable, Inc. v. Crisp, 467 U.S. 691, 699–700 (1984).

In light of these well-settled principles it is clear that the Court of Appeals misconceived the nature of its role in reviewing the regulations at issue. Once it determined, after its own examination of the legislation, that Congress did not actually have an intent regarding the applicability of the bubble concept to the permit program, the question before it was not whether in its view the concept is "inappropriate" in the general context of a program designed to improve air quality, but whether the Administrator's view that it is appropriate in the context of this particular program is a reasonable one. Based on the examination of the legislation and its history which follows, we agree with the Court of Appeals that Congress did not have a specific intention on the applicability of the bubble concept in these cases, and conclude that the EPA's use of that concept here is a reasonable policy choice for the agency to make.

III

[The Court then reviewed the legislative history at length, remarking that the issue before it concerned "one phase" of a "small portion" of "a lengthy, detailed, technical, complex, and comprehensive response to a major social issue," the Clean Air Act Amendments of 1977, that in turn was only part of a much larger statutory scheme under EPA's administration. "The legislative history of the portion of the 1977 Amendments dealing with nonattainment areas," it remarked, "does not contain any specific comment on the 'bubble concept' or the question whether a plantwide definition of a stationary source is permissible under the permit program. It does, however, plainly disclose that in the permit program Congress sought to accommodate the conflict between the economic interest in permitting capital improvements to continue and the environmental interest in improving air quality."

Turning to the administrative history of implementation, the Court noted that EPA had at first proposed interpretations like that under challenge.] . . .

VI

. . . In August 1980, however, the EPA adopted a regulation that, in essence, applied the basic reasoning of the Court of Appeals in these cases. The EPA took particular note of the two then-recent Court of Appeals decisions, which had created the bright-line rule that the "bubble concept" should be employed in a program designed to maintain air quality but not in one designed to enhance air quality. Relying heavily on those cases, EPA adopted a dual definition of "source" for nonattainment areas that required a permit whenever a change in either the entire plant, or one of its components, would result in a significant increase in emissions even if the increase was completely offset by reductions elsewhere in the plant. . . .

In 1981 a new administration took office and initiated a "Government-wide reexamination of regulatory burdens and complexities." 46 Fed. Reg. 16281. In the context of that review, the EPA reevaluated the various arguments that had been advanced in connection with the proper definition of the term "source" and concluded that the term should be given the same definition in both nonattainment areas and PSD areas.

In explaining its conclusion, the EPA first noted that the definitional issue was not squarely addressed in either the statute or its legislative history and therefore that the issue involved an agency "judgment as how to best carry out the Act." *Ibid.* It then set forth several reasons for concluding that the plantwide definition was more appropriate. . . .

VII

. . . Based on our examination of the legislative history, we agree with the Court of Appeals that it is unilluminating. The general remarks pointed to by respondents "were obviously not made with this narrow issue in mind and they cannot be said to demonstrate a Congressional desire. . . ." Jewell Ridge Coal Corp. v. Mine Workers, 325 U.S. 161, 168–169 (1945). . . . We find that the legislative history as a whole is silent on the precise issue before us. It is, however, consistent with the view that the EPA should have broad discretion in implementing the policies of the 1977 Amendments.

More importantly, that history plainly identifies the policy concerns that motivated the enactment; the plantwide definition is fully consistent with one of those concerns—the allowance of reasonable economic growth—and, whether or not we believe it most effectively implements the other, we must recognize that the EPA has advanced a reasonable explanation for its conclusion that the regulations serve the environmental objectives as well. Indeed, its reasoning is supported by the public record developed in the rulemaking process, as well as by certain private studies.[37]

Our review of the EPA's varying interpretations of the word "source"—both before and after the 1977 Amendments—convinces us that the agency primarily responsible for administering this important legislation has consistently interpreted it flexibly—not in a sterile textual vacuum, but in the context of implementing policy decisions in a technical and complex arena. The fact that the agency has from time to

---

[37] "Economists have proposed that economic incentives be substituted for the cumbersome administrative-legal framework. The objective is to make the profit and cost incentives that work so well in the marketplace work for pollution control. . . . [The 'bubble' or 'netting' concept] is a first attempt in this direction. By giving a plant manager flexibility to find the places and processes within a plant that control emissions most cheaply, pollution control can be achieved more quickly and cheaply." L. Lave & G. Omenn, Cleaning Air: Reforming the Clean Air Act 28 (1981) (footnote omitted).

time changed its interpretation of the term "source" does not, as respondents argue, lead us to conclude that no deference should be accorded the agency's interpretation of the statute. An initial agency interpretation is not instantly carved in stone. On the contrary, the agency, to engage in informed rulemaking, must consider varying interpretations and the wisdom of its policy on a continuing basis. Moreover, the fact that the agency has adopted different definitions in different contexts adds force to the argument that the definition itself is flexible, particularly since Congress has never indicated any disapproval of a flexible reading of the statute.

Significantly, it was not the agency in 1980, but rather the Court of Appeals that read the statute inflexibly to command a plantwide definition for programs designed to maintain clean air and to forbid such a definition for programs designed to improve air quality. The distinction the court drew may well be a sensible one, but our labored review of the problem has surely disclosed that it is not a distinction that Congress ever articulated itself, or one that the EPA found in the statute before the courts began to review the legislative work product. We conclude that it was the Court of Appeals, rather than Congress or any of the decisionmakers who are authorized by Congress to administer this legislation, that was primarily responsible for the 1980 position taken by the agency.

. . . In these cases, the Administrator's interpretation represents a reasonable accommodation of manifestly competing interests and is entitled to deference: the regulatory scheme is technical and complex, the agency considered the matter in a detailed and reasoned fashion, and the decision involves reconciling conflicting policies. Congress intended to accommodate both interests, but did not do so itself on the level of specificity presented by these cases. Perhaps that body consciously desired the Administrator to strike the balance at this level, thinking that those with great expertise and charged with responsibility for administering the provision would be in a better position to do so; perhaps it simply did not consider the question at this level; and perhaps Congress was unable to forge a coalition on either side of the question, and those on each side decided to take their chances with the scheme devised by the agency. For judicial purposes, it matters not which of these things occurred.

Judges are not experts in the field, and are not part of either political branch of the Government. Courts must, in some cases, reconcile competing political interests, but not on the basis of the judges' personal policy preferences. In contrast, an agency to which Congress has delegated policy-making responsibilities may, within the limits of that delegation, properly rely upon the incumbent administration's views of wise policy to inform its judgments. While agencies are not directly accountable to the people, the Chief Executive is, and it is entirely appropriate for this political branch of the Government to make such policy choices—resolving the competing interests which Congress itself either inadvertently did not resolve, or intentionally left to be resolved by the agency charged with the administration of the statute in light of everyday realities.

When a challenge to an agency construction of a statutory provision, fairly conceptualized, really centers on the wisdom of the agency's policy, rather than whether it is a reasonable choice within a gap left open by Congress, the challenge must fail. In such a case, federal judges—who have no constituency—have a duty to respect legitimate policy choices made by those who do. The responsibilities for assessing the wisdom of such policy choices and resolving the struggle between competing views of the public interest are not judicial ones: "Our Constitution vests such responsibilities in the political branches." TVA v. Hill, 437 U.S. 153, 195 (1978). . . . [R]eversed.

It is so ordered.

■ JUSTICE MARSHALL and JUSTICE REHNQUIST took no part in the consideration or decision of these cases.

■ JUSTICE O'CONNOR took no part in the decision of these cases.

NOTE: WHICH AGENCY INTERPRETATIONS WARRANT *CHEVRON* DEFERENCE?

Chevron thus introduced a formal, two-stage analysis for judicial review of agency interpretations: (1) has Congress expressed its intent clearly in the statute, or is the statute ambiguous as to the relevant provision?; and (2) if the statute is ambiguous, is the agency's interpretation a permissible construction of the provision? Under *Chevron*, if Congress has spoken clearly as to the provision's meaning, there is no place for a "stage two" inquiry, and the agency must carry out the clearly expressed intent of Congress. *Chevron* is among the Court's most-cited statutory interpretation decisions of the past four decades, but that does not mean its holding is always easily applied. Indeed, as Professor Richard Pierce noted shortly after *Chevron* was decided, the proper application of *Chevron* requires deciding first whether the question at issue is one of law or policy:

> In determining whether an agency's interpretation of a statute involves an issue of law or policy, it is useful to analyze and characterize the issue prior to Congress' enactment of the statute in question. For example, in *Chevron* most would agree that, prior to the enactment of the Clean Air Act, the question of whether to limit emissions at the plant level or the level of each piece of combustion equipment is a pure question of policy. This question is but one of hundreds of policy issues that some institution of government must resolve in order to implement any regulatory program to reduce air pollution. In the process of enacting the Clean Air Act, or any other regulatory statute, Congress invariably resolves some policy issues but leaves to some other institution of government the task of resolving many other policy issues.

As the Court recognized in *Chevron*, Congress declines to resolve policy issues for many different reasons: Congress simply may have neglected to consider the issue; Congress may have believed that the agency was in a better position to resolve the issue; or finally, Congress may not have been able to forge a coalition or simply may have lacked the political courage necessary to resolve the issue, given that a resolution either way might damage the political future of many members of Congress. The general proposition that Congress cannot and does not resolve all the policy issues raised by its creation of a regulatory scheme probably is not at all controversial.

A more controversial point, however, may be that Congress resolves very few issues when it enacts a statute empowering an agency to regulate. Rather, Congress typically leaves the vast majority of policy issues, including many of the most important issues, for resolution by some other institution of government. Congress accomplishes this through several different statutory drafting techniques, including the use of empty standards, lists of unranked decisional goals, and contradictory standards. Thus, Congress declines to resolve many policy issues by using statutory language that is incapable of meaningful definition and application.

Once a court realizes that it is reviewing an agency's resolution of a policy issue, rather than an issue of law, comparative institutional analysis demonstrates that the agency is a more appropriate institution than a court to resolve the controversy. Because agencies are more accountable to the electorate than courts, agencies should have the dominant role in policy making when the choice is between agencies and courts. A court's function in reviewing a policy decision made by an agency should be the same whether the agency policy decision is made by interpreting an ambiguous statutory provision or by any other means of agency policy making. The court should affirm the agency's policy decision, and hence its statutory interpretation, if the policy is "reasonable." The court should reverse the agency's policy decision if the policy is arbitrary and capricious. Of course, in deciding whether the agency's policy decision is "reasonable," the court should review the agency's decision making process by which the agency determined that its choice of policy was consistent with statutory goals and the contextual facts of the controversy in question.

Richard J. Pierce, Chevron *and Its Aftermath: Judicial Review of Agency Interpretations of Statutory Provisions*, 41 Vand. L. Rev. 301 (1988).

Yet a court's work is not done once it determines that a statutory question is one of law rather than policy. This is because *Chevron* did not provide clear guidelines concerning which types of agency interpretations of law warrant *Chevron* deference in the first place. After all, agency interpretations arising from formal and informal rulemaking offer the opportunity for notice and comment from affected members of the public, and often carry the force of law, while interpretive rules and other forms of agency guidance, while highly influential, may not. The decision was also silent as to whether *Skidmore* deference should remain in circumstances in which *Chevron* deference is *not* warranted, or if the *Chevron* framework supplanted *Skidmore* entirely. The Supreme Court directly touched upon these issues in **Christensen v. Harris**, 529 U.S. 576 (2000), when it considered whether Harris County, Texas, violated the Fair Labor Standards Act of 1938 (FLSA) by requiring its employees to schedule time off so as to reduce their accrued compensatory time resulting from overtime work—work for which employers are otherwise required to pay cash compensation. The Department of Labor had provided an opinion letter (a form of agency guidance that need not be promulgated through formal or informal rulemaking procedures under the APA) that supported the plaintiffs' interpretation of the FLSA concerning how employers may treat accrued compensatory time. Justice Thomas, writing for the majority, addressed the plaintiffs' claim that the Department's opinion letter was entitled to deference from the Court:

> . . . [Petitioners] argue that the agency opinion letter is entitled to deference under our decision in *Chevron* [citation]. In *Chevron,* we held that a court must give effect to an agency's regulation containing a reasonable interpretation of an ambiguous statute. [Citation.]

> Here, however, we confront an interpretation contained in an opinion letter, not one arrived at after, for example, a formal adjudication or notice-and-comment rulemaking. Interpretations such as those in opinion letters—like interpretations contained in policy statements, agency manuals, and enforcement guidelines, all of which lack the force of law— do not warrant *Chevron*-style deference. . . . Instead, interpretations contained in formats such as opinion letters are "entitled to respect" under our decision in *Skidmore v. Swift & Co.,* 323 U.S. 134, 140 (1944), but only to the extent that those interpretations have the "power to persuade[.]," [Citations.] As explained above, we find unpersuasive the agency's interpretation of the statute at issue in this case.

While the majority concluded that *Chevron* deference had not replaced *Skidmore* deference, Justice Scalia disagreed. Concurring in the judgement and in the majority opinion except for its discussion of *Chevron* and *Skidmore* deference, Justice Scalia argued that *Skidmore* deference to authoritative agency interpretations was "an anachronism" that had been entirely supplanted by the doctrine of *Chevron* deference. According to Justice Scalia, *Chevron* deference should be applied "not only to agency regulations, but [also] to authoritative agency positions set forth in a variety of other formats."

In his dissent, Justice Breyer explained that *Skidmore* and *Chevron* could coexist because *Chevron* was more an evolution of *Skidmore* as opposed to a revolution in judicial deference to agency interpretations:

> *Skidmore* made clear that courts may pay particular attention to the views of an expert agency where they represent "specialized experience," [citation], even if they do not constitute an exercise of delegated lawmaking authority. The Court held that the "rulings, interpretations and opinions of" an agency, "while not controlling upon the courts by reason of their authority, do constitute a body of experience and informed judgment to which courts and litigants may properly resort for guidance." [Citations.] As Justice Jackson wrote for the Court, those views may possess the "power to persuade," even where they lack the "power to control." [Citation.]

> *Chevron* made no relevant change. It simply focused upon an additional, separate legal reason for deferring to certain agency determinations, namely, that Congress had delegated to the agency the legal authority to make those determinations. [Citation.] And, to the extent there may be circumstances in which *Chevron*-type deference is inapplicable—*e.g.*, where one has doubt that Congress actually intended to delegate interpretive authority to the agency (an "ambiguity" that *Chevron* does not presumptively leave to agency resolution)—I believe that *Skidmore* nonetheless retains legal vitality. If statutes are to serve the human purposes that called them into being, courts will have to continue to pay particular attention in appropriate cases to the experience-based views of expert agencies.

While *Christensen* elaborated on the circumstances in which *Chevron* deference is warranted, the Court in *Christensen* did not provide a clear decisional rule for lower courts and agencies to follow when deciding whether a given agency interpretation would be likely to be accorded *Chevron* deference. In part, this is because *Christensen* introduced a new and related consideration: what constitutes an agency action undertaken with the "force of law?" The Court provided such a framework, now known as "*Chevron* Step Zero," one year later, in **United States v. Mead**, 533 U.S. 218 (2001). At issue in *Mead* was whether a tariff classification ruling by the U.S. Customs Service ("Customs") was eligible for *Chevron* deference. Customs promulgates the Harmonized Tariff Schedule of the United States (HTSUS), which defines merchandise classifications and assigns tariff rates to imported goods. Any of Customs' 46 port-of-entry offices of its Headquarters Office can issue "ruling letters" that "[represent] the official position of the Customs Service with respect to the particular transaction or issue described therein and is binding on all Customs Service personnel in accordance with the provisions of this section until modified or revoked." 19 CFR § 177.9(a).

The Respondent, the Mead Corporation, imported day planners described as "three-ring binders with pages having room for notes of daily schedules and phone numbers and addresses." At the time of the controversy, HTSUS heading 4820 and 4820.10.20, concerning "[r]egisters, account books, notebooks, order books, receipt books, letter pads, memorandum pads, diaries, and similar articles," provided that "[d]iaries, notebooks and address books, bound; memorandum pads, letter pads and similar articles" were subject to a 4% tariff, while under HTSUS subheading 4820.10.40, other items were duty-free. From 1989 to 1993, Customs considered respondent's day planners as "other" and did not charge an import duty. In 1993, however, Customs issued a ruling letter that concluded that respondent's day planners were of the type of articles subject to a 4% tariff. Mead challenged the application of the duty to its day planners.

Justice Souter, writing for the majority, found that *Chevron* deference was not warranted to the Customs' interpretation contained in its ruling letter:

> We have recognized a very good indicator of delegation meriting *Chevron* treatment in express congressional authorizations to engage in the process of rulemaking or adjudication that produces regulations or rulings for which deference is claimed. [Citations.] It is fair to assume generally that Congress contemplates administrative action with the effect of law when it provides for a relatively formal administrative procedure tending to foster the fairness and deliberation that should underlie a pronouncement of such force. [Citations.] Thus, the overwhelming number of our cases applying *Chevron* deference have reviewed the fruits of notice-and-comment rulemaking or formal adjudication. That said, and as significant as notice-and-comment is in pointing to *Chevron* authority, the want of that procedure here does not decide the case, for we have sometimes found reasons for *Chevron* deference even when no such administrative formality was required and none was afforded, [citation]. The fact that the tariff classification here was not a product of such formal process does not alone, therefore, bar the application of *Chevron*.

> There are, nonetheless, ample reasons to deny *Chevron* deference here. The authorization for classification rulings, and Customs's practice in making them, present a case far removed not only from notice-and-comment process, but from any other circumstances reasonably suggesting that Congress ever thought of classification rulings as deserving the deference claimed for them here.

The Court found no indication that Congress intended HTSUS "to delegate [the] authority to Customs to issue classification rulings with the force of law." That many different Customs offices could issue ruling letters, Customs issued 10 to 15 thousand letters each year, and the letters bound only the parties to the ruling all indicated an absence of the force of law and placed ruling letters "beyond the *Chevron* pale." Finally, as *Chevron* deference was not warranted, the Court remanded the case so that a lower court may determine if ruling letters warranted *Skidmore* deference.

In addressing objections raised by Justice Scalia (discussed below), the majority echoed Justice Breyer's dissent in *Christensen* and clarified that the *Chevron* and *Skidmore* doctrines coexist:

> Justice Scalia would pose the question of deference as an either-or choice. On his view ... *Chevron* rendered *Skidmore* anachronistic, [and] when courts owe any deference[,] it is *Chevron* deference that they owe. . . .

> The Court, on the other hand, said nothing in *Chevron* to eliminate *Skidmore*'s recognition of various justifications for deference depending on statutory circumstances and agency action; *Chevron* was simply a case recognizing that even without express authority to fill a specific statutory gap, circumstances pointing to implicit congressional delegation present a particularly insistent call for deference. Indeed, in holding here that *Chevron* left *Skidmore* intact and applicable where statutory circumstances indicate no intent to delegate general authority to make rules with force of law, or where such authority was not invoked, we hold nothing more than we said last Term in response to the particular statutory circumstances in *Christensen* . . . .

In his dissent, Justice Scalia claimed that the majority's "opinion makes an avulsive change in judicial review of federal administrative action." Justice Scalia was particularly concerned about the future impact of the majority's opinion:

> [A] general presumption of authority in agencies to resolve ambiguity in the statutes they have been authorized to enforce has been changed to a presumption of no such authority, which must be overcome by affirmative legislative intent to the contrary. And whereas previously, when agency authority to resolve ambiguity did not exist the court was free to give the statute what it considered the best interpretation, henceforth the court must supposedly give the agency view some indeterminate amount of so-called *Skidmore* deference. [Citation.] We will be sorting out the consequences of the *Mead* doctrine, which has today replaced the *Chevron* doctrine, [citation], for years to come. I would adhere to our established jurisprudence, defer to the reasonable interpretation the

Customs Service has given to the statute it is charged with enforcing, and reverse the judgment of the Court of Appeals.

Justice Scalia remained staunch in his position that *Chevron* required deference to *all* authoritative agency interpretations and argued that such a reading maintained the division of powers between Congress and the judiciary. To Justice Scalia, the majority's opinion allowed judges, not agencies, to resolve ambiguity in legislative instructions to those same agencies. Of particular concern for Justice Scalia was the majority's perceived emphasis on an agency's choice of procedure, which can range from case-by-case adjudication; to formal rulemaking in the form of a hearing with an administrative law judge and the presentation of evidence; to informal rulemaking in the form of a notice-and-comment period during which interested parties can comment on proposed agency rules. Adjudication is usually required by statute, whereas informal rulemaking is often authorized but not required. Justice Scalia was concerned that the majority's opinion hampered agency flexibility and would deny *Chevron* deference to some forms of informal rulemaking while granting deference only to adjudications, because only adjudications are specifically prescribed by law.

Justice Scalia envisioned a number of negative impacts resulting from the majority's decision in *Mead*:

1

The principal effect will be protracted confusion. . . . [T]he one test for *Chevron* deference that the Court enunciates is wonderfully imprecise: whether "Congress delegated authority to the agency generally to make rules carrying the force of law, . . . as by . . . adjudication[,] notice-and-comment rulemaking, or . . . some other [procedure] indicati[ng] comparable congressional intent." But even this description does not do justice to the utter flabbiness of the Court's criterion, since, in order to maintain the fiction that the new test is really just the old one, applied consistently throughout our case law, the Court must make a virtually open-ended exception to its already imprecise guidance: In the present case, it tells us, the absence of notice-and-comment rulemaking (and "[who knows?] [of] some other [procedure] indicati[ng] comparable congressional intent") is not enough to decide the question of *Chevron* deference, "for we have sometimes found reasons for *Chevron* deference even when no such administrative formality was required and none was afforded." . . . It is hard to know what the lower courts are to make of today's guidance.

2

Another practical effect of today's opinion will be an artificially induced increase in informal rulemaking. Buy stock in the

GPO.* Since informal rulemaking and formal adjudication are the only more-or-less safe harbors from the storm that the Court has unleashed; and since formal adjudication is not an option but must be mandated by statute or constitutional command; informal rulemaking—which the Court was once careful to make voluntary unless required by statute, [citations]—will now become a virtual necessity. . . . Surely the mere *conferral* of rulemaking authority demonstrates—if one accepts the Court's logic—a congressional intent to allow the agency to resolve ambiguities. . . .

3

Worst of all, the majority's approach will lead to the ossification of large portions of our statutory law. Where *Chevron* applies, statutory ambiguities remain ambiguities subject to the agency's ongoing clarification. They create a space, so to speak, for the exercise of continuing agency discretion. . . . For the indeterminately large number of statutes taken out of *Chevron* by today's decision, however, ambiguity (and hence flexibility) will cease with the first judicial resolution. *Skidmore* deference gives the agency's current position some vague and uncertain amount of respect, but it does not, like *Chevron, leave* the matter within the control of the Executive Branch for the future. Once the court has spoken, it becomes *unlawful* for the agency to take a contradictory position; the statute now *says* what the court has prescribed. . . .

4

And finally, the majority's approach compounds the confusion it creates by breathing new life into the anachronism of *Skidmore*. . . . Justice Jackson's eloquence notwithstanding, the rule of *Skidmore* deference is an empty truism and a trifling statement of the obvious: A judge should take into account the well-considered views of expert observers. . . .

To condemn a vast body of agency action to that regime (all except rulemaking, formal (and informal?) adjudication, and whatever else might now and then be included within today's intentionally vague formulation of affirmative congressional intent to "delegate") is irresponsible.

Justice Scalia concluded that applying *Chevron*'s "original formulation" would dispense with the central issue here: the Customs Service's interpretation was an authoritative view that resolved ambiguity Congress had placed within the agency's discretion. As such,

---

* Editors' Note: The Government Publishing Office publishes, among other things, the *Federal Register*, which contains official agency notices of proposed rulemaking and invitations for comment on proposed rules.

he maintained, the Court should accord *Chevron* deference to the agency's interpretation.

Nearly two decades on, it is unclear whether all of Justice Scalia's grim predictions as to the future of agency interpretation and deference have come to pass. An empirical study of all Supreme Court cases between its 1983 and 2005 terms found that there has been "haphazard application [of *Chevron*] over a more than twenty-year period, with the post-*Mead* era producing results exactly contrary to what the *Mead* decision announced." William N. Eskridge, Jr. & Lauren E. Baer, *The Continuum of Deference: Supreme Court Treatment of Agency Statutory Interpretations from Chevron to Hamdan*, 96 GEO. L.J. 1083, 1128 (2008). Professor Thomas Merrill, a leading administrative law scholar, has deduced that the *Mead* doctrine can best be "boil[ed] down to three factors: (1) whether Congress has prescribed relatively formal procedures; (2) whether Congress has authorized the agency to adopt rules or precedents that generalize to more than a single case; and (3) whether Congress has authorized the agency to prescribe legal norms that apply uniformly throughout its jurisdiction. Nevertheless, I readily admit that the number and correct characterization of the factors invoked in the majority opinion is open to debate." Thomas W. Merrill, *The Mead Doctrine: Rules and Standards, Meta-Rules and Meta-Standards*, 54 Admin. L. Rev. 807, 814 (2002).

Even if the federal courts continue to struggle with *Chevron*, *Mead*, and when to defer to agency interpretations, legislative drafters have apparently thoroughly incorporated the broader lessons of *Mead*. In a study based on interviews with 137 congressional counsels, *Mead* was a "big winner" for legislative staffer awareness: 88% of respondents indicated knowledge of the case and its takeaway that "the authorization of notice-and-comment rulemaking . . . is always or often relevant to whether drafters intend for an agency to have gap-filled authority." Abbe R. Gluck & Lisa Schultz Bressman, *Statutory Interpretation from the Inside—an Empirical Study of Congressional Drafting, Delegation, and the Canons: Part I*, 65 Stan. L. Rev. 901, 999 (2013).

The *Mead* factors Professor Merrill identifies raise a related dilemma: should a court defer to an agency's determination that the statutory delegation in question fulfills the *Chevron* Step Zero criteria? In other words, if the agency interprets an ambiguous statutory provision concerning the scope of the agency's jurisdiction to regulate under the statute, should a court defer to that determination? Who decides what the agency can decide?

City of Arlington v. Federal
Communications Commission

Supreme Court of the United States, 2013.
569 U.S. 290, 133 S.Ct. 1863, 185 L.Ed.2d 941.

■ JUSTICE SCALIA delivered the opinion of the Court[, in which JUSTICE THOMAS, JUSTICE GINSBURG, JUSTICE SOTOMAYOR, and JUSTICE KAGAN joined].

[Editors' Note: Wireless phone service providers must obtain zoning approval from state and local governments before they may construct wireless towers or attach wireless equipment to existing buildings. Although a 1996 amendment to the Communications Act of [date] required that state and local governments respond to zoning requests "within a reasonable period of time," 47 U.S.C.§ 332(c)(7)(B)(ii), zoning approval often proved a drawn-out process, severely delaying construction of the towers. In 2008, CTIA, a wireless service provider trade association, petitioned the FCC to clarify the meaning of "a reasonable period of time." In November 2009, the FCC issued a declaratory ruling that set time limits for zoning requests: 90 days for attachments to current buildings and 150 days for new structures.

In the declaratory ruling, the FCC reasoned that Congress' delegation to the FCC of the responsibility for administering the Communications Act also conferred authority to interpret the Act. The declaratory ruling specifically cited [§]4(i) of the Act, which stated that the FCC "may perform any and all acts, make such rules and regulations, and issue such orders, not inconsistent with this Act, as may be necessary in the execution of its functions." The declaratory ruling rejected the arguments of state and local governments, saying that "[the FCC's] interpretation of [§]332(c)(7) is not the imposition of new limitations, as it merely interprets the limits Congress already imposed on State and local governments."

The cities of Arlington and San Antonio, Texas, petitioned for review of the FCC's declaratory ruling, arguing that the FCC lacked legal authority either to interpret the law or to determine the extent of the legal authority that Congress allegedly delegated to the agency. In other words, the cities argued that agency interpretations of the scope of their jurisdiction and power should not be subject to *Chevron* deference. The Court of Appeals for the Fifth Circuit applied *Chevron* deference and upheld the FCC's decision as a permissible interpretation.

The Supreme Court granted certiorari to consider whether an agency's interpretation of a statutory ambiguity that concerns the scope of its regulatory authority (that is, its jurisdiction) is entitled to deference under *Chevron*.]

II

* * *

B

The question here is whether a court must defer under *Chevron* to an agency's interpretation of a statutory ambiguity that concerns the scope of the agency's statutory authority (that is, its jurisdiction). The argument against deference rests on the premise that there exist two distinct classes of agency interpretations: Some interpretations—the big, important ones, presumably—define the agency's "jurisdiction." Others—humdrum, run-of-the-mill stuff—are simply applications of jurisdiction the agency plainly has. That premise is false, because the distinction between "jurisdictional" and "nonjurisdictional" interpretations is a mirage. No matter how it is framed, the question a court faces when confronted with an agency's interpretation of a statute it administers is always, simply, *whether the agency has stayed within the bounds of its statutory authority.*

The misconception that there are, for *Chevron* purposes, separate "jurisdictional" questions on which no deference is due derives, perhaps, from a reflexive extension to agencies of the very real division between the jurisdictional and nonjurisdictional that is applicable to courts. In the judicial context, there *is* a meaningful line: Whether the court decided *correctly* is a question that has different consequences from the question whether it had the power to decide *at all.* Congress has the power (within limits) to tell the courts what classes of cases they may decide, [citations], but not to prescribe or superintend how they decide those cases, [citation]. A court's power to decide a case is independent of whether its decision is correct, which is why even an erroneous judgment is entitled to res judicata effect. Put differently, a jurisdictionally proper but substantively incorrect judicial decision is not ultra vires.

That is not so for agencies charged with administering congressional statutes. Both their power to act and how they are to act is authoritatively prescribed by Congress, so that when they act improperly, no less than when they act beyond their jurisdiction, what they do is ultra vires. Because the question—whether framed as an incorrect application of agency authority or an assertion of authority not conferred—is always whether the agency has gone beyond what Congress has permitted it to do, there is no principled basis for carving out some arbitrary subset of such claims as "jurisdictional." . . .

The label is an empty distraction because every new application of a broad statutory term can be reframed as a questionable extension of the agency's jurisdiction. . . . In sum, judges should not waste their time in the mental acrobatics needed to decide whether an agency's interpretation of a statutory provision is "jurisdictional" or "nonjurisdictional." . . .

C

Fortunately, then, we have consistently held "that *Chevron* applies to cases in which an agency adopts a construction of a jurisdictional provision of a statute it administers." [Citation.] One of our opinions explicitly says that no "exception exists to the normal [deferential] standard of review" for " 'jurisdictional or legal question[s] concerning the coverage' " of an Act. [Citation.] . . .

Our cases hold that *Chevron* applies equally to statutes designed to *curtail* the scope of agency discretion. . . . And we have applied *Chevron* where concerns about agency self-aggrandizement are at their apogee: in cases where an agency's expansive construction of the extent of its own power would have wrought a fundamental change in the regulatory scheme. In *FDA v. Brown & Williamson Tobacco Corp.*, 529 U.S. 120 (2000), the threshold question was the "appropriate framework for analyzing" the FDA's assertion of "jurisdiction to regulate tobacco products," [citation]—a question of vast "economic and political magnitude," [citation]. "Because this case involves an administrative agency's construction of a statute that it administers," we held, *Chevron* applied. [Citation.] . . .

The false dichotomy between "jurisdictional" and "nonjurisdictional" agency interpretations may be no more than a bogeyman, but it is dangerous all the same. Like the Hound of the Baskervilles, it is conjured by those with greater quarry in sight: Make no mistake—the ultimate target here is *Chevron* itself. Savvy challengers of agency action would play the "jurisdictional" card in every case. [Citation.] Some judges would be deceived by the specious, but scary-sounding, "jurisdictional"-"nonjurisdictional" line; others tempted by the prospect of making public policy by prescribing the meaning of ambiguous statutory commands. The effect would be to transfer any number of interpretive decisions—archetypal *Chevron* questions, about how best to construe an ambiguous term in light of competing policy interests—from the agencies that administer the statutes to federal courts. We have cautioned that "judges ought to refrain from substituting their own interstitial lawmaking" for that of an agency. [Citation.] That is precisely what *Chevron* prevents.

III

* * *

B

A few words in response to the dissent. The question on which we granted certiorari was whether "a court should apply *Chevron* to review an agency's determination of its own jurisdiction." Perhaps sensing the incoherence of the "jurisdictional-nonjurisdictional" line, the dissent does not even attempt to defend it, but proposes a much broader scope for *de novo* judicial review: Jurisdictional or not, and even where a rule is at issue and the statute contains a broad grant of rulemaking authority, the dissent would have a court search provision-by-provision to determine "whether [that] delegation covers the 'specific provision' and 'particular question' before the court."

The dissent is correct that *Mead,* [citation], requires that, for *Chevron* deference to apply, the agency must have received congressional authority to determine the particular matter at issue in the particular manner adopted. No one disputes that. But *Mead* denied *Chevron* deference to action, by an agency with rulemaking authority, that was not rulemaking. What the dissent needs, and fails to produce, is a single case in which a general conferral of rulemaking or adjudicative authority has been held insufficient to support *Chevron* deference for an exercise of that authority within the agency's substantive field. There is no such case, and what the dissent proposes is a massive revision of our *Chevron* jurisprudence.

Where we differ from the dissent is in its apparent rejection of the theorem that the whole includes all of its parts—its view that a general conferral of rulemaking authority does not validate rules for *all* the matters the agency is charged with administering. Rather, the dissent proposes that even when general rulemaking authority is clear, *every* agency rule must be subjected to a *de novo* judicial determination of whether *the particular issue* was committed to agency discretion. It offers no standards at all to guide this open-ended hunt for congressional intent (that is to say, for evidence of congressional intent more specific than the conferral of general rulemaking authority). It would simply punt that question back to the Court of Appeals, presumably for application of some sort of totality-of-the-circumstances test—which is really, of course, not a test at all but an invitation to make an ad hoc judgment regarding congressional intent. Thirteen Courts of Appeals applying a totality-of-the-circumstances test would render the binding effect of agency rules unpredictable and destroy the whole stabilizing purpose of *Chevron.* The excessive agency power that the dissent fears would be replaced by chaos. There is no need to wade into these murky waters. It suffices to decide this case that the preconditions to deference under *Chevron* are satisfied because Congress has unambiguously vested the FCC with general authority to administer the Communications Act through rulemaking and adjudication, and the agency interpretation at issue was promulgated in the exercise of that authority.

* * *

Those who assert that applying *Chevron* to "jurisdictional" interpretations "leaves the fox in charge of the henhouse" overlook the reality that a separate category of "jurisdictional" interpretations does not exist. The fox-in-the-henhouse syndrome is to be avoided not by establishing an arbitrary and undefinable category of agency decisionmaking that is accorded no deference, but by taking seriously, and applying rigorously, in all cases, statutory limits on agencies' authority. Where Congress has established a clear line, the agency cannot go beyond it; and where Congress has established an ambiguous line, the agency can go no further than the ambiguity will fairly allow. But in rigorously applying the latter rule, a court need not pause to puzzle over whether the interpretive question presented is "jurisdictional." If "the agency's answer is based on a permissible construction of the statute," that is the end of the matter. *Chevron,* [citation].

The judgment of the Court of Appeals is affirmed.

It is so ordered.

■ JUSTICE BREYER concurring in part and concurring in the judgment.

I agree with the Court that normally "the question a court faces when confronted with an agency's interpretation of a statute it administers" is, "simply, *whether the agency has stayed within the bounds of its statutory authority."* In this context, "the distinction between 'jurisdictional' and 'non-jurisdictional' interpretations is a mirage."

Deciding just what those statutory bounds are, however, is not always an easy matter, and the Court's case law abounds with discussion of the subject. . . . I say that the existence of statutory ambiguity is sometimes not enough to warrant the conclusion that Congress has left a deference-warranting gap for the agency to fill because our cases make clear that other, sometimes context-specific, factors will on occasion prove relevant. (And, given the vast number of government statutes, regulatory programs, and underlying circumstances, that variety is hardly surprising.) In *Mead,* for example, we looked to several factors other than simple ambiguity to help determine whether Congress left a statutory gap, thus delegating to the agency the authority to fill that gap with an interpretation that would carry "the force of law." [Citation.] Elsewhere, we have assessed

> "the interstitial nature of the legal question, the related expertise of the Agency, the importance of the question to administration of the statute, the complexity of that administration, and the careful consideration the Agency has given the question over a long period of time." [Citation.]

The subject matter of the relevant provision—for instance, its distance from the agency's ordinary statutory duties or its falling within the scope of another agency's authority—has also proved relevant. [Citations.]

Moreover, the statute's text, its context, the structure of the statutory scheme, and canons of textual construction are relevant in determining whether the statute is ambiguous and can be equally helpful in determining whether such ambiguity comes accompanied with agency authority to fill a gap with an interpretation that carries the force of law. [Citations.] Statutory purposes, including those revealed in part by legislative and regulatory history, can be similarly relevant. [Citations.]

Although seemingly complex in abstract description, in practice this framework has proved a workable way to approximate how Congress would likely have meant to allocate interpretive law-determining authority between reviewing court and agency. The question whether Congress has delegated to an agency the authority to provide an interpretation that carries the force of law is for the judge to answer independently. The judge, considering "traditional tools of statutory construction," [citation], will ask whether Congress has spoken unambiguously. If so, the text controls. If not, the judge will ask whether Congress would have intended the agency to resolve the resulting ambiguity. If so, deference is warranted. *See Mead,* [citation]. Even if not, however, sometimes an agency interpretation, in light of the agency's special expertise, will still have the "power to persuade, if lacking power to control," *Skidmore,* [citation].

The case before us offers an example. The relevant statutory provision requires state or local governments to act on wireless siting applications "within a reasonable period of time after" a wireless service provider files such a request. 47 U.S.C. § 332(c)(7)(B)(ii). The Federal Communications Commission (FCC) argued that this provision granted it a degree of leeway in determining the amount of time that is reasonable. Many factors favor the agency's view: (1) the language of the Telecommunications Act grants the FCC broad authority (including rulemaking authority) to administer the Act; (2) the words are open-ended—*i.e.* "ambiguous"; (3) the provision concerns an interstitial administrative matter, in respect to which the agency's expertise could have an important role to play; and (4) the matter, in context, is complex, likely making the agency's expertise useful in helping to answer the "reasonableness" question that the statute poses. [Citations.] . . .

For these reasons, I would reject petitioners' argument and conclude that § 332(c)(7)(B)(ii)—the "reasonableness" statute—leaves a gap for the FCC to fill. I would hold that the FCC's lawful efforts to do so carry "the force of law." *Mead,* [citation]. The Court of Appeals ultimately reached the same conclusion (though for somewhat different reasons), and the majority affirms the lower court. I consequently join the majority's judgment and such portions of its opinion as are consistent with what I have written here.

■ CHIEF JUSTICE ROBERTS, with whom JUSTICE KENNEDY and JUSTICE ALITO join, dissenting.

My disagreement with the Court is fundamental. It is also easily expressed: A court should not defer to an agency until the court decides, on its own, that the agency is entitled to deference. Courts defer to an agency's interpretation of law when and because Congress has conferred on the agency interpretive authority over the question at issue. An agency cannot exercise interpretive authority until it has it; the question whether an agency enjoys that authority must be decided by a court, without deference to the agency.

I

. . . The administrative state "wields vast power and touches almost every aspect of daily life." . . . [T]he citizen confronting thousands of pages of regulations—promulgated by an agency directed by Congress to regulate, say, "in the public interest"—can perhaps be excused for thinking that it is the agency really doing the legislating. And with hundreds of federal agencies poking into every nook and cranny of daily life, that citizen might also understandably question whether Presidential oversight—a critical part of the Constitutional plan—is always an effective safeguard against agency overreaching. It is against this background that we consider whether the authority of administrative agencies should be augmented even further, to include not only broad power to give definitive answers to questions left to them by Congress, but also the same power to decide when Congress has given them that power. . . .

The Court states that the question "is whether a court must defer under *Chevron* to an agency's interpretation of a statutory ambiguity that concerns the scope of the agency's statutory authority (that is, its jurisdiction)." That is fine—until the parenthetical. The parties, *amici*, and court below too often use the term "jurisdiction" imprecisely, which leads the Court to misunderstand the argument it must confront. That argument is not that "there exist two distinct classes of agency interpretations," some "big, important ones" that "define the agency's 'jurisdiction,'" and other "humdrum, run-of-the-mill" ones that "are simply applications of jurisdiction the agency plainly has." The argument is instead that a court should not defer to an agency on whether Congress has granted the agency interpretive authority over the statutory ambiguity at issue. . . .

II

"It is emphatically the province and duty of the judicial department to say what the law is." *Marbury v. Madison,* [citation]. The rise of the modern administrative state has not changed that duty. Indeed, the Administrative Procedure Act, governing judicial review of most agency action, instructs reviewing courts to decide "all relevant questions of law." [Citation.] We do not ignore that command when we afford an agency's statutory interpretation *Chevron* deference; we respect it. We give binding deference to permissible agency interpretations of statutory ambiguities *because* Congress has delegated to the agency the authority to interpret those ambiguities "with the force of law." *United States v. Mead Corp.,* [citations].

But before a court may grant such deference, it must on its own decide whether Congress—the branch vested with lawmaking authority under the Constitution—has in fact delegated to the agency lawmaking power over the ambiguity at issue. Agencies are creatures of Congress; "an agency literally has no power to act . . . unless and until Congress confers power upon it." [Citation.] Whether Congress has conferred such power is the "relevant question[ ] of law" that must be answered before affording *Chevron* deference. [Citation.] . . .

III

A

Our precedents confirm this conclusion—beginning with *Chevron* itself. . . . *Chevron*'s rule of deference was based on—and limited by—[a] congressional delegation. And the Court did not ask simply whether Congress had delegated to the EPA the authority to administer the Clean Air Act generally. We asked whether Congress had "delegat[ed] authority to the agency to elucidate a *specific provision* of the statute by regulation." [Citations] (discussing "the legislative delegation to an agency on a *particular question*" (emphasis added)). We deferred to the EPA's interpretation of "stationary sources" based on our conclusion that the agency had been "charged with responsibility for administering *the provision*." [Citation.] (emphasis added).

B

We have never faltered in our understanding of this straightforward principle, that whether a particular agency interpretation warrants *Chevron* deference turns on the court's determination whether Congress has delegated to the agency the authority to interpret the statutory ambiguity at issue. . . . We made the point perhaps most clearly in *Adams Fruit Co. v. Barrett,* 494 U.S. 638 (1990). In that case, the Department of Labor contended the Court should defer to its interpretation of the scope of the private right of action provided by the Migrant and Seasonal Agriculture Worker Protection Act (AWPA), 29 U.S.C. § 1854, against employers who intentionally violated the Act's motor vehicle safety provisions. We refused to do so. Although "as an initial matter" we rejected the idea that Congress left a "statutory 'gap' " for the agency to fill, we reasoned that if the "AWPA's language establishing a private right of action is ambiguous," the Secretary of Labor's interpretation of its scope did not warrant *Chevron* deference. [Citation.]

In language directly applicable to the question before us, we explained that "[a] precondition to deference under *Chevron* is a congressional delegation of administrative authority." [Citation.] Although "Congress clearly envisioned, indeed expressly mandated, a role for the Department of Labor in administering the statute by requiring the Secretary to promulgate *standards* implementing AWPA's *motor vehicle provisions*," we found "[n]o such delegation regarding AWPA's *enforcement provisions*." [Citation.] It would therefore be "inappropriate," we said, "to consult executive interpretations" of the enforcement provisions to resolve ambiguities "surrounding the scope of AWPA's judicially enforceable remedy." *Ibid.* Without questioning the principle that agency determinations "within the scope of delegated authority are entitled to deference," we explained that "it is fundamental 'that an agency may not bootstrap itself into an area in which it has no jurisdiction.'" [Citation.] . . .

[Chief Justice Roberts also pointed to the Court's decisions in *Mead* and *Gonzales v. Oregon*, 546 U.S. 243 (2006), *see infra* Section V.C.2, as examples of cases in which the question of *Chevron* deference depends on whether Congress has delegated interpretive authority to an agency.]

Adams Fruit, Mead, and *Gonzales* thus confirm that *Chevron* deference is based on, and finds legitimacy as, a congressional delegation of interpretive authority. An agency interpretation warrants such deference only if Congress has delegated authority to definitively interpret a particular ambiguity in a particular manner. Whether Congress has done so must be determined by the court on its own before *Chevron* can apply. [Citations.] In other words, we do not defer to an agency's interpretation of an ambiguous provision unless Congress wants us to, and whether Congress wants us to is a question that courts, not agencies, must decide. Simply put, that question is "beyond the *Chevron* pale." *Mead,* [citation.]

IV

Despite these precedents, the FCC argues that a court need only locate an agency and a grant of general rulemaking authority over a statute. *Chevron* deference then applies, it contends, to the agency's interpretation of any ambiguity in the Act, including ambiguity in a provision said to carve out specific provisions from the agency's general rulemaking authority. If Congress intends to exempt part of the statute from the agency's interpretive authority, the FCC says, Congress "can ordinarily be expected to state that intent explicitly."

If a congressional delegation of interpretive authority is to support *Chevron* deference, however, that delegation must extend to the specific statutory ambiguity at issue. The appropriate question is whether the delegation covers the "specific provision" and "particular question" before the court. [Citation.] A congressional grant of authority over some portion of a statute does not necessarily mean that Congress granted the agency interpretive authority over all its provisions. [Citation.]

An example that might highlight the point concerns statutes that parcel out authority to multiple agencies, which "may be the norm, rather than an exception." [Citations.] The Dodd-Frank Wall Street Reform and Consumer Protection Act, for example, authorizes rulemaking by at least eight different agencies. [Citation.] When presented with an agency's interpretation of such a statute, a court cannot simply ask whether the statute is one that the agency administers; the question is whether authority over the particular ambiguity at issue has been delegated to the particular agency.

By the same logic, even when Congress provides interpretive authority to a single agency, a court must decide if the ambiguity the agency has purported to interpret with the force of law is one to which the congressional delegation extends. A general delegation to the agency to administer the statute will often suffice to satisfy the court that Congress has delegated interpretive authority over the ambiguity at issue. But if Congress has exempted particular provisions from that authority, that exemption must be respected, and the determination whether Congress has done so is for the courts alone. . . .

VI

The Court sees something nefarious behind the view that courts must decide on their own whether Congress has delegated interpretative authority to an agency, before deferring to that agency's interpretation of law. What is afoot, according to the Court, is a judicial power-grab, with nothing less than "*Chevron* itself" as "the ultimate target."

The Court touches on a legitimate concern: *Chevron* importantly guards against the Judiciary arrogating to itself policymaking properly left, under the separation of powers, to the Executive. But there is another concern at play, no less firmly rooted in our constitutional structure. That is the obligation of the Judiciary not only to confine itself to its proper role, but to ensure that the other branches do so as well.

An agency's interpretive authority, entitling the agency to judicial deference, acquires its legitimacy from a delegation of lawmaking power from Congress to the Executive. Our duty to police the boundary between the Legislature and the Executive is as critical as our duty to respect that between the Judiciary and the Executive. [Citation.] . . . And it is heightened, not diminished, by the dramatic shift in power over the last 50 years from Congress to the Executive—a shift effected through the administrative agencies.

We reconcile our competing responsibilities in this area by ensuring judicial deference to agency interpretations under *Chevron*—but only after we have determined on our own that Congress has given interpretive authority to the agency. Our "task is to fix the boundaries of delegated authority," Monaghan, 83 Colum. L. Rev., at 27; that is not a task we can delegate to the agency. We do not leave it to the agency to decide when it is in charge.

* * *

In these cases, the FCC issued a declaratory ruling interpreting the term "reasonable period of time" in 47 U.S.C. § 332(c)(7) (B)(ii). The Fifth Circuit correctly recognized that it could not apply *Chevron* deference to the FCC's interpretation unless the agency "possessed statutory authority to administer § 332(c)(7)(B)(ii)," but it erred by granting *Chevron* deference to the FCC's view on that antecedent question. [Citation.] Because the court should have determined on its own whether Congress delegated interpretive authority over § 332(c)(7) (B)(ii) to the FCC before affording *Chevron* deference, I would vacate the decision below and remand the cases to the Fifth Circuit to perform the proper inquiry in the first instance.

I respectfully dissent.

QUESTIONS

1. Is the difference between the majority and the dissent as "fundamental" as the dissent proclaims? Don't all the Justices agree that the prerequisite to *Chevron* deference is ascertaining whether Congress left the question at issue to agency determination?

2. Justice Scalia wrote the opinion of the Court in this case. Yet Scalia also dissented in *Mead, supra,* chiefly because the *Mead* majority held that whether Congress has vested the agency with rulemaking authority that carries the force of law is a central inquiry in deciding whether *Chevron* deference is warranted. Are those positions consistent? Can you articulate the principle behind Justice Scalia's conclusions in *Mead* and *City of Arlington*?

3. The dissent appears to argue in Section III.B that only express congressional delegations of authority enable the agency to interpret with the expectation of *Chevron* deference. Is this a practical argument? Would such a requirement hamper Congress' ability to delegate authority to agencies in the first place? Can you think of language Congress could use to designate such delegations? Is there language in statutes you have already seen that might provide a ready example? If such a rule were adopted by a majority of the Court, what should be done about statutes enacted prior to the rule's adoption?

The *Chevron* framework contemplates the possibility of multiple permissible interpretations of a statute that delegates binding rulemaking authority to agencies. As you have already seen in *Chevron,* moreover, the preferable interpretation of that authority may evolve over time. *Chevron* therefore also implicates questions of temporality. For example, if a lower federal court first interprets an ambiguous statutory provision in one manner, and then the relevant agency subsequently regulates on the basis of a competing interpretation of the same provision, should a court reviewing the agency's interpretation adopt the lower court's interpretation because it came first in time, or adopt the agency's subsequent interpretation (assuming it warrants *Chevron* deference)? The next case addresses this question.

National Cable & Telecommunications Assoc. v. Brand X Internet Services

Supreme Court of the United States, 2005.
545 U.S. 967, 125 S.Ct. 2688, 162 L.Ed.2d 820.

■ JUSTICE THOMAS delivered the opinion of the Court[, in which CHIEF JUSTICE REHNQUIST, JUSTICE STEVENS, JUSTICE O'CONNOR, JUSTICE KENNEDY, and JUSTICE BREYER joined].

[Editors' Note: In the United States, internet connectivity is either dial-up (using telephone lines) or broadband, which includes cable modem (using television cable lines) and digital subscriber line (also called CDSL, using telephone lines). Dial-up offers slower connectivity than broadband solutions. Telephone and cable companies can function as Internet Service Providers, or ISPs by providing internet service over their lines, or they can lease transmission to independent ISPs.

This case concerns net neutrality, which is, generally, the principle that internet service providers (ISPs) treat all data they transmit equally. Net neutrality proponents were and continue to be concerned that cable companies that operate as ISPs could discriminate against online services that compete with their other revenue streams or that they find objectionable. For example, cable companies that also have an online streaming platform might slow down their ISP customers' Netflix connections, or they might block access to websites critical of the company.

Petitioners here, including Brand X and other small ISPs, believed that cable companies providing broadband service should be subject to common-carrier regulations, thereby ensuring that companies would be unable to discriminate against certain types of data that they transmit to their customers.]

Title II of the Communications Act of 1934, 48 Stat. 1064, as amended, 47 U.S.C. § 151 *et seq.*, subjects all providers of "telecommunications servic[e]" to mandatory common-carrier regulation, § 153(44). In the order under review, the Federal Communications Commission concluded that cable companies that sell broadband Internet service do not provide "telecommunications servic[e]" as the Communications Act defines that term, and hence are exempt from mandatory common-carrier regulation under Title II. We must decide whether that conclusion is a lawful construction of the Communications Act under *Chevron,* [citation], and the Administrative Procedure Act, 5 U.S.C. § 551 *et seq.* We hold that it is. . . .

II

At issue in these cases is the proper regulatory classification under the Communications Act of broadband cable Internet service. The Act, as amended by the Telecommunications Act of 1996, 110 Stat. 56, defines two categories of regulated entities relevant to these cases: telecommunications carriers and information-service providers. The Act regulates telecommunications carriers, but not information-service providers, as common carriers. Telecommunications carriers, for example, must charge just and reasonable, nondiscriminatory rates to their customers, 47 U.S.C. §§ 201–209, design their systems so that other carriers can interconnect with their communications networks, § 251(a)(1), and contribute to the federal "universal service" fund, § 254(d). These provisions are mandatory, but the Commission must forbear from applying them if it determines that the public interest requires it. §§ 160(a), (b). Information-service providers, by contrast, are not subject to mandatory common-carrier regulation under Title II, though the Commission has jurisdiction to impose additional regulatory obligations under its Title I ancillary jurisdiction to regulate interstate and foreign communications, see §§ 151–161.

These two statutory classifications originated in the late 1970's, as the Commission developed rules to regulate data-processing services offered over telephone wires. . . . The definitions of the terms "telecommunications service" and "information service" [were] established by the 1996 Act. . . . "Telecommunications service" . . . is "the offering of telecommunications for a fee directly to the public . . . regardless of the facilities used." 47 U.S.C. § 153(46). "Telecommunications" is "the transmission, between or among points specified by the user, of information of the user's choosing, without change in the form or content of the information as sent and received." § 153(43). "Telecommunications carrier[s]"—those subjected to mandatory Title II common-carrier regulation—are defined as "provider[s] of telecommunications services." § 153(44). And "information service" . . . is "the offering of a capability for generating, acquiring, storing, transforming, processing, retrieving, utilizing, or making available information via telecommunications. . . ." § 153(20).

In September 2000, the Commission initiated a rulemaking proceeding to, among other things, apply these classifications to cable companies that offer broadband Internet service directly to consumers. In March 2002, that rulemaking culminated in the *Declaratory Ruling* under review in these cases. In the *Declaratory Ruling,* the Commission concluded that broadband Internet service provided by cable companies is an "information service" but not a "telecommunications service" under the Act, and therefore not subject to mandatory Title II common-carrier regulation. In support of this conclusion, the Commission relied heavily on its *Universal Service Report.* [Citation.] The *Universal Service Report* classified "non-facilities-based" ISPs—those that do not own the transmission facilities they use to connect the end user to the Internet— solely as information-service providers. [Citation.] Unlike those ISPs, cable companies own the cable lines they use to provide Internet access. Nevertheless, in the *Declaratory Ruling,* the Commission found no basis in the statutory definitions for treating cable companies differently from non-facilities-based ISPs: Both offer "a single, integrated service that enables the subscriber to utilize Internet access service . . . and to realize the benefits of a comprehensive service offering." [Citation.] Because Internet access provides a capability for manipulating and storing information, the Commission concluded that it was an information service. [Citation.]

The integrated nature of Internet access and the high-speed wire used to provide Internet access led the Commission to conclude that cable companies providing Internet access are not telecommunications providers. This conclusion, the Commission reasoned, followed from the logic of the *Universal Service Report.* The *Report* had concluded that, though Internet service "involves data transport elements" because "an Internet access provider must enable the movement of information between customers' own computers and distant computers with which those customers seek to interact," it also "offers end users information-service capabilities inextricably intertwined with data transport." [Citation.] ISPs, therefore, were not "offering . . . telecommunications . . . directly to the public," § 153(46), and so were not properly classified as telecommunications carriers, [citation]. In other words, the Commission reasoned that consumers use their cable modems not to transmit information "transparently," such as by using a telephone, but instead to obtain Internet access.

The Commission applied this same reasoning to cable companies offering broadband Internet access. Its logic was that, like non-facilities-based ISPs, cable companies do not "offe[r] telecommunications service to the end user, but rather . . . merely us[e] telecommunications to provide end users with cable modem service." [Citation.] Though the Commission declined to apply mandatory Title II common-carrier regulation to cable companies, it invited comment on whether under its Title I jurisdiction it should require cable companies to offer other ISPs access to their facilities on common-carrier terms. [Citation.] Numerous parties petitioned for judicial review, challenging the Commission's conclusion that cable modem service was not telecommunications service. By judicial lottery, the Court of Appeals for the Ninth Circuit was selected as the venue for the challenge.

The Court of Appeals granted the petitions in part, vacated the *Declaratory Ruling* in part, and remanded to the Commission for further proceedings. In particular, the Court of Appeals vacated the ruling to the extent it concluded that cable modem service was not "telecommunications service" under the Communications Act. It held that the Commission could not permissibly construe the Communications Act to exempt cable companies providing Internet service from Title II regulation. [Citation.] Rather than analyzing the permissibility of that construction under the deferential framework of *Chevron,* [citation], however, the Court of Appeals grounded its holding in the *stare decisis* effect of *AT & T Corp. v. Portland,* 216 F.3d 871 (CA9 2000). [Citation.] *Portland* held that cable modem service was a "telecommunications service," though the court in that case was not reviewing an administrative proceeding and the Commission was not a party to the case. *See* 216 F. 3d, at 877–880. Nevertheless, *Portland's* holding, the Court of Appeals reasoned, overrode the contrary interpretation reached by the Commission in the *Declaratory Ruling.* [Citation.]

We granted certiorari to settle the important questions of federal law that these cases present. [Citation.]

III

We first consider whether we should apply *Chevron's* framework to the Commission's interpretation of the term "telecommunications service." We conclude that we should. We also conclude that the Court of Appeals should have done the same, instead of following the contrary construction it adopted in *Portland.*

A

The *Chevron* framework governs our review of the Commission's construction. Congress has delegated to the Commission the authority to "execute and enforce" the Communications Act, § 151, and to "prescribe such rules and regulations as may be necessary in the public interest to carry out the provisions" of the Act, § 201(b); [citation]. These provisions give the Commission the authority to promulgate binding legal rules; the Commission issued the order under review in the exercise of that authority; and no one questions that the order is within the Commission's jurisdiction. *See . . . Mead,* [citation]; *Christensen,* [citation]. Hence, as we have in the past, we apply the *Chevron* framework to the Commission's interpretation of the Communications Act. [Citations.]

Some of the respondents dispute this conclusion, on the ground that the Commission's interpretation is inconsistent with its past practice. We reject this argument. Agency inconsistency is not a basis for declining to analyze the agency's interpretation under the *Chevron* framework. . . . For if the agency adequately explains the reasons for a reversal of policy, "change is not invalidating, since the whole point of *Chevron* is to leave the discretion provided by the ambiguities of a statute with the implementing agency." [Citations]. "An initial agency interpretation is not instantly carved in stone. On the contrary, the agency . . . must consider varying interpretations and the wisdom of its policy on a continuing basis," *Chevron,* [citation], for example, in response to changed factual circumstances, or a change in administrations, see *State Farm,* [citation]. That is no doubt why in *Chevron* itself, this Court deferred to an agency interpretation that was a recent reversal of agency policy. [Citation.] We therefore have no difficulty concluding that *Chevron* applies.

B

The Court of Appeals declined to apply *Chevron* because it thought the Commission's interpretation of the Communications Act foreclosed by the conflicting construction of the Act it had adopted in *Portland. See*

345 F. 3d, at 1127–1132. It based that holding on the assumption that *Portland's* construction overrode the Commission's, regardless of whether *Portland* had held the statute to be unambiguous. 345 F. 3d, at 1131. That reasoning was incorrect.

A court's prior judicial construction of a statute trumps an agency construction otherwise entitled to *Chevron* deference only if the prior court decision holds that its construction follows from the unambiguous terms of the statute and thus leaves no room for agency discretion. This principle follows from *Chevron* itself. *Chevron* established a "presumption that Congress, when it left ambiguity in a statute meant for implementation by an agency, understood that the ambiguity would be resolved, first and foremost, by the agency, and desired the agency (rather than the courts) to possess whatever degree of discretion the ambiguity allows." [Citation.] Yet allowing a judicial precedent to foreclose an agency from interpreting an ambiguous statute, as the Court of Appeals assumed it could, would allow a court's interpretation to override an agency's. *Chevron's* premise is that it is for agencies, not courts, to fill statutory gaps. [Citation.] The better rule is to hold judicial interpretations contained in precedents to the same demanding *Chevron* step one standard that applies if the court is reviewing the agency's construction on a blank slate: Only a judicial precedent holding that the statute unambiguously forecloses the agency's interpretation, and therefore contains no gap for the agency to fill, displaces a conflicting agency construction.

A contrary rule would produce anomalous results. It would mean that whether an agency's interpretation of an ambiguous statute is entitled to *Chevron* deference would turn on the order in which the interpretations issue: If the court's construction came first, its construction would prevail, whereas if the agency's came first, the agency's construction would command *Chevron* deference. Yet whether Congress has delegated to an agency the authority to interpret a statute does not depend on the order in which the judicial and administrative constructions occur. The Court of Appeals' rule, moreover, would "lead to the ossification of large portions of our statutory law," *Mead,* [citation] (Scalia, J., dissenting), by precluding agencies from revising unwise judicial constructions of ambiguous statutes. Neither *Chevron* nor the doctrine of *stare decisis* requires these haphazard results.

The Court of Appeals derived a contrary rule from a mistaken reading of this Court's decisions. . . . Against this background, the Court of Appeals erred in refusing to apply *Chevron* to the Commission's interpretation of the definition of "telecommunications service," 47 U.S.C. § 153(46). Its prior decision in *Portland* held only that the *best* reading of § 153(46) was that cable modem service was a "telecommunications service," not that it was the *only permissible* reading of the statute. *See* 216 F. 3d, at 877–880. Nothing in *Portland* held that the Communications Act unambiguously required treating cable Internet providers as telecommunications carriers. Instead, the court noted that it was "not presented with a case involving potential deference to an administrative agency's statutory construction pursuant to the *Chevron* doctrine," *id.*, at 876; and the court invoked no other rule of construction (such as the rule of lenity) requiring it to conclude that the statute was unambiguous to reach its judgment. Before a judicial construction of a statute, whether contained in a precedent or not, may trump an agency's, the court must hold that the statute unambiguously requires the court's construction. *Portland* did not do so.

IV

We next address whether the Commission's construction of the definition of "telecommunications service," 47 U.S.C. § 153(46), is a permissible reading of the Communications Act under the *Chevron* framework. *Chevron* established a familiar two-step procedure for evaluating whether an agency's interpretation of a statute is lawful. At the first step, we ask whether the statute's plain terms "directly addres[s] the precise question at issue." [Citation.] If the statute is ambiguous on the point, we defer at step two to the agency's interpretation so long as the construction is "a reasonable policy choice for the agency to make." [Citation.] The Commission's interpretation is permissible at both steps.

A

We first set forth our understanding of the interpretation of the Communications Act that the Commission embraced. The issue before the Commission was whether cable companies providing cable modem service are providing a "telecommunications service" in addition to an "information service."

The Commission first concluded that cable modem service is an "information service," a conclusion unchallenged here. The Act defines "information service" as "the offering of a capability for generating, acquiring, storing, transforming, processing, retrieving, utilizing, or making available information via telecommunications . . . ." § 153(20). Cable modem service is an information service, the Commission reasoned, because it provides consumers with a comprehensive capability for manipulating information using the Internet via high-speed telecommunications. That service enables users, for example, to browse the World Wide Web, to transfer files from file archives available on the Internet via the "File Transfer Protocol," and to access e-mail and Usenet newsgroups. [Citations.] Like other forms of Internet service, cable modem service also gives users access to the Domain Name System (DNS). DNS, among other things, matches the Web page addresses that end users type into their browsers (or "click" on) with the Internet Protocol (IP) addresses of the servers containing the Web pages the users wish to access. [Citation.] All of these features, the Commission concluded, were part of the information service that cable companies provide consumers. [Citations.]

At the same time, the Commission concluded that cable modem service was not "telecommunications service." "Telecommunications service" is "the offering of telecommunications for a fee directly to the public." 47 U.S.C. § 153(46). "Telecommunications," in turn, is defined as "the transmission, between or among points specified by the user, of information of the user's choosing, without change in the form or content of the information as sent and received." § 153(43). The Commission conceded that, like all information-service providers, cable companies use "telecommunications" to provide consumers with Internet service; cable companies provide such service via the high-speed wire that transmits signals to and from an end user's computer. [Citation.] For the Commission, however, the question whether cable broadband Internet providers "offer" telecommunications involved more than whether telecommunications was one necessary component of cable modem service. Instead, whether that service also includes a telecommunications "offering" "turn[ed] on the nature of the functions the *end user* is offered," [citation] for the statutory definition of "telecommunications service" does not "res[t] on the particular types of facilities used," [citations.]

Seen from the consumer's point of view, the Commission concluded, cable modem service is not a telecommunications offering because the consumer uses the high-speed wire always in connection with the information-processing capabilities provided by Internet access, and because the transmission is a necessary component of Internet access: "As provided to the end user the telecommunications is part and parcel of cable modem service and is integral to its other capabilities." [Citation.] The wire is used, in other words, to access the World Wide Web, newsgroups, and so forth, rather than "transparently" to transmit and receive ordinary-language messages without computer processing or storage of the message. [Citation.] The integrated character of this offering led the Commission to conclude that cable modem service is not a "stand-alone," transparent offering of telecommunications. [Citation.]

B

This construction passes *Chevron's* first step. Respondents argue that it does not, on the ground that cable companies providing Internet service necessarily "offe[r]" the underlying telecommunications used to transmit that service. The word "offering" as used in § 153(46), however, does not unambiguously require that result. Instead, "offering" can reasonably be read to mean a "stand-alone" offering of telecommunications, *i.e.,* an offered service that, from the user's perspective, transmits messages unadulterated by computer processing. That conclusion follows not only from the ordinary meaning of the word "offering," but also from the regulatory history of the Communications Act.

1

Cable companies in the broadband Internet service business "offe[r]" consumers an information service in the form of Internet access and they do so "via telecommunications," § 153(20), but it does not inexorably follow as a matter of ordinary language that they also "offe[r]" consumers the high-speed data transmission (telecommunications) that is an input used to provide this service, § 153(46). We have held that where a statute's plain terms admit of two or more reasonable ordinary usages, the Commission's choice of one of them is entitled to deference. [Citation.] The term "offe[r]" as used in the definition of telecommunications service, § 153(46), is ambiguous in this way.

It is common usage to describe what a company "offers" to a consumer as what the consumer perceives to be the integrated finished product, even to the exclusion of discrete components that compose the product, as the dissent concedes. One might well say that a car dealership "offers" cars, but does not "offer" the integrated major inputs that make purchasing the car valuable, such as the engine or the chassis. It would, in fact, be odd to describe a car dealership as "offering" consumers the car's components in addition to the car itself. Even if it is linguistically permissible to say that the car dealership "offers" engines when it offers cars, that shows, at most, that the term "offer," when applied to a commercial transaction, is ambiguous about whether it describes only the offered finished product, or the product's discrete components as well. It does not show that no other usage is permitted.

The question, then, is whether the transmission component of cable modem service is sufficiently integrated with the finished service to make it reasonable to describe the two as a single, integrated offering. [Citation.] We think that they are sufficiently integrated, because "[a] consumer uses the high-speed wire always in connection with the information-processing capabilities provided by Internet access, and because the transmission is a necessary component of Internet access." [Citation.] In the telecommunications context, it is at least reasonable to describe companies as not "offering" to consumers each discrete input that is necessary to providing, and is always used in connection with, a finished service. We think it no misuse of language, for example, to say that cable companies providing Internet service do not "offer" consumers DNS, even though DNS is essential to providing Internet access. [Citation.] Likewise, a telephone company "offers" consumers a transparent transmission path that conveys an ordinary-language message, not necessarily the data-transmission facilities that also "transmi[t] . . . information of the user's choosing," § 153(43), or other physical elements of the facilities used to provide telephone service, like the trunks and switches, or the copper in the wires. What cable companies providing cable modem service and telephone companies providing telephone service "offer" is Internet service and telephone service respectively—the finished services, though they do so using (or "via") the discrete components composing the end product, including data transmission. Such functionally integrated components need not be described as distinct "offerings."

In response, the dissent argues that the high-speed transmission component necessary to providing cable modem service is necessarily "offered" with Internet service because cable modem service is like the offering of pizza delivery service together with pizza, and the offering of puppies together with dog leashes. The dissent's appeal to these analogies only underscores that the term "offer" is ambiguous in the way that we have described. The entire question is whether the products here are functionally integrated (like the components of a car) or functionally separate (like pets and leashes). That question turns not on the language of the Act, but on the factual particulars of how Internet technology works and how it is provided, questions *Chevron* leaves to the Commission to resolve in the first instance. . . .

We also do not share the dissent's certainty that cable modem service is so obviously like pizza delivery service and the combination of dog leashes and dogs that the Commission could not reasonably have thought otherwise. For example, unlike the transmission component of Internet service, delivery service and dog leashes are not integral components of the finished products (pizzas and pet dogs). One can pick up a pizza rather than having it delivered, and one can own a dog without buying a leash. By contrast, the Commission reasonably concluded, a consumer cannot purchase Internet service without also purchasing a connection to the Internet and the transmission always occurs in connection with information processing. In any event, we doubt that a statute that, for example, subjected offerors of "delivery" service (such as Federal Express and United Parcel Service) to common-carrier regulation would unambiguously require pizza-delivery companies to offer their delivery services on a common-carrier basis.

2

[The Court held that the regulatory history of the Communications Act confirms the ambiguous nature of "telecommunications service." The majority reasoned that "if the Act fails unambiguously to classify non-facilities-based information-service providers that use telecommunications inputs to provide an information service as "offer[ors]" of "telecommunications," then it also fails unambiguously to classify facilities-based information-service providers as telecommunications-service offerors . . . . That silence suggests, instead, that the Commission has the discretion to fill the consequent statutory gap."]

C

We also conclude that the Commission's construction was "a reasonable policy choice for the [Commission] to make" at *Chevron's* second step. [Citation.] . . .

V

[The majority rejected respondents' argument that the Commission's determination was arbitrary and capricious deviation from agency policy, citing the Commission's sufficiently reasoned decision for treating cable modem service differently from DSL service.]

* * *

The questions the Commission resolved in the order under review involve a "subject matter [that] is technical, complex, and dynamic." [Citation.] The Commission is in a far better position to address these questions than we are. Nothing in the Communications Act or the Administrative Procedure Act makes unlawful the Commission's use of its expert policy judgment to resolve these difficult questions. The judgment of the Court of Appeals is reversed, and the cases are remanded for further proceedings consistent with this opinion.

It is so ordered.

■ JUSTICE STEVENS, concurring.

While I join the Court's opinion in full, I add this caveat concerning Part III-B, which correctly explains why a court of appeals' interpretation of an ambiguous provision in a regulatory statute does not foreclose a contrary reading by the agency. That explanation would not necessarily be applicable to a decision by this Court that would presumably remove any pre-existing ambiguity.

[The concurring opinion of JUSTICE BREYER, contesting the dissent's characterization of *Mead*, has been omitted.]

■ JUSTICE SCALIA, with whom JUSTICE SOUTER and JUSTICE GINSBURG join as to Part I, dissenting.

The Federal Communications Commission (FCC or Commission) has once again attempted to concoct "a whole new regime of regulation (or of free-market competition)" under the guise of statutory construction. *MCI,* [citation]. . . . [T]he Commission has chosen to achieve this through an implausible reading of the statute, and has thus exceeded the authority given it by Congress.

I

The first sentence of the FCC ruling under review reads as follows: "Cable modem service provides high-speed access to the Internet, *as well as* many applications or functions that can be used with that access, over cable system facilities." [Citation.] Does this mean that cable companies "offer" high-speed access to the Internet? Surprisingly not, if the Commission and the Court are to be believed.

It happens that cable-modem service is popular precisely because of the high-speed access it provides, and that, once connected with the Internet, cable-modem subscribers often use Internet applications and functions from providers other than the cable company. Nevertheless, for purposes of classifying what the cable company does, the Commission (with the Court's approval) puts all the emphasis on the rest of the package (the additional "applications or functions"). It does so by claiming that the cable company does not "offe[r]" its customers high-speed Internet access because it offers that access only in conjunction with particular applications and functions, rather than "separate[ly]," as a "stand-alone offering." [Citation.] . . .

The Court concludes that the word "offer" is ambiguous in the sense that it has " 'alternative dictionary definitions' " that might be relevant. It seems to me, however, that the analytic problem pertains not really to the meaning of "offer," but to the identity of what is offered. The relevant question is whether the individual components in a package being offered still possess sufficient identity to be described as separate objects of the offer, or whether they have been so changed by their combination with the other components that it is no longer reasonable to describe them in that way.

Thus, I agree (to adapt the Court's example) that it would be odd to say that a car dealer is in the business of selling steel or carpets because the cars he sells include both steel frames and carpeting. Nor does the water company sell hydrogen, nor the pet store water (though dogs and cats are largely water at the molecular level). But what is sometimes true is not, as the Court seems to assume, *always* true. There are instances in which it is ridiculous to deny that one part of a joint offering is being offered merely because it is not offered on a " 'stand-alone' " basis.

If, for example, I call up a pizzeria and ask whether they offer delivery, both common sense and common "usage," would prevent them from answering: "No, we do not offer delivery—but if you order a pizza from us, we'll bake it for you and then bring it to your house." The logical response to this would be something on the order of, "so, you *do* offer delivery." But our pizza-man may continue to deny the obvious and explain, paraphrasing the FCC and the Court: "No, even though we bring the pizza to your house, we are not actually 'offering' you delivery, because the delivery that we provide to our end users is 'part and parcel' of our pizzeria-pizza-at-home service and is 'integral to its other capabilities.' " [Citations.] Any reasonable customer would conclude at that point that his interlocutor was either crazy or following some too-clever-by-half legal advice.

In short, for the inputs of a finished service to qualify as the objects of an "offer" (as that term is reasonably understood), it is perhaps a sufficient, *but surely not a necessary,* condition that the seller offer separately "each discrete input that is necessary to providing . . . a finished service." The pet store may have a policy of selling puppies only with leashes, but any customer will say that it *does* offer puppies— because a leashed puppy is still a puppy, even though it is not offered on a "stand-alone" basis.

Despite the Court's mighty labors to prove otherwise, the telecommunications component of cable-modem service retains such ample independent identity that it must be regarded as being on offer— especially when seen from the perspective of the consumer or the end user, which the Court purports to find determinative. The Commission's ruling began by noting that cable-modem service provides *both* "high-speed access to the Internet" *and* other "applications and functions," [citation], because that is exactly how any reasonable consumer would perceive it: as consisting of two separate things.

The consumer's view of the matter is best assessed by asking what other products cable-modem service substitutes for in the marketplace. Broadband Internet service provided by cable companies is one of the three most common forms of Internet service, the other two being dial-up access and broadband Digital Subscriber Line (DSL) service. In each of the other two, the physical transmission pathway to the Internet is sold—indeed, *is legally required* to be sold—separately from the Internet functionality. With dial-up access, the physical pathway comes from the telephone company, and the Internet service provider (ISP) provides the functionality. . . .

Since the delivery service provided by cable (the broad-band connection between the customer's computer and the cable company's computer-processing facilities) is downstream from the computer-processing facilities, there is no question that it merely serves as a conduit for the information services that have already been "assembled" by the cable company in its capacity as ISP. This is relevant because of the statutory distinction between an "information service" and "telecommunications." The former involves the capability of getting, processing, and manipulating information. § 153(20). The latter, by contrast, involves no "change in the form or content of the information as sent and received." § 153(43). When cable-company-assembled information enters the cable for delivery to the subscriber, the information service is already complete. The information has been (as the statute requires) generated, acquired, stored, transformed, processed, retrieved, utilized, or made available. All that remains is for the information in its final, unaltered form, to be delivered (via telecommunications) to the subscriber. . . .

Finally, I must note that, notwithstanding the Commission's self-congratulatory paean to its deregulatory largesse. . . . This is a wonderful illustration of how an experienced agency can (with some assistance from credulous courts) turn statutory constraints into bureaucratic discretions. The main source of the Commission's regulatory authority over common carriers is Title II, but the Commission has rendered that inapplicable in this instance by concluding that the definition of "telecommunications service" is ambiguous and does not (in its current view) apply to cable-modem service. It contemplates, however, altering that (unnecessary) outcome, not by changing the law (*i.e.*, its construction of the Title II definitions), but by reserving the right to change the facts. Under its undefined and sparingly used "ancillary" powers, the Commission might conclude that it can order cable companies to "unbundle" the telecommunications component of cable-modem service. And presto, Title II will then apply to them, because they will finally be "offering" telecommunications service! Of course, the Commission will still have the statutory power to forbear from regulating them under § 160 (which it has already tentatively concluded it would do, *Declaratory Ruling* 4847–4848, ¶¶ 94–95). Such Möbius-strip reasoning mocks the principle that the statute constrains the agency in any meaningful way. . . .

For that simple reason set forth in the statute, I would affirm the Court of Appeals.

II

In Part III-B of its opinion, the Court continues the administrative-law improvisation project it began four years ago in *Mead,* [citation]. To the extent it set forth a comprehensible rule, *Mead* drastically limited the categories of agency action that would qualify for deference under *Chevron,* [citation]. . . . This meant that many more issues appropriate for agency determination would reach the courts without benefit of an agency position entitled to *Chevron* deference, requiring the courts to rule on these issues de novo. As I pointed out in dissent, this in turn meant (under the law as it was understood until today) that many statutory ambiguities that might be resolved in varying fashions by successive agency administrations would be resolved finally, conclusively, and forever, by federal judges—producing an "ossification of large portions of our statutory law," [citation]. The Court today moves to solve this problem of its own creation by inventing yet another breathtaking novelty: judicial decisions subject to reversal by executive officers. . . .

Of course, like *Mead* itself, today's novelty in belated remediation of *Mead* creates many uncertainties to bedevil the lower courts. A court's interpretation is conclusive, the Court says, only if it holds that interpretation to be "the *only permissible* reading of the statute," and not if it merely holds it to be "the *best* reading." Does this mean that in future statutory-construction cases involving agency-administered statutes courts must specify (presumably in dictum) which of the two they are holding? And what of the many cases decided in the past, before this dictum's requirement was established? Apparently, silence on the point means that the court's decision is subject to agency reversal: "Before a judicial construction of a statute, whether contained in a precedent or not, may trump an agency's, the court must hold that the statute unambiguously requires the court's construction." (I have not made, and as far as I know the Court has not made, any calculation of how many hundreds of past statutory decisions are now agency-reversible because of failure to include an "unambiguous" finding. I suspect the number is very large.) How much extra work will it entail for each court confronted with an agency-administered statute to determine whether it has reached, not only the right ("best") result, but "the only permissible" result? Is the standard for "unambiguous" under the Court's new agency-reversal rule the same as the standard for "unambiguous" under step one of *Chevron?* (If so, of course, every case that reaches step two of *Chevron* will be agency-reversible.) Does the "unambiguous" dictum produce *stare decisis* effect even when a court is *affirming*, rather than *reversing*, agency action—so that in the future the agency *must adhere* to that affirmed interpretation? If so, does the victorious agency have the right to appeal a Court of Appeals judgment in its favor, on the ground that the text in question is in fact not (as the Court of Appeals held) unambiguous, so the agency should be able to change its view in the future?

It is indeed a wonderful new world that the Court creates, one full of promise for administrative-law professors in need of tenure articles and, of course, for litigators. I would adhere to what has been the rule in the past: When a court interprets a statute without *Chevron* deference to agency views, its interpretation (whether or not asserted to rest upon an unambiguous text) is the law. I might add that it is a great mystery why any of this is relevant here. *Whatever* the *stare decisis* effect of *Portland,* [citation], in the Ninth Circuit, it surely does not govern this Court's decision. And—despite the Court's peculiar, self-abnegating suggestion to the contrary—the Ninth Circuit would already be obliged to abandon *Portland's* holding in the face of *this Court's* decision that the Commission's construction of "telecommunications service" is entitled to deference and is reasonable. It is a sadness that the Court should go so far out of its way to make bad law.

I respectfully dissent.

NOTES AND QUESTIONS

1. *Brand X* highlights an additional complication in implementing *Chevron* deference: agencies will not necessarily be the first to reach and resolve an interpretive problem arising from a statute implemented under its authority. In *Brand X*, the lower federal court in a prior case, *AT & T Corp. v. Portland,* had ruled on the issue before the agency could. Not only did the *Portland* court lack the agency's formal participation as a party construing the statute, but the *Portland* court's interpretation conflicted with the agency's later final considered judgment. In such circumstances, what should the agency's recourse be if it is not a party to the lower court case? Unless it intervenes below, it cannot seek certiorari before the U.S. Supreme Court in order to assert its preferred interpretation and correct what it concludes was an erroneous decision below. And even if the agency does intervene, the Court might decline to take that case, for any number of reasons. In that event, why should a lower federal court's interpretation prevail over the agency's subsequent, more expert construction? Is the agency's only recourse to wait until it can litigate the issue through another circuit in the hopes the Court will eventually correct the first court's error? Do these considerations influence how satisfactory you find the dissent's response to the majority's approach?

2. Recall that *Chevron* applies only to questions of statutory *interpretation*; it does not guide courts in evaluating whether the agency's policy choice in implementing the statute was prudent and well-substantiated, or arbitrary and capricious—other doctrines in administrative law guide the review of those questions. Notwithstanding this distinction, does the question in *Brand X* seem to be one of pure *legal* interpretation? Consider, for example, the familiar tools of statutory interpretation. Which methods does the majority employ at *Chevron* Step One? At Step Two? Alternatively, might *Brand X* also stand for the notion that *Chevron* deference may be warranted not only when the statutory term itself is *inherently* ambiguous (as a matter of interpretation), but also when technological developments and changing circumstances demand that an agency adopt a policy response within its broad regulatory ambit, whether or not the specific circumstances were wholly foreseen by the statute's drafters, or formally addressed in by the text of the statute itself? If so, would it be incorrect to suggest that *Chevron* Step Two review may in fact be as much about ascertaining a reasonable *policy* rationale as a reasonable *interpretation*?

3. Recall the typology of interpretive methods, *supra* Section II.B.1. What was the basis for the interpretive claims the FCC and the majority made in order to conclude that Broadband Internet was not a telecommunications service? That Congress intended the term to exclude Broadband Internet from telecommunications services regulations when it enacted the statute? That the reasonable (and hyper-technically savvy) reader would not understand the term (as defined) to cover Broadband Internet? That Congress drafted the statute to leave the statutory distinction between telecommunications and information services purposefully broad so that the agency would have flexibility to respond to developing technologies? Or something else? Does it matter if the agency's rationale does not neatly fit within any of these categories? Where traditional judicial tools of statutory interpretation "run out," might this signal that deference to the agency's interpretation—within the "*Chevron* space"—is especially appropriate? Or, as referenced in question 2, *supra*, is this not really about legal interpretation at all, and therefore not really about *Chevron*?

4. In Section III.A of the majority's opinion, the majority rejects the notion that the agency's seeming "flip flop" over time should hurt its case for *Chevron* deference. Notwithstanding the dissent's other complaints with the majority's resolution, it was silent in response to this conclusion, suggesting that all members of the *Brand X* Court agreed that *Chevron* deference need not be limited to instances in which the agency's interpretive determination at Step Two has been consistent and long-standing. (Recall, after all, that *Chevron* itself concerned an agency's interpretive about-face.) Nevertheless, in cases decided prior to *Brand X*, the Court had suggested that "the consistency of an agency's position is a factor in assessing the weight that position is due." *Good Samaritan Hospital v. Shalala*, 508 U.S. 402, 417 (1993). Keep this tension in mind as you encounter the case studies of *FDA v. Brown & Williamson Tobacco*, *Gonzales v. Oregon*, and *Guedes v. ATF*, later in this chapter.

C. CASE STUDIES IN JUDICIAL REVIEW OF AGENCY INTERPRETATIONS

As the forgoing cases make all too clear, ascertaining the nature of a congressional delegation to an agency is often as vexing an interpretive question as deciding whether the agency's interpretation warrants deference under *Chevron*; as the majority in *City of Arlington* suggests, the two inquiries are often inextricably entwined. Nevertheless, agencies may be inclined to stretch the boundaries of their regulatory authority, so from time to time, courts will need to referee exercises of agency rulemaking. Courts thus often confront a nesting doll of questions concerning agency interpretations of statutes: did Congress delegate lawmaking authority to the agency? (*Chevron* Step Zero.) If so, does the agency's action fall within the category of activity Congress delegated to it, or is the action so sweeping in nature that only a clear delegation from Congress would permit such regulation? This is the "Major Questions" doctrine, discussed in *Brown & Williamson Tobacco, infra*.

Even if Congress *has* delegated to the agency the capacity to act with the force of law, has the agency taken the kind of interpretive action that warrants *Chevron* deference? This question arose in *Gonzales v. Oregon, infra*, in which the Attorney General sought to implement a statute via an interpretive (rather than legislative) rule, one that did not go through either formal or informal rulemaking—the kinds of agency activities *Mead* suggests are sufficient, though not always necessary, for triggering *Chevron* deference.

Finally, even if the agency does undertake notice-and-comment rulemaking, is the textual instruction from Congress sufficiently ambiguous (*Chevron* Step One) that the agency can choose from a range of permissible constructions (at *Chevron* Step Two)? That issue arose in *Babbitt v. Sweet Home*, in which the agency's proposed interpretation was both sweeping in consequence and changed in form between the proposed rule and its final rule. Nevertheless, Congress seemed to incorporate that rule into the statutory scheme when it subsequently amended the statute to establish a permitting system that would alleviate potential unforeseen (and undesirable) consequences of the agency's interpretation of the statute.

The cases in this section are prominent examples of the complex dynamics of legislative delegation, agency rulemaking, and judicial interpretation. For each, we have provided the text of the statutory delegation in question as well as the relevant portions of the agency rulemaking in question. Just as the adage, "Read the Statute! Read the Statute! Read the Statute!," applies to the interpretation of statutes, so too does it bear on the review of regulations interpreting and implementing statutes. Accordingly, a careful read of the regulation is often at least as important as of the underlying statute, and a lawyer advising clients as to regulatory matters should be equally adept at engaging in both interpretive endeavors.

1. CASE STUDY IN LEGISLATING ANSWERS TO MAJOR QUESTIONS: REGULATING TOBACCO UNDER THE FOOD AND DRUG ACT

This case study concerns the vexing, multi-decade challenge of appropriately regulating cigarettes and smokeless tobacco. As you work your way through the statutes and regulation at issue in *FDA v. Brown & Williamson Tobacco*, try to ascertain: what subject matter does the Food, Drug, and Cosmetic Act (FDCA) of 1938 cover, and what actions may the FDA take in connection with the subject matter it regulates? What is the relationship of the Federal Cigarette Labelling and Advertising Act of 1965 (FCLAA) to the FDCA? What is the relationship of the FDA Regulations Restricting the Sale and Distribution of Cigarettes and Smokeless Tobacco to Protect Children and Adolescents to the FCLAA? What is the Regulations' relationship the FDCA? Which provisions of the FDCA do the Regulations implement?

The Texts to Be Construed: The Food and Drug Act and Legislation and Regulation Related to Tobacco Sales and Advertising

From the introduction of *FDA v. Brown & Williamson Tobacco, infra*:

> In 1996, the Food and Drug Administration (FDA), after having expressly disavowed any such authority since its inception, asserted jurisdiction to regulate tobacco products. [Citation.] The FDA concluded that nicotine is a drug within the meaning of the Food, Drug, and Cosmetic Act (FDCA or Act), 52 Stat. 1040, as amended, 21 U.S.C. § 301 et seq., and that cigarettes and smokeless tobacco are combination products that deliver nicotine to the body. 61 Fed. Reg. 44397 (1996). Pursuant to this authority, it promulgated regulations intended to reduce tobacco consumption among children and adolescents. *Id.*, at 44615–44618. The agency believed that, because most tobacco consumers begin their use before reaching the age of 18, curbing tobacco use by minors could substantially reduce the prevalence of addiction in future generations and thus the incidence of tobacco-related death and disease. *Id.*, at 44398–44399.

Food, Drug, and Cosmetic Act of 1938

United States Code, Title 21, Chapter 9.

§ 321.   Definitions; generally

(g)(1)   The term "drug" means (A) articles recognized in the official United States Pharmacopœia, official Homœopathic Pharmacopœia of the United States, or official National Formulary, or any supplement to any of them; and (B) articles intended for use in the diagnosis, cure, mitigation, treatment, or prevention of disease in man or other animals; and (C) articles (other than food) intended to affect the structure or any function of the body of man or other animals; and (D) articles intended for use as a component of any article specified in clause (A), (B), or (C). . . .

(h) The term "device" . . . means an instrument, apparatus, implement, machine, contrivance, implant, in vitro reagent, or other similar or related article, including any component, part, or accessory, which is—

(1) recognized in the official National Formulary, or the United States Pharmacopeia, or any supplement to them,

(2) intended for use in the diagnosis of disease or other conditions, or in the cure, mitigation, treatment, or prevention of disease, in man or other animals, or

(3) intended to affect the structure or any function of the body of man or other animals, and

which does not achieve its primary intended purposes through chemical action within or on the body of man or other animals and which is not dependent upon being metabolized for the achievement of its primary intended purposes. The term "device" does not include software functions excluded pursuant to section 360j(*o*) of this title. . . .

(n) If an article is alleged to be misbranded because the labeling or advertising is misleading, then in determining whether the labeling or advertising is misleading there shall be taken into account (among other things) not only representations made or suggested by statement, word, design, device, or any combination thereof, but also the extent to which the labeling or advertising fails to reveal facts material in the light of such representations or material with respect to consequences which may result from the use of the article to which the labeling or advertising relates under the conditions of use prescribed in the labeling or advertising thereof or under such conditions of use as are customary or usual.

§ 360f. Banned devices

(a) General rule

Whenever the Secretary finds, on the basis of all available data and information that—

(1) a device intended for human use presents substantial deception or an unreasonable and substantial risk of illness or injury; and

(2) in the case of substantial deception or an unreasonable and substantial risk of illness or injury which the Secretary determined could be corrected or eliminated by labeling or change in labeling and with respect to which the Secretary provided written notice to the manufacturer specifying the deception or risk of illness or injury,

the labeling or change in labeling to correct the deception or eliminate or reduce such risk, and the period within which such labeling or change in labeling was to be done, such labeling or change in labeling was not done within such period;

he may initiate a proceeding to promulgate a regulation to make such device a banned device.

§ 360j. General provisions respecting control of devices intended for human use

(e) Restricted devices

(1) The Secretary may by regulation require that a device be restricted to sale, distribution, or use—

(A) only upon the written or oral authorization of a practitioner licensed by law to administer or use such device, or

(B) upon such other conditions as the Secretary may prescribe in such regulation,

if, because of its potentiality for harmful effect or the collateral measures necessary to its use, the Secretary determines that there cannot otherwise be reasonable assurance of its safety and effectiveness. . . . A device subject to a regulation under this subsection is a restricted device.

(2) The label of a restricted device shall bear such appropriate statements of the restrictions required by a regulation under paragraph (1) as the Secretary may in such regulation prescribe.

§ 393. Food and Drug Administration

(b) Mission

The Administration shall—

(1) promote the public health by promptly and efficiently reviewing clinical research and taking appropriate action on the marketing of regulated products in a timely manner;

(2) with respect to such products, protect the public health by ensuring that—

(A) foods are safe, wholesome, sanitary, and properly labeled;

(B) human and veterinary drugs are safe and effective;

(C) there is reasonable assurance of the safety and effectiveness of devices intended for human use;

(D) cosmetics are safe and properly labeled; and

(E) public health and safety are protected from electronic product radiation . . . .

Federal Cigarette Labelling and Advertising Act of 1965

United States Code, Title 15, Chapter 36.

§ 1331. Congressional declaration of policy and purpose

It is the policy of the Congress, and the purpose of this chapter, to establish a comprehensive Federal program to deal with cigarette labeling and advertising with respect to any relationship between smoking and health, whereby—

(1) the public may be adequately informed about any adverse health effects of cigarette smoking by inclusion of warning notices on each package of cigarettes and in each advertisement of cigarettes; and

(2) commerce and the national economy may be (A) protected to the maximum extent consistent with this declared policy and (B) not impeded by diverse, nonuniform, and confusing cigarette labeling and advertising regulations with respect to any relationship between smoking and health.

FDA Regulations Restricting the Sale and Distribution of Cigarettes and Smokeless Tobacco to Protect Children and Adolescents

61 Federal Register 44396 (2010).

This rule establishes regulations restricting the sale and distribution of cigarettes and smokeless tobacco to children and adolescents, implementing FDA's determination that it has jurisdiction over these products under the Federal Food, Drug, and Cosmetic Act (the act). . . . FDA has determined that cigarettes and smokeless tobacco are intended to affect the structure or function of the body, within the meaning of the act's definitions of "drug" and "device." The nicotine in cigarettes and smokeless tobacco is a "drug," which produces significant pharmacological effects in consumers, including satisfaction of addiction, stimulation, sedation, and weight control. Cigarettes and smokeless tobacco are combination products consisting of the drug nicotine and device components intended to deliver nicotine to the body.

FDA has chosen to regulate cigarettes and smokeless tobacco under the act's device authorities. This rule allows the continued marketing of these products, while employing measures to prevent future generations of Americans from becoming addicted to them. . . . [M]ost people who use cigarettes and smokeless tobacco begin their use before the age of 18 and, therefore, before they fully understand the addictive nature and serious health risks of these products. Even though the sale of tobacco products to minors is illegal in 50 States, the tobacco industry has adopted extensive marketing campaigns which appeal to children and adolescents. Therefore, the rule effects measures that would both complement the existing State restrictions on access and prevent tobacco companies from marketing their products to children and adolescents. . . .

Food and Drug Administration (FDA) has determined that cigarettes and smokeless tobacco are combination products consisting of a drug (nicotine) and device components intended to deliver nicotine to the body. The agency may regulate a drug/device combination product using the Federal Food, Drug, and Cosmetic Act's (the act's) drug authorities, device authorities, or both. The agency exercises its discretion to determine which authorities to apply in the regulation of combination products to provide the most effective protection to the public health. FDA has determined that tobacco products are most appropriately regulated under the device provisions of the act, including the restricted device authority in section 520(e) of the act (21 U.S.C. 360j(e)).

FDA v. Brown & Williamson Tobacco Corp.

Supreme Court of the United States, 2000.
529 U.S. 120, 120 S.Ct. 1291, 146 L.Ed.2d 121.

■ JUSTICE O'CONNOR delivered the opinion of the Court[, joined by CHIEF JUSTICE REHNQUIST, JUSTICE SCALIA, JUSTICE KENNEDY, and JUSTICE THOMAS].

This case involves one of the most troubling public health problems facing our Nation today: thousands of premature deaths that occur each year because of tobacco use. . . . Regardless of how serious the problem an administrative agency seeks to address, however, it may not exercise its authority in a manner that is inconsistent with the administrative structure that Congress enacted into law. [Citation.] And although agencies are generally entitled to deference in the interpretation of statutes that they administer, a reviewing court, as well as the agency, must give effect to the unambiguously expressed intent of Congress. *Chevron*, [citation]. In this case, we believe that Congress has clearly precluded the FDA from asserting jurisdiction to regulate tobacco products. Such authority is inconsistent with the intent that Congress has expressed in the FDCA's overall regulatory scheme and in the tobacco-specific legislation that it has enacted subsequent to the FDCA. In light of this clear intent, the FDA's assertion of jurisdiction is impermissible.

I

The FDCA grants the FDA, as the designee of the Secretary of Health and Human Services, the authority to regulate, among other items, "drugs" and "devices." *See* 21 U.S.C. §§ 321(g)–(h), 393 (1994 ed. and Supp. III). The Act defines "drug" to include "articles (other than food) intended to affect the structure or any function of the body." 21 U.S.C. § 321(g)(1)(C). It defines "device," in part, as "an instrument, apparatus, implement, machine, contrivance, . . . or other similar or related article, including any component, part, or accessory, which is . . . intended to affect the structure or any function of the body." § 321(h). The Act also grants the FDA the authority to regulate so-called "combination products," which "constitute a combination of a drug, device, or biological product." § 353(g)(1). The FDA has construed this provision as giving it the discretion to regulate combination products as drugs, as devices, or as both. *See* 61 Fed. Reg. 44400 (1996). . . .

Based on [its] findings [regarding the dangerousness of tobacco], the FDA promulgated regulations concerning tobacco products' promotion, labeling, and accessibility to children and adolescents. *See id.*, at 44615–44618. . . .

The FDA promulgated these regulations pursuant to its authority to regulate "restricted devices." *See* 21 U.S.C. § 360j(e). The FDA construed § 353(g)(1) as giving it the discretion to regulate "combination products" using the Act's drug authorities, device authorities, or both, depending on "how the public health goals of the act can be best accomplished." 61 Fed. Reg. 44403 (1996). Given the greater flexibility in the FDCA for the regulation of devices, the FDA determined that "the device authorities provide the most appropriate basis for regulating cigarettes and smokeless tobacco." *Id.*, at 44404. Under 21 U.S.C. § 360j(e), the agency may "require that a device be restricted to sale, distribution, or use . . . upon such other conditions as [the FDA] may prescribe in such regulation, if, because of its potentiality for harmful effect or the collateral measures necessary to its use, [the FDA] determines that there cannot otherwise be reasonable assurance of its safety and effectiveness." The FDA reasoned that its regulations fell within the authority granted by § 360j(e) because they related to the sale or distribution of tobacco products and were necessary for providing a reasonable assurance of safety. 61 Fed. Reg. 44405–44407 (1996).

Respondents, a group of tobacco manufacturers, retailers, and advertisers, filed suit in [federal district court. Citation.] They moved for summary judgment on the grounds that the FDA lacked jurisdiction to regulate tobacco products as customarily marketed, the regulations exceeded the FDA's authority under 21 U.S.C. § 360j(e). . . . The District Court granted respondents' motion in part and denied it in part. [Citation.] The court held that the FDCA authorizes the FDA to regulate tobacco products as customarily marketed and that the FDA's access and labeling regulations are permissible, but it also found that the agency's advertising and promotion restrictions exceed its authority under § 360j(e). [Citation.]

The Court of Appeals for the Fourth Circuit reversed, holding that Congress has not granted the FDA jurisdiction to regulate tobacco products. [Citation.] . . .

We granted the [Government's] petition for certiorari, [citation], to determine whether the FDA has authority under the FDCA to regulate tobacco products as customarily marketed.

II

The FDA's assertion of jurisdiction to regulate tobacco products is founded on its conclusions that nicotine is a "drug" and that cigarettes and smokeless tobacco are "drug delivery devices." . . .

A threshold issue is the appropriate framework for analyzing the FDA's assertion of authority to regulate tobacco products. Because this case involves an administrative agency's construction of a statute that it administers, our analysis is governed by *Chevron*. Under *Chevron*, a reviewing court must first ask "whether Congress has directly spoken to the precise question at issue." *Id.*, at 842. If Congress has done so, the inquiry is at an end; the court "must give effect to the unambiguously expressed intent of Congress." *Id.*, at 843 [other citations omitted]. But if Congress has not specifically addressed the question, a reviewing court must respect the agency's construction of the statute so long as it is permissible. [Citation]. Such deference is justified because [t]he responsibilities for assessing the wisdom of such policy choices and resolving the struggle between competing views of the public interest are not judicial ones, *Chevron*, [citation,] and because of the agency's greater familiarity with the ever-changing facts and circumstances surrounding the subjects regulated[, citation].

In determining whether Congress has specifically addressed the question at issue, a reviewing court should not confine itself to examining a particular statutory provision in isolation. The meaning—or ambiguity—of certain words or phrases may only become evident when placed in context. *See* Brown v. Gardner, 513 U.S. 115, 118 (1994) ("Ambiguity is a creature not of definitional possibilities but of statutory context"). It is a "fundamental canon of statutory construction that the words of a statute must be read in their context and with a view to their place in the overall statutory scheme." [Citation.] A court must therefore interpret the statute as a symmetrical and coherent regulatory scheme, [citation], and "fit, if possible, all parts into an harmonious whole," [citation]. Similarly, the meaning of one statute may be affected by other Acts, particularly where Congress has spoken subsequently and more specifically to the topic at hand. [Citations.] In addition, we must be guided to a degree by common sense as to the manner in which Congress is likely to delegate a policy decision of such economic and political magnitude to an administrative agency. [Citation.]

With these principles in mind, we find that Congress has directly spoken to the issue here and precluded the FDA's jurisdiction to regulate tobacco products.

A

Viewing the FDCA as a whole, it is evident that one of the Act's core objectives is to ensure that any product regulated by the FDA is safe and "effective" for its intended use. *See* 21 U.S.C. § 393(b)(2) (1994 ed., Supp. III) (defining the FDA's mission). . . . This essential purpose pervades the FDCA. For instance, 21 U.S.C. § 393(b)(2) (1994 ed., Supp. III) defines the FDA's "mission" to include "protect[ing] the public health by ensuring that . . . drugs are safe and effective and that there is reasonable assurance of the safety and effectiveness of devices intended for human use." The FDCA requires premarket approval of any new drug, with some limited exceptions, and states that the FDA "shall issue an order refusing to approve the application" of a new drug if it is not safe and effective for its intended purpose. §§ 355(d)(1)–(2), (4)–(5). If the FDA discovers after approval that a drug is unsafe or ineffective, it "shall, after due notice and opportunity for hearing to the applicant, withdraw approval" of the drug. 21 U.S.C. §§ 355(e)(1)–(3). The Act also requires the FDA to classify all devices into one of three categories. § 360c(b)(1). Regardless of which category the FDA chooses, there must be a "reasonable assurance of the safety and effectiveness of the device." 21 U.S.C. §§ 360c(a)(1)(A)(i), (B), (C) (1994 ed. and Supp. III); 61 Fed. Reg. 44412 (1996). Even the "restricted device" provision pursuant to which the FDA promulgated the regulations at issue here authorizes the agency to place conditions on the sale or distribution of a device specifically when "there cannot otherwise be reasonable assurance of its safety and effectiveness." 21 U.S.C. § 360j(e). Thus, the Act generally requires the FDA to prevent the marketing of any drug or device where "the potential for inflicting death or physical injury is not offset by the possibility of therapeutic benefit." United States v. Rutherford, 442 U.S. 544, 556 (1979).

In its rulemaking proceeding, the FDA quite exhaustively documented that tobacco products are unsafe, dangerous, and cause great pain and suffering from illness. 61 Fed. Reg. 44412 (1996). . . . These findings logically imply that, if tobacco products were devices under the FDCA, the FDA would be required to remove them from the market. Consider, first, the FDCA's provisions concerning the misbranding of drugs or devices. The Act prohibits "[t]he introduction or delivery for introduction into interstate commerce of any food, drug, device, or cosmetic that is adulterated or misbranded." 21 U.S.C. § 331(a). . . . Thus, were tobacco products within the FDA's jurisdiction, the Act would deem them misbranded devices that could not be introduced into interstate commerce. . . .

Congress, however, has foreclosed the removal of tobacco products from the market. A provision of the United States Code currently in force states that "[t]he marketing of tobacco constitutes one of the greatest basic industries of the United States with ramifying activities which directly affect interstate and foreign commerce at every point, and stable conditions therein are necessary to the general welfare." 7 U.S.C.

§ 1311(a). More importantly, Congress has directly addressed the problem of tobacco and health through legislation on six occasions since 1965. . . . Nonetheless, Congress stopped well short of ordering a ban. Instead, it has generally regulated the labeling and advertisement of tobacco products, expressly providing that it is the policy of Congress that "commerce and the national economy may be . . . protected to the maximum extent consistent with" consumers "be[ing] adequately informed about any adverse health effects." 15 U.S.C. § 1331. Congress' decisions to regulate labeling and advertising and to adopt the express policy of protecting "commerce and the national economy . . . to the maximum extent" reveal its intent that tobacco products remain on the market. Indeed, the collective premise of these statutes is that cigarettes and smokeless tobacco will continue to be sold in the United States. A ban of tobacco products by the FDA would therefore plainly contradict congressional policy. . . .

The dissent contends that our conclusion means that the FDCA requires the FDA to ban outright "dangerous" drugs or devices, and that this is a "perverse" reading of the statute. This misunderstands our holding. The FDA, consistent with the FDCA, may clearly regulate many "dangerous" products without banning them. Indeed, virtually every drug or device poses dangers under certain conditions. What the FDA may not do is conclude that a drug or device cannot be used safely for any therapeutic purpose and yet, at the same time, allow that product to remain on the market. Such regulation is incompatible with the FDCA's core objective of ensuring that every drug or device is safe and effective.

Considering the FDCA as a whole, it is clear that Congress intended to exclude tobacco products from the FDA's jurisdiction. . . . [I]f tobacco products were within the FDA's jurisdiction, the Act would require the FDA to remove them from the market entirely. But a ban would contradict Congress' clear intent as expressed in its more recent, tobacco-specific legislation. The inescapable conclusion is that there is no room for tobacco products within the FDCA's regulatory scheme. If they cannot be used safely for any therapeutic purpose, and yet they cannot be banned, they simply do not fit.

B

In determining whether Congress has spoken directly to the FDA's authority to regulate tobacco, we must also consider in greater detail the tobacco-specific legislation that Congress has enacted over the past 35 years. At the time a statute is enacted, it may have a range of plausible meanings. Over time, however, subsequent acts can shape or focus those meanings. The "classic judicial task of reconciling many laws enacted over time, and getting them to 'make sense' in combination, necessarily assumes that the implications of a statute may be altered by the implications of a later statute." United States v. Fausto, 484 U.S., at 453. This is particularly so where the scope of the earlier statute is broad but the subsequent statutes more specifically address the topic at hand. As we recognized recently in United States v. Estate of Romani, "a specific policy embodied in a later federal statute should control our construction of the [earlier] statute, even though it ha[s] not been expressly amended." 523 U.S., at 530–531.

Congress has enacted six separate pieces of legislation since 1965 addressing the problem of tobacco use and human health. *See supra*, at 1322. Those statutes, among other things, require that health warnings appear on all packaging and in all print and outdoor advertisements, see 15 U.S.C. §§ 1331, 1333, 4402; prohibit the advertisement of tobacco products through any medium of electronic communication subject to regulation by the Federal Communications Commission (FCC), see §§ 1335, 4402(f); require the Secretary of Health and Human Services (HHS) to report every three years to Congress on research findings concerning "the addictive property of tobacco," 42 U.S.C. § 290aa–2(b)(2); and make States' receipt of certain federal block grants contingent on their making it unlawful "for any manufacturer, retailer, or distributor of tobacco products to sell or distribute any such product to any individual under the age of 18," § 300x–26(a)(1).

In adopting each statute, Congress has acted against the backdrop of the FDA's consistent and repeated statements that it lacked authority under the FDCA to regulate tobacco absent claims of therapeutic benefit by the manufacturer. In fact, on several occasions over this period, and after the health consequences of tobacco use and nicotine's pharmacological effects had become well known, Congress considered and rejected bills that would have granted the FDA such jurisdiction. Under these circumstances, it is evident that Congress' tobacco-specific statutes have effectively ratified the FDA's long-held position that it lacks jurisdiction under the FDCA to regulate tobacco products. Congress has created a distinct regulatory scheme to address the problem of tobacco and health, and that scheme, as presently constructed, precludes any role for the FDA. . . .

Taken together, these actions by Congress over the past 35 years preclude an interpretation of the FDCA that grants the FDA jurisdiction to regulate tobacco products. We do not rely on Congress' failure to act—its consideration and rejection of bills that would have given the FDA this authority—in reaching this conclusion. Indeed, this is not a case of simple inaction by Congress that purportedly represents its acquiescence in an agency's position. To the contrary, Congress has enacted several statutes addressing the particular subject of tobacco and health, creating a distinct regulatory scheme for cigarettes and smokeless tobacco. In doing so, Congress has been aware of tobacco's health hazards and its pharmacological effects. It has also enacted this legislation against the background of the FDA repeatedly and consistently asserting that it lacks jurisdiction under the FDCA to regulate tobacco products as customarily marketed. Further, Congress has persistently acted to preclude a meaningful role for any administrative agency in making policy on the subject of tobacco and health. Moreover, the substance of Congress' regulatory scheme is, in an important respect, incompatible with FDA jurisdiction. Although the supervision of product labeling to protect consumer health is a substantial component of the FDA's regulation of drugs and devices, see 21 U.S.C. § 352 (1994 ed. and Supp. III), the FCLAA and the CSTHEA explicitly prohibit any federal agency from imposing any health-related labeling requirements on cigarettes or smokeless tobacco products, see 15 U.S.C. §§ 1334(a), 4406(a).

Under these circumstances, it is clear that Congress' tobacco-specific legislation has effectively ratified the FDA's previous position that it lacks jurisdiction to regulate tobacco. . . .

"It is hardly conceivable that Congress—and in this setting, any Member of Congress—was not abundantly aware of what was going on." [Citation.] Congress has affirmatively acted to address the issue of tobacco and health, relying on the representations of the FDA that it had no authority to regulate tobacco. It has created a distinct scheme to regulate the sale of tobacco products, focused on labeling and advertising, and premised on the belief that the FDA lacks such jurisdiction under the FDCA. As a result, Congress' tobacco-specific statutes preclude the FDA from regulating tobacco products as customarily marketed. . . .

[O]ur conclusion does not rely on the fact that the FDA's assertion of jurisdiction represents a sharp break with its prior interpretation of the FDCA. Certainly, an agency's initial interpretation of a statute that it is charged with administering is not "carved in stone." *Chevron*, [citations]. As we recognized in Motor Vehicle Mfrs. Assn. of United States, Inc. v. State Farm Mut. Automobile Ins. Co., 463 U.S. 29 (1983), agencies "must be given ample latitude to 'adapt their rules and policies to the demands of changing circumstances.' " *Id.*, at 42. The consistency of the FDA's prior position is significant in this case for a different reason: it provides important context to Congress' enactment of its tobacco-specific legislation. When the FDA repeatedly informed Congress that the FDCA does not grant it the authority to regulate tobacco products, its statements were consistent with the agency's unwavering position since its inception, and with the position that its predecessor agency had first taken in 1914. Although not crucial, the consistency of the FDA's prior position bolsters the conclusion that when Congress created a distinct regulatory scheme addressing the subject of tobacco and health, it understood that the FDA is without jurisdiction to regulate tobacco products and ratified that position.

The dissent also argues that the proper inference to be drawn from Congress' tobacco-specific legislation is "critically ambivalent." We disagree. In that series of statutes, Congress crafted a specific legislative response to the problem of tobacco and health, and it did so with the understanding, based on repeated assertions by the FDA, that the agency has no authority under the FDCA to regulate tobacco products. Moreover, Congress expressly preempted any other regulation of the labeling of tobacco products concerning their health consequences, even though the oversight of labeling is central to the FDCA's regulatory scheme. And in addressing the subject, Congress consistently evidenced its intent to preclude any federal agency from exercising significant policymaking authority in the area. Under these circumstances, we believe the appropriate inference—that Congress intended to ratify the FDA's prior position that it lacks jurisdiction—is unmistakable.

The dissent alternatively argues that, even if Congress' subsequent tobacco-specific legislation did, in fact, ratify the FDA's position, that position was merely a contingent disavowal of jurisdiction. Specifically, the dissent contends that "the FDA's traditional view was largely premised on a perceived inability to prove the necessary statutory 'intent' requirement." A fair reading of the FDA's representations prior to 1995, however, demonstrates that the agency's position was essentially unconditional. [Citation.] To the extent the agency's position could be characterized as equivocal, it was only with respect to the well-established exception of when the manufacturer makes express claims of therapeutic benefit. [Citation.] Thus, what Congress ratified was the FDA's plain and resolute position that the FDCA gives the agency no authority to regulate tobacco products as customarily marketed. . . .

C

Finally, our inquiry into whether Congress has directly spoken to the precise question at issue is shaped, at least in some measure, by the nature of the question presented. Deference under Chevron to an agency's construction of a statute that it administers is premised on the theory that a statute's ambiguity constitutes an implicit delegation from Congress to the agency to fill in the statutory gaps. *See Chevron,* [citation]. In extraordinary cases, however, there may be reason to hesitate before concluding that Congress has intended such an implicit delegation. Cf. Breyer, Judicial Review of Questions of Law and Policy, 38 Admin. L. Rev. 363, 370 (1986) ("A court may also ask whether the legal question is an important one. Congress is more likely to have focused upon, and answered, major questions, while leaving interstitial matters to answer themselves in the course of the statute's daily administration").

This is hardly an ordinary case. Contrary to its representations to Congress since 1914, the FDA has now asserted jurisdiction to regulate an industry constituting a significant portion of the American economy. In fact, the FDA contends that, were it to determine that tobacco products provide no "reasonable assurance of safety," it would have the authority to ban cigarettes and smokeless tobacco entirely. Owing to its unique place in American history and society, tobacco has its own unique political history. Congress, for better or for worse, has created a distinct regulatory scheme for tobacco products, squarely rejected proposals to give the FDA jurisdiction over tobacco, and repeatedly acted to preclude any agency from exercising significant policymaking authority in the area. Given this history and the breadth of the authority that the FDA has asserted, we are obliged to defer not to the agency's expansive construction of the statute, but to Congress' consistent judgment to deny the FDA this power.

Our decision in MCI Telecommunications Corp. v. American Telephone & Telegraph Co., 512 U.S. 218 (1994), is instructive. That case involved the proper construction of the term "modify" in § 203(b) of the Communications Act of 1934. The FCC contended that, because the Act gave it the discretion to "modify any requirement" imposed under the statute, it therefore possessed the authority to render voluntary the otherwise mandatory requirement that long distance carriers file their rates. [Citation.] We rejected the FCC's construction, finding "not the slightest doubt" that Congress had directly spoken to the question. [Citation.] In reasoning even more apt here, we concluded that "[i]t is highly unlikely that Congress would leave the determination of whether an industry will be entirely, or even substantially, rate-regulated to agency discretion—and even more unlikely that it would achieve that through such a subtle device as permission to 'modify' rate-filing requirements." [Citation.]

As in *MCI*, we are confident that Congress could not have intended to delegate a decision of such economic and political significance to an agency in so cryptic a fashion. To find that the FDA has the authority to regulate tobacco products, one must not only adopt an extremely strained understanding of "safety" as it is used throughout the Act—a concept central to the FDCA's regulatory scheme—but also ignore the plain implication of Congress' subsequent tobacco-specific legislation. It is therefore clear, based on the FDCA's overall regulatory scheme and the subsequent tobacco legislation, that Congress has directly spoken to the question at issue and precluded the FDA from regulating tobacco products. . . .

Reading the FDCA as a whole, as well as in conjunction with Congress' subsequent tobacco-specific legislation, it is plain that Congress has not given the FDA the authority that it seeks to exercise here. For these reasons, the judgment of the Court of Appeals for the Fourth Circuit is affirmed.

It is so ordered.

■ JUSTICE BREYER, with whom JUSTICE STEVENS, JUSTICE SOUTER, and JUSTICE GINSBURG join, dissenting.

The Food and Drug Administration (FDA) has the authority to regulate "articles (other than food) intended to affect the structure or any function of the body. . . ." Federal Food, Drug and Cosmetic Act (FDCA), 21 U.S.C. § 321(g)(1)(C). Unlike the majority, I believe that tobacco products fit within this statutory language.

In its own interpretation, the majority nowhere denies the following two salient points. First, tobacco products (including cigarettes) fall within the scope of this statutory definition, read literally. Cigarettes achieve their mood-stabilizing effects through the interaction of the chemical nicotine and the cells of the central nervous system. Both cigarette manufacturers and smokers alike know of, and desire, that chemically induced result. Hence, cigarettes are "intended to affect" the body's "structure" and "function," in the literal sense of these words.

Second, the statute's basic purpose—the protection of public health—supports the inclusion of cigarettes within its scope. *See* United States v. Article of Drug . . . Bacto-Unidisk, 394 U.S. 784, 798 (1969) (FDCA "is to be given *a liberal construction consistent with [its] overriding purpose to protect the public health*" (emphasis added)). Unregulated tobacco use causes [m]ore than 400,000 people [to] die each year from tobacco-related illnesses, such as cancer, respiratory illnesses, and heart disease. 61 Fed. Reg. 44398 (1996). Indeed, tobacco products kill more people in this country every year "than . . . AIDS, car accidents, alcohol, homicides, illegal drugs, suicides, and fires, *combined*." *Ibid.* (emphasis added).

Despite the FDCA's literal language and general purpose (both of which support the FDA's finding that cigarettes come within its statutory authority), the majority nonetheless reads the statute as excluding tobacco products for two basic reasons:

(1) the FDCA does not "fit" the case of tobacco because the statute requires the FDA to prohibit dangerous drugs or devices (like cigarettes) outright, and the agency concedes that simply banning the sale of cigarettes is not a proper remedy; and

(2) Congress has enacted other statutes, which, when viewed in light of the FDA's long history of denying tobacco-related jurisdiction and considered together with Congress' failure explicitly to grant the agency tobacco-specific authority, demonstrate that Congress did not intend for the FDA to exercise jurisdiction over tobacco.

In my view, neither of these propositions is valid. Rather, the FDCA does not significantly limit the FDA's remedial alternatives. And the later statutes do not tell the FDA it cannot exercise jurisdiction, but simply leave FDA jurisdictional law where Congress found it. . . .

The bulk of the opinion that follows will explain the basis for these latter conclusions. In short, I believe that the most important indicia of statutory meaning—language and purpose—along with the FDCA's legislative history (described briefly in Part I) are sufficient to establish that the FDA has authority to regulate tobacco. . . .

I

Before 1938, the federal Pure Food and Drug Act contained only two jurisdictional definitions of "drug":

"[1] medicines and preparations recognized in the United States Pharmacopoeia or National Formulary ... and [2] any substance or mixture of substances intended to be used for the cure, mitigation, or prevention of disease." Act of June 30, 1906, ch. 3915, § 6, 34 Stat. 769.

In 1938, Congress added a third definition, relevant here:

"(3) articles (other than food) intended to affect the structure or any function of the body. ..." Act of June 25, 1938, ch. 675, § 201(g), 52 Stat. 1041 (codified at 21 U.S.C. § 321(g)(1)(C)).

It also added a similar definition in respect to a "device." *See* § 201(h), 52 Stat. 1041 (codified at 21 U.S.C. § 321(h)). As I have mentioned, the literal language of the third definition and the FDCA's general purpose both strongly support a projurisdiction reading of the statute. *See supra*, at 1316.

The statute's history offers further support. The FDA drafted the new language, and it testified before Congress that the third definition would expand the FDCA's jurisdictional scope significantly. . . .

That Congress would grant the FDA such broad jurisdictional authority should surprise no one. In 1938, the President and much of Congress believed that federal administrative agencies needed broad authority and would exercise that authority wisely—a view embodied in much Second New Deal legislation. . . . Thus, at around the same time that it added the relevant language to the FDCA, Congress enacted laws granting other administrative agencies even broader powers to regulate much of the Nation's transportation and communication. [Citation.] Why would the 1938 New Deal Congress suddenly have hesitated to delegate to so well established an agency as the FDA all of the discretionary authority that a straightforward reading of the relevant statutory language implies?

Nor is it surprising that such a statutory delegation of power could lead after many years to an assertion of jurisdiction that the 1938 legislators might not have expected. Such a possibility is inherent in the very nature of a broad delegation. In 1938, it may well have seemed unlikely that the FDA would ever bring cigarette manufacturers within the FDCA's statutory language by proving that cigarettes produce chemical changes in the body and that the makers "intended" their product chemically to affect the body's "structure" or "function." Or, back then, it may have seemed unlikely that, even assuming such proof, the FDA actually would exercise its discretion to regulate so popular a product. *See* R. Kluger, Ashes to Ashes 105 (1997) (in the 1930's "Americans were in love with smoking . . .").

But it should not have seemed unlikely that, assuming the FDA decided to regulate and proved the particular jurisdictional prerequisites, the courts would rule such a jurisdictional assertion fully authorized. Cf. United States v. Southwestern Cable Co., 392 U.S. 157,

172 (1968) (reading Federal Communications Act as authorizing FCC jurisdiction to regulate cable systems while noting that "Congress could not in 1934 have foreseen the development of" advanced communications systems). After all, this Court has read more narrowly phrased statutes to grant what might have seemed even more unlikely assertions of agency jurisdiction. *See, e.g.,* Permian Basin Area Rate Cases, 390 U.S. 747, 774–777 (1968) (statutory authority to regulate interstate "transportation" of natural gas includes authority to regulate "prices" charged by field producers); Phillips Petroleum Co. v. Wisconsin, 347 U.S. 672, 677–684 (1954) (independent gas producer subject to regulation despite Natural Gas Act's express exemption of gathering and production facilities).

I shall not pursue these general matters further, for neither the companies nor the majority denies that the FDCA's literal language, its general purpose, and its particular legislative history favor the FDA's present jurisdictional view. Rather, they have made several specific arguments in support of one basic contention: even if the statutory delegation is broad, it is not broad enough to include tobacco. I now turn to each of those arguments.

II

A

The tobacco companies contend that the FDCA's words cannot possibly be read to mean what they literally say. The statute defines "device," for example, as "an instrument, apparatus, implement, machine, contrivance, implant, in vitro reagent, or other similar or related article . . . intended to affect the structure or any function of the body. . . ." 21 U.S.C. § 321(h). Taken literally, this definition might include everything from room air conditioners to thermal pajamas. The companies argue that, to avoid such a result, the meaning of "drug" or "device" should be confined to medical or therapeutic products, narrowly defined.

The companies may well be right that the statute should not be read to cover room air conditioners and winter underwear. But I do not agree that we must accept their proposed limitation. For one thing, such a cramped reading contravenes the established purpose of the statutory language. *See Bacto-Unidisk,* 394 U.S., at 798 (third definition is "clearly, broader than any strict medical definition"); 1 Leg. Hist. 108 (definition covers products "that cannot be alleged to be treatments for diseased conditions"). For another, the companies' restriction would render the other two "drug" definitions superfluous. *See* 21 U.S.C. §§ 321(g)(1)(A), (g)(1)(B) (covering articles in the leading pharmacology compendia and those "intended for use in the diagnosis, cure, mitigation, treatment, or prevention of disease").

Most importantly, the statute's language itself supplies a different, more suitable, limitation: that a "drug" must be a *chemical* agent. The

FDCA's "device" definition states that an article which affects the structure or function of the body is a "device" only if it "does *not* achieve its primary intended purposes through chemical action within . . . the body," and "is *not* dependent upon being metabolized for the achievement of its primary intended purposes." § 321(h) (emphasis added). One can readily infer from this language that at least an article that *does* achieve its primary purpose through chemical action within the body and that *is* dependent upon being metabolized is a "drug," provided that it otherwise falls within the scope of the "drug" definition. And one need not hypothesize about air conditioners or thermal pajamas to recognize that the chemical nicotine, an important tobacco ingredient, meets this test. . . .

B

The tobacco companies' principal definitional argument focuses upon the statutory word "intended." *See* 21 U.S.C. § 321(g)(1)(C). The companies say that "intended" in this context is a term of art. They assert that the statutory word "intended" means that the product's maker has made an express claim about the effect that its product will have on the body. Indeed, according to the companies, the FDA's inability to prove that cigarette manufacturers make such claims is precisely why that agency historically has said it lacked the statutory power to regulate tobacco.

The FDCA, however, does not use the word "claimed"; it uses the word "intended." And the FDA long ago issued regulations that say the relevant "intent" can be shown not only by a manufacturer's "expressions," but also "by the circumstances surrounding the distribution of the article." 41 Fed. Reg. 6896 (1976) (codified at 21 CFR § 801.4 (1999)); *see also* 41 Fed. Reg. 6896 (1976) ("objective intent" shown if "article is, with the knowledge [of its makers], offered and used" for a particular purpose). Thus, even in the absence of express claims, the FDA has regulated products that affect the body if the manufacturer wants, and knows, that consumers so use the product. *See, e.g.*, 60 Fed. Reg. 41527–41531 (1995) (describing agency's regulation of topical hormones, sunscreens, fluoride, tanning lamps, thyroid in food supplements, novelty condoms—all marketed without express claims); *see also* O'Reilly, Food and Drug Administration § 13.04, at 13–15 ("Sometimes the very nature of the material makes it a drug . . .").

Courts ordinarily reverse an agency interpretation of this kind only if Congress has clearly answered the interpretive question or if the agency's interpretation is unreasonable. *Chevron*, [citation]. The companies, in an effort to argue the former, point to language in the legislative history tying the word "intended" to a technical concept called "intended use." But nothing in Congress' discussion either of "intended" or "intended use" suggests that an express claim (which often shows intent) is always necessary. Indeed, the primary statement to which the companies direct our attention says only that a manufacturer can determine what kind of regulation applies—"food" or "drug"—because, through his representations in connection with its sale, [the manufacturer] can determine whether an article is to be used as a "food," as a "drug," or as "both." S. Rep. No. 361, 74th Cong., 1st Sess., 4 (1935), reprinted in 3 Leg. Hist. 696.

Nor is the FDA's "objective intent" interpretation unreasonable. It falls well within the established scope of the ordinary meaning of the word "intended." *See* Agnew v. United States, 165 U.S. 36, 53 (1897) (intent encompasses the known consequences of an act). And the companies acknowledge that the FDA can regulate a drug-like substance in the ordinary circumstance, *i.e.*, where the manufacturer makes an express claim, so it is not unreasonable to conclude that the agency retains such power where a product's effects on the body are so well known (say, like those of aspirin or calamine lotion), that there is no need for express representations because the product speaks for itself.

The companies also cannot deny that the evidence of their intent is sufficient to satisfy the statutory word "intended" as the FDA long has interpreted it. . . . With such evidence, the FDA has more than sufficiently established that the companies "intend" their products to "affect" the body within the meaning of the FDCA.

C

The majority nonetheless reaches the "inescapable conclusion" that the language and structure of the FDCA as a whole "simply do not fit" the kind of public health problem that tobacco creates. That is because, in the majority's view, the FDCA requires the FDA to ban outright "dangerous" drugs or devices (such as cigarettes); yet, the FDA concedes that an immediate and total cigarette-sale ban is inappropriate. *Ibid.*

This argument is curious because it leads with similarly "inescapable" force to precisely the opposite conclusion, namely, that the FDA does have jurisdiction but that it must ban cigarettes. More importantly, the argument fails to take into account the fact that a statute interpreted as requiring the FDA to pick a more dangerous over a less dangerous remedy would be a perverse statute, causing, rather than preventing, unnecessary harm whenever a total ban is likely the more dangerous response. And one can at least imagine such circumstances.

Suppose, for example, that a commonly used, mildly addictive sleeping pill (or, say, a kind of popular contact lens), plainly within the FDA's jurisdiction, turned out to pose serious health risks for certain consumers. Suppose further that many of those addicted consumers would ignore an immediate total ban, turning to a potentially more dangerous black-market substitute, while a less draconian remedy (say, adequate notice) would wean them gradually away to a safer product. Would the FDCA still force the FDA to impose the more dangerous remedy? For the following reasons, I think not.

First, the statute's language does not restrict the FDA's remedial powers in this way. The FDCA permits the FDA to regulate a "combination product"—*i.e.*, a "device" (such as a cigarette) that contains a "drug" (such as nicotine)—under its "device" provisions. 21 U.S.C. § 353(g)(1). And the FDCA's "device" provisions explicitly grant the FDA wide remedial discretion. For example, where the FDA cannot "otherwise" obtain "reasonable assurance" of a device's "safety and effectiveness," the agency may restrict by regulation a product's "sale, distribution, or use" upon "*such . . . conditions as the Secretary may prescribe.*" § 360j(e)(1) (emphasis added). And the statutory section that most clearly addresses the FDA's power to ban (entitled Banned devices) says that, where a device presents "an unreasonable and substantial risk of illness or injury," the Secretary "*may*"—not *must*—"initiate a proceeding . . . to make such device a banned device." § 360f(a) (emphasis added).

The tobacco companies point to another statutory provision which says that if a device "would cause serious, adverse health consequences or death, the Secretary *shall* issue" a cease distribution order. 21 U.S.C. § 360h(e)(1) (emphasis added). But that word "shall" in this context cannot mean that the Secretary must resort to the recall remedy *whenever* a device would have serious, adverse health effects. Rather, that language must mean that the Secretary "shall issue" a cease distribution order in compliance with the section's procedural requirements if the Secretary chooses *in her discretion* to use that particular subsection's recall remedy. Otherwise, the subsection would trump and make meaningless the same section's provision of other lesser remedies such as simple "notice" (which the Secretary similarly can impose if, but only if, she finds that the device "presents an unreasonable risk of substantial harm to the public"). § 360h(a)(1). And reading the statute to compel the FDA to "recall" every dangerous device likewise would conflict with that same subsection's statement that the recall remedy "shall be *in addition to* [the other] remedies provided" in the statute. § 360h(e)(3) (emphasis added).

The statute's language, then, permits the agency to choose remedies consistent with its basic purpose—the overall protection of public health.

The second reason the FDCA does not require the FDA to select the more dangerous remedy, is that, despite the majority's assertions to the contrary, the statute does not distinguish among the kinds of health effects that the agency may take into account when assessing safety. The Court insists that the statute only permits the agency to take into account the health risks and benefits of the "product itself" as used by individual consumers and, thus, that the FDA is prohibited from considering that a ban on smoking would lead many smokers to suffer severe withdrawal symptoms or to buy possibly stronger, more dangerous, black market cigarettes—considerations that the majority calls "the aggregate health effects of alternative administrative actions."

Ibid. But the FDCA expressly permits the FDA to take account of comparative safety in precisely this manner. *See, e.g.,* 21 U.S.C. § 360h(e)(2)(B)(i)(II) (no device recall "if risk of recall[l]" presents "a greater health risk than" no recall); § 360h(a) (notification "unless" notification "would present a greater danger" than "no such notification"). . . .

I concede that, as a matter of logic, one could consider the FDA's "safety" evaluation to be different from its choice of remedies. But to read the statute to forbid the agency from taking account of the realities of consumer behavior either in assessing safety or in choosing a remedy could increase the risks of harm—doubling the risk of death to each "individual user" in my example above. Why would Congress insist that the FDA ignore such realities, even if the consequent harm would occur only unusually, say, where the FDA evaluates a product (a sleeping pill; a cigarette; a contact lens) that is already on the market, potentially habit forming, or popular? I can find no satisfactory answer to this question. And that, I imagine, is why the statute itself says nothing about any of the distinctions that the Court has tried to draw. *See* 21 U.S.C. § 360c(a)(2) (instructing FDA to determine the safety and effectiveness of a "device" in part by weighing "any probable benefit to health . . . against *any* probable risk of injury or illness . . .") (emphasis added). . . .

In my view, where linguistically permissible, we should interpret the FDCA in light of Congress' overall desire to protect health. That purpose requires a flexible interpretation that both permits the FDA to take into account the realities of human behavior and allows it, in appropriate cases, to choose from its arsenal of statutory remedies. A statute so interpreted easily "fit[s]" this, and other, drug-and device-related health problems.

III

In the majority's view, laws enacted since 1965 require us to deny jurisdiction, whatever the FDCA might mean in their absence. But why? Do those laws contain language barring FDA jurisdiction? The majority must concede that they do not. Do they contain provisions that are inconsistent with the FDA's exercise of jurisdiction? With one exception, the majority points to no such provision. Do they somehow repeal the principles of law (discussed in Part II, *supra*) that otherwise would lead to the conclusion that the FDA has jurisdiction in this area? The companies themselves deny making any such claim. *See* Tr. of Oral Arg. 27 (denying reliance on doctrine of "partial repeal"). Perhaps the later laws "shape" and "focus" what the 1938 Congress meant a generation earlier. But this Court has warned against using the views of a later Congress to construe a statute enacted many years before. *See* Pension Benefit Guaranty Corporation v. LTV Corp., 496 U.S. 633, 650 (1990) (later history is "a 'hazardous basis for inferring the intent of an earlier' " Congress (quoting United States v. Price, 361 U.S. 304, 313 (1960))). And, while the majority suggests that the subsequent history "control[s] our construction" of the FDCA, this Court expressly has held that such subsequent views are not "controlling." Haynes v. United States, 390 U.S. 85, 87–88, n. 4 (1968); accord, Southwestern Cable Co., 392 U.S., at 170 (such views have "very little, if any, significance"); *see also* Sullivan v. Finkelstein, 496 U.S. 617, 632 (1990) (SCALIA, J., concurring) ("Arguments based on subsequent legislative history . . . should not be taken seriously, not even in a footnote.").

Regardless, the later statutes do not support the majority's conclusion. That is because, whatever individual Members of Congress after 1964 may have assumed about the FDA's jurisdiction, the laws they enacted did not embody any such "no jurisdiction" assumption. And one cannot automatically infer an antijurisdiction intent, as the majority does, for the later statutes are both (and similarly) consistent with quite a different congressional desire, namely, the intent to proceed without interfering with whatever authority the FDA otherwise may have possessed. *See, e.g.*, Cigarette Labeling and Advertising—1965: Hearings on H.R. 2248 et al. before the House Committee on Interstate and Foreign Commerce, 89th Cong., 1st Sess., 19 (1965) (hereinafter 1965 Hearings) (statement of Rep. Fino that the proposed legislation would not "erode" agency authority). . . . [Indeed], the subsequent legislative history is critically ambivalent, for it can be read either as (a) "ratif[ying]" a no-jurisdiction assumption, or as (b) leaving the jurisdictional question just where Congress found it. And the fact that both inferences are "equally tenable," [citations], prevents the majority from drawing from the later statutes the firm, antijurisdiction implication that it needs. . . .

IV

I now turn to the final historical fact that the majority views as a factor in its interpretation of the subsequent legislative history: the FDA's former denials of its tobacco-related authority.

Until the early 1990's, the FDA expressly maintained that the 1938 statute did not give it the power that it now seeks to assert. It then changed its mind. The majority agrees with me that the FDA's change of positions does not make a significant legal difference. *See also Chevron*, 467 U.S., at 863 ("An initial agency interpretation is not instantly carved in stone"); *accord*, Smiley v. Citibank (South Dakota), N. A., 517 U.S. 735, 742 (1996) ("[C]hange is not invalidating"). Nevertheless, it labels those denials "important context" for drawing an inference about Congress' intent. In my view, the FDA's change of policy, like the subsequent statutes themselves, does nothing to advance the majority's position.

When it denied jurisdiction to regulate cigarettes, the FDA consistently stated why that was so. In 1963, for example, FDA administrators wrote that cigarettes did not satisfy the relevant FDCA definitions—in particular, the "intent" requirement—because cigarette makers did not sell their product with accompanying "therapeutic claims." Letter to Directors of Bureaus, Divisions and Directors of Districts from FDA Bureau of Enforcement (May 24, 1963), in Public

Health Cigarette Amendments of 1971: Hearings on S. 1454 before the Consumer Subcommittee of the Senate Committee on Commerce, 92d Cong., 2d Sess., 240 (1972) (hereinafter FDA Enforcement Letter). And subsequent FDA Commissioners made roughly the same assertion. . . .

[A] fair reading of the FDA's denials suggests that the overwhelming problem was one of proving the requisite manufacturer intent. *See* Action on Smoking and Health v. Harris, 655 F.2d 236, 238–239 (C.A.D.C.1980) (FDA "comments" reveal its "understanding" that "the crux of FDA jurisdiction over drugs lay in manufacturers' representations as revelatory of their intent").

What changed? For one thing, the FDA obtained evidence sufficient to prove the necessary "intent" despite the absence of specific "claims." This evidence, which first became available in the early 1990's, permitted the agency to demonstrate that the tobacco companies knew nicotine achieved appetite-suppressing, mood-stabilizing, and habituating effects through chemical (not psychological) means, even at a time when the companies were publicly denying such knowledge.

Moreover, scientific evidence of adverse health effects mounted, until, in the late 1980's, a consensus on the seriousness of the matter became firm. . . .

Finally, administration policy changed. Earlier administrations may have hesitated to assert jurisdiction for the reasons prior Commissioners expressed. Commissioners of the current administration simply took a different regulatory attitude. Nothing in the law prevents the FDA from changing its policy for such reasons. . . .

The upshot is that the Court today holds that a regulatory statute aimed at unsafe drugs and devices does not authorize regulation of a drug (nicotine) and a device (a cigarette) that the Court itself finds unsafe. Far more than most, this particular drug and device risks the life-threatening harms that administrative regulation seeks to rectify. The majority's conclusion is counter intuitive. And, for the reasons set forth, I believe that the law does not require it.

Consequently, I dissent.

QUESTIONS

1.   The majority suggests that the FDA's current determination to regulate tobacco products is illegitimate in light of the agency's prior disavowals of authority. Is this consistent with the *Chevron* approach to agency policy changes? Are you persuaded by the majority that a meaningful distinction should be drawn between an agency changing its interpretation of a statutory provision clearly delegating authority to the agency, versus changing its interpretation of whether the statute grants it authority to regulate at all?

2.   The majority contends that, if the FDA has jurisdiction to regulate tobacco products at all, the FDA must ban them—it may not take lesser

measures. As Congress has given no indication that it wished tobacco products banned, it would follow that the FDA lacks jurisdiction over tobacco products. More typically, however, if a legislature grants authority to take "greater" actions (such as totally prohibiting), it also implicitly authorizes "lesser" responses (such as regulation). Should a "greater/lesser" argument prevail here? Why or why not?

3.   The dissent argues that the majority's conclusion requires looking to later laws as "shap[ing]" and "focus[ing]" what an earlier Congress meant, a problematic approach insofar as the Court has elsewhere "warned against using the views of a later Congress to construe a statute enacted many years before." Recall the typology of interpretive methods in Section II.B.1, *supra*. If one seeks to understand what Congress either objectively or subjectively intended in enacting a statute, is it appropriate to look to materials postdating the statute's enactment? On the other hand, could the statute itself be understood to invite an evolutionary approach to its interpretation, with its "shape" and "focus" evolving as social and technological changes require new approaches to regulation? Recall Judge Leval's distinction between "micromanager" and "delegating" statutes in Section III.B, *supra*. What textual evidence in the statute supports an interpretation of the FDCA as either a micromanager or delegating statute? Keep this question in mind as your read the case study on the Endangered Species Act in Section V.C.3, *infra*.

NOTE: INTERPRETING "MAJOR QUESTIONS"

Judge Leval's distinction between a "micromanager" statute and a "delegating" statute raises a related concern for judges interpreting statutes for which the relevant agency claims that Congress has delegated it lawmaking authority. How clear and specific must Congress's delegation be for the agency to warrant *Chevron* deference for its interpretations of the statute? And if the nature of the delegation itself remains ambiguous, who should prevail when the agency and the courts disagree about the statute's meaning? *City of Arlington, supra*, suggests that the court should often defer to the agency. But what if the agency's desired regulatory ambit seems to exceed the statutory delegation altogether? To resolve this question, the Supreme Court has on several occasions invoked what is known as the "major questions" doctrine, as well as the related "Elephants in Mouseholes" quasi-canon:

> The [major question] approach aims to address a long-standing challenge for courts—determining whether and to what degree Congress intended to delegate authority to federal agencies. Although the challenge is long-standing, the role of the major questions doctrine in addressing the challenge remains uncertain. . . .

> A 1986 law review article by then-First Circuit Judge Stephen Breyer examining the judicial deference and statutory interpretation in the aftermath of *Chevron* is credited as one of the early sources contributing to the development of the current major

questions doctrine. Breyer, writing in the immediate aftermath of *Chevron*, noted the tension between expecting federal judges to allow agencies to tackle complex problems, such as protecting public health and the environment on the one hand and the need for vigilant judicial oversight to ensure that administrators do not "exercise their broad powers [in a manner that] lead[s] to unwise policies or unfair or oppressive behavior" on the other. Breyer predicted that the doctrine calling for these conflicting judicial roles was "inherently unstable and likely to change." Attempting to reconcile the competing signals, Breyer concluded that "Congress is more likely to have focused upon, and answered, major questions, while leaving interstitial matters to answer themselves in the course of the statute's daily administration."

Another key source of the doctrine is *MCI*, in which the Court . . . drew a distinction between the FCC's authority to modify the form, content, and locations of required filings, as well as defer or waive filings in limited circumstances, versus making tariff filing optional. Because the latter would effectively introduce a new regulatory regime, the Court deemed the FCC's actions to be much more than a mere modification and therefore declined to defer to the Commission's interpretation. Instead, the Court concluded that the FCC violated its authority, reasoning that "It is highly unlikely that Congress would leave the determination of whether an industry will be entirely, or even substantially, rate-regulated to agency discretion—and even more unlikely that it would achieve that through such a subtle device as permission to 'modify' rate-filing requirements."

The Court explicitly articulated the major questions doctrine in *Brown & Williamson*, citing both *MCI* and Breyer's 1986 article. . . . Breyer dissented, contradicting his 1986 article by arguing that tobacco regulation is such a major political question that it is appropriately addressed by one of the politically-accountable branches—whether it be Congress or the Executive Branch—rather than the courts. Breyer reasoned that the public was well aware of such a controversial issue as tobacco use, and therefore the check on agency authority would come in the form of elections.

While Whitman v. American Trucking Ass'n[, 531 U.S. 457 (2001),] did not directly invoke the "major political and economic significance" language of *Brown & Williamson*, the holding articulated a similar standard under the *Chevron* doctrine: Congress does not "hide elephants in mouseholes." Evaluating whether the EPA could consider the costs of implementing National Ambient Air Quality Standards (NAAQS) under § 109(b)(1) of the Clear Air Act (CAA), the Court started with the section's plain language, which "instructs the EPA to set primary ambient air quality standards 'the attainment and maintenance of which . . . are requisite to protect the public health' with 'an adequate margin of safety.' " Relying on § 109 and the broader context of the NAAQS provisions, the Court noted the EPA's statutory mandate to "identify the maximum airborne concentration of a pollutant that the public health can tolerate, decrease the concentration to provide an 'adequate' margin of safety, and set the standard at that level" does not include consideration of "the costs of achieving such a standard [as] part of that initial calculation." Furthermore, numerous other sections of the CAA contained express grants of authorization that permit the EPA to consider costs. Citing *MCI*, the Court "[found] it implausible that Congress would give to the EPA through these modest words the power to determine whether implementation costs should moderate national air quality standards."

Five years after *American Trucking*, the Court again applied the major questions doctrine in a case considering whether the Controlled Substances Act allows the Attorney General to prohibit doctors from prescribing regulated drugs for use in physician-assisted suicide, notwithstanding a state law permitting the procedure. . . .

Jonas J. Monast, *Major Questions About the Major Questions Doctrine*, 68 Admin. L. Rev. 445 (2016).

Does the major questions doctrine seem to conflict with the holding in *City of Arlington*, *supra*? Recall the majority there rejected the "premise that there exist two distinct classes of agency interpretations: Some interpretations—the big, important ones, presumably—define the agency's 'jurisdiction.' Others—humdrum, run-of-the-mill stuff—are simply applications of jurisdiction the agency plainly has." Rather, "No matter how it is framed, the question a court faces when confronted with an agency's interpretation of a statute it administers is always, simply, *whether the agency has stayed within the bounds of its statutory authority*." Consider this tension as you engage with the following materials

2. CASE STUDY IN EXECUTIVE BRANCH INTERPRETATION: REGULATING PHYSICIAN-ASSISTED SUICIDE BY INTERPRETIVE RULE

In addition to policing agency actions that implicate "major questions" of law, courts also review the manner in which rules are promulgated by agencies. As the Court first clearly explained in Chrysler Corp. v. Brown, 441 U.S. 281 (1979), significant differences exist between legislative (also sometimes known as "substantive") rules and interpretive (or interpretative) rules, and the distinction also implicates whether the agency's interpretation warrants *Chevron* deference:

In order for a regulation to have the "force and effect of law," it must have certain substantive characteristics and be the product of certain procedural requisites. The central distinction among agency regulations found in the APA is that between "substantive rules" on the one hand and "interpretative rules, general statements of policy, or rules of agency organization, procedure, or practice" on the other. A "substantive rule" is not defined in the APA, and other authoritative sources essentially offer definitions by negative inference: [We have given some weight to the Attorney General's Manual on the Administrative Procedure Act (1947), since the Justice Department was heavily involved in the legislative process that resulted in the Act's enactment in 1946. . . . The Manual refers to substantive rules as rules that "implement" the statute. "Such rules have the force and effect of law." [Citation.] In contrast it suggests that "interpretive rules" and "general statements of policy" do not have the force and effect of law. Interpretive rules are "issued by an agency to advise the public of the agency's construction of the statutes and rules which it administers." [Citation.] General statements of policy are "statements issued by an agency to advise the public prospectively of the manner in which the agency proposes to exercise a discretionary power." [Citations.] But . . . we [have] noted a characteristic inherent in the concept of a "substantive rule." We [have] described a substantive rule— or a "legislative-type rule"—as one "affecting individual rights and obligations." This characteristic is an important touchstone for distinguishing those rules that may be "binding" or have the "force of law." [Citation.]

That an agency regulation is "substantive," however, does not by itself give it the "force and effect of law." The legislative power of the United States is vested in the Congress, and the exercise of quasi-legislative authority by governmental departments and agencies must be rooted in a grant of such power by the Congress and subject to limitations which that body imposes. . .: "Legislative, or substantive, regulations are 'issued by an agency pursuant to statutory authority and . . . implement the statute, as, for example, the proxy rules issued by the Securities and Exchange Commission. . . . Such rules have the force and effect of law.' "

Likewise the promulgation of these regulations must conform with any procedural requirements imposed by Congress. [Citation.] For agency discretion is limited not only by substantive, statutory grants of authority, but also by the procedural requirements which "assure fairness and mature consideration of rules of general application." [Citation.] The pertinent procedural limitations in this case are those found in the APA.

Id. at 301–03. At stake in determining whether an agency rule is legislative or interpretive is thus not only (often) whether the rule carries the force of law, but also (always) whether the rule's interpretation of the underlying statute warrants *Chevron* deference. So far, you have mostly encountered cases involving legislative rules promulgated through notice-and-comment rulemaking. However, as you will see in the next case, *Gonzales v. Oregon*, interpretive rules also have their advantages, for they permit the agency or, in this case, the Attorney General, to act with greater alacrity than the notice-and-comment rulemaking process usually affords (that process can sometimes drag on for *years*). Nevertheless, agencies that promulgate interpretive rules risk the possibility that their interpretation will not warrant *Chevron* deference, precisely the issue arising in *Gonzales*.

From the introduction to *Gonzales v. Oregon, infra*:

In 1994, Oregon became the first State to legalize assisted suicide when voters approved a ballot measure enacting the Oregon Death With Dignity Act (ODWDA). Ore.Rev.Stat. § 127.800 *et seq.* (2003). ODWDA, which survived a 1997 ballot measure seeking its repeal, exempts from civil or criminal liability state-licensed physicians who, in compliance with the specific safeguards in ODWDA, dispense or prescribe a lethal dose of drugs upon the request of a terminally ill patient.

The drugs Oregon physicians prescribe under ODWDA are regulated under a federal statute, the Controlled Substances Act (CSA or Act). 84 Stat. 1242, as amended, 21 U.S.C. § 801 *et seq*. The CSA allows these particular drugs to be available only by a written prescription from a registered physician. In the ordinary course the same drugs are prescribed in smaller doses for pain alleviation.

A November 9, 2001, Interpretive Rule issued by the Attorney General addresse[d] the implementation and enforcement of the CSA with respect to ODWDA. It determine[d] that using controlled substances to assist suicide is not a legitimate medical practice and that dispensing or prescribing them for this purpose is unlawful under the CSA. . . .

The Texts to Be Construed: The Controlled Substances Act and the Regulation of Substances Used in Physician-Assisted Suicide

a. RELEVANT STATUTORY PROVISIONS OF THE CONTROLLED SUBSTANCES ACT

As you work your way through the materials related to the Controlled Substances Act (CSA) and the Attorney General's effort in the early 2000s to prohibit physician-assisted suicide through implementation of the CSA, consider the following questions in connection with the statutory text:

1.   What do you think is the "principal evil" that the CSA addresses? What "lesser" or "related" evils could the CSA also be interpreted to address?

2.   Which, if any, of the CSA's provisions grant the Attorney General the authority to interpret the act? Which, if any, of the provisions limit the Attorney General's authority arising under the CSA? Which other agency officials, if any, seem to exercise shared authority over the statute alongside the Attorney General?

The Controlled Substances Act
United States Code, Title 21, Chapter 23.

§ 801.   Congressional findings and declarations: controlled substances

The Congress makes the following findings and declarations:

(1)   Many of the drugs included within this subchapter have a useful and legitimate medical purpose and are necessary to maintain the health and general welfare of the American people.

(2)   The illegal importation, manufacture, distribution, and possession and improper use of controlled substances have a substantial and detrimental effect on the health and general welfare of the American people.

(3)   A major portion of the traffic in controlled substances flows through interstate and foreign commerce. . . .

(6)   Federal control of the intrastate incidents of the traffic in controlled substances is essential to the effective control of the interstate incidents of such traffic. . . .

§ 802.   Definitions . . .

(6)   The term "controlled substance" means a drug or other substance, or immediate precursor, included in schedule I, II, III, IV, or V of [§ 812(b), *infra*] of this subchapter. . . .

(10) The term "dispense" means to deliver a controlled substance to an ultimate user or research subject by, or pursuant to the lawful order of, a practitioner, including the prescribing and administering of a controlled substance and the packaging, labeling or compounding necessary to prepare the substance for such delivery. The term "dispenser" means a practitioner who so delivers a controlled substance to an ultimate user or research subject. . . .

(21) The term "practitioner" means a physician, dentist, veterinarian, scientific investigator, pharmacy, hospital, or other person licensed, registered, or otherwise permitted, by the United States or the jurisdiction in which he practices or does research, to distribute, dispense, conduct research with respect to, administer, or use in teaching or chemical analysis, a controlled substance in the course of professional practice or research.

§ 841. Prohibited acts

(a) Unlawful acts

Except as authorized by this subchapter, it shall be unlawful for any person knowingly or intentionally—

(1) to manufacture, distribute, or dispense, or possess with intent to manufacture, distribute, or dispense, a controlled substance. . . .

§ 811. Authority and criteria for classification of substances

(a) Rules and regulations of Attorney General; hearing

The Attorney General shall apply the provisions of this subchapter to the controlled substances listed in the schedules established by section 812 of this title and to any other drug or other substance added to such schedules under this subchapter. Except as provided in subsections (d) and (e), the Attorney General may by rule—

(1) add to such a schedule or transfer between such schedules any drug or other substance if he—

   (A) finds that such drug or other substance has a potential for abuse, and

   (B) makes with respect to such drug or other substance the findings prescribed by subsection (b) of section 812 of this title for the schedule in which such drug is to be placed; or

(2) remove any drug or other substance from the schedules if he finds that the drug or other substance does not meet the requirements for inclusion in any schedule.

Rules of the Attorney General under this subsection shall be made on the record after opportunity for a hearing pursuant to the rulemaking procedures prescribed . . . .

(b) Evaluation of drugs and other substances

The Attorney General shall, before initiating proceedings under subsection (a) to control a drug or other substance or to remove a drug or other substance entirely from the schedules, and after gathering the necessary data, request from the Secretary [of Health and Human Services] a scientific and medical evaluation, and his recommendations, as to whether such drug or other substance should be so controlled or removed as a controlled substance. In making such evaluation and recommendations, the Secretary shall consider the factors listed in paragraphs (2), (3), (6), (7), and (8) of subsection (c) and any scientific or medical considerations involved in paragraphs (1), (4), and (5) of such subsection. The recommendations of the Secretary shall include recommendations with respect to the appropriate schedule, if any, under which such drug or other substance should be listed. . . . The recommendations of the Secretary to the Attorney General shall be binding on the Attorney General as to such scientific and medical matters, and if the Secretary recommends that a drug or other substance not be controlled, the Attorney General shall not control the drug or other substance. . . .

(c) Factors determinative of control or removal from schedules

In making any finding under subsection (a) of this section or under subsection (b) of section 812 of this title, the Attorney General shall consider the following factors with respect to each drug or other substance proposed to be controlled or removed from the schedules:

(1) Its actual or relative potential for abuse.

(2) Scientific evidence of its pharmacological effect, if known.

(3) The state of current scientific knowledge regarding the drug or other substance.

(4) Its history and current pattern of abuse.

(5) The scope, duration, and significance of abuse.

(6) What, if any, risk there is to the public health.

(7) Its psychic or physiological dependence liability.

(8) Whether the substance is an immediate precursor of a substance already controlled under this subchapter.

§ 812.   Schedules of controlled substances

(a) Establishment

There are established five schedules of controlled substances, to be known as schedules I, II, III, IV, and V. . . . . The schedules established by this section shall be updated and republished . . . .on an annual basis . . . .

(b) Placement on schedules; findings required

Except where control is required by United States obligations under an international treaty, convention, or protocol, in effect on October 27, 1970, and except in the case of an immediate precursor, a drug or other substance may not be placed in any schedule unless the findings required for such schedule are made with respect to such drug or other substance. The findings required for each of the schedules are as follows [in five schedules of decreasing restrictiveness, (1)–(5).] . . .

§ 821.   Rules and regulations

The Attorney General is authorized to promulgate rules and regulations and to charge reasonable fees relating to the registration and control of the manufacture, distribution, and dispensing of controlled substances and to listed chemicals.

§ 822.   Persons required to register

(a) Period of registration . . .

(1) Every person who manufactures or distributes any controlled substance or list I chemical, or who proposes to engage in the manufacture or distribution of any controlled substance or list I chemical, shall obtain annually a registration issued by the Attorney General in accordance with the rules and regulations promulgated by him.

(2) Every person who dispenses, or who proposes to dispense, any controlled substance, shall obtain from the Attorney General a registration issued in accordance with the rules and regulations promulgated by him. The Attorney General shall, by regulation, determine the period of such registrations. In no event, however, shall such registrations be issued for less than one year nor for more than three years.

(f) Research by practitioners; pharmacies; research applications . . .

The Attorney General shall register practitioners (including pharmacies, as distinguished from pharmacists) to dispense, or conduct research with, controlled substances in schedule II, III, IV, or V and shall modify the registrations of pharmacies so registered to authorize them to dispense controlled substances by means of the Internet, if the applicant is authorized to dispense, or conduct research with respect to, controlled substances under the laws of the State in which he practices. The Attorney General may deny an application for such registration or such modification of registration if the Attorney General determines that the issuance of such registration or modification would be inconsistent with the public interest. In determining the public interest, the following factors shall be considered:

(1) The recommendation of the appropriate State licensing board or professional disciplinary authority.

(2) The applicant's experience in dispensing, or conducting research with respect to controlled substances.

(3) The applicant's conviction record under Federal or State laws relating to the manufacture, distribution, or dispensing of controlled substances.

(4) Compliance with applicable State, Federal, or local laws relating to controlled substances.

(5) Such other conduct which may threaten the public health and safety. . . .

§ 824. Denial, revocation, or suspension of registration

(a) Grounds

A registration pursuant to section 823 of this title to manufacture, distribute, or dispense a controlled substance or a list I chemical may be suspended or revoked by the Attorney General upon a finding that the registrant—

(1) has materially falsified any application filed pursuant to or required by this subchapter or subchapter II;

(2) has been convicted of a felony under this subchapter or subchapter II or any other law of the United States, or of any State, relating to any substance defined in this subchapter as a controlled substance or a list I chemical;

(3) has had his State license or registration suspended, revoked, or denied by competent State authority and is no longer authorized by State law to engage in the manufacturing, distribution, or dispensing of controlled substances or list I chemicals or has had the suspension, revocation, or denial of his registration recommended by competent State authority;

(4) has committed such acts as would render his registration under section 823 of this title inconsistent with the public interest as determined under such section . . .

§ 829. Prescriptions

(a) Schedule II substances

Except when dispensed directly by a practitioner, other than a pharmacists, to an ultimate user, no controlled substance in schedule II, which is a prescription drug as determined under the Federal Food, Drug, and Cosmetic Act, may be dispensed without the written prescription of a practitioner, except that in emergency situations, as prescribed by the Secretary by regulation after consultation with the Attorney General, such drug may be dispensed upon oral prescription in accordance with section 503(b) of that Act. Prescriptions shall be retained in conformity with the requirements of section 827 of this title. No prescription for a controlled substance in schedule II may be refilled.

b. FEDERAL REGULATION GOVERNING THE PRESCRIPTION OF CONTROLLED SUBSTANCES UNDER THE CSA

The branch of the Department of Justice then known as the Bureau of Narcotics and Dangerous Drugs—now the Drug Enforcement Administration—undertook rulemaking in 1971 to implement Section 829 of the CSA in "Regulations Implementing the Comprehensive Drug Abuse Prevention and Control Act of 1970." Compare the text of Section 829 of the CSA, *supra*, with Rule § 1306.04, *infra*. What additional rules or limitations does the Rule overlay onto the statutory provision?

Drug Enforcement Administration Prescriptions, CFR §§ 1306.01, 1306.04

United States Code of Federal Regulations, Title 21, Chapter 2.*

§ 1306.01   Scope of Part 306.

Rules governing the issuance, filling, and filing of prescriptions pursuant to section 309 of the Act (21 U.S.C. 829) are set forth generally in that section and specifically by the sections of this part. . . .

§ 1306.04   Purpose of issue of prescription.

A prescription for a controlled substance to be effective must be issued for a legitimate medical purpose by an individual practitioner acting in the usual course of his professional practice. The responsibility for the proper prescribing and dispensing of controlled substances is upon the prescribing practitioner, but a corresponding responsibility rests with the pharmacist who fills the prescription. An order purporting to be a prescription issued not in the usual course of professional treatment or in legitimate and authorized research is not a prescription within the meaning and intent of section 309 of the Act (21 U.S.C. 829) and the person knowingly filling such a purported prescription, as well as the person issuing it, shall be subject to the penalties provided for violations of the provisions of law relating to controlled substances.

c.   THE ATTORNEY GENERAL'S INTERPRETIVE RULE PROHIBITING THE USE OF CONTROLLED SUBSTANCES IN PHYSICIAN-ASSISTED SUICIDE

In 2001, the Attorney General issued an interpretive rule, *Dispensing of Controlled Substances to Assist Suicide, infra.* As you read the interpretive rule, consider how the reasoning offered does (or does not) align with the CSA's grant of interpretive authority.

Dispensing of Controlled Substances to Assist Suicide (Fed. Reg. 2001)

66 Federal Register 56607–02 (Nov. 9, 2001).

Memorandum for Asa Hutchinson, Administrator, The Drug Enforcement Administration

From: John Ashcroft, Attorney General

Subject: Dispensing of Controlled Substances to Assist Suicide

As you are aware, the Supreme Court reaffirmed last term that the application of federal law regulating controlled substances is uniform

---

* Editors' Note: As excerpted, 21 C.F.R. § 1306.04 was enacted on April 24, 1971, *see* 36 Fed. Reg. 7799 (1971), and was the version in effect as of 2001.

throughout the United States and may not be nullified by the legislative decisions of individual States. *See* United States v. Oakland Cannabis Buyers' Coop., 532 U.S. 483 (2001). In light of this decision, questions have been raised about the validity of an Attorney General letter dated June 5, 1998, which overruled an earlier Drug Enforcement Administration (DEA) determination that narcotics and other dangerous drugs controlled by federal law may not be dispensed consistently with the Controlled Substances Act, [citation], to assist suicide in the United States. Upon review of the Oakland Cannabis decision and other relevant authorities, I have concluded that the DEA's original reading of the CSA—that controlled substances may not be dispensed to assist suicide—was correct. I therefore advise you that the original DEA determination is reinstated and should be implemented as set forth in greater detail below.

The attached Office of Legal Counsel opinion, entitled "Whether Physician-Assisted Suicide Serves a "Legitimate Medical Purpose" Under The Drug Enforcement Administration's Regulations Implementing the Controlled Substances Act" (June 27, 2001) ("OLC Opinion") (attached) sets forth the legal basis for my decision.

1.   Determination on Use of Federally Controlled Substances to Assist Suicide. For the reasons set forth in the OLC Opinion, I hereby determine that assisting suicide is not a "legitimate medical purpose" within the meaning of 21 CFR § 1306.04 (2001), and that prescribing, dispensing, or administering federally controlled substances to assist suicide violates the CSA. Such conduct by a physician registered to dispense controlled substances may "render his registration * * * inconsistent with the public interest" and therefore subject to possible suspension or revocation under 21 U.S.C. 824(a)(4). This conclusion applies regardless of whether state law authorizes or permits such conduct by practitioners or others and regardless of the condition of the person whose suicide is assisted. . . .

I hereby direct the DEA, effective upon publication of this memorandum in the Federal Register, to enforce and apply this determination, notwithstanding anything to the contrary in the June 5, 1998, Attorney General's letter. . . .

Dated: November 6, 2001.

John Ashcroft,

Attorney General.

d.   THE OFFICE OF LEGAL COUNSEL'S MEMORANDUM OPINION CONCERNING WHETHER PHYSICIAN-ASSISTED SUICIDE SERVES A "LEGITIMATE MEDICAL PURPOSE"

1.   The Attorney General's interpretive rule drew on a 2001 Memorandum Opinion from the Office of Legal Counsel, a subdivision of the Department of Justice that advises the Attorney General, the White

House, and executive branch agencies as to potential legal and constitutional issues that could arise from policy decisions under consideration. The Office's authority to issue legal opinions is by delegation of the Attorney General, see 28 C.F.R. § 0.25, who is empowered to provide legal advice to every executive branch agency upon request, see 28 U.S.C. §§ 511–513. Certain other functions of OLC, such as reviewing orders of the President or the Attorney General for legality, happen as a matter of course. *See* 28 C.F.R. § 0.25(b). How does the relevant OLC Memo, *Whether Physician-Assisted Suicide Serves a "Legitimate Medical Purpose" Under DEA Regulations*, address the question of interpretive authority?

2.   To what authorities does the Office of Legal Counsel refer when it reasons that physician-assisted suicide is not a "legitimate medical purpose"? How convincing are the authorities?

Office of Legal Counsel, Whether Physician-Assisted Suicide Serves a "Legitimate Medical Purpose" under DEA Regulations (2001)

Office of Legal Counsel, 25 Op. O.L.C. 135 (2001).

Memorandum Opinion for the Attorney General

I.   Background

You have asked for our opinion whether a physician who assists in a patient's suicide by prescribing a controlled substance has a "legitimate medical purpose" within the meaning of a regulation of the Drug Enforcement Administration (DEA), 21 C.F.R. § 1306.04(a) (2000), if the physician is immune from liability under a state law such as the Oregon "Death with Dignity Act" for assisting in a suicide in such a manner. In our view, assisting in suicide, even in a manner permitted by state law, is not a "legitimate medical purpose" under the DEA regulation, and accordingly dispensing controlled substances for this purpose violates the Controlled Substances Act, which the DEA regulation implements. . . .

II.   Physicians Are Regulated Under the Controlled Substances Act

Where a physician dispenses controlled substances without a "legitimate medical purpose" under 21 C.F.R. § 1306.04(a), the physician violates several provisions of the CSA, including §§ 829 and 841(a)(1). . . .

III.   Dispensing Controlled Substances to Assist in Suicide Does Not Serve a "Legitimate Medical Purpose"

In our opinion, assisting in suicide is not a "legitimate medical purpose" within the meaning of 21 C.F.R. § 1306.04(a) that would justify a physician's dispensing controlled substances. That interpretation . . . is the best reading of the regulatory language: it is firmly supported by the case law, by the traditional and current policies and practices of the

Federal government and of the overwhelming majority of the States, and by the dominant views of the American medical and nursing professions. . . .

B.   State and Federal Policy

As detailed in Washington v. Glucksberg, state law and policy, with the sole exception of Oregon's, emphatically oppose assisted suicide. Assisted suicide has long been prohibited at common law, [citation], and at least forty States and territories have laws explicitly prohibiting the practice. "In the two hundred and five years of our [national] existence no constitutional right to aid in killing oneself has ever been asserted and upheld by a court of final jurisdiction." [Citations.] The only state supreme court to decide the matter has rejected recognition of an enforceable right to assisted suicide under that State's constitution. Krischer v. McIver, 697 So.2d 97 (Fla. 1997). . . .

C.   Views of the Medical and Nursing Professions

The leading organizations of the American medical profession have repeatedly, and recently, expressed the profession's condemnation of physician-assisted suicide. The American Medical Association (AMA), joined by the American Nurses Association (ANA), the American Psychiatric Association, and 43 other national medical organizations, filed a brief in the Glucksberg case declaring that "[t]he ethical prohibition against physician-assisted suicide is a cornerstone of medical ethics" and that physician-assisted suicide is "'infundamentally incompatible with the physician's role as healer.'" More specifically, the AMA's Brief said:

The power to assist in intentionally taking the life of a patient is antithetical to the central mission of healing that guides both medicine and nursing. It is a power that most physicians and nurses do not want and could not control. Once established, the right to physician-assisted suicide would create profound danger for many ill persons with undiagnosed depression and inadequately treated pain, for whom physician-assisted suicide rather than good palliative care could become the norm. At greatest risk would be those with the least access to palliative care—the poor, the elderly, and members of minority groups. . . .

VII. The DEA Had the Authority to Promulgate and Interpret A Regulation Concerning Whether Dispensing a Controlled Substance Has a "Legitimate Medical Purpose"

The truth is that, far from being outside the Attorney General's mission under the CSA, addressing such questions is inherent in that mission. See Chevron, [citation]. If the CSA is to be administered effectively, the Attorney General must interpret its provisions so as to decide, e.g., whether prescribing of controlled substances in a particular class of cases takes place within the "course of professional practice," 21 U.S.C. § 802(21), whether a physician's conduct involving such substances "may threaten the public health and safety," *id.*, § 823(f)(5), and whether issuing a registration to an applicant would be "inconsistent with the public interest," *id.*, § 823(f). Of course such administrative determinations will require a judgment about public policy. . . . As a matter of administrative practice, there was nothing unusual or unauthorized in the fact that the DEA's interpretation implicated questions of public policy or morality. . . .

Based on the foregoing considerations, the conclusion that a physician's assisting suicide through the dispensing of a controlled substance does not serve a "legitimate medical purpose" within the meaning of 21 CFR § 1306.04 is the best reading of that regulation.

Sheldon Bradshaw
Deputy Assistant Attorney General

Robert J. Delahunty
Special Counsel
Office of Legal Counsel

Gonzales v. Oregon

Supreme Court of the United States, 2006.
546 U.S. 243, 126 S.Ct. 904, 163 L.Ed.2d 748.

■ JUSTICE KENNEDY delivered the opinion of the Court[, in which JUSTICE STEVENS, JUSTICE O'CONNOR, JUSTICE SOUTER, JUSTICE GINSBURG, and JUSTICE BREYER joined].

The question before us is whether the Controlled Substances Act allows the United States Attorney General [via the above excerpted Interpretive Rule] to prohibit doctors from prescribing regulated drugs for use in physician-assisted suicide, notwithstanding a state law permitting the procedure. As the Court has observed, "Americans are engaged in an earnest and profound debate about the morality, legality, and practicality of physician-assisted suicide." Washington v. Glucksberg, 521 U.S. 702, 735 (1997). The dispute before us is in part a product of this political and moral debate, but its resolution requires an inquiry familiar to the courts: interpreting a federal statute to determine whether executive action is authorized by, or otherwise consistent with, the enactment.

The Interpretive Rule's validity under the CSA is the issue before us.

I

A

We turn first to the text and structure of the CSA. Enacted in 1970 with the main objectives of combating drug abuse and controlling the legitimate and illegitimate traffic in controlled substances, the CSA creates a comprehensive, closed regulatory regime criminalizing the unauthorized manufacture, distribution, dispensing, and possession of substances classified in any of the Act's five schedules. . . .

The present dispute involves controlled substances listed in Schedule II, substances generally available only pursuant to a written, nonrefillable prescription by a physician. 21 U.S.C. § 829(a). A 1971 regulation promulgated by the Attorney General requires that every prescription for a controlled substance "be issued for a legitimate medical purpose by an individual practitioner acting in the usual course of his professional practice." 21 CFR § 1306.04(a) (2005).

To prevent diversion of controlled substances with medical uses, the CSA regulates the activity of physicians. To issue lawful prescriptions of Schedule II drugs, physicians must "obtain from the Attorney General a registration issued in accordance with the rules and regulations promulgated by him." 21 U.S.C. § 822(a)(2). The Attorney General may deny, suspend, or revoke this registration if, as relevant here, the physician's registration would be "inconsistent with the public interest." § 824(a)(4); § 822(a)(2). When deciding whether a practitioner's registration is in the public interest, the Attorney General "shall" consider: [see § 823(f), *supra*] . . .

The CSA explicitly contemplates a role for the States in regulating controlled substances, as evidenced by its pre-emption provision.

> "No provision of this subchapter shall be construed as indicating an intent on the part of the Congress to occupy the field in which that provision operates . . . to the exclusion of any State law on the same subject matter which would otherwise be within the authority of the State, unless there is a positive conflict between that provision . . . and that State law so that the two cannot consistently stand together." § 903.

B

Oregon voters enacted ODWDA in 1994. For Oregon residents to be eligible to request a prescription under ODWDA, they must receive a diagnosis from their attending physician that they have an incurable and irreversible disease that, within reasonable medical judgment, will cause death within six months. [Citations.] Attending physicians must also determine whether a patient has made a voluntary request, ensure a patient's choice is informed, and refer patients to counseling if they might be suffering from a psychological disorder or depression causing impaired judgment. [Citations.] A second "consulting" physician must examine the patient and the medical record and confirm the attending physician's conclusions. [Citation.] Oregon physicians may dispense or issue a prescription for the requested drug, but may not administer it. [Citations.]

. . . Physicians who dispense medication pursuant to ODWDA must also be registered with both the State's Board of Medical Examiners and the federal Drug Enforcement Administration (DEA). [Citation.] In 2004, 37 patients ended their lives by ingesting a lethal dose of medication prescribed under ODWDA. Oregon Dept. of Human Servs., Seventh Annual Report on Oregon's Death with Dignity Act 20 (Mar. 10, 2005).

C

In 1997, Members of Congress concerned about ODWDA invited the DEA to prosecute or revoke the CSA registration of Oregon physicians who assist suicide. They contended that hastening a patient's death is not legitimate medical practice, so prescribing controlled substances for that purpose violates the CSA. [Citation.] The letter received an initial, favorable response from the director of the DEA, [citation], but Attorney General Reno considered the matter and concluded that the DEA could not take the proposed action because the CSA did not authorize it to "displace the states as the primary regulators of the medical profession, or to override a state's determination as to what constitutes legitimate medical practice," [citation]. Legislation was then introduced to grant the explicit authority Attorney General Reno found lacking; but it failed to pass. *See* H.R. 4006, 105th Cong., 2d Sess. (1998); H.R. 2260, 106th Cong., 1st Sess. (1999).

In 2001, John Ashcroft was appointed Attorney General. Perhaps because Mr. Ashcroft had supported efforts to curtail assisted suicide while serving as a Senator, [citation], Oregon Attorney General Hardy Myers wrote him to request a meeting with Department of Justice officials should the Department decide to revisit the application of the CSA to assisted suicide. [Citation.] Attorney General Myers received a reply letter from one of Attorney General Ashcroft's advisers writing on his behalf, which stated:

"I am aware of no pending legislation in Congress that would prompt a review of the Department's interpretation of the CSA as it relates to physician-assisted suicide. Should such a review be commenced in the future, we would be happy to include your views in that review." [Citation.]

On November 9, 2001, without consulting Oregon or apparently anyone outside his Department, the Attorney General issued an Interpretive Rule announcing his intent to restrict the use of controlled substances for physician-assisted suicide. Incorporating the legal analysis of a memorandum he had solicited from his Office of Legal Counsel, the Attorney General ruled:

"[A]ssisting suicide is not a 'legitimate medical purpose' within the meaning of 21 CFR 1306.04 (2001), and that prescribing, dispensing, or administering federally controlled substances to assist suicide violates the Controlled Substances Act. Such conduct by a physician registered to dispense controlled

substances may 'render his registration . . . inconsistent with
the public interest' and therefore subject to possible suspension
or revocation under 21 U.S.C. 824(a)(4). The Attorney General's
conclusion applies regardless of whether state law authorizes or
permits such conduct by practitioners or others and regardless
of the condition of the person whose suicide is assisted." 66 Fed.
Reg. 56608 (2001).

There is little dispute that the Interpretive Rule would substantially
disrupt the ODWDA regime. Respondents contend, and petitioners do not
dispute, that every prescription filled under ODWDA has specified drugs
classified under Schedule II. A physician cannot prescribe the substances
without DEA registration, and revocation or suspension of the
registration would be a severe restriction on medical practice. Dispensing
controlled substances without a valid prescription, furthermore, is a
federal crime. [Citation.]

In response the State of Oregon, joined by a physician, a pharmacist,
and some terminally ill patients, all from Oregon, challenged the
Interpretive Rule in federal court. The United States District Court for
the District of Oregon entered a permanent injunction against the
Interpretive Rule's enforcement.

A divided panel of the Court of Appeals for the Ninth Circuit granted
the petitions for review and held the Interpretive Rule invalid. . . . We
granted the Government's petition for certiorari.

II

Executive actors often must interpret the enactments Congress has
charged them with enforcing and implementing. The parties before us
are in sharp disagreement both as to the degree of deference we must
accord the Interpretive Rule's substantive conclusions and whether the
Rule is authorized by the statutory text at all. Although balancing the
necessary respect for an agency's knowledge, expertise, and
constitutional office with the courts' role as interpreter of laws can be a
delicate matter, familiar principles guide us. An administrative rule may
receive substantial deference if it interprets the issuing agency's own
ambiguous regulation. *Auer v. Robbins,* 519 U.S. 452, 461–463 (1997). An
interpretation of an ambiguous statute may also receive substantial
deference. *Chevron,* [citation]. Deference in accordance with *Chevron,*
however, is warranted only "when it appears that Congress delegated
authority to the agency generally to make rules carrying the force of law,
and that the agency interpretation claiming deference was promulgated
in the exercise of that authority." *Mead,* [citation]. Otherwise, the
interpretation is "entitled to respect" only to the extent it has the "power
to persuade." *Skidmore,* [citation].

A

The Government first argues that the Interpretive Rule is an
elaboration of one of the Attorney General's own regulations, 21 CFR

§ 1306.04 (2005), which requires all prescriptions be issued "for a legitimate medical purpose by an individual practitioner acting in the usual course of his professional practice." As such, the Government says, the Interpretive Rule is entitled to considerable deference in accordance with *Auer*. In our view *Auer* and the standard of deference it accords to an agency are inapplicable here. . . . In *Auer,* the underlying regulations gave specificity to a statutory scheme the Secretary was charged with enforcing and reflected the considerable experience and expertise the Department of Labor had acquired over time with respect to the complexities of the Fair Labor Standards Act. Here, on the other hand, the underlying regulation does little more than restate the terms of the statute itself. The language the Interpretive Rule addresses comes from Congress, not the Attorney General, and the near equivalence of the statute and regulation belies the Government's argument for *Auer* deference. . . . Deference under *Auer* being inappropriate, we turn to the question whether the Interpretive Rule, on its own terms, is a permissible interpretation of the CSA.

B

Just as the Interpretive Rule receives no deference under *Auer,* neither does it receive deference under *Chevron*. If a statute is ambiguous, judicial review of administrative rulemaking often demands *Chevron* deference; and the rule is judged accordingly. All would agree, we should think, that the statutory phrase "legitimate medical purpose" is a generality, susceptible to more precise definition and open to varying constructions, and thus ambiguous in the relevant sense. *Chevron* deference, however, is not accorded merely because the statute is ambiguous and an administrative official is involved. To begin with, the rule must be promulgated pursuant to authority Congress has delegated to the official. [Citation.]

The Attorney General has rulemaking power to fulfill his duties under the CSA. The specific respects in which he is authorized to make rules, however, instruct us that he is not authorized to make a rule declaring illegitimate a medical standard for care and treatment of patients that is specifically authorized under state law.

The starting point for this inquiry is, of course, the language of the delegation provision itself. In many cases authority is clear because the statute gives an agency broad power to enforce all provisions of the statute. *See, e.g., Brand X Internet Services* . . . . The CSA does not grant the Attorney General this broad authority to promulgate rules.

The CSA gives the Attorney General limited powers, to be exercised in specific ways. His rulemaking authority under the CSA is described in two provisions: (1) "The Attorney General is authorized to promulgate rules and regulations and to charge reasonable fees relating to the registration and control of the manufacture, distribution, and dispensing of controlled substances and to listed chemicals," 21 U.S.C. § 821 (2000 ed., Supp.V); and (2) "The Attorney General may promulgate and enforce any rules, regulations, and procedures which he may deem necessary and appropriate for the efficient execution of his functions under this subchapter," 21 U.S.C. § 871(b). As is evident from these sections, Congress did not delegate to the Attorney General authority to carry out or effect all provisions of the CSA. Rather, he can promulgate rules relating only to "registration" and "control," and "for the efficient execution of his functions" under the statute.

Turning first to the Attorney General's authority to make regulations for the "control" of drugs, this delegation cannot sustain the Interpretive Rule's attempt to define standards of medical practice. Control is a term of art in the CSA. "As used in this subchapter," § 802—the subchapter that includes § 821—

> "The term 'control' means to add a drug or other substance, or immediate precursor, to a schedule under part B of this subchapter, whether by transfer from another schedule or otherwise." § 802(5).

To exercise his scheduling power, the Attorney General must follow a detailed set of procedures, including requesting a scientific and medical evaluation from the Secretary. *See* 21 U.S.C. §§ 811, 812 (2000 ed. and Supp.V). The statute is also specific as to the manner in which the Attorney General must exercise this authority: "Rules of the Attorney General under this subsection [regarding scheduling] shall be made on the record after opportunity for a hearing pursuant to the rulemaking procedures prescribed by [the Administrative Procedure Act, 5 U.S.C. § 553]." 21 U.S.C. § 811(a). The Interpretive Rule now under consideration does not concern the scheduling of substances and was not issued after the required procedures for rules regarding scheduling, so it cannot fall under the Attorney General's "control" authority.

Even if "control" in § 821 were understood to signify something other than its statutory definition, it would not support the Interpretive Rule. The statutory references to "control" outside the scheduling context make clear that the Attorney General can establish controls "against diversion," *e.g.,* § 823(a)(1), but do not give him authority to define diversion based on his view of legitimate medical practice. . . . [I]f "control" were given the expansive meaning required to sustain the Interpretive Rule, it would transform the carefully described limits on the Attorney General's authority over registration and scheduling into mere suggestions.

We turn, next, to the registration provisions of the CSA[, which] . . . allow the Attorney General to deny registration to an applicant "if he determines that the issuance of such registration would be inconsistent with the public interest." 21 U.S.C. § 823(f). Registration may also be revoked or suspended by the Attorney General on the same grounds. § 824(a)(4). In determining consistency with the public interest, the Attorney General must, as discussed above, consider five factors, including: the State's recommendation; compliance with state, federal, and local laws regarding controlled substances; and public health and safety. § 823(f).

The Interpretive Rule cannot be justified under this part of the statute. It does not undertake the five-factor analysis and concerns much more than registration. Nor does the Interpretive Rule on its face purport to be an application of the registration provision in § 823(f). It is, instead, an interpretation of the substantive federal law requirements (under 21 CFR § 1306.04 (2005)) for a valid prescription. It begins by announcing that assisting suicide is not a "legitimate medical purpose" under § 1306.04, and that dispensing controlled substances to assist a suicide violates the CSA. 66 Fed. Reg. 56608. Violation is a criminal offense, and often a felony, under 21 U.S.C. § 841 (2000 ed. and Supp. II). The Interpretive Rule thus purports to declare that using controlled substances for physician-assisted suicide is a crime, an authority that goes well beyond the Attorney General's statutory power to register or deregister.

The Attorney General's deregistration power, of course, may carry implications for criminal enforcement because if a physician dispenses a controlled substance after he is deregistered, he violates § 841. The Interpretive Rule works in the opposite direction, however: It declares certain conduct criminal, placing in jeopardy the registration of any physician who engages in that conduct. To the extent the Interpretive Rule concerns registration, it simply states the obvious because one of the five factors the Attorney General must consider in deciding the "public interest" is "[c]ompliance with applicable State, Federal, or local laws relating to controlled substances." 21 U.S.C. § 823(f)(4). The problem with the design of the Interpretive Rule is that it cannot, and does not, explain why the Attorney General has the authority to decide what constitutes an underlying violation of the CSA in the first place. The explanation the Government seems to advance is that the Attorney General's authority to decide whether a physician's actions are inconsistent with the "public interest" provides the basis for the Interpretive Rule.

By this logic, however, the Attorney General claims extraordinary authority. If the Attorney General's argument were correct, his power to deregister necessarily would include the greater power to criminalize even the actions of registered physicians, whenever they engage in conduct he deems illegitimate. This power to criminalize—unlike his power over registration, which must be exercised only after considering five express statutory factors—would be unrestrained. It would be anomalous for Congress to have so painstakingly described the Attorney General's limited authority to deregister a single physician or schedule a single drug, but to have given him, just by implication, authority to declare an entire class of activity outside "the course of professional practice," and therefore a criminal violation of the CSA. . . .

The authority desired by the Government is inconsistent with the design of the statute in other fundamental respects. The Attorney General does not have the sole delegated authority under the CSA. He must instead share it with, and in some respects defer to, the Secretary [of Health and Human Services], whose functions are likewise delineated and confined by the statute. The CSA allocates decisionmaking powers among statutory actors so that medical judgments, if they are to be decided at the federal level and for the limited objects of the statute, are placed in the hands of the Secretary. In the scheduling context, for example, the Secretary's recommendations on scientific and medical matters bind the Attorney General. The Attorney General cannot control a substance if the Secretary disagrees. 21 U.S.C. § 811(b). *See* H.R. Rep. No. 91–1444, pt. 1, p. 33 (1970), U.S. Code Cong. & Admin. News 1970, pp. 4566, 4600 (the section "is not intended to authorize the Attorney General to undertake or support medical and scientific research [for the purpose of scheduling], which is within the competence of the Department of Health, Education, and Welfare"). . . .

The structure of the CSA, then, conveys unwillingness to cede medical judgments to an executive official who lacks medical expertise. . . . The Government contends the Attorney General's decision here is a legal, not a medical, one. This generality, however, does not suffice. The Attorney General's Interpretive Rule, and the Office of Legal Counsel memo it incorporates, place extensive reliance on medical judgments and the views of the medical community in concluding that assisted suicide is not a "legitimate medical purpose." *See* 66 Fed. Reg. 56608 (noting the "medical" distinctions between assisting suicide and giving sufficient medication to alleviate pain); Memorandum from Office of Legal Counsel to Attorney General (June 27, 2001) [citation] (discussing the "Federal medical policy" against physician-assisted suicide), *id.*, at 124a–130a (examining views of the medical community). This confirms that the authority claimed by the Attorney General is both beyond his expertise and incongruous with the statutory purposes and design.

The idea that Congress gave the Attorney General such broad and unusual authority through an implicit delegation in the CSA's registration provision is not sustainable. "Congress, we have held, does not alter the fundamental details of a regulatory scheme in vague terms or ancillary provisions—it does not, one might say, hide elephants in mouseholes." *Whitman v. American Trucking Assns., Inc.*, 531 U.S. 457, 468 (2001); see *Brown & Williamson Tobacco Corp.*, [citation] ("[W]e are confident that Congress could not have intended to delegate a decision of such economic and political significance to an agency in so cryptic a fashion").

The importance of the issue of physician-assisted suicide, which has been the subject of an "earnest and profound debate" across the country, [citation], makes the oblique form of the claimed delegation all the more suspect. Under the Government's theory, moreover, the medical judgments the Attorney General could make are not limited to physician-assisted suicide. Were this argument accepted, he could decide whether any particular drug may be used for any particular purpose, or indeed whether a physician who administers any controversial treatment could be deregistered. This would occur, under the Government's view, despite the statute's express limitation of the Attorney General's authority to registration and control, with attendant restrictions on each of those functions, and despite the statutory purposes to combat drug abuse and prevent illicit drug trafficking. . . .

Since the Interpretive Rule was not promulgated pursuant to the Attorney General's authority, its interpretation of "legitimate medical purpose" does not receive *Chevron* deference. Instead, it receives deference only in accordance with *Skidmore*. . . . The deference here is tempered by the Attorney General's lack of expertise in this area and the apparent absence of any consultation with anyone outside the Department of Justice who might aid in a reasoned judgment. In any event, under *Skidmore,* we follow an agency's rule only to the extent it is persuasive, [citation]; and for the reasons given and for further reasons set out below, we do not find the Attorney General's opinion persuasive.

III

As we have noted before, the CSA "repealed most of the earlier antidrug laws in favor of a comprehensive regime to combat the international and interstate traffic in illicit drugs." [Citation.] In doing so, Congress sought to "conquer drug abuse and to control the legitimate and illegitimate traffic in controlled substances." [Citation.] It comes as little surprise, then, that we have not considered the extent to which the CSA regulates medical practice beyond prohibiting a doctor from acting as a drug " 'pusher' " instead of a physician. [Citation.] . . .

In deciding whether the CSA can be read as prohibiting physician-assisted suicide, we look to the statute's text and design. The statute and our case law amply support the conclusion that Congress regulates medical practice insofar as it bars doctors from using their prescription-writing powers as a means to engage in illicit drug dealing and trafficking as conventionally understood. Beyond this, however, the statute manifests no intent to regulate the practice of medicine generally. The silence is understandable given the structure and limitations of federalism, which allow the States " 'great latitude under their police powers to legislate as to the protection of the lives, limbs, health, comfort, and quiet of all persons.' " [Citation.]

The structure and operation of the CSA presume and rely upon a functioning medical profession regulated under the States' police powers. The Attorney General can register a physician to dispense controlled substances "if the applicant is authorized to dispense . . . controlled substances under the laws of the State in which he practices." 21 U.S.C. § 823(f). When considering whether to revoke a physician's registration, the Attorney General looks not just to violations of federal drug laws; but he "shall" also consider "[t]he recommendation of the appropriate State licensing board or professional disciplinary authority" and the registrant's compliance with state and local drug laws. *Ibid.* The very definition of a "practitioner" eligible to prescribe includes physicians "licensed, registered, or otherwise permitted, by the United States or the jurisdiction in which he practices" to dispense controlled substances. § 802(21). Further cautioning against the conclusion that the CSA effectively displaces the States' general regulation of medical practice is the Act's pre-emption provision, which indicates that, absent a positive conflict, none of the Act's provisions should be "construed as indicating an intent on the part of the Congress to occupy the field in which that provision operates . . . to the exclusion of any State law on the same subject matter which would otherwise be within the authority of the State." § 903.

Oregon's regime is an example of the state regulation of medical practice that the CSA presupposes. Rather than simply decriminalizing assisted suicide, ODWDA limits its exercise to the attending physicians of terminally ill patients, physicians who must be licensed by Oregon's Board of Medical Examiners. Ore. Rev. Stat. §§ 127.815, 127.800(10) (2003). The statute gives attending physicians a central role, requiring them to provide prognoses and prescriptions, give information about palliative alternatives and counseling, and ensure patients are competent and acting voluntarily. § 127.815. Any eligible patient must also get a second opinion from another registered physician, § 127.820, and the statute's safeguards require physicians to keep and submit to inspection detailed records of their actions, §§ 127.855, 127.865. . . .

In connection to the CSA, however, we find only one area in which Congress set general, uniform standards of medical practice. Title I of the Comprehensive Drug Abuse Prevention and Control Act of 1970, of which the CSA was Title II, provides:

> "[The Secretary], after consultation with the Attorney General and with national organizations representative of persons with knowledge and experience in the treatment of narcotic addicts, shall determine the appropriate methods of professional practice in the medical treatment of the narcotic addiction of various classes of narcotic addicts, and shall report thereon from time to time to the Congress." § 4, 84 Stat. 1241, codified at 42 U.S.C. § 290bb–2a.

This provision strengthens the understanding of the CSA as a statute combating recreational drug abuse, and also indicates that when Congress wants to regulate medical practice in the given scheme, it does so by explicit language in the statute.

In the face of the CSA's silence on the practice of medicine generally and its recognition of state regulation of the medical profession it is difficult to defend the Attorney General's declaration that the statute impliedly criminalizes physician-assisted suicide. This difficulty is compounded by the CSA's consistent delegation of medical judgments to the Secretary and its otherwise careful allocation of powers for enforcing the limited objects of the CSA. The Government's attempt to meet this challenge rests, for the most part, on the CSA's requirement that every Schedule II drug be dispensed pursuant to a "written prescription of a practitioner." 21 U.S.C. § 829(a). A prescription, the Government argues, necessarily implies that the substance is being made available to a patient for a legitimate medical purpose. The statute, in this view, requires an anterior judgment about the term "medical" or "medicine." The Government contends ordinary usage of these words ineluctably refers to a healing or curative art, which by these terms cannot embrace the intentional hastening of a patient's death. It also points to the teachings of Hippocrates, the positions of prominent medical organizations, the Federal Government, and the judgment of the 49 States that have not legalized physician-assisted suicide as further support for the proposition that the practice is not legitimate medicine. . . .

On its own, this understanding of medicine's boundaries is at least reasonable. The primary problem with the Government's argument, however, is its assumption that the CSA impliedly authorizes an Executive officer to bar a use simply because it may be inconsistent with one reasonable understanding of medical practice. Viewed alone, the prescription requirement may support such an understanding, but statutes "should not be read as a series of unrelated and isolated provisions." *Gustafson v. Alloyd Co.*, 513 U.S. 561, 570 (1995). The CSA's substantive provisions and their arrangement undermine this assertion of an expansive federal authority to regulate medicine.

The statutory criteria for deciding what substances are controlled, determinations which are central to the Act, consistently connect the undefined term "drug abuse" with addiction or abnormal effects on the nervous system. When the Attorney General schedules drugs, he must consider a substance's psychic or physiological dependence liability. 21 U.S.C. § 811(c)(7). To classify a substance in Schedules II through V, the Attorney General must find abuse of the drug leads to psychological or physical dependence. § 812(b). Indeed, the differentiation of Schedules II through V turns in large part on a substance's habit-forming potential: The more addictive a substance, the stricter the controls. *Ibid.* When Congress wanted to extend the CSA's regulation to substances not obviously habit forming or psychotropic, moreover, it relied not on executive ingenuity, but rather on specific legislation. *See* § 1902(a) of the Anabolic Steroids Control Act of 1990, 104 Stat. 4851 (placing anabolic steroids in Schedule III). . . .

The Interpretive Rule rests on a reading of the prescription requirement that is persuasive only to the extent one scrutinizes the provision without the illumination of the rest of the statute. [Citation.]

Viewed in its context, the prescription requirement is better understood as a provision that ensures patients use controlled substances under the supervision of a doctor so as to prevent addiction and recreational abuse. As a corollary, the provision also bars doctors from peddling to patients who crave the drugs for those prohibited uses. [Citation.] To read prescriptions for assisted suicide as constituting "drug abuse" under the CSA is discordant with the phrase's consistent use throughout the statute, not to mention its ordinary meaning.

The Government's interpretation of the prescription requirement also fails under the objection that the Attorney General is an unlikely recipient of such broad authority, given the Secretary's primacy in shaping medical policy under the CSA, and the statute's otherwise careful allocation of decisionmaking powers. Just as the conventions of expression indicate that Congress is unlikely to alter a statute's obvious scope and division of authority through muffled hints, the background principles of our federal system also belie the notion that Congress would use such an obscure grant of authority to regulate areas traditionally supervised by the States' police power. . . . For all these reasons, we conclude the CSA's prescription requirement does not authorize the Attorney General to bar dispensing controlled substances for assisted suicide in the face of a state medical regime permitting such conduct.

IV

The Government, in the end, maintains that the prescription requirement delegates to a single executive officer the power to effect a radical shift of authority from the States to the Federal Government to define general standards of medical practice in every locality. The text and structure of the CSA show that Congress did not have this far-reaching intent to alter the federal-state balance and the congressional role in maintaining it.

The judgment of the Court of Appeals is

Affirmed.

■ JUSTICE SCALIA, with whom CHIEF JUSTICE ROBERTS and JUSTICE THOMAS join, dissenting.

The Court concludes that the Attorney General lacked authority to declare assisted suicide illicit under the Controlled Substances Act (CSA), because the CSA is concerned only with "*illicit* drug dealing and trafficking" (emphasis added). This question-begging conclusion is obscured by a flurry of arguments that distort the statute and disregard settled principles of our interpretive jurisprudence.

Contrary to the Court's analysis, this case involves not one but *three* independently sufficient grounds for reversing the Ninth Circuit's judgment. First, the Attorney General's interpretation of "legitimate medical purpose" in 21 CFR § 1306.04 (2005) (hereinafter Regulation) is clearly valid, given the substantial deference we must accord it under *Auer*, [citation], and his two remaining conclusions follow naturally from this interpretation. Second, even if this interpretation of the Regulation is entitled to lesser deference or no deference at all, it is by far the most natural interpretation of the Regulation—whose validity is not challenged here. This interpretation is thus correct even upon *de novo* review. Third, even if that interpretation of the Regulation were incorrect, the Attorney General's independent interpretation of the *statutory* phrase "public interest" in 21 U.S.C. §§ 824(a) and 823(f), and his implicit interpretation of the statutory phrase "public health and safety" in § 823(f)(5), are entitled to deference under *Chevron*, [citation], and they are valid under *Chevron*. For these reasons, I respectfully dissent.

I

The Interpretive Rule issued by the Attorney General (hereinafter Directive) purports to do three distinct things: (1) to interpret the phrase "legitimate medical purpose" in the Regulation to exclude physician-assisted suicide; (2) to determine that prescribing, dispensing, and administering federally controlled substances to assist suicide violates the CSA; and (3) to determine that participating in physician-assisted suicide may render a practitioner's registration "inconsistent with the public interest" within the meaning of 21 U.S.C. §§ 823(f) and 824(a)(4) (which incorporates § 823(f) by reference). The Court's analysis suffers from an unremitting failure to distinguish among these distinct propositions in the Directive.

As an initial matter, the validity of the Regulation's interpretation of "prescription" in § 829 to require a "legitimate medical purpose" is not at issue. Respondents conceded the validity of this interpretation in the lower court, [citation], and they have not challenged it here. By its assertion that the Regulation merely restates the statutory standard of 21 U.S.C. § 830(b)(3)(A)(ii), the Court likewise accepts that the "legitimate medical purpose" interpretation for prescriptions is proper. [Citation.] It is beyond dispute, then, that a "prescription" under § 829 must issue for a "legitimate medical purpose."

A

Because the Regulation was promulgated by the Attorney General, and because the Directive purported to interpret the language of the Regulation, see 66 Fed. Reg. 56608, this case calls for the straightforward application of our rule that an agency's interpretation of its own regulations is "controlling unless plainly erroneous or inconsistent with the regulation." *Auer*, [citation]. The Court reasons that *Auer* is inapplicable because the Regulation "does little more than restate the terms of the statute itself." "Simply put," the Court asserts, "the existence of a parroting regulation does not change the fact that the question here is not the meaning of the regulation but the meaning of the statute."

To begin with, it is doubtful that any such exception to the *Auer* rule exists. . . . Even if there were an antiparroting canon, however, it would have no application here. The Court's description of 21 CFR § 1306.04 (2005) as a regulation that merely "paraphrase[s] the statutory language" is demonstrably false. In relevant part, the Regulation interprets the word "prescription" as it appears in 21 U.S.C. § 829, which governs the dispensation of controlled substances other than those on Schedule I (which may not be dispensed at all). Entitled "[p]rescriptions," § 829 requires, with certain exceptions not relevant here, "the written prescription of a practitioner" (usually a medical doctor) for the dispensation of Schedule II substances (§ 829(a)), "a written or oral prescription" for substances on Schedules III and IV (§ 829(b)), and no prescription but merely a "medical purpose" for the dispensation of Schedule V substances (§ 829(c)).

As used in this section, "prescription" is susceptible of at least three reasonable interpretations. First, it might mean any oral or written direction of a practitioner for the dispensation of drugs. [Citation.] Second, in light of the requirement of a "medical purpose" for the dispensation of Schedule V substances, see § 829(c), it might mean a practitioner's oral or written direction for the dispensation of drugs that the practitioner believes to be for a legitimate medical purpose. *See* Webster's New International Dictionary 1954 (2d ed.1950) (hereinafter Webster's Second) (defining "prescription" as "[a] written direction for the preparation and use of a *medicine*"); *id.,* at 1527 (defining "medicine" as "[a]ny substance or preparation used in *treating disease*") (emphasis added). Finally, "prescription" might refer to a practitioner's direction for the dispensation of drugs that serves an *objectively* legitimate medical purpose, regardless of the practitioner's *subjective* judgment about the legitimacy of the anticipated use. *See ibid.*

The Regulation at issue constricts or clarifies the statute by adopting the last and narrowest of these three possible interpretations of the undefined statutory term: "A prescription for a controlled substance to be effective must be issued for a legitimate medical purpose . . . ." 21 CFR § 1306.04(a) (2005). We have previously *acknowledged* that the Regulation gives added content to the text of the statute: "The medical purpose requirement explicit in subsection (c) [of § 829] could be implicit in subsections (a) and (b). Regulation § [1]306.04 makes it explicit." [Citation.]

The Court points out that the Regulation adopts some of the phrasing employed in unrelated sections of the statute. This is irrelevant. A regulation that significantly clarifies the meaning of an otherwise ambiguous statutory provision is not a "parroting" regulation, *regardless* of the sources that the agency draws upon for the clarification. . . .

Since the Regulation does not run afowl (so to speak) of the Court's newly invented prohibition of "parroting"; and since the Directive represents the agency's own interpretation of that concededly valid regulation; the only question remaining is whether that interpretation is "plainly erroneous or inconsistent with the regulation"; otherwise, it is "controlling." *Auer*, [citation]. This is not a difficult question. The Directive is assuredly valid insofar as it interprets "prescription" to require a medical purpose that is "legitimate" as a matter of *federal* law—since that is an interpretation of "prescription" that we ourselves have adopted. . . .

B

Even if the Regulation merely parroted the statute, and the Directive therefore had to be treated as though it construed the statute directly, the Directive would still be entitled to deference under *Chevron*. The Court does not take issue with the Solicitor General's contention that no alleged procedural defect, such as the absence of notice-and-comment rulemaking before promulgation of the Directive, renders *Chevron* inapplicable here. [Citation.] Instead, the Court holds that the Attorney General lacks interpretive authority to issue the Directive at all, on the ground that the explicit delegation provision, 21 U.S.C. § 821 (2000 ed., Supp. V), limits his rulemaking authority to "registration and control," which (according to the Court) are not implicated by the Directive's interpretation of the prescription requirement.

Setting aside the implicit delegation inherent in Congress's use of the undefined term "prescription" in § 829, the Court's reading of "control" in § 821 is manifestly erroneous. The Court urges, that "control" is a term defined in part A of the subchapter (entitled "Introductory Provisions") to mean "to add a drug or other substance . . . to a schedule *under part B of this subchapter*," 21 U.S.C. § 802(5) (emphasis added). But § 821 is not included in "part B of this subchapter," which is entitled "Authority to Control; Standards and Schedules," and consists of the sections related to *scheduling,* 21 U.S.C. §§ 811–814 (2000 ed. and Supp. V), where the statutory definition is uniquely appropriate. Rather, § 821 is found in *part C* of the subchapter, §§ 821–830, entitled "Registration of Manufacturers, Distributors, and Dispensers of Controlled Substances," which includes all and only the provisions relating to the "manufacture, distribution, and dispensing of controlled substances," § 821. The artificial definition of "control" in § 802(5) has no conceivable application to the use of that word in § 821. Under that definition, "control" must take a *substance* as its direct object, see 21 U.S.C. § 802(5) ("to add a drug or other substance . . . to a schedule")—and that is how "control" is consistently used throughout *part B. See, e.g.,* §§ 811(b) ("proceedings . . . to *control* a drug or other substance"), 811(c) ("each drug or other substance proposed to be *controlled* or removed from the schedules"), 811(d)(1) ("If *control* is required . . . the Attorney General shall issue an order *controlling* such drug . . ."), 812(b) ("Except where *control* is required . . . a drug or other substance may not be placed in any schedule . . .").

In § 821, by contrast, the term "control" has as its object, not "a drug or other substance," but rather the *processes* of "manufacture, distribution, and dispensing of controlled substances." It could not be clearer that the artificial definition of "control" in § 802(5) is inapplicable. It makes no sense to speak of "adding the manufacturing, distribution, and dispensing of substances to a schedule." We do not force term-of-art definitions into contexts where they plainly do not fit and produce nonsense. What is obviously intended in § 821 is the ordinary meaning of "control"—namely, "[t]o exercise restraining or directing influence over; to dominate; regulate; hence, to hold from action; to curb," Webster's Second 580. "Control" is regularly used in this ordinary sense elsewhere in *part C* of the subchapter. *See, e.g.,* 21 U.S.C. §§ 823(a)(1), (b)(1), (d)(1), (e)(1), (h)(1) ("maintenance of effective *controls* against diversion"); §§ 823(a)(5), (d)(5) ("establishment of effective *control* against diversion"); § 823(g)(2)(H)(i) ("to exercise supervision or *control* over the practice of medicine"); § 830(b)(1)(C) ("a listed chemical under the *control* of the regulated person"); § 830(c)(2)(D) ("chemical *control* laws") (emphasis added).

When the word is given its ordinary meaning, the Attorney General's interpretation of the prescription requirement of § 829 plainly "relat[es] to the ... *control* of the ... dispensing of controlled substances," 21 U.S.C. § 821 (2000 ed., Supp. V) (emphasis added), since a prescription is the chief requirement for "dispensing" such drugs, see § 829. The same meaning is compelled by the fact that § 821 is the first section not of part B of the subchapter, which deals entirely with "control" in the artificial sense, but of part C, every section of which relates to the "registration and control of the manufacture, distribution, and dispensing of controlled substances," § 821. *See* §§ 822 (persons required to register), 823 (registration requirements), 824 (denial, revocation, or suspension of registration), 825 (labeling and packaging), 826 (production quotas for controlled substances), 827 (recordkeeping and reporting requirements of registrants), 828 (order forms), 829 (prescription requirements), 830 (regulation of listed chemicals and certain machines). It would be peculiar for the first section of this part to authorize rulemaking for matters covered by the *previous* part. The only sensible interpretation of § 821 is that it gives the Attorney General interpretive authority over the provisions of part C, all of which "relat[e] to the registration and control of the manufacture, distribution, and dispensing of controlled substances." These provisions include *both* the prescription requirement of § 829, and the criteria for registration and deregistration of §§ 823 and 824 (as relevant below, see *infra* Part III).

C

In sum, the Directive's construction of "legitimate medical purpose" is a perfectly valid agency interpretation of its own regulation; and if not that, a perfectly valid agency interpretation of the statute. No one contends that the construction is "plainly erroneous or inconsistent with the regulation," [citation], or beyond the scope of ambiguity in the statute, see *Chevron,* [citation]. In fact, as explained below, the Directive provides *the most natural* interpretation of the Regulation and of the statute. The Directive thus definitively establishes that a doctor's order authorizing the dispensation of a Schedule II substance for the purpose of assisting a suicide is not a "prescription" within the meaning of § 829.

Once this conclusion is established, the other two conclusions in the Directive follow inevitably. . . . [W]riting prescriptions that are illegitimate under § 829 is certainly not "in the [usual] course of professional practice" under § 802(21) and thus not "authorized by this subchapter" under § 841(a). [Citation.] A doctor who does this may thus be prosecuted under § 841(a), and so it follows that such conduct "violates the Controlled Substances Act," 66 Fed. Reg. 56608. And since such conduct is thus not in "[c]ompliance with applicable . . . Federal . . . laws relating to controlled substances," 21 U.S.C. § 823(f)(4), and may also be fairly judged to "threaten the public health and safety," § 823(f)(5), it follows that "[s]uch conduct by a physician registered to dispense controlled substances *may* 'render his registration . . . inconsistent with the public interest' and therefore subject to *possible* suspension or revocation under 21 U.S.C. [§]824(a)(4)," 66 Fed. Reg. 56608 (emphasis added).

II

Even if the Directive were entitled to no deference whatever, the most reasonable interpretation of the Regulation and of the statute would produce the same result. Virtually every relevant source of authoritative meaning confirms that the phrase "legitimate medical purpose" does not include intentionally assisting suicide. "Medicine" refers to "[t]he science and art dealing with the prevention, cure, or alleviation of disease." Webster's Second 1527. The use of the word "legitimate" connotes an *objective* standard of "medicine," and our presumption that the CSA creates a uniform federal law regulating the dispensation of controlled substances, [citation], means that this objective standard must be a federal one. As recounted in detail in the memorandum for the Attorney General that is attached as an appendix to the Directive (OLC Memo), virtually every medical authority from Hippocrates to the current American Medical Association (AMA) confirms that assisting suicide has seldom or never been viewed as a form of "prevention, cure, or alleviation of disease," and (even more so) that assisting suicide is not a "legitimate" branch of that "science and art." . . . .

In the face of this "overwhelming weight of authority," the Court's admission that "[o]n its own, this understanding of medicine's boundaries is *at least reasonable*," (emphasis added), tests the limits of understatement. The only explanation for such a distortion is that the Court confuses the *normative* inquiry of what the boundaries of medicine *should be*—which it is laudably hesitant to undertake—with the *objective* inquiry of what the accepted definition of "medicine" *is*. The same confusion is reflected in the Court's remarkable statement that "[t]he primary problem with the Government's argument . . . is its assumption that the CSA impliedly authorizes an executive officer to bar a use simply because it may be inconsistent with *one reasonable understanding* of medical practice." The fact that many in Oregon believe that the boundaries of "legitimate medicine" *should be* extended to include assisted suicide does not change the fact that the overwhelming weight of authority (including the 47 States that condemn physician-assisted suicide) confirms that they have not yet been so extended. . . .

The Court contends that the phrase "legitimate medical purpose" *cannot* be read to establish a broad, uniform federal standard for the medically proper use of controlled substances. But it also rejects the most plausible alternative proposition, urged by the State, that any use authorized under state law constitutes a "legitimate medical purpose." (The Court is perhaps leery of embracing this position because the State candidly admitted at oral argument that, on its view, a State could exempt from the CSA's coverage the use of morphine to achieve euphoria.) Instead, the Court reverse-engineers an approach somewhere between a uniform national standard and a state-by-state approach, holding (with no basis in the CSA's text) that "legitimate medical purpose" refers to *all* uses of drugs unrelated to "addiction and recreational abuse." Thus, though the Court pays lipservice to state autonomy, its standard for "legitimate medical purpose" is in fact a hazily defined *federal* standard based on its purposive reading of the CSA, and extracted from obliquely relevant sections of the Act. . . .

Even assuming, however, that the *principal* concern of the CSA is the curtailment of "addiction and recreational abuse," there is no reason to think that this is its *exclusive* concern. We have repeatedly observed that Congress often passes statutes that sweep more broadly than the main problem they were designed to address. "[S]tatutory prohibitions often go beyond the principal evil to cover reasonably comparable evils, and it is ultimately the provisions of our laws rather than the principal concerns of our legislators by which we are governed." *Oncale v. Sundowner Offshore Services, Inc.*, 523 U.S. 75, 79 (1998). [Citation.]

III

Even if the Regulation did not exist and "prescription" in § 829 could not be interpreted to require a "legitimate medical purpose," the Directive's conclusion that "prescribing, dispensing, or administering federally controlled substances . . . by a physician . . . may 'render his registration . . . inconsistent with the public interest' and therefore subject to possible suspension or revocation under 21 U.S.C. [§]824(a)(4)," 66 Fed. Reg. 56608, would nevertheless be unassailable in this Court.

Sections 823(f) and 824(a) explicitly grant the Attorney General the authority to register and deregister physicians, and his discretion in exercising that authority is spelled out in very broad terms. He may refuse to register or deregister if he determines that registration is "inconsistent with the public interest," 21 U.S.C. § 823(f), after considering five factors, the fifth of which is "[s]uch other conduct which may threaten the public health and safety," § 823(f)(5). [Citation.] As the Court points out, these broad standards were enacted in the 1984 amendments for the specific purpose of *freeing* the Attorney General's discretion over registration from the decisions of state authorities. . . .

Three considerations make it perfectly clear that the statute confers authority to interpret these phrases upon the Attorney General. First, the Attorney General is solely and explicitly charged with administering the registration and deregistration provisions. *See* §§ 823(f), 824(a). . . . Second, even if explicit delegation were required, Congress provided it in § 821, which authorizes the Attorney General to "promulgate rules and regulations . . . relating to the *registration and control* of the manufacture, distribution, and dispensing of controlled substances . . . ." (Emphasis added.) Because "dispensing" refers to the delivery of a controlled substance "pursuant to the lawful order of, a practitioner," 21 U.S.C. § 802(10), the deregistration of such practitioners for writing impermissible orders "relat[es] to the registration . . . of the . . . dispensing" of controlled substances, 21 U.S.C. § 821 (2000 ed., Supp. V).

Third, § 821 also gives the Attorney General authority to promulgate rules and regulations "relating to the . . . control of the . . . dispensing of controlled substances." As discussed earlier, it is plain that the *ordinary* meaning of "control" must apply to § 821, so that the plain import of the provision is to grant the Attorney General rulemaking authority over all the provisions of part C of the CSA, §§ 821–830 (main ed. and Supp.2005). Registering and deregistering the practitioners who issue the prescriptions necessary for lawful dispensation of controlled substances plainly "relat[es] to the . . . control of the . . . dispensing of controlled substances." § 821 (Supp.2005).

The Attorney General is thus authorized to promulgate regulations interpreting §§ 823(f) and 824(a), both by implicit delegation in § 823(f) and by two grounds of explicit delegation in § 821. The Court nevertheless holds that this triply unambiguous delegation cannot be given full effect because "the design of the statute," *ante,* at 920, evinces the intent to grant the Secretary of Health and Human Services exclusive authority over scientific and medical determinations. This proposition is not remotely plausible. The Court cites as authority for the Secretary's exclusive authority two specific areas in which his medical determinations are said to be binding on the Attorney General—with regard to the "scientific and medical evaluation" of a drug's effects that precedes its scheduling, § 811(b), and with regard to "the appropriate methods of professional practice in the medical treatment of the narcotic addiction of various classes of narcotic addicts," 42 U.S.C. § 290bb–2a; *see also* 21 U.S.C. § 823(g) (2000 ed. and Supp. II). Far from establishing a general principle of Secretary supremacy with regard to all scientific and medical determinations, the fact that Congress granted the Secretary specifically defined authority in the areas of scheduling and addiction treatment, *without otherwise mentioning him* in the registration provisions, suggests, to the contrary, that Congress envisioned *no* role for the Secretary in that area—where, as we have said, interpretive authority was both implicitly and explicitly conferred upon the Attorney General. . . .

* * *

. . . The Court's decision today is perhaps driven by a feeling that the subject of assisted suicide is none of the Federal Government's business. It is easy to sympathize with that position. The prohibition or deterrence of assisted suicide is certainly not among the enumerated powers conferred on the United States by the Constitution, and it is within the realm of public morality *(bonos mores)* traditionally addressed by the so-called police power of the States. But then, neither is prohibiting the recreational use of drugs or discouraging drug addiction among the enumerated powers. From an early time in our national history, the Federal Government has used its enumerated powers, such as its power to regulate interstate commerce, for the purpose of protecting public morality—for example, by banning the interstate shipment of lottery tickets, or the interstate transport of women for immoral purposes. [Citations.] Unless we are to repudiate a long and well-established principle of our jurisprudence, using the federal commerce power to prevent assisted suicide is unquestionably permissible. The question before us is not whether Congress *can* do this, or even whether Congress *should* do this; but simply whether Congress *has* done this in the CSA. I think there is no doubt that it has. If the term "*legitimate* medical purpose" has any meaning, it surely excludes the prescription of drugs to produce death.

For the above reasons, I respectfully dissent from the judgment of the Court.

[The dissent of JUSTICE THOMAS, focusing on constitutional matters related to this case, has been omitted.]

NOTES AND QUESTIONS

1.   The majority makes much of the Attorney General's attempt to enforce the statute by interpretive rule, but it also notes that the AG's rule departed from longstanding interpretive practices on which the State of Oregon had relied in developing its physician-assisted suicide program. Recall the question in *Brand X, supra* Section V.B.1, about whether *Chevron* deference is warranted only (or especially) for agency interpretations that are long-standing and consistent. Should it matter to the reviewing court that the agency has changed course to the likely detriment of those who have formed reliance interests on the previous interpretation? Does drawing a distinction between interpretive rules (which do not, per the Court, warrant *Chevron* deference) and legislative rules (which generally do) remedy this concern, insofar as legislative rules must undergo formal or informal rulemaking that

affords all relevant stakeholders the opportunity to weigh in? Keep this question in mind as you read *Guedes v. ATF, infra.*

2.   Recall the Major Questions doctrine, discussed *supra.* The majority in *Gonzales* argues that if Congress had meant to grant medical judgments to the Attorney General—"an executive official who lacks medical expertise"—it would have done so clearly, quoting *Whitman*'s precept that "Congress . . . . does not alter the fundamental details of a regulatory scheme in vague terms or ancillary provisions—it does not, one might say, hide elephants in mouseholes." 531 U.S. at 468. Is it notable that Justice Scalia, a dissenter in *Gonzales*, wrote *Whitman*? Does his dissent in *Gonzales* satisfactorily address the majority's "Elephants in Mouseholes" argument? Does it matter if, technically speaking, narrow textual provisions seemingly permit the Attorney General to wield broad powers, as the dissent suggests? Or is that precisely the kind of technical loophole the canon was developed to close?

3.   Justice Scalia also wrote for the majority in *City of Arlington*, which seemed to abandon the Major Questions doctrine altogether by rejecting the distinction between giving deference to an agency's interpretation of "humdrum, run-of-the-mill stuff" but not of "big, important" issues. Can you identify a rationale that explains his position across his opinions in *Gonzales*, *Whitman*, and *City of Arlington*? Alternatively, do you think he overturned *Whitman*'s rule *sub silentio* in *City of Arlington*?

4.   Despite *City of Arlington*, the majority in *King v. Burwell, supra* Section III.A.1.a, seemed to revive the Major Questions doctrine a mere two years later. Recall that in rejecting the applicability of *Chevron* deference, the majority explained that "[i]n extraordinary cases . . . there may be reason to hesitate before concluding that Congress has intended such an implicit delegation." There, it concluded that whether the tax credits were available on federal exchanges was "a question of deep 'economic and political significance' that is central to this statutory scheme; had Congress wished to assign that question to an agency, it surely would have done so expressly." Can you state a rule or rationale that explains either (a) the Court's applications (and non-applications) of the Major Questions doctrine, or (b) Justice Scalia's occasional rejection of the doctrine?

5.   The Government in *Gonzales* relied on the interpretive rule of the Attorney General and the interpretive memorandum opinion of the Office of Legal Counsel (OLC) to bolster its proffered interpretation of the CSA. The status of the AG and OLC as authoritative interpreters of statutes highlights the inherent tension among executive branch lawyers who act both as "neutral expositors" of the law as well as advocates for the President's policy agenda. Now-Judge Randolph D. Moss of the U.S. District Court for the District of Columbia reflected on this tension during his time as Assistant Attorney General in the Office of Legal Counsel:

> Much has been written about the role of the courts in interpreting the law. In contrast, executive branch legal interpretation has received considerably less attention . . . [, which is] striking given the extraordinary breadth and significance of executive branch legal interpretation. In the process of executing

the laws, the executive branch is perpetually involved in giving the law meaning. . . .

Given the prevalence, importance, and frequent finality of executive branch legal interpretation, it is important to consider the standards governing that interpretative process. Among the far-ranging questions this subject raises are issues as fundamental as the extent to which the executive branch should consider judicial pronouncements (and judgments) controlling on its interpretation of the law . . .

I will focus here on the role of the executive branch lawyer, however, from the perspective of the lawyers in the Department of Justice's Office of Legal Counsel. When the views of the Office of Legal Counsel are sought on the question of the legality of a proposed executive branch action, those views are typically treated as conclusive and binding within the executive branch. The legal advice of the Office, often embodied in formal, written opinions, constitutes the legal position of the executive branch, unless overruled by the President or the Attorney General. It is in this sense—the sense of the lawyer who is responsible for making decisions on behalf of the government regarding the interpretation of the laws—that I use the phrase "executive branch lawyer" . . . .

[I]t is helpful to consider two fundamentally distinct conceptions of how executive branch lawyers might approach legal interpretation. Under the first model, the executive branch lawyer acts as an advocate, proffering any reasonable argument in support of his client's policy objectives. Only when no reasonable argument may be formed should the lawyer opine that action should not be taken. The lawyer may candidly assess the relative merits of competing arguments for his client, but ultimately should not stand as a roadblock to the effectuation of administration policy unless the legal hurdles are clearly insurmountable. Under the second model, the executive branch lawyer acts more as a judge than as an advocate. He rejects legal arguments, even if reasonable, that do not represent the best view of the law. Like a judge, the lawyer shuns consideration of his client's desired policy goals and acts instead with complete impartiality.

Each of these models is, of course, a caricature, both overstating and understating the obligations of the executive branch lawyer. The lawyer as advocate model overstates the lawyer's obligation to promote his client's policy objectives, and understates the obligation neutrally to interpret the law. The lawyer as neutral expositor model, in contrast, is too quick to equate the executive branch lawyer with an Article III judge. As developed below, in my view, the executive branch lawyer should work within the framework and tradition of executive branch legal interpretation and seek ways to further the legal and policy goals of the administration he serves. He should do so, however, within the framework of the best view of the law and, in that sense should take the obligation neutrally to interpret the law as seriously as a court. This is particularly so for to the Attorney General, and by delegation, the Office of Legal Counsel, who bear a distinct responsibility in executive branch legal interpretation. . . .

When Congress created the office of Attorney General in the final section of the Judiciary Act of 1789, it assigned to that office only two duties. . . [and a]lthough the duties of the Attorney General have undergone dramatic expansion, over two hundred years later she retains the duty to "give [her] advice and opinion on questions of law when required by the President," and to provide her "opinion . . . on questions of law arising in the administration of [a] department" when requested by the head of that department. . . .

The Attorney General has delegated . . . these responsibilities to the Office of Legal Counsel. Under Department regulations, the Office of Legal Counsel is authorized, among other things, to provide legal advice within the executive branch, to prepare and render legal opinions, and to advise "as to [the] form and legality [of proposed executive orders and proclamations] prior to their transmission to the President." Today, the Office of Legal Counsel renders all but a small portion of the formal legal opinions of the Department of Justice. . . .

One might first take issue with the premise that the role of the executive branch lawyer is, in any significant way, distinct from the role of a lawyer in private practice. Both have clients, and both have an obligation to provide their clients with candid, considered advice. Absent extraordinary circumstances, moreover, it is for the client to determine what advice to seek and to decide how to proceed in light of that advice. As one commentator has observed:

> Like clients in private practice, the President is responsible for his own decisions, and in fact he has the authority either to make his own legal determinations without consulting any particular lawyer or to proceed in the face of contrary advice from any lawyer he does consult. Accordingly, there is no obvious reason for him to have less freedom than private clients to require from his lawyers the kind of legal advice he thinks will be most useful to him. It is true that the President has legal obligations that are different from those of any private citizen, but they are his obligations, not those of his lawyers or other subordinates. [Nelson Lund, *Rational Choice at the Office of Legal Counsel*, 15 Cardozo L. Rev. 437, 449 (1993) (citations omitted).]

In short, the neutral expositor model is flawed, according to this counterargument, because it would support an arrogation of authority from client to lawyer. It is the President, and the agency heads based on his general direction, who must make the ultimate decision whether to go forward with particular initiatives, and it is the role of the lawyer merely to provide these clients with relevant information that will help them weigh the costs—including legal risks—and benefits of proposed actions. . . .

[However, t]he finality of the Department's views, whether legally required or merely observed in practice, dictates the standard that must govern when the Attorney General and the Office of Law Counsel render legal opinions. That role is distinct from that of the typical private attorney because, at least in practice, the Attorney General and the Office of Legal Counsel define, through their opinions, the meaning of the law for an entire branch of government, and that branch of government has an obligation to get the law right. . . .

Under the reasoning of the *Chevron* case, an executive branch lawyer might at times appropriately conclude that a statute that he or she has been asked to construe does not answer the question at issue, and that, within defined bounds, the question may be resolved based on the policy priorities of the administration. In practice, this approach at times can be a perilous one for the executive branch lawyer, who must insure that an articulated "gap" or "ambiguity" in a statute is a genuine one, and not the sort of ambiguity that a good lawyer can find in almost any statutory text. Where a true gap exists, *Chevron* analysis creates an express or implied delegation to the executive branch of authority to resolve a question as a matter of policy, and the lawyer should not usurp a decision that the Congress has committed to policymakers. More generally, the obligation to find the best view of the law includes the duty to identify where either the Constitution or a relevant statute vests the President or another executive branch official with a zone of discretion in which to act, and to avoid conflating questions of law and policy. . . .

[T]the executive branch lawyer can [also] serve the interest of democratic accountability, without departing from the best view of the law . . . [, for w]hen the lawyer concludes that a proposed course of action is not legally available, he or she can explore what legally available alternatives might exist. On almost a daily basis, the Office of Legal Counsel works with its clients to refine and reconceptualize proposed executive branch initiatives in the face of legal constraints. This dynamic process is only rarely evidenced in the Office of Legal Counsel's written opinions because the Office's formal opinions typically focus on the end product of any such process. It nonetheless constitutes a critical part of the work of the Office of Legal Counsel and provides a means by which the executive branch lawyer can contribute to the ability of the popularly-elected President and his administration to achieve important policy goals. In this manner, the executive branch lawyer can balance the duty to work within the framework of the best view of the law with the obligation to assist those who are most directly accountable to the People in achieving their policy objectives.

Randolph D. Moss, *Executive Branch Legal Interpretation: A Perspective from the Office of Legal Counsel*, 52 Admin. L. Rev. 1303 (2000).

Keep these considerations in mind when reading the next section, Agency Interpretations with Potential Criminal Consequences.

NOTE: "*AUER* DEFERENCE"—DEFERRING TO AGENCIES INTERPRETING THEIR OWN REGULATIONS

In *Gonzales*, the majority and dissent disagreed about the applicability of what the opinions refer to as *Auer* deference, the practice of courts deferring to an agency's interpretive rule that purports to interpret its own ambiguous regulation. The doctrine's name derives from the decision that formalized the modern version of a longstanding practice, Auer v. Robbins, 519 U.S. 451 (1997). *Auer* deference has sparked pointed criticism. In theory, *Auer* deference permits an agency, in promulgating a regulation from an already ambiguous statutory delegation, to draft that regulation with sufficient ambiguity as to evade the details of its enforcement. Again, in theory, the agency can then point to that earlier ambiguity as the basis for evolving policy choices implemented through interpretive rules of its own ambiguous regulation that do not require formal or informal rulemaking. Critics of *Auer* deference object that courts should not defer to the agency interpretations of their own ambiguous regulations when doing so creates perverse incentives and sidesteps participation from regulated parties.

To this end, recall that in *Gonzales* the majority invoked what the dissent derisively called the "anti-parroting canon" to deny deference to the AG's interpretation of his own rule, which merely parroted the underlying statutory text that a prior AG had informed the State of Oregon would not conflict with its physician-assisted suicide program. A strict application of *Auer* deference would have instructed a court to defer to the AG's interpretation of his own rule even when no such deference was warranted for his interpretation of the statutory provision it effectively reproduced. Although one might not guess it from his dissent in *Gonzales*, chief among critics of *Auer* deference to interpretive rules was Justice Scalia, who grew skeptical over the years of deference not only to interpretive rules generally, but especially when the interpretive rule interpreted an agency regulation rather than a statute. Somewhat ironically, Scalia was the opinion writer in *Auer*, and shortly before his death, he came to repudiate his creation, writing:

> [W]e have revolutionized the import of interpretive rules' exemption from notice-and-comment rulemaking. Agencies may now use these rules not just to advise the public, but also to bind them. After all, if an interpretive rule gets deference, the people are bound to obey it on pain of sanction, no less surely than they are bound to obey substantive rules, which are accorded similar deference. Interpretive rules that command deference do have the force of law. . . .

By giving . . . interpretive rules [that interpret the agency's own regulations] *Auer* deference, we do more than allow the agency to make binding regulations without notice and comment. Because the agency (not Congress) drafts the substantive rules that are the object of those interpretations, giving them deference allows the agency to control the extent of its notice-and-comment-free domain. To expand this domain, the agency need only write substantive rules more broadly and vaguely, leaving plenty of gaps to be filled in later, using interpretive rules unchecked by notice and comment. . . .

As I have described elsewhere, the rule of *Chevron*, if it did not comport with the APA, at least was in conformity with the long history of judicial review of executive action, where "[s]tatutory ambiguities . . . were left to reasonable resolution by the Executive." *Mead Corp.*, 533 U.S. at 243 (2001) (SCALIA, J., dissenting). I am unaware of any such history justifying deference to agency interpretations of its own regulations. And there are weighty reasons to deny a lawgiver the power to write ambiguous laws and then be the judge of what the ambiguity means. [Citation.] I would therefore restore the balance . . . The agency is free to interpret its own regulations with or without notice and comment; but courts will decide—with no deference to the agency—whether that interpretation is correct.

Perez v. Mortgage Bankers Ass'n, 135 S. Ct. 1199, 1212–13 (2015) (Scalia, J., concurring in the judgment).

Shortly after Justice Scalia's death, the Court had another opportunity to overrule *Auer* deference, in Kisor v. Wilkie, 139 S. Ct. 2400 (2019). While the Court declined the invitation, it did make clear why the hypothetical problem Justice Scalia identified was unlikely to be pervasive in practice. Justice Kagan, writing for the majority, set out several important preconditions for *Auer* deference:

To begin with, the regulatory interpretation must be one actually made by the agency. In other words, it must be the agency's "authoritative" or "official position," rather than any more ad hoc statement not reflecting the agency's views. [Citation.] That constraint follows from the logic of *Auer* deference—because Congress has delegated rulemaking power, and all that typically goes with it, to the agency alone. Of course, the requirement of "authoritative" action must recognize a reality of bureaucratic life: Not everything the agency does comes from, or is even in the name of, the Secretary or his chief advisers. . . . But there are limits. The interpretation must at the least emanate from those actors, using those vehicles, understood to make authoritative policy in the relevant context. [Citations.] If the interpretation does not do so, a court may not defer.

Next, the agency's interpretation must in some way implicate its substantive expertise. Administrative knowledge and experience largely "account [for] the presumption that Congress delegates interpretive lawmaking power to the agency." [Citation,] So the basis for deference ebbs when "[t]he subject matter of the [dispute is] distan[t] from the agency's ordinary" duties or "fall[s] within the scope of another agency's authority." *Arlington*, 569 U.S. at 309 (opinion of BREYER, J.). This Court indicated as much when it analyzed a "split enforcement" scheme, in which Congress divided regulatory power between two entities. [Citation.] To decide "whose reasonable interpretation" of a rule controlled, we "presum[ed] Congress intended to invest interpretive power" in whichever actor was "best position[ed] to develop" expertise about the given problem. [Citation.] The same idea holds good as between agencies and courts. "Generally, agencies have a nuanced understanding of the regulations they administer." That point is most obvious when a rule is technical . . . . Once again, though, there are limits. Some interpretive issues may fall more naturally into a judge's bailiwick. . . . When the agency has no comparative expertise in resolving a regulatory ambiguity, Congress presumably would not grant it that authority.

Finally, an agency's reading of a rule must reflect "fair and considered judgment" to receive *Auer* deference. [Citation,] That means, we have stated, that a court should decline to defer to a merely "convenient litigating position" or "post hoc rationalizatio[n] advanced" to "defend past agency action against attack." [Citation,] And a court may not defer to a new interpretation, whether or not introduced in litigation, that creates "unfair surprise" to regulated parties. [Citation.] That disruption of expectations may occur when an agency substitutes one view of a rule for another. We have therefore only rarely given *Auer* deference to an agency construction "conflict[ing] with a prior" one. [Citation.] Or the upending of reliance may happen without such an explicit interpretive change. This Court, for example, recently refused to defer to an interpretation that would have imposed retroactive liability on parties for longstanding conduct that the agency had never before addressed. [Citation.] Here too the lack of "fair warning" outweighed the reasons to apply *Auer*.

The upshot of all this goes something as follows. When it applies, *Auer* deference gives an agency significant leeway to say what its own rules mean. In so doing, the doctrine enables the agency to fill out the regulatory scheme Congress has placed under its supervision. But that phrase "when it applies" is important— because it often doesn't. As described above, this Court has cabined *Auer*'s scope in varied and critical ways—and in exactly that measure, has maintained a strong judicial role in interpreting rules. What emerges is a deference doctrine not quite so tame as some might hope, but not nearly so menacing as they might fear.

Id. at 2415–18. Applying the criteria Justice Kagan identifies as necessary for warranting *Auer* deference, consider whether *Auer* deference should have applied in *Gonzales*. Was it the agency's official position? Was the issue within the agency's "substantive expertise"? If the CSA divided regulatory power between the AG and HHS, whose substantive expertise should have controlled? Finally, was the AG's interpretation the "fair and considered judgment" as to the CSA's meaning? Or did it create an "unfair surprise" for the State of Oregon, given the AG's prior and publicly stated position?

3. CASE STUDY IN NOTICE-AND-COMMENT INTERPRETIVE RULEMAKING: PROTECTING ENDANGERED SPECIES AND THEIR HABITATS BY DEFINING THE TERMS OF THE STATUTE

The Texts to Be Construed: The Endangered Species Act and Related Regulations

a. RELEVANT STATUTORY PROVISIONS OF THE ENDANGERED SPECIES ACT

Congress enacted the Endangered Species Act (ESA) in 1973, relevant excerpts below. Can you articulate the "principal evil" Congress had in mind when it enacted the ESA? What related evils, if any, do you think the prohibitions set out in the act also cover?

The Endangered Species Act [An Overview]
United States Code, Title 16, Chapter 35.

§ 1531. Congressional findings and declaration of purposes and policy

(a) Findings

The Congress finds and declares that—

(1) various species of fish, wildlife, and plants in the United States have been rendered extinct as a consequence of economic growth and development untempered by adequate concern and conservation;

(2) other species of fish, wildlife, and plants have been so depleted in numbers that they are in danger of or threatened with extinction;

(3) these species of fish, wildlife, and plants are of esthetic, ecological, educational, historical, recreational, and scientific value to the Nation and its people;

(4) the United States has pledged itself as a sovereign state in the international community to conserve to the extent practicable the various species of fish or wildlife and plants facing extinction, . . .

(5) encouraging the States and other interested parties, through Federal financial assistance and a system of incentives, to develop and maintain conservation programs which meet national and international standards is a key to meeting the Nation's international commitments and to better safeguarding, for the benefit of all citizens, the Nation's heritage in fish, wildlife, and plants.

(b) Purposes

The purposes of this chapter are to provide a means whereby the ecosystems upon which endangered species and threatened species depend may be conserved, to provide a program for the conservation of such endangered species and threatened species, and to take such steps as may be appropriate to achieve the purposes of the treaties and conventions set forth in subsection (a) of this section.

§ 1532. Definitions

. . .

(19) The term "take" means to harass, harm, pursue, hunt, shoot, wound, kill, trap, capture, or collect, or to attempt to engage in any such conduct. . . .

§ 1536. Interagency cooperation

(a) Federal agency actions and consultations . . .

(2) Each Federal agency shall, in consultation with and with the assistance of the Secretary, insure that any action authorized, funded, or carried out by such agency . . . is not likely to jeopardize the continued existence of any endangered species or threatened species or result in the destruction or adverse modification of habitat of such species which is determined by the Secretary . . . to be critical . . .

§ 1538. Prohibited acts

(a) Generally

(1) . . . [I]t is unlawful for any person subject to the jurisdiction of the United States to—

(A) import any such species into, or export any such species from the United States;

(B) take any such species within the United States or the territorial sea of the United States;

(C) take any such species upon the high seas;

(D) possess, sell, deliver, carry, transport, or ship, by any means whatsoever, any such species taken in violation of subparagraphs (B) and (C);

(E) deliver, receive, carry, transport, or ship in interstate or foreign commerce, by any means whatsoever and in the course of a commercial activity, any such species;

(F) sell or offer for sale in interstate or foreign commerce any such species; or

(G) violate any regulation pertaining to such species or to any threatened species of fish or wildlife listed pursuant to section 1533 of this title and promulgated by the Secretary pursuant to authority provided by this chapter. . . .

§ 1540. Penalties and enforcement

(a) Civil penalties

(1) Any person who knowingly violates, and any person engaged in business as an importer or exporter of fish, wildlife, or plants who violates, any provision of this chapter, or any provision of any permit or certificate issued hereunder, or of any regulation issued in order to implement [relevant] subsection[s] . . . may be assessed a civil penalty by the Secretary of not more than $25,000 for each violation.

(b) Criminal violations

(1) Any person who knowingly violates any provision of this chapter, of any permit or certificate issued hereunder, or of any regulation issued in order to implement [relevant] subsection[s] . . . shall, upon conviction, be fined not more than $50,000 or imprisoned for not more than one year, or both.

b. NOTICE OF PROPOSED RULE INTERPRETING "HARM" IN THE DEFINITION OF "TAKE"

In 1975, the U.S. Fish and Wildlife Service, an agency within the Department of the Interior, promulgated a notice of proposed rulemaking that would, among other things, elaborate on the definition of the "take" prohibition's sub-definition of "harass." Can you identify methods of statutory interpretation the agency draws on to justify its interpretation of the take prohibition? What are possible counter-arguments to the agency's interpretation of "harass"?

U.S. Fish and Wildlife Serv., Proposal to Reclassify the American Alligator (Fed. Reg. 1975)

Federal Register, Vol. 40, No. 131—Tuesday, July 8, 1975.
28,712–28,714.

DEPARTMENT OF THE INTERIOR

Fish and Wildlife Service

[50 CFR Part 17]

ENDANGERED AND THREATENED WILDLIFE

Proposal to Reclassify the American Alligator

The Director, U.S. Fish and Wildlife Service, hereby issues a notice of proposed rulemaking which would reclassify the American Alligator (Alligator mississippiensis) from its present listing as Endangered throughout its entire range, . . .

DESCRIPTION OF THE PROPOSAL

Subpart A (Introduction and General Provisions) would be amended by adding a series of definitions necessary for the proper implementation of the Act. Of note are the definitions of "harass" and "industry and trade." These definitions are intended to clarify the scope of the Prohibition on taking, and on interstate commerce. . . .

Accordingly, it is hereby proposed to amend Part 17, Title 50 CFR as follows:

PART 17—ENDANGERED AND THREATENED WILDLIFE AND PLANTS

. . . 5. Add the following new §§ 17.3, 17.4, 17.5, 17.6, 17.7, and 17.8 to Subpart A, reading as follows:

§ 17.3   Definitions.

In addition to the definitions contained in Part 10 of this subchapter, and unless the context otherwise requires, in this Part 17:

"Act" means the Endangered Species Act of 1973 (16 U.S.C. 1531–1543; 87 Stat. 884); . . .

"Harass" in the definition of "take" in the Act means an act which either actually or potentially harms wildlife by killing or injuring it, or by annoying it to such an extent as to cause serious disruption in essential behavior patterns, such as feeding, breeding or sheltering; significant environmental modification or degradation which has such effects is included within the meaning of "harass"; . . .

SUBMITTAL OF WRITTEN COMMENTS

Interested persons may participate in this rulemaking by submitting written comments to the Director (FWS/LE) U.S. Fish and Wildlife Service, . . . All relevant comments received no later than September 8, 1975, will be considered. . . . Dated: June 27, 1975.

c.   FINAL RULE INTERPRETING "HARM" IN THE DEFINITION OF "TAKE"

In response to comments from members of the public, the agency's final rule modified its definition of the "take" prohibition. Can you identify the meaningful differences between this definition and the definition in the notice of proposed rulemaking? Why do you think the agency changed course? What arguments support the agency's alteration? What arguments might oppose it? Can you articulate what behaviors this regulation newly prohibits under the statute? What exceptions are there, if any, to those prohibitions?

U.S. Fish and Wildlife Serv., Final Rule: Reclassification of the American Alligator and Other Amendments (Fed. Reg. 1975)

Federal Register, Vol. 40, No. 188—Friday, September 26, 1975.
44,412–44,413.

Title 50—Wildlife and Fisheries

CHAPTER I—UNITED STATES FISH AND WILDLIFE
SERVICE, DEPARTMENT OF THE INTERIOR

SUBCHAPTER B—TAKING, POSSESSION, TRANSPORTATION,
SALE, PURCHASE, BARTER, EXPORTATION, AND
IMPORTATION OF WILDLIFE

PART 17—Endangered and Threatened
Wildlife and Plants

Reclassification of the American Alligator
and Other Amendments

On July 8, 1975, the Service proposed certain changes in regulations on endangered and threatened wildlife (40 FR 28712). The proposal would . . . add new provisions to Part 17 on similarity of appearance, on captive, self-sustaining populations, and on interpretations of prohibitions applicable to endangered and threatened wildlife. . . . With the changes noted in this preamble, this rulemaking accepts the proposal, effective September 26, 1975. . . .

PUBLIC COMMENTS

The proposed rulemaking was published in the FEDERAL REGISTER on July 8, 1975 (40 FR 28712). Interested persons were invited to submit written comments to the Director until September 8, 1975. The written responses are summarized, essentially, as follows:

(1)   26 Responses supported the proposed rulemaking;

(2)   17 Responses opposed any change in current classification of the American alligator as endangered throughout its entire range;

(3)   24 Responses generally approved the proposed rulemaking, but recommended one or more changes to reflect the writer's position;

(4) 4 Responses generally opposed the Proposed rulemaking, unless one or more changes are made in the final rules; and

(5) 17 Responses either were totally irrelevant or merely acknowledged receipt of the proposed rules and their transmittal to an appropriate official for further response . . . .

DESCRIPTION OF THE RULEMAKING

Following careful review and consideration of all written comments, the proposed rulemaking [has been] modified. . . .

(2) Changes from the proposal. Generally speaking, there is only one major change from the proposal, dealing with the status of the alligator. However, there are a number of editorial revisions for clarity, and some minor substantive changes to further define concepts set out in the proposal. . . . The differences between the proposal and this final rulemaking will be discussed subpart by subpart, below. . . .

SUBPART A (INTRODUCTION AND GENERAL PROVISIONS)

In the proposal, Subpart A contained a series of definitions necessary for proper implementation of the Act. Especially notable were the definitions of . . . "harass," which clarified the scope of the prohibition on taking. The definition of "harass" has been retained in a modified form in this final rulemaking, to make it applicable to actions or omissions with the potential for injury. The concept of environmental damage being considered a "taking" has been retained, but is now found in a new definition, of the word "harm." "Harm" covers actions or omissions which actually, (as opposed to potentially), cause injury. In addition, the definition of "harass" has been modified by restricting its application to acts or omissions which are done intentionally or negligently. In the proposal, "harass" would have applied to any action, regardless of intent or negligence. . . .

By moving the concept of environmental degradation to the definition of "harm," potential restrictions on environmental modifications are expressly limited to those actions causing actual death or injury to a protected species of fish or wildlife. The actual consequences of such an action upon a listed species is paramount.

These environmental restrictions represent a reasonable response to the habitat needs of listed species. Congress specifically acknowledged these needs by stating in the "Purposes" subsection of the Act: "The purposes of this Act are to provide a means whereby the ecosystems upon which endangered and threatened Species depend may be conserved . . ." (87 Stat. 885. Section 2 (b), 16 U.S.C. 1531 (b)). Furthermore, Congress acknowledged that a rational relationship existed between the protection of the needs of listed species and the public welfare: "The Congress finds and declares that . . . (3) these species of fish, wildlife, and plants are of esthetic, ecological, educational, historical, recreational and scientific value to the Nation and its people . . ." (87 Stat. 884, Section 2(a) (3), 16 U.S.C. Section 1541(3)).

It should be noted that this definition of "harm" which includes significant environmental modification, does not permanently limit the environmental modifications that are permissible for the habitat of a listed species of fish or wildlife. If the species was originally classified as endangered and made a significant recovery, it could be down-listed to threatened with regulations that don't prohibit "takings." Second, the species could recover completely and be delisted altogether. Finally, the species in question could abandon its use of the area. In all of these situations, the limited restrictions on environmental modification under the definition of "harm" would be removed . . . .

Accordingly, Part 17 of Chapter I, Title 50, Code of Federal Regulations, is amended as set forth below. This amendment is effective on September 26, 1975, . . .

Part 17, Title 50 Code of Federal Regulations is amended and republished as follows:

PART 17—ENDANGERED AND THREATENED WILDLIFE AND PLANTS

1. Retitle Part 17 of Subchapter B of CFR Chapter I to read as set forth above. . . .

3. Amend § 17.1 by deleting the present language and replacing it with the following:

§ 17.2   Scope of regulations.

(a) The regulations of this part apply only to endangered and threatened wildlife and plants. . . .

§ 17.3   Definitions.

In addition to the definitions contained in Part 10 of this subchapter, and unless the context otherwise requires, in this Part 17:

"Act" means the Endangered Species Act of 1973 (16 U.S.C. 1531–1543; 87 Stat. 884);

"Harass" in the definition of "take" in the Act means an intentional or negligent act or omission which creates the likelihood of injury to wildlife by annoying it to such an extent as to significantly disrupt normal behavioral patterns which include, but are not limited to, breeding, feeding or sheltering.

"Harm" in the definition of "take" in the Act means an act or omission which actually injures or kills wildlife, including acts which annoy it to such an extent as to significantly disrupt essential behavioral patterns, which include, but are not limited to, breeding, feeding or sheltering; significant environmental modification or degradation which has such effects is included within the meaning of "harm"; . . .

§ 17.21 Prohibitions.

(a) Except as provided in Subpart A of this part, or under permits issued pursuant to § 17.22 or § 17.23, it is unlawful for any person subject to the jurisdiction of the United States to commit, to attempt to commit, to solicit another to commit or to cause to be committed, any of the acts described in paragraphs (b) through (f) of this section in regard to any endangered wildlife. . . .

(c) Take. (1) It is unlawful to take endangered wildlife within the United States, within the territorial sea of the United States, or upon the high seas. . . .

(2) Notwithstanding paragraph (c) (1) of this section, any person may take endangered wildlife in defense of his own life or the lives of others.

(4) Any taking pursuant to paragraph[ ] (c) (2) . . . of this section must be reported in writing to the United States Fish and Wildlife Service, Division of Law Enforcement, P.O. Box 19183, Washington, D.C. 20036, within 5 days. The specimen may only be retained, disposed of, or salvaged in accordance with directions from the Service.

§ 17.22 Permits for scientific purposes or for the enhancement of propagation or survival.

Upon receipt of a complete application, the Director may issue a permit authorizing any activity otherwise prohibited by § 17.21, in accordance with the issuance criteria of this section, for scientific research or for enhancing the propagation or survival of endangered wildlife. (*See* § 17.32 for permits for threatened species.)

(a) Application requirements. Applications for permits under this section must be submitted to the Director by the person who wishes to engage in the activity prohibited by § 17.21. Each application must be submitted on an official application form. (Form 3-200) provided by. the Service, and must include as an attachment, all of the following information:

(1) The common and scientific names of the species sought to be covered by the permit, as well as the number, age, and sex of such species, and the activity sought to be authorized (such as taking, exporting, selling in interstate commerce, etc.);

(2) A statement as to whether, at the time of application, the wildlife sought to be covered by the permit (i) is still in the wild, (ii) has already been removed from the wild, or (iii) was born in captivity;

(3) A resume of the applicant's attempts to obtain the wildlife sought to be covered by the permit in a manner which would not cause the death or removal from the wild of such wildlife;

(4) If the wildlife sought to be covered by the permit has already been removed from the wild, the country and place where such

removal occurred; if the wildlife sought to be covered by the permit was raised in captivity, the country and place where such wildlife was born; . . .

d.   1982 AMENDMENTS TO THE ENDANGERED SPECIES ACT

Congress amended the ESA in 1982 to create the following permitting scheme. How is this permitting scheme distinct from the permit scheme identified in the Final Rule above? Can you identify how this permit scheme may affect the agency's "take" prohibition as defined by the Final Rule?

The Endangered Species Act [as Amended]
United States Code, Title 16, Chapter 35.

§ 1539. Exceptions

(a) Permits

(1) The Secretary may permit, under such terms and conditions as he shall prescribe—

(A) any act otherwise prohibited by section 1538 of this title for scientific purposes or to enhance the propagation or survival of the affected species, including, but not limited to, acts necessary for the establishment and maintenance of experimental populations pursuant to subsection (j); or

(B) any taking otherwise prohibited by section 1538(a)(1)(B) of this title if such taking is incidental to, and not the purpose of, the carrying out of an otherwise lawful activity.

(2)

(A) No permit may be issued by the Secretary authorizing any taking referred to in paragraph (1)(B) unless the applicant therefor submits to the Secretary a conservation plan that specifies—

(i)   the impact which will likely result from such taking;

(ii)   what steps the applicant will take to minimize and mitigate such impacts, and the funding that will be available to implement such steps;

(iii) what alternative actions to such taking the applicant considered and the reasons why such alternatives are not being utilized; and

(iv)   such other measures that the Secretary may require as being necessary or appropriate for purposes of the plan.

Babbitt v. Sweet Home Chapter of Communities for a Great Oregon

Supreme Court of the United States, 1995.
515 U.S. 687, 115 S.Ct. 2407, 132 L.Ed.2d 597.

■ JUSTICE STEVENS delivered the opinion of the Court[, in which JUSTICE KENNEDY, JUSTICE SOUTER, JUSTICE GINSBURG, and JUSTICE BREYER joined].

The Endangered Species Act of 1973 . . . makes it unlawful for any person to "take" any endangered or threatened species. The Secretary has promulgated a regulation that defines the statute's prohibition on takings to include "significant habitat modification or degradation where it actually kills or injures wildlife." This case presents the question whether the Secretary exceeded his authority under the Act by promulgating that regulation.

I

. . . Section 3(19) of the [Endangered Species] Act defines the statutory term "take":

"The term 'take' means to harass, harm, pursue, hunt, shoot, wound, kill, trap, capture, or collect, or to attempt to engage in any such conduct." 16 U.S.C. § 1532(19).

The Act does not further define the terms it uses to define "take." The Interior Department regulations that implement the statute, however, define the statutory term "harm":

"*Harm* in the definition of 'take' in the Act means an act which actually kills or injures wildlife. Such act may include significant habitat modification or degradation where it actually kills or injures wildlife by significantly impairing essential behavioral patterns, including breeding, feeding, or sheltering." 50 CFR § 17.3 (1994).

This regulation has been in place since 1975.[2]

A limitation on the § 9 "take" prohibition appears in § 10(a)(1)(B) of the Act, which Congress added by amendment in 1982. That section authorizes the Secretary to grant a permit for any taking otherwise prohibited by § 9(a)(1)(B) "if such taking is incidental to, and not the purpose of, the carrying out of an otherwise lawful activity." 16 U.S.C. § 1539(a)(1)(B). . . .

Respondents in this action are small landowners, logging companies, and families dependent on the forest products industries in the Pacific Northwest and in the Southeast, and organizations that represent their interests. They brought this declaratory judgment action against petitioners, the Secretary of the Interior and the Director of the Fish and

---

[2] The Secretary, through the Director of the Fish and Wildlife Service, originally promulgated the regulation in 1975 and amended it in 1981 to emphasize that actual death or injury of a protected animal is necessary for a violation. *See* 40 Fed. Reg. 44412, 44416 (1975); 46 Fed. Reg. 54748, 54750 (1981).

Wildlife Service, in the United States District Court for the District of Columbia to challenge the statutory validity of the Secretary's regulation defining "harm," particularly the inclusion of habitat modification and degradation in the definition. Respondents challenged the regulation on its face. Their complaint alleged that application of the "harm" regulation to the redcockaded woodpecker, an endangered species, and the northern spotted owl, a threatened species, had injured them economically.

. . . The District Court therefore entered summary judgment for petitioners and dismissed respondents' complaint. A divided panel of the Court of Appeals initially affirmed the judgment of the District Court. [Citation.] After granting a petition for rehearing, however, the panel reversed. . . .

II

Because this case was decided on motions for summary judgment, we may appropriately make certain factual assumptions in order to frame the legal issue. First, we assume respondents have no desire to harm either the red-cockaded woodpecker or the spotted owl; they merely wish to continue logging activities that would be entirely proper if not prohibited by the ESA. On the other hand, we must assume, *arguendo*, that those activities will have the effect, even though unintended, of detrimentally changing the natural habitat of both listed species and that, as a consequence, members of those species will be killed or injured. . . . The Secretary . . . submits that the § 9 prohibition on takings, which Congress defined to include "harm," places on respondents a duty to avoid harm that habitat alteration will cause the birds unless respondents first obtain a permit pursuant to § 10.

The text of the Act provides three reasons for concluding that the Secretary's interpretation is reasonable. First, an ordinary understanding of the word "harm" supports it. The dictionary definition of the verb form of "harm" is "to cause hurt or damage to: injure." Webster's Third New International Dictionary 1034 (1966). In the context of the ESA, that definition naturally encompasses habitat modification that results in actual injury or death to members of an endangered or threatened species.

Respondents argue that the Secretary should have limited the purview of "harm" to direct applications of force against protected species, but the dictionary definition does not include the word "directly" or suggest in any way that only direct or willful action that leads to injury constitutes "harm."[10] Moreover, unless the statutory term "harm"

---

[10] Respondents and the dissent emphasize what they portray as the "established meaning" of "take" in the sense of a "wildlife take," a meaning respondents argue extends only to "the effort to exercise dominion over some creature, and the concrete effect of [sic] that creature." . . . This limitation ill serves the statutory text, which forbids not taking "some creature" but "tak[ing] any [endangered] species"—a formidable task for even the most rapacious feudal lord. More importantly, Congress explicitly defined the operative term "take" in the ESA, no matter how much the dissent wishes otherwise . . . thereby obviating the need for us to probe its meaning as we must probe the meaning of the undefined subsidiary term "harm." Finally,

encompasses indirect as well as direct injuries, the word has no meaning that does not duplicate the meaning of other words that § 3 uses to define "take." A reluctance to treat statutory terms as surplusage supports the reasonableness of the Secretary's interpretation.[11] [Citation.]

Second, the broad purpose of the ESA supports the Secretary's decision to extend protection against activities that cause the precise harms Congress enacted the statute to avoid. . . . [W]e have described the Act as "the most comprehensive legislation for the preservation of endangered species ever enacted by any nation." [Citation.] Whereas predecessor statutes enacted in 1966 and 1969 had not contained any sweeping prohibition against the taking of endangered species except on federal lands, [citation,] the 1973 Act applied to all land in the United States and to the Nation's territorial seas. As stated in § 2 of the Act, among its central purposes is "to provide a means whereby the ecosystems upon which endangered species and threatened species depend may be conserved. . . ." 16 U.S.C. § 1531(b).

. . . Congress' intent to provide comprehensive protection for endangered and threatened species supports the permissibility of the Secretary's "harm" regulation.

Respondents advance strong arguments that activities that cause minimal or unforeseeable harm will not violate the Act as construed in the "harm" regulation. Respondents, however, present a facial challenge to the regulation. [Citation.] Thus, they ask us to invalidate the Secretary's understanding of "harm" in every circumstance, even when an actor knows that an activity, such as draining a pond, would actually result in the extinction of a listed species by destroying its habitat. Given Congress' clear expression of the ESA's broad purpose to protect endangered and threatened wildlife, the Secretary's definition of "harm" is reasonable.

Third, the fact that Congress in 1982 authorized the Secretary to issue permits for takings that § 9(a)(1)(B) would otherwise prohibit, "if such taking is incidental to, and not the purpose of, the carrying out of an otherwise lawful activity," 16 U.S.C. § 1539(a)(1)(B), strongly suggests that Congress understood § 9(a)(1)(B) to prohibit indirect as well as deliberate takings. [Citation.] The permit process requires the applicant

---

Congress' definition of "take" includes several words—most obviously "harass," "pursue," and "wound," in addition to "harm" itself—that fit respondents' and the dissent's definition of "take" no better than does "significant habitat modification or degradation."

[11] In contrast, if the statutory term "harm" encompasses such indirect means of killing and injuring wildlife as habitat modification, the other terms listed in § 3—"harass," "pursue," "hunt," "shoot," "wound," "kill," "trap," "capture," and "collect"—generally retain independent meanings. Most of those terms refer to deliberate actions more frequently than does "harm," and they therefore do not duplicate the sense of indirect causation that "harm" adds to the statute. In addition, most of the other words in the definition describe either actions from which habitat modification does not usually result (e.g., "pursue," "harass") or effects to which activities that modify habitat do not usually lead (e.g., "trap," "collect"). To the extent the Secretary's definition of "harm" may have applications that overlap with other words in the definition, that overlap reflects the broad purpose of the Act.

to prepare a "conservation plan" that specifies how he intends to "minimize and mitigate" the "impact" of his activity on endangered and threatened species, 16 U.S.C. § 1539(a)(2)(A), making clear that Congress had in mind foreseeable rather than merely accidental effects on listed species. No one could seriously request an "incidental" take permit to avert § 9 liability for direct, deliberate action against a member of an endangered or threatened species, but respondents would read "harm" so narrowly that the permit procedure would have little more than that absurd purpose. "When Congress acts to amend a statute, we presume it intends its amendment to have real and substantial effect." Stone v. INS, 514 U.S. 386, 397 (1995). Congress' addition of the § 10 permit provision supports the Secretary's conclusion that activities not intended to harm an endangered species, such as habitat modification, may constitute unlawful takings under the ESA unless the Secretary permits them.

The Court of Appeals made three errors in asserting that "harm" must refer to a direct application of force because the words around it do. First, the court's premise was flawed. Several of the words that accompany "harm" in the § 3 definition of "take," especially "harass," "pursue," "wound," and "kill," refer to actions or effects that do not require direct applications of force. Second, to the extent the court read a requirement of intent or purpose into the words used to define "take," it ignored § 11's express provision that a "knowin[g]" action is enough to violate the Act. Third, the court employed *noscitur a sociis* to give "harm" essentially the same function as other words in the definition, thereby denying it independent meaning. The canon, to the contrary, counsels that a word "gathers meaning from the words around it." [Citation.] The statutory context of "harm" suggests that Congress meant that term to serve a particular function in the ESA, consistent with, but distinct from, the functions of the other verbs used to define "take." The Secretary's interpretation of "harm" to include indirectly injuring endangered animals through habitat modification permissibly interprets "harm" to have "a character of its own not to be submerged by its association." [Citation.]

. . . We need not decide whether the statutory definition of "take" compels the Secretary's interpretation of "harm," because our conclusions that Congress did not unambiguously manifest its intent to adopt respondents' view and that the Secretary's interpretation is reasonable suffice to decide this case. *See generally Chevron*, [citation]. The latitude the ESA gives the Secretary in enforcing the statute, together with the degree of regulatory expertise necessary to its enforcement, establishes that we owe some degree of deference to the Secretary's reasonable interpretation. [Citation.][18]

---

[18] Respondents also argue that the rule of lenity should foreclose any deference to the Secretary's interpretation of the ESA because the statute includes criminal penalties. The rule of lenity is premised on two ideas: First, " 'a fair warning should be given to the world in

III

Our conclusion that the Secretary's definition of "harm" rests on a permissible construction of the ESA gains further support from the legislative history of the statute. The Committee Reports accompanying the bills that became the ESA do not specifically discuss the meaning of "harm," but they make clear that Congress intended "take" to apply broadly to cover indirect as well as purposeful actions. The Senate Report stressed that " '[t]ake' is defined . . . in the broadest possible manner to include every conceivable way in which a person can 'take' or attempt to 'take' any fish or wildlife." [Citation.] The House Report stated that "the broadest possible terms" were used to define restrictions on takings. [Citation.] The House Report underscored the breadth of the "take" definition by noting that it included "harassment, *whether intentional or not.*" [Citation.] The Report explained that the definition "would allow, for example, the Secretary to regulate or prohibit the activities of bird-watchers where the effect of those activities might disturb the birds and make it difficult for them to hatch or raise their young." [Citation.] These comments, ignored in the dissent's welcome but selective foray into legislative history, support the Secretary's interpretation that the term "take" in § 9 reached far more than the deliberate actions of hunters and trappers. . . .

[A floor amendment that added "harm" to the definition, noting that this and accompanying amendments would "help to achieve the purposes of the bill."] Respondents argue that the lack of debate about the amendment that added "harm" counsels in favor of a narrow interpretation. We disagree. An obviously broad word that the Senate went out of its way to add to an important statutory definition is precisely the sort of provision that deserves a respectful reading.

The definition of "take" that originally appeared in S. 1983 differed from the definition as ultimately enacted in one other significant respect: It included "the destruction, modification, or curtailment of [the] habitat or range" of fish and wildlife. [Citation.] Respondents make much of the fact that the Commerce Committee removed this phrase from the "take" definition before S. 1983 went to the floor. [Citation.] We do not find that fact especially significant. The legislative materials contain no indication why the habitat protection provision was deleted. That provision differed greatly from the regulation at issue today. Most notably, the habitat protection provision in S. 1983 would have applied far more broadly than the regulation does because it made adverse habitat modification a

---

language that the common world will understand, of what the law intends to do if a certain line is passed' "; second, "legislatures and not courts should define criminal activity." [Citations.] . . . We have never suggested that the rule of lenity should provide the standard for reviewing facial challenges to administrative regulations whenever the governing statute authorizes criminal enforcement. Even if there exist regulations whose interpretations of statutory criminal penalties provide such inadequate notice of potential liability as to offend the rule of lenity, the "harm" regulation, which has existed for two decades and gives a fair warning of its consequences, cannot be one of them.

categorical violation of the "take" prohibition, unbounded by the regulation's limitation to habitat modifications that actually kill or injure wildlife. The S. 1983 language also failed to qualify "modification" with the regulation's limiting adjective "significant." We do not believe the Senate's unelaborated disavowal of the provision in S. 1983 undermines the reasonableness of the more moderate habitat protection in the Secretary's "harm" regulation.

The history of the 1982 amendment that gave the Secretary authority to grant permits for "incidental" takings provides further support for his reading of the Act. The House Report expressly states that "[b]y use of the word 'incidental' the Committee intends to cover situations in which it is known that a taking will occur if the other activity is engaged in but such taking is incidental to, and not the purpose of, the activity." [Citation.] This reference to the foreseeability of incidental takings undermines respondents' argument that the 1982 amendment covered only accidental killings of endangered and threatened animals that might occur in the course of hunting or trapping other animals. Indeed, Congress had habitat modification directly in mind: both the Senate Report and the House Conference Report identified as the model for the permit process a cooperative state-federal response to a case in California where a development project threatened incidental harm to a species of endangered butterfly by modification of its habitat. [Citation.] Thus, Congress in 1982 focused squarely on the aspect of the "harm" regulation at issue in this litigation. Congress' implementation of a permit program is consistent with the Secretary's interpretation of the term "harm."

IV

When it enacted the ESA, Congress delegated broad administrative and interpretive power to the Secretary. *See* 16 U.S.C. §§ 1533, 1540(f). The task of defining and listing endangered and threatened species requires an expertise and attention to detail that exceeds the normal province of Congress. Fashioning appropriate standards for issuing permits under § 10 for takings that would otherwise violate § 9 necessarily requires the exercise of broad discretion. The proper interpretation of a term such as "harm" involves a complex policy choice. When Congress has entrusted the Secretary with broad discretion, we are especially reluctant to substitute our views of wise policy for his. *See Chevron,* 467 U.S., at 865–866. In this case, that reluctance accords with our conclusion, based on the text, structure, and legislative history of the ESA, that the Secretary reasonably construed the intent of Congress when he defined "harm" to include "significant habitat modification or degradation that actually kills or injures wildlife." . . .

The judgment of the Court of Appeals is reversed.

It is so ordered.

[The concurring opinion of JUSTICE O'CONNOR has been omitted.]

■ JUSTICE SCALIA, with whom . . . CHIEF JUSTICE [REHNQUIST] and JUSTICE THOMAS join, dissenting.

I think it unmistakably clear that the legislation at issue here (1) forbade the hunting and killing of endangered animals, and (2) provided federal lands and federal funds *for the acquisition of private lands,* to preserve the habitat of endangered animals. The Court's holding that the hunting and killing prohibition incidentally preserves habitat on private lands imposes unfairness to the point of financial ruin—not just upon the rich, but upon the simplest farmer who finds his land conscripted to national zoological use. I respectfully dissent.

I

. . . In my view . . . the regulation must fall—even under the test of *Chevron,* [citation]. . . . The regulation has three features which, for reasons I shall discuss at length below, do not comport with the statute.

First, it interprets the statute to prohibit habitat modification that is no more than the cause-in-fact of death or injury to wildlife. *Any* "significant habitat modification" that in fact produces that result by "impairing essential behavioral patterns" is made unlawful, regardless of whether that result is intended or even foreseeable, and no matter how long the chain of causality between modification and injury. . . . Second, the regulation does not require an "act"; the Secretary's officially stated position is that an *omission* will do. . . . The third and most important unlawful feature of the regulation is that it encompasses injury inflicted, not only upon individual animals, but upon populations of the protected species. "Injury" in the regulation includes "significantly impairing essential behavioral patterns, including *breeding,*" 50 CFR § 17.3 (1994) (emphasis added). Impairment of breeding does not "injure" living creatures; it prevents them from propagating, thus "injuring" *a population* of animals which would otherwise have maintained or increased its numbers. What the face of the regulation shows, the Secretary's official pronouncements confirm. The Final Redefinition of "Harm" accompanying publication of the regulation said that "harm" is not limited to "direct physical injury to an individual member of the wildlife species," [citation,] and refers to "injury *to a population,*" [citation] (emphasis added). . . .

None of these three features of the regulation can be found in the statutory provisions supposed to authorize it. The term "harm" in § 1532(19) has no legal force of its own. An indictment or civil complaint that charged the defendant with "harming" an animal protected under the Act would be dismissed as defective, for the only *operative* term in the statute is to "take." If "take" were not elsewhere defined in the Act, none could dispute what it means, for the term is as old as the law itself. To "take," when applied to wild animals, means to reduce those animals, by killing or capturing, to human control. *See, e.g.,* 11 Oxford English Dictionary (1933) ("Take . . . To catch, capture (a wild beast, bird, fish, etc.)"); Webster's New International Dictionary of the English Language

(2d ed. 1949) (take defined as "to catch or capture by trapping, snaring, etc., or as prey"); Geer v. Connecticut, 161 U.S. 519, 523, 16 S.Ct. 600, 602, 40 L.Ed. 793 (1896) ("[A]ll the animals which can be taken upon the earth, in the sea, or in the air, that is to say, wild animals, belong to those who take them") (quoting the Digest of Justinian); 2 W. Blackstone, Commentaries 411 (1766) ("Every man . . . has an equal right of pursuing and taking to his own use all such creatures as are *ferae naturae*"). This is just the sense in which "take" is used elsewhere in federal legislation and treaty. *See, e.g.,* Migratory Bird Treaty Act, 16 U.S.C. § 703 (1988 ed., Supp. V) (no person may "pursue, hunt, take, capture, kill, [or] attempt to take, capture, or kill" any migratory bird); Agreement on the Conservation of Polar Bears, Nov. 15, 1973, Art. I, 27 U.S.T. 3918, 3921, T.I.A.S. No. 8409 (defining "taking" as "hunting, killing and capturing"). And that meaning fits neatly with the rest of § 1538(a)(1), which makes it unlawful not only to take protected species, but also to import or export them (§ 1538(a)(1)(A)); to possess, sell, deliver, carry, transport, or ship any taken species (§ 1538(a)(1)(D)); and to transport, sell, or offer to sell them in interstate or foreign commerce (§§ 1538(a)(1)(E)(F)). The taking prohibition, in other words, is only part of the regulatory plan of § 1538(a)(1), which covers all the stages of the process by which protected wildlife is reduced to man's dominion and made the object of profit. It is obvious that "take" in this sense—a term of art deeply embedded in the statutory and common law concerning wildlife—describes a class of acts (not omissions) done directly and intentionally (not indirectly and by accident) to particular animals (not populations of animals).

The Act's definition of "take" does expand the word slightly (and not unusually), so as to make clear that it includes not just a completed taking, but the process of taking, and all of the acts that are customarily identified with or accompany that process ("to harass, harm, pursue, hunt, shoot, wound, kill, trap, capture, or collect"); and so as to include attempts. § 1532(19). The tempting fallacy—which the Court commits with abandon—is to assume that *once defined,* "take" loses any significance, and it is only the definition that matters. The Court treats the statute as though Congress had directly enacted the § 1532(19) definition as a self-executing prohibition, and had not enacted § 1538(a)(1)(B) at all. But § 1538(a)(1)(B) *is* there, and if the terms contained in the definitional section are susceptible of two readings, one of which comports with the standard meaning of "take" as used in application to wildlife, and one of which does not, an agency regulation that adopts the latter reading is necessarily unreasonable, for it reads the defined term "take"—the only operative term—out of the statute altogether.[2]

---

[2]   The Court suggests halfheartedly that "take" cannot refer to the taking of particular animals, because § 1538(a)(1)(B) prohibits "tak[ing] any [endangered] species." The suggestion is halfhearted because that reading obviously contradicts the statutory intent. It would mean no violation in the intentional shooting of a single bald eagle—or, for that matter, the intentional

That is what has occurred here. The verb "harm" has a *range* of meaning: "to cause injury" at its broadest, "to do hurt or damage" in a narrower and more direct sense. *See, e.g.,* 1 N. Webster, An American Dictionary of the English Language (1828) ("Harm, *v.t.* To hurt; to injure; to damage; *to impair soundness of body, either animal* or vegetable") (emphasis added); American College Dictionary 551 (1970) ("harm . . . *n.* injury; damage; hurt: *to do him bodily harm*"). In fact the more directed sense of "harm" is a somewhat more common and preferred usage; "*harm* has in it a little of the idea of specially focused hurt or injury, as if a personal injury has been anticipated and intended." J. Opdycke, Mark My Words: A Guide to Modern Usage and Expression 330 (1949). *See also* American Heritage Dictionary of the English Language (1981) ("*Injure* has the widest range. . . . *Harm* and *hurt* refer principally to what causes physical or mental distress to living things"). To define "harm" as an act or omission that, however remotely, "actually kills or injures" a population of wildlife through habitat modification, is to choose a meaning that makes nonsense of the word that "harm" defines— requiring us to accept that a farmer who tills his field and causes erosion that makes silt run into a nearby river which depletes oxygen and thereby "impairs [the] breeding" of protected fish, has "taken" or "attempted to take" the fish. It should take the strongest evidence to make us believe that Congress has defined a term in a manner repugnant to its ordinary and traditional sense.

Here the evidence shows the opposite. "Harm" is merely one of 10 prohibitory words in § 1532(19), and the other 9 fit the ordinary meaning of "take" perfectly. To "harass, pursue, hunt, shoot, wound, kill, trap, capture, or collect" are all affirmative acts (the provision itself describes them as "conduct," see § 1532(19)) which are directed immediately and intentionally against a particular animal—not acts or omissions that indirectly and accidentally cause injury to a population of animals. . . .

I am not the first to notice this fact, or to draw the conclusion that it compels. In 1981 the Solicitor of the Fish and Wildlife Service delivered a legal opinion on § 1532(19) that is in complete agreement with my reading:

> "The Act's definition of 'take' contains a list of actions that illustrate the intended scope of the term. . . . With the possible exception of 'harm,' these terms all represent forms of conduct that are directed against and likely to injure or kill *individual* wildlife. Under the principle of statutory construction, *ejusdem generis,* . . . the term 'harm' should be interpreted to include only those actions that are directed against, and likely to injure or kill, individual wildlife." Memorandum of April 17, 1981, reprinted in 46 Fed. Reg. 29490, 29491 (emphasis in original).

---

shooting of 1,000 bald eagles out of the extant 1,001. The phrasing of § 1538(a)(1)(B), as the Court recognizes elsewhere, is shorthand for "take any member of [an endangered] species."

I would call it *noscitur a sociis,* but the principle is much the same: the fact that "several items in a list share an attribute counsels in favor of interpreting the other items as possessing that attribute as well," [Citation.] The Court contends that the canon cannot be applied to deprive a word of all its "independent meaning." That proposition is questionable to begin with, especially as applied to long lawyers' listings such as this. If it were true, we ought to give the word "trap" in the definition its rare meaning of "to clothe" (whence "trappings")—since otherwise it adds nothing to the word "capture." *See* Moskal v. United States, 498 U.S. 103, 120 (1990) (Scalia, J., dissenting). . . .

The penalty provisions of the Act counsel this interpretation as well. Any person who "knowingly" violates § 1538(a)(1)(B) is subject to criminal penalties under § 1540(b)(1) and civil penalties under § 1540(a)(1); moreover, under the latter section, any person "who otherwise violates" the taking prohibition (*i.e.,* violates it *un* knowingly) may be assessed a civil penalty of $500 for each violation, with the stricture that "[e]ach such violation shall be a separate offense." This last provision should be clear warning that the regulation is in error, for when combined with the regulation it produces a result that no legislature could reasonably be thought to have intended: A large number of routine private activities—farming, for example, farming, ranching, roadbuilding, construction and logging—are subjected to strict-liability penalties when they fortuitously injure protected wildlife, no matter how remote the chain of causation and no matter how difficult to foresee (or to disprove) the "injury" may be (*e.g.,* an "impairment" of breeding). . . .

So far I have discussed only the immediate statutory text bearing on the regulation. But the definition of "take" in § 1532(19) applies "[f]or the purposes of this chapter," that is, it governs the meaning of the word *as used everywhere in the Act.* Thus, the Secretary's interpretation of "harm" is wrong if it does not fit with the use of "take" throughout the Act. And it does not. In § 1540(e)(4)(B), for example, Congress provided for the forfeiture of "[a]ll guns, traps, nets, and other equipment . . . used to aid the taking, possessing, selling, [etc.]" of protected animals. This listing plainly relates to "taking" in the ordinary sense. If environmental modification were part (and necessarily a major part) of taking, as the Secretary maintains, one would have expected the list to include "plows, bulldozers, and backhoes." As another example, § 1539(e)(1) exempts "the taking of any endangered species" by Alaskan Indians and Eskimos "if such taking is primarily for subsistence purposes"; and provides that "[n]on-edible byproducts of species taken pursuant to this section may be sold . . . when made into authentic native articles of handicrafts and clothing." Surely these provisions apply to taking only in the ordinary sense, and are meaningless as applied to species injured by environmental modification. The Act is full of like examples. [Citation.] "[I]f the Act is to be interpreted as a symmetrical and coherent regulatory scheme, one in which the operative words have a consistent meaning throughout," [citation,] the regulation must fall.

The broader structure of the Act confirms the unreasonableness of the regulation. Section 1536 provides:

> "Each Federal agency shall ... insure that any action authorized, funded, or carried out by such agency ... is not likely to jeopardize the continued existence of any endangered species or threatened species or *result in the destruction or adverse modification of habitat* of such species which is determined by the Secretary ... to be critical." 16 U.S.C. § 1536(a)(2) (emphasis added). ...

This means that the "harm" regulation also contradicts another principle of interpretation: that statutes should be read so far as possible to give independent effect to all their provisions. *See* Ratzlaf v. United States, 510 U.S. 135, 155. By defining "harm" in the definition of "take" in § 1538(a)(1)(B) to include significant habitat modification that injures populations of wildlife, the regulation makes the habitat-modification restriction in § 1536(a)(2) almost wholly superfluous.

II

The Court makes ... other arguments. First, "the broad purpose of the [Act] supports the Secretary's decision to extend protection against activities that cause the precise harms Congress enacted the statute to avoid." I thought we had renounced the vice of "simplistically ... assum[ing] that *whatever* furthers the statute's primary objective must be the law." [Citation.] Deduction from the "broad purpose" of a statute begs the question if it is used to decide by what *means* (and hence to what *length*) Congress pursued that purpose; to get the right answer to that question there is no substitute for the hard job (or, in this case, the quite simple one) of reading the whole text. "The Act must do everything necessary to achieve its broad purpose" is the slogan of the enthusiast, not the analytical tool of the arbiter. ...

III

In response to the points made in this dissent, the Court's opinion stresses two points, neither of which is supported by the regulation, and so cannot validly be used to uphold it. First, the Court and the concurrence suggest that the regulation should be read to contain a requirement of proximate causation or foreseeability, principally *because the statute does*—and "[n]othing in the regulation purports to weaken those requirements [of the statute]." I quite agree that the statute contains such a limitation, because the verbs of purpose in § 1538(a)(1)(B) denote action directed at animals. *But the Court has rejected that reading*. The critical premise on which it has upheld the regulation is that, despite the weight of the other words in § 1538(a)(1)(B), "the statutory term 'harm' encompasses indirect as well as direct injuries," (describing "the sense of indirect causation that 'harm' adds to the statute"); (stating that the Secretary permissibly interprets " 'harm' " to include "indirectly injuring endangered animals"). Consequently, unless there is some strange category of causation that is indirect and yet also proximate, the Court has already rejected its own basis for finding a proximate-cause limitation in the regulation. In fact "proximate" causation simply *means* "direct" causation. [Citation.] . . .

The only other reason given for finding a proximate-cause limitation in the regulation is that "by use of the word 'actually,' " the regulation clearly rejects speculative or conjectural effects, and thus itself invokes principles of proximate causation. . . . "actually" defines the requisite *injury*, not the requisite *causality*.

The regulation says (it is worth repeating) that "harm" means (1) an act that (2) actually kills or injures wildlife. If that does not dispense with a proximate cause requirement, I do not know what language would. And changing the regulation by judicial invention, even to achieve compliance with the statute, is not permissible. Perhaps the agency itself would prefer to achieve compliance in some other fashion. We defer to reasonable agency interpretations of ambiguous statutes precisely in order that agencies, rather than courts, may exercise policymaking discretion in the interstices of statutes. *See Chevron*, 467 U.S., at 843–845, 104 S. Ct., at 2782. Just as courts may not exercise an agency's power to adjudicate, and so may not affirm an agency order on discretionary grounds the agency has not advanced, [citation,] so also this Court may not exercise the Secretary's power to regulate, and so may not uphold a regulation by adding to it even the most reasonable of elements it does not contain.

The second point the Court stresses in its response seems to me a belated mending of its holding. It apparently *concedes* that the statute requires injury *to particular animals* rather than merely to populations of animals (referring to killing or injuring "*members of* [listed] species" (emphasis added)). The Court then rejects my contention that the regulation ignores this requirement, since, it says, "every term in the regulation's definition of 'harm' is subservient to the phrase 'an act which actually kills or injures wildlife.' " As I have pointed out, this reading is incompatible with the regulation's specification of impairment of "breeding" as one of the *modes* of "kill[ing] or injur[ing] wildlife." . . .

But since the Court is reading the regulation and the statute incorrectly in other respects, it may as well introduce this novelty as well—law à la carte. As I understand the regulation that the Court has created and held consistent with the statute that it has also created, habitat modification can constitute a "taking," but only if it results in the killing or harming of *individual animals,* and only if that consequence is the direct result of the modification. This means that the destruction of privately owned habitat that is essential, not for the feeding or nesting, but for the *breeding,* of butterflies, would not violate the Act, since it would not harm or kill any living butterfly. I, too, think it would not violate the Act—not for the utterly unsupported reason that habitat modifications fall outside the regulation if they happen not to kill or injure a living animal, but for the textual reason that only action directed at living animals constitutes a "take." . . .

The Endangered Species Act is a carefully considered piece of legislation that forbids all persons to hunt or harm endangered animals, but places upon the public at large, rather than upon fortuitously accountable individual landowners, the cost of preserving the habitat of endangered species. There is neither textual support for, nor even evidence of congressional consideration of, the radically different disposition contained in the regulation that the Court sustains. For these reasons, I respectfully dissent.

QUESTIONS

1.   The dissent emphasizes that the majority's interpretation of the harm cross-definition of "take" seems to read the ordinary meaning of "take" out of the statute altogether. Is this true? Does it matter whether a cross-definition seems to include conduct beyond what the ordinary meaning of the verb it defines usually conveys?

2.   The dissent contends that "[a]n indictment or civil complaint that charged the defendant with 'harming' an animal protected under the Act would be dismissed as defective, for the only *operative* term in the statute is to 'take.'" Does it seem reasonable to cabin a criminal prohibition only to a term's ordinary meaning, even if Congress elsewhere defined that term in a more expansive way? On the other hand, how much of a departure from the ordinary meaning of the term should be tolerated—either as a result of a definitions section or a cross-reference to other portions of the statute— before the statute might be thought defective in giving fair notice to members of the general public as to the conduct the statute criminalizes?

3.   Even if you find the dissent's concerns about the reach of potential criminal law applications of the "harm" regulation compelling, should that matter for the resolution of the legal question in *Sweet Home*, which concerned whether the plaintiffs were required to seek a permit to engage in incidental takings? Should courts consider every potential civil and criminal application of a statute when interpreting its meaning in a given case? Keep this question in mind when reading Section V.D, *infra*.

4.   The majority notes that Congress's 1982 amendments to the ESA seem to endorse the agency's incidental takings definition of harm by establishing a permitting system that would allow limited incidental takings notwithstanding the regulatory prohibition. Nevertheless, as the dissent notes, such an interpretation seriously complicates the meaning of "take" and "harm" as applied elsewhere in the statute. When such intra-statutory complications arise—especially with a statute that has been amended multiple times—what is the appropriate role of courts in reviewing challenges to the amended statute's application? Should courts attend to developing the most coherent interpretation of the statute as a whole, or

simply ensure the integrity of the specific statutory text at issue in the instant case or application?

D. AGENCY INTERPRETATIONS WITH POTENTIAL CRIMINAL CONSEQUENCES

The disagreement between Justices Stevens and Scalia in *Babbitt v. Sweet Home, supra,* illustrates an emerging tension for agency interpretations of statutes with potential criminal consequences. Historically, the interpretation of criminal prohibitions enacted by legislatures came by way of the formal criminal justice system. When prosecutors try cases, they must assert both at the charging stage and during trial or plea bargaining that the defendant's conduct fell within the statutory criminal prohibition. Such an interpretation may be provided in the charging instrument, in pre-trial motions, and in court-approved jury instructions that explain to the jury what the statutory prohibition means, as well as the elements the jury must find in order for the government to secure a conviction. The defendant may object to the prosecutor's proposed interpretation both by seeking a pre-trial dismissal of the indictment, or by appealing the conviction on the grounds that the court below misinterpreted the statute. Courses in Criminal Law, Criminal Procedure, and Federal Criminal Law often address the statutory interpretation problems implicated in this process.

Today, however, numerous administrative statutes contain both civil and criminal prohibitions, and the traditionally tidy distinctions no longer hold in all circumstances. As illustrated in *Babbitt v. Sweet Home,* agencies engaged in promulgating interpretations of civil prohibitions with adjacent criminal consequences may articulate an agency interpretation that can also have consequences for potential criminal prosecutions. And recall that in *United States v. Thompson/Center Arms* (1992), *supra* Section III.A.2.c, members of the Supreme Court disagreed about the propriety of applying the rule of lenity to interpret a statutory provision implicating civil tax consequences that in some potential future case might also have criminal statutory interpretation implications.

This section highlights cases that push the interpretive boundaries between civil and criminal sanctions further: what happens when an agency's interpretation may warrant *Chevron* deference but also has criminal consequences for future parties? Should the Court defer under *Chevron* when the statute is sufficiently ambiguous? Or, should such ambiguity demand application of the rule of lenity?

NOTE: IMMIGRATION STATUTES WITH POTENTIAL CRIMINAL CONSEQUENCES

In **Esquivel-Quintana v. Lynch**, 810 F.3d 1019 (6th. Cir. 2016), the Sixth Circuit considered whether a conviction under a California statute criminalizing sexual intercourse with a minor who is more than three years younger than the perpetrator constituted "sexual abuse of a minor" under the Immigration and Nationality Act (INA).

Juan Esquivel-Quintana, a Mexican citizen and lawful permanent resident, was convicted of statutory rape under California law. The prohibited conduct occurred over a five-month period in which the victim was 16 and Esquivel-Quintana was 20 or 21. After Esquivel-Quintana had relocated to Michigan, the Department of Homeland Security subsequently initiated removal proceedings against him under 8 U.S.C. § 1227(a)(2)(A)(iii), which states that an alien can be removed if he is convicted of an aggravated felony such as "sexual abuse of a minor." An immigration judge ordered Esquivel-Quintana's removal, which he appealed. The Board of Immigration Appeals ruled against him, concluding that "sexual abuse of a minor" includes convictions under the relevant California statute, and that "in the context of State statutory rape offenses, a statute that includes 16- or 17-year-olds must also contain a meaningful age differential to constitute 'sexual abuse of a minor.' " The Board did not specify exactly what constitutes a "meaningful" age differential, but it held that the age differential in California's statute—which requires an age gap of more than three years—was meaningful.

The members of the Sixth Circuit agreed that the INA provision, which did not provide a definition of "sexual abuse of a minor," was ambiguous, but they disagreed about whether *Chevron* or the rule of lenity should apply in resolving the ambiguity. While this was a civil case, the relevant statute drew on the definition of a predicate criminal offense. The majority concluded that *Chevron* should apply and deferred to the Board's interpretation:

> An increasingly emergent view asserts that the rule of lenity ought to apply in civil cases involving statutes that have both civil and criminal applications. [Citations.] This view is based on two principles. First, statutory terms should not have different meanings in different cases—"a statute is not a chameleon." [Citation.] Second, ambiguous statutes must be construed in favor of defendants under the rule of lenity. The rule of lenity ensures that the public has adequate notice of what conduct is criminalized, and preserves the separation of powers by ensuring that legislatures, not executive officers, define crimes. Taken together, these two principles lead to the conclusion that the rule of lenity should apply in civil cases involving ambiguous statutes with criminal applications.

> There are compelling reasons to apply the rule of lenity in such cases. Giving deference to agency interpretations of ambiguous laws with criminal applications would allow agencies to "create (and uncreate) new crimes at will, so long as they do not roam beyond ambiguities that the laws contain." [Citation.] Writing criminal laws is the legislature's prerogative, not the executive's. Furthermore, deferring to agency interpretations of criminal laws violates the principle that "criminal laws are for courts, not for the Government, to construe." [Citation.] Left unchecked, deference to

agency interpretations of laws with criminal applications threatens a complete undermining of the Constitution's separation of powers.

Nonetheless, while this view is increasing in prominence, the Supreme Court has not made it the law. To the contrary, the Court has reached the opposite conclusion. In *Babbitt*, the Court deferred to the Secretary of the Interior's definition of the term "take" in the Endangered Species Act of 1973, even though violations of the act could be enforced by criminal penalties. [Citation] The Court expressly considered and rejected the rule of lenity: "We have never suggested that the rule of lenity should provide the standard for reviewing facial challenges to administrative regulations whenever the governing statute authorizes criminal enforcement." [Citation.]. Since then, . . . the Court [has] suggested that the rule of lenity could apply if an ambiguity existed, but [has] had no occasion to apply it because the statute[s before the Court have been] unambiguous.

While the Court has begun to distance itself from *Babbitt*, we do not read dicta . . . [in] subsequent cases as overruling *Babbitt*, or requiring that we apply the rule of lenity here in Esquivel-Quintana's civil removal proceeding. As an "inferior" court, our job is to adhere faithfully to the Supreme Court's precedents. The Supreme Court has said that we must follow *Chevron* in cases involving the Board's interpretations of immigration laws. [Citations.] . . . *Chevron* applies.

Judge Jeffrey Sutton dissented in part, for in his view *Chevron* is inapplicable to criminal statutes and the rule of lenity should apply to statutes with both civil and criminal implications:

Chevron permits agencies to fill gaps in civil statutes that Congress has delegated authority to the agency to interpret. [Citation.] Under the doctrine, courts presume that, when Congress leaves an ambiguity in an agency-administered statute, it intends the agency to fill the gap. [Citation.] But *Chevron* has no role to play in construing criminal statutes. In 227 years and counting, the federal courts have never presumed that, when an ambiguity arises in a criminal statute, the congressional silence signals that Congress wants an executive-branch agency to fill the gap. For all of the theories of *Chevron* that have filled the U.S. Reports and the Federal Reporter, to say nothing of the law journals, the idea that *Chevron* is a tool for construing criminal statutes has yet to make an appearance. That is because criminal statutes "are for courts, not for the Government, to construe." [Citation.] The doctrine does not give the Department of Justice (or for that matter any other federal agency) implied gap-filling authority over ambiguous criminal statutes.

Otherwise, that would leave this distasteful combination: The prosecutor would have the explicit (executive) power to enforce the criminal laws, an implied (legislative) power to fill policy gaps in ambiguous criminal statutes, and an implied (judicial) power to interpret ambiguous criminal laws. [Citation.] And it would permit this aggregation of power in the one area where its division matters most: the removal of citizens from society. . . .

The application of *Chevron* to criminal laws also would leave no room for the rule of lenity, a rule that resolves ambiguities in criminal statutes in favor of the individual and a rule of construction that Chief Justice Marshall described as "perhaps not much less old than construction itself." United States v. Wiltberger, 18 U.S. (5 Wheat.) 76, 95 (1820). . . .

So far so good.

But what happens when the same statute has criminal and civil applications? May Congress sidestep these requirements by giving criminal statutes a civil application? The answer is no. The courts must give dual-application statutes just one interpretation, and the criminal application controls. Statutes are not "chameleon[s]" that mean one thing in one setting and something else in another. [Citation.] Because a single law should have a single meaning, the "lowest common denominator"—including all rules applicable to the interpretation of criminal laws—governs all of its applications. [Citation.] That explains why *United States v. Thompson/Center Arms Co.* applied the rule of lenity to a civil tax case that turned on language that had civil and criminal applications. [Citation.] Time, time, and time again, the Court has confirmed that the one-interpretation rule means that the criminal-law construction of the statute (with the rule of lenity) prevails over the civil-law construction of it (without the rule of lenity). When a single statute has twin applications, the search for the least common denominator leads to the least liberty-infringing interpretation. [Citations.]

The provision at issue in today's case is subject to the one-statute/one-interpretation rule because it has criminal and civil applications. The Immigration and Nationality Act makes a state or federal conviction for "sexual abuse of a minor" an "aggravated felony." 8 U.S.C. § 1101(a)(43)(A). The Act subjects aliens who have committed aggravated felonies (1) to civil consequences, most notably removal from the country, *id.* § 1227(a)(2)(A)(iii); *see also id.* § 1229b(a)(3), and (2) to criminal consequences, most notably increasing the maximum prison term for illegal reentry into the United States, *id.* § 1326(b)(2); *see also id.* § 1327. . . .

All clues considered, the phrase "sexual abuse of a minor" may, but may not, include convictions under California's § 261.5(c), and for that reason the rule of lenity should end the case in favor of the immigrant.

The application of *Chevron* to this ambiguity of course leads to a different result. A statute sufficiently ambiguous to invoke the rule of lenity assuredly is sufficiently ambiguous to trigger *Chevron* deference. And adjudicative decisions by the Board typically receive *Chevron* deference. [Citation.] That means, as the court explains, that the Board's decision that Esquivel-Quintana's § 261.5(c) conviction amounts to "sexual abuse of a minor" prevails under *Chevron* deference. But it also means, as the court explains, that this interpretation would not prevail under the rule of lenity, where "sexual abuse of a minor" would cover no more than those statutory-rape crimes that set the age of consent at sixteen or less.

Yet the application of *Chevron* in this setting, as the court acknowledges, "threatens a complete undermining of the Constitution's separation of powers," while the application of the rule of lenity "preserves" them by maintaining the legislature as the creator of crimes. Lenity also ensures fair notice of criminal consequences, precludes the same agency from altering criminal laws back and forth over time (even over conflicting judicial interpretations, see *Brand X Internet Servs.*, [citation], and even without input from Congress), and ensures that the same "[r]ules of interpretation bind all interpreters, administrative agencies included." [Citation.] Lenity also avoids several "uninvited oddities [that] arise if courts but not agencies must adhere to the rule of lenity." [Citation.] By applying lenity in this setting, last of all, courts would avoid incentivizing Congress to enact hybrid statutes that duck under lenity's imperatives, to say nothing of other imperatives in construing criminal laws.

Where I part ways with the court is over its conclusion that, even though the rule of lenity ought to control here, we must defer to the government's position under *Chevron* all the same.

The disagreement boils down to the meaning of one sentence in one footnote. [In *Babbitt*, t]he Supreme Court decided it "owe[d] some degree of deference" to the Department of Labor's interpretation, [citation], and cited *Chevron* in the process. Then, in a footnote, it said that it "ha[d] never suggested that the rule of lenity should provide the standard for reviewing facial challenges to administrative regulations whenever the governing statute authorizes criminal enforcement." [Citation.] This statement does not, as the court claims, require us to apply *Chevron*. If it did, the footnote would have (silently) overruled an entire line of cases that "hold that, if Congress wants to assign responsibility for crime definition to the executive, it must speak clearly." [Citations.] And the footnote expressly limits itself to "facial challenges," the sorts of claims that raise arguments—say that the regulation exceeded the agency's authority and thus was unenforceable in all of its applications—that have no connection to the rule of lenity. Today's case does not involve a facial challenge.

Whatever this footnote and its inscrutable reference to facial challenges meant then, cases since *Babbitt* have not followed the reading the court finds itself constrained to follow. . . .

Perhaps something else gives the court pause today—the potential sticker shock of transforming a government-always-wins canon (*Chevron*) into a government-always-loses canon (rule of lenity). But that may not be where the Court's cases necessarily lead. The Court's recent cases, as shown, just require two things: that the one-statute/one-interpretation rule governs dual-role statutes, and *Chevron* does not apply to that one interpretation. Those two requirements, however, may not dictate when the rule of lenity governs and when it does not. Yes, the rule of lenity frequently may dictate that one interpretation but that need not invariably be the case. Statutory "ambiguity" may mean one thing under *Chevron* and something else under the rule of lenity. If American Inuits have more than one way to describe snow, American lawyers may have more than one way to describe ambiguity. *See* Bill Bryson, The Mother Tongue 14–15 (2001). Under *Chevron*, courts will defer to an agency interpretation if the relevant statute "is silent or ambiguous with respect to the specific issue." [Citation]. It remains to be seen whether the same type of ambiguity triggers the rule of lenity. [Citation.] *Chevron's* domain and the rule of lenity's domain thus may not necessarily overlap in some cases.

What matters for present purposes is that *Chevron* has no role to play in construing hybrid statutes. Whether the rule of lenity necessarily will provide the answer in all of these cases is another matter, one for the Court ultimately to decide. In some settings, it may turn out, the Court simply will apply the normal rules of construction unaided by a zero-sum default rule, and will look to the rule of lenity only in the kinds of interpretive disputes that require it.

One last point. An exception to *Chevron* for dual-role statutes would not be the least bit unusual. Deference under that rule is categorically unavailable, the Supreme Court has held, in many settings: (1) agency interpretations of statutes the agency is not "charged with administering," Metro. Stevedore Co. v. Rambo, 521 U.S. 121, 137 n. 9 (1997); (2) agency interpretations of "the scope of the judicial power vested by [a] statute," such as the availability of a private right of action, Adams Fruit Co. v. Barrett, 494 U.S. 638, 649–50 (1990); [citation]; (3) agency interpretations that result from procedures that were not "in the exercise" of the agency's authority "to make rules carrying the force of law," *Mead.*, [citations]; (4) agency interpretations with respect to "extraordinary cases" where it is unlikely Congress "intended . . . an implicit delegation" to the agency, *King v. Burwell*, [citation]; and (5) agency interpretations of criminal statutes, Abramski, 134 S.Ct. at 2274. An exception for statutes with civil and criminal consequences fits easily alongside these exceptions and originates from the same place as the last one. Indeed, it is exceedingly difficult to understand how *Chevron* could prevail in a dual-statute case. Since the founding, it has been the job of Article III courts, not Article II executive-branch agencies, to have the final say over what criminal laws mean. I would honor that imperative here and reject the idea that Congress can end-run this principle by giving a criminal statute a civil application.

For these reasons, I concur with much of the court's reasoning but must disagree with its conclusion.

Esquivel-Quintana appealed his removal order to the Supreme Court, which granted cert, and, in **Esquivel-Quintana v. Sessions**, 137 S. Ct. 1562 (2017), unanimously reversed the Sixth Circuit's judgment. The Court held that the "generic" federal definition of "sexual abuse of a minor" requires that the victim be younger than 16, at least where sexual intercourse is considered abusive based solely on the ages of the participants. In reaching its decision, the Court sidestepped the question of whether *Chevron* or the rule or lenity should apply, finding that neither was applicable because the relevant INA provision, read in context, was unambiguous.

1. CASE STUDY: BANNING BUMP-STOCKS BY REGULATION

[From the introduction of *Guedes v. ATF, infra*:] In October 2017, a lone gunman armed with bump-stock-enhanced semiautomatic weapons murdered 58 people and wounded hundreds more in a mass shooting at a concert in Las Vegas, Nevada. In the wake of that tragedy, the Bureau of Alcohol, Tobacco, Firearms and Explosives ("Bureau") promulgated through formal notice-and-comment proceedings a rule that classifies bump-stock devices as machine guns under the National Firearms Act, 26 U.S.C. §§ 5801–5872. *See* Bump-Stock-Type Devices, 83 Fed. Reg. 66,514 (Dec. 26, 2018) ("Bump-Stock Rule"). The then-Acting Attorney General Matthew Whitaker initially signed the final Bump-Stock Rule, and Attorney General William Barr independently ratified it shortly after taking office.

The Texts to Be Construed: The National Firearms Act, the Gun Control Act, and the Bump-Stock Rule

Before you read the D.C. Circuit's disposition of a legal challenge to the Bump-Stock Rule in *Guedes v. Bureau of Alcohol, Tobacco, Firearms and Explosives* (D.C. Cir. 2019), review the following statutory provisions and regulatory interpretations, referenced in the majority and dissenting opinions, and consider these questions.

a. RELEVANT STATUTORY PROVISIONS

Drawing on the interpretive methods reviewed throughout this Casebook, consider whether the statutory definition of "machinegun" in the National Firearms Act ambiguous. If so, which parts of the definition are ambiguous? What canons or methods, if any, would support that conclusion?

Gun Control Act of 1968

United States Code, Title 18, Chapter 44.

Section 921.   Definitions...

(23) The term "machinegun" has the meaning given such term in section 5845(b) of the National Firearms Act of 1934 (26 U.S.C. 5845(b)). . . .

Section 922.   Unlawful Acts...

(*o*)(1)   Except as provided in paragraph (2), it shall be unlawful for any person to transfer or possess a machinegun.

    (2)   This subsection does not apply with respect to—

        (A)   a transfer to or by, or possession by or under the authority of, the United States or any department or agency thereof or a State, or a department, agency, or political subdivision thereof; or

        (B)   any lawful transfer or lawful possession of a machinegun that was lawfully possessed before the date this subsection takes effect.

National Firearms Act of 1934

United States Code, Title 26, Chapter 53.

Section 5845. Definitions

For the purpose of this chapter—

(a) **Firearm.**—The term "firearm" means (1) a shotgun having a barrel or barrels of less than 18 inches in length; (2) a weapon made from a shotgun if such weapon as modified has an overall length of less than 26 inches or a barrel or barrels of less than 18 inches in length; (3) a rifle having a barrel or barrels of less than 16 inches in length; (4) a weapon made from a rifle if such weapon as modified has an overall length of less than 26 inches or a barrel or barrels of less than 16 inches in length; (5) any other weapon, as defined in subsection (e); (6) a machinegun; (7) any silencer (as defined in section 921 of title 18, United States Code); and (8) a destructive device. The term "firearm" shall not include an antique firearm or any device (other than a machinegun or destructive device) which, although designed as a weapon, the Secretary finds by reason of the date of its manufacture, value, design, and other characteristics is primarily a collector's item and is not likely to be used as a weapon.

(b) **Machinegun.**—The term "machinegun" means any weapon which shoots, is designed to shoot, or can be readily restored to shoot, automatically more than one shot, without manual reloading, by a single function of the trigger. The term shall also include the frame or receiver of any such weapon, any part designed and intended solely and exclusively, or combination of parts designed and intended, for use in converting a weapon into a machinegun, and any combination of parts from which a machinegun can be assembled if such parts are in the possession or under the control of a person.

b.   THE BUMP-STOCK RULE'S REVISED DEFINITION OF MACHINE GUN

1.   As you read the revised definition of Machine gun provided by the Bump-Stock Rule, 27 CFR § 479.11, consider whether the ATF's interpretation and definition contradicts the statutory definition of "machinegun"? Why or why not?

2.   Recall the majority's argument in *Gonzales v. Oregon*, *supra*, that the Attorney General's regulatory definition simply parroted the statutory definition, and thus the rule elaborating on the regulatory definition constituted an interpretive rule not eligible for *Chevron* deference. Could the same be said of the regulation's definition of "machine gun" prior to the Bump-Stock Rule's promulgation? What about after it?

Machine Guns, Destructive Devices, and Certain Other Firearms, CFR § 479.11

United States Code of Federal Regulations, Title 27, Chapter 2.*

§ 479.11 Meaning of Terms. . . .

Machine gun. Any weapon which shoots, is designed to shoot, or can be readily restored to shoot, automatically more than one shot, without manual reloading, by a single function of the trigger. The term shall also include the frame or receiver of any such weapon, any part designed and intended solely and exclusively, or combination of parts designed and intended, for use in converting a weapon into a machine gun, and any combination of parts from which a machine gun can be assembled if such parts are in the possession or under the control of a person.

[Editors' Note: The following text, effective March 26, 2019, now follows the preceding paragraph:]

For purposes of this definition, the term "automatically" as it modifies "shoots, is designed to shoot, or can be readily restored to shoot," means functioning as the result of a self-acting or self-regulating mechanism that allows the firing of multiple rounds through a single function of the trigger; and "single function of the trigger" means a single pull of the trigger and analogous motions. The term "machine gun" includes a bump-stock-type device, *i.e.*, a device that allows a semi-automatic firearm to shoot more than one shot with a single pull of the trigger by harnessing the recoil energy of the semi-automatic firearm to

---

*   Editors' Note: The definition provided for the term "Machine gun" is identical in both 27 CFR § 479.11, which supplies definitions for the National Firearms Act, and 27 CFR § 478.11, which supplies definitions for the Gun Control Act.

which it is affixed so that the trigger resets and continues firing without
additional physical manipulation of the trigger by the shooter.

c. THE BUMP-STOCK RULE AND THE ATF'S INTERPRETATION OF THE
RELEVANT STATUTES

1. As you read the Bump-Stock Rule and its interpretation of the
relevant statutes, consider whether the Bump-Stock Rule constitutes a
"legislative" rule, for which *Chevron* deference may be warranted, or an
"interpretive" rule, for which it would not. What arguments could be
made either way?

2. Consider the interpretive methods the ATF cites to support its
interpretation, and recall the typology of interpretive methods in Section
II.B.1, *supra*. Which of these arguments are grounded in claims about
what Congress intended to accomplish when enacting the GCA and the
NFA? Which arguments are grounded in claims about how a reasonable
reader would understand the statute's meaning? Which arguments do
you find more persuasive, and why?

3. The ATF acknowledges that defining machine guns to include bump-
stock-type devices constitutes a departure from prior agency
interpretation and practice. What is the justification for the agency's
change of heart? Is it defensible, either as a matter of law or as a matter
of policy?

Bump-Stock Rule (Fed. Reg. 2018)
83 Fed. Reg. 66514 (2018).

Bump-Stock-Type Devices

AGENCY: Bureau of Alcohol, Tobacco, Firearms, and
Explosives; Department of Justice.

ACTION: Final rule.

I. Executive Summary

A. Summary of the Regulatory Action

The current regulations at §§ 447.11, 478.11, and 479.11 of title 27,
Code of Federal Regulations (CFR), contain definitions for the term
"machinegun." The definitions used in 27 CFR 478.11 and 479.11 match
the statutory definition of "machinegun" in the National Firearms Act of
1934 (NFA), as amended, and the Gun Control Act of 1968 (GCA), as
amended. . . .

In 2006, ATF concluded that certain bump-stock-type devices
qualified as machineguns under the NFA and GCA. Specifically, ATF
concluded that a device attached to a semiautomatic firearm that uses
an internal spring to harness the force of a firearm's recoil so that the
firearm shoots more than one shot with a single pull of the trigger is a
machinegun. Between 2008 and 2017, however, ATF also issued

classification decisions concluding that other bump-stock-type devices were not machineguns, primarily because the devices did not rely on internal springs or similar mechanical parts to channel recoil energy. Decisions issued during that time did not include extensive legal analysis relating to the definition of "machinegun." ATF undertook a review of its past classifications and determined that those conclusions did not reflect the best interpretation of "machinegun" under the NFA and GCA.

ATF decided to promulgate a rule that would bring clarity to the definition of "machinegun"—specifically with respect to the terms "automatically" and "single function of the trigger," as those terms are used to define "machinegun." As an initial step in the process of promulgating a rule, on December 26, 2017, the Department of Justice (Department) published in the Federal Register an advance notice of proposed rulemaking [citation].

The NPRM proposed to amend the regulations at 27 CFR 447.11, 478.11, and 479.11 to clarify that bump-stock-type devices are "machineguns" as defined by the NFA and GCA because such devices allow a shooter of a semiautomatic firearm to initiate a continuous firing cycle with a single pull of the trigger. Specifically, these devices convert an otherwise semiautomatic firearm into a machinegun by functioning as a self-acting or self-regulating mechanism that harnesses the recoil energy of the semiautomatic firearm in a manner that allows the trigger to reset and continue firing without additional physical manipulation of the trigger by the shooter. Hence, a semiautomatic firearm to which a bump-stock-type device is attached is able to produce automatic fire with a single pull of the trigger. [Citation.]

The NPRM proposed regulatory definitions for the statutory terms "single function of the trigger" and "automatically," and amendments of the regulatory definition of "machinegun" for purposes of clarity. Specifically, the NPRM proposed to amend the definitions of "machinegun" in §§ 478.11 and 479.11, define the term "single function of the trigger" to mean "single pull of the trigger," and define the term "automatically" to mean "as the result of a self-acting or self-regulating mechanism that allows the firing of multiple rounds through a single pull of the trigger." 83 FR at 13447–48. The NPRM also proposed to clarify that the definition of "machinegun" includes a device that allows a semiautomatic firearm to shoot more than one shot with a single pull of the trigger by harnessing the recoil energy of the semiautomatic firearm to which it is affixed so that the trigger resets and continues firing without additional physical manipulation of the trigger by the shooter (commonly known as bump-stock-type devices). *Id.* at 13447. Finally, the NPRM proposed to harmonize the definition of "machinegun" in § 447.11 with the definitions in 27 CFR parts 478 and 479, as those definitions would be amended. *Id.* at 13448.

The goal of this final rule is to amend the relevant regulatory definitions as described above. The Department, however, has revised the definition of "single function of the trigger" to mean "single pull of the trigger" and analogous motions, taking into account that there are other methods of initiating an automatic firing sequence that do not require a pull. This final rule also informs current possessors of bump-stock-type devices of the proper methods of disposal, including destruction by the owner or abandonment to ATF. . . .

III. Notice of Proposed Rulemaking

On March 29, 2018, the Department published in the Federal Register a notice of proposed rulemaking (NPRM) titled "Bump-Stock-Type Devices," 83 FR 13442 (ATF Docket No. 2017R-22), proposing changes to the regulations in 27 CFR 447.11, 478.11, and 479.11. The comment period for the proposed rule concluded on June 27, 2018.

C. *Proposed Definition of "Single Function of the Trigger"*

The Department proposed to interpret the phrase "single function of the trigger" to mean "a single pull of the trigger," as it considered it the best interpretation of the statute and because it reflected ATF's position since 2006. The Supreme Court in Staples v. United States, 511 U.S. 600, 602 n.1 (1994), indicated that a machinegun within the NFA "fires repeatedly with a single pull of the trigger." This interpretation is also consistent with how the phrase "single function of the trigger" was understood at the time of the NFA's enactment in 1934. For instance, in a congressional hearing leading up to the NFA's enactment, the National Rifle Association's then-president testified that a gun "which is capable of firing more than one shot by a single pull of the trigger, a single function of the trigger, is properly regarded, in my opinion, as a machine gun." [Citation.] Furthermore, . . . the Eleventh Circuit in *Akins* [*v. United States*] concluded that ATF's interpretation of "single function of the trigger" to mean a "single pull of the trigger" "is consonant with the statute and its legislative history." 312 F. App'x [197,] 200 [(11th Cir. 2009) (per curiam)]. No other court has held otherwise.

D. *Proposed Definition of "Automatically"*

The Department also proposed to interpret the term "automatically" to mean "as the result of a self-acting or self-regulating mechanism that allows the firing of multiple rounds through a single pull of the trigger." That interpretation reflects the ordinary meaning of that term at the time of the NFA's enactment in 1934. The word "automatically" is the adverbial form of "automatic," meaning "[h]aving a self-acting or self-regulating mechanism that performs a required act at a predetermined point in an operation[.]" Webster's New International Dictionary 187 (2d ed. 1934); *see also* 1 Oxford English Dictionary 574 (1933) (defining "Automatic" as "[s]elf-acting under conditions fixed for it, going of itself.").

Relying on these definitions, the United States Court of Appeals for the Seventh Circuit interpreted the term "automatically" as used in the NFA as "delineat[ing] how the discharge of multiple rounds from a weapon occurs: As the result of a self-acting mechanism . . . set in motion by a single function of the trigger and . . . accomplished without manual reloading." United States v. Olofson, 563 F.3d 652, 658 (7th Cir. 2009). So long as the firearm is capable of producing multiple rounds with a single pull of the trigger until the trigger finger is removed, the ammunition supply is exhausted, or the firearm malfunctions, the firearm shoots "automatically" irrespective of why the firing sequence ultimately ends. *Id.* ("[T]he reason a weapon ceased firing is not a matter with which § 5845(b) is concerned."). *Olofson* thus requires only that the weapon shoot multiple rounds with a single function of the trigger "as the result of a self-acting mechanism," not that the self-acting mechanism produces the firing sequence without any additional action by the shooter. This definition accordingly requires that the self-acting or self-regulating mechanism allows the firing of multiple rounds through a single function of the trigger.

E.   Proposed   Clarification   That   the   Definition   of "Machinegun" Includes Bump-Stock-Type Devices

The Department also proposed, based on the interpretations discussed above, to clarify that the term "machinegun" includes a device that allows a semiautomatic firearm to shoot more than one shot with a single pull of the trigger by harnessing the recoil energy of the semiautomatic firearm to which it is affixed so that the trigger resets and continues firing without additional physical manipulation of the trigger by the shooter. The Department explained that when a shooter who has affixed a bump-stock-type device to a semiautomatic firearm pulls the trigger, that movement initiates a firing sequence that produces more than one shot. And that firing sequence is "automatic" because the device harnesses the firearm's recoil energy in a continuous back-and-forth cycle that allows the shooter to attain continuous firing after a single pull of the trigger, so long as the trigger finger remains stationary on the device's ledge (as designed). Accordingly, these devices are included under the definition of "machinegun" and, therefore, come within the purview of the NFA.

F.   Amendment of 27 CFR 479.11

The regulatory definition of "machine gun" in 27 CFR 479.11 matches the statutory definition of "machinegun" in the NFA. The definition includes the terms "single function of the trigger" and "automatically," but those terms are not defined in the statutory text. The NPRM proposed to define these terms in order to clarify the meaning of "machinegun." Specifically, the Department proposed to amend the definition of "machine gun" in 27 CFR 479.11 by:

1.   Defining the term "single function of the trigger" to mean "single pull of the trigger";

2.   defining the term "automatically" to mean "as the result of a self-acting or self-regulating mechanism that allows the firing of multiple rounds through a single pull of the trigger"; and

3.   adding a sentence to clarify that a "machine gun" includes a device that allows a semiautomatic firearm to shoot more than one shot with a single pull of the trigger by harnessing the recoil energy of the semiautomatic firearm to which it is affixed so that the trigger resets and continues firing without additional physical manipulation of the trigger by the shooter (commonly known as a bump-stock-type device).

G.   Amendment of 27 CFR 478.11

The GCA and its implementing regulations in 27 CFR part 478 reference the NFA's definition of machinegun. Accordingly, the NPRM proposed to make the same amendments in 27 CFR 478.11 that were proposed for § 479.11.

H.   Amendment of 27 CFR 447.11

The Arms Export Control Act (AECA), as amended, does not define the term "machinegun" in its key provision, 22 U.S.C. 2778. However, regulations in 27 CFR part 447 that implement the AECA include a similar definition of "machinegun," and explain that machineguns, submachineguns, machine pistols, and fully automatic rifles fall within Category I(b) of the U.S. Munitions Import List when those defense articles are permanently imported. *See* 27 CFR 447.11, 447.21. Currently, the definition of "machinegun" in § 447.11 provides that "[a] 'machinegun', 'machine pistol', 'submachinegun', or 'automatic rifle' is a firearm originally designed to fire, or capable of being fired fully automatically by a single pull of the trigger." The NPRM proposed to harmonize the AECA's regulatory definition of machinegun with the definitions in 27 CFR parts 478 and 479, as those definitions would be amended by the proposed rule.

IV. Analysis of Comments and Department Responses for Proposed Rule . . .

f.   Lack of Statutory Authority . . .

A total of 47,863 commenters, most of whom sent form submissions opposed to the proposed rule, argued that ATF lacks statutory authority to regulate bump-stock-type devices. Many commenters said that ATF, by its own admission, repeatedly stated it could not regulate such devices. Commenters generally expressed the view that because bump-stock-type devices are not firearms, ATF has no authority under the NFA or GCA to regulate them. . . .

In addition, numerous commenters argued that, as the term "machinegun" is already clearly defined in the NFA, only Congress can make changes to the definition and regulate bump-stock-type devices. Furthermore, commenters stated that the agency's interpretation of the term "machinegun" would not be entitled to deference under *Chevron*, [citation].

Department Response

The Attorney General is responsible for enforcing the NFA, as amended, and the GCA, as amended. This includes the authority to promulgate regulations necessary to enforce the provisions of these statutes. *See* 18 U.S.C. 926(a); [citations]. 6 U.S.C. 531, . . . [a] provision of the Homeland Security Act of 2002, . . . transferred the powers the Secretary of the Treasury had with respect to ATF to the Attorney General when ATF was transferred to the Department of Justice. Accordingly, the Attorney General is now responsible for enforcing the NFA and GCA, and he has delegated the responsibility for administering and enforcing the NFA and GCA to the Director of ATF, subject to the direction of the Attorney General and the Deputy Attorney General. [Citation.]

"Because § 926 authorizes the [Attorney General] to promulgate those regulations which are 'necessary,' it almost inevitably confers some measure of discretion to determine what regulations are in fact 'necessary.' " Nat'l Rifle Ass'n v. Brady, 914 F.2d 475, 479 (4th Cir. 1990). In the original GCA implementing regulations, ATF provided regulatory definitions of the terms that Congress did not define in the statute. [Citation.] Since 1968, ATF has occasionally added definitions to the implementing regulations. [Citations.] Similarly, 26 U.S.C. 7805(a) states that "the [Attorney General] shall prescribe all needful rules and regulations for the enforcement of this title." As is the case with the GCA, ATF has provided regulatory definitions for terms in the NFA that Congress did not define, such as "frame or receiver" and "manual reloading." [Citation.] These definitions were necessary to explain and implement the statute, and do not contradict the statute. Federal courts have recognized ATF's authority to classify devices as "firearms" under Federal law. [Citations.]

This rule is based upon this authority. Further, ATF has provided technical and legal reasons why bump-stock-type devices enable automatic fire by a single function of the trigger, and thus qualify as machinegun conversion devices, not mere "accessories." ATF has regularly classified items as machinegun "conversion devices" or "combinations of parts," . . .

The Department agrees that regulatory agencies may not promulgate rules that conflict with statutes. However, the Department disagrees that the rule conflicts with the statutes or is in contravention of administrative-law principles. The rule merely defines terms used in the definition of "machinegun" that Congress did not—the terms "automatically" and "single function of the trigger"—as part of implementing the provisions of the NFA and GCA.

When a court is called upon to review an agency's construction of the statute it administers, the court looks to the framework set forth in *Chevron*, [citation]. The Department believes that this rule's interpretations of "automatically" and "single function of the trigger" in the statutory definition of "machinegun" accord with the plain meaning of those terms. . . . Although Congress defined "machinegun" in the NFA, 26 U.S.C. 5845(b), it did not further define the components of that definition. *See, e.g.*, United States v. One TRW, Model M14, 7.62 Caliber Rifle, 441 F.3d 416, 419 (6th Cir. 2006) (noting that the NFA does not define the phrases "designed to shoot" or "can be readily restored" in the definition of "machinegun"). Congress thus implicitly left it to the Department to define "automatically" and "single function of the trigger" in the event those terms are ambiguous. [Citation.] Courts have appropriately recognized that the Department has the authority to interpret elements of the definition of "machinegun" like "automatically" and "single function of the trigger." [Citations.]

Second, the Department's construction of those terms is reasonable under *Chevron*. . . . [T]he Department is clarifying its regulatory definition of "automatically" to conform to how that word was understood and used when the NFA was enacted in 1934. *See Olofson*, [citation]. And the Department is reaffirming that a single pull of the trigger is a single function of the trigger, consistent with the NFA's legislative history, ATF's previous determinations, and judicial precedent. *See, e.g., Akins*, [citation]. This rule is therefore lawful under the NFA and GCA even if the operative statutory terms are ambiguous.

Guedes v. Bureau of Alcohol, Tobacco, Firearms and Explosives

United States Court of Appeals, District of Columbia Circuit, 2019.
920 F.3d 1.

■ PER CURIAM [Before: HENDERSON, SRINIVASAN and MILLETT, CIRCUIT JUDGES]:

Bump-stock owners and advocates filed separate lawsuits in the United States District Court for the District of Columbia to prevent the Rule from taking effect. The district court denied the plaintiffs' motions for a preliminary injunction to halt the Rule's effective date. We affirm the denial of preliminary injunctive relief. . . .

B

1

Machine guns are generally prohibited by federal law. *See* 18 U.S.C. § 922(*o*). On the other hand, many firearms that require a distinct pull of the trigger to shoot each bullet are lawful. *See generally id.* § 922; 26 U.S.C. § 5845.

A "bump stock" is a device that replaces the standard stationary stock of a semiautomatic rifle—the part of the rifle that typically rests against the shooter's shoulder—with a non-stationary, sliding stock that allows the shooter to rapidly increase the rate of fire, approximating that of an automatic weapon. 83 Fed. Reg. at 66,516. A bump stock does so by channeling and directing the recoil energy from each shot "into the space created by the sliding stock (approximately 1.5 inches) in constrained linear rearward and forward paths." *Id.* at 66,518. In so doing, the bump stock "harnesses the firearm's recoil energy as part of a continuous back-and-forth cycle that allows the shooter to attain continuous firing" following a single pull of the trigger. *Id.* at 66,533. That design allows the shooter, by maintaining constant backward pressure on the trigger as well as forward pressure on the front of the gun, to fire bullets continuously and at a high rate of fire to "mimic" the performance of a fully automatic weapon. *Id.* at 66,516.

Exercising his regulatory authority, the Attorney General first included a bump-stock type device within the statutory definition of "machinegun" in 2006. *See* ATF Ruling 2006–2; [citation]. In later years, some other bumpstock devices were not categorized as machine guns. 83 Fed. Reg. at 66,514.

2

The Las Vegas massacre prompted an immediate outcry from the public and members of Congress. In response, President Trump "direct[ed] the Department of Justice, * * * as expeditiously as possible, to propose for notice and comment a rule banning all devices that turn legal weapons into machineguns." [Citation.] The Bureau then revisited the status of bump stocks and addressed the variation in its prior positions. [Citations.] . . . The Bureau promulgated its final rule on December 26, 2018. With respect to the statutory definition of machine gun, the Bump-Stock Rule provided that the National Firearms Act's use of "the term 'automatically' as it modifies 'shoots, is designed to shoot, or can be readily restored to shoot,'" 26 U.S.C. § 5845(b), "means functioning as the result of a self-acting or self-regulating mechanism that allows the firing of multiple rounds through a single function of the trigger." 83 Fed. Reg. at 66,553–66,554 (codified at 27 C.F.R. §§ 447.11, 478.11, 479.11). The Rule further defined "single function of the trigger," 26 U.S.C. § 5845(b), to mean "a single pull of the trigger and analogous motions." 83 Fed. Reg. at 66,553–66,554 (codified at 27 C.F.R. §§ 447.11, 478.11, 479.11).

In light of those definitions, the Bump-Stock Rule concluded that the statutory term " 'machinegun' includes a bump-stock-type device"—that is, "a device that allows a semiautomatic firearm to shoot more than one shot with a single pull of the trigger by harnessing the recoil energy of the semiautomatic firearm to which it is affixed so that the trigger resets and continues firing without additional physical manipulation of the trigger by the shooter." 83 Fed. Reg. at 66,553–66,554 (codified at 27 C.F.R. §§ 447.11, 478.11, 479.11).

In adopting the Bump-Stock Rule, the Bureau relied on both the "plain meaning" of the statute and the agency's charge to implement the National Firearms Act and the Gun Control Act. [Citations.] The Bureau explained that the Bump-Stock Rule both "accord[s] with the plain meaning" of the statute, and "rests on a reasonable construction of" any "ambiguous" statutory terms. [Citation.] In the Bureau's view, by not further defining the terms "automatically" and "single function of the trigger," Congress "left it to the [Attorney General] to define [them] in the event those terms are ambiguous." [Citations.]

The Bureau was explicit that the Bump-Stock Rule would only become "effective" on March 26, 2019, ninety days after promulgation. [Citation.] The Bureau further assured that individuals would be subject to "criminal liability only for possessing bump-stock-type devices *after* the effective date of regulation, not for possession before that date." [Citation] (providing that the Rule "criminalize[s] only future conduct, not past possession of bump-stock-type devices that ceases by the effective date"); [citation] ("To the extent that owners timely destroy or abandon these bumpstock-type devices, they will not be in violation of the law[.]"). Bump-stock owners were directed to destroy their devices or leave them at a Bureau office by March 26, 2019. *Id.* at 66,514. . . .

C

Three groups of bump-stock owners and advocates filed suit in the United States District Court for the District of Columbia to prevent the Bump-Stock Rule from taking effect. As relevant here, the Guedes plaintiffs ("Guedes") and the Codrea plaintiffs ("Codrea") argued that the Bureau promulgated the Bump-Stock Rule in violation of the Administrative Procedure Act, 5 U.S.C. § 500 *et seq.* . . . The district court denied all three motions for a preliminary injunction. The district court concluded that Guedes [and] Codrea . . . had not demonstrated a likelihood of success on the merits. The court first held that "[m]ost of the plaintiffs' administrative law challenges are foreclosed by the *Chevron* doctrine," and the Rule "adequately explained" the agency's decision to classify bump-stock-type devices as machine guns. . . . [A]ll appealed. . . .

III

* * *

B

We next consider the plaintiffs' contention that the Bureau lacked statutory authority to promulgate the Bump-Stock Rule. Specifically, Guedes and Codrea argue that the statutory definition of "machinegun" cannot be read to include bumpstock devices. Guedes and Codrea have not demonstrated a substantial likelihood of success on that claim.

1

At the outset, we must determine the standard by which to assess the Rule's conclusion that bump-stock devices amount to "machineguns" under the statutory definition. In particular, should we examine the Rule's conclusion to that effect under the *Chevron* framework, or is *Chevron* inapplicable? . . . [N]one of the parties presents an argument for applying the *Chevron* framework (the plaintiffs contend that *Chevron* is inapplicable and the government does not argue otherwise), [so] we devote considerable attention to the question of *Chevron*'s applicability to the Bump-Stock Rule. We conclude that the Rule warrants consideration under *Chevron*.

a

The applicability of *Chevron* materially depends on what kind of rule the Bump-Stock Rule represents. There is a "central distinction" under the Administrative Procedure Act between legislative rules and interpretive rules. *Chrysler Corp v. Brown*, 441 U.S. 281, 301 (1979); *see* 5 U.S.C. § 553(b), (d). And that distinction centrally informs the applicability of *Chevron*. "Legislative rules generally receive *Chevron* deference," *Nat'l Mining Ass'n v. McCarthy*, 758 F.3d 243, 251 (D.C. Cir. 2014), whereas "interpretive rules * * * enjoy no *Chevron* status as a class," *Mead*, [citations].

Legislative rules result from an agency's exercise of "delegated legislative power" from Congress. [Citation.] Accordingly, legislative rules have the "force and effect of law." *Encino Motorcars, LLC v. Navarro*, 136 S.Ct. 2117, 2122 (2016). Interpretive rules, on the other hand, are "issued by an agency to advise the public of the agency's construction of the statutes and rules which it administers." *Shalala v. Guernsey Mem'l Hosp.*, 514 U.S. 87, 99 (1995). Because they are not an exercise of delegated legislative authority, interpretive rules "do not have the force and effect of law and are not accorded that weight in the adjudicatory process." *Id.* While legislative rules generally require notice and comment, interpretive rules need not issue pursuant to any formalized procedures. *See* 5 U.S.C. § 553(b). To determine whether a rule is legislative or interpretive, we ask whether the agency "intended" to speak with the force of law. [Citations.] Central to the analysis is the "language actually used by the agency." [Citation.] We also consider "whether the agency has published the rule in the Code of Federal Regulations" and "whether the agency has explicitly invoked its general legislative authority." [Citation.]

All pertinent indicia of agency intent confirm that the Bump-Stock Rule is a legislative rule. The Rule unequivocally bespeaks an effort by the Bureau to adjust the legal rights and obligations of bump-stock owners . . . . The Bureau further evinced its intent to exercise legislative authority by expressly invoking the *Chevron* framework and then elaborating at length as to how *Chevron* applies to the Rule. . . . [And o]ne consideration under our decisions is "whether the agency has explicitly invoked its general legislative authority." [Citation.] The Rule does exactly that, invoking two separate delegations of legislative authority. [Citation.] The first is 18 U.S.C. § 926(a), which empowers the Attorney General to "prescribe only such rules and regulations as are necessary to carry out the provisions of [the Gun Control Act]." The second is 26 U.S.C. § 7805(a), which grants the Attorney General authority to "prescribe all needful rules and regulations" for the enforcement of the National Firearms Act. [Citation.] . . . [Finally, t]he Rule's publication in the Code of Federal Regulations also indicates that it is a legislative rule. [Citation.] By statute, publication in the Code of Federal Regulations is limited to rules "having general applicability and *legal effect*." 44 U.S.C. § 1510 (emphasis added). . . . In short, the Rule confirms throughout, in numerous ways, that it intends to speak with the force of law. . . .

Notwithstanding all of that, the government's litigating position in this case seeks to reimagine the Rule as merely interpretive. The government's briefing says that the Rule is "not an act of legislative rulemaking," and that the Rule instead only "sets forth the agency's interpretation of the best reading of the statutory definition of 'machinegun.' "

The government's position to that effect has highly significant implications for owners of bump-stock devices. Whereas a legislative rule, as an exercise of delegated lawmaking authority, can establish a new legal rule going forward, an interpretive rule by nature simply communicates the agency's interpretation of what a statute has always meant. So here, if the Bump-Stock Rule is merely interpretive, it conveys the government's understanding that bump-stock devices have always been machine guns under the statute. The government says exactly that in its brief, observing that, per the interpretation set out in the Rule, "any bump stock made after 1986 has *always* been a machinegun."

That in turn would mean that bump-stock owners have been committing a felony for the entire time they have possessed the devices. Under 18 U.S.C. § 922(*o*)(1), it is "unlawful for any person to transfer or possess a machinegun," and violators "shall be fined [or] imprisoned not more than 10 years, or both," *id*. § 924(a)(2). As the government acknowledges, under the view it espouses in its brief that the Rule is interpretive, the possession of bump stocks "has *always* been banned." And that would be so notwithstanding a number of prior contrary interpretations by the agency. *See* 83 Fed. Reg. at 13,444–13,446.

The government's account of the Rule in its brief—including its position that bump-stock owners have always been felons—is incompatible with the Rule's terms. The Rule gives no indication that bump stocks have always been machine guns or that bump-stock owners have been committing a felony for the entire time they have possessed the device. The Rule in fact says the opposite. After all, it establishes an effective date, *after* which (and only after which) bump-stock possession will be prohibited. 83 Fed. Reg. at 66,523. A future effective date of that kind cannot be reconciled with a supposed intent to convey that bump-stock possession "has *always* been banned."

The government now characterizes the Rule's effective date as merely marking the end of a period of discretionary withholding of enforcement, in that the Rule informs the public that the Department will "not pursue enforcement action against individuals who sold or possessed bump stocks prior to the effective date." Once again, that is not what the Rule says. The government engages in enforcement discretion when it voluntarily refrains from prosecuting a person *even though he is acting unlawfully*. The Rule, by contrast, announces that a person "in possession of a bumpstock type device *is not acting unlawfully* unless they fail to relinquish or destroy their device *after* the effective date of this regulation." 83 Fed. Reg. at 66,523 (emphases added). That is the language of a legislative rule establishing when bump-stock possession will become unlawful, not an interpretive rule indicating it has always been unlawful.

In short, the government cannot now, in litigation, reconceive the Bump-Stock Rule as an interpretive rule. The character of a rule depends on the agency's intent when issuing it, not on counsel's description of the rule during subsequent litigation. *See Encino Motorcars*, [citation]; cf. SEC v. Chenery Corp., 318 U.S. 80, 87–88 (1943). Here, that intent is unmistakable: the Bump-Stock rule is a legislative rule.

b

Ordinarily, legislative rules receive *Chevron* deference. [Citation.] This legislative rule is no different. . . . First, we know Congress intended a delegation of legislative authority to the agency because Congress made the relevant delegations express. As noted, the Attorney General has the power to prescribe "such rules and regulations as are necessary to carry out the provisions of" the Gun Control Act. 18 U.S.C. § 926(a). And the Attorney General "shall prescribe all needful rules and regulations for the enforcement of" the National Firearms Act. 26 U.S.C. § 7805(a); *see id.* § 7801(a)(2)(A). "[A] general conferral of rulemaking authority" of that variety "validate[s] rules for *all* the matters the agency is charged with administering." *City of Arlington*, [citation]. . . .

Second, we know that the Bureau promulgated the Bump-Stock Rule "in the exercise of that authority" to "make rules carrying the force of law" because that criterion is the defining characteristic of a legislative rule. *Mead*, [citation]. And we have already determined that the Rule is legislative in character. We are then firmly within *Chevron*'s domain.

Nonetheless, the parties protest the applicability of *Chevron* on several grounds. The plaintiffs first argue that *Chevron* deference has been waived or forfeited by the government. Next, the parties (including the government) submit that *Chevron* deference is inapplicable in the context of criminal statutes. And finally, Guedes contends that *Chevron* deference for criminal statutes is displaced by the rule of lenity. None of those objections to applying *Chevron*, we conclude, is likely to succeed in the context of the Bump-Stock Rule.

(i)

To the extent *Chevron* treatment can be waived, we assume that the government's posture in this litigation would amount to a waiver rather than only a forfeiture. *See Wood v. Milyard*, 566 U.S. 463, 470 n.4 (2012) ("A waived claim or defense is one that a party has knowingly and intelligently relinquished; a forfeited plea is one that a party has merely failed to preserve."). But our court has yet to address whether, when an agency promulgates a rule that would otherwise plainly occasion the application of *Chevron*, agency counsel could nonetheless opt to effect a waiver of *Chevron* treatment when later defending against a challenge to the rule.

We have, however, held that an agency's lawyers cannot *forfeit* the applicability of *Chevron* deference unless the underlying agency action fails to "manifests its engagement in the kind of interpretive exercise to which review under *Chevron* generally applies—*i.e.*, interpreting a statute it is charged with administering in a manner (and through a process) evincing an exercise of its lawmaking authority." *SoundExchange, Inc. v. Copyright Royalty Bd.*, 904 F.3d 41, 54 (D.C. Cir. 2018). We grounded our holding in the principle that "it is the expertise of the agency, not its lawyers," that underpins *Chevron*. [Citations.] We see no reason that the same limitations on forfeiture of *Chevron* should not also govern waiver of *Chevron*.

Forfeiture and waiver involve, respectively, a failure to invoke, or an affirmative decision not to invoke, a party's "right or privilege." [Citation.] But *Chevron* is not a "right" or "privilege" belonging to a litigant. It is instead a doctrine about statutory meaning—specifically, about how courts should construe a statute. If a statute contains ambiguity, *Chevron* directs courts to construe the ambiguity as "an implicit delegation from Congress to the agency to fill in the statutory gaps." *Brown & Williamson Tobacco*, [citation]. If there is ambiguity, the meaning of the statute becomes whatever the agency decides to fill the gaps with, as long as the agency's interpretation is reasonable and "speak[s] with the force of law." *Mead*, [citation]. And insofar as *Chevron* concerns the meaning of a statute, it is an awkward conceptual fit for the doctrines of forfeiture and waiver.

We, for example, would give no mind to a litigant's failure to invoke interpretive canons such as *expressio unius* or constitutional avoidance even if she intentionally left them out of her brief. "[T]he court is not limited to the particular legal theories advanced by the parties, but rather retains the independent power to identify and apply the proper construction of governing law." [Citation.] The "independent power" to identify and apply the correct law presumably includes application of the *Chevron* framework when determining the meaning of a statute.

Allowing an agency to freely waive *Chevron* treatment in litigation also would stand considerably in tension with basic precepts of administrative law. As we have explained, a legislative rule qualifying for *Chevron* deference remains legislative in character even if the agency claims during litigation that the rule is interpretive: *Chenery* instructs that the proper subject of our review is what the agency actually did, not what the agency's lawyers later say the agency did. *See* 318 U.S. at 87–88. Accordingly, we have held that a particular rule is legislative rather than interpretive over the protestations of the agency. [Citation.] And once we conclude that a rule is legislative, it follows that we generally review the rule's validity under the *Chevron* framework. [Citation.]

A waiver regime, moreover, would allow an agency to vary the binding nature of a legislative rule merely by asserting in litigation that the rule does not carry the force of law, even though the rule speaks to the public with all the indicia of a legislative rule. Agency litigants then could effectively amend or withdraw the legal force of a rule without undergoing a new notice-and-comment rulemaking. That result would enable agencies to circumvent the Administrative Procedure Act's requirement "that agencies use the same procedures when they amend or repeal a rule as they used to issue the rule in the first instance." [Citation.] And an agency could attempt to secure rescission of a policy it no longer favors without complying with the Administrative Procedure Act, or perhaps could avoid the political accountability that would attend its own policy reversal by effectively inviting the courts to set aside the rule instead.

We thus conclude, consistent with *SoundExchange*'s approach to forfeiture of *Chevron*, that an agency's lawyers similarly cannot waive *Chevron* if the underlying agency action "manifests its engagement in the kind of interpretive exercise to which review under *Chevron* generally applies." *SoundExchange*, [citation]. In that event, we "apply *Chevron* * * * even if there is no invocation of *Chevron* in the briefing in our court." [Citation.]

In this case, the Bump-Stock Rule plainly indicates the agency's view that it was engaging in a rulemaking entitled to *Chevron* deference. . . . The Rule expressly defends the agency's reading of the statute as an interpretive exercise implicating *Chevron*. Agency counsel's later litigating decision to refrain from invoking *Chevron* thus affords no basis for our denying the Rule *Chevron* status.

(ii)

Next, the plaintiffs submit that *Chevron* deference has no application to regulations interpreting statutes like the National Firearms Act and the Gun Control Act because they impose criminal penalties on violators. *Chevron* deference in the context of such statutes, the plaintiffs urge, would flout an understanding that "criminal laws are for courts, not for the Government, to construe." *Abramski v. United States*, 573 U.S. 169, 191 (2014). And the plaintiffs are not the only parties who question *Chevron*'s salience in the criminal context. The government's decision to refrain from invoking *Chevron* in this litigation appears to stem from the same concerns.

Guedes and Codrea, however, have failed to demonstrate a likelihood of success in establishing a general rule against applying *Chevron* to agency interpretations of statutes that have criminal-law implications. To the contrary, precedent says otherwise.

Start with *Chevron* itself. At issue in *Chevron* was the meaning of the term "stationary source" in the Clean Air Act. *See Chevron*, [citation]. The scope of that term defined the statutory obligation of private parties, under state implementation plans, to obtain permits for the construction and operation of "new or modified major stationary sources of air pollution." [Citation.] But at the time, any person who knowingly violated any requirement of a state implementation plan (after notice from the EPA) faced a fine of $25,000 a day or imprisonment for up to a year, or both. [Citation.] Nevertheless, the *Chevron* Court established the decision's namesake deference.

For another example, consider the securities laws. The SEC's interpretation of those laws regularly receives *Chevron* treatment, [citations], even though their violation often triggers criminal liability. The Securities Exchange Act, for instance, imposes criminal sanctions for willful violations of "any provision" of the Act or "any rule or regulation thereunder the violation of which is made unlawful." 15 U.S.C. § 78ff(a). Yet in *United States v. O'Hagan*—a criminal case—the Supreme Court accorded *Chevron* deference to an SEC rule that interpreted a provision of the Act in a manner rendering the defendant's conduct a crime. 521 U.S. 642, 667 (1997) (citing *Chevron*, [citation]). The Court noted that Congress had authorized the Commission "to prescribe legislative rules," and held that the rule in question, issued in an exercise of that authority, should receive "controlling weight" under *Chevron*. [Citation.]

While the Court in *O'Hagan* applied *Chevron* in a criminal case, it (like *Chevron* itself) did not specifically address whether the criminal context should have afforded a basis for denying deference to the agency's interpretation. But the Court engaged with that precise issue in *Babbitt*, [citation]. There, the Court reviewed a regulation interpreting the term "take" in the Endangered Species Act. The challengers argued that *Chevron* deference was inappropriate because the Endangered Species Act included criminal penalties for certain violations. [Citation.] The Court disagreed, holding that, notwithstanding the statute's criminal penalties, it would defer "to the Secretary's reasonable interpretation" under *Chevron*. [Citation.] . . .

To be sure, the Supreme Court has signaled some wariness about deferring to the government's interpretations of criminal statutes. . . . But those statements were made outside the context of a *Chevron*-eligible interpretation—that is, outside the context of an agency "speak[ing] with the force of law." *Mead*, [citation]. In *Abramski*, the Court declined to extend deference to informal guidance documents published by the Bureau. [Citation.] And in *Apel*, the Court declined to defer to an interpretation contained in "Executive Branch documents" that were "not intended to be binding." 571 U.S. at 368. When directly faced with the question of *Chevron*'s applicability to an agency's interpretation of a statute with criminal applications through a full-dress regulation, the Court adhered to *Chevron. See Babbitt*, [citation].

That holding, and our court's precedents, govern us here and call for the application of *Chevron*. The parties have identified no distinction between the provision at issue in this case and the provisions with criminal penalties to which *Chevron* deference has been applied. The briefing contains nary a word suggesting any distinction between this case and prior decisions applying *Chevron* in criminal contexts. And neither Guedes nor counsel for the government offered any distinction even when specifically asked at oral argument.

Nothing in the relevant statutory delegations of authority, moreover, suggests a basis for denying *Chevron* treatment for agency actions with criminal implications[.] The Supreme Court has instructed that the inquiry turns on whether the "language of the delegation provision" is sufficiently "broad" such that it is "clear * * * the statute gives [the] agency * * * power to enforce *all* provisions of the statute." *Gonzales*, [citation] (emphasis added). . . .

The statutory context bolsters the inference that Congress intended those delegations to encompass regulations with criminal implications. The Gun Control Act, found at Chapter 44 of Title 18,* is a purely criminal statute. [Citation.] Yet § 926(a) expressly delegates to the Attorney General the power to promulgate "such rules and regulations as are necessary to carry out the provisions of th[at] chapter." Similarly, the National Firearms Act, found at Chapter 53 of Title 26, has criminal applications. [Citations.] . . .

The plaintiffs rely on *Thompson/Center Arms Co.*, in which the Supreme Court applied the rule of lenity to an ambiguous provision of the National Firearms Act. [Citation.] But *Babbitt* later made clear that the Court in *Thompson/Center* had no occasion to apply *Chevron*: *Thompson/Center*, the *Babbitt* Court explained, "rais[ed] a narrow question concerning the application of a statute that contain[ed] criminal sanctions * * * *where no regulation was present.*" *Babbitt*, [citations] (emphasis added). If anything, then, *Babbitt* implies that *Chevron* should apply in a case—like this one—involving an interpretation of the National Firearms Act where a regulation *is* present. . . .

In short, Congress delegated authority to administer the National Firearms Act and the Gun Control Act to the Attorney General, and the Attorney General promulgated a legislative rule in the exercise of that

---

* Editors' Note: Title 18 of the U.S. Code, Crimes and Criminal Procedure, contains most of the federal statutory criminal prohibitions.

authority. Under binding precedent, Guedes and Codrea have failed to demonstrate a likelihood of success on their claim that the Rule is invalid just because of its criminal-law implications.

(iii)

Relatedly, Guedes argue that *Chevron* is inapplicable because a different canon of interpretation, the rule of lenity, should control instead. Under the rule of lenity, "ambiguity concerning the ambit of criminal statutes should be resolved in favor of lenity." [Citation.] Guedes reasons that because *Chevron* is premised on the existence of statutory ambiguity, and because the rule of lenity resolves ambiguity in favor of the defendant, there is no remaining ambiguity to which *Chevron* can apply.

It is true that the rule of lenity generally applies to the interpretation of the National Firearms Act and the Gun Control Act. But in circumstances in which *both Chevron* and the rule of lenity are applicable, the Supreme Court has never indicated that the rule of lenity applies first. In fact, the Court has held to the contrary. In *Babbitt*, the Court squarely rejected the argument that "the rule of lenity should foreclose any deference to the Secretary's interpretation of the ESA because the statute includes criminal penalties." [Citation.] The Court observed that it had "never suggested that the rule of lenity should provide the standard for reviewing facial challenges to administrative regulations whenever the governing statute authorizes criminal enforcement." [Citation.] The Court proceeded to apply *Chevron* deference. [Citation.] . . .

[Our court's] precedents are in line with the Supreme Court's characterization of the rule of lenity as a canon of "last resort." The Court has instructed that "[t]he rule comes into operation at the end of the process of construing what Congress has expressed, not at the beginning as an overriding consideration of being lenient to wrongdoers." [Citation.] Accordingly, the rule of lenity applies only "when the ordinary canons of statutory construction have revealed no satisfactory construction." *Lockhart v. United States*, ___ U.S. ___, 136 S.Ct. 958, 968 (2016). And *Chevron* is a rule of statutory construction, insofar as it is a doctrine that "constru[es] what Congress has expressed." [Citation.]

Finally, our approach coheres with the rule of lenity's purposes. The doctrine serves to ensure that "legislatures and not courts [are] defin[ing] criminal activity" and to secure "fair warning" about the content of criminal law. [Citation.] *Chevron* deference vindicates both purposes.

First, *Chevron* is consistent with the separation of powers, including for regulations defining criminal activity, because delegations of legislative authority in the criminal sphere are constitutional. [Citation.] The parties would have us disregard Congress's textual delegations to the agency and do the interpretive work instead. That course, though, would not respect the notion that "legislatures and not courts" should take the lead. [Citation.]

Second, *Chevron* promotes fair notice about the content of criminal law. It applies only when, at Congress's direction, agencies have followed "relatively formal administrative procedure tending to foster the fairness and deliberation that should underlie a pronouncement of such force." *Mead*, [citation]. Importantly, such procedures, which generally include formal public notice and publication in the Federal Register, do not "provide such inadequate notice of potential liability as to offend the rule of lenity." *Babbitt*, [citation]. Tellingly, there is no suggestion of inadequate notice here. Rather, if the Rule is a valid legislative rule, all are on notice of what is prohibited. . . .

2

Having concluded that the *Chevron* framework is applicable, we now proceed to examine the Bump-Stock Rule under it. We first ask whether the agency-administered statute is ambiguous on the "precise question at issue." [Citation.] . . .

a

At *Chevron*'s first step, two features of the statutory definition of "machinegun" render it ambiguous. The first is the phase "single function of the trigger." The second is the word "automatically." We discuss them in that order.

(i)

As the district court recognized, the statutory phrase "single function of the trigger" admits of more than one interpretation. It could mean "a mechanical act of the trigger." Or it could mean "a single pull of the trigger from the perspective of the shooter."

The first interpretation would tend to exclude bump-stock devices: while a semiautomatic rifle outfitted with a bump stock enables a continuous, high-speed rate of fire, it does so by engendering a rapid bumping of the trigger against the shooter's stationary finger, such that each bullet is fired because of a distinct mechanical act of the trigger. The second interpretation would tend to include bump-stock devices: the shooter engages in a single pull of the trigger with her trigger finger, and that action, via the operation of the bump stock, yields a continuous stream of fire as long she keeps her finger stationary and does not release it. [Citation.]

Neither of those interpretations is compelled (or foreclosed) by the term "function" in "single function of the trigger." The word "function" focuses our attention on the "mode of action," 4 Oxford English Dictionary 602 (1933), or "natural * * * action," Webster's New International Dictionary 876 (1933), by which the trigger operates. But the text is silent on the crucial question of *which perspective* is relevant. A mechanical perspective, for instance, might focus on the trigger's release of the hammer, which causes the release of a round. From that perspective, a "single function of the trigger" yields a single round of fire when a bump-stock device moves the trigger back and forth. By contrast, from the perspective of the shooter's action, the function of pulling the trigger a single time results in repeated shots when a bump-stock device is engaged. From that perspective, then, a "single function of the trigger" yields multiple rounds of fire. In light of those competing, available interpretations, the statute contains a "gap for the agency to fill." [Citation.] . . .

At *Chevron*'s first step, we do not ask which of those interpretations is the better reading of the statute. Rather, we ask whether either of those interpretations is unambiguously "compel[led]" by the statute, to the exclusion of the other one. [Citation.] Here, we think the answer is no. . . .

(ii)

Similarly, the statutory term "automatically" admits of multiple interpretations. The statute speaks in terms of a "weapon which shoots * * * automatically more than one shot, without manual reloading, by a single function of the trigger." 26 U.S.C. § 5845(b); [citation]. The term "automatically" does not require that there be *no* human involvement to give rise to "more than one shot." Rather, the term can be read to require only that there be *limited* human involvement to bring about more than one shot. *See, e.g.,* Webster's New International Dictionary 157 (defining "automatically" as the adverbial form of "automatic"); *id.* at 156 (defining "automatic" as "self-acting or self-regulating," especially applied to "machinery or devices which perform *parts* of the work formerly or usually done by hand" (emphasis added)). But how much human input in the "self-acting or self-regulating" mechanism is too much?

The plaintiffs would read the phrase "by a single function of the trigger" to provide "the starting and the ending point of just how much human input is allowable." In their view, then, a gun cannot be said to fire "automatically" if it requires both a single pull of the trigger *and* constant pressure on the gun's barrel, as a bump-stock device requires. We are unpersuaded. After all, a quite common feature of weapons that indisputably qualify as machine guns is that they require both a single pull of the trigger *and* the application of constant and continuing pressure on the trigger after it is pulled. We know, therefore, that the requirement of some measure of additional human input does not render a weapon nonautomatic. To purloin an example from the district court: an "automatic" sewing machine still "requires the user to press a pedal *and* direct the fabric."

That workaday example illustrates another, perhaps more natural, reading of "automatically": the "automatic[ ]" mechanism need only be *"set in motion"* by a single function of the trigger. *Olofson*, [citation] (emphasis added); *see also United States v. Evans*, 978 F.2d 1112, 1113 n.2 (9th Cir. 1992) (" '[B]y a single function of the trigger' describes the action that enables the weapon to 'shoot automatically without manual reloading, not the 'trigger' mechanism." (ellipses omitted)). That is, rather than reading the phrase "by a single function of the trigger" to mean "by *only* a single function of the trigger," the phrase can naturally be read to establish only the preconditions for setting off the "automatic" mechanism, without foreclosing some further degree of manual input such as the constant forward pressure needed to engage the bump stock in the first instance. And if so, then the identified ambiguity endures. How much further input is permitted in the mechanism set in motion by the trigger? The statute does not say.

In sum, the statutory definition of "machinegun" contains two central ambiguities, both of which the agency has attempted to construe. We therefore proceed to *Chevron*'s second step.

b

At the second step, "the question for the court is whether the agency's [construction] is based on a permissible construction of the statute." *Chevron*, [citation]. . . . The Bureau's interpretation of "single function of the trigger" to mean "single pull of the trigger" is a permissible reading of the statute. The Bureau is better equipped than we are to make the pivotal policy choice between a mechanism-focused and shooter-focused understanding of "function of the trigger." And the Bureau's interpretation comports with how some courts have read the statute, which is a strong sign of reasonableness. In *Akins*, [citation], for example, the Eleventh Circuit held that the Bureau's reading of "single function of the trigger" to mean "single pull of the trigger" was "consonant with the statute and its legislative history." [Citation.] The court relied on that definition to conclude that an "Accelerator"—a type of bump stock—was reasonably classified as a machine gun. [Citation.] And "single pull of the trigger" has been the definition the agency has employed since 2006. *See* 83 Fed. Reg. at 66,543. The Rule's interpretation also accords with how the phrase "single pull of the trigger" was understood at the time of the enactment of the National Firearms Act. *See* 83 Fed. Reg. at 66,518. . . .

The Bureau's interpretation of "automatically" is permissible too. The Rule's requirement of a "self-acting or self-regulating mechanism" demands a significant degree of autonomy from the weapon without mandating a firing mechanism that is completely autonomous. That definition accords with the everyday understanding of the word "automatic." And it focuses the inquiry about what needs to be automated right where the statute does: the ability of the trigger function to produce "more than one shot, without manual reloading." 26 U.S.C. § 5845(b). It also tracks the interpretation reached by the Seventh Circuit in *Olofson*, [citation], in which the court interpreted the term to require a "self-acting mechanism" without requiring more, [citation].

The plaintiffs argue that the Bureau's definition of "machinegun" is unreasonable because it has the effect of reaching all semiautomatic rifles. Because "virtually all" semiautomatic rifles can be "bump-fired" with the use of common household items, the plaintiffs contend, the Bureau's definition covers even unmodified semiautomatic rifles, which renders it unreasonable.

The Rule explains why the plaintiff's understanding is incorrect, and the Rule's explanation in that regard is reasonable. *See* 83 Fed. Reg. at 66,532–66,534. The Bureau acknowledges that bump firing—a technique using a stable point like a belt loop to approximate the function of a bump stock—is possible with semiautomatic weapons. *See id.* at 66,533. But even when a semiautomatic weapon is bump fired using an object like a belt loop or a rubber band, the Bureau explained, the weapon does not fire "automatically" because there is no "self-acting or self-regulating mechanism." Rubber bands and their ilk do not "capture and direct the recoil energy" to "harness[ ] [it] as part of a continuous back-and-forth cycle." *Id.* at 66,533. Rather, "the shooter must do so" herself. *Id.* Bump firing without the aid of a bump-stock-type device is therefore "more difficult" because it relies solely on the shooter "to control the distance that the firearm recoils and the movement along the plane on which the firearm recoils." *Id.*

Bump stocks, on the other hand, are specifically designed to "direct[ ] the recoil energy of the discharged rounds * * * in constrained linear rearward and forward paths." *Id.* at 66,532. By capturing the recoil energy of the gun and directing it through a specified "distance" and along a specified "plane," bump stocks "incorporate[ ] a self-acting or self-regulating component" that would otherwise be absent. *Id.* at 66,533. Thus, belt loops, unlike bump stocks, do not transform semiautomatic weapons into statutory "machineguns." Or so the Bureau reasonably concluded in the Rule. . . . Here, the Bump-Stock Rule sets forth a permissible interpretation of the statute's ambiguous definition of "machinegun." It therefore merits our deference. . . .

* * * * *

The plaintiffs have failed to establish a likelihood of success . . . for their objections to the substantive validity of the Rule. For the foregoing reasons, we affirm the district court's denial of a preliminary injunction.

So ordered.

■ KAREN LECRAFT HENDERSON, CIRCUIT JUDGE, concurring in part and dissenting in part:

. . . Despite the parties' agreement that the *de novo* standard of review applies, my colleagues, like the district court, nonetheless review the ATF's interpretation under the two-step framework set out in *Chevron*, [citation]. But the United States Supreme Court has recently clarified whether the *Chevron* framework applies to a statute—and, by extension a rule—enforced by a criminal sanction. *United States v. Apel*, 571 U.S. 359, 369 (2014) ("[W]e have never held that the Government's reading of a criminal statute is entitled to any deference."). In another recent decision, *Abramski v. United States*, the ATF had taken one view of 18 U.S.C. § 922(a)(6) for "almost two decades," concluding that a straw purchaser's "misrepresentation" counted as "material" under the statute notwithstanding the true buyer could legally possess a gun. [Citation.] The defendant pointed out that the ATF had until 1995 taken the opposite position, requiring the true buyer to be ineligible to possess a gun in order to make the straw purchaser's misrepresentation "material." *Id.* The Supreme Court responded that the "ATF's old position [is] no more relevant than its current one—which is to say, not relevant at all." *Id.* Indeed, "[w]hether the Government interprets a criminal statute too broadly (as it sometimes does) or too narrowly (as the ATF used to in construing § 922(a)(6)), a court has an obligation to correct its error." *Id.* In its *Apel* and *Abramski* decisions, then, "[t]he Supreme Court has expressly instructed us *not* to apply *Chevron* deference when an agency seeks to interpret a criminal statute." [Citation.]

My colleagues believe that this case is different because the 26 U.S.C. § 5845(b) definition of "machinegun" has both civil and criminal enforcement implications. They reach their conclusion regarding the applicable standard of review based in part on a footnote in *Babbitt*, [citation]. . . . The majority reads *Babbitt*—and some of our precedent—to establish a bright-line rule that any regulation with both civil and criminal enforcement provisions merits *Chevron* deference. [Citations.]

With respect, I am not convinced that my colleagues' reading of *Babbitt* as the last word on this topic is correct. [Citation.] The Supreme Court's most recent decisions indicate, as the ATF and the plaintiffs argue here, that *Chevron* review does not apply to a statute/rule with criminal sanctions. [Citations.] And if *Chevron* review does not apply to a statute/rule with criminal sanctions, *Chevron* cannot apply to a statute/rule with *both* criminal *and* civil sanctions. [Citations.] [*Babbitt*] suggests, I submit, that a regulation with a criminal sanction *can* violate the rule of lenity but concluded that the regulation at issue, with its longstanding definition of "harm," did not do so. [Citation.] My reading allows *Babbitt* to be harmonized with more recent decisions: *Chevron* does not apply to a regulation enforced both civilly and criminally unless the regulation gives fair warning sufficient to avoid posing a rule of lenity problem. The ATF's interpretation of "machinegun" gives anything but fair warning—instead, it does a *volte-face* of its almost eleven years' treatment of a non-mechanical bump stock as not constituting a "machinegun."

Although I do not dispute that the ATF has been delegated general rulemaking authority to implement section 5845(b), *inter alia*, I am less certain than my colleagues that we owe deference to the ATF's interpretation of section 5845(b). "Deference under *Chevron* to an agency's construction of a statute that it administers is premised on the theory that a statute's ambiguity constitutes an implicit delegation from Congress to the agency to fill in the statutory gaps." *Brown & Williamson*

Tobacco Corp., [citation]. Statutory ambiguity, if it exists, does not necessarily constitute an implicit delegation. *King v. Burwell*, [citations]. The Congress must, for instance, "speak clearly if it wishes to assign to an agency decisions of vast economic and political significance." [Citation.] There is good reason to believe that a similar clear-statement rule applies in the criminal law context. Under longstanding separation-of-powers principles, the Congress defines the criminal law and must speak distinctly to delegate its responsibility. [Citations.] Unlike with civil statutes, then, ambiguity in the criminal law is presumptively for the Congress—not the ATF—to resolve. [Citation.] Accordingly, I would treat an ambiguous criminal statute to be of "vast economic and political significance" and apply *Chevron* only if the Congress expressly delegates its lawmaking responsibility. [Citation.] The Congress has made no such clear statement; instead the ATF relies solely on its general rulemaking power and statutory ambiguity. 18 U.S.C. § 926(a); 26 U.S.C. §§ 7801(a)(2)(A), 7805(a). *Chevron* is inapplicable. [Citation.]

I believe the applicable standard of review is de novo and therefore we should go "the old-fashioned" route and "decide for ourselves the best reading" of "machinegun." [Citation.] As is always the case in construing a statute, the inquiry focuses on "the plain meaning of the text, looking to the 'language itself, the specific context in which that language is used, and the broader context of the statute as a whole.' " [Citation.] The Bump Stock Rule declares that any bump stock device qualifies as a "machinegun." Although the Rule—in my view—correctly interprets "single function of the trigger," it misreads "automatically." Moreover, it misapplies its interpretation of "single function of the trigger" to bump stock type devices.

B. "Single Function of the Trigger"

The Rule determines that "single function of the trigger" within the statutory definition of "machinegun" means "single pull of the trigger and analogous motions." [Citation.] To me, the "function" of the trigger means "action" of the trigger. Webster's New International Dictionary 1019 (2d ed. 1934). According to the section 5845(b) definition, the trigger function "shoots" the firearm. 26 U.S.C. § 5845(b) ("The term 'machinegun' means any weapon which shoots . . . automatically more than one shot, without manual reloading, by a single function of the trigger."); [citation]. "Pull of the trigger," then, describes *how* the trigger works. [Citations.] The Rule recognizes that not all firearms feature a pull trigger; some involve "fire initiated by voice command, electronic switch, swipe on a touchscreen or pad, or any conceivable number of interfaces." [Citation]. To include these non-pull methods used to shoot a firearm, the Rule includes the phrase "and analogous motions." [Citation.]

The plaintiffs claim that the Rule's interpretation of "single function" impermissibly shifts the statutory focus from the trigger's action to the trigger finger's action. But the Rule defines "single function" to mean "single pull of the trigger and analogous motions." The Rule's definition describes the "motion" of the trigger, not of the trigger finger. [Citation.] Indeed, nothing in the Rule's definition refers to a shooter's finger or a volitional action. [Citation.] The plaintiffs challenge the Rule because the ATF determines therein that a bump stock device allows the firearm to shoot more than one shot with only a single pull. But that is a question of application, not definition. As for the definition, I believe the Rule correctly reads "function" by focusing on how the trigger acts—that is, through a pull.

C.   "Automatically"

The Bump Stock Rule defines "automatically" to mean "as the result of a self-acting or self-regulating mechanism that allows the firing of multiple rounds through a single pull of the trigger." [Citation.] The plaintiffs challenge this definition because it does not account for the additional physical input the shooter must provide in the firing sequence to make a firearm with a bump stock shoot more rapidly. That "pull plus" action, they say, invalidly expands the statutory text: a " 'single function of the trigger' is the starting and the ending point of [making] a firearm automatic." I agree.

The Rule's fatal flaw comes from its "adding to" the statutory language in a way that is—at least to me—plainly *ultra vires*. [Citations.] "Automatically" cannot be read in isolation. On the contrary, it is modified—that is, limited—by the clause "by a single function of the trigger." 26 U.S.C. § 5845(b); Webster's New International Dictionary 307 (2d ed. 1934) (defining "by" as "through the means of"). Section 5845(b)'s awkward syntax does not equal ambiguity, as illustrated by the lost art of diagramming. "Automatically . . . by a single function of the trigger" is the sum total of the *action necessary* to constitute a firearm a "machinegun." 26 U.S.C. § 5845(b). A "machinegun," then, is a firearm that shoots more than one round by a single trigger pull without manual reloading. The statutory definition of "machinegun" does not include a firearm that shoots more than one round "automatically" by a single pull of the trigger **AND THEN SOME** (that is, by "constant forward pressure with the non-trigger hand"). *Bump-Stock-Type Devices*, 83 Fed. Reg. at 66,532. By including more action than a single trigger pull, the Rule invalidly expands section 5845(b), as the ATF itself recognized in the rulemaking. *See id.* (shooter "maintain[s] constant forward pressure with the non-trigger hand on the barrel-shroud or fore-grip of the rifle," *and* "maintain[s] the trigger finger on the device's extension ledge with constant rearward pressure.").

My reading of the statute comports with the common sense meaning of the language used. Suppose an advertisement declares that a device performs a task "automatically by a push of a button." I would understand the phrase to mean pushing the button activates whatever function the device performs. It would come as a surprise, I submit, if the device does not operate until the button is pushed *and* some other action is taken—a pedal pressed, a dial turned and so on. Although the device might be "automatic" under some definition, it would not fit the advertised definition of "automatic": by a push of a button period.

More importantly, my reading of the statute—unlike the ATF's reading—maintains the longstanding distinction between "automatic" and "semiautomatic" in the firearms context. The original definition of "machinegun" in the 1934 Act included a firearm that shoots more than one round "automatically or semiautomatically." 26 U.S.C. § 2733(b) (1940). At the time, an "automatic gun" was understood to be "[a] firearm which, after the first round is exploded, by gas pressure or force of recoil automatically extracts and ejects the empty case, loads another round into the chamber, fires, and repeats the above cycle, until the ammunition in the feeding mechanism is exhausted, or pressure on the trigger is released." Webster's New International Dictionary 187 (2d ed. 1934). A "semiautomatic gun" was (and is) "[a] firearm in which part, but not all, of the operations involved in loading and firing are performed automatically, as when the recoil is used to open the breech and thus prepare for reloading by hand." Webster's New International Dictionary 187 (2d ed. 1934). At the time of the 1934 Act's enactment, then, the difference between an "automatic" and a "semiautomatic" gun depended on whether the shooter played a manual role in the loading and firing process. My interpretation fits the historical context by limiting "automatic[ ]" to a firearm that shoots more than one round by a single trigger pull with no additional action by the shooter. By contrast, the Bump Stock Rule reinterprets "automatically" to mean what "semiautomatically" did in 1934—a pull of the trigger *plus*. The Congress deleted "semiautomatically" from the statute in 1968 and the ATF is without authority to resurrect it by regulation.

The ATF insists that my interpretation renders "automatically" superfluous—a result inconsistent with the well-established principle that " '[a] statute should be construed so that effect is given to all its provisions, so that no part will be inoperative or superfluous, void or insignificant.' " [Citations.] Not even close. "[A]utomatically" means that the firearm shoots more than one shot as the result of a self-acting mechanism effected by a single pull of the trigger. Thus, the combination of "automatically" and "by a single pull" explains *how* the shooter accomplishes the firing sequence of a "machinegun." Under my reading, "automatically" *excludes* a "machinegun" that uses a self-acting firing sequence effected by action in addition to a single pull of the trigger.

Finally, the ATF, as well as the district court, posits that the Bump Stock Rule meets one ordinary meaning of "automatically"—that is, "perform[s] parts of the work formerly or usually done by hand." Webster's New International Dictionary 187 (2d ed. 1934). Both believe that a bump stock "makes it easier to bump fire because it controls the distance the firearm recoils and ensures that the firearm moves linearly—two tasks the shooter would ordinarily have to perform manually." Maybe so. But the Rule does not use the "formerly done by hand" meaning of "automatically." *Bump-Stock-Type Devices*, 83 Fed. Reg. at 66,519. It defines "automatically" to mean "as the result of a self-acting or self-regulating mechanism." *Id.* Whether *that* definition is consistent with section 5845(b)'s definition is the question before us.

D.   Is a Bump Stock a "Machinegun?"

Having interpreted "automatically" and "single function of the trigger," the Rule declares that a " 'machinegun' includes a bump-stock-type device, *i.e.*, a device that allows a semiautomatic firearm to shoot more than one shot with a single pull of the trigger by harnessing the recoil energy of the semiautomatic firearm to which it is affixed so that the trigger resets and continues firing without additional physical manipulation of the trigger by the shooter." [Citation.] There are at least two defects in this classification. It ignores the fact that a non-mechanical bump stock—a type of bump stock device covered by the Rule—does not allow the firearm to shoot more rapidly with a single pull of the trigger because the shooter must provide "constant forward pressure with the non-trigger hand" for the device to function. *Id.* at 66,532. It also erroneously determines that a bump stock allows a semiautomatic rifle to fire more than one round with a single pull of the trigger. For these reasons, I agree with the plaintiffs that a bump stock is not a "machinegun."

First, a firearm equipped with a non-mechanical bump stock does not fire "automatically" because the shooter must also provide constant forward pressure with his non-shooting hand. The Rule's very description of a non-mechanical bump stock manifests that its proscription is *ultra vires*:

> [Bump stock] devices replace a rifle's standard stock and free the weapon to slide back and forth rapidly, harnessing the energy from the firearm's recoil either through a mechanism like an internal spring or in conjunction with the shooter's maintenance of pressure (typically constant forward pressure with the non-trigger hand on the barrel-shroud or fore-grip of the rifle, and constant rearward pressure on the device's extension ledge with the shooter's trigger finger).

Id. at 66,516 (emphases added). This description covers two types of bump stocks, one that includes a mechanism like an internal spring and the other that requires the shooter to maintain pressure with his non-trigger hand. *Id.* The first type, including the original Akins Accelerator, has been classified as a "machinegun" and hence illegal since 2006. *Id.* at 66,517. The Rule must—and does—aim at the second type—the non-mechanical bump stock—which operates only in conjunction with the shooter's added physical pressure. But that added physical pressure is inconsistent with the statutory definition of a "machinegun," which fires multiple rounds with a self-acting mechanism effected through a single pull of the trigger *simpliciter*. In short, the statute uses "pull" and the Rule—invalidly—uses "pull *plus*."

Other parts of the Rule expose the ATF's error. . . . [T]he ATF describes the firing process of a firearm with a bump stock as follows: "the shooter 'pulls' the trigger once and allows the firearm and attached bump-stock-type device to operate until the shooter releases the trigger finger *or* the constant forward pressure with the non-trigger hand." *Id.* at 66,532 (emphasis added). In my view, this assertion is an explicit recognition that a bump stock device *does not* continue shooting rounds with a single trigger pull if the shooter does not maintain "constant forward pressure with the non-trigger hand." *Id.* at 66,532.

Moreover, I find it difficult to ignore the ATF's repeated earlier determinations that non-mechanical bump stocks do not initiate an automatic firing sequence. Three ATF determination letters from 2010 to 2013 explained why non-mechanical bump stocks are not "machineguns":

> [Our] evaluation confirmed that the submitted stock (see enclosed photos) does attach to the rear of an AR-15 type rifle which has been fitted with a sliding shoulder-stock type buffer-tube assembly. The stock has no automatically functioning mechanical parts or springs and performs no automatic mechanical function when installed. In order to use the installed device, the shooter must apply constant forward pressure with the non-shooting hand and constant rearward pressure with the shooting hand.

[Citation.] The Rule does not fairly treat the ATF's repeated determinations that a non-mechanical bump stock "performs no automatic mechanical function when installed." [Citation.] Instead, it rejects its previous reading as based on an incomplete *legal* definition of "automatically." [Citation.] But those determinations made *factual findings* that the non-mechanical bump stock operates only if the shooter applies "constant forward pressure with the non-shooting hand and constant rearward pressure with the shooting hand." [Citation.]

Second, a semiautomatic rifle equipped with a bump stock *cannot* fire more than one round with a *single* function of the trigger. The plaintiffs argue—and the ATF does not dispute—that the trigger of a semiautomatic rifle must release the hammer for each individual discharge. Nor is there any dispute that a semiautomatic rifle cannot fire again until the trigger is released, which causes the hammer to reset. . . .

Still, the ATF insists that a bump stock allows a firearm to shoot multiple shots with a single pull. [Citation.] The ATF focuses on whether the shooter must pull his index finger more than once to fire multiple shots. Because a bump stock allows the firearm to fire more than once with a single pull of the index finger, the ATF concludes that a bump stock is a "machinegun." Remember, however, section 5845(b) uses "single function of the trigger," not single function of the shooter's trigger finger... With a bump stock, however, the shooter—after the initial pull—maintains backward pressure on the trigger and puts forward pressure on the barrel with his non-shooting hand; these manual inputs cause the rifle to slide and result in the shooter's *stationary* finger pulling the trigger. [Citation.] The bump stock therefore affects whether the shooter *pulls* his trigger finger or keeps it *stationary*. It does not change the movement of the trigger itself, which "must be released, reset, and fully pulled rearward before [a] subsequent round can be fired." [Citation.]

Like countless other Americans, I can think of little legitimate use for a bump stock. That thought, however, has nothing to do with the legality of the Bump Stock Rule. For the reasons detailed *supra*, I believe the Bump Stock Rule expands the statutory definition of "machinegun" and is therefore *ultra vires*. In my view, the plaintiffs are likely to succeed on the merits of their challenge and I would grant them preliminary injunctive relief.

Accordingly, I respectfully dissent.

NOTES AND QUESTIONS

1. Recall the discussion of dictionaries and the controversy surrounding *Webster's Third* in Section III.B.3.a, *supra*. In theory, when courts cite to dictionaries from earlier eras, they do so in order to understand linguistic meaning at the time of the statute's enactment. Yet this inquiry becomes problematic when statutes (or statutory amendments) incorporate statutory language enacted in an earlier era. In *Guedes*, the dissent cites *Webster's Second* in interpreting the ordinary meaning of the statutory text at issue—the prohibition on the possession of machineguns from the Gun Control Act of 1968, which itself incorporated its definition of the Firearms Control Act of 1934. *Webster's Third*, published in 1961, was published less than a decade before the Gun Control Act was enacted, while *Webster's Second* was published in 1934, the same year as the passage of the Firearms Control Act. Would *Webster's Third* better capture the ordinary usage of a word at the time of enactment of the statutory prohibition? Or should courts presume the 1968 Congress to have understood the ordinary meaning in 1934 of the term "machinegun"? Justice Scalia's 2006 dissent in *Gonzales v. Oregon*, *supra*, also referenced *Webster's Second*, even though the statute involved—the Controlled Substances Act—was enacted in 1970, much closer to the publication of Webster's Third. By contrast, in *Babbitt v. Sweet Home*, *supra*, decided in 1995, the Supreme Court cited *Webster's Third* in its interpretation of provisions of the Endangered Species Act, enacted in 1975. Given what you know about *Webster's Third's* controversial reception, why do you think Judge Henderson and Justice Scalia declined to use it? If a court seeks the term's ordinary meaning at the time of the statute's enactment, shouldn't the dictionary whose publication came closest to the statutory enactment prevail? Keep these questions in mind as you read *New Prime Inc. v. Oliveira* and *Bostock v. Clayton County*, *infra* Section VI.A.

2. The preceding question illustrates that in at least some circumstances, a proper "textual" interpretation of a statute may require a rather extensive excursion into the statute's enactment history and subsequent amendments.

Is such an approach susceptible to the same criticisms that some textualists lodge at interpretive approaches that rely on a statute's legislative history? Why or why not?

3.   Plaintiffs filed an interlocutory appeal before the Supreme Court, which denied cert. Justice Gorsuch provided the following statement accompanying the denial:

> Does owning a bump stock expose a citizen to a decade in federal prison? For years, the government didn't think so. But recently the Bureau of Alcohol, Tobacco, Firearms and Explosives changed its mind. Now, according to a new interpretive rule* from the agency, owning a bump stock is forbidden by a longstanding federal statute that outlaws the "possession [of] a machinegun." [Citation.] Whether bump stocks can be fairly reclassified and effectively outlawed as machineguns under existing statutory definitions, I do not know and could not say without briefing and argument. Nor do I question that Congress might seek to enact new legislation directly regulating the use and possession of bump stocks. But at least one thing should be clear: Contrary to the court of appeals's decision in this case, *Chevron*, [citation], has nothing to say about the proper interpretation of the law before us.
>
> In the first place, the government expressly waived reliance on *Chevron*. The government told the court of appeals that, if the validity of its rule (re)interpreting the machinegun statute "turns on the applicability of *Chevron*, it would prefer that the [r]ule be set aside rather than upheld." [Citation.] Yet, despite this concession, the court proceeded to uphold the agency's new rule *only* on the strength of *Chevron* deference. Think about it this way. The executive branch and affected citizens asked the court to do what courts usually do in statutory interpretation disputes: supply its best independent judgment about what the law means. But, instead of deciding the case the old-fashioned way, the court placed an uninvited thumb on the scale in favor of the government.
>
> That was mistaken. This Court has often declined to apply *Chevron* deference when the government fails to invoke it. [Citing law review articles.] Even when *Chevron* deference is sought, this Court has found it inappropriate where "the Executive seems of two minds" about the result it prefers. *Epic Systems Corp. v. Lewis*, 138 S.Ct. 1612, 1630 (2018). Nor is it a surprise that the government can lose the benefit of *Chevron* in situations like these and ours. If the justification for *Chevron* is that " 'policy choices' should be left to executive branch officials 'directly accountable to the people,' " *Epic Systems*, [citation], then courts must equally respect the Executive's decision *not* to make policy choices in the interpretation of Congress's handiwork.

---

*   Editors' Note: Note that although Justice Gorsuch's dissent from the denial of cert refers to the Bump-Stock Rule as an "interpretive rule," as indicated *supra*, the D.C. Circuit below had held that the rule is a legislative rule and thus should be accorded *Chevron* deference.

To make matters worse, the law before us carries the possibility of criminal sanctions. And, as the government itself may have recognized in offering its disclaimer, whatever else one thinks about *Chevron*, it has no role to play when liberty is at stake. Under our Constitution, "[o]nly the people's elected representatives in the legislature are authorized to 'make an act a crime.'" *United States v. Davis*, 139 S.Ct. 2319, 2325 (2019) (quoting *United States v. Hudson*, 7 Cranch 32, 34, 3 L.Ed. 259 (1812)). Before courts may send people to prison, we owe them an independent determination that the law actually forbids their conduct. A "reasonable" prosecutor's say-so is cold comfort in comparison. That's why this Court has "never held that the Government's reading of a criminal statute is entitled to any deference." *Apel*, [citation]. Instead, we have emphasized, courts bear an "obligation" to determine independently what the law allows and forbids. *Abramski*, [citation]; *see also* 920 F.3d at 39–40 (opinion of Henderson, J.); *Esquivel-Quintana v. Lynch*, 810 F.3d 1019, 1027–1032 (C.A.6 2016) (Sutton, J., concurring in part and dissenting in part). That obligation went unfulfilled here.

Chevron's application in this case may be doubtful for other reasons too. The agency used to tell everyone that bump stocks don't qualify as "machineguns." Now it says the opposite. The law hasn't changed, only an agency's interpretation of it. And these days it sometimes seems agencies change their statutory interpretations almost as often as elections change administrations. How, in all this, can ordinary citizens be expected to keep up—required not only to conform their conduct to the fairest reading of the law they might expect from a neutral judge, but forced to guess whether the statute will be declared ambiguous; to guess again whether the agency's initial interpretation of the law will be declared "reasonable"; and to guess *again* whether a later and opposing agency interpretation will *also* be held "reasonable"? And why should courts, charged with the independent and neutral interpretation of the laws Congress has enacted, defer to such bureaucratic pirouetting?

Despite these concerns, I agree with my colleagues that the interlocutory petition before us does not merit review. The errors apparent in this preliminary ruling might yet be corrected before final judgment. Further, other courts of appeals are actively considering challenges to the same regulation. Before deciding whether to weigh in, we would benefit from hearing their considered judgments—provided, of course, that they are not afflicted with the same problems. But waiting should not be mistaken for lack of concern.

It is notable that nearly four decades after *Chevron* was first decided—unanimously—its viability, applicability, and workability are increasingly contentious topics, both inside and outside the judiciary. Yet despite numerous calls for the Court to abolish the doctrine, *Chevron* continues to be popular among many lower court judges confronted with complex regulatory implementations and interpretations of statutes, especially judges on the D.C. Circuit, who encounter numerous such questions in their daily work. *See* Abbe R. Gluck & Richard A. Posner, *Statutory Interpretation on the Bench: A Survey of Forty-Two Judges on the Federal Court of Appeals*, 131 Harv. L. Rev. 1298 (2018) (contrasting the strong support for *Chevron* among D.C. Circuit judges with its more uneven reception elsewhere among the federal appellate courts).

PART VI

TEMPORAL ISSUES IN STATUTORY ENACTMENT AND INTERPRETATION

A. APPLYING OLD STATUTES TO CHANGING CIRCUMSTANCES

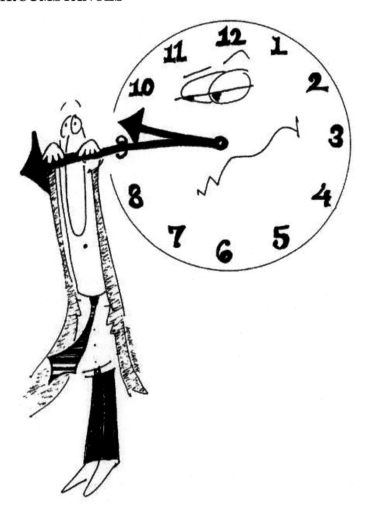

Whether or not legislative drafters have in mind "an evil to be remedied" when enacting a statute, the resulting statute nevertheless will likely apply to circumstances beyond those considered at the time of its enactment. The cases in this section raise issues about the interpretation and application of statutes in changing circumstances and over time.

Commonwealth v. Maxwell

Supreme Court of Pennsylvania, 1921.
271 Pa. 378, 114 A. 825.

■ Opinion by MR. JUSTICE SCHAFFER. In this case, the court below quashed an indictment, charging the defendants with murder, because a woman served on the grand jury which found the bill. The Commonwealth has appealed; and this brings before us the important question whether women are eligible as jurors in Pennsylvania.

It is conceded that, under the 19th Amendment to the Constitution of the United States, women are given the right to vote, and are therefore electors; but the oyer and terminer held that the provision of our Constitution (article I, section 6),—"Trial by jury shall be as heretofore and the right thereof remain inviolate,"—preserves in this State trial by jury as it existed at common law, and that neither the federal amendment nor its effect upon the Act of April 10, 1867, P.L. 62, providing for the selection of jurors, alters the ancient rule that men only may serve.

Let it be noted that what we are called upon to determine is the composition of juries, so far as the qualifications of jurors are concerned, not the conduct of trials before such a body nor the kinds of cases which under the Constitution must be decided by that character of tribunal.

At the time the provision we are considering was placed in Pennsylvania's first Constitution, in 1776, justice had been administered in the Commonwealth according to English forms for about a century. Does the word "heretofore" refer to jury trials as conducted in England or in Pennsylvania? We find the method of selecting juries and the qualifications of jurors, at the time of the promulgation of this Constitution, September 28, 1776, was regulated in Pennsylvania and in England by legislation and not by the common law, in the latter country by the Act of 3 George II, c. 25; 3 Blackstone 361. . . .

Under the Act of April 10, 1867, P.L. 62, section 2, (2 Purdon 2062, placitum 2), which expressly applies to each of the counties in the Commonwealth, except Philadelphia, the jury commissioners are required to select "from the *whole qualified electors* of the respective county, at large, a number," such as shall be designated by the court of common pleas, "of sober, intelligent and judicious persons, to serve as jurors in the several courts of such county during that year." The seventh section of this act exempts Philadelphia from its provisions. The statutory enactment which covers Philadelphia is section 2 of the Act of April 20, 1858, P.L. 354 (2 Purdon 2077, placitum 94); it sets forth: "That prior to the first day of December in each and every year, the receiver of public taxes of the said city shall lodge with the said sheriff, for the use of the said board [of judges], a duly certified list of *all taxable inhabitants of the said city,* setting out their names, places of residence and occupation; and, prior to the tenth day of December in each and every year, it shall be the duty of the said board, or a quorum thereof, to assemble together and select from the said list of taxables a sufficient number of sober, healthy and discreet citizens, to constitute the several panels of jurors, grand and petit, that may be required for service in the several courts for the next ensuing year, in due proportion from the several wards of the said city and the principal avocations."

It will thus be seen that since 1805, when the Constitution of 1790 was in force, the persons charged with the duty of jury service have been fixed, from time to time, by the legislature and have been "taxable citizens," "white male taxable citizens," "male taxable citizens," "taxable inhabitants" and "qualified electors." . . .

Without feeling called upon to determine what other matters the word "heretofore" in the Constitution of 1873 refers to, we do say that when that instrument was adopted the uniform method of selecting jurors and determining their qualification was by legislation, both here and in England. This was known to the framers of the first and all succeeding Constitutions, in the first being specifically recognized, and, in guaranteeing the right of trial by jury, it and all the others did not in any way limit the legislature from determining from time to time how juries should be composed.

We have then the Act of 1867, constitutionally providing that the jury commissioners are required to select "from the *whole qualified electors* of the respective county . . . persons to serve as jurors in the several courts of such county," and the 19th Amendment to the federal Constitution putting women in the body of electors. "The term 'elector' is a technical, generic term, descriptive of a citizen having constitutional and statutory qualifications that enable him to vote, and including not only those who vote, but also those who are qualified yet fail to exercise the right of franchise": 20 Corpus Juris 58. If the Act of 1867 is prospective in operation, and takes in new classes of electors as they come to the voting privilege from time to time, then necessarily women being electors are eligible to jury service. That the Act of 1867 does cover those who at any time shall come within the designation of electors there can be no question. "Statutes framed in general terms apply to new cases that arise, and to new subjects that are created from time to time, and which come within their general scope and policy. It is a rule of statutory construction that legislative enactments in general and comprehensive terms, prospective in operation, apply alike to all persons, subjects and business within their general purview and scope coming into existence subsequent to their passage": 25 Ruling Case Law 778.

Summing up, we conclude, (1) there was no absolute and fixed qualification of jurors at common law, and from very ancient times their qualifications were fixed by act of parliament; (2) the qualification of jurors was not the thing spoken of by the section of the Constitution under consideration; (3) the words "as heretofore" in that section refer to the kinds of cases triable before juries and the trial, not the qualifications of the jurors; (4) the designation "qualified elector" embraces all electors at the time jurors are selected from the body of electors; (5) the term "electors" embraces those who may be added to the electorate from time to time. . . .

The pending case calls for the immediate decision only of the right of women to serve as jurors in those counties which are covered by the Act of 1867. We entertain no doubt, however, that women are eligible to serve as jurors in all the Commonwealth's courts.

The order quashing the indictment is reversed, and the indictment is reinstated with direction to the court below to proceed with the trial of the defendants in due course.

Commonwealth v. Welosky

Supreme Court of Massachusetts, 1931.
276 Mass. 398, 177 N.E. 656.

Complaint, received and sworn to in the District Court of Chelsea on July 9, 1930, charging the defendant with keeping and exposing intoxicating liquor with intent unlawfully to sell the same.

Upon appeal to the Superior Court, the complaint was tried before *Hayes, J.*, a judge of a district court sitting in the Superior Court under statutory provisions. The defendant's challenge to the array is described in the opinion. The judge sustained a replication by the Commonwealth thereto. The defendant was found guilty and alleged exceptions.

■ RUGG, C.J.[, joined by CROSBY, CARROLL, WAIT, and FIELD, JJ.] As the jurors were about to be empaneled for the trial of this complaint, the defendant filed a challenge to the array. Issue of law was joined thereon. [Citation.] The ground on which that challenge rests is that there were no women on the lists from which the jurors were drawn.

1.   The first question to be decided is whether the statutes of this Commonwealth require that the names of women otherwise qualified be placed upon jury lists so that they may be drawn for service as jurors.

It is plain that women could not rightly serve as jurors, save in the rare instances where a jury of matrons was called, under the Constitution and laws of this Commonwealth prior to the adoption of the Nineteenth Amendment to the Constitution of the United States. The terms of the statute, in the light of the Constitution, express decisions, universal understanding, and unbroken practice, forbid any other view. The trial by jury of the common law and that contemplated by both the Constitution of this Commonwealth and that of the United States were by a jury of twelve composed exclusively of men. [Citation.]

The statute to be interpreted is G.L. c. 234, § 1. Its relevant language is: "A person qualified to vote for representatives to the general court shall be liable to serve as a juror," with exceptions not here material.

The words of a statute are the main source for the ascertainment of a legislative purpose. They are to be construed according to their natural import in common and approved usage. The imperfections of language to express intent often render necessary further inquiry. Statutes are to be interpreted, not alone according to their simple, literal or strict verbal meaning, but in connection with their development, their progression through the legislative body, the history of the times, prior legislation, contemporary customs and conditions and the system of positive law of which they are part, and in the light of the Constitution and of the common law, to the end that they be held to cover the subjects presumably within the vision of the Legislature and, on the one hand, be not unduly constricted so as to exclude matters fairly within their scope, and, on the other hand, be not stretched by enlargement of signification to comprehend matters not within the principle and purview on which they were founded when originally framed and their words chosen. General expressions may be restrained by relevant circumstances showing a legislative intent that they be narrowed and used in a particular sense. [Citation.]

It is clear beyond peradventure that the words of G.L. c. 234, § 1, when originally enacted could not by any possibility have included or been intended by the General Court to include women among those liable to jury duty. The Constitution forbade the words, "A person qualified to vote for representatives to the general court," to comprehend women. Women have been qualified to vote in this Commonwealth only since the adoption of the Nineteenth Amendment to the Constitution of the United States. It is not argued in behalf of the defendant that the terms of the statutes preceding G.L. c. 234, § 1, that is to say of R.L. c. 176, § 1, and its predecessors in substantially the same words since a time before the adoption of the Constitution, could possibly have imposed jury duty upon women. The argument on this point is twofold: (A) that the phrase of the statute is general and therefore was intended automatically to include women if their constitutional inhibitions were ever removed; and (B) that, since the General Laws were enacted in December, 1920, after the ratification of the Nineteenth Amendment, the statute was intended to include women. These arguments will be considered in turn.

A. The Nineteenth Amendment was, on August 26, 1920, proclaimed to have been duly ratified. That amendment declared that "The right of citizens of the United States to vote shall not be denied or abridged by the United States or by any state on account of sex." It became forthwith binding upon the people and the several departments of this Commonwealth. By its own self-executing force it struck from the Constitution of this Commonwealth the word "male" wherever it occurred as a limitation upon the right to vote. . . .

Statutes framed in general terms commonly look to the future and may include conditions as they arise from time to time not even known at the time of enactment, provided they are fairly within the sweep and the meaning of the words and falling within their obvious scope and purpose. But statutes do not govern situations not within the reason of their enactment and giving rise to radically diverse circumstances presumably not within the dominating purpose of those who framed and enacted them. [Citation.]

As matter of strict and abstract verbal interpretation, apart from context, circumstances, and contemporary and antecedent history, the language of G.L. c. 234, § 1, is broad enough to comprise women. The word "person" when used in an unrestricted sense includes a woman. It has been said that "The word 'persons,' in its natural and usual signification, includes women as well as men." *Opinion of the Justices,* 136 Mass. 578, 580. Binney v. Globe National Bank, 150 Mass. 574. "The natural and obvious meaning of the word 'person' is a living human being." Sawyer v. Mackie, 149 Mass. 269, 270. Madden v. Election Commissioners of Boston, 251 Mass. 95, 98. The word "person," like many other words, has no fixed and rigid signification, but has different meanings dependent upon contemporary conditions, the connection in which it is used, and the result intended to be accomplished. It has been said to be "an ambiguous word" and may refer to those of either or both sexes. Nairn v. University of St. Andrews, [1909] A.C. 147, 162. . . . Yet it was held not to include corporations upon the facts in Commonwealth v. Phoenix Bank, 11 Met. 129, 149. Notwithstanding Pub.Sts. c. 3, § 3, Sixteenth, (G.L. c. 4, § 7, Twenty-third) to the effect that the word "person" in construing statutes shall include corporations, it was held not thus inclusive in Steel Edge Stamping & Retinning Co. v. Manchester Savings Bank, 163 Mass. 252. It has also been held not to include a woman. Mashburn v. State, 65 Fla. 470, 474. Several cases have arisen where the question was whether the word "person," when used respecting the right to hold office or to exercise the franchise, included women. In Nairn v. University of St. Andrews, [1909] A.C. 147, it appeared that, by Acts of Parliament of 1868 and 1881, the university franchise was conferred upon "every person" whose name was on the register and on whom degrees had been conferred. At that time women were not admitted to graduation and could not receive degrees. In 1889, a further act was passed for the appointment of commissioners with extensive regulatory powers over universities. These commissioners adopted an ordinance enabling the universities to confer degrees on women for satisfactory academic accomplishments. The appellants, having received degrees upon graduation, contended that they had the right to vote. In rejecting that contention, it was said by Lord Loreburn, at page 161: "It proceeds upon the supposition that the word 'person' in the Act of 1868 did include women, though not then giving them the vote, so that at some later date an Act purporting to deal only with education might enable commissioners to admit them to the degree, and thereby also indirectly confer upon them the franchise. It would require a convincing demonstration to satisfy me that Parliament intended to effect a constitutional change so momentous and far-reaching by so furtive a process. It is a dangerous assumption to suppose that the Legislature foresees every possible result that may ensue from the unguarded use of a single word, or that the language used in statutes is so precisely accurate that you can pick out from various Acts this and that expression and, skillfully piecing them together, lay a safe foundation for some remote inference." It was held that the statutory word "person" did not in these circumstances include women. It was held in *Viscountess Rhondda's Claim,* [1922] 2 A.C. 339, that an Act of Parliament passed in 1919, providing that "A person shall not be disqualified by sex or marriage from the exercise of any public function," did not entitle a peeress of the United Kingdom in her own right to receive the writ of summons to Parliament. Doubtless, as an abstract conception, it is a public function to sit in the House of Lords and to exercise the prerogatives of a member. But it was held by ten out of twelve law lords sitting in the case, among whom were the most eminent judges of the day, that the word "person" as used in the act could not rightly be interpreted to include women in those entitled to sit in the House of Lords. It was said by Lord Birkenhead in the course of an exhaustive statement reviewing many decisions, at page 369: ". . . a long stream of cases has established that general words are to be construed so as, in an old phrase, 'to pursue the intent of the makers of statutes' . . . and so as to import all those implied exceptions which arise from a close consideration of the mischiefs sought to be remedied and of the state of the law at the moment, when the statute was passed." At pages 372–373, the words of Lord Loreburn in Nairn v. University of St. Andrews, [1909] A.C. 147, at pages 160, 161, to which reference has already been made, were quoted with high commendation.

This brief review of authorities demonstrates that "person" by itself is an equivocal word. Its meaning in a statute requires interpretation. The statute here under examination (G.L. c. 234, § 1) is a reenactment of a long line of statutes of the Commonwealth running back to a time shortly after the adoption of the Constitution as well as through all intermediate revisions dealing with qualifications for jury service. Laws of the Colony and of the Province are in effect the same. In the earlier and later statutes, the same essential and almost the identical words have been employed. The word "person" occurs in them all. The selection of jurors has constantly been required to be from those qualified to vote. Qualifications for voting have been continuously established by the Constitution. By the words of that instrument and its amendments (apart from the effect of the Nineteenth Amendment to the Federal Constitution) the right to vote was confined to male inhabitants, male persons, and finally to male citizens, until the word "male" was stricken out in 1924 by Amendment 68. *See* c. 1, § 2, art. 2; c. 1, § 3, art. 4; arts. 3 and 32 of the Amendments. Manifestly, therefore, the intent of the

Legislature must have been, in using the word "person" in statutes concerning jurors and jury lists, to confine its meaning to men. . . .

Possession of property of specified value and payment of taxes, as qualifications for voters, were required in earlier days and from time to time, but these were gradually eliminated by amendments to the Constitution until the last of such limitations disappeared with the approval of Amendment 32 in 1891. When the suffrage has been thus widened among male citizens, there has followed, without further legislation and without change in the phrase of the statute, a like extension of citizens liable to service as jurors. These concurring enlargements of those liable to jury service were simply an extension to larger numbers of the same classification of persons. Since the word "person" in the statutes respecting jurors meant men, when there was an extension of the right to vote to other men previously disqualified, the jury statutes by specific definition included them. No amendment to the statute can be conceived which could have made that meaning more clear. . . .

Changes in suffrage and in liability for jury service in the past differ in kind from the change here urged.

The Nineteenth Amendment to the Federal Constitution conferred the suffrage upon an entirely new class of human beings. It did not extend the right to vote to members of an existing classification theretofore disqualified, but created a new class. It added to qualified voters those who did not fall within the meaning of the word "person" in the jury statutes. No member of the class thus added to the body of voters had ever theretofore in this Commonwealth had the right to vote for candidates for offices created by the Constitution. The change in the legal status of women wrought by the Nineteenth Amendment was radical, drastic and unprecedented. While it is to be given full effect in its field, it is not to be extended by implication. It is unthinkable that those who first framed and selected the words for the statute now embodied in G.L. c. 234, § 1, had any design that it should ever include women within its scope. It is equally inconceivable that those who from time to time have reenacted that statute had any such design. When they used the word "person" in connection with those qualified to vote for members of the more numerous branch of the General Court, to describe those liable to jury service, no one contemplated the possibility of women becoming so qualified. The same is true in general of those who from time to time reenacted the statute in substantially the same words. No intention to include women can be deduced from the omission of the word male. That word was imbedded in the Constitution of the Commonwealth as a limitation upon those citizens who might become voters and thereby members of a class from which jurors might be drawn. It would have been superfluous also to insert that word in the statute. The words of Chief Justice Gray in *Robinson's Case,* 131 Mass. 376, at pages 380, 381, are equally pertinent to the case at bar: "Whenever the Legislature has intended to make a change in the legal rights or capacities of women, it has used words clearly manifesting its intent and the extent of the change intended. . . . In making innovations upon the long-established system of law on this subject, the Legislature appears to have proceeded with great caution, one step at a time; and the whole course of legislation precludes the inference that any change in the legal rights or capacities of women is to be implied, which has not been clearly expressed."

The conclusion is irresistible that, according to sound principles of statutory construction, it cannot rightly be held that the scope of R.L. c. 176, § 1, the statute in force on August 26, 1920, now G.L. c. 234, § 1, was extended by the ratification of the Nineteenth Amendment so as to render women liable to jury duty. To reach that result would be directly contrary to every purpose and intent of the General Court in enacting that law. . . .

NOTES AND QUESTIONS

1. The statutory text construed in *Maxwell* directed that jurors were to be drawn "from the whole qualified electors . . ." In *Welosky,* the statute designated "persons qualified to vote . . ." Does the different statutory language explain the different outcomes in the two cases?

2. *Maxwell*'s approach to statutory interpretation seems consistent with the "plain meaning rule," while *Welosky*'s interpretive techniques recall a variety of other devices to ascertain legislative intent. Do those devices seem more problematic here than, for example, in *Johnson v. Southern Pacific Co., supra* Section II.B.2?

3. Is it relevant that the different outcomes on the composition of juries permitted the convictions in both cases to be sustained?

4. Once women obtained the right to vote, many hoped the Nineteenth Amendment would guarantee equal citizenship in all aspects of civic life. Because many states' jury duty statutes, like those in *Maxwell* and *Welosky*, linked jury duty with the franchise, lawsuits in many states tested the scope of women's legal equality by urging that women voters were as subject to jury service as male voters. Most of these challenges failed; the majority of state courts ruled that the Nineteenth Amendment had no effect beyond the specific domain of voting. *See* Gretchen Ritter, *Jury Service and Women's Citizenship before and after the Nineteenth Amendment*, 20 L. & Hist. Rev. 479, 507–09 (2002).

New Prime Inc. v. Oliveira

Supreme Court of the United States, 2019.
139 S.Ct. 532, 202 L.Ed.2d 536.

■ JUSTICE GORSUCH delivered the opinion of the Court[, in which all other Members joined, except JUSTICE KAVANAUGH, who took no part in the consideration or decision of the case.].

The Federal Arbitration Act requires courts to enforce private arbitration agreements. But like most laws, this one bears its qualifications. Among other things, § 1 says that "nothing herein" may be used to compel arbitration in disputes involving the "contracts of employment" of certain transportation workers. 9 U.S.C. § 1. And that qualification has sparked these questions: When a contract delegates questions of arbitrability to an arbitrator, must a court leave disputes over the application of § 1's exception for the arbitrator to resolve? And does the term "contracts of employment" refer only to contracts between employers and employees, or does it also reach contracts with independent contractors? . . .

New Prime is an interstate trucking company and Dominic Oliveira works as one of its drivers. But, at least on paper, Mr. Oliveira isn't an employee; the parties' contracts label him an independent contractor. Those agreements also instruct that any disputes arising out of the parties' relationship should be resolved by an arbitrator—even disputes over the scope of the arbitrator's authority.

Eventually, of course, a dispute did arise. In a class action lawsuit in federal court, Mr. Oliveira argued that New Prime denies its drivers lawful wages. The company may call its drivers independent contractors. But, Mr. Oliveira alleged, in reality New Prime treats them as employees and fails to pay the statutorily due minimum wage. In response to Mr. Oliveira's complaint, New Prime asked the court to invoke its statutory authority under the Act and compel arbitration according to the terms found in the parties' agreements.

That request led to more than a little litigation of its own. Even when the parties' contracts mandate arbitration, Mr. Oliveira observed, the Act doesn't *always* authorize a court to enter an order compelling it. In particular, § 1 carves out from the Act's coverage "contracts of employment of . . . workers engaged in foreign or interstate commerce." And at least for purposes of this collateral dispute, Mr. Oliveira submitted, it doesn't matter whether you view him as an employee or independent contractor. Either way, his agreement to drive trucks for New Prime qualifies as a "contract[ ] of employment of . . . [a] worker[ ] engaged in . . . interstate commerce." Accordingly, Mr. Oliveira argued, the Act supplied the district court with no authority to compel arbitration in this case.

Naturally, New Prime disagreed. Given the extraordinary breadth of the parties' arbitration agreement, the company insisted that any question about § 1's application belonged for the arbitrator alone to resolve. Alternatively and assuming a court could address the question, New Prime contended that the term "contracts of employment" refers only to contracts that establish an employer-employee relationship. And because Mr. Oliveira is, in fact as well as form, an independent contractor, the company argued, § 1's exception doesn't apply; the rest of the statute does; and the district court was (once again) required to order arbitration.

Ultimately, the district court and the First Circuit sided with Mr. Oliveira. [Citation] . . . . [T]he court of appeals held . . . that . . . § 1's exclusion of certain "contracts of employment" removes from the Act's coverage not only employer-employee contracts but also contracts involving independent contractors. So under any account of the parties' agreement in this case, the court held, it lacked authority under the Act to order arbitration. . . .

Did the First Circuit correctly resolve the merits of the § 1 challenge in this case? . . . What does the term "contracts of employment" mean? If it refers only to contracts that reflect an employer-employee relationship, then § 1's exception is irrelevant and a court is free to order arbitration, just as New Prime urges. But if the term *also* encompasses contracts that require an independent contractor to perform work, then the exception takes hold and a court lacks authority under the Act to order arbitration, exactly as Mr. Oliveira argues. . . .

In taking up this question, we bear an important caution in mind. "[I]t's a 'fundamental canon of statutory construction' that words generally should be 'interpreted as taking their ordinary . . . meaning . . . at the time Congress enacted the statute.'" [Citation.] After all, if judges could freely invest old statutory terms with new meanings, we would risk amending legislation outside the "single, finely wrought and exhaustively considered, procedure" the Constitution commands. [Citation.] We would risk, too, upsetting reliance interests in the settled meaning of a statute. [Citation.] Of course, statutes may sometimes refer to an external source of law and fairly warn readers that they must abide that external source of law, later amendments and modifications included. [Citation.] But nothing like that exists here. Nor has anyone suggested any other appropriate reason that might allow us to depart from the original meaning of the statute at hand.

That, we think, holds the key to the case. To many lawyerly ears today, the term "contracts of employment" might call to mind only agreements between employers and employees (or what the common law sometimes called masters and servants). Suggestively, at least one recently published law dictionary defines the word "employment" to mean "the relationship between master and servant." Black's Law Dictionary 641 (10th ed. 2014). But this modern intuition isn't easily squared with evidence of the term's meaning at the time of the Act's adoption in 1925. At that time, a "contract of employment" usually meant nothing more than an agreement to perform work. As a result, most people then would have understood § 1 to exclude not only agreements between employers and employees but also agreements that require independent contractors to perform work.

What's the evidence to support this conclusion? It turns out that in 1925 the term "contract of employment" wasn't defined in any of the (many) popular or legal dictionaries the parties cite to us. And surely that's a first hint the phrase wasn't then a term of art bearing some specialized meaning. It turns out, too, that the dictionaries of the era consistently afforded the word "employment" a broad construction, broader than may be often found in dictionaries today. Back then, dictionaries tended to treat "employment" more or less as a synonym for "work." Nor did they distinguish between different kinds of work or workers: All work was treated as employment, whether or not the common law criteria for a master-servant relationship happened to be satisfied.[1]

What the dictionaries suggest, legal authorities confirm. This Court's early 20th-century cases used the phrase "contract of employment" to describe work agreements involving independent contractors. Many state court cases did the same.[3] So did a variety of federal statutes. And state statutes too. We see here no evidence that a "contract of employment" necessarily signaled a formal employer-employee or master-servant relationship.

More confirmation yet comes from a neighboring term in the statutory text. Recall that the Act excludes from its coverage "contracts of employment of . . . any . . . class of *workers* engaged in foreign or interstate commerce." 9 U.S.C. § 1 (emphasis added). Notice Congress didn't use the word "employees" or "servants," the natural choices if the term "contracts of employment" addressed them alone. Instead, Congress spoke of "workers," a term that everyone agrees easily embraces

---

[1]   *See, e.g.,* 3 J. Murray, A New English Dictionary on Historical Principles 130 (1891) (defining "employment" as, among other things, "[t]he action or process of employing; the state of being employed. The service (of a person). That on which (one) is employed; business; occupation; a special errand or commission. A person's regular occupation or business; a trade or profession"); 3 The Century Dictionary and Cyclopedia 1904 (1914) (defining "employment" as "[w]ork or business of any kind"); W. Harris, Webster's New International Dictionary 718 (1st ed. 1909) (listing "work" as a synonym for "employment"); Webster's Collegiate Dictionary 329 (3d ed. 1916) (same); Black's Law Dictionary 422 (2d ed. 1910) ("an engagement or rendering services" for oneself or another); 3 Oxford English Dictionary 130 (1933) ("[t]hat on which (one) is employed; business; occupation; a special errand or commission").

[3]   *See, e.g., Lindsay v. McCaslin (Two Cases),* 123 Me. 197, 200, 122 A. 412, 413 (1923) ("When the contract of employment has been reduced to writing, the question whether the person employed was an independent contractor or merely a servant is determined by the court as a matter of law"); *Tankersley v. Webster,* 116 Okla. 208, 210, 243 P. 745, 747 (1925) ("[T]he contract of employment between Tankersley and Casey was admitted in evidence without objections, and we think conclusively shows that Casey was an independent contractor"); *Waldron v. Garland Pocahontas Coal Co.,* 89 W.Va. 426, 427, 109 S.E. 729 (1921) (syllabus) ("Whether a person performing work for another is an independent contractor depends upon a consideration of the contract of employment, the nature of the business, the circumstances under which the contract was made and the work was done"); *see also* App. to Brief for Respondent 1a–12a (citing additional examples).

independent contractors. That word choice may not mean everything, but it does supply further evidence still that Congress used the term "contracts of employment" in a broad sense to capture any contract for the performance of *work* by *workers*. . . .

What does New Prime have to say about the case building against it? Mainly, it seeks to shift the debate from the term "contracts of employment" to the word "employee." Today, the company emphasizes, the law often distinguishes between employees and independent contractors. Employees are generally understood as those who work "in the service of another person (the employer) under an express or implied contract of hire, under which the employer has the right to control the details of work performance." Black's Law Dictionary, at 639. Meanwhile, independent contractors are sometimes described as those "entrusted to undertake a specific project but who [are] left free to do the assigned work and to choose the method for accomplishing it." *Id.*, at 888. New Prime argues that, by 1925, the words "employee" and "independent contractor" had already assumed these distinct meanings. And given that, the company contends, the phrase "contracts of *employment*" should be understood to refer only to relationships between *employers and employees*.

Unsurprisingly, Mr. Oliveira disagrees. He replies that, while the term "employment" dates back many centuries, the word "employee" only made its first appearance in English in the 1800s. *See* Oxford English Dictionary (3d ed., Mar. 2014), www.oed.com/view/Entry/61374 (all Internet materials as last visited Jan. 9, 2019). At that time, the word from which it derived, "employ," simply meant to "apply (a thing) to some definite purpose." 3 J. Murray, A New English Dictionary on Historical Principles 129 (1891). And even in 1910, Black's Law Dictionary reported that the term "employee" had only "become somewhat naturalized in our language." Black's Law Dictionary 421 (2d ed. 1910).

Still, the parties do share some common ground. They agree that the word "employee" eventually came into wide circulation and came to denote those who work for a wage at the direction of another. They agree, too, that all this came to pass in part because the word "employee" didn't suffer from the same "historical baggage" of the older common law term "servant," and because it proved useful when drafting legislation to regulate burgeoning industries and their labor forces in the early 20th century. The parties even agree that the development of the term "employee" may have come to influence and narrow our understanding of the word "employment" in comparatively recent years and may be why today it might signify to some a "relationship between master and servant."

But if the parties' extended etymological debate persuades us of anything, it is that care is called for. The words "employee" and "employment" may share a common root and an intertwined history. But they also developed at different times and in at least some different ways.

The only question in this case concerns the meaning of the term "contracts of *employment*" in 1925. And, whatever the word "employee" may have meant at that time, and however it may have later influenced the meaning of "employment," the evidence before us remains that, as dominantly understood in 1925, a contract of *employment* did not necessarily imply the existence of an employer-employee or master-servant relationship.

When New Prime finally turns its attention to the term in dispute, it directs us to Coppage v. Kansas, 236 U.S. 1, 13 (1915). There and in other cases like it, New Prime notes, courts sometimes used the phrase "contracts of employment" to describe what today we'd recognize as agreements between employers and employees. But this proves little. No one doubts that employer-employee agreements to perform work qualified as "contracts of employment" in 1925—and documenting that fact does nothing to negate the possibility that "contracts of employment" *also* embraced agreements by independent contractors to perform work. Coming a bit closer to the mark, New Prime eventually cites a handful of early 20th-century legal materials that seem to use the term "contracts of employment" to refer *exclusively* to employer-employee agreements. But from the record amassed before us, these authorities appear to represent at most the vanguard, not the main body, of contemporaneous usage.

New Prime's effort to explain away the statute's suggestive use of the term "worker" proves no more compelling. The company reminds us that the statute excludes "contracts of employment" for "seamen" and "railroad employees" as well as other transportation workers. And because "seamen" and "railroad employees" included *only* employees in 1925, the company reasons, we should understand "any other class of workers engaged in . . . interstate commerce" to bear a similar construction. But this argument rests on a precarious premise. At the time of the Act's passage, shipboard surgeons who tended injured sailors were considered "seamen" though they likely served in an independent contractor capacity. Even the term "railroad employees" may have swept more broadly at the time of the Act's passage than might seem obvious today. In 1922, for example, the Railroad Labor Board interpreted the word "employee" in the Transportation Act of 1920 to refer to anyone "engaged in the customary work directly contributory to the operation of the railroads." And the Erdman Act, a statute enacted to address disruptive railroad strikes at the end of the 19th century, seems to evince an equally broad understanding of "railroad employees." . . .

When Congress enacted the Arbitration Act in 1925, the term "contracts of employment" referred to agreements to perform work. No less than those who came before him, Mr. Oliveira is entitled to the benefit of that same understanding today. Accordingly, his agreement with New Prime falls within § 1's exception, the court of appeals was correct that it lacked authority under the Act to order arbitration, and the judgment is

Affirmed.

■ JUSTICE GINSBURG, concurring.

"[W]ords generally should be 'interpreted as taking their ordinary . . . meaning . . . at the time Congress enacted the statute.' " The Court so reaffirms, and I agree. Looking to the period of enactment to gauge statutory meaning ordinarily fosters fidelity to the "regime . . . Congress established." MCI Telecommunications Corp. v. American Telephone & Telegraph Co., 512 U.S. 218, 234 (1994).

Congress, however, may design legislation to govern changing times and circumstances. *See, e.g.*, Kimble v. Marvel Entertainment, LLC, 135 S.Ct. 2401, 2412 (2015) ("Congress . . . intended [the Sherman Antitrust Act's] reference to 'restraint of trade' to have 'changing content,' and authorized courts to oversee the term's 'dynamic potential.' " (quoting Business Electronics Corp. v. Sharp Electronics Corp., 485 U.S. 717, 731– 732 (1988))); SEC v. Zandford, 535 U.S. 813, 819 (2002) (In enacting the Securities Exchange Act, "Congress sought to substitute a philosophy of full disclosure for the philosophy of caveat emptor . . . . Consequently, . . . the statute should be construed not technically and restrictively, but flexibly to effectuate its remedial purposes." (internal quotation marks and paragraph break omitted)); H.J. Inc. v. Northwestern Bell Telephone Co., 492 U.S. 229, 243 (1989) ("The limits of the relationship and continuity concepts that combine to define a [Racketeer Influenced and Corrupt Organizations] pattern . . . cannot be fixed in advance with such clarity that it will always be apparent whether in a particular case a 'pattern of racketeering activity' exists. The development of these concepts must await future cases. . . ."). As these illustrations suggest, sometimes, "[w]ords in statutes can enlarge or contract their scope as other changes, in law or in the world, require their application to new instances or make old applications anachronistic." West v. Gibson, 527 U.S. 212, 218 (1999).

NOTE: "ORIGINAL" STATUTORY MEANING

The majority's approach in *Oliveira* has an intuitive appeal for its apparent connection to meaning at the moment of the statute's enactment. Nevertheless, its temporally-oriented inquiry may result in potential uncertainties if applied more broadly to statutory interpretation questions of first impression.

First, an approach that seeks the original ordinary (or "public") meaning of a statutory term raises interesting methodological problems. First, the problem of notice: in *Oliveira*, the majority gave the term "contracts of employment" its "original" meaning "at the time Congress enacted the statute," and suggested that even if the *ordinary* meaning of a term "drifts" over time, the statute's *legal* meaning should not change. (Though note, as you will see in *Bostock v. Clayton County, infra*, that the inverse may sometimes be true as well.) Does this approach raise rule-of-law issues if the "ordinary meaning" of a statutory term as commonly used and understood *today* is not what it *legally* means according to courts? Can you imagine circumstances where this approach could undermine the capacity for the statute to give notice to those it regulates?

Second, recall the typology of interpretive methods in Section III.B.1, *supra*. Broadly speaking, courts employ interpretive methods to determine one of three (potentially overlapping) meanings of a statutory term or phrase:

(1) the drafters' intended meaning;

(2) the meaning as understood by the reasonable reader of the statute; and/or

(3) the meaning that, for rule of law reasons, is the best *legal* meaning to be attributed to that statutory term or phrase.

Most textualists resist attributing to a statutory term its meaning *as intended by the statute's drafters*. (Contrast this approach with Chief Justice Rugg's conviction in *Welosky*, *supra*, that the Massachusetts legislators who enacted the statute governing jury duty could not possibly have intended that women serve as jurors.) Some textualists argue that any evidence of the drafters' intentions in the legislative history may be inherently unreliable as a source of statutory meaning. Others who are skeptical of interpretive methods revealing the "legislative intent" have noted that "Congress is a they, not an it," so a legislative body cannot have a single coherent intention concerning any given term's "intended" meaning. Most textualists thus generally rule out the drafters' intentions as a basis for deciding on the meaning of ambiguous statutory text.

Instead, textualists generally seek to attribute to a statutory term its *"ordinary"* meaning, the meaning as understood by the reasonable reader. But recall that the "reasonable reader's understanding" may refer either to (a) the *original* reasonable reader's understanding at the time of the statute's enactment; or (b) the *contemporary* reasonable reader's understanding at the time the interpretive problem arises. According to the majority in *Oliveira*, where the original and contemporary readers' understandings might conflict, the original reader's understanding should prevail over the contemporary reader's. What is the basis for limiting a statute's meaning to the meaning understood by the reasonable reader *at the time of enactment*? The majority in *Oliveira* references the possibility of reliance issues. However, in any case of first impression, the term's meaning may be *inherently* unsettled; absent authoritative guidance from relevant agency officials or courts, *either* party could make a claim of legal reliance based on *its* understanding of what the statute meant at the time of enactment. Reliance interests, then, can carry only so much weight.

Relatedly, if the term's legal meaning has not remained fixed over time, why should the historical reader's understanding prevail over the contemporary reasonable reader's? Arguably, the enacting-era reasonable reader would understand better than today's readers what the statute was supposed to mean at the time it was enacted. But whose intended meaning was that? The legislative drafters'! Unless the term was indisputably clear at the time of enactment, is there reason to think that a (potentially haphazard) collection of historical sources of ordinary usage will furnish more reliable indicia of intended meaning than the legislative history of the statute?

The same temporality quandary may arise when divining the drafters' intentions about whether the statute's meaning and potential applications should evolve over time. On some occasions, evidence suggests the legislative drafters intended the meaning of the statutory provision to stay fixed at the time of its enactment (as the *Welosky* court claimed). Other times, legislators select an open-ended term precisely so the statutory provision can be interpreted dynamically over time, as social problems and practices evolve (as the *Maxwell* court determined). In the latter circumstances, would a judge be an "unfaithful" agent of the legislature if she imposed a temporally-fixed meaning on a statutory term that the legislature intended to evolve over time? What clues in the statutory text might indicate that a particular term or provision should be given a dynamic rather than static meaning? For example, should common-law terms of art presumptively be given more dynamic meanings than other statutory terms that do not have common-law origins? (*Cf.* State Oil Co. v. Khan, 522 U.S. 3, 21 (1997) ("[T]he term 'restraint of trade', as used in § 1 [of the Sherman Act], also invokes the common law itself, and not merely the static content that the common law had assigned to the term in 1890." (internal quotation marks omitted)). Recall also the Court's interpretation of the "falsely made" security prohibition in *Moskal, supra* Section IV.A. Was the majority's approach in that case at odds with the majority in *Oliveira*? Why or why not?

Third, the majority's approach also raises potential epistemological problems, because the "original reasonable reader's understanding" is a hypothetical construct developed by contemporary judges, not an actual historical person's real understanding. But actual persons often disagree about meaning, even at the time of enactment. Recall the legal question in *King v. Burwell* in Section III.A.2.a, *supra*: whether the phrase "an Exchange established by the State" as used in the Affordable Care Act included an Exchange established by the federal government (on behalf of a State). That question arose in the years immediately after the ACA's enactment, and it was heavily contested by both opponents and supporters of the law. Prior to the Supreme Court's decision in *King*, would it have made sense to say that a settled "ordinary" meaning of that statutory phrase existed? What about "carry[ing] a firearm," as in *Muscarello*? If a term or phrase's meaning was heavily contested even at the time of the statute's enactment, would it be reasonable to conclude that *any* future court's quest for an original ordinary meaning will necessarily be an exercise in frustration, or at least in subjectivity?

Finally, consider how, methodologically, a court is supposed to derive the original ordinary meaning of a statutory term or phrase. In *Oliveira*, the majority notes that the term "contract of employment" had no settled *legal* meaning, but that courts during the relevant period tended to include among "contract[s] of employment" any contracts that involved independent contractors. If there was no settled legal meaning, but *some* interpreters in exclusively *legal* settings attributed a particular meaning to the term, is that adequate evidence to establish a statutory term's *ordinary* meaning at that time? Note also that the contemporary interpreter must often weigh competing evidence of historical usage and meaning to decide which of two or more hypothetical historical readings is more reasonable. How much evidence of agreement about original ordinary meaning at the time of enactment must be found to conclude there *was* an established ordinary meaning? Are judges and lawyers—as opposed to historians or linguists— well-suited to engage in such inquiries?

1. CASE STUDY IN PREVENTING SEX DISCRIMINATION IN EMPLOYMENT

Tensions in statutory interpretation can arise not only from changes in linguistic meaning and evolving social mores, but also as a result of experience applying the statute to a range of behaviors and practices. As a result, courts sometimes apply statutes to circumstances unlikely to have been "central" to the legislators' objectives in enacting the statute (in other words, to circumstances which may not correspond to the *principal* evil to be remedied), but which fit somewhat comfortably (or uncomfortably) within the broader ambit of both the statutory scheme and the specific textual instruction at issue. Consider, for example, Justice Scalia's statement in Oncale v. Sundowner Offshore Services, Inc., 523 U.S. 75, 79–80 (1998). In *Oncale*, the Court addressed whether workplace harassment against an employee of the same sex as the harasser can violate Title VII's prohibition against "discriminat[ion] . . . because of . . . sex," 42 U.S.C. § 2000e–2(a)(1). Justice Scalia, writing for the Court, concluded that:

> We see no justification in the statutory language or our precedents for a categorical rule excluding same-sex harassment claims from the coverage of Title VII. As some courts have observed, male-on-male sexual harassment in the workplace was assuredly not the principal evil Congress was concerned with when it enacted Title VII. But statutory prohibitions often go beyond the principal evil to cover reasonably comparable evils, and it is ultimately the provisions of our laws rather than the principal concerns of our legislators by which we are governed. Title VII prohibits "discriminat[ion] . . . because of . . . sex" in the "terms" or "conditions" of employment. Our holding that this includes sexual harassment must extend to sexual harassment of any kind that meets the statutory requirements.

Scalia's observations in *Oncale* took on new life, as litigants pressed courts to confront whether one of the "principal evil[s]" Title VII seeks to prohibit—discrimination against women "because of . . . sex"—would also prohibit employment discrimination against LGBTQ individuals. This case study examines the evolving applications of Title VII as the statute has been interpreted over time.

The Texts to Be Construed: Title VII and Executive Branch Enforcement Guidance

a.   RELEVANT STATUTORY PROVISIONS PROHIBITING
     DISCRIMINATION IN EMPLOYMENT

Civil Rights Act of 1964
United States Code, Title 42, Chapter. 21.

§ 2000e–2   [Section 703 of the Act]. Unlawful employment practices

(a) Employer practices

It shall be an unlawful employment practice for an employer—

(1) to fail or refuse to hire or to discharge any individual, or otherwise to discriminate against any individual with respect to his compensation, terms, conditions, or privileges of employment, because of such individual's race, color, religion, sex, or national origin; or

(2) to limit, segregate, or classify his employees or applicants for employment in any way which would deprive or tend to deprive any individual of employment opportunities or otherwise adversely affect his status as an employee, because of such individual's race, color, religion, sex, or national origin. . . .

§ 2000e [Section 701 of the Act]. Definitions

For the purposes of this chapter—. . .

(k) The terms "because of sex" or "on the basis of sex" include, but are not limited to, because of or on the basis of pregnancy, childbirth, or related medical conditions; and women affected by pregnancy, childbirth, or related medical conditions shall be treated the same for all employment—related purposes, including receipt of benefits under fringe benefit programs, as other persons not so affected but similar in their ability or inability to work, and nothing in section 2000e–2(h) of this title [section 703(h), seniority or merit system] shall be interpreted to permit otherwise. . . . [Added to Title VII by the Pregnancy Discrimination Act of 1978, Pub. L. 95–555.]

b.   A JUDICIAL INTERPRETATION OF TITLE VII THAT ELICITS
     CONGRESSIONAL RESPONSE

A decade after Title VII's enactment as part of the Civil Rights Act of 1964, the Supreme Court upheld an employee health plan that covered all employee medical conditions, except pregnancy. Although the majority acknowledged that only women could become pregnant, it ruled that the plan's discrimination because of pregnancy was not "because of sex." Writing for a five-member majority, with Justice Blackmun concurring in part, Justice Rehnquist echoed the Court's then-recent pronouncement in Geduldig v. Aiello, 417 U.S. 484 (1974), which ruled that "a strikingly similar disability plan" for California state employees did not violate the equal protection clause of the 14th amendment:

> "[T]his case is thus a far cry from cases like Reed v. Reed, 404 U.S. 71 (1971), and Frontiero v. Richardson, 411 U.S. 677 (1973), involving discrimination based upon gender as such. The California insurance program does not exclude anyone from benefit eligibility because of gender but merely removes one physical condition—pregnancy—from the list of compensable disabilities. While it is true that only women can become pregnant, it does not follow that every legislative classification concerning pregnancy is a sex-based classification like those considered in *Reed*, and *Frontiero*. Normal pregnancy is an objectively identifiable physical condition with unique characteristics. Absent a showing that distinctions involving pregnancy are mere pretexts designed to effect an invidious discrimination against the members of one sex or the other, lawmakers are constitutionally free to include or exclude pregnancy from the coverage of legislation such as this on any reasonable basis, just as with respect to any other physical condition.
>
> > "The lack of identity between the excluded disability and gender as such under this insurance program becomes clear upon the most cursory analysis. The program divides potential recipients into two groups—pregnant women and nonpregnant persons. While the first group is exclusively female, the second includes members of both sexes." [Citation.]
>
> The quoted language from *Geduldig* leaves no doubt that our reason for rejecting appellee's equal protection claim in that case was that the exclusion of pregnancy from coverage under California's disability-benefits plan was not in itself discrimination based on sex.

Outcry over the Court's interpretation of "because of sex" led Congress to pass, less than two years later, the Pregnancy Discrimination Act of 1978, adding to Title VII the definition in section 701(k) quoted above. (For further discussion of *Gilbert* and the PDA, *see Newport News Shipbuilding and Dry Dock v. EEOC* and *AT&T Corp. v. Noreen Hulteen, infra* Sections VII.C.2 and 3.)

c.   EXECUTIVE BRANCH GUIDANCE: CONFLICTING 2014 AND 2017
ATTORNEY GENERAL MEMORANDA REGARDING THE TREATMENT
OF TRANSGENDER EMPLOYMENT DISCRIMINATION CLAIMS UNDER
TITLE VII

In 2014 the Department of Justice, under the Obama administration, issued an interpretive memorandum construing Title VII to cover claims of sex discrimination by transgender employees. In 2017, the Trump administration reversed that position, and stated that "Title VII does not prohibit discrimination based on gender identity *per se*." The two memoranda follow. Based on the materials you studied in Part V, *supra*, how much, if any, deference do you think is due either document?

Office of the Attorney General [2014 Memorandum re: Transgender Employment Discrimination Claims]

December 15, 2014.

TO: UNITED STATES ATTORNEYS

             HEADS OF DEPARTMENT COMPONENTS

FROM: THE ATTORNEY GENERAL

SUBJECT: Treatment of Transgender Employment Discrimination
             Claims Under Title VII of the Civil Rights Act of 1964

Title VII of the Civil Rights Act of 1964 makes it unlawful for employers to discriminate in the employment of an individual "because of such individual's ... sex." 42 U.S.C. § 2000e2(a) (prohibiting discrimination by private employers and by state and local governments); 42 U.S.C. § 2000e–16(a) (providing that personnel actions by federal agencies "shall be made free from any discrimination based on ... sex"). Title VII's prohibition of sex discrimination is a strong and vital principle that underlies the integrity of our workforce. In a variety of judicial and administrative contexts, however, questions have arisen concerning the appropriate legal standard for establishing claims of gender identity discrimination, including discrimination claims raised by transgender employees.[1]

Many courts have recognized that gender identity discrimination claims may be established under a "sex-stereotyping" theory. Following the Supreme Court's decision in Price Waterhouse v. Hopkins, 490 U.S. 228 (1989), courts have interpreted Title VII's prohibition of discrimination because of "sex" as barring discrimination based on a perceived failure to conform to socially constructed characteristics of males and females. [Citations.] But courts have reached varying

---

[1] Guidance from the Office of Personnel Management states that "[t]ransgender individuals are people with a gender identity that is different from the sex assigned to them at birth," and defines "gender identity" as an individual's "internal sense of being male or female." *See* http://www.opm.gov/diversity/Transgender/Guidance.asp.

conclusions about whether discrimination based on gender identity in and of itself—including transgender status—constitutes discrimination based on sex. [Citations.]

The federal government's approach to this issue has also evolved over time. In 2006, the Department stated in litigation that Title VII's prohibition of discrimination based on sex did not cover discrimination based on transgender status or gender identity per se; the district court rejected that position. [Citation.] Subsequently, in 2011, the Office of Personnel Management issued guidance announcing that the federal government's policy of providing a workplace free of discrimination based on sex includes a prohibition against discrimination based on gender identity. In 2012, the Equal Employment Opportunity Commission ruled that discrimination on the basis of gender identity is discrimination on the basis of sex. Macy v. Holder, Appeal No. 0120120821 (EEOC April 20, 2012). More recently, the President announced that discrimination based on gender identity is prohibited for purposes of federal employment and government contracting. *See* Executive Order 13672 (July 21, 2014); *see also* U.S. Dep't of Labor Directive 2014–02 (August 19, 2014).

After considering the text of Title VII, the relevant Supreme Court case law interpreting the statute, and the developing jurisprudence in this area, I have determined that the best reading. of Title VII's prohibition of sex discrimination is that it encompasses discrimination based on gender identity, including transgender status. The most straightforward reading of Title VII is that discrimination "because of . . . sex" includes discrimination because an employee's gender identification is as a member of a particular sex, or because the employee is transitioning, or has transitioned, to another sex. As the Court explained in *Price Waterhouse*, by using "the simple words 'because of,' . . . Congress meant to obligate" a Title VII plaintiff to prove only "that the employer relied upon sex-based considerations in coming to its decision." 490 U.S. at 241–242. It follows that, as a matter of plain meaning, Title VII's prohibition against discrimination "because of . . . sex" encompasses discrimination founded on sex-based considerations, including discrimination based on an employee's transitioning to, or identifying as, a different sex altogether. Although Congress may not have had such claims in mind when it enacted Title VII, the Supreme Court has made clear that Title VII must be interpreted according to its plain text, noting that "statutory prohibitions often go beyond the principal evil to cover reasonably comparable evils, and it is ultimately the provisions of our laws rather than the principal concerns of our legislators by which we are governed." Oncale v. Sundowner Offshore Servs., 523 U.S. 75, 79 (1998).

For these reasons, the Department will no longer assert that Title VII's prohibition against discrimination based on sex does not encompass gender identity per se (including transgender discrimination).[2] This memorandum is not intended to otherwise prescribe the course of litigation or defenses that should be raised in any particular employment discrimination case. The application of Title VII to any given case will necessarily turn on the specific facts at hand. My hope, however, is that this clarification of the Department's position will foster consistent treatment of claimants throughout the government, in furtherance of this Department's commitment to fair and impartial justice for all Americans. If you have questions about this memorandum or its application in a case, please contact your Civil Chief or your Component's Front Office.

Office of the Attorney General [2017 Memorandum re: Revised Treatment of Transgender Employment Discrimination Claims]

October 4, 2017.

TO: UNITED STATES ATTORNEYS

HEADS OF DEPARTMENT COMPONENTS

FROM: THE ATTORNEY GENERAL

SUBJECT: Revised Treatment of Transgender Employment Discrimination Claims Under Title VII of the Civil Rights Act of 1964

Title VII of the Civil Rights Act of 1964 makes it unlawful for employers to discriminate in the employment of an individual "because of such individual's . . . sex." 42 U.S.C. § 2000e–2(a) (prohibiting discrinlination by private employers and by state and local governments); 42 U.S.C. § 2000e–16(a) (providing that personnel actions by federal agencies "shall be made free from any discrimination based on . . . sex"). Title VII's prohibition of sex discrimination is a strong and vital principle that underlies the integrity of our workforce.

The question of whether Title VII's prohibition on sex discrimination encompasses discrimination based on gender identity per se, including discrimination against transgender individuals, arises in a variety of contexts. In a December 15, 2014, memorandum, Attorney General Holder concluded that Title VII does encompass such discrimination, based on his view that Title VII prohibits employers from taking into account "sex-based considerations." Memo. at 2; *see also id.* at n.1 (defining "gender identity" and "transgender individuals").

Although federal law, including Title VII, provides various protections to transgender individuals, Title VII does not prohibit discrimination based on gender identity *per se*. This is a conclusion of law, not policy. The sole issue addressed in this memorandum is what

---

[2] "Sex-stereotyping" remains an available theory under which to bring a Title VII claim, including a claim by a transgender individual, in cases where the evidence supports that theory.

conduct Title VII prohibits by its terms, not what conduct should be prohibited by statute, regulation, or employer action. As a law enforcement agency, the Department of Justice must interpret Title VII as written by Congress.

Title VII expressly prohibits discrimination "because of . . . sex" and several other protected traits, but it does not refer to gender identity. "Sex" is ordinarily defined to mean biologically male or female. [Citations.] Congress has confirmed this ordinary meaning by expressly prohibiting, in several other statutes, "gender identity" discrimination, which Congress lists in addition to, rather than within, prohibitions on discrimination based on "sex" or "gender." *See, e.g.*, 18 U.S.C. § 249(a)(2); 42 U.S.C. § 13925(b)(13)(A). Furthermore, the Supreme Court has explained that "[t]he critical issue, Title VII's text indicates, is whether members of one sex are exposed to disadvantageous terms or conditions of employment [or other employment actions] to which members of the other sex are not exposed." *Oncale v. Sundowner Offshore Servs., Inc.*, 523 U.S. 75, 80 (1998). Although Title VII bars "sex stereotypes" insofar as that particular sort of "sex-based consideration[ ]" causes "disparate treatment of men and women," *Price Waterhouse v. Hopkins*, 490 U.S. 228, 242, 251 (1989) (plurality op.), Title VII is not properly construed to proscribe employment practices (such as sex-specific bathrooms) that take account of the sex of employees but do not impose different burdens on similarly situated members of each sex. [Citation.]

Accordingly, Title VII's prohibition on sex discrimination encompasses discrimination between men and women but does not encompass discrimination based on gender identity per se, including transgender status. Therefore, as of the date of this memorandum, which hereby withdraws the December 15, 2014, memorandum, the Department of Justice will take that position in all pending and future matters (except where controlling lower-court precedent dictates otherwise, in which event the issue should be preserved for potential further review).

The Justice Department must and will continue to affirm the dignity of all people, including transgender individuals. Nothing in this memorandum should be construed to condone mistreatment on the basis of gender identity, or to express a policy view on whether Congress should amend Title VII to provide different or additional protections. Nor does this memorandum remove or reduce the protections against discrimination on the basis of sex that Congress has provided all individuals, including transgender individuals, under Title VII. In addition, the Matthew Shepard and James Byrd, Jr., Hate Crimes Prevention Act and the Violence Against Women Reauthorization Act prohibit gender identity discrimination along with other types of discrimination in certain contexts. 18 U.S.C. § 249(a)(2); 42 U.S.C. § 13925(b)(13)(A). The Department of Justice has vigorously enforced such laws, and will continue to do so, on behalf of all Americans, including transgender Americans.

If you have questions about this memorandum or its application in a case, please contact your Civil Chief or your Component's Front Office.

Bostock v. Clayton County

Supreme Court of the United States, 2020.
140 S.Ct. 1731, 207 L.Ed.2d 218.

■ JUSTICE GORSUCH delivered the opinion of the Court[, in which CHIEF JUSTICE ROBERTS, JUSTICE GINSBURG, JUSTICE BREYER, JUSTICE SOTOMAYOR, and JUSTICE KAGAN joined].

Sometimes small gestures can have unexpected consequences. Major initiatives practically guarantee them. In our time, few pieces of federal legislation rank in significance with the Civil Rights Act of 1964. There, in Title VII, Congress outlawed discrimination in the workplace on the basis of race, color, religion, sex, or national origin. Today, we must decide whether an employer can fire someone simply for being homosexual or transgender. The answer is clear. An employer who fires an individual for being homosexual or transgender fires that person for traits or actions it would not have questioned in members of a different sex. Sex plays a necessary and undisguisable role in the decision, exactly what Title VII forbids.

Those who adopted the Civil Rights Act might not have anticipated their work would lead to this particular result. Likely, they weren't thinking about many of the Act's consequences that have become apparent over the years, including its prohibition against discrimination on the basis of motherhood or its ban on the sexual harassment of male employees. But the limits of the drafters' imagination supply no reason to ignore the law's demands. When the express terms of a statute give us one answer and extratextual considerations suggest another, it's no contest. Only the written word is the law, and all persons are entitled to its benefit.

I

Few facts are needed to appreciate the legal question we face. Each of the three cases before us started the same way: An employer fired a long-time employee shortly after the employee revealed that he or she is homosexual or transgender—and allegedly for no reason other than the employee's homosexuality or transgender status.

Gerald Bostock worked for Clayton County, Georgia, as a child welfare advocate. Under his leadership, the county won national awards for its work. After a decade with the county, Mr. Bostock began participating in a gay recreational softball league. Not long after that, influential members of the community allegedly made disparaging comments about Mr. Bostock's sexual orientation and participation in the league. Soon, he was fired for conduct "unbecoming" a county employee.

Donald Zarda worked as a skydiving instructor at Altitude Express in New York. After several seasons with the company, Mr. Zarda mentioned that he was gay and, days later, was fired.

Aimee Stephens worked at R.G. & G.R. Harris Funeral Homes in Garden City, Michigan. When she got the job, Ms. Stephens presented as a male. But two years into her service with the company, she began treatment for despair and loneliness. Ultimately, clinicians diagnosed her with gender dysphoria and recommended that she begin living as a woman. In her sixth year with the company, Ms. Stephens wrote a letter to her employer explaining that she planned to "live and work full-time as a woman" after she returned from an upcoming vacation. The funeral home fired her before she left, telling her "this is not going to work out." . . .

II

This Court normally interprets a statute in accord with the ordinary public meaning of its terms at the time of its enactment. After all, only the words on the page constitute the law adopted by Congress and approved by the President. If judges could add to, remodel, update, or detract from old statutory terms inspired only by extratextual sources and our own imaginations, we would risk amending statutes outside the legislative process reserved for the people's representatives. And we would deny the people the right to continue relying on the original meaning of the law they have counted on to settle their rights and obligations. *See* New Prime Inc. v. Oliveira, 586 U.S. ___, ___–___, 139 S.Ct. 532, 538–539 (2019).

With this in mind, our task is clear. We must determine the ordinary public meaning of Title VII's command that it is "unlawful . . . for an employer to fail or refuse to hire or to discharge any individual, or otherwise to discriminate against any individual with respect to his compensation, terms, conditions, or privileges of employment, because of such individual's race, color, religion, sex, or national origin." § 2000e–2(a)(1). To do so, we orient ourselves to the time of the statute's adoption, here 1964, and begin by examining the key statutory terms in turn before assessing their impact on the cases at hand and then confirming our work against this Court's precedents.

A

The only statutorily protected characteristic at issue in today's cases is "sex"—and that is also the primary term in Title VII whose meaning the parties dispute. Appealing to roughly contemporaneous dictionaries, the employers say that, as used here, the term "sex" in 1964 referred to "status as either male or female [as] determined by reproductive biology." The employees counter by submitting that, even in 1964, the term bore a broader scope, capturing more than anatomy and reaching at least some norms concerning gender identity and sexual orientation. But because nothing in our approach to these cases turns on the outcome of the parties' debate, and because the employees concede the point for argument's sake, we proceed on the assumption that "sex" signified what the employers suggest, referring only to biological distinctions between male and female.

Still, that's just a starting point. The question isn't just what "sex" meant, but what Title VII says about it. Most notably, the statute prohibits employers from taking certain actions "because of" sex. And, as this Court has previously explained, "the ordinary meaning of 'because of' is 'by reason of' or 'on account of.' " [Citations.] In the language of law, this means that Title VII's "because of" test incorporates the " 'simple' " and "traditional" standard of but-for causation. [Citation.] That form of causation is established whenever a particular outcome would not have happened "but for" the purported cause. [Citation.] In other words, a but-for test directs us to change one thing at a time and see if the outcome changes. If it does, we have found a but-for cause.

No doubt, Congress could have taken a more parsimonious approach. As it has in other statutes, it could have added "solely" to indicate that actions taken "because of" the confluence of multiple factors do not violate the law. [Citation.] Or it could have written "primarily because of" to indicate that the prohibited factor had to be the main cause of the defendant's challenged employment decision. [Citation.] But none of this is the law we have. If anything, Congress has moved in the opposite direction, supplementing Title VII in 1991 to allow a plaintiff to prevail merely by showing that a protected trait like sex was a "motivating factor" in a defendant's challenged employment practice. Civil Rights Act of 1991, § 107, 105 Stat. 1075, codified at 42 U.S.C. § 2000e–2(m). Under this more forgiving standard, liability can sometimes follow even if sex *wasn't* a but-for cause of the employer's challenged decision. Still, because nothing in our analysis depends on the motivating factor test, we focus on the more traditional but-for causation standard that continues to afford a viable, if no longer exclusive, path to relief under Title VII. § 2000e–2(a)(1).

As sweeping as even the but-for causation standard can be, Title VII does not concern itself with everything that happens "because of" sex. The statute imposes liability on employers only when they "fail or refuse to hire," "discharge," "or otherwise ... discriminate against" someone because of a statutorily protected characteristic like sex. *Ibid.* The employers acknowledge that they discharged the plaintiffs in today's cases, but assert that the statute's list of verbs is qualified by the last item on it: "otherwise ... discriminate against." By virtue of the word *otherwise*, the employers suggest, Title VII concerns itself not with every discharge, only with those discharges that involve discrimination.

Accepting this point, too, for argument's sake, the question becomes: What did "discriminate" mean in 1964? As it turns out, it meant then roughly what it means today: "To make a difference in treatment or favor (of one as compared with others)." Webster's New International Dictionary 745 (2d ed. 1954). To "discriminate against" a person, then, would seem to mean treating that individual worse than others who are similarly situated. [Citation.] In so-called "disparate treatment" cases like today's, this Court has also held that the difference in treatment based on sex must be intentional. [Citation.] So, taken together, an employer who intentionally treats a person worse because of sex—such as by firing the person for actions or attributes it would tolerate in an individual of another sex—discriminates against that person in violation of Title VII.

At first glance, another interpretation might seem possible. Discrimination sometimes involves "the act, practice, or an instance of discriminating categorically rather than individually." Webster's New Collegiate Dictionary 326 (1975); [citation]. On that understanding, the statute would require us to consider the employer's treatment of groups rather than individuals, to see how a policy affects one sex as a whole versus the other as a whole. That idea holds some intuitive appeal too. Maybe the law concerns itself simply with ensuring that employers don't treat women generally less favorably than they do men. So how can we tell which sense, individual or group, "discriminate" carries in Title VII?

The statute answers that question directly. It tells us three times— including immediately after the words "discriminate against"—that our focus should be on individuals, not groups: Employers may not "fail or refuse to hire or ... discharge any *individual,* or otherwise ... discriminate against any *individual* with respect to his compensation, terms, conditions, or privileges of employment, because of such *individual's* ... sex." § 2000e–2(a)(1) (emphasis added). And the meaning of "individual" was as uncontroversial in 1964 as it is today: "A particular being as distinguished from a class, species, or collection." Webster's New International Dictionary, at 1267. Here, again, Congress could have written the law differently. It might have said that "it shall be an unlawful employment practice to prefer one sex to the other in hiring, firing, or the terms or conditions of employment." It might have said that there should be no "sex discrimination," perhaps implying a focus on differential treatment between the two sexes as groups. More narrowly still, it could have forbidden only "sexist policies" against women as a class. But, once again, that is not the law we have.

The consequences of the law's focus on individuals rather than groups are anything but academic. Suppose an employer fires a woman for refusing his sexual advances. It's no defense for the employer to note that, while he treated that individual woman worse than he would have treated a man, he gives preferential treatment to female employees overall. The employer is liable for treating *this* woman worse in part because of her sex. Nor is it a defense for an employer to say it discriminates against both men and women because of sex. This statute works to protect individuals of both sexes from discrimination, and does so equally. . . .

B

From the ordinary public meaning of the statute's language at the time of the law's adoption, a straightforward rule emerges: An employer violates Title VII when it intentionally fires an individual employee based in part on sex. It doesn't matter if other factors besides the plaintiff's sex contributed to the decision. And it doesn't matter if the employer treated women as a group the same when compared to men as a group. If the employer intentionally relies in part on an individual employee's sex when deciding to discharge the employee—put differently, if changing the employee's sex would have yielded a different choice by the employer—a statutory violation has occurred. Title VII's message is "simple but momentous": An individual employee's sex is "not relevant to the selection, evaluation, or compensation of employees." Price Waterhouse v. Hopkins, 490 U.S. 228, 239 (1989) (plurality opinion).

The statute's message for our cases is equally simple and momentous: An individual's homosexuality or transgender status is not relevant to employment decisions. That's because it is impossible to discriminate against a person for being homosexual or transgender without discriminating against that individual based on sex. Consider, for example, an employer with two employees, both of whom are attracted to men. The two individuals are, to the employer's mind, materially identical in all respects, except that one is a man and the other a woman. If the employer fires the male employee for no reason other than the fact he is attracted to men, the employer discriminates against him for traits or actions it tolerates in his female colleague. Put differently, the employer intentionally singles out an employee to fire based in part on the employee's sex, and the affected employee's sex is a but-for cause of his discharge. Or take an employer who fires a transgender person who was identified as a male at birth but who now identifies as a female. If the employer retains an otherwise identical employee who was identified as female at birth, the employer intentionally penalizes a person identified as male at birth for traits or actions that it tolerates in an employee identified as female at birth. Again, the individual employee's sex plays an unmistakable and impermissible role in the discharge decision.

That distinguishes these cases from countless others where Title VII has nothing to say. Take an employer who fires a female employee for tardiness or incompetence or simply supporting the wrong sports team. Assuming the employer would not have tolerated the same trait in a man, Title VII stands silent. But unlike any of these other traits or actions, homosexuality and transgender status are inextricably bound up with sex. Not because homosexuality or transgender status are related to sex in some vague sense or because discrimination on these bases has some disparate impact on one sex or another, but because to discriminate on these grounds requires an employer to intentionally treat individual employees differently because of their sex.

Nor does it matter that, when an employer treats one employee worse because of that individual's sex, other factors may contribute to the decision. Consider an employer with a policy of firing any woman he discovers to be a Yankees fan. Carrying out that rule because an employee is a woman *and* a fan of the Yankees is a firing "because of sex" if the employer would have tolerated the same allegiance in a male employee. Likewise here. When an employer fires an employee because she is homosexual or transgender, two causal factors may be in play— *both* the individual's sex *and* something else (the sex to which the individual is attracted or with which the individual identifies). But Title VII doesn't care. If an employer would not have discharged an employee but for that individual's sex, the statute's causation standard is met, and liability may attach.

Reframing the additional causes in today's cases as additional intentions can do no more to insulate the employers from liability. Intentionally burning down a neighbor's house is arson, even if the perpetrator's ultimate intention (or motivation) is only to improve the view. No less, intentional discrimination based on sex violates Title VII, even if it is intended only as a means to achieving the employer's ultimate goal of discriminating against homosexual or transgender employees. There is simply no escaping the role intent plays here: Just as sex is necessarily a but-for *cause* when an employer discriminates against homosexual or transgender employees, an employer who discriminates on these grounds inescapably *intends* to rely on sex in its decisionmaking. Imagine an employer who has a policy of firing any employee known to be homosexual. The employer hosts an office holiday party and invites employees to bring their spouses. A model employee arrives and introduces a manager to Susan, the employee's wife. Will that employee be fired? If the policy works as the employer intends, the answer depends entirely on whether the model employee is a man or a woman. To be sure, that employer's ultimate goal might be to discriminate on the basis of sexual orientation. But to achieve that purpose the employer must, along the way, intentionally treat an employee worse based in part on that individual's sex.

An employer musters no better a defense by responding that it is equally happy to fire male *and* female employees who are homosexual or transgender. Title VII liability is not limited to employers who, through the sum of all of their employment actions, treat the class of men differently than the class of women. Instead, the law makes each instance of discriminating against an individual employee because of that individual's sex an independent violation of Title VII. So just as an employer who fires both Hannah and Bob for failing to fulfill traditional sex stereotypes doubles rather than eliminates Title VII liability, an employer who fires both Hannah and Bob for being gay or transgender does the same.

At bottom, these cases involve no more than the straightforward application of legal terms with plain and settled meanings. For an employer to discriminate against employees for being homosexual or transgender, the employer must intentionally discriminate against individual men and women in part because of sex. That has always been prohibited by Title VII's plain terms—and that "should be the end of the analysis." 883 F.3d at 135 (Cabranes, J., concurring in judgment).

C

If more support for our conclusion were required, there's no need to look far. All that the statute's plain terms suggest, this Court's cases have already confirmed. Consider three of our leading precedents.

In *Phillips v. Martin Marietta Corp.*, 400 U.S. 542 (1971) (*per curiam*), a company allegedly refused to hire women with young children, but did hire men with children the same age. Because its discrimination depended not only on the employee's sex as a female but also on the presence of another criterion—namely, being a parent of young children—the company contended it hadn't engaged in discrimination "because of" sex. The company maintained, too, that it hadn't violated the law because, as a whole, it tended to favor hiring women over men. Unsurprisingly by now, these submissions did not sway the Court. That an employer discriminates intentionally against an individual only in part because of sex supplies no defense to Title VII. Nor does the fact an employer may happen to favor women as a class.

In *Los Angeles Dept. of Water and Power v. Manhart*, 435 U.S. 702 (1978), an employer required women to make larger pension fund contributions than men. The employer sought to justify its disparate treatment on the ground that women tend to live longer than men, and thus are likely to receive more from the pension fund over time. By everyone's admission, the employer was not guilty of animosity against women or a "purely habitual assumptio[n] about a woman's inability to perform certain kinds of work"; instead, it relied on what appeared to be a statistically accurate statement about life expectancy. *Id.*, at 707–708. Even so, the Court recognized, a rule that appears evenhanded at the group level can prove discriminatory at the level of individuals. True, women as a class may live longer than men as a class. But "[t]he statute's focus on the individual is unambiguous," and any individual woman might make the larger pension contributions and still die as early as a man. *Id.*, at 708. Likewise, the Court dismissed as irrelevant the employer's insistence that its actions were motivated by a wish to achieve classwide equality between the sexes: An employer's intentional discrimination on the basis of sex is no more permissible when it is prompted by some further intention (or motivation), even one as prosaic as seeking to account for actuarial tables. *Ibid.* . . .

In Oncale v. Sundowner Offshore Services, Inc., 523 U.S. 75 (1998), a male plaintiff alleged that he was singled out by his male co-workers for sexual harassment. The Court held it was immaterial that members of the same sex as the victim committed the alleged discrimination. Nor did the Court concern itself with whether men as a group were subject to discrimination or whether something in addition to sex contributed to the discrimination, like the plaintiff's conduct or personal attributes. "[A]ssuredly," the case didn't involve "the principal evil Congress was concerned with when it enacted Title VII." *Id.*, at 79. But, the Court unanimously explained, it is "the provisions of our laws rather than the principal concerns of our legislators by which we are governed." *Ibid.* Because the plaintiff alleged that the harassment would not have taken place but for his sex—that is, the plaintiff would not have suffered similar treatment if he were female—a triable Title VII claim existed.

The lessons these cases hold for ours are by now familiar.

First, it's irrelevant what an employer might call its discriminatory practice, how others might label it, or what else might motivate it. In *Manhart*, the employer called its rule requiring women to pay more into the pension fund a "life expectancy" adjustment necessary to achieve sex equality. In *Phillips*, the employer could have accurately spoken of its policy as one based on "motherhood." In much the same way, today's employers might describe their actions as motivated by their employees' homosexuality or transgender status. But just as labels and additional intentions or motivations didn't make a difference in *Manhart* or *Phillips*, they cannot make a difference here. When an employer fires an employee for being homosexual or transgender, it necessarily and intentionally discriminates against that individual in part because of sex. And that is all Title VII has ever demanded to establish liability.

Second, the plaintiff's sex need not be the sole or primary cause of the employer's adverse action. In *Phillips*, *Manhart*, and *Oncale*, the defendant easily could have pointed to some other, nonprotected trait and insisted it was the more important factor in the adverse employment outcome. So, too, it has no significance here if another factor—such as the sex the plaintiff is attracted to or presents as—might also be at work, or even play a more important role in the employer's decision.

Finally, an employer cannot escape liability by demonstrating that it treats males and females comparably as groups. As *Manhart* teaches, an employer is liable for intentionally requiring an individual female employee to pay more into a pension plan than a male counterpart even if the scheme promotes equality at the group level. Likewise, an employer who intentionally fires an individual homosexual or transgender employee in part because of that individual's sex violates the law even if the employer is willing to subject all male and female homosexual or transgender employees to the same rule.

III

What do the employers have to say in reply? For present purposes, they do not dispute that they fired the plaintiffs for being homosexual or transgender. Sorting out the true reasons for an adverse employment decision is often a hard business, but none of that is at issue here. Rather, the employers submit that even intentional discrimination against employees based on their homosexuality or transgender status supplies no basis for liability under Title VII.

The employers' argument proceeds in two stages. Seeking footing in the statutory text, they begin by advancing a number of reasons why discrimination on the basis of homosexuality or transgender status doesn't involve discrimination because of sex. But each of these arguments turns out only to repackage errors we've already seen and this Court's precedents have already rejected. In the end, the employers are left to retreat beyond the statute's text, where they fault us for ignoring the legislature's purposes in enacting Title VII or certain expectations about its operation. They warn, too, about consequences that might follow a ruling for the employees. But none of these contentions about what the employers think the law was meant to do, or should do, allow us to ignore the law as it is.

A

Maybe most intuitively, the employers assert that discrimination on the basis of homosexuality and transgender status aren't referred to as sex discrimination in ordinary conversation. If asked by a friend (rather than a judge) why they were fired, even today's plaintiffs would likely respond that it was because they were gay or transgender, not because of sex. According to the employers, that conversational answer, not the statute's strict terms, should guide our thinking and suffice to defeat any suggestion that the employees now before us were fired because of sex.

But this submission rests on a mistaken understanding of what kind of cause the law is looking for in a Title VII case. In conversation, a speaker is likely to focus on what seems most relevant or informative to the listener. So an employee who has just been fired is likely to identify the primary or most direct cause rather than list literally every but-for cause. To do otherwise would be tiring at best. But these conversational conventions do not control Title VII's legal analysis, which asks simply whether sex was a but-for cause. In *Phillips*, for example, a woman who was not hired under the employer's policy might have told her friends that her application was rejected because she was a mother, or because she had young children. Given that many women could be hired under the policy, it's unlikely she would say she was not hired because she was a woman. But the Court did not hesitate to recognize that the employer in *Phillips* discriminated against the plaintiff because of her sex. Sex wasn't the only factor, or maybe even the main factor, but it was one but-for cause—and that was enough. You can call the statute's but-for causation test what you will—expansive, legalistic, the dissents even dismiss it as wooden or literal. But it is the law.

Trying another angle, the defendants before us suggest that an employer who discriminates based on homosexuality or transgender status doesn't *intentionally* discriminate based on sex, as a disparate treatment claim requires. But, as we've seen, an employer who discriminates against homosexual or transgender employees necessarily and intentionally applies sex-based rules. An employer that announces it will not employ anyone who is homosexual, for example, intends to penalize male employees for being attracted to men and female employees for being attracted to women.

What, then, do the employers mean when they insist intentional discrimination based on homosexuality or transgender status isn't intentional discrimination based on sex? Maybe the employers mean they don't intend to harm one sex or the other as a class. But as should be clear by now, the statute focuses on discrimination against individuals, not groups. Alternatively, the employers may mean that they don't perceive themselves as motivated by a desire to discriminate based on sex. But nothing in Title VII turns on the employer's labels or any further intentions (or motivations) for its conduct beyond sex discrimination. In *Manhart*, the employer intentionally required women to make higher pension contributions only to fulfill the further purpose of making things more equitable between men and women as groups. In *Phillips*, the employer may have perceived itself as discriminating based on motherhood, not sex, given that its hiring policies as a whole *favored* women. But in both cases, the Court set all this aside as irrelevant. The employers' policies involved intentional discrimination because of sex, and Title VII liability necessarily followed.

Aren't these cases different, the employers ask, given that an employer could refuse to hire a gay or transgender individual without ever learning the applicant's sex? Suppose an employer asked homosexual or transgender applicants to tick a box on its application form. The employer then had someone else redact any information that could be used to discern sex. The resulting applications would disclose which individuals are homosexual or transgender without revealing whether they also happen to be men or women. Doesn't that possibility indicate that the employer's discrimination against homosexual or transgender persons cannot be sex discrimination?

No, it doesn't. Even in this example, the individual applicant's sex still weighs as a factor in the employer's decision. Change the hypothetical ever so slightly and its flaws become apparent. Suppose an employer's application form offered a single box to check if the applicant is either black or Catholic. If the employer refuses to hire anyone who checks that box, would we conclude the employer has complied with Title VII, so long as it studiously avoids learning any particular applicant's race or religion? Of course not: By intentionally setting out a rule that makes hiring turn on race or religion, the employer violates the law, whatever he might know or not know about individual applicants.

The same holds here. There is no way for an applicant to decide whether to check the homosexual or transgender box without considering sex. To see why, imagine an applicant doesn't know what the words homosexual or transgender mean. Then try writing out instructions for who should check the box without using the words man, woman, or sex (or some synonym). It can't be done. Likewise, there is no way an employer can discriminate against those who check the homosexual or transgender box without discriminating in part because of an applicant's sex. By discriminating against homosexuals, the employer intentionally penalizes men for being attracted to men and women for being attracted to women. By discriminating against transgender persons, the employer unavoidably discriminates against persons with one sex identified at birth and another today. Any way you slice it, the employer intentionally refuses to hire applicants in part because of the affected individuals' sex, even if it never learns any applicant's sex.

Next, the employers turn to Title VII's list of protected characteristics—race, color, religion, sex, and national origin. Because homosexuality and transgender status can't be found on that list and because they are conceptually distinct from sex, the employers reason, they are implicitly excluded from Title VII's reach. Put another way, if Congress had wanted to address these matters in Title VII, it would have referenced them specifically.

But that much does not follow. We agree that homosexuality and transgender status are distinct concepts from sex. But, as we've seen, discrimination based on homosexuality or transgender status necessarily entails discrimination based on sex; the first cannot happen without the second. Nor is there any such thing as a "canon of donut holes," in which Congress's failure to speak directly to a specific case that falls within a more general statutory rule creates a tacit exception. Instead, when Congress chooses not to include any exceptions to a broad rule, courts apply the broad rule. And that is exactly how this Court has always approached Title VII. "Sexual harassment" is conceptually distinct from sex discrimination, but it can fall within Title VII's sweep. *Oncale*, 523 U.S. at 79–80. Same with "motherhood discrimination." *See Phillips*, 400 U.S. at 544. Would the employers have us reverse those cases on the theory that Congress could have spoken to those problems more specifically? Of course not. As enacted, Title VII prohibits all forms of discrimination because of sex, however they may manifest themselves or whatever other labels might attach to them.

The employers try the same point another way. Since 1964, they observe, Congress has considered several proposals to add sexual orientation to Title VII's list of protected characteristics, but no such amendment has become law. Meanwhile, Congress has enacted other statutes addressing other topics that do discuss sexual orientation. This postenactment legislative history, they urge, should tell us something.

But what? There's no authoritative evidence explaining why later Congresses adopted other laws referencing sexual orientation but didn't amend this one. Maybe some in the later legislatures understood the impact Title VII's broad language already promised for cases like ours and didn't think a revision needed. Maybe others knew about its impact but hoped no one else would notice. Maybe still others, occupied by other concerns, didn't consider the issue at all. All we can know for certain is that speculation about why a later Congress declined to adopt new legislation offers a "particularly dangerous" basis on which to rest an interpretation of an existing law a different and earlier Congress did adopt. [Citations]; *Sullivan v. Finkelstein,* 496 U.S. 617, 632 (1990) (Scalia, J., concurring) ("Arguments based on subsequent legislative history . . . should not be taken seriously, not even in a footnote").

That leaves the employers to seek a different sort of exception. Maybe the traditional and simple but-for causation test should apply in all other Title VII cases, but it just doesn't work when it comes to cases involving homosexual and transgender employees. The test is too blunt to capture the nuances here. The employers illustrate their concern with an example. When we apply the simple test to Mr. Bostock—asking whether Mr. Bostock, a man attracted to other men, would have been fired had he been a woman—we don't just change his sex. Along the way, we change his sexual orientation too (from homosexual to heterosexual). If the aim is to isolate whether a plaintiff's sex caused the dismissal, the employers stress, we must hold sexual orientation constant—meaning we need to change both his sex and the sex to which he is attracted. So for Mr. Bostock, the question should be whether he would've been fired if he were a woman attracted to women. And because his employer would have been as quick to fire a lesbian as it was a gay man, the employers conclude, no Title VII violation has occurred.

While the explanation is new, the mistakes are the same. The employers might be onto something if Title VII only ensured equal treatment between groups of men and women or if the statute applied only when sex is the sole or primary reason for an employer's challenged adverse employment action. But both of these premises are mistaken. Title VII's plain terms and our precedents don't care if an employer treats men and women comparably as groups; an employer who fires both lesbians and gay men equally doesn't diminish but doubles its liability. Just cast a glance back to *Manhart,* where it was no defense that the employer sought to equalize pension contributions based on life expectancy. Nor does the statute care if other factors besides sex contribute to an employer's discharge decision. Mr. Bostock's employer might have decided to fire him only because of the confluence of two factors, his sex and the sex to which he is attracted. But exactly the same might have been said in *Phillips*, where motherhood was the added variable.

Still, the employers insist, something seems different here. Unlike certain other employment policies this Court has addressed that harmed only women or only men, the employers' policies in the cases before us have the same adverse consequences for men and women. How could sex be necessary to the result if a member of the opposite sex might face the same outcome from the same policy?

What the employers see as unique isn't even unusual. Often in life and law two but-for factors combine to yield a result that could have also occurred in some other way. Imagine that it's a nice day outside and your house is too warm, so you decide to open the window. Both the cool temperature outside and the heat inside are but-for causes of your choice to open the window. That doesn't change just because you also would have opened the window had it been warm outside and cold inside. In either case, no one would deny that the window is open "because of" the outside temperature. Our cases are much the same. So, for example, when it comes to homosexual employees, male sex and attraction to men are but-for factors that can combine to get them fired. The fact that female sex and attraction to women can *also* get an employee fired does no more than show the same outcome can be achieved through the combination of different factors. In either case, though, sex plays an essential but-for role.

At bottom, the employers' argument unavoidably comes down to a suggestion that sex must be the sole or primary cause of an adverse employment action for Title VII liability to follow. And, as we've seen, that suggestion is at odds with everything we know about the statute. Consider an employer eager to revive the workplace gender roles of the 1950s. He enforces a policy that he will hire only men as mechanics and only women as secretaries. When a qualified woman applies for a mechanic position and is denied, the "simple test" immediately spots the discrimination: A qualified man would have been given the job, so sex was a but-for cause of the employer's refusal to hire. But like the employers before us today, this employer would say not so fast. By comparing the woman who applied to be a mechanic to a man who applied to be a mechanic, we've quietly changed two things: the applicant's sex and her trait of failing to conform to 1950s gender roles. The "simple test" thus overlooks that it is really the applicant's bucking of 1950s gender roles, not her sex, doing the work. So we need to hold that second trait constant: Instead of comparing the disappointed female applicant to a man who applied for the same position, the employer would say, we should compare her to a man who applied to be a secretary. And because that jobseeker would be refused too, this must not be sex discrimination.

No one thinks *that*, so the employers must scramble to justify deploying a stricter causation test for use only in cases involving discrimination based on sexual orientation or transgender status. Such a rule would create a curious discontinuity in our case law, to put it mildly. Employer hires based on sexual stereotypes? Simple test. Employer sets pension contributions based on sex? Simple test. Employer fires men who do not behave in a sufficiently masculine way around the office? Simple test. But when that same employer discriminates against women who are attracted to women, or persons identified at birth as women who later identify as men, we suddenly roll out a new and more rigorous standard? Why are *these* reasons for taking sex into account different from all the rest? Title VII's text can offer no answer.

B

Ultimately, the employers are forced to abandon the statutory text and precedent altogether and appeal to assumptions and policy. Most pointedly, they contend that few in 1964 would have expected Title VII to apply to discrimination against homosexual and transgender persons. And whatever the text and our precedent indicate, they say, shouldn't this fact cause us to pause before recognizing liability?

It might be tempting to reject this argument out of hand. This Court has explained many times over many years that, when the meaning of the statute's terms is plain, our job is at an end. The people are entitled to rely on the law as written, without fearing that courts might disregard its plain terms based on some extratextual consideration. [Citation.] Of course, some Members of this Court have consulted legislative history when interpreting *ambiguous* statutory language. But that has no bearing here. "Legislative history, for those who take it into account, is meant to clear up ambiguity, not create it." *Milner v. Department of Navy*, 562 U.S. 562, 574 (2011). And as we have seen, no ambiguity exists about how Title VII's terms apply to the facts before us. To be sure, the statute's application in these cases reaches "beyond the principal evil" legislators may have intended or expected to address. *Oncale*, 523 U.S. at 79. But " 'the fact that [a statute] has been applied in situations not expressly anticipated by Congress' " does not demonstrate ambiguity; instead, it simply " 'demonstrates [the] breadth' " of a legislative command. [Citation.] And "it is ultimately the provisions of" those legislative commands "rather than the principal concerns of our legislators by which we are governed." *Oncale*, 523 U.S. at 79; *see also* A. Scalia & B. Garner, Reading Law: The Interpretation of Legal Texts 101 (2012) (noting that unexpected applications of broad language reflect only Congress's "presumed point [to] produce general coverage—not to leave room for courts to recognize ad hoc exceptions").

Still, while legislative history can never defeat unambiguous statutory text, historical sources can be useful for a different purpose: Because the law's ordinary meaning at the time of enactment usually governs, we must be sensitive to the possibility a statutory term that means one thing today or in one context might have meant something else at the time of its adoption or might mean something different in another context. And we must be attuned to the possibility that a statutory phrase ordinarily bears a different meaning than the terms do when viewed individually or literally. To ferret out such shifts in linguistic usage or subtle distinctions between literal and ordinary meaning, this Court has sometimes consulted the understandings of the law's drafters as some (not always conclusive) evidence. For example, in the context of the National Motor Vehicle Theft Act, this Court admitted that the term "vehicle" in 1931 could literally mean "a conveyance working on land, water or air." *McBoyle v. United States*, 283 U.S. 25, 26 (1931). But given contextual clues and "everyday speech" at the time of the Act's adoption in 1919, this Court concluded that "vehicles" in that statute included only things "moving on land," not airplanes too. *Ibid.* Similarly, in *New Prime*, we held that, while the term "contracts of employment" today might seem to encompass only contracts with employees, at the time of the statute's adoption the phrase was ordinarily understood to cover contracts with independent contractors as well. 139 S.Ct., at 538–540.

The employers, however, advocate nothing like that here. They do not seek to use historical sources to illustrate that the meaning of any of Title VII's language has changed since 1964 or that the statute's terms, whether viewed individually or as a whole, ordinarily carried some message we have missed. To the contrary, as we have seen, the employers *agree* with our understanding of all the statutory language— "discriminate against any individual . . . because of such individual's . . . sex." Nor do the competing dissents offer an alternative account about what these terms mean either when viewed individually or in the aggregate. Rather than suggesting that the statutory language bears some other *meaning*, the employers and dissents merely suggest that, because few in 1964 expected today's *result*, we should not dare to admit that it follows ineluctably from the statutory text. When a new application emerges that is both unexpected and important, they would seemingly have us merely point out the question, refer the subject back to Congress, and decline to enforce the plain terms of the law in the meantime.

That is exactly the sort of reasoning this Court has long rejected. Admittedly, the employers take pains to couch their argument in terms of seeking to honor the statute's "expected applications" rather than vindicate its "legislative intent." But the concepts are closely related. One could easily contend that legislators only intended expected applications or that a statute's purpose is limited to achieving applications foreseen at the time of enactment. However framed, the employer's logic impermissibly seeks to displace the plain meaning of the law in favor of something lying beyond it.

If anything, the employers' new framing may only add new problems. The employers assert that "no one" in 1964 or for some time after would have anticipated today's result. But is that really true? Not long after the law's passage, gay and transgender employees began filing Title VII complaints, so at least *some* people foresaw this potential application. *See, e.g.,* Smith v. Liberty Mut. Ins. Co., 395 F. Supp. 1098, 1099 (ND Ga. 1975) (addressing claim from 1969); Holloway v. Arthur Andersen & Co., 566 F. 2d 659, 661 (CA9 1977) (addressing claim from 1974). And less than a decade after Title VII's passage, during debates over the Equal Rights Amendment, others counseled that its language—which was strikingly similar to Title VII's—might also protect homosexuals from discrimination. *See, e.g.,* Note, The Legality of Homosexual Marriage, 82 Yale L. J. 573, 583–584 (1973).

Why isn't that enough to demonstrate that today's result isn't totally unexpected? How many people have to foresee the application for it to qualify as "expected"? Do we look only at the moment the statute was enacted, or do we allow some time for the implications of a new statute to be worked out? Should we consider the expectations of those who had no reason to give a particular application any thought or only those with reason to think about the question? How do we account for those who change their minds over time, after learning new facts or hearing a new argument? How specifically or generally should we frame the "application" at issue? None of these questions have obvious answers, and the employers don't propose any. . . .

If we applied Title VII's plain text only to applications some (yet-to-be-determined) group expected in 1964, we'd have more than a little law to overturn. Start with *Oncale.* How many people in 1964 could have expected that the law would turn out to protect male employees? Let alone to protect them from harassment by other male employees? As we acknowledged at the time, "male-on-male sexual harassment in the workplace was assuredly not the principal evil Congress was concerned with when it enacted Title VII." 523 U.S. at 79. Yet the Court did not hesitate to recognize that Title VII's plain terms forbade it. Under the employer's logic, it would seem this was a mistake.

That's just the beginning of the law we would have to unravel. As one Equal Employment Opportunity Commission (EEOC) Commissioner observed shortly after the law's passage, the words of " 'the sex provision of Title VII [are] difficult to . . . control.' " [Citation.] The "difficult[y]" may owe something to the initial proponent of the sex discrimination rule in Title VII, Representative Howard Smith. On some accounts, the congressman may have wanted (or at least was indifferent to the possibility of) broad language with wide-ranging effect. Not necessarily because he was interested in rooting out sex discrimination in all its forms, but because he may have hoped to scuttle the whole Civil Rights Act and thought that adding language covering sex discrimination would serve as a poison pill. [Citation.] Certainly nothing in the meager legislative history of this provision suggests it was meant to be read narrowly.

Whatever his reasons, thanks to the broad language Representative Smith introduced, many, maybe most, applications of Title VII's sex provision were "unanticipated" at the time of the law's adoption. In fact, many now-obvious applications met with heated opposition early on, even among those tasked with enforcing the law. In the years immediately following Title VII's passage, the EEOC officially opined that listing men's positions and women's positions separately in job postings was simply helpful rather than discriminatory. [Citation.] Some courts held that Title VII did not prevent an employer from firing an employee for refusing his sexual advances. [Citation.] And courts held that a policy against hiring mothers but not fathers of young children wasn't discrimination because of sex. [Citation.]

Over time, though, the breadth of the statutory language proved too difficult to deny. By the end of the 1960s, the EEOC reversed its stance on sex-segregated job advertising. [Citation.] In 1971, this Court held that treating women with children differently from men with children violated Title VII. *Phillips*, 400 U.S. at 544. And by the late 1970s, courts began to recognize that sexual harassment can sometimes amount to sex discrimination. [Citation.] While to the modern eye each of these examples may seem "plainly [to] constitut[e] discrimination because of biological sex," (ALITO, J., dissenting), all were hotly contested for years following Title VII's enactment. And as with the discrimination we consider today, many federal judges long accepted interpretations of Title VII that excluded these situations. *Cf. post*, at ___–___ (KAVANAUGH, J., dissenting) (highlighting that certain lower courts have rejected Title VII claims based on homosexuality and transgender status). Would the employers have us undo every one of these unexpected applications too?

The weighty implications of the employers' argument from expectations also reveal why they cannot hide behind the no-elephants-in-mouseholes canon. That canon recognizes that Congress "does not alter the fundamental details of a regulatory scheme in vague terms or ancillary provisions." *Whitman*, [citation]. But it has no relevance here. We can't deny that today's holding—that employers are prohibited from firing employees on the basis of homosexuality or transgender status—is an elephant. But where's the mousehole? Title VII's prohibition of sex discrimination in employment is a major piece of federal civil rights legislation. It is written in starkly broad terms. It has repeatedly produced unexpected applications, at least in the view of those on the receiving end of them. Congress's key drafting choices—to focus on discrimination against individuals and not merely between groups and to hold employers liable whenever sex is a but-for cause of the plaintiff's injuries—virtually guaranteed that unexpected applications would emerge over time. This elephant has never hidden in a mousehole; it has been standing before us all along.

With that, the employers are left to abandon their concern for expected applications and fall back to the last line of defense for all failing statutory interpretation arguments: naked policy appeals. If we were to apply the statute's plain language, they complain, any number of undesirable policy consequences would follow. [Citation.] Gone here is any pretense of statutory interpretation; all that's left is a suggestion we should proceed without the law's guidance to do as we think best. But that's an invitation no court should ever take up. The place to make new legislation, or address unwanted consequences of old legislation, lies in Congress. When it comes to statutory interpretation, our role is limited to applying the law's demands as faithfully as we can in the cases that come before us. As judges we possess no special expertise or authority to declare for ourselves what a self-governing people should consider just or wise. And the same judicial humility that requires us to refrain from adding to statutes requires us to refrain from diminishing them.

What are these consequences anyway? The employers worry that our decision will sweep beyond Title VII to other federal or state laws that prohibit sex discrimination. And, under Title VII itself, they say sex-segregated bathrooms, locker rooms, and dress codes will prove unsustainable after our decision today. But none of these other laws are before us; we have not had the benefit of adversarial testing about the meaning of their terms, and we do not prejudge any such question today. Under Title VII, too, we do not purport to address bathrooms, locker rooms, or anything else of the kind. The only question before us is whether an employer who fires someone simply for being homosexual or transgender has discharged or otherwise discriminated against that individual "because of such individual's sex." As used in Title VII, the term " 'discriminate against' " refers to "distinctions or differences in treatment that injure protected individuals." [Citation.] Firing employees because of a statutorily protected trait surely counts. Whether other policies and practices might or might not qualify as unlawful discrimination or find justifications under other provisions of Title VII are questions for future cases, not these. . . .

*

Some of those who supported adding language to Title VII to ban sex discrimination may have hoped it would derail the entire Civil Rights Act. Yet, contrary to those intentions, the bill became law. Since then, Title VII's effects have unfolded with far-reaching consequences, some likely beyond what many in Congress or elsewhere expected.

But none of this helps decide today's cases. Ours is a society of written laws. Judges are not free to overlook plain statutory commands on the strength of nothing more than suppositions about intentions or guesswork about expectations. In Title VII, Congress adopted broad language making it illegal for an employer to rely on an employee's sex when deciding to fire that employee. We do not hesitate to recognize today a necessary consequence of that legislative choice: An employer who fires an individual merely for being gay or transgender defies the law. . . .

It is so ordered.

■ JUSTICE ALITO, with whom JUSTICE THOMAS joins, dissenting.

There is only one word for what the Court has done today: legislation. The document that the Court releases is in the form of a judicial opinion interpreting a statute, but that is deceptive.

Title VII of the Civil Rights Act of 1964 prohibits employment discrimination on any of five specified grounds: "race, color, religion, sex, [and] national origin." 42 U.S.C. § 2000e–2(a)(1). Neither "sexual orientation" nor "gender identity" appears on that list. For the past 45 years, bills have been introduced in Congress to add "sexual orientation" to the list, and in recent years, bills have included "gender identity" as well. But to date, none has passed both Houses. . . .

Because no such amendment of Title VII has been enacted in accordance with the requirements in the Constitution (passage in both Houses and presentment to the President, Art. I, § 7, cl. 2), Title VII's prohibition of discrimination because of "sex" still means what it has always meant. But the Court is not deterred by these constitutional niceties. . . .

The Court tries to convince readers that it is merely enforcing the terms of the statute, but that is preposterous. Even as understood today, the concept of discrimination because of "sex" is different from discrimination because of "sexual orientation" or "gender identity." And in any event, our duty is to interpret statutory terms to "mean what they conveyed to reasonable people *at the time they were written*." A. Scalia & B. Garner, Reading Law: The Interpretation of Legal Texts 16 (2012) (emphasis added). If every single living American had been surveyed in 1964, it would have been hard to find any who thought that discrimination because of sex meant discrimination because of sexual orientation—not to mention gender identity, a concept that was essentially unknown at the time.

The Court attempts to pass off its decision as the inevitable product of the textualist school of statutory interpretation championed by our late colleague Justice Scalia, but no one should be fooled. The Court's opinion is like a pirate ship. It sails under a textualist flag, but what it actually represents is a theory of statutory interpretation that Justice Scalia excoriated—the theory that courts should "update" old statutes so that they better reflect the current values of society. [Citation.] If the Court finds it appropriate to adopt this theory, it should own up to what it is doing.

Many will applaud today's decision because they agree on policy grounds with the Court's updating of Title VII. But the question in these cases is not whether discrimination because of sexual orientation or gender identity *should be* outlawed. The question is *whether Congress did that in 1964*. It indisputably did not.

I

A

Title VII, as noted, prohibits discrimination "because of . . . sex," § 2000e–2(a)(1), and in 1964, it was as clear as clear could be that this meant discrimination because of the genetic and anatomical characteristics that men and women have at the time of birth. Determined searching has not found a single dictionary from that time that defined "sex" to mean sexual orientation, gender identity, or "transgender status." . . .

In [unabridged] dictionaries [used in the 1960s], the primary definition of "sex" was essentially the same as that in the then-most recent edition of Webster's New International Dictionary 2296 (def. 1) (2d ed. 1953): "[o]ne of the two divisions of organisms formed on the distinction of male and female." *See also* American Heritage Dictionary 1187 (def. 1(a)) (1969) ("The property or quality by which organisms are classified according to their reproductive functions"); Random House Dictionary of the English Language 1307 (def. 1) (1966) (Random House Dictionary) ("the fact or character of being either male or female"); 9 Oxford English Dictionary 577 (def. 1) (1933) ("Either of the two divisions of organic beings distinguished as male and female respectively").

The Court does not dispute that this is what "sex" means in Title VII, although it coyly suggests that there is at least some support for a different and potentially relevant definition. (I address alternative definitions below. *See* Part I-B-3, *infra*.) But the Court declines to stand on that ground and instead "proceed[s] on the assumption that 'sex' . . . refer[s] only to biological distinctions between male and female."

If that is so, it should be perfectly clear that Title VII does not reach discrimination because of sexual orientation or gender identity. If "sex" in Title VII means biologically male or female, then discrimination because of sex means discrimination because the person in question is biologically male or biologically female, not because that person is sexually attracted to members of the same sex or identifies as a member of a particular gender.

How then does the Court claim to avoid that conclusion? The Court tries to cloud the issue by spending many pages discussing matters that are beside the point. The Court observes that a Title VII plaintiff need not show that "sex" was the sole or primary motive for a challenged employment decision or its sole or primary cause; that Title VII is limited to discrimination with respect to a list of specified actions (such as hiring, firing, etc.); and that Title VII protects individual rights, not group rights.

All that is true, but so what? In cases like those before us, a plaintiff must show that sex was a "motivating factor" in the challenged employment action, 42 U.S.C. § 2000e–2(m), so the question we must decide comes down to this: if an individual employee or applicant for employment shows that his or her sexual orientation or gender identity was a "motivating factor" in a hiring or discharge decision, for example, is that enough to establish that the employer discriminated "because of . . . sex"? Or, to put the same question in different terms, if an employer takes an employment action solely because of the sexual orientation or gender identity of an employee or applicant, has that employer necessarily discriminated because of biological sex?

The answers to those questions must be no, unless discrimination because of sexual orientation or gender identity inherently constitutes discrimination because of sex. The Court attempts to prove that point, and it argues, not merely that the terms of Title VII *can* be interpreted that way but that they *cannot reasonably be interpreted any other way*. According to the Court, the text is unambiguous.

The arrogance of this argument is breathtaking. . . . [T]here is not a shred of evidence that any Member of Congress interpreted the statutory text that way when Title VII was enacted. But the Court apparently thinks that this was because the Members were not "smart enough to realize" what its language means. Hively v. Ivy Tech Community College of Ind., 853 F.3d 339, 357 (CA7 2017) (Posner, J., concurring). The Court seemingly has the same opinion about our colleagues on the Courts of Appeals, because until 2017, every single Court of Appeals to consider the question interpreted Title VII's prohibition against sex discrimination to mean discrimination on the basis of biological sex. [Citation.] And for good measure, the Court's conclusion that Title VII unambiguously reaches discrimination on the basis of sexual orientation and gender identity necessarily means that the EEOC failed to see the obvious for the first 48 years after Title VII became law. Day in and day out, the Commission enforced Title VII but did not grasp what discrimination "because of . . . sex" unambiguously means. [Citation.]

The Court's argument is not only arrogant, it is wrong. It fails on its own terms. "Sex," "sexual orientation," and "gender identity" are different concepts, as the Court concedes. *Ante*, ("homosexuality and transgender status are distinct concepts from sex"). And neither "sexual orientation" nor "gender identity" is tied to either of the two biological sexes. *See ante*, (recognizing that "discrimination on these bases" does not have "some disparate impact on one sex or another"). Both men and women may be attracted to members of the opposite sex, members of the same sex, or members of both sexes. And individuals who are born with the genes and organs of either biological sex may identify with a different gender.

Using slightly different terms, the Court asserts again and again that discrimination because of sexual orientation or gender identity inherently or necessarily entails discrimination because of sex. . . . Contrary to the Court's contention, discrimination because of sexual orientation or gender identity does not in and of itself entail discrimination because of sex. We can see this because it is quite possible for an employer to discriminate on those grounds without taking the sex of an individual applicant or employee into account. An employer can have a policy that says: "We do not hire gays, lesbians, or transgender individuals." And an employer can implement this policy without paying any attention to or even knowing the biological sex of gay, lesbian, and transgender applicants. In fact, at the time of the enactment of Title VII, the United States military had a blanket policy of refusing to enlist gays or lesbians, and under this policy for years thereafter, applicants for enlistment were required to complete a form that asked whether they were "homosexual." . . .

At oral argument, the attorney representing the employees, a prominent professor of constitutional law, was asked if there would be discrimination because of sex if an employer with a blanket policy against hiring gays, lesbians, and transgender individuals implemented that policy without knowing the biological sex of any job applicants. Her candid answer was that this would "not" be sex discrimination. And she was right.

The attorney's concession was necessary, but it is fatal to the Court's interpretation, for if an employer discriminates against individual applicants or employees without even knowing whether they are male or female, it is impossible to argue that the employer intentionally discriminated because of sex. An employer cannot intentionally discriminate on the basis of a characteristic of which the employer has no knowledge. And if an employer does not violate Title VII by discriminating on the basis of sexual orientation or gender identity without knowing the sex of the affected individuals, there is no reason why the same employer could not lawfully implement the same policy even if it knows the sex of these individuals. If an employer takes an adverse employment action for a perfectly legitimate reason—for example, because an employee stole company property—that action is not converted into sex discrimination simply because the employer knows the employee's sex. As explained, a disparate treatment case requires proof of intent—*i.e.*, that the employee's sex motivated the firing. In short, what this example shows is that discrimination because of sexual orientation or gender identity does not inherently or necessarily entail discrimination because of sex, and for that reason, the Court's chief argument collapses.

Trying to escape the consequences of the attorney's concession, the Court offers its own hypothetical:

"Suppose an employer's application form offered a single box to check if the applicant is either black or Catholic. If the employer refuses to hire anyone who checks that box, would we conclude the employer has complied with Title VII, so long as it studiously avoids learning any particular applicant's race or religion? Of course not."

How this hypothetical proves the Court's point is a mystery. A person who checked that box would presumably be black, Catholic, or both, and refusing to hire an applicant because of race or religion is prohibited by Title VII. Rejecting applicants who checked a box indicating that they are homosexual is entirely different because it is impossible to tell from that answer whether an applicant is male or female.

The Court follows this strange hypothetical with an even stranger argument. The Court argues that an applicant could not answer the question whether he or she is homosexual without knowing something about sex. If the applicant was unfamiliar with the term "homosexual," the applicant would have to look it up or ask what the term means. And because this applicant would have to take into account his or her sex and that of the persons to whom he or she is sexually attracted to answer the question, it follows, the Court reasons, that an employer could not reject this applicant without taking the applicant's sex into account.

This is illogical. Just because an applicant cannot say whether he or she is homosexual without knowing his or her own sex and that of the persons to whom the applicant is attracted, it does not follow that an employer cannot reject an applicant based on homosexuality without knowing the applicant's sex.

While the Court's imagined application form proves nothing, another hypothetical case offered by the Court is telling. But what it proves is not what the Court thinks. The Court posits:

"Imagine an employer who has a policy of firing any employee known to be homosexual. The employer hosts an office holiday party and invites employees to bring their spouses. A model employee arrives and introduces a manager to Susan, the employee's wife. Will that employee be fired? If the policy works as the employer intends, the answer depends entirely on whether the model employee is a man or a woman."

This example disproves the Court's argument because it is perfectly clear that the employer's motivation in firing the female employee had nothing to do with that employee's sex. The employer presumably knew that this employee was a woman before she was invited to the fateful party. Yet the employer, far from holding her biological sex against her, rated her a "model employee." At the party, the employer learned something new, her sexual orientation, and it was this new information that motivated her discharge. So this is another example showing that discrimination because of sexual orientation does not inherently involve discrimination because of sex.

In addition to the failed argument just discussed, the Court makes two other arguments, more or less in passing. The first of these is essentially that sexual orientation and gender identity are closely related to sex. The Court argues that sexual orientation and gender identity are "inextricably bound up with sex," and that discrimination on the basis of sexual orientation or gender identity involves the application of "sex-based rules." This is a variant of an argument found in many of the briefs filed in support of the employees and in the lower court decisions that agreed with the Court's interpretation. All these variants stress that sex, sexual orientation, and gender identity are related concepts. The Seventh Circuit observed that "[i]t would require considerable calisthenics to remove 'sex' from 'sexual orientation.'" *Hively*, 853 F.3d at 350. The Second Circuit wrote that sex is necessarily "a factor in sexual orientation" and further concluded that "sexual orientation is a function of sex." 883 F.3d 100, 112–113 (CA2 2018) (en banc). Bostock's brief and those of *amici* supporting his position contend that sexual orientation is "a sex-based consideration." Other briefs state that sexual orientation is "a function of sex" or is "intrinsically related to sex." Similarly, Stephens argues that sex and gender identity are necessarily intertwined: "By definition, a transgender person is someone who lives and identifies with a sex different than the sex assigned to the person at birth."

It is curious to see this argument in an opinion that purports to apply the purest and highest form of textualism because the argument effectively amends the statutory text. Title VII prohibits discrimination because of *sex itself,* not everything that is related to, based on, or defined with reference to, "sex." Many things are related to sex. Think of all the nouns other than "orientation" that are commonly modified by the adjective "sexual." Some examples yielded by a quick computer search are "sexual harassment," "sexual assault," "sexual violence," "sexual intercourse," and "sexual content."

Does the Court really think that Title VII prohibits discrimination on all these grounds? Is it unlawful for an employer to refuse to hire an employee with a record of sexual harassment in prior jobs? Or a record of sexual assault or violence?

To be fair, the Court does not claim that Title VII prohibits discrimination because of *everything* that is related to sex. The Court draws a distinction between things that are "inextricably" related and those that are related in "some vague sense." Apparently the Court would graft onto Title VII some arbitrary line separating the things that are related closely enough and those that are not. And it would do this in the name of high textualism. An additional argument made in passing also fights the text of Title VII and the policy it reflects. The Court proclaims that "[a]n individual's homosexuality or transgender status is not relevant to employment decisions." That is the policy view of many people in 2020, and perhaps Congress would have amended Title VII to implement it if this Court had not intervened. But that is not the policy embodied in Title VII in its current form. Title VII prohibits discrimination based on five specified grounds, and neither sexual orientation nor gender identity is on the list. As long as an employer does not discriminate based on one of the listed grounds, the employer is free to decide for itself which characteristics are "relevant to [its] employment decisions." By proclaiming that sexual orientation and gender identity are "not relevant to employment decisions," the Court updates Title VII to reflect what it regards as 2020 values.

The Court's remaining argument is based on a hypothetical that the Court finds instructive. In this hypothetical, an employer has two employees who are "attracted to men," and "*to the employer's mind*" the two employees are "materially identical" except that one is a man and the other is a woman. *Ante*, at ___ (emphasis added). The Court reasons that if the employer fires the man but not the woman, the employer is necessarily motivated by the man's biological sex. After all, if two employees are identical in every respect but sex, and the employer fires only one, what other reason could there be?

The problem with this argument is that the Court loads the dice. That is so because in the mind of an employer who does not want to employ individuals who are attracted to members of the same sex, these two employees are not materially identical in every respect but sex. On the contrary, they differ in another way that the employer thinks is quite material. And until Title VII is amended to add sexual orientation as a prohibited ground, this is a view that an employer is permitted to implement. As noted, other than prohibiting discrimination on any of five specified grounds, "race, color, religion, sex, [and] national origin." 42 U.S.C. § 2000e–2(a)(1), Title VII allows employers to decide whether two employees are "materially identical." Even idiosyncratic criteria are permitted; if an employer thinks that Scorpios make bad employees, the employer can refuse to hire Scorpios. Such a policy would be unfair and foolish, but under Title VII, it is permitted. And until Title VII is amended, so is a policy against employing gays, lesbians, or transgender individuals.

Once this is recognized, what we have in the Court's hypothetical case are two employees who differ in *two* ways—sex and sexual orientation—and if the employer fires one and keeps the other, all that can be inferred is that the employer was motivated either entirely by sexual orientation, entirely by sex, or in part by both. We cannot infer with any certainty, as the hypothetical is apparently meant to suggest, that the employer was motivated even in part by sex. The Court harps on the fact that under Title VII a prohibited ground need not be the sole motivation for an adverse employment action, but its example does not show that sex necessarily played *any* part in the employer's thinking.

The Court tries to avoid this inescapable conclusion by arguing that sex is really the only difference between the two employees. This is so, the Court maintains, because both employees "are attracted to men." Of course, the employer would couch its objection to the man differently. It would say that its objection was his sexual orientation. So this may appear to leave us with a battle of labels. If the employer's objection to the male employee is characterized as attraction to men, it seems that he is just like the woman in all respects except sex and that the employer's disparate treatment must be based on that one difference. On the other hand, if the employer's objection is sexual orientation or homosexuality, the two employees differ in two respects, and it cannot be inferred that the disparate treatment was due even in part to sex.

The Court insists that its label is the right one, and that presumably is why it makes such a point of arguing that an employer cannot escape liability under Title VII by giving sex discrimination some other name. That is certainly true, but so is the opposite. Something that is *not* sex discrimination cannot be converted into sex discrimination by slapping on that label. So the Court cannot prove its point simply by labeling the employer's objection as "attract[ion] to men." Rather, the Court needs to show that its label is the correct one.

And a labeling standoff would not help the Court because that would mean that the bare text of Title VII does not unambiguously show that its interpretation is right. The Court would have no justification for its stubborn refusal to look any further.

As it turns out, however, there is no standoff. It can easily be shown that the employer's real objection is not "attract[ion] to men" but homosexual orientation.

In an effort to prove its point, the Court carefully includes in its example just two employees, a homosexual man and a heterosexual woman, but suppose we add two more individuals, a woman who is attracted to women and a man who is attracted to women. (A large employer will likely have applicants and employees who fall into all four categories, and a small employer can potentially have all four as well.) We now have the four exemplars listed below, with the discharged employees crossed out:

Man attracted to men

Woman attracted to men

Woman attracted to women

Man attracted to women

The discharged employees have one thing in common. It is not biological sex, attraction to men, or attraction to women. It is attraction to members of their own sex—in a word, sexual orientation. And that, we can infer, is the employer's real motive.

In sum, the Court's textual arguments fail on their own terms. The Court tries to prove that "it is impossible to discriminate against a person for being homosexual or transgender without discriminating against that individual based on sex," but as has been shown, it is entirely possible for an employer to do just that. "[H]omosexuality and transgender status are distinct concepts from sex," *ante*, at ___, and discrimination because of sexual orientation or transgender status does not inherently or necessarily constitute discrimination because of sex. The Court's arguments are squarely contrary to the statutory text.

But even if the words of Title VII did not definitively refute the Court's interpretation, that would not justify the Court's refusal to consider alternative interpretations. The Court's excuse for ignoring everything other than the bare statutory text is that the text is unambiguous and therefore no one can reasonably interpret the text in any way other than the Court does. Unless the Court has met that high standard, it has no justification for its blinkered approach. And to say that the Court's interpretation is the only possible reading is indefensible. . . .

II

A

So far, I have not looked beyond dictionary definitions of "sex," but textualists like Justice Scalia do not confine their inquiry to the scrutiny of dictionaries. . . . Leading proponents of Justice Scalia's school of textualism have expounded on this principle and explained that it is grounded on an understanding of the way language works. As Dean John F. Manning explains, "the meaning of language depends on the way a linguistic community uses words and phrases in context." *What Divides Textualists From Purposivists?* 106 Colum. L. Rev. 70, 78 (2006). "[O]ne can make sense of others' communications only by placing them in their appropriate social and linguistic context," *id.*, at 79–80, and this is no less true of statutes than any other verbal communications. "[S]tatutes convey meaning only because members of a relevant linguistic community apply shared background conventions for understanding how particular words are used in particular contexts." Manning, *The Absurdity Doctrine*, 116 Harv. L. Rev. 2387, 2457 (2003). Therefore, judges should ascribe to the words of a statute "what a reasonable person conversant with applicable social conventions would have understood them to be adopting." Manning, 106 Colum. L. Rev., at 77. Or, to put the point in slightly different terms, a judge interpreting a statute should ask " 'what one would ordinarily be understood as saying, given the circumstances in which one said it.' " Manning, 116 Harv. L. Rev., at 2397–2398. . . .

Thus, when textualism is properly understood, it calls for an examination of the social context in which a statute was enacted because this may have an important bearing on what its words were understood to mean at the time of enactment. Textualists do not read statutes as if they were messages picked up by a powerful radio telescope from a distant and utterly unknown civilization. Statutes consist of communications between members of a particular linguistic community, one that existed in a particular place and at a particular time, and these communications must therefore be interpreted as they were understood by that community at that time.

For this reason, it is imperative to consider how Americans in 1964 would have understood Title VII's prohibition of discrimination because of sex. To get a picture of this, we may imagine this scene. Suppose that, while Title VII was under consideration in Congress, a group of average Americans decided to read the text of the bill with the aim of writing or calling their representatives in Congress and conveying their approval or disapproval. What would these ordinary citizens have taken "discrimination because of sex" to mean? Would they have thought that this language prohibited discrimination because of sexual orientation or gender identity? . . .

The answer could not be clearer. In 1964, ordinary Americans reading the text of Title VII would not have dreamed that discrimination because of sex meant discrimination because of sexual orientation, much less gender identity. The *ordinary meaning* of discrimination because of "sex" was discrimination because of a person's biological sex, not sexual orientation or gender identity. The possibility that discrimination on either of these grounds might fit within some exotic understanding of sex discrimination would not have crossed their minds.

In 1964, the concept of prohibiting discrimination "because of sex" was no novelty. It was a familiar and well-understood concept, and what it meant was equal treatment for men and women. [Citing state statutes and constitutional provisions of and before the era.] . . . Discrimination "because of sex" was not understood as having anything to do with discrimination because of sexual orientation or transgender status. Any such notion would have clashed in spectacular fashion with the societal norms of the day.

For most 21st-century Americans, it is painful to be reminded of the way our society once treated gays and lesbians, but any honest effort to understand what the terms of Title VII were understood to mean when enacted must take into account the societal norms of that time. And the plain truth is that in 1964 homosexuality was thought to be a mental disorder, and homosexual conduct was regarded as morally culpable and worthy of punishment.

In its then-most recent Diagnostic and Statistical Manual of Mental Disorders (1952) (DSM-I), the American Psychiatric Association (APA) classified same-sex attraction as a "sexual deviation," a particular type of "sociopathic personality disturbance," *id.*, at 38–39, and the next edition, issued in 1968, similarly classified homosexuality as a "sexual deviatio[n]," Diagnostic and Statistical Manual of Mental Disorders 44 (2d ed.) (DSM-II). It was not until the sixth printing of the DSM-II in 1973 that this was changed.

Society's treatment of homosexuality and homosexual conduct was consistent with this understanding. Sodomy was a crime in every State but Illinois, *see* W. Eskridge, Dishonorable Passions 387–407 (2008), and in the District of Columbia, a law enacted by Congress made sodomy a felony punishable by imprisonment for up to 10 years and permitted the indefinite civil commitment of "sexual psychopath[s]," [citation].

This view of homosexuality was reflected in the rules governing the federal work force. In 1964, federal "[a]gencies could deny homosexual men and women employment because of their sexual orientation," and this practice continued until 1975. [Citations.] In 1964, individuals who were known to be homosexual could not obtain security clearances, and any who possessed clearances were likely to lose them if their orientation was discovered. . . .

To its credit, our society has now come to recognize the injustice of past practices, and this recognition provides the impetus to "update" Title VII. But that is not our job. Our duty is to understand what the terms of Title VII were understood to mean when enacted, and in doing so, we must take into account the societal norms of that time. We must therefore ask whether ordinary Americans in 1964 would have thought that discrimination because of "sex" carried some exotic meaning under which private-sector employers would be prohibited from engaging in a practice that represented the official policy of the Federal Government with respect to its own employees. We must ask whether Americans at that time would have thought that Title VII banned discrimination against an employee for engaging in conduct that Congress had made a felony and a ground for civil commitment.

The questions answer themselves. Even if discrimination based on sexual orientation or gender identity could be squeezed into some arcane understanding of sex discrimination, the context in which Title VII was enacted would tell us that this is not what the statute's terms were understood to mean at that time. To paraphrase something Justice Scalia once wrote, "our job is not to scavenge the world of English usage to discover whether there is any possible meaning" of discrimination because of sex that might be broad enough to encompass discrimination because of sexual orientation or gender identity. [Citation.] Without strong evidence to the contrary (and there is none here), our job is to ascertain and apply the "*ordinary* meaning" of the statute. And in 1964, ordinary Americans most certainly would not have understood Title VII to ban discrimination because of sexual orientation or gender identity. . . .

D

1

. . . In arguing that we must put out of our minds what we know about the time when Title VII was enacted, the Court relies on Justice Scalia's opinion for the Court in *Oncale v. Sundowner Offshore Services, Inc.*, 523 U.S. 75 (1998). But *Oncale* is nothing like these cases, and no one should be taken in by the majority's effort to enlist Justice Scalia in its updating project.

The Court's unanimous decision in *Oncale* was thoroughly unremarkable. The Court held that a male employee who alleged that he had been sexually harassed at work by other men stated a claim under

Title VII. Although the impetus for Title VII's prohibition of sex discrimination was to protect women, anybody reading its terms would immediately appreciate that it applies equally to both sexes, and by the time *Oncale* reached the Court, our precedent already established that sexual harassment may constitute sex discrimination within the meaning of Title VII. [Citation.] Given these premises, syllogistic reasoning dictated the holding.

What today's decision latches onto are *Oncale*'s comments about whether " 'male-on-male sexual harassment' " was on Congress's mind when it enacted Title VII. The Court in *Oncale* observed that this specific type of behavior "was assuredly not the *principal evil* Congress was concerned with when it enacted Title VII," but it found that immaterial because "statutory prohibitions often go beyond the *principal evil* to cover reasonably comparable evils, and it is ultimately the provisions of our laws rather than the *principal concerns* of our legislators by which we are governed." [Citation.]

It takes considerable audacity to read these comments as committing the Court to a position on deep philosophical questions about the meaning of language and their implications for the interpretation of legal rules. These comments are better understood as stating mundane and uncontroversial truths. Who would argue that a statute applies only to the "principal evils" and not lesser evils that fall within the plain scope of its terms? Would even the most ardent "purposivists" and fans of legislative history contend that congressional intent is restricted to Congress's "*principal* concerns"?

Properly understood, *Oncale* does not provide the slightest support for what the Court has done today. For one thing, it would be a wild understatement to say that discrimination because of sexual orientation and transgender status was not the "principal evil" on Congress's mind in 1964. Whether we like to admit it now or not, in the thinking of Congress and the public at that time, such discrimination would not have been evil at all.

But the more important difference between these cases and *Oncale* is that here the interpretation that the Court adopts does not fall within the ordinary meaning of the statutory text as it would have been understood in 1964. To decide for the defendants in *Oncale*, it would have been necessary to carve out an exception to the statutory text. Here, no such surgery is at issue. Even if we totally disregard the societal norms of 1964, the text of Title VII does not support the Court's holding. And the reasoning of *Oncale* does not preclude or counsel against our taking those norms into account. They are relevant, not for the purpose of creating an exception to the terms of the statute, but for the purpose of better appreciating how those terms would have been understood at the time.

2

The Court argues that two other decisions—Phillips v. Martin Marietta Corp., 400 U.S. 542 (1971) (*per curiam*), and Los Angeles Dept. of Water and Power v. Manhart, 435 U.S. 702 (1978)—buttress its decision, but those cases merely held that Title VII prohibits employer conduct that plainly constitutes discrimination because of biological sex. In *Philips*, the employer treated women with young children less favorably than men with young children. In *Manhart*, the employer required women to make larger pension contributions than men. It is hard to see how these holdings assist the Court.

The Court extracts three "lessons" from *Phillips*, *Manhart*, and *Oncale*, but none sheds any light on the question before us. The first lesson is that "it's irrelevant what an employer might call its discriminatory practice, how others might label it, or what else might motivate it." This lesson is obviously true but proves nothing. As to the label attached to a practice, has anyone ever thought that the application of a law to a person's conduct depends on how it is labeled? Could a bank robber escape conviction by saying he was engaged in asset enhancement? So if an employer discriminates because of sex, the employer is liable no matter what it calls its conduct, but if the employer's conduct is not sex discrimination, the statute does not apply. Thus, this lesson simply takes us back to the question whether discrimination because of sexual orientation or gender identity is a form of discrimination because of biological sex. For reasons already discussed, it is not.

It likewise proves nothing of relevance here to note that an employer cannot escape liability by showing that discrimination on a prohibited ground was not its sole motivation. So long as a prohibited ground was a motivating factor, the existence of other motivating factors does not defeat liability.

The Court makes much of the argument that "[i]n *Phillips*, the employer could have accurately spoken of its policy as one based on 'motherhood.' " But motherhood, by definition, is a condition that can be experienced only by women, so a policy that distinguishes between motherhood and parenthood is necessarily a policy that draws a sex-based distinction. There was sex discrimination in *Phillips*, because women with children were treated disadvantageously compared to men with children.

Lesson number two—"the plaintiff's sex need not be the sole or primary cause of the employer's adverse action"—is similarly unhelpful. The standard of causation in these cases is whether sex is necessarily a "motivating factor" when an employer discriminates on the basis of sexual orientation or gender identity. 42 U.S.C. § 2000e–2(m). But the essential question—whether discrimination because of sexual orientation or gender identity constitutes sex discrimination—would be the same no matter what causation standard applied. The Court's extensive discussion of causation standards is so much smoke.

Lesson number three—"an employer cannot escape liability by demonstrating that it treats males and females comparably as groups"— is also irrelevant. There is no dispute that discrimination against an individual employee based on that person's sex cannot be justified on the ground that the employer's treatment of the average employee of that sex is at least as favorable as its treatment of the average employee of the opposite sex. Nor does it matter if an employer discriminates against only a subset of men or women, where the same subset of the opposite sex is treated differently, as in *Phillips*. That is not the issue here. An employer who discriminates equally on the basis of sexual orientation or gender identity applies the same criterion to every affected *individual* regardless of sex. . . .

* * *

The updating desire to which the Court succumbs no doubt arises from humane and generous impulses. Today, many Americans know individuals who are gay, lesbian, or transgender and want them to be treated with the dignity, consideration, and fairness that everyone deserves. But the authority of this Court is limited to saying what the law *is*.

The Court itself recognizes this:

"The place to make new legislation . . . lies in Congress. When it comes to statutory interpretation, our role is limited to applying the law's demands as faithfully as we can in the cases that come before us."

It is easy to utter such words. If only the Court would live by them.

I respectfully dissent.

[The appendices accompanying Justice Alito's opinion have been omitted. They provide enacting-era dictionary definitions of "sex"; set out additional federal statutes prohibiting sex discrimination; and evince prior sexual-orientation-based discrimination in federal employment procedures and forms.]

■ JUSTICE KAVANAUGH, dissenting.

Like many cases in this Court, this case boils down to one fundamental question: Who decides? Title VII of the Civil Rights Act of 1964 prohibits employment discrimination "because of" an individual's "race, color, religion, sex, or national origin." The question here is whether Title VII should be expanded to prohibit employment discrimination because of sexual orientation. Under the Constitution's separation of powers, the responsibility to amend Title VII belongs to Congress and the President in the legislative process, not to this Court.

The political branches are well aware of this issue. In 2007, the U.S. House of Representatives voted 235 to 184 to prohibit employment discrimination on the basis of sexual orientation. In 2013, the U.S.

Senate voted 64 to 32 in favor of a similar ban. In 2019, the House again voted 236 to 173 to outlaw employment discrimination on the basis of sexual orientation. Although both the House and Senate have voted at different times to prohibit sexual orientation discrimination, the two Houses have not yet come together with the President to enact a bill into law.

The policy arguments for amending Title VII are very weighty. The Court has previously stated, and I fully agree, that gay and lesbian Americans "cannot be treated as social outcasts or as inferior in dignity and worth." Masterpiece Cakeshop, Ltd. v. Colorado Civil Rights Comm'n, 138 S. Ct. 1719, 1727 (2018).

But we are judges, not Members of Congress. And in Alexander Hamilton's words, federal judges exercise "neither Force nor Will, but merely judgment." The Federalist No. 78, p. 523 (J. Cooke ed. 1961). Under the Constitution's separation of powers, our role as judges is to interpret and follow the law as written, regardless of whether we like the result. [Citation.] Our role is not to make or amend the law. As written, Title VII does not prohibit employment discrimination because of sexual orientation.[1] . . .

I

For several decades, Congress has considered numerous bills to prohibit employment discrimination based on sexual orientation. But as noted above, although Congress has come close, it has not yet shouldered a bill over the legislative finish line.

In the face of the unsuccessful legislative efforts (so far) to prohibit sexual orientation discrimination, judges may not rewrite the law simply because of their own policy views. Judges may not update the law merely because they think that Congress does not have the votes or the fortitude. Judges may not predictively amend the law just because they believe that Congress is likely to do it soon anyway.

If judges could rewrite laws based on their own policy views, or based on their own assessments of likely future legislative action, the critical distinction between legislative authority and judicial authority that undergirds the Constitution's separation of powers would collapse, thereby threatening the impartial rule of law and individual liberty. . . .

Because judges interpret the law as written, not as they might wish it were written, the first 10 U.S. Courts of Appeals to consider whether Title VII prohibits sexual orientation discrimination all said no. Some 30 federal judges considered the question. All 30 judges said no, based on the text of the statute. 30 out of 30.

---

[1]   Although this opinion does not separately analyze discrimination on the basis of gender identity, this opinion's legal analysis of discrimination on the basis of sexual orientation would apply in much the same way to discrimination on the basis of gender identity.

But in the last few years, a new theory has emerged. To end-run the bedrock separation-of-powers principle that courts may not unilaterally rewrite statutes, the plaintiffs here (and, recently, two Courts of Appeals) have advanced a novel and creative argument. They contend that discrimination "because of sexual orientation" and discrimination "because of sex" are actually not separate categories of discrimination after all. Instead, the theory goes, discrimination because of sexual orientation always qualifies as discrimination because of sex: When a gay man is fired because he is gay, he is fired because he is attracted to men, even though a similarly situated woman would not be fired just because she is attracted to men. According to this theory, it follows that the man has been fired, at least as a literal matter, because of his sex.

Under this literalist approach, sexual orientation discrimination automatically qualifies as sex discrimination, and Title VII's prohibition against sex discrimination therefore also prohibits sexual orientation discrimination—and actually has done so since 1964, unbeknownst to everyone. Surprisingly, the Court today buys into this approach.

For the sake of argument, I will assume that firing someone because of their sexual orientation may, as a very literal matter, entail making a distinction based on sex. But to prevail in this case with their literalist approach, the plaintiffs must *also* establish one of two other points. The plaintiffs must establish that courts, when interpreting a statute, adhere to literal meaning rather than ordinary meaning. Or alternatively, the plaintiffs must establish that the ordinary meaning of "discriminate because of sex"—not just the literal meaning—encompasses sexual orientation discrimination. The plaintiffs fall short on both counts.

First, courts must follow ordinary meaning, not literal meaning. And courts must adhere to the ordinary meaning of phrases, not just the meaning of the words in a phrase.

There is no serious debate about the foundational interpretive principle that courts adhere to ordinary meaning, not literal meaning, when interpreting statutes. As Justice Scalia explained, "the good textualist is not a literalist." A. Scalia, A Matter of Interpretation 24 (1997). Or as Professor Eskridge stated: The "prime directive in statutory interpretation is to apply the meaning that a reasonable reader would derive from the text of the law," so that "for hard cases as well as easy ones, the *ordinary meaning* (or the 'everyday meaning' or the 'commonsense' reading) of the relevant statutory text is the anchor for statutory interpretation." W. Eskridge, Interpreting Law 33, 34–35 (2016) (footnote omitted). Or as Professor Manning put it, proper statutory interpretation asks "how a reasonable person, conversant with the relevant social and linguistic conventions, would read the text in context. This approach recognizes that the literal or dictionary definitions of words will often fail to account for settled nuances or background conventions that qualify the literal meaning of language and, in particular, of legal language." Manning, *The Absurdity Doctrine*, 116 Harv. L. Rev. 2387, 2392–2393 (2003). . . .

Judges adhere to ordinary meaning for two main reasons: rule of law and democratic accountability. A society governed by the rule of law must have laws that are known and understandable to the citizenry. And judicial adherence to ordinary meaning facilitates the democratic accountability of America's elected representatives for the laws they enact. Citizens and legislators must be able to ascertain the law by reading the words of the statute. Both the rule of law and democratic accountability badly suffer when a court adopts a hidden or obscure interpretation of the law, and not its ordinary meaning.

Consider a simple example of how ordinary meaning differs from literal meaning. A statutory ban on "vehicles in the park" would literally encompass a baby stroller. But no good judge would interpret the statute that way because the word "vehicle," in its ordinary meaning, does not encompass baby strollers.

The ordinary meaning principle is longstanding and well settled. Time and again, this Court has rejected literalism in favor of ordinary meaning. Take a few examples:

The Court recognized that beans may be seeds "in the language of botany or natural history," but concluded that beans are not seeds "in commerce" or "in common parlance." Robertson v. Salomon, 130 U.S. 412, 414 (1889).

The Court explained that tomatoes are literally "the fruit of a vine," but "in the common language of the people," tomatoes are vegetables. Nix v. Hedden, 149 U.S. 304, 307 (1893).

The Court stated that the statutory term "vehicle" does not cover an aircraft: "No doubt etymologically it is possible to use the word to signify a conveyance working on land, water or air . . . . But in everyday speech 'vehicle' calls up the picture of a thing moving on land." McBoyle v. United States, 283 U.S. 25, 26 (1931).

The Court pointed out that "this Court's interpretation of the three-judge-court statutes has frequently deviated from the path of literalism." Gonzalez v. Automatic Employees Credit Union, 419 U.S. 90, 96 (1974).

The Court refused a reading of "mineral deposits" that would include water, even if "water is a 'mineral,' in the broadest sense of that word," because it would bring about a "major . . . alteration in established legal relationships based on nothing more than an overly literal reading of a statute, without any regard for its context or history." Andrus v. Charlestone Stone Products Co., 436 U.S. 604, 610, 616 (1978).

The Court declined to interpret "facilitating" a drug distribution crime in a way that would cover purchasing drugs, because the "literal sweep of 'facilitate' sits uncomfortably with common usage." Abuelhawa v. United States, 556 U.S. 816, 820 (2009). . . .

Those cases exemplify a deeply rooted principle: When there is a divide between the literal meaning and the ordinary meaning, courts must follow the ordinary meaning.

Next is a critical point of emphasis in this case. The difference between literal and ordinary meaning becomes especially important when—as in this case—judges consider *phrases* in statutes. (Recall that the shorthand version of the phrase at issue here is "discriminate because of sex.")3 Courts must heed the ordinary meaning of the *phrase as a whole*, not just the meaning of the words in the phrase. That is because a phrase may have a more precise or confined meaning than the literal meaning of the individual words in the phrase. Examples abound. An "American flag" could literally encompass a flag made in America, but in common parlance it denotes the Stars and Stripes. A "three-pointer" could literally include a field goal in football, but in common parlance, it is a shot from behind the arc in basketball. A "cold war" could literally mean any wintertime war, but in common parlance it signifies a conflict short of open warfare. A "washing machine" could literally refer to any machine used for washing any item, but in everyday speech it means a machine for washing clothes.

This Court has often emphasized the importance of sticking to the ordinary meaning *of a phrase*, rather than the meaning of words in the phrase. [*See supra* Section III.B.3] FCC v. AT&T Inc., 562 U.S. 397 (2011) . . . .

Justice Scalia explained the extraordinary importance of hewing to the ordinary meaning of a phrase: "Adhering to the *fair meaning* of the text (the textualist's touchstone) does not limit one to the hyperliteral meaning of each word in the text. In the words of Learned Hand: 'a sterile literalism . . . loses sight of the forest for the trees.' The full body of a text contains implications that can alter the literal meaning of individual words." A. Scalia & B. Garner, Reading Law 356 (2012) (footnote omitted). Put another way, "the meaning of a sentence may be more than that of the separate words, as a melody is more than the notes." Helvering v. Gregory, 69 F.2d 809, 810–811 (CA2 1934) (L. Hand, J.). Judges must take care to follow ordinary meaning "when two words combine to produce a meaning that is not the mechanical composition of the two words separately." Eskridge, Interpreting Law, at 62. Dictionaries are not "always useful for determining the ordinary meaning of word clusters (like 'driving a vehicle') or phrases and clauses or entire sentences." *Id.*, at 44. And we must recognize that a phrase can cover a "dramatically smaller category than either component term." *Id.*, at 62. . . .

In other words, this Court's precedents and longstanding principles of statutory interpretation teach a clear lesson: Do not simply split statutory phrases into their component words, look up each in a dictionary, and then mechanically put them together again, as the majority opinion today mistakenly does. . . .

A literalist approach to interpreting phrases disrespects ordinary meaning and deprives the citizenry of fair notice of what the law is. It destabilizes the rule of law and thwarts democratic accountability. For phrases as well as terms, the "linchpin of statutory interpretation is *ordinary meaning*, for that is going to be most accessible to the citizenry desirous of following the law *and* to the legislators and their staffs drafting the legal terms of the plans launched by statutes *and* to the administrators and judges implementing the statutory plan." Eskridge, Interpreting Law, at 81; *see* Scalia, A Matter of Interpretation, at 17.

Bottom line: Statutory Interpretation 101 instructs courts to follow ordinary meaning, not literal meaning, and to adhere to the ordinary meaning of phrases, not just the meaning of the words in a phrase.

Second, in light of the bedrock principle that we must adhere to the ordinary meaning of a phrase, the question in this case boils down to the ordinary meaning of the phrase "discriminate because of sex." Does the ordinary meaning of that phrase encompass discrimination because of sexual orientation? The answer is plainly no.

On occasion, it can be difficult for judges to assess ordinary meaning. Not here. Both common parlance and common legal usage treat sex discrimination and sexual orientation discrimination as two distinct categories of discrimination—back in 1964 and still today.

As to common parlance, few in 1964 (or today) would describe a firing because of sexual orientation as a firing because of sex. . . .

Contrary to the majority opinion's approach today, this Court has repeatedly emphasized that common parlance matters in assessing the ordinary meaning of a statute, because courts heed how "most people" "would have understood" the text of a statute when enacted. [Citations.]

Consider the employer who has four employees but must fire two of them for financial reasons. Suppose the four employees are a straight man, a straight woman, a gay man, and a lesbian. The employer with animosity against women (animosity based on sex) will fire the two women. The employer with animosity against gays (animosity based on sexual orientation) will fire the gay man and the lesbian. Those are two distinct harms caused by two distinct biases that have two different outcomes. To treat one as a form of the other—as the majority opinion does—misapprehends common language, human psychology, and real life. [Citation.]

It also rewrites history. Seneca Falls was not Stonewall. The women's rights movement was not (and is not) the gay rights movement, although many people obviously support or participate in both. So to think that sexual orientation discrimination is just a form of sex discrimination is not just a mistake of language and psychology, but also a mistake of history and sociology.

Importantly, an overwhelming body of federal law reflects and reinforces the ordinary meaning and demonstrates that sexual orientation discrimination is distinct from, and not a form of, sex discrimination. Since enacting Title VII in 1964, Congress has *never* treated sexual orientation discrimination the same as, or as a form of, sex discrimination. Instead, Congress has consistently treated sex discrimination and sexual orientation discrimination as legally distinct categories of discrimination. . . . That longstanding and widespread congressional practice matters. When interpreting statutes, as the Court has often said, we "usually presume differences in language" convey "differences in meaning." *Wisconsin Central*, 585 U.S., at ___, 138 S. Ct., at 2071 (internal quotation marks omitted). When Congress chooses distinct phrases to accomplish distinct purposes, and does so over and over again for decades, we may not lightly toss aside all of Congress's careful handiwork. . . .

So it is here. As demonstrated by all of the statutes covering sexual orientation discrimination, Congress knows how to prohibit sexual orientation discrimination. So courts should not read that specific concept into the general words "discriminate because of sex." . . . Where possible, we also strive to interpret statutes so as not to create undue surplusage. It is not uncommon to find some scattered redundancies in statutes. But reading sex discrimination to encompass sexual orientation discrimination would cast aside as surplusage the numerous references to sexual orientation discrimination sprinkled throughout the U.S. Code in laws enacted over the last 25 years.

The story is the same with bills proposed in Congress. Since the 1970s, Members of Congress have introduced many bills to prohibit sexual orientation discrimination in the workplace. . . . [T]he proposed bills are telling because they, like the enacted laws, further demonstrate the widespread usage of the English language in the United States: Sexual orientation discrimination is distinct from, and not a form of, sex discrimination.

Presidential Executive Orders reflect that same common understanding. [Citing examples.] . . . Federal regulations likewise reflect that same understanding. [Citing examples.] . . . The States have proceeded in the same fashion. A majority of States prohibit sexual orientation discrimination in employment, either by legislation applying to most workers, an executive order applying to public employees, or both. Almost every state statute or executive order proscribing sexual orientation discrimination expressly prohibits sexual orientation discrimination separately from the State's ban on sex discrimination. . . . That common usage in the States underscores that sexual orientation discrimination is commonly understood as a legal concept distinct from sex discrimination.

And it is the common understanding in this Court as well. [Citations.] Over the last several decades, the Court has also decided many cases involving sexual orientation. But in those cases, the Court never suggested that sexual orientation discrimination is just a form of sex discrimination. All of the Court's cases . . . would have been far easier to analyze and decide if sexual orientation discrimination were just a form of sex discrimination and therefore received the same heightened scrutiny as sex discrimination under the Equal Protection Clause. [Citations.]

Did the Court in all of those sexual orientation cases just miss that obvious answer—and overlook the fact that sexual orientation discrimination is actually a form of sex discrimination? That seems implausible. Nineteen Justices have participated in those cases. Not a single Justice stated or even hinted that sexual orientation discrimination was just a form of sex discrimination and therefore entitled to the same heightened scrutiny under the Equal Protection Clause. . . .

In sum, all of the usual indicators of ordinary meaning—common parlance, common usage by Congress, the practice in the Executive Branch, the laws in the States, and the decisions of this Court—overwhelmingly establish that sexual orientation discrimination is distinct from, and not a form of, sex discrimination. The usage has been consistent across decades, in both the federal and state contexts. . . .

To tie it all together, the plaintiffs have only two routes to succeed here. Either they can say that literal meaning overrides ordinary meaning when the two conflict. Or they can say that the ordinary meaning of the phrase "discriminate because of sex" encompasses sexual orientation discrimination. But the first flouts long-settled principles of statutory interpretation. And the second contradicts the widespread ordinary use of the English language in America.

II

Until the last few years, every U.S. Court of Appeals to address this question concluded that Title VII does not prohibit discrimination because of sexual orientation. So what changed from the situation only a few years ago . . .? Not the text of Title VII. The law has not changed. Rather, the judges' decisions have evolved. . . .

In judicially rewriting Title VII, the Court today cashiers an ongoing legislative process, at a time when a new law to prohibit sexual orientation discrimination was probably close at hand. . . . In 2019, the House voted 236 to 173 to amend Title VII to prohibit employment discrimination on the basis of sexual orientation. H.R. 5, 116th Cong., 1st Sess. It was therefore easy to envision a day, likely just in the next few years, when the House and Senate took historic votes on a bill that would prohibit employment discrimination on the basis of sexual orientation. It was easy to picture a massive and celebratory Presidential signing ceremony in the East Room or on the South Lawn.

It is true that meaningful legislative action takes time—often too much time, especially in the unwieldy morass on Capitol Hill. But . . . [t]he proper role of the Judiciary in statutory interpretation cases is "to apply, not amend, the work of the People's representatives," even when the judges might think that "Congress should reenter the field and alter the judgments it made in the past." [Citation.]

Instead of a hard-earned victory won through the democratic process, today's victory is brought about by judicial dictate—judges latching on to a novel form of living literalism to rewrite ordinary meaning and remake American law. Under the Constitution and laws of the United States, this Court is the wrong body to change American law in that way. . . . And the implications of this Court's usurpation of the legislative process will likely reverberate in unpredictable ways for years to come.

Notwithstanding my concern about the Court's transgression of the Constitution's separation of powers, it is appropriate to acknowledge the important victory achieved today by gay and lesbian Americans. Millions of gay and lesbian Americans have worked hard for many decades to achieve equal treatment in fact and in law. They have exhibited extraordinary vision, tenacity, and grit—battling often steep odds in the legislative and judicial arenas, not to mention in their daily lives. They have advanced powerful policy arguments and can take pride in today's result. Under the Constitution's separation of powers, however, I believe that it was Congress's role, not this Court's, to amend Title VII. I therefore must respectfully dissent from the Court's judgment.

QUESTIONS

1. In his famous essay setting out the dueling "thrust/parry" canons of statutory construction, excerpted in Section II.B.3, *supra*, Professor Karl Llewellyn also addressed the problem of statutes whose "language is called upon to deal with circumstances utterly uncontemplated at the time of its passage":

> Here the quest is not properly for the sense originally intended by the statute, for the sense sought originally to be put into it, but rather for the sense which can be quarried out of it in the light of the new situation. Broad purposes can indeed reach far beyond details known or knowable at the time of drafting. . . . But for all that, the sound quest does not run primarily in terms of historical intent. It runs in terms of what the words can be made to bear, in making sense in the light of the unforeseen.

Karl N. Llewellyn, *Remarks on the Theory of Appellate Decision and the Rules or Canons About How Statutes Are to be Construed*, 3 Vand. L. Rev. 395 (1950).

Justice Gorsuch's opinion seems to follow the prescription to "quarr[y] out of" Title VII a meaning that "because of sex" can be "made to bear." But does the last element of Llewellyn's formula belie the apparent rigor of the rest? To whom should the words "mak[e] sense in light of the unforeseen"? Is it possible that the extent to which the words make sense turns on normative agreement with the result?

2. Why do you think neither of the dissenters cited Congress's overruling of *General Electric Co. v Gilbert* by enacting the Pregnancy Discrimination Act? When the Supreme Court announced a blinkered view of "because of sex," Congress made clear that pregnancy discrimination was sex discrimination. By contrast, Congress didn't overrule the 30 appellate court decisions holding that sexual orientation discrimination wasn't sex discrimination. Does the history of the PDA make Congress' inaction more probative? Or does it matter that, on the one hand, Congress was correcting a definitive Supreme Court interpretation of the statute in *Gilbert*, while on the other, until *Bostock* the Court had not clearly announced a uniform and final interpretation of Title VII's meaning with respect to sexual orientation or gender identity?*

3. In his dissent, Justice Kavanaugh refers to, but does not define, "literal meaning." What kind of meaning do you think "literal meaning" refers to? Consider, for example, the discussion in the Note on "Corpus Linguistics" in Section III.B.3.b, *supra*, about the range of potential meanings that could be considered a kind of linguistic meaning: these include a linguistically *possible* meaning, a *common* meaning, the *most frequent* meaning, and an *exclusive* meaning. Which of these, if any, do you think best describes what Justice Kavanaugh refers to as "literal" meaning? Which do you think best describes what he refers to as "ordinary" meaning? Does it matter?

4. Justice Kavanaugh's dissent rejects the application of the "literal" meaning of statutory terms by invoking Justice Scalia's admonition against rote, literalist textualism. If "literal" meaning is simply the application of any *permissible* meaning, can you think of other instances in this Casebook in which the "literal" meaning was promoted by one or more Justices? Consider, for example, the dissent's interpretation of "an Exchange established by the state" in *King v. Burwell, supra* Section III.A.2.a; the dissent's interpretation of "*any* tangible object" in *Yates v. United States, supra* Section III.A.1; or the majority's interpretation of the prohibition on "harm[ing]" endangered species in *Babbitt v. Sweet Home, supra* Section V.C.3. Would you describe any of these interpretations as "literal?" Why or why not?

5. What is "living literalism"? Can "literalism" be both "living" and "sterile," as Justice Kavanaugh charges?

6. If "because of sex" always encompassed discrimination against gay and transgender people, why did it take over 50 years to realize that? What about those 30 federal judges Justice Kavanaugh asserted all rejected the application of Title VII to claims of discrimination based on sexual orientation?

7. In addition to deciding whether to attribute to a statutory term its "original" or, instead, its "present-day" meaning, a court may often confront an additional temporal issue: how to interpret the statute's meaning in light

---

*   Editors' Note: To our knowledge, Congress has never enacted a statutory amendment with the aim to override the judgment of a lower federal court without the Supreme Court first upholding that judgment. For more on congressional overrides of Supreme Court precedents, *see infra* Section VII.C.2, "Note: Overriding Supreme Court Precedents."

of prior related judicial interpretations of the *legal* meaning of the provision
at issue. As Section VII.B will explore, courts often must interpret a statute
in light of past courts' prior interpretations; this application of their prior
interpretations resembles the synthesis of common-law precedents applied
to new circumstances. But the common law is not fixed in text; its inherent
fluidity allows it to evolve. By contrast, the words of a statute do not change
by judicial fiat (judges are not supposed to rewrite statutes). Yet statutory
interpretation, like common-law analysis, is an essentially accretive
exercise. Given this, can a statute be said to continue to convey an "ordinary"
and "original" meaning (*i.e.*, the meaning the term or phrase conveyed in
ordinary linguistic usage at the time of the statute's passage) once the
statute has acquired a different legal meaning through repeated applications
over time? As Title VII's long and tortuous interpretive (and amendment)
history reveals, both courts and Congress have elaborated on the meaning of
the term "because of sex" in ways that give the term a *legal* meaning distinct
from the term's probable *ordinary* meaning at the time of the statute's
passage. If, for example, it is unlikely that Congress intended (or the
reasonable reader of 1964 understood) Title VII's prohibition of
discrimination "because of sex" to apply to instances of same-sex harassment
or to discrimination on the basis of sex-stereotyping, can the original
ordinary meaning continue to be the touchstone for future applications of the
statute? And could the "literal" meaning Justice Kavanaugh suggests Justice
Gorsuch has applied also be considered the statute's "legal" meaning in light
of prior precedents? Why or why not?

B. APPLYING NEW STATUTES TO ONGOING CIRCUMSTANCES

Landgraf v. USI Film Products

Supreme Court of the United States, 1994.
511 U.S. 244, 114 S.Ct. 1483, 128 L.Ed.2d 229.

■ JUSTICE STEVENS delivered the opinion of the Court[, in which CHIEF
JUSTICE REHNQUIST, JUSTICE O'CONNOR, JUSTICE SOUTER, and JUSTICE
GINSBURG joined].

The Civil Rights Act of 1991 (1991 Act or Act) creates a right to
recover compensatory and punitive damages for certain violations of Title
VII of the Civil Rights Act of 1964. *See* Rev. Stat. § 1977A(a), 42 U.S.C.
§ 1981a(a), as added by § 102 of the 1991 Act, Pub. L. 102–166, 105 Stat.
1071. The Act further provides that any party may demand a trial by jury
if such damages are sought. We granted certiorari to decide whether
these provisions apply to a Title VII case that was pending on appeal
when the statute was enacted. We hold that they do not.

I

From September 4, 1984, through January 17, 1986, petitioner
Barbara Landgraf was employed in the USI Film Products (USI) plant in
Tyler, Texas. She worked the 11 p.m. to 7 a.m. shift operating a machine

that produced plastic bags. A fellow employee named John Williams repeatedly harassed her with inappropriate remarks and physical contact. Petitioner's complaints to her immediate supervisor brought her no relief, but when she reported the incidents to the personnel manager, he conducted an investigation, reprimanded Williams, and transferred him to another department. Four days later petitioner quit her job.

Petitioner filed a timely charge with the Equal Employment Opportunity Commission (EEOC or Commission). The Commission determined that petitioner had likely been the victim of sexual harassment creating a hostile work environment in violation of Title VII of the Civil Rights Act of 1964, 42 U.S.C. § 2000e et seq., but concluded that her employer had adequately remedied the violation. Accordingly, the Commission dismissed the charge and issued a notice of right to sue.

On July 21, 1989, petitioner commenced this action against USI, its corporate owner, and that company's successor-in-interest. After a bench trial, the District Court found that Williams had sexually harassed petitioner causing her to suffer mental anguish. However, the court concluded that she had not been constructively discharged. The court said:

> "Although the harassment was serious enough to establish that a hostile work environment existed for Landgraf, it was not so severe that a reasonable person would have felt compelled to resign. This is particularly true in light of the fact that at the time Landgraf resigned from her job, USI had taken steps . . . to eliminate the hostile working environment arising from the sexual harassment. Landgraf voluntarily resigned from her employment with USI for reasons unrelated to the sexual harassment in question." App. to Pet. for Cert. B-3–4.

Because the court found that petitioner's employment was not terminated in violation of Title VII, she was not entitled to equitable relief, and because Title VII did not then authorize any other form of relief, the court dismissed her complaint.

On November 21, 1991, while petitioner's appeal was pending, the President signed into law the Civil Rights Act of 1991. The Court of Appeals rejected petitioner's argument that her case should be remanded for a jury trial on damages pursuant to the 1991 Act. Its decision not to remand rested on the premise that "a court must 'apply the law in effect at the time it renders its decision, unless doing so would result in manifest injustice or there is statutory direction or legislative history to the contrary.' Bradley [v. Richmond School Bd., 416 U.S. 696, 711 (1974)]." 968 F.2d 427, 432 (C.A.5 1992). Commenting first on the provision for a jury trial in § 102(c), the court stated that requiring the defendant "to retry this case because of a statutory change enacted after the trial was completed would be an injustice and a waste of judicial resources. We apply procedural rules to pending cases, but we do not invalidate procedures followed before the new rule was adopted." 968

F.2d, at 432–433. The court then characterized the provision for compensatory and punitive damages in § 102 as "a seachange in employer liability for Title VII violations" and concluded that it would be unjust to apply this kind of additional and unforeseeable obligation to conduct occurring before the effective date of the Act. *Ibid.* Finding no clear error in the District Court's factual findings, the Court of Appeals affirmed the judgment for respondents.

We granted certiorari and set the case for argument with Rivers v. Roadway Express, Inc., 507 U.S. 908 (1993). Our order limited argument to the question whether § 102 of the 1991 Act applies to cases pending when it became law. 507 U.S. 908 (1993). Accordingly, for purposes of our decision, we assume that the District Court and the Court of Appeals properly applied the law in effect at the time of the discriminatory conduct and that the relevant findings of fact were correct. We therefore assume that petitioner was the victim of sexual harassment violative of Title VII, but that the law did not then authorize any recovery of damages even though she was injured. We also assume, arguendo, that if the same conduct were to occur today, petitioner would be entitled to a jury trial and that the jury might find that she was constructively discharged, or that her mental anguish or other injuries would support an award of damages against her former employer. Thus, the controlling question is whether the Court of Appeals should have applied the law in effect at the time the discriminatory conduct occurred, or at the time of its decision in July 1992.

II

Petitioner's primary submission is that the text of the 1991 Act requires that it be applied to cases pending on its enactment. Her argument, if accepted, would make the entire Act (with two narrow exceptions) applicable to conduct that occurred, and to cases that were filed, before the Act's effective date. Although only § 102 is at issue in this case, we therefore preface our analysis with a brief description of the scope of the 1991 Act.

The Civil Rights Act of 1991 is in large part a response to a series of decisions of this Court interpreting the Civil Rights Acts of 1866 and 1964. Section 3(4) expressly identifies as one of the Act's purposes "to respond to recent decisions of the Supreme Court by expanding the scope of relevant civil rights statutes in order to provide adequate protection to victims of discrimination." That section, as well as a specific finding in § 2(2), identifies Wards Cove Packing Co. v. Atonio, 490 U.S. 642 (1989), as a decision that gave rise to special concerns.[3] Section 105 of the Act,

---

[3] Section 2(2) finds that the Wards Cove decision "has weakened the scope and effectiveness of Federal civil rights protections," and § 3(2) expresses Congress' intent "to codify" certain concepts enunciated in "Supreme Court decisions prior to Wards Cove Packing Co. v. Atonio, 490 U.S. 642 [109 S.Ct. 2115, 104 L.Ed.2d 733] (1989)." We take note of the express references to that case because it is the focus of § 402(b), on which petitioner places particular reliance.

entitled "Burden of Proof in Disparate Impact Cases," is a direct response to Wards Cove.

Other sections of the Act were obviously drafted with "recent decisions of the Supreme Court" in mind. [citations omitted]. A number of important provisions in the Act, however, were not responses to Supreme Court decisions. For example, § 106 enacts a new prohibition against adjusting test scores "on the basis of race, color, religion, sex, or national origin"; § 117 extends the coverage of Title VII to include the House of Representatives and certain employees of the Legislative Branch; and §§ 301–325 establish special procedures to protect Senate employees from discrimination. Among the provisions that did not directly respond to any Supreme Court decision is the one at issue in this case, § 102.

Entitled "Damages in Cases of Intentional Discrimination," § 102 provides in relevant part:

(a) Right of Recovery.—

(1) Civil Rights.—In an action brought by a complaining party under section 706 or 717 of the Civil Rights Act of 1964 (42 U.S.C. 2000e–5) against a respondent who engaged in unlawful intentional discrimination (not an employment practice that is unlawful because of its disparate impact) prohibited under section 703, 704, or 717 of the Act (42 U.S.C. 2000e–2 or 2000e–3), and provided that the complaining party cannot recover under section 1977 of the Revised Statutes (42 U.S.C. 1981), the complaining party may recover compensatory and punitive damages ... in addition to any relief authorized by section 706(g) of the Civil Rights Act of 1964, from the respondent....

(c) Jury Trial.—If a complaining party seeks compensatory or punitive damages under this section—

(1) any party may demand a trial by jury.

Before the enactment of the 1991 Act, Title VII afforded only "equitable" remedies. The primary form of monetary relief available was backpay. Title VII's back pay remedy, modeled on that of the National Labor Relations Act, 29 U.S.C. § 160(c), is a "make-whole" remedy that resembles compensatory damages in some respects. *See* Albemarle Paper Co. v. Moody, 422 U.S. 405, 418–422 (1975). However, the new compensatory damages provision of the 1991 Act is "in addition to," and does not replace or duplicate, the backpay remedy allowed under prior law. Indeed, to prevent double recovery, the 1991 Act provides that compensatory damages "shall not include backpay, interest on backpay, or any other type of relief authorized under section 706(g) of the Civil Rights Act of 1964." § 102(b)(2).

Section 102 significantly expands the monetary relief potentially available to plaintiffs who would have been entitled to backpay under prior law....

Section 102 also allows monetary relief for some forms of workplace discrimination that would not previously have justified any relief under Title VII. As this case illustrates, even if unlawful discrimination was proved, under prior law a Title VII plaintiff could not recover monetary relief unless the discrimination was also found to have some concrete effect on the plaintiff's employment status, such as a denied promotion, a differential in compensation, or termination. Section 102, however, allows a plaintiff to recover in circumstances in which there has been unlawful discrimination in the "terms, conditions, or privileges of employment," 42 U.S.C. § 2000e–2(a)(1), even though the discrimination did not involve a discharge or a loss of pay. In short, to further Title VII's "central statutory purposes of eradicating discrimination throughout the economy and making persons whole for injuries suffered through past discrimination," Albemarle Paper Co., 422 U.S., at 421, 95 S.Ct., at 2373, § 102 of the 1991 Act effects a major expansion in the relief available to victims of employment discrimination.

In 1990, a comprehensive civil rights bill passed both Houses of Congress. Although similar to the 1991 Act in many other respects, the 1990 bill differed in that it contained language expressly calling for application of many of its provisions, including the section providing for damages in cases of intentional employment discrimination, to cases arising before its (expected) enactment.[8] The President vetoed the 1990

---

[8] The relevant section of the Civil Rights Act of 1990, S. 2104, 101st Cong., 1st Sess. (1990), provided:

"SEC. 15. APPLICATION OF AMENDMENTS AND TRANSITION RULES.

    "(a) APPLICATION OF AMENDMENTS.—The amendments made by—

        (1) section 4 shall apply to all proceedings pending on or commenced after June 5, 1989 [the date of Wards Cove Packing Co. v. Atonio, 490 U.S. 642, 109 S.Ct. 2115];

        "(2) section 5 shall apply to all proceedings pending on or commenced after May 1, 1989 [the date of Price Waterhouse v. Hopkins, 490 U.S. 228, 109 S.Ct. 1775];

        "(3) section 6 shall apply to all proceedings pending on or commenced after June 12, 1989 [the date of Martin v. Wilks, 490 U.S. 755, 109 S.Ct. 2180];

        "(4) sections 7(a)(1), 7(a)(3) and 7(a)(4), 7(b), 8 [providing for compensatory and punitive damages for intentional discrimination], 9, 10, and 11 shall apply to all proceedings pending on or commenced after the date of enactment of this Act;

        "(5) section 7(a)(2) shall apply to all proceedings pending on or after June 12, 1989 [the date of Lorance v. AT & T Technologies, Inc., 490 U.S. 900, 109 S.Ct. 2261]; and

        "(6) section 12 shall apply to all proceedings pending on or commenced after June 15, 1989 [the date of Patterson v. McLean Credit Union, 491 U.S. 164, 109 S.Ct. 2363].

    "(b) TRANSITION RULES.—

        "(1) IN GENERAL.—Any orders entered by a court between the effective dates described in subsection (a) and the date of enactment of this Act that are inconsistent with the amendments made by sections 4, 5, 7(a)(2), or 12, shall be vacated if, not later than 1 year after such date of enactment, a request for such relief is made.

        "(3) FINAL JUDGMENTS.—Pursuant to paragraphs (1) and (2), any final judgment entered prior to the date of the enactment of this Act as to which the rights of any of the parties thereto have become fixed and vested, where the time for seeking further judicial review of such judgment has otherwise expired pursuant to title 28 of the United States Code, the Federal Rules of Civil Procedure, and the Federal Rules of Appellate Procedure, shall be vacated in whole or in part if justice requires pursuant to rule 60(b)(6) of the Federal Rules of Civil Procedure or other legislation, however, citing the bill's "unfair retroactivity rules" as one reason for his disapproval.[9] Congress narrowly failed to override the veto. *See* 136 Cong. Rec. S16589 (Oct. 24, 1990) (66–34 Senate vote in favor of override.) . . .

The absence of comparable language in the 1991 Act cannot realistically be attributed to oversight or to unawareness of the retroactivity issue. Rather, it seems likely that one of the compromises that made it possible to enact the 1991 version was an agreement not to include the kind of explicit retroactivity command found in the 1990 bill.

The omission of the elaborate retroactivity provision of the 1990 bill—which was by no means the only source of political controversy over that legislation—is not dispositive because it does not tell us precisely where the compromise was struck in the 1991 Act. . . . Our first question, then, is whether the statutory text on which petitioner relies manifests an intent that the 1991 Act should be applied to cases that arose and went to trial before its enactment.

III

Petitioner's textual argument relies on three provisions of the 1991 Act: §§ 402(a), 402(b), and 109(c). Section 402(a), the only provision of the Act that speaks directly to the question before us, states:

> Except as otherwise specifically provided, this Act and the amendments made by this Act shall take effect upon enactment.

That language does not, by itself, resolve the question before us. A statement that a statute will become effective on a certain date does not even arguably suggest that it has any application to conduct that occurred at an earlier date.[10] Petitioner does not argue otherwise. Rather, she contends that the introductory clause of § 402(a) would be

---

appropriate authority, and consistent with the constitutional requirements of due process of law."

[9] *See* President's Message to the Senate Returning Without Approval the Civil Rights Act of 1990, 26 Weekly Comp.Pres.Doc. 1632–1634 (Oct. 22, 1990), reprinted in 136 Cong. Rec. S16418, 16419 (Oct. 22, 1990). The President's veto message referred to the bill's "retroactivity" only briefly; the Attorney General's Memorandum to which the President referred was no more expansive, and may be read to refer only to the bill's special provision for reopening final judgments, *see* n. 8, *supra*, rather than its provisions covering pending cases.

[10] The history of prior amendments to Title VII suggests that the "effective-upon-enactment" formula would have been an especially inapt way to reach pending cases. When it amended Title VII in the Equal Employment Opportunity Act of 1972, Congress explicitly provided:

"The amendments made by this Act to section 706 of the Civil Rights Act of 1964 shall be applicable with respect to charges pending with the Commission on the date of enactment of this Act and all charges filed thereafter." Pub. L. 92–261, § 14, 86 Stat. 113. In contrast, in amending Title VII to bar discrimination on the basis of pregnancy in 1978, Congress provided:

"Except as provided in subsection (b), the amendment made by this Act shall be effective on the date of enactment." § 2(a), 92 Stat. 2076.

The only Courts of Appeals to consider whether the 1978 amendments applied to pending cases concluded that they did not. [Citations omitted].

superfluous unless it refers to §§ 402(b) and 109(c), which provide for prospective application in limited contexts.

The parties agree that § 402(b) was intended to exempt a single disparate impact lawsuit against the Wards Cove Packing Company. Section 402(b) provides:

> (b) CERTAIN   DISPARATE   IMPACT   CASES.—
> Notwithstanding any other provision of this Act, nothing in this Act shall apply to any disparate impact case for which a complaint was filed before March 1, 1975, and for which an initial decision was rendered after October 30, 1983.

Section 109(c), part of the section extending Title VII to overseas employers, states:

> (c) APPLICATION OF AMENDMENTS.—The amendments made by this section shall not apply with respect to conduct occurring before the date of the enactment of this Act.

According to petitioner, these two subsections are the "other provisions" contemplated in the first clause of § 402(a), and together create a strong negative inference that all sections of the Act not specifically declared prospective apply to pending cases that arose before November 21, 1991.

Before addressing the particulars of petitioner's argument, we observe that she places extraordinary weight on two comparatively minor and narrow provisions in a long and complex statute. Applying the entire Act to cases arising from preenactment conduct would have important consequences, including the possibility that trials completed before its enactment would need to be retried and the possibility that employers would be liable for punitive damages for conduct antedating the Act's enactment. Purely prospective application, on the other hand, would prolong the life of a remedial scheme, and of judicial constructions of civil rights statutes, that Congress obviously found wanting. Given the high stakes of the retroactivity question, the broad coverage of the statute, and the prominent and specific retroactivity provisions in the 1990 bill, it would be surprising for Congress to have chosen to resolve that question through negative inferences drawn from two provisions of quite limited effect.

Petitioner, however, invokes the canon that a court should give effect to every provision of a statute and thus avoid redundancy among different provisions. Unless the word "otherwise" in § 402(a) refers to either § 402(b) or § 109(c), she contends, the first five words in § 402(a) are entirely superfluous. Moreover, relying on the canon "[e]xpressio unius est exclusio alterius," petitioner argues that because Congress provided specifically for prospectivity in two places (§§ 109(c) and 402(b)), we should infer that it intended the opposite for the remainder of the statute. [citations omitted].

Petitioner emphasizes that § 402(a) begins: "Except as otherwise specifically provided." A scan of the statute for other "specific provisions" concerning effective dates reveals that §§ 402(b) and 109(c) are the most likely candidates. Since those provisions decree prospectivity, and since § 402(a) tells us that the specific provisions are exceptions, § 402(a) should be considered as prescribing a general rule of retroactivity. Petitioner's argument has some force, but we find it most unlikely that Congress intended the introductory clause to carry the critically important meaning petitioner assigns it. Had Congress wished § 402(a) to have such a determinate meaning, it surely would have used language comparable to its reference to the predecessor Title VII damages provisions in the 1990 legislation: that the new provisions "shall apply to all proceedings pending on or commenced after the date of enactment of this Act." S. 2104, 101st Cong., 1st Sess. § 15(a)(4) (1990).

It is entirely possible that Congress inserted the "otherwise specifically provided" language not because it understood the "takes effect" clause to establish a rule of retroactivity to which only two "other specific provisions" would be exceptions, but instead to assure that any specific timing provisions in the Act would prevail over the general "take effect on enactment" command. The drafters of a complicated piece of legislation containing more than 50 separate sections may well have inserted the "except as otherwise provided" language merely to avoid the risk of an inadvertent conflict in the statute.[11] If the introductory clause of § 402(a) was intended to refer specifically to §§ 402(b), 109(c), or both, it is difficult to understand why the drafters chose the word "otherwise" rather than either or both of the appropriate section numbers.

We are also unpersuaded by petitioner's argument that both §§ 402(b) and 109(c) merely duplicate the "take effect upon enactment" command of § 402(a) unless all other provisions, including the damages provisions of § 102, apply to pending cases. That argument depends on the assumption that all those other provisions must be treated uniformly for purposes of their application to pending cases based on preenactment conduct. That thesis, however, is by no means an inevitable one. It is entirely possible—indeed, highly probable—that, because it was unable to resolve the retroactivity issue with the clarity of the 1990 legislation, Congress viewed the matter as an open issue to be resolved by the courts. Our precedents on retroactivity left doubts about what default rule would apply in the absence of congressional guidance, and suggested that some provisions might apply to cases arising before enactment while others might not.[12] [citations omitted]. The only matters Congress did not leave

---

[11] There is some evidence that the drafters of the 1991 Act did not devote particular attention to the interplay of the Act's "effective date" provisions. Section 110, which directs the EEOC to establish a "Technical Assistance Training Institute" to assist employers in complying with antidiscrimination laws and regulations, contains a subsection providing that it "shall take effect on the date of enactment of this Act." § 110(b). That provision and § 402(a) are unavoidably redundant.

[12] This point also diminishes the force of petitioner's "expressio unius" argument. Once one abandons the unsupported assumption that Congress expected that all of the Act's provisions would be treated alike, and takes account of uncertainty about the applicable default rule, § 109(c) and 402(b) do not carry the negative implication petitioner draws from them. We do not

to the courts were set out with specificity in § 109(c) and 402(b). Congressional doubt concerning judicial retroactivity doctrine, coupled with the likelihood that the routine "take effect upon enactment" language would require courts to fall back upon that doctrine, provide a plausible explanation for both §§ 402(b) and 109(c) that makes neither provision redundant.

Turning to the text of § 402(b), it seems unlikely that the introductory phrase ("Notwithstanding any other provision of this Act") was meant to refer to the immediately preceding subsection. Since petitioner does not contend that any other provision speaks to the general effective date issue, the logic of her argument requires us to interpret that phrase to mean nothing more than "Notwithstanding § 402(a)." Petitioner's textual argument assumes that the drafters selected the indefinite word "otherwise" in § 402(a) to identify two specific subsections and the even more indefinite term "any other provision" in § 402(b) to refer to nothing more than § 402(b)'s next-door neighbor—§ 402(a). Here again, petitioner's statutory argument would require us to assume that Congress chose a surprisingly indirect route to convey an important and easily expressed message concerning the Act's effect on pending cases.

The relevant legislative history of the 1991 Act reinforces our conclusion that §§ 402(a), 109(c) and 402(b) cannot bear the weight petitioner places upon them. The 1991 bill as originally introduced in the House contained explicit retroactivity provisions similar to those found in the 1990 bill.[13] However, the Senate substitute that was agreed upon omitted those explicit retroactivity provisions. The legislative history discloses some frankly partisan statements about the meaning of the final effective date language, but those statements cannot plausibly be read as reflecting any general agreement. The history reveals no evidence that Members believed that an agreement had been tacitly struck on the controversial retroactivity issue, and little to suggest that Congress understood or intended the interplay of §§ 402(a), 402(b) and 109(c) to have the decisive effect petitioner assigns them. Instead, the history of the 1991 Act conveys the impression that legislators agreed to disagree about whether and to what extent the Act would apply to preenactment conduct.

Although the passage of the 1990 bill may indicate that a majority of the 1991 Congress also favored retroactive application, even the will of the majority does not become law unless it follows the path charted in Article I, § 7, cl. 2 of the Constitution. [citation omitted] In the absence of

---

read either provision as doing anything more than definitively rejecting retroactivity with respect to the specific matters covered by its plain language.

[13] *See, e.g.*, H.R. 1, 102d Cong., 1st Sess. § 113 (1991), reprinted in 137 Cong. Rec. H3924–H3925 (Jan. 3, 1991). The prospectivity proviso to the section extending Title VII to overseas employers was first added to legislation that generally was to apply to pending cases. *See* H.R. 1, 102d Cong., 1st Sess. § 119(c) (1991), reprinted in 137 Cong. Rec. H3925–H3926 (June 5, 1991). Thus, at the time its language was introduced, the provision that became § 109(c) was surely not redundant.

the kind of unambiguous directive found in § 15 of the 1990 bill, we must look elsewhere for guidance on whether § 102 applies to this case.

IV

It is not uncommon to find "apparent tension" between different canons of statutory construction. As Professor Llewellyn famously illustrated, many of the traditional canons have equal opposites.[16] In order to resolve the question left open by the 1991 Act, federal courts have labored to reconcile two seemingly contradictory statements found in our decisions concerning the effect of intervening changes in the law. Each statement is framed as a generally applicable rule for interpreting statutes that do not specify their temporal reach. The first is the rule that "a court is to apply the law in effect at the time it renders its decision," *Bradley*, 416 U.S., at 711. The second is the axiom that "[r]etroactivity is not favored in the law," and its interpretive corollary that "congressional enactments and administrative rules will not be construed to have retroactive effect unless their language requires this result." *Bowen*, 488 U.S., at 208. . . .

[W]e turn to the "apparent tension" between the two canons mindful of another canon of unquestionable vitality, the "maxim not to be disregarded that general expressions, in every opinion, are to be taken in connection with the case in which those expressions are used." Cohens v. Virginia, 6 Wheat. 264, 399 (1821).

A

As Justice Scalia has demonstrated, the presumption against retroactive legislation is deeply rooted in our jurisprudence, and embodies a legal doctrine centuries older than our Republic. Elementary considerations of fairness dictate that individuals should have an opportunity to know what the law is and to conform their conduct accordingly; settled expectations should not be lightly disrupted. For that reason, the "principle that the legal effect of conduct should ordinarily be assessed under the law that existed when the conduct took place has timeless and universal appeal." [citation omitted]. In a free, dynamic society, creativity in both commercial and artistic endeavors is fostered by a rule of law that gives people confidence about the legal consequences of their actions.

It is therefore not surprising that the antiretroactivity principle finds expression in several provisions of our Constitution [including the

---

[16] *See* Llewellyn, *Remarks on the Theory of Appellate Decision and the Rules or Canons about How Statutes are to be Construed*, 3 Vand. L. Rev. 395 (1950). Llewellyn's article identified the apparent conflict between the canon that

> "[a] statute imposing a new penalty or forfeiture, or a new liability or disability, or creating a new right of action will not be construed as having a retroactive effect;"

and the countervailing rule that

> "[r]emedial statutes are to be liberally construed and if a retroactive interpretation will promote the ends of justice, they should receive such construction." *Id.*, at 402 (citations omitted).

Ex Post Facto, Takings, and Due Process Clauses and the prohibition on Bills of Attainder]. . . . The Constitution's restrictions, of course, are of limited scope. Absent a violation of one of those specific provisions, the potential unfairness of retroactive civil legislation is not a sufficient reason for a court to fail to give a statute its intended scope. . . .

A statute does not operate "retrospectively" merely because it is applied in a case arising from conduct antedating the statute's enactment, *see* Republic Nat. Bank of Miami v. United States, 506 U.S. 80, ___, 113 S.Ct. 554, 556–557 (1992) (THOMAS, J., concurring in part and concurring in judgment), or upsets expectations based in prior law.[24] Rather, the court must ask whether the new provision attaches new legal consequences to events completed before its enactment. The conclusion that a particular rule operates "retroactively" comes at the end of a process of judgment concerning the nature and extent of the change in the law and the degree of connection between the operation of the new rule and a relevant past event. Any test of retroactivity will leave room for disagreement in hard cases, and is unlikely to classify the enormous variety of legal changes with perfect philosophical clarity. However, retroactivity is a matter on which judges tend to have "sound . . . instinct[s]," *see* Danforth v. Groton Water Co., 178 Mass. 472, 476, 59 N.E. 1033, 1034 (1901) (Holmes, J.), and familiar considerations of fair notice, reasonable reliance, and settled expectations offer sound guidance.

Since the early days of this Court, we have declined to give retroactive effect to statutes burdening private rights unless Congress had made clear its intent. . . . The presumption against statutory retroactivity has consistently been explained by reference to the unfairness of imposing new burdens on persons after the fact.

The largest category of cases in which we have applied the presumption against statutory retroactivity has involved new provisions affecting contractual or property rights, matters in which predictability and stability are of prime importance. The presumption has not, however, been limited to such cases. At issue in Chew Heong v. United States, 112 U.S. 536 (1884), for example, was a provision of the "Chinese Restriction Act" of 1882 barring Chinese laborers from reentering the United States without a certificate prepared when they exited this country. We held that the statute did not bar the reentry of a laborer who had left the United States before the certification requirement was promulgated. Justice Harlan's opinion for the Court observed that the

---

[24] Even uncontroversially prospective statutes may unsettle expectations and impose burdens on past conduct; a new property tax or zoning regulation may upset the reasonable expectations that prompted those affected to acquire property; a new law banning gambling harms the person who had begun to construct a casino before the law's enactment or spent his life learning to count cards. *See* Fuller 60 ("If every time a man relied on existing law in arranging his affairs, he were made secure against any change in legal rules, the whole body of our law would be ossified forever"). Moreover, a statute "is not made retroactive merely because it draws upon antecedent facts for its operation." [citations omitted].

law in effect before the 1882 enactment had accorded laborers a right to re-enter without a certificate, and invoked the "uniformly" accepted rule against "giv[ing] to statutes a retrospective operation, whereby rights previously vested are injuriously affected, unless compelled to do so by language so clear and positive as to leave no room to doubt that such was the intention of the legislature." *Id.*, at 559.

Our statement in *Bowen* that "congressional enactments and administrative rules will not be construed to have retroactive effect unless their language requires this result," 488 U.S., at 208, 109 S.Ct., at 471, was in step with this long line of cases. *Bowen* itself was a paradigmatic case of retroactivity in which a federal agency sought to recoup, under cost limit regulations issued in 1984, funds that had been paid to hospitals for services rendered earlier, *see id.*, at 207; our search for clear congressional intent authorizing retroactivity was consistent with the approach taken in decisions spanning two centuries.

. . . Requiring clear intent assures that Congress itself has affirmatively considered the potential unfairness of retroactive application and determined that it is an acceptable price to pay for the countervailing benefits. Such a requirement allocates to Congress responsibility for fundamental policy judgments concerning the proper temporal reach of statutes, and has the additional virtue of giving legislators a predictable background rule against which to legislate.

B

Although we have long embraced a presumption against statutory retroactivity, for just as long we have recognized that, in many situations, a court should "apply the law in effect at the time it renders its decision," *Bradley*, 416 U.S., at 711, even though that law was enacted after the events that gave rise to the suit. There is, of course, no conflict between that principle and a presumption against retroactivity when the statute in question is unambiguous. . . .

Even absent specific legislative authorization, application of new statutes passed after the events in suit is unquestionably proper in many situations. When the intervening statute authorizes or affects the propriety of prospective relief, application of the new provision is not retroactive. Thus, in American Steel Foundries v. Tri-City Central Trades Council, 257 U.S. 184 (1921), we held that § 20 of the Clayton Act, enacted while the case was pending on appeal, governed the propriety of injunctive relief against labor picketing. In remanding the suit for application of the intervening statute, we observed that "relief by injunction operates in futuro," and that the plaintiff had no "vested right" in the decree entered by the trial court.

We have regularly applied intervening statutes conferring or ousting jurisdiction, whether or not jurisdiction lay when the underlying conduct occurred or when the suit was filed. . . . Changes in procedural rules may often be applied in suits arising before their enactment without raising concerns about retroactivity. . . .[29]

When a case implicates a federal statute enacted after the events in suit, the court's first task is to determine whether Congress has expressly prescribed the statute's proper reach. If Congress has done so, of course, there is no need to resort to judicial default rules. When, however, the statute contains no such express command, the court must determine whether the new statute would have retroactive effect, *i.e.*, whether it would impair rights a party possessed when he acted, increase a party's liability for past conduct, or impose new duties with respect to transactions already completed. If the statute would operate retroactively, our traditional presumption teaches that it does not govern absent clear congressional intent favoring such a result.

V

We now ask whether, given the absence of guiding instructions from Congress, § 102 of the Civil Rights Act of 1991 is the type of provision that should govern cases arising before its enactment. . . . [T]he new compensatory damages provision would operate "retrospectively" if it were applied to conduct occurring before November 21, 1991. Unlike certain other forms of relief, compensatory damages are quintessentially backward-looking. Compensatory damages may be intended less to sanction wrongdoers than to make victims whole, but they do so by a mechanism that affects the liabilities of defendants. They do not "compensate" by distributing funds from the public coffers, but by requiring particular employers to pay for harms they caused. The introduction of a right to compensatory damages is also the type of legal change that would have an impact on private parties' planning.[35] In this

---

[29] Of course, the mere fact that a new rule is procedural does not mean that it applies to every pending case. A new rule concerning the filing of complaints would not govern an action in which the complaint had already been properly filed under the old regime, and the promulgation of a new rule of evidence would not require an appellate remand for a new trial. Our orders approving amendments to federal procedural rules reflect the common-sense notion that the applicability of such provisions ordinarily depends on the posture of the particular case [citations omitted]. Contrary to Justice SCALIA's suggestion, we do not restrict the presumption against statutory retroactivity to cases involving "vested rights." (Neither is Justice Story's definition of retroactivity, so restricted.) Nor do we suggest that concerns about retroactivity have no application to procedural rules.

[35] As petitioner and amici suggest, concerns of unfair surprise and upsetting expectations are attenuated in the case of intentional employment discrimination, which has been unlawful for more than a generation. However, fairness concerns would not be entirely absent if the damages provisions of § 102 were to apply to events preceding its enactment, as the facts of this case illustrate. Respondent USI's management, when apprised of the wrongful conduct of petitioner's coworker, took timely action to remedy the problem. The law then in effect imposed no liability on an employer who corrected discriminatory work conditions before the conditions became so severe as to result in the victim's constructive discharge. Assessing damages against respondents on a theory of *respondeat superior* would thus entail an element of surprise. Even when the conduct in question is morally reprehensible or illegal, a degree of unfairness is inherent whenever the law imposes additional burdens based on conduct that occurred in the past. *Cf.* Weaver, 450 U.S., at 28–30, 101 S.Ct., at 963–965 (Ex Post Facto Clause assures fair notice and governmental restraint, and does not turn on "an individual's right to less punishment"). The new damages provisions of § 102 can be expected to give managers an added

case, the event to which the new damages provision relates is the discriminatory conduct of respondents' agent John Williams; if applied here, that provision would attach an important new legal burden to that conduct. The new damages remedy in § 102, we conclude, is the kind of provision that does not apply to events antedating its enactment in the absence of clear congressional intent.

In cases like this one, in which prior law afforded no relief, § 102 can be seen as creating a new cause of action, and its impact on parties' rights is especially pronounced. Section 102 confers a new right to monetary relief on persons like petitioner who were victims of a hostile work environment but were not constructively discharged, and the novel prospect of damages liability for their employers. Because Title VII previously authorized recovery of backpay in some cases, and because compensatory damages under § 102(a) are in addition to any backpay recoverable, the new provision also resembles a statute increasing the amount of damages available under a preestablished cause of action. Even under that view, however, the provision would, if applied in cases arising before the Act's effective date, undoubtedly impose on employers found liable a "new disability" in respect to past events. *See Society for Propagation of the Gospel*, 22 F.Cas., at 767. The extent of a party's liability, in the civil context as well as the criminal, is an important legal consequence that cannot be ignored.[36] Neither in *Bradley* itself, nor in any case before or since in which Congress had not clearly spoken, have we read a statute substantially increasing the monetary liability of a private party to apply to conduct occurring before the statute's enactment. [citations omitted].[37]

It will frequently be true, as petitioner and amici forcefully argue here, that retroactive application of a new statute would vindicate its purpose more fully. That consideration, however, is not sufficient to rebut

---

incentive to take preventive measures to ward off discriminatory conduct by subordinates before it occurs, but that purpose is not served by applying the regime to preenactment conduct.

[36] The state courts have consistently held that statutes changing or abolishing limits on the amount of damages available in wrongful death actions should not, in the absence of clear legislative intent, apply to actions arising before their enactment. *See, e.g.*, Dempsey v. State, 451 A.2d 273 (R.I.1982) ("Every court which has considered the issue . . . has found a subsequent change as to the amount or the elements of damage in the wrongful-death statute to be substantive rather than procedural or remedial, and thus any such change must be applied prospectively"); . . . Mihoy v. Proulx, 113 N.H 698, 701, 313 A.2d 723, 725 (1973) ("To apply the increased limit after the date of the accident would clearly enlarge the defendant's liability retrospectively. In the absence of an express provision, we cannot conclude that the legislature intended retrospective application"). [citations omitted].

[37] We have sometimes said that new "remedial" statutes, like new "procedural" ones, should presumptively apply to pending cases. *See, e.g.*, Ex parte Collett, 337 U.S., at 71, and n. 38, 69 S.Ct., at 952–953, and n. 38 ("Clearly, § 1404(a) is a remedial provision applicable to pending actions"); Beazell, 269 U.S., at 171, 46 S.Ct., at 69 (Ex Post Facto Clause does not limit "legislative control of remedies and modes of procedure which do not affect matters of substance"). While that statement holds true for some kinds of remedies, we have not classified a statute introducing damages liability as the sort of "remedial" change that should presumptively apply in pending cases. "Retroactive modification" of damage remedies may "normally harbo[r] much less potential for mischief than retroactive changes in the principles of liability," Hastings v. Earth Satellite Corp., 628 F.2d 85, 93 (C.A.D.C.), cert. denied, 449 U.S. 905, 101 S.Ct. 281, 66 L.Ed.2d 137 (1980), but that potential is nevertheless still significant.

the presumption against retroactivity. Statutes are seldom crafted to pursue a single goal, and compromises necessary to their enactment may require adopting means other than those that would most effectively pursue the main goal. A legislator who supported a prospective statute might reasonably oppose retroactive application of the same statute. Indeed, there is reason to believe that the omission of the 1990 version's express retroactivity provisions was a factor in the passage of the 1991 bill. Section 102 is plainly not the sort of provision that must be understood to operate retroactively because a contrary reading would render it ineffective.

The presumption against statutory retroactivity is founded upon sound considerations of general policy and practice, and accords with long held and widely shared expectations about the usual operation of legislation. We are satisfied that it applies to § 102. Because we have found no clear evidence of congressional intent that § 102 of the Civil Rights Act of 1991 should apply to cases arising before its enactment, we conclude that the judgment of the Court of Appeals must be affirmed.

It is so ordered.

■ Justice Scalia, with whom Justice Kennedy and Justice Thomas join, concurring in the judgments.

I

I of course agree with the Court that there exists a judicial presumption, of great antiquity, that a legislative enactment affecting substantive rights does not apply retroactively absent clear statement to the contrary. *See generally* Kaiser Aluminum & Chemical Corp. v. Bonjorno, 494 U.S. 827, 840 (1990) (Scalia, J., concurring). The Court, however, is willing to let that clear statement be supplied, not by the text of the law in question, but by individual legislators who participated in the enactment of the law, and even legislators in an earlier Congress which tried and failed to enact a similar law. For the Court not only combs the floor debate and committee reports of the statute at issue, the Civil Rights Act of 1991, Pub. L. 102–166, 105 Stat. 1071, but also reviews the procedural history of an earlier, unsuccessful, attempt by a different Congress to enact similar legislation, the Civil Rights Act of 1990, S. 2104, 101st Cong., 1st Sess. (1990).

This effectively converts the "clear statement" rule into a "discernible legislative intent" rule—and even that understates the difference. The Court's rejection of the floor statements of certain Senators because they are "frankly partisan" and "cannot plausibly be read as reflecting any general agreement" reads like any other exercise in the soft science of legislative historicizing,[1] undisciplined by any

---

[1] In one respect, I must acknowledge, the Court's effort may be unique. There is novelty as well as irony in his supporting the judgment that the floor statements on the 1991 Act are unreliable by citing Senator Danforth's floor statement on the 1991 Act to the effect that floor statements on the 1991 Act are unreliable.

distinctive "clear statement" requirement. If it is a "clear statement" we are seeking, surely it is not enough to insist that the statement can "plausibly be read as reflecting general agreement"; the statement must clearly reflect general agreement. No legislative history can do that, of course, but only the text of the statute itself. That has been the meaning of the "clear statement" retroactivity rule from the earliest times. [citations omitted]. I do not deem that clear rule to be changed by the Court's dicta regarding legislative history in the present case. . . .

III

My last, and most significant, disagreement with the Court's analysis of this case pertains to the meaning of retroactivity. The Court adopts as its own the definition crafted by Justice Story in a case involving a provision of the New Hampshire Constitution that prohibited "retrospective" laws: a law is retroactive only if it "takes away or impairs vested rights acquired under existing laws, or creates a new obligation, imposes a new duty, or attaches a new disability, in respect to transactions or considerations already past." Society for Propagation of the Gospel v. Wheeler, 22 F.Cas. 756, 767 (No. 13,516) (CCNH 1814) (Story, J.). . . .

The seemingly random exceptions to the Court's "vested rights" (substance-vs.-procedure) criterion must be made, I suggest, because that criterion is fundamentally wrong. It may well be that the upsetting of "vested substantive rights" was the proper touchstone for interpretation of New Hampshire's constitutional prohibition, as it is for interpretation of the United States Constitution's ex post facto Clauses. But I doubt that it has anything to do with the more mundane question before us here: absent clear statement to the contrary, what is the presumed temporal application of a statute? For purposes of that question, a procedural change should no more be presumed to be retroactive than a substantive one. The critical issue, I think, is not whether the rule affects "vested rights," or governs substance or procedure, but rather what is the relevant activity that the rule regulates. Absent clear statement otherwise, only such relevant activity which occurs after the effective date of the statute is covered. Most statutes are meant to regulate primary conduct, and hence will not be applied in trials involving conduct that occurred before their effective date. But other statutes have a different purpose and therefore a different relevant retroactivity event. A new rule of evidence governing expert testimony, for example, is aimed at regulating the conduct of trial, and the event relevant to retroactivity of the rule is introduction of the testimony. Even though it is a procedural rule, it would unquestionably not be applied to testimony already taken—reversing a case on appeal, for example, because the new rule had not been applied at a trial which antedated the statute.

The inadequacy of the Court's "vested rights" approach becomes apparent when a change in one of the incidents of trial alters substantive entitlements. The opinion classifies attorney's fees provisions as procedural and permits "retroactive" application (in the sense of application to cases involving pre-enactment conduct). It seems to me, however, that holding a person liable for attorney's fees affects a "substantive right" no less than holding him liable for compensatory or punitive damages, which the Court treats as affecting a vested right. If attorney's fees can be awarded in a suit involving conduct that antedated the fee-authorizing statute, it is because the purpose of the fee award is not to affect that conduct, but to encourage suit for the vindication of certain rights—so that the retroactivity event is the filing of suit, whereafter encouragement is no longer needed. Or perhaps because the purpose of the fee award is to facilitate suit—so that the retroactivity event is the termination of suit, whereafter facilitation can no longer be achieved.

* * *

Finally, statutes eliminating previously available forms of prospective relief provide another challenge to the Court's approach. Courts traditionally withhold requested injunctions that are not authorized by then-current law, even if they were authorized at the time suit commenced and at the time the primary conduct sought to be enjoined was first engaged in [citations omitted]. The reason, which has nothing to do with whether it is possible to have a vested right to prospective relief, is that "obviously, this form of relief operates only in futuro," *Deering, ibid.* Since the purpose of prospective relief is to affect the future rather than remedy the past, the relevant time for judging its retroactivity is the very moment at which it is ordered.

I do not maintain that it will always be easy to determine, from the statute's purpose, the relevant event for assessing its retroactivity. As I have suggested, for example, a statutory provision for attorney's fees presents a difficult case. Ordinarily, however, the answer is clear—as it is in both *Landgraf* and *Rivers.* Unlike the Court, I do not think that any of the provisions at issue is "not easily classified." They are all directed at the regulation of primary conduct, and the occurrence of the primary conduct is the relevant event.

■ JUSTICE BLACKMUN, dissenting.

. . . the Court rejects the "most logical reading," of the Civil Rights Act of 1991, 105 Stat. 1071 (Act), and resorts to a presumption against retroactivity. This approach seems to me to pay insufficient fidelity to the settled principle that the "starting point for interpretation of a statute 'is the language of the statute itself,'" and extends the presumption against retroactive legislation beyond its historical reach and purpose. [citations omitted].

A straightforward textual analysis of the Act indicates that § 102's provision of compensatory damages and its attendant right to a jury trial apply to cases pending on appeal on the date of enactment. This analysis begins with § 402(a) of the Act, 105 Stat. 1099: "Except as otherwise specifically provided, this Act and the amendments made by this Act shall take effect upon enactment." Under the "settled rule that a statute must, if possible, be construed in such fashion that every word has operative effect," § 402(a)'s qualifying clause, "[e]xcept as otherwise specifically provided," cannot be dismissed as mere surplusage or an "insurance policy" against future judicial interpretation. Instead, it most logically refers to the Act's two sections "specifically providing" that the statute does not apply to cases pending on the date of enactment: (a) § 402(b), 105 Stat. 1099, which provides, in effect, that the Act did not apply to the then pending case of Wards Cove Packing Co. v. Atonio, 490 U.S. 642 (1989), and (b) § 109(c), 105 Stat. 1078, which states that the Act's protections of overseas employment "shall not apply with respect to conduct occurring before the date of the enactment of this Act." Self-evidently, if the entire Act were inapplicable to pending cases, §§ 402(b) and 109(c) would be "entirely redundant.". Thus, the clear implication is that, while § 402(b) and § 109(c) do not apply to pending cases, other provisions—including § 102—do. " 'Absent a clearly expressed legislative intention to the contrary, [this] language must ... be regarded as conclusive.' " The legislative history of the Act, featuring a welter of conflicting and "some frankly partisan" floor statements, but no committee report, evinces no such contrary legislative intent.[2] Thus, I see no reason to dismiss as "unlikely," the most natural reading of the statute, in order to embrace some other reading that is also "possible[.]" [citations omitted].

Even if the language of the statute did not answer the retroactivity question, it would be appropriate under our precedents to apply § 102 to pending cases. The well-established presumption against retroactive legislation, which serves to protect settled expectations, is grounded in a respect for vested rights.[citation omitted]. This presumption need not be applied to remedial legislation, such as § 102, that does not proscribe any conduct that was previously legal [citations omitted].

At no time within the last generation has an employer had a vested right to engage in or to permit sexual harassment; " 'there is no such thing as a vested right to do wrong.' " [citations omitted]. Section 102 of the Act expands the remedies available for acts of intentional discrimination, but does not alter the scope of the employee's basic right to be free from discrimination or the employer's corresponding legal duty. There is nothing unjust about holding an employer responsible for

---

[2] Virtually every Court of Appeals to consider the application of the 1991 Act to pending cases has concluded that the legislative history provides no reliable guidance. *See, e.g.,* Gersman v. Group Health Ass'n, Inc., 975 F.2d 886 (C.A.D.C.1992); Mozee v. American Commercial Marine Service Co., 963 F.2d 929 (C.A.7 1992). The absence in the Act of the strong retroactivity language of the vetoed 1990 legislation, which would have applied the new law to final judgments as well as to pending cases, [citations omitted] is not instructive of Congress' intent with respect to pending cases alone. Significantly, Congress also rejected language that put pending claims beyond the reach of the 1990 or 1991 Act. *See* 136 Cong. Rec. H6747 (daily ed. Aug. 3, 1990) [citations omitted].

injuries caused by conduct that has been illegal for almost 30 years. Accordingly, I respectfully dissent.

NOTE AND QUESTIONS

1.   The majority makes a point of noting that the presumption against statutory retroactivity is "founded upon sound considerations of general policy and practice, and accords with long held and widely shared expectations about the usual operation of legislation." Recall the typology of interpretive methods in Section II.B.1, *supra*. What kind of interpretive method is this presumption, and what is the source of its legitimacy? Should it matter whether such a presumption is "long held" and accords to "widely shared expectations"? Should it matter whether legislators and their drafting staffers are among those who hold such expectations? Or whether they draft on the basis of those expectations?

2.   What is the temporal effect of restorative statutes, where the intent of the statute is to correct a wrong judicial interpretation? This question was addressed in Rivers v. Roadway Express, Inc., 511 U.S. 298 (1994), decided on the same day as *Landgraf*.

In *Rivers,* the petitioners alleged they had been wrongfully dismissed from their jobs based on their race. They sued under 42 U.S.C. § 1981. Before the trial, the Supreme Court issued Patterson v. McLean, 491 U.S. 164 (1989), holding that 42 U.S.C. § 1981 prohibited discrimination only in the making and enforcement of contracts and therefore did not prohibit racial discrimination in the *termination* of the contract. This interpretation precluded the *Rivers* claim. The District Court therefore dismissed the case. While the petitioner's appeal was pending, Congress passed § 101 of the Civil Rights Act of 1991, "overruling" the Supreme Court's decision in *Patterson*. According to the *Rivers* plaintiffs, § 1981, correctly understood, always covered race discrimination in terminations of employment; in "overruling" *Patterson*, Congress was not changing the law, it was reinstating the correct *status quo ante*. The Court of Appeals nonetheless ruled that the Civil Rights Act of 1964 as interpreted by *Patterson*, not new § 101, governed the *Rivers* case.

The Supreme Court affirmed. Applying its reasoning in *Landgraf,* the Court ruled that "Congress' decision to alter the rule of law established in one of our cases . . . does not, by itself, reveal whether Congress intends the 'overruling' statute to apply retroactively to events." The Court noted that a proposed version of § 101 included explicitly retroactive language not contained in the enacted version. Its elimination from the final version strongly suggested that Congress did not intend for the amended statute to apply to pending cases. As a result, *Patterson*, albeit repudiated, continued to provide the rule of decision for cases arising before the effective date of the Civil Rights Act of 1991.

Keep in mind issues related to the restorative nature of statutes as you read *Newport News Shipbuilding and Dry Dock, infra* Section VII.C.2, and *AT&T Corp. v. Noreen Hulteen, infra* Section VII.C.3.

Martin v. Hadix

Supreme Court of the United States, 1999.
527 U.S. 343, 119 S.Ct. 1998, 144 L.Ed.2d 347.

■ JUSTICE O'CONNOR delivered the opinion of the Court.

Section 803(d)(3) of the Prison Litigation Reform Act of 1995 (PLRA or Act), 110 Stat. 1321–66, 42 U.S.C. § 1997e(d)(3) (1994 ed., Supp. II), places limits on the fees that may be awarded to attorneys who litigate prisoner lawsuits. We are asked to decide how this section applies to cases that were pending when the PLRA became effective on April 26, 1996. We conclude that § 803(d)(3) limits attorney's fees with respect to postjudgment monitoring services performed after the PLRA's effective date but it does not so limit fees for postjudgment monitoring performed before the effective date.

I

The fee disputes before us arose out of two class action lawsuits challenging the conditions of confinement in the Michigan prison system. The first case, which we will call *Glover*, began in 1977 when a now-certified class of female prisoners filed suit under Rev. Stat. § 1979, 42 U.S.C. § 1983 (1994 ed., Supp. II), in the United States District Court for the Eastern District of Michigan. The Glover plaintiffs alleged that the defendant prison officials had violated their rights under the Equal Protection Clause of the Fourteenth Amendment by denying them access to vocational and educational opportunities that were available to male prisoners. . . . The second case at issue here, *Hadix*, began in 1980. At that time, male prisoners at the State Prison of Southern Michigan, Central Complex (SPSM-CC), filed suit under 42 U.S.C. § 1983 in the United States District Court for the Eastern District of Michigan claiming that the conditions of their confinement at SPSM-CC violated the First, Eighth, and Fourteenth Amendments to the Constitution. . . .

In 1985, the parties agreed to, and the District Court entered, an order providing that the plaintiffs were entitled to attorney's fees for postjudgment monitoring of the defendants' compliance with the court's remedial decrees. [Citation.] This order also established the system for awarding monitoring fees that was in place when the present dispute arose. Under this system, the plaintiffs submit their fee requests on a semiannual basis, and the defendants then have 28 days to submit any objections to the requested award. The District Court resolves any disputes. In an appeal from a subsequent dispute over the meaning of this order, the Court of Appeals for the Sixth Circuit affirmed that the plaintiffs were entitled to attorney's fees, at the prevailing market rate, for postjudgment monitoring. The prevailing market rate has been adjusted over the years, but it is currently set at $150 per hour. [Citation]. . . .

The fee landscape changed with the passage of the PLRA on April 26, 1996. The PLRA, as its name suggests, contains numerous provisions governing the course of prison litigation in the federal courts. It provides, for example, limits on the availability of certain types of relief in such suits, *see* 18 U.S.C. § 3626(a)(2) (1994 ed., Supp. III), and for the termination of prospective relief orders after a limited time, § 3626(b). The section of the PLRA at issue here, § 803(d)(3), places a cap on the size of attorney's fees that may be awarded in prison litigation suits:

"(d) Attorney's fees

"(1) In any action brought by a prisoner who is confined to any jail, prison, or other correctional facility, in which attorney's fees are authorized under [42 U.S.C. § 1988], such fees shall not be awarded, except to the extent [authorized here]. . . .

"(3) No award of attorney's fees in an action described in paragraph (1) shall be based on an hourly rate greater than 150 percent of the hourly rate established under [18 U.S.C. § 3006A (1994 ed. and Supp. III)], for payment of court-appointed counsel." § 803(d), 42 U.S.C. § 1997e(d) (1994 ed., Supp. II).

Court-appointed attorneys in the Eastern District of Michigan are compensated at a maximum rate of $75 per hour, and thus, under § 803(d)(3), the PLRA fee cap for attorneys working on prison litigation suits translates into a maximum hourly rate of $112.50.

Questions involving the PLRA first arose in both *Glover* and *Hadix* with respect to fee requests for postjudgment monitoring performed before the PLRA was enacted. In both cases, in early 1996, the plaintiffs submitted fee requests for work performed during the last half of 1995. These requests were still pending when the PLRA became effective on April 26, 1996. In both cases, the District Court concluded that the PLRA fee cap did not limit attorney's fees for services performed in these cases prior to the effective date of the Act. [Citation.] . . . Fee requests next were filed in both *Glover* and *Hadix* for services performed between January 1, 1996, and June 30, 1996, a time period encompassing work performed both before and after the effective date of the PLRA. As relevant to this case, the defendant state prison officials argued that these fee requests were subject to the fee cap found in § 803(d)(3) of the PLRA, and the District Court accepted this argument in part. In nearly identical orders issued in the two cases, the court reiterated its earlier conclusion that the PLRA does not limit fees for work performed before April 26, 1996, but concluded that the PLRA fee cap does limit fees for services performed after the effective date. . . .

In this Court, the *Hadix* and *Glover* plaintiffs are respondents, and the defendant prison officials from both cases are petitioners.

II

Petitioners contend that the PLRA applies to *Glover* and *Hadix*, cases that were pending when the PLRA was enacted. This fact pattern presents a recurring question in the law: When should a new federal statute be applied to pending cases? [Citation.] To answer this question, we ask first "whether Congress has expressly prescribed the statute's proper reach." Landgraf v. USI Film Products, 511 U.S. 244, 280 (1994). If there is no congressional directive on the temporal reach of a statute, we determine whether the application of the statute to the conduct at issue would result in a retroactive effect. *Ibid.* If so, then in keeping with our "traditional presumption" against retroactivity, we presume that the statute does not apply to that conduct. *Ibid.*

A

1

Congress has not expressly mandated the temporal reach of § 803(d)(3). Section 803(d)(1) provides that "in any action brought by a prisoner who is confined [to a correctional facility] . . . attorney's fees . . . shall not be awarded, except" as authorized by the statute. Section 803(d)(3) further provides that "no award of attorney's fees . . . shall be based on an hourly rate greater than 150 percent of the hourly rate established under [18 U.S.C. § 3006A], for payment of court-appointed counsel." Petitioners contend that this language—particularly the phrase "in *any* action *brought* by a prisoner who *is* confined," § 803(d)(1) (emphasis added)—clearly expresses a congressional intent that § 803(d) apply to pending cases. They argue that "any" is a broad, encompassing word, and that its use with "brought," a past-tense verb, demonstrates congressional intent to apply the fees limitations to all fee awards entered after the PLRA became effective, even when those awards were for services performed before the PLRA was enacted. They also contend that § 803(d)(3), by its own terms, applies to all "awards"—understood as the actual court order directing the payment of fees—entered after the effective date of the PLRA, regardless of when the work was performed.

The fundamental problem with all of petitioners' statutory arguments is that they stretch the language of § 803(d) to find congressional intent on the temporal scope of that section when we believe that § 803(d) is better read as setting substantive limits on the award of attorney's fees. Section 803(d)(1), for example, prohibits fee awards unless those fees were "directly and reasonably incurred" in the suit, and unless those fees are "proportionately related" to or "directly and reasonably incurred in enforcing" the relief ordered. 42 U.S.C. § 1997e(d)(1). Similarly, § 803(d)(3) sets substantive limits by prohibiting the award of fees based on hourly rates greater than a specified rate. In other words, these sections define the substantive availability of attorney's fees; they do not purport to define the temporal reach of these substantive limitations. This language falls short of demonstrating a "clear congressional intent" favoring retroactive application of these fees limitations. *Landgraf*, 511 U.S. at 280. It falls short, in other words, of the "unambiguous directive" or "express command" that the statute is to be applied retroactively. *Id.*, at 263, 280.

In any event, we note that "brought," as used in this section, is not a past-tense verb; rather, it is the participle in a participial phrase modifying the noun "action." And although the word "any" is broad, it stretches the imagination to suggest that Congress intended, through the use of this one word, to make the fee limitations applicable to all fee awards. Finally, we do not believe that the phrase "no award" in § 803(d)(3) demonstrates congressional intent to apply that section to all fee awards (*i.e.*, fee payment orders) entered after the PLRA's effective date. Had Congress intended § 803(d)(3) to apply to all fee orders entered after the effective date, even when those awards compensate for work performed before the effective date, it could have used language more obviously targeted to addressing the temporal reach of that section. It could have stated, for example, that "No award entered after the effective date of this Act shall be based on an hourly rate greater than the ceiling rate."

The conclusion that § 803(d) does not clearly express congressional intent that it apply retroactively is strengthened by comparing § 803(d) to the language that we suggested in *Landgraf* might qualify as a clear statement that a statute was to apply retroactively: "The new provisions shall apply to all proceedings pending on or commenced after the date of enactment." *Id.*, at 260 (internal quotation marks omitted). This provision, unlike the language of the PLRA, unambiguously addresses the temporal reach of the statute. With no such analogous language making explicit reference to the statute's temporal reach, it cannot be said that Congress has "expressly prescribed" § 803(d)'s temporal reach. *Id.*, at 280. . . .

According to respondents, a comparison of §§ 802 and 803 of the PLRA leads to the conclusion that § 803(d) should only apply to cases filed after its enactment. The attorney's fees provisions are found in § 803 of the PLRA, and, as described above, this section contains no explicit directive that it should apply to pending cases. By contrast, § 802— addressing "appropriate remedies" in prison litigation—explicitly provides that it applies to pending cases: "[This section] shall apply with respect to all prospective relief whether such relief was originally granted or approved before, on, or after the date of the enactment of this title." § 802(b)(1), note following 18 U.S.C. § 3626 (1994 ed., Supp. III). . . .

Because §§ 802 and 803 address wholly distinct subject matters, [a] negative inference does not arise from the silence of § 803. Section 802 addresses "appropriate remedies" in prison litigation, prohibiting, for example, prospective relief unless it is "narrowly drawn" and is "the least intrusive means necessary to correct the violation." § 802(a), 18 U.S.C. § 3626(a)(1)(A) (1994 ed., Supp. III). That section also creates new standards designed to encourage the prompt termination of prospective relief orders, providing, for example, for the "immediate termination of any prospective relief if the relief was approved or granted in the absence of a finding by the court that the relief is narrowly drawn, extends no further than necessary to correct the violation of the Federal right, and is the least intrusive means necessary to correct the violation of the

Federal right." § 802(a), 18 U.S.C. § 3626(b)(2). Section 803(d), by contrast, does not address the propriety of various forms of relief and does not provide for the immediate termination of ongoing relief orders. Rather, it governs the award of attorney's fees. Thus, there is no reason to conclude that if Congress was concerned that § 802 apply to pending cases, it would "have been just as concerned" that § 803 apply to pending cases.

Finally, we note that respondents' reliance on the legislative history overstates the inferences that can be drawn from an ambiguous act of legislative drafting. Even if respondents are correct about the legislative history, the inference that respondents draw from this history is speculative. It rests on the assumption that the reason the fees provisions were moved was to move them away from the language applying § 802 to pending cases, when they may have been moved for a variety of other reasons. This weak inference provides a thin reed on which to rest the argument that the fees provisions, by negative implication, were intended to apply prospectively.

B

Because we conclude that Congress has not "expressly prescribed" the proper reach of § 803(d)(3), *Landgraf*, 511 U.S. at 280, we must determine whether application of this section in this case would have retroactive effects inconsistent with the usual rule that legislation is deemed to be prospective. The inquiry into whether a statute operates retroactively demands a common sense, functional judgment about "whether the new provision attaches new legal consequences to events completed before its enactment." *Id*. at 270. This judgment should be informed and guided by "familiar considerations of fair notice, reasonable reliance, and settled expectations." *Ibid*.

1

For postjudgment monitoring performed before the effective date of the PLRA, the PLRA's attorney's fees provisions, as construed by the respondents, would have a retroactive effect contrary to the usual assumption that congressional statutes are prospective in operation. . . . The PLRA, as applied to work performed before its effective date, would alter the fee arrangement post hoc by reducing the rate of compensation. To give effect to the PLRA's fees limitations, after the fact, would "attach new legal consequences" to completed conduct. *Landgraf, supra*, at 270.

. . . While it may be possible to generalize about types of rules that ordinarily will not raise retroactivity concerns, *see, e.g., id*. at 273–275, these generalizations do not end the inquiry. For example, in *Landgraf*, we acknowledged that procedural rules may often be applied to pending suits with no retroactivity problems, *id*. at 275, but we also cautioned that "the mere fact that a new rule is procedural does not mean that it applies to every pending case," *id*. at 275, n. 29. We took pains to dispel the "suggestion that concerns about retroactivity have no application to procedural rules." *Ibid.* [Citation.] When determining whether a new statute operates retroactively, it is not enough to attach a label (*e.g.*, "procedural," "collateral") to the statute; we must ask whether the statute operates retroactively.

Moreover, petitioners' reliance on our decision in Bradley v. School Bd. of Richmond, 416 U.S. 696, 40 L. Ed. 2d 476, 94 S.Ct. 2006 (1974), to support their argument that attorney's fees provisions can be applied retroactively is misplaced. In *Bradley*, the District Court had awarded attorney's fees, based on general equitable principles, to a group of parents who had prevailed in their suit seeking the desegregation of the Richmond schools. While the case was pending on appeal, Congress passed a statute specifically authorizing the award of attorney's fees for prevailing parties in school desegregation cases. The Court of Appeals held that the new statute could not authorize fee awards for work performed before the effective date of the new law, but we reversed, holding that the fee award in that case was proper. Because attorney's fees were available, albeit under different principles, before passage of the statute, and because the District Court had in fact already awarded fees invoking these different principles, there was no manifest injustice in allowing the fee statute to apply in that case. *Id.*, at 720–721. We held that the award of statutory attorney's fees did not upset any reasonable expectations of the parties. [Citation.] In this case, by contrast, from the beginning of these suits, the parties have proceeded on the assumption that 42 U.S.C. § 1988 would govern. The PLRA was not passed until well after respondents had been declared prevailing parties and thus entitled to attorney's fees. To impose the new standards now, for work performed before the PLRA became effective, would upset the reasonable expectations of the parties.

2

With respect to postjudgment monitoring performed after the effective date of the PLRA, by contrast, there is no retroactivity problem. On April 26, 1996, through the PLRA, the plaintiffs' attorneys were on notice that their hourly rate had been adjusted. From that point forward, they would be paid at a rate consistent with the dictates of the law. After April 26, 1996, any expectation of compensation at the pre-PLRA rates was unreasonable. There is no manifest injustice in telling an attorney performing postjudgment monitoring services that, going forward, she will earn a lower hourly rate than she had earned in the past. If the attorney does not wish to perform services at this new, lower, pay rate, she can choose not to work. In other words, as applied to work performed after the effective date of the PLRA, the PLRA has future effect on future work; this does not raise retroactivity concerns.

Respondents contend that the PLRA has retroactive effect in this context because it attaches new legal consequences (a lower pay rate) to conduct completed before enactment. The pre-enactment conduct that respondents contend is affected is the attorney's initial decision to file suit on behalf of the prisoner clients.... [R]espondents' argument assumes that once an attorney files suit, she must continue working on that case until the decree is terminated. Respondents provide no support for this assumption, however. They allude to ethical constraints on an attorney's ability to withdraw from a case midstream, *see* Brief for Respondents 29 ("And finally, it is at that time that plaintiffs' counsel commit themselves ethically to continued representation of their clients to ensure that the Constitution is honored, a course of conduct that cannot lightly be altered"), but they do not seriously contend that the attorneys here were prohibited from withdrawing from the case during the postjudgment monitoring stage. It cannot be said that the PLRA changes the legal consequences of the attorneys' pre-PLRA decision to file the case.

C

In sum, we conclude that the PLRA contains no express command about its temporal scope. Because we find that the PLRA, if applied to postjudgment monitoring services performed before the effective date of the Act, would have a retroactive effect inconsistent with our assumption that statutes are prospective, in the absence of an express command by Congress to apply the Act retroactively, we decline to do so. *Landgraf*, 511 U.S. at 280. With respect to postjudgment monitoring performed after the effective date, by contrast, there is no retroactive effect, and the PLRA fees cap applies to such work. Accordingly, the judgment of the Court of Appeals for the Sixth Circuit is affirmed in part and reversed in part.

It is so ordered.

■ JUSTICE SCALIA, concurring in part and concurring in the judgment....

I agree with the Court that the [PLRA's] intended temporal application is not set forth in the text of the statute, and that the outcome must therefore be governed by our interpretive principle that, in absence of contrary indication, a statute will not be construed to have retroactive application, *see Landgraf*. But that leaves open the key question: retroactive in reference to what? The various options in the present case include (1) the alleged violation upon which the fee-imposing suit is based (applying the new fee rule to any case involving an alleged violation that occurred before the PLRA became effective would be giving it "retroactive application"); (2) the lawyer's undertaking to prosecute the suit for which attorney's fees were provided (applying the new fee rule to any case in which the lawyer was retained before the PLRA became effective would be giving it "retroactive application"); (3) the filing of the suit in which the fees are imposed (applying the new fee rule to any suit brought before the PLRA became effective would be giving it "retroactive application"); (4) the doing of the legal work for which the fees are payable (applying the new fee rule to any work done before the PLRA became effective would be giving it "retroactive application"); and (5) the actual award of fees in a prisoner case (applying the new fee rule to an award rendered before the PLRA became effective would be giving it "retroactive application").

My disagreement with the Court's approach is that, in deciding which of the above five reference points for the retroactivity determination ought to be selected, it seems to me not much help to ask which of them would frustrate expectations. In varying degrees, they all would. As I explained in my concurrence in *Landgraf*, 511 U.S. at 286 (opinion concurring in judgments), I think the decision of which reference point (which "retroactivity event") to select should turn upon which activity the statute was intended to regulate. If it was intended to affect primary conduct, No. 1 should govern; if it was intended to induce lawyers to undertake representation, No. 2—and so forth.

In my view, the most precisely defined purpose of the provision at issue here was to reduce the previously established incentive for lawyers to work on prisoners' civil rights cases. If the PLRA is viewed in isolation, of course, its purpose could be regarded as being simply to prevent a judicial award of fees in excess of the referenced amount—in which case the relevant retroactivity event would be the award. In reality, however, the PLRA simply revises the fees provided for by § 1988, and it seems to me that the underlying purpose of that provision must govern its amendment as well—which purpose was to provide an appropriate incentive for lawyers to work on (among other civil rights cases) prisoner suits. That being so, the relevant retroactivity event is the doing of the work for which the incentive was offered. All work rendered in reliance upon the fee assurance contained in the former § 1988 will be reimbursed at those rates; all work rendered after the revised fee assurance of the PLRA became effective will be limited to the new rates. The District Court's announcement that it would permit future work to be billed at a higher rate operated in futuro; it sought to regulate future conduct rather than adjudicate past. It was therefore no less subject to revision by statute than is an injunction. Pennsylvania v. Wheeling & Belmont Bridge Co., 59 U.S. 421, 18 How. 421, 436 (1856).

For these reasons, I concur in the judgment of the Court and join all but Part II-B of its opinion.

■ JUSTICE GINSBURG, with whom JUSTICE STEVENS joins, concurring in part and dissenting in part.

I agree with the Court's determination that § 803(d) of the Prison Litigation Reform Act of 1995, (PLRA or Act), does not "limit fees for postjudgment monitoring performed before the [Act's] effective date," and with much of the reasoning set out in Parts I, II-A-1, and II-B-1 of the Court's opinion. I disagree, however, with the holding that § 803(d) "limits attorney's fees with respect to postjudgment monitoring services performed after . . . the effective date." *Ibid.* I do not find in the PLRA's text or history a satisfactory basis for concluding that Congress meant to order a midstream change, placing cases commenced before the PLRA became law under the new regime. I would therefore affirm in full the judgment of the Court of Appeals for the Sixth Circuit, which held § 803(d) inapplicable to cases brought to court prior to the enactment of the PLRA. . . .

II

. . . As the Court recognizes . . . § 803(d)'s "any action brought" language refers to the provision's substantive scope, not its temporal reach; "any" appears in the text only in proximity to provisions identifying the law's substantive dimensions. Had Congress intended that § 803(d) apply retroactively, it might easily have specified, as the Court suggests, that all post-enactment awards shall be subject to the limitation, or prescribed that the provision "shall apply in all proceedings pending on or commenced after the date of enactment of this Act." Congress instead left unaddressed § 803(d)'s temporal reach.

Comparison of § 803(d)'s text with that of a neighboring provision, § 802(b)(1) of the PLRA, is instructive for the retroactivity question we face. Section 802(b)(1), which governs "appropriate remedies" in prison litigation, applies expressly to "all prospective relief whether such relief was originally granted or approved before, on, or after the date of the enactment of this title." 110 Stat. 1321–70, note following 18 U.S.C. § 3626. "Congress [thus] saw fit to tell us which part of the Act was to be retroactively applied," *i.e.*, § 802. Jensen v. Clarke, 94 F.3d 1191, 1203 (C.A.8 1996). While I agree with the Court that the negative implication created by these two provisions is not dispositive, Congress' silence nevertheless suggests that § 803(d) has no carryback thrust.

Absent an express statutory command respecting retroactivity, *Landgraf* teaches, the attorney's fees provision should not be applied to pending cases if doing so would "have retroactive effect." 511 U.S. at 280. As the Court recognizes, application of § 803(d) to work performed before the PLRA's effective date would be impermissibly retroactive. Instead of the court-approved market-based fee that attorneys anticipated for work performed under the old regime, counsel would be limited to the new statutory rate. We long ago recognized the injustice of interpreting a statute to reduce the level of compensation for work already performed. [Citation.]

III

In my view, § 803(d) is most soundly read to cover all and only representations undertaken after the PLRA's effective date. Application of § 803(d) to representations commenced before the PLRA became law would "attach new legal consequences to [an] event completed before [the statute's] enactment"; hence the application would be retroactive under *Landgraf*, 511 U.S. at 270. The critical event effected before the PLRA's effective date is the lawyer's undertaking to prosecute the client's civil rights claim. Applying § 803(d) to pending matters significantly alters the consequences of the representation on which the lawyer has embarked. Notably, attorneys engaged before passage of the PLRA have little leeway to alter their conduct in response to the new legal regime; an attorney who initiated a prisoner's rights suit before April 26, 1996 remains subject to a professional obligation to see the litigation through to final disposition. *See* American Bar Association Model Rules of Professional Conduct, Rule 1.3, and Comment [3] (1999) ("[A] lawyer should carry through to conclusion all matters undertaken for a client."). Counsel's actions before and after that date are thus "inextricably part of a course of conduct initiated prior to the law." Inmates of D. C. Jail v. Jackson, 332 U.S. App. D.C. 451, 158 F.3d 1357, 1362 (C.A.D.C.1998) (Wald, J., dissenting).

While the injustice in applying the fee limitations to pending actions may be more readily apparent regarding work performed before the PLRA's effective date, application of the statute to work performed thereafter in pending cases also frustrates reasonable reliance on prior law and court-approved market rates. Consider, for example, two attorneys who filed similar prison reform lawsuits at the same time, pre-PLRA. Both attorneys initiated their lawsuits in the expectation that, if they prevailed, they would earn the market rate anticipated by pre-PLRA law. In one case, the lawsuit progressed swiftly, and labor-intensive pretrial discovery was completed before April 26, 1996. In the other, the suit lagged through no fault of plaintiff's counsel, pending the court's disposition of threshold motions, and the attorney was unable to pursue discovery until after April 26, 1996. Both attorneys have prosecuted their claims with due diligence; both were obliged, having accepted the representations, to perform the work for which they seek compensation. There is scarcely greater injustice in denying pre-PLRA compensation for pretrial discovery in the one case than the other. Nor is there any reason to think that Congress intended these similarly situated attorneys to be treated differently.

The Court avoids a conclusion of retroactivity by dismissing as an unsupported assumption the attorneys' assertion of an obligation to continue their representations through to final disposition. It seems to me, however, that the assertion has secure support.

Like the ABA's Model Rules, the Michigan Rules of Professional Conduct, which apply to counsel in both *Hadix* and *Glover, see* Rule 83.20(j) (1999), provide that absent good cause for terminating a representation, "a lawyer should carry through to conclusion all matters undertaken for a client." Mich. Rules of Prof. Conduct, Rule 1.3 Comment (1999) It is true that withdrawal may be permitted where "the representation will result in an unreasonable financial burden on the lawyer," Rule 1.16(b)(5), but explanatory comments suggest that this exception is designed for situations in which "the client refuses to abide by the terms of an agreement relating to the representation, such as an agreement concerning fees," Rule 1.16 Comment Consistent with the Michigan Rules, counsel for petitioners affirmed at oral argument their ethical obligation to continue these representations to a natural conclusion. *See* Tr. of Oral Arg. 43 ("[Continuing the representation] does involve ethical concerns certainly, especially in these circumstances."). There is no reason to think counsel ethically could have abandoned these representations in response to the PLRA fee limitation, nor any basis to believe the trial court would have permitted counsel to withdraw. *See* Rule 1.16(c) ("When ordered to do so by a tribunal, a lawyer shall continue representation."). As I see it, the attorneys' pre-PLRA pursuit of the civil rights claims thus created an obligation, enduring post-PLRA, to continue to provide effective representation.

Accordingly, I conclude that the Sixth Circuit soundly resisted the "sophisticated construction," 143 F.3d at 252, that would split apart, for fee award purposes, a constant course of representation. "The triggering event for retroactivity purposes," I am persuaded, "is when the lawyer undertakes to litigate the civil rights action on behalf of the client." *Inmates of D. C. Jail*, 158 F.3d at 1362 (Wald, J. dissenting).

Landgraf's lesson is that Congress must speak clearly when it wants new rules to govern pending cases. Because § 803(d) contains no clear statement on its temporal reach, and because the provision would operate retroactively as applied to lawsuits pending on the Act's effective date, I would hold that the fee limitation applies only to cases commenced after April 26, 1996.

QUESTIONS

1.   In *Martin v. Hadix*, the history of the case and of the legislation suggests several "retroactivity events." What are they, and at what point could the legislation, if effective as of that event, be said to have "genuinely retroactive" effect? What activity is the statute endeavoring to address and change? Which event implicates fairness concerns (such as reliance)?

2.   Was anything left of the *Bradley* presumption after *Landgraf*? After *Martin v. Hadix*? Can you articulate a meaningful distinction between "substance" and "procedure"? One that will afford guidance in a future case?

Vartelas v. Holder

Supreme Court of the United States, 2012.
566 U.S. 257, 132 S.Ct. 1479, 182 L.Ed.2d 473.

■ JUSTICE GINSBURG delivered the opinion of the Court.

Panagis Vartelas, a native of Greece, became a lawful permanent resident of the United States in 1989. He pleaded guilty to a felony (conspiring to make a counterfeit security) in 1994, and served a prison sentence of four months for that offense. Vartelas traveled to Greece in 2003 to visit his parents. On his return to the United States a week later, he was treated as an inadmissible alien and placed in removal proceedings. Under the law governing at the time of Vartelas' plea, an alien in his situation could travel abroad for brief periods without jeopardizing his resident alien status. *See* 8 U.S.C. § 1101(a)(13) (1988 ed.), as construed in Rosenberg v. Fleuti, 374 U.S. 449 (1963).

In 1996, Congress enacted the Illegal Immigration Reform and Immigrant Responsibility Act (IIRIRA), 110 Stat. 3009–546. That Act effectively precluded foreign travel by lawful permanent residents who had a conviction like Vartelas'. Under IIRIRA, such aliens, on return from a sojourn abroad, however brief, may be permanently removed from the United States. *See* 8 U.S.C. §§ 1101(a)(13)(C)(v); § 1182(a)(2).

This case presents a question of retroactivity not addressed by Congress: As to a lawful permanent resident convicted of a crime before the effective date of IIRIRA, which regime governs, the one in force at the time of the conviction, or IIRIRA? If the former, Vartelas' brief trip abroad would not disturb his lawful permanent resident status. If the latter, he may be denied reentry. We conclude that the relevant provision of IIRIRA, § 1101(a)(13)(C)(v), attached a new disability (denial of reentry) in respect to past events (Vartelas' pre-IIRIRA offense, plea, and conviction). Guided by the deeply rooted presumption against retroactive legislation, we hold that § 1101(a)(13)(C)(v) does not apply to Vartelas' conviction. The impact of Vartelas' brief travel abroad on his permanent resident status is therefore determined not by IIRIRA, but by the legal regime in force at the time of his conviction.

I

A

Before IIRIRA's passage, United States immigration law established "two types of proceedings in which aliens can be denied the hospitality of the United States: deportation hearings and exclusion hearings." *Landon v. Plasencia*, 459 U.S. 21, 25 (1982). Exclusion hearings were held for certain aliens seeking entry to the United States, and deportation hearings were held for certain aliens who had already entered this country. *See ibid.*

Under this regime, "entry" into the United States was defined as "any coming of an alien into the United States, from a foreign port or place." 8 U.S.C. § 1101(a)(13) (1988 ed.). The statute, however, provided an exception for lawful permanent residents; aliens lawfully residing here were not regarded as making an "entry" if their "departure to a foreign port or place . . . was not intended or reasonably to be expected by [them] or [their] presence in a foreign port or place . . . was not voluntary." *Ibid.* Interpreting this cryptic provision, we held in *Fleuti*, 374 U.S., at 461–462, that Congress did not intend to exclude aliens long resident in the United States upon their return from "innocent, casual, and brief excursion[s] . . . outside this country's borders." Instead, the Court determined, Congress meant to rank a once-permanent resident as a new entrant only when the foreign excursion "meaningfully interrupt[ed] . . . the alien's [U.S.] residence." *Id.*, at 462. Absent such "disrupti[on]" of the alien's residency, the alien would not be "subject . . . to the consequences of an 'entry' into the country on his return." *Ibid.*

In IIRIRA, Congress abolished the distinction between exclusion and deportation procedures and created a uniform proceeding known as "removal." *See* 8 U.S.C. §§ 1229, 1229a; *Judulang v. Holder*, 565 U.S. ___, ___, 132 S.Ct. 476 (2011). Congress made "admission" the key word, and defined admission to mean "the lawful entry of the alien into the United States after inspection and authorization by an immigration officer." § 1101(a)(13)(A). This alteration, the Board of Immigration Appeals (BIA) determined, superseded *Fleuti*. *See In re Collado-Munoz*, 21 I. & N. Dec. 1061, 1065–1066 (1998) (en banc). Thus, lawful permanent residents returning post-IIRIRA, like Vartelas, may be required to " 'see[k] an admission' into the United States, without regard to whether the alien's departure from the United States might previously have been ranked as 'brief, casual, and innocent' under the Fleuti doctrine." *Id.*, at 1066.

An alien seeking "admission" to the United States is subject to various requirements, *see, e.g.*, § 1181(a), and cannot gain entry if she is deemed "inadmissible" on any of the numerous grounds set out in the immigration statutes, *see* § 1182. Under IIRIRA, lawful permanent residents are regarded as seeking admission into the United States if they fall into any of six enumerated categories. § 1101(a)(13)(C). Relevant here, the fifth of these categories covers aliens who "ha[ve] committed an offense identified in section 1182(a)(2) of this title." § 1101(a)(13)(C)(v). Offenses in this category include "a crime involving moral turpitude (other than a purely political offense) or an attempt or conspiracy to commit such a crime." § 1182(a)(2)(A)(i).

In sum, before IIRIRA, lawful permanent residents who had committed a crime of moral turpitude could, under the *Fleuti* doctrine, return from brief trips abroad without applying for admission to the United States. Under IIRIRA, such residents are subject to admission procedures, and, potentially, to removal from the United States on grounds of inadmissibility.

B

Panagis Vartelas, born and raised in Greece, has resided in the United States for over 30 years. Originally admitted on a student visa issued in 1979, Vartelas became a lawful permanent resident in 1989. He currently lives in the New York area and works as a sales manager for a roofing company.

In 1992, Vartelas opened an auto body shop in Queens, New York. One of his business partners used the shop's photocopier to make counterfeit travelers' checks. Vartelas helped his partner perforate the sheets into individual checks, but Vartelas did not sell the checks or receive any money from the venture. In 1994, he pleaded guilty to conspiracy to make or possess counterfeit securities, in violation of 18

U.S.C. § 371. He was sentenced to four months' incarceration, followed by two years' supervised release.

Vartelas regularly traveled to Greece to visit his aging parents in the years after his 1994 conviction; even after the passage of IIRIRA in 1996, his return to the United States from these visits remained uneventful. In January 2003, however, when Vartelas returned from a week-long trip to Greece, an immigration officer classified him as an alien seeking "admission." The officer based this classification on Vartelas' 1994 conviction. *See* United States ex rel. Volpe v. Smith, 289 U.S. 422 (1933) (counterfeiting ranks as a crime of moral turpitude).

At Vartelas' removal proceedings, his initial attorney conceded removability, and requested discretionary relief from removal under the former § 212(c) of the Immigration and Nationality Act (INA). *See* 8 U.S.C. § 1182(c) (1994 ed.) (repealed 1996). This attorney twice failed to appear for hearings and once failed to submit a requested brief. Vartelas engaged a new attorney, who continued to concede removability and to request discretionary relief. The Immigration Judge denied the request for relief, and ordered Vartelas removed to Greece. The BIA affirmed the Immigration Judge's decision.

In July 2008, Vartelas filed with the BIA a timely motion to reopen the removal proceedings, alleging that his previous attorneys were ineffective for, among other lapses, conceding his removability. He sought to withdraw the concession of removability on the ground that IIRIRA's new "admission" provision, codified at § 1101(a)(13), did not reach back to deprive him of lawful resident status based on his pre-IIRIRA conviction. The BIA denied the motion, declaring that Vartelas had not been prejudiced by his lawyers' performance, for no legal authority prevented the application of IIRIRA to Vartelas' pre-IIRIRA conduct.

The U.S. Court of Appeals for the Second Circuit affirmed the BIA's decision, agreeing that Vartelas had failed to show he was prejudiced by his attorneys' allegedly ineffective performance. Rejecting Vartelas' argument that IIRIRA operated prospectively and therefore did not govern his case, the Second Circuit reasoned that he had not relied on the prior legal regime at the time he committed the disqualifying crime. *See* 620 F.3d 108, 118–120 (2010).

In so ruling, the Second Circuit created a split with two other Circuits. The Fourth and Ninth Circuits have held that the new § 1101(a)(13) may not be applied to lawful permanent residents who committed crimes listed in § 1182 (among them, crimes of moral turpitude) prior to IIRIRA's enactment. [Citation.] We granted certiorari to resolve the conflict among the Circuits.

II

As earlier explained, pre-IIRIRA, a resident alien who once committed a crime of moral turpitude could travel abroad for short durations without jeopardizing his status as a lawful permanent resident. Under IIRIRA, on return from foreign travel, such an alien is treated as a new arrival to our shores, and may be removed from the United States. Vartelas does not question Congress' authority to restrict reentry in this manner. Nor does he contend that Congress could not do so retroactively. Instead, he invokes the principle against retroactive legislation, under which courts read laws as prospective in application unless Congress has unambiguously instructed retroactivity. *See* Landgraf v. USI Film Products, 511 U.S. 244 (1994).

The presumption against retroactive legislation, the Court recalled in *Landgraf*, "embodies a legal doctrine centuries older than our Republic." *Id.*, at 265. Several provisions of the Constitution, the Court noted, embrace the doctrine, among them, the *Ex Post Facto* Clause, the Contract Clause, and the Fifth Amendment's Due Process Clause. *Id.*, at 266. Numerous decisions of this Court repeat the classic formulation Justice Story penned for determining when retrospective application of a law would collide with the doctrine. It would do so, Story stated, when such application would "tak[e] away or impai[r] vested rights acquired under existing laws, or creat[e] a new obligation, impos[e] a new duty, or attac[h] a new disability, in respect to transactions or considerations already past." [Citation.]

Vartelas urges that applying IIRIRA to him, rather than the law that existed at the time of his conviction, would attach a "new disability," effectively a ban on travel outside the United States, "in respect to [events] . . . already past," *i.e.*, his offense, guilty plea, conviction, and punishment, all occurring prior to the passage of IIRIRA. In evaluating Vartelas' argument, we note first a matter not disputed by the Government: Congress did not expressly prescribe the temporal reach of the IIRIRA provision in question, 8 U.S.C. § 1101(a)(13). . . .

Vartelas presents a firm case for application of the antiretroactivity principle. Neither his sentence, nor the immigration law in effect when he was convicted and sentenced, blocked him from occasional visits to his parents in Greece. Current § 1101(a)(13)(C)(v), if applied to him, would thus attach "a new disability" to conduct over and done well before the provision's enactment.

Beyond genuine doubt, we note, the restraint § 1101(a)(13)(C)(v) places on lawful permanent residents like Vartelas ranks as a "new disability." Once able to journey abroad to fulfill religious obligations, attend funerals and weddings of family members, tend to vital financial interests, or respond to family emergencies, permanent residents situated as Vartelas is now face potential banishment. We have several times recognized the severity of that sanction. [Citation.]

It is no answer to say, as the Government suggests, that Vartelas could have avoided any adverse consequences if he simply stayed at home in the United States, his residence for 24 years prior to his 2003 visit to his parents in Greece. . . . Loss of the ability to travel abroad is itself a harsh penalty, made all the more devastating if it means enduring separation from close family members living abroad. *See* Brief for Asian American Justice Center et al. as *Amici Curiae* 16–23 (describing illustrative cases). We have rejected arguments for retroactivity in similar cases, and in cases in which the loss at stake was less momentous.

In *Chew Heong v. United States*, 112 U.S. 536 (1884), a pathmarking decision, the Court confronted the "Chinese Restriction Act," which barred Chinese laborers from reentering the United States without a certificate issued on their departure. The Court held the reentry bar inapplicable to aliens who had left the country prior to the Act's passage and tried to return afterward without a certificate. The Act's text, the Court observed, was not "so clear and positive as to leave no room to doubt [retroactive application] was the intention of the legislature." *Id.*, at 559.

In *Landgraf*, the question was whether an amendment to Title VII's ban on employment discrimination authorizing compensatory and punitive damages applied to pre-enactment conduct. The Court held it did not. No doubt the complaint against the employer charged discrimination that violated the Act at the time it occurred. But compensatory and punitive damages were not then available remedies. The later provision for such damages, the Court determined, operated prospectively only, and did not apply to employers whose discriminatory conduct occurred prior to the amendment. *See* 511 U.S., at 280–286. And in Hughes Aircraft [v. United States ex rel. Schumer, 520 U.S. 939 (1997)], the Court held that a provision removing an affirmative defense to *qui tam* suits* did not apply to pre-enactment fraud. As in *Landgraf*, the provision attached "a new disability" to past wrongful conduct and therefore could not apply retrospectively unless Congress clearly manifested such an intention. *Hughes Aircraft*, 520 U.S., at 946–950.

Most recently, in [*INS* v.] *St. Cyr*, the Court took up the case of an alien who had entered a plea to a deportable offense. At the time of the plea, the alien was eligible for discretionary relief from deportation. IIRIRA, enacted after entry of the plea, removed that eligibility. The Court held that the IIRIRA provision in point could not be applied to the alien, for it attached a "new disability" to the guilty plea and Congress had not instructed such a result. 533 U.S. 289, 321–23 (2001).

III

The Government, echoed in part by the dissent, argues that no retroactive effect is involved in this case, for the Legislature has not attached any disability to past conduct. Rather, it has made the relevant event the alien's post-IIRIRA act of returning to the United States. We find this argument disingenuous. Vartelas' return to the United States occasioned his treatment as a new entrant, but the reason for the "new

---

* Editors' Note: A *qui tam* action is a statutorily-authorized civil suit brought by a private citizen (often a "whistleblower") seeking a penalty to be shared with the government against a person or entity who has violated a government regulation or contract.

disability" imposed on him was not his lawful foreign travel. It was, indeed, his conviction, pre-IIRIRA, of an offense qualifying as one of moral turpitude. That past misconduct, in other words, not present travel, is the wrongful activity Congress targeted in § 1101(a)(13)(C)(v).

The Government observes that lower courts have upheld Racketeer Influenced and Corrupt Organizations Act prosecutions that encompassed pre-enactment conduct. [Citation.] But those prosecutions depended on criminal activity, *i.e.*, an act of racketeering occurring *after* the provision's effective date. Section 1101(a)(13)(C)(v), in contrast, does not require any showing of criminal conduct postdating IIRIRA's enactment.

Fernandez-Vargas v. Gonzales, 548 U.S. 30 (2006), featured by the Government and the dissent, is similarly inapposite. That case involved 8 U.S.C. § 1231(a)(5), an IIRIRA addition, which provides that an alien who reenters the United States after having been removed can be removed again under the same removal order. We held that the provision could be applied to an alien who reentered illegally before IIRIRA's enactment. Explaining the Court's decision, we said: "[T]he conduct of remaining in the country . . . is the predicate action; the statute applies to stop *an indefinitely continuing violation.* . . . It is therefore the alien's choice *to continue his illegal presence* . . . *after* the effective date of the new la[w] that subjects him to the new . . . legal regime, not a past act that he is helpless to undo." 548 U.S., at 44 (emphasis added). Vartelas, we have several times stressed, engaged in no criminal activity after IIRIRA's passage. He simply took a brief trip to Greece, anticipating a return without incident as in past visits to his parents. No "indefinitely continuing" crime occurred; instead, Vartelas was apprehended because of a pre-IIRIRA crime he was "helpless to undo." *Ibid.*

The Government further refers to lower court decisions in cases involving 18 U.S.C. § 922(g), which prohibits the possession of firearms by convicted felons. [Citation.] "[L]ongstanding prohibitions on the possession of firearms by felons," District of Columbia v. Heller, 554 U.S. 570 (2008), however, target a present danger, *i.e.*, the danger posed by felons who bear arms. *See, e.g.*, United States v. Pfeifer, 371 F. 3d, 430, at 436 (CA8 2004) (hazardous conduct that statute targets "occurred after enactment of the statute"); Omnibus Crime Control and Safe Streets Act of 1968, § 1201, 82 Stat. 236 (noting hazards involved when felons possess firearms).[7]

---

[7]   The dissent, notes two statutes of the same genre: laws prohibiting persons convicted of a sex crime against a victim under 16 years of age from working in jobs involving frequent contact with minors, and laws prohibiting a person "who has been adjudicated as a mental defective or who has been committed to a mental institution" from possessing guns, 18 U.S.C. § 922(g)(4). The dissent is correct that these statutes do not operate retroactively. Rather, they address dangers that arise postenactment: sex offenders with a history of child molestation working in close proximity to children, and mentally unstable persons purchasing guns. The act of flying to Greece, in contrast, does not render a lawful permanent resident like Vartelas hazardous. Nor is it plausible that Congress' solution to the problem of dangerous lawful

Nor do recidivism sentencing enhancements support the Government's position. Enhanced punishment imposed for the later offense " 'is not to be viewed as . . . [an] additional penalty for the earlier crimes,' but instead, as a 'stiffened penalty for the latest crime, which is considered to be an aggravated offense because [it is] a repetitive one.' " Witte v. United States, 515 U.S. 389, 400 (1995) (quoting Gryger v. Burke, 334 U.S. 728, 732 (1948)). In Vartelas' case, however, there is no "aggravated . . . repetitive" offense. There is, in contrast, no post-IIRIRA criminal offense at all. Vartelas' travel abroad and return are "innocent" acts, see Fleuti, 374 U.S., at 462, burdened only because of his pre-IIRIRA offense.

In sum, Vartelas' brief trip abroad post-IIRIRA involved no criminal infraction. IIRIRA disabled him from leaving the United States and returning as a lawful permanent resident. That new disability rested not on any continuing criminal activity, but on a single crime committed years before IIRIRA's enactment. The antiretroactivity principle instructs against application of the new proscription to render Vartelas a first-time arrival at the country's gateway.

IV

The Second Circuit homed in on the words "committed an offense" in § 1101(a)(13)(C)(v) in determining that the change IIRIRA wrought had no retroactive effect. 620 F. 3d, at 119–121. It matters not that Vartelas may have relied on the prospect of continuing visits to Greece in deciding to plead guilty, the court reasoned. "[I]t would border on the absurd," the court observed, "to suggest that Vartelas committed his counterfeiting crime in reliance on the immigration laws." Id., at 120. This reasoning is doubly flawed.

As the Government acknowledges, "th[is] Court has not required a party challenging the application of a statute to show [he relied on prior law] in structuring his conduct." In Landgraf, for example, the issue was the retroactivity of compensatory and punitive damages as remedies for employment discrimination. "[C]oncerns of . . . upsetting expectations are attenuated in the case of intentional employment discrimination," the Court noted, for such discrimination "has been unlawful for more than a generation." 511 U.S., at 282, n. 35. But "[e]ven when the conduct in question is morally reprehensible or illegal," the Court added, "a degree of unfairness is inherent whenever the law imposes additional burdens based on conduct that occurred in the past." Id., at 283, n. 35. . . .

---

permanent residents would be to pass a law that would deter such persons from ever leaving the United States.

As for student loans, it is unlikely that the provision noted by the dissent, 20 U.S.C. § 1091(r), would raise retroactivity questions in the first place. The statute has a prospective thrust. It concerns "[s]uspension of eligibility" when a student receiving a college loan commits a drug crime. The suspension runs "from the date of th[e] conviction" for specified periods, e.g., two years for a second offense of possession. Moreover, eligibility may be restored before the period of ineligibility ends if the student establishes, under prescribed criteria, his rehabilitation.

The operative presumption, after all, is that Congress intends its laws to govern prospectively only. "It is a strange 'presumption,'" the Third Circuit commented, "that arises only on . . . a showing [of] actual reliance." Ponnapula v. Ashcroft, 373 F.3d 480, 491 (2004). The essential inquiry, as stated in *Landgraf*, 511 U.S., at 269–270, is "whether the new provision attaches new legal consequences to events completed before its enactment." That is just what occurred here.

In any event, Vartelas likely relied on then-existing immigration law. While the presumption against retroactive application of statutes does not require a showing of detrimental reliance, *see Olatunji*, 387 F. 3d, at 389–395, reasonable reliance has been noted among the "familiar considerations" animating the presumption, *see Landgraf*, 511 U.S., at 270 (presumption reflects "familiar considerations of fair notice, reasonable reliance, and settled expectations"). Although not a necessary predicate for invoking the antiretroactivity principle, the likelihood of reliance on prior law strengthens the case for reading a newly enacted law prospectively. *See Olatunji*, 387 F. 3d, at 393 (discussing *St. Cyr*).

St. Cyr is illustrative. That case involved a lawful permanent resident who pleaded guilty to a criminal charge that made him deportable. Under the immigration law in effect when he was convicted, he would have been eligible to apply for a waiver of deportation. But his removal proceeding was commenced after Congress, in IIRIRA, withdrew that dispensation. Disallowance of discretionary waivers, the Court recognized, "attache[d] a new disability, in respect to transactions or considerations already past." 533 U.S., at 321 (internal quotation marks omitted). Aliens like St. Cyr, the Court observed, "almost certainly relied upon th[e] likelihood [of receiving discretionary relief] in deciding [to plead guilty, thereby] forgo[ing] their right to a trial." *Id.*, at 325.[9] Hence, applying the IIRIRA withdrawal to St. Cyr would have an "obvious and severe retroactive effect." *Ibid.* Because Congress made no such intention plain, *ibid.*, n. 55, we held that the prior law, permitting relief from deportation, governed St. Cyr's case.

As to retroactivity, one might think Vartelas' case even easier than St. Cyr's. St. Cyr could seek the Attorney General's *discretionary* dispensation. Vartelas, under *Fleuti*, was free, without seeking an official's permission, to make trips of short duration to see and assist his parents in Greece.[10] The Second Circuit thought otherwise, compounding

---

[9] "There can be little doubt," the Court noted in *St. Cyr*, "that, as a general matter, alien defendants considering whether to enter into a plea agreement are acutely aware of the immigration consequences of their convictions." 533 U.S., at 322. Indeed, "[p]reserving [their] right to remain in the United States may be more important to [them] than any potential jail sentence." *Ibid.* (internal quotation marks omitted). *See Padilla v. Kentucky*, 130 S.Ct. 1473, 1478–80 (2010) (holding that counsel has a duty under the Sixth Amendment to inform a noncitizen defendant that his plea would make him eligible for deportation).

[10] Armed with knowledge that a guilty plea would preclude travel abroad, aliens like Vartelas might endeavor to negotiate a plea to a nonexcludable offense—in Vartelas' case, *e.g.*, possession of counterfeit securities—or exercise a right to trial.

its initial misperception (treating reliance as essential to application of the antiretroactivity principle). . . .

Satisfied that Vartelas' case is at least as clear as St. Cyr's for declining to apply a new law retroactively, we hold that *Fleuti* continues to govern Vartelas' short-term travel.

For the reasons stated, the judgment of the Court of Appeals for the Second Circuit is reversed, and the case is remanded for further proceedings consistent with this opinion.

It is so ordered.

■ JUSTICE SCALIA, with whom JUSTICE THOMAS and JUSTICE ALITO join, dissenting.

As part of the Illegal Immigration Reform and Immigrant Responsibility Act of 1996 (IIRIRA), Congress required that lawful permanent residents who have committed certain crimes seek formal "admission" when they return to the United States from abroad. 8 U.S.C. § 1101(a)(13)(C)(v). This case presents a straightforward question of statutory interpretation: Does that statute apply to lawful permanent residents who, like Vartelas, committed one of the specified offenses before 1996, but traveled abroad after 1996? Under the proper approach to determining a statute's temporal application, the answer is yes.

I

The text of § 1101(a)(13)(C)(v) does not contain a clear statement answering the question presented here. So the Court is correct that this case is governed by our longstanding interpretive principle that, in the absence of a contrary indication, a statute will not be construed to have retroactive application. *See, e.g.,* Landgraf v. USI Film Products, 511 U.S. 244, 280 (1994). The operative provision of this text—the provision that specifies the act that it prohibits or prescribes—says that lawful permanent residents convicted of offenses similar to Vartelas's must seek formal "admission" before they return to the United States from abroad. Since Vartelas returned to the United States after the statute's effective date, the application of that text to his reentry does not give the statute a retroactive effect.

In determining whether a statute applies retroactively, we should concern ourselves with the statute's actual operation on regulated parties, not with retroactivity as an abstract concept or as a substitute for fairness concerns. It is impossible to decide whether a statute's application is retrospective or prospective without first identifying a reference point—a moment in time to which the statute's effective date is either subsequent or antecedent. (Otherwise, the obvious question— retroactive in reference to what?—remains unanswered.) In my view, the identity of that reference point turns on the activity a statute is intended to regulate. For any given regulated party, the reference point (or "retroactivity event") is the moment at which the party does what the statute forbids or fails to do what it requires. *See* Martin v. Hadix, 527

U.S. 343, 362–363 (1999) (SCALIA, J., concurring in part and concurring in judgment); *Landgraf, supra,* at 291 (SCALIA, J., concurring in judgments). With an identified reference point, the retroactivity analysis is simple. If a person has engaged in the primary regulated activity *before* the statute's effective date, then the statute's application *would* be retroactive. But if a person engages in the primary regulated activity *after* the statute's effective date, then the statute's application is prospective only. In the latter case, the interpretive presumption against retroactivity does not bar the statute's application.

Under that commonsense approach, this is a relatively easy case. Although the *class* of aliens affected by § 1101(a)(13)(C)(v) is defined with respect to past crimes, the *regulated activity* is reentry into the United States. By its terms, the statute is all about controlling admission at the border. It specifies six criteria to identify lawful permanent residents who are subject to formal "admission" procedures, most of which relate to the circumstances of departure, the trip itself, or reentry. The titles of the statutory sections containing § 1101(a)(13)(C)(v) confirm its focus on admission, rather than crime: The provision is located within Title III of IIRIRA ("Inspection, Apprehension, Detention, Adjudication, and Removal of Inadmissible and Deportable Aliens"), under Subtitle A ("Revision of Procedures for Removal of Aliens"), and § 301 ("Treating Persons Present in the United States Without Authorization as Not Admitted"). 110 Stat. 3009–575. And the specific subsection of IIRIRA at issue (§ 301(a), entitled " 'Admission' Defined") is an amendment to the definition of "entry" in the general "Definitions" section of the Immigration and Nationality Act (INA). The original provision told border officials how to regulate admission—not how to punish crime— and the amendment does as well.

Section 1101(a)(13)(C)(v) thus has no retroactive effect on Vartelas because the reference point here—Vartelas's readmission to the United States after a trip abroad occurred years after the statute's effective date. Although Vartelas cannot change the fact of his prior conviction, he could have avoided *entirely* the consequences of § 1101(a)(13)(C)(v) by simply remaining in the United States or, having left, remaining in Greece. That § 1101(a)(13)(C)(v) had no effect on Vartelas until he performed a post-enactment activity is a clear indication that the statute's application is purely prospective. *See Fernandez-Vargas v. Gonzales,* 548 U.S. 30, 45, n. 11, 46 (2006) (no retroactive effect where the statute in question did "not operate on a completed preenactment act" and instead turned on "a failure to take timely action that would have avoided application of the new law altogether").

II

The Court avoids this conclusion by insisting that "[p]ast misconduct, ... not present travel, is the wrongful activity Congress targeted" in § 1101(a)(13)(C)(v). That assertion does not, however, have any basis in the statute's text or structure, and the Court does not pretend otherwise. Instead, the Court simply asserts that Vartelas's "lawful foreign travel" surely could not be the "reason for the 'new disability' imposed on him." *Ibid.* . . . But the *reason* for a prohibition has nothing to do with whether the prohibition is being applied to a past rather than a future act. It may be relevant to other legal inquiries—for example, to whether a legislative act violates one of the *Ex Post Facto* Clauses in Article I, [citation,] or one of the Due Process Clauses in the Fifth and Fourteenth Amendments, *see, e.g.,* Williamson v. Lee Optical of Okla., Inc., [citation,] or the Takings Clause in the Fifth Amendment, [citation,] or the Obligation of Contracts Clause in Article I [citation omitted]. But it has no direct bearing upon whether the statute is retroactive.

The Court's failure to differentiate between the statutory-interpretation question (whether giving certain effect to a provision would make it retroactive and hence presumptively unintended) and the validity question (whether giving certain effect to a provision is unlawful) is on full display in its attempts to distinguish § 1101(a)(13)(C)(v) from similar statutes. Take, for example, the Court's discussion of the Racketeer Influenced and Corrupt Organizations Act (RICO). That Act, which targets "patterns of racketeering," *expressly* defines those "patterns" to include some pre-enactment conduct. *See* 18 U.S.C. § 1961(5). Courts interpreting RICO therefore need not consider the presumption against retroactivity; instead, the cases cited by the majority consider whether RICO violates the *Ex Post Facto* Clause. [Citation.] The Government recognized this distinction and cited RICO to make a point about the *Ex Post Facto* Clause rather than the presumption against retroactivity; the Court evidently does not.

The Court's confident assertion that Congress surely would not have meant this statute to apply to Vartelas, whose foreign travel and subsequent return to the United States were innocent events, simply begs the question presented in this case. Ignorance, of course, is no excuse *(ignorantia legis neminem excusat)*; and his return was entirely lawful only if the statute before us did not render it unlawful. Since IIRIRA's effective date in 1996, lawful permanent residents who have committed crimes of moral turpitude are forbidden to leave the United States and return without formally seeking "admission." *See* § 1101(a)(13)(C)(v). As a result, Vartelas's numerous trips abroad and "uneventful" reentries into the United States after the passage of IIRIRA were lawful only *if* § 1101(a)(13)(C)(v) does not apply to him—which is, of course, precisely the matter in dispute here.

The Court's circular reasoning betrays its underlying concern: Because the Court believes that reentry after a brief trip abroad *should* be lawful, it will decline to apply a statute that clearly provides otherwise for certain criminal aliens. . . . The Court's test for retroactivity—asking whether the statute creates a "new disability" in "respect to past events"—invites this focus on fairness. Understandably so, since it is derived from a Justice Story opinion interpreting a provision of the New Hampshire Constitution that *forbade* retroactive laws—a provision comparable to the Federal Constitution's *ex post facto* prohibition and bearing no relation to the presumption against retroactivity. What is unfair or irrational (and hence should be forbidden) has nothing to do with whether applying a statute to a particular act is prospective (and thus presumptively intended) or retroactive (and thus presumptively unintended). On the latter question, the "new disability in respect to past events" test provides no meaningful guidance.

I can imagine countless laws that, like § 1101(a)(13)(C)(v), impose "new disabilities" related to "past events" and yet do not operate retroactively. For example, a statute making persons convicted of drug crimes ineligible for student loans. *See, e.g.*, 20 U.S.C. § 1091(r)(1). Or laws prohibiting those convicted of sex crimes from working in certain jobs that involve repeated contact with minors. *See, e.g.*, Cal. Penal Code Ann. § 290.95(c) (West Supp. 2012). Or laws prohibiting those previously committed for mental instability from purchasing guns. *See, e.g.*, 18 U.S.C. § 922(g)(4). The Court concedes that it would not consider the last two laws inapplicable to pre-enactment convictions or commitments. The Court does not deny that these statutes impose a "new disability in respect to past events," but it distinguishes them based on the *reason* for their enactment: These statutes "address dangers that arise postenactment." So much for the new-disability-in-respect-to-past-events test; it has now become a new-disability-not-designed-to-guard-against-future-danger test. But why is guarding against future danger the *only* reason Congress may wish to regulate future action in light of past events? It obviously is not. So the Court must invent yet another doctrine to address my first example, the law making persons convicted of drug crimes ineligible for student loans. According to the Court, that statute differs from § 1101(a)(13)(C)(v) because it "has a prospective thrust." I cannot imagine what that means, other than that the statute regulates post-enactment conduct. But, of course, so does § 1101(a)(13)(C)(v). Rather than reconciling any of these distinctions with Justice Story's formulation of retroactivity, the Court leaves to lower courts the unenviable task of identifying new-disabilities-not-designed-to-guard-against-future-danger-and-also-lacking-a-prospective-thrust.

And anyway, is there any doubt that § 1101(a)(13)(C)(v) is intended to guard against the "dangers that arise postenactment" from having aliens in our midst who have shown themselves to have proclivity for crime? Must that be rejected as its purpose simply because Congress has not sought to achieve it by all possible means—by ferreting out such dangerous aliens and going through the expensive and lengthy process of deporting them? At least some of the post-enactment danger can readily be eliminated by forcing lawful permanent residents who have committed certain crimes to undergo formal "admission" procedures at our borders. Indeed, by limiting criminal aliens' opportunities to travel and then return to the United States, § 1101(a)(13)(C)(v) may encourage self-deportation. But all this is irrelevant. The positing of legislative "purpose" is always a slippery enterprise compared to the simple determination of whether a statute regulates a future event—and it is that, rather than the Court's pronouncement of some forward-looking *reason*, which governs whether a statute has retroactive effect. . . .

This case raises a plain-vanilla question of statutory interpretation, not broader questions about frustrated expectations or fairness. Our approach to answering that question should be similarly straightforward: We should determine what relevant activity the statute regulates (here, reentry); absent a clear statement otherwise, only such relevant activity which occurs after the statute's effective date should be covered (here, post-1996 re-entries). If, as so construed, the statute is unfair or irrational enough to violate the Constitution, that is another matter entirely, and one not presented here. Our interpretive presumption against retroactivity, however, is just that—a tool to ascertain what the statute means, not a license to rewrite the statute in a way the Court considers more desirable.

I respectfully dissent.

QUESTIONS

1.   In *Vartelas*, which "retroactivity event"—the past guilty plea or re-entry into the United States—makes more sense in analyzing the effect of the amended statute? If the statute is effective as of that event, could the statute be said to have "genuinely retroactive" effect? What activity is the statute endeavoring to address and change?

2.   What are the concerns underlying the antiretroactivity principle? Which approach in *Vartelas*, the majority's or dissent's, better addresses those concerns?

3.   What do you make of the dissent's statement in *Vartelas* that "[if] the statute is unfair or irrational enough to violate the Constitution, that is another matter entirely, and one not presented here." Does this statement suggest that fairness concerns are to be addressed only by means of a constitutional challenge? What, then, of the doctrine of "constitutional avoidance," which enables a court to reject a proposed statutory interpretation on the ground that, so read, the statute would be unconstitutional? Is not the anti-retroactivity principle an attempt to address fairness concerns without engaging in constitutional interpretation?

PART VII

THE RELATIONSHIPS BETWEEN STATUTES, AND AMONG JUDICIAL INTERPRETATIONS OF THOSE STATUTES

A. WHEN THE LEGISLATURE PROVIDES INSTRUCTIONS FOR JUDICIAL INTERPRETATION

Would the task of statutory construction be facilitated if Congress simply enacted a general statute *telling* courts how to interpret their enactments? The definition sections that legislatures often provide for specific statutes, already encountered in Section III.B.2, are far from full guides to statutory interpretation. Similarly, as discussed earlier in Parts II.B.3 and III.B.1, legislatures may pass laws against a backdrop of canons of construction, but these are judge-made devices (and are susceptible of varied application); they are not legislated codes of construction. How advisable might such a code be? Consider the following:

1. ACT INTERPRETATION ACTS

The interpretative status quo is cacophonous. Every judge and scholar has his own theory of how best to interpret statutes, and this diversity renders the interpretative project unpredictable. Each theory may have its own merits, and some may be better than others, but these differences ultimately may matter less

than a central imperative of statutory interpretation: a single,
predictable, coherent set of rules. The Supreme Court, with its
nine competing perspectives and its jurisdictional restriction to
cases and controversies, will never be able to achieve this
coherence alone.

Nicholas Quinn Rosenkrantz, *Federal Rules of Statutory Interpretation*,
115 Harv. L. Rev. 2085, 2088 (2002).

Acts Interpretations Acts are statutes that codify rules for
interpreting statutes. The preeminent example of such codification is the
Vienna Convention on the Law of Treaties, which in Article 31.1 sets out
a general rule for the interpretation of treaties between states: "A treaty
shall be interpreted in good faith in accordance with the ordinary
meaning given to the terms of the treaty in context and in light of its
object and purpose." Article 32 authorizes recourse to extrinsic
information in certain circumstances.

As you have seen, in common-law systems, interpretation rules have
traditionally evolved through judge-made canons of construction. Where
they exist, interpretation statutes displace the canons. In practice,
however, the canons interplay with the statutory rules by filling any gaps
left open. In this way, interpretation statutes can sometimes expand,
rather than restrict, debate as to the proper meaning of legislation.
Although many federal statutes contain definitions sections and
sometimes also purpose clauses to aid in interpretation, and the
Dictionary Act provides a small number of definitions for terms as used
throughout the U.S. Code, no general U.S. federal interpretation act
exists. By contrast, all fifty states and the District of Columbia have
interpretative codes which, while not fully-blown interpretation acts,
provide more detailed instructions on interpretation than anything
appearing in the U.S. Code.[1] The reason these interpretative codes are
not "fully-blown" is that, instead of setting out general interpretative
rules (such as those found in the Vienna Convention), the state codes
tend to provide only technical guidance for the interpretation of
particular terms.[2] For instance, the Michigan code provides a rule for the
computation of time under any statute or administrative rule.[3] Even
more specifically, the Florida code defines the word "writing" to include
"handwriting, printing, typewriting, and all other methods and means of

---

[1]   *See* the legislation cited in Nicholas Quinn Rosenkrantz, *Federal Rules of Statutory
Interpretation*, 115 Harv. L. Rev. 2085, 2089 n.10 (2002).

[2]   The comprehensive New York code is an exception to this principle and does contain
some general guidance. *See for instance* N.Y. Stat. Law § 76 (McKinney 1971 & Supp. 2001–
2002): "Where words of a statute are free from ambiguity and express plainly, clearly and
distinctly the legislative intent, resort may not be had to other means of interpretation." *See
generally* §§ 71–424.

[3]   Mich. Comp. Laws § 8.6 (1979). The rule is that the first day of the period is excluded
and the last day is included, unless the last day of the period is a Saturday, Sunday or legal
holiday (in which case the period is extended to include the next working day).

forming letters and characters upon paper, stone, wood, or other materials."[4]

Unlike judicial canons of construction, interpretation statutes dictate the rules for constructing the legislature's own enactments. Rather than leaving it to courts to devise an interpretive methodology, the legislature tells the court how to undertake the interpretive task. Of course, this sometimes requires courts to interpret not only the statute in question, but also the act interpretation act, as the next case study illustrates:

2. CASE STUDY IN ACT INTERPRETATION ACTS: INTERPRETING STATE TORT LAW ACCORDING TO AN ACT INTERPRETATION ACT

The Texts to Be Construed: Pennsylvania Vehicular Tort Statutes and Statutory Rules of Statutory Construction

a. RELEVANT STATE VEHICULAR REGISTRATION AND TORT STATUTES

Like most states, Pennsylvania's tort law is largely governed by statute, and those statutory rules often draw on related regulatory rules. Consider the interplay between the statutory provisions that govern vehicle insurance coverage and liability in Pennsylvania.

Vehicles, Registration and Title
Pennsylvania Statutes and Consolidated Statutes, Title 75, Part II, Chapter 17.

§ 1705. Election of tort options

(a) Financial responsibility requirements.—

(1) Each insurer . . . shall notify in writing each named insured of the availability of two alternatives of full tort insurance . . . The notice shall be a standardized form adopted by the commissioner and shall include the following language: . . .

A. "Limited Tort" Option—The laws of the Commonwealth of Pennsylvania give you the right to choose a form of insurance that limits your right and the right of members of your household to seek financial compensation for injuries caused by other drivers. Under this form of insurance, you and other household members covered under this policy may seek recovery for all medical and other out-of-pocket expenses, but not for pain and suffering or other nonmonetary damages unless the injuries suffered fall within the definition of "serious injury" as set forth in

---

[4] Fla. Stat. ch. 1.01 (2001).

the policy or unless one of several other exceptions noted in the policy applies. . . .

B. "Full Tort" Option—The laws of the Commonwealth of Pennsylvania also give you the right to choose a form of insurance under which you maintain an unrestricted right for you and the members of your household to seek financial compensation for injuries caused by other drivers. Under this form of insurance, you and other household members covered under this policy may seek recovery for all medical and other out-of-pocket expenses and may also seek financial compensation for pain and suffering and other nonmonetary damages as a result of injuries caused by other drivers. . . .

(5) An owner of a currently registered private passenger motor vehicle who does not have financial responsibility shall be deemed to have chosen the limited tort alternative.

(b) Application of tort options.—

(1) The tort option elected by a named insured shall apply to all private passenger motor vehicle policies of the named insured issued by the same insurer and shall continue in force as to all subsequent renewal policies, replacement policies and any other private passenger motor vehicle policies under which the individual is a named insured until the insurer, or its authorized representative, receives a properly executed form electing the other tort option.

(2) The tort option elected by a named insured shall apply to all insureds under the private passenger motor vehicle policy who are not named insureds under another private passenger motor vehicle policy. In the case where more than one private passenger motor vehicle policy is applicable to an insured and the policies have conflicting tort options, the insured is bound by the tort option of the policy associated with the private passenger motor vehicle in which the insured is an occupant at the time of the accident if he is an insured on that policy and bound by the full tort option otherwise.

(3) An individual who is not an owner of a currently registered private passenger motor vehicle and who is not a named insured or insured under any private passenger motor vehicle policy shall not be precluded from maintaining an action for noneconomic loss or economic loss sustained in a motor vehicle accident as the consequence of the fault of another person pursuant to applicable tort law.

(c) Full tort alternative.—Each person who is bound by the full tort election remains eligible to seek compensation for noneconomic loss claimed and economic loss sustained in a motor vehicle accident as the consequence of the fault of another person pursuant to applicable tort law.

(d) Limited tort alternative.—Each person who elects the limited tort alternative remains eligible to seek compensation for economic loss sustained in a motor vehicle accident as the consequence of the fault of another person pursuant to applicable tort law. Unless the injury sustained is a serious injury, each person who is bound by the limited tort election shall be precluded from maintaining an action for any noneconomic loss . . .

(f) Definitions.—As used in this section, the following words and phrases when used in this section shall have the meanings given to them in this subsection unless the context clearly indicates otherwise:

"Insured." Any individual residing in the household of the named insured who is:

(1) a spouse or other relative of the named insured; or

(2) a minor in the custody of either the named insured or relative of the named insured.

"Named insured." Any individual identified by name as an insured in a policy of private passenger motor vehicle insurance.

QUESTIONS

1. From § 1705(a)(1), can you articulate the salient differences between the "limited tort" and "full tort" options? What are the consequences of those choices?

2. Can you articulate how these options affect different individuals in distinct ways? Can you identify any ambiguities in the application of these combined provisions?

b. PENNSYLVANIA'S ACT INTERPRETATION ACT

As is true of every state in the Union, the Pennsylvania legislature has provided its state courts with an act interpretation act that instructs state courts how to interpret Pennsylvania statutes.

Statutory Construction: Rules of Construction

Pennsylvania Statutes and Consolidated Statutes, Title 1, Part V, Chapter 19.

§ 1921. Legislative intent controls

(a) The object of all interpretation and construction of statutes is to ascertain and effectuate the intention of the General Assembly. Every statute shall be construed, if possible, to give effect to all its provisions.

(b) When the words of a statute are clear and free from all ambiguity, the letter of it is not to be disregarded under the pretext of pursuing its spirit.

(c) When the words of the statute are not explicit, the intention of the General Assembly may be ascertained by considering, among other matters:

    (1) The occasion and necessity for the statute.

    (2) The circumstances under which it was enacted.

    (3) The mischief to be remedied.

    (4) The object to be attained.

    (5) The former law, if any, including other statutes upon the same or similar subjects.

    (6) The consequences of a particular interpretation.

    (7) The contemporaneous legislative history.

    (8) Legislative and administrative interpretations of such statute.

§ 1922. Presumptions in ascertaining legislative intent

In ascertaining the intention of the General Assembly in the enactment of a statute the following presumptions, among others, may be used:

(1) That the General Assembly does not intend a result that is absurd, impossible of execution or unreasonable. . . .

(5) That the General Assembly intends to favor the public interest as against any private interest.

§ 1928. Rule of strict and liberal construction

(a) The rule that statutes in derogation of the common law are to be strictly construed, shall have no application to the statutes of this Commonwealth enacted finally after September 1, 1937.

(b) All provisions of a statute of the classes hereafter enumerated shall be strictly construed:

    (1) Penal provisions.

    (2) Retroactive provisions.

    (3) Provisions imposing taxes.

    (4) Provisions conferring the power of eminent domain.

    (5) Provisions exempting persons and property from taxation.

    (6) Provisions exempting property from the power of eminent domain.

    (7) Provisions decreasing the jurisdiction of a court of record.

    (8) Provisions enacted finally prior to September 1, 1937 which are in derogation of the common law.

(c) All other provisions of a statute shall be liberally construed to effect their objects and to promote justice.

§ 1932. Statutes in pari materia

(a) Statutes or parts of statutes are in pari materia when they relate to the same persons or things or to the same class of persons or things.

(b) Statutes in pari materia shall be construed together, if possible, as one statute.

QUESTION

What criteria should an interpreter use to decide whether statutes are *in pari materia*? What would you consider is "the same class of persons?" Vehicle owners? Insured Drivers? Passengers? *Any* occupant of a vehicle?

Holland v. Marcy

Supreme Court of Pennsylvania, 2005.
584 Pa. 195, 883 A.2d 449.

■ JUSTICE BAER, joined by CAPPY, C.J., and SAYLOR, J.

This Court granted review of this case in order to address ... following question of law: Whether full tort remedies are available to children of an owner of a registered but uninsured vehicle or whether they, like their parent, may only pursue limited tort remedies pursuant to Section 1705 of the Motor Vehicle Financial Responsibility Law (the "MVFRL"), 75 Pa.C.S. § 1705? ... [T]he Superior Court held that the plain language of Section 1705 dictates that children injured in their parent's registered but uninsured vehicle may obtain full tort remedies under subsection (b)(3) because the language of subsection (a)(5) only specifies that the uninsured *owner* is deemed to have chosen limited tort coverage. [Citation.] Similarly, the Superior Court previously concluded that full tort remedies were available to the wife of the owner of a registered but uninsured vehicle when the wife did not have any ownership interest in the vehicle. [Citation.] Conversely, when addressing a similar fact pattern, the Commonwealth Court looked at the legislative intent of the 1990 amendments to the MVFRL, which included Section 1705, and at the language of subsections (a)(5) and (b)(2) to determine that children of an owner of a registered but uninsured vehicle were bound by their parent's deemed selection of limited tort. [Citation.] For the following reasons, we hold that Section 1705 does not bind the children of an owner of a registered but uninsured vehicle to limited tort remedies despite the fact that their parent is deemed to have chosen the limited tort option.

The facts of the case are straightforward and uncontested. Theresa Holland and Joel R. Holland were divorced, and the parents of minor Appellees, Joel and Heather Holland. Theresa owned the car involved in the accident leading to this case. At the time of the accident, Joel R. was driving, accompanied by Theresa and the children, Joel and Heather. Prior to the time of the accident, Theresa had purchased two insurance policies on the subject automobile. At the time of each purchase, Theresa elected the limited tort option. Both policies had expired prior to the time of the accident, and thus, while Theresa continued to own the registered car when the accident occurred, she was uninsured.

This incident happened when Appellant Edward E. Marcy, while traveling in an easterly direction on State Route 20 in Erie County, made an abrupt left turn from the right hand lane and collided with the Hollands' car which was traveling in the same direction in the left hand lane. The children received treatment for injuries resulting from the accident.

The Hollands filed suit against Marcy to recover economic and non-economic damages. [The trial court entered summary judgment for Marcy, a divided Superior Court reversed.] [Before this Court], Marcy argues that Section 1705(a)(5) and (b)(2) bind the children of an owner of a registered but uninsured vehicle to the owner's deemed election of the limited tort option. He asserts that to permit them to recover non-economic damages would be in violation of the intent and policy underlying the MVFRL, in that it would provide an incentive to parents who decide consciously to remain uninsured in order to provide their children with full tort remedies. Moreover, . . . he argues that it would provide the children of registered but uninsured owners with benefits in excess of those provided to responsible parents who choose the limited tort option. In contrast, the Hollands assert that the Superior Court . . . correctly determined that the clear and unambiguous language of Section 1705 did not limit the Holland children to limited tort recovery, but rather provided for recovery of non-economic damages pursuant to subsection (b)(3) because the children were not owners, named insureds or insureds.

As all the parties have conceded, the issue before the Court is a question of statutory interpretation and thus is a pure question of law subject to our plenary review. [Citation.] As in all cases of statutory interpretation, our goal is to ascertain the intent of the General Assembly in adopting the statute. 1 Pa.C.S. § 1921(a). In doing so, we must, if possible, give effect to all the provisions of a statute. 1 Pa.C.S. §§ 1921, 1922. "When the words of a statute are clear and free from all ambiguity, the letter of it is not to be disregarded under the pretext of pursuing its spirit." 1 Pa.C.S. § 1921(b). Only when the words are ambiguous may we look to the general purposes of the statute, legislative history, and other sources in an attempt to determine the legislative intent. 1 Pa.C.S. § 1921(c). In construing a statute, the courts must attempt to give meaning to every word in a statute as we cannot assume that the legislature intended any words to be mere surplusage. Furthermore, we should avoid construing a statute in such a way as would lead to an absurd result. 1 Pa.C.S. § 1922. Additionally, statutes which apply to the same class of persons should be read, where possible, in *pari materia*. 1 Pa.C.S. § 1932. As with all statutes not contained in the categories

pari materia = on the same subject or matter

described in 1 Pa.C.S. § 1928(b), the MVFRL must be liberally construed to give effect to its purposes and promote justice. 1 Pa.C.S. § 1928(c).

We agree with the Superior Court's conclusion that the language of Section 1705 is clear and unambiguous. . . [and] conclude that the language of subsection (a)(5) only applies to "[a]n owner of a currently registered private passenger motor vehicle who does not have financial responsibility." 75 Pa.C.S. § 1705(a)(5). . . . Section 1705(f) specifically defines a "named insured" as "[a]ny individual identified by name as an insured in a policy of private passenger motor vehicle insurance." 75 Pa.C.S. § 1705(f). Had the legislature intended to equate the two terms ["owner" and "named insured"] they could have specified such in either subsection (a)(5) or (f) by defining a "named insured" to include both individuals actually named in an insurance policy and those deemed to have chosen the limited tort option pursuant to 1705(a)(5), or by specifying that an uninsured owner will be deemed to be a named insured in a limited tort insurance policy. This Court may not amend the statute but instead must examine the statute as drafted by the legislature. We, thus, refuse to expand the meaning of the words used by the legislature which clearly state that the owner is "deemed to have chosen the limited tort alternative" to mean that the owner is deemed to be a "named insured" on a limited tort insurance policy so as to trigger subsection (b)(2) and bind the children of the owner to the limited tort option. Therefore, the children clearly fall within Section 1705 (b)(3) and may pursue economic and non-economic damages in that the parties do not dispute that the children were not owners of an uninsured vehicle and that neither child was a named insured or insured under any other actual private passenger motor vehicle policy.

Not only is the language clear, but it is consistent with other provisions of the MVFRL which punish only the owner. *See* 75 Pa.C.S. §§ 1714 ("An owner of a currently registered motor vehicle who does not have financial responsibility . . . cannot recover first party benefits."), 1752 (preventing recovery from the Assigned Claims Plan by owners), 1786(d) and (f) (punishing owners of uninsured vehicles by suspending the registration of the vehicle, the operating privileges of the owner, and imposing a $300 fine for a summary criminal offense). . . .

Although the clarity of the language does not require us to look to the purposes of the statute, we observe that the language is entirely consistent with such purposes. This Court has previously interpreted subsections of Section 1705 and noted that a primary concern of the legislature in passing the MVFRL was the rising cost of consumer automobile insurance "created in part by the substantial number of uninsured motorists who contributed nothing to the pool of insurance funds from which claims were paid." [Citation.] Section 1705(a)(5) rectifies this problem by providing a disincentive to uninsured owners in that they will be deemed to have chosen the limited tort option. The restriction on the owner in (a)(5) is but one of a number of disincentives that clearly outweigh the suggestion that the children of uninsured owners will be "better off" than children of parents who choose the limited tort option. In cases such as the present where the uninsured owner-parent is not at fault in the accident, the parent and the children would not have an insurer from which they could recover benefits provided by uninsured/underinsured coverage in the event that the tortfeasor was not insured. . . . Moreover, the owner would be subject to the penalties, including criminal charges, fines, and suspension of operating privileges, under Section 1786. These disincentives could result in significant costs to the uninsured owner, which would in turn cause hardships on the family. . . .

Additionally, we note that this Court has previously concluded that the MVFRL should be "accorded a liberal construction, in favor of the insured" and that the legislative history suggests that the General Assembly made a "conscious attempt to rule in favor of the full tort alternative" when there was a question as to which coverage applied. [Citation.] Therefore, although we need not resort to statutory construction due to the clear language of the statute, we are further satisfied that the clear language is not contrary to the purposes of the MVFRL or to the majority of the decisions applying the MVFRL. For all the foregoing reasons, we hold, under the facts of this case, that 1705(a)(5) does not preclude the children of an owner of a registered but uninsured vehicle from maintaining actions for non-economic damages and affirm the decision of the Superior Court reversing the trial court's grant of summary judgment in favor of appellee-defendant Marcy and remanding for further proceedings.

■ JUSTICE NEWMAN [files a concurring opinion in which JUSTICE NIGRO joins].

This is a situation where applying the plain language of one section of a statute leads to an absurd result, which is dissonant with the purpose of the statutory scheme in its entirety. I join in the result that the Majority reaches because of the unambiguous words of Section 1705(b)(3) of Motor Vehicle Financial Responsibility Law (MVFRL), 75 Pa.C.S. § 1705(b)(3). By holding that the children of an owner of a registered but uninsured vehicle are not bound to limited tort remedies despite the fact that their parent is deemed to have chosen the limited tort option, this Court confers greater benefits on children of parents who have not maintained financial responsibility than on those with financially responsible parents. Nevertheless, as the Majority states, "the clarity of the language does not require us to look to the purposes of the statute." I write separately to express my opinion that I find it difficult to believe that the legislature could have intended this outcome when it provided for the election of tort options and financial responsibility at Section 1705 of the MVFRL.

I believe that our holding today produces a result that directly opposes the goal of the MVFRL. We have held that "the legislative history of the MVFRL indicates that the primary concerns of the General Assembly in repealing the No-fault Act and enacting the MVFRL were the spiraling cost of automobile insurance and the resultant increase in the number of uninsured motorists driving on public highways. [Citations.] Had Theresa Holland complied with the mandate of the financial responsibility law, and purchased insurance with the limited tort option, her children would have been limited by her choice and unable to pursue noneconomic damages. Because Holland drove without insurance, and paid no premium whatsoever, her children are now entitled to pursue noneconomic damages, in the same way they would have had their mother bought the full tort option. Stated most simply, the direct result of the Majority's decision is to encourage and reward failure to comply with the law, an outcome that the legislature surely did not intend when it implemented the MVFRL.

Section 1705(b)(3) states that **"[a]n individual who is not an owner of a currently registered ... vehicle and who is not a named insured ... shall not be precluded from maintaining an action for noneconomic loss ...."** 75 Pa.C.S. § 1705(b)(3) (emphasis added). The Majority applied the literal wording of this Section, which is the only way this Court can read it because the words are clear. This requires us to determine that the Holland children are entitled to the full tort option because they do not own a car and are not named insureds, since their mother drove an uninsured car. Because it is true that the Holland children did not own the registered uninsured car, they are not precluded from maintaining an action for noneconomic loss.

I believe that ... two conflicting determinations [by the Superior Court and the Commonwealth Court in earlier cases] reflect the dilemma that this matter presents—applying the literal words of one section of the statute yields a result that the legislature likely did not intend to govern the outcome in the instant case. . . Although the clear wording of Section 1705(b)(3) calls for the result that the Majority articulates, I believe that the legislature did not intend this outcome, because the legislature "does not intend a result that is absurd, impossible of execution, or unreasonable." 1 Pa.C.S. § 1922(1). It is my opinion that the legislature likely designed this Section to apply only to individuals who have no connection to either cars or insurance and who, however, have had the misfortune of being involved in an accident that was the fault of another. . . .

■ JUSTICE EAKIN [files a dissenting opinion in which JUSTICE CASTILLE joins].

I respectfully disagree with the majority's determination that the language of the MVFRL clearly determined this question, which obviously is not addressed by the statute itself. I believe the majority's decision produces a result contrary to both the legislative intent of the MVFRL and the canons of statutory construction. While the meaning of the words in § 1705 might appear unambiguous when each subsection is plucked from the statute and read in isolation, statutes are not to be interpreted in such a manner. . . .

Statutes are considered to be *in pari materia* when they relate to the same persons or things, and statutes or parts of statutes *in pari materia* shall be construed together, if possible. 1 Pa.C.S. § 1932. Courts are required, if possible, to give effect to each provision or subsection of the statute. *Id.,* § 1921(a). I believe the majority looks at the statute through an overly narrow lens, and by doing so it overlooks the ambiguity that arises when each provision of this statute is given effect. The words of § 1705 lack clarity when its parts are read *in pari materia,* and since the goal of judicial interpretation of this void in the statute is to ascertain and give effect to the legislative intent, we are required to ascertain that intent and to interpret the statute in a manner consistent therewith.

. . . [The] spiraling auto insurance costs and the resultant increase in the number of uninsured motorists [were] the foremost reasons for the 1990 amendments to the MVFRL. [Citations.] Pursuant to the MVFRL, only a "named insured" under an insurance policy can choose a tort option. By indicating that an uninsured automobile owner is considered to "have chosen" the limited tort option, the legislature intended the uninsured vehicle owner to be treated like a named insured under an insurance policy. When read *in pari materia,* 75 Pa.C.S. § 1705(a)(5) and § 1705(d) support such an interpretation of the MVFRL. . . . Clearly, this language evinces an intent by the legislature to create the legal fiction of an insurance policy where the uninsured owner of a vehicle stands in the shoes of a named insured. [Citation.]

An uninsured parent who is deemed to have chosen the limited tort alternative pursuant to § 1705(a)(5) must be treated the same as a "named insured" on a limited tort insurance policy. Therefore, pursuant to § 1705(b)(2), the limited tort option also applies to the minor children of the "named insured." I would reverse the determination of the Superior Court . . . .

QUESTIONS

1.   The majority notes that Pennsylvania's Rules of Construction provide for a number of instructions, including to "give effect to all the provisions of a statute"; that when clear "the letter of it is not to be disregarded under the pretext of pursuing its spirit"; that only "when the words are ambiguous may we look to the general purposes of the statute, legislative history, and other sources in an attempt to determine the legislative intent"; that courts should "avoid construing a statute in such a way as would lead to an absurd result"; that "statutes which apply to the same class of persons should be read, where possible, *in pari materia*"; and that (with some exceptions) statutes "be liberally construed to give effect to its purposes and promote justice." As the dissent's reasoning implies, some of these instructions seem to be at odds with other instructions, depending on the provision at issue. For instance, the dissent suggests that when the vehicular tort law provisions in question

are read together, *in pari materia*, they "lack clarity," even if they are less ambiguous when read individually. Do you think Pennsylvania's Rules of Construction provide a rule of decision in such circumstances? If so, how would you articulate it?

2. Recall Karl Llewellyn's thrust/parry critique of the canons of construction in Section II.B.3—that every canon has a counter-canon that applies to similar circumstances but yields an opposite result. Does the same critique apply to act interpretation acts such as Pennsylvania's Rules of Construction? Does it make any difference that act interpretation acts, unlike canons of construction, are often indicated numerically? Would it be reasonable to conclude that when two act interpretation act provisions conflict, the one appearing first in lexical order should prevail over the one appearing second? *I.e.*, in this case, should an interpretation that satisfies § 1921(b) always prevail over one resulting from the application of § 1921(c)? And if the application of § 1921(a) yields a result at odds with the interpretation that satisfies § 1921(b), should the former application prevail over the latter? Why or why not?

B. WHEN THE LEGISLATURE PROVIDES INSTRUCTIONS FOR SEVERING PROBLEMATIC STATUTORY PROVISIONS

In addition to instructing courts as to the interpretation of statutes, legislatures also sometimes provide guidance in the event portions of a statute prove to be constitutionally troublesome or otherwise void. This practice, known as the severability doctrine, enables courts to spare unproblematic portions of the statute when striking down a statute as void. Often, however, legislatures either fail to give such instructions, or their instructions are not as straightforward to apply as expected. Severability analysis also can raise other problems, as highlighted in the following case.

Barr v. American Association of Political Consultants

Supreme Court of the United States, 2020.
140 S.Ct. 2335, 207 L.Ed.2d 784.

■ JUSTICE KAVANAUGH announced the judgment of the Court and delivered an opinion, in which THE CHIEF JUSTICE and JUSTICE ALITO join, and in which JUSTICE THOMAS joins as to Parts I and II.

Americans passionately disagree about many things. But they are largely united in their disdain for robocalls. The Federal Government receives a staggering number of complaints about robocalls—3.7 million complaints in 2019 alone. The States likewise field a constant barrage of complaints.

For nearly 30 years, the people's representatives in Congress have been fighting back. As relevant here, the Telephone Consumer Protection

Act of 1991, known as the TCPA, generally prohibits robocalls to cell phones and home phones. But a 2015 amendment to the TCPA allows robocalls that are made to collect debts owed to or guaranteed by the Federal Government, including robocalls made to collect many student loan and mortgage debts.

This case concerns robocalls to cell phones. Plaintiffs in this case are political and nonprofit organizations that want to make political robocalls to cell phones. Invoking the First Amendment, they argue that the 2015 government-debt exception unconstitutionally favors debt-collection speech over political and other speech. As relief from that unconstitutional law, they urge us to invalidate the entire 1991 robocall restriction, rather than simply invalidating the 2015 government-debt exception.

Six Members of the Court today conclude that Congress has impermissibly favored debt-collection speech over political and other speech, in violation of the First Amendment. . . . Applying traditional severability principles, seven Members of the Court conclude that the entire 1991 robocall restriction should not be invalidated, but rather that the 2015 government-debt exception must be invalidated and severed from the remainder of the statute. . . . As a result, plaintiffs still may not make political robocalls to cell phones, but their speech is now treated equally with debt-collection speech. . . .

I

A

In 1991, Congress passed and President George H. W. Bush signed the Telephone Consumer Protection Act. The Act responded to a torrent of vociferous consumer complaints about intrusive robocalls. A growing number of telemarketers were using equipment that could automatically dial a telephone number and deliver an artificial or prerecorded voice message. At the time, more than 300,000 solicitors called more than 18 million Americans every day. [Citation.] Consumers were "outraged" and considered robocalls an invasion of privacy "regardless of the content or the initiator of the message." [Citation.] . . .

In enacting the TCPA, Congress found that banning robocalls was "the only effective means of protecting telephone consumers from this nuisance and privacy invasion." [Citation.] . . .

In plain English, the TCPA prohibited almost all robocalls to cell phones.

Twenty-four years later, in 2015, Congress passed and President Obama signed the Bipartisan Budget Act. In addition to making other unrelated changes to the U. S. Code, that Act amended the TCPA's restriction on robocalls to cell phones. It stated:

"(a) IN GENERAL.—Section 227(b) of the Communications Act of 1934 (47 U. S. C. 227(b)) is amended—

(1) in paragraph (1)—

(A) in subparagraph (A)(iii), by inserting ', unless such call is made solely to collect a debt owed to or guaranteed by the United States' after 'charged for the call.' " 129 Stat. 588.[2]

In other words, Congress carved out a new government-debt exception to the general robocall restriction. . . .

II

[In this Part, JUSTICE KAVANAUGH explains why the provision in question violates the First Amendment.]

III

Having concluded that the 2015 government-debt exception created an unconstitutional exception to the 1991 robocall restriction, we must decide whether to invalidate the entire 1991 robocall restriction, or instead to invalidate and sever the 2015 government-debt exception. . . .

[T]he question before the Court is whether (i) to invalidate the entire 1991 robocall restriction, as plaintiffs want, or (ii) to invalidate just the 2015 government-debt exception and sever it from the remainder of the statute, as the Government wants.

We agree with the Government that we must invalidate the 2015 government-debt exception and sever that exception from the remainder of the statute. To explain why, we begin with general severability principles and then apply those principles to this case.

1

When enacting a law, Congress sometimes expressly addresses severability. For example, Congress may include a severability clause in the law, making clear that the unconstitutionality of one provision does not affect the rest of the law. [Citations.] Alternatively, Congress may include a nonseverability clause, making clear that the unconstitutionality of one provision means the invalidity of some or all of the remainder of the law, to the extent specified in the text of the nonseverability clause. [Citation.]

Of course, when enacting a law, Congress often does not include either a severability clause or a nonseverability clause.

---

[2] After the 2015 amendment, § 227(b)(1) now provides:

"It shall be unlawful for any person within the United States, or any person outside the United States if the recipient is within the United States—

(A) to make any call (other than a call made for emergency purposes or made with the prior express consent of the called party) using any automatic telephone dialing system or an artificial or prerecorded voice— . . .

(iii) to any telephone number assigned to a paging service, cellular telephone service, specialized mobile radio service, or other radio common carrier service, or any service for which the called party is charged for the call, *unless such call is made solely to collect a debt owed to or guaranteed by the United States*." (Emphasis added.)

In those cases, it is sometimes said that courts applying severability doctrine should search for other indicia of congressional intent. For example, some of the Court's cases declare that courts should sever the offending provision unless "the statute created in its absence is legislation that Congress would not have enacted." Alaska Airlines, 480 U. S., at 685. But experience shows that this formulation often leads to an analytical dead end. That is because courts are not well equipped to imaginatively reconstruct a prior Congress's hypothetical intent. In other words, absent a severability or nonseverability clause, a court often cannot really know what the two Houses of Congress and the President from the time of original enactment of a law would have wanted if one provision of a law were later declared unconstitutional.

The Court's cases have instead developed a strong presumption of severability. The Court presumes that an unconstitutional provision in a law is severable from the remainder of the law or statute. For example, in Free Enterprise Fund v. Public Company Accounting Oversight Bd., the Court set forth the "normal rule": "Generally speaking, when confronting a constitutional flaw in a statute, we try to limit the solution to the problem, severing any problematic portions while leaving the remainder intact." 561 U. S. 477, 508 (2010) (internal quotation marks omitted); [citation.] . . . .

The Court's power and preference to partially invalidate a statute in that fashion has been firmly established since Marbury v. Madison. There, the Court invalidated part of § 13 of the Judiciary Act of 1789. 5 U.S. 137 (1803). The Judiciary Act did not contain a severability clause. But the Court did not proceed to invalidate the entire Judiciary Act. As Chief Justice Marshall later explained, if any part of an Act is "unconstitutional, the provisions of that part may be disregarded while full effect will be given to such as are not repugnant to the constitution of the United States." Bank of Hamilton v. Lessee of Dudley, 27 U.S. 492 (1829); [citations.] From Marbury v. Madison to the present, apart from some isolated detours mostly in the late 1800s and early 1900s, the Court's remedial preference after finding a provision of a federal law unconstitutional has been to salvage rather than destroy the rest of the law passed by Congress and signed by the President. The Court's precedents reflect a decisive preference for surgical severance rather than wholesale destruction, even in the absence of a severability clause.

The Court's presumption of severability supplies a workable solution—one that allows courts to avoid judicial policymaking or de facto judicial legislation in determining just how much of the remainder of a statute should be invalidated. The presumption also reflects the confined role of the Judiciary in our system of separated powers—stated otherwise, the presumption manifests the Judiciary's respect for Congress's legislative role by keeping courts from unnecessarily disturbing a law apart from invalidating the provision that is unconstitutional. Furthermore, the presumption recognizes that plaintiffs who successfully challenge one provision of a law may lack standing to challenge other provisions of that law. [Citation.]

Those and other considerations, taken together, have steered the Court to a presumption of severability. Applying the presumption, the Court invalidates and severs unconstitutional provisions from the remainder of the law rather than razing whole statutes or Acts of Congress. Put in common parlance, the tail (one unconstitutional provision) does not wag the dog (the rest of the codified statute or the Act as passed by Congress). Constitutional litigation is not a game of gotcha against Congress, where litigants can ride a discrete constitutional flaw in a statute to take down the whole, otherwise constitutional statute. . . . If the rule were otherwise, the entire Judiciary Act of 1789 would be invalid as a consequence of Marbury v. Madison.

Before severing a provision and leaving the remainder of a law intact, the Court must determine that the remainder of the statute is "capable of functioning independently" and thus would be "fully operative" as a law. [Citations.] But it is fairly unusual for the remainder of a law not to be operative.

2

We next apply those general severability principles to this case.

Recall how this statute came together. Passed by Congress and signed by President Franklin Roosevelt in 1934, the Communications Act is codified in Title 47 of the U. S. Code. The TCPA of 1991 amended the Communications Act by adding the robocall restriction, which is codified at § 227(b)(1)(A)(iii) of Title 47. The Bipartisan Budget Act of 2015 then amended the Communications Act by adding the government-debt exception, which is codified along with the robocall restriction at § 227(b)(1)(A)(iii) of Title 47.

Since 1934, the Communications Act has contained an express severability clause: "If any provision of this chapter or the application thereof to any person or circumstance is held invalid, the remainder of the chapter and the application of such provision to other persons or circumstances shall not be affected thereby." 47 U. S. C. § 608 (emphasis added). The "chapter" referred to in the severability clause is Chapter 5 of Title 47. And Chapter 5 in turn encompasses § 151 to § 700 of Title 47, and therefore covers § 227 of Title 47, the provision with the robocall restriction and the government-debt exception.[10]

Enacted in 2015, the government-debt exception added an unconstitutional discriminatory exception to the robocall restriction. The text of the severability clause squarely covers the unconstitutional government-debt exception and requires that we sever it.

---

[10] A codifier's note explains a change in wording from the original Public Law: "This chapter, referred to in text, was in the original 'this Act', meaning act June 19, 1934, ch. 652, 48 Stat. 1064, known as the Communications Act of 1934, which is classified principally to this chapter." Note following 47 U. S. C. § 608.

To get around the text of the severability clause, plaintiffs point out that the Communications Act's severability clause was enacted in 1934, long before the TCPA's 1991 robocall restriction and the 2015 government-debt exception. But a severability clause must be interpreted according to its terms, regardless of when Congress enacted it. [Citation.]

Even if the severability clause did not apply to the government-debt provision at issue in this case (or even if there were no severability clause in the Communications Act), we would apply the presumption of severability as described and applied in cases such as Free Enterprise Fund. And under that presumption, we likewise would sever the 2015 government-debt exception, the constitutionally offending provision.

With the government-debt exception severed, the remainder of the law is capable of functioning independently and thus would be fully operative as a law. Indeed, the remainder of the robocall restriction did function independently and fully operate as a law for 20-plus years before the government-debt exception was added in 2015. . . .

In sum, the text of the Communications Act's severability clause requires that the Court sever the 2015 government-debt exception from the remainder of the statute. And even if the text of the severability clause did not apply here, the presumption of severability would require that the Court sever the 2015 government-debt exception from the remainder of the statute.

3

One final severability wrinkle remains. This is an equal-treatment case, and equal-treatment cases can sometimes pose complicated severability questions. . . .

When the constitutional violation is unequal treatment, as it is here, a court theoretically can cure that unequal treatment either by extending the benefits or burdens to the exempted class, or by nullifying the benefits or burdens for all. [Citation.] Here, for example, the Government would prefer to cure the unequal treatment by extending the robocall restriction and thereby proscribing nearly all robocalls to cell phones. By contrast, plaintiffs want to cure the unequal treatment by nullifying the robocall restriction and thereby allowing all robocalls to cell phones.

When, as here, the Court confronts an equal-treatment constitutional violation, the Court generally applies the same commonsense severability principles described above. If the statute contains a severability clause, the Court typically severs the discriminatory exception or classification, and thereby extends the relevant statutory benefits or burdens to those previously exempted, rather than nullifying the benefits or burdens for all. In light of the presumption of severability, the Court generally does the same even in the absence of a severability clause. The Court's precedents reflect that preference for extension rather than nullification. [Citations.] . . .

[H]ere, we need not tackle all of the possible hypothetical applications of severability doctrine in equal-treatment cases. The government-debt exception is a relatively narrow exception to the broad robocall restriction, and severing the government-debt exception does not raise any other constitutional problems. . . .

Therefore, we apply traditional severability principles. And as we have explained, severing the 2015 government-debt exception cures the unequal treatment and constitutes the proper result under the Court's traditional severability principles. In short, the correct result in this case is to sever the 2015 government-debt exception and leave in place the longstanding robocall restriction.

4

JUSTICE GORSUCH's well-stated separate opinion makes a number of important points that warrant this respectful response.

JUSTICE GORSUCH suggests that our decision provides "no relief" to plaintiffs. We disagree. Plaintiffs want to be able to make political robocalls to cell phones, and they have not received *that* relief. But the First Amendment complaint at the heart of their suit was unequal treatment. Invalidating and severing the government-debt exception fully addresses that First Amendment injury.[13] JUSTICE GORSUCH further suggests that plaintiffs may lack standing to challenge the government-debt exception, because that exception merely favors others. But the Court has squarely held that a plaintiff who suffers unequal treatment has standing to challenge a discriminatory exception that favors others. [Citations.]

JUSTICE GORSUCH also objects that our decision today "harms strangers to this suit" by eliminating favorable treatment for debt collectors. But that is necessarily true in many cases where a court cures unequal treatment by, for example, extending a burden or nullifying a benefit. [Citations.]

Moreover, JUSTICE GORSUCH's approach to this case would not solve the problem of harming strangers to this suit; it would just create a different and much bigger problem. His proposed remedy of injunctive relief, plus *stare decisis*, would in effect allow all robocalls to cell phones—notwithstanding Congress's decisive choice to prohibit most robocalls to cell phones. That is not a judicially modest approach but is more of a wolf in sheep's clothing. That approach would disrespect the democratic process, through which the people's representatives have made crystal clear that robocalls must be restricted. JUSTICE GORSUCH's remedy would end up harming a different and far larger set of strangers to this suit—the tens of millions of consumers who would be bombarded

---

[13] Plaintiffs suggest that parties will not have incentive to sue if the cure for challenging an unconstitutional exception to a speech restriction is to eliminate the exception and extend the restriction. But many individuals and organizations often have incentive to challenge unequal treatment of speech, especially when a competitor is regulated less heavily.

every day with nonstop robocalls notwithstanding Congress's clear prohibition of those robocalls.

JUSTICE GORSUCH suggests more broadly that severability doctrine may need to be reconsidered. But when and how? As the saying goes, John Marshall is not walking through that door. And this Court, in this and other recent decisions, has clarified and refined severability doctrine by emphasizing firm adherence to the text of severability clauses, and underscoring the strong presumption of severability. The doctrine as so refined is constitutionally well-rooted, *see, e.g.,* Marbury v. Madison, 5 U.S. 137 (Marshall, C. J.), and can be predictably applied. True, there is no magic solution to severability that solves every conundrum, especially in equal-treatment cases, but the Court's current approach as reflected in recent cases . . . is constitutional, stable, predictable, and commonsensical.

[The opinion of JUSTICE SOTOMAYOR concurring in the judgment and discussing the proper form of scrutiny for assessing content-based speech restrictions, has been omitted.]

[The opinion of JUSTICE BREYER, in which JUSTICE GINSBURG and JUSTICE KAGAN joins, concurring in the judgment with respect to severability and dissenting with respect to the First Amendment holding, has been omitted.]

■ JUSTICE GORSUCH, with whom JUSTICE THOMAS joins as to Part II, concurring in the judgment in part and dissenting in part.

I agree with JUSTICE KAVANAUGH that the provision of the Telephone Consumer Protection Act before us violates the First Amendment. Respectfully, however, I disagree about why that is so and what remedial consequences should follow.

I

[In this part, JUSTICE GORSUCH explained why the provision in question violates the First Amendment.]

II

Because the challenged robocall ban unconstitutionally infringes on their speech, I would hold that the plaintiffs are entitled to an injunction preventing its enforcement against them. This is the traditional remedy for proven violations of legal rights likely to work irreparable injury in the future. Preventing the law's enforcement against the plaintiffs would fully address their injury. And going this far, but no further, would avoid "short circuit[ing] the democratic process" by interfering with the work of Congress any more than necessary. [Citation.]

JUSTICE KAVANAUGH's opinion pursues a different course. Invoking "severability doctrine," it declares the government-debt exception void and severs it from the statute. As revised by today's decision, the law prohibits nearly all robocalls to cell phones, just as it did back in 1991. In support of this remedy, we are asked to consider cases involving equal protection violations, where courts have sometimes solved the problem of unequal treatment by leveling others "down" to the plaintiff's status rather than by leveling the plaintiff "up" to the status others enjoy.

I am doubtful of our authority to rewrite the law in this way. Many have questioned the propriety of modern severability doctrine, and today's case illustrates some of the reasons why. To start, it's hard to see how today's use of severability doctrine qualifies as a remedy at all: The plaintiffs have not challenged the government-debt exception, they have not sought to have it severed and stricken, and far from placing "unequal treatment" at the "heart of their suit," they have never complained of unequal treatment as such. [Citation.] The plaintiffs point to the government-debt exception only to show that the government lacks a compelling interest in restricting their speech. It isn't even clear the plaintiffs would have standing to challenge the government-debt exception. They came to court asserting a right to speak, not a right to be free from other speakers. Severing and voiding the government-debt exception does nothing to address the injury they claim; after today's ruling, federal law bars the plaintiffs from using robocalls to promote political causes just as stoutly as it did before. What is the point of fighting this long battle, through many years and all the way to the Supreme Court, if the prize for winning is no relief at all?

A severance remedy not only fails to help the plaintiffs, it harms strangers to this suit. Just five years ago, Congress expressly authorized robocalls to cell phones to collect government-backed debts. Yet, today, the Court reverses that decision and outlaws the entire industry. It is highly unusual for judges to render unlawful conduct that Congress has explicitly made lawful—let alone to take such an extraordinary step without warning to those who have ordered their lives and livelihoods in reliance on the law, and without affording those individuals any opportunity to be heard. This assertion of power strikes me as raising serious separation of powers questions, and it marks no small departure from our usual reliance on the adversarial process.

Nor does the analogy to equal protection doctrine solve the problem. That doctrine promises equality of treatment, whatever that treatment may be. The First Amendment isn't so neutral. It pushes, always, in one direction: against governmental restrictions on speech. Yet, somehow, in the name of vindicating the First Amendment, our remedial course today leads to the unlikely result that not a single person will be allowed to speak more freely and, instead, more speech will be banned.

In an effort to mitigate at least some of these problems, JUSTICE KAVANAUGH suggests that the ban on government-debt collection calls announced today might be applied only prospectively. But prospective decisionmaking has never been easy to square with the judicial power. [Citations.] And a holding that shields *only* government-debt collection callers from past liability under an admittedly unconstitutional law would wind up endorsing the very same kind of content discrimination we say we are seeking to eliminate.

Unable to solve the problems associated with its preferred severance remedy, today's decision seeks at least to identify "harm[s]" associated with mine. In particular, we are reminded that granting an injunction in this case would allow the plaintiffs' (unpopular) speech, and that could induce others to seek injunctions of their own, resulting in still more (unpopular) speech. But this "harm" is hardly comparable to the problems associated with using severability doctrine: Having to tolerate unwanted speech imposes no cognizable constitutional injury on anyone; it is life under the First Amendment, which almost always invoked to protect speech some would rather not hear.

*

In the end, I agree that 47 U. S. C. § 227(b)(1)(A)(iii) violates the First Amendment, though not for the reasons JUSTICE KAVANAUGH offers. Nor am I able to support the remedy the Court endorses today. Respectfully, if this is what modern "severability doctrine" has become, it seems to me all the more reason to reconsider our course.

QUESTIONS

1. The dissent highlights how severability analysis will sometimes fail the parties to the suit and also harm non-parties. Should the nature of the specific plaintiff and the relief sought matter if the statute itself is categorically void for *all* such applications?

2. The dissent suggests that the majority's approach to severability raises "serious separation of powers questions," because "it is highly unusual for judges to render unlawful conduct that Congress has explicitly made lawful." When Congress provides instructions for severing the provision in question as a failsafe in the event it has overreached its authority, what exactly are those separation of powers questions?

3. The 1991 TCPA contained a severability clause that the majority applied to sever the problematic 2015 amendment. If, by contrast, a later amendment introduced a severability clause absent from the original statute, should that make a difference? Imagine if the 1991 TCPA lacked a severability clause; would the subsequent clause apply only to portions of the statute added contemporaneously with that severability clause?

C. Interpreting a Statute in Light of Prior Judicial Interpretations of That Statute

1. Case Study in Five Little Words

The Texts to Be Construed: 18 U.S.C. § 924 and Related Provisions

Recall that in *Johnson, supra* Section III.A.2.c, the Supreme Court had repeated difficulty interpreting 18 U.S.C. § 924(e)(2)(B)'s residual clause definition of a crime of violence before finally, on the fifth round, declaring it void for vagueness. A different provision of the same statute has raised a related difficulty: when the Court's interpretation of a particular provision as applied to one kind of behavior solves the present interpretive conundrum, only to create new problems applying it to a different kind of behavior.

The following cases interpret neighboring words in the same provision at issue in *Johnson* and *Muscarello, supra* Section III.B.3.b. Although the Court in *Muscarello* focused only on the meaning of "carries

a firearm" in 18 U.S.C. § 924(c), the statute also increased by five years
the duration of a sentence if the defendant "during and in relation to any
crime of violence or drug trafficking crime . . . , *uses* or carries a firearm."
(emphasis added). Thus, in a related set of cases, the Court had to decide
what it means to "use" a firearm. To place that provision in context, we
reproduce the full section, and other pertinent sections as they appeared
in the statute at the time the Court decided these cases. (As indicated in
Muscarello, supra, Congress has subsequently amended the statute.)

Crimes—Firearms

United States Code, Title 18, Chapter 44.

§ 924.   Penalties

. . . **(b)** Whoever, with intent to commit therewith an offense
punishable by imprisonment for a term exceeding one year, or with
knowledge or reasonable cause to believe that an offense punishable
by imprisonment for a term exceeding one year is to be committed
therewith, ships, transports, or receives a firearm or any
ammunition in interstate or foreign commerce shall be fined under
this title, or imprisoned not more than ten years, or both.

(c) **(1)** Whoever, during and in relation to any crime of violence or drug
trafficking crime (including a crime of violence or drug trafficking
crime which provides for an enhanced punishment if committed by
the use of a deadly or dangerous weapon or device) for which he may
be prosecuted in a court of the United States, uses or carries a
firearm, shall, in addition to the punishment provided for such crime
of violence or drug trafficking crime, be sentenced to imprisonment
for five years, and if the firearm is a short-barreled rifle, short-
barreled shotgun, or semiautomatic assault weapon, to
imprisonment for ten years, and if the firearm is a machinegun, or a
destructive device, or is equipped with a firearm silencer or firearm
muffler, to imprisonment for thirty years. In the case of his second
or subsequent conviction under this subsection, such person shall be
sentenced to imprisonment for twenty years, and if the firearm is a
machinegun, or a destructive device, or is equipped with a firearm
silencer or firearm muffler, to life imprisonment without release.
Notwithstanding any other provision of law, the court shall not place
on probation or suspend the sentence of any person convicted of a
violation of this subsection, nor shall the term of imprisonment
imposed under this subsection run concurrently with any other term
of imprisonment including that imposed for the crime of violence or
drug trafficking crime in which the firearm was used or carried.

(d) **(1)** Any firearm or ammunition involved in or used in any knowing
violation of [various provisions], or willful violation of any other
provision of this chapter or any rule or regulation promulgated
thereunder, or any violation of any other criminal law of the United

States, or any firearm or ammunition intended to be used in any offense referred to in paragraph (3) of this subsection, where such intent is demonstrated by clear and convincing evidence, shall be subject to seizure and forfeiture, ...

(3) The offenses referred to in paragraphs (1) and (2)(C) of this subsection are—. . .

> **(D)** any offense described in section 922(d) of this title [making it "unlawful for any person to sell or otherwise dispose of any firearm or ammunition to any person knowing or having reasonable cause to believe that such person" is one of specified classes of persons, including convicted felons and persons under restraining orders for domestic violence] where the firearm or ammunition is intended to be used in such offense by the transferor of such firearm or ammunition; . . .

§ 922. Unlawful acts

(g) It shall be unlawful for any [specified category of] person[s] . . . to ship or transport in interstate or foreign commerce, or possess in or affecting commerce, any firearm or ammunition; or to receive any firearm or ammunition which has been shipped or transported in interstate or foreign commerce. . . .

(j) It shall be unlawful for any person to receive, possess, conceal, store, barter, sell, or dispose of any stolen firearm or stolen ammunition, or pledge or accept as security for a loan any stolen firearm or stolen ammunition, which is moving as, which is a part of, which constitutes, or which has been shipped or transported in, interstate or foreign commerce, either before or after it was stolen, knowing or having reasonable cause to believe that the firearm or ammunition was stolen.

Smith v. United States

Supreme Court of the United States, 1993.
508 U.S. 223, 113 S.Ct. 2050, 124 L.Ed.2d 138.

■ JUSTICE O'CONNOR delivered the opinion of the Court, [in which CHIEF JUSTICE REHNQUIST, JUSTICE WHITE, JUSTICE BLACKMUN, JUSTICE KENNEDY, and JUSTICE THOMAS joined].

We decide today whether the exchange of a gun for narcotics constitutes "use" of a firearm "during and in relation to . . . [a] drug trafficking crime" within the meaning of 18 U.S.C. § 924(c)(1). We hold that it does.

I

Petitioner John Angus Smith and his companion went from Tennessee to Florida to buy cocaine; they hoped to resell it at a profit. While in Florida, they met petitioner's acquaintance, Deborah Hoag.

Hoag agreed to, and in fact did, purchase cocaine for petitioner. She then accompanied petitioner and his friend to her motel room, where they were joined by a drug dealer. While Hoag listened, petitioner and the dealer discussed petitioner's MAC-10 firearm, which had been modified to operate as an automatic. The MAC-10 apparently is a favorite among criminals. It is small and compact, lightweight, and can be equipped with a silencer. Most important of all, it can be devastating: A fully automatic MAC-10 can fire more than 1,000 rounds per minute. The dealer expressed his interest in becoming the owner of a MAC-10, and petitioner promised that he would discuss selling the gun if his arrangement with another potential buyer fell through.

Unfortunately for petitioner, Hoag had contacts not only with narcotics traffickers but also with law enforcement officials. In fact, she was a confidential informant. Consistent with her post, she informed the Broward County Sheriff's Office of petitioner's activities. The Sheriff's Office responded quickly, sending an undercover officer to Hoag's motel room. Several others were assigned to keep the motel under surveillance. Upon arriving at Hoag's motel room, the undercover officer presented himself to petitioner as a pawnshop dealer. Petitioner, in turn, presented the officer with a proposition: He had an automatic MAC-10 and silencer with which he might be willing to part. Petitioner then pulled the MAC-10 out of a black canvas bag and showed it to the officer. The officer examined the gun and asked petitioner what he wanted for it. Rather than asking for money, however, petitioner asked for drugs. He was willing to trade his MAC-10, he said, for two ounces of cocaine. The officer told petitioner that he was just a pawnshop dealer and did not distribute narcotics. Nonetheless, he indicated that he wanted the MAC-10 and would try to get the cocaine. The officer then left, promising to return within an hour.

Rather than seeking out cocaine as he had promised, the officer returned to the Sheriff's Office to arrange for petitioner's arrest. But petitioner was not content to wait. The officers who were conducting surveillance saw him leave the motel room carrying a gun bag; he then climbed into his van and drove away. The officers reported petitioner's departure and began following him. When law enforcement authorities tried to stop petitioner, he led them on a high-speed chase. Petitioner eventually was apprehended.

Petitioner, it turns out, was well armed. A search of his van revealed the MAC-10 weapon, a silencer, ammunition, and a "fast-feed" mechanism. In addition, the police found a MAC-11 machine gun, a loaded .45 caliber pistol, and a .22 caliber pistol with a scope and homemade silencer. Petitioner also had a loaded 9 millimeter handgun in his waistband.

A grand jury sitting in the District Court for the Southern District of Florida returned an indictment charging petitioner with, among other offenses, two drug trafficking crimes—conspiracy to possess cocaine with intent to distribute and attempt to possess cocaine with intent to distribute in violation of 21 U.S.C. §§ 841(a)(1), 846, and 18 U.S.C. § 2. Most important here, the indictment alleged that petitioner knowingly used the MAC-10 and its silencer during and in relation to a drug trafficking crime. Under 18 U.S.C. § 924(c)(1), a defendant who so uses a firearm must be sentenced to five years' incarceration. And where, as here, the firearm is a "machinegun" or is fitted with a silencer, the sentence is 30 years. See § 924(c)(1) ("If the firearm is a machinegun, or is equipped with a firearm silencer," the sentence is "thirty years"); § 921(a)(23), 26 U.S.C. § 5845(b) (term "machinegun" includes automatic weapons). The jury convicted petitioner on all counts.

On appeal, petitioner argued that § 924(c)(1)'s penalty for using a firearm during and in relation to a drug trafficking offense covers only situations in which the firearm is used as a weapon. According to petitioner, the provision does not extend to defendants who use a firearm solely as a medium of exchange or for barter. The Court of Appeals for the Eleventh Circuit disagreed. 957 F.2d 835 (1992). The plain language of the statute, the court explained, imposes no requirement that the firearm be used as a weapon. Instead, any use of "the weapon to facilitate *in any manner* the commission of the offense" suffices.

Shortly before the Eleventh Circuit decided this case, the Court of Appeals for the District of Columbia Circuit arrived at the same conclusion. [Citation.] [H]owever, the Court of Appeals for the Ninth Circuit held that trading a gun in a drug-related transaction could not constitute use of a firearm during and in relation to a drug trafficking offense within the meaning of § 924(c)(1). We granted certiorari to resolve the conflict among the Circuits. We now affirm.

II

Section 924(c)(1) requires the imposition of specified penalties if the defendant, "during and in relation to any crime of violence or drug trafficking crime[,] uses or carries a firearm." By its terms, the statute requires the prosecution to make two showings. First, the prosecution must demonstrate that the defendant "use[d] or carrie[d] a firearm." Second, it must prove that the use or carrying was "during and in relation to" a "crime of violence or drug trafficking crime." Petitioner argues that exchanging a firearm for drugs does not constitute "use" of the firearm within the meaning of the statute. He points out that nothing in the record indicates that he fired the MAC-10, threatened anyone with it, or employed it for self-protection. In essence, petitioner argues that he cannot be said to have "use[d]" a firearm unless he used it as a weapon, since that is how firearms most often are used. See 957 F.2d at 837 (firearm often facilitates drug offenses by protecting drugs or protecting or emboldening the defendant). Of course, § 924(c)(1) is not limited to those cases in which a gun is used; it applies with equal force whenever a gun is "carrie[d]." In this case, however, the indictment alleged only that petitioner "use[d]" the MAC-10. Accordingly, we do not consider whether the evidence might support the conclusion that petitioner carried the MAC-10 within the meaning of § 924(c)(1). Instead we confine our discussion to what the parties view as the dispositive issue in this case: whether trading a firearm for drugs can constitute "use" of the firearm within the meaning of § 924(c)(1).

When a word is not defined by statute, we normally construe it in accord with its ordinary or natural meaning. [Citation.] Surely petitioner's treatment of his MAC-10 can be described as "use" within the everyday meaning of that term. Petitioner "used" his MAC-10 in an attempt to obtain drugs by offering to trade it for cocaine. Webster's defines "to use" as "to convert to one's service" or "to employ." Webster's New International Dictionary 2806 (2d ed. 1950). Black's Law Dictionary contains a similar definition: "to make use of; to convert to one's service; to employ; to avail oneself of; to utilize; to carry out a purpose or action by means of." Black's Law Dictionary 1541 (6th ed. 1990). Indeed, over 100 years ago we gave the word "use" the same gloss, indicating that it means " 'to employ' " or " 'to derive service from.' " *Astor v. Merritt*, 111 U.S. 202, 213 (1884). Petitioner's handling of the MAC-10 in this case falls squarely within those definitions. By attempting to trade his MAC-10 for the drugs, he "used" or "employed" it as an item of barter to obtain cocaine; he "derived service" from it because it was going to bring him the very drugs he sought.

In petitioner's view, § 924(c)(1) should require proof not only that the defendant used the firearm, but also that he used it *as a weapon*. But the words "as a weapon" appear nowhere in the statute. Rather, § 924(c)(1)'s language sweeps broadly, punishing any "use" of a firearm, so long as the use is "during and in relation to" a drug trafficking offense. See *United States v. Long*, 284 U.S. App. D.C. 405, 409–410, 905 F.2d 1572, 1576–1577 (Thomas, J.) (although not without limits, the word "use" is "expansive" and extends even to situations where the gun is not actively employed), cert. denied, 498 U.S. 948 (1990). Had Congress intended the narrow construction petitioner urges, it could have so indicated. It did not, and we decline to introduce that additional requirement on our own.

Language, of course, cannot be interpreted apart from context. The meaning of a word that appears ambiguous if viewed in isolation may become clear when the word is analyzed in light of the terms that surround it. Recognizing this, petitioner and the dissent argue that the word "uses" has a somewhat reduced scope in § 924(c)(1) because it appears alongside the word "firearm." Specifically, they contend that the average person on the street would not think immediately of a guns-for-drugs trade as an example of "us[ing] a firearm." Rather, that phrase normally evokes an image of the most familiar use to which a firearm is put—use as a weapon. Petitioner and the dissent therefore argue that the statute excludes uses where the weapon is not fired or otherwise employed for its destructive capacity. Indeed, relying on that argument— and without citation to authority—the dissent announces its own, restrictive definition of "use." "To use an instrumentality," the dissent argues, "ordinarily means to use it for its intended purpose."

There is a significant flaw to this argument. It is one thing to say that the ordinary meaning of "uses a firearm" *includes* using a firearm as a weapon, since that is the intended purpose of a firearm and the example of "use" that most immediately comes to mind. But it is quite another to conclude that, as a result, the phrase also *excludes* any other use. Certainly that conclusion does not follow from the phrase "uses . . . a firearm" itself. As the dictionary definitions and experience make clear, one can use a firearm in a number of ways. That one example of "use" is the first to come to mind when the phrase "uses . . . a firearm" is uttered does not preclude us from recognizing that there are other "uses" that qualify as well. In this case, it is both reasonable and normal to say that petitioner "used" his MAC-10 in his drug trafficking offense by trading it for cocaine; the dissent does not contend otherwise.

The dissent's example of how one might "use" a cane, suffers from a similar flaw. To be sure, "use" as an adornment in a hallway is not the first "use" of a cane that comes to mind. But certainly it does not follow that the *only* "use" to which a cane might be put is assisting one's grandfather in walking. Quite the opposite: The most infamous use of a cane in American history had nothing to do with walking at all, see J. McPherson, Battle Cry of Freedom 150 (1988) (describing the caning of Senator Sumner in the United States Senate in 1856); and the use of a cane as an instrument of punishment was once so common that "to cane" has become a verb meaning "to beat with a cane." Webster's New International Dictionary, *supra*. In any event, the only question in this case is whether the phrase "uses . . . a firearm" in § 924(c)(1) is most reasonably read as *excluding* the use of a firearm in a gun-for-drugs trade. The fact that the phrase clearly *includes* using a firearm to shoot someone, as the dissent contends, does not answer it. . . .

We are not persuaded that our construction of the phrase "uses . . . a firearm" will produce anomalous applications. § 924(c)(1) requires not only that the defendant "use" the firearm, but also that he use it "during and in relation to" the drug trafficking crime. As a result, the defendant who "uses" a firearm to scratch his head, or for some other innocuous purpose, would avoid punishment for that conduct altogether: Although scratching one's head with a gun might constitute "use," that action cannot support punishment under § 924(c)(1) unless it facilitates or furthers the drug crime; that the firearm served to relieve an itch is not enough. Such a defendant would escape the six-point enhancement provided in USSG § 2B3.1(b)(2)(B) as well. . . .

In any event, the "intended purpose" of a firearm is not that it be used in any offensive manner whatever, but rather that it be used in a particular fashion—by firing it. The dissent's contention therefore cannot be that the defendant must use the firearm "as a weapon," but rather that he must fire it or threaten to fire it, "as a gun." Under the dissent's approach, then, even the criminal who pistol-whips his victim has not used a firearm within the meaning of § 924(c)(1), for firearms are intended to be fired or brandished, not used as bludgeons. It appears that the dissent similarly would limit the scope of the "other use[s]" covered by USSG § 2B3.1(b) (2)(B). The universal view of the courts of appeals, however, is directly to the contrary. No court of appeals ever has held that using a gun to pistol-whip a victim is anything but the "use" of a firearm; nor has any court ever held that trading a firearm for drugs falls short of being the "use" thereof. [Citation.]

To the extent there is uncertainty about the scope of the phrase "uses ... a firearm" in § 924(c)(1), we believe the remainder of § 924 appropriately sets it to rest. Just as a single word cannot be read in isolation, nor can a single provision of a statute. As we have recognized:

> "Statutory construction ... is a holistic endeavor. A provision that may seem ambiguous in isolation is often clarified by the remainder of the statutory scheme—because the same terminology is used elsewhere in a context that makes its meaning clear, or because only one of the permissible meanings produces a substantive effect that is compatible with the rest of the law." [Citation.]

Here, Congress employed the words "use" and "firearm" together not only in § 924(c)(1), but also in § 924(d)(1), which deals with forfeiture of firearms. [Citation.] Under § 924(d)(1), any "firearm or ammunition intended to be used" in the various offenses listed in § 924(d)(3) is subject to seizure and forfeiture. Consistent with petitioner's interpretation, § 924(d)(3) lists offenses in which guns might be used as offensive weapons. See §§ 924(d)(3)(A), (B) (weapons used in a crime of violence or drug trafficking offense). But it also lists offenses in which the firearm is *not* used as a weapon but instead as an item of barter or commerce. For example, any gun intended to be "used" in an interstate "transfer, sale, trade, gift, transport, or delivery" of a firearm prohibited under § 922(a)(5) where there is a pattern of such activity, see § 924(d)(3)(C), or in a federal offense involving "the exportation of firearms," § 924(d)(3)(F), is subject to forfeiture. In fact, none of the offenses listed in four of the six subsections of § 924(d)(3) involves the bellicose use of a firearm; each offense involves use as an item in commerce.* Thus, it is clear from

---

* Section 924(d)(3)(C) lists four offenses: unlicensed manufacture of or commerce in firearms, in violation of § 922(a)(1); unlicensed receipt of a weapon from outside the State, in violation of § 922(a)(3); unlicensed transfer of a firearm to a resident of a different State, in violation of § 922(a)(5); and delivery of a gun by a licensed entity to a resident of a State that is not the licensee's, in violation of § 922(b)(3). Section 924(d)(3)(D) mentions only one offense, the transfer or sale of a weapon to disqualified persons, such as fugitives from justice and felons, in violation of § 922(d). Under § 924(d)(3)(E), firearms are subject to forfeiture if they are intended to be used in any of five listed offenses: shipping stolen firearms, in violation of § 922(i); receipt of stolen firearms, in violation of § 922(j); importation of firearms, in violation of § 922(*l*); shipment of a firearm by a felon, in violation of § 922(n); and shipment or receipt of a firearm with intent to commit a felony, in violation of § 924(b). Finally, § 924(d)(3)(F) subjects to forfeiture any firearm intended to be used in any offense that may be prosecuted in federal court if it involves the exportation of firearms.

§ 924(d)(3) that one who transports, exports, sells, or trades a firearm "uses" it within the meaning of § 924(d)(1)—even though those actions do not involve using the firearm as a weapon. Unless we are to hold that using a firearm has a different meaning in § 924(c)(1) than it does in § 924(d)—and clearly we should not—we must reject petitioner's narrow interpretation.

The evident care with which Congress chose the language of § 924(d)(1) reinforces our conclusion in this regard. Although § 924(d)(1) lists numerous firearm-related offenses that render guns subject to forfeiture, Congress did not lump all of those offenses together and require forfeiture solely of guns "used" in a prohibited activity. Instead, it carefully varied the statutory language in accordance with the guns' relation to the offense. For example, with respect to some crimes, the firearm is subject to forfeiture not only if it is "used," but also if it is "involved in" the offense. § 924(d)(1). Examination of the offenses to which the "involved in" language applies reveals why Congress believed it necessary to include such an expansive term. One of the listed offenses, violation of § 922(a)(6), is the making of a false statement material to the lawfulness of a gun's transfer. Because making a material misstatement in order to acquire or sell a gun is not "use" of the gun even under the broadest definition of the word "use," Congress carefully expanded the statutory language. As a result, a gun with respect to which a material misstatement is made is subject to forfeiture because, even though the gun is not "used" in the offense, it is "involved in" it. Congress, however, did not so expand the language for offenses in which firearms were "intended to be used," even though the firearms in many of those offenses function as items of commerce rather than as weapons. Instead, Congress apparently was of the view that one could use a gun by trading it. In light of the common meaning of the word "use" and the structure and language of the statute, we are not in any position to disagree.

The dissent suggests that our interpretation produces a "strange dichotomy" between "using" a firearm and "carrying" one. We do not see why that is so. Just as a defendant may "use" a firearm within the meaning of § 924(c)(1) by trading it for drugs *or* using it to shoot someone, so too would a defendant "carry" the firearm by keeping it on his person whether he intends to exchange it for cocaine or fire it in self-defense. The dichotomy arises, if at all, only when one tries to extend the phrase " 'uses . . . a firearm' " to any use " 'for any purpose whatever.' " For our purposes, it is sufficient to recognize that, because § 924(d)(1) includes both using a firearm for *trade* and using a firearm as a *weapon* as "us[ing] a firearm," it is most reasonable to construe § 924(c)(1) as encompassing both of those "uses" as well. . . .

■ JUSTICE SCALIA, with whom JUSTICE STEVENS and JUSTICE SOUTER join, dissenting.

Section 924(c)(1) mandates a sentence enhancement for any defendant who "during and in relation to any crime of violence or drug

trafficking crime . . . uses . . . a firearm." 18 U.S.C. § 924(c)(1). The Court
begins its analysis by focusing upon the word "use" in this passage, and
explaining that the dictionary definitions of that word are very broad. It
is, however, a "fundamental principle of statutory construction (and,
indeed, of language itself) that the meaning of a word cannot be
determined in isolation, but must be drawn from the context in which it
is used." That is particularly true of a word as elastic as "use," whose
meanings range all the way from "to partake of" (as in "he uses tobacco")
to "to be wont or accustomed" (as in "he used to smoke tobacco"). See
Webster's New International Dictionary 2806 (2d ed. 1950).

In the search for statutory meaning, we give nontechnical words and
phrases their ordinary meaning. [Citation.] To use an instrumentality
ordinarily means to use it for its intended purpose. When someone asks,
"Do you use a cane?," he is not inquiring whether you have your
grandfather's silver-handled walking stick on display in the hall; he
wants to know whether you *walk* with a cane. Similarly, to speak of
"using a firearm" is to speak of using it for its distinctive purpose, *i.e.*, as
a weapon. To be sure, "one can use a firearm in a number of ways,"
including as an article of exchange, just as one can "use" a cane as a hall
decoration—but that is not the ordinary meaning of "using" the one or
the other.[1] The Court does not appear to grasp the distinction between
how a word *can be* used and how it *ordinarily is* used. It would, indeed,
be "both reasonable and normal to say that petitioner 'used' his MAC-10
in his drug trafficking offense by trading it for cocaine." *Ibid.* It would
also be reasonable and normal to say that he "used" it to scratch his head.
When one wishes to describe the action of employing the instrument of a
firearm for such unusual purposes, "use" is assuredly a verb one could
select. But that says nothing about whether the *ordinary* meaning of the
phrase "uses a firearm" embraces such extraordinary employments. It is
unquestionably *not* reasonable and normal, I think, to say simply "do not
use firearms" when one means to prohibit selling or scratching with
them. . . .

The Court seeks to avoid this conclusion by referring to the next
subsection of the statute, § 924(d), which does not employ the phrase
"uses a firearm," but provides for the confiscation of firearms that are
"used in" referenced offenses which include the crimes of transferring,
selling, or transporting firearms in interstate commerce. The Court
concludes from this that *whenever* the term appears in this statute, "use"
of a firearm must include nonweapon use. I do not agree. We are dealing
here not with a technical word or an "artfully defined" legal term, *cf.*

---

[1]   The Court asserts that the "significant flaw" in this argument is that "to say that the
ordinary meaning of 'uses a firearm' *includes* using a firearm as a weapon" is quite different
from saying that the ordinary meaning "also *excludes* any other use." The two are indeed
different—but it is precisely the latter that I assert to be true: The ordinary meaning of "uses a
firearm" does *not* include using it as an article of commerce. I think it perfectly obvious, for
example, that the objective falsity requirement for a perjury conviction would not be satisfied if
a witness answered "no" to a prosecutor's inquiry whether he had ever "used a firearm," even
though he had once sold his grandfather's Enfield rifle to a collector.

Dewsnup v. Timm, 502 U.S. 410, 423, 116 L. Ed. 2d 903, 112 S.Ct. 773 (1992) (SCALIA, J., dissenting), but with common words that are, as I have suggested, inordinately sensitive to context. Just as adding the direct object "a firearm" to the verb "use" *narrows* the meaning of that verb (it can no longer mean "partake of"), so also adding the modifier "in the offense of transferring, selling, or transporting firearms" to the phrase "use a firearm" *expands* the meaning of that phrase (it then includes, as it previously would not, nonweapon use). But neither the narrowing nor the expansion should logically be thought to apply to *all* appearances of the affected word or phrase. Just as every appearance of the word "use" in the statute need not be given the narrow meaning that word acquires in the phrase "use a firearm," so also every appearance of the phrase "use a firearm" need not be given the expansive connotation that phrase acquires in the broader context "use a firearm in crimes such as unlawful sale of firearms." When, for example, the statute provides that its prohibition on certain transactions in firearms "shall not apply to the loan or rental of a firearm to any person for temporary use for lawful sporting purposes," 18 U.S.C. §§ 922(a)(5)(B), (b)(3)(B), I have no doubt that the "use" referred to is *only* use as a sporting *weapon*, and not the use of pawning the firearm to pay for a ski trip. Likewise when, in § 924(c)(1), the phrase "uses . . . a firearm" is not employed in a context that necessarily envisions the unusual "use" of a firearm as a commodity, the normally understood meaning of the phrase should prevail.

Another consideration leads to the same conclusion: § 924(c)(1) provides increased penalties not only for one who "uses" a firearm during and in relation to any crime of violence or drug trafficking crime, but also for one who "carries" a firearm in those circumstances. The interpretation I would give the language produces an eminently reasonable dichotomy between "using a firearm" (as a weapon) and "carrying a firearm" (which in the context "uses or carries a firearm" means carrying it in such manner as to be ready for use as a weapon). The Court's interpretation, by contrast, produces a strange dichotomy between "using a firearm for any purpose whatever, including barter," and "carrying a firearm."[3] . . .

QUESTIONS

1. Consider the arguments for and against implying the "as a weapon" condition on "uses." Which do you find most persuasive? Why?

2. 15 U.S.C. § 1644(a) imposes criminal liability on any person who:

knowingly in a transaction affecting interstate or foreign commerce, uses or attempts or conspires to use any counterfeit,

---

[3] The Court responds to this argument by abandoning all pretense of giving the phrase "uses a firearm" even a *permissible* meaning, much less its ordinary one. There is no problem, the Court says, because it is not contending that "uses a firearm" means "uses for *any* purpose," only that it means "uses as a weapon or for trade." Unfortunately, that is not one of the options that our mother tongue makes available. "Uses a firearm" can be given a broad meaning ("uses for any purpose") or its more ordinary narrow meaning ("uses as a weapon"); but it can not possibly mean "uses as a weapon or for trade."

fictitious, altered, forged, lost, stolen, or fraudulently obtained credit card to obtain money, goods, services, or anything else of value which within any one-year period has an aggregating value of $1,000 or more.

"Credit card" is defined as "any card, plate, coupon book or other credit device existing for the purpose of obtaining money, property, labor, or services on credit." 15 U.S.C. § 1702(k). Can a person be convicted under this statute if the government can show that the defendant made use of a credit card number, but not the credit card itself? See United States v. Bice-Bey, 701 F.2d 1086 (4th Cir.1983).

Bailey v. United States

Supreme Court of the United States, 1995.
516 U.S. 137, 116 S.Ct. 501, 133 L.Ed.2d 472.

■ JUSTICE O'CONNOR delivered the [unanimous] opinion of the Court.

These consolidated petitions each challenge a conviction under 18 U.S.C. § 924(c)(1). In relevant part, that section imposes a 5-year minimum term of imprisonment upon a person who "during and in relation to any crime of violence or drug trafficking crime . . . uses or carries a firearm." We are asked to decide whether evidence of the proximity and accessibility of a firearm to drugs or drug proceeds is alone sufficient to support a conviction for "use" of a firearm during and in relation to a drug trafficking offense under 18 U.S.C. § 924(c)(1).

I

In May 1989, petitioner Roland Bailey was stopped by police officers after they noticed that his car lacked a front license plate and an inspection sticker. When Bailey failed to produce a driver's license, the officers ordered him out of the car. As he stepped out, the officers saw Bailey push something between the seat and the front console. A search of the passenger compartment revealed one round of ammunition and 27 plastic bags containing a total of 30 grams of cocaine. After arresting Bailey, the officers searched the trunk of his car where they found, among a number of items, a large amount of cash and a bag containing a loaded 9-mm. pistol.

Bailey was charged on several counts, including using and carrying a firearm in violation of 18 U.S.C. § 924(c)(1). A prosecution expert testified at trial that drug dealers frequently carry a firearm to protect their drugs and money as well as themselves. Bailey was convicted by the jury on all charges, and his sentence included a consecutive 60-month term of imprisonment on the § 924(c)(1) conviction.

The Court of Appeals for the District of Columbia Circuit rejected Bailey's claim that the evidence was insufficient to support his conviction under § 924(c)(1). United States v. Bailey, 995 F.2d 1113 (C.A.D.C.1993). The court held that Bailey could be convicted for "using" a firearm during and in relation to a drug trafficking crime if the jury could reasonably infer that the gun facilitated Bailey's commission of a drug offense. *Id.*, at 1119. In Bailey's case, the court explained, the trier of fact could reasonably infer that Bailey had used the gun in the trunk to protect his drugs and drug proceeds and to facilitate sales. Judge Douglas H. Ginsburg, dissenting in part, argued that prior circuit precedent required reversal of Bailey's conviction.

In June 1991, an undercover officer made a controlled buy of crack cocaine from petitioner Candisha Robinson. The officer observed Robinson retrieve the drugs from the bedroom of her one-bedroom apartment. After a second controlled buy, the police executed a search warrant of the apartment. Inside a locked trunk in the bedroom closet, the police found, among other things, an unloaded, holstered .22-caliber Derringer, papers and a tax return belonging to Robinson, 10.88 grams of crack cocaine, and a marked $20 bill from the first controlled buy.

Robinson was indicted on a number of counts, including using or carrying a firearm in violation of § 924(c)(1). A prosecution expert testified that the Derringer was a "second gun," *i.e.*, a type of gun a drug dealer might hide on his or her person for use until reaching a "real gun." The expert also testified that drug dealers generally use guns to protect themselves from other dealers, the police, and their own employees. Robinson was convicted on all counts, including the § 924(c)(1) count, for which she received a 60-month term of imprisonment. The District Court denied Robinson's motion for a judgment of acquittal with respect to the "using or carrying" conviction and ruled that the evidence was sufficient to establish a violation of § 924(c)(1).

A divided panel of the Court of Appeals reversed Robinson's conviction on the § 924(c)(1) count. *United States v. Robinson,* 997 F.2d 884 (C.A.D.C.1993). The court determined, "[g]iven the way section 924(c)(1) is drafted, even if an individual intends to use a firearm in connection with a drug trafficking offense, the conduct of that individual is not reached by the statute unless the individual actually uses the firearm for that purpose." *Id.*, at 887. The court held that Robinson's possession of an unloaded .22-caliber Derringer in a locked trunk in a bedroom closet fell significantly short of the type of evidence the court had previously held necessary to establish actual use under § 924(c)(1). The mere proximity of the gun to the drugs was held insufficient to support the conviction. Judge Henderson dissented, arguing among other things that the firearm facilitated Robinson's distribution of drugs because it protected Robinson and the drugs during sales.

In order to resolve the apparent inconsistencies in its decisions applying § 924(c)(1), the Court of Appeals for the District of Columbia Circuit consolidated the two cases and reheard them en banc. In a divided opinion, a majority of the court held that the evidence was sufficient to establish that each defendant had used a firearm in relation to a drug trafficking offense and affirmed the § 924(c)(1) conviction in each case. 36 F.3d 106 (C.A.D.C.1994) (en banc).

The majority . . . "[held] that one uses a gun, *i.e.*, avails oneself of a gun, and therefore violates [§ 924(c)(1)], whenever one puts or keeps the gun in a particular place from which one (or one's agent) can gain access to it if and when needed to facilitate a drug crime." *Id.*, at 115. The court applied this new standard and affirmed the convictions of both Bailey and Robinson. In both cases, the court determined that the gun was sufficiently accessible and proximate to the drugs or drug proceeds that the jury could properly infer that the defendant had placed the gun in order to further the drug offenses or to protect the possession of the drugs.

Judge Wald, [dissented]. . . . Judge Williams, joined by Judges Silberman and Buckley, also dissented. He explained his understanding that "use" under § 924(c)(1) denoted active employment of the firearm "rather than possession with a contingent intent to use." *Id.*, at 121. "[B]y articulating a 'proximity' plus 'accessibility' test, however, the court has in effect diluted 'use' to mean simply possession with a floating intent to use." *Ibid.*

As the debate within the District of Columbia Circuit illustrates, § 924(c)(1) has been the source of much perplexity in the courts. The Circuits are in conflict both in the standards they have articulated, compare *United States v. Torres-Rodriguez*, 930 F.2d 1375, 1385 (C.A.9 1991) (mere possession sufficient to satisfy § 924(c)) with *United States v. Castro-Lara*, 970 F.2d 976, 983 (C.A.1 1992), cert. denied, 508 U.S. 962 (1993) (mere possession insufficient); and in the results they have reached, compare *United States v. Feliz-Cordero*, 859 F.2d 250, 254 (C.A.2 1988) (presence of gun in dresser drawer in apartment with drugs, drug proceeds, and paraphernalia insufficient to meet § 924(c)(1)) with *United States v. McFadden*, 13 F.3d 463, 465 (C.A.1 1994) (evidence of gun hidden under mattress with money, near drugs, was sufficient to show "use") and *United States v. Hager*, 969 F.2d 883, 889 (C.A.10), cert. denied, 506 U.S. 964 (1992) (gun in boots in living room near drugs was "used"). We granted certiorari to clarify the meaning of "use" under § 924(c)(1). 514 U.S. 1062 (1995).

II

Section 924(c)(1) requires the imposition of specified penalties if the defendant, "during and in relation to any crime of violence or drug trafficking crime . . . uses or carries a firearm." Petitioners argue that "use" signifies active employment of a firearm. Respondent opposes that definition and defends the proximity and accessibility test adopted by the Court of Appeals. We agree with petitioners, and hold that § 924(c)(1) requires evidence sufficient to show an *active employment* of the firearm by the defendant, a use that makes the firearm an operative factor in relation to the predicate offense.

This case is not the first one in which the Court has grappled with the proper understanding of "use" in § 924(c)(1). In *Smith*, we faced the question whether the barter of a gun for drugs was a "use," and concluded that it was. *Smith v. United States*, 508 U.S. 223 (1993). As the debate in *Smith* illustrated, the word "use" poses some interpretational difficulties because of the different meanings attributable to it. Consider the paradoxical statement: "I *use* a gun to protect my house, but I've never had to *use* it." "Use" draws meaning from its context, and we will look not only to the word itself, but also to the statute and the sentencing scheme, to determine the meaning Congress intended.

We agree with the majority below that "use" must connote more than mere possession of a firearm by a person who commits a drug offense. [Citation.] Had Congress intended possession alone to trigger liability under § 924(c)(1), it easily could have so provided. This obvious conclusion is supported by the frequent use of the term "possess" in the gun-crime statutes to describe prohibited gun-related conduct. *See, e.g.*, §§ 922(g), 922(j), 922(k), 922(o)(1), 930(a), 930(b).

Where the Court of Appeals erred was not in its conclusion that "use" means more than mere possession, but in its standard for evaluating whether the involvement of a firearm amounted to something more than mere possession. Its proximity and accessibility standard provides almost no limitation on the kind of possession that would be criminalized; in practice, nearly every possession of a firearm by a person engaged in drug trafficking would satisfy the standard, "thereby eras[ing] the line that the statutes, and the courts, have tried to draw." *United States v. McFadden, supra*, at 469 (Breyer, C.J., dissenting). Rather than requiring actual use, the District of Columbia Circuit would criminalize "simpl[e] possession with a floating intent to use." 36 F.3d, at 121 (Williams, J., dissenting). The shortcomings of this test are succinctly explained in Judge Williams' dissent:

> "While the majority attempts to fine-tune the concept of facilitation (and thereby, use) through its twin guideposts of proximity and accessibility, the ultimate result is that possession amounts to 'use' because possession enhances the defendant's confidence. Had Congress intended that, all it need have mentioned is possession. In this regard, the majority's test is either so broad as to assure automatic affirmance of any jury conviction or, if not so broad, is unlikely to produce a clear guideline." *Id.*, at 124–125 (citations omitted).

An evidentiary standard for finding "use" that is satisfied in almost every case by evidence of mere possession does not adhere to the obvious congressional intent to require more than possession to trigger the statute's application.

This conclusion—that a conviction for "use" of a firearm under § 924(c)(1) requires more than a showing of mere possession—requires us to answer a more difficult question. What must the Government show, beyond mere possession, to establish "use" for the purposes of the statute? We conclude that the language, context, and history of

§ 924(c)(1) indicate that the Government must show active employment of the firearm.

We start, as we must, with the language of the statute. See United States v. Ron Pair Enterprises, Inc., 489 U.S. 235, 241 (1989). The word "use" in the statute must be given its "ordinary or natural" meaning, a meaning variously defined as "[t]o convert to one's service," "to employ," "to avail oneself of," and "to carry out a purpose or action by means of." *Smith, supra,* at 228–229, 113 S.Ct., at 2054 (slip op., at 5) (internal quotation marks omitted) (citing Webster's New International Dictionary of English Language 2806 (2d ed. 1949) and Black's Law Dictionary 1541 (6th ed. 1990)). These various definitions of "use" imply action and implementation. *See also McFadden,* 13 F.3d, at 467 (Breyer, C.J., dissenting) ("the ordinary meanings of the words 'use and carry' . . . connote activity beyond simple possession").

We consider not only the bare meaning of the word but also its placement and purpose in the statutory scheme. " '[T]he meaning of statutory language, plain or not, depends on context.' " [Citation.] Looking past the word "use" itself, we read § 924(c)(1) with the assumption that Congress intended each of its terms to have meaning. "Judges should hesitate . . . to treat [as surplusage] statutory terms in any setting, and resistance should be heightened when the words describe an element of a criminal offense." Ratzlaf v. United States, 510 U.S. 135 (1994) (slip op., at 5–6). Here, Congress has specified two types of conduct with a firearm: "uses" or "carries."

Under the Government's reading of § 924(c)(1), "use" includes even the action of a defendant who puts a gun into place to protect drugs or to embolden himself. This reading is of such breadth that no role remains for "carry." The Government admits that the meanings of "use" and "carry" converge under its interpretation, but maintains that this overlap is a product of the particular history of § 924(c)(1). Therefore, the Government argues, the canon of construction that instructs that "a legislature is presumed to have used no superfluous words," [citation] is inapplicable. We disagree. Nothing here indicates that Congress, when it provided these two terms, intended that they be understood to be redundant.

We assume that Congress used two terms because it intended each term to have a particular, nonsuperfluous meaning. While a broad reading of "use" undermines virtually any function for "carry," a more limited, active interpretation of "use" preserves a meaningful role for "carries" as an alternative basis for a charge. Under the interpretation we enunciate today, a firearm can be used without being carried, *e.g.,* when an offender has a gun on display during a transaction, or barters with a firearm without handling it; and a firearm can be carried without being used, *e.g.,* when an offender keeps a gun hidden in his clothing throughout a drug transaction.

This reading receives further support from the context of § 924(c)(1). As we observed in *Smith,* "using a firearm" should not have a "different meaning in § 924(c)(1) than it does in § 924(d)." 508 U.S., at 235 (slip op., at 11). *See also United Savings Assn. v. Timbers of Inwood Forest Assocs., Ltd.,* 484 U.S. 365, 371 (1988) ("A provision that may seem ambiguous in isolation is often clarified by the remainder of the statutory scheme"). Section 924(d)(1) provides for the forfeiture of any firearm that is "used" or "intended to be used" in certain crimes. In that provision, Congress recognized a distinction between firearms "used" in commission of a crime and those "intended to be used," and provided for forfeiture of a weapon even before it had been "used." In § 924(c)(1), however, liability attaches only to cases of actual use, not intended use, as when an offender places a firearm with the intent to use it later if necessary. The difference between the two provisions demonstrates that, had Congress meant to broaden application of the statute beyond actual "use," Congress could and would have so specified, as it did in § 924(d)(1).

The amendment history of § 924(c) casts further light on Congress' intended meaning. The original version, passed in 1968, read:

"(c) Whoever—

"(1) uses a firearm to commit any felony which may be prosecuted in a court of the United States, or

"(2) carries a firearm unlawfully during the commission of any felony which may be prosecuted in a court of the United States, shall be sentenced to a term of imprisonment for not less than one year nor more than 10 years." § 102, 82 Stat. 1224.

The phrase "uses . . . to commit" indicates that Congress originally intended to reach the situation where the firearm was actively employed during commission of the crime. This original language would not have stretched so far as to cover a firearm that played no detectable role in the crime's commission. For example, a defendant who stored a gun in a nearby closet for retrieval in case the deal went sour would not have "use[d] a firearm to commit" a crime. This version also shows that "use" and "carry" were employed with distinctly different meanings.

Congress' 1984 amendment to § 924(c) altered the scope of predicate offenses from "any felony" to "any crime of violence," removed the "unlawfully" requirement, merged the "uses" and "carries" prongs, substituted "during and in relation to" the predicate crimes for the earlier provisions linking the firearm to the predicate crimes, and raised the minimum sentence to five years. § 1005(a), 98 Stat. 2138–2139. The Government argues that this amendment stripped "uses" and "carries" of the qualifications ("to commit" and "unlawfully during") that originally gave them distinct meanings, so that the terms should now be understood to overlap. Of course, in *Smith* we recognized that Congress' subsequent amendments to § 924(c) employed "use" expansively, to cover both use as a weapon and use as an item of barter. But there is no evidence to indicate that Congress intended to expand the meaning of "use" so far as to swallow up any significance for "carry." If Congress had intended to deprive "use" of its active connotations, it could have simply substituted a more appropriate term—"possession"—to cover the conduct it wished to reach.

The Government nonetheless argues that our observation in *Smith* that "§ 924(c)(1)'s language sweeps broadly," 508 U.S. at 229 (slip op., at 5), precludes limiting "use" to active employment. But our decision today is not inconsistent with *Smith*. Although there we declined to limit "use" to the meaning "use as a weapon," our interpretation of § 924(c)(1) nonetheless adhered to an active meaning of the term. In *Smith*, it was clear that the defendant had "used" the gun; the question was whether that particular use (bartering) came within the meaning of § 924(c)(1). *Smith* did not address the question we face today of what evidence is required to permit a jury to find that a firearm had been used at all.

To illustrate the activities that fall within the definition of "use" provided here, we briefly describe some of the activities that fall within "active employment" of a firearm, and those that do not.

The active-employment understanding of "use" certainly includes brandishing, displaying, bartering, striking with, and most obviously, firing or attempting to fire, a firearm. We note that this reading compels the conclusion that even an offender's reference to a firearm in his possession could satisfy § 924(c)(1). Thus, a reference to a firearm calculated to bring about a change in the circumstances of the predicate offense is a "use," just as the silent but obvious and forceful presence of a gun on a table can be a "use."

The example given above—"I *use* a gun to protect my house, but I've never had to *use* it"—shows that "use" takes on different meanings depending on context. In the first phrase of the example, "use" refers to an ongoing, inactive function fulfilled by a firearm. It is this sense of "use" that underlies the Government's contention that "placement for protection"—*i.e.,* placement of a firearm to provide a sense of security or to embolden—constitutes a "use." It follows, according to this argument, that a gun placed in a closet is "used," because its mere presence emboldens or protects its owner. We disagree. Under this reading, mere possession of a firearm by a drug offender, at or near the site of a drug crime or its proceeds or paraphernalia, is a "use" by the offender, because its availability for intimidation, attack, or defense would always, presumably, embolden or comfort the offender. But the inert presence of a firearm, without more, is not enough to trigger § 924(c)(1). Perhaps the nonactive nature of this asserted "use" is clearer if a synonym is used: storage. A defendant cannot be charged under § 924(c)(1) merely for storing a weapon near drugs or drug proceeds. Storage of a firearm, without its more active employment, is not reasonably distinguishable from possession.

A possibly more difficult question arises where an offender conceals a gun nearby to be at the ready for an imminent confrontation. *Cf.* 36 F.3d, at 119 (Wald, J., dissenting) (discussing distinction between firearm's accessibility to drugs or drug proceeds, and its accessibility to defendant). Some might argue that the offender has "actively employed" the gun by hiding it where he can grab and use it if necessary. In our view, "use" cannot extend to encompass this action. If the gun is not disclosed or mentioned by the offender, it is not actively employed, and it is not "used." To conclude otherwise would distort the language of the statute as well as create an impossible line-drawing problem. How "at the ready" was the firearm? Within arm's reach? In the room? In the house? How long before the confrontation did he place it there? Five minutes or 24 hours? Placement for later active use does not constitute "use." An alternative rationale for why "placement at the ready" is a "use"—that such placement is made with the intent to put the firearm to a future active use—also fails. As discussed above, § 924(d)(1) demonstrates that Congress knew how to draft a statute to reach a firearm that was "intended to be used." In § 924(c)(1), it chose not to include that term, but instead established the five-year mandatory minimum only for those defendants who actually "use" the firearm.

While it is undeniable that the active-employment reading of "use" restricts the scope of § 924(c)(1), the Government often has other means available to charge offenders who mix guns and drugs. The "carry" prong of § 924(c)(1), for example, brings some offenders who would not satisfy the "use" prong within the reach of the statute. And Sentencing Guidelines § 2D1.1(b)(1) provides an enhancement for a person convicted of certain drug-trafficking offenses if a firearm was possessed during the offense. United States Sentencing Commission, Guidelines Manual § 2D1.1(b)(1) (Nov. 1994). But the word "use" in § 924(c)(1) cannot support the extended applications that prosecutors have sometimes placed on it, in order to penalize drug-trafficking offenders for firearms possession.

The test set forth by the Court of Appeals renders "use" virtually synonymous with "possession" and makes any role for "carry" superfluous. The language of § 924(c)(1), supported by its history and context, compels the conclusion that Congress intended "use" in the active sense of "to avail oneself of." To sustain a conviction under the "use" prong of § 924(c)(1), the Government must show that the defendant actively employed the firearm during and in relation to the predicate crime.

III

Having determined that "use" denotes active employment, we must conclude that the evidence was insufficient to support either Bailey's or Robinson's conviction for "use" under § 924(c)(1).

The police stopped Bailey for a traffic offense and arrested him after finding cocaine in the driver's compartment of his car. The police then found a firearm inside a bag in the locked car trunk. There was no evidence that Bailey actively employed the firearm in any way. In Robinson's case, the unloaded, holstered firearm that provided the basis for her § 924(c)(1) conviction was found locked in a footlocker in a bedroom closet. No evidence showed that Robinson had actively employed the firearm. We reverse both judgments.

Bailey and Robinson were each charged under both the "use" and "carry" prongs of § 924(c)(1). Because the Court of Appeals did not consider liability under the "carry" prong of § 924(c)(1) for Bailey or Robinson, we remand for consideration of that basis for upholding the convictions.

It is so ordered.

Questions

1. Do you understand why the term "use" as used in 18 U.S.C. § 924(c)(1) does not encompass all the meanings the term used to have?

2. Are you persuaded by the court's attempt to reconcile *Bailey* with *Smith*? Should the Court simply have overruled *Smith*? *See infra Watson v. United States.*

Watson v. United States

Supreme Court of the United States, 2007.
552 U.S. 74, 128 S.Ct. 579, 169 L.Ed.2d 472.

■ Justice Souter delivered the opinion of the Court[, in which Chief Justice Roberts, Justice Stevens, Justice Scalia, Justice Kennedy, Justice Thomas, Justice Breyer, and Justice Alito joined].

The question is whether a person who trades his drugs for a gun "uses" a firearm "during and in relation to . . . [a] drug trafficking crime" within the meaning of 18 U.S.C. § 924(c)(1)(A). We hold that he does not.

I

A

Section 924(c)(1)(A) sets a mandatory minimum sentence, depending on the facts, for a defendant who, "during and in relation to any crime of violence or drug trafficking crime[,] . . . uses or carries a firearm."[2] The statute leaves the term "uses" undefined, though we have spoken to it twice before.

Smith v. United States, 508 U.S. 223, 113 S.Ct. 2050, 124 L. Ed. 2d 138 (1993) raised the converse of today's question, and held that "a criminal who trades his firearm for drugs 'uses' it during and in relation to a drug trafficking offense within the meaning of § 924(c)(1)." We rested

---

[2]   Any violation of § 924(c)(1)(A), for example, demands a mandatory minimum sentence of 5 years. *See* 18 U.S.C. § 924(c)(1)(A)(i). If the firearm is brandished, the minimum goes up to 7 years, *see* § 924(c)(1)(A)(ii); if the firearm is discharged, the minimum jumps to 10 years, *see* § 924(c)(1)(A)(iii).

primarily on the "ordinary or natural meaning" of the verb in context, and understood its common range as going beyond employment as a weapon: "it is both reasonable and normal to say that petitioner 'used' his MAC-10 in his drug trafficking offense by trading it for cocaine."

Two years later, the issue in *Bailey v. United States*, 516 U.S. 137, 116 S.Ct. 501, 133 L. Ed. 2d 472 (1995) was whether possessing a firearm kept near the scene of drug trafficking is "use" under § 924(c)(1). We looked again to "ordinary or natural" meaning, and decided that mere possession does not amount to "use": "§ 924(c)(1) requires evidence sufficient to show an *active employment* of the firearm by the defendant, a use that makes the firearm an operative factor in relation to the predicate offense."[3]

B

This third case on the reach of § 924(c)(1)(A) began to take shape when petitioner, Michael A. Watson, told a Government informant that he wanted to acquire a gun. On the matter of price, the informant quoted no dollar figure but suggested that Watson could pay in narcotics. Next, Watson met with the informant and an undercover law enforcement agent posing as a firearms dealer, to whom he gave 24 doses of oxycodone hydrocholoride (commonly, OxyContin) for a .50 caliber semiautomatic pistol. When law enforcement officers arrested Watson, they found the pistol in his car, and a later search of his house turned up a cache of prescription medicines, guns, and ammunition. Watson said he got the pistol "to protect his other firearms and drugs."

A federal grand jury indicted him for distributing a Schedule II controlled substance and for "using" the pistol during and in relation to that crime, in violation of § 924(c)(1)(A). Watson pleaded guilty across the board, reserving the right to challenge the factual basis for a § 924(c)(1)(A) conviction and the added consecutive sentence of 60 months for using the gun. The Court of Appeals affirmed, [citation,] on Circuit precedent foreclosing any argument that Watson had not "used" a firearm. [Citation.]

We granted certiorari to resolve a conflict among the Circuits on whether a person "uses" a firearm within the meaning of 18 U.S.C. § 924(c)(1)(A) when he trades narcotics to obtain a gun. We now reverse.

II

A

The Government's position that Watson "used" the pistol under § 924(c)(1)(A) by receiving it for narcotics lacks authority in either precedent or regular English. To begin with, neither *Smith* nor *Bailey* implicitly decides this case. While *Smith* held that firearms may be

---

[3] In 1998, Congress responded to *Bailey* by amending § 924(c)(1). The amendment broadened the provision to cover a defendant who "in furtherance of any [crime of violence or drug trafficking] crime, possesses a firearm." 18 U.S.C. § 924(c)(1)(A). The amendment did not touch the "use" prong of § 924(c)(1).

"used" in a barter transaction, even with no violent employment, the case
addressed only the trader who swaps his gun for drugs, not the trading
partner who ends up with the gun. *Bailey*, too, is unhelpful, with its rule
that a gun must be made use of actively to satisfy § 924(c)(1)(A), as "an
operative factor in relation to the predicate offense." The question here is
whether it makes sense to say that Watson employed the gun at all;
Bailey does not answer it.

With no statutory definition or definitive clue, the meaning of the
verb "uses" has to turn on the language as we normally speak it; there is
no other source of a reasonable inference about what Congress
understood when writing or what its words will bring to the mind of a
careful reader. So, in *Smith* we looked for "everyday meaning," revealed
in phraseology that strikes the ear as "both reasonable and normal."
[Citation.] *See also Bailey, supra*. This appeal to the ordinary leaves the
Government without much of a case.

The Government may say that a person "uses" a firearm simply by
receiving it in a barter transaction, but no one else would. A boy who
trades an apple to get a granola bar is sensibly said to use the apple, but
one would never guess which way this commerce actually flowed from
hearing that the boy used the granola. *Cf. United States v. Stewart*, 345
U.S. App. D.C. 384, 246 F.3d 728, 731 (CADC 2001) ("When a person pays
a cashier a dollar for a cup of coffee in the courthouse cafeteria, the
customer has not used the coffee. He has only used the dollar bill"). So,
when Watson handed over the drugs for the pistol, the informant or the
agent "used" the pistol to get the drugs, just as *Smith* held, but regular
speech would not say that Watson himself used the pistol in the trade.
"A seller does not 'use' a buyer's consideration," *United States v.
Westmoreland*, 122 F.3d 431, 436 (CA7 1997), and the Government's
contrary position recalls another case; [we previously] rejected the
Government's interpretation of 18 U.S.C. § 924(c)(2) because "we do not
normally speak or write the Government's way."[7]

B

The Government would trump ordinary English with two
arguments. First, it relies on *Smith* for the pertinence of a neighboring
provision, 18 U.S.C. § 924(d)(1), which authorizes seizure and forfeiture
of firearms "intended to be used in" certain criminal offenses listed in
§ 924(d)(3). Some of those offenses involve receipt of a firearm,[8] from

---

[7] Dictionaries confirm the conclusion. "Use" is concededly "elastic," *Smith* v. *United
States*, 508 U.S. 223, 241, 113 S.Ct. 2050, 124 L. Ed. 2d 138 (1993) (SCALIA, J., dissenting), but
none of its standard definitions stretch far enough to reach Watson's conduct, *see, e.g.*, Webster's
New International Dictionary of the English Language 2806 (2d ed. 1939) ("to employ"); The
Random House Dictionary of the English Language 2097 (2d ed. 1987) (to "apply to one's own
purposes"; "put into service; make use of"); Black's Law Dictionary 1541 (6th ed. 1990) ("to avail
oneself of; . . . to utilize"); *see also Smith, supra*, at 228–229, 241, 113 S.Ct. 2050, 124 L. Ed. 2d
138 (listing various dictionary definitions).

[8] *See, e.g.*, 18 U.S.C. § 922(j) (prohibiting, *inter alia*, the receipt of a stolen firearm in
interstate commerce); § 924(b) (prohibiting, *inter alia*, the receipt of a firearm in interstate
commerce with the intent to commit a felony).

which the Government infers that "use" under § 924(d) necessarily includes receipt of a gun even in a barter transaction. *Smith* is cited for the proposition that the term must be given the same meaning in both subsections, and the Government urges us to import "use" as "receipt in barter" into § 924(c)(1)(A).

We agree with the Government that § 924(d) calls for attention; the reference to intended use in a receipt crime carries some suggestion that receipt can be "use" (more of a hint, say, than speaking of intended "use" in a crime defined as exchange). But the suggestion is a tepid one and falls short of supporting what is really an attempt to draw a conclusion too specific from a premise too general.

The *Smith* majority rested principally on ordinary speech in reasoning that § 924(c)(1) extends beyond use as a weapon and includes use as an item of barter, [citation,] and the *Smith* opinion looks to § 924(d) only for its light on that conclusion. It notes that the "intended to be used" clause of § 924(d)(1) refers to offenses where "the firearm is *not* used as a weapon but instead as an item of barter or commerce," [citation,] with the implication that Congress intended "use" to reach commercial transactions, not just gun violence, in § 924(d) generally. It was this breadth of treatment that led the *Smith* majority to say that, "unless we are to hold that using a firearm has a different meaning in § 924(c)(1) than it does in § 924(d)—and clearly we should not—we must reject petitioner's narrow interpretation"; [citation] *see also Bailey, supra* ("Using a firearm should not have a different meaning in § 924(c)(1) than it does in § 924(d)" (internal quotation marks omitted)).

The Government overreads *Smith*. While the neighboring provision indicates that a firearm is "used" nonoffensively, and supports the conclusion that a gun can be "used" in barter, beyond that point its illumination fails. This is so because the utility of § 924(d)(1) is limited by its generality and its passive voice; it tells us a gun can be "used" in a receipt crime, but not whether both parties to a transfer use the gun, or only one, or which one. The nearby subsection (c)(1)(A), however, requires just such a specific identification. It provides that a person who uses a gun in the circumstances described commits a crime, whose perpetrator must be clearly identifiable in advance.

The agnosticism on the part of § 924(d)(1) about who does the using is entirely consistent with common speech's understanding that the first possessor is the one who "uses" the gun in the trade, and there is thus no cause to admonish us to adhere to the paradigm of a statute "as a symmetrical and coherent regulatory scheme, . . . in which the operative words have a consistent meaning throughout," *Gustafson v. Alloyd Co.*, 513 U.S. 561, 569, 115 S.Ct. 1061, 131 L. Ed. 2d 1 (1995), or to invoke the "standard principle of statutory construction . . . that identical words and phrases within the same statute should normally be given the same meaning," *Powerex Corp. v. Reliant Energy Servs.*, 551 U.S. 224, 127 S.Ct. 2411, 168 L. Ed. 2d 112 (2007) Subsections (d)(1) and (c)(1)(A) as we read them are not at odds over the verb "use"; the point is merely that in the two subsections the common verb speaks to different issues in different voices and at different levels of specificity. The provisions do distinct jobs, but we do not make them guilty of employing the common verb inconsistently.[9]

C

The second effort to trump regular English is the claim that failing to treat receipt in trade as "use" would create unacceptable asymmetry with *Smith*. At bottom, this atextual policy critique says it would be strange to penalize one side of a gun-for-drugs exchange but not the other: "the danger to society is created not only by the person who brings the firearm to the drug transaction, but also by the drug dealer who takes the weapon in exchange for his drugs during the transaction," Brief for United States 23.

The position assumes that *Smith* must be respected, and we join the Government at least on this starting point. A difference of opinion within the Court (as in *Smith*) does not keep the door open for another try at statutory construction, where *stare decisis* has "special force [since] the legislative power is implicated, and Congress remains free to alter what we have done." What is more, in 14 years Congress has taken no step to modify *Smith*'s holding, and this long congressional acquiescence "has enhanced even the usual precedential force" we accord to our interpretations of statutes,

The problem, then, is not with the sturdiness of *Smith* but with the limited malleability of the language *Smith* construed, and policy-driven symmetry cannot turn "receipt-in-trade" into "use." Whatever the tension between the prior result and the outcome here, law depends on respect for language and would be served better by statutory amendment (if Congress sees asymmetry) than by racking statutory language to cover a policy it fails to reach.

The argument is a peculiar one, in fact, given the Government's take on the current state of § 924(c)(1)(A). It was amended after *Bailey* and now prohibits not only using a firearm during and in relation to a drug trafficking crime, but also possessing one "in furtherance of" such a crime. 18 U.S.C. § 924(c)(1)(A); *see* n. 3, *supra*. The Government is confident that "a drug dealer who takes a firearm in exchange for his drugs generally will be subject to prosecution" under this new possession prong. Brief for United States 27; see Tr. of Oral Arg. 41 (Watson's case

---

[9] For that matter, the Government's argument that "use" must always have an identical meaning in §§ 924(c)(1)(A) and 924(d)(1) would upend *Bailey* v. *United States*, 516 U.S. 137, 116 S.Ct. 501, 133 L. Ed. 2d 472 (1995). One of the relevant predicate offenses referred to by § 924(d)(1) is possession of "any stolen firearm . . . [in] interstate or foreign commerce." 18 U.S.C. § 922(j). If we were to hold that all criminal conduct covered by the "intended to be used" clause in § 924(d)(1) is "use" for purposes of § 924(c)(1)(A), it would follow that mere possession is use. But that would squarely conflict with our considered and unanimous decision in *Bailey* that " 'use' must connote more than mere possession of a firearm." 516 U.S., at 143, 116 S.Ct. 501, 133 L. Ed. 2d 472.

"could have been charged as possession"); *cf. United States v. Cox*, 324 F.3d 77, 83, n. 2 (CA2 2003) ("For defendants charged under § 924(c) after [the post-*Bailey*] amendment, trading drugs for a gun will probably result in . . . possession [in furtherance of a drug trafficking crime]"). This view may or may not prevail, and we do not speak to it today, but it does leave the appeal to symmetry underwhelming in a contest with the English language, on the Government's very terms.

Given ordinary meaning and the conventions of English, we hold that a person does not "use" a firearm under § 924(c)(1)(A) when he receives it in trade for drugs. The judgment of the Court of Appeals is reversed, and the case is remanded for further proceedings consistent with this opinion.

■ JUSTICE GINSBURG, concurring in the judgment.

It is better to receive than to give, the Court holds today, at least when the subject is guns. Distinguishing, as the Court does, between trading a gun for drugs and trading drugs for a gun, for purposes of the 18 U.S.C. § 924(c)(1) enhancement, makes scant sense to me. I join the Court's judgment, however, because I am persuaded that the Court took a wrong turn in *Smith v. United States*, 508 U.S. 223, 113 S.Ct. 2050, 124 L. Ed. 2d 138 (1993), when it held that trading a gun for drugs fits within § 924(c)(1)'s compass as "use" of a firearm "during and in relation to any . . . drug trafficking crime." For reasons well stated by JUSTICE SCALIA in his dissenting opinion in *Smith*, 508 U.S., at 241, 113 S.Ct. 2050, 124 L. Ed. 2d 138, I would read the word "use" in § 924(c)(1) to mean use as a weapon, not use in a bartering transaction. Accordingly, I would overrule *Smith*, and thereby render our precedent both coherent and consistent with normal usage. *Cf. Henslee v. Union Planters Nat. Bank & Trust Co.*, 335 U.S. 595, 600, 69 S.Ct. 290, 93 L. Ed. 259, 1949–1 C.B. 223 (1949) (Frankfurter, J., dissenting) ("Wisdom too often never comes, and so one ought not to reject it merely because it comes late.").

QUESTIONS

1. Is *Smith* still good law after *Watson*? Under what circumstances might employment of a firearm for any purpose other than as a weapon still warrant application of the § 924(c) sentence enhancer?

2. How should the court's interpretation of "uses" to mean "actively employs" affect the understanding of "or carries" in the same statutory section? Is there a risk that a broad interpretation of "uses" could swallow any independent meaning to the term "or carries?" See *Muscarello v. United States, supra*.

D. INTERPRETING LEGISLATIVE RESPONSES TO PRIOR JUDICIAL INTERPRETATIONS

1. WHEN THE LEGISLATURE DECLINES, OR FAILS, TO RESPOND

Girouard v. United States

Supreme Court of the United States, 1946.
328 U.S. 61, 66 S.Ct. 826, 90 L.Ed. 1084.

Certiorari to the United States Circuit Court of Appeals for the First Circuit.

■ MR. JUSTICE DOUGLAS delivered the opinion of the Court[, in which JUSTICE BLACK, JUSTICE MURPHY, JUSTICE RUTLEDGE, and JUSTICE BURTON joined].

In 1943 petitioner, a native of Canada, filed his petition for naturalization in the District Court of Massachusetts. He stated in his application that he understood the principles of the government of the United States, believed in its form of government, and was willing to take the oath of allegiance (54 Stat. 1157, 8 U.S.C.A. § 735(b)), which reads as follows:

"I hereby declare, on oath, that I absolutely and entirely renounce and abjure all allegiance and fidelity to any foreign prince, potentate, state, or sovereignty of whom or which I have heretofore been a subject or citizen; that I will support and defend the Constitution and laws of the United States of America against all enemies, foreign and domestic; that I will bear true faith and allegiance to the same; and that I take this obligation freely without any mental reservation or purpose of evasion: So help me God."

To the question in the application "If necessary, are you willing to take up arms in defense of this country?" he replied, "No (Noncombatant) Seventh Day Adventist." He explained that answer before the examiner by saying "it is a purely religious matter with me, I have no political or personal reasons other than that." He did not claim before his Selective Service board exemption from all military service, but only from combatant military duty. At the hearing in the District Court petitioner testified that he was a member of the Seventh Day Adventist denomination, of whom approximately 10,000 were then serving in the armed forces of the United States as non-combatants, especially in the medical corps; and that he was willing to serve in the army but would not bear arms. The District Court admitted him to citizenship. The Circuit Court of Appeals reversed, one judge dissenting. 1 Cir., 149 F.2d 760. It took that action on the authority of United States v. Schwimmer, 279 U.S. 644, 49 S.Ct. 448, 73 L.Ed. 889; United States v. Macintosh, 283 U.S. 605, 51 S.Ct. 570, 75 L.Ed. 1302, and United States v. Bland, 283

U.S. 636, 51 S.Ct. 569, 75 L.Ed. 1319, saying that the facts of the present case brought it squarely within the principles of those cases. The case is here on a petition for a writ of certiorari which we granted so that those authorities might be re-examined.

The *Schwimmer, Macintosh* and *Bland* cases involved, as does the present one, a question of statutory construction. At the time of those cases, Congress required an alien, before admission to citizenship, to declare on oath in open court that "he will support and defend the Constitution and laws of the United States against all enemies, foreign and domestic, and bear true faith and allegiance to the same." It also required the court to be satisfied that the alien had during the five year period immediately preceding the date of his application "behaved as a man of good moral character, attached to the principles of the Constitution of the United States, and well disposed to the good order and happiness of the same." Those provisions were reenacted into the present law in substantially the same form.

While there are some factual distinctions between this case and the *Schwimmer* and *Macintosh* cases, the *Bland* case on its facts is indistinguishable. But the principle emerging from the three cases obliterates any factual distinction among them. As we recognized in In re Summers, 325 U.S. 561, 572, 577, 65 S.Ct. 1307, 1313, 1316, they stand for the same general rule—that an alien who refuses to bear arms will not be admitted to citizenship. As an original proposition, we could not agree with that rule. The fallacies underlying it were, we think, demonstrated in the dissents of Mr. Justice Holmes in the *Schwimmer* case and of Mr. Chief Justice Hughes in the *Macintosh* case.

The oath required of aliens does not in terms require that they promise to bear arms. Nor has Congress expressly made any such finding a prerequisite to citizenship. To hold that it is required is to read it into the Act by implication. But we could not assume that Congress intended to make such an abrupt and radical departure from our traditions unless it spoke in unequivocal terms.

The bearing of arms, important as it is, is not the only way in which our institutions may be supported and defended, even in times of great peril. Total war in its modern form dramatizes as never before the great cooperative effort necessary for victory. The nuclear physicists who developed the atomic bomb, the worker at his lathe, the seaman on cargo vessels, construction battalions, nurses, engineers, litter bearers, doctors, chaplains—these, too, made essential contributions. And many of them made the supreme sacrifice. Mr. Justice Holmes stated in the *Schwimmer* case, 279 U.S. at page 655, 49 S.Ct. at page 451, 73 L.Ed. 889, that "the Quakers have done their share to make the country what it is." And the annals of the recent war show that many whose religious scruples prevented them from bearing arms, nevertheless were unselfish participants in the war effort. Refusal to bear arms is not necessarily a sign of disloyalty or a lack of attachment to our institutions. One may serve his country faithfully and devotedly though his religious scruples make it impossible for him to shoulder a rifle. Devotion to one's country can be as real and as enduring among non-combatants as among combatants. One may adhere to what he deems to be his obligation to God and yet assume all military risks to secure victory. The effort of war is indivisible; and those whose religious scruples prevent them from killing are no less patriots than those whose special traits or handicaps result in their assignment to duties far behind the fighting front. Each is making the utmost contribution according to his capacity. The fact that his role may be limited by religious convictions rather than by physical characteristics has no necessary bearing on his attachment to his country or on his willingness to support and defend it to his utmost.

Petitioner's religious scruples would not disqualify him from becoming a member of Congress or holding other public offices. While Article VI, Clause 3 of the Constitution provides that such officials, both of the United States and the several States, "shall be bound by Oath or Affirmation, to support this Constitution," it significantly adds that "no religious Test shall ever be required as a Qualification to any Office or public Trust under the United States." The oath required is in no material respect different from that prescribed for aliens under the Naturalization Act. It has long contained the provision "that I will support and defend the Constitution of the United States against all enemies, foreign and domestic; that I will bear true faith and allegiance to the same; that I take this obligation freely, without any mental reservation or purpose of evasion." R.S. § 1757, 5 U.S.C.A. § 16. As Mr. Chief Justice Hughes stated in his dissent in the *Macintosh* case, 283 U.S. at page 631, "the history of the struggle for religious liberty, the large number of citizens of our country from the very beginning who have been unwilling to sacrifice their religious convictions, and in particular, those who have been conscientiously opposed to war and who would not yield what they sincerely believed to be their allegiance to the will of God"—these considerations make it impossible to conclude "that such persons are to be deemed disqualified for public office in this country because of the requirement of the oath which must be taken before they enter upon their duties."

There is not the slightest suggestion that Congress set a stricter standard for aliens seeking admission to citizenship than it did for officials who make and enforce the laws of the nation and administer its affairs. It is hard to believe that one need forsake his religious scruples to become a citizen but not to sit in the high councils of state.

As Mr. Chief Justice Hughes pointed out (United States v. Macintosh, *supra*, 283 U.S. at page 633), religious scruples against bearing arms have been recognized by Congress in the various draft laws. This is true of the Selective Training and Service Act of 1940, 54 Stat. 889, 50 U.S.C.A. Appendix, § 305(g), as it was of earlier acts. He who is inducted into the armed services takes an oath which includes the provision "that I will bear true faith and allegiance to the United States of America; that I will serve them honestly and faithfully against all their enemies whomsoever." 41 Stat. 809, 10 U.S.C.A. § 1581. Congress has thus recognized that one may adequately discharge his obligations as a citizen by rendering non-combatant as well as combatant services. This respect by Congress over the years for the conscience of those having religious scruples against bearing arms is cogent evidence of the meaning of the oath. It is recognition by Congress that even in time of war one may truly support and defend our institutions though he stops short of using weapons of war.

That construction of the naturalization oath received new support in 1942. In the Second War Powers Act, 56 Stat. 176, 182, 8 U.S.C.A. § 1001, Congress relaxed certain of the requirements for aliens who served honorably in the armed forces of the United States during World War II and provided machinery to expedite their naturalization. Residence requirements were relaxed, educational tests were eliminated, and no fees were required. But no change in the oath was made; nor was any change made in the requirement that the alien be attached to the principles of the Constitution. Yet it is clear that these new provisions cover non-combatants as well as combatants. If petitioner had served as a non-combatant (as he was willing to do), he could have been admitted to citizenship by taking the identical oath which he is willing to take. Can it be that the oath means one thing to one who has served to the extent permitted by his religious scruples and another thing to one equally willing to serve but who has not had the opportunity? It is not enough to say that petitioner is not entitled to the benefits of the new Act since he did not serve in the armed forces. He is not seeking the benefits of the expedited procedure and the relaxed requirements. The oath which he must take is identical with the oath which both non-combatants and combatants must take. It would, indeed, be a strange construction to say that "support and defend the Constitution and laws of the United States of America against all enemies, foreign and domestic" demands something more from some than it does from others. That oath can hardly be adequate for one who is unwilling to bear arms because of religious scruples and yet exact from another a promise to bear arms despite religious scruples.

Mr. Justice Holmes stated in the *Schwimmer* case, 279 U.S. at pages 654, 655: "if there is any principle of the Constitution that more imperatively calls for attachment than any other it is the principle of free thought—not free thought for those who agree with us but freedom for the thought that we hate. I think that we should adhere to that principle with regard to admission into, as well as to life within this country." The struggle for religious liberty has through the centuries been an effort to accommodate the demands of the State to the conscience of the individual. The victory for freedom of thought recorded in our Bill of Rights recognizes that in the domain of conscience there is a moral power higher than the State. Throughout the ages men have suffered death rather than subordinate their allegiance to God to the authority of the State. Freedom of religion guaranteed by the First Amendment is the product of that struggle. As we recently stated in United States v. Ballard, 322 U.S. 78, 86, "Freedom of thought, which includes freedom of religious belief, is basic in a society of free men. West Virginia State Board of Education v. Barnette, 319 U.S. 624." The test oath is abhorrent to our tradition. Over the years Congress has meticulously respected that tradition and even in time of war has sought to accommodate the military requirements to the religious scruples of the individual. We do not believe that Congress intended to reverse that policy when it came to draft the naturalization oath. Such an abrupt and radical departure from our traditions should not be implied. See Schneiderman v. United States, 320 U.S. 118, 132. Cogent evidence would be necessary to convince us that Congress took that course.

We conclude that the *Schwimmer, Macintosh* and *Bland* cases do not state the correct rule of law.

We are met, however, with the argument that even though those cases were wrongly decided, Congress has adopted the rule which they announced. The argument runs as follows: Many efforts were made to amend the law so as to change the rule announced by those cases; but in every instance the bill died in committee. Moreover, in 1940 when the new Naturalization Act was passed, Congress reenacted the oath in its pre-existing form, though at the same time it made extensive changes in the requirements and procedure for naturalization. From this it is argued that Congress adopted and reenacted the rule of the *Schwimmer, Macintosh*, and *Bland* cases. *Cf.* Apex Hosiery Co. v. Leader, 310 U.S. 469, 488, 489.

We stated in Helvering v. Hallock, 309 U.S. 106, 119, that "It would require very persuasive circumstances enveloping Congressional silence to debar this Court from re-examining its own doctrines." It is at best treacherous to find in Congressional silence alone the adoption of a controlling rule of law. We do not think under the circumstances of this legislative history that we can properly place on the shoulders of Congress the burden of the Court's own error. The history of the 1940 Act is at most equivocal. It contains no affirmative recognition of the rule of the *Schwimmer, Macintosh* and *Bland* cases. The silence of Congress and its inaction are as consistent with a desire to leave the problem fluid as they are with an adoption by silence of the rule of those cases. But for us, it is enough to say that since the date of those cases Congress never acted affirmatively on this question but once and that was in 1942. At that time, as we have noted, Congress specifically granted naturalization privileges to noncombatants who like petitioner were prevented from bearing arms by their religious scruples. That was affirmative recognition that one could be attached to the principles of our government and could support and defend it even though his religious convictions prevented him from bearing arms. And, as we have said, we cannot believe that the oath was designed to exact something more from one person than from another. Thus the affirmative action taken by Congress in 1942 negatives any inference that otherwise might be drawn from its silence when it re-enacted the oath in 1940.

Reversed.

■ MR. JUSTICE JACKSON took no part in the consideration or decision of this case.

■ MR. CHIEF JUSTICE STONE dissenting.

I think the judgment should be affirmed, for the reason that the court below, in applying the controlling provisions of the naturalization statutes, correctly applied them as earlier construed by this Court, whose construction Congress has adopted and confirmed.

In three cases decided more than fifteen years ago, this Court denied citizenship to applicants for naturalization who had announced that they proposed to take the prescribed oath of allegiance with the reservation or qualification that they would not, as naturalized citizens, assist in the defense of this country by force of arms or give their moral support to the government in any war which they did not believe to be morally justified or in the best interests of the country. See United States v. Schwimmer, 279 U.S. 644; United States v. Macintosh, 283 U.S. 605; United States v. Bland, 283 U.S. 636.

In each of these cases this Court held that the applicant had failed to meet the conditions which Congress had made prerequisite to naturalization by § 4 of the Naturalization Act of June 29, 1906, c. 3592, 34 Stat. 596, the provisions of which, here relevant, were enacted in the Nationality Act of October 14, 1940. See c. 876, 54 Stat. 1137, as amended by the Act of March 27, 1942, c. 199, 56 Stat. 176, 182, 183, and by the Act of December 7, 1942, c. 690, 56 Stat. 1041, 8 U.S.C.A. §§ 707, 723a, 735, 1001 et seq. Section 4 of the Naturalization Act of 1906, paragraph "Third", provided that before the admission to citizenship the applicant should declare on oath in open court that "he will support and defend the Constitution and laws of the United States against all enemies, foreign and domestic, and bear true faith and allegiance to the same." And paragraph "Fourth" required that before admission it be made to appear "to the satisfaction of the court admitting any alien to citizenship" that at least for a period of five years immediately preceding his application the applicant "has behaved as a man of good moral character, attached to the principles of the Constitution of the United States, and well disposed to the good order and happiness of the same." In applying these provisions in the cases mentioned, this Court held only that an applicant who is unable to take the oath of allegiance without the reservations or qualifications insisted upon by the applicants in those cases manifests his want of attachment to the principles of the Constitution and his unwillingness to meet the requirements of the oath, that he will support and defend the Constitution of the United States and bear true faith and allegiance to the same, and so does not comply with the statutory conditions of his naturalization. No question of the constitutional power of Congress to withhold citizenship on these grounds was involved. That power was not doubted. See Selective Draft Law Cases [(Arver v. United States)], 245 U.S. 366; Hamilton v. Regents, 293 U.S. 245. The only question was of construction of the statute which Congress at all times has been free to amend if dissatisfied with the construction adopted by the Court.

With three other Justices of the Court I dissented in the *Macintosh* and *Bland* cases, for reasons which the Court now adopts as ground for overruling them. Since this Court in three considered earlier opinions has rejected the construction of the statute for which the dissenting Justices contended, the question, which for me is decisive of the present case, is whether Congress has likewise rejected that construction by its subsequent legislative action, and has adopted and confirmed the Court's earlier construction of the statutes in question. A study of Congressional action taken with respect to proposals for amendment of the naturalization laws since the decision in the *Schwimmer* case, leads me to conclude that Congress has adopted and confirmed this Court's earlier construction of the naturalization laws. For that reason alone I think that the judgment should be affirmed.

The construction of the naturalization statutes, adopted by this Court in the three cases mentioned, immediately became the target of an active, publicized legislative attack in Congress which persisted for a period of eleven years, until the adoption of the Nationality Act in 1940. Two days after the *Schwimmer* case was decided, a bill was introduced in the House, H.R. 3547, 71st Cong., 1st Sess., to give the Naturalization Act a construction contrary to that which had been given to it by this Court and which, if adopted, would have made the applicants rejected by this Court in the *Schwimmer, Macintosh* and *Bland* cases eligible for citizenship. This effort to establish by Congressional action that the construction which this Court had placed on the Naturalization Act was not one which Congress had adopted or intended, was renewed without success after the decision in the Macintosh and Bland cases, and was continued for a period of about ten years. All of these measures were of substantially the same pattern as H.R. 297, 72d Cong., 1st Sess., introduced December 8, 1931, at the first session of Congress, after the decision in the Macintosh case. It provided that no person otherwise qualified "shall be debarred from citizenship by reason of his or her religious views or philosophical opinions with respect to the lawfulness of war as a means of settling international disputes, but every alien admitted to citizenship shall be subject to the same obligation as the native-born citizen." H.R. 3547, 71st Cong., 1st Sess., introduced immediately after the decision in the *Schwimmer* case, had contained a like provision, but with the omission of the last clause beginning "but every alien." Hearings were had before the House Committee on Immigration and Naturalization on both bills at which their proponents had stated clearly their purpose to set aside the interpretation placed on the oath of allegiance by the *Schwimmer* and *Macintosh* cases. There was opposition on each occasion. Bills identical with H.R. 297 were introduced in three later Congresses. None of these bills were reported out of Committee. The other proposals, all of which failed of passage . . ., had the same purpose and differed only in phraseology.

Thus, for six successive Congresses, over a period of more than a decade, there were continuously pending before Congress in one form or another proposals to overturn the rulings in the three Supreme Court decisions in question. Congress declined to adopt these proposals after full hearings and after speeches on the floor advocating the change. 72 Cong. Rec. 6966–7; 75th Cong. Rec. 15354–7. In the meantime the decisions of this Court had been followed in Clarke's Case, 301 Pa. 321, 152 A. 92; Beale v. United States, 8 Cir., 71 F.2d 737; In re Warkentin, 7 Cir., 93 F.2d 42. In Beale v. United States, *supra*, [71 F.2d 737] the court pointed out that the proposed amendments affecting the provisions of the statutes relating to admission to citizenship had failed saying: "We must conclude, therefore, that these statutory requirements as construed by the Supreme Court have Congressional sanction and approval."

Any doubts that such were the purpose and will of Congress would seem to have been dissipated by the reenactment by Congress in 1940 of Paragraphs "Third" and "Fourth" of § 4 of the Naturalization Act of 1906, and by the incorporation in the Act of 1940 of the very form of oath which had been administratively prescribed for the applicants in the *Schwimmer, Macintosh* and *Bland* cases. See Rule 8(c), Naturalization Regulations of July 1, 1929.

The Nationality Act of 1940 was a comprehensive, slowly matured and carefully considered revision of the naturalization laws. The preparation of this measure was not only delegated to a Congressional Committee, but was considered by a committee of Cabinet members, one of whom was the Attorney General. Both were aware of our decisions in the *Schwimmer* and related cases and that no other question pertinent to the naturalization laws had been as persistently and continuously before Congress in the ten years following the decision in the *Schwimmer* case. The modifications in the provisions of Paragraphs "Third" and "Fourth" of § 4 of the 1906 Act show conclusively the careful attention which was given to them.

In the face of this legislative history the "failure of Congress to alter the Act after it had been judicially construed, and the enactment by Congress of legislation which implicitly recognizes the judicial construction as effective, is persuasive of legislative recognition that the judicial construction is the correct one. This is the more so where, as here, the application of the statute . . . has brought forth sharply conflicting views both on the Court and in Congress, and where after the matter has been fully brought to the attention of the public and the Congress, the latter has not seen fit to change the statute." [Citations.] It is the responsibility of Congress, in reenacting a statute, to make known its purpose in a controversial matter of interpretation of its former language, at least when the matter has, for over a decade, been persistently brought to its attention. In the light of this legislative history, it is abundantly clear that Congress has performed that duty. In any case it is not lightly to be implied that Congress has failed to perform it and has delegated to this Court the responsibility of giving new content to language deliberately readopted after this Court has construed it. For us to make such an assumption is to discourage, if not to deny, legislative responsibility. By thus adopting and confirming this Court's construction of what Congress had enacted in the Naturalization Act of 1906 Congress gave that construction the same legal significance as though it had written the very words into the Act of 1940.

The only remaining question is whether Congress repealed this construction by enactment of the 1942 amendments of the Nationality Act. That Act extended special privileges to applicants for naturalization who were aliens and who have served in the armed forces of the United States in time of war, by dispensing with or modifying existing requirements, relating to declarations of intention, period of residence, education, and fees. It left unchanged the requirements that the applicant's behavior show his attachment to the principles of the Constitution and that he take the oath of allegiance. In adopting the 1942 amendments Congress did not have before it any question of the oath of allegiance with which it had been concerned when it adopted the 1940 Act. In 1942 it was concerned with the grant of special favors to those seeking naturalization who had worn the uniform and rendered military service in time of war and who could satisfy such naturalization requirements as had not been dispensed with by the amendments. In the case of those entitled to avail themselves of these privileges, Congress left it to the naturalization authorities, as in other cases, to determine whether, by their applications and their conduct in the military service they satisfy the requirements for naturalization which had not been waived.

It is pointed out that one of the 1942 amendments, 8 U.S.C.A. § 1004, provided that the provisions of the amendment should not apply to "any conscientious objector who performed no military duty whatever or refused to wear the uniform." It is said that the implication of this provision is that conscientious objectors who rendered noncombatant service and wore the uniform were, under the 1942 amendments, to be admitted to citizenship. From this it is argued that since the 1942 amendments apply to those who have been in noncombatant, as well as combatant, military service, the amendment must be taken to include some who have rendered noncombatant service who are also conscientious objectors and who would be admitted to citizenship under the 1942 amendments, even though they made the same reservations as to the oath of allegiance as did the applicants in the *Schwimmer, Macintosh* and *Bland* cases. And it is said that although the 1942 amendments are not applicable to petitioner, who has not been in military service, the oath cannot mean one thing as to him and another as to those who have been in the noncombatant service.

To these suggestions there are two answers. One is that if the 1942 amendment be construed as including noncombatants who are also conscientious objectors, who are unwilling to take the oath without the reservations made by the applicants in the *Schwimmer, Macintosh* and *Bland* cases, the only effect would be to exempt noncombatant conscientious objectors from the requirements of the oath, which had clearly been made applicable to all objectors, including petitioner, by the Nationality Act of 1940, and from which petitioner was not exempted by the 1942 amendments. If such is the construction of the 1942 Act, there is no constitutional or statutory obstacle to Congress' taking such action. Congress if it saw fit could have admitted to citizenship those who had rendered noncombatant service, with a modified oath or without any oath at all. Petitioner has not been so exempted.

Since petitioner was never in the military or naval forces of the United States, we need not decide whether the 1942 amendments authorized any different oath for those who had been in noncombatant service than for others. The amendments have been construed as requiring the same oath, without reservations, from conscientious objectors, as from others. In re Nielsen, D.C., 60 F.Supp. 240. Not all of those who rendered noncombatant service were conscientious objectors. Few were. There were others in the noncombatant service who had announced their conscientious objections to combatant service, who may have waived or abandoned their objections. Such was the experience in the First World War. See "Statement Concerning the Treatment of Conscientious Objectors in the Army", prepared and published by direction of the Secretary of War, June 18, 1919. All such could have taken the oath without the reservations made by the applicants in the *Schwimmer, Macintosh* and *Bland* cases and would have been entitled to the benefits of the 1942 amendments provided they had performed military duty and had not refused to wear the uniform. The fact that Congress recognized by indirection, in 8 U.S.C.A. § 1004, that those who had appeared in the role of conscientious objectors, might become citizens by taking the oath of allegiance and establishing their attachment to the principles of the Constitution, does not show that Congress dispensed with the requirements of the oath as construed by this Court and plainly confirmed by Congress in the Nationality Act of 1940. There is no necessary inconsistency in this respect between the 1940 Act and the 1942 amendments. Without it repeal by implication is not favored. United States v. Borden Co., 308 U.S. 188, 198, 199, 203–206, 60 S.Ct. 182, 188, 189, 190–192, 84 L.Ed. 181; State of Georgia v. Pennsylvania

R. Co., 324 U.S. 439, 457, 65 S.Ct. 716, 726; United States Alkali Export Ass'n v. United States, 325 U.S. 196, 209, 65 S.Ct. 1120, 1128. The amendments and their legislative history give no hint of any purpose of Congress to relax, at least for persons who had rendered no military service, the requirements of the oath of allegiance and proof of attachment to the Constitution as this Court had interpreted them and as the Nationality Act of 1940 plainly required them to be interpreted. It is not the function of this Court to disregard the will of Congress in the exercise of its constitutional power.

■ MR. JUSTICE REED and MR. JUSTICE FRANKFURTER join in this opinion.

QUESTION

How pointed must Congress's non-response to a controversial statutory interpretation be before Congress should be deemed to have "ratified" that interpretation? Would it matter if no bills to amend the statute to "overrule" the judicial interpretation were ever proposed? If bills were repeatedly submitted, but no action taken? Submitted and hearings held? Submitted and committee reports issued? Voted on but failed to pass? Is this kind of inquiry helpful at all?

2.   WHEN THE LEGISLATURE DOES RESPOND

Newport News Shipbuilding and Dry Dock Co. v. EEOC

Supreme Court of the United States, 1983.
462 U.S. 669, 103 S.Ct. 2622, 77 L.Ed.2d 89.

■ JUSTICE STEVENS delivered the opinion of the Court[, in which CHIEF JUSTICE BURGER, JUSTICE BRENNAN, JUSTICE WHITE, JUSTICE MARSHALL, JUSTICE BLACKMUN, and JUSTICE O'CONNOR joined].

In 1978 Congress decided to overrule our decision in General Electric Co. v. Gilbert, 429 U.S. 125 (1976), by amending Title VII of the Civil Rights Act of 1964 "to prohibit sex discrimination on the basis of pregnancy."[1] On the effective date of the Act, petitioner amended its health insurance plan to provide its female employees with hospitalization benefits for pregnancy-related conditions to the same extent as for other medical conditions.[2] The plan continued, however, to

---

[1] Pub. L. 95–555, 92 Stat. 2076 (quoting title of 1978 Act). The new statute (the Pregnancy Discrimination Act) amended the "Definitions" section of Title VII, 42 U.S.C. § 2000e, to add a new subsection (k) reading in pertinent part as follows: "The terms 'because of sex' or 'on the basis of sex' include, but are not limited to, because of or on the basis of pregnancy, childbirth, or related medical conditions; and women affected by pregnancy, childbirth, or related medical conditions shall be treated the same for all employment-related purposes, including receipt of benefits under fringe benefit programs, as other persons not so affected but similar in their ability or inability to work, and nothing in section 2000e–2(h) of this title shall be interpreted to permit otherwise. . . ." § 2000e(k) (1976 ed., Supp. V).

[2] The amendment to Title VII became effective on the date of its enactment, October 31, 1978, but its requirements did not apply to any then-existing fringe benefit program until 180

provide less favorable pregnancy benefits for spouses of male employees. The question presented is whether the amended plan complies with the amended statute.

Petitioner's plan provides hospitalization and medical-surgical coverage for a defined category of employees and a defined category of dependents. Dependents covered by the plan include employees' spouses . . . . Prior to April 29, 1979, the scope of the plan's coverage for eligible dependents was identical to its coverage for employees. All covered males, whether employees or dependents, were treated alike for purposes of hospitalization coverage. All covered females, whether employees or dependents, also were treated alike. Moreover, with one relevant exception, the coverage for males and females was identical. The exception was a limitation on hospital coverage for pregnancy that did not apply to any other hospital confinement.

After the plan was amended in 1979, it provided the same hospitalization coverage for male and female employees themselves for all medical conditions, but it differentiated between female employees and spouses of male employees in its provision of pregnancy-related benefits. . . .

On September 20, 1979, one of petitioner's male employees filed a charge with the EEOC alleging that petitioner had unlawfully refused to provide full insurance coverage for his wife's hospitalization caused by pregnancy; a month later the United Steelworkers filed a similar charge on behalf of other individuals. App. 15–18. Petitioner then commenced an action in the United States District Court for the Eastern District of Virginia, challenging the Commission's guidelines and seeking both declaratory and injunctive relief. . . . Concluding that the benefits of the new Act extended only to female employees, and not to spouses of male employees, the District Court held that petitioner's plan was lawful and enjoined enforcement of the EEOC guidelines relating to pregnancy benefits for employees' spouses. 510 F.Supp. 66 (1981). It also dismissed the EEOC's complaint. App. to Pet. for Cert. 21a. The two cases were consolidated on appeal.

A divided panel of the United States Court of Appeals for the Fourth Circuit reversed, reasoning that since "the company's health insurance plan contains a distinction based on pregnancy that results in less complete medical coverage for male employees with spouses than for female employees with spouses, it is impermissible under the statute." 667 F.2d, at 451. After rehearing the case en banc, the court reaffirmed the conclusion of the panel over the dissent of three judges who believed the statute was intended to protect female employees "in their ability or inability to work," and not to protect spouses of male employees. 682 F.2d 113 (1982). Because the important question presented by the case had

---

days after enactment—April 29, 1979. 92 Stat. 2076. The amendment to petitioner's plan became effective on April 29, 1979.

been decided differently by the United States Court of Appeals for the Ninth Circuit, EEOC v. Lockheed Missiles & Space Co., 680 F.2d 1243 (1982), we granted certiorari 459 U.S. 1069 (1982).

Ultimately the question we must decide is whether petitioner has discriminated against its male employees with respect to their compensation, terms, conditions, or privileges of employment because of their sex within the meaning of § 703(a)(1) of Title VII.[11] Although the Pregnancy Discrimination Act has clarified the meaning of certain terms in this section, neither that Act nor the underlying statute contains a definition of the word "discriminate." In order to decide whether petitioner's plan discriminates against male employees because of *their* sex, we must therefore go beyond the bare statutory language. Accordingly, we shall consider whether Congress, by enacting the Pregnancy Discrimination Act, not only overturned the specific holding in General Electric Co. v. Gilbert, 429 U.S. 125 (1976), but also rejected the test of discrimination employed by the Court in that case. We believe it did. Under the proper test petitioner's plan is unlawful, because the protection it affords to married male employees is less comprehensive than the protection it affords to married female employees.

I

At issue in *General Electric Co. v. Gilbert* was the legality of a disability plan that provided the company's employees with weekly compensation during periods of disability resulting from nonoccupational causes. Because the plan excluded disabilities arising from pregnancy, the District Court and the Court of Appeals concluded that it discriminated against female employees because of their sex. This Court reversed.

After noting that Title VII does not define the term "discrimination," the Court applied an analysis derived from cases construing the Equal Protection Clause of the Fourteenth Amendment to the Constitution. *Id.,* at 133. The *Gilbert* opinion quoted at length from a footnote in Geduldig v. Aiello, 417 U.S. 484 (1974), a case which had upheld the constitutionality of excluding pregnancy coverage under California's disability insurance plan.[12] "Since it is a finding of sex-based

---

[11] Section 703(a), 42 U.S.C. § 2000e–2(a), provides in pertinent part:

"It shall be an unlawful employment practice for an employer—

"(1) to fail or refuse to hire or discharge any individual, or otherwise to discriminate against any individual with respect to his compensation, terms, conditions, or privileges of employment, because of such individual's race, color, religion, sex, or national origin. . . ."

Although the 1978 Act makes clear that this language should be construed to prohibit discrimination against a female employee on the basis of her own pregnancy, it did not remove or limit Title VII's prohibition of discrimination on the basis of the sex of the employee—male or female—which was already present in the Act. As we explain *infra*, petitioner's plan discriminates against male employees on the basis of their sex.

[12] " 'While it is true that only women can become pregnant, it does not follow that every legislative classification concerning pregnancy is a sex-based classification like those considered in *Reed* [*v. Reed*, 404 U.S. 71 (1971)], and *Frontiero* [*v. Richardson*, 411 U.S. 677 (1973)]. Normal

discrimination that must trigger, in a case such as this, the finding of an unlawful employment practice under § 703(a)(1)," the Court added, "*Geduldig* is precisely in point in its holding that an exclusion of pregnancy from a disability-benefits plan providing general coverage is not a gender-based discrimination at all." 429 U.S., at 136.

The dissenters in *Gilbert* took issue with the majority's assumption "that the Fourteenth Amendment standard of discrimination is coterminous with that applicable to Title VII." *Id.*, at 154, n. 6 (Brennan, J., dissenting); *id.*, at 160–161 (Stevens, J., dissenting). As a matter of statutory interpretation, the dissenters rejected the Court's holding that the plan's exclusion of disabilities caused by pregnancy did not constitute discrimination based on sex. As Justice Brennan explained, it was facially discriminatory for the company to devise "a policy that, but for pregnancy, offers protection for all risks, even those that are 'unique to' men or heavily male dominated." *Id.*, at 160. It was inaccurate to describe the program as dividing potential recipients into two groups, pregnant women and nonpregnant persons, because insurance programs "deal with future *risks* rather than historic facts." Rather, the appropriate classification was "between persons who face a risk of pregnancy and those who do not." *Id.*, at 161–162, n. 5 (Stevens, J., dissenting). The company's plan, which was intended to provide employees with protection against the risk of uncompensated unemployment caused by physical disability, discriminated on the basis of sex by giving men protection for all categories of risk but giving women only partial protection. Thus, the dissenters asserted that the statute had been violated because conditions of employment for females were less favorable than for similarly situated males.

When Congress amended Title VII in 1978, it unambiguously expressed its disapproval of both the holding and the reasoning of the Court in the *Gilbert* decision. It incorporated a new subsection in the "definitions" applicable "[f]or the purposes of this subchapter." 42 U.S.C. § 2000e (1976 ed., Supp. V). The first clause of the Act states, quite simply: "The terms 'because of sex' or 'on the basis of sex' include, but are not limited to, because of or on the basis of pregnancy, childbirth, or

---

pregnancy is an objectively identifiable physical condition with unique characteristics. Absent a showing that distinctions involving pregnancy are mere pretexts designed to effect an invidious discrimination against the members of one sex or the other, lawmakers are constitutionally free to include or exclude pregnancy from the coverage of legislation such as this on any reasonable basis, just as with respect to any other physical condition.

" 'The lack of identity between the excluded disability and gender as such under this insurance program becomes clear upon the most cursory analysis. The program divides potential recipients into two groups—pregnant women and nonpregnant persons. While the first group is exclusively female, the second includes members of both sexes.' [417 U.S.], at 496–497, n. 20." 429 U.S., at 134–135.

The principal emphasis in the text of the *Geduldig* opinion, unlike the quoted footnote, was on the reasonableness of the State's cost justifications for the classification in its insurance program.

related medical conditions." § 2000e(k).[14] The House Report stated: "It is the Committee's view that the dissenting Justices correctly interpreted the Act."[15] Similarly, the Senate Report quoted passages from the two dissenting opinions, stating that they "correctly express both the principle and the meaning of title VII."[16] Proponents of the bill repeatedly emphasized that the Supreme Court had erroneously interpreted congressional intent and that amending legislation was necessary to reestablish the principles of Title VII law as they had been understood prior to the *Gilbert* decision. Many of them expressly agreed with the views of the dissenting Justices.[17]

As petitioner argues, congressional discussion focused on the needs of female members of the work force rather than spouses of male employees. This does not create a "negative inference" limiting the scope of the Act to the specific problem that motivated its enactment. See United States v. Turkette, 452 U.S. 576, 591 (1981). *Cf.* McDonald v. Santa Fe Trail Transp. Co., 427 U.S. 273, 285–296 (1976).[18] Congress apparently assumed that existing plans that included benefits for dependents typically provided no less pregnancy-related coverage for the

---

[14] The meaning of the first clause is not limited by the specific language in the second clause, which explains the application of the general principle to women employees.

[15] H.R. Rep. No. 95–948, p. 2 (1978), Legislative History of the Pregnancy Discrimination Act of 1978 (Committee Print prepared for the Senate Committee on Labor and Human Resources), p. 148 (1979) (hereinafter Leg. Hist.).

[16] S. Rep. No. 95–331, pp. 2–3 (1977), Leg. Hist., at 39–40.

[17] *Id.*, at 7–8 ("the bill is merely reestablishing the law as it was understood prior to *Gilbert* by the EEOC and by the lower courts"); H.R. Rep. No. 95–948, *supra*, at 8 (same); 123 Cong. Rec. 10581 (1977) (remarks of Rep. Hawkins) ("H.R. 5055 does not really add anything to title VII as I and, I believe, most of my colleagues in Congress when title VII was enacted in 1964 and amended in 1972, understood the prohibition against sex discrimination in employment. For, it seems only commonsense, that since only women can become pregnant, discrimination against pregnant people is necessarily discrimination against women, and that forbidding discrimination based on sex therefore clearly forbids discrimination based on pregnancy"); *id.*, at 29387 (remarks of Sen. Javits) ("this bill is simply corrective legislation, designed to restore the law with respect to pregnant women employees to the point where it was last year, before the Supreme Court's decision in *Gilbert* . . ."); *id.*, at 29647; *id.*, at 29655 (remarks of Sen. Javits) ("What we are doing is leaving the situation the way it was before the Supreme Court decided the Gilbert case last year"); 124 Cong. Rec. 21436 (1978) (remarks of Rep. Sarasin) ("This bill would restore the interpretation of title VII prior to that decision").

For statements expressly approving the views of the dissenting Justices that pregnancy discrimination is discrimination on the basis of sex, *see* Leg. Hist., at 18 (remarks of Sen. Bayh, Mar. 18, 1977, 123 Cong. Rec. 8144); 24 (remarks of Rep. Hawkins, Apr. 5, 1977, 123 Cong. Rec. 10582); 67 (remarks of Sen. Javits, Sept. 15, 1977, 123 Cong. Rec. 29387); 73 (remarks of Sen. Bayh, Sept. 16, 1977, 123 Cong. Rec. 29641); 134 (remarks of Sen. Mathias, Sept. 16, 1977, 123 Cong. Rec. 29663–29664); 168 (remarks of Rep. Sarasin, July 18, 1978, 124 Cong. Rec. 21436). *See also* Discrimination on the Basis of Pregnancy, 1977, Hearings on S. 995 before the Subcommittee on Labor of the Senate Committee on Human Resources, 95th Cong., 1st Sess., 13 (1977) (statement of Sen. Bayh); *id.*, at 37, 51 (statement of Assistant Attorney General for Civil Rights Drew S. Days).

[18] In *McDonald*, the Court held that 42 U.S.C. § 1981, which gives "[a]ll persons within the jurisdiction of the United States . . . the same right in every State and Territory to make and enforce contracts . . . as is enjoyed by white citizens," protects whites against discrimination on the basis of race even though the "immediate impetus for the bill was the necessity for further relief of the constitutionally emancipated former Negro slaves." 427 U.S., at 289.

wives of male employees than they did for female employees. . . .[19] Proponents of the legislation stressed throughout the debates that Congress had always intended to protect *all* individuals from sex discrimination in employment—including but not limited to pregnant women workers.[21] Against this background we review the terms of the amended statute to decide whether petitioner has unlawfully discriminated against its male employees.

II

Section 703(a) makes it an unlawful employment practice for an employer to "discriminate against any individual with respect to his compensation, terms, conditions, or privileges of employment, because of such individual's race, color, religion, sex, or national origin. . . ." 42 U.S.C. § 2000e–2(a)(1). Health insurance and other fringe benefits are "compensation, terms, conditions, or privileges of employment." Male as well as female employees are protected against discrimination. Thus, if a private employer were to provide complete health insurance coverage for the dependents of its female employees, and no coverage at all for the dependents of its male employees, it would violate Title VII. Such a practice would not pass the simple test of Title VII discrimination that we enunciated in Los Angeles Dept. of Water & Power v. Manhart, 435 U.S. 702, 711 (1978), for it would treat a male employee with dependents " 'in a manner which but for that person's sex would be different.' " The same result would be reached even if the magnitude of the discrimination were smaller. For example, a plan that provided complete hospitalization coverage for the spouses of female employees but did not cover spouses of male employees when they had broken bones would violate Title VII by discriminating against male employees.

Petitioner's practice is just as unlawful. Its plan provides limited pregnancy-related benefits for employees' wives, and affords more extensive coverage for employees' spouses for all other medical conditions

---

[19] This, of course, was true of petitioner's plan prior to the enactment of the statute. *See supra*, at 672. *See* S. Rep. No. 95–331, *supra* n. 16, at 6, Leg. Hist., at 43 ("Presumably because plans which provide comprehensive medical coverage for spouses of women employees but not spouses of male employees are rare, we are not aware of any Title VII litigation concerning such plans. It is certainly not this committee's desire to encourage the institution of such plans"); 123 Cong. Rec. 29663 (1977) (remarks of Sen. Cranston); Brief for Respondent 31–33, n. 31.

[21] *See, e.g.,* 123 Cong. Rec. 7539 (1977) (remarks of Sen. Williams) ("the Court has ignored the congressional intent in enacting title VII of the Civil Rights Act—that intent was to protect all individuals from unjust employment discrimination, including pregnant workers"); *id.,* at 29385, 29652. In light of statements such as these, it would be anomalous to hold that Congress provided that an employee's pregnancy is sex-based, while a spouse's pregnancy is gender-neutral.

During the course of the Senate debate on the Pregnancy Discrimination Act, Senator Bayh and Senator Cranston both expressed the belief that the new Act would prohibit the exclusion of pregnancy coverage for spouses if spouses were otherwise fully covered by an insurance plan. *See id.,* at 29642, 29663. Because our holding relies on the 1978 legislation only to the extent that it unequivocally rejected the *Gilbert* decision, and ultimately we rely on our understanding of general Title VII principles, we attach no more significance to these two statements than to the many other comments by both Senators and Congressmen disapproving the Court's reasoning and conclusion in *Gilbert*. *See* n. 17, *supra*.

requiring hospitalization. Thus the husbands of female employees receive a specified level of hospitalization coverage for all conditions; the wives of male employees receive such coverage except for pregnancy-related conditions. Although *Gilbert* concluded that an otherwise inclusive plan that singled out pregnancy-related benefits for exclusion was nondiscriminatory on its face, because only women can become pregnant, Congress has unequivocally rejected that reasoning. The 1978 Act makes clear that it is discriminatory to treat pregnancy-related conditions less favorably than other medical conditions. Thus petitioner's plan unlawfully gives married male employees a benefit package for their dependents that is less inclusive than the dependency coverage provided to married female employees.

There is no merit to petitioner's argument that the prohibitions of Title VII do not extend to discrimination against pregnant spouses because the statute applies only to discrimination in employment. A two-step analysis demonstrates the fallacy in this contention. The Pregnancy Discrimination Act has now made clear that, for all Title VII purposes, discrimination based on a woman's pregnancy is, on its face, discrimination because of her sex. And since the sex of the spouse is always the opposite of the sex of the employee, it follows inexorably that discrimination against female spouses in the provision of fringe benefits is also discrimination against male employees. *Cf.* Wengler v. Druggists Mutual Ins. Co., 446 U.S. 142, 147 (1980). By making clear that an employer could not discriminate on the basis of an employee's pregnancy, Congress did not erase the original prohibition against discrimination on the basis of an employee's sex.

In short, Congress' rejection of the premises of *General Electric Co. v. Gilbert* forecloses any claim that an insurance program excluding pregnancy coverage for female beneficiaries and providing complete coverage to similarly situated male beneficiaries does not discriminate on the basis of sex. Petitioner's plan is the mirror image of the plan at issue in *Gilbert*. The pregnancy limitation in this case violates Title VII by discriminating against male employees.

The judgment of the Court of Appeals is

Affirmed.

■ JUSTICE REHNQUIST, with whom JUSTICE POWELL joins, dissenting.

In *General Electric Co. v. Gilbert,* 429 U.S. 125 (1976), we held that an exclusion of pregnancy from a disability-benefits plan is not discrimination "because of [an] individual's . . . sex" within the meaning of Title VII of the Civil Rights Act of 1964, § 703(a)(1), 78 Stat. 255, 42 U.S.C. § 2000e–2(a)(1). . . . Under our decision in *Gilbert,* petitioner's otherwise inclusive benefits plan that excludes pregnancy benefits for a male employee's spouse clearly would not violate Title VII. For a different result to obtain, *Gilbert* would have to be judicially overruled by this

Court or Congress would have to legislatively overrule our decision in its entirety by amending Title VII.

Today, the Court purports to find the latter by relying on the Pregnancy Discrimination Act of 1978, Pub.L. 95–555, 92 Stat. 2076, 42 U.S.C. § 2000e(k) (1976 ed., Supp. V), a statute that plainly speaks only of female employees affected by pregnancy and says nothing about spouses of male employees. Congress, of course, was free to legislatively overrule *Gilbert* in whole or in part, and there is no question but that the Pregnancy Discrimination Act manifests congressional dissatisfaction with the result we reached in *Gilbert*. But I think the Court reads far more into the Pregnancy Discrimination Act than Congress put there, and that therefore it is the Court, and not Congress, which is now overruling *Gilbert*.

In a case presenting a relatively simple question of statutory construction, the Court pays virtually no attention to the language of the Pregnancy Discrimination Act or the legislative history pertaining to that language. The Act provides in relevant part:

"The terms 'because of sex' or 'on the basis of sex' include, but are not limited to, because of or on the basis of pregnancy, childbirth, or related medical conditions; and women affected by pregnancy, childbirth, or related medical conditions shall be treated the same for all employment-related purposes, including receipt of benefits under fringe benefit programs, as other persons not so affected but similar in their ability or inability to work. . . ." 42 U.S.C. § 2000e(k) (1976 ed., Supp. V).

The Court recognizes that this provision is merely definitional and that "[u]ltimately the question we must decide is whether petitioner has discriminated against its male employees . . . because of their sex within the meaning of § 703(a)(1)" of Title VII. Section 703(a)(1) provides in part:

"It shall be an unlawful employment practice for an employer . . . to fail or refuse to hire or to discharge any individual, or otherwise to discriminate against any individual with respect to his compensation, terms, conditions, or privileges of employment, because of such individual's race, color, religion, sex, or national origin. . . ." 42 U.S.C. § 2000e–2(a)(1).

It is undisputed that in § 703(a)(1) the word "individual" refers to an employee or applicant for employment. As modified by the first clause of the definitional provision of the Pregnancy Discrimination Act, the proscription in § 703(a)(1) is for discrimination "against any individual . . . because of such individual's . . . pregnancy, childbirth, or related medical conditions." This can only be read as referring to the pregnancy of an employee.

That this result was not inadvertent on the part of Congress is made very evident by the second clause of the Act, language that the Court essentially ignores in its opinion. When Congress in this clause further explained the proscription it was creating by saying that "women affected by pregnancy . . . shall be treated the same . . . as other persons not so affected but *similar in their ability or inability to work*" it could only have been referring to *female employees*. The Court of Appeals below stands alone in thinking otherwise. . . .

The plain language of the Pregnancy Discrimination Act leaves little room for the Court's conclusion that the Act was intended to extend beyond female employees. The Court concedes that "congressional discussion focused on the needs of female members of the work force rather than spouses of male employees." In fact, the singular focus of discussion on the problems of the *pregnant worker* is striking.

When introducing the Senate Report on the bill that later became the Pregnancy Discrimination Act, its principal sponsor, Senator Williams, explained:

> "Because of the Supreme Court's decision in the *Gilbert* case, this legislation is necessary to provide fundamental protection against sex discrimination for our Nation's 42 million *working women*." . . .

. . . [T]he Congressional Record is overflowing with similar statements by individual Members of Congress expressing their intention to ensure with the Pregnancy Discrimination Act that working women are not treated differently because of pregnancy. Consistent with these views, all three Committee Reports on the bills that led to the Pregnancy Discrimination Act expressly state that the Act would require employers to treat pregnant employees the same as "other employees."

The Court tr[ie]s to avoid the impact of this legislative history by saying that it "does not create a 'negative inference' limiting the scope of the Act to the specific problem that motivated its enactment." This reasoning might have some force if the legislative history was silent on an arguably related issue. But the legislative history is not silent. . . .

Under our decision in *General Electric Co. v. Gilbert,* petitioner's exclusion of pregnancy benefits for male employees' spouses would not violate Title VII. Since nothing in the Pregnancy Discrimination Act even arguably reaches beyond female employees affected by pregnancy, *Gilbert* requires that we reverse the Court of Appeals. Because the Court concludes otherwise, I dissent.

QUESTIONS

1.   The *Newport News* majority held that Congress, in enacting the 1978 pregnancy discrimination amendments, rejected the rationale of the *Gilbert* decision. There, Justice Rehnquist identified two classes of individuals, pregnant persons, and non-pregnant persons. This was not sex discrimination, according to the majority, because the second class consisted of both women and men. While the pregnancy discrimination amendments prohibited classifications based on pregnancy by subsuming them under sex discrimination, do those amendments discredit other classification exercises of the *Gilbert* variety?

2. Consider how the Pregnancy Discrimination Act (PDA) would function in a different context (see the relevant text of the PDA in note 1 of *Newport News*, *supra*, and in section § 2000e(k) of the Civil Rights Act of 1964, *supra* Section VI.A.1). Suppose that a company provides health care benefits to its employees. The plan includes coverage of routine physical exams and other preventative measures such as immunization shots, but it excludes both male and female contraceptive methods, prescription and non-prescription, when used for the sole purpose of contraception. A female employee of child-bearing age brings a suit against the company claiming that the company discriminates against its female employees under the PDA by not providing coverage of contraception.

Is contraception "related" to pregnancy under the PDA? Does it make a difference that both male and female contraception is excluded under the health plan? Does it make a difference that prescription contraception is currently available only for women?

The PDA was enacted to amend Title VII of the Civil Rights Act, which states generally that "[i]t shall be an unlawful employment practice for an employer . . . to discriminate against any individual with respect to his compensation, terms, conditions, or privileges of employment, because of such individual's . . . sex." Suppose that the health plan discussed above covers prescription drugs, devices, and services that are used to prevent the occurrence of medical conditions that occur only in men, such as prostate cancer and male-pattern baldness. How does this affect the female employee's claim?

Suppose that female contraception is a lot more expensive than male contraception. Therefore, women have greater out-of-pocket expenses than men on the same plan. How would a claim based on this fact fare under Title VII? *See* In re Union Pacific Railroad Employment Practices Litigation, 479 F.3d 936 (8th Cir. 2007).

3. The majority took as a given that "since the sex of the spouse is always the opposite of the sex of the employee, it follows inexorably that discrimination against female spouses in the provision of fringe benefits is also discrimination against male employees." In 2015, in Obergefell v. Hodges, 135 S.Ct. 2584 (2015), the Supreme Court ruled that couples of the same-sex may not be deprived of the right to marry. By that time, several dozen state legislatures had already enacted laws permitting same-sex marriage. In the wake of these developments, does the *Newport News* majority's assumption still hold? If it does not, can an employee benefits policy of the kind at issue in *Newport News* still be said to discriminate on the basis of sex?

4. After *Bostock*, *supra* Section VI.A.1, may an employer exclude from its employees' health insurance package coverage of medical and surgical treatment for gender-reassignment? May it do so if it declines to cover any "voluntary" procedures? Are medical costs associated with pregnancy "voluntary"?

NOTE: OVERRIDING SUPREME COURT PRECEDENTS

Gilbert is but one of dozens of instances in which Congress has not taken kindly to the Supreme Court's treatment of its work product. As Professor William Eskridge noted nearly three decades ago, Congress has often overridden Supreme Court precedents that interpret and apply federal statutes in a manner with which Congress disagrees:

> Based on . . . comprehensive empirical evidence documenting congressional responses to the Court's statutory interpretation decisions, . . . Congress and its committees are aware of the Court's statutory decisions, devote significant efforts toward analyzing their policy implications, and override those decisions with a frequency heretofore unreported. Congressional overrides are most likely when a Supreme Court interpretation reveals an ideologically fragmented Court, relies on the text's plain meaning and ignores legislative signals, and/or rejects positions taken by federal, state, or local governments.

> . . . [A] dynamic game exists between the Court, the relevant congressional committees, Congress, and the President. In this game, ultimate statutory policy is set through a sequential process by which each player—including the Court—tries to impose its policy preferences. The game is a dynamic one because each player is responsive to the preferences of other players and because the preferences of the players change as information is generated and distributed in the game. . . .

> Descriptively, a central theme is that the Court's statutory interpretation decisions are more responsive to the expectations of the current Congress than to those of the enacting Congress. But the Court is also responsive to its own institutional and personal preferences—especially its preference for coherence and predictability in the law. . . . If the Court is more responsive to the preferences of the current Congress than to those of the enacting Congress, the question remains: Should the Court be playing such a game? To lawyers, this game may seem like an "unjudicial," if not highly irregular, way for the Court to carry out its statutory interpretation duties, which have in the legal literature traditionally been characterized as a search for Congress' "intent" or application of a statute's "plain meaning." . . .

> According to traditional political theory, the Court's willingness to consider current legislative preferences and its desire to avoid legislative overrides rests upon a specific and widely held ideology regarding the Court's role in our political system. Under this ideology, the Court is part of our nation's pluralist political system, just as Congress and the President are. Like the other branches, the Court plays a specialized role in the overall lawmaking process, but a role that facilitates rather than obstructs the operation of the pluralist system. The Court is, therefore, not normally "countermajoritarian," though sometimes it may push our

pluralism to make adjustments ensuring the participation of relevant groups (and hence the perpetuation of pluralism and the stability it brings). This vision sees a limited but important role for the Court as constitutional interpreter and a most important role for the Court as statutory interpreter. As statutory interpreter, the Court is a faithful agent of majoritarian policymaking and carries out statutory policies as Congress desires.

An ambiguity rests in the lessons of this traditional ideology. If the Court is to be a facilitator of majoritarian policies, it is unclear which majority it should obey. Should it obey the congressional majority that enacted the statute or the majority in the current Congress, which may not be willing to enact anything like the original statute? The Court cannot ignore either Congress. It needs to pay attention to the preferences of the enacting Congress, not just to assert "rule of law" values, but also to reassure interest groups that, when they receive legislation from Congress, their legislative deal will not entirely collapse over time. But the Court also needs to pay attention to the preferences of the current Congress, to facilitate the efficient operation of pluralism. If the Court completely ignored current legislative preferences and interest group configurations, Congress would have to revisit statutes constantly to update them-a job the Court can perform more efficiently for a wide range of issues. Because most of the statutory issues decided by the Court are those for which there is no completely verifiable "deal" in the enacting Congress, the preferences of the current Congress are usually more important for the Court than are the preferences of the enacting Congress.

The evidence suggests that during the time frame of this Article (1967–90), the Court has tacitly followed the ideology just described. This may be changing, however. Voices within the Court itself are openly questioning this traditional ideology, and academics and judges writing about issues of statutory interpretation are criticizing the Court for its practices in the pluralist system. A discussion of the normative desirability of the Court's pluralist ideology first should focus upon the now-ascendant "formalist" ideology. Formalism offers both a critique of the Court's traditional approach and an affirmative new approach. The difficulties with formalism suggest a different, "normative" critique, which argues that the Court ought to challenge the pluralist system more often to protect values not protected by normal politics.

Formalism argues that constitutional "rule of law" values require the Court to follow only the statutory language as understood by both Congress and the President at the time of enactment. . . . The formalist group on the Court is not interested in the preferences of the current Congress. Thus, they have vigorously attacked the traditional doctrines by which the Court has explicitly considered post-enactment congressional preferences. . . . Not surprisingly, Congress is more likely to override Supreme Court statutory decisions following such a formalist approach. . . .

While aware that the Court has often followed the preferences of current Congresses, formalists believe the Court is doing the country a greater service when it ignores evidence of subsequent congressional purposes and attitudes. They argue that the Court should refuse to do Congress' job. . . . Formalism raises important questions about the Court's traditional accommodationist approach to statutory interpretation and makes an attractive case for a more confrontational approach. However, there are several problems with such a strategy of confrontation. One problem arises out of the nature of formalist reasoning and raises the question of whether the Court's formalists have really made out a case for rejecting the Court's traditional accommodationist attitude. To make its case, formalism must root its argument in an authoritative source. The obvious source for the Court's formalism is the Constitution, but the Constitution offers little if any support for such a vision of statutory interpretation. Nothing in the text of the Constitution provides reliable support for formalism. . . .

A second problem with the formalist critique is that it requires the Court to act in a more countermajoritarian manner than its traditional approach. Both traditional and formalist ideologies view the Court as Congress' "agent" in statutory interpretation. Like commercial agents in the real world, the Court's role is a subordinate one, implementing directives issued by the principal (Congress) over time. Like principals in the real world, Congress makes the big choices and expects its agent to implement them. The question then becomes one of who is a better agent, the accommodationist who keeps one eye on the principal's current as well as historical preferences, or the formalist, who only has eyes for the principal's original intent or for the plain terms of the written directives? Obviously the principal would rather have the agent who follows the dynamic purpose of his directives, rather than their strict, literal meaning. . . .

This difficulty is compounded by the democratic process' reliance on the Court's past practice. Since 1937, it appears that the Court has generally been in sync with the pluralist political process in statutory interpretation. During this period, Congress has enacted thousands of statutes, which were surely written and implemented with the baseline assumption that the Court (or, increasingly, an agency) would interpret the statutes over time to carry out Congress' overall goals in a practical fashion. If, as formalists such as Justice Scalia suggest, the Court in the 1990's were to replace its accommodationist philosophy with a more confrontational one, the Court's move would be tantamount to a game of "bait and switch"-one that lures the mark into enacting a statute by holding out the promise of helpful dynamic interpretation (bait), but then eviscerates the statute over time by stingy interpretation (switch). . . .

William N. Eskridge, Jr., *Overriding Supreme Court Statutory Interpretation Decisions*, 101 Yale L.J. 331 (1991).

During the period Professor Eskridge first observed, both Congress and the Court seemed relatively responsive to the work product of the other, although Eskridge and a co-author anticipated the possibility that the Court might take on a more antagonistic attitude toward the work product of Congress.

[O]ur current study updates the 1991 Eskridge study, bringing the overrides record forward twenty years (so accounting for overrides 1967–2011) . . . [T]he 1990s was actually the golden age of overrides, with an unprecedented explosion of statutes resetting statutory policy in important ways. After 1998, however, we found that overrides declined as dramatically as they had ascended, though they have not (yet) "fallen to almost none." . . .

Overrides never went away, but the climate for overrides has changed. . . . The most-publicized overrides, such as the 1991 CRA, are what we call restorative overrides: maintaining that the Supreme Court has reneged on historic legislative commitments, Congress "restores" what it considers the correct understanding of the statutory scheme, often the understanding that an agency had implemented before being rejected by the Court. Restorative overrides such as the 1991 CRA are an important phenomenon and include other landmark statutes, such as the Pregnancy Discrimination Act of 1978, the Voting Rights Act Amendments of 1982 and the Voting Rights Act Reauthorization and Amendments Act of 2006, the ADA Amendments Act of 2008, the Lilly Ledbetter Fair Pay Act of 2009, and the Family Smoking Prevention and Tobacco Control Act. [For example,] Justice Ginsburg's dissent in *Vance* [*v. Ball State University*, 570 U.S. 421 (2013),]* urged Congress to restore the proper law for Title VII precisely along these lines. Most restorative overrides involve high-salience issues of public law, such as civil and political rights. Many of them divide Congress along strict party lines—more so today than twenty years ago. . . .

[T]he large majority of overrides are not well-publicized restorative overrides like the 1991 CRA—but are instead more routine policy-updating overrides, namely, override statutes frequently supported by bipartisan majorities in Congress that have as their stated goal the updating of public law, rather than "correction" of judicial mistakes. Updating overrides often occur

---

* Editors' Note: *Vance* concerned whether a coworker who is vested with the authority to oversee the daily work of another worker could be considered a supervisor for the purpose of determining employer liability for harassment under Title VII. By a 5–4 split, a majority of the Court concluded that, for the purposes of liability for workplace harassment under Title VII, the definition of a "supervisor" is limited to a person empowered to take tangible employment action against the victim.

years, decades, or, in two cases, centuries, after the Supreme Court decisions being overridden and do not reflect ideological rebuffs of the Court. Landmark statutes such as the Copyrights Act of 1976, the Bankruptcy Reform Act of 1978, the Judicial Improvements Act of 1990, the Antiterrorism and Effective Death Penalty Act (AEDPA) of 1996, the Illegal Immigration Reform and Immigrant Responsibility Act of 1996, the Telecommunications Act of 1996, and the IRS Restructuring and Reform Act of 1998, are just some examples of broad bipartisan laws that ambitiously reset statutory policies and, in the process, override bushels of Supreme Court opinions. Notably, it is these policy-updating overrides, and not so much the restorative ones, that have dried up most dramatically after 1998. . . . We do not offer a causal account, only a strong set of correlations . . . . If the past is any guide, the Court's interpretation of Title VII in *Vance* ought to be vulnerable to a congressional override. A failure of Congress to override *Vance* in this decade would support the hypothesis that the current downturn in override activity is a long-term trend and will persist . . . .

The big override winners are governmental institutions . . . . Federal agencies win almost seventy percent of their cases before the Supreme Court, and Congress is much less likely to override the Court when a federal agency defends the Court's decision. Conversely, when the Court rejects a federal agency interpretation, that decision is much more likely to be overridden by Congress than the average Supreme Court decision, much less a decision supported by the agency. More generally, we found that the Department of Justice or another federal agency was noticeably involved in seventy percent of the 275 overrides reported in our study—and the agency view prevailed with Congress in three-quarters of those overrides. . . .

What values and goals does an override potentially serve? Do overrides actually serve those goals? We consider three important public-regarding goals: the predictable operation of the rule of law, democratic legitimacy, and institutional efficiency and good public policy. Especially when adopted through an open and deliberative process, overrides most clearly serve democratic legitimacy goals—but we were surprised that overrides also frequently advanced rule of law values. Tentatively, from an empirical perspective, our study also supports the proposition that most overrides often advance the goal of "good" public policy—and almost always update public policy to reflect current values and priorities. . . .

For Congress, the central lesson of our study is that overrides are a sign of health for the greatest legislature in history: when Congress is churning out overrides of Supreme Court statutory decisions, it is making solid contributions to the legitimate evolution of public policy and even the rule of law. We are impressed with the ability of Congress to advance public projects

after a transparent and deliberative process in which leading
stakeholding groups and institutions are well represented. Indeed,
one of the most surprising features of our study is that *Carolene*[25]
groups and women fare better in the legislative process than in the
judicial one. Another surprising feature is that conservative
policies fare almost as well as liberal ones when Congress overrides
the Court—so there is no necessary partisan political reason to
reject or denigrate overrides. . . .

Matthew R. Christiansen & William N. Eskridge, Jr., *Congressional
Overrides of Supreme Court Statutory Interpretation Decisions, 1967–2011*,
92 Tex. L. Rev. 1317 (2014).

NOTE AND QUESTIONS

1. Was it surprising to learn that federal agencies not only prevail more
often before the Court, but also in the congressional overrides process? What
about "*Carolene* groups"? Who might this suggest are the winners and losers
if Congress overrides Supreme Court statutory interpretation precedents
with decreasing frequency?

2. Christiansen and Eskridge distinguish "restorative" overrides from
"routine policy-updating" overrides, and note that the decline in observed
congressional override behavior can be traced primarily to the decreasing
frequency with which Congress has engaged in routine policy-updating
overrides. What factors might you identify for a decline in routine policy-
updating overrides?

3. Christiansen and Eskridge predict that if the Congress of the 2010s
behaved as past Congresses had, the Court's interpretation in *Vance* ought
to be vulnerable to override. As of late-2020, however, Congress has yet to
mount a serious effort to override *Vance*.

3. WHEN LEGISLATIVE RESPONSES TO JUDICIAL INTERPRETATIONS TAKE EFFECT

When Congress overrides a Supreme Court statutory interpretation
precedent as in the case of the 1978 Pregnancy Discrimination Act, new
problems can arise. To what conduct does the new legislation apply? Only
to events occurring after enactment, or to prior events (at least within
the statute of limitations) as well? If the statute does not apply to prior
events, Congress will not fully have corrected the Supreme Court's error,
see, e.g., Rivers v. Roadway Express, supra Section VI.B. But complete
correction potentially entails the retroactive application of a new law,
and therefore raises fairness (or due process) concerns, if the new law
would change the legal consequences of prior conduct to the detriment of
the prior actor. On the other hand, as we have seen, *supra* Section VI.B,
not every statutory correction of, or change to, a past legal standard is
"genuinely retroactive" in this sense. As the ensuing case illustrates, in

---

[25] United States v. Carolene Prods. Co., 304 U.S. 144, 152 n.4 (1938) (articulating more
aggressive judicial review for laws harming "discrete and insular minorities").

order to assess whether a statute has retroactive effect, it is necessary to identify what conduct Congress sought to impact.

Congress may in any event specify the temporal application of a new statute, including one that corrects past judicial errors. Interpretive problems arise when Congress fails to make clear its intention (if any, and if so, to what extent) to confer retrospective effect on new legislation. Courts must then search the text and related sources for clues. In the absence or insufficiency of indicia of Congressional intent, courts will generally construe a new or a corrective enactment only prospectively. (Contrast this rule of construction with the general common-law rule that judge-made rules apply not only forward but also backward in time.) The Supreme Court considered the temporal effect of the Pregnancy Discrimination Act in *AT&T Corp. v. Noreen Hulteen et al.*

AT&T Corp. v. Noreen Hulteen et al.

Supreme Court of the United States, 2009.
556 U.S. 701, 129 S.Ct. 1962, 173 L.Ed.2d 898.

■ JUSTICE SOUTER delivered the opinion of the Court[, in which CHIEF JUSTICE ROBERTS, JUSTICE STEVENS, JUSTICE SCALIA, JUSTICE KENNEDY, JUSTICE THOMAS, and JUSTICE ALITO joined].

The question is whether an employer necessarily violates the Pregnancy Discrimination Act (PDA), 42 U.S.C. § 2000e(k), when it pays pension benefits calculated in part under an accrual rule, applied only prior to the PDA, that gave less retirement credit for pregnancy leave than for medical leave generally. We hold there is no necessary violation; and the benefit calculation rule in this case is part of a bona fide seniority system under § 703(h) of Title VII of the Civil Rights Act of 1964, 42 U.S.C. § 2000e–2(h), which insulates it from challenge.

I

Since 1914, AT&T Corporation (then American Telephone & Telegraph Company) and its Bell System Operating Companies, including Pacific Telephone and Telegraph Company (hereinafter, collectively, AT&T), have provided pensions and other benefits based on a seniority system that relies upon an employee's term of employment, understood as the period of service at the company minus uncredited leave time.

In the 1960s and early to mid-1970s, AT&T employees on "disability" leave got full service credit for the entire periods of absence, but those who took "personal" leaves of absence received maximum service credit of 30 days. Leave for pregnancy was treated as personal, not disability. AT&T altered this practice in 1977 by adopting its Maternity Payment Plan (MPP), entitling pregnant employees to disability benefits and service credit for up to six weeks of leave. If the absence went beyond six weeks, however, it was treated as personal leave, with no further benefits or credit, whereas employees out on disability unrelated to pregnancy continued to receive full service credit for the duration of absence. This differential treatment of pregnancy leave, under both the pre-1977 plan and the MPP, was lawful: in *General Elec. Co. v. Gilbert*, 429 U.S. 125 (1976), this Court concluded that a disability benefit plan excluding disabilities related to pregnancy was not sex-based discrimination within the meaning of Title VII of the Civil Rights Act of 1964, 78 Stat. 253, as amended, 42 U.S.C. § 2000e *et seq.*

In 1978, Congress amended Title VII by passing the PDA, 92 Stat. 2076, 42 U.S.C. § 2000e(k), which superseded *Gilbert* so as to make it "clear that it is discriminatory to treat pregnancy-related conditions less favorably than other medical conditions." *Newport News Shipbuilding & Dry Dock Co. v. EEOC*, 462 U.S. 669, 684 (1983). On April 29, 1979, the effective date of the PDA, AT&T adopted its Anticipated Disability Plan which replaced the MPP and provided service credit for pregnancy leave on the same basis as leave taken for other temporary disabilities. AT&T did not, however, make any retroactive adjustments to the service credit calculations of women who had been subject to the pre-PDA personnel policies.

Four of those women are named respondents in this case. Each of them received less service credit for pregnancy leave than she would have accrued on the same leave for disability: seven months less for Noreen Hulteen; about six months for Eleanora Collet; and about two for Elizabeth Snyder and Linda Porter. Respondents Hulteen, Collet, and Snyder have retired from AT&T respondent Porter has yet to. If her total term of employment had not been decreased due to her pregnancy leave, each would be entitled to a greater pension benefit.

Eventually, each of the individual respondents and respondent Communications Workers of America (CWA), the collective-bargaining representative for the majority of AT&T's nonmanagement employees, filed charges of discrimination with the Equal Employment Opportunity Commission (EEOC), alleging discrimination on the basis of sex and pregnancy in violation of Title VII. In 1998, the EEOC issued a Letter of Determination finding reasonable cause to believe that AT&T had discriminated against respondent Hulteen and "a class of other similarly-situated female employees whose adjusted [commencement of service] date has been used to determine eligibility for a service or disability pension, the amount of pension benefits, and eligibility for certain other benefits and programs, including early retirement offerings." The EEOC issued a notice of right to sue to each named respondent and the CWA (collectively, Hulteen), and Hulteen filed suit in the United States District Court for the Northern District of California.

On dueling motions for summary judgment, the District Court held itself bound by a prior Ninth Circuit decision, *Pallas v. Pacific Bell*, 940 F.2d 1324 (1991), which found a Title VII violation where post-PDA retirement eligibility calculations incorporated pre-PDA accrual rules that differentiated on the basis of pregnancy. [Citation.] The Circuit, en banc, affirmed and held that *Pallas*'s conclusion that "calculation of service credit excluding time spent on pregnancy leave violates Title VII was, and is, correct." 498 F.3d 1001, 1003 (2007).

The Ninth Circuit's decision directly conflicts with the holdings of the Sixth and Seventh Circuits that reliance on a pre-PDA differential accrual rule to determine pension benefits does not constitute a current violation of Title VII. *See Ameritech Benefit Plan Comm. v. Communication Workers of Am.*, 220 F.3d 814 (CA7 2000) (finding no actionable Title VII violation given the existence of a bona fide seniority system); *Leffman v. Sprint Corp.*, 481 F.3d 428 (CA6 2007) (characterizing claim as challenging the continuing effects of past discrimination rather than alleging a current Title VII violation). We granted certiorari in order to resolve this split, 554 U.S. ___, 128 S.Ct. 2957 (2008), and now reverse the judgment of the Ninth Circuit.

II

Title VII makes it an "unlawful employment practice" for an employer "to discriminate against any individual with respect to his compensation, terms, conditions, or privileges of employment, because of such individual's . . . sex." 42 U.S.C. § 2000e–2(a)(1). Generally, a claim under Title VII must be filed "within one hundred and eighty days after the alleged unlawful employment practice occurred," § 2000e–5(e)(1). In this case, Hulteen has identified the challenged practice as applying the terms of AT&T's seniority system to calculate and pay pension benefits to women who took pregnancy leaves before April 29, 1979. She says the claim is timely because the old service credit differential for pregnancy leave was carried forward through the system's calculations so as to produce an effect in the amount of the benefit when payments began.

There is no question that the payment of pension benefits in this case is a function of a seniority system, given the fact that calculating benefits under the pension plan depends in part on an employee's term of employment. As we have said, "[a] 'seniority system' is a scheme that, alone or in tandem with non-'seniority' criteria, allots to employees ever improving employment rights and benefits as their relative lengths of pertinent employment increase." *California Brewers Assn. v. Bryant*, 444 U.S. 598, 605–606 (1980) (footnote omitted). Hulteen is also undoubtedly correct that AT&T's personnel policies affecting the calculation of any employee's start date should be considered "ancillary rules" and elements of the system, necessary for it to operate at all, being rules that "define which passages of time will 'count' towards the accrual of seniority and which will not." *Id.*, at 607.

But contrary to Hulteen's position, establishing the continuity of a seniority system whose results depend in part on obsolete rules entailing disadvantage to once-pregnant employees does not resolve this case. Although adopting a service credit rule unfavorable to those out on pregnancy leave would violate Title VII today, a seniority system does not necessarily violate the statute when it gives current effect to such rules that operated before the PDA. "[S]eniority systems are afforded special treatment under Title VII," *Trans World Airlines, Inc. v. Hardison*, 432 U.S. 63, 81 (1977), reflecting Congress's understanding that their stability is valuable in its own right. Hence, § 703(h):

> "Notwithstanding any other provision of this subchapter, it shall not be an unlawful employment practice for an employer to apply different standards of compensation, or different terms, conditions, or privileges of employment pursuant to a bona fide seniority . . . system . . . provided that such differences are not the result of an intention to discriminate because of race, color, religion, sex, or national origin . . . ." 42 U.S.C. § 2000e–2(h).

Benefit differentials produced by a bona fide seniority-based pension plan are permitted unless they are "the result of an intention to discriminate." *Ibid.*

In *Teamsters v. United States*, 431 U.S. 324 (1977), advantages of a seniority system flowed disproportionately to white, as against minority, employees, because of an employer's prior discrimination in job assignments. We recognized that this "disproportionate distribution of advantages does in a very real sense operate to freeze the status quo of prior discriminatory employment practices[,] [b]ut both the literal terms of § 703(h) and the legislative history of Title VII demonstrate that Congress considered this very effect of many seniority systems and extended a measure of immunity to them." *Id.*, at 350 (internal quotation marks omitted). "[T]he unmistakable purpose of § 703(h) was to make clear that the routine application of a bona fide seniority system would not be unlawful under Title VII." *Id.*, at 352. The seniority system in *Teamsters* exemplified a bona fide system without any discriminatory terms (the discrimination having occurred in executive action hiring employees and assigning jobs), so that the Court could conclude that the system "did not have its genesis in . . . discrimination, and . . . has been maintained free from any illegal purpose." *Id.*, at 356.

AT&T's system must also be viewed as bona fide, that is, as a system that has no discriminatory terms, with the consequence that subsection (h) controls the result here, just as in *Teamsters*. It is true that in this case the pre-April 29, 1979 rule of differential treatment was an element of the seniority system itself; but it did not taint the system under the terms of subsection (h), because this Court held in *Gilbert* that an accrual rule limiting the seniority credit for time taken for pregnancy leave did not unlawfully discriminate on the basis of sex. As a matter of law, at that time, "an exclusion of pregnancy from a disability-benefits plan providing general coverage [was] not a gender-based discrimination at all." 429 U.S., at 136. Although the PDA would have made it discriminatory to continue the accrual policies of the old rule, AT&T amended that rule as of the effective date of the Act, April 29, 1979; the new one, treating pregnancy and other temporary disabilities the same way, remains a part of AT&T's seniority system today. . . .

The only way to conclude here that the subsection would not support the application of AT&T's system would be to read the PDA as applying retroactively to recharacterize the acts as having been illegal when done, contra *Gilbert*. But this is not a serious possibility. As we have said,

> "Because it accords with widely held intuitions about how statutes ordinarily operate, a presumption against retroactivity will generally coincide with legislative and public expectations. Requiring clear intent assures that Congress itself has affirmatively considered the potential unfairness of retroactive application and determined that it is an acceptable price to pay for the countervailing benefits." *Landgraf v. USI Film Products*, 511 U.S. 244, 272–273 (1994).

There is no such clear intent here, indeed, no indication at all that Congress had retroactive application in mind; the evidence points the other way. Congress provided for the PDA to take effect on the date of enactment, except in its application to certain benefit programs, as to which effectiveness was held back 180 days. Act of Oct. 31, 1978, § 2(b), 92 Stat. 2076, note following 42 U.S.C. § 2000e(k) (1976 ed. Supp. III). The House Report adverted to these benefit schemes:

> "As the *Gilbert* decision permits employers to exclude pregnancy-related coverage from employee benefit plans, [the bill] provides for [a] transition period of 180 days to allow employees *[sic]* to comply with the explicit provisions of this amendment. It is the committee's intention to provide for an orderly and equitable transition, with the least disruption for employers and employees, consistent with the purposes of the bill." H. R. Rep. No. 95–948, p. 8 (1978), U.S. Code Cong. & Admin. News 1978, pp. 4749, 4756.

This is the language of prospective intent, not retrospective revision.

Hulteen argues that she nonetheless has a challenge to AT&T's current payment of pension benefits under § 706(e)(2) of Title VII, believing (again mistakenly) that this subsection affects the validity of any arrangement predating the PDA that would be facially discriminatory if instituted today. Brief for Respondents 27–29. Section 706(e)(2) provides that

> "an unlawful employment practice occurs, with respect to a seniority system that has been adopted for an intentionally discriminatory purpose in violation of this subchapter (whether or not that discriminatory purpose is apparent on the face of the seniority provision), when the seniority system is adopted, when an individual becomes subject to the seniority system, or when a person aggrieved is injured by the application of the seniority system or provision of the system." 42 U.S.C. § 2000e–5(e)(2).

But, as the text makes clear, this subsection determines the moments at which a seniority system violates Title VII only if it is a system "adopted for an intentionally discriminatory purpose in violation of this subchapter." As discussed above, the Court has unquestionably held that the feature of AT&T's seniority system at issue was not discriminatory when adopted, let alone intentionally so in violation of this subchapter. That leaves § 706(e)(2) without any application here. . . .

III

We have accepted supplemental briefing after the argument on the possible effect on this case of the recent amendment to § 706(e) of Title VII, adopted in response to *Ledbetter v. Goodyear Tire & Rubber Co.*, 550 U.S. 618 (2007), and dealing specifically with discrimination in compensation:

> "For purposes of this section, an unlawful employment practice occurs, with respect to discrimination in compensation in violation of this title, when a discriminatory compensation decision or other practice is adopted, when an individual becomes subject to a discriminatory compensation decision or other practice, or when an individual is affected by application of a discriminatory compensation decision or other practice, including each time wages, benefits, or other compensation is paid, resulting in whole or in part from such a decision or other practice." Lilly Ledbetter Fair Pay Act of 2009, Pub. L. 111–2, § 3(A), 123 Stat. 5–6.

Hulteen argues that payment of the pension benefits at issue in this case marks the moment at which she "is affected by application of a discriminatory compensation decision or other practice," and she reads the statute as providing that such a "decision or other practice" may not be applied to her disadvantage.

But the answer to this claim is essentially the same as the answer to Hulteen's argument that § 706(e)(2) helps her. For the reasons already discussed, AT&T's pre-PDA decision not to award Hulteen service credit for pregnancy leave was not discriminatory, with the consequence that Hulteen has not been "affected by application of a discriminatory compensation decision or other practice." § 3(A), 123 Stat. 6.

IV

Bona fide seniority systems allow, among other things, for predictable financial consequences, both for the employer who pays the bill and for the employee who gets the benefit. [Citation.] As § 703(h) demonstrates, Congress recognized the salience of these reliance interests and, where not based upon or resulting from an intention to discriminate, gave them protection. Because the seniority system run by AT&T is bona fide, the judgment of the Court of Appeals for the Ninth Circuit is reversed.

It is so ordered.

■ JUSTICE STEVENS, concurring.

Today my appraisal of the Court's decision in *General Elec. Co. v. Gilbert*, 429 U.S. 125 (1976), is the same as that expressed more than 30 years ago in my dissent. I therefore agree with much of what JUSTICE GINSBURG has to say in this case. Nevertheless, I must accept *Gilbert*'s interpretation of Title VII as having been the governing law until Congress enacted the Pregnancy Discrimination Act. Because this case involves rules that were in force only prior to that Act, I join the Court's opinion.

■ JUSTICE GINSBURG, with whom JUSTICE BREYER joins, dissenting.

In *General Elec. Co. v. Gilbert*, 429 U.S. 125 (1976), this Court held that a classification harmful to women based on pregnancy did not qualify as discrimination "because of . . . sex" prohibited by Title VII of the Civil Rights Act of 1964. 42 U.S.C. § 2000e–2(a)(1). Exclusion of pregnancy from an employer's disability benefits plan, the Court ruled, "is not a gender-based discrimination at all." 429 U.S., at 136. *See also id.*, at 138 (describing G. E.'s plan as "facially nondiscriminatory" and without "any gender-based discriminatory effect"). In dissent, JUSTICE STEVENS wondered how the Court could come to that conclusion, for "it is the capacity to become pregnant which primarily differentiates the female from the male." *Id.*, at 162.

Prior to *Gilbert*, all Federal Courts of Appeals presented with the question had determined that pregnancy discrimination violated Title VII. Guidelines issued in 1972 by the Equal Employment Opportunity Commission (EEOC or Commission) declared that disadvantageous classifications of employees based on pregnancy-related conditions are "in prima facie violation of Title VII." 37 Fed. Reg. 6837 (1972). In terms closely resembling the EEOC's current Guideline, *see* 29 CFR § 1604.10 (2008), the Commission counseled:

> "Written and unwritten employment policies and practices involving . . . the accrual of seniority and other benefits and privileges . . . shall be applied to disability due to pregnancy or childbirth on the same terms and conditions as they are applied to other temporary disabilities." 37 Fed. Reg. 6837.

The history of women in the paid labor force underpinned and corroborated the views of the lower courts and the EEOC. In generations preceding—and lingering long after—the passage of Title VII, that history demonstrates, societal attitudes about pregnancy and motherhood severely impeded women's employment opportunities. [Citation.]

Congress swiftly reacted to the *Gilbert* decision. Less than two years after the Court's ruling, Congress passed the Pregnancy Discrimination Act of 1978 (PDA or Act) to overturn *Gilbert* and make plain the legislators' clear understanding that discrimination based on pregnancy *is* discrimination against women. The Act amended Title VII to require that women affected by pregnancy "be treated the same for all employment-related purposes, including receipt of benefits under fringe benefit programs, as other persons not so affected but similar in their ability or inability to work." 42 U.S.C. § 2000e(k).

The PDA does not require redress for past discrimination. It does not oblige employers to make women whole for the compensation denied them when, prior to the Act, they were placed on pregnancy leave, often while still ready, willing, and able to work, and with no secure right to return to their jobs after childbirth.[4] But the PDA does protect women, from and after April 1979, when the Act became fully effective, against repetition or continuation of pregnancy-based disadvantageous treatment.

Congress interred *Gilbert* more than 30 years ago, but the Court today allows that wrong decision still to hold sway. The plaintiffs (now respondents) in this action will receive, for the rest of their lives, lower pension benefits than colleagues who worked for AT&T no longer than they did. They will experience this discrimination not simply because of the adverse action to which they were subjected pre-PDA. Rather, they are harmed today because AT&T has refused fully to heed the PDA's core command: Hereafter, for "*all* employment-related purposes," disadvantageous treatment "on the basis of pregnancy, childbirth, or related medical conditions" must cease. 42 U.S.C. § 2000e(k) (emphasis added). I would hold that AT&T committed a current violation of Title VII when, post-PDA, it did not totally discontinue reliance upon a pension calculation premised on the notion that pregnancy-based classifications display no gender bias.

I

Enacted as an addition to the section defining terms used in Title VII, the PDA provides:

"The terms 'because of sex' or 'on the basis of sex' include, but are not limited to, because of or on the basis of pregnancy, childbirth, or related medical conditions; and women affected by pregnancy, childbirth, or related medical conditions shall be treated the same for all employment-related purposes, including receipt of benefits under fringe benefit programs, as other persons not so affected but similar in their ability or inability to work. . . ." 42 U.S.C. § 2000e(k).

---

[4] For examples of once prevalent restrictions, see *Turner* v. *Utah Dept. of Employment Security*, 423 U.S. 44, 96 S.Ct. 249, 46 L. Ed. 2d 181 (1975) *(per curiam)* (state statute made pregnant women ineligible for unemployment benefits for a period extending from 12 weeks before the expected date of childbirth until six weeks after childbirth); *Cleveland Bd. of Ed.* v. *LaFleur*, 414 U.S. 632, 634–635, 94 S.Ct. 791, 39 L. Ed. 2d 52 (1974) (school board rule forced pregnant public school teachers to take unpaid maternity leave five months before the expected date of childbirth, with no guarantee of re-employment). *Cf. Nev. Dep't of Human Res.* v. *Hibbs*, 538 U.S. 721, 736–737, 123 S.Ct. 1972, 155 L. Ed. 2d 953 (2003) (sex discrimination, Congress recognized, is rooted, primarily, in stereotypes about "women when they are mothers or mothers-to-be" (internal quotation marks omitted)).

The text of the Act, this Court has acknowledged, "unambiguously expressed [Congress'] disapproval of both the holding and the reasoning of the Court in the *Gilbert* decision." *Newport News Shipbuilding & Dry Dock Co. v. EEOC*, 462 U.S. 669, 678 (1983). "Proponents of the [PDA]," the Court observed, "repeatedly emphasized that the Supreme Court had erroneously interpreted congressional intent and that amending legislation was necessary to reestablish the principles of Title VII law as they had been understood prior to the *Gilbert* decision." *Id.*, at 679. *See also California Federal Sav. & Loan Ass'n v. Guerra*, 479 U.S. 272, 284–285 (1987) (explaining that "the first clause of the PDA reflects Congress' disapproval of the reasoning in *Gilbert*," while "the second clause . . . illustrate[s] how discrimination against pregnancy is to be remedied"). *Cf. Newport News*, 462 U.S., at 694 (Rehnquist, J., dissenting) (criticizing the Court for concluding that the PDA "renders all of *Gilbert* obsolete").

Today's case presents a question of time. As the Court comprehends the PDA, even after the effective date of the Act, lower pension benefits perpetually can be paid to women whose pregnancy leaves predated the PDA. As to those women, the Court reasons, the disadvantageous treatment remains as *Gilbert* declared it to be: "facially nondiscriminatory," and without "any gender-based discriminatory effect," 429 U.S., at 138.

There is another way to read the PDA, one better attuned to Congress' "unambiguou[s] . . . disapproval of both the holding and the reasoning" in *Gilbert*. *Newport News*, 462 U.S., at 678. On this reading, the Act calls for an immediate end to any pretense that classification on the basis of pregnancy can be "facially nondiscriminatory." While the PDA does not reach back to redress discrimination women encountered before Congress overruled *Gilbert*, the Act instructs employers forthwith to cease and desist: From and after the PDA's effective date, classifications treating pregnancy disadvantageously must be recognized, "for all employment-related purposes," including pension payments, as discriminatory both on their face and in their impact. So comprehended, the PDA requires AT&T to pay Noreen Hulteen and others similarly situated pension benefits untainted by pregnancy-based discrimination.

II

The Court's rejection of plaintiffs' claims to pension benefits undiminished by discrimination "because of [their] sex," 42 U.S.C. § 2000e–2(h), centers on § 703(h) of Title VII, as construed by this Court in *Teamsters v. United States*, 431 U.S. 324 (1977). Section 703(h) permits employers "to apply different standards of compensation . . . pursuant to a bona fide seniority . . . system." 42 U.S.C. § 2000e–2(h). Congress enacted § 703(h), *Teamsters* explained, to "exten[d] a measure of immunity" to seniority systems even when they "operate to 'freeze' the status quo of prior discriminatory employment practices." 431 U.S., at 350 (quoting *Griggs v. Duke Power Co.*, 401 U.S. 424, 430 (1971)).

Teamsters involved a seniority system attacked under Title VII as perpetuating race-based discrimination. Minority group members ranked low on the seniority list because, pre-Title VII, they were locked out of the job category in question. But the seniority system itself, the Court reasoned, "did not have its genesis in ... discrimination," contained no discriminatory terms, and applied "equally to all races and ethnic groups," 431 U.S., at 355–356. Therefore, the Court concluded, § 703(h) sheltered the system despite its adverse impact on minority group members only recently hired for, or allowed to transfer into, more desirable jobs. *See id.*, at 356.

This case differs from *Teamsters* because AT&T's seniority system itself was infected by an overt differential. ("[R]ule of differential treatment was an element of the seniority system itself . . . ."). One could scarcely maintain that AT&T's scheme was "neutral on [its] face and in intent," discriminating against women only "in effect." *Cf. Teamsters*, 431 U.S., at 349. Surely not a term fairly described as "equally [applicable] to all," *id.*, at 355, AT&T's prescription regarding pregnancy leave would gain no immunity under § 703(h) but for this Court's astonishing declaration in *Gilbert:* "[E]xclusion of pregnancy from a disability-benefits plan providing general coverage," the Court decreed, "[was] not a gender-based discrimination at all." 429 U.S., at 136. *See ante*, (because of *Gilbert*, AT&T's disadvantageous treatment of pregnancy leave "did not taint the system under the terms of [§ 703(h)]").

Were the PDA an ordinary instance of legislative revision by Congress in response to this Court's construction of a statutory text, I would not dissent from today's decision. But Congress made plain its view that *Gilbert* was not simply wrong about the character of a classification that treats leave necessitated by pregnancy and childbirth disadvantageously. In disregarding the opinions of other courts, of the agency that superintends enforcement of Title VII and, most fundamentally, the root cause of discrimination against women in the paid labor force, this Court erred egregiously. Congress did not provide a remedy for pregnancy-based discrimination already experienced before the PDA became effective. I am persuaded by the Act's text and legislative history, however, that Congress intended no continuing reduction of women's compensation, pension benefits included, attributable to their placement on pregnancy leave.

III

A few further considerations influence my dissenting view. Seeking equal treatment only from and after the PDA's effective date, plaintiffs present modest claims. As the Court observes, they seek service credit, for pension benefit purposes, for the periods of their pregnancy leaves. For the named plaintiffs, whose claims are typical, the uncounted leave days are these: "seven months . . . for Noreen Hulteen; about six months for Eleanora Collet; and about two for Elizabeth Snyder and Linda Porter." [Citation.] Their demands can be met without disturbing settled expectations of other workers, the core concern underlying the shelter § 703(h) provides for seniority systems. *See Franks v. Bowman Transp. Co.*, 424 U.S. 747, 766, 773, and n. 33 (1976) (" 'benefit' seniority," unlike " 'competitive status' seniority," does not conflict with economic interests of other employees).

Furthermore, as Judge Rymer explained in her opinion dissenting from the Ninth Circuit's initial panel opinion, 441 F.3d 653, 665–666 (2006), the relief plaintiffs request is not retroactive in character. Plaintiffs request no backpay or other compensation for past injury. They seek pension benefits, now and in the future, equal to the benefits received by others employed for the same length of time. The actionable conduct of which they complain is AT&T's denial of equal benefits to plaintiffs "in the post-PDA world." *Id.*, at 667.

Nor does it appear that equal benefits for plaintiffs during their retirement years would expose AT&T to an excessive or unmanageable cost. The plaintiffs' class is not large; it comprises only women whose pregnancy leaves predated April 29, 1979 and whose employment continued long enough for their pensions to vest. The periods of service involved are short—several weeks or some months, not years. And the cost of equal treatment would be spread out over many years, as eligible women retire.

IV

Certain attitudes about pregnancy and childbirth, throughout human history, have sustained pervasive, often law-sanctioned, restrictions on a woman's place among paid workers and active citizens. This Court so recognized in *Nev. Dep't of Human Res. v. Hibbs*, 538 U.S. 721 (2003). *Hibbs* rejected challenges, under the Eleventh and Fourteenth Amendments, to the Family and Medical Leave Act of 1993, 107 Stat. 6, 29 U.S.C. § 2601 *et seq.*, as applied to state employees. The Court's opinion featured Congress' recognition that,

> "[h]istorically, denial or curtailment of women's employment opportunities has been traceable directly to the pervasive presumption that women are mothers first, and workers second. This prevailing ideology about women's roles has in turn justified discrimination against women when they are mothers or mothers-to-be." Joint Hearing before the Subcommittee on Labor-Management Relations and the Subcommittee on Labor Standards of the House Committee on Education and Labor, 99th Cong., 2d Sess., 100 (1986) (quoted in *Hibbs*, 538 U.S., at 736).

Several of our own decisions, the opinion in *Hibbs* acknowledged, 538 U.S., at 729, exemplified the once "prevailing ideology." [Citation.] The *Hibbs* opinion contrasted [those decisions] with more recent opinions: Commencing in 1971, the Court had shown increasing awareness that traditional sex-based classifications confined or depressed women's opportunities. 538 U.S., at 728–730. . . .

Gilbert is aberrational not simply because it placed outside Title VII disadvantageous treatment of pregnancy rooted in "stereotype-based beliefs about the allocation of family duties," *Hibbs*, 538 U.S., at 730; *Gilbert* also advanced the strange notion that a benefits classification excluding some women ("pregnant women") is not sex-based because other women are among the favored class ("nonpregnant persons"). . . .

Grasping the connection *Gilbert* failed to make, a District Court opinion pre-*Gilbert*, *Wetzel v. Liberty Mut. Ins. Co.*, 372 F. Supp. 1146 (WD Pa. 1974), published this deft observation. In response to an employer's argument that its disadvantageous maternity leave and pregnancy disability income protection policies were not based on sex, the court commented: "[I]t might appear to the lay mind that we are treading on the brink of a precipice of absurdity. Perhaps the admonition of Professor Thomas Reed Powell to his law students is apt; 'If you can think of something which is inextricably related to some other thing and not think of the other thing, you have a legal mind.'" *Id.*, at 1157.

Congress put the Court back on track in 1978 when it amended Title VII to repudiate *Gilbert*'s holding and reasoning. *See Newport News*, 462 U.S., at 678; *California Fed.*, 479 U.S., at 284–285; *supra*, at 4–5. Congress' swift and strong repudiation of *Gilbert*, the Court today holds, does not warrant any redress for the plaintiffs in this case. They must continue to experience the impact of their employer's discriminatory—but, for a short time, *Gilbert*-blessed—plan. That outcome is far from inevitable. It is at least reasonable to read the PDA to say, from and after the effective date of the Act, no woman's pension payments are to be diminished by the pretense that pregnancy-based discrimination displays no gender bias.

I would construe the Act to embrace plaintiffs' complaint, and would explicitly overrule *Gilbert* so that the decision can generate no more mischief. . . .

For the reasons stated, I would affirm the Ninth Circuit's judgment.

QUESTIONS

1. How does AT&T's pension system perpetuate pregnancy discrimination?

2. Is Hulteen demanding back pay to cover the period of her uncompensated maternity leave?

3. Imagine a timeline from the date of the *Gilbert* decision, the dates of Hulteen's maternity leave, the PDA's effective date, and the date Ms. Hulteen began collecting her pension. If retroactivity changes the consequences of past conduct, what is the conduct the PDA changes, and when did it occur?

E. THE RELATIONSHIP BETWEEN CONGRESS AND THE COURTS, REVISITED

Arguments raised in the preceding materials have suggested that both Congress and the courts would benefit from greater understanding of how the other branch operates, something Chief Judge Robert A. Katzmann of the U.S. Court of Appeals for the Second Circuit has reflected on in *Judging Statutes*:

> My experience as a judge only reinforces my view that at some basic level, each institution—that is, the courts and the legislature—could benefit from a deeper appreciation of how the other operates. Congress, which enacts the laws, should find it useful to learn more about how the judiciary interprets its laws; and the judiciary, for its part, could learn more about the legislative process to better equip judges to interpret those laws. The lineage of jurists with legislative experience is a distinguished one, including England's Lord Mansfield in the eighteenth century. Today—in contrast to a generation ago— only two federal judges have served as members of Congress. And in Congress, there is only one former federal judge and one state supreme court justice, though some federal legislators clerked for judges.

> To aid the judiciary in understanding Congress, some entity such as the Congressional Research Service of the Library of Congress, perhaps in conjunction with the legislative counsels' offices in both legislative chambers, could sponsor periodic seminars for judges and law clerks about the legislative process, perhaps developing a manual and videos about the lawmaking process. A start on this task is a pamphlet for judges on legislative drafting conventions by M. Douglass Bellis, longtime member of the House legislative counsel's office. . . . [T]here may be ways for Congress to help clarify legislative meaning, through both the drafting and the statutory revision processes, as well as the development of more reliable legislative histories that could aid judges as they undertake their work. . . .

> Ideally, legislators and their staffs should make greater use of the skilled legislative drafters in their offices of legislative counsel. If all legislative drafting were funneled through those offices, which apply accepted linguistic conventions and standards, then courts would have an easier time interpreting statutes. But that is not the reality of the legislative process. For those who do not avail themselves of the legislative drafting services, a checklist of common issues might be prepared—for example, dealing with such matters as attorneys' fees, private rights of action, preemption, statutes of limitations, effective dates, and exhaustion of administrative remedies. There have

already been several proposals for such a checklist. When not addressed in the law, such issues are resolved in court. While such a checklist would not prevent strategic, deliberate omissions, it could be useful in avoiding drafting oversights, clarifying legislative intent, and reducing burdens on the courts.

Similarly, the offices of legislative counsel could prepare a drafting guidebook for members and staffs. Law schools or some other neutral body could organize seminars with legislative counsels and judges to discuss problems of drafting and interpretation. Law school courses and continuing legal education programs on drafting would also be helpful, not only for those who work in Congress, but also for those in interest groups and organizations urging legislators and staffs to introduce bills for which they have crafted language.

Finally, to provide more precision, Congress might resort more to default rules, which would become effective when the legislative branch has not dealt with the particular issue in question in a specific substantive statute. For example, a statute may not explicitly provide for the time period in which a lawsuit must commence after the alleged violation of the law occurs. The failure to do so could lead to litigation, calling on courts to determine that time period. But a default rule enacted by Congress, as to civil statutes, solves the problem in circumstances where the specific law does not address the issue: "Except as otherwise provided by law, a civil action arising under an Act of Congress enacted after the date of the enactment of this section may not be commenced later than 4 years after the cause of action accrues." Hence, the default position is triggered if a particular statute has not addressed the time limitations on the commencement of civil actions arising under it.

The flip side of drafting before bills are enacted is the statutory revision process. Interbranch understanding of statutes can also be enhanced through the process of statutory revision. Supreme Court justices will from time to time identify an opinion meriting further congressional attention, as Justice Ginsburg did, to prominent effect, in the Lilly Ledbetter case. Congress is generally aware of Supreme Court decisions, as evidenced by legislative reversals of decisions of our highest tribunal. But the first branch tends to give little attention to the large number of statutory opinions of the lower courts. This lack of attention, while understandable given Congress's workload, is curious in view of the role that those courts play in construing statutes. Since the Supreme Court hears about eighty cases a year, the decisions made in the federal appellate courts are especially consequential. "Most of the work currently done by

federal courts, including the Supreme Court," commented
Justice Ginsburg, "involves not grand constitutional principle,
but the interpretation and application of laws passed by
Congress, laws that are sometimes ambiguous or obscure. She
further observed:

> When Congress is not clear, courts often invite, and are glad
> to receive, legislative correction. The law Congress declares,
> as the Chief Justice recently stated, is by and large the law
> federal courts apply. When Congress has been Delphic or
> dense, or simply imprecise, legislative clarification can
> ward off further confusion.

Nearly five decades ago, Judge Henry J. Friendly of the
Second Circuit, writing about the importance of statutory law,
lamented "the problems posed by defective draftsmanship,"
especially in uncontroversial legislation. He wrote about "the
occasional statute in which the legislature has succeeded in
literally saying something it probably did not mean," observed
that "even the best draftsman is likely to have experienced the
occasional shock of finding that what he wrote was not at all
what he meant," and commented on the legislative time
pressures that result in "neglect of the undramatic type of
legislative activity." Three decades later, another circuit judge,
James L. Buckley of the D.C. Circuit and also a former senator,
remembered that in Congress, "[w]ith time often the enemy,
mistakes—problems of grammar, syntax, and punctuation—are
made in the drafting of statutes and affect the meaning of
legislation." . . .

In an era when Congress passes large omnibus bills that
encompass a large number of diverse, often unrelated subjects,
making legislative history more reliable is all the more
important. To better signal a statute's meaning, legislative
leadership could more clearly identify legislative history that
courts should take into account. For instance, where feasible,
the floor managers of a bill could indicate what constitutes the
definitive legislative history, including floor statements and
colloquies. Such signaling would simplify a court's task in
reviewing the Congressional Record. Steven Charnovitz has
suggested that the enrolled bill—the final copy of a bill or joint
resolution which has passed both chambers in identical form,
signed by the appropriate House and Senate officers and
submitted to the President for signature—could also be a vehicle
for conveying legislative history. In other words, accompanying
the enrolled bill would be an official listing of legislative history,
although, of course, the President would not be asked to sign the
legislative history.

Another idea relates to the use of THOMAS, online resource of the Library of Congress, launched by the leadership of the 104th Congress, to make federal legislative information freely available to the public. Under the direction of Congress, THOMAS could add a section, "Legislative History" that would consist, for example, of specific links to committee reports, relevant colloquies and floor statements, making it easier for courts to sift through such history.

Moreover, as Stephen F. Ross proposed several years ago, having committee members sign committee reports, with signature sheets attached to the document, could effectively meet the charge that those reports are not endorsed by a majority of the committee. This could address the concern that committee members are not aware of the reports, or just do not read them. At present, generally only those offering additional views sign the reports. Identifying authoritative legislative history, moreover, will make it easier for courts to assess amicus briefs of legislators that are filed to persuade the courts about what Congress meant in passing the statute. For legislators to try to achieve through such briefs what they could not in Congress itself is something Representative Kastenmeier deemed "a questionable procedure." The more authoritative the legislative history is, the more likely it is that courts can review amicus briefs and interpret statutes in ways that do not result in what Senator Hatch called " 'slippage' from agreements reached in Congress."

Congress and courts are together engaged in an ongoing venture. The better understood the legislature makes its laws through text and accompanying materials, the more likely that the judiciary will interpret those laws in ways consonant with congressional meaning. . . .

There you have it: the views of a judge, judging statutes. In the end, my points are simply these. In our constitutional system in which Congress, the people's branch, is charged with enacting laws, how Congress makes its purposes known— through text and reliable accompanying materials—should be respected, lest the integrity of legislation be undermined. The experience of the executive branch in interpreting statutes can be helpful to courts. And practical ways should be pursued to further the objective of promoting statutory understanding. With greater sensitivity to the workings of the branches in the lawmaking process, we will be closer to realizing Publius's (most likely Madison's) vision in The Federalist No. 62: "A good government implies two things: first, fidelity to the object of government, which is the happiness of the people[;] secondly, a knowledge of the means by which the object can be best attained." Statutes, after all, are expressions by the people's representatives of this nation's aspirations, its challenges, and approaches to those challenges. That has been so throughout our country's experience, across a whole range of issues, mundane and dramatic, bearing on the very fabric of our values. That has been true as Congress enacted laws, for example, addressing civil rights, the environment, health care, voting rights, the economy, national security, and gender discrimination. When judges interpret the words of statutes, they are not simply performing a task. They are maintaining an unspoken covenant with the citizenry on whose trust the authority and vitality of an independent judiciary depend, to render decisions that strive to be faithful to the work of the people's representatives memorialized in statutory language. To have a part in that system of constitutional governance is a great privilege, indeed.

Robert A. Katzmann, Judging Statutes 92–105 (2014).

HOW JUDGES UNDERSTAND THE RELATIONSHIP BETWEEN LEGAL METHODS OF INTERPRETATION, LEGISLATION, AND THE LEGISLATIVE PROCESS

Relatedly, Professor Abbe Gluck and former Seventh Circuit Judge Richard A. Posner recently interviewed several dozen federal appeals court judges to understand how they think about questions of statutory interpretation, including the role that knowledge of the legislative process plays, if any, in how the engage in interpretation:

> ... This Article reports the results of a survey of forty-two federal appellate judges regarding their approaches to statutory interpretation, including their consideration of statutory text, dictionaries, the canons of construction, legislative history, and purpose. We also asked them about, among other things, pragmatism, the role of administrative agencies in statutory interpretation, and the value to judges of understanding how Congress works. . . .

> Several major themes emerge from the responses. First, what divides judges is not what academics and judges think divides judges. None of the judges is a "textualist" in the extreme sense of that word, or even in the version of textualism that was practiced by Justice Scalia. Very few judges told us they read the entire statute, or even begin their analysis of statutory cases with the text of the statute. All of the judges use legislative history. Dictionaries are mostly disfavored. Even when asked to provide one word to describe their interpretive approaches, not one judge was willing to self-describe as "textualist" without qualification. Even the text-centric judges described themselves in such terms as "textualist-pragmatist" or "textualist-contextualist." Our findings reveal the

academic cliché de mode—"we are all textualists now"—to be an overstatement.

At the other end of the spectrum, however, there were no extreme purposivists either, in the sense of the purposivism that has been textualism's foil. No judge stated that purpose was a more important tool than statutory text, and only one judge claimed to begin analysis of a statutory case with the statute's purpose. Even those judges who emphasized the importance of purpose as an interpretive tool made clear they still would not use purpose to push a statute's interpretation beyond the limits of its text.

And when it comes to tools of decision, the biggest divisions among the judges interviewed had nothing to do with text, legislative history, or canons—the topics that dominate and divide Supreme Court opinions and academic discourse. Also, no significant differences could be found simply by looking at the political party of the President who had appointed the judge, or at other personal factors such as the judge's gender or race, at least based on our limited sample. Among the judges we interviewed, the greatest divisions resulted from the three factors . . .: the judge's age, whether he or she sits on the D.C. Circuit, and prior experience working on Capitol Hill. These factors have received almost no theoretical attention.

1.   *The Judge's Generation.*—The judges over the age of seventy, regardless of political affiliation, were much more focused on questions about the inherent power and duty of the federal courts in statutory cases than on any interpretive dogmas. [W]e call[ ] these judges the "legal process institutionalists." They were more forthright about the quasi-legislative activity that statutory interpretation by judges entails, and discussed openly whether gaps in statutes could be understood as delegation by Congress to the courts. This position gels with Posner's work, which has emphasized that statutory interpretation, in reality, often entails more than merely searching for original meaning. Posner identifies two additional general categories of statutory interpretation: giving meaning to "unexpressed intent" and "giving a fresh meaning to a statement" by "making old law satisfy modern needs and understandings." In such situations, the judge's function is, realistically, more legislative than interpretive. Many of the older judges recognized this, especially with regard to unexpressed intent (we encountered more resistance to the idea of updating . . .).

The younger judges, on the other hand, many of whom went to law school in the 1980s or later, advanced a more rule-oriented approach. These are who we call the "canonists." Most of them, as noted, are very familiar with the canons of construction, either through their legal education or their litigation and advocacy experience—and have them at the forefront of their thinking. They do not seem to focus on the big-picture questions about the judicial role and inherent authority that we heard emphasized by the older judges—indeed, they seem more insecure than the older judges that they even have such authority. This is not a division that tracks the political party of the nominating President. Instead, the general influence of formalism on this generation of judges seems to carry across the board. We heard Justice Scalia's and textualism's influences emphasized by younger judges of all political backgrounds. . .

Trends in legal education, including the new courses in statutory interpretation that tend to highlight the influence of textualism on the field, alongside the virtual disappearance of legal process theory from most American law school curricula, are likely playing an important role in this generational shift. . . .

2. *The D.C. Circuit Is Different.*—A second major theme that emerges is that the D.C. Circuit judges appear different from the others. They have drunk the *Chevron* Kool-Aid—the decisionmaking framework that requires judges to defer to reasonable agency interpretations of ambiguous statutes. They find comfort in that framework and consider the question of the agency's role to be the first and most important question in statutory cases. In contrast, the vast majority of the non-D.C. Circuit judges we spoke with seriously questioned the wisdom and even legality of *Chevron*, especially in regard to legal questions that are not within an agency's expertise.

3. *Previous Experience Working in the Federal Government.*—Previous experience working in the legislative or executive branch of the federal government, or even a state government, appears to have a significant impact on a judge's approach to statutory interpretation, at least in our sample. We found that judges with previous Capitol Hill experience are less likely to embrace many of the interpretive assumptions favored by the current Supreme Court that depend on the fiction that Congress is perfect, consistent, and omniscient.

Indeed, these "ex-staffer" judges are more likely to accept a broader judicial role, taking the view that no statutory drafter can ever foresee and encompass the full range of possible statutory applications. These judges—again regardless of political affiliation—were more interested in legislative history, understanding how Congress works, giving Congress the benefit of the doubt, and even repairing Congress's mistakes. For these reasons, unlike conventional textualists, many of these judges— even those who are publicly associated with a text-centric approach—did not put much of a premium on reading statutes to be consistent, internally coherent, nonredundant, and so on—the kinds of canons that are most favored by the Scalia/Garner treatise but that bear little resemblance to how Congress actually drafts. . . .

Our overarching impression across all of the categories of judges was one of widespread eclecticism. For some judges, the eclecticism seemed intentional, as a way to make the judge confident of having reached the "correct result." One judge, known widely as a textualist, put it this way: "I just keep reading until I get comfortable. If I have to start reading a secondary text . . . I will. I don't necessarily rely on everything I have read but I do keep reading." Others said that looking at all the materials is about ensuring "[we] are doing what the legislature wanted" and "to the extent judges believe it is their job to find out what Congress meant, being eclectic is inevitable." Another said: "Nobody endorses any other method! That's like asking me why I look at a map to get where I am going. It's the only way that makes any sense." We found these perspectives interesting and not well represented in most current scholarship about statutory interpretation.

Some judges did seem more at sea. For these, a preference for eclecticism seems to stem from an eagerness to grasp at whatever supports are available to reinforce a conclusion and to help to explain decisions in ways that are both acceptable to colleagues of different political persuasions, and that also sound sufficiently "opinion-like" for the general public. Indeed, we heard a lot about statutory interpretation doctrine as a way to express results in opinions, rather than as a tool that actually decides cases. . . .

Another judge defended the eclecticism we saw on the ground this way: "That is the essence of being a judge." He said: "You could give someone a computer and they could do our job, you could feed in all the canons, rules, etc., and it could spit out an opinion. But the essence of being a judge is the human factor."

Only a few judges articulated any general theory of their own interpretive approach. Most resisted the very question—that is, resisted the idea that their practice is driven by any organized theory. Instead they told us they move case by case, in almost a common law fashion.

Although eclecticism may not seem a particularly exciting finding, our findings may dispel some misconceptions about judging in statutory cases and may also help shift the intellectual debate to newer and more fruitful topics than the now very tired "textualism versus purposivism" debate. We think it more interesting to focus on such questions as why the canons endure and why judges are uncomfortable writing opinions without them even if they do not really use them in decisionmaking. We also find more interesting questions concerning how judges think about who (Congress? The Supreme Court?) can control their own interpretive approach; what they think their role is in helping Congress, such as correcting its mistakes; and how judges should relate to agencies that issue judicially reviewable decisions.

We can acknowledge that judges use a mixture of interpretive tools and then finally move past the evidentiary issue to questions like why they write opinions the way they do, and whether it undermines legitimacy that many judges do not seem to have a consistent or identifiable interpretive approach. To the extent that appellate judges are doing more common law-type judging in the statutory context than previously assumed, pragmatism may be playing a bigger role than most judges (Posner excluded) have previously publicly acknowledged. . . .

Twenty-four of the judges we interviewed reported that they begin statutory interpretation with the words of the statute. But there was disagreement as to what that meant. For two of the judges, reading the statute is a pro forma exercise, apparently for "cover" in opinion writing. Both told us that they begin with the text "because the Supreme Court has told us many times we have to," but both then move quickly to other considerations, including purpose and consequences. . . .

In the end, both the judges who start with the words of the statute and those who do not seem to us to engage in essentially the same mode of contextual analysis, which defies categorization as either textualist or purposivist. They begin by trying to understand the statute, the problem the statute addresses, and the issue in the case at a broad level of generality. This broad lens often seems necessary to understand what lengthy and complex modern statutes mean. None of the judges we spoke with was formalist about this process. . . .

Of the forty-two judges whom we interviewed, only seventeen advocated using dictionaries, even though dictionaries are a favored interpretive tool of the current Supreme Court. The others told us that they rarely consulted dictionaries, or preferred to consult them in two types of circumstances: (1) to ascertain technical or specialized meaning; or (2) to determine if a word has multiple meanings, which they might do by consulting several dictionaries. We asked about the use of dictionaries after we asked the judges where they begin their analysis in statutory cases and the role that "plain meaning" plays in their decisions, because dictionaries are often trotted out by the Court to substantiate a textual reading before moving on to canons or nontextual tools. Although textualists may be responsible for elevating the importance of dictionaries, the Court's liberals now use dictionaries almost as often as the Court's conservatives. As Professors James Brudney and Lawrence Baum have documented, in a subset of cases likely to require statutory interpretation between 2005 and 2010 Chief Justice Roberts cited a dictionary in 35.7% of majority opinions; Justice Scalia in 30.8%; Justice Kennedy in 23.1%; Justice Thomas in 35.7%; Justice Ginsburg in 23.5%; Justice Breyer in 28.0%; Justice Alito in 33.3%; Justice Sotomayor in 25.0%; and Justice Kagan in 50.0%.

Yet dictionaries strike us as an odd interpretive tool. As the Gluck-Bressman study found, congressional drafters do not consult dictionaries when drafting. Dictionaries are "extrinsic" interpretive aids—aids outside of the statutory text—much as legislative history is, but dictionaries have not received the same critical scrutiny. Scholars have long pointed out that dictionaries tend to lag behind the real-life evolution of language. Indeed, a judge today who wishes to determine ordinary usage might be better off consulting Google. And as one of our respondents told us, if usage is truly ordinary, the judge does not need a dictionary to discover it. . . .

All but one of our six respondents on the D.C. Circuit made clear that *Chevron U.S.A. Inc. v. Natural Resources Defense Council, Inc.*—the case in which the Court declared that reasonable agency interpretations of ambiguous statutes should receive deference from courts—defines their interpretive approach more than anything else. The first thing these judges think about is not what the fight is about, or what the statute is meant to do, or what the statute says, but simply whether the statute invites an agency interpretation and whether the statute is ambiguous. Administrative law cases implicating these questions dominate the D.C. Circuit docket. . . .

The dominance of the *Chevron* inquiry also makes D.C. Circuit judges less interpretively pluralistic. In response to our follow-up question on the defensibility of interpretive eclecticism, one D.C. Circuit judge said:

Judges on this court might be different from other judges because so much of our work relates to *Chevron*. Most cases we have on statutory interpretation if the statute is ambiguous we don't have to go further. For us, when we are reviewing statutes *de novo*, like in the criminal context, it's a completely different thing, in terms of your list of eclectic considerations . . . . But most of the time we are looking at it through the *Chevron* lens. . . .

We saw much more agreement about the general approach than disagreement, and more emphasis on context and pragmatics than either plain text or purpose. Some of the most illuminating answers in this regard came to our question, asked toward the end of the survey, whether there was a "single word" to describe the judges' interpretive approach. We offered the descriptive terms "textualist," "purposivist," "pragmatist," "contextualist," or "anything else" as options they might choose. We provide these responses here to set the stage for the more detailed findings that follow.

Not one judge was willing to describe him or herself as a textualist without qualification. Every judge who included textualist in his or her self-description qualified the description in ways along the following lines: "some word that is on the continuum between textualist and contextualist"; "pragmatist but constraining"; "closer to textualist but not unmindful of practical consequences"; "textualist, but I would include being a contextualist"; or "textual pragmatism."

At the other extreme, only two judges out of the forty-two characterized themselves as "purposivist" without qualification (one appointed by each of the two political parties). Only four additional judges mentioned purpose at all, but with qualifications that they are both textualist and purposivist, or contextualist and purposivist. Three judges refused to answer this question, saying no single word or phrase could capture their approach. . . .

These findings should bolster our effort to open the door to new debates in statutory interpretation because they give rise to new questions. What does it mean to be "contextualist"? Some prominent academic textualists have used the contextual label, but their reference to context often means only canons, statutory structure and surrounding words. Our judges took a much broader view. Pragmatism was also an important theme. Is pragmatism in statutory interpretation consistent with legislative supremacy or the role of the courts in a democracy? Are there legal doctrines that could guide interpretive pragmatism? These kinds of questions have not received the attention they deserve. . . .

Every judge we spoke with, except for one, told us he or she uses legislative history. Recognizing that we do not have a representative sample of judges, one of the most salient findings of our study is that the most common way of categorizing different judicial approaches—through a judge's choice of interpretive rules and materials—is not a feasible sorting technique in the lower courts because it appears that many judges use all the available tools. . . .

Purpose seems to be another straw man, relevant only to academic (and perhaps artificial) divisions in the Court. Only four of the forty-two judges we spoke with did not mention purpose as an appropriate tool of statutory interpretation. The judges we spoke with interpreted the search for purpose in terms of "the mischief" or "the problem that gave rise to the statute in the first place." One described it as follows: "What are they trying to accomplish? Absolutely I use it."

No judge advocated the so-called sin of the *Holy Trinity* (referring to the infamous and much-maligned 1892 decision that first sanctioned using a statute's "spirit" to trump clear text). *Holy Trinity* has long been used as a foil by textualists to argue that textualism offers a more objective approach. But the judges with whom we spoke use purpose as part of the background context, together with other evidence, including text. . . .

It is sometimes assumed that purposivist judges use legislative history, while textualist judges use canons. That assumption should be put to rest. All of our forty-two judges use both tools to some extent and there does not seem to be any link between their canon use and the political party of their nominating Presidents, or their denominations as conservative or liberal. . . .

Even though the judges we interviewed certainly use canons, their reasons for doing so did not approach anything close to [a deep] level of analysis. The notion that the canons may need a connection to how statutory language works to be legitimate did not seem a concern for most of the judges (with a few exceptions); nor did the judges recognize canons as judge-made policy. Most judges also did not seem to appreciate that learning about the legislative process might debunk certain canons from common usage (for instance, why apply the rule against superfluities if legislative drafters are often intentionally redundant?). At the same time, the judges we spoke with had no other articulated reason for why they would use the canons, even if they did not reflect congressional understanding or practice. This is not to say there might not be such justifications; simply that none was offered.

While these results were not surprising, they are disappointing, given the heavy use of the canons by lawyers and even these same judges. Is the mere fact that canons may provide a common language for parties in the legal system to talk about statutory cases enough to justify their use, even if judges do not really have a justification for which ones are used and why? One of us (Posner) thinks emphatically "no."

1. *Canons as Tools of Persuasion, Not Decision.—"Like an Old Song."*—Roughly one third of the judges told us that the canons are "tools to make your arguments more persuasive or to persuade colleagues." For these judges, the canons are primarily tools of opinion writing. Linguistic canons especially, as opposed to policy canons, seem to be of this "window dressing" variety. . .

2. *Canons as Useful Decision Tools, Planted in the Judge's Mind.*—Twenty-six judges, including some who also said that the canons were useful for opinion-writing purposes, reported at least some canons to be genuinely useful to their decisionmaking processes. Several of the younger judges seemed to realize that they referenced the canons almost unconsciously, largely because they were educated about them in law school. One of these judges told us that he uses canons because he "feel[s] obliged to use them," thanks to learning them in law school as the field's doctrines. This, he explained, has both made him view the canons as "a tool you have to deploy" and also shaped his thinking about statutes in ways that cannot be consciously undone: "I try to think about what [a statute] means and these things [canons] are popping into my mind. If I had been educated differently maybe other things would pop into my mind. I can't help it." Another younger judge told us that as a practicing lawyer, statutory cases were his favorite cases to "brief and argue because I liked the fact there was a relatively

closed set of tools and cases to work through. It was like a puzzle." Another told us she had been given a list of the canons "at baby judge school" and kept them on her desk her first few years on the bench. In her view, the canons are "helpful to cabin our role and limit our discretion. Yes, I do think they help make decisions."

The Gluck-Bressman empirical study of congressional drafting suggests that there may be a difference in canon awareness between younger legislative drafters and older ones. Similarly, there appears to be a generational effect among the judges we interviewed with respect to how entrenched the canons are in their thinking that tracks the dramatic rise of legislation courses in law schools over the past three decades. . . .

3.   *Lenity and Avoidance Are Special.*—Some canons seem special. Thirteen judges—some of whom find most canons useful only as post-hoc window dressing and some of whom find canons more generally useful—singled out lenity and/or constitutional avoidance as "actual rules" and distinguished them from the other canons, in terms of their mandatory application. They told us that these presumptions are "not canons" but rather are "substantive law." Some judges seemed to believe these doctrines derived their special status simply because the Supreme Court said they did. (This observation, to us, implies a view that the Supreme Court could designate more canons to have this special status. Nevertheless, and inconsistent with this observation, many of these same judges later told us that the Supreme Court could not control lower-court interpretive methodology when we asked that question.) A few judges did not see these canons as deriving their power from the Supreme Court, but rather from the Constitution (for example, that lenity derives from the constitutional concept that federal judges cannot create crimes).

4.   *Canons in Opinions.*—Many canons other than lenity and avoidance permeate judicial opinions, regardless of what judges say about them. There are some useful observations to draw from this. First, we think the role of the lawyers and the law clerks with respect to canon citation practice cannot be overstated. As one judge told us:

Often [judges] get a bench memo and the bench memo cites canons. They may be taken from the briefs. But then by the time they get to conference I can't remember anyone using canons to justify their vote, but they will end up in the opinion. Why? I don't know. Maybe [judges] go back to the bench memos.

If lawyers and law clerks argue in canons, judges who draw on briefs or law-clerk work for opinion writing may be referencing canons in their decisions too, even if those canons did not actually inform the judges' decisions.

We also think that the framing role that lawyers play in making salient the key canons for each case has been underappreciated. As noted, our random study of opinions from the judges we interviewed revealed that many canons used in the opinions were introduced by the briefs. Professor William Eskridge and Lauren Baer have similarly demonstrated, in the administrative deference context, that the Court relies heavily—sometimes quite literally—on the rationales provided in the briefing in applying the deference canons (for instance, *Chevron* [or] *Skidmore* . . .) and that the regime chosen generally defines the case. . . .

All but seven of the judges we interviewed told us that understanding Congress is valuable for statutory interpretation. Many of these judges had experience working on Capitol Hill earlier in their careers. They told us that this background informed their views and gave them a comfort level in working with statutes. For example, one judge commented, "I feel I have a good insight on how the legislative process works and it is helpful. By contrast, I don't know squat on how the legislative process works [in the state capital] . . . . So when I get a question about state legislation I feel less certain . . . ." Several judges mentioned the idea of a Federal Judicial Center (FJC) training program on the legislative process for judges.

Yet, in another puzzle, even among the judges with an interest in how Congress works and a belief that such information is relevant to the task of judging, very few had ever considered examples like the one we raised (about not applying the presumption of consistency to statutes drafted by multiple noncoordinating drafters), or had thought much about applying knowledge of the legislative process to evaluating other legislative presumptions. . . .

Puzzlingly, a handful of judges told us they were interested in how Congress works specifically (and it seems only) because they thought it helped debunk the case for legislative history. As the Gluck-Bressman study illustrated, however, congressional drafters from both parties tend to insist that legislative history is essential to understanding statutes. It is thus ironic that some of the judges told us that understanding Congress is useful only to make the case against legislative materials. None of the judges who reported this interest also told us that understanding Congress could shed light on other interpretive questions or the applicability of widely accepted canons, like presumptions of statutory perfection, that are not linked to how Congress actually drafts.

Previous legislative experience may be more relevant to a judge's general—often more forgiving—approach to statutes than to his or her use of specific canons. Those with Capitol Hill experience emphasized how the practical understandings that come from knowing how Congress works help with statutory interpretation cases. One judge explained:

You can't answer everything in a statute. You can see all of
this in the U.C.C. Originally there were fifty-nine provisions.
Now there are 119. They are trying to answer all the questions
but you can't. The codes get longer and longer and longer.
When that happens, when the statute is vague, you have to
work it out. You never say that we are doing the drafting but,
in some ways, you become a shadow legislator. You have to
supply the answer. We say we are doing interpretation and we
aren't trying to be activist but you become a shadow legislator.

Understanding that statutes cannot cover every situation
gives this judge a sense of his role as "shadow legislator"; it
legitimizes to his mind the judge's gap-filling function. Another
judge of the younger generation said that her Capitol Hill
experience made her skeptical about statutory interpretation tools
that assume legislative perfection or omniscience:

I am no master of the intricacies about how Congress works
but I do have a healthy understanding. You need to
understand there is a slapdash quality to what happens. You
should not expect a level of precision in statutes that isn't
there. It is a healthy understanding to have to understand
stuff that comes out of the process. No one has thought so
much about comma placement, etc.

These sentiments were echoed by a judge of the older
generation who also worked on the Hill:

I think the public thinks that the process of statutory
interpretation is much easier than it actually is and that
judges should have a much smaller role. But Congress has its
own problems in drafting. That is difficult. It is almost an
impossible task to cover the waterfront and have it work
forever. Sometimes there is a disconnect between what the
Court thinks and the processes of what judges are doing.
Scalia's idea of legislative supremacy and judges just trying to
carry out known directives is just not the fact.

Another judge agreed that understanding more about
Congress could assist appellate judges because briefs in the courts
of appeals are not always sufficiently sophisticated to tell the
complex story of how statutes are put together. "Maybe by the time
you get to the Supreme Court you have various amicus briefs," he
said, "but it is useful to know about the legislative process. Why a
statute looks the way it does."

Four judges expressed no interest at all in how Congress
works. Two other judges thought it would just be too difficult for
judges to use such knowledge. They argued that the process would
be "essentially impenetrable by judges"; that "interpreting in light
of a realistic understanding of how legislative 'sausage' is made
would somehow invade legislative prerogatives, as well as confuse
judges." Another judge, in response to the information about how

multiple committee drafters defeat assumptions of consistency, said:

> For me that's a "whoa" moment, but if judges start worrying about that we are asking for trouble. It's the statute that's enacted and we have to live with it. It's a terrible mistake if we start fooling around with that info. Congress has got to understand how we are going to operate even if these assumptions are fictitious.

> Another said, "we'll always be amateurs." One judge referred to the arguments by textualists that statutes are made up of impenetrable compromises. As a result, "learning the process won't help judges with that essential problem of not being able to get into the statutory deals," he said. "All you can do is look at the text agreed on. I agree with John Manning on this."

Abbe R. Gluck & Richard Posner, *Statutory Interpretation on the Bench: A Survey of Forty-Two Judges on the Federal Courts of Appeals*, 131 Harv. L. Rev. 1298 (2018).

QUESTIONS

1. Several of the judges that Gluck and Posner interviewed indicated that the legislative process may simply be too complex for judges to master at a level that would inform their interpretations of statutes. Is this an indictment of interpretive approaches that require such knowledge? Of the federal lawmaking process? Of the training and expertise of the federal bench?

2. Chief Judge Katzmann lamented that in contrast to past eras, when many judges had prior legislative experience and vice versa, today only two federal judges previously served as members of Congress, and only two members of Congress have previous state or federal judicial experience. Should we be concerned about the near-total lack of overlap between the branches? Why or why not? What difference could it make were a legislator to have served as a federal law clerk, or a judge to have worked as a legislative staffer?

3. Gluck & Posner found that while many judges do not decide cases on the basis of the canons of construction, they are happy to invoke the canons in their written opinions. Are these canons simply window dressing? As a matter of method, could articulating legal rationales in the form of canons provide a disciplining effect on the legal reasoning? Or are they more likely to obfuscate the real reasons for the decision? As the judicial opinions in this Casebook show, judges are not likely to invoke canons to reach a decision they said they were otherwise disinclined to support. Under those circumstances, wasn't Karl Llewellyn right that canons have only as much weight as the underlying rationales that otherwise support the outcome the canons reach?

4. If neither insights from the legislative process nor the canons of construction determine judges' decisions in statutory interpretation cases, and few judges would call themselves either hardened textualists or unswerving purposivists, what do you think drives outcomes in individual statutory interpretation cases? Consider, once more, the typology of interpretive methods, *supra* Section II.B.1. Is it possible that interpretive methods grounded in rule-of-law values do more work than most judges will openly acknowledge?

5. Finally, look back to this Casebook's preface's call to remain mindful, while working through the excerpted cases, of whether the interplay among legislative, administrative, and judicial remedies has yielded a socially desirable result. How do the judicial reflections in the preceding excerpts inform your view of the dynamics between the federal courts and Congress, and the federal courts and administrative agencies? What reforms, if any, might enhance the capacity for the branches to understand each other's procedures, customs, and work product? Should those considerations affect how statutes are drafted and interpreted? Keep these questions in mind as you adopt the role of the legislative drafter in the next chapter.

PART VIII

THE DRAFTING OF STATUTES: OVERVIEW AND EXERCISES

ADINE VARAH

Having come this far, the reader might reasonably question both the judgment and ability of legislative drafters, given the numerous problems, ambiguities, and occasionally obvious errors in statutes that the previous chapters of this Casebook revealed. This Part serves as something of a rejoinder: as you will encounter firsthand, drafting a statute is no easier than interpreting one, and often harder.

A. OVERVIEW OF LEGISLATIVE DRAFTING

1. THE PROBLEM OF DRAFTING UNAMBIGUOUS RULES

In Part I of this casebook, we described the process by which a bill becomes law, and the many hurdles such a bill faces along the way. To be sure, successfully navigating a bill through various "vetogates" and unorthodox procedures is no easy feat. Yet drafting statutory language that adequately addresses the social problem the legislation seeks to remedy is not a simple task, either! Recall Problem Case No. 2 in Part II.A.1, in which the concise and apparently clear command, "Pedestrians only. No bikes," in practice revealed multiple ambiguities. The amended version including pictograms resolved some uncertainties, but introduced others. How would you draft a direction to pedestrians, bike riders, and others regarding the use of public paths? Your first task, of course, is to determine which uses to permit and which to prohibit. Then consider the words that will activate those policy choices. Bear in mind that if the policy choices themselves lack clarity, the words will inevitably be as murky as the unclear rules they express. In practice (but not in your drafting efforts!), substantive ambiguity may reflect a considered choice: legislators might agree on the broad policy objective but not about every specific application. Thus, drafting in broad strokes and "punting" as to the precise conduct to be prohibited or allowed—either to an administrative agency to resolve through rulemaking, or to a court to resolve through subsequent case decisions—can be an effective way to achieve the consensus necessary to enact law.

Nevertheless, every word matters, and subtle differences in language can produce a radical disjuncture in outcomes. A look at the drafting history of various statutes will show that legislators have debated at length about seemingly simple words, such as "and" and "or." Below is part of the legislative history of what was then known as "An Act prescribing the Form of the enacting and resolving Clauses of Acts and Resolutions of Congress, and Rules for the Construction thereof," now known as the Dictionary Act of 1871, 1 U.S.C. § 1 et seq. The Dictionary Act appears in the first few sections of the United States Code, and it provides definitions for certain common words that appear throughout the Code. [For cases applying the Dictionary Act, see Part III.B.2, *supra*.]

In this portion of the legislative history, several Senators discussed the proposed definition for the words "insane person" and "lunatic." The definition, as then proposed, provided: "the words 'insane person' and 'lunatic' shall include every idiot, *non compos*, lunatic, insane, and distracted person."* Perhaps unsurprisingly, ambiguity in meaning often results from lack of clarity in intention. Consider whether the Senators' difficulties derive from disagreement over which words best express a legislative policy, or from substantive discord over who the definition should cover, or both:

> Mr. Bayard. I should like to ask the chairman of the Judiciary Committee whether he does not consider the word

---

*   The current definition reads: "the words 'insane' and 'insane person' and 'lunatic' shall include every idiot, lunatic, insane person, and person non compos mentis." 1 U.S.C. § 1.

"distracted" . . ., is one of rather general meaning, and of application too general for law of this kind?

Mr. Trumbull. That is a word which is used in some of the States.

Mr. Sherman. In what connection is it used?

Mr. Bayard. The bill reads "the words 'insane person' and 'lunatic' shall include every idiot, *non compos*, lunatic, insane, and distracted person."

Mr. Conkling. The definition of that word is very broad. . . .

Mr. Bayard. It occurs to me that there are occasions in the history of this body when that phrase might be held to embrace a large portion of this body. [Laughter.]

Mr. Conkling. It would embrace the minority a good deal of the time. [Laughter.]

Mr. Bayard. When we come to the cause of all this, of course we can understand it.

Mr. Trumbull. I will say . . . that that is a portion of the bill as it came from the House. I suppose the meaning of the word as it is introduced here would not be very different from that of "insane" or "lunatic." I understand that word is used in some States to mean about the same thing. I should not be particular about the word at all; but it is in the bill. I do not suppose it will effect [sic] it one way or the other; but if the Senator thinks it is calculated to embrace too many persons, let it be stricken out.

Mr. Bayard. I submit that the word "deranged" would be far better.

Mr. Trumbull. Would not "lunatic" and "insane" embrace the whole of them?

Mr. Bayard. Exactly. I move to strike out the words "and distracted" in the seventh line of the second edition.

The amendment was agreed to.

Mr. Trumbull. Now the word "and" should be inserted between the words "lunatic" and "insane" in that line.

The VICE PRESIDENT. That amendment will be made it being merely verbal.

Mr. Thurman. I suggest to the chairman that the word "or" should be inserted before "insane," and not "and," to make good grammar.

Mr. Trumbull. I think not. I think "and" is the right word. The language is: "the words 'insane person' and 'lunatic' shall include every idiot, *non compos*, lunatic, and insane person." I think "and" is the right word.

Mr. Thurman. I do not wish to go into a question of grammar here, but I must insist that good grammar requires the word "or" instead of "and;" because if we put in the word "and" it implies that a person must be all of these, whereas it is really intended to apply if he is any one of them.

The VICE PRESIDENT. Does the Senator from Ohio make that motion?

Mr. Thurman. Yes, sir; I move to insert the word "or" instead of "and."

Mr. Trumbull. "And" is the right word, I submit to my friend from Ohio, grammatically and literally. "Or" would be the wrong word.

Mr. Hamlin. That is a question that ought to be deliberately discussed. [Laughter.]

Mr. Williams. I think one of these Senators had better parse this sentence. [Laughter.]

Mr. Bayard. The word "or," if inserted, should precede the word "insane," in order to make good grammar and sense.

Mr. Thurman. The Senator from Illinois moved to insert the word "and" before the word "insane." I suggest to him that the word "or" is the proper one. However, I am indifferent about it. I do not care about making any motion in regard to it, unless he is willing to refer the question to the Committee on Education and Labor. [Laughter].

The VICE PRESIDENT. The Senator from Ohio does not insist on the amendment.

Cong. Globe, 41st Cong., 3rd Sess. 776 (1871).

2.   CONSIDERATIONS FOR LEGISLATIVE DRAFTING

The U.S. House of Representatives' Office of Legislative Counsel has prepared and regularly updates a guide to drafting legislation, which provides an introductory overview of the considerations that go into both the pragmatic and technical components of drafting legislation. Below is an excerpt setting out a number of relevant questions for legislative drafters to consider:

[I].   The legislative thought process

A.   *The need for legislation*

The first step in the legislative thought process is identifying the problem to be solved. What is the end goal?

The next step is articulating a policy for achieving that goal. By what specific means will the problem be solved? Sometimes, a legislative solution will not be appropriate because of the difficulty of stating a policy with enough specificity, insurmountable problems with enforcement, or constitutional limitations. Additionally, the policy may already be accomplished by existing statutes or regulations, or it may be more appropriate to try to persuade an agency to enforce existing law in a different way than to pass new legislation. If new, binding legislation is not appropriate or desirable but Congress still wants to express its views on a policy, it may do so through a nonbinding resolution or sense of Congress provision.

B.   Key drafting questions

Once the decision has been made to proceed with new, binding legislation, the following key questions should be answered to produce a draft that accomplishes the intended policy and avoids unintended consequences:

- What is the scope of the policy—To whom or what does it apply?
  - For example, does a policy that applies to the States also apply to the territories and the District of Columbia? Does a policy that applies to "Federal funds" apply to Federal loan guarantees? Does a policy that applies to individuals also apply to corporations?
  - Should there be any exceptions or special rules for particular persons or things?
- Questions of administration—Who will be responsible for carrying out the policy?
  - Are the States or the Federal Government responsible?
  - If the Federal Government, which particular entity in the Federal Government?
    - Will the policy be administered by one entity or many?
    - Should a new entity be created to administer the policy?
- Questions of enforcement—What if the policy is not followed?
  - Will people be encouraged to follow the policy through incentives or punished for violating it (carrots versus sticks)?
    - If there are going to be penalties, should they be criminal or civil?
- Questions of timing
  - Should the policy take effect on the date of enactment or at some later time?

- o   How much lead-time will agencies or private actors need to prepare to implement the policy?

- o   Are there constitutional or other legal restrictions on applying the policy immediately?

- o   Should the policy apply to different persons or things at different times?

- o   If the policy affects current programs or current behavior, should there be any transitional rules?

- •   What is the relation between the policy and existing law— Must existing law be amended to avoid conflicts with the policy? . . .

[II]. Use of particular legislative provisions

A.   Purpose and findings provisions

The Office discourages the use of a statement of purpose that merely summarizes the specific matters covered by a bill. At a minimum, such a statement is redundant if the operative text of the bill already states exactly what is required, permitted, or prohibited. More importantly, any differences between such a statement and the operative text may be construed in ways that are difficult to anticipate. There may be cases, however, where a statement of the objective of a particularly complex provision may be useful in clarifying Congress's intent behind the provision. . . .

C.   Effective date provisions

Unless otherwise provided, a bill takes effect on the date of its enactment. An effective date provision should only be included if another effective date is intended. In a bill making amendments, any effective date provision with respect to when the amendments take effect should be stated, outside the quotes, as applying to "the amendments made by this [provision]", not the provision itself.

[III]. Three important conventions

A.   The terms "means" and "includes"

The basic distinction between these two terms is that "means" is exclusive while "includes" is not. If a definition says that "the term 'X' means A, B, and C", then X means only A, B, and C and cannot also mean D or E. If a definition says that "the term 'X' includes A, B, and C", then X must include A, B, and C, but it may also include D or E, or both. Thus, the phrase "includes, but is not limited to" is redundant. In fact, using it in some places out of an abundance of caution could cause a limitation to be read into places where it is not used.

B. The terms "shall" and "may"

The term "shall" means that an action is required; the term "may" means that it is permitted but not required. While this might seem obvious, a common misconception concerns the phrase "may not", which is mandatory and is the preferred language for denying a right, power, or privilege (*e.g.*, "The Secretary may not accept an application after April 1, 2011."). "Shall not" perhaps sounds stronger and is usually construed to have the same meaning, but it is subject to some (rather arcane) interpretations that are best avoided.

C. Use of the singular preferred

In general, provisions should be drafted in the singular to avoid the ambiguity that plural constructions can create. Take, for example, this provision: "Drivers may not run red lights.". It is ambiguous as to whether there is any violation unless multiple drivers run multiple red lights. This problem can be avoided by rewriting the provision as follows: "A driver may not run a red light."....

Drafting Legislation, Office of Legislative Council, U.S. House of Representatives, last revised Jan. 13, 2019, *available at* https://legcounsel.house.gov/holc-guide-legislative-drafting.

3. ORGANIZING A BILL

As with many states, in Oregon the Legislature's Legislative Counsel's office provides a manual for legislators and their staff members, providing an overview on how, among other things, to structure proposed legislation. Oregon's manual provides one example of best practices for organizing statutory drafting:

TYPICAL ORDER OF SECTIONS.

Although a bill does not always fit a uniform pattern, the order described below is recommended unless there are valid reasons for departing from the order in drafting a particular bill. Not all sections are required, or even recommended, and a drafter should consult the explanations of the sections in other chapters of this manual.

Sections of a bill ordinarily should be arranged as follows:

(1) Act names (rare).

(2) Definitions.

(3) Policy and purpose statements (rare).

(4) Legislative findings (rare).

(5) The leading purpose of the bill.

(6) Subordinate provisions (*i.e.*, conditions, exceptions and special cases important enough to be stated as separate sections).

(7) Administrative provisions (*i.e.*, authority and responsibility for administration and procedure).

(8) Subordinate (or "housekeeping") amendments . . .

(9) Saving clause (rare).

(10) Temporary and transitional provisions.

(11) Penalties.

(12) Repeals.

(13) Operative or applicable date.

(14) Emergency clause or nonstandard effective date.

(15) Referendum clause. . . .

DEFINITIONS.

The use of definitions should be considered when drafting a bill. If the drafter desires a particular word to have a particular meaning, a definition is essential. The length of bills can be reduced and the bill made clearer through the use of definitions. However, a word should *not* be defined if it is not used in the bill.

Definitions are useful to:

1. Limit or extend the meaning of a word, particularly if the word is used in a rarely employed sense or is ambiguous.

2. Translate technical terms or words of art into common language. . . .

As a general rule, definitions should not be used for a word when that word has a clear and definite dictionary meaning and that meaning is the one intended. A statutory definition is unnecessary and could lead to confusion. On the other hand, if a word has a well-defined legal meaning (that is, one well-defined in case law) and there is no statutory definition, the court will assume that the well-defined legal meaning is what the Legislative Assembly intended. If there is a well-defined legal meaning, and the Legislative Assembly intends that the definition of the term actually be something else, the drafter should define the term whether or not the intended meaning is identical to the dictionary definition.

The [Oregon] appellate courts [have said they] will use *Webster's Third New International Dictionary, Unabridged,* to determine the meaning of a word if there is no statutory definition or well-defined legal meaning. When resorting to dictionary definitions of a term it is important to consider the form of the word. For example, when a statute uses a word in its noun form, the definitions applicable to the verb form of the same word don't apply.

A definition should not be used to twist a word into meaning something *wholly* foreign to its dictionary meaning. For example, "dog" should not be defined to mean "cat." After a word is defined, the defined word should be used rather than the definition.

The drafter should take care not to place substantive matter in a definition. To do so makes the substantive matter hard to locate and usually detracts from the clarity of the definition. . . . Definitions should never be phrased in the alternative unless the use of the defined terms in the bill does not require judgment as to which alternative applies; for example, "commission means XYZ Commission **or** ABC Commission" may be acceptable, but not if the reader has to make a judgment as to which agency fits the definition each time the term "commission" is used. Acronyms and abbreviations should be used sparingly in bill drafts, and only if previously defined. . . .

Definitions usually begin with a reference to the particular sections in the bill that rely on those definitions: "As used in sections x to y of this (year) Act . . ." or "As used in sections 2, 3 and 10 of this (year) Act . . . ." Consider whether a penalty section is likely to be codified at the back of an ORS chapter. If no defined terms are used in the penalty section, consider whether omitting the penalty section from the definition reference will avoid the creation of a split series. Housekeeping or amended sections at the end of the bill may not depend on the definitions, so "As used in this (year) Act" should not be used. The ORS editors substitute all sections in an Act for references to "this (year) Act." If only a few sections depend on the definition, the substitution is confusing.

When writing a section of definitions, the drafter should place each definition in a separate subsection or paragraph. The defined words must be placed in quotation marks and arranged in alphabetical order. Disregard spaces when alphabetizing defined terms.

"Means" is used in the definition if the definition restricts or limits the meaning of a word. "Includes" is used if the definition extends the meaning. The combination "means and includes" should *never* be used, even if the combination is split into more than one sentence. A doubt is raised as to whether the definition is intended to be restrictive or extensive. The singular form of "means" or "includes" is used even if the term being defined is plural because the subject of "means" or "includes" is "the word"; *e.g.*, [the word] "Toys" includes teddy bears.

In some cases a drafter may not want to define a word or phrase completely and exactly, yet may want to make certain that the word or phrase *includes* all the specific cases in mind. . . .

Oregon Legislative Counsel Committee, Bill Drafting Manual (18th ed. 2018).

4. DRAFTING FOR STYLE

The U.S. House of Representatives' Office of Legislative Counsel has also published a manual on drafting style, which provides useful guidance in choices of language and word choice:

. . . Sec. 102. Main Message—. . .

    (b) USE SHORT SIMPLE SENTENCES.—

      (1) . . . Use short simple sentences.

      (2) . . . A listener survey was conducted recently. The median listener tunes out after the 12th word.

      (3) Break up complex and compound sentences.— Most complex and compound sentences should be broken up into 2 or more sentences. Often the offending sentence contains—

        (A) an unresolved policy issue; or

        (B) both a general rule and 1 or more exceptions and special rules. . . .

    (d) CHOOSE WORDS CAREFULLY.—

      (1) . . . Choose each word as if it were an integral part of the Taj Mahal you are building. There is 1 best word to get across each thought. To find that word, use the dictionary and bounce words and drafts off any member of the office who will listen. What a word means to you may not be what it means to the next person. . . .

      (4) Use same word over and over.—If you have found the right word, don't be afraid to use it again and again. In other words, don't show your pedantry by an ostentatious parade of synonyms. Your English teacher may be disappointed, but the courts and others who are straining to find your meaning will bless you.

      (5) Avoid utraquistic* subterfuges.—Do not use the same word in 2 different ways in the same draft (unless you give the reader clear warning.)

    (e) DEFINE YOUR TERMS.—

      (1) . . . Check to see if the use of 1 or more defined terms will improve the draft. Often a skillful use of definitions will promote clarity, brevity, and consistency. . .

---

    * Editors' Note: The term "utraquistic" appears to derive from the Latin "utraque" meaning "both" or "whichever," "no matter which," or "one or other." "Because legal documents are for the most part nonemotive, it is presumed that the author's language has been used, not for its artistic or emotional effect, but for its ability to convey ideas. Accordingly, it is presumed that the author has not varied his terminology unless he has changed his meaning, and has not changed his meaning unless he has varied his terminology; that is, that he has committed neither 'elegant variation' nor 'utraquistic subterfuge.' This is the rebuttable presumption of formal consistency. [Fn. refs. omitted.]" Reed Dickerson, The Interpretation of Statutes 224 (1975).

(f) PART OF YOUR JOB IS TO GET THE MESSAGE ACROSS.—

(1) . . .Your client comes to you because of wanting to send a message to 1 or more of the following:

(A) The world.

(B) The American people.

(C) Fellow legislators.

(D) Legislative staff.

(E) Administrators.

(F) Courts.

(G) Constituents.

(H) The media.

(I) Others.

(2) IDENTIFY THE AUDIENCE.—Decide who is supposed to get the message.

(3) Draft should be readable and understandable.—In almost all cases, the message has a better chance of accomplishing your client's goal if it readable and understandable. It should be written in English for real people. . . .

Office of Legislative Council, U.S. House of Representatives, Nov. 1995, *available* at https://legcounsel.house.gov/sites/legcounsel.house.gov/files/documents/draftstyle.pdf

B. DRAFTING EXERCISES

After studying the texts and cases in the previous Parts of the casebook, you may be tempted to think, "How could Congress have drafted such a mess?! Surely, anyone with half a brain could do better." In this section, you will have several opportunities to try your hand at drafting your own statutes: see if you can avert incoherence and avoid creating mischief of your own.

1. EXERCISE NO. 1: DRAFTING A REMEDY TO THE MISCHIEF

The following is an extract from the Minutes of an English Borough Council Meeting*:

Councillor Trafford took exception to the proposed notice at the entrance of South Park: "No dogs must be brought to this Park except on a lead." He pointed out that this order would not

---

* Reprinted by permission of Random House, Inc. from The Reader Over Your Shoulder by Robert Graves and Alan Hodge. Copyright 1943 by Robert Graves and Alan Hodge.

prevent an owner from releasing his pets, or pet, from a lead when once safely inside the Park.

The Chairman (Colonel Vine): What alternative wording would you propose, Councillor?

Councillor Trafford: "Dogs are not allowed in this Park without leads."

Councillor Hogg: Mr. Chairman, I object. The order should be addressed to the owners, not to the dogs.

Councillor Trafford: That is a nice point. Very well then: "Owners of dogs are not allowed in this Park unless they keep them on leads."

Councillor Hogg: Mr. Chairman, I object. Strictly speaking, this would prevent me as a dog-owner from leaving my dog in the back-garden at home and walking with Mrs. Hogg across the Park.

Councillor Trafford: Mr. Chairman, I suggest that our legalistic friend be asked to redraft the notice himself.

Councillor Hogg: Mr. Chairman, since Councillor Trafford finds it so difficult to improve on my original wording, I accept. "Nobody without his dog on a lead is allowed in this Park."

Councillor Trafford: Mr. Chairman, I object. Strictly speaking, this notice would prevent me, as a citizen who owns no dog, from walking in the Park without first acquiring one.

Councillor Hogg (with some warmth): Very simply, then: "Dogs must be led in this Park."

Councillor Trafford: Mr. Chairman, I object: this reads as if it were a general injunction to the Borough to lead their dogs into the Park.

Councillor Hogg interposed a remark for which he was called to order; upon his withdrawing it, it was directed to be expunged from the Minutes.

The Chairman: Councillor Trafford, Councillor Hogg has had three tries; you have had only two * * *.

Councillor Trafford: "All dogs must be kept on leads in the Park."

The Chairman: I see Councillor Hogg rising quite rightly to raise another objection. May I anticipate him with another amendment: "All dogs in this Park must be kept on the lead."

This draft was put to the vote and carried unanimously, with two abstentions.

———————

Having seen the travails of the English Borough Council, try your hand at drafting a municipal ordinance:

At a recent city council meeting of Metropolis, in the state of New Hazard, numerous residents of the city complained bitterly about the proliferation of aggressive and harassing panhandlers on the subway platforms in all sectors of the city. They demanded an outright ban on soliciting money on subway property. Some of the specific concerns raised were:

1) People soliciting money on subway platforms are often perceived as threatening to subway patrons, either in their appearance or in their behavior.

2) Some panhandlers will not leave a customer alone if the customer refuses to give money.

3) The overall appearance of the subway and desirability of using the subway are diminished by the presence of panhandlers.

Countering the complaints of those citizens opposed to panhandlers are several important constituencies whose views must also be addressed in resolving this problem. First, there are a number of "legitimate" charities, such as the Salvation Army, who solicit donations on subway platforms. Without this source of income, their ability to feed and shelter the homeless would be severely curtailed. Second, there are the musicians and other artists who perform on subway platforms. For many, this is their sole source of income, and customers of the subway enjoy the range and diversity of talent these artists bring to the underground. Lastly, there are several groups who advocate on behalf of the homeless who argue that most panhandlers in the subway have nowhere else to go, that many patrons of the subway do voluntarily agree to give them money, and to that turn them out simply on esthetic grounds would be unfair and unjust.

Council Representative Compassion, Transit President Law and Mayor Order have asked you, a legislative aide, to draft an ordinance addressing the concerns of the subway patrons and community interests of Metropolis. Do not ignore or slight the concerns of the various constituencies. Keep in mind not only the definition of the conduct you determine to regulate, but the means of enforcement of the ordinance. Your draft ordinance should address the following issues:

WHO does the statute target?

WHAT conduct does the statute address?

WHEN—the statute should take into account the time of day in which the acts to be regulated occur.

WHERE—the statute should take into account where the acts to be regulated occur.

HOW will the statute be enforced?

Metropolis has a long-standing reputation of drafting legislation in plain English. Therefore, you know that any ordinance you draft on the Council's behalf must address the issues completely, but should be as clear and simple as possible. In addition, the Metropolis municipal court carefully polices municipal ordinances for prohibitions that may be so vague as to be voidable. Thus, keep in mind backdrop considerations of unconstitutionally vague statutory prohibitions discussed in Part III.A.2.c, *supra*, as well as statutory severability savings clauses discussed in Part VII.B, *supra*. And if the Metropolis court were to find one or more of your ordinance's prohibitions void for vagueness, how might you draft the ordinance to signal which portions should be spared?

PROBLEMS

Assume that your ordinance is now in effect. The following events have transpired since.

a.   It is rush hour in August, and the subway platform in the heart of Metropolis is packed. Hot and sticky commuters wait for a train that has been delayed. In the middle of the subway platform, a reasonably well-dressed, slightly disheveled looking woman named Billie removes a deformed horn from her bag. She places it to her lips, and a sudden, piercing din begins to emanate from the instrument. Everyone immediately looks up. Most of the people near Billie start to edge away, although two or three jazz-punk-heavy-metal fusion fans converge and urge her to continue the performance.

Billie tosses her hat upturned onto the ground and shouts the following words to the crowded platform:

EXCUSE ME LADIES AND GENTLEMEN. I APOLOGIZE FOR THE INTERRUPTION. I AM HOMELESS. I AM HUNGRY. I CANNOT AFFORD TO REPAIR MY HORN WITHOUT YOUR HELP. IF YOU GIVE GENEROUSLY, I PROMISE TO PLAY MY HORN SOMEWHERE ELSE.

A few tentative hands toss quarters and bills into the hat. However, Billie is disappointed with the response, and she lifts the horn threateningly to her mouth. Suddenly, two transit officers arrive and escort Billie away. She is charged under your new ordinance.

Disillusioned with the political process, you have quit your job as a legislative aide, and you now work at a Legal Aid Clinic. Billie has hired you to defend her. Based on the ordinance you have drafted, what do you think Billie's best arguments would be? Would she be convicted? On the basis of Billie's case, is there any provision of the ordinance you would amend?

b.   The Metropolis Transit Authority has given permission to the Metropolis Animal Shelter to set up a booth where uniformed volunteers may accept donations. On a slow evening not long ago, Don, one of the Shelter's volunteers, was told to find some way to solicit donations more actively. Having little experience in such matters, Don decided to buy a cup of coffee and hope an idea would occur to him. Suddenly, an older woman walked by Don, who was decked out in a distinctive Animal Shelter uniform, and dropped two dimes into his coffee. The dimes sank to the bottom of Don's cup, still half-filled with coffee. Other subway patrons followed suit, though Don did not say a word. Delighted, Don walked back and forth on the platform, until the cup was about to burst. As he returned to the Shelter's booth, two transit officers detained him. Don has been charged under your ordinance.

This time you are no longer a legislative aide, nor a Legal Aid attorney; you have now moved on to greener, private practice pastures. The Metropolis Animal Shelter has hired you to defend Don. Based on the ordinance you have drafted, what would Don's best arguments be? Would he be convicted? On the basis of the Animal Shelter's case, is there any provision of the ordinance you would amend?

2. EXERCISE NO. 2: DRAFTING IN LIGHT OF OTHER REMEDIES TO THE MISCHIEF

For most areas of policy, legislators and their aides (and lobbyists!) do not draft against a blank slate: many statutes adapt previously enacted statutes from other jurisdictions. In the course of developing your bill, your research has turned up the following panhandling ordinances from three other jurisdictions. To ascertain how they would work, review and assess them using the Who? What? Etc. template above. Consider whether the ordinances fully address the concerns of the various constituents. Consider also whether they may bring about unintended consequences. Finally, scrutinize whether any of the provisions seem to be impermissibly vague.

New York City Panhandling Ordinance
New York City Administrative Code, Title 10, Chapter 1.

§ 10–136 Prohibition against certain forms of aggressive solicitation.

a. *Definitions.* For purposes of this section:

  (1) "Aggressive manner" shall mean:

  (a) Approaching or speaking to a person, or following a person before, during or after soliciting, asking or begging, if that conduct is intended or is likely to cause a reasonable person to (i) fear bodily harm to oneself or to another, damage to or loss of property, or the commission of any offense as defined in section ten of the penal law upon oneself or another, or (ii) otherwise be intimidated into giving money or other thing of value, or (iii) suffer unreasonable inconvenience, annoyance or alarm;

  (b) Intentionally touching or causing physical contact with another person or an occupied vehicle without that person's consent in the course of soliciting, asking or begging;

    (c) Intentionally blocking or interfering with the safe or free passage of a pedestrian or vehicle by any means, including unreasonably causing a pedestrian or vehicle operator to take evasive action to avoid physical contact; or

    (d) Using violent or threatening gestures toward a person solicited.

(2) "Solicit, ask or beg" shall include using the spoken, written, or printed word, or bodily gestures, signs or other means with the purpose of obtaining an immediate donation of money or other thing of value or soliciting the sale of goods or services.

(3) "Public place" shall mean a place to which the public or a substantial group of persons has access, and includes, but is not limited to, any street, highway, parking lot, plaza, transportation facility, school, place of amusement, park, playground, and any hallway, lobby and other portion of an apartment house or hotel not constituting.

(4) "Bank" shall mean any banking corporation as defined in section 11–164 of the code.

(5) "Check cashing business" shall mean any person duly licensed by the superintendent of banks to engage in the business of cashing checks, drafts or money orders for consideration pursuant to the provisions of article 9-A of the banking law.

(6) "Automated teller machine" shall mean a device, linked to a financial institution's account records, which is able to carry out transactions, including, but not limited to: account transfers, deposits, cash withdrawals, balance inquiries, and mortgage and loan payments.

(7) "Automated teller machine facility" shall mean the area comprised of one or more automated teller machines, and any adjacent space which is made available to banking customers after regular banking hours.

b. *Prohibited acts.*

(1) No person shall solicit, ask or beg in an aggressive manner in any public place.

(2) No person shall solicit, ask or beg within ten feet of any entrance or exit of any bank or check cashing business during its business hours or within ten feet of any automated teller machine during the time it is available for customers' use. Provided, however, that when an automated teller machine is located within an automated teller machine facility, such distance shall be measured from the entrance or exit of the automated teller machine facility. Provided further that no person shall solicit, ask or beg within an automated teller machine facility where a reasonable person would or should know that he or she does not

have the permission to do so from the owner or other person lawfully in possession of such facility. Nothing in this paragraph shall be construed to prohibit the lawful vending of goods and services within such areas.

(3) No person shall approach an operator or other occupant of a motor vehicle while such vehicle is located on any street, for the purpose of either performing or offering to perform a service in connection with such vehicle or otherwise soliciting the sale of goods or services, if such approaching, performing, offering or soliciting is done in an aggressive manner as defined in paragraph one of subdivision a of this section. Provided, however, that this paragraph shall not apply to services rendered in connection with the lawful towing of such vehicle or in connection with emergency repairs requested by the operator or other occupant of such vehicle.

c. *Exemptions.* The provisions of this section shall not apply to any unenclosed automated teller machine located within any building, structure or space whose primary purpose or function is unrelated to banking activities, including but not limited to supermarkets, airports and school buildings, provided that such automated teller machine shall be available for use only during the regular hours of operation of the building, structure or space in which such machine is located.

d. *Penalties.* Any violation of the provisions of this section shall constitute a misdemeanor punishable by imprisonment for not more than sixteen days or by a fine not to exceed one hundred dollars, or by both.

Orlando Panhandling Ordinance
Code of the City of Orlando, Florida, Subtitle A.

Sec. 43.88.—Sitting/Lying on Sidewalks in the Downtown Core District Prohibited.

(1) *Definitions.*

Sidewalk—An improved walkway intended primarily for pedestrians, usually running parallel to one or both sides of the pavement of a street and public transit waiting areas located within the public right-of-way.

Downtown Core District—An area in the City of Orlando, Florida described as: [identifying the applicable portion of the downtown core district.]

(2) *Prohibition.* It is unlawful for any person, after having been notified by a law enforcement officer of the prohibition in this section, to sit or lie down upon a public sidewalk or upon a blanket, chair, stool, or

any other object placed upon a public sidewalk, in the Downtown Core District.

(3) *Affirmative Defenses.* It is an affirmative defense to the prohibition in this section if it is shown that:

(a) Sitting or lying down on a public sidewalk is due to a medical emergency; or

(b) As a result of age, infirmity or disability a person utilizes a wheelchair, walker, stroller, or similar device to move about a public sidewalk; or

(c) The person is operating or patronizing a commercial establishment conducted on the public sidewalk pursuant to a street use or similar permit: or a person participating in or attending a parade, festival, performance, rally, demonstration, meeting or similar event conducted on a public sidewalk pursuant to a street use or other applicable permit; or

(d) The person is sitting on a chair or bench located on the public sidewalk which is supplied by a public or private agency or by the abutting private property owner; or

(e) The sitting or lying is while waiting in an orderly line for entry to any building, including shelters, or awaiting social services such as provision of meals; or outside a box office to purchase tickets to any sporting event, concert, performance, or other special event; or

(f) The sitting or lying is an integral part of a planned, publicized protest by ten (10) or more people accompanied by incidents of speech such as signs and literature explaining the protest, for which proper city permits have been obtained.

Sec. 45.02.—Prohibitions.

(1) It is unlawful for any individual solicitor, agent or peddler as defined in this Chapter to:

(a) Enter the premises of a private resident for the purpose of selling or soliciting orders for goods, wares or merchandise, personal services or information when a "No Solicitors" sign is posted;

(b) Remain upon any residential premises after the owner occupant requests the solicitor to depart;

(c) Conduct business between 5:00 p.m. and 9:00 a.m. or at any time on Sundays;

(d) To approach back or rear doors or the sides or rear of residential premises;

(e) To refuse or fail to exhibit his solicitor's permit identification card upon request by any law enforcement officer or citizen solicited;

(f) Intentionally make any physical contact with or touch the person solicited without that person's consent;

(g) Block the free passage of the person being solicited;

(h) Intentionally approach in such a manner or use obscene or abusive language or gestures intended to or likely to cause a reasonable person to be intimidated into responding affirmatively to the solicitation.

Sec. 51.02.—Exemptions from Registration Requirements.

Notwithstanding the provisions of Section 51.01, registration shall not be required in connection with a solicitation, sale or offer for sale where such activity:

(1) Is conducted by an organization within its own membership.

(2) Is conducted by a school, college, or university or by some organization sponsored by or affiliated with such school, college, or university.

(3) Is conducted by a governmental agency acting within the scope of its governmental authority.

(4) Is conducted by a candidate for election pursuant to Florida Statutes.

(5) Is a constitutionally guaranteed exercise of First Amendment rights.

Sec. 51.06–1.—Prohibitions.

(1) *Definitions.*

(a) "Harass" means to make any threats or demands that place the person solicited in reasonable fear of harm to his or her person or damage to his or her property.

(b) "Solicit" means to directly or indirectly request or attempt to request by spoken, written or printed word, money, donations of money, property or financial assistance of any kind, or to sell or offer for sale any article, tag, service, emblem, publication, ticket, advertisement, subscription or any thing of value on the pleas or representation that such solicitation or sale, or the proceeds thereof, is for a charitable, patriotic, public, 364 philanthropic or political purpose.

(c) "Vehicle" means every device in, upon, or by which any person or property is or may be transported or drawn upon a highway, except devices used exclusively upon stationary rails or tracks.

(2) *Aggressive Solicitation—Violation.* It is unlawful for any person to intentionally solicit in any of the following manners:

(a) By blocking any legal parking area or structure such that vehicles cannot enter or exit that parking area.

(b) By harassing the person solicited.

(c) By following an individual or group of persons with the intent to harass that individual or group.

(d) By continuing to actively solicit a captive audience after receiving a clear refusal.

(e) By soliciting an individual while that person is operating an automated teller machine (ATM).

(f) By entering the premises of private property for the purpose of soliciting when a "No Solicitors" sign is posted.

(3) *False or Misleading Solicitation—Violation.* It is unlawful for any person to knowingly and intentionally make any false or misleading representations in the course of soliciting a donation. False or misleading representations include, but are not limited to, the following:

(a) Stating that the contribution is needed to meet a need which does not exist;

(b) Use of any makeup, clothing or device to simulate any deformity, handicap or disability that does not exist;

(c) Representations or misleading statements that any other person or organization sponsors or endorses such solicitation, approves its purpose, or is connected therewith, when that person or organization has not given written consent to the use of its name;

(d) Use of any name, symbol, emblem, device, or printed matter so closely related or similar to that used by another charitable organization or sponsor that the use thereof would mislead the public; or

(e) Using or exploiting the fact of registration so as to lead any person to believe that such registration in any manner constitutes an endorsement or approval by the City.

(4) *Expenditure of Funds Solicited—Violation.* It is unlawful for any person to solicit a contribution stating that the funds are needed for a specific purpose with the intent to spend or distribute the funds received for a different purpose.

Sec. 51.087.—Penalty.

Any person violating any of the provisions of this article shall, upon conviction, be punished as provided in Section 1.08 of this Code.

Sec. 1.08.—General Penalty . . .

(3) Except as otherwise provided by law or ordinance, a person found guilty of violating any provision of this Code may be sentenced to pay a fine not to exceed $500.00 and may be sentenced to a definite term of imprisonment not to exceed sixty (60) days, or by both such fine and imprisonment.

(4) In addition to, or as an alternative to, the penalties hereinabove provided, a person found guilty of violating any provision of this Code may be sentenced to or otherwise be:

   (a) placed on supervised probation by the Court in accordance with the terms of Sections 1.13 through 1.20 of this Code;

   (b) ordered by the Court to pay restitution in accordance with Florida Statutes chs. 775 and 921;

   (c) ordered by the Court to perform public service in accordance with Florida Statutes chs. 775 and 921;

   (d) allowed to participate in the pretrial intervention program as set forth in Florida Statutes ch. 948, if such violator meets the qualifications enumerated therein and participation in the program is approved by the City Prosecutor's Office;

   (e) ordered by the Court to undergo psychiatric, psychological and/or drug and alcohol abuse evaluation treatment and/or counseling;

   (f) ordered by the Court to undergo testing for the Human Immunodeficiency Virus (HIV) and/or sexually transmitted disease (STD);

   (g) ordered by the Court to comply with the terms and provisions of any authorized and legal sentence.

(5) With regard to violations of this Code that are continuous with respect to time, each day the violation continues is and constitutes a separate offense.

(6) The City may, but is not limited to, enforce its Code and ordinances through the issuance of a citation, a summons, a notice to appear in County Court, or arrest as provided for in Florida Statutes ch. 901. . . .

St. Louis Panhandling Ordinance

St. Louis, Missouri, Code of Ordinances, Title 15.

15.44   AGGRESSIVE BEGGING

15.44.010—Definitions.

A. The following definitions shall apply to the provisions of this ordinance:

   (1) "Aggressive Panhandling" means panhandling in the following manner:

      a. To approach or speak to a person in such a manner as would cause a reasonable person to believe that the person is being threatened with:

         1. Imminent bodily injury; or

       2.   The commission of a criminal act upon the person or another person, or upon property in the person's immediate possession;

    b.   To persist in panhandling after the person solicited has given a negative response;

    c.   To block, either individually or as part of a group of persons, the passage of a solicited person;

    d.   To touch a solicited person without the person's consent;

    e.   To render any service to a motor vehicle, including but not limited to any cleaning, washing, protecting, guarding or repairing of said vehicle or any portion thereof, without the prior consent of the owner, operator or occupant of such vehicle, and thereafter asking, begging or soliciting alms or payment for the performance of such service, regardless of whether such vehicle is stopped, standing or parked on a public street or upon other public or private property; or

    f.   To engage in conduct that would reasonably be construed as intended to intimidate, compel or force a solicited person to make a donation.

(2)   "Charitable Organization" means any nonprofit community organization, fraternal, benevolent, educational, philanthropic, or service organization, or governmental employee organization, which solicits or obtains contributions solicited from the public for charitable purposes or holds any assets solely for charitable purposes.

(3)   "Panhandling" means any solicitation in person, by a person, other than a charitable organization, for an immediate grant of money, goods or any other form of gratuity from another person(s) when the person making the request is not known to the person(s) who is the subject of the request. The term "panhandling" shall not mean the act of passively standing or sitting with a sign or other indicator that a donation of money, goods or any other form of gratuity is being sought without any vocal request other than a response to an inquiry by another person.

15.44.020—Prohibitions.

A. It shall be unlawful for any person to engage in aggressive panhandling.

B. It shall be unlawful for any person to engage in the act of panhandling when either the panhandler or the person being solicited is located in, on, or at any of the following locations:

(1)   In any public transportation vehicle;

(2) Within 50 feet of an automatic teller machine or entrance to a bank;

(3) Within 30 feet of a point of entry to or exit from any building open to the public, including commercial establishments;

(4) At any sidewalk café;

(5) Within 50 feet of any public or private school;

(6) At any bus stop, train stop, or cab stand;

(7) Within 20 feet of any crosswalk;

(8) Within any municipal or government owned building, park, golf course, or playground.

C. It shall be unlawful for any person to engage in the act of panhandling on private property or inside a business without written permission from the owner.

D. It shall be unlawful for any person to engage in the act of panhandling after 8:00 p.m. and before 7:00 a.m. during any dates on which Daylight Saving Time is in effect; or after 7:00 p.m. and before 7:00 a.m. during any dates on which Daylight Saving Time is not in effect.

E. It shall be unlawful for any person to panhandle in a group of two (2) or more persons.

15.44.030—Penalty for violation.

A. Every person issued a citation under this section shall be offered immediate referral and direction to an appropriate community outreach service program.

B. Penalties for violations of this section shall be as follows:

(1) First violation: Upon a first violation, the person accused of violating this Ordinance shall be issued a warning ticket, which shall not include a summons to appear before a court of proper jurisdiction.

(2) Second violation:

a. Upon a second violation, the person accused of violating this Ordinance shall be issued a written citation, including a summons to appear before a court of proper jurisdiction for disposition of the case.

b. Upon conviction for a second violation, the violator may be sentenced to one or more of the following: the performance of up to 30 days of community service, mandatory enrollment and completion of a community outreach services program, and/or a monetary fine not less than Fifty ($50.00) Dollars but no more than Five Hundred ($500.00) Dollars.

    c.   The court should consider completion of a community outreach service program in determining the appropriate sentence.

(3) Third violation, and subsequent violations:

    a.   Upon a third violation, and subsequent violations, the person accused of violating this Ordinance shall be issued a written citation, including a summons to appear before a court of proper jurisdiction for disposition of the case.

    b.   Upon conviction for a third offense, and subsequent offenses, the violator may be sentenced to one or more of the following: the performance of up to 30 days community service, mandatory enrollment and completion of a community outreach service program, a monetary fine not to exceed Five Hundred ($500.00) Dollars; and/or imprisonment not to exceed 30 days.

    c.   The court should consider completion of a community outreach service program in determining the appropriate sentence.

PROBLEMS

1. Albert is cited for aggressive panhandling after a witness reports that he has asked at least five people for money in a shopping center over the course of one hour. What sort of penalties could Albert face in New York City? In Orlando? In St. Louis?

2. Barbara approaches a man on the subway and asks for money. The man says nothing and does not make eye contact. Barbara asks again, and the man puts earphones in and looks down at his phone. Barbara continues to repeat her request for money for several minutes, and the man continues to exhibit no response. Does this constitute "aggressive panhandling" in New York City? In Orlando? In St. Louis?

3. Conrad approaches a woman sitting in a car at a red light. While the car is stopped, he sprays the windshield with liquid and begins to wipe it. The woman shakes her head violently and wags her finger. Conrad stops several seconds later and looks expectantly through the woman's driver's window. He extends an open palm. The light turns green, and Conrad steps clear of the car. Does this constitute "aggressive panhandling" in New York City? In Orlando? In St. Louis?

4. Denise is asking patrons for money as they enter the front door of a grocery store. Just inside the front door is an ATM, around ten feet from where Denise is standing. Does this constitute "aggressive panhandling" in New York City? In Orlando? In St. Louis?

5. Edgar is approaching a man on a sidewalk who is holding a sign that asks for donations. As Edgar approaches, he trips on a rock and lightly bumps into the man. Does this constitute "aggressive panhandling" in New York City? In Orlando? In St. Louis?

Now that you have reviewed the three ordinances and considered their practical application to several hypothetical questions, try writing your own. For example, consider whether (and how) to provide a statutory definitions section; whether to set out all prohibited acts under a single subheading; as well as the specificity of both the conduct to be avoided and the penalties for violations therein. Feel free to "borrow" from the three ordinances, but you must not simply cut-and-paste. Think about which, if any, of the preexisting provisions sufficiently address the varied, and sometimes conflicting, concerns of your constituents. Then test your statute against the hypothetical questions posed after the three municipal ordinances, as well as against the fact patterns applied to the statute you drafted before encountering the three municipal ordinances. Be sure to keep in mind potential vagueness challenges.

3. EXERCISE NO. 3: DRAFTING TO BALANCE COMPETING MISCHIEFS

As you by now no doubt appreciate, drafting a remedy to the mischief is difficult enough even when the relevant stakeholders broadly agree about what the mischief is and how it should be remedied. In the real world, however, one stakeholder's "mischief" is another stakeholder's preferred state of affairs—rarely do all legislators agree on the ideal solution. Thus, statutory drafting entails not only the careful craft of drafting, but also the deft art of negotiation, as the following group drafting exercise will reveal:

You serve as a city council member on the Metropolis City Council (MCC) in the state of New Hazard. At a recent council meeting, numerous citizens complained about the usage of four adjacent parts of Metropolis Park: the lawns, picnic area, playground, and sports areas. The park is 16 acres, with each part of the park adjacent to the other three (*see park map, below*).

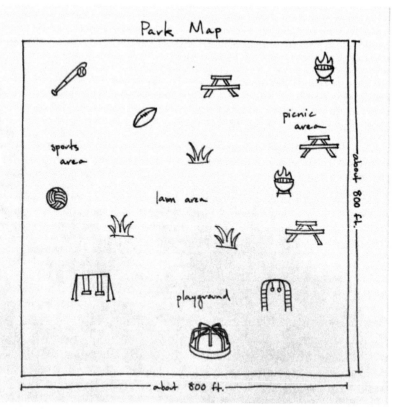

Map by Andrea Nishi, Columbia Law School Class of 2020. Used with permission.

Some of the specific concerns raised by those who use the park or live near it were:

1. The high demand for the lawns and sports areas from recreational league teams, school teams, and informally organized pick-up games; competing demands have created uncertainty about which users should have priority, and when different groups could use these areas.

2. The improper use of vehicles and sports equipment, as well as disruptive conduct from roaming pets and boisterous teenagers, in all areas of the park, but especially in the playground where young children play, and on the lawns, where retirees want to stroll in a peaceful, pedestrian-only area.

3. Issues related to noise, smells, and trash—from food and beverage vendors in all areas of the park; from too many parties, family gatherings, and social events in and around the BBQ pits in the picnic area; and from city festivals that use the picnic area and lawns of the park, often spilling into adjacent areas of the park and continuing well after sundown.

Countering those complaints were several important constituencies whose views must also be addressed in resolving the problem. *First,* a number of city sports leagues and clubs that regularly use the lawns and sports areas also informally help to maintain them, and the Metropolis Parks & Recreation Department (MPRD) collects use fees from these leagues that are vital to funding park operations. *Second,* several parents testified that the park is one of the safest places for their teenagers to socialize outside. They believe having such a space for teens to congregate and engage cycling, roller skating, skateboarding, drone piloting, and other activities helps to keep teens out of trouble. They worry that restricting park use too extensively will drive their teens to more dangerous parts of the city. *Last,* many families, including large, multi-generational families, regularly use the park—particularly the picnic areas and playground—for family gatherings, weddings, and other social events involving music, food, drinking, and dancing. The city is concerned that any complex or burdensome administrative scheme regulating these kinds of social activities will either breed scofflaws who ignore the rules entirely or else drive away these groups, which form an important and lasting part of the community. The Police Department is also eager for rules that can be easily enforced and that don't raise law enforcement problems.

As the MCC, you have decided to draft an ordinance to address concerns related to how the parts of Metropolis Park may be used, and also to set out how the MPRD will enforce the ordinance. You are to draft an ordinance, in plain English, that identifies the kinds of conduct that, for each of the four constituent parts of the Park (the lawns, picnic area, playground, and sports areas), is (1) allowed at all times; (2) prohibited at all times; and (3) permitted by the MPRD under certain circumstances, and if so, what those circumstances should be.

Keep in mind not only the definition of the conduct you seek to regulate, but also your ordinance's implementation—specifically, how the MPRD, which supervises the park, should enforce your ordinance. The ordinance should identify what permitting and enforcement powers the MPRD will have, and the criteria that should guide how it exercises them. Citizens of Metropolis value its prudent fiscal management, so be sure to consider the allocation of resources and personnel that your enforcement scheme may necessitate. Note that your legislative authority does not extend to allowing you to make physical modifications to the park.

Your draft ordinance should address the following issues:

WHOSE interests does the ordinance address? How does it address competing priorities?

WHAT conduct does the ordinance regulate?

WHEN should particular activities be permitted, regulated, or conditionally allowed under the ordinance?

WHERE in the park should the ordinance permit particular activities to take place?

HOW will the ordinance be enforced?

Metropolis has a long-standing reputation for drafting legislation in plain English. Therefore, any ordinance you draft must address the issues completely, but it should be as clear and simple as possible. In addition, the Metropolis municipal court carefully polices municipal ordinances for prohibitions that may be so vague as to be voidable. Thus, keep in mind backdrop considerations of unconstitutionally vague statutory prohibitions discussed in Part III.A.2.c, *supra*, as well as statutory severability savings clauses discussed in Part VII.B, *supra*. And if the Metropolis court were to find one or more of your ordinance's prohibitions void for vagueness, how might you draft the ordinance to signal which portions should be spared?

[Editors' Note: Your instructor may provide each of you with assignments concerning specific constituencies you are to represent in the legislative drafting process. If so, you must also ensure your constituency's desires and concerns are reflected in the park ordinance you produce.]

INDEX

References are to Pages